Short Story
Criticism

Guide to Thomson Gale Literary Criticism Series

For criticism on	Consult these Thomson Gale series
Authors now living or who died after December 31, 1999	*CONTEMPORARY LITERARY CRITICISM (CLC)*
Authors who died between 1900 and 1999	*TWENTIETH-CENTURY LITERARY CRITICISM (TCLC)*
Authors who died between 1800 and 1899	*NINETEENTH-CENTURY LITERATURE CRITICISM (NCLC)*
Authors who died between 1400 and 1799	*LITERATURE CRITICISM FROM 1400 TO 1800 (LC)* *SHAKESPEAREAN CRITICISM (SC)*
Authors who died before 1400	*CLASSICAL AND MEDIEVAL LITERATURE CRITICISM (CMLC)*
Authors of books for children and young adults	*CHILDREN'S LITERATURE REVIEW (CLR)*
Dramatists	*DRAMA CRITICISM (DC)*
Poets	*POETRY CRITICISM (PC)*
Short story writers	*SHORT STORY CRITICISM (SSC)*
Literary topics and movements	*HARLEM RENAISSANCE: A GALE CRITICAL COMPANION (HR)* *THE BEAT GENERATION: A GALE CRITICAL COMPANION (BG)* *FEMINISM IN LITERATURE: A GALE CRITICAL COMPANION (FL)* *GOTHIC LITERATURE: A GALE CRITICAL COMPANION (GL)*
Asian American writers of the last two hundred years	*ASIAN AMERICAN LITERATURE (AAL)*
Black writers of the past two hundred years	*BLACK LITERATURE CRITICISM (BLC)* *BLACK LITERATURE CRITICISM SUPPLEMENT (BLCS)*
Hispanic writers of the late nineteenth and twentieth centuries	*HISPANIC LITERATURE CRITICISM (HLC)* *HISPANIC LITERATURE CRITICISM SUPPLEMENT (HLCS)*
Native North American writers and orators of the eighteenth, nineteenth, and twentieth centuries	*NATIVE NORTH AMERICAN LITERATURE (NNAL)*
Major authors from the Renaissance to the present	*WORLD LITERATURE CRITICISM, 1500 TO THE PRESENT (WLC)* *WORLD LITERATURE CRITICISM SUPPLEMENT (WLCS)*

Volume 95

Short Story Criticism

Criticism of the Works of Short Fiction Writers

Jelena Krstović
Project Editor

THOMSON
GALE

Detroit • New York • San Francisco • New Haven, Conn. • Waterville, Maine • London

Short Story Criticism, Vol. 95

Project Editor
Jelena Krstović

Editorial
Kathy D. Darrow, Jeffrey W. Hunter, Michelle Lee, Thomas J. Schoenberg, Noah Schusterbauer, Lawrence J. Trudeau, Russel Whitaker

Data Capture
Frances Monroe, Gwen Tucker

Indexing Services
Factiva®, a Dow Jones and Reuters Company

Rights and Acquisitions
Margaret Abendroth, Margaret Chamberlain-Gaston, Edna Hedblad

Imaging and Multimedia
Dean Dauphinais, Leitha Etheridge-Sims, Lezlie Light, Mike Logusz, Dan Newell, Christine O'Bryan, Kelly A. Quin, Denay Wilding, Robyn Young

Composition and Electronic Capture
Gary Oudersluys

Manufacturing
Rhonda Dover

Associate Product Manager
Marc Cormier

LIBRARY OF CONGRESS CATALOG CARD NUMBER 88-641014

ISBN-13: 978-0-7876-8892-9

ISBN-10: 0-7876-8892-4
ISSN 0895-9439

Printed in the United States of America
10 9 8 7 6 5 4 3 2 1

Contents

Preface vii

Acknowledgments xi

Literary Criticism Series Advisory Board xiii

Preface

*S*hort Story Criticism (SSC) presents significant criticism of the world's greatest short-story writers and provides supplementary biographical and bibliographical materials to guide the interested reader to a greater understanding of the authors of short fiction. This series was developed in response to suggestions from librarians serving high school, college, and public library patrons, who had noted a considerable number of requests for critical material on short-story writers. Although major short-story writers are covered in such Thomson Gale series as *Contemporary Literary Criticism* (*CLC*), *Twentieth-Century Literary Criticism* (*TCLC*), *Nineteenth-Century Literature Criticism* (*NCLC*), and *Literature Criticism from 1400 to 1800* (*LC*), librarians perceived the need for a series devoted solely to writers of the short-story genre.

Scope of the Series

SSC is designed to serve as an introduction to major short-story writers of all eras and nationalities. Since these authors have inspired a great deal of relevant critical material, *SSC* is necessarily selective, and the editors have chosen the most important published criticism to aid readers and students in their research.

Approximately three to six authors, works, or topics are included in each volume, and each entry presents a historical survey of the critical response to the work. The length of an entry is intended to reflect the amount of critical attention the author has received from critics writing in English and from foreign critics in translation. Every attempt has been made to identify and include the most significant essays on each author's work. In order to provide these important critical pieces, the editors sometimes reprint essays that have appeared elsewhere in Thomson Gale's Literary Criticism Series. Such duplication, however, never exceeds twenty percent of an *SSC* volume.

Organization of the Book

An *SSC* entry consists of the following elements:

- The **Author Heading** cites the name under which the author most commonly wrote, followed by birth and death dates. Also located here are any name variations under which an author wrote, including transliterated forms for authors whose native languages use nonroman alphabets. If the author wrote consistently under a pseudonym, the pseudonym will be listed in the author heading and the author's actual name given in parentheses on the first line of the biographical and critical introduction. Uncertain birth or death dates are indicated by question marks. Single-work entries are preceded by the title of the work and its date of publication.

- The **Introduction** contains background information that introduces the reader to the author and the critical debates surrounding his or her work.

- The list of **Principal Works** is ordered chronologically by date of first publication and lists the most important works by the author. The first section comprises short-story collections, novellas, and novella collections. The second section gives information on other major works by the author. For foreign authors, the editors have provided original foreign-language publication information and have selected what are considered the best and most complete English-language editions of their works.

- Reprinted **Criticism** is arranged chronologically in each entry to provide a useful perspective on changes in critical evaluation over time. All short-story, novella, and collection titles by the author featured in the entry are printed in boldface type. The critic's name and the date of composition or publication of the critical work are given at the beginning of each piece of criticism. Unsigned criticism is preceded by the title of the source in which it appeared. Footnotes are reprinted at the end of each essay or excerpt. In the case of excerpted criticism, only those footnotes that pertain to the excerpted texts are included.

- Critical essays are prefaced by brief **Annotations** explicating each piece.

- A complete **Bibliographical Citation** of the original essay or book precedes each piece of criticism. Source citations in the Literary Criticism Series follow University of Chicago Press style, as outlined in *The Chicago Manual of Style,* 15th ed. (Chicago: The University of Chicago Press, 2006).

- An annotated bibliography of **Further Reading** appears at the end of each entry and suggests resources for additional study. In some cases, significant essays for which the editors could not obtain reprint rights are included here. Boxed material following the further reading list provides references to other biographical and critical sources on the author in series published by Thomson Gale.

Indexes

A **Cumulative Author Index** lists all of the authors that appear in a wide variety of reference sources published by Thomson Gale, including *SSC*. A complete list of these sources is found facing the first page of the Author Index. The index also includes birth and death dates and cross references between pseudonyms and actual names.

A **Cumulative Nationality Index** lists all authors featured in *SSC* by nationality, followed by the number of the *SSC* volume in which their entry appears.

An alphabetical **Title Index** lists all short-story, novella, and collection titles contained in the *SSC* series. Titles of short-story collections, separately published novellas, and novella collections are printed in italics, while titles of individual short stories are printed in roman type with quotation marks. Each title is followed by the author's last name and corresponding volume and page numbers where commentary on the work is located. English-language translations of original foreign-language titles are cross-referenced to the foreign titles so that all references to discussion of a work are combined in one listing.

In response to numerous suggestions from librarians, Thomson Gale also produces an annual paperbound edition of the SSC cumulative title index. This annual cumulation, which alphabetically lists all titles reviewed in the series, is available to all customers. Additional copies of this index are available upon request. Librarians and patrons will welcome this separate index; it saves shelf space, is easy to use, and is recyclable upon receipt of the next edition.

Citing *Short Story Criticism*

When citing criticism reprinted in the Literary Criticism Series, students should provide complete bibliographic information so that the cited essay can be located in the original print or electronic source. Students who quote directly from reprinted criticism may use any accepted bibliographic format, such as University of Chicago Press style or Modern Language Association (MLA) style. Both the MLA and the University of Chicago formats are acceptable and recognized as being the current standards for citations. It is important, however, to choose one format for all citations; do not mix the two formats within a list of citations.

The examples below follow recommendations for preparing a bibliography set forth in *The Chicago Manual of Style,* 15th ed. (Chicago: The University of Chicago Press, 2006); the first example pertains to material drawn from periodicals, the second to material reprinted from books:

Morrison, Jago. "Narration and Unease in Ian McEwan's Later Fiction." *Critique* 42, no. 3 (spring 2001): 253-68. Reprinted in *Short Story Criticism.* Vol. 57, edited by Jelena Krstovic, 212-20. Detroit: Gale, 2003.

Brossard, Nicole. "Poetic Politics." In *The Politics of Poetic Form: Poetry and Public Policy,* edited by Charles Bernstein, 73-82. New York: Roof Books, 1990. Reprinted in *Short Story Criticism.* Vol. 57, edited by Jelena Krstovic, 3-8. Detroit: Gale, 2003.

The examples below follow recommendations for preparing a works cited list set forth in the *MLA Handbook for Writers of Research Papers,* 6th ed. (New York: The Modern Language Association of America, 2003); the first example pertains to material drawn from periodicals, the second to material reprinted from books:

Morrison, Jago. "Narration and Unease in Ian McEwan's Later Fiction." *Critique* 42.3 (spring 2001): 253-68. Reprinted in *Short Story Criticism.* Ed. Jelena Krstovic. Vol. 57. Detroit: Gale, 2003. 212-20.

Brossard, Nicole. "Poetic Politics." *The Politics of Poetic Form: Poetry and Public Policy.* Ed. Charles Bernstein. New York: Roof Books, 1990. 73-82. Reprinted in *Short Story Criticism.* Ed. Jelena Krstovic. Vol. 57. Detroit: Gale, 2003. 3-8.

Suggestions are Welcome

Readers who wish to suggest new features, topics, or authors to appear in future volumes, or who have other suggestions or comments are cordially invited to call, write, or fax the Associate Product Manager:

Associate Product Manager, Literary Criticism Series
Thomson Gale
27500 Drake Road
Farmington Hills, MI 48331-3535
1-800-347-4253 (GALE)
Fax: 248-699-8054

Acknowledgments

The editors wish to thank the copyright holders of the excerpted criticism included in this volume and the permissions managers of many book and magazine publishing companies for assisting us in securing reproduction rights. Following is a list of the copyright holders who have granted us permission to reproduce material in this volume of *SSC*. Every effort has been made to trace copyright, but if omissions have been made, please let us know.

COPYRIGHTED MATERIAL IN *SSC,* VOLUME 95, WAS REPRODUCED FROM THE FOLLOWING PERIODICALS:

American Literature, v. 72, March, 2000; v. 72, September, 2000; v. 76, June, 2004. Copyright 2000, 2004 Duke University Press. All rights reserved. All used by permission of the publisher.—*American Review of Canadian Studies*, v. 30, autumn, 2000. Reproduced by permission.—*ANQ*, v. 13, summer, 2000; v. 16, winter, 2003; v. 18, spring, 2005. Copyright © 2000, 2003, 2005 by Helen Dwight Reid Educational Foundation. All reproduced with permission of the Helen Dwight Reid Educational Foundation, published by Heldref Publications, 1319 18th Street, NW, Washington, DC 20036-1802.— *Antigonish Review*, autumn, 1998 for "An Inner Bell That Rings: The Craft of Alice Munro" by Judith Maclean Miller. Copyright 1998 by the author. Reproduced by permission of the publisher and the author.—*ARIEL*, v. 29, April, 1998 for "Alice Munro's &lsdquo;Day of the Butterfly': An American Source" by Darlene Kelly. Copyright 1998 The Board of Governors, The University of Calgary. Reproduced by permission of the publisher and the author.—*Arizona Quarterly*, v. 62, spring, 2006 for "The Temporality of Allegory: Melville's &lsdquo;The Lightning-Rod Man'" by Sean R. Silver. Copyright © 2006 by the Regents of the University of Arizona. Reproduced by permission of the publisher and the author.— *ATQ*, v. 17, March, 2003. Copyright © 2003 by The University of Rhode Island. Reproduced by permission.—*The Baker Street Journal*, v. 15, September, 1965; v. 27, June, 1977; v. 3, 1948; v. 33, June, 1983; v. 34, September, 1984; v. 40, September, 1990. © Copyright 1965, 1977, 1983, 1984, 1990 by The Baker Street Journal. All rights reserved. All reproduced by permission.—*Contemporary Literature*, v. 44, spring, 2003. Copyright © 2003 by the Board of Regents of the University of Wisconsin System. Reproduced by permission.—*Critique*, v. 36, winter, 1995. Copyright © 1995 by Helen Dwight Reid Educational Foundation. Reproduced with permission of the Helen Dwight Reid Educational Foundation, published by Heldref Publications, 1319 18th Street, NW, Washington, DC 20036-1802.—*Dalhousie Review*, v. 78, autumn, 1998 for "Private Scandals/Public Selves: The Education of a Gossip in *Who Do You Think You Are?*" by Brian Johnson. © 2000. Reproduced by permission of the publisher and the author.—*Explicator*, v. 62, summer, 2004; v. 64, fall, 2005. Copyright © 2004, 2005 by Helen Dwight Reid Educational Foundation. Both reproduced with permission of the Helen Dwight Reid Educational Foundation, published by Heldref Publications, 1319 18th Street, NW, Washington, DC 20036-1802.—*Iowa Journal of Literary Studies*, v. 4, winter, 1983. Reproduced by permission.—*Journal of Canadian Studies*, v. 33, summer, 1998. Reproduced by permission.—*Journal of Modern Literature*, v. 20, summer, 1996. Copyright © Indiana University Press. Reproduced by permission.—*Journal of the Short Story in English*, spring, 2002; autumn, 2003. Copyright © 2002, 2003 by Presses de l'Université d'Angers. Reproduced by permission.—*Mosaic*, v. 35, December, 2000. Copyright © Mosaic 2000. Acknowledgment of previous publication is herewith made.—*Papers on Language and Literature*, v. 38, winter, 2002. Copyright © 2002 by The Board of Trustees, Southern Illinois University at Edwardsville. Reproduced by permission.—*Poetics Today*, v. 13, 1992. Copyright, 1992, Porter Institute for Poetics and Semiotics, Tel Aviv University. All rights reserved. Used by permission of the publisher.—*Publishers Weekly*, v. 244, December 15, 1997. Copyright © 1997 by Reed Publishing USA. Reproduced from Publishers Weekly, published by the Bowker Magazine Group of Cahners Publishing Co., a division of Reed Publishing USA, by permission.—*Queen's Quarterly*, v. 112, summer, 2005 for "Alice Munro: A Life in Writing, A Conversation with Eleanor Wachtel" by Alice Munro and Eleanor Wachtel. Copyright © 2005 by Alice Munro and Eleanor Wachtel. Reproduced by permission from Eleanor Wachtel and the William Morris Agency, Inc., on behalf of Alice Munro. (A version of this interview was broadcast on CBC Radio's "Writers & Company.")—*South Central Review*, v. 13, spring, 1996. Copyright © 1996 The Johns Hopkins University Press. Reproduced by permission.— *Studies in American Fiction*, v. 30, autumn, 2002; v. 31, spring, 2003. Copyright © 2002, 2003 Northeastern University. Both reproduced by permission.—*Studies in Short Fiction*, v. 35, summer, 1998. Copyright © 1998 by Studies in Short Fiction. Reproduced by permission.—*Style*, v. 35, spring, 2001. Copyright © Style, 2001. All rights reserved. Reproduced by permission of the publisher.—*University of Toronto Quarterly*, v. 71, summer, 2002. Copyright © University of Toronto Press 2002. Reproduced by permission of the University of Toronto Press Incorporated.—*Utopian Studies*, v. 11, spring, 2000. Copyright 2000 Society for Utopian Studies. Reproduced by permission.—*Wascana Review of Contemporary Poetry and Short Fiction*, v. 38, spring, 2003 for "Wilderness Stations: Peregrination and Homesickness in Alice Munro's *Open Secrets*" by Ella Soper-Jones. Copyright © by The University of Regina. Reproduced by permission of the author.

Thomson Gale Literature Product Advisory Board

The members of the Thomson Gale Literature Product Advisory Board—reference librarians from public and academic library systems—represent a cross-section of our customer base and offer a variety of informed perspectives on both the presentation and content of our literature products. Advisory board members assess and define such quality issues as the relevance, currency, and usefulness of the author coverage, critical content, and literary topics included in our series; evaluate the layout, presentation, and general quality of our printed volumes; provide feedback on the criteria used for selecting authors and topics covered in our series; provide suggestions for potential enhancements to our series; identify any gaps in our coverage of authors or literary topics, recommending authors or topics for inclusion; analyze the appropriateness of our content and presentation for various user audiences, such as high school students, undergraduates, graduate students, librarians, and educators; and offer feedback on any proposed changes/enhancements to our series. We wish to thank the following advisors for their advice throughout the year.

"The Adventure of the Speckled Band"

Arthur Conan Doyle

The following entry presents criticism of Doyle's short story "The Adventure of the Speckled Band" (1892). For discussion of Doyle's complete short fiction career, see *SC*, Volumes 12 and 83.

INTRODUCTION

Cited by Doyle as his favorite Sherlock Holmes mystery, "The Adventure of the Speckled Band" is one of the most widely read stories of the Victorian era. Originally published in *Strand* magazine in 1892 and collected in *The Adventures of Sherlock Holmes* (1892) that same year, "The Adventure of the Speckled Band" has inspired a number of successful stage, film, and television adaptations. Beloved among fans of the detective genre, Doyle's classic tale of suspense continues to spur reinterpretation and speculation by modern scholars.

PLOT AND MAJOR CHARACTERS

Like nearly all of the Sherlock Holmes tales, "The Adventure of the Speckled Band" is narrated by Dr. Watson, Holmes's sidekick and loyal friend. Watson explains that the events of the narrative actually took place years earlier, in 1883, while the two men were roommates on Baker Street. One morning Holmes invites Watson to join him for a meeting with a prospective client, Miss Helen Stoner. Visibly shaken, Helen proceeds to explain her background and the reason for her visit.

Helen's stepfather, Dr. Grimesby Roylott, married Helen's widowed mother after having met her in India, where Roylott had practiced medicine and Helen's father had served in the military. Roylott is descended from a once-prestigious English family whose wealth has been squandered, and had recently served a prison sentence for murdering a servant whom he had suspected of theft. By marrying Helen's mother, Roylott gained access to a sizable fortune. A portion of the money, however, had been set aside as a dowry for Helen and her twin sister, Julia. After Helen's mother died in a car accident, Roylott took the girls to live with him at Stoke Moral, his desolate family manor in the British countryside. Roylott became increasingly ill-tempered and strange after the move, frequently allowing gypsies to live on his property and occasionally wandering away with them on their journeys. He also imported a baboon and a cheetah from India, permitting the animals to roam the manor grounds.

After enduring a bleak, isolated existence at Stoke Moral for six years, Julia met and became engaged to a major in the military. Not long afterward, Helen was awakened in the middle of the night by the sounds of a struggle in her sister's bedroom. She recalls having heard a low whistle and the clanging of metal as she rushed to Julia's aid. Having found her sister on the verge of unconsciousness, Helen heard her last words: "It was the band! The speckled band!" Just before dying, Julia had also gestured toward their stepfather's bedroom.

Two years after Julia's strange demise, Helen has come to Holmes. She, too, has recently become engaged, and fears for her life. Helen suspects that the gypsies may have played a role in her sister's death. She has also recently heard the suspicious low whistle that she detected on the night of her sister's death. Holmes and Watson agree to travel to Stoke Moral later that day. Just as Helen leaves, Roylott appears at Holmes's door. He has followed his stepdaughter to the detectives, and warns the two men to stay away. He proceeds to twist a metal poker out of shape and throw it into the fire. Holmes and Watson are not intimidated, making their way to Roylott's home as planned. Once there, they investigate the room in which Julia was killed—the same room that Helen now occupies. Holmes finds a bell-pull, but is puzzled to learn that it is not attached to a bell. The detective also notes the ventilator in the wall that opens into the adjoining room. Next, they inspect Roylott's room, where Holmes finds a large safe with a saucer of milk resting on top. A small, looped dog leash sits on the corner of Roylott's bed. Sensing that the young woman is in danger, Holmes suggests that he and Watson stay in Helen's room overnight. Hours pass as they sit in the darkened room, until they finally hear the low whistle. Holmes lights a match and begins swinging his cane in the direction of the bell-rope. A ghastly scream comes from Roylott's room, and the two men rush in to find Roylott dead with a speckled snake wrapped around his forehead. Holmes uses Roylott's dog leash to grab the snake and throw it into the nearby safe. Watson concludes the narrative by providing Holmes's explanation for the deadly chain of events. Roylott had attempted to murder Helen to prevent her marriage and subsequent inheritance. By training an exotic Indian snake to crawl through the ventilator, inch across the bell-rope, and plummet onto the bed, he had hoped that its venomous bite would kill his stepdaughter while remaining undetected by the coroner. The leash, milk, and whistle had been used to train the animal, which was contained in the safe during the day. Holmes assures Watson that the death of Roylott will not bother the detective's conscience.

MAJOR THEMES

One of the prominent themes in "The Adventure of the Speckled Band" is that of greed. Just as the Roylott family fortune was eventually dissipated by gambling, so Dr. Roylott's marriage to Helen's mother and subsequent murder of Julia were also inspired by monetary gain. Additionally, Dr. Roylott embodies oppressive patriarchal authority, while Holmes, Watson, and the sisters' suitors typify the positive, benevolent potential of male authority. "The Adventure of the Speckled Band" also depicts fear of the exotic. As members of a community generally regarded as "foreign," the gypsies serve as a natural scapegoat for Roylott's misdeeds and add a general air of suspiciousness to his character by association. The wild animals that roam around Stoke Moral likewise suggest increased danger and mystery by virtue of their origins in India. Finally, the story serves as an example of the superiority of intellect and reason over brute strength. Though Roylott's imposing physicality and feats of strength are well-documented in the text, he is ultimately thwarted by Holmes's powers of deduction.

CRITICAL RECEPTION

An abundance of scholarly attention has focused on the snake in "The Adventure of the Speckled Band." Asserting that the physical agility required by the snake matches no known species, reviewers have suggested that Roylott may have bred the animal with another kind of reptile. Roylott's possible method for training the snake has been scrutinized, as has the symbolic significance of the serpent. "Rather than holding up the serpentine staff of the physician," observed commentator Michael Atkinson, "Dr. Roylott manipulates his snake with a whip." Scholars have also questioned Roylott's guilt, alleging that Helen Stoner may have orchestrated the events of the story in order to secure her inheritance. Furthermore, critics have discussed issues of class sensitivity and the mistreatment of women in the story. Doyle's overall narrative structure has been subject to analysis as well, particularly for its relevance to mystery fiction in general. According to scholar John

A. Hodgson, "The Adventure of the Speckled Band" "is not about detecting a crime, but about defining a crime-detecting genre."

PRINCIPAL WORKS

Short Fiction

The Adventures of Sherlock Holmes 1892
The Memoirs of Sherlock Holmes 1894
Round the Red Lamp: Being Facts and Fancies of Medical Life 1894
The Exploits of Brigadier Gerard 1896
Round the Fire Stories 1902
The Adventures of Gerard 1903
The Return of Sherlock Holmes 1905
His Last Bow: A Reminiscence of Sherlock Holmes 1917
The Case Book of Sherlock Holmes 1927
The Professor Challenger Stories 1952
The Annotated Sherlock Holmes: The Four Novels and the Fifty-Six Short Stories Complete 1967
Uncollected Stories: The Unknown Conan Doyle 1982
The Uncollected Sherlock Holmes 1983
The Collected Brigadier Gerard Stories 1995
Sherlock Holmes: The Complete Illustrated Short Stories 2000

Other Major Works

A Study in Scarlet (novel) 1888
Micah Clarke (novel) 1889
The Sign of Four (novel) 1890
The Stark Munro Letters (novel) 1895
The Hound of the Baskervilles (novel) 1902
The Lost World (novel) 1912
The Valley of Fear (novel) 1914
Memories and Adventures (memoirs) 1924
Sherlock Holmes: The Complete Illustrated Novels (novels) 2001

*Contains the novel *The Lost World*; the novella *The Poison Belt*; the novel *The Land of Mist*; and the short stories "The Disintegration Machine" and "When the World Screamed."

CRITICISM

Laurence M. Klauber (essay date 1948)

SOURCE: Klauber, Laurence M. "The Truth about the Speckled Band." *Baker Street Journal* 3, no. 2 (1948): 149-57.

[*In the following essay, Klauber explores Dr. Watson's role in "The Adventure of the Speckled Band."*]

To any student of the Writings one of the most disturbing elements is the frequency with which Dr. Watson has carelessly, and with obvious inaccuracy, recorded some statement of the Master. From such have resulted those uncertainties of explanation so puzzling to his reverential following. They must, certainly, have been shocking to one like Holmes, who treasured, above all, lucidity of thought and directness of conclusion. One may picture him pacing among his bee-hives, torn between loyalty to his old associate and a natural desire to protect his own great name. Since he has not yet come forward to correct the curious aberrancies with which Watson's careless writing has saddled him, we can only assume that he has decided on the nobler course.

Nowhere is there a wider discrepancy between Watson's record of a Holmes statement and what was actually said than in **"The Adventure of the Speckled Band."** Here is one of the most important chapters of the Canon; in fact the one most often chosen[1] as the perfect exemplification of all those qualities that have placed the Writings on their deserved pinnacle. Yet the *dénouement,* as given us by Watson, is so fantastically impossible that some other explanation must be forthcoming. We must go beyond the Watsonian transcription for a knowledge of what really happened.

As to my own position in this matter, I had previously concluded that to divulge the facts would lead to results no one could contemplate with composure. To have spoken before would have jeopardized the marital happiness of many a newly appointed Civil servant boarding a P. and O. boat, outward bound for Madras. But now that the British have withdrawn from India, I feel free to disclose the truth. In the past we had been told of "Young ladies refusing eligible matrimonial alliances because they did not like to go to a place [India] so full of snakes."[2] And how much more frequent would have been these blasted weddings, had the prospective brides been aware of hazards more terrible than any snake, whether met within the formal gardens at Benares, or the dank morass of the jungle at Inner Madaripur. At last I welcome the privilege of speaking, now that skilled natives, rather than unaccustomed Europeans, will be called upon to deal with the menace initiated by that calculating scoundrel, the late Dr. Grimesby Roylott of Stoke Moran.

The nature of the creature that snuffed out the life of Julia Stoner, and, two years later, her unlamented stepfather, has long been a puzzle to herpetologists. They have not been satisfied with the accusation leveled at the "swamp adder, the deadliest snake in India" for, of course, there is no such reptile. How Holmes must have recoiled at the Watsonian version of his identification of the creature that glared at the intruders from its vantage point on Dr. Roylott's brow. That, in fact, Holmes did recognize it for what it was, testifies to his profound knowledge of ophiology, a matter of no surprise; for medical jurisprudence abounds in cases of both simulated and disguised snake-bite, with all of which the great detective was familiar. We know that the Holmes library was particularly complete on every phase of toxicology.[3] As of April, 1883, it must have contained such recent works as *The Reptiles of British India,* by Albert C. L. G. Guenther, The Ray Society, London, 1864; *Indian Snakes: An Elementary Treatise on Ophiology,* second edition, by Edward Nicholson, Madras, 1874; *Report on . . . Indian and Australian Snake Poisoning and the Physiological, Chemical, and Microscopical Nature of Snake-Poisons,* by The Commission,[4] "Appointed to Investigate the Subject," Calcutta, 1874; *Descriptive Catalogue of the Reptiles of British India,* by William Theobald, Calcutta, 1876; *The Poisonous Snakes of India [Prepared] for the Use of the Officials and Others Residing in the Indian Empire,* by Joseph Ewart, London, 1878; *Destruction of Life by Snakes, Hydrophobia, etc., in Western India,* by an Ex-Commissioner,[5] London, 1880; and *Indian Snake Poisons, Their Nature and Effects,* by A. J. Wall, London, 1883. But especially Holmes would have had recourse to that authoritative work, published in folio with magnificent colored illustrations by Hindu artists, *The Thanatophidia of India: Being a Description of the Venomous Snakes of the Indian Peninsula,* by J. (afterwards Sir Joseph) Fayrer; London, 1872; second edition, revised and enlarged, London, 1874.

Now the important point is that in none of these more than adequate works in the Holmes library is there any mention of a swamp adder or, indeed, of any kind of adder[6] in India. It might be reasoned that Holmes, with his encyclopedic knowledge in those fields related to crime and death, had lately heard of some snake in India not yet recorded in the scientific treatises of the time. But even today the latest and most authoritative work on the subject[7] fails to mention such a creature.

That the causative agent in the deaths of Julia Stoner and Dr. Roylott could have been no "adder" is immediately apparent to anyone having even the most superficial knowledge of ophiology. It has been carelessly suggested that the reptile was the common Indian snake variously known as Russell's viper, tic-polonga, or daboia (*Vipera russelli russelli*).[8] Nothing could be more incredible. The daboia is a bulky, lethargic snake growing to a length of 5½ feet. We are told by Malcolm Smith (*loc. cit.,* p. 484) that 5-foot specimens are not unusual. Roylott's pet was an adult, for he had kept it in his room not less than 3 years, allowing for a year of training and experimentation prior to the death of Julia Stoner; and these snakes become adults, although they do not reach maximum size, at the age of 3 years. An adult Russell's viper would weigh 4 or 5 pounds, with a bulk that would more than fill a gallon jar. For such a large snake to balance itself on Dr. Roylott's head would be impossible; if for no other reason the weight would have tipped the head back, as "his chin was cocked upward," and the snake would have rested on, and completely hidden, his face, which, we know, was not the case, as "his eyes were fixed in a dreadful, rigid stare."

Nor does this snake answer to the description: "round his brow he had a peculiar yellow band, with brownish speckles"—for Russell's viper is brown, with black-edged dorsal and lateral blotches, as can be seen from Fayrer's plate 11. It is unthinkable that even Watson would have so distorted the description merely to achieve a better title than "The Adventure of the Black-edged Brown-blotched Band." Finally, the symptoms, whether in the case of Julia or the doctor, are not those of daboia poisoning, as may be noted by anyone who cares to consult the authorities for example cases involving some rather gruesome details.[9]

But these discrepancies in the choice of some specific snake are immaterial compared with the basic fact that the culprit could not, by any possibility, have been a snake at all. Consider these obvious absurdities: The creature lives on milk, not the natural food of any snake, and one that it will accept only rarely as a substitute for water, if the latter be unobtainable. It is recalled to the doctor's room by a whistle: how could this be when it is well known that snakes are quite deaf? It is true that they are extraordinarily sensitive to vibrations of the substratum upon which they rest, so they often appear to hear sounds of sufficient magnitude to affect such a vibrator as a box in which they may be kept; but this could not be the case with a snake clinging tenuously to a flimsy bell-rope. Finally, while admitting that a snake might slide down a bell-rope, it could certainly not climb up one, particularly with the lower end swinging loose above the fatal bed. For snakes do not climb—as many think—by twining themselves around an object; they climb by wedging their bodies into any crannies and interstices, taking advantage of every irregularity or protrusion upon which a loop of body may be hooked. It is by this method that they progress rapidly up the rough bark of branching trees or the tangled skein of a vine. And, to add to the difficulty of the Roylott snake, it is required to climb on a cold night, for one tragedy took place when the "wind was howling outside, and the rain was beating and splashing against the windows" and the other when there was "a chill wind blowing in our faces." Central heating, of course, was unheard of then; and we know that no grate fire[10] was burning in either room at the time of the final fatality because Holmes insisted "We must sit without a light. He [Roylott] would see it through the ventilator"; and after midnight, when the doctor's stealthy activities began, there was a "momentary gleam of light up in the direction of the ventilator." So we have a creature performing the—for it—impossible feat of climbing a loose bell-rope at a temperature at which an ectothermic ani-

mal, such as a snake, would be practically comatose. There are eleven other reasons, evident to any beginner in ophiology, why the theory of a snake having caused either death is untenable, but I shall not labor the subject. A small work of my own upon the principles involved can be seen at the British Museum.

It will be remembered that, after the departure of the pugnacious doctor from Baker Street, when Holmes had straightened the poker again, he set off for Doctors' Commons. He returned at one o'clock and reported to Watson upon some unimportant details of the late Mrs. Roylott's will. Now obviously he would have had this from the Recorder's office. Then why Doctors' Commons; what did he learn there of the sinister doctor's Indian career? Did he only verify Miss Stoner's tale of the robberies in the house and the death of the butler?

Were it not for a fortunate coincidence, I should be as much at sea as Watson, but now I know that Holmes had been engaged in more definitive researches. Not long ago I was ferreting out the literature of reptile hybridization preparatory to reporting on a captive-bred hybrid rattlesnake,[11] when a name attached to an old reference in the Zoological Abstracts caught my eye. Roylott, G. appeared familiar, but I could not place the connection. The title "Hybridization on the Suborder Level" seemed near enough to my field of interest to warrant study, and after some correspondence I found myself in possession of a bibliofilm copy of the doctoral thesis of Griscom[12] Roylott (Cand. Med.), 1855. I shall not weary the reader with technicalities; let it suffice that Roylott was an advanced worker in the field of hybridization barriers. Some of his experiments in artificial fertilization were amazing for that day, and there was to be noted a flair for involved research that made one wonder why the name Roylott was not more frequently met in the bibliographies. How curious are the patterns of memory! It was at a concert devoted to the di Lasso motets that I first connected this Roylott with the Canon. I need hardly say that despite the late hour I had the film threaded into the reading machine, and the Writings open at **"The Adventure of the Speckled Band"** as soon as I reached home.

Space does not permit my citing the confirmatory evidence found in the thesis except that the author concludes, in detailing the results of some experiments with the European green lizard and the grass snake: "and the fact that a viable embryo made its appearance would lead to the belief that the hybridization of even such diverse animals as *Heloderma horridum*[13] and *Naia tripudians*[14] is by no means impossible. What a creature that would be!"

How Roylott was enabled to carry on his researches after his arrival in India we do not know. Without question the gypsies formed the line of communication through which he secured his Mexican specimens. We may look with doubt upon the report of his beating his butler to death because of "robberies which had been perpetrated in the house"; clearly the butler had learned of the success of the doctor's frightful experiments and was engaged in blackmail. And as to that poor girl, the young widow of Major-General Stoner, we can only imagine her loathing upon discovering the character of her second husband. We may even visualize the true nature of the so-called accident that led to her untimely demise on the railway near Crewe.

Whether some of the offspring of the foul miscegenation perpetrated by Dr. Roylott ever escaped and became established in the wild is not definitely known, but there are three evidences that they did: First, Sherlock Holmes had heard rumors of some such creature and verified its existence by his fortunate find of a copy of the thesis on a tip from Doctors' Commons. Secondly, we know that Roylott secured one or more specimens after his release from prison, and was able to bring them to England; these must have resulted from the pre-confinement experiments. And, finally, there are reports of deaths from the bite of an exceedingly active and venomous lizard emanating from an ever-widening circle of localities around Ghatal, including Kharar, Khirpai, and even as far west as Chandrakona. No doubt it was somewhere in this vicinity, not far from Calcutta, that Dr. Roylott maintained his laboratories.

It is to be hoped that the new Government will take the necessary steps to extirpate this menace. For we have here a sinister combination—a creature uniting the intelligence and agility of the lizard with the inimical disposition of the snake. It has fangs in the upper jaw inherited from one parent, and in the lower jaw from the other,[15] and a venom incomparably strengthened by hybridization, thus assuring the almost instant demise of any victim. Here we have an animal that would feed on the batter that was mistaken for milk, for so does its parent, the Gila monster; one with ears like any lizard, wherewith to hear a whistle; and one whose legs and claws permitted it to run up a bell-rope as readily as down, especially when it knew there was the warmth of a coal-oil dark lantern awaiting its return to the doctor's room. Here was a reptile that would be handled with a noose on a dog switch; whereas any snake handler would have used a stick terminated with a hook. And, above all, when we combine the cobra and heloderm the result is certain to assume the likeness of a speckled band.

Which brings us at last to the explanation of all the inexplicable points in the Canon—Watson's characteristic inaccuracies. What Holmes didn't say was, as reported by Watson: "It is a swamp adder, the deadliest snake in India." On the contrary, what he did say was "It is a *samp-aderm*,[16] the deadliest skink[17] in India." Watson

evidently transliterated Holmes's words on the theory that what seemed to him a slurred pronunciation was the result of Holmes's horror at sight of the speckled band. But Holmes, as usual, was being coldly accurate in employing a composite name for a hybrid creature not yet known to science.

Notes

1. *The Baker Street Journal,* Vol. I, p. 457. Here it is placed at the top of the merit lists of both Watson's literary agent, Canon Doyle, and the Baker Street Irregulars.

2. Surgeon-General W. B. Beatson, discussing the paper entitled "On Serpent-Worship and on the Venomous Snakes of India and the Mortality Caused by Them" read by Sir Joseph Fayrer before the Victoria Institute, 7 March, 1892 [*vide* Trans. Vict. Inst., Vol. 26, p. 106].

3. "Well up . . . in poisons generally." *A Study in Scarlet.*

4. Composed of J. Ewart, Pres., Vincent Richards, and S. Coull Mackenzie. Richards subsequently published *The Landmarks of Snake-Poison Literature,* Calcutta, 1885; second edition, 1886. Of the earlier edition I have a copy, indited on the title page "Edwin O. Milward, M.A., Surgeon Medical Staff, Camp V/B, R.H.d., Mustaphabad, Punjab, Dec. 1885." Milward was somewhat skeptical of Richards' conclusions, certain of his marginal notes reading "Draw it mild old chappie," "yah-yah," and "pulling his leg." His last raucous comment was induced by Richards' having repeated the ancient story of the lady who awoke one morning to find her infant pushed aside by a snake that had replaced the child at her breast. Richards, of course, didn't believe this myth and merely repeated it as having been told him by an Englishman who did. Milward was frankly skeptical that anyone could be so simple-minded as this anonymous Englishman. This leads us to conclude that Milward's and Watson's paths had never crossed in India, despite the similarity of their callings.

5. My copy of this work contains this dedication written on the fly-leaf: "To the Misses Winch from the Author." Why the continued anonymity, even with his friends the Winches? Can this be connected with the reasons for his being an Ex? Has anyone the Winch address so I may make further enquiries?

6. A rather loose term at best. The European vipers (*Vipera berus*) are often called adders, as are the African venomous snakes of the genera *Causus* and *Bitis*. In Australia there is the death adder (*Acanthophis antarcticus*). In the United States the harmless hog-nose snakes (*Heterodon*) are frequently referred to as puff or blowing adders.

7. *The Fauna of British India, Ceylon and Burma. Reptilia and Amphibia, Vol. III, Serpentes,* by Malcolm A. Smith, London, 1943.

8. "Dr. Roylott's Wily Fillip" by Rolfe Boswell, *The Baker Street Journal,* Vol. 1, p. 307.

9. George Lamb and William Hanna: "Some Observations on the Poison of Russell's Viper"; Scientific Memoirs by Officers of the Medical and Sanitary Departments of the Government of India, no. 3, Calcutta, 1903 (see p. 37); Hideo Noguchi: *Snake Venoms,* Washington, 1909 (see pp. 108, 135); Major Frank Wall: *The Poisonous Terrestrial Snakes of Our British Indian Dominions (including Ceylon) and How to Recognize Them. With Symptoms of Snake Poisoning and Treatment,* fourth edition, Bombay, 1928 (see pp. 102-114).

10. There was a grate in each room; that in Miss Stoner's room is referred to as "a gaping fireplace" and the doctor's room was a duplicate.

11. *Crotalus viridis oreganus* x *Crotalus ruber.* The result looks surprisingly like *Crotalus scutulatus scutulatus.* See also "An Integeneric Hybrid Rattlesnake" by Reeve M. Bailey, in *American Naturalist,* Vol. 76, pp. 376-385, 1942.

12. I am unable to explain this discrepancy; Watson, again, I presume.

13. The Mexican Gila monster; with *Heloderma suspectum,* the Arizona Gila monster, the only known poisonous lizards.

14. The spectacled or Indian cobra, now known as *Naja naja naja.*

15. Strangely, the Gila monster's venom glands and fangs are in the lower jaw, thus differing from all poisonous snakes.

16. May be translated "snake-Gila-monster." *Samp,* is Hindustani for snake; for example, the banded krait is *raj samp* (Fayrer, *loc. cit.,* p. 10) and the Indian cobra *nag samp* (Nicholson, *loc. cit.* p. 133). Richards (*loc. cit.*) refers to snake catchers as *samp-wallahs* (p. 34), and to the mythical two-headed snake as *do morkhka samp* (p. 21), which Milward, in a marginal note, corrects to *do mookha ka samp.* The derivation of the suffix *aderm* from heloderm, the common or vernacular name of the Gila monster generally used by European naturalists, is self-evident.

17. Skinks are smooth-scaled lizards of the family Scincidae, many of which are swift in movement and snake-like in form. The little blue-tailed skink of the United States is often mistaken for a snake, but has well-developed legs.

William Baring-Gould (essay date September 1965)

SOURCE: Baring-Gould, William. "The Problem of the Speckled Band." *Baker Street Journal* 15, no. 3 (September 1965): 167-73.

[*In the following essay, Baring-Gould outlines the speculations of several prominent Sherlock Holmes scholars concerning the exact species of the snake in Doyle's short story.*]

"'It is a swamp adder!' cried Holmes—'the deadliest snake in India.'"

"Unfortunately, the name 'swamp adder' is not now in common use. It may be an obsolete vernacular name from some early work of natural history now forgotten; or it may be a purely local name, acquired by Holmes from one of his cosmopolitan acquaintances, in which case it is unlikely to appear in any standard work of reference. The identity of the snake must therefore be deduced from such information as we possess on its appearance and behaviour."—*Sherlock Holmes; Catalogue of an Exhibition Held at Abbey House, Baker Street, London, May-September 1951,* pp. 24-25.

Let us therefore consider the data describing Dr. Roylott's messenger of death, as Watson has recorded it [in **"The Adventure of the Speckled Band"**], and the conclusions that certain eminent Sherlockians have reached after studying that data.

1. HOLMES CALLED THE SNAKE AN INDIAN SWAMP ADDER

"There is a widespread belief that [the puff adder, *Bitis Arietans*] was the snake intended. The fact that it is African in origin does not disqualify it, since there is only circumstantial evidence that the snake was Indian. (In this connection it should be noted that Dr. Roylott also kept a baboon; apart from the small black baboon (*Cynopithecus niger*) of Celebes, baboons are confined to Africa and Arabia.) However, the lethargic nature of this snake, its relatively slow-acting venom, and its striking markings (which could not reasonably be described, even by Julia Stoner immediately after being bitten, as speckled) seem to rule it out. Apart from the sea-snakes (*Hydrophiidae*) of the Indian coasts, whose flat oar-like tails would seem to preclude them from negotiating bell-ropes, there are no truly aquatic venemous snakes in India. Holmes's use of the term 'swamp adder' has caused some investigators to suggest the damp-loving river-jack vipers of the African rain-forests (*Bitis nasicornis* and *B. gabonica*); but these must be ruled out for precisely the same reasons as the puff adder."—*Abbey House Catalogue.*

2. ITS FANGS LEFT "TWO LITTLE DARK PUNCTURES" IN ITS VICTIMS

"The only snakes that kill by poison fangs in India are divided . . . into two families—the *Elapidae* and the

Viperidie. One of the major differences between those families is the difference in the poison fangs. In *Elapidae* the relatively short fangs lie in the front of the jaw, and, on contact, eject poison into the victim—*but not in killing amounts.* After the ejection of the poison, the series of frontal teeth and four half-jaws pull the drugged victim closer to its attacker, and the poison fangs, embedded repeatedly, eject new quantities of poison at each contact. The result to an observer is that a victim of *Elapidae*'s poison has a series of marks where the poison fangs have embedded themselves time and again. In *Viperidie,* the poison fangs are much larger, and when not in use lie in the roof of the mouth at the back of the head. When the Viper attacks, these poison fangs extend beyond the mouth and make the first contact with the victim; and only one contact. . . . Thus a victim poisoned by *Viperidie* has only two puncture marks, and this was what Holmes and Watson found when they examined the body of Dr. Roylott. We have therefore established that Dr. Roylott's messenger of death was an Indian viper."—Douglas Lawson, "The Speckled Band—What Is It?" BSJ [*Baker Street Journal*] (NS) 4:12-20, 1954.

3. In Color It Was Yellow with Brown Specks

"Of the numerous Viper families throughout the world, there are but two poisonous varieties in India . . . the Russell's Viper [*Russelli Elegans*] and [the saw-scaled viper] *Echis Carinata.* Of these two snakes, the most prolific and the most featured in Indian snake-lore is the Russell's viper—consider the popularity of its names: Tic Polonga, *Daboia Russelli, Daboia Elegans,* Chain Viper, Uloo Borra, Siahchunder Amata—and Russell's Viper. In contrast, Echis Carinata has only one pseudonym. The descriptions differ slightly, *Echis Carinata* being described by Dr. [Raymond Lee] Ditmars (*Snakes of the World,* New York: The Macmillan Co., 1931) as: 'The body is browning-gray with three longitudinal series of whitish black-edged spots,' whereas *Russelli Elegans* is described as a pale brown body, with three longitudinal series of black rings, centered with a chocolate brown and ringed in a frame of white and yellow. Nevertheless, to the layman, a young Tic Polonga would be identical with a full-grown *Echis Carinata.* . . . To the uninitiated, a close study [of pictures of the two reptiles] would still leave you in doubt, so closely are their markings identical."—Lawson, pp. 17-18, 20.

"Its [Russell's Viper's] markings, however, seem unsuitable: the characteristic rings are unmistakable and, while Julia Stoner might conceivably have described it as 'spotted,' it can hardly be regarded as speckled. Moreover, it is not naturally a climber; it . . . is lethargic in habit, and, though if pushed through the ventilator it would no doubt have climbed *down* the bell-rope, it is most improbable that it would ever have climbed up again."—*Abbey House Catalogue,* p. 25.

"[*Echis Carinata*], though typically a desert snake, is also a possibility, if only because its marking is less striking than that of Russell's viper. It shares, however, the same disadvantages: its slow-acting venom and its disinclination to climb."—*Abbey House Catalogue,* p. 25.

"[*Bungarus magnimaculatus,* the krait] possesses a 'neurotoxic' venom, one that acts on the nervous system, and acts in consequence more quickly [than does 'haemotoxic' venom, *i.e.,* one that acts on the blood system; both the Russell's Viper and *Echis Carinata* have haemotoxic venom]; death could well occur within an hour of being bitten and might, if accompanied by severe shock, be even more rapid. The striking banded design does not necessarily debar it from consideration, since . . . the lighter bands may themselves show dark specks: the snake may in fact be said to be marked with a series of speckled bands. This would not, however, tally with Watson's 'Round his brow he had a peculiar yellow band, with brownish speckles . . .'; furthermore, though the krait must perhaps be regarded as a serious possibility, it is doubtful whether its behaviour would be appropriate."—*Abbey House Catalogue,* p. 26.

4. Its Hiss Was "Gentle" and "Soothing, Like That of a Small Jet of Steam Escaping from a Tea-Kettle"

"Russell's Viper hisses with each inhalation and expulsion of its breath, and contrary to Dr. Watson's testimony, it's a very loud hiss. . . . Actually, this savage and relentless alarm is audible thirty feet away."—Rolfe Boswell, "Dr. Roylott's Wily Fillip," BSJ (OS) 1:307-311, 1946.

"The Russell's Viper is silent until thoroughly aroused, and then hisses violently on both the outgo and intake of its breath. The hissing of a Tic Polonga would have boomed on the Doctor's eardrums. Therefore, the Doctor did *not* hear the hissing of a Russell's Viper. However, the ophidologists agree on one snake that answers the description as though it were a tape recording: *Echis Carinata* probably does not hiss at all, but in any excitement, he emits a sibilant sound by the constant rubbing together of his scales as he coils and twists his lithe body, and the sound to the listener is 'that of steam escaping from a tea kettle.'"—Lawson, p. 19.

5. It Was Perhaps Three Feet in Length

"The average length of a Russell's Viper is a strong four to five feet. Since the circumference of Dr. Roylott's head probably was not more than 27 inches, it would seem that a Russell's Viper must have encircled that head twice, still allowing room to park its neck in the Roylott scalp. Surely Dr. Watson would not have described such a voluminous headpiece as a 'speckled band.' What, then, could he have seen? The *Echis Cari-nata,* attaining a length of two to three feet, and a very much thinner snake than its bigger counterpart, would have answered photographically Dr. Watson's descrip-tion."—Lawson, pp. 19-20.

6. ITS BITE CAUSED DEATH "WITHIN TEN SECONDS" IN THE CASE OF DR. ROYLOTT

"The murderous medico's fatal reaction to the virulent venom appears to have been quicker than is to be ex-pected."—Boswell, p. 309.

"It was impossible for Dr. Roylott to have died in the time allotted him in the Saga from the bite of *any* known species of snake. . . . We now reach our final picture—the terrible killer, sitting with his dark lantern, tensely waiting to find out if he had killed again. Sud-denly the silence is shattered by Holmes's cries and the slashing at the bell-rope. Through the darkened hole slithers the venomous head of the enraged viper. It draws back to strike, and Dr. Roylott's heart, already enfeebled by angina pectoris, suffers the convulsion of a tremendous thrombosis, calling forth a scream of agony heard round the village—and the *Echis Carinata* embeds its fangs in a dead man."—Lawson, pp. 18-19, 20.

"No snake-bite would kill in so short a time as ten sec-onds; and we may say with complete confidence that Dr. Roylott must still have been alive when Holmes and Watson entered his room. It would be most interesting to know what remedial steps, if any, Watson took, and why he has thought fit to suppress any reference to his actions in this respect."—*Abbey House Catalogue,* p. 27.

7. BUT DR. ROYLOTT'S DEATH "WITHIN TEN SECONDS" IS INCONSISTENT WITH THE FATE OF JULIA STONER, WHO "SLOWLY SANK AND DIED WITHOUT HAVING RECOVERED HER CONSCIOUSNESS"

"The reader of the Saga will note how carefully Dr. Watson has avoided a time-table of the death scene; but we may speak with authority when we state that it was some hours after the attack before she succumbed. . . . A quick demise for Julia . . . is in no way borne out by the written word."—Lawson, p. 18.

"There had presumably been no change in snake."—*Abbey House Catalogue,* p. 27.

"Why was Dr. Roylott's death so much more rapid than Miss Stoner's? Was it, perhaps, the less-toxic bamboo viper which had killed the step-daughter, then suc-cumbed to England's steak-and-kidney-pie climate, only to be replaced later by the deadlier Russell's Viper?"—Boswell, p. 309.

"In spite of the sloppy work of the local coroner, Julia Stoner unquestionably died from the poison of a viper, for in every report which I have examined, the bite of the *Echis Carinata* would not bring death to animal or human. In that the bite of *Echis Carinata* is not fatal, and in that the whole description, slightly dandified for the reading public of 1890, is that of a person struck by the poison fangs of a *Tic Polonga,* we can say without fear of contradiction that we have established that Julia Stoner was killed by the bite of a Russell's Viper. . . . The snake which struck Dr. Roylott was not the *Rus-selli Elegans* which had killed Julia Stoner two years previously. For, as a clincher, we have no record of a Russell's Viper living more than a year in captivity."—Lawson, pp. 18, 19-20.

8. IT HAD A "SQUAT, DIAMOND-SHAPED HEAD"

"This is true to a greater or lesser extent of practically all snakes."—*Abbey House Catalogue,* p. 25.

9. IT HAD A "PUFFED NECK"

"[*Naja naja,* the cobra] must be regarded as the most probable solution. The cobra is extremely variable in colour, but forms with brown speckles on a yellow background are common. It is a ubiquitous animal and though not typically aquatic might well enter swamps in search of food. It is an extremely active and—as snakes go—intelligent snake; it would be quite likely not only to climb down the bell-rope but also up again—it is in fact one of the very few snakes that might be expected so to behave. It too has a neurotoxic venom. Finally, we may return to Watson's descrip-tion. . . . The habit of rearing almost vertically when roused is very characteristic of the cobra. In general, it would appear that the cobra is the only snake which completely satisfies the requirements."—*Abbey House Catalogue,* p. 26.

"Unfortunately for [Dr. Watson's] accuracy, neither the Russell's Viper nor *Echis Carinata* is capable of enlarg-ing its short, squat neck other than to swallow its vic-tims. How, then, could the Doctor say he had seen such a manifestation? Obviously, through self-hypnosis. . . . [The performance of the Indian snake-charmers] must have been seen by Dr. Watson so many times that he came to associate all the snakes in the basket with the more prominent dancing of the hooded cobras."—Law-son, pp. 16-17.

10. IT FED ON MILK

"No snake drinks milk from choice, though it may do so if it is thirsty and water is not available; Dr. Roylott evidently shared the popular misapprehension in this matter."—*Abbey House Catalogue,* p. 27.

"[Milk is] not the natural food of any snake, and one that it will accept only rarely as a substitute for water, if the latter be unobtainable."—Laurence M. Klauber, "The Truth about the Speckled Band," BSJ (OS) 3: 149-157, 1948.

"I asked Dr. [William M.] Mann [curator of the Zoological Park in Washington, D.C.] the direct question: 'Will a snake in captivity drink milk?' He seemed very surprised and said, 'Why, certainly.' I then said, 'Dr. Mann, can you state this on your personal knowledge?' He said, 'Why, of course I can. I have seen dozens of them drink milk.'"—Lawson, p. 14.

11. It Climbed up and down a Bell-Pull

"The temple-vipers (species of *Trimeresurus*) have . . . been suggested by some authorities, since they are tree-climbers with prehensile tails. They are, however, brilliantly-coloured creatures (often green, sometimes with red tails), and such colouring could hardly have escaped attention."—*Abbey House Catalogue*, p. 26.

"While admitting that a snake might slide down a bell-rope, it could certainly not climb up one, particularly with the lower end swinging loose above the fatal bed. For snakes do not climb—as many think—by twining themselves around an object; they climb by wedging their bodies into any crannies and interstices, taking advantage of every irregularity or protrusion upon which a loop of body may be hooked. It is by this method that they progress rapidly up the rough bark of branching trees or the tangled skein of a vine. And, to add to the difficulty of the Roylott snake, it is required to climb on a cold night. . . . An ectothermic animal, such as a snake, would be practically comatose."—Klauber, pp. 153-154.

12. It Responded to a Whistle

"This is most improbable; for snakes are deaf to ordinary sounds, and will only respond to relatively violent vibration. However, Dr. Roylott was evidently remarkably gifted in the care and handling of snakes. It could be no easy matter to keep a cobra alive and well for some months in an iron safe, an environment which even to so adaptable an animal as the cobra must be regarded as distinctly abnormal; and his practice of depositing it therein and withdrawing it at will must have required considerable skill and some agility if he was not himself to be bitten."—*Abbey House Catalogue*, p. 27.

"[The snake] is recalled to the doctor's room by a whistle: how could this be when it is well known that snakes are quite deaf? It is true that they are extraordinarily sensitive to vibrations of the substratum upon which they rest, so they often appear to hear sounds of

sufficient magnitude to affect such a vibrator as a box in which they may be kept; but this could not be the case with a snake clinging tenuously to a flimsy bell-rope."—Klauber, p. 153.

* * *

We may sum up the opinions of these authorities thus:

	Death of Julia Stoner	Death of Dr. Roylott
Abbey House	Cobra	Cobra
Mr. Boswell	Bamboo Viper	Russell's Viper
Mr. Lawson	Russell's Viper	Saw-scaled Viper (*Echis Carinata*)

It is nevertheless apparent that *no known species of snake satisfies all the requirements.*

Mr. Klauber, who believes that "when you have eliminated the impossible, whatever remains, *however improbable,* must be the truth," has suggested that the animal that killed Julia Stoner and Dr. Roylott was a *hybrid,* bred by the Doctor in India. Holmes, he maintains, said, not "swamp-adder," but "samp-aderm": "*Samp* is Hindustani for snake, . . . the suffix *aderm* [derives] from *heloderm,* the common or vernacular name of the Gila monster generally used by European naturalists. . . . For here we have a sinister combination—a creature uniting the intelligence and agility of the lizard with the inimical disposition of the snake. It has fangs in the upper jaw inherited from one parent, and in the lower jaw from the other, and a venom incomparably strengthened by hybridization, thus assuring the almost instant demise of any victim. Here we have an animal that would feed on the batter that was mistaken for milk, for so does its parent, the Gila monster; one with ears like any lizard, wherewith to hear a whistle; and one whose legs and claws permitted it to run up a bell-rope as readily as down" (p. 156).

T. F. Foss and J. M. Linsenmeyer (essay date June 1977)

SOURCE: Foss, T. F. and J. M. Linsenmeyer. "Look to the Lady." *Baker Street Journal* 27, no. 2 (June 1977): 79-85.

[*In the following essay, Foss and Linsenmeyer maintain that the character Helen Stoner, Dr. Roylott's stepdaughter, staged the events of "The Adventure of the Speckled Band" to secure her inheritance of the family estate.*]

Few villains of the double-dyed variety came to a more deserved end at the hands of Holmes than the unspeakable Dr. Roylott in **"The Speckled Band."**. Or was that so? Was the good Doctor (Roylott, not Watson) one of the most sinister sinners in Victorian times? Let us analyse the story his step-daughter Helen Stoner told Holmes.

For a start, Helen's mother married Dr. Roylott 30 years prior to the interview with Holmes, when her twin daughters by her first husband, Major-General Stoner, were 2 years old. With his usual inattention to detail, Watson puts the age of Helen Stoner as being 30 at the time of the interview, although Helen subsequently disclosed her twin sister, Julia, died at the age of 30, just two years before *l'affaire Speckled Band,* which would then make Helen 32.

We do not quite know when, according to Helen, Dr. Roylott's uncontrollable temper caused him to beat his "native butler" to death, but it is reasonable to assume from the ages of his twin stepdaughters and the length of his post-imprisonment stay in England that it would have been within three or four years after his marriage. For his crime he received a long imprisonment, having narrowly missed hanging. Under section 302 of the Indian Penal Code[1] the punishment he was given could not have been less than life, in reality 20 years,[2] and with his arrogant attitude it is unlikely that he would have earned any remission and would have served the whole sentence. Yet during all this time Mrs. Roylott and her two daughters stayed in India until they all returned Home *en famille* some 20 or more years later.

This strange fidelity on the part of Mrs. Roylott inspired the authors to make a far more critical examination of Helen's whole story to Holmes. It is fair to say that this examination quickly raised a host of problems, to the extent that it seems clear that Holmes was in fact humbugged by Miss Stoner.

The first minor puzzle in her saga is why Helen Stoner referred to the slain servant as a "native butler." She had lived in India most of her life, and in the argot of the sahibs the chief servant in a household was the "bearer." A young miss-sahib who had spent the whole of her life up to young womanhood in India would think and refer to an upper servant as such. Had she used the term "native butler" for Holmes's enlightenment it was quite unnecessary, since at hand was John H. Watson, M.D., late Indian Army,[3] to effect the necessary translation.

But, as frequently occurs, this minor discrepancy merely calls attention to the fatal flaws in her tale.

A second puzzle, of psychological import, is why Mrs. Roylott stayed in India when her husband was languishing in jail. It was not for financial reasons. In prison her husband would have no means of supporting her while she, on the other hand, was well-off with an income of over a thousand pounds per year, presumably derived from dividends from the capital her first husband, the Major-General, had invested. (Her annual income would not include the military pension of a General Officer's widow as that would cease on her remarriage.) This indicates that she had a substantial capital sum for the 1880's, the interest from which she bequeathed to her second husband in its entirety provided a certain sum was set aside for her two daughters in the event of their marriage. Why, in heaven's name? It is quite impossible to believe she continued to be besotted by him after he had shown his true colours. Love is all very well, but there are limits. Admittedly divorce carried a severe social stigma in the 1880's, but it must have been preferable to being tied to a brutal killer. If she had taken the plunge and instituted divorce proceedings she would have received much sympathy as the innocent wronged party. Anyhow, even if she had shrunk from divorce, she had the means to have left her cad of a husband mouldering in an Indian jail while she returned to the U.K. with her daughters to live in reasonable comfort in Cheltenham, Budleigh, Slaterton, or Camberley.

Think of the miserable life she and her daughters must have lived in the narrow and censorious confines of Calcutta European society, where *burra memsahibs* were few and gossip was the main means of passing the time. If she had not been completely ostracised the best she could have hoped for would be innuendoes or patronising protestations of sympathy every time she appeared in the European clubs, which were the only places she could have gone if she was not always to stay in her own bungalow. Women were, no doubt, expected to be submissive to their lords and masters, but Mrs. Roylott's attitude to hers was (the word is used advisedly) ridiculous. Not only did she cling, but she made him free of her cash as well. That a lady of such a weak will ever existed even in Victorian times is hard to believe. It says little for what Watson calls his friend's "rapid deductions, as swift as intuitions, yet always founded on a logical basis"[4] that Holmes did not probe deeper into this aspect of Helen Stoner's tale.

Then again there was that incredible remark of Helen's that after her mother's death there seemed no obstacle to her and her sister "living in happiness" with her step-father. Happiness indeed, with a man who (according to Helen's own story) was not only a brutal killer but who had returned to England "morose" and "disappointed" and was a ruffian "notorious in the county." She must have been as feeble-witted as her mother to have thought that.

Clearly, however, the single most peculiar feature of Helen's story was the alleged instrumentality of two deaths, the snake called the Speckled Band.

First, let us consider the tragic death of Miss Julia Stoner two years earlier. According to Helen, her passing was marked by the "whistle" and the metallic "clanging" (of the iron safe) which Holmes quickly and in melodramatic terms associated with the snake. Moreover, said Helen, the authorities were so suspicious of the circumstances of the death that they examined the body for poison and examined the walls and the foundations of the house for secret passages. The coroner allegedly conducted a detailed *post mortem*; in Helen's words:

> He investigated the case with great care, for Dr. Roy-lott's conduct had long been notorious in the county, but he was unable to find any satisfactory cause of death. . . . Besides, there were no marks of any violence upon her.

Now just a minute! One does not have to be Sir Bernard Spillsbury to know that there is a little more to a fatal snake bite than "the two little dark punctures" Holmes suggested.

All snake venom is either neurotoxic or haemotoxic. Most types of venom are haemotoxic, and act through blood cell destruction, visceral haemorrhage and liquification or alteration of capillaries. Thus, cases of snake bite involving haemotoxic venom are marked by very severe local reactions, including swelling and ecchymosis (vivid black-and-blue discoloration), as well as by haemorrhages from mucosal linings of the mouth, bladder, viscera, and even eyes. Of course, in cases where the bite is severe enough to be fatal, these symptoms would be *more* prominent and, it seems fair to say, hard to miss.

The proteroglyphous snakes (those having fixed as opposed to hinged fangs), including the whole cobra family, have neurotoxic venom, which acts somewhat more quickly than the haemotoxic. But the symptoms are likewise unmistakable, involving severe systemic reactions unlikely in natural illness, including facial and ocular muscle paralysis and excess salivation.

In addition, all snake venoms contain bacteria, particularly including tetanus and gas gangrene, which are not present at the normal natural death.

Yet Helen would have Holmes (and us) believe that a mature woman was killed by snakebite; the symptoms went unnoticed despite (*a*) the "great care" with which the coroner "investigated" the death, and (*b*) the "medical aid from the village" prior to her death. Surely this is unlikely.

But the worst anomalies come in the account of Dr. Roylott's *mode d'emploi* of his deadly pet. According to Helen's deductions, the snake—

(1) lived in an iron safe *which had no airholes or other openings*;[5]

(2) was apparently odourless—those accustomed to the aroma of reptiles living in confined quarters would doubtless give much to learn the secret by which a three-foot-long snake was kept in a box (safe or not) in a bedroom without producing olfactory evidence thereof;

(3) drank milk;

(4) answered to his owner's whistle;

(5) scurried up and down a bell-rope;

(6) was apparently so tractable that its owner could handle him (even with a noose) without being bitten, yet would bite a sleeping girl!

At this point, it seemed only too clear that Helen's entire story was a farrago of nonsense, designed for the obvious purpose of covering up her own criminal enterprises.[6] According to the experts, the snake described by Helen is impossible by reason of its rope-climbing, its diet, and its instantaneous deadliness.[7] But just as it seemed to the authors that Helen was hoist with her own petard, the following account came to light, from an irreproachable source. Frank Richards wrote an account of his Great War experiences called *Old Soldiers Never Die*, which was such a success that Robert Graves, the Poet Laureate, persuaded him to write a similar account of his experiences in the Army in India. This book, *Old Soldier Sahib*, contains the following account of the purchase by Richards' friends, from an Indian bazaar rascal, of what was supposed to be a harmless grass-snake as a pet:

> In anticipation of the snake's arrival Yank had a small wooden box made at the Pioneer's shop, with a sliding glass side and holes punched in the top. He also *bought some milk to give it a feed,* as he thought it would be hungry after its capture. . . . Yank said that Abdullah, who had arrived with it in a cloth just after seven, had told him that according to the snake-catcher it was a very rare variety of grass-snake and dirt-cheap at a rupee. *It seemed listless at first but after a feed of milk it grew lively* and in less than no time Yank was handling it as if he had had it for years.

> . . . Just after the Battalion had moved off to church I persuaded Yank to bring his pet along to a man called Ogden [who] . . . was an authority on snakes and could reel off the names of the different species and varieties as easy as a child with its A.B.C.

> As soon as Ogden saw it, his face changed colour and he took a few quick paces backward. Then he said: "For Heaven's sake, Corporal, don't ask me any questions, but do exactly as I tell you. Put that thing back in your handkerchief. Now lay it under your heel and crush it to death."

> Ogden's frightened face put the wind up me, but Yank kept his nerve. Without a word of protest he did exactly as he was told. When he removed his heel we found that he had crushed the little snake's head to a pulp.

After Ogden had examined the corpse he said: "Well, Corporal, I don't know how the hell you are still alive, but I am very glad that you are. I have handled live cobras in my time but I would not have attempted to handle this pretty little thing, not while it was alive, for all the wealth in the world. *Look, it's no thicker than my little finger but it's one of the deadliest creatures in the whole of India. If it had bitten you, you would have been dead in less than two minutes. It's rare, too.* I first heard of the species about ten years ago from an old snake-charmer, but I never saw a specimen until to-day. I recognized the markings at once, from an illustrated book on snakes I have, that cost me a lot of money to buy." He went inside the Canteen and brought the book out to us. Then he found us the picture of the snake (the name of which I have forgotten) which corresponded in every detail with the one that had just been killed. The writing underneath said: "One of the rarest and deadliest of Oriental snakes" [emphasis added].

Clearly, then, a case against Helen cannot be predicated simply upon the non-existence of the snake. But proper consideration of the facts only provides a deeper appreciation of her cleverness. Coroners might be duped (as in the case of Julia's death[8]) by ersatz snake bites, but not Holmes. This points up an important distinction: Holmes knew a great deal about forensic medicine (remember Stamford's horror at his attempts to produce *post mortem* lividity), but he knew absolutely nothing about India. He could quickly determine whether a death was caused by snake venom, but he had no opportunity to learn what Indian snakes can or cannot do.

Helen was acute enough to recognize this and so produced a genuine snake, but duped Holmes with the whole rest of the story. Snakes are deaf, so they cannot answer whistles. Snakes do not climb by looping themselves around an object but by wedging their bodies into crannies and interstices, so this snake could not scurry up and down a bell-pull.

The amazing thing is not that the young Holmes[9] was deceived by the snake business, but that he appears never to have suspected the obvious culprit, based on motive. He virtually cackles at his discovery that under Mrs. Stoner Roylott's will the good Doctor would lose £250 if Helen married, and calls this "the very strongest motive." But by the same will, all these deaths led to Helen's collecting the whole inheritance! For all that Helen appeared "weary and haggard," something about her must have appealed to the great misogynist.

In conclusion, then, it is obvious that Dr. Grimesby Roylott, unpleasant character as he undoubtedly was, was not the villain of the piece, but the innocent victim of Helen herself. And the word "obvious" was chosen intentionally: think of what Holmes and Watson saw and heard in the bedrooms of Stoke Moran Manor House the night Roylott came to his untimely end, even forgetting for the moment who would gain from his death. Helen was a woman of 32 and not a particularly attractive one at that. Even the well-known admirer of feminine beauty, Watson, had little to say about her looks. ("Her face was drawn and grey . . . her hair was shot with premature grey . . . her expression was weary and haggard.") For a plain single woman of 32 in Victorian days this was not a happy state of affairs. The ultimate ambition of every middle-class woman was matrimony. Unless Helen was careful she would find herself on the shelf. Then out of the blue, her boy friend of many years, Percy Armitage, had asked her to marry him. She must have had something more than plainness of features to have made him do that. Money, of course. The £750 a year to which her mother's fortune had now shrunk would be a nice little bait for a second son who could expect little at his father's death and would have to earn his bread by the sweat of his brow in the biblical sense. Three times as big a bait as the £250 a year she would have got if her father remained alive. Not only that, Helen could reasonably have expected to inherit Stoke Moran House on her stepfather's death. The temptation to achieve marital status was irresistible even if it did mean murdering the doctor as well as her sister Julia (for that is what she also did) and possibly her mother as well. Her story of Mrs. Roylott's death in a train crash near Crewe, accepted and unquestioned, is as weak as the rest of her tale. However, on this last point, we will give her the benefit of the doubt. It may well be that her mother's death first put the idea into her head of disposing of her sister and stepfather, the only two lives that stood between her and the whole of her mother's fortune.

And now consider what happened that fateful night at Stoke Moran. Apart from a glimpse of Grimesby Roylott through the window of the Crown Inn at Stoke Moran neither Holmes nor Watson had seen him after his poker-bending efforts at 221B Baker Street. All that remained was to seat the snake on him and then arrange a convincing tableau of death to suggest that Dr. Roylott's plot had backfired. What did Holmes see on entering Dr. Roylott's bedroom? The unfortunate doctor with a swamp adder coiled around his head. Helen first disposed of her stepfather by persuading him to drink an extra strong chota-peg (no difficult task to get a retired Anglo-Indian to do this) which she had dosed with some drug. Then, wearing thick leather gloves, she could have procured the appropriate bite and then tastefully draped the "speckled band" around the dead doctor's brow to await its discovery by a credulous detective.

Apart from anything else, Dr. Roylott's innocence is shown by the iron safe in which the snake was supposed to live. For it to have done so would have meant yet one more unlikely physical attribute to this already extraordinary reptile: its ability to live without air when the iron door of the safe was closed. It will also be remembered that after Holmes had knocked at the doctor's bedroom door he turned the handle and entered. In other words, Roylott had not bothered to lock the door. How singularly careless for a man about to perpetrate a complicated murder to have risked the secrecy this demanded by omitting to lock his bedroom door.

Then there were those off-stage noises heard from Helen's bedroom: as if steam was issuing from the spout of a kettle, a whistle and finally the hoarse yell of pain, fear and anger. The boiling kettle and the whistling could well have had the explanation previously offered, that they were made by the gipsies camped in the grounds who had just returned from a little nocturnal poaching and were brewing-up their supper. As for the yell sounding like fear, pain, and anger, this was clearly made by one of the doctor's other pets, the baboon. It is also clear that this noise never came from inside the Manor House, for it was heard down in the village and in the distant parsonage, raising sleepers from their beds. Obviously it must have been made in the open air, probably by a bored, angry, or possibly lovesick baboon.

There is no need to worry unduly about the end of Dr. Grimesby Roylott. Holmes did not, neither need we. His life-style showed that he deserved all he got. On the other hand, had Holmes delved more logically into Helen's original story it need never have happened. What is worrying is what eventually happened to Percy Armitage after he had married Helen. He would be saddled with a wife who would not think twice of murder if her married life turned out to be not the bed of roses she had expected.

Notes

1. "Whoever commits murder shall be punished with death, or imprisonment for life. . . ." The normal punishment for murder under the Code has always been death, unless extenuating circumstances are present, *Gourishankar v. Gov't*, 68 Bombay Law Reptr. 236 (Bombay High Ct. 1965).

2. "In calculating fractions of terms of imprisonment, imprisonment for life shall be reckoned as equivalent to imprisonment for twenty years." Indian Penal Code, sec. 57.

3. "Thor Bridge" ["The Problem of Thor Bridge"].

4. Strictly speaking, of course, Holmes was almost always logical; his major errors were the product of ignorance or misinformation. On no topic was this archetypical Victorian less informed than on the languages, peoples, places, and doings of the Indian Empire. Stated otherwise, Holmes's syllogisms were impeccable, but his premises were wrong.

5. Regardless of whether he was from time to time humbugged, there can be no doubt that Holmes was a meticulous observer. That the safe was with-

out airholes is ineluctable: if they were on the top or sides, he would have noticed them, and if they were on the bottom, he would have noticed the snake's excreta on the floor. Elementary!

6. While this paper was in the process of preparation, Edward F. Clark, Esq., called the authors' attention to a purported confession by Helen Stoner that she had in fact murdered Roylott, her sister, her mother and her Armitage in-laws [see "An Amazing Epistle—Fact or Forgery?" by Jennifer Chorley, BSJ [*Baker Street Journal*] (NS) 15:165-166, (September) 1965]. Its authenticity is, however, uncertain, so the authors have not in any way relied thereon for authority.

7. See the authorities collected in "It is . . . the Deadliest Snake in India" in Baring-Gould's *Annotated Sherlock Holmes*, Vol. I, pp. 263-66; see also M. Dakin, *A Sherlock Holmes Commentary* (David & Charles, 1972) at pp. 76-79 and S. Moran, *Vermin of Central Hindustan* (Bangalore: Mookerjee Press, 1878).

8. At this distant remove, it is impossible to say just how Julia was killed—a gentle pillow over the face would suffice. Helen's mother, of course, "fell" into the path of a train, so Julia was doubtless leery of railway platforms, at least when her sister was around.

9. Watson himself dates the affair in April 1883, so Holmes was just 29.

Bruce Harris (essay date June 1983)

SOURCE: Harris, Bruce. "You Can Teach a Speckled Band New Tricks." *Baker Street Journal* 33, no. 2 (June 1983): 95-6.

[*In the following essay, Harris concentrates on the techniques Dr. Roylott might have used to train the snake in "The Adventure of the Speckled Band."*]

At the conclusion of **"The Speckled Band,"** Sherlock Holmes recounted to Dr. Watson, "Then I thought of the whistle. Of course [Roylott] must recall the snake before the morning light revealed it to the victim. He had trained it, probably by the use of the milk which we saw, to return to him when summoned." Although much has been written on Roylott's infamous serpent, there has been no response to Rolfe Boswell's query, "How Dr. Roylott succeeded in training his specimen with a small saucer of milk is yet another problem in snakecharming."[1] The purpose of this paper is to shed some light on the possible snakecharming (training) methods of the late Dr. Grimesby Roylott of Stoke Moran.

First, let us speculate how Roylott managed to get the swamp adder into Julia Stoner's room and onto her bed. These steps, I propose, would not require any training. The bell-rope in Julia's room was fastened to a hook just above the opening for the ventilator, and hung down beside the bed, with the tassel actually lying on the pillow. Roylott, using the dog-whip, probably carried the snake at arm's length (the same way Holmes returned it to its den) from the iron safe to the ventilator. Since snakes do not like confinement,[2] the beast would eagerly go through the ventilator opening and down the bell-rope.

The training process involved getting the snake to climb up the bell-rope and into Roylott's room when summoned by the whistle.[3] In order to understand the procedure Roylott invoked, a brief review of two recent laboratory experiments would be helpful. Psychologist Paul Kleinginna[4] investigated the question of whether or not snakes could be trained to touch a wire and eventually press a key. By giving the snake water after each appropriate wire touch and key press, Kleinginna successfully trained his snake within thirty-eight days to press the key. In a second experiment,[5] he demonstrated that snakes can be trained to press a key when a light was illuminated and to ignore the key when the light was off. Again, water was used as the reward and the training process took several weeks.

We can surmise that Roylott employed similar training procedures and used milk to reward his snake for appropriate behaviour. Specifically, I propose that the training process began before the bell-rope was hung in Julia Stoner's room, and occurred in several stages. The first step would be to give the snake milk any time it came close to the rope. Once this behaviour was learned, Roylott would administer the milk when the snake touched the bell-rope. After that phase of training had taken place, simply touching the rope would no longer be sufficient for the serpent to receive the milk. It would have to climb up the rope in order to get the reward. In the final stage, the milk would be administered only when the snake climbed the rope after Roylott blew the whistle. Climbing the rope before the whistle was blown would not result in the snake's receiving milk. That way, Roylott was certain that the snake would not prematurely climb up the rope before he called for it. Based on the time involved in Kleinginna's experiments, it is conceivable that Roylott completed his training programme in less than two months.

The preceding should not suggest that snakes learn quickly and are easily trained. In fact, snakes take longer to train than other laboratory animals.[6] And published reports of successful training experiments with snakes are scarce. Still, the research of Paul Kleinginna empirically demonstrates that snakes can be trained. By applying this knowledge to **"The Speckled Band,"**

some insight is provided into the snakecharming practices of Dr. Grimesby Roylott.

Notes

1. Rolfe Boswell, "Dr. Roylott's Wily Fillip," BSJ [*Baker Street Journal*] (os) 1 (July 1946) 307-11.

2. Paul R. Kleinginna, Jr., "Operant Conditioning in the Indigo Snake," *Psychonomic Science,* 18 (10 January 1970) 53-55.

3. This point is puzzling as snakes are deaf. The problem has been addressed by Laurence M. Klauber, "The Truth About the Speckled Band," BSJ (os) 3 (April 1948) 149-57, but the question is still unanswered.

4. Kleinginna, *supra.*

5. Paul R. Kleinginna, Jr. and Joe Seamens, "Discrimination in the Eastern Kingsnake *Lampropeltis getulus getulus*," *Journal of General Psychology,* 102 (January 1980) 153-54.

6. *Ibid.*

Lionel Needleman (essay date September 1984)

SOURCE: Needleman, Lionel. "Unravelling 'The Speckled Band.'" *Baker Street Journal* 34, no. 3 (September 1984): 139-49.

[*In the following essay, Needleman contends that Sherlock Holmes's interpretation of the events in "The Adventure of the Speckled Band" is faulty and inconsistent with the evidence of the tale.*]

Holmes's interpretation of the events in the case of **"The Speckled Band"** cannot be the true explanation of what happened. His interpretation is built upon assumptions and inferences that are either implausible or are in conflict with the facts. In this paper, we first show how and where Holmes erred, and then attempt to provide an alternative explanation of the events that is consistent with the evidence.

DID DR. ROYLOTT MURDER JULIA STONER?

Holmes believed that Dr. Grimesby Roylott killed his stepdaughter Julia by training a poisonous snake to crawl through a ventilator into Julia's bedroom, slide down a bell-pull onto the pillow of her bed, bite the sleeping woman, and then return up the bell-pull when summoned by a low whistle from the next-door room. But the autopsy findings rule out snakebite as the cause of death. Holmes assumed that there were bite marks on the body but that they were missed, and explained that "It would be a sharp-eyed coroner indeed who could distinguish the two little dark punctures which would show where the poison fangs had done their work." But the speckled band was almost certainly a cobra or a viper, and the bite marks of either kind of snake would have been highly conspicuous, particularly if the bite were on the face or hands, as would be expected if the snake bit Julia immediately after dropping onto her pillow. The face and hands of possible murder victims are always inspected minutely at post-mortem examinations. In this case, as Helen Stoner told Holmes, the doctors who examined Julia's body searched with great care for marks of violence and for poisons as "Dr. Roylott's conduct had long been notorious in the county," but no sign was found of either. They found nothing, evidently, because there was nothing to find; Julia had not been bitten.

If Dr. Roylott had wished to murder his stepdaughter, and we have no reason to suppose that he did, it is most unlikely he would have chosen a method that could hardly have succeeded and would almost certainly have led to his being accused of attempted murder. The method is preposterous, first, because it is doubtful if snakes can be trained to bite a sleeping person—they normally only attack if they are threatened. Second, the snake could not possibly be recalled by a whistle from Dr. Roylott's room because snakes are deaf to airborne noises, though extremely sensitive to vibrations that they can feel.[1] Finally, even if a signal to return could have been conveyed to the snake, no snake resembling the speckled band would have been able to crawl up the vertical bell-rope—only constrictors or tree snakes with prehensile tails are capable of this feat.[2]

Not only would the method have been unreliable, it would also have been extremely risky. Holmes speculated that Dr. Roylott might have had to have sent the snake into Julia's room every night for a week before it would bite its victim. But Julia was a light sleeper. If, on hearing the snake in her room, she raised the alarm before it could attack her, Dr. Roylott would immediately be suspected of having put it there. Even if the snake did bite her and then returned in some way to the next-door room, Julia would probably not have been seriously harmed. A leading authority on snakebite has pointed out: "We can say with every confidence that when poisonous snakes bite man, over one-half the victims will escape without poisoning. . . . Snakebite in humans is a defensive reaction, which rarely results in the injection of much venom."[3] But even if the bite were fatal, Julia would normally have remained conscious for several hours, and would have had plenty of time to tell the household that she had been bitten by a snake. Finally, in the extremely unlikely event that she fainted on being bitten and never regained consciousness, the post-mortem examination, as we have seen, would almost certainly have revealed the cause of death.

If Dr. Roylott, whom Holmes judged to be a clever man, had contemplated murdering Julia Stoner, he would surely have employed a safer and surer method, and would have been less obvious in his timing. Apart from all the problems involved in using a snake, he had the further complications of constructing a ventilator that did not ventilate, of hanging a bell-pull that did not ring, and of clamping Julia's bed to the floor. To make all these suspicious alterations shortly before committing a murder, and then for none of them to be noticed by Julia, Helen, the police, or the coroner, would have been extraordinary luck. But, having against all the odds escaped detection the first time, to attempt to murder his remaining step-daughter two years later, again shortly before her marriage, again using a trained snake, and as a final manic touch, to attempt the crime within twenty-four hours of his victim's visiting Sherlock Holmes, would suggest a confidence so overweening as to amount to insanity.

Apart from the suggested means being absurdly impractical, the motive was lacking. Holmes supposed Dr. Roylott to be entirely dependent on the income left to him by his wife, which in April 1883, when the investigation took place, amounted to £750 a year, and which would have been reduced by £250 for each stepdaughter who married. The implication was that Dr. Roylott committed murder to prevent his wife's will from being implemented. But that is implausible because we know that Dr. Roylott must have approved the will. Before the Married Women's Property Act of 1882, a woman disposing of income by means of a will made after her marriage had to obtain her husband's consent to its terms. If Dr. Roylott had thought that the loss of £500 a year would have seriously inconvenienced him, he could have insisted that his wife leave him the money unconditionally. He did not insist, because he had no need to. In 1875, when his wife died, he would have had a substantial income even without his wife's legacy.

We know that he established a large practice in Calcutta, probably before 1853, when he married Mrs. Stoner. At that time she was a young widow with an income of not less than £1,000 a year. A poor man, even of ancient family, could not have aspired to her hand, and we may suppose that his income was already comparable to hers. It would not be at all unusual for a successful doctor in a major Indian city in the 1850s to be earning well in excess of £1,000 a year. We would expect a physician with a large private practice to earn more than one who was an employee of a company, even of *the* Company. But Dr. Thomas Key, who died an octogenarian in 1880 after many years as a doctor employed by the East India Company in Madras, must have been earning substantially more than £1,000 annually because he retired on a pension of £600 to £700 a year.[4]

From 1853 onwards, Dr. Roylott's annual income, including that of his wife, would probably have amounted to well over £2,000, from which at least £1,000 could have been saved. He returned to England with his family in 1875 after serving what Helen Stoner described as a "long term" imprisonment for beating his native butler to death. But it is unlikely that he would have served more than seven years for such an offence, so that we may assume that his high-income period ended no earlier than 1867. Nevertheless, even ignoring any savings made before his marriage, if he had saved £1,000 each year since 1853, and had invested it so as to bring in no more than the five percent that the British Government guaranteed on investments in Indian railways throughout the second half of the nineteenth century,[5] by 1867 his capital would have accumulated to £19,600. Assuming that he and his family lived on his wife's ample income while he was in jail, by 1875 when they all returned to England, his wealth would have grown to £28,950. If this were invested so as to yield five percent, his income after 1875, ignoring any income from his ancestral estates, would have amounted to about £1,450 a year without his wife's legacy, and to at least £2,200 with it. The loss of £250, or even of £500 a year if both his stepdaughters were to marry, would barely affect his standard of living, and would certainly not be a convincing motive for murder.

Dr. Roylott's behaviour when Julia collapsed also points to his innocence. He tried to revive his unconscious stepdaughter with brandy and, significantly, he "sent for medical aid from the village." But that would have been a very risky thing to do had he been responsible for a snake's biting her. The village doctor might have spotted the bite marks, or have heard her, if she regained consciousness, say that she had been bitten by a snake. Nor was there any need to call in outside medical assistance; Dr. Roylott was competent to attend to Julia himself. But he was prudent as well as innocent, so that when Julia collapsed for no apparent reason, knowing how eager his many enemies in the neighbourhood would be to discredit him if the opportunity arose, for his own protection he ensured that Julia should be cared for by another physician.

The Cause of Julia Stoner's Death

If Julia Stoner did not die as a consequence of snakebite, what did she die of? Her symptoms of sudden collapse, delirium, convulsions, and coma are consistent with several neurological conditions, the commonest of which would be a stroke. Her reference to a speckled band suggests that on the night she died she saw a snake similar to the one that later bit Dr. Roylott. But we should not infer that it attacked her, or even that she saw it in her room. On leaving her sister Helen's room that night, instead of going immediately to her own room, she could have called on her stepfather for some reason—possibly to discuss the next day's menus, or even to request him to put out his malodorous Indian cigar. On entering his room, she might have found him

looking into a large box or basket, and before he could close it, she could have glimpsed a yellow speckled band within, though not clearly enough to be able to identify it as a snake. It would be in character for Dr. Roylott to refuse to tell her what the band was, and she may have returned to her room and fallen asleep puzzling over the mystery. On suffering a stroke in the middle of the night, it would not be surprising that she should refer to the last thing that was in her mind before falling asleep—the speckled band.

Did Dr. Roylott Attempt to Murder Helen Stoner?

If, as we have argued, Dr. Roylott had no motive for murdering Julia Stoner, then he also had none for attempting to murder her sister. But Watson in his narrative claimed that Dr. Roylott did try to kill Helen Stoner at least twice—on the night before she consulted Holmes, and also on the following night. Let us examine what happened on each occasion.

During the first night, Helen Stoner lay awake thinking over her sister's end when she heard a low, clear whistle, just as Julia had done before her death. She sprang out of bed and lit the lamp, but saw nothing unusual in the room. It will be recalled that when Julia originally mentioned that she always heard the whistle at about three o'clock in the morning, but could not tell where it came from, Helen commented that the gipsies in the plantation must have been responsible, and Julia agreed that it was possible. Holmes, however, confused as he was as to the abilities of snakes, believed that the whistle was used as a recall signal. But even if the snake had been capable both of hearing and of climbing, Holmes should have deduced that it was unlikely that the whistle had been used to recall the snake on either night.

If Holmes had been correct in his suspicions, on the first night Dr. Roylott would have released the snake into the next-door bedroom while Helen was asleep. Some time later she woke up, and was awake when she heard the "recall" whistle. But in order for the snake to return to Dr. Roylott's room it would have had to have crawled onto Helen's bed, within inches of her face, to get to the bell-rope, the bottom of which rested on her pillow, while she was awake, without her noticing it. Nor, after she leapt out of bed, could the snake have reached the pillow, ascended the bell-rope and disappeared through the ventilator in the few seconds she spent lighting the lamp. Even snakes that can climb ropes cannot do so quickly. But after she lit the lamp she saw nothing amiss in the room. She then dressed and waited in the room until it was daylight.

Where was the snake all the while? It could not have returned before Helen woke up, or she would not have heard the "recall" whistle. Nor could it have returned after she awoke, or she would have noticed it. But if the snake had not returned, to suppose that it was still in the room, as Holmes's theory required, would imply that on that one occasion the snake conveniently ignored the whistle to return, secreted itself noiselessly in some corner out of sight, kept completely still for a few hours until Helen left the room, and then returned to its master. A far more likely explanation of her not seeing the snake is that it never entered the room in which she slept. But if the snake were not put into her room, then the whistle she heard could not have been intended to recall it.

Let us now examine the happenings of the following night. Holmes and Watson were sitting in complete darkness and silence, waiting. Just after three o'clock a lantern was lit in Dr. Roylott's room; then, about half an hour later, a soft hissing noise was heard. Watson records: "The instant that we heard it, Holmes sprang from the bed, struck a match, and lashed furiously with his cane at the bell-pull."

"'You see it, Watson?' he yelled. 'You see it?'"

A strange question to ask. If the snake had been on the bell-pull when Holmes struck, Watson would have seen it. A snake coiled round a rope cannot suddenly disappear. It could, of course, have fallen on to the floor, in which case Watson would have heard it fall, or it could, as Holmes believed, have crawled back up the bell-pull, when again Watson would have observed it. Holmes's eagerness for Watson's confirmation may have reflected his own uncertainty as to whether there really was a snake on the bell-pull.

Watson's comment on the curious incident is revealing. "But I saw nothing," he wrote. "At the moment when Holmes struck the light I heard a low, clear whistle, but the sudden glare flashing into my weary eyes made it impossible for me to tell what it was at which my friend lashed so savagely." Impossible? But the eye adjusts to the glare of a match in a fraction of a second. Watson's loyalty to his friend forbade him to protest that there had been no snake on the bell-pull, but his honesty prevented him from giving the reassurance that Holmes sought.

Once more the mysterious whistling sound is noted, and once more there are difficulties in accepting that it could have been a recall signal. If, when Holmes lit the match and the whistle was heard, the snake were on the bell-pull, it would have been descending, having only entered the bedroom a few moments before. But if Dr. Roylott were bent on murdering Helen Stoner, why should he recall the snake before it had time to bite her? He would not have done so merely because a match had been struck. According to Holmes's reconstruction, on the night Julia died she had also lit a match

after the snake had entered her room; but the whistle was not heard until after her screams proclaimed that she had been bitten.

After the snake had been struck, Holmes claimed that it fled through the ventilator and bit its master on the other side. When Holmes and Watson entered Dr. Roylott's room, they found him sitting in a chair, apparently dead, with the snake round his head and the dog whip on his lap. But if Dr. Roylott had acted as Holmes supposed, the whip could not have been where it was found. In the absence of a bell-rope or anything similar in Dr. Roylott's room, the snake could have descended only with its master's assistance. Presumably, as soon as the snake appeared at the opening, Dr. Roylott would have thrown the noose over its head and carried it over to its container. At no time would he have sat down while carrying the snake. So, if the snake had bitten him soon after it returned, he would have been standing at the time. On being bitten he would have dropped the whip, and then possibly have collapsed into the chair. The whip would subsequently have been found on the floor. But, in fact, the whip was found on his lap, where it could only have been if it had been placed there by Dr. Roylott after he sat down, but before he was bitten—a sequence inconsistent with Holmes's hypothesis.

Unfortunately, in this case Holmes several times leapt to conclusions that were either unsupported or were at variance with the facts known to him. He even ignored his own warnings against reasoning from insufficient data, for he told Watson that he had arrived at the correct conclusions as to the method used to kill Julia Stoner before even entering Dr. Roylott's room.

When he did enter, he found what he considered to be confirmation of his theory in a saucer of milk, a large iron safe, a dog whip with the cord tied in a loop, and some marks on the seat of a wooden chair. He assumed that the saucer of milk was for the snake. But it appears that most snakes do not drink milk. He also assumed, incredibly, that the snake was kept in the safe, which would have been a most unsuitable home. The ventilation would have been inadequate, and the safe would have been difficult to keep clean. Furthermore, the vibrations produced when the door was slammed would have acutely distressed the snake, and could have made it very dangerous to handle. The looped dog-whip could have been used for picking up many small creatures apart from snakes. But the item he examined with the greatest attention was the seat of the wooden chair.

Holmes concluded from his inspection that Dr. Roylott "had been in the habit of standing on it, which, of course, would be necessary in order that he should reach the ventilator." But Dr. Roylott did not need to stand on the chair to get to the ventilator. His room and those of his two stepdaughters were all on the ground floor of the same wing of the house, and would presumably all have been of the same height. Watson described the middle bedroom as having a low ceiling, which in a seventeenth-century building could hardly have been more than seven feet six inches high. Moreover, the ventilator, which was in the dividing wall between the two rooms, was below the ceiling, as the bell-pull was fastened to a hook *above* the opening of the ventilator. Now, Dr. Roylott was described as a huge man, so tall that his hat brushed the crossbar of the outer doorway of the 221B sitting room (which presumably did not have a low ceiling). Assuming that the crossbar was seven feet high, Dr. Roylott would have been about six feet six inches tall. A man of that stature would not need to step on a chair to reach a ventilator less than a foot above his head. He could do it far more comfortably standing on the floor. It is clear that whatever Dr. Roylott was doing when he stood on the chair, it was not putting a snake through the ventilator.

Furthermore, the marks on the seat of the chair weaken rather than support the snake-poisoning hypothesis. If Dr. Roylott had stood on the chair to put a snake through the radiator in the small hours of the morning, he would have been barefoot or wearing his red heel-less Turkish slippers, and so would have left no traces. The presence of marks indicated that he stood on the chair in his boots or shoes, and that he did so during normal waking hours, and hence, once more, for reasons other than introducing snakes into his stepdaughter's bedroom.

DR. ROYLOTT'S SECRET

If Dr. Roylott had no plans to murder his stepdaughter Julia using a poisonous snake, we have to explain why he arranged for the sham ventilator to be built, with the dummy bell-pull hanging by it, and for the bed to be clamped into place beside the bell-pull. The simplest explanation consistent with all the facts is that Dr. Roylott was a voyeur.

He was a lonely man; his wife had died some years before; he had no female friends of his own class, and he would have had difficulty in acquiring any. His age, appearance, and explosive temperament would have made him distinctly unattractive to most women. Given his circumstances, he might have hoped to obtain some sexual gratification from spying on his stepdaughter Julia. The ventilator—no doubt, with widely splayed openings to increase the field of view—would have been designed as a peephole through which he could observe Julia dressing and undressing, and possibly bathing in a portable bath in front of the fire. . . .

We may suppose that Julia was in the habit of putting on and taking off her stockings while seated on the bed. If watching this spectacle gave Dr. Roylott a special

thrill, he might have tried to ensure that she did not move out of his view through, for example, transferring her bed to where the chest of drawers was, by clamping the bed in the corner by the ventilator. The thick bell-rope would have been placed so as to conceal part of the ventilator opening to lessen the chance that Julia would notice him spying on her from a few feet away. We can now see why the doctor needed to stand on the wooden chair—so as to be able to observe his step-daughter at her toilette.

WHAT REALLY HAPPENED?

Dr. Roylott was probably as shocked by Julia's sudden death as Helen was, and he may well have felt deeply ashamed of his conduct towards her. He managed, apparently, to control his obsession for the next two years, but finally yielded to it, and arranged for his surviving stepdaughter, Helen, to move into her sister's room, where he could spy on her.

Helen was aware that her stepfather persistently watched her—she exclaimed that he was so cunning that she never knew when she was safe from him, that is, when she was free from his surveillance. But she did not explain what she thought his motives were for keeping her under observation. There was no hint that she suspected him of having any sexual interest in her—she would surely have been horrified by the suggestion. Nor did she think of him as an ogre who intended to harm her. It was Holmes who accused Dr. Roylott of being cruel, and who referred to him as a brute; Helen Stoner was usually protective towards her stepfather, and tried to conceal or to excuse much of his conduct. Thus, after he had assaulted the local blacksmith she attempted to buy the man off, apparently using her own money to do so. She hid the bruises her stepfather inflicted on her, and when Holmes accused her of screening him, at first she pretended ignorance, and then, blushing deeply, explained that Dr. Roylott did not know his own strength, thereby implying that he did not mean to hurt her. She blushed for him, and attempted to cover up his excesses, presumably because she cared for him and believed that in spite of his irascibility and fits of violence he cared for her. He was, after all, the only father she had ever known.

The second night after Helen moved into her new room he would have noticed that she became very restless. She lit her lamp in the small hours and did not return to sleep. Clearly she was agitated about something. He would have known that he had alarmed her when he grasped her wrist too passionately a day or two earlier, and he may also have been worried that, unobservant though she normally was, she had spotted him eyeing her through the ventilator when she was undressing prior to going to bed that night. At daybreak she hurried off to London. He followed close behind, and was doubtless appalled to find her consulting a well-known private detective. He naturally assumed that she had been talking about him, and so warned Holmes: "Don't you dare to meddle with my affairs." Finding that he was being laughed at, and concerned that the warnings of an elderly voyeur might not be taken seriously, he tried to impress Holmes with his strength and virility by bending a steel poker in half.

On returning home that evening, he found that Helen was avoiding him, which would have confirmed his suspicions that she had discovered his secret. Saddened, he may have attempted to lose himself in his work on poisonous snakes. We do not know the precise nature of his studies, but they clearly involved extracting venom—perhaps he was working on an antidote to some kinds of snakebite. He would have gone to the conservatory, or wherever he kept his snakes, and brought one back to his room in a secure container. He did not, of course, keep a snake in the safe, though he probably did keep his equipment for handling snakes and extracting venom there. He would not have wanted his stepdaughters when they cleaned his room to see his implements and then to bother him with their questions.

We may speculate as to the identity of the snake he brought back to his room that evening and which later bit him. Watson's description of its puffed neck suggests that it was a cobra. Holmes, however, claimed that it was an Indian swamp adder, and that its bite would leave two small punctures. Cobra bites are much more noticeable. But there is no evidence that Holmes actually saw any bite marks, and he could easily have been mistaken about the snake's identity. A man who does not know that snakes are deaf, who believes that the speckled band could climb up a rope, and who asserts that its bite would kill within ten seconds, can hardly be accepted as an authority on the subject.

The common cobra of India, *Naja naja,* is sometimes yellowish, though it is not speckled. But it is a large, heavy creature, and even a young one would be too thick-bodied to be aptly described as a band. However, the yellow cobra of Africa, *Naja nivea,* appears to fit the description perfectly: "A relatively small and slender cobra. . . . Dorsal coloration extremely variable, usually yellowish to reddish brown . . . light color sometimes speckled with dark."[6] The African origin of the snake is not a problem. Dr. Roylott's correspondent in India might well have exchanged animals with a collector in Africa, and so have been able to send to Dr. Roylott not only the African cheetah and baboon that we know he supplied, but African snakes as well.

For some reason Dr. Roylott did not extract any venom that evening. Perhaps he was too distressed, or he may have felt unwell—he was almost certainly in poor health. Watson described his face as "burned yellow

with the sun." But Dr. Roylott had returned from India eight years before, and his tropical tan would have faded soon afterwards. Nor would the Surrey sun in April have restored it. The most likely explanation of his yellow face and bileshot eyes is that he had jaundice, which is a symptom of many diseases, including some—for example gonococcal endocarditis—that affect the heart.

After a few hours' sleep he woke at about three o'clock, and may then have decided to continue with his work. He lit a lantern and prepared himself for the delicate task of extracting venom. We may assume that he lifted the snake from the container with the looped dog-whip, and brought the reptile over to the lantern on the table. Seating himself on the wooden chair, he would have grasped the snake firmly behind the head, while with his other hand he would have withdrawn the dog-whip and laid it on his lap. Perhaps he held the snake too firmly, for it showed its irritation by hissing. Soon afterwards he heard the familiar sound of one of the gipsies signalling his return to the encampment with a low whistle. Then suddenly, from the room next door in which he believed Helen to be sleeping, he heard the sickening thuds of repeated blows, followed by a man's voice shouting. Horrified and distracted by what sounded like a frenzied assault on his sleeping stepdaughter, he may momentarily have relaxed his hold on the snake, which promptly bit him. He gave a despairing cry of pain and frustration and tried to rise from the chair, but failed to do so. The shock of the bite, coming so soon after what he believed to be a brutal attack on his stepdaughter, triggered a massive heart attack, from which he dies before Holmes and Watson could assure him that his stepdaughter was unharmed and he could convince them of his innocence.

Notes

1. Lorus and Margery Milne, *The Senses of Animals and Men* (Harmondsworth: Penguin, 1965), p. 80.

2. Carl Gans, "How Snakes Move," *Scientific American* 222 No. 6 (June 1970), 82-96 at 93.

3. H. Alistair Reid, "Symptomatology, Pathology, and Treatment of Land Snakebite in India and Southeast Asia," in *Venomous Animals and Their Venoms,* ed. Wolfgang Bücherl, Eleanor E. Buckley, and Venancio Deulofeu (New York: Academic Press, 1968), I 611-42 at 614.

4. W. H. Carey, *The Good Old Days of Honorable John Company,* ed. Amendra Nath Mookerji (Calcutta: Quins Book Co., 1964), p. 252.

5. *The Cambridge Economic History of India,* ed. Dharma Kumar (Cambridge: Cambridge University Press, 1983), II 738-41.

6. U.S. Department of the Navy, *Poisonous Snakes of the World* (Washington, D.C.: Government Printing Office, 1968), p. 96.

Pierre Pratte (essay date September 1990)

SOURCE: Pratte, Pierre. "The Uncelebrated Accomplice of the Speckled Band." *Baker Street Journal* 40, no. 3 (September 1990): 144-48.

[*In the following essay, Pratte analyzes the idea that another creature, possibly a mammal, was used to assist in the murders, thereby explaining common misperceptions of the serpent in Doyle's story.*]

In **"The Adventure of the Speckled Band,"** a snake was implicated as the sole means of a rather unsavory man's demise. Sherlock Holmes exclaimed that the speckled viper encircling the deceased's head was a "swamp adder." Since the publication of this case, many attempts have been made to identify this particular serpent. In fact, the various Indian snakes which have been deemed as likely culprits are surprisingly few. The consensus favors *Echis carinata,* the saw-scaled viper, as the most likely suspect (Baring-Gould 264). Yet there remain certain characteristics of this mysterious animal which are inconsistent with the saw-scaled viper. Indeed, there are attributes ascribed to this serpent which are unlike any ability generally imputed to snakes.

Snakes are reptiles and would not be able to digest cow's milk with efficiency. Indeed, such a food source would undoubtedly bring about the *viper*'s demise, in a most unpleasant manner. The milk would curdle and the multitudes of bacteria existing in the serpent's gastro-intestinal tract would proliferate, and, if capable of thought, would wonder if they had somehow entered paradise. Their celebration would cause profuse diarrhea, dehydration, and death. Rather than milk, whole dead mice are recommended for this snake's weekly repast (Cooper 180).

Mammals are noted for their acute hearing, in contrast to their cold-blooded relatives whose ability to discern sound is greatly inferior. The main anatomical difference between these groups is the middle ear. Mammals have one; reptiles do not. Not only are snakes limited in this way, but among their scaly peers, they occupy the lowest level of hearing ability. Indeed, they are practically deaf, having no external ear or ear drum. They may be able to detect low-frequency sounds, such as thunder, if the amplitude is sufficiently high (Cooper 179).

Although there are snakes which inhabit the branches of trees, even such adroit climbers could not conquer a bell-rope. These creatures squeeze along crannies in bark and branches, but coiling up a rope would clearly be an impossibility. It should be noted, however, that climbing down a rope would be possible. According to Mr. Raymond Massey, who portrayed Sherlock Holmes in the movie version of **"The Speckled Band,"** the snake used in that production: ". . . climbed down the bell-rope with a realism which I think satisfied the most rabid Holmes fan" (Baring-Gould 265).

Finally, these creatures are noted for their lack of cerebral aptitude, and an intelligent, trainable viper would be rarer than a hen's premolar.

There seems to be little doubt that a snake bite did bring about the demise of Julia Stoner and her evil step-father. After all, we have both Holmes and Watson describing the viper. We even have a victim's last words decrying a "speckled band."

Yet, if the milk and the low whistle were not intended for the snake, then what indeed was their purpose? And if the snake could not ascend the rope, then how came it to reside atop Dr. Roylott's crown; or, for that matter, quit Miss Stoner's room undetected? To determine the answer to this conundrum, it is necessary first to describe a creature which is consistent with the evidence. Once that task is accomplished, this entire episode may be viewed in an unbiased light. It is important to get the right clue from the beginning and not to be unduly influenced by the multiple eye-witness accounts. Many times, a great quantity of evidence may induce intellectual myopia.

The mystery animal enjoys milk. It must possess good, mammalian-like hearing. The supposed reason for these auditory and gustatory stimuli is related to the training of the creature for some arduous task. If it is simply assumed that this animal must possess the intellectual prowess to learn novel behavior, then at least its taxonomic class may be discovered. In short, this creature should possess mammalian tastes, hearing, and trainability. It is almost embarrassingly obvious that it is a mammal.

It is known that the evil Dr. Roylott fancied animals from India. The baboon, cheetah, and saw-scaled viper were all imported from that country. Most probably, our mystery mammal also involuntarily emigrated from India.

But to uncover the creature's complete identity, its *raison d'être* must be revealed. What was the thing's role? Why have it? How was it employed? To answer these questions, the events must be reconstructed with attention paid to the speckled serpent's movements.

In the dark bedroom of the would-be victim waited our heroes for the appearance of the would-be slayer. There was a brief light at the ventilator. A burnt odor, testifying to the use of a dark-lantern, permeated the room. An anxious thirty minutes passed. A hiss was heard. Holmes struck at the bell-rope, and presently a snake was found coiled about a dead man's head. Surely it was let down the rope. It would have made the descent in less than a minute. It was incapable of reversing its direction and escaping the room, yet it ended up on the bad doctor's bean. Clearly it was *conveyed* to that position. What vehicle is better suited than our mysterious Indian mammal, for not only is it capable of climbing up and down a rope, it is competent in the handling of poisonous snakes? Most certainly, the mystery mammal is a mongoose.

The impossible has been eliminated, and what is left is not only possible but highly probable. Armed with this new insight, the events of this episode may be properly described.

Dr. Roylott, being a man of violent tastes, purchased antagonistic animals of Indian origin. A baboon and cheetah were acquired and allowed to roam his estate. It is hardly an intuitive leap to describe the baboon's existence as nervous. Indeed when approached by the detecting duo, the unfortunate creature dashed away in terror. Later, the cheetah's soft murmurs could be heard as it stalked its would-be snack. The doctor enjoyed such cruel displays of fear and aggression, yet he had to infer most of the pair's activity, for it would be a rare chance to see a nightly confrontation. And so to slake his depraved appetite, he again purchased a pair of natural enemies: a saw-scaled viper and a mongoose. One can only shudder at the interplay between these forbidding foes. Perhaps such spectacles gave the evil man hours of enjoyment. Yet, surely he found his expenses for replacement snakes to be prohibitory. And so he hit upon a splendid idea. He would train the furry, fleet-footed animal to retrieve the serpent without fatal injury (". . . snake-catcher is what I call them . . ." [CROO]). The intelligent snake-smiter learned to bring the incapacitated reptile to Roylott when a low whistle was blown. And his reward for such a feat would be a drink of milk. These gladiators continued to demonstrate their skills to this lone despotic spectator and perhaps occasionally to his gypsy friends. Conceivably, he picked up some spending money on wagers made foretelling the outcome of the pair's sport. Such entertainment, although unsavory, remained innocuous until Julia Stoner fell in love and openly contemplated marriage.

Grimesby Roylott, an intelligent man of ruthless character, conceived a diabolical means to continue his financial status quo. He already had a "snake-catcher," trained to respond to an auditory signal. It would have been difficult, but not impossible, to train the mongoose to ascend a rope with his foe securely immobilized in his jaws. Since the conditioning process had already been utilized for one task, this second bit of gymnastics would be learned readily.

On the night preceding Julia Stoner's murder, the snake was allowed access to the rope, which it slid down quickly. In thirty minutes, the eager snake-retrieving

mammal was sent down. The ventilator proved a tight fit, for Watson claimed ". . . that a rat would hardly pass through." Only a streamlined pole-cat such as a ferret, stoat, or, in this case, mongoose could navigate the aperture with aplomb. In a minute or so, the whistle was blown, and presently a fatigued but expectant mongoose appeared with a slithery prize.

The next evening, the same sequence of events took place, but unfortunately Roylott's step-daughter became involved in a deadly encounter. Miss Stoner, after receiving a fatal bite, probably voiced her surprise, which alerted the evil doctor who immediately allowed the mongoose access to the rope. As the poor woman groped for matches, a whistle softly permeated the still night, and the murder weapon was seized by its neck. Presently, she struck a match and observed a speckled band being transported up the bell-rope. Indeed, she probably did not recognize the creature as a snake; yet, what woman would have failed to recognize a colored, tubular, slithering creature as a snake? Miss Stoner felt a better description of the unexpected apparition to be an inanimate band. Such a mistake would be understandable, if the creature were immobilized and being transported involuntarily by a dark furtive thing which ascended the rope.

Two years later, the same room now contained a consulting detective and a medical doctor, who nervously sat in complete darkness awaiting the arrival of a most uncommon murder weapon. Again the snake was sent down. And again, about half an hour passed, and a confident pole-cat descended the rope. This "first of criminals" waited a minute and calmly whistled. What followed this simple action must have greatly alarmed the sinister doctor.

As the muscular sleek mammal confronted his scaly opponent, the slithery foe became agitated and twisted and coiled its lithe body, emitting a sibilant sound like that of steam escaping from a tea-kettle (Baring-Gould 264). Suddenly a tall lean man struck a match. Watson stated: ". . . I heard only a low whistle when the match was struck. . . ." Surely by the time Dr. Roylott reacted to the sudden illumination, unless his reactions were faster than his furry accomplice's, his whistle would have been drowned by the detective's exclamations and activity.

There remains still another inconsistency with Watson's recollection of the timing of the whistle. For the sake of argument, let it be accepted that a snake may be fitted with a hearing aid, artificial limbs, and frontal cerebral lobes. What, pray tell, is this bionic serpent doing hanging about the bell-pull for half an hour? The serpent should slide down the rope within a couple of minutes and wander about the bed. Yet we find it on the rope soon after the hiss is heard. Either it took thirty minutes to descend the bell-pull partially, or the snake, after mulling about, decided to climb the rope before the proper signal was given.

Clearly, neither alternative is very likely. On the other hand, if the whistle preceded the lighting of the match, then a fleet-footed mammal might have had enough opportunity to gain the bell-pull, before it was beaten from reach. With the excitement that evening, especially at this most intense time, it is excusable for Dr. Watson to have confused the order of events.

As the low whistle pierced the still night, the mongoose struck and seized the serpent's neck, and if an observer were to have the misfortune to blink, he would have missed the attack completely. The creatures gained access to the bell-pull, as the gentleman, match in hand, approached the rope. Whether Holmes merely thrashed wildly at the rope, imploring his colleague to describe the thing, or whether the questions, frantically asked, were merely exclamations of his own perceptions, seems to be questionable, but not terribly important. It seems plausible that he expected the more usual image of a writhing snake, and instead perceived a dark tubular form, with a speckled stole draped about its shoulders. It is not surprising that the perplexed sleuth shouted to his companion to verify the confusing apparition. Whether Watson's inability to discern the escaping pair was due to blindness from the bright light, or as some claim, a vitamin A deficiency, remains speculative. That he saw nothing, and consequently his description of the events can only be second hand, is well founded.

In any event, the bell-pull, and a couple of creatures clinging to it, received a thrashing. To the hapless mongoose, the sudden appearance of the tall man venting his fury on the bell-rope must have been particularly disconcerting. It would take all the agility and tenacity for which this furry carnivore is famous to maintain its grip, and not lose hold of the squirming trophy. But the poor mammal was struck upon the back with such force as to make it forget any thought but that of escape. Upon reaching the ventilator, it dropped its burden, and, bounding off the shoulder of an alarmed Dr. Roylott, the frightened creature made its escape. A confused Dr. Roylott found that he was now in intimate contact with the enraged serpent, and received a fatal wound, which precipitated a heart attack or allergic shock (Baring-Gould 265). His last sound pierced the night and, collapsing into his chair, he expired. His killer slithered its way to his head and, encircling his brow, awaited the detective and his Boswell. The mongoose, dark and silent, remained concealed under a piece of furniture, probably the camp bed. He bided his time and, unseen, quit the room, as well as the house. No doubt the hapless animal gained access to the outdoors and lived for a time (I would like to believe a long time) in the gardens and copses feeding on rodents and hares.

It remains a mystery as to whether Sherlock Holmes did indeed deduce that another animal, probably a mongoose, was an unwitting accomplice in this business and did not express himself clearly to Watson or whether the sleuth merely botched the case's conclusion. I prefer the former explanation. I also prefer to believe that the furry pole-cat lived the rest of its days in some wooded retreat. Perhaps it met up with Watson's bull-pup, and they spent the sunny afternoons regaling each other with their respective yarns.

Bibliography

Baring-Gould, William S. "It Is . . . the Deadliest Snake in India." *Annotated* [*The Annotated Sherlock Holmes*], I, 263-66.

Cooper, John, Maureen Hutchison, Oliphant Jackson, and R. Julian Maurice. *Manual of Exotic Pets.* Cheltenham: B.S.A. V.A., 1985. Pp. 179-85.

John A. Hodgson (essay date 1992)

SOURCE: Hodgson, John A. "The Recoil of 'The Speckled Band': Detective Story and Detective Discourse." In *Sherlock Holmes: The Major Stories with Contemporary Critical Essays,* edited by John A. Hodgson, pp. 335-52. Boston: Bedford Books of St. Martin Press, 1994.

[*In the following essay, originally published in 1992, Hodgson characterizes "The Adventure of the Speckled Band" as "an invitation to detection" and suggests that the story's "incongruities and impossibilities" are intentional violations of the detective fiction and realism genres.*]

> "You seem to know a lot about [Sherlock Holmes]."
>
> "On the contrary, any Sherlockian would tell you I know nothing about him, except what I picked up as a child reading. . . . Do you think Charlotte Lucas sleeps below a false vent, and is visited nightly by a dangerous snake who responds to whistles?"
>
> "What a memory you have."
>
> "Everyone remembers that."
>
> —AMANDA CROSS, *No Word from Winifred,* 1986

I

"If you ask the ordinary reader which of the Sherlock Holmes short stories he likes best," Jacques Barzun observes in *The Delights of Detection,* "the chances are that he will say: '**The Speckled Band**'" (Barzun 1980 [1961]: 150). There is much evidence to support Barzun's guess. Perhaps the true Holmes aficionado is no ordinary reader; if you ask him or her this same question, though, the chances are very good that you will

get the same answer. Thus readers of the *Strand* magazine, where the Sherlock Holmes stories originally appeared, ranked **"The Adventure of the Speckled Band"**
first among the forty-four stories by then collected in
book form in 1927; in the same year readers of the *Observer* ranked it first among all of the adventures, short
stories, and novels; the Baker Street Irregulars, in a
1944 poll of members, also placed it first and, at their
1959 "one hundredth anniversary" dinner, again named
the story as far and away their first choice; also in that
year, a survey taken by the *Baker Street Journal* produced the same result (Bigelow 1976: 47-50; Baring-
Gould 1967: I, 262).

Such enthusiasm for the story is not surprising, for certainly **"The Speckled Band"** has its power. "The vision of the snake coming down the bell pull is the utmost thrill [the ordinary reader] expects from detection,"
Barzun sniffs, himself disappointed that in this adventure Doyle let "sensationalism" dominate "the detective
interest" (Barzun 1980 [1961]: 150). But this hardly
does justice to the story, which has its strong detective
interest, too. Still, that detective interest seems remarkably uncharacteristic of Conan Doyle in some unsettling ways. The appeal of Sherlock Holmes, after all,
comes from his method and his skillful application of
it. Holmes is the master reasoner, diagnostician, interpreter: he not only sees (Watson can do as much), he
makes sense of what he sees, thanks to his vast store of
useful, if often esoteric, knowledge and his highly developed powers of inference. But in **"The Speckled
Band"** Holmes makes nonsense of what he sees; here,
to a degree unmatched elsewhere in the canon, his
method is not merely shaky, but overtly and devastatingly flawed.[1] As a recent writer for the popular press
only begins to summarize:

> Snakes don't have ears, so they cannot hear a low
> whistle. Snakes can't climb ropes. Snakes can't survive
> in an airtight safe. There's no such thing as an Indian
> swamp adder. No snake poison could have killed a
> huge man like Grimesby Roylott instantly.
>
>   (Murphy 1987: 65)

That such extravagances of plot and errors of fact, many
of them howlers, should not particularly trouble that
poor straw man, the ordinary reader, is no surprise. It is
mildly surprising, perhaps, that the Irregulars and other
Holmes enthusiasts should not balk at them. But that
Conan Doyle, who took pride in having created "a scientific detective who solved cases on his own merits
and not through the folly of the criminal" (Doyle 1924:
21), should have himself ranked the story as his very
best—which he explicitly did, listing it first (both "in
popular favor and in my own esteem") on the "twelve
best" list he drew up for the June 1927 issue of the
Strand (Doyle 1980 [1927]: 209)—is very surprising
indeed. How could so absurd a solution have pleased so
analytical a writer?

The very question, of course, is itself an invitation to
detection. As Holmes says in *The Hound of the Baskervilles,* "The more *outré* and grotesque an incident is, the
more carefully it deserves to be examined," and, in
"The Boscombe Valley Mystery," "Singularity is almost invariably a clue" (p. 91).[2] The singular, exaggerated badness of **"The Speckled Band"**'s solution is
worth investigating. And indeed, its incongruities and
impossibilities so violate the laws of the detective-story
genre as to be criminal. Perhaps they are.

Does not **"The Adventure of the Speckled Band"** itself warn us of this? "When a doctor does go wrong he
is the first of criminals. He has nerve and he has knowledge" (p. 169). So Holmes—whose creator, Conan
Doyle, was himself a doctor—suggests of Dr. Grimesby
Roylott, the villain of this story (and the only villainous
doctor in the Holmes canon). The possible parallel of
life with literature here is intriguing. What if a master
writer of detective stories should "go wrong"? Perhaps
we should not too quickly dismiss as mere bumbling
what might well be the work of the first of literary
criminals.

                                        II

When I speak of **"The Adventure of the Speckled
Band"** as criminally violating the laws of its genre, I
refer above all to the laws, not merely of detective fiction, but of realism itself. In this story Holmes does not
merely diagnose more acutely and interpret more
shrewdly than an untrained and less knowledgeable observer, such as Watson, might. Rather, he reasons—
illogically—from the available evidence to infer the existence of a deadly serpent that not only does not "in
fact" exist, but that cannot even presumably exist. This
is a far different case from the kind of mistake central
to Dorothy Sayers's *Documents in the Case*. In Sayers's work the detection turns on the fact that the organic and synthetic versions of poisons occurring naturally in toadstools can be distinguished by their different
light-polarizing properties. As "a very polite professor
of chemistry" informed Sayers soon after the book's
appearance, however, "[her] general theory was quite
all right, but Muscarin [the particular poison featured in
her plot] was an exception. Natural Muscarin didn't
play fair. It didn't twist the ray of the polarised light
any more than the synthetic kind" (Guillard 1981: 8).
So the crucial act of detection in Sayers's plot is invalid; yet it seems credible, and indeed Sayers herself
and her scientific collaborator, Robert Eustace (Dr. Eustace Robert Barton), took pains to make it so. Conan
Doyle's deadly serpent, however, is not merely farfetched, but epistemically impossible.[3] Even granting
Holmes's (and Roylott's) fantastic knowledge, unshared
by all zoologists then and since, of a snake of such unprecedented poisonousness, a snake that can survive
(apparently for more than two years, since the time of

Julia Stoner's engagement and death) in an iron safe, a snake that drinks from a saucer of milk, still we cannot grant those additional premises upon which all of Holmes's conjecture depends—that the snake could hear a low whistle and could climb back up a Victorian bell-pull. No snake, however exotic, could do these things, any more than it could fly. The knowledge of these snakish limitations, moreover, is not esoteric (indeed, the snake's deafness is proverbial: cf. Psalms 58: 4-5); even a Watson might well know, at the very least, that snakes don't have external ears and can't hear low whistles.[4]

Thus **"The Adventure of the Speckled Band,"** like its villain, is fatally wounded by its own deadly serpent. But is this wounding a crime, rather than an error? What kind of "going wrong" is it? There are rules for these critical detections, too, and perhaps it will be objected that I am myself behaving unlawfully as a critic by positing the criminality of the author. On the contrary: my analogy lies at the very heart of the detective-story genre.

There are two vitally balanced relationships central to the detective story. The first, central indeed to an even larger range of literature, is that obtaining between detective and criminal, pursuer and pursued. Opposed though they may be, these characters have, as is widely recognized, much in common. At the very least, detection often depends upon the detective's imaginative ability to identify with his opponent, if only temporarily. Thus Poe's Auguste Dupin solves the mystery of "The Purloined Letter" by identifying his own intellect with that of his opponent (Poe 1978: III, 984); and Holmes similarly reminds Watson (in **"The Musgrave Ritual"**), "You know my method in such cases . . . I put myself in the man's place, and having first gauged his intelligence, I try to imagine how I should myself have proceeded under the same circumstances" (p. 210). Toward the extreme—or the epitome—of the genre, detective and criminal approach very close to a shared identity. So it is with Holmes and his great adversary, Professor Moriarty. "What will [Moriarty] do?" Watson asks, in **"The Final Problem."** Holmes knows the answer: "What I should do. . . . Moriarty will again do what I should do" (p. 223). And so it is in "The Purloined Letter" with Dupin and the villainous Minister D—, who are pointedly doubles of each other, perhaps even brothers (Wilbur 1962: 380; Babener 1987 [1972]: 46-50; Hoffman 1972: 131-32; Derrida 1975: 109). At the very extreme, finally, detective and criminal are one and the same. Although both Ronald Knox, in his "Detective Story Decalogue," and S. S. Van Dine, in his "Twenty Rules for Writing Detective Stories," presumed to forbid this, insisting that "the detective must not himself commit the crime" (Knox 1946 [1929]: 196; cf. Van Dine 1946 [1928]: 190), the commandment has come to seem not only narrow-minded but even mis-

guided; witness Robin Winks's flat statement, "The ideal detective story is one in which the detective hero discovers that he (or she) is the criminal" (Winks 1980: 5).[5] The classic instance of the detective as the criminal, of course, is Oedipus. But even at the beginnings of detection proper, in the *Mémoires* of François Vidocq (the former criminal who became chief of detectives in Paris), the pattern recurs: once Vidocq, as a police spy, was assigned to investigate a crime which he himself had committed.[6] Similarly, in Wilkie Collins's *The Moonstone*, the first English detective novel, Franklin Blake initiates and sustains the search for the stolen moonstone until, to his astonishment, "I had discovered Myself as the Thief" (Collins 1966 [1868]: 359). And in Israel Zangwill's important early detective story *The Big Bow Mystery*, the famous retired detective George Grodman concludes his investigation of the murder by confessing his own guilt, intending that his confession should "form the basis of an appendix to the twenty-fifth edition . . . of my book, *Criminals I Have Caught*" (Zangwill 1986 [1891]: 148). A variation on the pattern also informs "The Purloined Letter," as Dupin solves the original crime by duplicating it—and was perhaps the author of the originally purloined letter, even as he was of its replacement (Hoffman 1972: 131).

The second vital relationship of the detective story exists in a curious equilibrium with the first. This second relationship is that obtaining between the author and the reader. As writers, readers, and critics of classic detective fiction have generally agreed, the detective story is a veritable game between two players, the author and the reader: hence the widespread interest in "the rules of the game" (Haycraft 1946: 187; Van Dine 1946 [1928]: 189; Knox 1946 [1929]: 194; Caillois 1983 [1941]; Heissenbutel 1983 [1963]), and the continual recurrence by critics and apologists to chess and even sporting events to explain the genre's appeal (Nicolson 1946 [1929]: 118-22; Van Dine 1946 [1928]: 189, 191; Knox 1946 [1929]: 194-96). The "game" analogy, of course, comes directly from Poe's "Murders in the Rue Morgue" (on the mere complexity and "elaborate frivolity" of chess versus the profundity of draughts and whist [Poe 1978 [1841]: II, 528-30]) and from "The Purloined Letter" (on the game of "even and odd" [ibid. [1845]: III, 984])—where it is, however, a model for the relationship of the criminal and the detective. But the transition to the second relationship is a natural one, for reading is itself a form of detection. The analogousness of reader to detective is thus central to any poetics of the genre. As Kathleen Klein and Joseph Keller note,

> The criminal's truth generates a fiction, an allegory whose key is hidden, an illusion of which the alibi is an important if not the most important part. The detective's method results in an interpretation of this fiction, a hermeneutic.
>
> (Klein and Keller 1986: 162)

But if the reader is a detective, what is the author? Sherlock Holmes himself insinuates the answer to Watson when he alludes, at the beginning of a case (**"The Crooked Man"**), to

> the effect of some of these little sketches of yours, which is entirely meretricious, depending as it does upon your retaining in your own hands some factors in the problem which are never imparted to the reader. Now, at present I am in the position of these same readers, for I hold in this hand several threads of one of the strangest cases which ever perplexed a man's brain, and yet I lack the one or two which are needful to complete my theory.

Dorothy Sayers drove her *Omnibus of Crime* at this point almost sixty years ago when she noted that the seasoned reader of detective stories, "instead of detecting the murderer . . . is engaged in detecting the writer" (Sayers 1946 [1929]: 108); Tzvetan Todorov similarly implies it in observing that "we have no need to follow the detective's ingenious logic to discover the killer—we need merely refer to the much simpler law of the author of murder mysteries" (Todorov 1977 [1971]: 86). As Dennis Porter notes, criminal and detective "stand in relation to each other as a problem maker to a problem solver and thus repeat inside the novel the relationship that exists between author and reader" (Porter 1981: 88). The analogy insists on the author's being a type of the criminal.

We tend to regard "bad" writing as simply uncontrolled or inexpert (hence our usual figurative labels for it— "clumsy," "careless," "crude," "awkward," "immature," "inconsistent," "overwrought," "silly"), and we do not usually think of a story as committing a kind of crime. But sometimes it does; and one of our terms for such a crime is "hoax." I hesitate to suggest that **"The Adventure of the Speckled Band"** is a hoax, exactly. Roylott's speckled serpent is no red herring—although it may be something of a gold bug. Yet neither is it simply that absurd swamp adder, which does not and cannot "really" exist. The story's more significant crime, I would propose, is not the impossible crime that it ostensibly recounts, but the crime that it commits; yet for this crime, too, Doyle offers a resolution, although on an entirely different level of narrative.

III

The doubleness of **"The Adventure of the Speckled Band"**—a story about twins—is already implicit in its ambivalent title. Here we find another of those singularities which Holmes himself thinks so important as clues. This is the only story in the canon, I believe, that involves a pun in its title. "O, my God! Helen! It was the band! The speckled band!" are the dying Julia Stoner's last words (p. 158). "What did you gather from this allusion to a band—a speckled band?" Holmes asks

Helen Stoner, and she guesses "that it may have referred to some band of people, perhaps to these very gypsies in the plantation," many of whom wear spotted handkerchiefs over their heads (p. 159). Holmes, of course, is dissatisfied; nevertheless, he too is misled:

> I had . . . come to an entirely erroneous conclusion, which shows, my dear Watson, how dangerous it always is to reason from insufficient data. The presence of the gipsies, and the use of the word "band," which was used by the poor girl, no doubt, to explain the appearance which she had caught a hurried glimpse of by the light of her match, were sufficient to put me upon an entirely wrong scent.
>
> (p. 172)

Thus "the speckled band"—not the serpent but the phrase—*is* a false scent, a red herring. But, curiously, Helen Stoner's wrong guess is partly righted by the snake's final appearance: bound tightly around Roylott's brow, the snake is indeed a spotted headband. Thus the title is effectively, rhetorically misleading; yet the "entirely wrong scent" fortuitously recrosses "the right track" (p. 172). Just so does it happen with the story itself.

In keeping with its doubly significant title, **"The Adventure of the Speckled Band"** contains within itself two paradigms—one active, one discursive—for its story. The first of these we may call the story's synecdochic[7] paradigm: it constitutes part of the story itself, rather than of the discourse only. This episode occurs when Dr. Roylott tries to warn Holmes off of the case:

> "I am a dangerous man to fall foul of! See here." He stepped swiftly forward, seized the poker, and bent it into a curve with his huge brown hands.
>
> "See that you keep yourself out of my grip," he snarled, and hurling the twisted poker into the fireplace, he strode out of the room.
>
> "He seems a very amiable person," said Holmes, laughing. "I am not quite so bulky, but if he had remained I might have shown him that my grip was not much more feeble than his own." As he spoke he picked up the steel poker, and with a sudden effort straightened it out again.
>
> (p. 162)

Here is encapsulated the typical plan of the detective story: the detective counters and reverses the actions of the criminal, restoring matters to their proper state, making straight what the criminal has made crooked. At the same time, though, here is another red herring. Roylott is indeed a violent, fierce-tempered "man of immense strength," who leaves the mark of his grip on his stepdaughter's wrist, who recently "hurled the local blacksmith over a parapet into a stream," and who once, in India, "beat his native butler to death" (p. 155). But he is most dangerous to his stepdaughters not as a brute, but as a doctor; his deepest villainy is not confrontational but subtle. This episode, then, is seriously misleading as a clue to Roylott's dangerousness.

The second paradigm of **"The Speckled Band"** is not mimetic but metaphoric: it comprises part of the discourse but not of the story. This paradigm takes shape in a number of hints, culminating in Holmes's postmortem summation. After Roylott "trace[s]" Helen Stoner to Holmes's sitting room (p. 161), Holmes reassures her, "He must guard himself, for he may find that there is someone more cunning than himself upon his track" (pp. 163-64). That evening, after investigating Miss Stoner's room and discovering Roylott's plot, Holmes notes, "This man strikes even deeper [than earlier doctor-criminals], but I think, Watson, that we shall be able to strike deeper still" (p. 169). And finally, after Roylott is killed by his own serpent, Holmes moralizes, "Violence does, in truth, recoil upon the violent, and the schemer falls into the pit which he digs for another" (pp. 171-72). Here is the apter paradigm for the story of this particular detection—retaliation by repetition: the crime is not merely undone but redone, the criminal not only defeated but victimized by his own devices. From Poe's "Purloined Letter" (if not, indeed, from Dante), Conan Doyle learned how a detection, no less than a punishment, could duplicate a crime. In **"The Adventure of the Speckled Band,"** he offers his own version of this significant redundancy.

IV

The breakthrough for Holmes's detection in **"The Adventure of the Speckled Band"** comes when he tugs on the bellpull in Julia Stoner's bedroom and makes an interesting discovery: "Why, it's a dummy" (p. 165). Roylott's plot involves many such devices: "dummy bell-ropes, and ventilators which do not ventilate" (p. 166), and a safe which contains, rather than excludes, danger. Holmes solves the case when he sees through the figuratively innocuous disguises of these accessories to discern their deadly actual uses. We, in turn, in order to discover the deeper, satisfactory resolution of this apparently flawed story, must read its literal clues figuratively, recognizing them as features not of an actual scene, but of a textual one.

The real dummy of this suspicious story, the apparently murderous device which proves to be only figuratively deadly, is that impossible snake, whose insinuation into the story constitutes Doyle's literary crime. Our recognition of the snake as mere figure enables our own interpretive breakthrough. Once we can realize, "why, *it's* a dummy," we, like Holmes, are finally "on the right track" (p. 172).

That track, like the very different one Holmes follows, soon leads us to "one or two very singular points" (p. 165) about the scene. There is, to begin with, the matter

of those oddly unfamiliar names. "Grimesby Roylott," especially: what manner of name is this? Even Donald Redmond, in his exhaustive (nearly 400 pages) source study of "the personal names . . . with which Conan Doyle christened his cast" (Redmond 1982: xiv), draws a rare blank here: "The oddest thing about his name is that neither part of it can be found anywhere" (ibid.: 52). Does "Grimesby" simply suggest "grim"? (In placing **"The Speckled Band"** first on his top-twelve list for the *Strand,* Doyle called it "a grim snake story" [Doyle 1927: 209].) "Grime?" "Crime?" (Grimesby Roylott = "Crimes by Roylott"?) "Stoke Moran," we might also note, contains an anagrammatic "snake" (even a "snake o' mort"). And indeed, Watson's initial presentation of the names, the "Roylotts of Stoke Moran," permutes itself anagrammatically into "snake story tomfool rot."

Such Poesque name games are not typical of Conan Doyle—although we might, after all, sense a faintly Poesque self-reflexiveness in Doyle's emphasis on Holmes's "Bohemian soul" in **"A Scandal in Bohemia,"** or his siting "a manufactory of artificial kneecaps" at one dead end of the story (**"The Red-headed League"**) that stresses the evidence afforded by a suspect's knees. The anagram, accordingly, is by itself more curious than convincing. But similarly subversive hints infuse many other aspects of the story as well. Consider, for example, how the secondary instruments of Roylott's criminal plot figuratively evoke the generic plot of detective fiction itself. Roylott's ventilator does not ventilate, his bellpull will not ring any bell, his safe is dangerous. But Holmes, in figuring out Roylott's real devices, realizes Roylott's figures: the dummy bellpull, although useless for calling the foolish housekeeper who was so easily gotten out of the way, "rings a bell" of summons and alarm in Holmes's mind; he "ventilates" Roylott's scheme; he acts to make all truly "safe." Roylott's dummies are Doyle's truths, just as Roylott's truth (the snake) is Doyle's dummy.

A sense of ambivalent self-awareness also resonates within the narrative's two paradigms of its own action. Both paradigms allude pointedly to biblical contexts. The first, synecdochic paradigm, mimetic but misleading—Roylott threateningly bends and twists the poker, and Holmes "straighten[s] it out again"—sports with a Solomonic aphorism. "That which is crooked cannot be made straight" (Eccles. 1:15), the Preacher of Ecclesiastes insists; more accurately, as both John the Baptist and his antitype Isaiah declare, he who makes crooked things straight is God (Isa. 40:4, 42:16; Luke 3:5). But what if an author himself makes something crooked? The Preacher knows of such things—"Consider the work of God: for who can make that straight, which he hath made crooked?" (Eccles. 7:13). And the Scriptures elsewhere specify "that . . . which he hath made crooked": "his hand hath formed the crooked serpent" (Job 26:13).

For the second, metaphorical paradigm of the story, showing the criminal victimized by his own devices, Holmes himself leads us directly to the biblical source. "The schemer falls into the pit which he digs for another," he moralizes to Watson. The wisdom is again Solomon's: "He that diggeth a pit shall fall into it" (Eccles. 10:8; see also Proverbs 26:27). And here again, the text points to the snake, for the verse from Ecclesiastes continues, "And whoso breaketh a hedge, a serpent shall bite him."

Thus, if **"The Adventure of the Speckled Band"** commits a literary crime by breaking the laws of its genre, it nevertheless works also to detect this crime and to resolve it—which is to say, it remains true to its genre. But this resolution, appropriately, is itself strictly a literary one. While Conan Doyle has "plotted" against his readers (to read the story literally is to be victimized), he has also dug deeper again than his own deep digging; and at this level he has not, after all, broken the "hedge," the limits and rules, of his chosen genre.

"The Speckled Band" is, then, something like a critical work masquerading as a literary one: it is not about detecting a crime, but about defining a crime-detecting genre. Seeming to violate and thus to undermine that genre, Conan Doyle actually respects it and, at a deeper level, remains true to it. And surely he enjoyed thus cutting deeper than his protagonist's cultists could ever plow. As Holmes says of Moriarty in **"The Final Problem,"** "My horror at his crimes was lost in my admiration at his skill" (p. 217). Conan Doyle had good reason to admire **"The Adventure of the Speckled Band"** as the best of his stories.

V

So **"The Speckled Band,"** like certain works by such notable enthusiasts of detective fiction as Borges and Nabokov, tells two very different stories, or rather two very different versions of a single story. It operates to contradictory effect at two different levels, telling alternatively of Roylott's crime or of Doyle's, offering alternatively a narrated or an incompatible "literary" detection and resolution.

These two levels have other names, names that I have already introduced without comment. They correspond exactly to what narratology discriminates as "story" (or *histoire*, or *fabula*—"the content plane of narrative . . . the 'what' of a narrative") versus "discourse" (or *sjužhet*—"the expression plane of narrative . . . the 'how' of a narrative") (Prince 1987: 91, 21; see also Culler 1981: 169-71). Indeed, theorists of narrative

have taken a particular interest in detective stories precisely because such fiction isolates these two levels so starkly as "the story of the crime" (story, *fabula*) and "the story of the investigation" (discourse, *sjužhet*) (Todorov 1977 [1971]: 45); as Peter Brooks notes, "Narrative always makes the implicit claim to be in a state of repetition, as a going over again of a ground already covered: a *sjužhet* repeating the *fabula,* as the detective retraces the tracks of the criminal" (Brooks 1985 [1984]: 97). But if detective fiction typically suggests "a laying-bare of the structure of all narrative in that it dramatizes the role of *sjužhet* and *fabula* and the nature of their relation" (ibid.: 25), **"The Adventure of the Speckled Band"** also particularly dramatizes a complicating and blurring of these roles.

Consider again the tale's two paradigms of its own action. The first of these, the episode of the twisted and untwisted poker, I have labeled "active" and "synecdochic" because it is an enactment that is part of the story itself; we might equally well call it a "story-paradigm." The second paradigm, the motif of retaliation by repetition ("This man strikes even deeper, but I think, Watson, that we shall be able to strike deeper still"; "Violence does, in truth, recoil upon the violent, and the schemer falls into the pit which he digs for another"), is in contrast "discursive" and "metaphoric": it recounts rather than enacts, and it proposes a similarity between different signifieds, this paradigm not being part of the story. We can call this one a "discourse-paradigm." These two particular paradigms of detection are figuratively quite dissimilar, almost opposite—a straightening out versus a doubling under or back or around, reversal versus repetition, the crime undone versus the crime redone—but nonetheless entirely compatible with each other, like the two sides of a single door. Indeed, to some degree the patterns of both paradigms—in the former, reversal; in the latter, repetition—will always be present in detective fiction, since these correspond to the dual movement (backward to causes or origins, forward to effects or conclusions) of detective-fiction hypothesis and hypothesis-testing (Sebeok and Umiker-Sebeok 1983: 19-28, 39-41; Truzzi 1983 [1973]: 61-71; Bonfantini and Proni 1983: 119-28). But how then can we dismiss the former paradigm as a false trail, a red herring, in **"The Speckled Band"**? It is false or misleading, we recognize, with reference to the story; with reference to the detection, the discourse, it is apt. The story-paradigm of **"The Speckled Band"** is paradigmatic of the discourse.

The discourse-paradigm of **"The Speckled Band,"** on the other hand, is paradigmatic of the story. It is not, however, paradigmatic of the discourse, which follows no such pattern of retaliation by repetition—not paradigmatic of the discourse, that is, *unless* we entertain some such notion of that discourse's duplicity as I have been advancing here. To do this is also to read Doyle's (not Watson's) "story" as an exercise in distorting and restoring its genre—a meta-story for which the story-paradigm now becomes fitting.

Jonathan Culler has noted that every narrative involves an "irreconcilable opposition, a conflict between two logics" (Culler 1981: 187) founded alternatively on the assumed precedence of story or of discourse: in one, "the discourse is seen as a representation of events which must be thought of as independent of that particular representation," while in the other, "the so-called events are thought of as the postulates or products of a discourse" (ibid.: 186). "One logic assumes the primacy of events; the other treats the events as the products of meanings" (ibid.: 178). **"The Adventure of the Speckled Band"** not only illustrates this conflict, but points up some of its deeper implications.

A discourse tells a story in a double sense, Culler is arguing: it recounts or relates a prior and independent sequence of events, but then again it shapes these events by its "demands of signification" (ibid.: 175), "suggesting by its implicit claims to significance that these events are justified by their appropriateness to a thematic structure" (ibid.: 178). This doubleness, we might add, suggests one way of understanding how a story can have many discourses (cf. Chatman 1978: 123): the different tellings advance different claims to significance. But this double logic of narrative also suggests—and a narrative such as **"The Adventure of the Speckled Band"** confirms—that, just as a story may have more than one discourse, so may a discourse have more than one story. The story of the discourse may not be simply or exclusively identifiable with the discoursed story.

VI

A final problem: In 1894, so the familiar anecdote goes, feeling that he had fallen into a literary rut and anxious to devote himself to grander fictions, Arthur Conan Doyle decided to put an end to his Sherlock Holmes tales by killing off his protagonist. Accordingly, he wrote for the *Strand* and for the conclusion of *Memoirs of Sherlock Holmes* a valedictory and epitaphic tale, **"The Final Problem,"** recounting Holmes's to-the-death struggle with his archenemy, Moriarty, at the Falls of Reichenbach. The tale recalls **"The Adventure of the Speckled Band"** in several interesting respects. Like **"The Speckled Band,"** wherein Watson counters the "widespread rumours as to the death of Dr. Grimesby Roylott which tend to make the matter even more terrible than the truth" (p. 152), **"The Final Problem"** professes to be an alternative retelling of a story: two "extremely condensed" accounts have appeared in the press, and now, Watson says, "my hand has been forced . . . by the recent letters in which Colonel James Moriarty defends the memory of his brother" through

"an absolute perversion of the facts" that "endeavoured to clear his memory by attacks upon" Holmes (pp. 214, 229). While the slender, ascetic-looking Professor Moriarty is superficially quite different from the huge and brutish Dr. Roylott, he is nevertheless what Holmes calls Roylott, "the first of criminals" (p. 169): "He is the Napoleon of crime, Watson," and stands "on a pinnacle in the records of crime" (p. 216). Like Roylott, Moriarty personally calls on Holmes to warn him off. Moriarty's "curiously reptilian fashion" of oscillating his face from side to side (p. 218) and the deadly threat of his presence recall Roylott's serpent; and his warning, "You must stand clear, Mr. Holmes, or be trodden under foot" (p. 219), especially in this context of a final, supreme struggle, invokes (inversely, from Holmes's point of view) the prophecy made to the serpent in Genesis 3:15: "It shall bruise thy head, and thou shalt bruise his heel." The motif of the pursuer pursued also recurs in the later story ("One would think that we were the criminals," Watson grumbles about the precautions that Holmes deems necessary for evading Moriarty [p. 223]), as does the very imagery of retaliatory undercutting ("He cut deep," Holmes says of his intellectual contest with Moriarty, "and yet I just undercut him" [p. 217]).

But the discourse of **"The Final Problem,"** like that of **"The Speckled Band,"** has another story. What appears to be a dead end ("The path has been cut half-way round the [Reichenbach] fall to afford a complete view, but it ends abruptly, and the traveller has to return as he came" [p. 226]) is not.

"I alone know the absolute truth of the matter," Watson announces (p. 214). He has arrived at the dénouement of this truth by following Holmes's example. What had happened, he wonders, when Moriarty overtook Holmes?

> I stood for a minute or two to collect myself, for I was dazed with the horror of the thing. Then I began to think of Holmes's own methods and to try to practise them in reading this tragedy. It was, alas! only too easy to do.
>
> (p. 227)

All signs of that meeting and struggle, including a brief farewell note from Holmes, indicate that

> a personal contest between the two men ended, as it could hardly fail to end in such a situation, in their reeling over, locked in each other's arms. Any attempt at recovering the bodies was absolutely hopeless, and there, deep down in that dreadful cauldron of swirling water and seething foam, will lie for all time the most dangerous criminal and the foremost champion of the law of their generation.
>
> (pp. 228-29)

Nine years later, however, in response to immense and sustained popular demand (and strong financial inducements), Conan Doyle brought Sherlock Holmes back to literary life. As he later commented, "I had fully determined at the conclusion of ***The Memoirs*** [***The Memoirs of Sherlock Holmes***] to bring Holmes to an end. . . . I did the deed, but fortunately no coroner had pronounced upon the remains, and so, after a long interval, it was not difficult for me to . . . explain my rash act away." But in doing so he thereby made a mockery of Watson's essay in detection at the end of the story, where Watson reads the signs of Holmes's struggle with Moriarty to mean that his friend is surely dead. ***The Memoirs of Sherlock Holmes*** thus ends, wittily (although its wittiness may—or may not!—be retroactive), with a false detection. The discourse has more than one story.

Notes

1. Thus in a recent, impressive collection of scholarly essays bearing on Conan Doyle's and Holmes's methods, *The Sign of Three: Dupin, Holmes, Peirce* (Eco and Sebeok 1983), "The Speckled Band" goes almost entirely unnoticed. This is rather like the famously "curious incident of the dog in the night-time" recounted in "Silver Blaze" (curious, in that "the dog did nothing in the night-time" [p. 190]): it seems noteworthy that this particularly popular story contributes nothing to the evidence of Holmes's method.

2. Here again "The Speckled Band" invites particular attention: of all the cases in which he has studied Holmes's methods, Watson tells us, "I cannot recall any which presented more singular features than that which was associated with the well-known Surrey family of the Roylotts of Stoke Moran" (p. 152).

3. "Epistemically impossible": I recur to Michel Foucault (1970 [1966]: xxii et passim) for the concept, but the phrase is also used by Robert Champigny (1977: 22).

4. Thus a contemporaneous edition of the *Encyclopædia Britannica* notes: "The structure of the ear in serpents seems to demonstrate that these creatures are dull in their sense of hearing" (8th ed., s.v. "serpents").

5. Winks seems to be following Charles Rycroft's 1957 remark: "In the ideal detective story, the detective or hero would discover that he himself is the criminal for whom he has been seeking" (quoted in Symons 1972: 7). See also Helmut Heissenbuttel (1983 [1963]: 91). As early as 1933, Sayers's Peter Wimsey is alluding casually to "those detective stories where the detective turns out to be the villain" (Sayers 1967 [1933]: 185). The prologue to Julian Symons's 1949 *Bland Beginning* suggests how conventional this identification had already become: "Posit Willshard/

Glibbery, the great detective, as the murderer. Commonplace? Perhaps—but let his murderous identity stay unrevealed, let him be a schizophrene making the most urgent efforts with Detectial Personality Number 1 to unravel the tangle made for him by Murderous Personality Number 2" (Symons 1987 [1949]: vii).

6. Cited by Gavin Lambert (1980 [1975]: 50). (This passage does not appear in the heavily revised, 1976 American edition of Lambert's book.) Cf. Ian Ousby (1976: 13, citing in particular Jonathan Wild).

7. *synecdochic*: A synecdoche is a figure of speech substituting a part for the whole, or vice versa. [Editor's note]

References

Babener, Liahna 1987 [1972] "The Shadow's Shadow: The Motif of the Double in Edgar Allan Poe's 'The Purloined Letter,'" in *Literary Theory in Praxis,* edited by Shirley F. Staton, 42-53 (Philadelphia: University of Pennsylvania Press).

Baring-Gould, William S., ed. 1967 *The Annotated Sherlock Holmes,* 2 vols. (New York: Clarkson N. Potter).

Barzun, Jacques 1980 [1961] "Detection and the Literary Art," from *The Delights of Detection,* in Winks 1980: 144-53.

Bigelow, S. Tupper 1976 "An Assessment and Valuation of the Ten Best Canonical Stories, with Some Observations on Those Somewhat Less Deserving of Praise," in *Beyond Baker Street: A Sherlockian Anthology,* edited by Michael Harrison, 45-54 (Indianapolis and New York: Bobbs-Merrill).

Bonfantini, Massimo A., and Giampaolo Proni 1983 "To Guess or Not to Guess?" in Eco and Sebeok 1983: 119-34.

Brooks, Peter 1985 [1984] *Reading for the Plot: Design and Intention in Narrative* (New York: Vintage).

Caillois, Roger 1983 [1941] "The Detective Novel as Game," translated by William W. Stowe, in *The Poetics of Murder: Detective Fiction and Literary Theory,* edited by Glenn W. Most and William W. Stowe, 1-12 (New York: Harcourt Brace Jovanovich).

Champigny, Robert 1977 *What Will Have Happened: A Philosophical and Technical Essay on Mystery Stories* (Bloomington: Indiana University Press).

Chatman, Seymour 1978 *Story and Discourse: Narrative Structure in Fiction and Film* (Ithaca: Cornell University Press).

Collins, Wilkie 1966 [1868] *The Moonstone,* edited by J. I. M. Stewart (London: Penguin).

Culler, Jonathan 1981 "Story and Discourse in the Analysis of Narrative," *The Pursuit of Signs: Semiotics, Literature, Deconstruction,* 169-87 (Ithaca: Cornell University Press).

Derrida, Jacques 1975 "The Purveyor of Truth," translated by Willis Domingo, James Hulbert, Moshe Ron, and Marie-Rose Logan, *Yale French Studies* 52: 31-113.

Doyle, Arthur Conan 1924 *Memories and Adventures* (London: Hodder and Stoughton). 1980 [1927] "The Sherlock Holmes Prize Competition—How I Made My List," in *A Sherlock Holmes Compendium,* edited by Peter Haining, 208-10 (London: W. H. Allen).

Eco, Umberto, and Thomas A. Sebeok, eds. 1983 *The Sign of Three: Dupin, Holmes, Peirce* (Bloomington: Indiana University Press).

Foucault, Michel 1970 [1966] *The Order of Things: An Archaeology of the Human Sciences* (New York: Random House).

Guillard, Dawson 1981 *Dorothy L. Sayers* (New York: Ungar).

Haycraft, Howard, ed. 1946 *The Art of the Mystery Story* (New York: Simon and Schuster).

Heissenbuttel, Helmut 1983 [1963] "Rules of the Game of the Crime Novel," translated by Glenn W. Most and William W. Stowe, in *The Poetics of Murder: Detective Fiction and Literary Theory,* edited by Glenn W. Most and William W. Stowe, 79-92 (New York: Harcourt Brace Jovanovich).

Hoffman, Daniel 1972 *Poe Poe Poe Poe Poe Poe Poe* (Garden City, NY: Doubleday).

Klein, Kathleen Gregory, and Joseph Keller 1986 "Deductive Detective Fiction: The Self-Destructive Genre," *Genre* 19(2): 155-72.

Knox, Ronald A. 1946 [1929] "A Detective Story Decalogue," in Haycraft 1946: 194-96.

Lambert, Gavin 1980 [1975] "Prologue," *The Dangerous Edge,* in Winks 1980: 47-52.

Murphy, Cait 1987 "The Game's Still Afoot," *The Atlantic* 259(3): 58-62, 64-66.

Nicolson, Marjorie 1946 [1929] "The Professor and the Detective," in Haycraft 1946: 110-27.

Ousby, Ian 1976 *Bloodhounds of Heaven: The Detective in English Fiction from Godwin to Doyle* (Cambridge, MA: Harvard University Press).

Poe, Edgar Allan 1978 *Collected Works of Edgar Allan Poe,* edited by Thomas Ollive Mabbott. Vols. 2 and 3, *Tales and Sketches* (Cambridge, MA: Harvard University Press).

Porter, Dennis 1981 *The Pursuit of Crime: Art and Ideology in Detective Fiction* (New Haven: Yale University Press).

Prince, Gerald 1987 *A Dictionary of Narratology* (Lincoln and London: University of Nebraska Press).

Redmond, Donald A. 1982 *Sherlock Holmes: A Study in Sources* (Kingston and Montreal: McGill-Queen's University Press).

Sayers, Dorothy L. 1946 [1929] "Introduction," from *The Omnibus of Crime,* in Haycraft 1946: 71-109. 1967 [1933] *Murder Must Advertise* (New York: Avon).

Sebeok, Thomas A., and Jean Umiker-Sebeok 1983 "'You Know My Method': A Juxtaposition of Charles S. Peirce and Sherlock Holmes," in Eco and Sebeok 1983: 11-54.

Symons, Julian 1972 *Mortal Consequences, A History: From the Detective Story to the Crime Novel* (New York: Schocken). 1987 [1949] *Bland Beginning* (New York: Carroll and Graf).

Todorov, Tzvetan 1977 [1971] *The Poetics of Prose,* translated by Richard Howard (Ithaca: Cornell University Press).

Truzzi, Marcello 1983 [1973] "Sherlock Holmes: Applied Social Psychologist," in Eco and Sebeok 1983: 55-80.

Van Dine, S. S. 1946 [1928] "Twenty Rules for Writing Detective Stories," in Haycraft 1946: 189-93.

Wilbur, Richard 1962 "Edgar Allan Poe," in *Major Writers of America,* edited by Perry Miller, 1:369-82 (New York: Harcourt Brace Jovanovich).

Winks, Robin W., ed. 1980 *Detective Fiction: A Collection of Critical Essays* (Englewood Cliffs, NJ: Prentice-Hall).

Zangwill, Israel 1986 [1891] *The Big Bow Mystery* (New York: Carroll and Graf).

Rosemary Jann (essay date 1995)

SOURCE: Jann, Rosemary. "'Cherchez la femme.'" In *The Adventures of Sherlock Holmes: Detecting Social Order,* pp. 103-26. New York: Twayne Publishers, 1995.

[*In the following excerpt, Jann examines notions of class in "The Adventure of the Speckled Band," focusing on Sherlock Holmes's attempts to shield the Roylott family from scandal.*]

In **"The Speckled Band"** we find the father-daughter contest transposed into a much more somber key and painted in the heightened colors of the Gothic thriller. Helen and Julia Stoner are purely innocent and ignorant victims of a larger-than-life villain, helpless and abused maidens imprisoned in a gloomy, decaying mansion, threatened by strange beasts and sinister gypsies, in need not just of a detective, but of one who "can see deeply into the manifold wickedness of the human heart" (**SPEC** ["**The Adventure of the Speckled Band**"] 1:349). Here the stepdaughter is conveniently doubled, so that one twin can die the mysterious midnight death demanded by the Gothic plot, while the other can be saved for the happy marriage she so justly deserves. With melodramatic insistence, the stepfather's evil is overdetermined by a piling up of contributing causes: he is not merely greedy but insane, the last link in a degenerate aristocratic family, suffering from a hereditary "violence of temper approaching to mania" that has been further intensified by many years in the feverish tropics. Colossal strength and size are thrown in for good measure (1:350). Sherlock Holmes plays much the same role in this melodrama that he will in the later *Hound of the Baskervilles,* another tale in which terrors verging on the supernatural are ultimately reduced to the work of quite real, if exotic, animals. As the agent of scientific reason and modern justice, Holmes cuts mystery and horror down to size, revealing the usual sordid economic motives at their heart and ensuring that the rightful heirs will be able to enjoy their property.

Jasmine Yong Hall and others noted that the implicitly incestuous pressures that stepfathers bring to bear on stepdaughters are in this story suggested by the imagery of the snake attack as a kind of rape; after "piercing" the wall of Helen's bedroom (1:354), Roylott has her sleep in a bed bolted to the floor so that she cannot escape his snake when it crawls through the hole in the ceiling.[1] Notwithstanding their importance in motivating crime, however, the sisters function as little more than props in this story, where the real contest is once again between the detective and the "male relative," Roylott. On one level, this contest is conducted in the same phallic imagery: Holmes straightens out the poker bent by Roylott and thrashes the doctor's snake with his own bamboo cane (Hall, 300-301), thus proving himself to be the stronger man. But their opposition is figured in class terms as well. Grimesby Roylott is on one level a degenerate aristocrat, traditional enemy to middle-class prerogatives. His violent behavior is the sign of a hereditary weakness as well as a manifestation of the feudal indifference to the rights of others, including his own stepdaughters. His denunciation of Holmes as "the Scotland Yard Jack-in-office" (1:356) is the aristocrat's typical put-down of middle-class workers as vulgar and officious drudges and is of course considered particularly insolent because it denies Holmes his status as a gentleman amateur. But Roylott has also adopted the middle-class lesson of enterprise and self-help. Realizing that, given his family's dwindling fortunes, he "must adapt himself to the new conditions" or waste away as an "aristocratic pauper" (1:349), he obtained a medical degree and went out to the colonies to earn his fortune. There, by virtue of "his professional skill and force of character," he succeeded in establish-

ing a large practice, although he cannot keep it up because of his disorderly conduct. Holmes never denies his intellectual power. Indeed, it is precisely his professional status that makes Roylott so dangerous: "When a doctor does go wrong he is the first of criminals. He has nerve and he has knowledge" (1:364). Nothing is so destabilizing to social order, this implies, as the professional who uses the very skills that afford him status to betray his most sacred responsibilities. Having abandoned his respectable profession to return to Stoke Moran and play the squire on his wife's money, Roylott draws on his formidable mental resources to plot diabolical murders when that income is threatened by his stepdaughters' marriages. Perhaps it is because of his dangerous corruption of both aristocratic and middle-class ideals that Roylott must die, the only criminal in the ***Adventures*** [***The Adventures of Sherlock Holmes***] whom we see meet such an end. Such an outsized melodrama villain cannot finally be contained by the law, and he finds his death in a sensational revenge, as the snake he has trained turns on him (with a little encouragement from Sherlock Holmes).

Holmes reestablishes social order not only by helping to eliminate the evil stepfather but also by ensuring that Helen Stoner and her independent income are confided to the care of her new husband, notwithstanding Mr. Armitage's failure to take seriously the threats against her earlier (1:349). And despite Roylott's egregious criminality, Holmes and Watson play their typical role of suppressing scandal against prominent families. They take care to conceal their true identities from the coachman who drives them to Stoke Moran (1:358) and suppress the truth about Roylott's death until after Helen's death, revealing it then only to squelch rumors that attributed even greater villainy to him (1:346). Unworthy aristocrats and corrupt professionals are self-defeating, the story implies, and the technicalities of the law (such as testifying truthfully about the full circumstances of mysterious deaths) should be bent occasionally in order to protect the reputation and position of the innocent.

Note

1. Jasmin Yong Hall, "Ordering the Sensational: Sherlock Holmes and the Female Gothic," *Studies in Short Fiction* 28 (1991): 298.

Michael Atkinson (essay date 1996)

SOURCE: Atkinson, Michael. "The Subtle Serpent in 'The Adventure of the Speckled Band.'" In *The Secret Marriage of Sherlock Holmes and Other Eccentric Readings,* pp. 23-38. Ann Arbor: The University of Michigan Press, 1996.

[*In the following essay, Atkinson views the snake in "The Adventure of the Speckled Band" as a symbol of Indian yogi philosophy.*]

> The idea . . . was just such a one as would occur to a clever and ruthless man who had had an Eastern training.

Asked to name his favorite Sherlock Holmes tale, Conan Doyle couldn't remember the title and called it simply "the one about the snake." That story was **"The Adventure of the Speckled Band,"** and most readers favor it as well—with good reason. Conan Doyle was thoroughly right to call it "the one about the snake," for the story touches just about every form the serpent takes in our conscious and unconscious imaginations. His forgetting the title, too, was "right"—for it points us toward the reason Holmes at first failed to comprehend the significance of those mysterious words, "the speckled band," and then toward the curious way in which Holmes at last came to grasp their meaning.

With the passing of time, the title may not be the only feature one forgets, even in so vivid a tale as this, so here is a review of the salient details.

* * *

> Working as he did rather for the love of his art than for the acquirement of wealth, he refused to associate himself with any investigation which did not tend towards the unusual, and even the fantastic.

Of all Holmes's cases, Watson "cannot recall any which presented more singular features" than this one. "It is possible that I might have placed them upon record before, but a promise of secrecy was made at the time, from which I have only been freed during the last month by the untimely death of the lady to whom the pledge was given."

The adventure begins when that lady, a young but graying Helen Stoner, arrives shaken at 221-B Baker Street. She has heard that Holmes "can see deeply into the manifold wickedness of the human heart," and she comes to seek his help in resolving fears that even her fiancé dismisses as "the fancies of a nervous woman."

She has good cause for fear. Her stepfather, Dr. Grimesby Roylott, is a violent-tempered physician who once beat his native butler to death while serving in India. There he also married the recently widowed mother of two-year-old Helen and her twin, Julia. Shortly after the family returned to his ancestral home in England, Helen's mother was killed in a railway accident, leaving Dr. Roylott in charge of her considerable fortune until such time as the girls might marry. The grounds of their remote estate are now oddly populated with living memoirs of India—a cheetah and a baboon—as well as a troupe of wandering gypsies who have become the hot-tempered Roylott's only associates.

Two years earlier, Helen's sister Julia had accepted a proposal of marriage, and her stepfather raised no objection. But a fortnight before the wedding, she died.

The night of her death, Julia had complained to Helen of the scent of cigar smoke from Roylott's adjacent room, and she reported hearing a low, clear whistle for the previous three nights. Later, both girls locked themselves in their respective rooms (as one would on an estate hosting wild animals and gypsies) and retired to sleep.

Helen heard the "wild scream of a terrified woman," and as she opened her door, she "seemed to hear a low whistle, such as [her] sister described, and a few moments later a clanging sound, as if a mass of metal had fallen." Her sister's door opened, and Helen saw Julia fall to the ground in convulsions, shrieking "O, my God! Helen! It was the band! The speckled band!" and pointing toward the doctor's room. Dr. Roylott arrived on the scene, administered brandy and summoned further medical aid from the village, but all efforts to revive her were in vain. Julia's demise was all the more mysterious because the room was sealed tight, there were no marks of violence on her body, and the village coroner could detect no trace of poison. "It is [Helen's] belief that she died of pure fear and nervous shock, though what it was which frightened her I cannot imagine."

Helen's life has disturbing parallels to her twin sister Julia's. She, too, has recently become engaged, and, though her stepfather again offered no opposition to the match, he undertook house repairs that required Helen to put herself in a very uncomfortable position:

> my bedroom wall has been pierced, so that I have had to move into the chamber in which my sister died, and to sleep in the very bed in which she slept. Imagine, then, my thrill of terror when last night, as I lay awake, thinking over her terrible fate, I suddenly heard in the silence of the night the low whistle which had been the herald of her own death.

Holmes agrees the matter is most urgent. Both he and Helen suspect the band of gypsies. Before they can leave for the estate, Holmes and Watson are confronted in their Baker Street rooms by Dr. Roylott himself, who has come to warn the pair not to meddle in his affairs. He demonstrates the strength of his rage by seizing the poker and bending it with his bare hands. Though Holmes, not to be bested, nonchalantly straightens the poker out again, it is clear Roylott is a dangerous character.

Holmes and Watson leave for the estate, posing as architects. They agree the repairs are just excuses to move the young lady from her room. Trying the shutters from outside, Holmes discovers they cannot be forced and must discard his initial theory that gypsies entered the room from without. Inside the fatal room, noticing the bed is clamped to the floor, Holmes focuses on the "bell-rope which hung down beside the bed, the tassel actually lying upon the pillow." He is told the bellpull was "only put there a couple of years ago." With a brisk jerk, Holmes discovers it is a dummy. "The rope— for so we may call it, since it was clearly never meant for a bell-pull," was "fastened only to a hook just above . . . the little opening of the ventilator"—also installed just two years ago, shortly before Julia's death.

The investigation proceeds to Dr. Roylott's room, in which Holmes takes note of a large metal safe, a saucer of milk, and a dog leash tied in a loop. Holmes explains that when night falls he and Watson will wait outside for Helen to signal that Roylott has retired. Then they will take her place in the fateful chamber, while she goes to her own proper room, even though it is in disrepair. Clearly Holmes thinks the danger lies not outside the house, but within. Soon the signal lamp gleams, and they advance. Just before they enter the window, "out from a clump of laurel bushes there darted what seemed to be a hideous and distorted child, who threw itself on the grass with writhing limbs, and then ran swiftly across the lawn into the darkness." Watson, like the reader, is struck by the full horror of the image, which Holmes only partly dispels by explaining that what they saw was a baboon.

In the fatal room, they keep a dark and silent vigil. At last they hear a low whistle.

> The instant that we heard it, Holmes sprang from the bed, struck a match, and lashed furiously with his cane at the bell-pull. . . . [H]is face was deadly pale, and filled with horror and loathing. . . .
>
> Suddenly there broke from the silence of the night the most horrible cry to which I have ever listened. It swelled up louder and louder, a hoarse yell of pain and fear and anger all mingled in the one dreadful shriek. . . .
>
> "What can it mean?" I gasped.
>
> "It means that it is all over," Holmes answered.

Entering Roylott's room, they find him sitting quite dead beside the open safe, the dog leash in his lap.

> Round his brow he had a peculiar yellow band, with brownish speckles. . . .
>
> "The band! the speckled band!" whispered Holmes.
>
> . . . In an instant his strange head-gear began to move, and there reared itself from among his hair the squat diamond-shaped head and puffed neck of a loathsome serpent.
>
> "It is a swamp adder!" cried Holmes "—the deadliest snake in India. He has died within ten seconds of being bitten. Violence does, in truth, recoil upon the violent."

Using the dog whip as a noose, Holmes replaces the serpent in the safe and closes the door. The terrified Helen is sent off to "the care of her good aunt at Harrow," and police are left to infer that the doctor died while "indiscreetly playing with a dangerous pet."

Holmes admits he was led down the path of error by the presence of the gypsies and Julia's peculiar use of the word "*band*." When he realized the apparent bell-pull was just a rope, the idea of a snake instantly occurred to him—a source of a poison so exotic as not to register in the tests of a country coroner. The snake was trained to return to the sound of a whistle and fetch its reward of milk, and the metallic clang was the sound of the closing safe that served to cage the serpent. Every night the doctor "would put it through the ventilator . . . with the certainty that it would crawl down the rope, and land on the bed. It might or might not bite the occupant, perhaps she might escape every night for a week, but sooner or later she must fall a victim."

Attacking the serpent with his cane, Holmes drove it back through the ventilator and "roused its snakish temper, so that it flew upon the first person it saw. In this way I am no doubt indirectly responsible for Dr. Grimesby Roylott's death, and I cannot say that it is likely to weigh very heavily upon my conscience."

*   *   *

> The idea of a snake instantly occurred to me, and when I coupled it with my knowledge that the Doctor was furnished with a supply of creatures from India, I felt that I was probably on the right track.

Since this is "the one about the snake," it will pay to have a closer look at that serpent. In concocting a snake that responds to a whistle (snakes are deaf), drinks milk (at the very bottom of a serpent's dietary choices), climbs both up and down ropes (!), and produces a venom that kills in ten seconds if the victim is male and immoral, several minutes if she is female and innocent (whereas the fastest death caused by any known species of snake is measured in hours, no matter what your mother told you)—in concocting such a snake, Conan Doyle reveals himself to have skipped the research in writing his favorite story.

Nor did Holmes himself consult (or write) an expert's monograph on herpetology to clarify the case. That has not, however, prevented many readers from essaying naturalistic speculations of their own. After reviewing the possibilities exhaustively, ***The Annotated Sherlock Holmes*** concludes, "It would seem, regretfully, that no known species of snake fully satisfies all the requirements of 'the speckled band.'" But finally, with an eloquence striking for one whose tongue is lodged firmly in his cheek, the editor endorses this possibility:

> the creature was a horrible hybrid, bred by Dr. Roylott—a sinister combination of the Mexican Gila monster (*Heloderma horridum*) and the spectacled or Indian cobra, now known as *Naja naja naja.* It would have fangs in the upper jaw inherited from one parent, and in the lower jaw from the other, and a venom in-

comparably strengthened by hybridization, thus assuring the almost instant demise of any victim. Here we have an animal . . . with ears like any lizard, wherewith to hear a whistle; and one whose legs and claws permitted it to run up a bell-rope as easily as down.[1]

Admirable as we may find such ingenuity, it may be more to the point to put the Indian cobra's name into the language of the gila monster's Mexico and call it *nada, nada, nada*—an airy nothing, a fine hippogriff, a worthy entry in imagination's bestiary. Conan Doyle shut his eyes to facts and concocted an outrageous beast that could do *his* bidding as well as Dr. Roylott's, one that could assure that violence would punningly "recoil" upon the violent.

Now since this is literature, not natural history, and since, as Aristotle reminds us, art is more philosophical than history, we would do better to look to philosophy for the nature of this snake. Conan Doyle made it an Indian snake, so we quite naturally turn to Indian philosophy. Conan Doyle had Holmes see a snake where others saw only a rope, and that almost gives the game away. Here is how the famous trope is put in one of yogic philosophy's central texts, Shankara's celebrated *Crest-Jewel of Discrimination*:

> For example, [in the moonlight] you see a rope and think it is a snake. As soon as you realize that the rope is a rope, your false perception of a snake ceases, and you are no longer distracted by the fear which it inspired. Therefore, the wise man who wishes to break his bondage must know the Reality.[2]

In this story of things Indian transported to English soil, Conan Doyle uses the well-known Indian formula by reversing it. Like the meditating yogi, Holmes keeps a still and silent vigil to await his revelation. But whereas the Indian sage sees what looks like a snake and knows it to be just a rope, the great detective sees a "mere" rope and knows it will bear a snake. The result of this knowledge is not to banish fear, but to increase the shudder of terror we feel. In short, the Indian wisdom is present, but, like a proper yogi, stood on its head.[3]

Roylott committed his crime by bringing an Indian serpent to England. Utilizing the time-honored method of identifying with the criminal's mind in order to resolve the case, I would like to follow Roylott's lead and import to the good English soil of the Holmes canon another distinctively Indian serpent to do some work for me—to indicate how *many* manifestations of the serpent turn up in this story and give such power to "the one about the snake." Using the arcana of Hindu philosophy in the way Holmes employs treatises on tattoos and deep-sea fishes to clarify his cases, I would like to introduce the fabled kundalini serpent into this reading of **"The Adventure of the Speckled Band."**

Classical yogic philosophy envisions the mystical kundalini to be a serpent of subtle substance lying coiled inside the base of the spine, from which position it can be roused, through meditation, to move up through and to awaken the seven chakras, or energy centers, positioned along the spine at different levels of the psychic body. These centers represent different physical and psychological energies, as well as a sequence of distinct ways of viewing any reality. Here is a little schema of the chakras, their corresponding bodily areas, and the styles of outlook associated with them, moving traditionally from the bottom up. . . .

The Seven Chakras of Kundalini Yoga

7 Sahasrara (crown chakra): transcendent enlightenment

6 Ajna (third eye chakra): compassionate wisdom

5 Visshuda (throat chakra): articulation, discrimination

4 Anahata (heart chakra): healing, reconciled dualities

3 Manipura (navel chakra): ego identity, willed action

2 Svadisthana (genital chakra): sexuality, procreation

1 Muladhara (anal chakra): hoarding, retention

At the lowest—the anal—chakra, one simply holds on to the necessities of life, grasping and hoarding, never letting go. Here, the human spirit is shrunk to its most constricted. The second chakra, associated with the genital region, sees everything in sexual terms. Don Juan and Freud live here, and some students think their English professors do too. The third chakra, located in the navel region, is the center of ego and identity. At its best, this center is represented by the questing hero who defines a new identity by undertaking adventures. The fourth chakra's name is Anahata, literally "no hit" or "not striking." Here opposites are unified and reconciled, healing the divisions that tear at the heart. At the throat is the fifth chakra, articulation and purified discrimination. Here, one can not only see things as they are, but speak them as well. The famous third eye is the sixth chakra. From its vantage, one sees with complete compassion and wisdom. And the seventh chakra, at the crown of the head, represents the opening of the mind to cosmic consciousness, beyond the mundane experience of everyday life. As the yogi purifies mind and heart, the energy represented by the kundalini serpent moves up the chakras, shifting the concerns of life upward, from just holding on to what one has, toward opening to the fullness of the divine.

For centuries these centers, through which the subtle energy of the kundalini ascends, have represented stages of spiritual evolution. They can also help us to read literature more richly. For each story, even each image, can be seen from these differing perspectives, considerably enhancing our reading. Take the literary and mythological image of the serpent itself. At the first chakra lies the dragon serpent who guards the treasure hoard and holds the maiden captive. The second chakra gives us the familiar phallic serpent of Freud. At the third chakra, the hero's emerging identity is well imaged by the snake shedding its skin. The serpents winding up the physician's staff or caduceus embody the healing spirit of the fourth chakra. At the fifth chakra, discrimination is the key, and one is able to distinguish snake from rope, illusion from reality. We are wise as serpents, if not as gentle as doves. The serpent of the Ajna chakra (or third eye) is strikingly embodied in the cobra who peers from the forehead of the pharaoh's crown. And the seventh chakra is well represented by the great hooded serpent who rose above the Buddha to shelter him during the storm preceding his enlightenment.

It is remarkable how many of these serpents figure in **"The Speckled Band"** and amplify its power. Let us have a look, taking the second chakra first.

A snake is certainly a most unusual murder weapon, but it is more than that. Dr. Roylott's unsettling ingenuity suggests a motive scarcely to be measured by the simple desire to preserve his ancestral estate. If on the conscious level this is a story of a stepfather who wants to retain control of his stepdaughters' fortunes, at the unconscious level we have a picture of the father who simply wants his daughters. (Physically, Helen bears the marks of abuse: the doctor's grip has left bruises on her wrist. In Conan Doyle's original manuscript, Helen Stoner was Helen Roylott and Dr. Roylott was her natural father.)⁴ This subliminal incest theme is one of the things that makes us uneasy as we read. Certainly the image of a (step)father penetrating the walls of his daughter's room so as to slip his serpent in has both the power and the indirectness to activate our response without awakening us entirely to what is there. We see the rope and not the snake, as it were, and yet we find it disturbing. The same is true when Holmes and Watson glimpse what seems "a hideous and distorted child, who threw itself on the grass with writhing limbs"—a nightmare vision of incestuous offspring, realistically explained away as a baboon, after its unsettling impression has been made.

It takes only a shift of perspective (from the second chakra to the first and the third) to see here the clear outline of heroic romance, traditionally typified by St. George and the dragon. The first, or anal, chakra is the home of the tyrant holdfast and the hoard-guarding dragon. Dr. Roylott is the retentive tyrant who holds the maiden and the money captive in the wasteland, and the swamp adder is a miniature of the dragon-serpent who guards the treasure. Its lair is a metal safe, no less. With his faithful companion Watson, Holmes is the knight errant who risks his own life to do battle with the dragon and rescue the maiden, wriggling out of a near-death situation, once again to establish his particular heroic identity.

The other chakras, and their serpentine representatives, play roles here as well, though perversely. Rather than holding up the serpentine staff of the physician, Dr. Roylott manipulates his snake with a whip. He has abandoned the art of healing and taken up the cruel science of poisons. At the adventure's end, the striking image of the snake's head rearing out from his hair presents a gruesome parody of the sacred cobra head that gazes out from the pharaoh's crown. Here is wisdom gone awry, caught in a grotesque image that stays with us long after we close the book. The life-giving third eye of wisdom has become the vacant stare of death.

The seventh, all-protecting serpent of enlightenment quite transcends any heights this story might reach, even subliminally, and so it is absent. But the fifth chakra of discrimination and articulation, distinguishing snake from rope and eloquently elucidating the mystery, is the presiding genius of this tale, well embodied in the measured phrases of Holmes explaining all at the story's end.

Though Holmes himself would likely have shrugged off comparisons to the dragon slayer, the path of the kundalini makes clear just how richly and variously the serpent archetype and its associated characters manifest themselves here. To reduce a story like this to mere iterations of old patterns would be a mistake, but to miss the serpent's diverse archetypal presences would be to ignore a significant source of the tale's vitality—a force so compelling that we are quite willing to overlook all the contrivances and loose ends and fall gladly under its spell.

* * *

> "I had," said he, "come to an entirely erroneous conclusion. . . . The presence of the gipsies, and the use of the word 'band' . . . were sufficient to put me upon an entirely wrong scent."

Conan Doyle too was under the spell of the serpent, as his faulty memory reveals. To cast the snake into the formula of a Sherlock Holmes adventure, he had to put it into a puzzle that the intellect could solve. So Helen Stoner brings Sherlock Holmes a rational puzzle—a classic sealed-room mystery—accompanied by a verbal clue, Julia's dying phrase: "It was the band! The speckled band!" But years later, recalling the powerful climactic scene in which the innocent-looking rope conveys the venomous snake toward the waiting detective in the dark of night, it is no wonder that Conan Doyle forgot the word *band*—such an improbable word for serpent, at least as contrived as the talents the snake required to enter and leave the apparently sealed room. The word itself left no mark on its author. It faded like the setup of a joke too intricate to remember.

Holmes himself does not solve the mystery of the word *band* in language, but by a series of migrations. His understanding of the word, like ours, goes through several turns: the group of gypsies, the gypsies' headdress, and only finally (and most improbably) the snake. Significantly, his understanding changes only as he himself changes positions in the story—a strategy that is deeply appropriate to a story in which so many things migrate, taking one another's places. Dr. Roylott takes the place of Major General Stoner, the late husband and father, and then moves the family from India back to England. After his wife's death, Helen and Julia replace their mother as Roylott's access to wealth. Within the manor, Helen fears that by moving to Julia's room she will take her sister's place as a victim as well.

Holmes's migrations begin when he steps into the role Helen's fiancé should play, believing in the young woman's fear and coming quickly to her aid, even spending the night in her room. At the climax, he stands in for the intended victim of the crime. In taking Helen's place, he also "becomes" Julia, waiting in her room, immobile on her bed, striking a match as she did, seeing the same snake she saw, and finally speaking her very words—"the band! the speckled band!" Only then does he understand. Holmes, often so oracular himself, is here perplexed by oracular words until he has moved through the spaces and confronted the images that give the words meanings, images that linger long after the words have ceased to puzzle. Like Oedipus wandering the circuit of Corinth, Delphi, and Thebes—the round of son, stranger, and husband—Holmes decodes the prophecy not as a sequence of words to be defined, but as a series of roles to be taken on: fiancé, sister, victim. He cannot investigate the mystery lexically; he must live it out. Confronting the speckled band, he too experiences the terror: he is "deadly pale, and filled with horror and loathing."

Holmes's migration does not stop with his taking the victim's place. He moves through the role of villain as well. When Dr. Roylott visited Baker Street and bent the poker in a show of strength, Holmes was quick to step into his place and bend the poker back again. In the end, rousing the snakish temper of the swamp adder and driving it back through the ventilator, Holmes is as much a killer as Roylott, as he admits to Watson. No wonder he is content to mislead the police about how Roylott came to be bitten by the snake: in covering the doctor's crime, he covers his own.

The path to Holmes's understanding the word *band* is as sinuous and changing as the route of the kundalini serpent itself. Contrary to the image Holmes cultivates as the detached investigator, here he does not stand inviolate, a Cartesian experimenter untouched by what he contemplates. Victor, victim, and villain, he is thoroughly involved, even implicated, in the crimes.

* * *

"It is not cold which makes me shiver," said the woman. . . . "[I]t is fear, Mr. Holmes. It is terror."

Conan Doyle uses a host of means to make sure the reader, like Holmes, experiences the frightfulness of the crime as well as the elegance of its solution. The very distance and coolness that Holmes abandons, Conan Doyle gives to Roylott, who stands outside the scene he would affect. The image of detached reason he presents is chilling. It makes his crime all the more unsettling. As Holmes puts it, "When a doctor does go wrong he is the first of criminals. He has nerve and he has knowledge." A violent man who has turned all his strength to cruel calculation, Roylott is all the more frightening in his restraint. Constructing his elegant plan, letting a snake do his work for him, he presents us with a demonic mirror of the detachment we usually attribute to Holmes (and thus foreshadows the archvillain Moriarty). The patience with which Dr. Roylott put the adder down the rope night after night, waiting until it chose to strike, is a sinister version of the charged vigils Holmes keeps in this and other stories. Knowing of the snake's nightly visits (as Julia and Helen did not), we shudder at the peril to which such innocents were repeatedly exposed. Roylott's clamping the bed to the floor intensifies the sense of immobilized helplessness we feel for his victims. When, upon reflection, we realize that since killing Julia, he has for two years kept the snake in readiness for Helen, his coldness of mind seems all the more horrible.

In addition to the disturbing strategies of the doctor, Conan Doyle increases the story's sense of fear by charging the other characters with it as well. Fear has already shot gray through young Helen's hair, and her firm belief that fear itself killed her sister only adds to the general atmosphere of gothic terror. To increase the shudder brought by Roylott's death cry—a "hoarse yell of pain and fear and anger all mingled in the one dreadful shriek"—Conan Doyle makes it a haunting part of the region's folklore: "They say that away down in the village, and even in the distant parsonage, that cry raised the sleepers from their beds."

These sympathetic resonances of fear combine with the many forms of the serpent archetype to make this one of the most exciting and memorable adventures, and they keep our understanding of the mystery, like Holmes's, from being merely intellectual. As the speckled band moves through the shadows and slithers down the bellpull toward Julia, toward Helen, toward Holmes, that serpent can be fully understood only when it gives a shudder to detective and reader alike.

* * *

"Hum!" said he, scratching his chin in some perplexity, "my theory certainly presents some difficulties. . . . I can only claim the merit that I instantly reconsidered my position."

Arriving at the meaning and experiencing the frisson of "the speckled band" are so satisfying that Conan Doyle can leave the original purposes of the investigation dangling. After all, Holmes takes on Helen Stoner's case to save her life and free her to marry. Yet at the end of the story, she is packed off to the care of her "good aunt at Harrow" with not a word of fiancé or marriage. What's more, Watson frames the tale by saying that Helen's untimely death has at last freed him to tell it, but leaves us ignorant of how she met her premature demise just a few years after Holmes saved her from being killed. It may be that ragged stories are best served by eccentric readers, willing to shift ground as the opportunities arise, gypsies like those that thread their way through this adventure.

Holmes himself is something of a gypsy here. Erroneous as well as errant, Holmes first suspects the "band" of gypsies, then says his "only . . . merit" is that he was quite ready to change his mind, abandon his position. So, as we move through these stories, we too can be willing to camp for a while in Hindu or Nietzschean philosophy, in psychology or economics, deconstruction or myth, not seeking a final destination, a conclusive style of interpreting to call home. Like the gypsies who come to town, or the knight errant of romance who stands behind the figure of Sherlock Holmes, we will live off what we find at hand when we arrive.

Certainly it would be folly to cling to the stories' much advertised logic. A close, well-illuminated look is fatal to that illusion. As Holmes discovered the danger of an innocent bellpull—seeing the snake rather than the rope—so we find that these detective stories are more slippery, more interesting and more dangerous to our settled ideas than we had imagined—which is perhaps the first and final lesson of "the one about the snake."

Notes

1. Baring-Gould, *The Annotated Sherlock Holmes,* 1:266.

2. Shankara, *Crest-Jewel of Discrimination (Viveka-Chudamani),* 90-91.

3. In heading for India, which figured in more than a dozen of Conan Doyle's stories, I realize we are skipping over the Levant and the possibility of a biblical interpretation. Certainly an Edenic parallel might be tempting, with a Satanic Dr. Roylott bringing physical rather than spiritual death to a young woman by means of a snake in the midst of his fallen estate. However, the woman in question is not tempted but frightened and repelled. An Adam (her fiancé?) seems rather far off stage, though Holmes might well serve as a Christological figure, arriving late in the story, just in time to effect a salvation. In all, such a line of argument would be much less comprehensive and satisfying than the more geographically eccentric Indian proposition I would like to put forth. Readers in-

terested in Old and New Testament parallels in the Holmes stories should consult Wayne Wall, *God and Sherlock Holmes: A Study in the Life and Literature of Arthur Conan Doyle.*

4. See *The Annotated Sherlock Holmes,* 1:246.

Joseph A. Kestner (essay date 1997)

SOURCE: Kestner, Joseph A. "The Victorian Holmes: *The Adventures of Sherlock Holmes.*" In *Sherlock's Men: Masculinity, Conan Doyle, and Cultural History,* pp. 73-98. Aldershot, England: Ashgate, 1997.

[*In the following excerpt, Kestner discusses the mistreatment and neglect of women by male authority figures in "The Adventure of the Speckled Band."*]

Doyle's most incisive examination of the abuse of women by males in authority is **"The Speckled Band"** of February 1892. The case involves Helen Stoner, whose twin sister Julia had died mysteriously, soon before her marriage, uttering the exclamation 'the speckled band'. Helen Stoner tells Holmes that from her mother's legacy 'a certain annual sum should be allowed to each of us in the event of our marriage' (175) and that 'in a month or two I shall be married, with the control of my own income' (173). The sisters have been living with their stepfather, Dr Grimesby Roylott, 'the last survivor of one of the oldest Saxon families in England' (174). Roylott is nevertheless prone to aberrant behaviour and criminality. While in India, 'he beat his native butler to death, and narrowly escaped a capital sentence. As it was, he suffered a long term of imprisonment, and afterwards returned to England' (175).

Not only is Roylott guilty of murder when he returns from the colonies; the family is tainted genetically as well. It is of 'a dissolute and wasteful disposition. . . . Violence of temper approaching to mania has been hereditary in the men of the family, and in my stepfather's case it had, I believe, been intensified by his long residence in the tropics. . . . He is a man of immense strength, and absolutely uncontrollable in his anger' (174-5), Helen Stoner advises Holmes. As events reveal, Roylott had killed Julia Stoner by causing a swamp adder to slide through a ventilator down the bellrope to bite her while she slept in a bed affixed to the floor, adjacent to Roylott's bedroom. Roylott has now commanded Helen, on the eve of her marriage, to sleep in the same bed. Holmes and Watson hide in the room, prevent this second murder, and the serpent returns to infect Roylott, who dies.

Male desire in the figure of Roylott is a source of moral anarchy in **"The Speckled Band."** The fact that Helen and Julia Stoner are Roylott's stepdaughters raises the spectre of incest in the domestic sphere, a circumstance made apparent by the phallic nature of the death instrument, a snake, which indicates the intended crime is that of incestuous rape. Furthermore, the fact that the mode of death, an 'Indian swamp adder', originates from Roylott's contact with the colonies, condemns the colonial enterprise, as does the presence of a cheetah and a baboon from India on the grounds of Stoke Moran, indicating Roylott's savage and uncivilized disposition. In the tale, two forms of masculinity are juxtaposed: the colonial, eastern, aristocratic model of Roylott, and the middle-class gentlemanly nature of Holmes and Watson. Doyle thematizes this contrast of masculinities when Roylott bends a poker at 221B; Holmes 'picked up the steel poker, and with a sudden effort straightened it out again' (183), re-establishing a normative phallic order and underscoring the perversion of maleness by Roylott.

Two elements complicate the narrative. One is that both Holmes and Watson engage in secrecy regarding the events. Watson notes: 'It is possible that I might have placed them upon record before, but a promise of secrecy was made at the time, from which I have only been freed during the last month by the untimely death of the lady to whom the pledge was given' (171). In effect, Helen Stoner, despite her marriage to Percy Armitage after Roylott's death, died young as a result of these traumas. Here, as in **"A Case of Identity,"** the public exposure of the events is forestalled. Holmes both supports women's property rights and, at the same time, indicates that women cannot survive without male protection: the narrative thus questions the morality of male authority without suggesting it can be eliminated.

The tale also reveals the pandemic nature of crime in England. As Watson and Holmes drive to Stoke Moran, Watson observes

> the lovely Surrey lanes. It was a perfect day, with a bright sun and a few fleecy clouds in the heavens. . . . To me at least there was a strange contrast between the sweet promise of the spring and this sinister quest upon which we were engaged.
>
> (184)

To readers of the *Strand* passing through the suburbs, the significance of the locale and the implications of the narrative could be viewed from the train windows. As Hennessy and Mohan (1994) remark:

> Holmes's position as opponent to the traditional patriarch defines him as a 'new' man, but . . . this 'newness' is more a re-articulation than a transformation of the sexual economy of patriarchy. . . . The construction of woman in the public space as object of desire in need of protection helped tame the threat independent women posed to the family.
>
> (395, 401)

The narrative thus interrogates masculinity from various perspectives: the abuse of male authority, the commodification of the female body as an object of exchange or

possession among males, the strong incest motif, and the dangerous effects of contamination by colonial experience. 'The Home-Counties setting of many of these stories, plus the common presence of an innocent daughter, suggests an imagery of the crimes of Empire coming home to roost in the respectable heartland' (Priestman, 1990, 80). Doyle demonstrates that intransigent and reactionary masculinity is self-destructive for men.

Catherine Wynne (essay date 2002)

SOURCE: Wynne, Catherine. "Libidinal Encounters and Imperial Resistance: Knight Errant and Aberrant Serpent." In *The Colonial Conan Doyle: British Imperialism, Irish Nationalism, and the Gothic,* pp. 115-41. Westport, Conn.: Greenwood Press, 2002.

[*In the following excerpt, Wynne concludes that Doyle "inverts the process of patriarchal colonization" in "The Adventure of the Speckled Band," noting that the snake is symbolic of feminine principles in the tale.*]

FERTILITY, FEMININITY, AND THE SNAKE:
IMPERIAL IMPOSITION AND COLONIAL DISSENT

It is significant that the imperial contest in **"The Speckled Band"** centers on the sisters' wealth. In ancient and primitive societies the symbol of the snake is suffused with female sexuality, fecundity, landscape, and fertility rituals.[1] Green proposes, for example, that "the idea of sovereignty personified as a divine female is an extremely persistent tradition in early Irish myth. She was the goddess of the land, the spirit or essence of Ireland itself, and on her depended the fortunes, fertility and prosperity of her territory."[2] The image that accompanies the female deity is frequently that of a snake, "which may curl round a tree, encircle the goddess' arm or be fed from a bowl of fruit which she offers it."[3] In *Heart of Darkness* the sovereignty of the warrior queen is elided with the landscape:

> She carried her head high; her hair was done in the shape of a helmet; she had brass leggings to the knees, brass wire gauntlets to the elbow, a crimson spot on her tawny cheek, innumerable necklaces of glass beads on her neck. . . . She was savage and superb, wild-eyed and magnificent; there was something ominous and stately in her deliberate progress. And in the hush that had fallen suddenly upon the whole sorrowful land, the immense wilderness, the colossal body of the fecund and mysterious life seemed to look at her, pensive, as though it had been looking at the image of its own tenebrous and passionate soul.[4]

She is at the same time associated with the Congo River. Earlier, Marlow recalls his childhood fascination with the map of Africa in which the Congo is perceived as "an immense snake uncoiled, with its head in the sea, its body at rest curving afar over a vast country, and its tail lost in the depths of the land."[5] As the steamer departs with the dying Kurtz, the warrior queen "stretched tragically her bare arms after us over the sombre and glittering river."[6] The preimperial landscape is conflated with the feminine.

Similarly, in Irish myth the goddess of the land is represented by Macha, whose name means "field" or "plain," indelibly associating her with the land. Macha was the divine bride of Chrunnchu. Her husband boasted that she could outrun the king's horses, whereupon she was summoned to race. Macha, who was nine months' pregnant, begged that she abstain from the race until she had given birth. Refused this request, the heavily pregnant woman competed and won but died giving birth to twins. Before her death, she left an appropriate curse on the warriors of Ulster. Henceforth, they would suffer the pangs of childbirth for five days (mirroring the menstrual cycle), which was to leave them helpless whenever their strength was most needed. Green notes:

> Macha's role is complex and interlinked: she was a warrior, ruler, prophet, matriarch, guardian and benefactress of the land, careful of Ireland's well-being but vengeful if wronged at the hands of mortals. . . . But she was clearly a goddess associated with sovereignty in all its aspects. Some scholars see the downfall of Macha in the various stories as akin to "crushing the serpent," the overthrowing by men of female domination.[7]

Macha's conflict with the Ulster warriors can be read as the erosion of a matrifocal culture. "The Goddess," notes Mary Condren, "was one of the hardest images for Western culture to eradicate, and it can be said that only by killing the Serpent, severing the natural cycle of life and death, could dualistic patriarchal culture come into being."[8] In *Heart of Darkness,* the power and sovereignty of the warrior queen are depleted by imperialistic onslaught, and in **"The Speckled Band,"** the twins are of childbearing age, but one is murdered, and the other's visible and premature ageing denotes her sterility. Similar to **"The Speckled Band,"** it is significant that the ultimate eradication of the Serpent/Goddess and the concomitant imposition of a patriarchal culture are figured as a series of quasi-imperialistic conquests. Condren notes: "St. George kills the dragon, and in Ireland St. Patrick is credited with banishing the reptiles. . . . Crushing the Serpent/Goddess, therefore, symbolized the overthrow of these societies, together with their religions, which were matricentered."[9]

"Our Lady of Death" (1887) resurrects the conflict of faith and culture in an imperial context.[10] Here the snake is endowed with ambiguous symbolism. Miss Warrender, the orphaned daughter of an Indian chieftain and an Englishwoman, becomes governess to a Yorkshire family. Hugh Lawrence, a medical student and possibly a

Holmesian prototype, visits to spend some time with his friend John Thurston and is intrigued by the dislocation between Warrender's veneer of English civility and what he sees as her more primitive outbursts. The house becomes a scene of strange occurrences. The youngest child, Ethel, is found dead in bushes, and the housekeeper is awakened by a mysterious visitation during the night. It transpires that Warrender is performing human sacrifice in obedience, as Lawrence testifies, to the dictates of her Thugee religion.

> The Thugs! I had heard of the wild fanatics of that name who were found in the central part of India, and whose distorted religion represents murder as being the highest and purest of all the gifts which a mortal can offer to the Creator. I remember an account of them . . . the terrible power which their homicidal craze has over every other mental or moral faculty. I even recalled now that the roomal—a word which I had heard her mention more than once—was the sacred handkerchief with which they were wont to work their diabolical purpose.[11]

Her secret sacrifice of Ethel is discovered by the secretary of Thurston's Uncle Jeremy. Copperthorne then uses this knowledge to try to induce Warrender to kill Jeremy in a similar manner—the old man's death would suit Copperthorne's purposes, as he has previously inveigled his employer to draw up a will in his favor. However perverse Warrender's beliefs may be, she is opposed to deliberately using them for profitable murder—thus embodying a disjunction between an exploitative and patriarchal imperialism signified by Copperthorne and the indigenous religious practices of Warrender. However, the fact that the governess' rituals involve murder complicates the nature of the encounter. The narrative depicts the moral ambiguity in the convergence of the imperial and the colonized. Lawrence imparts the sense that Warrender is trapped by her faith and that the ritual incitement of her homicidal traits is, despite her Western education, innate. If the text betrays its racial stereotyping, it is also more complex in its examination of the dynamics of identity. At the heart of an imperial engagement, the image of the snake emerges. For example, Warrender becomes suitably venomous in her hatred of Copperthorne:

> "I don't wish ever to hear his name," she cried, passionately. "I hate it and I hate him. Oh, if I had only some one who loved me—that is, as men love away over the seas in my own land, I know what I should say to him."
>
> "What would you say?" I asked, astonished at this extraordinary outburst.
>
> She leaned forward until I seemed to feel the quick pants of her warm breath upon my face.
>
> "Kill Copperthorne," she said. "That is what I should say to him. Kill Copperthorne. Then you can come and talk of love to me."

Nothing can describe the intensity of fierceness with which she hissed these words out from between her white teeth. She looked so venomous as she spoke that I involuntarily shrank away from her. Could this pythoness be the demure young lady who sat every day so primly and quietly at the table of Uncle Jeremy?[12]

The governess later arranges Copperthorne's murder by inducing one of her kinsmen to kill him. Immediately prior to the attack, Lawrence witnesses the Indian slithering down the tree:

As I gazed I became conscious that down this luminous branch something was crawling—a flickering, inchoate something almost indistinguishable from the branch itself, and yet slowly and steadily writhing its way down it. My eyes, as I looked, became more accustomed to the light, and then this indefinite something took form and substance. It was a human being—a man—the Indian whom I had seen in the village. With his arms and legs twined round the great limb, he was shuffling his way down as silently and almost as rapidly as one of his native snakes.[13]

This episode is reminiscent of **"The Speckled Band"** in the phallic nature of the assault. Copperthorne, who becomes a Thugee sacrifice, is symbolically emasculated as punishment for his attempted control and perversion of Warrender's beliefs and for his own lecherous desire.

"Our Lady of Death" is read as an articulation of the complexities of Warrender's diasporic identity in a colonial context: English and Indian, governess and Thugee—these conflicting allegiances reside uneasily in Warrender's consciousness. It is pertinent that the governess is figured as a snake. For Doyle, the snake motif is central to the representation of otherness, cultural and religious conflict, murderous intent and libidinous excess.[14] The snake is a problematic trope in these fictions. It often articulates the impotence of the colonial enterprise. In its lack of fixedness and control, the snake also embodies the constant negotiation and renegotiation of position and identity. Indeed, the story's title asserts its perverse Christian antithesis: **"Our Lady of Death"** can be read as an inversion of the Christian appellation for the mother of God. Such convergence of Christian and Thugee associations in the story's title further signifies the conflict in Warrender's makeup.

The Christian allusions in the story's title beg further interpretation. Peter Cherici argues that the spread of Christianity in Western Europe was impeded by the "secret devotion to the female fertility principle personified as a goddess with various names. The quasi-deification of Mary provided a partial solution to the problem, allowing pagans to transfer their veneration of a local goddess to a Christian demi-goddess."[15] Mary is a contained and constructed female symbol. Indeed, Cherici continues that "many of the later medieval statues of

Mary showed her crushing a snake beneath her foot. . . . By stepping on the snake, Mary demonstrated her victory over the competing female principles found in pagan beliefs."[16] The power of the fertility goddess was initially harnessed and redeployed by patriarchy. Condren notes one such method:

In pre-Christian rites . . . the king, as kings did throughout the ancient world, participated in an annual rite of sacred marriage. The king "mated" with the Goddess, ensuring fertility for the land and for its people in the year to come. . . . But in patriarchal mythology, the future king had to find the Goddess, not in her form as the main source of creativity, but in the form of a hideous old hag, whom he would then have to embrace. The "old hag" then miraculously would turn into a young and beautiful woman, symbolizing the land of Ireland. Fertility would be restored, justice would reign, and the rightful king, having proved his wisdom, would be installed.

In this version of the myth the king rather than the Goddess became the main agent of fertility. Nevertheless, there are remnants of the matricentred religious worldview. The future king was not a brash, brazen hero who obtained his power through conquest. Indeed, the king was expected not to seek for individual glory but to manifest all the qualities of wisdom necessary to take care of the welfare of his kingdom.[17]

Thus, in the imperialist adventure romance *King Solomon's Mines* (1885), Umbopa proclaims: "'*I am Ignosi, rightful King of the Kukuanas!*'"[18] As proof of this, he disrobes to show the blazon of the eldest son: "[H]e pointed to the mark of a great snake tattooed in blue round his middle, its tail disappearing in its open mouth just above where the thighs are set into the body."[19] The coiled serpent represents the goddess of fertility. Ignosi must depose his despotic half brother's perverse union with the goddess and destroy the power of the witch hag Gagool in order to accede to his birthright. Transferred into the context of the late nineteenth-century world of the English middle class of **"The Speckled Band,"** land is replaced by wealth, in this instance the wealth that the girls have inherited from their mother. Like Ignosi's half brother, Roylott is a despot. He rules over a depleted estate "crushed under a heavy mortgage." Its impending collapse has been initiated by "four successive heirs [who] were of a dissolute and wasteful disposition."[20] Ignosi's return to his rightful lineage represents the union of the goddess and kingship, and the stepdaughter's reappropriation of her wealth signifies the redeployment of a matrilineal heritage that will be eventually united in marriage to a benign patriarchy.

A rereading of **"The Speckled Band"** as matrifocal problematizes the phallic identification of the earlier interpretation. At the end of both story and play we are presented with the image of the dying Roylott with the coiled serpent on his head. The coiling is significant.

"The image of the Serpent," argues Condren, "because of its association with life, rejuvenation, fertility, and regeneration, was a symbol of immortality. The coiled Serpent with its tail in its mouth was a circle of infinitude indicating omnipotence and omniscience."[21] Roylott's misuse of the snake and his attempt to subvert the female principle result in his annihilation, as the coiled serpent transforms into a symbol of death. Watson notes the snake's pose:

> Round his brow he had a peculiar yellow band, with brownish speckles, which seemed to be bound tightly round his head. As we entered he made neither sound nor motion.
>
> "The band! The speckled band!" whispered Holmes.
>
> I took a step forward. In an instant his strange headgear began to move, and there reared itself from among his hair the squat diamond-shaped head and puffed neck of a loathsome serpent.[22]

Frank interprets this as a Medusa head and argues: "The Medusa myth and western constructions of the Orient inform [Roylott's] fantasy, for active sexuality suggests the power of the Medusa and the ungovernable fecundity of the East. . . . In rearing itself from the dead Roylott's hair, the adder reveals the source of the Medusa story in male fantasies about the female body and the terror such fantasies evoke."[23] Following such an interpretation, Frank relegates the importance of the coiling of the snake on Roylott's head: "The headband suggests, of course, a turban, indicating, as do the slippers, Roylott's taste for things oriental."[24] Contrary to such an interpretation, the coiling of the snake provides deeper significance. It does not represent a destructive female sexuality but rather that the snake will ultimately thwart the perversion of its positive feminine symbolism, its union with healing, fertility, and rebirth. Thus, the snake's attack and its final coiling demonstrate its ultimate subversion of the patriarchal and imperial mission.

As a species of colonial literature, **"The Adventure of the Speckled Band"** shares certain features with *The Hound of the Baskervilles*. The cheetah and baboon that roam the gardens in the original story are replaced in the play version by a hound. Aptly, the hound is called Siva, thus sharing its name with the Hindu god symbolized as the destroyer and reproducer of life. If the dog shares this aspect with the snake, he also shares another one. The snake is used symbolically to rape the girls, and the hound safeguards Enid's incarceration in Stoke Moran, invoking the similar plight of the girl in the Baskerville legend. The latter escapes but is pursued over the moor by Sir Hugo's hound to facilitate, should she be captured, his master's intended rape. The name of the hound in the play teases out the ambiguous connotations of the creature in *The Hound of the Baskervilles*. If the baronet's hounds are initially used to trap the fleeing yeoman's daughter, the hell-hound revenges her death. In a colonial context, the message is evident. Sir Hugo, as debauched landlord, covets and attempts to possess his tenants. In an environment without political or legal recourse for the colonized, the supernatural and superstition serve to allay the threat of the aggressor. Seen in this context, the hound of the play equally sheds new light on the purpose of the baboon of the original story. The creature's sexually transgressive import is underlined by the political cartoons of popular British journals, which often depicted a weak and feminine Ireland threatened by a simianized, reptilian, and undoubtedly virile Fenianism.[25] Curtis clarifies the point:

> Lurking in most of these images of a Fenian monster threatening a pure and helpless Erin is the fantasy of ape rape. For centuries monkeys and apes have served men well as symbols of both male and female sexuality . . . the great apes became (silver-backed) screens onto which men projected their erotic and violent fantasies . . . the sheer size and strength of the great apes translated easily into phallic power or hypervirility in the minds of those who regarded them as not just capable but downright desirous of raping women.[26]

It could be conjectured that Doyle removed the baboon from the play because images of the simianized Fenian had peaked during the Irish Land War of the 1880s. Such a libidinized symbol would have been more readily identifiable to the 1892 *Strand* readers than to a 1910 theater audience. If we remember that the name of the house, Stoke Moran, carries Irish connotations, this story emerges as a metaphor for a post-Parnellian Ireland still unable to escape the nightmare of its colonial condition.

However, the narrative of **"The Speckled Band"** is ostensibly about the imperial experience at the heart of the British bourgeoisie. Roylott's imported Indian colony is a displaced one, a displacement that questions the validity, and demonstrates the absurdity, of the imperial enterprise. As Casement watched this play in 1910, the Belgian Congo must have preoccupied his thoughts. One wonders if it invoked any thoughts of a colonized Ireland, which was to increasingly engage the remaining years of his life. In any event, Casement could draw analogies between the symbol of serpent and imperial abuse. In his 1902 Congo inquiry he draws on an African proverb to describe his mission: "A man doesn't go among thorns unless a snake's after him—or he's after a snake," and in a direct allusion to Leopold he appends the remark: "I'm after a snake and please God I'll scotch it."[27]

In its concomitant identification with masculine and feminine sexuality in **"The Speckled Band,"** the snake can be perceived as gynandromorphic. Perverted to the role of destroyer, it ultimately subverts Roylott and seems to assert its final allegiance to the female principle as the serpent coils around the head of his master, thus leaving the dog-whip to lie redundantly on Roylott's lap. Yet the creature retains its ambiguity. Significantly, Julia Stoner is unable to name her attacker and is forced to resort to an enigmatic metaphor, the "speckled band." It is interesting that Julia refers to it as a band, invoking its coiling aspect, reminiscent of female-identified principles. The snake's natural proclivities are usurped by a phallic, penetrative, and destructive male sexuality. But Julia's inability to identify it also demonstrates that this aberrant creature refuses to be named and thus controlled. Holmes undergoes a similar experience with the elusive serpent. As he flails the bell-rope in the dark, he calls on Watson to identify the creature: "'You see it, Watson?' he yelled. "You see it?' But I saw nothing. At the moment when Holmes struck the light I heard a low clear, whistle, but the sudden glare flashing into my weary eyes made it impossible for me to tell what it was at which my friend lashed so savagely.'[28] A fitting symbol of a libidinized colonial Gothic, this nebulous creature retains its ambiguity to the end.

In **"The Speckled Band"** Doyle inverts the process of patriarchal colonization. The narrative resurrects the snake's female-identified principles, its elision of female sexuality, land, and fertility and presents the combat between this and a patriarchal and imperial culture that treats the serpent as a phallic symbol of control and dominance. In a colonial context, the conflict is a tense one as the snake—gothic, libidinal, and evasive—becomes an agent of disruption that simultaneously engages with processes of colonization and counter-colonization.

Notes

1. For a discussion of this, see Miranda Jane Green, *Celtic Myths: The Legendary Past* (London: British Museum Press, 1993) 58; Green, *Celtic Goddesses* 169-71; Stuart Gordon, *The Encyclopaedia of Myths and Legends* (London: Headline, 1993) 415-16; Lara Owen, *Her Blood Is Gold: Reclaiming the Power of Menstruation* (London: Aquarian/Thorsons, 1993) 40-41.

2. Green, *Celtic Goddesses* 70.

3. Ibid. 169.

4. Conrad, *Heart of Darkness* 100-101.

5. Ibid. 33.

6. Ibid. 101.

7. Green, *Celtic Goddesses* 77.

8. Mary Condren, *The Serpent and the Goddess: Women, Religion, and Power in Celtic Ireland* (San Francisco: Harper and Row, 1989) 24.

9. Ibid.

10. This story was first published with the title "Uncle Jeremy's Household" in *Boy's Own Paper* in 1887. Its domestic title parallels it with the concerns of *The Moonstone,* in which the household is threatened by the arrival of an Indian moonstone. Both narratives unveil "domestic" degeneracy; therefore, criminal "otherness" is immanent.

11. A Conan Doyle, *The Doings of Raffles Haw* and *Our Lady of Death* (London: Heinemann and Balestier, 1892) 227.

12. Ibid. 204-5.

13. Ibid. 236-37.

14. Lawrence's sympathy for Warrender, despite her murderous proclivities, parallels the sympathy for cultural and religious otherness that permeates Doyle's work. This is evident in his portrayal of the forced exile of the Huguenots from the France of Louis XIV in *The Refugees: A Tale of Two Continents,* 3 vols. (London: Longmans, Green, 1893); in the Puritans of the Monmouth rebellion of *Micah Clarke* (London: Longmans, Green, 1889); and in the Buddhists of *The Mystery of Cloomber.*

15. Peter Cherici, *Celtic Sexuality: Power, Paradigms and Passion* (1994; London: Gerald Duckworth, 1995) 104.

16. Ibid.

17. Condren, *Serpent* 23-24.

18. H. Rider Haggard, *King Solomon's Mines* (London: Cassell, 1885) 153.

19. Ibid. 154.

20. Doyle, "The Adventure of the Speckled Band" 259.

21. Condren, *Serpent* 8.

22. Doyle, "The Adventure of the Speckled Band" 272.

23. Frank, "Dreaming the Medusa" 71.

24. Ibid. 70.

25. See L. Perry Curtis Jr., *Apes and Angels: The Irishman in Victorian Caricature,* rev. ed. (Washington, DC: Smithsonian Institution Press, 1997) 39, 41, 44, 51, 135-74.

26. Ibid. 171.

27. Quoted in Hochschild, *King Leopold's Ghost* 200.

28. Doyle, "The Adventure of the Speckled Band" 271-72.

FURTHER READING

Criticism

Boswell, Rolfe. "Dr. Roylott's Wily Fillip: With a Proem on Veneration of Vipers." *Baker Street Journal* 1, no. 3 (1946): 307-11.

Illustrates the inconsistent effects of the snake's deadly venom.

Hennessy, Rosemary, and Rajeswari Mohan. "The Construction of Woman in Three Popular Texts of Empire: Towards a Critique of Materialist Feminism." *Textual Practice* 3, no. 3 (winter 1989): 323-59.

Analyzes the portrayal of women as property in "The Adventure of the Speckled Band."

Hoffer, Phil. "Julia Stoner as the First 'Woman.'" *Baker Street Journal* 29, no. 2 (June 1979): 106-07.

Suggests a romantic interest between Sherlock Holmes and Julia Stoner.

Lawson, Douglas. "The Speckled Band—What Is It?" *Baker Street Journal* n.s. 4, no. 1 (January 1954): 12-20.

Argues that two different snakes were used by Dr. Roylott against his stepdaughters.

Lozynsky, Artem. "The Scientific Fairy Tales of Sherlock Holmes." *Baker Street Journal* 42, no. 2 (June 1992): 78-83.

Provides a Freudian reading of the Sherlock Holmes mysteries.

Rodin, Alvin E., and Jack D. Key. "'The Speckled Band': Poisonous Snakes and Evil Doctors." In *The Baker Street Dozen*, edited by P. J. Doyle and E. W. McDiarmid, pp. 22-7. New York: Congdon & Weed, 1987.

Deems "The Adventure of the Speckled Band" one of Doyle's most accomplished stories.

————. "A Murderous Medical Trio: Doctors Roylott, Palmer, and Pritchard." *Baker Street Journal* 43, no. 4 (December 1993): 208-17.

Discusses two historically factual doctors mentioned in "The Adventure of the Speckled Band."

Wynne, Catherine. "Philanthropies and Villainies: The Conflict of the Imperial and the Anti-Imperial in Conan Doyle." In *The Devil Himself: Villainy in Detective Fiction and Film*, edited by Stacy Gillis and Philippa Gates, pp. 69-80. Westport, Conn.: Greenwood Press, 2002.

Centers on the snake as a symbol of British colonialism.

Additional coverage of Doyle's life and career is contained in the following sources published by Thomson Gale: *Authors and Artists for Young Adults,* **Vol. 14;** *British Writers Supplement,* **Vol. 2;** *Beacham's Encyclopedia of Popular Fiction: Biography & Resources,* **Vol. 1;** *Beacham's Guide to Literature for Young Adults,* **Vols. 4, 5, 11;** *Children's Literature Review,* **Vol. 106;** *Concise Dictionary of British Literary Biography,* **1890-1940;** *Contemporary Authors,* **Vols. 104, 122;** *Contemporary Authors New Revision Series,* **Vol. 131;** *Dictionary of Literary Biography,* **Vols. 18, 70, 156, 178;** *DISCovering Authors; DISCovering Authors: British Edition; DISCovering Authors: Canadian Edition; DISCovering Authors: Most-Studied Authors* **and** *Novelists; DISCovering Authors 3.0; Exploring Short Stories; Literature and Its Times,* **Vol. 2;** *Literature Resource Center; Major 20th-Century Writers,* **Eds. 1, 2;** *Major 21st-Century Writers,* **eBook 2005;** *Mystery and Suspense Writers; Reference Guide to English Literature,* **Ed. 2;** *Reference Guide to Short Fiction,* **Ed. 2;** *St. James Guide to Crime & Mystery Writers,* **Vol. 4;** *St. James Guide to Horror, Ghost & Gothic Writers; St. James Guide to Science Fiction Writers,* **Ed. 4;** *St. James Guide to Young Adult Writers; Science Fiction Writers,* **Eds. 1, 2;** *Short Stories for Students,* **Vol. 2;** *Short Story Criticism,* **Vols. 12, 83;** *Something about the Author,* **Vol. 24;** *Twayne's English Authors; Twentieth-Century Literary Criticism,* **Vol. 7;** *20th Century Romance and Historical Writers; World Literature and Its Times,* **Ed. 4;** *World Literature Criticism* **Vol. 2;** *Writers for Children;* **and** *Writers for Young Adults.*

James Alan McPherson
1943-

American short story writer, essayist, and memoirist.

The following entry provides an overview of McPherson's short fiction.

INTRODUCTION

Winner of the Pulitzer Prize for Fiction, McPherson is a prominent voice in African American literature. Like his mentor, Ralph Ellison, McPherson has followed an aesthetic of inclusion, drawing attention to both the universal and the unique in the American experience. Comparisons to such authors as Stanley Crouch and Charles Johnson attest to the provocative nature of McPherson's stories, while his articulate, thoughtful prose encourages readers to contemplate the complex nature of racial identity without providing easy answers. Although he has produced only two volumes of short fiction, McPherson's vision of human nature remains vital and compelling.

BIOGRAPHICAL INFORMATION

McPherson was born in a lower-class neighborhood of Savannah, Georgia, to James Allen McPherson, an electrician, and Mabel McPherson, a housekeeper. The public schools of his youth were racially segregated. He received his B.A. from Morris Brown College in Atlanta, Georgia, in 1965, having also attended Morgan College, a primarily black school in Baltimore, Maryland. McPherson's short story "Gold Coast" won an award from *Atlantic Monthly* while he was studying law at Harvard University. He received a law degree in 1968 and earned an M.F.A. in creative writing from the University of Iowa the next year. McPherson's first collection of stories, *Hue and Cry,* was published in 1969, at which time he became a contributing editor for *Atlantic Monthly.* He was awarded a Guggenheim fellowship in 1972 and a MacArthur fellowship in 1981. His second volume of short fiction, *Elbow Room* (1977), garnered the Pulitzer Prize. Additionally, four of McPherson's stories have won the prestigious O. Henry Prize. He was inducted into the American Academy of Arts and Sciences in 1995. Throughout his career, McPherson has taught at such institutions as the University of California, the University of Virginia, and Harvard University. He has served on the faculty of the Iowa Writers'

Workshop at the University of Iowa since 1981. McPherson published a memoir—entitled *Crabcakes*—in 1998, followed by a collection of essays, *A Region Not Home,* in 2000. In 2002 McPherson received a Lannan Literary Fellowship.

MAJOR WORKS OF SHORT FICTION

McPherson's work deals with friction between people of varying economic classes, educational backgrounds, races, and social strata. His debut volume of stories, *Hue and Cry,* received the endorsement of celebrated African American author Ralph Ellison, who praised McPherson's ability to highlight universal themes of human discord without relying solely upon racial or political points of view. For example, in "A Solo Song: For Doc" an older, experienced waiter offers advice to a young waiter on the nobility of perfecting one's craft. Though both characters are black men employed in the service industry, the story acts as a metaphor for pride and individuality as it pertains to any art form. In *Elbow Room,* McPherson continued to explore themes of selfhood and communication while emphasizing the function of language and narrative perspective in the storytelling process. "The Story of a Dead Man" recounts the misadventures of a local hoodlum whose escapades have taken on a legendary quality within the African American community. Told from the perspective of the man's educated cousin, the story hearkens to the tradition of black folk-hero tales by revealing the mundane reality behind the central figure's larger-than-life reputation. At the same time, the cousin's class-based prejudices are suggested by the haughty tone of his narration. Similar concerns with identity and reputation are displayed in "The Silver Bullet." The protagonist of this story attempts to establish a sense of self by joining the ranks of two different criminal gangs, both of which discourage individuality while perceiving the world around them according to negative stereotypes. "Problems of Art" features an attorney who believes that he has assessed the true nature of his client by evaluating the superficial aspects of her life. An elderly black woman accused of drunken driving, the client is acquitted on a technicality, but the lawyer later discovers that he had misjudged both her character and her culpability. In "The Story of a Scar," the African American narrator also incorrectly presumes to understand human nature based upon shallow preconceptions. As in "The Story of a Dead Man," the narrator's analytical and erudite command of language masks his thinly veiled disdain for people of a lower class, though all parties concerned are of the same race. The narrator of "Just Enough for the City" also uses language as a distancing mechanism, insisting that the nature of love be verbally defined before he can permit an emotional involvement with the world. Like "Problems of Art," "A Sense of Story" focuses on the legal system and its tendency to force classifications upon individuals. When a black man accused of murdering his boss startles the courtroom by openly declaring his guilt, the presiding judge is forced to pore over transcripts of the trial to decide if the prosecution proved its case. The judge's own biases influence his interpretation of the court documents as he attempts to make sense of the defendant's life. The title story details the attempts of an African American writer to pen a factual account of an interracial couple. "Elbow Room" is filled with interjections from a white editor imploring the writer to clarify aspects of the piece. By mirroring the interracial couple with the black writer and white editor, the story emphasizes the difficulty of explaining the essential nature of racial identification, and the futility of forcing human beings into simple categories.

CRITICAL RECEPTION

McPherson's stories are generally lauded for their intelligent and subtle consideration of race and interpersonal communication. Scholars have focused on his ability to demonstrate the anxiety of his characters by drawing attention to their manipulation of language. For instance, critic Jon Wallace has asserted that through their speech patterns, McPherson's characters "seek a space within which they can defend themselves against the claims of intimacy." Other reviewers have studied McPherson's treatment of racial stereotypes, maintaining that he has intentionally challenged commonly held misconceptions stemming from fear, ignorance, and an overall lack of self-awareness. McPherson's appropriation of African American folklore has likewise been analyzed, and his perspective on the psychology of cultural assimilation has been contrasted with that of author James Baldwin. Moreover, the postmodern element of McPherson's writing has been interpreted from a cultural perspective, leading commentator Wahneema Lubiano to assert that his fiction "derails narrative conventions in order to specify a connection between aesthetics and politics."

PRINCIPAL WORKS

Short Fiction

Hue and Cry: Short Stories 1969
Elbow Room: Stories 1977

Other Major Works

Railroad: Trains and Train People in American Culture [editor; with Miller Williams] (nonfiction) 1976
Crabcakes (memoir) 1998
A Region Not Home: Reflections from Exile (essays) 2000

CRITICISM

James Alan McPherson and Bob Shacochis (interview date winter 1983)

SOURCE: McPherson, James Alan, and Bob Shacochis. "Interview with James Alan McPherson." *Iowa Journal of Literary Studies* 4, no. 1 (winter 1983): 6-33.

[*In the following interview, McPherson discusses the situation of modern African American writers, his experiences at law school and as a university instructor, and the complex nature of identity.*]

[*Shacochis*]: *You agreed to give this interview because you said you were "tired of running." Running from what?*

[McPherson]: Well, not running, really. I think I speak as honestly as I can to people, but once you begin taking yourself too seriously, you get trapped in a persona, and if you start embellishing your persona by talking out of it, you get locked into that role, and often you get institutionalized. Some writers become institutions themselves. This is not the way I want to live. The price is too high. So I don't talk much, except in the classroom.

Will you talk about how success has affected you? Is fame a curse for a writer? Has it made you self-conscious when you work? Is it something that must be overcome or could it be embraced?

I think it depends on the life habits of the individual. I used to do what I could to maintain my privacy. I read, at one period of my life, most of the time. There's nothing wrong with embracing success as long as you don't let it change the consistency of your life habits. I don't know whether I embrace it or not. If anything, success hasn't changed my life—it's teaching, more than anything else. Having to teach different courses, having to be on top of things. I was thinking today in the car, I tend to intellectualize too much, and that comes from having taught for so long. I have to stay away from that way of thinking. A writer slows down when that happens.

Would you prefer not to teach, to be free of university sponsorship?

This is the irony. Where would a black writer go in this society? Or, as you say, a black man who writes—where would he go? He can't gain access to a community of people. He needs a community of people who share his interests, and I think a university area provides this. A black community, while it's proud of its people who do write, provides very few places where it can nurture you as a writer.

So this environment does nurture you?

Yeah.

Isn't it possible just to live in such a community without having to teach? And still get the same benefits that you came there for?

I imagine it is.

Could you do that? Are you burned out on teaching?

I think I am. In a special sense. I don't like to repeat myself, and if I have to do the same course over, the same way, without taking new ideas in, it'll be boring. One thing I disliked about Virginia was having to teach undergraduates, whereas here it's not the same kind of academic situation.

Even though Iowa does not seem to you as oppressive as that, do you find yourself having to be repetitious in the Workshop?

No, because the students are so interested, and different. They don't make the same mistakes. The quality of the work is high. They're almost professionals themselves.

The university atmosphere seems to be a very closed world. A lot of writers have trouble seeing beyond it.

I have no problems with that. As a matter of fact, I learned rather early that you need a support system that's normal, and so wherever I've gone I've always tried to make connections outside of the literary environment. I can still be comfortable with farmers, or blue-collar workers, without pretending or trying to act condescending to those people. When you can't, that's when you're in trouble. I'm not just talking about blue-collar workers. If you can't find something human to relate to in a person who is not doing something you're doing, then you're lost.

What about in the Workshop?

Well, the workshop is a greedy institution. I'm not putting it down, but it's an institution that tends to give one his total identity. I was surprised at how much of a burden the students are ready to impose on the Workshop, just in terms of things you could do for yourself outside of that context. But the reputation and the efficiency of the place sometimes make a student believe that all else is forthcoming. You go to Workshop parties, think of yourself as a Workshop person—fiction or poetry, you know—and it gets so specialized. *Who are you? Are you part of it all or are you nobody?*

Something else I've heard you say is that your work has not yet reached a mass audience or a popular market, that you weren't really successful—I don't fully understand what you mean by that, because of course you are, but is it really true that your work only reaches a small audience?

I don't know. I don't even recall saying that. But I don't try to reach a mass audience. That was never my ambition. I did a book on railroads with Miller Williams. We fought like cats and dogs because Miller wanted to cut out lots of stuff in order to make sure that the book would be popular, and I wanted to keep certain things in that I thought were interesting. No, I'm satisfied. What I want is to do better each step, do something different, and not just repeat myself.

Would it be bad for your work to be accepted by a mass audience? Would that be in some way lethal?

No. No, it's just that I'm not trying for that. Oh, I've turned down a lot of opportunities to capitalize on my work along the avenues that allow that. I'd rather not do it. I'm not frustrated by lusting after a mass audience. What I'm frustrated about is lusting after getting something accomplished that I'm proud of. Once it gets beyond me I don't care what happens to it as long as it survives. That's what I want. I'm not looking for mass acceptance. I'm neutral. That's the best way I can answer your question.

Frankly, the question is fuzzy to me. It might be more of a question about the nature of a mass audience, because to me, I don't know what would keep your work from having wide acceptance. I don't understand why you don't have a mass audience, whether you want it or not.

I don't think about it. I do think that certain books can be good and still have a mass audience, like Warren's *All the King's Men*. There are certain novels that are technically beautiful but are still popular. I think Warren's books are good enough and interesting enough to attract a large audience. When I saw him in Connecticut, he talked about writing things that everybody could read. I think this was his way of democratizing literature. Can we go on?

Yeah, but it gets tougher, because I've been leading into a sensitive question. You're a rare occurrence—a successful short story writer who is black. I don't know how much you want to talk about it. For me, questions of race are difficult because I never know exactly how to word them, and I'm not sure, ultimately, what their significance is. But I want to know your feelings about these things. To open it up, Western literature is more or less dominated by maleness and whiteness. Do you think it will ever change? I wanted to ask that about mass audience too. Are we beginning to assimilate? Do you think being a black writer prevents you from having popular acceptance? It certainly doesn't for somebody like Toni Morrison or James Baldwin.

No, I don't think it does. This is a tricky thing. Ralph Ellison is doing alright because his work is so great. Baldwin, I think, is a preacher. You mentioned Toni Morrison, but let's stick with Baldwin and Ellison. I think Ellison questions, and he analyzes, and he tends to get to the root of the problem. He functions more like a European intellectual. He can connect the condition of black Americans with something larger. He sees things in context. Baldwin is sort of a preacher who pronounces a last judgment on white America. I think that serves as a kind of titillation periodically for people who are secure in their power. But anybody who questions the basic assumptions is not going to reach that broad an audience. A man like Ellison, who asks those basic questions and can't be bluffed into an emotional stance—he's not a black, he's an anomaly. I think people would rather he weren't around. And I guess my ambition is to be in the same position.

You've often been compared to Ellison.

That's because Ellison has been supportive of me. But you don't achieve mass acceptance in this culture without being diffused. Unless you are diffused, then you're likely to be limited in your appeal. It's so easy, you know. But then you end up without your self. That's the way the whole thing is set up. It's not just blacks, it's anybody. They've got to be diffused. If you can't be, then you've got a price to pay just because you question what's normal, what's right and what's wrong, what's the truth and what's a lie. But in the case of black Americans, I think, asking those basic questions is almost obligatory. In a sense, your life depends on it. You're living in a crazy country that's paranoid, in a large part because of your presence in it, and if you have a view of the whole thing, it's because you're outside, and you say "This is where I fit in, and this is where things get warped."

This is the most difficult question I have to ask. I am sensitive to the issue, and I hope you'll forgive me for asking it. Two parts—do you ever feel that you're a token to a white literary establishment, or do you ever feel resentment from more radical black writers because of your evenhandedness?

I don't see myself as a token. I fought—I had too many fights with certain people. I'll say this, the people I fought with I wound up respecting, although I might not agree with them. But if I were a token, I'd be much more at ease and comfortable than I am now. But beyond that, Bob, my work is good. What I do is good. I teach, I write—nobody gave that to me. As for the responses of black people, no, surprisingly enough, the best review I ever got was in *Essence* and a black woman said, "Somebody out there's watching us, somebody out there's on to us." I'm in the tradition, I'm still in the core culture. I'm not explaining it to white folk. I don't think I'm using it to titillate whites. I've never gotten any negative criticism from black people—I never have.

Have you from white people?

A few nuts, but no, only from the Grand Kleagle of the California Klan, and even he tried to be gracious, sending his letterhead in a separate envelope. I can't think of any—I had a bad time with a student at Virginia who hated me—a white man. He would always disrupt my classes, always try to cause a sensation. He was sick. But that's the only time I really encountered hatred of me as a writer. Maybe it's because I use a form that everybody else avoids as much as possible. I leave the meat to the white boys (laughs).

The meat to the white boys?

I mean the novel. But I can't say I've gotten that much negative feedback from white people. Usually the response is indifference. People have been gracious to me, all down the line. I've been lucky in that respect. I never wrote for money. I never wrote for propaganda purposes. Well, to go back to your question about my feelings about the marketplace and my color, I will just say that there are very few short story writers who end up in paperback, and very few who get a Pulitzer Prize, and very, very few who ever get popular. So I ain't complaining, I ain't complaining.

What do you feel about minorities and their causes, and their different approaches to equality? You seem to react against angry voices and clenched fists.

I clench my fists now and then—it's healthy for your fist (laughs). I look for situations where there's a meshing, and I try to look at the values that come into conflict there. I'm going to be called a black writer until I die. But the point is that when I write at my best I try to look for the *human* situation, and I think whites have an obligation to do the same when writing about black folk, if they choose to write about black folk. What I'm trying to say is that there's an institutionalized classification. I used the phrase "greedy institution" a while back. That's really what those classifications come down to—institutions. They tend to define general groups in the population and assign character traits to them.

There is an institution of literature that we're both involved in, by choice.

That's where most of the exchange should take place. There's never been a time in this country when there was not at least some exchange between artists and intellectuals. There has to be some communication. Even in South Africa that has to happen. Somebody said he once saw a white South African admire the work of a black South African artist. He wanted to look at it closer, so he reached his hand through a fence and had the fellow come up and hand the thing to him so he could look at it. But he had to have that institutional protection.

It has to change. There are two obvious ways, perhaps. One is through artistic influence, and the other one is through the power of the gun. Will either of these change it?

I'm not a communist (laughs). I don't know. I know you set me up to be a commentator on race relations, and I don't mean to be that.

I don't know if I set you up to be that, but it was sort of inevitable, don't you think?

I don't have a gun. I never owned a gun. I think I don't use my writing as a gun. Any real and worthwhile change will probably come through aesthetic rather than political processes. As for radical change, I imagine the Second Coming of Christ, coming back to earth on a radical mission, and he looks at the white group, and looks at the black group, and just starts laughing. (Laughs.) A great cosmic laugh.

So it will be a miracle that will change us.

It would have to be a miracle, I imagine. But somebody has to laugh at this. Don't you think it's funny?

Well, I do. Yes. I laugh at it. But I also feel like crying about it too.

Yeah, yeah.

It's inevitable that you are going to become a racial commentator. That's part of what you buy into, I guess.

No, you can resist that.

You can resist it, but it's an important—

It's important only when the people who ask the questions are sincere. But I've seen too much of this stuff where the Ladies Auxiliary wants to do something, they invite a black person and say, "What can we do? How can we help the poor Negro?"

That's tokenism. But I don't know how you can avoid being a spokesman.

Well, there's money in it. It's a growth industry. (Laughs.) It's really a ritual. It's a ritual drama with its own mythology. If you learn how to play the game, you can get very rich off it. What happens is that when it's in everybody's interest that things don't explode, especially at a time when you think they might, a certain commentator is needed. So that, as soon as the first riot starts, people say, "Well, we need to find out why." So they hire somebody to consult with them. Suddenly the planes get full with black people who are going to consult, consult, consult. (Laughs.) You are well paid and a few people read your report: "Ah, this is why," and then they kick you in the ass again. It's so manipulative. I don't want to participate in it again. It's like a wall, and everything that has been learned, even common sense, is shut off. So you start with zero-based consciousness. You start from zero all over again. And then the same questions, the same people, the same responses—and then there's no threat anymore. Close down shop. Back to normal, so to speak. It's schizophrenia is what it is. I was wondering why Ellison was sitting on Riverside Drive all through the Sixties without saying a word. He'd seen all that in the Thirties!

Reviewers have said that you've never taken the color of your skin as an excuse for not learning the craft of fiction.

Ralph Ellison said that.

*Yeah. This reviewer borrowed it from a bigger quote from Ellison on **Hue and Cry** that said: "McPherson promises to move right past those talented but misguided writers of Negro American culture who take being black as a privilege for being obscenely secondrate, and who regard their social predicament as Negroes as exempting them from the necessity of mastering the crafts and forms of fiction." Those are strong words.*

Yeah.

Do you think they are unfair?

That thing has haunted me. I'll try to explain what happened, okay? I didn't know Ralph Ellison at the time. I never met him. But when I finished the book in '68, my editor asked if there was anybody I would like to get a blurb from. And I said, well, Ralph Ellison. I respected him a lot, because I had read his work. So, he sent the manuscript to Ellison and Ellison sent back a letter. I thought he was attaching a message to my back, so to speak. But I had nothing to do with it. I met him several years later, but that came back to haunt me. Ishmael Reed picked it up, and Ishmael said I was Ellison's heir apparent and things like that. But it wasn't that way at all. That's Ellison's statement, not mine. I've not since asked anybody for a blurb.

Do you think what he was saying was unfair?

I don't want to go back to that. It would just revive old hurts and we have enough trouble as it is. But I thought that he was responding to the kinds of material that were finding their way through in the Sixties, like Cleaver. All that stuff that titillated. I've got some records here by some guys I met in Watts named the Watts Prophets. I spent about two weeks in Watts and met one of these guys. They were some of the most beautiful people I had ever met in my life, he and his wife. They were very spiritual people. And another guy from Alabama who was untutored in a technical way but wrote some beautiful poetry about his children and the things that mattered to him. But on the records they said, "I'm black in a white world and I'm gonna kill, kill!" And I said, "Anthony, who do you think is buying this stuff? The same kind of people who live up there in Beverly Hills getting high on heroin or speed and this is just the stuff they're getting their jollies off of." That's the kind of thing, see, so if you appeal to that group, then you alienate people who are sincere about doing what they can to solve the problem. And I think that courtship of the reductive image during the late Sixties has something to do with Ellison's comment.

Who are your favorite authors? What are your fictional roots?

I like popular novels, popular storytellers. Some people don't like to admit this, but I read John O'Hara religiously. I did. I read all his stories. I read Hemingway and Fitzgerald. I read all of Damon Runyon. Jack Leggett was talking about a popular novel named *Anthony Adverse.* I read it four times. I read all the popular novels of Mika Waltari. He did one book called *The Egyptian,* one called *The Etruscan,* one called *The Wanderer.* I read everything he wrote. I'm still evolving. My goal this winter is to read all the Russians. I mean all of Dostoevski.

So you would point to the paperback rack in the drugstore for providing your impetus and inspiration.

Yeah. A lot of guys won't admit it, but that's where they started out too.

I'll admit it for myself.

I know I used to go to the Salvation Army to buy copies of Balzac and I used to buy comic books there, and Maupaussant, people like that. But you begin in a drugstore, buying a novel that has a pretty picture on the cover, something that attracts you. Then you say to the public, "I never read anything but Proust anyway." But it's not true.

You said you think some of your stories in **Hue and Cry** *or* **Elbow Room** *are slight. Which ones are your favorites? Which ones mean the most to you?*

"A Solo Song: For Doc" is my favorite story. About railroad waiters.

How autobiographical is that? How much imagination is there, how much observation?

That's completely made up. Made up in the sense that— well, I worked on the railroad for four summers during college. Just sitting around the table after breakfast, after lunch, all the waiters would talk, they'd tell all these stories. They'd just get into it—it's tradition being passed on. You don't think about it, but at some point it'll come back to you. There were about one hundred or two or three hundred stories I knew from them, that I just picked up listening to the waiters talking.

You refuse to be a propagandist in your writing—

So far I have. I just may try and do some (laughs).

Do you have any causes you support, in or out of fiction, besides honesty and humanism?

No. I don't like to see people hurt. A therapist told me I had a neurotic need to rescue. I don't like to see anybody get shafted. I remember one time I was walking down the street in Baltimore and I saw a street auction. All these sharks with these tailfin Cadillacs parked in the slums. They were about to bid on this house rented by an older black couple who were sitting on the porch. All the sharks were white, as was the auctioneer, and the people sitting on the porch were dressed in their best clothes. I said to myself, "Just look at this. This is what slavery was like." It wasn't like a buck on the auction block all greased down, muscles rippling. It was people in their best clothes, and they were placed in the hands of people who didn't care about them. I didn't have a penny but I walked into the crowd anyway, and the bidding started. I started bidding, raising the amount by five hundreds. The guys thought I was a shill placed there. Somebody would say $4,000. I'd say $4,500. So they'd back off. There I was stuck with this house that I couldn't pay for. I did it instinctively. The therapist says that's neurosis. I don't believe in causes, but I don't like to see that kind of thing happen.

Just in terms of technique or approach, in fiction at least, introspection seems to be a cause of yours. Does that make sense?

What else can anyone be but introspective?

I'm not sure. Isn't it more or less the opposite of realism? Realism would be more journalistic, objective— observing something and writing it down. Introspection would be the opposite approach. The writer or narrator exploring his own self, rather than examining the outside world. I know you are certainly realistic in your—

No, I've been criticized for that. It's been said that I see outside things only in relation to what I am. But that can't be helped. I wasn't aware of it, but that's the way my life is. I'm an individual, so that's what I do. Not consciously, perhaps.

Why did you go to Harvard and enter law school?

Why not?

Did you want to be a lawyer?

I had a disadvantage. I promised my grandmother I'd become a minister. That's why she helped me go to college. And I thought law was even better. But I had an illusionary perception of what the law really was. I really thought that a lawyer was a good guy who helped people. And then, I couldn't refuse the opportunity to go to Harvard. At that time I was trying to figure out what was going on. I took courses in the legal process and in jurisprudence. The teacher was a fast talker and talked about all these abstract issues. I sat next to a man from Wisconsin named Jim Himmer. During one lecture I turned to him and said, "Jim, I don't understand what the teacher just said concerning the issue." Jim said, "Don't you understand, man? This is all bullshit." You know, he meant the courses in jurisprudence and legal process. The meat and potatoes was taxation, corporate law, estate planning. You see, the school I attended brought in the sons and daughters of the middle class to perfect their skills to be moved into law firms to help those great fortunes pass from one generation to the next. I was being trained for that—unhappily. I didn't know any black folk who had money (laughs). So I thought I'd be a minister of law, but you can't do that, so I got out. Where are you going to help people?

Criminal law?

That's what I wanted to be. I prosecuted for a little while in the Boston courts. It was my last year in law school. They had a student D.A. project. I went down to the court and I was allowed to prosecute a case or two. I remember there was this Italian kid who had stolen a Cadillac and driven it from Boston to the suburbs and they caught him. I was in the conference room when the arresting officer came in and said, "We've got this kid cold. So now, you ask me this and this and this and I'll say this and this and this. And we'll get it over with." The kid had a lawyer with him. He came up and said to me, "He got lonely and wanted to see his mother. He got drunk and stole the car to go see his mother." Well, I could believe that. I could understand that. My

policeman just had the facts, but I could see the things that motivated the kid to do that. So I couldn't stand things like that.

What about defense?

You can't make a living defending people. It drives you crazy, because the system is so set up that it's automatic. Oh, I did a long article on housing discrimination in Chicago back in 1973. It took up almost an entire issue of *Atlantic*. That article probably took about a year of my life. Nobody read it and people condemned me for writing it. But one of the issues was these people, black people, were confronted by discrimination institutionalized by the FHA, which said that anytime more than a few black people come into a neighborhood, it's changing and banks should not risk any loan money there. That was its policy since the Thirties. They couldn't get mortgages. I mean, if you come up from the South, and the Southside is full of black folk, where are you going to go? So blockbusters moved in and scared the whites out of other areas. But since the area is changing, there's no mortgage money, so they sell the house to people on contract. They will buy a house that's worth maybe $50,000, pay $5,000 for it, and sell it for $65,000 to a black person on contract. It's like the easy payment plan. You know, you don't get any equity. If you miss one payment they take it all back from you. You're like a slave. So the people finally challenged this. They went on strike and refused to pay. And one of the issues was the seller took them to court to obtain payment, and the people said, "Well, we want to pay, but our case is in court. Let us pay the money in escrow. Anything but to give the money directly to these sellers who are cheating us." The judge said "No. The only issue is, 'Do you owe?' If you owe, why haven't you paid? If you haven't paid, get out of the house." So you had all these mass evictions of people. But the issue was a human one, and the legal system can't take that into account.

It can't. It's process.

Right. It's all process. It's all nuts and bolts. Why would I want to work in that kind of mess?

But you thought you did. After all, you did go to law school.

Um hmm. One of the things I got out of law school that I really value was meeting a man named Paul Freund. He was a great man, a great teacher. He was a Carl M. Loeb University Professor. That meant he was qualified to teach in any department of the university. He didn't just teach constitutional law. When he talked about censorship, he would bring in *Ulysses*. He knew the book well. He would talk about art! He wrote articles on law and art. He was a great man. I saw him in the hall. I said, "Professor Freund, I just wanted to say hello to you." He said, "What's your name?" I said McPherson. He said "Oh, you're the one who writes for *Atlantic.*" I said yes. He said, "You've gone *beyond* the law." And that's all he said to me. Then, last summer when I was here I got a note from a lady in Richmond. She said she had been to an ABA meeting and she had dinner with Professor Freund. And he made her swear to tell me that he had written a letter for me to get the MacArthur Award. When I look back on my law school career, the best thing that happened to me was encountering Paul Freund because he's the kind of man who would say, "We have very bright students who know all of the answers, but none of the questions." It's that kind of mind that you run across just once in your lifetime. And that makes you think that it's possible to do something "beyond the law," so to speak.

You were already writing for the Atlantic Monthly *when you were in law school.*

I sold my first two stories to them the last month I was there.

How old were you?

Twenty-four.

Why did you decide to become a writer?

Why not?

It was already in your mind there in law school. Let me rephrase it so I can get something out of you. What made you *think you could become a writer?*

What made *you* think you could become a writer?

Well, that's still in doubt.

No, you're a writer, but what made you think you could become one?

I suppose because I seemed to do it well, and there was joy in that.

All right, there's that. And being able to use my imagination. I remember I had a job in high school. All through high school I would have to go to work, after school from 3:30 to 7:30 at night and all day Saturday, bagging potatoes, putting Irish potatoes in five-pound and ten-pound bags. That was my job in produce. And so I never had time for dates. But what I did was use my imagination, because you can't do nothing but work and not use your imagination, or you die. I think it was looking at people, or just thinking, that kept me alive, so to speak, in my imagination. I suppose to find a way of expressing that, I chose writing.

The freedom of it is also something that attracted me. Not that being tied to your typewriter or pen and paper day after day is especially a free occupation, but there is a lot of freedom, room to move and grow, inherent in the profession of writing. Or rather lifestyle, not profession.

Yeah, if you can publish. But it's also a way of dealing with things. You asked me why I'm introspective. A lot of mean things have happened to me, and the only way I can deal with them, or beat them, is to take it inside myself, turn it over and look at it and try to humanize the experience, try to understand why it happened. I have that capacity, and I think without that capacity, you go out and shoot people or things like that.

Do you think the role of the writer extends beyond that personal process?

You mean into society? Well, I'd have to give an ideological answer. I think that because I'm classified as a black writer, and because I come from a group of people who are largely inarticulate and because society has erected certain norms and walls and ways of distorting their image, I sort of have an obligation not to write propaganda but to re-create them the way I know they are, because they can't do it for themselves. And that's something we shouldn't have to do. I wish I didn't have to struggle to understand black people who hurt me. But I have to understand why this happened, and what warped them a certain way.

There isn't always a sociological explanation for individuals, or for injustice, is there?

I should say so. That's true. Evil is—I never understood it until these last two or three years. It's smooth, and it's ever-vigilant. It's always on the case. I didn't really believe in evil until this last year or so, but it's steady on the case.

Have you read Anthony Burgess' Earthly Powers*?*

No. I want to, though.

It's an excellent evocation of good versus evil.

But I will say categorically that evil is a dirty muthafucker (laughs).

It's there, and it's something that—sociology or not—is there and working. It might matter if your mother beat the shit out of you when you were a kid, but I don't think it matters whether you're black or white or middle-class or upper-class or whatever.

I've got two copies of the *Daily Word* over there on the table. Mrs. Julia Smith got me to subscribe to it. And I said to her back in the Fall, "Well, I'm glad I moved to

Iowa City. I don't have any enemies there." She said, "How do you know?" She said, "You can't run from trouble. Some people are going to dislike you just for their own personal reasons." But she said if you read the Bible and think good thoughts, God will place a shield around you and they can't harm you. It's like evil is not in any one place, it's everywhere, and you have to do all you can to protect yourself from it. And sometimes I think probably prayer, or at least having the faith that God will protect you, is the only thing you can do. I went to church this morning. I was very depressed. But after communion when you come back to your seat, before you sit down you say a prayer, pray what you have to pray. A church is no real sanctuary against that, but it's good for you to be sharing something positive with other people. But once you become aware that evil does exist, you get frightened. You realize that what we call reality is just a stage, with invisible props. You push a little bit and you see those props.

Fear is the better vantage point to have than simply naïveté. It prepares you to deal with adversity.

Yeah.

It's also something that can help strengthen. You're a religious man. Does that have any effect on your writing?

No, I'm not a religious man.

You find value in religion, true?

I think not in organized religion. I think that if you maintain a belief in a divine principle it can make life easier for you. Easier in the sense that you don't tax yourself by trying to account for what happens to your life. You accept the possibility of mystery in human events. And that gives you a certain amount of peace. If I didn't have that I probably wouldn't be around now. It's not religion in the sense that I would say I'm a Baptist or a Methodist or an Episcopalian or I believe in a virgin birth. It's just that I believe that if there is no mystery, if life is what they say it is, I don't want to be around. I can't explain it better than that.

I share the same belief but I wouldn't go to a church to affirm it.

I just started going to church last year in Charlottesville. I didn't go to church from the time I finished college until then. But these are hard times, pal. Hard times in the sense that—oh, you see all this viciousness, this random evil. It's like people have lost the capacity to make moral distinctions. I saw on the news last week that a kid out in California raped and killed his girlfriend and then took his classmates to see the body. And nobody said a word. It's like they lost the capacity to feel guilt or remorse, and it scares me.

Is it really so extensive, or is it just that it is so publicized now, the media are so omniscient and effective, and that the population is now so big, so that the proportion is the same, and these acts have always been committed, that society has always been this way?

No. One thing that happened during the Sixties was that the humanities got pushed aside. Science and technology took ascendancy. The unrestrained, unrefined human soul is a vicious thing, it really is. And I think that that excess, when the discipline of the humanities was neglected and allowed technology to gain the upper hand, unhumanized technology. So now you go over to the mall—right next to the movie house, there's a little room where you got pinball machines, but they got these machines where little kids learn how to hit a pedestrian, you know, or shoot somebody. What's that doing to them? All that home video stuff, what's that doing to people?

Ferdinand Marcos just outlawed video games in the Philippines.

Did he?

It's a twelve-year sentence if you have one or are caught playing one. Hardly an appropriate answer to the problem.

I had a student in Virginia who was just a rotten kid. I talked to him and asked, "Don't you feel anything?" He said, "No, I don't feel anything." It's out there, people who lack the emotional depth to feel guilt, to have a conscience. That's why when you asked me about guilt the other day, I chuckled. I don't see much of it around. I don't.

Nevertheless, a lot of people I know seem to be almost crippled by guilt. I'm not talking about racial guilt—just guilt as a reaction to behaving irrationally and hurting other people.

I feel that kind of guilt myself.

Okay, let's move on. You came right from Harvard to the Iowa Writer's Workshop. Why? What did you hope to accomplish here? What had happened? You were in law school, you abandoned that and made a commitment to be a writer and came to Iowa.

I didn't abandon it. I finished law school. I finished in June of '68 and came here in September.

Right. But most graduates from your class in the Harvard Law School in September of '68 had taken their bars and were in practice. You changed commitments. Or finally made a commitment.

Yeah, well, I wanted to write. I had just sold two stories to *Atlantic*. I remember, I went up to see George Hughes, he was a classmate of mine. He was a year ahead of me, had finished the year before. Now this is not invention, it's the truth. I was wrestling with whether I should try my hand at writing or go ahead and become a lawyer. And I went up to see George—he lived out near Watertown. He had just got married and his parents were there. So we were talking in his apartment, you know, saying what we were going to do. George had gone to Yale and had gotten over-refined and he was really prissy. But his father was an old working-class Irish Catholic. And the old man said, "Well, Jim, do what you want to do, what's best for you." I was walking back to Cambridge and I passed a graveyard. I was looking at the gravestones, and one gravestone said on it *McPherson*. I said, "That's a sign. I'm going to end up there anyway (laughs)—might as well do something that's meaningful to me." So I spent that whole summer writing and came here in September.

Who were your teachers here?

Bill Fox, Richard Yates, people like that.

Do you think teachers in the Workshop have a great influence on their students?

Well, you can, if you don't watch yourself. I don't want to influence anybody except to get them thinking about certain things. In terms of style, I guess you can, because some students are also caught up with trying to imitate. So you have to be careful about pushing your own sense of style. But yeah, it stands to reason, anybody standing behind a desk has—I make a point in my classes of not sitting at the place where the power center is supposed to be. I want to be as democratic as possible. But if you insist on that prerogative, you run the risk of undermining the development of the student's own sense of style. You can add to it, but it has to be the student's own.

Do students influence teachers?

That's a good question. (Pauses.) Only if they're pretty (laughs).

What did the Workshop mean to you as a student?

I didn't have much contact with the writers here. I knew a few, but I sort of had my own life. But it did—not the Workshop but the Rhetoric Program—give me the opportunity to go into a classroom and teach for the first time. And I began to develop skills there that allowed me to teach in other places. It gave me that. It also gave me a base, a home base in Iowa City. Oh, a friend of mine in Boston, when I told him I was coming back

here—he was my old teacher, a man named Alan Liebowitz, he teaches at Tufts now. He taught me at Harvard when I was a law student, and we've been communicating since about '68, when I was first here—he told me he had been looking through all my letters, and that he had seen that Iowa City was the one place where I was happiest. So there was something here that allowed me to feel at ease.

Teaching Rhetoric is something that can influence and help your own writing since it compels you to analyze the process of writing. Do you feel that your writing benefited from the Workshop itself, or was it just a place to be?

Well, I had published a book before I ever came here.

Hue and Cry*?*

Yeah. But it did give me exposure to a critical process, the way students responded to manuscripts in class. And I suppose it gave me what Cambridge did not give me, and that was access to a community of writers, people who were doing the same thing. That's something that you need, I think, sometime.

*You wrote **Hue and Cry** when you were a law student then?*

I wrote that book my last summer in Cambridge.

You wrote it during the summer—one summer's work?

Yes.

(Laughs.) It takes an entire summer for me to write one story.

I couldn't do it any more, but I did it. I had a tremendous amount of energy in those days.

To what extent can a writer, or a student/writer, become a product of a workshop?

I don't think it's as simple as the Workshop influencing your style. I don't think that's possible. I think that if you come in hoping to get an MFA so you can teach, you are now a product of the Workshop. But as far as writing goes, I don't see how it can do that.

Then the Workshop, in your opinion, doesn't have a tendency to homogenize, or create schools of writing, as in schools of thought or schools of poetry. There are schools of poetry, aren't there? The Robert Lowell School, the Donald Justice School, the Philip Levine School of Poetry. They each influence other poets in the traditions and style and aesthetics they themselves established or worked with.

Yeah.

Does that happen in fiction writing?

Not in an institutional way. It happens because the teacher is there, not because of the institution. There's a great quote I used one time from André Malraux. It says, "The individual stands in opposition to society but he is nourished by it. And it is less important to understand him than to know on what he feeds." Every writer is an individual; he has to be. And every writer is going to look around for models. And models are never institutions. They're always other writers. I was accused of being Ralph Ellison's protégé, but what Ellison was was a mentor. He gave me certain ideas that made me proud to be a black American. I mean it's as simple as that. He was saying our influence is everywhere. And he hasn't propagandized anything. So I said, "Well damn, here's the perspective I've been looking for." The ideas I got from him I've used, I think, but my style is my own.

What is the role of the teacher/writer in teaching new writers? Is it a bogus role? Is it just to be close by, is it just proximity?

I suppose it is. I don't know. I know that if you study the lives of great writers you see that they've always had contact with writers that inspired them. And I suppose that since there are no salons in this country, places where writers can get together, the university tends to provide a facsimile of that.

What are the pitfalls of that trend, and also, what are the advantages?

One pitfall is that you get your ego stroked by students to such an extent that you stop writing. That's the worst thing. Another pitfall is that you can get comfortable. You can get so comfortable that you get institutionalized, and you start turning out these novels dealing with the academy.

Workshop stories?

Well, not workshop stories, but novels dealing specifically with college life, university life. The thing you want to do is maintain your separateness. Be a traveller. Get on a bus and go someplace. Walk the streets, just to learn something. If you become too much a part of the academic community, you run the risk of closing out the rest of the world and seeing life only as it's played out in that small arena. There are advantages in a university job—I can think of no other employment that allows you a month off for Christmas, summers off, and you go in about two days a week, and you read books. The man is going to pay you to talk about books!

Hurray for the university.

Yeah. I mean, I'm going to read books anyway, and a man's going to give me money to do that!!??

Tell me this. What's the most important lesson for a student writer to learn?

I don't know. What is the most important lesson?

I don't know for sure but—

Why'd you ask me that silly shit (laughs)?

Well, it might not be silly. What could you say?

Dot your i's. I don't know.

I'm not sure that it's a silly question.

Well, I want to say, try to tell the truth.

That answer makes it not silly any more.

But that's a cliché, because the world will hate you if you tell the truth. I mean the truth as you perceive it. I'm not saying that you have the monopoly on truth, but if you say what you see, people hate you for it. I think anybody who wants can tell the truth. When I say truth I mean, what you really think and what you really feel, what's important to you at the time.

Well, you see, that's taken away the silliness of the question.

No, because you set me in a position of offering advice to writers, which I would prefer not to do. I just said that because that's what I would want somebody to tell me.

You are in as much of a position to offer advice to writers as anybody. Even more so—you're getting paid for it.

Hemingway told somebody—it's the same advice—he said you should have a built-in shit detector with a manual crank in case it malfunctions. That's good advice.

The form of a story seems to be crucial to you. What are your motives in choosing a form, or experimenting with form?

I think that every story has its own form. It's just one way a story can be told. But if you try something the wrong way, you're not going to get all you can get out of it. So what I do is start by trying to find a point of view that best tells the story. That's hard. That's the hardest part about it. A story can be worked for years, but if you don't have the point of view, it won't be written. Let me think of a story—the one called **"The Story of a Scar."** I tried to write that story in California right after I got out of the hospital. I saw this woman with a scar and I couldn't figure out how she got cut that way. What I wrote was like, um, trash. It was like trying to account for a lower class way of life I didn't know anything about. Then some time later my sister told me about a man who cut his girlfriend in the post office. The two things came together, and I could write the story then. In fact, I gave my sister half the money I got for it.

Well, that completed the logic of the story. But did that really—let's say form *just in terms of the structure of the prose—did it affect that?*

Well, when you think back on yourself, sitting in California, writing a story about life among the lowly, and then you, or that persona that you were, becomes a character in the story who's condescending to people who have their own reality, you see. And that stems from a problem with language—like high language presuming to judge a low language.

A lot of your narrators seem quite affluent. Are they actually alienated from the other characters they encounter?

Affluent?

Yeah. Or affluent and well, distant. They have a distance, whether it's an affluent distance or a—

Linguistic difference.

Linguistic distance, or an intellectual distance.

That's what I was concentrating on. You're talking about **Elbow Room,** right? What I was working with there—I had taken a course from Henry Nash Smith at Berkeley when I was out in California. One thing he dealt with in his books was the relationship between vernacular language and social structure. That is, the American vernacular, the common speech, evolved and considered itself in opposition to the formal and certified mode of speech. Now, each level of speech contains its own values, its own value system. And it was fun to be able to trace the development of that language from its origins in the pre-Revolutionary War period to the time when it received its celebration in Mark Twain, in *Huckleberry Finn*. But the issue, and it's still unresolved, is whether vernacular language and the values it seems to affirm, are really as solid as the values presented in high speech. So what I was doing in **Elbow Room** was seeing it in terms of "high" linguistic habits and the values embodied in those habits, put in opposition to the linguistic habits of vernacular speech and its

values. Most people saw it in terms of the black middle class and the black lower class. It wasn't that way at all. I was just trying to show the presumptiveness and the arrogance of that high speech, especially when it confronts the reality presented by the low speech, which is more valid. Now the danger is that the low speech can be just as condescending and reductive as the high speech. What do you do when you get a Huckleberry Finn who speaks the vernacular, and you're about to celebrate those values and about to dramatize the decadence of the learned values, and you run into the Duke and Dauphin, those confidence men, who are also vernacular characters? You see what I'm trying to say? That was Twain's problem. What do you do? So you stop the novel, and you wreck the raft, and you put Huck ashore away from Jim, and he goes and tries to get back to this traditional community. And then Twain says, Well no, it's still decadent, so you go back, resurrect the raft, you find Jim and take him back. You see, but you can't resolve it. So in the end you say—I won't work out the implications of this because I can't, but I'll just end the novel with another melodrama and have everything come out fine. Jim is freed by his owner, Tom Sawyer appears, and Huck Finn reverts to being a boy again because he couldn't see anything better in the values represented by the common speech. That was Mark Twain's dilemma. There's a big thing in *Huckleberry Finn* where, in the midst of celebrating the common speech and the values it's supposed to convey, Huck goes to an Arkansas town and a drunk man named Boggs comes through and he says, "Where's Colonel Sherburn? I'm going to kill him because he insulted me." He arrives at the Colonel's house and says, "Come on out." And the Colonel, an old Southern aristocrat, comes out and he says to Boggs, "If you're in town when I come out again, I'll shoot you down." And he walked back into his house. Then people told Boggs he'd better leave town. He was just about to leave, I think, when the Colonel comes out again and shoots him. Then he goes back in his house. The townspeople are outraged. They gather together in a lynch mob and go to the Colonel's house. He comes out and says, "The idea of *you*, lynching *anybody.* I've lived in the North and in the South, and I know the average all around. The average man is a coward." And then they all left and he went back in his house. Well now, that's Twain. That's the same persona that later appears in *The Man That Corrupted Hadleyburg* and *The Whole Damn Human Race*. That's Twain.

His arrogance?

Well, it's not so much arrogance as it is a confession that although the values implied by the proper speech of his day didn't quite fit reality, the speech and the values of the vernacular class weren't necessarily any improvement. What are you going to do? You wreck the raft.

Well, it made him a cynic. Is it making you a cynic also, or are you finding that the values do fit better than Twain realized?

They don't fit better, but what I find is that it's not one or the other. It's not a class thing or a speech thing. What's needed is a kind of civility, a code of manners.

A code of decency.

All manners are a stylization of tension. Like in the South, even in the worst, most racist communities, people both white and black say to each other, "How are you?" "Nice day." You know. It's a way of acknowledging your presence, and also acknowledging that you have to cope because you're living together. That's what's needed, and it's not just needed between black and white; it's needed between white and white, black and black, and men and women, too. We need a code, some kind of civility.

Talk about the short story as a form itself.

The short story is the only indigenous American form. You don't have any great novels coming out of this country because it's too fragmented, made up of too many different groups. Who can see the whole picture? All you can do is give little reports from this section, that section.

Do you think the short story again will go under, or do you think it's up for good? It seems exceptionally strong now as a form. And, like jazz, we're heralding it as truly American.

I think that when people are in trouble—this country is in trouble—you always go back to your basic premise. And I think jazz will always be here, just because it grew as a form out of our basic American spirit. If you go into a record store you can see a whole wall full of rock and new wave and that kind of stuff, and that's for a decreasing piece of the audience, and the other stuff, jazz, is still around. I think the same is true for the short story form. People have to get some grounding, some sense of what the culture's basic orientation is. So you go back to familiar forms. That's all I can say.

How important are the small literary magazines?

They're very important, and they always have been important. This thing I read on Williams Carlos Williams—he never got a single poem published in any commercial publication. And this was a master! He had to rely on the small magazines all the time. They allow a lot of people to survive. The good thing about National Endowment is that it allows those magazines to live, so that there's room now for work that will not be touched by commercial publishers.

How did you get involved in the book Railroad *that you edited with Miller Williams?*

In '73 and '74, I was living in Rhode Island. This was a time of extreme racial reaction, and I had been trying to convince somebody, an editor, that it was in everybody's best interests if the country could decrease its polarization, if he could take a Bicentennial stance to affirm those things that we all had in common. And I said, "All we have in common that I know about is the Constitution, and our memory of the railroad, and if I can write something for you that could feed everybody into that central symbol and show you how it looks, maybe you will take the idea." So I wrote—that's when I was trying to save the world—I wrote a long long long essay, feeding everything into it; and he finally, after some long delays, said, "I don't know what you're talking about." So the essay sort of laid around. And I felt a lot of shame because here I was, a colored boy from Savannah, trying to say, "We have things in common that can hold us together as a people, as Americans." Anyway, later on when I was in Spokane, a year or so later, I met Miller Williams. We started trading railroad stories so we decided to do a book together. We got some money from Random House. If you look at the essay in the book, the form is that of a train, even with a caboose. I just had fun doing that. To answer your question another way, the real inspiration for it was my attempt to argue with a book by Leo Marx, a book called *The Machine in the Garden.* It was a study of the pastoral ideal. The idea of the pastoral comes down from the Greeks. The conflict was between this old world notion of the sublime and the hard facts of American technology in the eighteenth and nineteenth centuries. Marx's idea was that nineteenth century American writers had great difficulty reconciling the pastoral, which we inherited from the Greeks, with the hard facts of an industrial democracy. And I said, "Yeah, but whenever there's a conflict, a thesis and antithesis, there's always a synthesis someplace." And I said, "Well, what about the central symbol of nineteenth century industrial technology—the railroad. What do we do about that?" And then I began going through the literature and looking at the vernacular response to that artifact. What the common, untutored people had to say about it, not the people who had preconceived notions about the nature of art. People who had no choice— what *they* had to say. And I found that they had an instinctive fear of it, and also an instinctive desire to recontextualize it, to take it apart and redefine, reinvest it, with things that had meaning and value. And that was a kind of art. And that's why I wrote the long essay and edited the book. But who am I to argue with Leo Marx?

You're a voice, just as he's a voice. Who's anybody to argue with you?

I was proud of that book because I had the capacity to write about things beyond the immediate experience of my color. And that's what I love, because I found that I could master a certain amount of material. But then the message comes back, "Stick with what you know."

That's an ignorant message. You know that.

But if most people think that, it's reality.

I don't think most people think that.

Um hmm. Well that's what I really want. That period was the best in my life when I think back on it. I had all these books from Brown University library. I was reading them and I was really beginning to put Marx's, Leo Marx's, ideas into the American context. He's really *European.* I was able to say to myself, "I'm an American. This is *mine.*" And I was saying to him, "There's something you don't understand about being an American." It was like an expansion of my mind, so to speak. And I envision, maybe a hundred years from now, if the country lasts that long, a black American who wants to write a book on *anything* will have the freedom to do that without people saying, "How does this relate to your color?" That's what I really want to see.

Are you interested at all in the Third World? Is there any moral obligation, because writers use moral ammunition, is there any moral obligation for an American writer to look beyond his own house? Considering the way the world is today?

Well there's a lot of change going on outside of this country, but inside this country we can't seem to get a handle on it. I don't know what the Third World is. I think it's fiction.

It's just a convenient term.

This is dangerous to say, but if the Third World has any power, it's politically advantageous for black Americans to say, "I'm Third World." Well I'm not after power myself. I just want to see things. There's an old Negro saying, "You may be my color, but you ain't my kind." I guess what I want to do is find my kind. It has nothing to do with color.

If you insist on color, and the Third World continues to develop the way it is, that would be a very interesting revelation for white America, because the stronger the Third World becomes, the more voice they have, the more they expose themselves to white America, the more white America has to come to terms with themselves as the minority, the global minority.

Then that means doomsday for black Americans because we are the scapegoats for all the frustrations, you see, and the color fears they have for what's out there.

That's taken out on black Americans. You know what sustains me, what used to sustain me, is the story in the Bible about Joseph and his brothers. If there is a God, He must have had some reason for the sale of Africans to Europeans over here. If you think about it, we're the only people who didn't come here voluntarily. I mean, we had to make our own way. And there must be some part of God's plan that accounts for that. When Andrew Young was making these statements, he was trying to create a bridge between this country and Africa, this country and the Third World, and they shut him up. They didn't want to hear it.

Some people listened to Young. At least that's a step.

All those guys in the foreign service should be thrown out and they should put in some old dining car waiters (laughs).

In your article "On Becoming an American Writer," published in the Atlantic Monthly, *you say that you're the product of a contractual process. What does that statement mean?*

If I recall that article, I think when I was writing it, I recalled that my mother and father never did talk about the mean treatment that they received from white people. I remember my mother saying that her father was a sharecropper on a white man's plantation. She said that the owner fired the white overseer and gave her father the job. And she said the man that was fired swore he'd come back and kill her father. She said she remembered her father sitting on the porch all night with a gun in his lap waiting for the man to come back. That's the one thing she talked about. Another thing was that she was telling me when I was a child about World War II, and about how the Japanese would be hiding in trees to catch the Americans. And it came to me later that she was talking tongue-in-cheek about Reconstruction, about what the white South did to reclaim its power. But she had put it in a context that she could deal with. My father never talked about it. Well, there was a reason for that. It was grounded in, I think, a religious belief in progress and the correctability of people. And they refused to burden the younger generation with the baggage of their own frustrations. What they did was they crippled you, in ways that were well-meaning. When I say crippled I mean—Oh, I read a book last summer, a book called *Dry-Long-So.* It's an oral history of the core culture. But in that book the old people said, "There's nothing in the world as vicious and mean as a cracker. A cracker's the meanest thing." I mean, who are these people? This is what they held in, you see. "White people ought to be ashamed, all the energy they put into trying to keep us down." Things like that. But by holding it in and not passing it on, they sort of made a covenant with the future, and by virtue of that, of peace with white people in the future.

So that they said, "I would rather see my children that naive. Let this bitterness hurt me but not them. In the hope that the same things won't happen again in the future." That was it—the contractual process, that was the initial giving or withholding with the consideration that the future has to give something back to you. That's what I meant when I said I was the result of a contractual process. And it works, it works well during times of racial peace, so to speak, because if the antagonism never resumes, you cancel what's due to you. But when there's no racial peace, you look back on those folks and say, "They were right." And it hurts you. It hurts you.

You also said that the process led to people grasping for a provisional identity to hold on to. If the older generation starts the contractual process, protecting the next generation from the experiences they've had, and then when the young grow up and start having their own conflicts—how does a provisional identity fit into that?

I was talking about race. Now this is going to sound kind of silly, I guess. One thing that Ralph Ellison taught me, not taught me, but affirmed for me in a very prideful and manly way, was that I need make no apology for my color or for where I came from. That I was a multi-generational American, and if you didn't know that you were also an American, even though your color was different, that was your problem. You belonged here. This was my country and no Grand Kleagle of the California Klan could say it was not. Now I'm not talking about ideology now, or patriotism. I'm talking about a basic identity that is anybody's by birth, but that black Americans have to struggle for much more than white Americans. They have heavier dues. But what do you do when you let go of those moorings in the black community, the things that are worked out in terms of how you deal with white folk when there's no guidance there, because the situation is new? You have to figure out some new way to survive. In Cambridge, for example, I saw a lot of black guys becoming studs because that was an easy fashion. But you could not have an identity outside the role of a stud. Or, if you went to Harvard, you became Harvardized. Your identity became that of a Harvard man. But you couldn't bring in anything else with you. On the white side you saw the white students, or young white people, identifying with some of the most shallow aspects of black American tradition. Adopting the language, becoming theatrical revolutionaries. You see what I'm trying to say? The props were there. You take those props and construct something, but it's just illusions, just part way along the process, the process being an endless one because we were going to be lawyers, but also something more given the uniqueness of our experience. The point is that every generation of black Americans is torn between going back to the certainties of their ancestral identity, and they're goaded by the norms and clubs of society saying "You are a black," and the desire to go ahead and finish that contractual process. That's what I was talking about. Does that make sense to you?

Yeah, it does. The provisional identity is the mid-way point. See if this makes sense to you. It's a devil's advocate question. Is writing a provisional identity, or is it the antithesis of that?

I guess for me, all I can be is a writer. I'll be that in my spare time no matter what else I do.

So it's the antithesis.

That's the way I wound up.

Provisional identities are sort of like adolescent behavior. You play a role because the role makes you more secure in some way. And then after awhile you stop playing the role because you're more sure about yourself and you have a better awareness of who you are. So it's adolescent behavior in a way. Being a writer is a decision against that, it's the antithesis of provisional identity, at least for most serious writers. How do most people overcome their provisional identities, or do they?

They don't. They don't. That's why the entire American tradition is one of the theater. When American society is most American is when it's theatrical. It goes back to your question—we were talking earlier about an upper class: who is there to provide a model? What's out there? Who are your heroes? Football players. Basketball players. There are no models. If you look at the bestseller list now, you get the autobiographies of movie stars. A star is an actor, he's a craftsman. The roles are great—*he*'s not great. What is that for a model?

Most good models are usually very vulnerable and get their asses kicked.

Um hmm. I'm just saying that the country's still in process. It doesn't really know who it is because it has no sense of what it is. We're just trying to string along in order to get to the third act where things will be resolved. This country has no tragic sense because it has been nurtured by musical comedy and the soap opera. In American drama everything's resolved before the last scene. What do you do when things can't be resolved? You either grow or you die. I mean, when there are no traditions that make things meaningful before the last commercial comes on, you either say, "I don't understand, I give up," or you develop a tragic sense. And until the country develops that, it will lack maturity. We're just waiting for some excitement so we can sort of improvise a make-do ending.

Right. We seem very addicted to the decadence of excitement. Okay, let me ask one more question. What do you hope for in the years ahead as a writer and as a person?

Well, my hopes are for myself as a person. I hope to master the art of being closer to other people who should be in my life, to help raise my daughter and give her all the love I can, to learn from the mistakes I've made in the past. Right now I want personal happiness more than I want to write a bestseller.

There's a narrator in **"Just Enough for the City"** *who says, "Lately I've been trying for a simple definition of love." Have you found one yet? I know that's a narrator speaking in a story, but—*

No, because I don't think it can be that simple. But I think I've found it, just in human terms with my daughter Rachel, and even trying to see it in terms of a mate. But I learned this much. You don't look for it. If it's due you, it will come to you. I can't be any more profound than this.

Ruthe T. Sheffey (essay date 1985)

SOURCE: Sheffey, Ruthe T. "Antaeus Revisited: James A. McPherson and *Elbow Room.*" In *Amid Visions and Revisions: Poetry and Criticism on Literature and the Arts,* edited by Burney J. Hollis, pp. 122-31. Baltimore, Md.: Morgan State University Press, 1985.

[*In the following essay, Sheffey investigates elements of the Southern African American folk tradition in McPherson's* Elbow Room.]

The Academy in awarding Isaac Bashevis Singer the Nobel award in 1978 reported that Singer's stories of Jewish life were of east European Jewry "such as it was lived in cities and villages, in poverty and persecution, and imbued with sincere piety and rights combined with blind faith and superstition." The Academy added that these stories display "a redeeming melancholy, sense of humor, and a clear-sightedness free of illusion." This latter statement should certainly be affirmed also of James Alan McPherson's 1978 Pulitzer Award-winning book of short stories, **Elbow Room. Elbow Room** mines the deep vein of Afro-American folk-lore, unearthing its wry subtleties, its salty language, its aphoristic parables, and its rich humor. Where **Hue and Cry,** McPherson's first collection of short stories, was tentative, groping and uncertain, **Elbow Room** uses the one black eye of the title story to "peep around corners," in short to explore the joy and anguish of the Negro in America.

Contrary to Robie McCauley's *New York Times* note that he was a writer and black but not a "Black writer," McPherson does write of ethnic patterns and themes, although he does insist on the act of imagination and integrity required to understand the total human condi-

tion. The protagonists in these twelve stories are almost all black with the exception of the husband in the story **"Elbow Room"** who is a white Kansan student and a conscientious objector, married to a black girl from Tennessee, a former member of the Peace Corps. These two try in the face of familial hostilities and the misunderstanding of peers for a merger that will solve the human equation of love and which will obliterate racial distinction:

> Wouldn't it have been something to be a nigger that could relate to white and black and everything else in the world out of self as big as the world is . . . ? That would have been some nigger![1]

Virginia, the wife, goes on to say that at least she had been able to see through the fog. The narrator answers, "you were game all right." Interestingly enough this dialogue proceeds as if the experiment had failed. Instructively the narrator, perhaps the writer as artist, comments:

> Inside myself I suddenly felt a coolness as light as the morning against my skin. Then I realized that I was acting. I did not care about them and their problems any more. I did not think they had a story worth telling. I looked away from her and said, "Life is tough, all right."

> (p. 273)

Virginia's comment "But didn't I make some elbow room though?" as she tapped her temple with her forefinger, "I mean up here!" gives the title story and the book its name. In keeping with much black fiction, the narrator realizes that the world source of his desperation is even worse off than he. His view of the white world is that it is a weak, dull, colorless and morally improverished world. The narrator in **"Elbow Room"** says: "The people we saw seemed resigned, anemic, vaguely haunted by lackluster ghosts. My own eyes seemed drawn to black people" (p. 238).

The opening story, **"Why I Like Country Music"** has the wry humor and nostalgic reminiscence of childhood innocence and love, explicated with the pathos of the born loser. It is Totie Fields, Phyllis Diller, Bill Cosby, and Richard Pryor synthesized and distilled. The story's particularity is a part of its strength. To spice this narrative, McPherson reveals through subtleties of thought and feeling, black regional differences—what he calls North-lore and South-lore. The narrator has difficulty in convincing his third generation, Northern-born black wife that he likes country music. "She can see the blues, be-bop, even a little buck dancing. But not blue grass." With a nice sense of having come full circle at the end of the story, the wife, Gloria, maintains "I can see the hustle, the bump, maybe even Ibo highlife. But not hillbilly." Gloria, who was born in New York, still believes in the Stock Exchange as an index of economic health.

The writer counters "My perceptions were shaped in South Carolina and long ago I learned there, as a waiter in private clubs to gauge economic flux by the tips people give." The writer continues "What I do know is that while the two of us are black, the distance between us is sometimes as great as that between Ibo and Yoruba." Afro-American regionalism—even tribalism—is pinpointed in a way largely unparalleled in contemporary black fiction.

The mythic proportions of North-lore brought to the South are enlarged by stories of these new dances which invariably came from up North and were brought to town by people returning to rap on the good life said to exist in those far Northern places:

> They prowled our dirt streets in rented Cadillacs; paraded our brick sidewalks exhibiting styles abstracted from the fullness of life in Harlem, South Philadelphia, Roxbury, Baltimore and the South Side of Chicago. They confronted our provincial clothes merchants with the arrogant reminder, "But people ain't wearin' this in New Yorkkk!" Each of their movements, as well as their world-weary smoothness, told us locals meaningful tales of what was missing in our lives. Unfortunately, those of us under strict parental supervision, or those of us without Northern connections, could only stand at a distance and worship these envoys of culture. We stood on the sidelines—styleless, gestureless, danceless, doing nothing more than an improvised one-butt-shuffle—hoping for one of them to touch our lives. It was my good fortune, during my tenth year on the sidelines, to have one of these Northerners introduce me to the square dance.

(p. 5)

The warm memories of this cherished Northerner are of a pretty chocolate brown girl with dark brown eyes and two long black braids. He remembered the rainbow of deep rich colors in which she lived and her magical perfume smelling just slightly of fresh-cut lemons. These memories tantalize him even today. "Whenever I smell fresh lemons, whether in the market or at home, I look around me—not for Gweneth Lawson, but for some quiet corner where I can revive in private certain memories of her. And in pursuing these memories across such lemony bridges, I rediscovered that I loved her." Although a part of this magnificent North-lore, there was no condescension in Gweneth's manner. The city, in the youth of the narrator, was still the Eldorado which early black writers envisioned, and not the Minoan maze that it became in Ellison and in other new black writers.

> Only someone who understands what London meant to Dick Whittington, or how California and the suburbs function in the national mind could appreciate the mythical dimensions of this North-lore.

(p. 6)

This passion for Gweneth went not unnoticed by their fourth grade teacher, the round full-breasted strict disciplinarian Mrs. Esther Clay Boswell. Particularly hard

on the daydreamers she posted a sign under the electric clock, "Notice to all clockwatchers, time passes. Will You?" Her terse lessons left the more emotional among the students, including the narrator, in tears. Slapping a thick homemade ruler against the flat of her brown palm, she would recite:

> There ain't no babies in here. Thaap! Anybody thinks he's still a baby . . . Thaap! . . . should crawl back home to his mama's titty. Thaap! You little bunnies shed you last water . . . Thaap! From now on, you g'on do all your cryin' . . . Thaap! (in church!) . . . Now you little brown bunnies and you black buck rabbits and you few cottontails mixed in, some of you starting to smell yourselves under the arms without knowing what it's all about. . . . Now I know your mamas already made you think life is a bed of roses, but in my classroom you got to know the footpaths through the sticky parts of the rosebed.

(p. 7)

One of these cryptic lessons preceded the announcement of the traditional celebration of the arrival of Spring on May first by both the ritual plaiting of the May Pole and square dancing. When the narrator was placed with the square dancers instead of among the pole-plaiters with the beauteous Gweneth, he resolved not to square dance at all. After much persuasion the narrator's daddy wrote, "My boy does not square dance. Please excuse him as I am afraid he will break down and cry and mess up the show. Yours truly. . . ." The wily Mrs. Boswell agrees to let the narrator plait the pole but sends Gweneth to join the square dancers. He had been outdone. All he really wanted was "one moment to swing Gweneth Lawson in his arms."

Only Leon Pugh's arrogance and the vanity of his wearing silver spurs on the heels of his boots saved the day. Leon is sent, as the square dance is being called, to take off his dangerous spurs. The narrator is sent in to the ball as Gweneth's noon-hour prince. In seventh heaven, the narrator had no memory of moving but only of standing with Gweneth at the center of the yard. Told later that he made an allemande right instead of left, he had no memory of the mistake. He can only recall the warm brown eyes of Gweneth smiling at him.

> I smiled with lemonness of her and the loving of her pressed deep into those saving places of my private self. It was my plan to savor these, and I did savor them. . . . But I think sometimes of Gweneth now when I hear country music. And although it is difficult to explain to you, I still maintain that I am no mere arithmetician in the art of the square dance. I am in to the calculus of it.

(p. 21)

Like Zora Neale Hurston, McPherson probes deeply into American folklore and translates his findings into richly human stories. The second story titled, **"The**

Story of A Dead Man," becomes the ballad of "Wild Nigger Bill from Red Pepper Hill who never did die and never will." The unhurried and laconic quality of folk language is brilliantly preserved in this story. Verisimilitude has been managed no better, and all of the pungency of American folk heroes from John Henry to High John de Conquer is encapsulated in the story of Billy Renfro, the narrator's cousin. **"The Story of a Dead Man"** begins dramatically:

> It is not true that Billy Renfro was killed during that trouble in Houston. The man is an accomplished liar and likes to keep his enemies nervous. It was he who spread this madness. The truth of what happened, he told me in Chicago, was this: After tracking the debtor to a rented room, Billy Renfro's common sense was overwhelmed by the romantic aspects of the adventure. That was why he kicked open the door, charged boldly into the room and shouted, "Monroe Ellis, give-up Mr. Floyd's Cadillac that you done miss nine payments on!" Unhappily for Billy, neither Monroe Ellis nor the woman with him was in the giving-up mood. The woman fired first, aiming underneath Ellis on the bed. Contrary to most reports, that bullet only wounded Billy's arm. It was one of the subsequent blasts from Monroe's .38 that entered Billy's side. But this wound did not slow Billy's retreat from the room, the rooming house, or the city of Houston. He was alive and fully recovered when I saw him in Chicago, on his way back from Harvey after reclaiming a defaulted Chevy.
>
> (p. 23)

Zora Hurston says of High John that the old people frequently shook their heads and said, "That old High John he a case." Similarly Billy's mother's refrain is "Ah, Billy! He just won't do!" Beneath the movingly wry humor we slowly discover a deep sense of personal despair, masked by Billy's flamboyance. His strange uncaring demon laughter bragged of his urge to self-destruct. The narrator knew as did his mother, that Billy was doomed. And yet this story evades, with its bubbling humor, a sense of doom or despair. The lost left eye about which Billy spun such fascinating stories, a different one each time, was a symbol of his insouciance, of his outrageous charm. The narrator assures us that as Billy's cousin and honor bound to love him as he really is, he had the obligation to, "Deflate the mean rumors circulated by his enemies, cut through the fat of Billy's own lies, and lay bare the muscle of his life." The saga of the upwardly mobile narrator cousin who wins a church scholarship to college, an important job, and later an upper-middle-class "family-backed, efficiency-minded girl" is an enormously comic counterpoint to the story of his cousin who is in and out of jail and who flirts with death daily as a car repossessor for Mr. Dillingham. Mr. Dillingham is described as a liberal man who had negotiated with the state for Billy's release.

> The job was to track down Negroes who had defaulted on their car payments. No white man would even consider such employment. I do believe that Dillingham

wanted a Negro with a reputation for ruthlessness sufficient to strike fear into the hearts of the deadbeats. In the inevitable tug between desire and justice, some of Dillingham's clients had been known to kill. Paid agents do not grow old in such an enterprise.

> (p. 31)

The humor mounts when Billy arrives on a visit to his affluent cousin in Chicago. The narrator is almost plaintive in his demurrers. He insists that it is not true that he refuses to see Billy in his office. "I do not call the man a liar but I do say his imagination is a stranger to the truth. . . . It may be he was not dressed properly for the occasion. . . . On my honor as a member of the family I did not deny the bond." Looking closely at Billy's face, the narrator sees death walking. "The single red eye inspected him, and the left eye socket hollow was no more than a shriveled piece of flesh pressed grimly against his skull." Billy's stories begin again, all lifted directly from the richest vein of Afro-American folk-lore. Indeed, one could compose a dictionary of folk expressions from this book, although they are never obtrusive. Billy speaks in passing of Newark house rent parties, of the highlights of a fish fry in Baltimore, and of the economics of picking beans in New Jersey, if one is stranded there in August without cash.

> Billy recited his contributions to bus-depot graffiti, inscribed on stalls in Memphis, Little Rock, Phoenix and Los Angeles, and observed that practitioners of this art become more assertive, sexually and politically, the farther West one went. I heard his accounts of fights, poker games, epic bouts of wrestling, with recalcitrant claimers of defaulted cars.
>
> (p. 35)

Finally carried to meet his successful cousin's upper-class in-laws-to-be and dressed in the cousin's best suit and blue sunshades, shielding the eye socket from inspection, Billy gave, initially, the appearance of a publicity shy banker. In answer to a query about his business, he simply murmurs "Automotives." Billy is all elegance on the purple settee, his legs crossed and a glass of sherry held aloft. Late in the evening when Mr. Raymond becomes expansive and pulls out his cigars and bourbon, Billy can no longer contain himself but begins to offer tales about his own exploits on the coast. Hearing of the adventures of a hustling bellhop named "Swifty," Billy leaned forward, pounded the table, and shouted, "Damn if I don't know that Nigger. He in Detroit now, still just as crazy as a bedbug." Mrs. Raymond coughed violently and left the room, and the evening deteriorated rapidly from that point onward. The upwardly mobile cousin tries hilariously and without avail to save the situation. In a stunning denouement, Billy strips off glasses, coat, vest, and polka-dot tie. He lets the sky blue shirt fall to the floor. "Standing broad shouldered and brown in a ragged yellow undershirt, he directed all of our eyes to the welt-like scars on his arms and neck. These here come from running around the country," he grinned. "And I'll keep running till the pork chops get thicker and they give me two dollars more." As he laughed wickedly, Mrs. Raymond clutched her chest. The climax has the bride-to-be shouting. "You common *street nigger*!" Billy holds out his naked arm as if he were a ringmaster introducing an act. "And this here is my cousin William."

The narrator, comically crushed at this point, pathetically insists that it is not true that Billy Renfro is not welcome in his home. "The man is, after all, my cousin. It is a point of family pride." After his startlingly heroic gesture of self-revelation, Billy Renfro is one with "Wild Nigger Bill from Pepper Hill who never did die and who never will. But as things stand now, he is still someplace out there with a single eye flickering over open roadways, in his careless search for an exciting death. Ah! Billy!" (p. 43)

The humor in this story and others in the collection like **"The Story of a Scar"** and **"The Silver Bullet"** derives from a folkloric tall-tale tradition, told in a deliberately low-keyed, unhurried, matter-of-fact voice, at direct odds with the violence of the content. Laughter is the heroes' perfect mechanism for escape from the confinement of their blackness. The humor is wry, ironic, often in-group, a device for coping with and surviving in an oppressive system. As effective as it may be, some critics have maintained that laughter is a mechanism rarely used in black writing. On this subject Ossie Davis wrote:

> The Negro in this county has to protest, because he is protestant. He can't help but be. He cannot accept the situation in which he finds himself, so therefore he is driven to scream out against the oppression that surrounds him, that suffocates him.

He continues that one form of protest may take the form of Negro folk humor, for, in addition to being unjust, the situation may also be ridiculous:

> We can show that it is ridiculous, perhaps even laughable, and therefore not worthy of the behavior of educated, culturally advanced human beings, such as must be the kind of people, both black and white, who inhabit America at this late date. That stream of humor had to carry our sense of self, our sense of history, our hope of the future, our religious concern about man's relationship to man.

If a black man stood and said "I, too, am a man," he could be killed. He could assert his manhood through his folk humor. Ossie Davis, in *Purlie* and elsewhere, has attempted as he tells us "to give back to the Negro people the humor they themselves created, in the form in which they created it, and to let it begin, once again, to serve the function for which it was originally created." Langston Hughes succeeded in this mission with

Jesse B. Semple. But as far as I am able to determine, no one writing black fiction today has succeeded more magnificently in this wish than James Alan McPherson.

Roger Rosenblatt maintains in *Black Fiction,* "White convention has always held that Black people do a great deal of laughing in the hope that the tag of humor like the tag of rhythm might imply happiness and grant the oppressors absolution." Perhaps black writers may have felt like the Psalmists beside the rivers of Babylon, forced to provide everything else for their masters and also to provide hilarity:

> They that carried us away captive required of us a song;
> and they that wasted us required of us mirth, saying,
> Sing us one of the songs of Zion. How shall we sing the Lord's song in a strange land?
>
> (Psalm 137)

Yet urban folk heroes in literature like Langston Hughes' Semple, who foresees a second coming in which Jesus gets rid of all white people except Mrs. Eleanor Roosevelt, continue to laugh at the rigidity and inflexibility of white programmed responses to blacks and also at the comic adaptations of some blacks. Felton in **"Silver Bullet"** is a new style black ghetto conman who puffs his cheeks, looks enraged and who, before he strongarms a neighborhood bartender, speaks tritely in 1960s rhetoric of "the profound problems that relate to community structure that have to be challenged through the appropriate agency," and of "the dynamics of our organization vis-a-vis the community, as the only legitimate and viable group to operate in this sphere." Declaring the business nationalized and demanding ten percent of the profits to be paid on Friday mornings, R. V. Felton intones, "We support the Community dynamic, and together we all know what's going down. That is our dynamic. Dig it." In a later visit R. V. blusters as he looks down Jones' gun barrel:

> Let me run something down for you brother. First of all we are a non-profit community based grass roots organization, totally responsive to the needs of the community. Second, we think the community would be very interested in the Articulation of the total proceeds of this joint vis-a-vis the average income for this area. Third you don't want to mess with us, we got the support of the College Students.
>
> (p. 55)

Unimpressed by this rhetorical display, Jones levels his shotgun and says:

> Well I ain't never been to college myself but I can count to ten. And if you punks ain't down the block when I finish, the street out there is gonna be full of hamburger meat. He lifted the gun. And one last thing; I'm already past five.
>
> (p. 56)

"A Sense of Story," the penultimate story in *Elbow Room,* dramatically begins with another surprising self-revelation. On trial for murder, "Robert L. Charles, after having sat four days in silence while his court appointed lawyers pleaded for him, rose suddenly from his chair and faced the jurors. 'It wasn't no accident,' he told them in a calm voice. 'I had me nine bullets and a no good gun. Gentlemens, the onliest thing I regret is the gun broke before I could pump six more slugs into the sonofabitch.' Thus ensuring his doom the defendant sat down."

By flashback, the story which emerges is of a treacherous white supervisor who steals the defendant's invented formula for a lubricant, the device by which he had desperately hoped to rise in his work world. From the testimony of the arresting officer, to the Judge's abstracts, to the summation of the defense counsel, we come to know the deep frustration of this man whom the author calls:

> An illiterate Southern Black, socialized in an environment of violence and who possessed a single cherished skill. He is a man who acted out of motives beyond the competence of this witness, and of most white people to know.

> (p. 200)

The story is at the same time a quiet parody and satire on all the professionals who attempt to explain the Negro's condition. The absurdities of the psychiatrist are quoted at length, as are those of a *Michigan Study,* and of a sociologist who carries a tape recorder.

Robie McCauley's *New York Times* review of *Elbow Room* falls short of the critical mark when it maintains that McPherson is a black and a writer but not necessarily a black writer. Similarly, the reporter who wrote the Pulitzer award story about McPherson, and who picked the McCauley remark about McPherson refusing to fall into a color or ethnic-code saying that this was the opinion of critics, did the work a disservice. It is certainly true that what we expect to find in modern world literature, we get in McPherson: the complexity of expression, the allusiveness of meaning, the opposition to traditional social and esthetic systems, the tendency towards fragmentation as a method of development, the elements of violence, the permanence of subjectivity (sensed as loss or dislocation of main character). They are all here. The Pulitzer prize was, however, rightfully awarded to a book which goes far beyond these mere mechanics.

For, like Antaeus in mythology, the giant wrestler, son of Poseidon and Earth, who lived in Libya, and who was made stronger when thrown, by his mother, the Earth, McPherson has moved beyond the unresolved contradictions, the despair, and the nihilism of his first book *Hue and Cry.* He has moved beyond the mere wish to raise a hue and cry about the black man's pride and injury. For the first title was taken from Pollack and Maitland's *History of English Law.* The passage after the title page of *Hue and Cry* goes:

> When a felony is committed, the hue and cry (hutesium et clamor) should be raised. If, for example, a man comes upon a dead body and omits to raise the hue, he commits an amerciable offense, besides laying himself open to ugly suspicions. Possibly the proper cry is "Out! Out!"

Like the giant Antaeus, McPherson has at last touched the ground of his own being in his wryly comic and serious Afro-American folk-tales. As a literary artist, he has imitated his favorite theme of violently stripping off the mask and completely exposing himself, sometimes in the diabolically mocking manner of Billy Renfro in the inner sanctum of the Raymonds' polite circle, sometimes with the proud resignation to fate of Robert L. Charles' avowal of guilt in a **"Sense of Story."**

In as full a sense as that Isaac Bashevic Singer's literary strength derives from deep and honest probing beneath the lives of East European Jewry, so McPherson's great power is drawn from the deep substratum of Southern Afro-American perception. What emerges is clear sighted, honest, humorous, and free of illusion.

The literary tradition—the shared American experience—is there for all to savor. No whit less present is the undeniable uniqueness of the black experience in America. To capture the richness and the diversity of that experience (its flux and its earthy pathos) and at the same time to crystallize the discernible norms and patterns of that unique life-style is a prize-worthy achievement.

Like Antaeus, James Alan McPherson[4] will continue to be nourished by his roots in Southern soil and will continue to grow, to raise the hue and cry when man's inhumanity to his fellows is discovered, and to give vehement voice to the anguish and the paradox of the black man's existence in America.

Notes

1. James Alan McPherson, *Elbow Room* (Boston: Little Brown and Company, 1977), pg. 237. Subsequent references are to this edition.

2. Ossie Davis, "The Wonderful World of Law and Order," *Anger and Beyond,* ed. Herbert Hill (New York: Harper and Row, 1966) p. 157.

3. Roger Rosenblatt, *Black Fiction* (Cambridge: Harvard University Press, 1974), p. 101.

4. James McPherson was a student in Dr. Sheffey's Advanced Composition class at Morgan State University.

Jon Wallace (essay date 1992)

SOURCE: Wallace, Jon. "Making It Official: James Alan McPherson's *Elbow Room*." In *The Politics of Style: Language as Theme in the Fiction of Berger, McGuane, and McPherson,* pp. 123-59. Durango, Colo.: Hollowbrook Publishing, 1992.

[*In the following essay, Wallace outlines the significance of narrative perspective and stylistic shifts in* Elbow Room, *noting that many social and psychological aspects of the characters are revealed through their use of language.*]

"I'm black," declares Virginia Frost in the title story of James Alan McPherson's Pulitzer Prize winning book ***Elbow Room.***

> 'I've accepted myself as that. But didn't I make some elbow room though?' She tapped her temple with her forefinger. 'I mean up *here!*' Then she laughed bitterly and sipped her tea. 'When times get tough, *anybody* can pass for white. Niggers been doing *that* for *centuries,* so it ain't nothing new. But shit, wouldn't it of been something to be a nigger that could relate to white and black and everything else in the world out of a self as big as the world is?' She laughed. Then she said, 'That would have been *some* nigger!'
>
> (author's italics 281)

As a seeker of personal space, of the elbow room she needs to develop herself and a sympathetic understanding of other human beings, Virginia represents one end of a moral and psychological continuum within the book. At the opposite end stand other characters who also seek elbow room but for antithetical reasons. Unlike Virginia, who wants room to grow, the protagonists of **"The Story of a Dead Man," "The Story of a Scar"** and **"Just Enough for the City"** seek a space within which they can defend themselves against the claims of intimacy, human involvement and personal history. Masters of what is primarily a white linguistic code, they attempt to look out at the world from deep within the safety of conventional institutions and ideologies that implicitly justify their failure to see beyond them. In their mouths Standard English becomes a defensive weapon—a means of self-protection that, like Standard English in the mouths of defensive Whites, enables them to "hold the floor" at the expense of speakers of other codes who want, and often desperately need, to be heard. Characters in **"Problems of Art"** and **"A Sense of Story"** and the narrator of **"Elbow Room"** are similarly limited by their commitment to useful but highly restrictive official structures such as law, logic and, surprisingly, conventional literary form. In all six stories, the wayfarer-official distinction is useful as a means of understanding basic stylistic and thematic issues in a book that argues for Virginia's kind of transcultural and transracial selfhood, most often by dramatizing its ab-

sence. Read as such, ***Elbow Room,*** like *The Trial,* consists of so many official paragraphs designed to achieve a wayfaring end.

"It is not true," announces William, the narrator of **"The Story of a Dead Man,"** "that Billy Renfro was killed during that trouble in Houston" (32). Thus begins a narrative written to accomplish in fiction what the dramatic monologue accomplishes in poetry: unconscious self-revelation. The difference between most first-person fiction and the dramatic monologue, however, is that in the latter the identity of the audience is known, and of course relevant to what the speaker is revealing and why. In **"The Story of a Dead Man"** McPherson does not identify William's audience, but he continually reminds us that William is speaking or writing to someone and that his motive is to defend himself against stories told by Billy about the latter's heroic adventures on the road and to rumors about William's mistreatment of him.

Both the stories and the rumors threaten William: the rumors for obvious reasons, the stories because they expose the staid pointlessness of William's very conventional life. "Neither is it true," William tells us in the second paragraph, "as certain of his enemies have maintained, that Billy's left eye was lost during a rumble with that red-neck storekeep outside Limehouse, South Carolina" (33). At this point William seems to be interested in establishing the truth about his cousin. He says as much shortly thereafter: "I bother to refute these rumors because the man is my cousin, and I am honor-bound to love him as I know he really is" (34). In this wonderfully rationalized construction, we discover William's underlying motive and the identity of the audience he is addressing. He speaks not of love but of an obligation that requires love. He speaks also of Billy as "he really is." Given his "honor-bound to love him" expression, his casual fusing of love as an obligation, we have to infer that William is both unable and unwilling to give us his wildly mythic cousin as "he really is"— that what we will get instead is a formal attempt to demythify Billy in the interests of William's very unmythical values.

And this is exactly what William does. Thus, when he asserts at the end of the story that "it is not true, contrary to rumors circulating in my family, that Billy Renfro is unwelcome in my home" (54), we appreciate the distinction between "not unwelcome" and "welcome"; and we know that William does also, for he is nothing if not a stickler for distinctions—a highly literate explainer restoring to the precisions of standard language in an attempt to defend his bourgeois commitments, and a personal identity based on them, against the claims of the past and the present. His presumed audience is those who would not find anything objectionable in the candid but cautious fluency of the following lines:

In contrast to [Billy], I moved wesw:ard [sic], but only as far as Chicago, and settled in against this city's soul-killing winter winds. I purged from my speech all traces of the South and warmed myself by the fire of my thirty-year plan. Employment was available in the credit reference section of the Melrose Department Store, and there I established, though slowly, a reputation for efficiency and tact. Because I got along, I began moving up. In my second year in Chicago, I found and courted Chelseia Raymond, a family-backed, efficiency-minded girl. She was the kind of woman I needed to make my children safe. Her family loved me, and had the grace to overlook the fact that I had once been a poor migrant from the South. Third-generation Chicagoans, they nonetheless opened their hearts and home to me, as if I had been native to their city. With their backing, I settled into this rough-and-tumble city and learned to dodge all events detracting attention from the direction in which I had determined to move. From time to time, trudging through the winter slush on Michigan, I would pause to explore a reflection of myself in a store window. By my fifth year in Chicago, I became satisfied that no one could have mistaken me for a refugee from the South.

This was my situation when Billy Renfro came to visit.

(42)

Here the main social and linguistic issues of the story are made clear. In the second sentence, William explicitly notes the relevance of language to identity, or at least to social success; moreover, his metaphor reveals how willingly he yielded his native dialect in order to succeed in Chicago—a sacrifice we can understand, even endorse, except perhaps in cases where such a sacrifice, made in the interests of efficiency and tact, leads to a more costly sacrifice of human feeling.

That William has made such a sacrifice is implied throughout the story, more or less explicitly in the passages in which he tries to justify his handling of Billy and implicitly in the language of the above paragraph. For example, note the way William unknowingly modifies, at his own expense, the meaning of such honorific words as "loved," "grace" and "hearts." The context clearly suggests that the relationship between William and the Raymonds is a contingent and convenient one based on a respect for efficiency, tact and social status. These three words therefore mean something less here than they mean in most religious contexts—something less spiritual and more commercial. It is a distinction easily missed in a paragraph in which the words seem to fit so naturally. But just as we can hear lines such as "let's not be so philosophical" without being aware of the enormous difference in meaning between the adjective in this sentence and the same word in, say, Plato, so we can easily miss the secularization of William's terms. They seem descriptive but are in fact argumentative: subtle predications intended to affirm the middle-class values by which William and the Raymonds live.

At the end of the paragraph, William returns to the identity issue to acknowledge his determination "to

dodge all events detracting attention from the direction in which I had determined to move." His narrative reveals that some of the events he dodged involved non-commercial love, grace and matters of the heart.

After establishing William as the voice of black middle-class propriety, McPherson goes on to dramatize the primary conflict of the story, William's struggle to de-mythify (that is, to kill, make into a dead man) Billy within a new of Standard English and the presuppositions it embodies. In reference to Billy's losing his eye in a rumble, William says, "That eye, I now have reason to believe, was lost during domestic troubles" (33). In the minds of most middle-class readers, especially those interested in efficiency and tact, a man who has "reason to believe," who can make such a point in a nonrestrictive clause and then follow it with alliterative and euphemistic phrases is certainly going to seem more reliable than a man allegedly given to rumbling with storekeeps. Such readers would also be inclined to accept William's conclusion that Billy was essentially nothing more than a liar. "We are no longer young men," says an avuncular William to Billy.

> 'The foam has settled down into the beer. I, myself, no longer chase women, speak hotly, challenge opinions too far different from my own. I have learned it is to my advantage to get along. . . . In short, Billy, in my manhood I have become aware of complexity. You owe it to the family, and to the memory of your mother, to do the same.'
>
> Billy swished his Scotch and drank it down, then rapped the glass on the table to alert the barmaid. When she looked, he pointed two fingers downward toward our glasses and kissed at her. Then, turning to focus his single, red-rimmed eye on my face, he said, 'Bullshit!'
>
> He was dressed in the black gabardine suit of an undertaker. Dried purple-black blood streaked his coat sleeves, his black string tie, and the collar of the dirty white shirt he wore.
>
> 'People change, Billy,' I said.
>
> 'Bullshit!' Billy Renfro said.
>
> I looked closely at him and saw a gangster. He was not the kind of man I wanted to meet my family. I glanced at my watch and sipped my drink. I listened to his stories.
>
> Billy spun his usual lies.

(34-5)

We do not know how many of Billy's stories are pure fiction and how many, if any, are authentic. The blood he carries on his clothes implies that some of the violent ones are probably based on fact. In any case, it doesn't matter. It doesn't even matter if Billy is all lies, as William believes, at least not as far as our reading of the story is concerned, because what distinguishes William and Billy is not their allegiance to truth but their relation to white middle-class values.

As they are, both men are incomplete: two halves of a whole that would add up to Virginia's "self as big as the world." One half, William, has defined himself in collective terms; the other, Billy, stands in opposition to them. Each therefore has exaggerated a truth: William the truth that we need to be *a part* of the collective, Billy that we need to be *apart*—individualized, to some extent alone. In a moral sense, then, they are equally limited. Linguistically, however, they are not, for William commands the power code, the "transparent" language of the middle- and upper-class through which they control the circulation and credibility of alternative stories.

The man who sought to purge all traces of the South from his speech is sensitive to this stylistic opposition, to the fact that his and Billy's "vocabularies were growing rapidly apart" (37), and he resolves to use the difference to his advantage. Billy resists, simply but eloquently and not without humor. During one of his jail visits, William attempts to communicate "some sense of the broader options available to the man in possession of salable knowledge." Billy listens for awhile, then interrupts:

> 'Looka here,' he said. 'How 'bout runnin' cross the road and get me a hot sausage sandwich, heavy on the mustard, and a big orange soda.'
>
> I looked hard at him and wanted to weep. 'Is that *all* you want?' I asked.
>
> Billy chewed steadily. 'No,' he answered, looking out over the crowded room. 'Bring me a side of fries, hold the salt.'
>
> (author's italics 40)

Different codes involve different frames of reference, supplying different criteria for judging their truth. Within a scientific framework, truth is verifiable as objective fact; within a spiritual or poetic frame, truth is often subjective, a matter of feeling and intuition. As such, it may or may not be measured or verified by disinterested observers. What makes Billy and William's exchange especially significant is that it reveals, simply and comically, the basic issue of the story: the stylistic expression of ideological differences.

Though fond of metaphor ("The foam has settled down into the beer."), and sensitive to concrete realities such as the winter slush on Michigan Avenue, William lives mainly in a world of abstract terms and values and speaks an elaborate referential code in which the most useful truth is the most generalized. Thus he is inclined to talk about "thirty-year plans" and life goals, efficiency and tact, purged languages and a verifiable truth. Billy, on the other hand, lives in a concrete reality, constrained by immediate and mundane demands; he speaks a relatively simple expressive language in which the most valuable truth is the most personal, an expression

of heart and imagination. To him, most abstractions are bullshit indeed, as is the scientific assumption that a respect for truth obliges us to be "accurate" and objective in our claims about the world and ourselves.

The answer he gives to William's pompous question is therefore not only funny but true given Billy's frame of reference. And so are his stories, for they represent attempts at mythical self-definition and assertion in a culture dominated by white and black Williams speaking what amounts to an anti-Billy language. Within its frame of reference, he is nothing but a gangster, spinning not personalized alternatives but lies.

And so it goes, William trying to extinguish Billy linguistically, and Billy linguistically resisting, as when William begins to wax sentimental about the death of Billy's mother, who had taken care of him when he was a child. Not surprisingly, he has chosen to believe that her death was due to Billy's failure to settle down. After William refers to her "martyred life," Billy turns to him and asks, "What *you* cryin' for, *motherfucker*? . . . It's *my* mama!" (41).

By such means, Billy defeats William, even though he must do so within William's narrative. But it is only by hearing them as wayfarer and official respectively that we can understand the underlying conflicts in the first place. One is that to which I referred: the stylistic-ideological opposition between them. Another is the primary conflict within William that compels him, a black man, to use a standard white code against his cousin, his own reluctance to discover the "Billy" within him. Because of this reluctance, William also becomes a dead man, oblivious to "all events detracting attention" from his chosen path, oblivious as well to the fact that he must tell unmythical, face-saving lies in order to maintain his fragile social ego.

In the concluding scene of the story, Billy gets drunk during dinner with the Raymonds and begins to tell stories about his exploits on the Coast, entertaining Mr. Raymond but offending the women. When Chelseia insults him, Billy bristles. William then steps in

> to save the situation, although Billy has maintained that I turned on him. The man is a notorious liar, and likes to keep the family jumpy. Here is the truth of what happened: I moved quickly to Billy's side. I put my hand on his shoulder. I faced the Raymonds for the two of us. I said, 'Thank you for a splendid evening.' But all my tact was introduced too late. With a purposeful shrug, Billy separated his shoulder from my hand. All our eyes were on him. Only Mr. Raymond, sitting drooped and still in his chair, seemed distracted by thoughts of other matters.
>
> Someone had to take control. I took it as best I could. 'A red-neck down in South Carolina shot out Billy's eye,' I said. 'Billy is too proud to speak of it.'

'*Bullshit!*' Billy said.

By this one word, and through his subsequent actions, Billy himself completely severed what was left of our family bond.

(51)

William presumes to speak with authority about the truth of Billy's stories, but he has given us no reason to believe he knows the truth—or would tell it if he did. Furthermore, as the passive construction "was introduced too late" suggests, his tact was too false and too late. William's actual intent in this scene is to play the well-intentioned but helpless cousin to Billy's social and legal outlaw. His gestures and speech are contrived to assuage the Raymonds, not to defend Billy, who he knew at the outset would not be able to engage in civil discourse with a family like the Raymonds for very long.

In the concluding lines of the story, William hopes that he and Chelseia will one day be able to "reconstruct" Billy:

I say it is just a matter of time. We are, after all, the same age. Yet I have already charted my course. I have settled into Chicago, against the winter whippings of this city's winds. He can do the same. But as things stand now, he is still someplace out there, with a single eye flickering over open roadways, in his careless search for an exciting death. Ah, *Billy*!

(55)

The final exclamation recalls the last words of another upholder of the ideological status quo who was equally determined to live a safe and easy life. "Ah, Bartleby! Ah, Humanity!" cries the narrator of Melville's "Bartleby the Scrivener," expressing an understanding much deeper and sadder than Williams's. But the stories have more in common than their concluding lament. In each the narrator tries to ignore a troublesome outsider, for spiritual as well as commercial reasons. Billy's misadventures might not imply the existence of a Melvillian "organic ill," but he does represent a radical alternative to William's thirty-year plan. He reminds us that there is a dimension of the self that must be accommodated if human beings are ever to achieve selves "as big as the world."

In **"The Story of a Scar"** we meet a narrator as pompous as, but even more presumptuous than, William:

Since Dr. Wayland was late and there were no recent newsmagazines in the waiting room, I turned to the other patient and said: 'As a concerned person, and as your brother, I ask you, without meaning to offend, how did you get that scar on the side of your face?'

(118)

The sentence reveals the narrator as a liar who protects himself through intimidation. By demonstrating a fluent command of standard-to-formal English, he asserts his presumed superiority to most of his listeners, speakers of a black dialect. Safely ensconced within its conventional definitions and assumptions, he can look out upon a world of inferiors whom he need not get close to, especially since, or so he believes, he knows all he needs to know about them.

His quotation marks separate his private reality from his public image by revealing that he is far more interested in accumulating information, preferably in print, than in making social connections. Unable to find it, he resorts not to social intercourse but to interrogation, which enables him to speak without involvement, risk or concern. Contrary to his claim, therefore, he is not speaking as a brother, and he does wish to offend in order to put his auditor on the defensive and so avoid the perils of intimacy. In another formulation, he speaks as a detached reader of human texts:

I studied her approvingly. Such women have a natural leaning toward the abstract expression of themselves. Their styles have private meanings, advertise secret distillations of their souls. Their figures, and their figurations, make meaningful statements. . . . Such craftsmen must be approached with subtlety if they are to be deciphered.

(120)

It is no coincidence that the narrator describes the woman as a craftsman, thus missing, in language anyway, one of the most important facts about her. It is no coincidence because although everything he says is true, he has neither the subtlety nor the sensitivity to decipher anyone's soul.

And she knows it. "I *knowed* you'd get back around to that," she says, when he asks her again about her scar. "Black guys like you with them funny eyeglasses are a real trip. You got to know everything. You sit in corners and watch people." Unperturbed, he continues to press for an answer. But shortly after she begins to talk about where she was when it happened, and about the men she had been working with, the narrator interrupts what he calls "her tiresome ramblings" to demand "Which one of them cut you?"

Her face flashed a wall of brown fire. 'This here's *my* story!' she muttered, eyeing me up and down with suspicion. 'You dudes cain't stand to hear the whole of anything. You want everything broken down in little pieces.'

(121-2)

In one sense, she is wrong. The narrator isn't as interested in breaking things down as he is in discovering and imposing patterns on the world that suit *his* needs by corroborating *his* story about himself and his relation to everyone else. In Chapter One we considered Lakoff and Johnson's claim that therapy "involves the constant construction of new coherences . . . that give new meaning to old experiences. The process of self-understanding is the continual development of new life stories" (232-3).

But McPherson's official narrator cares not at all about self-understanding or development; what he wants is the continual validation of already established coherences (i.e., his ideology or life story) that confirm his superiority. This becomes clear later when he again interrupts to answer his own question. While listening to the woman tell about her growing disenchantment with Billy Crawford, a bookish, Williamesque boyfriend, and her growing interest in a jive-talking newcomer to the post office named Teddy Johnson, whom she proclaims "the last *true* son of the Great McDaddy," the narrator loses control:

> 'Sister,' I said quickly, overwhelmed suddenly by the burden of insight. 'I *know* the man of whom you speak. There is no time for this gutter-patter and indirection. Please, for my sake and for your own, avoid stuffing the shoes of the small with mythic homilies. This man was a bum, a hustler and a small-time punk. He broke up your romance with Billy, then he lived off you, cheated on you, and cut you when you confronted him.' So pathetic and gross seemed her elevation of the fellow that I abandoned all sense of caution. 'Is your mind so *dead,*' I continued, 'did his switchblade slice so *deep,* do you have so little *respect* for yourself, or at least for the idea of *proportion* in this sad world, that you'd sit here and *praise* this brute!?'
>
> (127)

The "proportion" the narrator is referring to is the coherence and meaning, or the ideological presuppositions and stereotypes, that support his sense of superiority to practically everyone else. Like Billy Crawford, he is threatened by the sexual power of the Great McDaddy's of the world, and by earthy, voluptuous women who know what he is beneath his elaborate, carefully articulated verbal shell. This is why he is so unnerved by her response. He tells us that while she looked at him through the smoke of her cigarette, he "watched her nervously, recognizing the evidence of past destructiveness, yet fearing the imminent occurrence of more. But it was not her temper or the potential strength of her flesh arm that I feared" (128). It is her insight through his intellectual defenses into his frail, impotent heart.

For unspecified reasons the narrator cannot, or will not, love. Language is his means of keeping this fact from others and from himself. When the woman does reveal that it was Billy Crawford and not Teddy Johnson who knifed her, he is astounded. The situation is made worse when the woman begins to speak as a "sister" in need:

> 'This here's the third doctor I been to see. The First one stitched me up like a turkey and left this scar. The second one refused to touch me.' She paused and wet her lips again. 'This man fixed your nose for you,' she said softly. 'Do you think he could do somethin' about this scar?'

The narrator's subsequent behavior reveals him to be a fearful wordman whose last refuge is print and abstract, impersonal rights—forms designed to compensate for the absence of human feeling:

> I searched the end table next to my couch for a newsmagazine, carefully avoiding her face. 'Dr. Wayland is a skilled man,' I told her. 'Whenever he's not late. I think he may be able to do something for you.'
>
> She sighed heavily and seemed to tremble. 'I don't expect no miracle or nothin',' she said. 'If he could just fix the part around my eye I wouldn't expect nothin' else. People say the rest don't look too bad.'
>
> I clutched a random magazine and did not answer. Nor did I look at her. The flesh around my nose began to itch, and I looked toward the inner office door with the most extreme irritation building in me. . . . I resolved to put aside all notions of civility and go into the office before her, as was my right.
>
> (135-6)

Needing desperately to escape the threat of intimacy, the narrator at first seeks protection behind a magazine. Then another idea occurs to him, a question that seems personal, that in another context could be personal but that here is merely another defensive tactic—the narrator's way of keeping his distance by reducing intimate discourse to a merely formal pursuit of factual information. "And then I remembered the most important question," he says,

> without which the entire exchange would have been wasted. I turned to the woman, now drawn together in the red plastic chair, as if struggling to sleep in a cold bed. 'Sister,' I said, careful to maintain a casual air. 'Sister . . . what is your name?'
>
> (136)

The narrator of **"Just Enough for the City"** is also determined to resist human involvement. After being visited in his apartment by fundamentalists, he speculates on the nature of love and concludes that just enough love for the city—and the people therein—is not very much. Or more than he is willing to give. Appropriately enough, he has an ear for language. Were it not for their accents, he tells us, he would not let the Germans in his apartment. Once they are in, however, they accomplish little, since he has nothing to give them but questions to which he expects no answers; for he, too, is an interrogator trying to avoid self-revelation. "They both watch and wait for me to disclose myself," he says. "Backed into a corner, I have no choice but to shift their focus. 'Where do you get your money?' I asked them. 'Who finances your operation?' They go away" (214). On this occasion, the narrator defends himself with relatively simple, factual questions. At other times, he resorts to complex conundrums designed to end uncomfortable discussions about religion and morality and love. By means of such elaborate verbosity, he avoids living the simple truths that most of his visitors present. "Der simple problem," one visitor declares, "is dat vee do not luff one another." Faced with such a baldly undeniable but demanding statement, the narrator does what all of McPherson's officials do so often: transform a spiritual or interpersonal issue into linguistic or aesthetic categories. "I agree with this," says the narrator. "But I insist that they define for me the term" (216).

Developing a simple definition of love is a goal the narrator has set for himself. Here is his first attempt:

> I think love must be the ability to suspend one's intelligence for the sake of something. At the basis of love therefore must live imagination. Instead of thinking 'I am I,' to love one must be able to feelingly conjugate the verb to be. Intuition must be part of the circuitous pathway leading ultimately to love. I wish I could ask someone.
>
> (216)

Within the story proper, the narrative of physical events, we see a narrator behaving in ways wholly at odds with his intellectual insights: intimidating people with his precise but distancing and at times baffling language. Together, his meditations on the theme of love and his narrative of his human relations, show him to be a sensitive and intelligent but emotionally sterile man who knows what he should be but who cannot be it—despite the depth and eloquence of his conclusions. "Love must be a going outward from the self," he writes, "from the most secret of safe positions. God is no more than the most secret place from which such emanations can be sent" (220). Eloquence need not be incompatible with action, but in McPherson's story it is an official substitute for the experience, as if in writing about it well, the narrator could justify his failure to love. In the following passage, the narrator uses metaphor to translate love into grammar. The result is eloquence in the service of an isolated and arid ego:

> If one is not too strict in his conjugation of the verb *to be,* he might wind up with a sense of living in the present. I believe that love exists at just that point when the first person singular moves into the plural estate: I am, you are, he is, she is, *we are.* . . . The saying of it requires a going out of oneself, of breath as well as confidence. Its image is of expansiveness, a taking roundly into and putting roundly out of oneself. Or perhaps another word should be used, one invented or one transported from another context: I am, you are, he is, she is, *we be.* . . . Or again, perhaps a beat of silence suggesting the burden of subjectivity: I am, you are, he is, she is, they are. . . .
>
> (222)

The possibilities proliferate, as official speculation often does, into mere words—Ionesco's chatter: "Words are literary. They are an escape. They stop silence from speaking. . . . Instead of being action, they comfort you as best they can for your inaction" (107).

Eventually the narrator decides that he need not entertain visitors at all. "I am refusing these days to bow on my knees and cry holy" (224). It is the beginning of the end. In response to the realization that he has seen deep into the eyes of a young haunted woman, he is tempted to speak to her:

> I want to say, but do not dare to say, that I saw briefly in her face the shadow of a human soul.
>
> *I am.* . . .
>
> (226)

Though still unable to feelingly conjugate the second-person singular, he nevertheless discovers that there is more to human experience than artful formulations. In an exchange with two ministers, he tells the story of a man who "Suspecting now that words were of little importance, he found himself watching gestures and facial expressions, listening to the rhythms of voices and not to the words spoken, for telltale insights into the true nature of reality . . ." (227). But like the man in his story, who later became "unable . . . to believe in any words" and "retreated into a room, questioning even the character behind his own name" (228), the narrator ends up isolated within a semantic universe that protects him against love by a wall of metaphor:

> Something breathes quickly against the cobwebs inside me. But because I fear what I feel is love, I turn my face away.
>
> *Tu es* . . .
>
> I am becoming sufficient.
>
> (230)

Read as correct French, *tu es* indicates that the narrator is once again attempting to conjugate the verb "to be"; read as incorrect Spanish (the disjunction of a second-person pronoun with a third-person verb), *tu es* indicates that the narrator cannot, or will not, "go outward from the most secret of safe positions," which in this case is not God, apparently, but his own fragile self: a matter of words contrived as defense. The disjunction expresses his inability to connect with the human world. In either interpretation, he isn't really in the world of human relations; he is somewhere else, making use of what Pearce sees as a distinguishing characteristic of literate culture: an "infinite capacity for rationalization" (64). It is just about all that he has and is: words, words, words, spoken not to overcome but to preserve the boundaries that define and protect a profoundly insufficient self.

Like the narrator of **"The Story of a Scar,"** the narrator of **"Just Enough for the City"** is literate to a fault, a compulsive semiotician determined to read people as if they were texts, or bundles of signs collected for the perusal of distant readers who tend to be more comfortable with linguistic categories and, in the case of **"The Story of a Scar,"** social stereotypes than with complex and demanding human realities.

Attorney Corliss Milford of **"Problems of Art"** appears to be another such reader. Assigned by Project Gratis to defend an older black woman against a charge of drunk driving, Milford pays her a visit. As he waits for her to return from an errand, he begins to read her living room, where he finds

> the imprint of a mind as meticulous as his own. Every item seemed in place; every detail meshed into an overriding suggestion of order. This neatness did no damage to the image of Mrs. Farragot he had assembled, even before visiting her home. Her first name was Mary, and she was thin and severe of manner. He recalled that her walnut-brown face betrayed few wrinkles; her dark eyes were quick and direct without being forceful; her thin lips, during conversation, moved with precision and resolve. Even her blue summer dress, with pearl-white buttons up its front, advertised efficiency of character. The bare facts of her personal life, too, argued neatness and restraint; he had them down on paper, and the paper rested on his knee. . . .
>
> (94-5)

Milford is no fool. It occurs to him that everything could have been contrived, that there could be an "undisclosed reality" in the room that Mrs. Farragot intended to keep from him. Evidence for such a conclusion is, he thinks, a portrait of Jesus on the wall, one with a valentine-shaped heart in the middle of the chest. To Milford, it

> conveyed the poverty of the artist's imagination and tended to undermine the sophistication of those who purchased such dimensionless renditions. Did not the Latin poor build great cathedrals? Even country Baptists wheeled their preachers about in Cadillacs. Why then, Milford asked himself, would a poor black woman compound an already bleak existence by worshipping before a dime-store rendition of a mystery? He recalled having heard someplace something about the function of such images, but could not recall exactly what he had heard.
>
> (95)

Milford is a neat, efficient, highly educated man who can be comforted by knowing that he has something "down on paper." He is in fact a lawyer who must work within strict rules of inference and procedure that determine what information he can accept as useful. As a graduate of Harvard Law School, McPherson himself has detailed knowledge of these restrictions; as a fiction writer, he appreciates how most people operate, albeit unconsciously, within similar rules of inference and procedure imposed upon them not by law but by culture.

Because Milford seems to accept such rules so uncritically, he makes an exemplary official. What complicates life for him (and other McPherson attorneys) is that he

is also, like Berger's Henry Webster Melrose in *Killing Time,* intrigued by aesthetic as well as legal form. For him it becomes a way of *not* keeping in touch with an untidy but very human world.

Fortunately for Milford, his problems of art turn out to be minor. He misreads Mrs. Farragot. Deriving the signified "efficiency of character" from her facial expression, and the signifieds "neatness and restraint" from the facts of her personal life, Milford tentatively concludes that she cannot be an alcoholic. The Jesus portrait seems inconsistent with this conclusion, for reasons only a preoccupied formalist could accept ("Why . . . would a poor black woman compound an already bleak existence . . . ?"); but he decides that he must reinterpret the portrait when he discovers a photograph of her husband saluting the flag while pointing one toe toward a bugle standing upright on its mouth in the lower corner, as if he were about to kick it. Because the man "reeks of irresponsibility," Milford reasons, the photo explains why Mrs. Farragot had so much difficulty getting someone to corroborate her claim of innocence. She had, after all, been arrested in her own neighborhood in front of numerous witnesses. Most of them were probably as irresponsible as her husband. Returning to the Jesus portrait, this time "with more understanding," Milford interprets it as a vulgar but nonetheless meaningful icon for a woman hungering for depth in a culture of shallow and boyish males.

Armed with these self-satisfying conclusions, Milford interviews Mrs. Farragot and her one supporting witness, Clarence Winfield, a verbose black man who possesses "a certain rough style"—despite "the imprecision of his language" (108). It is a concession easy for an efficient attorney to make, for he is operating by liberal rules of inference, or, more specifically, by liberal stereotypes that structure the context and hence the meaning of the signs within Mrs. Farragot's house. Combined with his interest in aesthetic form, they blind Milford to aspects of Mrs. Farragot and Winfield that are more to the point of the legal issue at hand. While Winfield spoke

> Milford sat transfixed. He leaned forward on the sofa, oblivious to anything but the big man in the brown seersucker suit standing quietly in the center of the room. He did not notice Mrs. Farragot, seated in the armchair beneath the picture of Jesus, draw her crossed arms tighter about her breasts.
>
> (105)

As the alcoholic we will discover her to be, Mrs. Farragot is thinking here about more than her legal defense. For the moment, however, she poses beneath the melodramatic picture and lets Winfield go on in a black vernacular colorful enough to warm any liberal's heart: "Mary's brake lights come on fast and red; there was a real loud *scruunch*!; and Big Boy scream, 'Mother-*fuck*!'" (104).

Convinced that Winfield is honest and Mrs. Farragot therefore innocent, Milford takes them to the hearing, winces at the painfully fluent allegations of the arresting officer, also black, then wins the case on a technicality by noting that the officer had not given Mrs. Farragot a choice of intoxication tests. It is only afterward at a drinking fountain that he learns the truth. "Many's the time," says Winfield, "I told Miss Mary about that drinkin'." When Milford admits that he assumed she drank beer, Winfield chuckles: "Man, Miss Mary don't drink no *beer*! . . . She don't drink nothin' but Maker's Mark. . . . I thought you *knowed* that" (116).

In **"A Sense of Story"** the consequences of an official's interest in reading are far more serious. The narrative begins in a courtroom during the murder trial of Robert Charles, a black man accused of shooting Frank Johnson, the white manager of the garage where he worked. While his court-appointed counsel is pleading his case, Charles rises from his chair and declares that the shooting was no accident; he only regrets that "the gun broke before I could pump six slugs into the sonofabitch" (231). The judge quickly calls the attorneys to the bench, where they decide that he ought to examine the record to determine "whether a preponderance of the evidence had already tipped the scales of justice against the defendant, making his confession of insignificant weight" (232). The judge then enters his chambers. The rest of the story consists mainly of sections of prior testimony that he chooses to read. He is occasionally interrupted by his secretary, who brings him lunch and notes from his clerk urging him, for political reasons, to be on time for a judges' conference.

Although the narrator describes him as a "thoughtful, pains-taking man," the transcript qualifies the claim. When the prosecuting attorney accuses him of dozing off, the judge insists that he was not asleep, only weighing the evidence in a complicated trial (249). We have no way of knowing whether the charge is true, but the transcript does reveal another detail about the judge that suggests that he was less than attentive to the real—or at least the most sympathetic—story of Robert Charles. In his explanation to Franklin Grant, Charles' attorney, as to why he is allowing testimony Grant has objected to, the judge says, "perhaps I am wrong, but my intuition tells me there is a sense of story here" (239). Later, in a passage that recalls Melrose's desire "to exploit the possibilities within the [legal] discipline, as a poet using the constricting form of the sonnet," the judge announces to the courtroom:

> I feel I must apologize to you for these lengthy excursions. I have attempted to grant leeway to counsel for both sides, because it seemed to me that my own decisions, based solely on the rules of evidence as I know them, would prevent your hearing the cross-light of competing views, which I consider essential to the adversary process. But it seems now that this trial has

> lost its direction. Still, in my mind, law is an art, and my function here should ideally be no different than that of a literary critic.

> (250)

The context of his apology and odd appeal to literary standards is significant. A fellow employee of Charles, a black man named Pinkett, has been testifying as a witness for the prosecution. After describing the good character of the victim, Pinkett is asked to elaborate on an earlier statement he had made about Charles going "soft." Grant, the defense attorney, objects but is overruled. Pinkett continues by talking about how Charles had taken "his own sweet time on a repair job." Pinkett contends that he did it just "to devil Mr. Johnson" and so was in part responsible for the antagonism that flared up between them. Grant objects and the judge sustains him with comments that define some of the official constrictions of legal form:

> Mr. Pinkett, I must warn you to refrain from making value judgments. By that I mean you are not being asked to assess whether the defendent in your opinion was a good or bad man, or whether he engineered his own failures. You must tell what you know that bears on the issue in contention here.

> MR. PINKETT: Contention?

> COURT: I must remind you, Mr. Pinkett, that you have been recalled as a prosecution witness. You must refrain, sir, from voicing opinions not solicited by counsel. You may not be aware of this, but Mr. Lindenberry [the prosecutor] is responsible to the rules of evidence, and not to you. You must answer directly the specific questions put to you by him. Do you understand, sir?

> (249-50)

Mr. Pinkett answers yes, and the judge proceeds to make his apology to the jury, apparently oblivious to the fact that he is speaking what is for Pinkett an alien language ("Contention?") about an alien world where it is forbidden to give opinions about good and bad, and where attorneys are responsible not to people but to abstract rules of evidence, to formal requirements that may or may not be just.

The above exchange reveals the difficulty of discovering the complex truth (of the degree of guilt or innocence, goodness or badness) of Robert Charles within the neat and official categories, rules and regulations of legal procedure—or, more to the literary point, within conventional literary forms: the kind that involve the "cross-light of competing interests" and a coherent direction (complete with complication, rising action, crisis). After all, coherence is not an objective fact but a perceptual judgment—directly proportional to the degree of conformity between the story and the reader's system of belief. A *deus ex machina* resolution, for example, is incoherent or unbelievable to atheists. "It is in the [kind] of 'tricks of the trade' employed by the author," writes Denis de Rougemont, "that the real plot of a given piece of fiction is disclosed, and a reader condones these tricks precisely to the extent that he shares the author's intentions" (36)—or values.

Unlike conspicuous crises in bad fiction, the crisis in **"A Sense of Story"** is understated. It occurs when the judge decides not to accept the narrative tricks of defense counsel Grant, precisely because Grant's moral design is so palpable. Although testimony has established that Charles was not drunk at the time of the shooting, Grant attempts to convince the jury that liquor was to blame. Worse, he tries to do so artlessly. Here is the section of Grant's appeal that the judge returns to in his chambers. He begins to read in midsentence:

> . . . worth very little to the ideal of justice if you, ladies and gentlemen of the jury, as the conscience of the community, cannot envision in your minds, and find room in your hearts, for an illiterate black. Here is a man, descended from slaves, who, on the day of his son's graduation from high school, did the habitual thing for the celebration. He had a drink. We all do it on the Fourth of July. Why can't he? . . . But linked in his mind with drinking was that other custom, that other part of the ritual of celebration so honored among blacks in the South. But he is in the city and feels restrained. So he puts a gun in his pocket. Then, a man of habit, he goes to work. There, knowing his boss takes an interest in the families of his employees, he goes into the office with the news. But he has had a nip. And in retelling the good news, there is a lapse of logic in his mind. Perhaps remembering past friction, but more likely in celebration of the event, the defendent takes the gun and accidentally. . . .
>
> (254-5)

It is this incredible and wearisome melodrama that Charles himself stands to interrupt with his confession, perhaps because he is as outraged by the bad storytelling as is the judge, who decides, immediately after reading it, that Charles is guilty as charged. His verdict is therefore a formal one not only in the sense that it is based on legal requirements in a court of law, but also in the sense that it derives in part from a literary judgment about the aesthetic value of Grant's story. He found Charles guilty of murder *because* Grant failed to create his half of an engaging and coherent "crosscurrent of competing views."

Charles' confession and Grant's words indicate that both verdicts are fair. But there is another story in the testimony, one that the judge misses even though it is inferable from the style and the content of other sections of the transcript. Had he widened his interpretive interests to include them, the judge might have found another Robert Charles who, as a poor Southern black, was denied access not only to fame and fortune but to the language code of the dominant class in white America: Standard Written English.

Because this other story requires a sensitivity not only to the aesthetic but also to the psychological and political dimensions of language, it is not obvious to language users inclined to look through language at a presumably non-verbal world, or to more sophisticated readers more interested in form and structure than in the relationship of language, reality and the self. With this relationship in mind, we can detect something other than piety in the transparently ordinary formulations of Mr. Rogers, the white owner of the garage:

> Sometimes you get an employee whose talent does not match his ambition. This is a painful truth, one of which most fair employers have to be aware. The Good Lord did not distribute talents equally, that's in the Bible. But some employees find it hard to accept their lot. They agitate and see offense where none was intended.
>
> (240)

There is nothing intrinsically wrong with such language; the problem is its value as information. In relation to the context, it is almost entirely predictable. Based on Biblical commonplaces about inequality, it conveniently supports the social superiority of the speaker—and whoever else he needs to justify. The words constitute a formula, useless because predetermined: the utterance of a speaker playing a role.

Which is not to say that this testimony is irrelevant to Charles' guilt. Of that there is no doubt. What is in doubt is the extent of his guilt and the appropriate punishment.

Here is another self-supporting linguistic sample from the transcript, the testimony of Dr. Walter R. Thorne, a psychiatrist:

> One must begin by first noting the peculiarities of the area of the subject's earliest socialization, for insight into his emotional background. . . . As you will recall, during the period of his childhood the South practiced rather crude and often vicious methods of caste segregation. The effects of this on the human personality, especially the concomitant violence, are inestimable. Coupled with this were the traumata of an abrupt move. . . .
>
> (242-3)

Thorne's abstract and impersonal language may contain statistical truths, may even be pertinent in a general way to Charles' story; but it misses the personal connections implicit in the vernacular, inexpert testimony of those closest to Charles: those black friends who, innocent of theory and the pressure to defend a political position, speak a simple, concrete language that gives us a Robert Charles neither Rogers, Thorne nor the judge can see. Here is Pinkett again, this time talking about how Charles

> had given up on life. He said he didn't understand things he thought he understood. We were in the john at the time. I was taking a pee and he was in the stall. I

couldn't see his face but I could hear him. He said, 'Mr. Johnson has hurt me so bad, Otis, till I don't want to live.' He said to me, 'There ain't nothing more I want than to get out of life.'

(247)

The fact that Pinkett later goes on to praise Frank Johnson and give equally convincing testimony that Charles' attorney construes as damaging to his client reinforces the impression of him as a simple, honest man who, as he puts it, is "not trying to take sides."

The Reverend Blake conveys the same impression in words that flesh out the other story of Robert Charles—in English that is every bit as conventional as Rogers' but without defensive platitudes, only insights into Charles' plight as a father ashamed of his lack of formal education and deeply afraid that he was losing the respect of his oldest son, who he believed was experimenting with drugs. Missing the point and the real story once again, Grant translates Blake's testimony into ineffectually general terms:

> MR. GRANT: You are saying then, Reverend, that he was a concerned parent?
>
> MR. BLAKE: Yes, sir. He was very concerned. He wanted me to talk with Robert, Jr. He wanted me to help him get the boy involved with boys his own age who had more positive activities. He asked me if I knew boys who read books.
>
> MR. LINDENBERRY: Your Honor, with all due respect to the Reverend, I must say that this is not getting us anywhere. The jails are full of homicidal maniacs who like to read books.

(252)

Grant objects to Lindenberry's oversimplification and is sustained by the judge, who then asks him what his intention is. Grant replies that he wanted to show that Charles placed "much value on his boy's progress. If I may, I would like to build on something" (252)—namely, on Charles' drinking problem, not on the related problems of his son's disrespect and his own illiteracy.

The possibility that illiteracy (here understood as the inability to speak, read and write a language respected by employers, judges, sons and oneself) could lead to violent despair does not seem to occur to any of the literal or figurative officials in McPherson's story, even the literary-minded one. So the illiterate Charles goes unheard, while the more ideologically convenient Charles, the murderer, is condemned to pay the full penalty for his crime. In the final paragraphs, we read that the judge

> rose from the chair and walked to the window and looked out. Down in the parking lot, against a backdrop of concrete driving ramps, dozens of cars shone in the sunlight like metal, multicolored animals. From this

> height they looked like toys. He puffed his pipe and looked up. The specially treated glass in the picture window made the sky seem more bright and blue than it really was. The judge straightened his tie. He flicked a spot of ash from the sleeve of his blue coat. Then he went into the bathroom and washed his face and hands.

(254)

From the height of an upper floor, that is, from the aesthetic distance available to a literary critic, what is wanted is form: a sky a little bluer than nature permits, an overall tidiness that satisfies the human need for legal and aesthetic order. The danger, however, is that an interest in form will become an end in itself and so diminish the interest in human contact and understanding—the only kind of understanding that can keep judges from washing their hands of the formless, untidy many who struggle, ant-like, below them.

In the last story in the collection, **"Elbow Room,"** McPherson again returns to the theme of storytelling. As an epigraph, he quotes William Carlos Williams' contention that one challenge faced by American pioneers was to settle a new land without relying entirely on old values. "Boone's genius," says Williams, "was to recognize the difficulty as neither material nor political but one purely moral and aesthetic" (136).[1] Like Boone, McPherson recognizes the importance of moral and aesthetic problems, especially when it comes to storytelling, which he considers a very important business indeed. In fact, another quotation that would be useful as an introduction to **"Elbow Room"** is Joan Didion's insight that "We tell ourselves stories in order to live" (11).

In much of McPherson's work and in Didion's essay, "story" can be read to refer simultaneously to fictional narratives and to systems of belief or myths that we use to order experience and define ourselves. Although such systems or myths can be expressed in the form of a coherent series of assumptions about the nature of the world and persons (e.g., the worldview of modern science), they generally take the form of dramatic narratives that serve as embodiments of abstract belief. Hence the relevance of morality and aesthetics, for what McPherson implies in **"Elbow Room"** is that neither meaning nor identity should be considered material or political matters, structures *necessarily* imposed upon us from without by external "realities." Instead, they should be recognized for what they always are: human constructions whose value must be measured in part by the sense of coherent and compelling purpose that they provide. Furthermore, as de Rougement observes, the plausibility of a given story or myth does not derive from its relation to an objective reality but from its relation to the "intentions" (convictions and beliefs) of the audience. We don't accept a story simply because we believe its central theme or idea is true to the facts;

we accept it because it appeals to us as a satisfying "new coherence" made aesthetically as well as morally cogent by the rhetorical power of art.

All of which is to say that the protagonist of **"Elbow Room"** is neither the white Paul Frost nor the black Virginia Valentine, about whom the narrator has so much to say; nor is the real story their struggle to live sanely and lovingly in a racist culture. The protagonist is the narrator himself, and the central story is his struggle to find a form for their story, a form that will be morally satisfying insofar as it will do justice to them as human beings seeking to define themselves in their own terms, and aesthetically satisfying insofar as it will engage and sustain our attention. The tempting alternative, one that the narrator succumbs to several times, is to create what amounts to an official version of them that explains and exploits them in terms consistent with *his* interests, not theirs.

McPherson dramatizes his narrator's moral and aesthetic struggle in both the frame and story-within-a-story of **"Elbow Room."** In the frame, the narrator rejects the conventional demands of an editor, who declares in his introduction that the

> Narrator is unmanageable. Demonstrates a disregard for form bordering on the paranoid. Questioned closely, he declares himself the open enemy of conventional narrative categories. When pressed for reasons, narrator became shrill in insistence that 'borders,' 'structures,' 'frames,' 'order,' and even 'form' itself are regarded by him with the highest suspicion.
>
> (256)

The editor's official status is clear, arguing as he does for the translation of unconventional people and perspectives into terms compatible with the "intentions" or expectations of ordinary readers. The narrator's wayfaring commitments are equally clear, arguing as he does for creative freedom from conventional constraints. This opposition is established in their first exchange. The narrator is describing a time when, following a short period of freedom (presumably in the Sixties), "caste curtains" were again drawn, "resegregating all imaginations" (261) and forcing him to go out in search of stories "to complete my sense of self." This search was often risky due to the distrust that was then separating people.

> Yet not to do this was to default on my responsibility to narrate fully. There are stories that *must* be told, if only to be around when fresh dimensions are needed. But in the East, during that time, there was no thought of this. A narrator cannot function without new angles of vision. I needed new eyes, regeneration, fresh forms, and went hunting for them out in the territory.

Apparently confused by such aspirations, the editor interrupts to request

A point of information. What has form to do with caste restrictions?

Everything.

You are saying you want to be white?

A narrator needs as much access to the world as the advocates of that mythology.

You are ashamed then of being black?

Only of not being nimble enough to dodge other people's straightjackets.

Are you not too much obsessed here with integration?

I was cursed with a healthy imagination.

What have caste restrictions to do with imagination?

Everything.

A point of information. What is your idea of personal freedom?

Unrestricted access to new stories forming.

Have you paid strict attention to the forming of this present one?

Once upon a time there was a wedding in San Francisco.

(261-2)

Insofar as he asserts the need for new angles and new eyes, fresh forms and unrestricted access, the narrator speaks as a wayfarer attempting to escape the editor's official straightjackets.

But when we leave the frame and enter the story of the wedding couple, Paul Frost and Virginia Valentine, we find the narrator becoming an official in his turn—a sensitive but egocentric artist committed primarily to form, not to people embedded in time trying to live sanely and lovingly.[2] "Virginia I valued for her stock of stories," he writes. "I was suspicious of Paul Frost for claiming first right to these. They were a treasure I felt sure he would exploit" (262). Here the narrator's moral and aesthetic interests clash. Good stories should be both moral (purposive, idealistic) and aesthetic (dramatically engaging); but, McPherson would have us remember, so should storytellers, for social if not aesthetic reasons.

As sensitive as the narrator is to his own sense of self, he nevertheless fails to relate to others without intruding, without trying literally to write them into his own story. For example, after listening to Virginia talk about how Paul's father had refused to accept their marriage, the narrator confesses that "It was not my story, but I could not help intruding upon its materials. It seemed to me to lack perspective" (270). He then pontificates on the themes of time, media and selfhood in a language hardly intended to express or encourage sympathetic understanding:

Time out here is different from time in the East. When we say "Good afternoon" here, in the East people are saying "Good night." It's a matter of distance, not of values. Ideas that start in the East move very fast in media, but here the diversity tends to slow them down. Still, a mind needs media to reinforce a sense of self. There are no imaginations pure enough to be self-sustaining.

(270)

Angered by what he takes as condescension, Paul says that he doesn't know what the narrator is talking about. Once again in McPherson's book we encounter a defensive protagonist attempting to structure the world to his satisfaction in order to escape its human entanglements. Aesthetic to a fault, his main goal seems to be to transform Paul and Virginia into a self-satisfying work of art.

Shortly after this exchange, the narrator again intrudes, this time as an interrogator. Pointing to an African mask on the wall of Paul and Virginia's apartment, he asks if Paul thinks it is beautiful. Paul answers, "It's very nice. Ginny bought it from a trader in Ibadan. There's a good story behind it." The narrator repeats the question. Growing angry, Paul says yes. The narrator then poses a problem:

> You are a dealer in art. You have extraordinary taste. But your shop is in a small town. You want to sell this mask by convincing your best customer it is beautiful and of interest to the eye. Every other dealer in town says it is ugly. How do you convince the customer and make a sale?

(271)

As useful as this question might be on an essay examination in a course in aesthetics and race, it is hardly an appropriate one for Paul, who simply wants to survive as a man and husband. The narrator know this but offers little help. Instead, he continues to overwhelm a bewildered Paul with heavy truths. "You have enlisted in a psychological war," he tells Paul, shortly before the latter orders him to leave. Later the narrator rationalizes the experience: "I left them alone with their dinner. It was not my story. It was not ripe for telling until they had got it under better control" (272).

Psychological war is everyone's story in **"Elbow Room."** At bottom the conflict involves a struggle of self-creation in which individuals oppose the power of culture in an attempt to transcend its limiting definitions. Immediately after the above scene the editor interrupts, declaring that an

> *Analysis of this section is needed. It is too subtle and needs to be more clearly explained.*
>
> I tried to enter his mind and failed.
>
> *Explain.*

I had confronted him with color and he became white.

Unclear. Explain.

There was a public area of personality in which his 'I' existed. The nervous nature of this is the basis of what is miscalled arrogance. In reality it was the way his relationship with the world was structured. I attempted to challenge this structure by attacking its assumptions too directly and abruptly. He sensed the intrusion and reacted emotionally to protect his sense of form. He simply shut me out of his world.

Unclear. Explain.

I am I. I am we. You are.

Clarity is essential on this point. Explain.

(272)

Like officials we have met elsewhere (e.g., Kraepelin and Hinsie), McPherson's editor cannot absorb the information he is receiving because it is incompatible with ideological assumptions that define and legitimize him. Unlike most of them, he does not dismiss the narrator's answers as nonsense, but his recurrent demands for an explanations suggest that he is communicating not to achieve insight and understanding but to preserve his collective identity and the reality upon which it is based; hence, he can only be confused when his reality or "sense of form" is challenged. The narrator's "I am I. I am we. You are" is unclear to him because the editor believes that he lives in a world of discrete and unique entities ("I am I. You are."). To ask him to think otherwise, to accept the intervening and, from his point of view, contradictory "I am we," which acknowledges the fact that unique individuals on one conceptual level are interdependent parts of a universal whole on another, is to ask him to accept an alien conception of human identity.

The narrator confronts Paul with a similar challenge. Naturally Paul resists, not only because adopting a black frame of reference threatens his white identity, but also because the challenge is phrased in patronizing terms that reveal the official agenda in what otherwise appears to be a wayfaring text. By patronizing Paul, the narrator encourages him to end the dialogue and order him out of the apartment. Thus rejected, the narrator can then lament Paul's limitations rather than come to terms with the fact that Paul and Virginia's story is challenging *his* assumptions, especially his belief that his storytelling "I" has the right to violate Paul and Virginia's "You are" in order to "ripen" their story, that is, make it consistent with his own sense of form.

Unable to achieve this end, the narrator eventually loses interest. After a conversation with Virginia in which she talks about her ideal of selfhood, he writes:

> Inside myself I suddenly felt a coolness as light as the morning mist against my skin. Then I realized that I

was acting. I did not care about them and their problems any more. I did not think they had a story worth telling. I looked away from her and said, 'Life is tough, all right.'

(281)

With a cliche he writes them off, convinced that they and their child have only two choices: black isolation or self-destructive compromise with white people who would entrap them within conventional social categories. His decision reveals the extent of his own isolation, his own defensive commitment to aesthetic rather than moral values. Losing interest in Paul's and Virginia's ability to live "fresh forms," the narrator walks away in despair, "convinced there were no new stories in the world" (284).

But Paul and Virginia, committed as they are to each other and to moral ideals of selfhood, succeed in proving him wrong. Broadened and deepened by her flight into the hearts of other countries and other people, Virginia becomes "a magic woman" who can speak "with her whole presence in very complicated ways. She was unique. She was a classic kind of narrator" (263). Virginia is also a woman capable of human intimacy and commitment, a trait evident in her relation to Paul, whom she resolves to protect against all psychological dangers. Paul is equally impressive in his own subdued Kansas way. Willing to confront "the hidden dimension of his history" (275) in order "to unstructure and flesh out his undefined 'I'" (279), Paul marries Virginia, fathers a son, and eventually persuades his father to accept his family. More importantly, at least as far as the theme of the story is concerned, he constantly grapples with the issue of his identity, realizing that the question "Who am I?" can never be answered conclusively. "And many times," writes the narrator, speculating about how he might help Paul answer it,

> watching him conceal his aloneness, I wanted to answer, 'The abstract white man of mythic dimensions, if being that will make you whole again.' But the story was still unfinished, and I did not want to intrude on its structure again. The chaos was his alone, as were the contents he was trying desperately to reclaim from an entrenched and determined form. But to his credit it must be said that, all during this time, I never once heard him say to Virginia, 'I don't understand.' For the stoic nature of this silence, considering the easy world waiting behind those words, one could not help but love him.

(279-80)

At the end of the story, the narrator describes his response to a photograph of Paul and Virginia that they had sent to him. It includes their baby, Paul's parents and, on the back, the announcement that the child "will be a *classic* kind of nigger." When the editor demands another explanation, the narrator says that he cannot give it.

It was from the beginning not my story. I lack the insight to narrate its complexities. But it may still be told. The mother is, after all, a country raconteur with cosmopolitan experience. The father sees clearly with both eyes. And when I called Kansas they had already left for the backwoods of Tennessee, where the baby has an odd assortment of relatives. I will wait. The mother is a bold woman. The father has a sense of how things should be. But while waiting, I will wager my reputation on the ambition, if not the strength, of the boy's story.

Comment is unclear. Explain. Explain.

(286)

Edified by Paul and Virginia's experience, the narrator realizes that there is no explanation beyond the story of **"Elbow Room"** itself, beyond the texture of its language, images, tone, syntax—in the feel of verbal formulations designed to make new eyes and new selves by modifying old forms, social and linguistic. Or, in terms of another metaphor, there is no explanation beyond the play of opposites that is the story: the editor and the narrator, the narrator and Paul, Paul and Virginia, male and female, and even the aesthetic and moral dimensions of stories that interact to generate a meaningful form. Paul? His son? Both? can become "classic" only by going beyond such antithetical classifications to a synthesis that subsumes them. Since such a synthesis does not yet exist, we cannot explain it, only sense it as a possibility somewhere beyond or between the lines of our current public and private stories, where there is room for everyone.

Notes

1. Williams goes on to write: "For the problem of the New World was, as every new comer soon found out, an awkward one, on all sides the same: how to replace from the wild land that which, at home, they had scarcely known the Old World meant to them; through difficulty and even brutal hardship to find a ground to take the place of England. They could not do it. They clung, one way or another, to the old, striving the while to pull off pieces to themselves from the fat of the new bounty."

2. The first names were possibly derived from Bernardin de Saint-Pierre's famous romance *Paul et Virginie* (1787), in which the title characters, who have loved each other since childhood, suffer a final separation when she refuses to remove her petticoats after a shipwreck and allow a naked sailor to swim her ashore. Integrity intact, she drowns, thus demonstrating "the imperfection of human life when it departs from nature" (Harvey and Haseltine 544). The edge of McPherson's irony might be turned against those who see mixed marriages as equally "unnatural."

Works Cited

Berger, Thomas. *Killing Time.* New York: Delta, 1967.

Didion, Joan. *The White Album.* New York: Simon & Schuster, 1979.

Harvey, Sir Paul and J. E. Haseltine. *The Oxford Companion to French Literature.* Oxford: Clarendon Press, 1959.

Ionesco, Eugene. *Fragments of a Journal.* New York: Atheneum, 1967.

Kafka, Franz. *The Trial.* Trans. Willa and Edwin Muir. New York: The Modern Library, 1956.

Lakoff, George, and Mark Johnson. *Metaphors We Live By.* Chicago, Ill.: Chicago UP, 1980.

McPherson, James Alan. *Elbow Room.* New York: Fawcett Crest, 1972.

Rougemont, Denis de. *Love in the Western World.* New York: Pantheon, 1956.

Williams, William Carlos. *In the American Grain.* New York: New Directions, 1933.

James Alan McPherson and Calvin Reid (interview date 15 December 1997)

SOURCE: McPherson, James Alan, and Calvin Reid. "James Alan McPherson: A Theater of Memory." *Publishers Weekly* 244, no. 51 (15 December 1997): 36-7.

[*In the course of the following interview, McPherson's discusses his life and career.*]

When James Alan McPherson was a dining-car waiter for the Great Northern Railroad in the 1960s, he would ride the trains out of the south to Chattanooga, along the Mason-Dixon line. He tells what would happen when the trains stopped to change engines: "The man would come on serving sandwiches and coffee in the black coach and he'd say, 'y'all can go up front.' Nobody moved. Why would you go against your whole tradition? Suddenly the whole car was white and you're sitting next to a white person for the first time in your life. When I was about 18 I went to St. Paul, about 1962, and went in a restaurant and ordered a hamburger. I sat near a white woman and her child and it was like committing a crime. I was ashamed of that feeling. I wanted to see more of the world."

McPherson has followed through on that promise. Sitting with *PW* in a quiet, comfortably isolated alcove towards the rear of a small Greek restaurant just off Sixth Avenue in Manhattan, he is soft-spoken and immediately engaging. This former janitor and dining-car waiter—who emerged from the segregated South to earn a law degree from Harvard, a "genius" grant from the MacArthur foundation and the 1978 Pulitzer Prize for his short-story collection *Elbow Room*—is chatting with *PW* about living in Iowa and his new writing projects. While he's at it, he defines several personally meaningful terms from Latin and Japanese, two languages that figure prominently in his new memoir, *Crabcakes,* out next month from Simon & Schuster (Forecasts, Nov. 17). McPherson is visiting New York from Stanford, where he is on a year's fellowship working on what he calls "an experimental novel" and compiling a collection of his essays.

Under a decidedly worn, and clearly cherished, black straw Kangol cap, McPherson's face, a rich burnished bronze, is animated and quick to smile. His speaking voice, a whispery, staccato rasp, is restrained at first, but quickly builds to a flurry of erudite observations delivered with a combination of professorial precision and the inflections and convivial intimacy typical of black Southern speech.

In 1969, Atlantic Monthly Press published *Hue and Cry,* his first collection of stories, which won the National Institute of Arts and Letters Award for Literature. He followed this auspicious debut with *Railroad: Trains and People in American Culture* (co-written with Miller Williams and acquired by Toni Morrison at Random House), which, like all of his books so far, quickly went out of print and is very nearly impossible to find. *Elbow Room* followed in 1977. McPherson taught at the University of California at Santa Cruz and at the University of Virginia before joining the faculty of the Writers Workshop in Iowa (where he received his M.F.A. in 1971). He is divorced, with a daughter about to enter college.

Whether he's writing about the elite black railroad waiters during the golden age of the passenger train (as in the story **"A Solo Song: For Doc Craft,"** from *Hue and Cry*), re-creating the world of a young child growing up in the South (as in **"A Matter of Vocabulary,"** also from *Hue and Cry*) or conjuring up the comic urban mythologies of small-time black hoodlums (in stories like **"The Story of a Deadman"** or **"The Silver Bullet,"** both from *Elbow Room*), McPherson presents a wonderfully precise social tableau full of vivid characters and dialogue so lively and true it seems taped. And it's all delivered within narratives so universal and directly meaningful that the stories aspire to the mythic realm of folklore and legend. "If that's there," McPherson says of his fiction's folkloric power, "I learned it from writers like Albert Murray and Ralph Ellison." His stories can also be heady experiential parables like **"Gold Coast,"** a poignant tale in *Hue and Cry* about a young black student working as a janitor and the slow disintegration of the elderly, Boston-Irish super he has been hired to replace. The story is crafted with a succession of disparate, affecting events that immerses the reader in an emotional pool of understanding (an approach to writing McPherson likes to call "tap dancing on the synapses").

Although he has written numerous essays, McPherson has not published fiction in nearly 20 years and, for the most part, has been barely visible on the literary horizon. He has a reputation for disliking interviews—and the promotional side of book publishing in general—and cheerfully admits he's submitting to this one at the prompting of his agent, Faith Childs. He's quick to credit Childs (recommended to him by his friend, the recently deceased and highly respected Chicago-born novelist Leon Forrest) with reviving editors' interest in the manuscript for *Crabcakes,* a sometimes difficult but urgently affecting work that inventively explores McPherson's sense of pervasive social dysfunction and a period in his life of deep personal despair.

McPherson was born in Savannah, Ga., in 1943 ("it was segregated but you were aware of its great history," he says). His father was one of the few licensed black electricians with his own business, "but he could not hold on to it." His mother, says McPherson, was "withdrawn. Her father actually managed Sears and Roebucks stores on a plantation in Florida." And although he has written of growing up in "extreme poverty," McPherson comes from a rather accomplished family. One sister is a corporate librarian, a younger one lives in Atlanta and his brother is an airplane mechanic. He has an aunt in Congress representing a rural district in North Carolina, and his cousin, Leonard Brisbon, is the copilot of Air Force One. "Not bad," says McPherson. He attended Morris Brown College, an historically black college founded in Georgia by the African Methodist Episcopal church in 1881, working as a janitor as well as a dining-car waiter on the railroads and graduating in 1965. He mentions both his family and time at Morris Brown with a cheerful pride. "People are surprised that I advanced as far as I have coming from a small private black college," he says. "But I got my start there. I had some teachers who loved literature and they passed that on to me."

Inspired by those train rides out of the South and his uneasy introduction into the world of whites, he decided to attend Harvard Law School after graduating from Morris Brown. Much like those train rides, McPherson says, the law seemed to him to represent "access to another world. I had traveled to Chicago, to St. Paul, Seattle, the whole Northwest, and I wanted to see more. The law represented the same kind of exploration."

At Harvard, he continued to work as a janitor while studying the law and also continued to write; and it now seems that all his occupations have had an impact

on his later work. Indeed, working as a janitor was a good job for a writer-in-training. "I paid my rent that way, but it was also an opportunity to see how ordinary people lived in Cambridge. You see one point of view going to law school. If you work as a janitor, you see another. I have always been wary of limiting my perspective."

During summers in Cambridge, McPherson took writing courses—instead of law internships—and began to think of publishing. "I knew the Atlantic Monthly was in Cambridge and I knew they would accept submissions over the transom," says McPherson. Much like the young student protagonist of **"Gold Coast,"** he was working as a janitor in Cambridge when he dropped off a manuscript of that story at the offices of the Atlantic Monthly Press in 1968. "Just before New Year's I left the manuscript at the front desk and said it was special delivery from Cambridge. I couldn't bring myself to say it was from me at the time. I looked like a bum, you see."

Of course the house lost his manuscript, but it materialized three months later (it was under the receptionist's desk), and editor-in-chief Edward Weeks immediately called to ask McPherson "if I had any more stories. I said I have many of them. So Ed Weeks and I worked all that summer on the book called **Hue and Cry.**" Critical response was swift. Weeks had asked Ralph Ellison to read the manuscript, and Ellison submitted a glowing endorsement for the book's jacket. "After Ellison endorsed **Hue and Cry,** I interviewed him for the *Atlantic Monthly* in 1970. I met Albert Murray around the same time at the American Academy. They both became mentors to me."

MEMORIES OF DEEP MOMENTS

Like his fiction, *Crabcakes* "tap dances on the synapses," presenting a procession of seemingly isolated social interactions separated by time and space and finding subtle psychic connections among them. In *Crabcakes,* McPherson examines the dehumanizing, prosaic regularity (and postmodern reinvigoration) of American racism; Western versus Eastern spiritual values and a disabling "standardization" of the language used to describe the most terrible events of our time. He creates a theater of memory, revisiting Baltimore, in 1976 and subsequent years, to examine his past acts. He recalls visits to old neighborhoods and to Baltimore's old Lexington Market, the place to get the best Maryland crabcakes. "What runs through the book is a sense of deep moments," says McPherson, "A sense of time that is circular. That what goes around comes around."

The book episodically charts McPherson's own period of depression and social withdrawal, beginning in the late 1970s, and his slow re-emergence into the world through the humane, lyrically simple precepts of Japanese culture and Buddhism. Despite his successes, it was the beginning of an emotionally trying period.

"In the 1980s I retreated from everything. My sister would say, 'What are you doing out there in Iowa with all of those white people?' But it was a haven for me so that I could get away from things that were giving me hell," McPherson recalls. "For the last 16 years," he says, "I've lived a very fragmented experience." He wasn't trying to write a memoir, he says. "It just came out that way. It strikes me that the forms in which we write, the conventional forms, have lost their vitality. I wanted a sense of wholeness. No matter what I had to do to get it. So I used all kinds of mundane forms—the sound bite, the folk tale, letters. I tried to use them with something meaningful for myself."

The first half of the book is a meditation on a house in Baltimore that McPherson bought in 1976 to prevent the eviction of an elderly black couple—an act he examines and reexamines. The second part of the book details an ongoing dialogue between McPherson and two Japanese friends, Kiyohiro Mirua, a writer and teacher, and Takeo Hammamoto, a scholar of black literature, that attempts to translate his life and American culture into terms that they might understand. It is also an attempt to apologize to his friends for an insulting social indiscretion he committed—an indiscretion later revealed to be an act of humane care and racial transcendence. To explain, he uses the language and rituals of Buddhism. "I was trying to explain, to a man with no understanding of the complexities of the black/white situation, why I had slighted him."

By the end of *Crabcakes*, McPherson does manage to achieve a sense of peace, emotional wholeness and a revived engagement with life. Two delightful, ironically symbolic events serve to evoke his emotional resurrection: a bee sting he received in the physical and emotionally hermetic isolation of his Iowa house, and an act of simple kindness from a Japanese woman, an acquaintance, during a train trip through Japan. He explains these events using the Buddhist term *ninjo,* a genuineness or "natural feeling" that indicates a close, communal association that transcends racial identity. "Christianity might work for some. Buddhist codes might work. I'm searching for codes that might work for black people today. I'm not trying to put down Western civilization," he says, smiling. "But Western civilization could use a little more *ninjo.*"

Wahneema Lubiano (essay date 1997)

SOURCE: Lubiano, Wahneema. "Shuckin' off the African-American Native Other: What's 'Po-Mo' Got to Do with It?" In *Dangerous Liaisons: Gender, Nation,* *and Postcolonial Perspectives,* edited by Anne McClintock, Aamir Mufti, and Ella Shohat, pp. 204-29. Minneapolis: University of Minnesota Press, 1997.

[*In the following essay, Lubiano analyzes postmodern motifs of narrative resistance and political suggestion in McPherson's short story "Elbow Room," contrasting African American with European American notions of literary realism.*]

> Remember the time when stories had a beginning, a middle, and an end?
>
> In that order . . .
>
> Three things made Britain great. A strong navy. The white race. And narrative closure. Don't let's throw them away.
>
> The *Sun,* June 12, 1988

> When Goebbels, the brain behind Nazi propaganda, heard culture being discussed, he brought out his revolver. That shows that the Nazis—who were and are the most tragic expression of imperialism—. . . had a clear idea of the value of culture as a factor of resistance to foreign domination.
>
> Amilcar Cabral

> Minority texts, like all literary texts, exist simultaneously as determinate objects and as rhetorical practices. . . . However, in the context of the neutralizing hegemonic pressures, they will never become effective rhetorical practices until a minority critical discourse articulates them as such.
>
> Abdul R. JanMohamed

First, a polemic: in this moment, postmodern or not, African-American literature and cultural production are being read, consumed, and criticized against a cacophony of voices, from various points of the U.S. academy's political spectrum, bleating that "theory," "postmodernism," and "critiques of race, gender, class, and sexuality" (subtract class from the left version of this complaint) have gone too far. I've tried to understand what such disparate voices might have in common, and it seems to me that what I've been hearing is some version of old narratives (from the right and the left) that delimit the discursive or material space available for particular concerns that are held not to matter by the speakers compared to other concerns that just as obviously do matter. Those speaking, I presume, know who (or what) at any moment has "gone too far." And who (or that which) has gone too far is always some variety of the marginalized, unwilling to stay out of the "center," who transgresses, who "goes too far," who behaves, in this moment, as though she or he has a right to lay claim to a place in the discursive spotlight. While reading my way angrily through the mountains of prose that demand my silence, demand it in the name of the "others" of my group (the "real" others I suppose, since the minute I speak I stop being one) who "cannot speak" (at least not in forums where academics listen) because they (and not I) live in the "real" world, I was stopped cold by a sentence (of Jon Wiener's): "Tell that to the veterans of foreign texts."[1] Because some of the voices complaining of "things" (racialized persons, women, gays, and lesbians?) having "gone too far" evoke a "real" world—much in the way that Wiener's language does—I felt myself drawn into these discussions out of my conviction that African-American cultural practices, texts that come out of those cultural practices, and interpretations/readings of those texts are things that do matter. They matter in the academy and in a "real" world of prisons and bombs. Besides, if the other "others" cannot speak, and I (who at least under some circumstances used to be an "other") allow myself to be admonished into silence, then who is left speaking? And who or what will interrupt business-as-usual?

This essay explores why the debates around postmodernism, "theory," and particular kinds of critiques matter; it uses as an exemplar of the theoretical possibilities of African-American postmodern literary production a short story that scripts the relation of aesthetic notions to raw events of power, the aesthetic as the gloss for an imperializing moral certainty. That story and this essay are answers to the demand implied by "tell that to the veterans of foreign texts": the demand that texts be made as "real" as war.

Gayatri Chakravorty Spivak articulates in "The Postmodern Condition: The End of Politics?" a similar response in more general terms:

> But when they [Derrida, etc.] talk about there is nothing but text, etc., they are talking about a network, a weave—you can put names on it—politico-psycho-sexual-socio, you name it. . . . The moment you name it, there is a network broader than that. . . . [That] is very different from saying that everything is language. And to an extent if we are exterminated within the next 5 minutes, it will be a textual event, because it would not come about without the history that we are speaking of at great length here. And if that is not a text, nothing is.
>
> (25)

It is perhaps arrogant to suggest that a short story, talking about a short story, is a way to insist that one is "talking back to history," but I am reminded by Spivak and Bruce Robbins that an intellectual grounds herself specifically because there is work to be done in institutions and because the split between the academy and the "real" world is an imposition that keeps nostalgically before us all a harking back to those golden never-never-land moments when "we" were either all working-class, white, revolutionary men storming the Winter Palace or white culture-aristocrats properly mindful of the sacredness of ivory towers. Robbins (in *Intellectuals: Aesthetics, Politics, Academics*) states:

> In the context of gender politics, it requires no paranoia to see attacks on the inadequate "publicness" of the contemporary academy from left and right as a covert means of undermining the specific (though still fragile) gains scored by feminism there. Such attacks are understandable enough from the right, but there is no excuse for anyone else. As if for women, even getting out of the home and into the labor market (not to speak of getting into the academy, *where so much of the content of socialization is determined*) were not to take even the smallest step in a "public" direction! Even in the worst instance, professionalization is always partly achievement from below as well as co-optation from above.
>
> (xviii; my emphasis)

I would add only that what Robbins holds for gender politics, for women, holds also for African-Americans. African-American studies (in both its "on and off campus eras"—as Russell Adams terms it) has operated for roughly two hundred years on the assumption that wherever the sites for knowledge production, reproduction, and dissemination were, those were the places on which to take a stand, for oneself and for one's group. An old African-American truism runs thusly: being where they give out education must mean something or they (whites) wouldn't try so hard to keep us out. Of course, getting an education must be extended to giving one too: so I begin here with the debate around postmodernism as an ubiquitous presence from which African-American voices have been largely absent.

Generally, I derive much pleasure at the discursive spectacle of men out of control—even if "real" power and wealth have not yet been redistributed across gender and race as well as class lines—so, if for no other reason than that, postmodernism, as a sign of that lack of control, seems like a good idea to me. That this talk of a "crisis" is now routine makes compelling Alice Jardine's argument for the name that she gives it: "Gynesis"—"a movement away from" identity in the direction of "a concern with difference," that is, a name for males "acting out" anxiety over constraints that have always trapped women (36).

With displays of typical patriarchal arrogance, however, some men continue to agonize over postmodernism's implications: "What is to be done?" (although a more honest version of this question would be "What can *I* do?" or, "Where am *I* in all of this?") is the rallying cry that results from their realization that authority is not stable. A response articulated by feminists, and shared by African-Americans, is to figure out what happens when the idea of metanarratives is up for grabs. One must try to understand what differences do, although in the midst of this kind of postmodernist project African-American men have to re/learn the idea that "difference" for African-Americans includes gender. Still, it is necessary to be able to see when color hangs us all as well as when gender or sexuality adds weight to the tree limb. Such is the political African-American postmodernist project.[2]

I

for the embattled
there is no place
that cannot be
home
nor is

Audre Lorde, "School Note"

Postmodernism is, according to Dick Hebdige, "a term that gets stretched in all directions across different debates"—from interior design through the "collective chagrin and morbid projections of a post-War generation of baby boomers" to "discussions of global media consumer commodifications" (181-82). While I am not interested in rehearsing everything that has gone on in the debate over postmodernism, nor in staking out a particular yet comprehensive position on a general postmodernism, negotiating with the term is a way to draw attention to where African-American texts write themselves and are written (or are not) in the midst of this debate, especially given the "worldliness" of postmodernism, as Jonathan Arac puts it (281). He adds the caveat, however, that postmodernist criticism is not "urbane" because "this is not a world in which one can or should be too easily at home" (281). What a difference race makes! Given the inhospitality of the United States to African-Americans, there are few of us who need such a reminder. Perhaps that is one of the things that an African-American presence in postmodernism generally can offer: constantly reinvigorated caution.

In his very useful study *The Condition of Postmodernity,* David Harvey warns us against postmodernism's abuses:

> Worst of all, while it opens up a radical prospect by acknowledging the authenticity of other voices, postmodernist thinking immediately shuts off those other voices from access to more universal sources of power by ghettoizing them within an opaque otherness, the specificity of this or that language game. It thereby disempowers those voices (of women, ethnic and racial minorities, colonized peoples, the unemployed, youth, etc.) in a world of lopsided power-relations. The language game of a cabal of international bankers may be impenetrable to us, but that does not put it on par with the equally impenetrable language of inner-city blacks from the standpoint of power-relations.

(117)

Prior to postmodernism, however, what or who was responsible for ghettoizing African-Americans—inner-city and otherwise? Was modernism so good to/for/ about us? When Gayatri Spivak says "you might want to entertain the notion that you cannot consider all other subjects [and] you should look at your own subjective investment in the narrative that is being produced," she is speaking to those who seek to stand confidently on those "more *universal* sources of power" (29; my emphasis).

Harvey is somewhat attentive to the ways in which postmodernism, according to him, "fits in with the emergence since 1970 of a fragmented politics of divergent special and regional interest groups" (302). But he warns that "regional resistances," bound as they are to particular *spaces* and to the work of "oppositional groups—racial minorities, colonized people, women, etc."—while "excellent bases for political action, . . . cannot bear the burden of radical historical change alone. 'Think globally and act locally' was the revolutionary slogan of the 1960s. It bears repeating" (303). Certainly. What also bears sustained attention are the particularities, the specifics, of what that slogan means applied to those groups whose politics are delimited by the description "regional resistances." Some "racial minorities, colonized people, women, etc." have proven themselves able to "think globally and act locally"— Frantz Fanon, Amilcar Cabral, Anna Cooper, W. E. B. Du Bois, Malcolm X, Angela Davis, and even Jesse Jackson (despite the constraints that have accompanied his attempt to act in the realm of electoral politics) come most immediately to mind—at the same time they were acting on regional concerns: whether focused on the specifics of colonialism, as was the case with Cabral and Fanon, or on domestic political resistance, cultural internationalism, and the relation between U.S. foreign policy and domestic racism, as has been the case with the others.

Nonetheless, one can make the argument that global metanarratives, "master" narratives (like modernism), have been used to recognize, make a place for, and engage with the specifics of African-Americans, at particular moments. Two cases in point: in "The Dilemma of the Black Intellectual," Cornel West argues that the "Marxist model, despite its shortcomings, is more part of the solution than part of the problem for black intellectuals" (119), and Robin Kelly (in "Comrades, Praise Gawd for Lenin and Them!") examines a period when African-Americans in Alabama manipulated or transformed Marxism in such a way as to make it part of African-American cultural practice, connecting Communist Party analysis and practice with local concerns, mores, and manners, including religious beliefs and practices.

Metanarratives, including Marxism, however, have also often "translated" those who make up "regional resistances" into more politically "universal" categories as part of their more general political deployments. The record on "racism" among those who have articulated their theories and strategies from modernism, Marxism, or other metanarratives has been problematic, as even Harvey is at pains to delineate throughout his study.

Against Harvey's questioning of "regional resistances" with their *space* emphases, Robert Fox has argued that "perhaps it is only minority strategies that can offer an alternative, that can preserve spaces in which difference may operate" (10). Perhaps this is because within the context of postmodernism, those of us who are part of marginalized groups and who also occupy institutional space within the academy are able to consider, in more intent fashion than before, the announcement of postmodernism, *how* difference operates, as opposed to only considering *what* difference is, and want to do so as a way to spread and share the burden of radical change to which Harvey alludes.

Still, in his attempt to be fair to the possibilities of postmodernism and about the problems of metanarratives, Harvey lists the horrors that shattered the optimism of believers in the Enlightenment and modernism, such as the writers Condorcet and Jürgen Habermas, respectively (13). But his list of *twentieth*-century horrors ("with its death camps and death squads, its militarism and two world wars, its threat of nuclear annihilation and its experience of Hiroshima and Nagasaki") passes over slavery and the genocide of the indigenous American population—examples of the on-the-ground facts of history for two marginalized groups in the United States, which means that at least 350 years ago some of us were already in training to be both cynical about the Enlightenment and less than optimistic about modernism.

My awareness of this history, then, tempers any enthusiasm I might feel either for those harangues against postmodernism that want simply to recuperate the idea of metanarratives or for celebrations of postmodernism that, as Cornel West puts it, want to replace modernism with a celebration of "everybody's" marginality: "American attacks on universality in the name of differences, these postmodern issues of 'Otherness' (Afro-Americans, Native Americans, women, gays) are in fact an implicit critique of certain French postmodern discourses about Otherness that really serve to hide and conceal the power of voices and movements of Others" (see Stephanson, 273).[3] West here is concerned with what I call another manifestation of the privileged's ability to exoticize themselves selectively. Against this new universal "otherness," West wants to remind us that specific postmodernisms cost specific "others" their lives, such as African-Americans existing in the cauldron of inner cities or, sometimes (regardless of place, or price, of residence), stopped by the police for traffic violations. Craig Owens also warns against the idea of postmodernism as a kind of free-floating pluralism—a pluralism that "reduces us to being an other among others" and, therefore, "interchangeable" (58). Hal Foster

reminds us, however, that seeing postmodernism as pluralism is simplistic, although he too recognizes differing positions in and deployments of postmodernism (xi).

Owens fastens his argument against pluralist postmodernism to recognition of the political edge that inheres in unequal, in politically loaded and oppressed, difference. He argues that feminism recognizes not just "difference" but politics (77). Owens's discussion of feminism and postmodernism is a considerable advance over the thinly disguised hostility toward feminism (and other sites of "regional resistances") that emerges from Harvey's criticism of postmodernism's privileging of difference (about which I say more below). It is an advance called for by Nancy Fraser and Linda Nicholson, who argue that postmodernism and feminism have much to learn from each other (84). Such an advance, however, also comes close, as Laura Kipnis puts it, to colonizing feminism as the currently politically empowering, peripheral "other" against the "center" of patriarchal Marxism (161).

The pitfalls of postmodernist celebration seem easy to fall into: Fox moves to a too general celebration of African-American postmodernism when he says that it has a "strong ethical basis rooted in the demand for, the need for justice" (8) and that "nowhere in the universe of black writing is there such a thing as a purely amoral text" (8). One needs to exercise caution in the matter of affirmations of general ideas of justice—especially "within the group," as many of us who are African-American women would be happy to attest—and morality: morality for whom, when, and under what circumstances? It seems to me more useful to think of African-American postmodernism as a way to negotiate particular material circumstances in order to attempt some constructions of justice.

Nonetheless, while I am cynical about some aspects of postmodernism, about the alleged "newness" of postmodernism's break with the past, for example, it is a "name" that allows certain of us African-Americans to organize our response to modernism's blind spot in regard to people of color, at least as part of a new attention to the politics of difference.

Stuart Hall argues that postmodernism says "this is the end of the world. History stops with us and there is no place to go after this" (47). Perhaps. Maybe for a certain subset of Euro-Americans with privilege to protect, which both stems from history and insulates them from the vacillations of the present, it is possible to say postmodernism and mean what Hall says—although Foster argues that one must not make of postmodernism a conservative monolith. African-American postmodernism, however, insists on the representation of history in the present moment.

But to return to Harvey's cautionary notes: he warns that "any postmodern novel focuses on masks without commenting directly on social meanings other than the activity of masking itself" (101). Well, there's masking and there's masking; within the terms of African-American vernacular, which often moves along lines of indirection—what we can call verbal masking—*commenting directly on* has often been a luxury denied us and, in the mouths of others, has meant being the object of a particular convention's imposition, a convention ignorant of, or which ignores the uses (depending on historical moment and circumstances) of, indirect commentary. Further, African masks, for example, exist in the world as commodities *and* as cultural markers with a wide range of meanings—again, both within specific groups and as political practices "speaking back to" or against domination and hegemony. Double deployment constitutes a primary mode of African-American masking in language and behavior, although as a strategy it is available for misuse as well: one "masks" oneself sometimes to live—striking poses, resisting other poses—and, unfortunately, one sometimes injures with or is injured by poses.

We can consider African-American postmodernism as not simply a historical moment when modernism's intellectual and cultural hegemony is at least being questioned, but as a general epistemological standpoint for engaging/foregrounding what has been left out of larger discourses, a consideration of certain kinds of difference and the reasons for their historical absences. It theorizes ways that prevent engagement with differences from concretizing into intellectually and politically static categories. That is to say, my interest, along with that of others—Hortense Spillers's "Mama's Baby, Papa's Maybe" comes to my mind—is in working over the conflicted ground of discourse genealogies in order to prevent difference from cohering into essentials that are then placed in the service of someone's theorizing.

I insist that African-American postmodernism has to include the kind of narrative flexibility demonstrated by James Alan McPherson's **"Elbow Room."** So, while I find West's discussion of postmodernism generally excellent and useful, he occasionally gives in to modernist nostalgia: "There used to be a set of stories that could convince people that their absurd situation was one worth coping with, but the passivity is now overwhelming" (in Stephanson, 286). Both passivity and active oppositionality historically have been part of African-American cultural and political practice and are present now. Our presence in this postmodern moment, our deployments of postmodern strategies, and our interventions in postmodern discourse will allow us to complicate those stories in the histories being written now.

I find useful Diane Elam's description of Foster's postmodernism, a postmodernist theorizing that

> allows us to recognize the limitations of the critic's own political role, a limitation we recognize as Foster goes on to explain what he means by postmodernism's

resistance. [Instead of] proposing a "reality" outside of ideology, . . . Foster argues for a theory of resistance that would consider the historical circumstances, the context in which we are necessarily located, at the same time as it acknowledges the difficulty of defining those circumstances.

(217)

"Think globally, act locally," then, in cultural resistance terms, might require some lack of sureness, confidence, some awareness of what Spivak calls "vulnerability" (18), or, to paraphrase Foster, a willingness to recognize that a representation may "mean" differently in place, in moment, and in particular minds.

The African-American presence in this postmodern moment is not a given. When Fredric Jameson (in his most recent and massive study of postmodernism) describes those postmodern productions of which he is a "relatively enthusiastic consumer," he lists, among other things, the novel, "the weaker of the new cultural areas," but states that the "subgeneric narratives, however, are very good, indeed; *in the Third World of course all this falls out very differently*" (*Postmodernism*, 298; my emphasis). Where does African-American fiction fit in this? Are we part of the category named by Third World, by subgeneric narrative? His assertion, in an earlier essay, "Modernism and Imperialism," more accurately places some African-American fiction:

> [W]e have come to think of the emergence of an internal Third World and of internal Third World voices, as in black women's literature or Chicano literature for example. When the other speaks, he or she becomes another subject, which must be consciously registered as a problem by the imperial or metropolitan subject—whence the turn of what are still largely Western theories of imperialism in a new direction, toward that other, and toward the structures of underdevelopment and dependency for which we are responsible.

(49)

Jameson is not required to talk about the complexities of "internal Third World" cultural production or politics, but what is interesting for my purposes is that the discourse of postmodernism presents itself as a site for thinking about difference—it is possible, then, for some of us to elbow our way onto that site. And if postmodernism marks an "incredulity toward metanarratives" (Lyotard, xxiv), it is certainly an appropriate name for African-Americans (whose "status" in Eurocentric metanarratives has been at least more problematic than not and at worst has justified our repression): our histories show that we've maintained a fairly consistent level of incredulity; perhaps it is time that the "West" caught up with us.

No, the ending of various kinds of cultural authorities (Jameson in his *New Left Review* article) is not a crisis for African-Americans. First slavery and then the continuing manifestation and operation of racism—a meta- or master narrative on the ground of the United States— have demanded that African-Americans see themselves as incapable of constructing and complicating their subjectivity, of positing some versions of value. Objecting to and/or resisting meta- or master narratives—either as part of a project that reconstructs more specific narratives or as practitioners of cultural practices that resemble what is called "postmodernist"—allow us to be seen as postmodernist, although we can call, and have called, what we do by other names. In other words, depending upon where I find myself, I might both articulate and complicate "African-American cultural practices" or notions of "African-American literary traditions."

An African-American feminist postmodernism, a name for internal critiques of African-American postmodernism, is attuned to valorizing African-American cultural practices but is not blind to their transgressions against within-the-group differences. African-American postmodernism, then, to be politically nuanced in a radical way, has to focus on such differences' implications, especially in moments of oppositional transgressions: it is not just attention to assertions of presence, but attentiveness to responsibilities and strategies that have to change *given* certain presences.

Our experience of history as sloppily and inconsistently, but saliently, present in this moment, as Toni Morrison's *Beloved* so thoroughly demonstrates, suggests that the collage modality of postmodernism is one way to refuse the dangerous pleasures of coherence by instead demanding constant reconstructing.

If we are willing to consider *a* postmodernist (I am again being careful here not to try to account for a general postmodernism) concern with deconstructing the hegemonic ideologies of the West, insofar as they construct a universal human subject, metaphysical grounding, and "truth," then African-American cultural practice and cultural artifacts can be "read" within such an economy. And that is the claim I make for **"Elbow Room."**

I chose this male-authored and largely male-centered text to discuss because it represents marriage and families as the ground for rereading, deconstructing, the relationship between power and aesthetics. In the story's dramatization (1) of a deconstruction of narrative convention, (2) of complications of social constructions of race, and (3) of the nexus of the political and the personal, its representation of a struggle over aesthetic imperialism and its agenda for certain "native others" offer a reason to read and talk about African-American literature, a reason that goes beyond positivist "pluralist" reasons, that is, variations of the position that texts of marginalized groups should be read because we read those of the dominant group.

"Elbow Room" is both a specific theoretical text and an exemplar that functions to expose the way in which Eurocentric, particularly Enlightenment/modernist, gatekeepers have read/framed African-American texts. Thus, it suggests itself as a site for engagement with at least one project of the African-American theoretical discourse: exploration of counter-hegemonic possibilities of narrative construction and interpretation that a minority critical discourse can address along the lines that JanMohamed articulates in "Humanism and Minority Literature: Toward a Definition of Counter-hegemonic Discourse" (quoted in the epigraph). It is an example of politically engaged African-American postmodernism that derails narrative conventions in order to specify a connection between aesthetics and politics.

II

"Elbow Room" revolves around four people: an unnamed African-American male narrator, a married couple—including Virginia, an African-American woman, and Paul, a Euro-American man—and an editor. The plot follows the narrator's intervention into the couple's lives, his editorial battles with the editor, and the interstices between the couple's personal details and families, the issue of race, and literary/aesthetic convention. The story is framed by an epigraph that equates Daniel Boone's conquest of Kentucky with aesthetic morality; the plot follows the narrator's resistance to the editor's attempts to impose a particular set of conventions in perusing the narrator's final draft. In this way, the reader "sees" the mechanics of "literary gatekeeping" via the editor's demands for overexplanation and repeated insistence that the narrator delete crucial segments "impeding" (in the editor's opinion) the "realistic narrative flow" of the story. His[4] inability to "read" the narrator's story is paralleled by Paul's inability to "read" race. **"Elbow Room"** foregrounds the means of its own production—demystifying the aesthetic against which it intervenes.

The text foregrounds indeterminacy as an act of resistance to external pressure to translate and nail down racial consciousness; it delegitimates the master codes of narrative in the power struggle between the black narrator and the white editor; it parodies conventional literary modes in its play with the representations of romance; and it consistently draws attention to itself as a narrative in its metacommentary on the structure, demands, expectations, and failures of storytelling. The story exploits the political possibilities of postmodernist technique by juxtaposing problems of racism and imperialism (cultural and material) with arguments about aesthetics and narrative form.

At the same time that **"Elbow Room"** subverts expectations of traditional concepts of narrative, its language and structure provide a site for seeing the interplay between the discourse of colonialism and anticolonialism and the discourse of the African-American literary-critical tradition. In this regard my study draws on the terms that Houston Baker delineates.[5] And when I speak of African-American texts and African-Americans in terms of colonialist discourse, I am drawing on Frantz Fanon's theory that African-American culture has the same relationship to the dominant culture as a colonialized culture has to the colonialists, a relationship that he describes in *The Wretched of the Earth*:

> The Negroes who live in the United States . . . experience the need to attach themselves to a cultural matrix. Their problem is not fundamentally different from that of the Africans. The whites of America did not mete out to them any different treatment from that of the whites who ruled over the Africans. We have seen that the whites were used to putting all Negroes in the same bag.
>
> (215)

The story foregrounds the material struggles generally glossed over in the name of aesthetics by placing a matrix of overdeterminations—racial identity, racism, territoriality, a discussion of internal and external aesthetics, societal relations, and political upheavals—at the heart of what is also an almost ruthlessly formulaic story of boy meets girl, boy marries girl, boy and girl have baby, all against a background of parental disapproval. It also explores the pervasiveness and perniciousness of ideas of "race" and the "racial other," exemplifying the ways in which African-American texts (and marginalized texts generally) undermine notions of the world constructed according to, and by, the hegemonic culture of Euro-America. Through explicit and implicit problematizing of the possible range of meanings of "nigger," the story also "signifies" (in the vernacular sense)[6] on the terms of the discourse of African-American literary-critical tradition.[7]

What I find most interesting about **"Elbow Room,"** however, is the fact that it is one of the very few male-authored African-American texts to center on what has historically been trivialized as "women's concerns"—the realm of marriage, domesticity, and private relations. Things conventionally considered public and political—race and imperialism—cohere in that private and personal realm. This text combines an anticolonialist reimagining of the world with content that embodies the tie between sexual attraction and politics. That tie manifests itself, within this narrative, in the construction of an interracial marriage; the tension implicit in the politics of aesthetics is embodied in the problematized domesticity of the protagonists of this story.

Feminist theory has argued for decades that the split between the personal and the political was always a chimera, and feminist practice has made the personal another site for political engagement—hence the slogan that equates the two. And while Arac has argued that "one reason the personal has become the political is because of the agitation for public remedies in areas long considered private" (306), I would add that the political (or public) is both reified and made "real" in the realm of the personal or private, that the "chickens" of the public/political come "home" to roost in the personal (or private). The story dramatizes this.

III

According to JanMohamed, "race" or racial difference is transformed "into a moral and even metaphysical difference" within the logocentric system of the Western tradition or culture ("Economy," 80). He argues that "colonialist literature is an exploitation and a representation of a world at the boundaries of 'civilization,' . . . [a world] perceived as uncontrollable, chaotic, unattainable, and ultimately evil" (83). Within this economy a civilizing project is demanded that introduces the "native" to the benefits of Western culture (63).

"Elbow Room" turns such traditional and colonialist propositions of "race" or the "racial other" on their heads through the vehicle of the narrator, who appropriates the "civilizing function" in regard both to the editor of the story and to the story's white male protagonist, while he repeatedly interrupts the attempts of the editor to impose conventional narrative form on this story. At the same time, the story itself decenters traditional realistic narrative forms by replacing such forms, and reader expectation of such modes of presentation, with a narration that only initially suggests itself as "native other" to the expectations of the editor, but ultimately subverts both that editor's and its own potential control of the content. And through its explicit questioning of narrative form, and its implicit questioning of what is meant by "art," the story addresses the terms of the discourse of the African-American literary-critical tradition.

"Elbow Room" encourages theoretical analysis because it narrates a story of rebellion against imposed form as an analogue to its other, more customarily political, subject matters. The story refuses to explain itself, and that refusal critiques the "civilizing function" of such self-commentary. That is to say, its break with such forms is analogous to disrupting the colonizer positions such forms maintain in the literature of the colonized. The story represents a struggle that Hazel Carby (drawing on Hall) has described as "the struggle within and over language" that reveals "the nature of the struggle of social relations and the hierarchy of power" (17). I argue that this narrative is explicitly and implicitly a resisting narrative. In order to frame the issues at stake in this narrative, however, it is necessary to juxtapose African-American literary history to the larger Euro-American literary history.

IV

The idea of realism as the proper mode of narration goes back, at least, to Aristotle and comes down to us via the articulation of any number of critics and writers in the Western tradition. In "The Art of Fiction," for example, Henry James places the logocentric seal of approval on representation and its marriage to realism: "[T]he only reason for the existence of a novel [and, by extension, fiction] is that it represents life" (378). And, as John Ruskin asserts, the painter [or poet]

> must always have two great and distinctive ends: the first, to induce in the spectator's [reader's] mind the faithful conception of any natural objects; . . . the second, to guide the spectator's mind to those objects most worthy of its contemplation, and to inform him of the thoughts and feelings with which these were regarded by the artist himself.
>
> (133)

We get the point. Realistic technique is its own system of universal morality. What Ruskin's language does not admit is that such morality depends upon acceptance of a larger narrative that "explains" what is "worthy." Realism, then, according to Catherine Belsey, "evokes a world we already seem to know" and "offers itself as transparent"—thus performing the work of ideology, offering consistent subjects who originate meaning (51-52). Such realism, described by Wilson Harris as "obsessive centrality," can be subverted by the exercise of language, or as Harris asserts, the imposed centrality of something called realism can be undermined by the properties of language itself, an "interior and active expedition through and beyond what is already known" (77). I am talking here not about specific representations of a particular "real" but about a notion that a truthful, consensual real exists, a notion that is loaded with unacknowledged ideology about realism.

Of course, the privileging of realism is not restricted to British and Euro-American literary discourse; the effect of hegemony is that the concerns of the dominant culture are internalized, to some extent, by the "others." So it follows that African-American literary critics of the first two eras of African-American criticism, the integrationist poetics critics and the black aesthetic critics, also privilege realism as the key mode for narration without reflecting on their hegemonic compliance. Both eras of critics internalized to some degree the demands of Euro-American culture: the integrationist critics in their assumption that the forms of English and American literature had universal application, and the black aesthetic critics, black cultural nationalists, in their insistence upon the imposition of another "truth," another realism—a monolithic, absolutist, and essentialist "black truth" or "black reality" to counteract the big white "lies" about black culture and history. James Stewart (in Larry Neal and Amiri Baraka's *Black Fire*) puts it

bluntly indeed: "The Black artist must construct models which correspond to his [*sic*] reality" (3) because "the [other] reality model was incongruous. It was a white reality model" (8).

I do not ignore here the constraints of material and historical oppression. The critics of both eras were beset by vicious distortions of African-Americans and their culture on the part of the dominant culture—distortions that had to be addressed. I agree with West when he states: "The fight for representation and recognition highlighted moral judgements regarding Black 'positive' images over and against White supremacist stereotypes" ("New Cultural Politics," 103). I refer only to the fact that their attempts at correction often responded in terms that remained on the ground of the racist and sexist Euro-American discourse. Edward Said argues: "[T]hat is one problem with nationalism: its results are written across the formerly colonized world, usually in the fabrics of newly independent states whose pathologies of power, as Eqbal Ahmad has called them, bedevil political life even as we speak" (74). While African-Americans as a group are not trying to constitute themselves as a state (although some African-Americans do rally around such a desire)—here African-American nationalism is a cultural strategy and desire—Said's language does describe, to some degree, the traps built into uncomplicated African-American cultural nationalism.

Not an easily assimilable text for either integrationist or black nationalist readings, **"Elbow Room"** intervenes against preconstructions. Of course, the text has its own "real," its own world. And in that world characters are given histories by the text. Nonetheless, its narrator's insistence, within that "world," that he is looking for stories is the way in which the text attempts, at least, not to lay claim to a single monolithic "reality," a way to suggest that narrative is multiple, that others construct them also. **"Elbow Room"** calls the narrative conventions of monolithic or stable ideas of representation and realism into question from its beginning by refusing to state a "truth," a "general" truth in a form that pretends to be disinterested—although the editor never admits that any form he demands comes out of a particular aesthetic history. The narrator not only resists editorial authority—he shatters the illusion of accurate and controlled representation by interrupting the story to argue *against* the imposition of a single narrative form, reminding the reader that he is not telling his story along the lines or within the boundaries that would reassure the editor or reinstate a "white" aesthetic in "black" face. Additionally, by the end of the story, he even admits out loud his own narrative inadequacy in the face of storytelling "material" as complex as racialized human beings in their particularity.

This narrative constantly resists attempts to be read as a *unified* and organized whole even as it flagrantly displays the trappings of linear plot. It starts and stops as a result of false beginnings, vicissitudes of the friendship between the narrator and the characters, the editor's and narrator's passages of arms, and, most importantly, as a result of the difficulties, limitations, inadequacies, and intricacies of narration itself. The compromised omniscient, playful knowledge and interventions of the narrator of **"Elbow Room"** violate James's manifesto of the importance of intensity of illusion and pretense of bewilderment in constructing realistic prose that presents itself as unmediated (*Art of the Novel,* 66). It is not that the narrator has no investment in realism at all; rather, it is that he refuses to pretend that the stories he recounts are uninformed by his mediation, a mediation that takes a different form from that which the editor attempts to impose. The narrator continually reminds us of his presence as narrator through his decisions to continue the indirect mode of his "political" subtext. McPherson, as author, will not stay out of this text, nor will that narrator fall back within the lines the editor continually draws. The story interrupts the pretense of an "unauthored" narrative (Belsey, 52). While narrative interruptions are not inherently antirealistic, his interruptions shatter the illusion that the story is going on under its own momentum.

The idea of form confronted in the text is an analogue for the idea of Western civilization and its ideology of beauty and morality. The first lines of the text set up the struggle:

> Narrator is unmanageable. Demonstrates a disregard for form bordering on the paranoid. Questioned closely, he declares himself the open enemy of conventional narrative categories. When pressed for reasons, narrator became shrill in insistence that "border," "structures," "frames," "order," and even "form" itself are regarded by him with the highest suspicion. Insists on unevenness as a virtue. Flaunts an almost barbaric disregard for the moral mysteries, or integrities, of traditional narrative modes.

(215)

The disapproving voice of the editor ties conventions to morality—disregard of form is "almost barbaric" disregard for "moral mysteries" or "integrities" of traditional narrative form. The message is clear: certain aesthetics equal moral good. Indeed, these lines are a parody of received ideas about the sacredness of form. The editor goes on to assume the role of the civilizer who will present the refined "essence" of the story: "Editor speaks here of a morality of morality, of that necessary corroboration between unyielding material and the discerning eye of absolute importance in the making of a final draft. This is the essence of what he said" (256). The story itself, however, comes from the hands (or mouth) of an "unmanageable" black narrator and as such relentlessly undermines its own authority. The opening frame, however, is spoken by the nonnarrating editorial voice and sets up a journalistic distance; that

editor attempts to make the reader complicit in prejudgment of the narrator, and while disavowing his ownership of the narration, the editor retains the power to deliver the "essence"—a crude reduction—of that story. He attempts to repeat the colonizer's trope: "native" caricature.

The "story" begins with a microhistory of two individuals it then places immediately in the larger political history of their time. In fact, we know the time and the characters in terms of political and social oppression. By the end of the story, we realize that through this narration of a microhistory (a "personal" relationship), we've been "reading" the macro- ("political") history of the construction of race in America.

But the confusion evoked by the story's refusal to "behave" makes it hard for the editor to read the words on the page: expectations of some forthcoming clarity get in the way. The editor finally can "see" neither the story taking shape before him nor the relationship between that failure and his "duty" to restrain the story and the "barbaric" narrator. Ironically, then, given the history of "whites'" encounters with "blacks," the narrator is there to "civilize" the editor, who has tried to set up a civilizing project directed at the narrative: an inversion of the colonialist ur-text. The text and the narrator, in African-American vernacular terms, deconstruct the terms of history. The two "talk back" and turn the tables, then, on a dynamic that Said describes as "one of the salient traits of modern imperialism," that "in most places it set out quite consciously to modernize, develop, instruct, and civilize the natives" (74).

The narration proper begins from an omniscient point of view (an omniscience that has been problematized already by the text and challenged by the editor), introducing characters and questions, presenting plausible information within conventional-enough metaphors—in short, setting us up to expect something or some things recognizable in symbolic terms we already understand:

> Paul Frost was one of thousands of boys who came out of those little Kansas towns back during that time.
>
> Virginia Valentine had come out of Warren some ten years before, on the crest of that great wave of jail-breaking peasants. . . . Virginia's quest was an epic of idealism.

(215-17)

We are introduced in greater detail to Paul, who represents the quintessential liberal humanist whose war protest took the form of conscientious objection and whose personal political statement takes the form of interracial marriage with Virginia, a black peasant, who, while on a voyage of international "discovery" (the typical romantic quest adventure made atypical and political by its context, the Peace Corps), had made an important finding not usually part of the conventional apparatus of the conventional "hero": a perspective that makes the sign "nigger" a symbol of self-affirmation (217), an inversion of an old hierarchy.

The temporal setting of the story focuses on the 1960s and a temporary new international egalitarianism (in some quarters) that could not, however, be sustained. The egalitarianism is undermined by reassertions of old conventions at home and forces Virginia and Paul out to the territory—to California—for new possibilities, just as the narrator is forced to the territory because he needs to find new narratives.

From the beginning, Virginia and Paul's marriage inverts the conventional hierarchy: Virginia, child of a rural African-American Tennessee farmer family, is the "rural lumpen" aristocrat, and Paul, the child of a Euro-American bourgeois, entrepreneurial family, is the consort who needs remaking. The inverted hierarchy here is based on political consciousness.

Almost immediately, however, the control of the narrative breaks down. The stories that had allowed for the beginning of connection among people begin to disappear, and a nascent internationalist perception (an internationalism that had empowered Virginia) recedes back into simplistic divisions of "black and white" (218), back into conventionalism—imperialist "form" inscribed in the flesh of individuals.

It is then that we are lulled by the entrance of the black, male, first-person narrator—no more customary (but behind-the-scenes) authorial omniscience guides the story—who seems to be the "native other" to the editor. This "I" "tells" the remainder of the narration, but his assumption of control has been complicated by the editor's prior presentation of him—the reader hears the echo of the words "unmanageable," "barbaric," and "uncontrollable" at his entrance; the struggle between these two voices is set up. The reader steps into a tug-of-war between the editor, who insists upon closure, and the narrator, holding out for indeterminacy or (in some cases) a turnabout of form and meaning.

This would-be civilizing function of the editor is manifested in his attempt to control the story: the narrator's story generates "too much" indeterminacy, which in turn threatens to undermine the certainty of conventional symbols and constructs. The editor's attempt, however, is turned on its head. His demand for narrative clarity and traditionally stated realism is decentered. In the first interruption (following the various beginnings of the story) the editor questions and the narrator answers with a nonanswer that nonetheless foregrounds the hidden demand made on the text by the editor:

A point of information. What has form to do with caste restrictions?

Everything.

You are saying you want to be white?

A narrator needs as much access to the world as the advocates of that mythology.

You are ashamed then of being black?

Only of not being nimble enough to dodge other people's straight-jackets.

Are you not too much obsessed here with integration?

I was cursed with a healthy imagination.

What have caste restrictions to do with imagination?

Everything.

A point of information. What is your idea of personal freedom?

Unrestricted access to new stories forming.

Have you paid sufficient attention to the forming of this present one?

Once upon a time there was a wedding in San Francisco.

(220)

The editor's first interruption asks a question about explicit statements, about explicit explanations, that the narrator refuses to make. Throughout such interruptions, the narrator carries out both his resistance to the attempts of the editor to impose form on him as well as his own more subtle civilizing project in regard to the editor. The resistance itself, as in this case, often takes the shape of what seems to be a non sequitur, a seemingly direct answer that nonetheless refuses to answer the question: "Once upon a time there was a wedding in San Francisco"—a response so direct that it skips the metalanguage of an answer to the editor's question and goes so directly to a conventional narrative form that it parodies the demand of the editor's question. After all, what does "once upon a time" mean? Is it here? Is it true? Is it now? What could "there was" possibly mean in this context? It introduces a "dummy" topic that demonstrates that conventional and privileged forms do not "tell" us anything and that suppresses the principals of the wedding while introducing a conventional ritual in place of answering the editor's demand to make the story conventional. It cuts off a discussion with a narrative "red herring."

Here and elsewhere, the narrator, while resisting the pressure to impose control on this narrative and to clarify it, "teaches" the editor. While refusing to alter his mode of discourse, he forces the editor either to accept his own ignorance (his inability to "read" the narrator's language) or to "read" (or at least indicate his consciousness of) the narrator's indirectness. By the end of the story the editor's inability to do either makes him break down into unanswered hysteria. His final line (and that of the story also) is one last reiteration of his customary refrain: "Comment is unclear. Explain. Explain" (241). To this exhortation there is no response. The editor is outside of the text's discourse—left in the darkness of his uninterrogated whiteness. The editor "believes in" conventional form and can't accept the narrator's advocacy of other constructs; he refuses to acknowledge the surfacing of formerly repressed "otherness."

The narrator's more directly civilizing project comes into play with his interaction with Paul, the white male protagonist who is the new "native other," who needs the "light" of darkness, of knowledge of black people, of black culture. The narrator reverses the colonizer/native relationship and describes Paul in the protective language (normally associated with the "other") reminiscent of that which Ralph Ellison uses in order to establish invisibility as a beachhead for subversive activity. The narrator (now the black colonizer) sets out to the "territory," to the frontier—to California—repeating in North American terms the journey across the borders of civilization to a more fluid, less civilized place, a place where social formations have not yet cohered into the "old ways."

It is here, in the territory's fluid possibilities, that the text turns a spotlight on the tendency of members of the dominant group to turn an exoticizing and commodifying gaze on the "native" and artifacts of that "native's" culture—a gaze that nonetheless remains completely blind to the political and material reality of the "native." Paul, a man of the prairie, with "dead Indians living in his eyes" (263), must remake himself in international terms in order to see past his own exoticizing gaze. He has to learn to "see" Virginia (get an earlier set of dead "natives" out of his eyes) in order to save his marriage to her—a black figure of power, a teller of stories with an international flavor, and the figure who names and defines.

The narrator undertakes to bring to Paul's attention the assumptions underlying his way of seeing and his refusal of sight—an intrasubjective evaluation. Such politicization is absolutely necessary if the marriage is to withstand the pressure from Paul's conventionally racist father. The narrator attempts a warning:

> I said, "Someone is coming here to claim you. Soon you may surprise even yourself. While there is still time, you must force the reality of your wife into your father's mind and run toward whatever cover it provides."

I felt bad for having intruded into his story, but there was a point I wanted very much for him to see. I pointed toward a Nigerian ceremonial mask nailed to the wall just over the kitchen door. The white light from the bulbs above us glowed on the brown polished wood of the mask. "Do you think it's beautiful?" I asked.

Paul sipped his wine. He said, "It's very nice. Ginny bought it from a trader in Ibadan. There's a very good story behind it." I said, "But do you think it's beautiful?"

Then he looked at me with great emotion in his eyes. "It's nice," he said. I said, "You are a dealer in art. You have extraordinary taste. But your shop is in a small town. You want to sell this mask by convincing your best customer it is beautiful and of interest to the eye. Every other dealer in town says it is ugly. How do you convince the customer and make a sale?"

I said to Paul, "You have enlisted in a psychological war."

(228)

Paul fails. At that time, he could not remake his aesthetic judgment even within the terms of commodity culture. He would attempt to "sell" the mask by virtue of an exotic narrative—it has "a very good story behind it"—but his "values" do not allow him to "see" that it is beautiful. By allegorical extension, Paul fails to communicate Virginia's value to his middle-class, provincial father. Out of his frustration and anger he asks the narrator what "nigger" *really* means to him and hangs up angrily when the narrator answers: "A descendant of Proteus, an expression of the highest form of freedom" (233). The narrator has responded with a version of the truth: there isn't *one* or *a* nigger, but a Protean mass of definitions, a historically specific set of deployable constructions. Yet Paul must generate a narrative about the mask (or, at least, generate a sales pitch) that can explain its beauty, so as to teach his entrepreneurial father to complicate his notions of "blackness," to "see" Virginia.

Paul's making of himself represents more than a bourgeois individualistic journey to a better self. His racial politicization, which is the thing at stake here, is part of the text's attempt to deconstruct his "innocence," the political privilege of the powerful—an innocence that allows the ideology of white racial stratification to remain unchallenged while certain white individuals simply parade their idiosyncratic tolerance, a tolerance incongruent with racism's history. The explicit ground upon which Paul's remaking is engaged is the need for him to understand and communicate a new set of aesthetics. A system of aesthetics, however, is only the artistic arm of the dominant culture's law. At stake in his increased consciousness is the undermining of the construction of race.

The narrative foregrounds the sign "nigger" as an ideological construction and reclaims it as a sign of affirmation. Aimé Césaire describes a similar moment in his explanation of the origins of "negritude": "That's when we adopted the word negre, as a term of defiance. It was a defiant name. To some extent it was a reaction of enraged youth. Since there was shame about the word negre, we chose the word negre" (74). Reconstructing "nigger" is part of the landscape of African-American self-imagining and an indication of deployments of rhetorical art. When Paul shouts accusingly at the narrator that "nigger" is what the narrator is when he thinks of himself as a work of art, Paul is speaking more truth than he knows. Yes, "nigger" is art, participatory art, creative manipulation of available materials with political intent. The focus is not on what a "nigger" is (classic or otherwise) but on what a "nigger" does—definition by practice, by relation to sociopolitical requirements. In a sharp piece of vernacular indirection, the text tells us that "nigger" equals art, a notion that eventually literally "gags" the editor.

Paul must act in this discursive work or his and Virginia's domesticity, as well as what their domesticity represents—a personally and politically engaged world order—is threatened. He has to learn to be part of a meditation that can form the necessary background for a "classic kind of nigger" and to be a fit consort for Virginia—a woman complicated enough to resist the reification implied in the state of "honorary whiteness" for her soon-to-be-born child, a state offered by the stringently conditioned initial response to her of Paul's father (281). She realizes her own ability to "make enough elbow room" for herself and for her complexities, including her blackness (281), and it is she who decenters the colonial sign "nigger," but she alone cannot make that marriage.

Virginia, Paul, and their relationship are part of the text's play with notions of "star-crossed lovers" (a category into which interracial mésalliances conventionally fall). The narrator attempts to alert Paul to the conventional narrative formulas for such relationships: "I can understand your father's worry. According to convention, one of you is supposed to die, get crippled for life, or get struck down by a freak flash of lightning while making love on a sunny day" (226). But what resonates are the political ramifications and possibilities represented by an interracial marriage. The text ironically presents the ingredients of the old formula with a fascinating twist: the black, male narrator, while aware of his own vulnerabilities in matters of storytelling, still attempts to mold the white male's political consciousness in order to help this couple maintain the kind of relationship that foregrounds some of black and white America's most salient fears in order to subvert those

fears. Within the terms of white supremacy, what is race, finally, if it is not completely delineated and contained by biological difference? An interracial relationship that results in children is at least the heterosexual deconstruction of a false metanarrative. Moving outside of that economy, the story asks another question: What is the meaning of race as a legal and geographical construct? And, given race as a construct, what is being represented in an interracial marriage and its issue—the mulatto? This relationship is the troubled ground for a consideration of the effects of the public and political hegemonic pressure of racism (and its manifestation in aesthetics) on something as private and personal as a romantic relationship, and for a consideration of the demands on private identity of increased racial consciousness. At the same time, the story critiques individual postures of defensive reaction. When Paul snaps at the narrator in anger, "You think I'm a racist," reinscribing a conventional political narrative, the required response is far more complicated than a simple yes or no could be.

V

The story's deliberate subversion of itself remains constant. Within its frame, stories have potential to save lives and allow for connection. But the narrative self-consciously admits its own inadequacies as well as the narrator's own inadequacies and occasional lack of vision or interest: "I did not think they had a story worth telling," he says at one point (227). In the face of his inadequacy, he falls back on an assertion of disdain based on personal aesthetics. He tries to pull back from the narration, at the point where Virginia reduces her own history to conventional rugged bourgeois individualism, by recourse to the prop of all inept narrators—a cliché: "Life is tough all right" (237).

Neither this narrative nor this narrator is part of a pattern for unproblematic and centered control, for a unified subject. The story is, however, a sure ground for exploration, for problematizing, and for decentering. The narrative decenters the authority of Western tradition and declines to replace it with another authority, not even narrative authority. It suggests, instead, the power and problems of attempts to create indeterminate space for the enactment of human imagination.

"Elbow Room" is not only an anticolonialist text that deconstructs the Manichaean dichotomies that posit the "native other" as a savage in need of the civilizing benefits of Western culture; it does so within the African-American vernacular "signifying" structure to which I referred above. Such a structure undoes the idea of a narrative even as it generates one; it engages the notion of a narrator telling a story that is the site of struggle within an editor.

Finally, who is telling this story? The narrator? Or the editor, who is attempting to deliver the "essence" of a story told by a black narrator about an interracial marriage, a story that questions notions of racial essence? Trying to both deliver and restrain something as slippery as essence is tricky, and the editor delivers more than he knows. And whose story is it? That of the protagonists? That of the editor, who demands constant translation, clarification, and commentary? Does the story belong to the narrator who resists certain narrative demands and questions even as he signifies on those demands and delivers, after a fashion, a story? Or does it slip out of everyone's grasp?

VI

From the idea that the self is not given to us, I think that there is only one practical consequence: we have to create ourselves as a work of art.

Michel Foucault

Indirection and playfulness characterize African-American signifying and the story **"Elbow Room."** The story constitutes the ground on which the battle over narrative aesthetics is yet another staging area for the same imperialist appropriations that govern land seizures and racial constructions. It indirectly states its intention of challenging the power of dynamics of conquest and aesthetics in the beginning with the epigraph taken from William Carlos William's "The Discovery of Kentucky":

Boone's genius was to recognize the difficulty as neither material nor political but one purely moral and aesthetic.

Where this epigraph argues that questions of aesthetics not only are morally binding but are the *only real* questions, the *Sun*'s language (quoted at the beginning of this essay) gives the game away: stories with narrative closure are as responsible for maintaining power as navies and white supremacy. And **"Elbow Room"** signifies on the idea of "Boone's genius" and unmasks it as a gloss for appropriation; to consider questions of aesthetics, or race, and not admit the power dynamics or material imperialism masked by such considerations—the message of Boone's discovery—is to leave the metanarrative unchallenged.

The nexus of class power and aesthetics is thematized at the point where the narrator, after visiting a recent prison parolee who has internalized prison, attends a prison reform party given by a female member of the bourgeoisie:

This woman looked me straight in the eye while denouncing prisons with a passionate indignation. Periodically, she swung her empty martini glass in a confi-

dent arc to the right of her body. There, as always, stood a servant holding a tray at just the point where, without ever having to look, my hostess knew a perfect arc and a flat surface were supposed to intersect. . . . I began to laugh.

(233-34)

The passage emphasizes the lock that order and constraint have on the interaction between the privileged and the objects of their largess, between aesthetics and politics. In other words, **"Elbow Room"** brings together narrative conventions, racial construction, aesthetics, and the dynamic of imperialist appropriativeness that is their subtext.

And this story vernacularly "loudtalks" in the presence of "the man"—the powerful white restrictor of other-than-conventional forms. The narrator addresses race issues that literally are outside the purview of this white gaze, a gaze finally made powerless because, while the editor simply does not "get it" (does not understand), the story is told anyway.

The narrative comments indirectly on imposed notions of reality and argues against the imposition of form, doing so by parodying such form: "Once upon a time there was a wedding." As part of its mode of indirection, it signifies on or revises tropes of other African-American texts.[8] From the beginning, **"Elbow Room"** pays tribute to Ralph Ellison's theorizing about the stranglehold of apolitical American modernism when it restates the phrase "morality of technique" (taken from Ellison's "Twentieth Century Fiction and the Black Mask of Humanity") in order to foreground form as the aesthetic arm of Anglo-American hegemony. Further, it tropes or revises the unnamed narrator of *Invisible Man* by making its own unnamed narrator the vehicle of other persons' stories while keeping him extraordinarily and didactically visible, and makes of "nigger"—the Protean shape-changer—a revised trope of Ellison's "invisibility": "nigger" here is "an expression of freedom." The idea of a Protean "nigger" is the theoretical equivalent of Ellison's Rinehart. And finally, the narrative revises Ishmael Reed's *Mumbo Jumbo* by unnaming the Western tradition parodied more directly by Reed: the Wallflower Order, the Atonists. In this text, however, that tradition is never described in its various named (or even renamed) aspects; it is left conspiratorially anonymous, but fought as the shadow everyone always already knows.

"Elbow Room" signifies on the concerns of the earlier integrationist poetic critics whose guiding assumption was that black content could be simply reclothed in traditional (i.e., Euro-American "civilized") forms. In the terms of **"Elbow Room"** such cross-dressing would be tantamount to the designation of Virginia Valentine's baby as an "honorary white." Instead, the narrative rejects the elimination of the black-white problem via black transformation into "honorary status."

The story indirectly calls into question the concerns of the black aesthetic critics by complicating notions of "blackness" or "nigger" and suggesting instead that such ideas rest on more than simple reaction to white culture or tradition. True to its decentering mode, however, **"Elbow Room"** does not offer an answer, only grounds for the discussion of component parts.

The narrative speaks more directly to the concerns of African-American theorists as it questions the big issues addressed above in terms of material about which we can theorize within or outside the form of a text. And it explores the materials in terms of who is, or what social categories are, changed by the form. The phrase written on the back of the photograph of the American family gothic turned on its head (black woman, white male, mulatto child)—"He will be a *classic* kind of nigger"—theorizes about intentionality, artisticness.

If "nigger" is a societal construct, then "classic kind of nigger" reconstructs, or unfixes, what "nigger" has been in the heart of the hegemonic culture. "Nigger," according to Kimberly Benston, "is a mechanism of control" that "subsumes the complexities of human existence into a tractable sign" (156-57). Reclaiming "nigger," reconstructing it by unmasking its constructedness, is a way to unmake the category; it is what Virginia does. "Classic kind of nigger" is both a new and an old story, a result of a dialectical engagement with political history. It alludes to the classic grandfather of *Invisible Man* who knew the power of folk wisdom to create, within a racist culture, a screen behind which maneuverability was possible. But the phrase also alludes to the consequences of a new attempt to resist definitions: a "classic kind of nigger." It is a discursive entity that encourages an examination of the question behind the pretense of a shared history, a mythology about the American black "other." "Classic kind of nigger" subverts the expectations evoked by the sign "nigger" by forcing an awareness of intentioned difference: a black undermining of a Eurocentric sense of what such a sign represents. It also takes "nigger" back to its older (i.e., African) terrain not as the nostalgic nationalist dream against which Fanon warns, but as a way, as *Beloved* puts it, to re-remember a particular history and its implication: a classic tenacity like that of African-Americans who lived through centuries of slavery or faced down racist sheriffs, attack dogs, and tear gas; a classicism like that of the African mask—one that demands a change in the gaze of the onlooker for recogni-

tion to occur, the kind of change apparent in Paul at the end, a father "who sees with both eyes." Classic niggers can see around corners. **"Elbow Room"** is paradigmatic in its exploration of the subversive possibilities that inhere in its reappropriation.

If interracial sexual relations have been the nightmare that embodies the sexual and racial paranoia of a white patriarchal society, then the "happy family" ending is vernacular signifying at its most surgical. The mulatto is reclaimed by the black half of the newly constructed interracial "family" as "nigger," and the notion of race as a societal construction is further complicated by biological combination. Or, as Hazel Carby argues in regard to Frances E. Harper's *Iola Leroy*: "[H]istorically the mulatto, as narrative figure, has two primary functions: as a vehicle for an exploration of the relationship between the races and, at the same time, an *expression* of the relationship between the races. The figure of the mulatto should be understood and analyzed as a narrative device of mediation" (89). The mulatto is finally a sign. The representation of a possibly nontragic mulatto allows the issue of race to escape the containment implied by physical difference and permits a burlesque of the Manichaean dichotomy of colonizer subject and colonized other, especially ironic in view of the historical context of the black woman as the producer of the essential slave "goods." Virginia Valentine, herself an heir to the complicated, rhetorically powerful, and subversive African-American populist techniques of folk culture, produces, in the context of American racial politics, the embodiment of semantic and material complexity: a mulatto child born into his mother's troping possibility—"a classic kind of nigger."

Naming this child Daniel, then, is the text's mulatto reappropriation of the imperialistic mission of Daniel Boone, which was referred to in the epigraph that begins the story. It is an act that expropriates the explorer/conqueror position and name and that underscores the text's "play" with Euro-American territorial and cultural will to power. Daniel Boone, the great American mythic, imperialist figure who is domesticated by this text, becomes Daniel P. Frost, a "classic nigger" who deconstructs "nigger" as a social construction—classic in expressing the relationship between the two parts of the racial dyad. Daniel Frost = Daniel Boone is an equation that describes an act of counterimperialism: taking back the group's consciousness and the "white" father's patrimony as well.

VII

According to Homi Bhabha, within the colonialist/European literary tradition, it is the discovery of the book that marks the intrusion of light into darkness; the world of God, truth, or art creates the conditions for a beginning, a practice of history of narrative (145).⁹ Within the terms of this economy, the book is the supreme signifier of authority, culture, light, and reason (146). **"Elbow Room"** is not the "book," the narrative, the ur-text. It is antinarrative if by narrative we mean a form that poses as its own supreme signifier.

Houston Baker has written: "Fixity is a function of power. Those who maintain place, who decide what takes place and dictate what has taken place, are power brokers of the traditional. The 'placeless,' by contrast, are translators of the non-traditional. . . . Their lineage is fluid, nomadic, transitional" (202). **"Elbow Room"** is a text of such flux; it moves along an axis of guerrilla-like mobility.

I refer to "shuckin' off" in my title. By that I mean the story shrugs aside, refocuses, jive talks the *narrative* other, complicates the "native other," and, in fact, reconstitutes that "other" object as shifting and fragmentary subject, all of which deconstructs the grounds for attribution of an "other" as a form or as an idea that results from the imposition of civilization. In *other* words, the texts makes some elbow room for the work of resisting the imperialism disguised in aesthetics.

VIII

"Elbow Room" is, in many ways, still a text about boys talking to boys and about competing to be "father"; while the narrator seems to revere Virginia, the real skeleton of this text comprises the narrator, the editor, Paul, and his father. It is, however, more complicated than—or at least different from—a buddy cop film. One does not need to call it counterhegemonic in the fullest sense to be able to map its resistances. It has its own limitations: as I pointed out earlier, while it does focus on a romantic and domestic heterosexual relationship as a site for political representation, the male narrator *assists* the female in *her* nurturing—after her marriage he does not imagine her doing anything else. And while it tropes bourgeois entrepreneurial capitalism by continuing the flow of Paul's father's "capital" through a mulatto grandson—thereby representing a moment of revenge against white-supremacist, patriarchal anxieties about the purity of "bloodlines," ironically twisting the patrimonial procession of flesh and assets—it stops short of any radical, general redistribution of the wealth. Paul and Virginia exist in an opaque world that excludes both the details of their respective employments and their reactions to the possibility of inheritance from the father. Still, the end of the "story" places them in rural Tennessee, where Virginia's folks live—the rural lumpen—and leaves open its and their resolution.

My intention in "reading" this story was to reclaim an underread (even within African-American literary circles) literary artifact as a way of describing possible African-American deployments of postmodernism in cultural practice as well as African-American strategies for revising a discourse that, notwithstanding the tendentiousness of voices on all its sides, has yet to speak to various differences as much as it speaks "about" the idea of them.

Notes

1. Weiner's piece was originally written for the *Nation* as part of his discussion of the Paul de Man affair. Weiner's language was recently repeated by Lipsitz.

2. I am not always sanguine about that project: I understand the motivating force behind Michele Wallace's question, "[C]an black women survive another dose of 'Black Pride?'" (106)—or, I might add, another dose of black male anxiety over the loss (and for them it was always illusory) of their authority?

3. While I agree with West generally, I do not draw the line that divides politically inflected and non-politically inflected postmodernism at national boundaries—we have homegrown conservative postmodernist villains, and I cannot believe that the French do not number among them those engaged in politically inflected postmodernism.

4. I choose to gender the editor as male, given that the function of the editor in this text is colonizer of the narrative and gatekeeper for literary master tropes, keeper of the word(s).

5. These are Baker's categories. He describes the first era of African-American critical tradition as the era of "integrationist poetics," an era that privileged African-American literary formal indistinguishability from Euro-American literature as the proper mode for African-American production. The second era of the critical tradition was that of the black aesthetic critics who privileged representation of the lower and working classes of African-American people as the source and core of black art. This era represented an important paradigm shift, according to Baker, in which "blackness" was posed as a fundamental condition of "artisticness." The third and current era is that of the "reconstructionist" critics who involve themselves with cultural, anthropological, historical, and language matters in terms of theoretical frameworks. These three eras of criticism are, of course, strategies and responses to hegemonic culture and politics. I use "hegemony" here to mean a state of affairs in which the "natives" (or the

"native others") accept and participate in, to varying degrees, some version of the colonizer's system of values, attitudes, morality, and institutions. The first era (albeit with some important exceptions) centered on an internalization of Euro-American aesthetics and the second (again, with important exceptions) on confrontation with those aesthetics and attempts to work out alternatives from the marginalized perspective. The third and present era, it seems to me, is one in which many critics of African-American literature are attempting to delineate counterhegemonic literary poetics that do not reduce themselves to celebrations of romantic essentials of a single African-American cultural practice or tradition.

6. I refer here to Henry Louis Gates's history, delineation, and theory of African-American signifying articulated in *The Signifying Monkey*. Gates's analysis is useful as a way to specify African-American cultural practice, although he places his analysis in the service primarily of uncovering intertextual "histories" while I am also interested in using vernacularity as a way to describe African-American language play as theory-making in this text and in others. Additionally, Gates's study glosses over the politics of the vernacular both between African- and Euro-American cultures and within African-American culture—across gender lines, for example.

7. That the African-American literary-critical tradition has been male-centered, predominantly male-articulated, and male-restrictive in terms of literary production and criticism has been a truism the complexities of which critics such as Hazel Carby, Hortense Spillers, Gloria Hull, Deborah McDowell, Mary Helen Washington, and others are presently exploring.

8. Lee Quinby's work on American aesthetics brought the epigraph from Foucault to my attention. I think it especially apt here.

9. See Gates, *The Signifying Monkey*, for explanation of tropes of African-American intertextual revision.

10. I find this aspect of Bhabha's work very useful, although I agree generally with JanMohamed that this study does not take seriously enough the power differentials between colonial subject and colonial "object" or "native other."

Works Cited

Arac, Jonathan. *Critical Genealogies: Historical Situations for Postmodern Literary Studies.* New York: Columbia University Press, 1987.

Baker, Houston. *Blues, Ideology, and Afro-American Literature.* Chicago: University of Chicago Press, 1984.

Belsey, Catherine. "Constructing the Subject: Deconstructing the Text." In *Feminist Criticism and Social Change,* ed. Judith Newton and Deborah Rosenfelt, 45-64. New York: Methuen, 1985.

Benston, Kimberly. "I Yam What I Yam: The Topos of (Un)naming in Afro-American Literature." In *Black Literature and Literary Theory,* ed. Henry Louis Gates Jr., 151-72. New York: Methuen, 1984.

Bhabha, Homi. "Signs Taken for Wonders: Questions of Ambivalence and Authority under a Tree Outside Delhi, May 1817." *Critical Inquiry* 12, no. 1 (1985): 145-65.

Cabral, Amilcar. *Return to the Source: Selected Speeches of Amilcar Cabral.* Ed. African Information Service. New York: Monthly Review, 1973.

Carby, Hazel V. *Reconstructing Womanhood: The Emergence of the Afro-American Woman Novelist.* New York: Oxford University Press, 1987.

Césaire, Aimé. *Discourse on Colonialism.* Trans. John Pinkham. New York: Monthly Review, 1972.

Elam, Diane. "Irresistible Resistance." *Novel: A Forum for Fiction* 23, no. 2 (winter 1990): 212-17.

Fanon, Frantz. *The Wretched of the Earth.* New York: Grove, 1968.

Foster, Hal, ed. *The Anti-aesthetic: Essays on Postmodern Culture.* Port Townsend, Wash.: Bay, 1983.

Fox, Robert. *Conscientious Sorcerers: The Black Postmodernist Fiction of LeRoi Jones/Amiri Baraka, Ishmael Reed, and Samuel R. Delaney.* Westport, Conn.: Greenwood Press, 1987.

Fraser, Nancy, and Linda Nicholson. "Social Criticism without Philosophy: An Encounter between Feminism and Postmodernism." In *Universal Abandon: The Politics of Postmodernism,* ed. Andrew Ross, 83-104. Minneapolis: University of Minnesota Press, 1988.

Gates, Henry Louis, Jr. *The Signifying Monkey: A Theory of Afro-American Literary Criticism.* New York: Oxford University Press, 1988.

Hall, Stuart. "On Postmodernism and Articulation: An Interview with Stuart Hall." *Journal of Communication Inquiry* 10, no. 2 (summer 1986): 45-60.

Harris, Wilson. "Fossil and Psyche." In *Explorations: A Selection of Talks and Articles, 1966-1981,* ed. Hena Maes-Jelinek, 96-112. Mundelstrup, Denmark: Dangaroo, 1981.

Harvey, David. *The Condition of Postmodernity: An Inquiry into the Origins of Cultural Change.* Cambridge: Basil Blackwell, 1989.

Hebdige, Dick. *Hiding in the Light: On Images and Things.* New York: Routledge, 1988.

James, Henry. "The Art of Fiction." In *Partial Portraits,* 377-408. Westport, Conn.: Greenwood Press, 1970.

———. *The Art of the Novel: Critical Prefaces.* Ed. R. P. Blackmur. London: Scribner's, 1948.

Jameson, Fredric. "Modernism and Imperialism." In *Nationalism, Colonialism, and Literature,* ed. Terry Eagleton, Fredric Jameson, and Edward W. Said, 43-68. Minneapolis: University of Minnesota Press, 1990.

———. *Postmodernism; Or, the Cultural Logic of Late Capitalism.* Durham, N.C.: Duke University Press, 1991.

———. "Postmodernism: Or, the Cultural Logic of Late Capitalism." *New Left Review* 146, no. 1 (July-August 1984): 53-92.

JanMohamed, Abdul. "The Economy of Manichean Allegory: The Function of Racial Difference in Colonialist Literature." In *"Race," Writing, and Difference.* Ed. Henry Louis Gates Jr. Chicago: University of Chicago Press, 1986.

———. "Humanism and Minority Literature: Toward a Definition of Counter-hegemonic Discourse." *Boundary 2* 13, no. 1 (1984): 281-99.

Jardine, Alice. *Gynesis: Configurations of Woman and Modernity.* Ithaca, N.Y.: Cornell University Press, 1985.

Kelly, Robin G. "'Comrades, Praise Gawd for Lenin and Them!' Ideology and Culture among Black Communists in Alabama, 1930-1935." *Science and Society* 52, no. 1 (spring 1988): 59-82.

Kipnis, Laura. "Feminism: The Political Conscience of Postmodernism?" In *Universal Abandon: The Politics of Postmodernism,* ed. Andrew Ross, 149-66. Minneapolis: University of Minnesota Press, 1988.

Lipsitz, George. "Listening to Learn and Learning to Listen: Popular Culture, Cultural Theory, and American Studies." *American Quarterly* 2, no. 4 (December 1990): 615-36.

Lyotard, Jean-François. *The Postmodern Condition: A Report on Knowledge.* Trans. Geoff Bennington and Brian Massumi. Minneapolis: University of Minnesota Press, 1984.

McPherson, James Alan. *Elbow Room.* Boston: Little, Brown, and Co., 1977.

Neal, Larry, and Amiri Baraka, eds. *Black Fire: An Anthology of Afro-American Writing.* New York: William Morrow, 1968.

Owens, Craig. "The Discourse of Others: Feminists and Postmodernism." In *The Anti-aesthetic: Essays on Postmodern Culture,* ed. Hal Foster, 57-82. Port Townsend, Wash.: Bay Press, 1983.

Robbins, Bruce, ed. *Intellectuals: Aesthetics, Politics, Academics.* Minneapolis: University of Minnesota Press, 1990.

Ruskin, John. *The Works of John Ruskin.* Vol. 3. Ed. E. T. Cook and Alexander Wedderburn. London: George Allen; New York: Longman, Green, 1903.

Said, Edward W. "Yeats and Decolonialization." *Nationalism, Colonialism, and Literature,* ed. Terry Eagleton, Fredric Jameson, and Edward W. Said, 69-95. Minneapolis: University of Minnesota Press, 1990.

Spillers, Hortense J. "Mama's Baby, Papa's Maybe: An American Grammar Book." *Diacritics* 17, no. 2 (summer 1987): 65-81.

Spivak, Gayatri. "The Post-modern Condition: The End of Politics?" In *The Post-colonial Critic: Interviews, Strategies, Dialogues,* ed. Sarah Harasym, 17-34. New York: Routledge, 1990.

Stephanson, Anders. "Interview with Cornel West." In *Universal Abandon? The Politics of Postmodernism,* ed. Andrew Ross, 269-87. Minneapolis: University of Minnesota Press, 1988.

Wallace, Michele. "Michael Jackson, Black Modernisms and 'The Ecstasy of Communication.'" In *Invisibility Blues: From Pop to Theory,* 77-110. New York: Verso, 1990.

West, Cornel. "The Dilemma of the Black Intellectual." *Cultural Critique* 1 (fall 1985): 109-24.

———. "The New Cultural Politics of Difference." *October* 53 (summer 1990): 93-109.

FURTHER READING

Criticism

Beavers, Herman. *Wrestling Angels into Song: The Fictions of Ernest J. Gaines and James Alan McPherson.* Philadelphia: University of Pennsylvania Press, 1995, 275 p.

    Book-length collection of essays on McPherson's fiction.

Champion, Laurie. "Assimilation versus Celebration in James McPherson's 'The Story of a Dead Man' and James Baldwin's 'Sonny's Blues.'" *Short Story* 8, no. 2 (fall 2000): 94-106.

Compares McPherson's portrayal of self-destructive lifestyles and familial relationships in "The Story of a Dead Man" with James Baldwin's in "Sonny's Blues."

Cox, Joseph T. "James Alan McPherson (1943-)." In *Contemporary Fiction Writers of the South: A Bio-Bibliographical Sourcebook,* edited by Joseph M. Flora and Robert Bain, pp. 311-19. Westport, Conn.: Greenwood Press, 1993.
　　Examines McPherson's background and his primary thematic concerns.

Kurtzleben, James. "James Alan McPherson." In *A Reader's Companion to the Short Story in English,* ed-

ited by Erin Fallon, et al., pp. 269-74. Westport, Conn.: Greenwood Press, 2001.
　　Focuses on the critical response to McPherson's stories.

Masiki, Trent. "The Burden of Insight: Dramatic Irony and the Rhetoric of Illumination in Selections from *Elbow Room*." *Short Story* 9, no. 1 (spring 2001): 78-87.
　　Considers the function of naïveté and the values of liberal humanism in McPherson's *Elbow Room.*

Vauthier, Simone. "A Modern Version of the Confidence Game: James Alan McPherson's 'Problems of Art.'" *Amerikastudien* 27, no. 2 (1982): 141-55.
　　Focuses on trickery in "Problems of Art."

Additional coverage of McPherson's life and career is contained in the following sources published by Thomson Gale: *Black Literature Criticism Supplement; Black Writers,* **Eds. 1, 3;** *Contemporary Authors,* **Vols. 25-28R;** *Contemporary Authors Autobiography Series,* **Vol. 17;** *Contemporary Authors New Revision Series,* **Vols. 24, 74, 140;** *Contemporary Literary Criticism,* **Vols. 19, 77;** *Contemporary Novelists,* **Eds. 3, 4, 5, 6;** *Contemporary Southern Writers; Dictionary of Literary Biography,* **Vols. 38, 244;** *Encyclopedia of World Literature in the 20th Century,* **Ed. 3;** *Literature Resource Center; Major 20th-Century Writers,* **Eds. 1, 2;** *Major 21st-Century Writers,* **eBook 2005;** *Reference Guide to American Literature,* **Ed. 4;** *Reference Guide to Short Fiction,* **Ed. 2; and** *Short Stories for Students,* **Vol. 23.**

Herman Melville
1819-1891

American short fiction writer, novelist, poet, and non-fiction author.

The following entry provides an overview of Melville's short fiction. For additional information on his short fiction career, see *SSC*, Volume 1; for discussion of the short story "Bartleby the Scrivener," see *SSC*, Volume 17; for discussion of the novella *Billy Budd*, see *SSC*, Volume 46.

INTRODUCTION

Best known as the author of the epic maritime novel *Moby-Dick* (1851), Melville also wrote powerfully rendered short stories that anticipate some of the themes and strategies characteristic of modern American fiction. His stories were among the earliest literary representations to focus on the experiences of people largely ignored by most members of his generation. Melville's tales explore the social and ethical implications of capitalism, slavery, patriarchy, and imperialism in American culture. A fierce but subtle advocate for social justice, Melville typically developed those concerns in his stories through allegory, irony, oblique points of view, and allusive, circuitous language. In this way, Melville managed to insinuate into his narratives unwelcome truths about different forms of oppression. Moreover, rather than appeal to his readers' ideological sympathies and literary expectations, Melville deliberately exploited his contemporaries' misapprehensions and prejudices about class, race, and gender as key elements of his art in order to expose their folly. Melville's writings achieved neither critical nor popular recognition during the author's lifetime or in the decades after his death, but scholars since the 1920s have made Melville one of the most written-about American authors and a major figure of world literature.

BIOGRAPHICAL INFORMATION

The third of eight children, Melville was born in New York City to Maria Gansevoort and Allan Melvill (Maria later added an e to their surname), an importer who managed to give his family a comfortable life. As a boy, Melville attended grammar school in Manhattan until his father's business went bankrupt in 1830 and the family relocated to Albany, New York, where

Melville entered the Albany Academy. His father suffered a mental collapse after another financial failure and died in 1832. Consequently, Melville had to quit school and seek work to help support the family. For the next several years, he held a series of low-paying jobs as a bank clerk, farmhand, store clerk, and rural schoolteacher. In 1838 the family moved upstate to Lansingburgh where Melville completed a surveying course at the local academy with hopes of securing work on the Erie Canal. When that effort failed, Melville found work on the docks of New York City as a cabin-boy on a four-month voyage to Liverpool, England, aboard the merchant ship *St. Lawrence*. Returning in 1840, he searched for work as far west as Illinois and the Mississippi River only to return to the sea. In 1841 Melville shipped out from New Bedford, Massachusetts, aboard the whaling ship *Acushnet*, bound for the South Pacific. In 1842, after eighteen months of brutal working conditions as a whaler, Melville and a shipmate jumped ship at the Marquesas Islands, where they were seized by Typee "cannibals," who dealt with them more humanely than did their superiors aboard the ship. Despite the tribe's kindness, Melville embarked on another whaling expedition a month later. The crew mutinied near Tahiti and Melville was promptly jailed on the island. After escaping, Melville roamed around Tahiti and nearby Eimeo for several weeks until he shipped aboard another whaler, which discharged him in Hawaii. In 1843 he signed on the homeward-bound naval frigate *United States* and arrived in Boston in 1844.

Melville returned to his mother's house, where he began to write fictionalized accounts of his maritime experiences, which resulted in his first novel, *Typee* (1846), and its sequel *Omoo* (1847). These novels proved instantly successful and Melville gained entry into New York's literary circles, regularly contributing reviews and other pieces to leading magazines. In 1847 he married Elizabeth Shaw, the daughter of Massachusetts Supreme Court Chief Justice Lemuel Shaw. In 1849 Melville experimented with formal literary conventions in a third novel about the South Seas, *Mardi*, but this allegorical work baffled reviewers and the public alike, as they expected another realistic novel. Melville complied and quickly published *Redburn* (1849), a novel based on his first sea voyage to Liverpool. In 1850 Melville moved his family to "Arrowhead" farm near Pittsfield, Massachusetts, where author Nathaniel Hawthorne lived. Melville forged an intense relationship with Hawthorne, whom he called "the American Shakespeare" in his essay "Hawthorne and His Mosses." Their friendship eventually waned but not before Hawthorne encouraged Melville to revise his draft of a narrative detailing a whale hunt into an allegorical novel. Heeding his mentor's advice, Melville perfected his technique of fusing fact and symbol in *Moby-Dick,* which became his masterpiece despite drawing little critical notice and meager financial reward. Desperate for both, however, Melville quickly wrote the novel *Pierre* (1852), which also failed critically and commercially. However, Melville found modest success with short stories, most notably publishing "Bartleby the Scrivener," "The Encantadas, or Enchanted Isles," "Benito Cereno," and a serialized novel, *Israel Potter* (1855), all of which first appeared in *Putnam's Monthly.* After the publication of *The Piazza Tales* (1856) and the novel *The Confidence-Man* (1857), Melville published no other prose fiction. Demoralized by what he perceived as the erosion of the public's intellectual rigor by the influence of popular culture, he lost his creative energy and gradually withdrew. In 1856 his father-in-law financed a year abroad in Europe and the Middle East to restore his health. Upon returning to the United States in 1857, he tried to support his family by lecturing on the national circuit until the Civil War erupted. The inheritance he received after his father-in-law died two years later allowed him to move his family to New York City in 1863. In 1866 Melville reluctantly took a political appointment as a customs inspector for the port of New York, a post he held for the next nineteen years. During this time, Melville's wife began to question his sanity and their eldest son committed suicide in 1867. For the rest of his life Melville lived in obscurity although he published some poetry, including *Battle-Pieces* (1866) and the eighteen-thousand-line poem *Clarel* (1876). When he retired from his customs-house work in 1886, Melville continued to write poetry, producing *John Marr and Other Sailors* (1888) and *Timoleon* (1891). More significantly, he began writing fiction again. After Melville died of heart failure in 1891, a nearly complete manuscript of the novella *Billy Budd,* which remained unpublished until 1924, was found among his papers.

MAJOR WORKS OF SHORT FICTION

Most of Melville's short fiction first appeared individually in either *Putnam's Monthly* or *Harper's Monthly* magazines between 1850 and 1856. His stories display the creative tension between the prevailing literary dictum of "art for art's sake" and his own belief that literature is "the Great Art of Telling the Truth" by deliberately subverting formalist conventions. His allegorical tales about the victims of hypocrisy and materialism wrought by capitalism, slavery, imperialism, and patriarchy are often told from the perspective of oblivious narrators who represent genteel society and its smug, elitist, and pious attitudes. Moreover, Melville's fiction aims to unsettle prejudices concerning class, race, and gender by encouraging readers to identify with the narrators. In *The Piazza Tales,* the only collection of short stories published during Melville's career, the tone and purpose of the volume is established by its title story, which was written exclusively to introduce the stories that follow. In "The Piazza Tale," the landlocked sailor narrator, who prefers to filter the ordinary realities of the world around him through the romantic ideals of his imagination, journeys to see Marianna, whom he considers his life's destiny. When he arrives, he finds Marianna impoverished—a circumstance he is ultimately unable to reconcile with his idealism—so he abandons her and returns home without ever admitting the inherent flaws of his approach to living. The next story, "Bartleby the Scrivener," ranks among Melville's most important short fiction. Reflecting Melville's pessimism about his own career at the time of its composition, this story explores the relation between individuality and social responsibility, juxtaposing the capitalistic ethic of Wall Street against the Christian work ethic illustrated by the parable of the talents in St. Matthew's gospel. Narrated by a Wall Street lawyer, "Bartleby the Scrivener" follows the career of the title character, whom the narrator hires to transcribe legal documents. At first, Bartleby quietly works hard at his job, but one day he simply utters "I would prefer not to" when asked to proofread. Bartleby eventually responds to all requests with the same reply, which irritates his colleagues and employer, who speculate about Bartleby's inscrutable behavior. The narrator eventually fires Bartleby, who refuses to accept responsibility for anything and ultimately starves to death in jail, a vagrant.

Another important piece in Melville's canon, "Benito Cereno" is one of the first literary works to treat violent race relations in the Americas. This third-person account is mostly narrated from the perspective of Amasa Delano, the captain of a seal-hunting ship who comes upon a slave revolt off the coast of Chile aboard the *San Dominick,* captained by the title character (though his role as captain is withheld until the story's end when Cereno gives his "Deposition"). At first, Delano misinterprets the situation onboard because of his racism, which the rebels also use to their advantage to prevent discovery of their real identities. Delano realizes the truth of what is happening in time to rescue Cereno and his crew and to help suppress the insurrection. Many critics have attributed the circuitous form of "Benito Cereno," which appeared at the height of the antebellum slavery controversy, to Melville's father-in-law's views on racial segregation and fugitive slaves. One of Melville's most popular stories in his lifetime, "The Lightning-Rod Man" centers on the beliefs and practices of American Christians by manipulating the conventions of the salesman-story genre. Narrated by a

New England bachelor, the allegorical tale recounts the sales pitch of a traveling lightning-rod peddler who, as the story begins, interrupts the narrator in the midst of a reverie on the grandeur of thunder. In the dialogue that ensues, their conversation circles around ethical questions about religion. In the end, the narrator declines to make a purchase following a theological discourse on the history of inoculation.

Originally published under the pseudonym Salvator R. Tarnmoor, "The Encantadas, or Enchanted Isles" comprises ten travel sketches of the Galapagos Islands, which Melville visited once during his time at sea. The general movement of the sketches progresses from a topographical overview through portrayals of particular flora, fauna, and natural phenomena, to accounts of human inhabitants. The narrator often endows the desolate, isolated landscape of the islands with human attributes, lending psychological depth to the sketches. In three of the pieces, the narrator recounts fictional incidents about various humans who temporarily inhabited the islands and their responses to its adverse conditions. These castaways include a Creole adventurer from Cuba, who brutally rules his colonists until they revolt and banish him; a biracial widow named Hunilla, who displays patience, fortitude, and humility until an American ship rescues her; and the evil hermit Oberlus, who cruelly enslaves mutinous sailors until their captains arrive to dispense justice.

A second collection of short stories, *The Apple-Tree Table* (1922), contains most of his other short fiction as well as an essay on the status of American literature, "Hawthorne and His Mosses." The title story, an allegory about two insects that emerge from the dead wood of an old piece of furniture, examines traditional ideas about gender roles perpetrated by patriarchy. Throughout the story the narrator's wife avoids domestic tasks associated with such "feminine" virtues as piety, submissiveness, hospitality, and frugality, attending instead to activities corresponding to "masculine" traits. Reflecting Melville's preoccupation with Hawthorne's literary strategies during the 1850s, "I and My Chimney" concerns the money-hungry ambitions of a wife intent on liquidating architectural elements of her husband's ancestral home, which symbolizes his personal and family identity. After overhearing a rumor about treasure concealed in the chimney, she plots to demolish the house along with the chimney, but the husband ultimately prevails and preserves the house. A parable about social inequality, "Cock-A-Doodle-Doo!" chronicles the narrator's increasing obsession with acquiring his poor neighbor's rooster, Signor Beneventano. After the neighbor rejects multiple offers to purchase the rooster, the narrator resorts to verbal abuse, which then escalates to physical threats. In the end, the neighbor dies under suspicious circumstances as the narrator descends into madness. Another allegorical critique of industrial capitalism and patriarchy, "The Paradise of Bachelors and the Tartarus of Maids" explores the dehumanizing work experiences of two diverse groups of laborers—the bachelor attorneys sequestered in London's Temple-Bar and the factory girls confined in New England's paper mills. In the "Paradise" section, the bachelors indulge their pleasures, engaging in life vicariously through conversation and producing nothing meaningful except obstructions to justice. The narrator's passive tone, slow pace, and indistinct rhetorical purpose in this sketch mirror the bachelors' hollow existence and establish a pattern to which the next story constantly refers. In the "Tartarus" section, the factory girls work for the pleasure of others, endlessly tending insatiable machines and creating reams of new paper to benefit the industry. However, the girls' working conditions provoke a visceral reaction in the narrator, whose allusive language in this section—particularly the dual connotations of the girls' status as "maids" and the animal symbolism alternately associated with both the girls and the machines—reflects the misery and horror of the factory girls' plight.

Set at sea during a war between England and France in the late 1790s, *Billy Budd* recounts the circumstances surrounding an alleged mutiny and the tragic death of a young man. The title character is a handsome, charismatic sailor, whose innocence endears him to his shipmates but also agitates them, especially the ruthless master-at-arms, John Claggart. When he falsely implicates Billy in a supposed conspiracy to mutiny, Billy accidentally kills him. Although Captain Vere sympathizes with Billy's predicament, he fears a real mutiny if he absolves Billy, so he orders a court-martial, which ultimately sentences Billy to hang for murder. Billy willingly accepts the verdict, shouting "God bless Captain Vere" as he plummets from the yardarm. He assumes religious significance for the crew, who view his death in a saintly light. In the novella's resolution, the captain mutters Billy's name as he dies during a battle with the French. Among Melville's most frequently anthologized pieces, *Billy Budd* offers a critique of militarism and the dehumanization it engenders as well as a meditation on the conflict between individuality and social responsibility.

CRITICAL RECEPTION

Melville was initially deemed a minor figure of American literature, but since the 1920s critics have enthusiastically recognized his short fiction as a major factor in the development of the modern short story. Beginning with the publication of *Billy Budd* in 1924 and a number of critical biographies, Melvillian scholarship has elevated the author to canonical status as a leading representative of American letters. Consequently, critics have pursued biographical, historical, cultural, and ideological analysis of his short stories in vast quantities. Among biographical studies, commentators have explored the role and significance of mental illness in Melville's plots and characterizations and have investigated the influence of his friendship with Hawthorne upon his literary technique and themes. Critics have examined the relationship among various elements of Melville's style and thought, particularly the ways his allusive, circuitous language and penchant for allegory engage readers and invest his characterizations with psychological depth. Others have studied Melville's contributions to the nineteenth-century debate among American writers about the defining characteristics of an authentic national literature, and some have focused on attributing to Melville a number of anonymous or pseudonymous stories by comparing their motifs or symbols to those recurring in his novels. Cultural critics have explored his stories within such historical contexts as the economic conditions of the 1840s, the exploitation of workers at the dawn of the industrial era, and the racial injustice perpetrated by American slavery. Historical scholarship has also produced studies linking Melville's themes to contemporaneous political and theological discourse. Although much commentary on Melville's fiction has traditionally perceived misogynistic tendencies, feminist critics have shown how his sympathy for people neglected by society also extends to women as victims of patriarchy. Many critics have attributed the fascination with Melville's writings to his prescient insight into a myriad of problems afflicting contemporary American society ranging from alienation, racism, and violence to ignorance, prejudice, and oppression.

PRINCIPAL WORKS

Short Fiction

The Piazza Tales 1856
The Apple-Tree Table, and Other Sketches 1922
Billy Budd, and Other Prose Pieces 1924
The Portable Melville 1952
The Writings of Herman Melville. 15 vols. 1968-89
Melville's Short Novels: Authoritative Texts, Contexts, Criticism [edited by Dan McCall] 2002

Other Major Works

Typee: A Peep at Polynesian Life, During a Four Months' Residence in a Valley of the Marquesas (novel) 1846

Omoo: A Narrative of Adventures in the South Seas (novel) 1847
Mardi; and a Voyage Thither (novel) 1849
Redburn: His First Voyage; Being the Sailor-Boy Confessions and Reminiscences of the Son-of-a-Gentleman, in the Merchant Service (novel) 1849
White-Jacket; or, The World in a Man-of-War (novel) 1850
Moby-Dick; or, The Whale (novel) 1851
Pierre; or, The Ambiguities (novel) 1852
Israel Potter: His Fifty Years of Exile (novel) 1855
The Confidence-Man: His Masquerade (novel) 1857
Battle-Pieces, and Aspects of the War (poetry) 1866
Clarel: A Poem and Pilgrimage in the Holy Land (poetry) 1876
John Marr and Other Sailors, with Some Sea-Pieces (poetry) 1888
Timoleon, Etc. (poetry) 1891
Journal of a Visit to London and the Continent (journals) 1948
Journal of a Visit to Europe and the Levant (journals) 1955
The Letters of Herman Melville (letters) 1960
Journals (journals) 1989
Correspondence (letters) 1993

CRITICISM

John Allison (essay date spring 1996)

SOURCE: Allison, John. "Conservative Architecture: Hawthorne in Melville's 'I and My Chimney.'" *South Central Review* 13, no. 1 (spring 1996): 17-25.

[*In the following essay, Allison investigates the nature of Melville's preoccupation with Nathaniel Hawthorne, outlining thematic similarities between "I and My Chimney" and three of Hawthorne's tales focusing on patriarchal models of individual, familial, and cultural identity.*]

In *Pierre* (1852) Melville advises his semi-autobiographical writer/protagonist to "thoroughly study architecture." From 1850-1863 Melville lived with one dominating architectural presence—the chimney at Arrowhead. Little wonder, then, that the "realities of architecture" in **"I and My Chimney"** (1856) provoke speculations concerning identity, representation, and meaning in Melville's story.[1] Heavy allusions to three of Hawthorne's sketches of domestic architecture and life—"The Old Manse," "Peter Goldthwaite's Treasure," and "Fire Worship"—suggest that Melville meant to endorse Hawthorne's special brand of conservatism and to maintain a role as Hawthorne's cultural ally.[2] In opposition to intrusive, exploitative, reformist, feminist, and Transcendentalist tendencies that both writers associate with modern times, the writers privilege relics of material culture that represent and preserve a patrician and patriarchal model of individual, familial, and cultural identity. As we shall see, Melville's tale both enshrines Hawthorne as literary mentor and advocates a rhetoric of evasion and resistance against forces of cultural innovation that threaten the self and the symbolic extensions of the self.

In 1970 Edward Rosenberry was the first to highlight a connection between Melville's **"I and My Chimney"** and Hawthorne's work. In "Melville and His Mosses," an article of just four pages, Rosenberry parallels Melville's conclusory words ("for it is resolved between me and my chimney, that I and my chimney will never surrender") with Hawthorne's steadfast defense of "the traditional rallying point" of the hearths near the end of "Fire Worship" and "The Old Manse" (377).[3] While all studies pursuing the Hawthorne/Melville relationship in **"I and My Chimney"** are indebted to Rosenberry, only two of the four pages of the article are devoted to Melville's tale; the article barely suggests the extent and nature of Melville's preoccupation with Hawthorne, a preoccupation at the very heart of Melville's role as creative writer and cultural critic during the mid-1850s.

More specifically, pursuing additional connections is worthwhile for two reasons. First, Melville's story clarifies what Richard Brodhead identifies—in Hawthorne's language—as a crucial determinant of the later Melville's rhetoric of evasion and resistance: to "'hide the man, instead of displaying him'"; the writer becomes a "bearer not of revelation but of mystery itself."[4] This strategy assures the power of text and author not by seeking to "penetrate the depths of more essential reality" but by preserving "power through the secrets" of a sustained mystery.[5] While Brodhead does not examine **"I and My Chimney,"** his description fits the procedure of Melville's narrator rather precisely. A second reason to pursue intertextual connections is that the story places a Hawthornesque rhetoric of evasion and resistance within a larger context of Melville's deep suspicion of the agents of cultural innovation. The victorious narrator continuously evades and resists confidence games meant to strip him of his identity as a traditional male. He wishes to preserve a traditional self-image during a time that, as David Leverenz explains, threatened patrician and patriarchal values with "middle-class male norms of practicality and competitiveness and a suddenly visible female audience."[6] Just as the chimney (which for the narrator is taboo) enshrines Hawthorne, so too it enshrines traditional notions of self, family, and nation.

Rosenberry was right to associate Hawthorne's "The Old Manse" with Melville's **"I and My Chimney."** "The Old Manse" is the prefatory sketch to *Mosses from an Old Manse,* the work which inspired Melville's reverence for Hawthorne's genius. In the sketch, Hawthorne deems the Manse itself "worthy to have been one of the time-honored parsonages of England" (4). Following Hawthorne's peculiar trans-Atlantic conservatism and architectural metaphor of the self, Melville's narrator asserts that "the proper place" for the "old chimney is ivied old England" (356). Here both speakers wish to locate their architectural reference points and patrician identities in a uniquely conservative space—in a country of genealogical and cultural origins. As Robert Ferguson notes, many conservative men of culture in America were threatened by "the dynamism of the expanding nation" and its endless social and intellectual innovations.[7] In response to such threats, many male authors sought refuge in what David Leverenz calls a "posture of meditative laziness, not hardworking ambition."[8] Hawthorne extols the value of "peace and quiet"; he offers readers "rest—rest, in a life of trouble" created by "Young visionaries" and "grayheaded theorists" whose determination to find a "clue" from Emerson makes life a "labyrinth around them" (30). Likewise, Melville's narrator feels a "sabbatical horror of industry" and evades the bustle of his grayheaded wife who, with an "infatuate juvenility," champions a range of trendy theories: "Swedenborgianism, the Spirit Rapping philosophy, with other new views," all symbolized by her plans for architectural innovation (364). While in "The Old Manse" Hawthorne despises "the triteness of novelty" and longs for the "world" to be "petrified and rendered immovable" (32), Melville's narrator abominates an absurd "itch after recently-discovered prospects" (362) and devotes himself to preserve forever "the one grand permanence" (365) symbolized by his "vast square of masonry"—the whole weight of a patriarchal past (357). Each writer yearns for a substantial, impervious, material culture that resists insubstantial, theoretical grounds for change.

Drawing on the plots of three of Hawthorne's tales, Melville sums up the supreme threat to conservative views. The result is a bogus treasure hunt threatening every available relic to satisfy the curiosity, greed, and vanity of a commercial, progressive order. The plot of **"I and My Chimney"** corresponds most obviously to Hawthorne's "Peter Goldthwaite's Treasure" (from *Twice-Told Tales*). Both stories feature treasure seekers determined to convert the ancestry and architecture of a family house into hard cash. Peter Goldthwaite believes that his deceased grandfather and "namesake" had hidden "treasure enough" for a grand modernity in a secret "burial place" within the family mansion (388). As far as Peter is concerned, the "'sooner we have it [house and chimney] all down the better,'" but the agent of conservatism, his old nurse Tabitha, guards the chimney

(387). She declares that she will never feel content with a house lacking a "'chimney corner'" not yet "'black with smoke'" (387). Heedless of her wishes, Goldthwaite breaks into a secret chamber near the chimney, locates a worthless treasure of old commercial papers, and calls for the ruin of his structurally weakened house with the words "'Let it fall!'" (406).

Although **"I and My Chimney"** shifts the genders of seeker and protector and arranges for a happier outcome, the plot and its implications bear remarkable similarity to those of Hawthorne's story. Acting on behalf of the narrator's treasure-hungry wife, Hiram Scribe announces to the narrator that the area of the chimney harbors a "secret chamber" for the "concealment of treasure" (369). This treasure, rumor has it, had been "hidden" by the narrator's "late kinsman," Julian Dacres (369), whose last name is clearly an anagram for "sacred." Like the aged Peter, a person of "high hopes" whose "youth" persists even in the "old embers and ashes" of advanced age (528), the narrator's aged wife "doesn't believe in old age" (361). She entertains little regard for "the realities of architecture" that the narrator appreciates, and she would gladly "demolish" chimney and house to achieve her pecuniary ambitions (360). There are other parallels. Just as Peter explores his "garret" (528), so the wife with "ambition of a mounting order" ascends to the "attic" (363). And just as Peter longs to violate the back kitchen wherein Tabitha presides over the chimney and sustains domestic life by cooking the meals, so the wife yearns to penetrate the chimney "all the way into the dining room in the remote rear of the mansion" (363). Tabitha fails to restrain Peter's destructive drive, but the narrator preserves his home out of respect for its "profound mystery" and "equally profound masonry" (370), which obviously represent his personal and family identity. This outcome testifies, I believe, to the later Melville's wish to champion Hawthorne's conservatism, just as the earlier Melville had wished to champion Hawthorne's "genius" in *Moby-Dick*.

The resonances between "Peter Goldthwaite's Treasure" and **"I and My Chimney"** suggest Melville's concurrence with at least two ideas implied by Hawthorne's tale: the traditional and familial origins of identity, and the visible representation of identity in material culture, especially architecture. A rhetoric of evasion and resistance shields both identity and its symbolic representation. This idea is especially probable in light of correspondences between **"I and My Chimney"** and another of Hawthorne's works, "Fire Worship" (from *Mosses from an Old Manse*). Given the anagram associated with Melville's chimney, the "sacred" character, or "spiritual essence," associated with the hearth in "Fire Worship" deserves special attention (139-40). The sacred character of the hearth, probably based on the actual hearth at the Old Manse, receives repeated amplifi-

cation; for Hawthorne's narrator it represents "the God" of the "fathers" (140). In **"I and My Chimney,"** the attributes of a patriarchal God are hard to miss: the chimney possesses "pre-eminence" (352); it receives the "first fruits" (352); it reigns as the "one great domineering object" (353); it displays "magnitude" and fills an "abundance of space" (355); it "stands upon an independent foundation of its own" (356); it inspires the narrator's temporary but fanatical search for "the light of heaven" within it (357); it opposes the "perverse magic" of destructive innovators (362). Significantly, both narrators bemoan a religious declension accompanied by an emergent cash culture symptomizing apostasy from traditional, patriarchal values. Hawthorne's narrator worries that the innovation of a stove, a cost-saving device, betrays "the sacred trust of the household fire" (145). The consequence of such betrayal is the scattering of the family tribe; "there will be nothing to attract" the "children" of new generations to "one center" (146). In **"I and My Chimney,"** Melville's narrator, victorious where Hawthorne's narrator fails, glories that "one grand central chimney" orients family members, even when they occupy opposing rooms, so that "their feet point to one center" (358).

Both narrators extend an obligation to defend the symbol of sacred patriarchy to the nation as a whole. Outraged that our modern "task" has been "to uproot the hearth," Hawthorne's narrator reminds us that "hearths," like "altars," embody both "a divine idea" and a "mortal truth" inspiring "defiant patriotism"; the hearth becomes a rallying point which "all subsequent ages" ought to "protect with force" (146-47). Employing the obvious rhetoric of politicians concerned about approaching civil war, Melville's narrator similarly defends his "federal stock in the middle of the house" (354); "standing guard" with patriotic fervor, he vows, "I and my chimney will never surrender" (377)[9]

Again drawing on Hawthorne, Melville's narrator clearly resists the temptation to sacrifice patrician privacy to satisfy the public's prying and demystifying curiosity. Here again he echoes Hawthorne. In "The Old Manse," at first Hawthorne describes himself as yet another modern seeker after "intellectual treasure in the old Manse, well worth those hoards of long-hidden gold, which people seek for in moss-grown houses" (4-5). Not unlike the enterprising wife of Melville's tale, Hawthorne believes for a time that "the rear of the house" is promising (5). What he really searches for, of course, is material "for a novel" with "physical substance enough to stand alone" (5), a structure looking forward to the narrator's chimney, which "stands upon an independent basis of its own" (356). In quest of literary materials to satisfy the public's curiosity and to support his family, Hawthorne at one point longs to "open a grave" that is "marked by a small, moss-grown fragment of stone" at the "head" and "feet" of two British soldiers (10). No desecration is beyond him. In **"I and My Chimney,"** the effort to penetrate a "profound mystery" is also linked to both "ingots" and "skulls"—grave robbing (370), and the Hawthorne persona's peculiar eagerness to rummage and dig in the first half of "The Old Manse" is matched by the narrator's temporarily insane impulse to begin "digging round the foundation" in hopes of "striking upon some old, earth-worn memorial" (357) of genealogical origins. Momentarily sharing the tendencies of their communities, both speakers are tempted to rob graves, to violate the material remnants of the self.

Hawthorne's and Melville's narrators, however, come to their senses out of respect for the concealed mystery of sacred interiors—the tombs of the patriarchy. Observing the "rude masonry of chimneys in the garret," Hawthorne grows "too reverent" of the chamber's "dust and cobwebs" to wrest the "secrets" of the place from "obscurity," particularly when he considers the "white-washed apartment," or "Saints' Chamber," where the presence of deceased "holy men seems to linger" (16-17). Here in the Saints' Chamber, complete with its own "fireplace" and "closet," Hawthorne reflects that "a young man might inspire himself with holy enthusiasm and saintly dreams" without invading the actual secrets of the past (17). Similarly, the narrator in **"I and My Chimney"** describes an episode in which he "ascends" to a "gallery," where he confesses "a weakness" identical to Hawthorne's: he cannot help but "cherish the cobwebs" (359). Seeming to mount within "a kind of soaring tower," he draws attention to a "mysterious closet" near the chimney, a closet that quite literally contains spirits—"cordials" benefitting from the chimney's "nurturing" (360). Melville may have in mind the "Manse" passage, as well as the passage in which Peter Goldthwaite locates the one valuable treasure in an otherwise abortive hunt: a "cordial" that Peter's deceased kinsman had walled up in "an old oven" for "unborn" generations to enjoy (401). But whether the allusion is specific or not, like Hawthorne, the narrator eventually concludes that insistent prying is "profane"—"a church-robbing" which can never compensate for loss of reverence (376).

The two works stress that the origins and extensions of the patrician self require protection from exploitative attempts to uncover it. Repeatedly Hawthorne associates the Manse with a "sanctity" conferred by his identification with a "succession of holy occupants"—all ministers (3). A mere "lay occupant" himself, he nevertheless remains keenly aware that "a priest had built" the Manse (3), and although Hawthorne pointedly rejects theological hairsplitting in the former occupant's sermons and tracts, he counts himself "none the less a Christian" in rejecting any simplistic, gnostic "'Open Sesame'" to "disclose treasures, hidden in some unsuspected cave of Truth" (20-21). The sacred, he comes to

realize, is symbolized by the structure, while the sacred itself lives within his capacity to invest objects (and persons) with sacred mystery, his own capacity for reverence. Accordingly, he abandons his search, respecting the "sacred" character of the Manse as a dwelling, a "home" (25) whose treasure at the moment is the Hawthornes themselves, the familial identity "enveloped" by the paradoxical "accessible seclusion" of that home (4). Like his dwelling, Hawthorne carefully withholds "anything too sacredly individual"; that is, he refuses entry to his "inner chambers," where readers might examine his "treasures or rubbish" (32). He "draws to the fireside" as long as possible to resist the "abomination" of a modern stove (29), and he absolutely rejects the modern vogue of self-revelation, the temptation to emulate "one of those supremely hospitable people, who serve up their own hearts delicately fried" (32-33). He becomes a patrician who denies access to a curious and innovating public.

Just as Hawthorne ridicules those who believe that they "have gone wandering, hand in hand with [him], through the inner passages of [his] being" (32), so the narrator in **"I and My Chimney"** ridicules those who become lost in what to them remains a "labyrinthine" architecture—an idiosyncratic "philosophical system" in which they seem "forever going somewhere, and getting nowhere" (364). As all readers of the story know, he takes particular delight in describing the "embarrassed air" of a fashionable suitor who without guidance has "very effectually succeeded in backing himself into a dark pantry, where he carefully shut himself up" (364). But the narrator practices his most deft evasion and resistance on Hiram Scribe, who seeks $500 by tempting the narrator with prospects of a treasure in the chimney. As in "The Old Manse," treasure and family are linked to writing since the name of the popular domestic architect, Hiram Scribe, is both a pun on the character's desires (in a rural accent—"hire 'em") and a reference to the profitable duties of a writer—a "scribe," or clerk, or copyist who writes for a price. Scribe entices the narrator with the possibility of a "secret chamber" harboring a legacy from the narrator's genealogical past (368-69). But, like Hawthorne, the narrator declines the role of an "'eaves-dropping varlet'" who exposes and consumes the "'heart'" of domestic and personal identity (376). Bribing the pecuniary Scribe for a note testifying to the absence of any interior chamber, the narrator determines that, "even if there were a secret closet, secret it should remain, and secret it shall" (376). Interesting in this connection is the fact that Melville died convinced that Hawthorne had always "concealed some great secret, which would, were it known, explain all the mysteries" of Hawthorne's "career."[10] How appropriate that the secret, if one existed, escaped Melville and us.

In none of these works do the writers encourage belief in some literal, indwelling spirit within the projections of the self—architecture, writing, and history. Rather, both writers wish to protect the patrician, authorial self that creates and identifies with such structures. In "The Old Manse," as long as Hawthorne persists in his ironic search for "intellectual treasure," he finds nothing, a point that he stresses: "I found no such treasure; all was dead alike" (19). Melville's narrator develops a similarly skeptical attitude about the supposed contents of his chimney. He suggests that only the knowledge of mortality awaits seekers who madly strike through the wall, as the following exchange between the narrator and his wife indicates:

> "You will get your death one of these days, exploring all about as you do. But supposing there be a secret closet, what then?"
>
> "What then? why what should be in the secret closet but—"
>
> "Dry bones, wife," broke in I with a puff, while the sociable old chimney broke in with another.
>
> (372)

The narrator senses, as Hawthorne had long before, that "no sign of the hidden work" within the work exists (373). In *Pierre,* the protagonist discovers precisely the same emptiness when he searches for the secret of his "soul" and the "world" within his writing; he enters the "central room" of the symbolic "pyramid" and raises the "lid" of the "sarcophagus" to find "no body"—only an absence "appallingly vacant as vast" (284-85). To look for presence within the structure is to misplace the source of meaning and subsequently to devalue the symbol, one's self, and the world.

Melville's narrator in **"I and My Chimney,"** following Hawthorne's lead in "The Old Manse," locates ultimate value not within the literal interior of some symbolic structure but rather within the ego's capacity to project sentiment, significance, and wonder. Hawthorne in "The Old Manse" writes that the "stately edifice" with "its gray, homely aspect" is "sacred" because

> it had been a home, for many years, in spite of all; it was my home, too—and, with these thoughts, it seemed to me that all the artifice and conventionalism of life was but an impalpable thinness on its surface, and that the depth below was none the worse for it.
>
> (25)

To reinforce his idea that things and even persons derive their value for him by virtue of an obscured, overlayered self-projection ("it seemed to me"), Hawthorne goes on to invest the "figure" of a "cloud" with the domestic signification of a household "hound keeping guard" over the Manse (25-26). This sentimental, almost comic image of defense in his sketch of a home

results not only in a cliché of domestic conservatism but, more profoundly, in a completed projection of reverence and act of enshrinement that Leon Chai has found in many other writings by Hawthorne.[11] Hawthorne ends his eulogy of domestic life as follows: "Gazing at this symbol [the cloud/dog above the house], I prayed that the upper influences might long protect the institutions that had grown out of the heart of mankind" (26). Although he apologizes for playing the "egotist" in celebrating his "moss-grown country parsonage" (32), it is his ego, his "I," which informs his dwelling and environs with a domestic and personal significance.

The narrator in **"I and My Chimney"** may allude to Hawthorne's domestic imagery and elusive self-projection at the conclusion of **"I and My Chimney."** In language recalling Hawthorne's cloud/dog, the narrator declares that he is no "misanthrope"; he is "simply standing guard over [his] mossy old chimney," not unlike a faithful household dog (377). Of course, this particular connection may be strained, but in light of the many more credible connections between the writers' works, the parallel is tempting. In any case, a more important connection is the conservative habit of mind shared by the two writers. Whether or not a particular allusion is intended, the narrator, like Hawthorne, invests the chimney and the house it supports with a sacred sentiment. Melville's narrator is determined to preserve the objective representation of his warm, interior self, a determination that is clear in the following description, where his personal, familial, and even sexual identification with the chimney is complete: "I and my chimney are settling together, and shall keep settling, too, till, as in a great feather bed, we shall have settled away clean out of sight" (372-73). A "dozy old dreamer," he enjoys his capacity for self-projection and self-concealment, and his chimney continues to represent the "warm heart" (360). Wishing to share this sensibility, he shuns visitants who want to live in "double houses"—who lack "a proper fraternal feeling" (353).

* * *

When Melville wrote **"I and My Chimney,"** as a thinker and a writer he was alone. His conclusion to the story carries an unmistakable lesson of his isolation. The "world" could not care less about his "philosophical jabber," however impassioned or brilliant (376). As his letter to Hawthorne in February 1851 shows, Melville relished the "pleasure" of Hawthorne's presence when the two men—two smokers—would "discuss the Universe with a bottle of brandy & cigars."[12] In May of the same year, Sophia Hawthorne fondly described how Melville would "speak his innermost about God, the Devil & Life" to Hawthorne and how Melville would "dash his tumultuous waves of thought against Mr. Hawthorne's great, genial, comprehending silences." Hawthorne himself recalled staying up "pretty late into the night" to hear Melville talk of "all possible and impossible matters." Melville loved nothing more than "smoking and talking metaphysics" with Hawthorne.[13]

In **"I and My Chimney"** it may be that permanent figuration of Hawthorne in the story enabled Melville to imaginatively sustain a profoundly reassuring relationship with his mentor, as the narrator's description of his nocturnal companionship with the chimney suggests: "And sitting up so late as we do at it [philosophizing], a mighty smoke it is that we two smoky old philosophers make" (188). In another of Melville's letters to Hawthorne in the earlier halcyon years, Melville considers having "a paper mill established at one end of the house" so that he might "write a thousand—a million—billion thoughts, all under the form of a letter" to Hawthorne.[14] **"I and My Chimney"** is probably one of the most important of Melville's letters, one in which public evasion is the envelope of private revelation.

Notes

1. Melville, *Pierre; or, the Ambiguities* (Evanston, Ill.: Northwestern University Press, 1971), 257; further references appear parenthetically in the text. "I and My Chimney," in *The Piazza Tales and Other Prose Pieces* (Evanston, Ill.: Northwestern University Press, 1987), 360. Again, all further references appear parenthetically in the text.

2. All references to the three sketches by Hawthorne may be found in Volume X of *The Centenary Edition of the Works of Nathaniel Hawthorne* (Columbus: Ohio State University Press, 1962).

3. Edward Rosenberry, "Melville and His *Mosses*," *American Transcendental Quarterly* 7 (Summer 1970): 51-55.

4. See Richard Brodhead's chapter "Hawthorne, Melville, and the Fiction of Prophecy," in *The School of Hawthorne* (New York: Oxford University Press, 1986), 17-47. As Brodhead argues, Melville in "Hawthorne and His Mosses" (1851) had "made Hawthorne the guarantor of his [Melville's] literary-prophetic identity" (32) while getting Hawthorne "just totally wrong . . . as an authorial model" for a fiction of revelation (43). Brodhead traces Melville's later, painful discovery of Hawthorne's actual project as "bearer not of revelation but of mystery itself" (47). As Brodhead argues, the shift in Melville's understanding of Hawthorne's purposes accounts in part for the more cryptic, elusive quality of Melville's later work.

5. Ibid., 47.

6. David Leverenz, *Manhood in the American Renaissance* (Ithaca: Cornell University Press, 1989), 16.

7. Robert Ferguson, *Law and Letters in American Culture* (Cambridge: Harvard University Press, 1986), 279-80.

8. Leverenz, 21.

9. For a good account of the story's political implications, see Allan Moore Emory's "The Political Significance of Melville's Chimney," *The New England Quarterly: A Historical Review of New England Life and Letters,* 55, no. 2 (1982): 201-28.

10. *The Melville Log: A Documentary Life of Herman Melville, with a New Supplementary Chapter,* ed. Jay Leyda (New York: Gordian Press, 1969), 2: 782.

11. See Leonard Chai's "Part III: The Secularization of Religion," in *The Romantic Foundations of the American Renaissance* (Ithaca: Cornell University Press, 1987), 194-207. In his account of the "psychologically miraculous" in Hawthorne's personal and public writing, Chai explains how the "theme of grace undergoes for Hawthorne a transposition from the theological to the psychological plane"; the sense of grace "depends on the possibility of a return in memory to an 'object of the affections of the past'" (194-97) and, in other cases, on the individual's capacity to render a person or thing "an object of the affections rather than perception," an object "created by the mind (or heart) itself" (207). In his interpretation of Chillingworth's consecration of the heart by placing Hester imaginatively in the "household fire," Chai clarifies a process whereby the chimney becomes a sacrosanct repository of the deceased kinsman, Julian Dacres (206-07).

12. Here I quote from *The Letters of Herman Melville,* ed. Merrill R. Davis and William H. Gilman (New Haven: Yale University Press, 1960), 121.

13. Melville, *Log,* 2: 926, 1: 419 and 407.

14. Melville, *Log,* 1: 436.

John D. Cloy (essay date summer 1998)

SOURCE: Cloy, John D. "Fatal Underestimation—Sue's *Atar-Gull* and Melville's 'Benito Cereno.'" *Studies in Short Fiction* 35, no. 3 (summer 1998): 241-49.

[*In the following essay, Cloy analyzes the characterizations of the black protagonists in "Benito Cereno" and Eugène Sue's* Atar-Gull, *detailing how each work handles the white characters' assumptions about race.*]

Eugène Sue and Herman Melville make strong racial statements in their nautical works, *Atar-Gull*[1] and **"Benito Cereno."** These pieces, published in 1831 and

1855, respectively, appeared with settings that antedate the abolition of the slave trade. For most whites, both American and European, blacks were a class apart, viewed as little more than cattle or other agricultural property. When considered as human by more liberal thinkers, their mental and emotional capacities were almost universally undervalued. Sue and Melville present in *Atar-Gull* (a novel) and **"Benito Cereno"** (a short story) blacks who are superior to most of their white neighbors in intelligence, cunning, patience, and fortitude. These black characters—the eponymous Atar-Gull of Sue's book and Babo in Melville's fiction—are slaves who make effectual use of whites' tendency to underestimate their abilities in order to take diabolical advantage of situations for vengeful purposes. By presenting loyal and subservient exteriors to gullible Caucasians, Atar-Gull, and Babo craftily execute murderous revenge on those who enslave them.

Although Babo and Atar-Gull use similar stratagems, their results markedly differ. Babo, who has taken over the vessel commanded by the flaccid Spanish aristocrat, Benito Cereno, fails to complete his plot to capture American captain Amasa Delano's ship and slaughter its crew. Cereno foils the scheme after Delano boards his slaver to relieve the want of the black and white sufferers who have nearly starved in a devastating calm that has paralyzed their movement for several weeks. When Delano launches his boat to return to his own ship, the *Bachelor's Delight,* Cereno leaps overboard into the skiff to warn the American. Babo follows with homicidal intent, but is captured by Delano's men, who then recapture Cereno's vessel. Babo is executed at Lima for his crimes after his treachery and criminal organizational skill are brought to light. Atar-Gull, however, is totally successful. When his father, an old slave incapable of working, is wrongfully executed by Tom Wil, his English owner, the slave vows revenge. He insinuates himself into the good graces of Wil and his family by assiduous and obsequious services. With the aid of the ferocious Jamaican Maroons, he ruins Wil's crops, has his stock killed, orchestrates his daughter's death from snakebite (which results in his wife's demise from grief), and accompanies his master on a return trip to Europe after his financial ruin. The two settle in Paris, cheaper than Wil's native England, where the old man suffers a paralytic stroke that deprives him of speech. Atar-Gull then reveals his true colors to his horrified owner. Keeping neighbors at bay through a pretense of over-protection, the former slave is viewed by all as a saint, while fiendishly torturing his former master with his gloating hatred and vindictiveness. When Wil mercifully dies, the disappointed Atar-Gull is given a medal by the French citizenry, who are still unaware of his Mephesophelean machinations.[2]

Babo and Atar-Gull belie contemporary notions of blacks' intelligence, implicitly revealing the attitudes of

Melville and Sue toward slavery and the supposed inferiority of non-white people.[3] These black characters allow themselves to be perceived as good-natured, harmless, loyal body servants to the white men they both hate and intend to destroy. By far the most resourceful and strongest figures in these works, they bide their time and reinforce their positions through seemingly assiduous care of the intended victims. Melville's American captain, Amasa Delano, reflects the then-current view of most whites regarding slaves as lesser entities.[4] He sees the "peculiar institution" as part of the established order of things: conventional and therefore unalterable, certainly not requiring alteration. The demarcation between black and white is so great that Delano cannot even conceive of an equal association between the races. When he initially becomes uneasy at the strange happenings aboard Cereno's vessel (perhaps suggesting some evil collusion between Babo and the Spanish captain), the *San Dominick,* the American reassures himself by some "rational" reasoning:

> The whites, too, by nature, were the shrewder race. A man with some evil design, would not he be likely to speak well of that stupidity which was blind to his depravity, and malign that intelligence from which it might be hidden? Not unlikely, perhaps. But if the whites had dark secrets concerning Don Benito, could then Don Benito be any way in complicity with the blacks? But they were too stupid. Besides, who ever heard of a white so far a renegade as to apostatize from his very species almost, by leaguing in against it with negroes?

(**"Benito Cereno"** 45)

In a twist of racial position and power, both black characters become essentially the masters of their white overlords. Babo and his mutineers hold Cereno and the crew of the *San Dominick* hostage, their lives dependent on their good behavior while Delano and his men are aboard. Since the Spaniards have seen graphic samples of the Africans' handiwork on some of their less fortunate shipmates, they fearfully acquiesce. Atar-Gull's domination of Wil is more subtle. He succeeds by guile, and not until the old colonist is paralyzed and rendered mute by a stroke does his former bondsman declare himself. After cataloging for the horrified old invalid all the evils he has perpetrated, Atar-Gull delivers his masterstroke:

> Au-dehors je serai loué, montré, fêté, comme le modèle des serviteurs, et je te soignerai, et je soutiendrai ta vie, car elle m'est precieuse, ta vie . . . plus que la mienne, vois-tu; il faut que tu vives longtemps pour moi, pour ma vengeance . . . oh! Bien longtemps . . . l'éternité, si je pouvais . . . Et si un étranger entrait ici . . . ce serait pour te dire mes louanges, te vanter mon devouement a moi, qui ai tué . . . tué ta famille . . . qui t'ai rendu muet et misérable . . . car c'est moi . . . c'est moi, entends-tu, Tom Wil . . . c'est moi seule qui ai tout fait . . . moi seul. . . .[5]

(*Atar-Gull* 261)

The obtuseness of the white characters in these works borders on the unbelievable. In the American captain's case, his density probably saves him.[6] Only after Cereno jumps into his boat as the visitors leave the *San Dominick* does Delano start to grasp the true nature of the drama around him. He still suspects the Spanish captain of perfidy at this point (grabbing him to restrain possible violence), and, until Babo leaps after his victim, attempting to poignard him, Delano is still confused. In Sue's novel, it seems unlikely that Wil and his family would not have missed Atar-Gull's overnight absences to confer with the Maroons in the mountains of Jamaica, since he was an omnipresent body-servant. Also, when one misfortune after another strikes the planter's family, the slave is never far off, in attendance at the house when Wil's daughter Jenny has her fatal encounter with the snake. Wil himself suspects nothing until Atar-Gull reveals himself in Paris as his tormentor. Neither do the neighbors in the run-down building where the two reside entertain doubts of the black's fidelity. The vastly higher intelligence and cunning of these black characters make a powerful and radical statement about Sue and Melville's beliefs in the supposed superiority of the white race.

The invidious depth of the blacks' revenge on their white owners is an accurate measure of their hatred. Both authors stress the slaves' pagan religion and foreign outlandish practices. The loosely interpreted European Christianity that allowed for the enslavement of fellow beings is contrasted with the more primal beliefs of the Africans. For the blacks, vengeance is an accepted part of their culture. The more barbarous the atrocities (including cannibalism) committed against enemies, the more successful the balancing of cosmic accounts. Thus Babo and his compatriots brutally slay the Spaniards aboard the *San Dominick*—by drowning, bludgeoning, and hacking them to death. In a particularly brutal twist, the slaves kill Don Alexandro Aranda, their former master, and install his skeleton (implying cannibalism) as figurehead on the ship, accompanied by the derisive motto "seguid vuestro jefe" (follow your leader). Atar-Gull is equally ruthless with Wil and his family, sparing no member of the Wil household. Sue and Melville subtly point out the slight distance between the ownership and degradation of slavery perpetrated by the whites to the wanton butchery of their enemies by the blacks. There seem to be no authentic Christians among the characters of either narrative, despite the claims of some of the whites themselves.[7] After Delano has rescued Cereno from the mutineers and they are safely ashore, the Spaniard tells the American captain that he considers their passage through the adventure unscathed as a case of divine intervention:

> "Nay, my friend," rejoined the Spaniard, courteous even to the point of religion, "God charmed your life, but you saved mine. To think of some things you did—

those smilings and chattings, rash pointings and gesturings. For less than these, they slew my mate, Raneds; but you had the Prince of Heaven's safe conduct through all ambuscades."

(**"Benito Cereno"** 103)

Benoit, whom Sue describes as a chaste and proper Catholic family man who is prone to moralizing, tries to keep his sailors in line as much as possible. When Simon, the *Catherine*'s mate, starts to blaspheme, Benoit sadly remonstrates with the offender:

> Simon . . . Simon . . . tu recommences, je n'aime pas a t'entendre blasphemer comme un païen; tu fais le philosophe, et ça te jouera un tour . . . tu verras.[8]

(*Atar-Gull* 18)

Though concerned with the language of his crew, Benoit nonetheless can live with the lucrative practice of slave trafficking, calling his cargo "bois d'ébene" (ebony wood), a particularly dehumanizing (and unchristian) appellation for human beings. The whites' religion seems to teem with convenient unstated precepts that allow them to act in many ways without moral restraint.

Irony figures prominently in both these fictions.[9] Atar-Gull's receiving a prize from the Academy for his "virtuous" treatment of his master is perhaps as ironic as any event in Western literature. He emerges unscathed from his crime, like Montresor in Poe's "The Cask of Amontillado," and, like the Italian character, he gloats over his victory. Delano's dullness contains an odd variety of irony in Melville's story. That Babo and his cohorts are able to hoodwink the "superior" white captain while masquerading as slaves to their victims presents an irony of a special kind. The American's sneering attitude toward African mentality (and, to a lesser degree, that of Latins) insures his failure to perceive correctly the situation aboard the *San Dominick*. Delano is a prime example of the limitations that result from the practice of what Herbert Spencer terms "contempt prior to investigation."

The intention of the Africans in both the French and American fictions is as much concerned with control of their destinies (and their former controllers) as it is with revenge.[10] Atar-Gull tries his mightiest to keep Tom Wil alive in order to prolong his torture (the black's sadistic control over him). Babo is willing to sacrifice his own life by leaping into Delano's boat in pursuit of Cereno; he goes to any lengths to retain his hold on the Spaniard. While Atar-Gull is devastated by Wil's death and does not long survive the Englishman, Babo dies on the scaffold for his crimes, unrepentant and silent to the last. However, his control over his victim extends beyond his death, since Cereno withdraws to a monastery, where, shattered in mind and body by his ordeal and haunted by the memory of Babo, he soon expires. Significantly, when Delano attempts to cheer the Spaniard after his rescue and the slaves' trial, the former captain's last words in the narrative (save those required at the hearing) refer to his physical and psychic captor:

> "You are saved, Don Benito," cried Captain Delano, more and more astonished and pained; "you are saved; what has cast a shadow upon you?"
>
> "The negro."

("Benito Cereno" 104)

The casual reader might be initially tempted to associate the dark skin of the Africans Babo and Atar-Gull with evil, the lighter hue of Benito Cereno and Tom Wil with virtue. However, both Sue and Melville employ the black characters as justified revenge figures, although not totally positive characters. Their enslavement by whites permits the extremity of the slaves' actions, though the barbarity of their retaliation revolts modern readers. The writers sought to demonstrate a more "civilized" barbarity on the part of whites in the practice of chattel bondage. Melville's travels as a merchant seaman (and presumably Sue's as a naval physician) gave him a tolerant attitude toward people of all races. The New York writer professed sympathy with "people of all shades of color, and all degrees of intellect, rank, and social worth."[11] Sue's republicanism has been described by detractors as opportunistic, embraced at a later period of his life after failing in an attempt at acceptance by the aristocracy. While the truth of this charge is doubtless impossible to prove after so long a period, Sue's implied sympathy with Atar-Gull and lack of empathy with Wil and his family in the novel speak volumes. Throughout the narrative the reader gets the sense that the slave is not only condoned in his vengeance by the author, but also tacitly approved.

Gothic elements are present in these sea narratives.[12] Melville's story contains structures that exude gothic characteristics—the *San Dominick* is called a "whitewashed monastery" in the narrative, and the official buildings in Lima where the rebels are tried resemble castles. The shadowy atmosphere of unreality that pervades the work supports a gothic theme; even the thickwitted Captain Delano senses that strange forces are at work. Sue's novel also features a slave vessel with many compartments, analogous to a medieval fortress. The many-storied dwelling where Atar-Gull and Wil come to live in Paris is a classic gothic house, with a concierge and numerous neighbors of various social complexions. The hint of magic involved in Atar-Gull's associations with the Maroons in the West Indies gives an added element of the macabre to this bizarre tale of ferocious revenge. Both works are shaded with religious overtones. Melville calls the slaves "black friars," and the entrance of Cereno into a monastery at the

book's end is no accident. Sue's choice of a Catholic country (France) to end his story is not coincidental. The pious neighbors and associates of the odd Englishman and his black servant confer honors on the fiendish hypocrite after Wil's demise. This implied criticism of Roman blindness to reality and preoccupation with externals parallels Sue's more overt condemnation of Catholicism in *The Wandering Jew,* a scathing denunciation of the Society of Jesus. One also gets the impression that Sue does not judge too harshly the African religion that the slaves continue to embrace covertly, since the whites' faith does little to console their misery and isolation. Indeed, European Christianity viewed blacks as benighted inferiors, leaving the slaves little opportunity for an acceptable existence within the rigid hierarchical confines of the eighteenth-century great chain of being.

The surprisingly tolerant attitudes that Sue and Melville display in these works exemplify an emerging societal concern and democratization of feeling for people of color. The American Civil War was only six years away at the time of the publication of "Benito Cereno," and the French were to free their remaining slaves in the Western hemisphere in 1848, 17 years after the appearance of *Atar-Gull.* French and American ideas on freedom and personal liberty had long coincided; though the Gallic presence in the American Revolution was largely one of moral support (save for notable examples like the Marquis de Lafayette), there is little doubt that the earlier French rebellion had encouraged the British colonies to revolt. These affinities of thought enabled such dissimilar authors as Melville and Sue to reach similar conclusions on the issue of racial equality—that men must be judged by their abilities alone, not their ethnic heritages.

Notes

1. Nora Atkinson states that *Atar-Gull* (1831) was inspired by two earlier voyages that Sue had made to the Antilles. She dates his sobriquet "Cooper français" from the appearance of *Plik et Plok* (1831), a pirate tale and claims for Sue the honor of the first maritime novelist in France (84). Eugène de Mirecourt's rather unflattering sketch of Sue nonetheless classes Atar-Gull as a resounding success in the new French maritime genre. He declares that Sue wrote the book, along with *Plik et Plok, la Salamandre,* and *la Vigie de Koatven,* to replenish his depleted coffers after he had squandered his paternal inheritance on fashionable women (69-70). Americo Bertuccioli also gives Sue credit for producing the first sea novels in French (65). He sees Atar-Gull as a stronger novel than *Plik et Plok,* and names it the deciding factor in the establishment of Sue's career (92-93). Bertuccioli goes on to cite Ernest Legouvé (*Soixante Ans de Souvenirs,* 1886) on the popular reception

of the book: "Ce mélange d'audace dramatique et de sarcasme, ces scènes pathétiques or gracieuses terminées par le plus insolent de dénouements, ce prix de vertu donné par l'Académie a ce nègre meurtrier et empoisonneur, tout cela scandalisa, exaspera, enthousiasma et donna lieu a un fait caracteristique" (93). [My translation: This audacious mixture of drama and sarcasm, these pathetic or gracious scenes terminated by the most insolent of endings, that prize of virtue given by the Academy to this murderous Negro poisoner, all this scandalized, exasperated, and enthused, giving occasion to an anticipated praise].

L. Durand-Dessert, in his entry on Sue for *Dictionnaire des Littératures de Langue Française* (Beaumarchais 4: 2391), mentions the popularity of Atar-Gull, noting that *le Monde* republished it as a summer serial in 1980.

2. Jean Louis Bory points out Atar-Gull's diabolical cunning (127-28). In speaking of his horrific punishment of Wil, Bory says that Atar-Gull, ". . . le torture si habilement qu'il l'achève et reçcoit pour son dévouement le prix Montyon de l'Académie française. Et 'Atar-Gull mourut bientôt, nostalgique et chrétien.'" [My translation: . . . torturing him so ably that he finishes him and receives for his devotion the Montyon prize of the French Academy. And Atar-Gull dies soon afterwards, nostalgic and Christian]. That the former slave ends his days in peace and comfort, a supposed member of his former owner's own religious sect borders on the fantastic, proving Atar-Gull's nearly superhuman intelligence and patient cunning.

3. Laurie Robertson-Lorant makes an interesting case for Melville as abolitionist. She suggests that his message to readers implies that the rebel Africans were as patriotic as his own forebears, throwing off the yoke of British servitude (350-51). However, Hershel Parker paints a more moderate picture of the author regarding the slavery question. He states that while Melville hated slavery as a tyrannical practice, he abstained from active participation in the abolitionist question, viewing American slavery as just another branch of a larger cosmic evil (831-32). Sue's position on slavery has not been discussed specifically by biographers or critics. His disapproval of the institution is evident in Atar-Gull and his later adoption of populist and republican principles is consistent with this train of thought. It seems reasonable to assert that the opinions attributed to Sue by Alain Pessin are applicable to blacks as well as whites. Pessin regards Sue as a progressive who saw the poor in France as disenfranchised by misery—low wages, high food prices, and lack of education, fundamental benefits that would help them emerge from their mire of degradation. He saw revolution as a last resort and Pessin feels that Sue intended for the poor to doctor themselves (le peuple médecin; 127-40).

4. William D. Richardson notes that Delano's paternalistic mindset is evident when he offers to purchase Babo from Benito Cereno in what he regards as a magnanimous compliment to the black's sterling qualities. Richardson observes that Delano considers his offer to buy the slave as evidence of his highest esteem. Such dehumanizing action from a man as "good" as the American mariner goes far in delineating the common perception among whites of the innate inferiority of blacks (78-79). A similar strain, though emerging from the opposite pole, is apparent in *Atar-Gull* when Wil allows himself to be persuaded to eliminate the unprofitable old slave, Job, when the ancient black becomes incapable of further work.

5. My translation:

> Moreover, I will be praised, exhibited, celebrated as a model of servants. And I will care for you and support your life, because it is precious to me, your life . . . more than my own, you see. You must live a long time for me, for my vengeance. Oh! A very long time . . . for eternity, if I can manage it. And if a stranger comes here . . . it will be in order to sing you my praises, to boast to you of my devotion; me, who has killed . . . killed your family . . . who has rendered you mute and miserable . . . because it's me . . . it's me, do you understand, Tom Wil . . . it's me alone who has done it all . . . me alone. . . .

6. David Kirby states that Delano's mental sluggishness is what saves him from butchery in "Benito Cereno." He feels that a more observant witness would have grasped the situation much more quickly and been slaughtered by Babo and his minions (149).

7. Amasa Delano looks upon his own faith as superior to that of the blacks and sees himself as a true follower of Christ, though he is not too modest to claim credit for his own abilities. He tells Cereno at the end of the tale that "Yes, all is owing to Providence, I know; but the temper of my mind that morning was more than commonly pleasant, while the sight of so much suffering—more apparent than real—added to my good nature, compassion, and charity, happily interweaving the three" (103). His condoning of the slave trade somewhat belies the notion of his devout religiosity. Captain Benoit, original owner of the *Catherine* before its seizure by the pirate Brulart, considers himself a pious man, though a slaver. He is given up by Brulart to a hostile tribe and falls victim to cannibalism. Ian Pickup states accurately that Atar-Gull

is not graced with characters who successfully embody Christian morality.

8. My translation: "Simon, Simon, you're starting again. I don't like to hear you blaspheme like a pagan. You're playing the philosopher, and that will give you a bad turn—you will see."

9. Paul Ginisty notes the overwhelming presence of irony in Atar-Gull. He mentions that, when the novel was adapted for the stage, it was toned down by making the main character more human. In the dramatic version, Atar-Gull falls in love with another of Wil's daughters, then kills himself out of remorse. Ginisty speculates that Sue was probably amused at this French concession to the Grundyism of the middle classes (76-77).

10. Cereno's utter destruction by Babo and his fellow mutineers is remarked by Tyrus Hillway, who observes that Babo's head, placed on a stake facing the monastery, continues to monitor the unfortunate Spaniard's movements until his death (118).

11. Sealts (105) cited in Garner (24). Garner terms Melville as "politically negligent," though he sees the writer as basically Republican in principles and opposed to slavery.

12. Charles Berryman makes a case for the presence of gothic trappings in "Benito Cereno" (159-61).

Works Cited

Atkinson, Nora. *Eugène Sue et le Roman-Feuilleton.* Paris: Nizet & Bastard, 1929.

Beaumarchais, Jean-Pierre de, et al. *Dictionnaire des Litteratures de Langue Française.* Paris: Bordas, 1987. 4 vols.

Berryman, Charles. "'Benito Cereno' and the Black Friars." *Studies in American Fiction* 18 (1990): 159-70.

Bertuccioli, Americo. *Les Origines du Roman Maritime Français.* S. Belforte, 1937.

Bory, Jean Louis. *Eugène Sue: Dandy Mais Socialist.* Paris: Hachette, 1962.

Garner, Stanton. *The Civil War World of Herman Melville.* Lawrence: UP of Kansas, 1993.

Ginisty, Paul. *Eugène Sue.* Paris: Editions Berger-Levrault, 1929.

Hillway, Tyrus. *Herman Melville.* Boston: Twayne, 1963.

Kirby, David. *Herman Melville.* New York: Continuum, 1993.

Melville, Herman. "Benito Cereno." *Shorter Novels of Herman Melville.* New York: Liveright, 1928. 1-106.

Mirecourt, Eugène de. "Eugène Sue." *Les Contemporains.* Paris: Havard, 1855.

Parker, Hershel. *Herman Melville: A Biography, Volume 1, 1819-1851.* Baltimore: Johns Hopkins UP, 1996.

Pessin, Alain. "Eugène Sue et le Peuple Malade." *Le Mythe du Peuple et la Société Française du XIXe Siècle.* Paris: Presses Universitaires de France, 1992. 127-40.

Pickup, Ian. "Eugène Sue." *Dictionary of Literary Biography.* 119: 303.

Richardson, William D. *Melville's "Benito Cereno": An Interpretation with Annotated Text and Concordance.* Durham, North Carolina: Carolina Academic P, 1987.

Robertson-Lorant, Laurie. *Melville: A Biography.* New York: Clarkson Potter, 1996.

Sealts, Merton M. *Melville as Lecturer.* Cambridge: Harvard UP, 1957.

Sue, Eugène. *Atar-Gull.* Verviers: Bibliothèque Marabout, 1975.

Barbara Foley (essay date March 2000)

SOURCE: Foley, Barbara. "From Wall Street to Astor Place: Historicizing Melville's 'Bartleby.'" *American Literature* 72, no. 1 (March 2000): 87-116.

[*In the following essay, Foley describes the political and historical contexts informing "Bartleby the Scrivener," focusing on the subliminal role played by the Astor Place riot of 1849 in the consciousness of both the narrator and Melville.*]

In recent years critics have been calling for a regrounding of mid-nineteenth-century American literature—of the romance in particular—in politics and history. John McWilliams applauds the contemporary "challenge to the boundaryless and abstract qualities of the older idea of the Romance's neutral territory." George Dekker notes that recent attempts to "rehistoricize the American romance" have entailed an "insist[ence]" that our major romancers have always been profoundly concerned with what might be called the mental or ideological 'manners' of American society, and that their seemingly anti-mimetic fictions both represent and criticize those manners."[1] But Herman Melville's **"Bartleby, the Scrivener: A Story of Wall Street"** (1853) has to this point been exempted from a thoroughgoing historical recontextualization; its subtitle remains to be fully explained.

Not all readings of the tale, to be sure, have been "boundaryless and abstract." Critics interested in the tale's autobiographical dimension have interpreted it as an allegory of the writer's fate in a market society, noting specific links with Melville's own difficult authorial career. Scholars concerned with the story's New York setting have discovered some important references to contemporaneous events. Marxist critics have argued that **"Bartleby"** [**"Bartleby the Scrivener"**] offers a portrait of the increasing alienation of labor in the rationalized capitalist economy that took shape in the mid-nineteenth-century United States.[2] But such critical enterprises have remained largely separate, with the result that biography, historical contextualization, and ideological analysis have been pursued in different registers. Moreover, criticism of **"Bartleby"** has rarely explored Melville's interest or involvement in current social conflicts and political discourses; "Wall Street" has thus functioned largely as metonymy rather than as constitutive context and locale.

In this essay I shall argue that a familiarity with mid-nineteenth-century class struggles in New York—and with the contemporaneous discourse about these struggles—is indispensable to a complete understanding of **"Bartleby."** In order to historicize the tale fully, however, it is necessary to engage in a certain amount of political—and, it turns out, psychoanalytic—detective work. History in **"Bartleby"** must be reconstructed from what has been repressed, fragmented, and displaced to the margins of the text. Certain of the narrator's passing references—to John Jacob Astor, to Trinity Church, to "fears of a mob," to paying rent and taxes—suggest a historical subtext that the Wall Street lawyer can only subliminally acknowledge. The tale's very abstractness, then—its apparently "anti-mimetic" quality—is part of its object of critique; the "mental and ideological manners" that Melville represents include the narrator's inability to see social relations as constituted by relations of economic power. But repression is working in **"Bartleby"** on another level as well. The Astor Place riot of 1849, I hypothesize, provides a covert historical subtext—one that is denied not so much by the narrator as by the author himself. In its ironic display of the narrator's attempts to rationalize his acts in relation to his employee, **"Bartleby"** offers Melville's critique of the workings of ideology; in its disguised paradigmatic plot of betrayal and guilt, the tale reveals Melville's own attempt to contend with the return of the political unconscious.

* * *

"Bartleby" takes place some time in the 1840s—although exactly when, as Charles Swann points out, is somewhat difficult to determine.[3] The story is narrated retrospectively, leaving the impression that a significant period has intervened between the lawyer's interactions with his intransigent employee and his later reflections on these events. The narration itself obviously occurs sometime before 1853 (the text's date of publication)

and after 1848 (the year of the death of John Jacob Astor, whose "rounded and orbicular" name the narrator "love[s] to repeat" because it "rings like unto bullion"; Astor is referred to as the "*late* John Jacob Astor" [italics added]).[4] The events constituting the story itself are somewhat harder to place, however. The narrator mentions that he hired Bartleby to help handle the increased workload accruing to the lawyer's assumption of the position of Master of Chancery; he complains, however, that he enjoyed the benefits of this position for "only a few short years" because of the "sudden and violent abrogation" of the office by "the new Constitution" (14). The New York State Constitution was revised in 1846, providing for the abolition of the equity courts in the following year. If we figure that Bartleby spends about six months in the lawyer's employ, and that "a few short years" intervene before 1847, the pallid scrivener probably appears on the lawyer's doorstep around 1843 or 1844. This dating is supported by the narrator's comparison of his emotional state with that of the businessman John C. Colt, who, in an uncontrolled rage, murdered the printer Samuel Adams in Adams's office. It would seem that the famous case, which was brought to trial in 1842, is in fairly recent memory.[5]

But this 1843-1844 dating is made problematic by the narrator's mention of his intended visit to Trinity Church on the Sunday when he finds Bartleby "keeping bachelor's hall all by himself" (27) in the office at No.__ Wall Street. Trinity was consecrated, with great fanfare, in May of 1846; yet Melville's lawyer makes no mention of its even being new. Moreover, when Bartleby ends up in the Tombs, the grub-man brings up the name of the "gentleman forger" Monroe Edwards, who, he remarks, "died of consumption at Sing Sing" (44). Edwards—a flamboyant criminal who, David Reynolds remarks, "decorated his cell in the Tombs elegantly, like a parlor" and became something of a criminal folk hero—died in prison in 1847.[6] If we date the events in **"Bartleby"** backwards from the abolition of the Courts of Chancery, and forwards from the consecration of Trinity and the death of Edwards, we immediately see that the story could not, strictly speaking, have taken place at all.

Perhaps it seems trivial to point up Melville's errors in setting up the chronology for his tale, particularly when we recognize that others of Melville's works—*Moby-Dick,* for example—manifest comparable discrepancies in time schemes.[7] I draw attention to these mistakes, however, because they suggest that Melville's imaginative process in **"Bartleby"** required him to blend events from the early 1840s with events occurring later in the decade and perhaps into the 1850s. What sorts of social developments and historical occurrences might have been crowding themselves into Melville's consciousness and compelling him to distort the historical record?

In the early 1840s, writes Sean Wilentz, the New York labor movement, which had been drastically set back by the panic of 1837, was relatively quiescent. By mid-decade, however, there was a labor resurgence: "A burst of strikes hit the city's bookbinding, upholstering, shoe-making, and tailoring shops; at the peak of what turned out to be a successful five-week strike, the tailors mounted a torchlight procession two thousand strong, led by two musical bands and men carrying the republican banners of old."[8] In 1849 striking Hudson River Railroad workers attacked and killed several scabs;[9] by 1850 there was continual conflict between police and bands of striking tailors, culminating in the August 1850 demonstrations in which two tailors were killed. By midcentury "there had been such a revival in the local labor movement that the *Tribune* could term it a 'general uprising,' . . . and the *Herald* warned workers against 'socialists,' 'Red Republicans,' and Horace Greeley."[10] Walt Whitman, observing the spirit of revolt among New York's workers, wrote in 1850 that "in all of them burns, almost with a fierceness, the divine fire which more or less, during all ages, has only waited a chance to leap forth and confound the calculations of tyrants, hunkers, and all their tribe. At this moment, New York is the most radical city in America."[11]

Class struggles in the streets of New York never attained the level of class consciousness or discipline that characterized the urban workers' uprisings of 1848 in Europe. By comparison, the New York riots and rebellions were, Luc Sante observes, "rampages, headless and tailless and flailing about."[12] Moreover, even in the 1840s and 1850s the politics of New York working-class movements were colored by the nativism and racism that would culminate in the 1863 Draft Riot. Nonetheless, the growing labor movement drew sustenance from a rhetoric of class warfare. As early as 1829, agrarian radical Thomas Skidmore had averred that "men have no right to their property (as they call it) when they use it, for the purpose of converting their fellow beings into slaves to labor for their use." Calling for a state constitutional convention that would abolish all rights of inheritance through wills, Skidmore called for an "equal division" of existing property among all state residents—including Indians.[13] In the late 1840s, writes David Reynolds, such expressions of radical class consciousness became more polemical: "The labor theory of value, which had been discussed rather abstractly by the rational socialists of the 1820s, now was vivified in increasingly lurid exposés detailing the vices of the wealthy 'upper ten' and the miseries of the oppressed 'lower million.'"[14] A representative of the striking tailors, for example, proclaimed that the workers' goal must be "to prevent the growth of an unwholesome aristocracy, whose only aim is to acquire wealth by robbery of the toiling masses; to place themselves in a position to successfully combat capital; to bring labor up to its proper elevation and take that position which God

intended man should fill—truly independent of his fellows, and above the position of a mere 'wage slave.'" Mike Walsh, an omnipresent radical of the 1840s, condemned "the slavery of wages" and proclaimed that "an overbearing employer" or a "tyrannical landlord" was "no democrat." He concluded, "No man can be a good political democrat without he's a good social democrat."[15] Any New York City resident aware of current political debates—as Melville certainly was—could not have been oblivious to the omnipresent language of class polarization.

To be sure, **"Bartleby"** is not precisely a story about labor unrest. Turkey and Nippers, while driven to alcoholism and ulcers by low wages and psychologically debilitating work, do not possess the "divine fire" of rebellion.[16] Bartleby, if arguably engaged in a "strange, mute sit-in,"[17] hardly exudes proletarian class consciousness or "leaps forth" Whitman-style against his employer. Indeed, it has been argued that the social relations in the lawyer's office are in some ways more reflective of an earlier, more paternalist phase of capitalist development than of full-blown market capitalism.[18] The narrator's various suggestions that the tale takes place in the early 1840s, a time of low ebb in class struggle, reinforce his view of the office as a seamless, organic, "natural" community. The narrator craves the good opinion of his employees and wishes to consider both himself and them as "sons of Adam" (28). His final sigh—"Ah, Bartleby! Ah, humanity!" (45)—reveals his desire to articulate an abstract humanism that will include both himself and the scrivener.

If **"Bartleby"** does not depict class struggle directly, it is, as David Kuebrich has pointed out, very much about ideological struggle as well as alienation; indeed, the conflict between Bartleby and his boss cannot be understood apart from the contemporaneous discourse about class polarization. The narrator treats his employees like wage slaves: he erects screens and barriers between himself and them; he views them as "useful" and "valuable"; and he reduces individuality to idiosyncrasy, viewing the scriveners' peculiarities (including their poverty) as intrinsic rather than caused by their relation to him. He offers charity rather than higher wages and, when pressed to the wall (as it were), invokes property rights; fearing both social upheaval and the bad opinion of his professional peers, he allows state power to take its course and to cart Bartleby off to the Tombs of capitalist justice. That the lawyer is in some ways a kind and well-meaning man only reinforces the tale's critique of ideology as justificatory practice: his "doctrine of assumptions" takes as a premise the legitimacy and necessity of capitalist social relations.[19]

Marxist critics of **"Bartleby"** have at times been faulted for super-imposing upon the tale anachronistic conceptions of class antagonism and false consciousness.[20] A consideration of the political discourses of the 1840s, however, reveals that Melville's characterizations do invoke the familiar contemporaneous categories of the false democrat and the wage slave. Moreover, the tale's various indications of being set in the late 1840s or even the early 1850s suggest that the narrator's vague paranoia (his "fears . . . of a mob," [40]) belies his paternalistic complacency and registers the increasingly violent street activity and strident rhetoric that characterized the class struggles of this later period.[21] But "Bartleby"'s links to the contemporaneous critique of the "upper ten" consist in more than its invocation of a generalized discourse of class warfare. The narrator's opening paean to John Jacob Astor unequivocally associates the teller of Melville's tale with the figure who more than any other symbolized in the popular mind the obscenity of great wealth. Mike Walsh singled out Astor for blistering attack:

> [I]t would take thirty-five hundred men, working twenty years . . . three hundred days in each year, without being sick or out of employment an hour during the whole time, and getting a dollar a day without spending a cent, but living with their families on air like chameleons [*sic*], sleeping in the parks and going naked: yes! 3,500 men working that length of time, living in that manner and receiving that much wages, it would take to *earn* what Mr. John Jacob Astor has *saved* from what the world calls "his industry."[22]

Astor, variously dubbed "Old Hunks," "Old Skinflint," and "the richest man in the country,"[23] was, Stephen Zelnick concludes, "probably the most hated man in New York when he died in 1848."[24] Already in possession of most of lower Manhattan by the 1830s, Astor bought up much of what is now midtown Manhattan at bargain prices during the depression of 1837 and extended his domain beyond the island. When the lawyer in "Bartleby" flees his office for day trips in his rockaway, the places he visits are, significantly, all Astor terrain: Hoboken, across the Hudson River in New Jersey, was the site of the Astor mansion, while Astoria, across the East River in Queens, bears the name of its overlord.[25] By 1848 Astor was collecting $200,000 a year in rents. Asked shortly before his death whether he had invested too much in real estate, Astor responded, "Could I begin life again, knowing what I now know, and had money to invest, I would buy every foot of land on the Island of Manhattan." When Astor died, his fortune was estimated at some twenty to thirty million.[26]

Astor's right to his wealth by no means went unchallenged. In the mid-1800s, taxes were not imposed on income, and property taxes were, by present standards, very low. In 1850, for example, William B. Astor, John Jacob's primary inheritor, paid $29,579.26 on property "assessed at $2.6 million but probably worth ten times as much."[27] While some radicals, like Skidmore, advocated the abolition of all transfers of property through

wills, inheritance taxes were generally seen as the principal means to prevent the development of a homegrown aristocracy. The obituaries on Astor were thus vocal in their demands that Astor's estate pay the taxes its founder had managed not to pay for so many years. Greeley's *Tribune* supported the movement to impose a massive tax on Astor's estate. It was unfair, the *Tribune* death notice stated, for the government to "protect Mr. Astor's houses, lands, ships, stocks, etc., and yet exact no direct taxes from him according to his income."[28] James Gordon Bennett's *Herald,* ordinarily anything but a radical paper, nonetheless invoked a loose version of the labor theory of value in its observation that

> [d]uring the last fifty years of the life of John Jacob Astor, his property had been augmented and increased in value by the aggregate intelligence, industry, enterprise, and commerce of New York, fully to the amount of one-half its value. The farms and lots of ground which he bought forty, twenty, and ten and five years ago, have all increased in value entirely by the industry of the citizens of New York. Of course, it is plain as that two and two make four, that the half of his immense estate, in its actual value, has accrued to him by the industry of the community.[29]

"Astor" rang unto bullion for many New Yorkers, but they ordinarily repeated the name not to venerate it but to revile it.

What the debate over Astor's "right" to his millions reveals is that the critique of great wealth was inextricably tied to the critique of land ownership; the capitalist and the landlord were closely linked in the radical imaginary of the 1840s and 1850s. Correlatively, demands for an end to wage slavery were frequently conjoined with demands for land reform. The glutted labor market, radicals argued, depressed wages: if urban workers had the option to farm rural homesteads, the labor market would expand and wages would rise. Even though the movement for land reform in New York State targeted the patroons' large holdings upstate, its headquarters were in the Bowery in the 1840s. As Wilentz notes, "[B]y the mid-1840s, land reform had captured the imagination of almost every labor radical still active in New York."[30] George Evans, former editor of the *Working Man's Advocate,* declared in 1841 that "if any man has a right on earth, he has a right to land enough to raise a habitation on. If he has a *right to live,* he has a right to land enough for his subsistence. Deprive anyone of these rights, and you place him at the mercy of those who possess them." "An End to Land Monopoly" and "Our Public Lands: The Workingmen's Remedy" were toasts proposed at labor's 1843 Thomas Paine day celebrations. At the same time, land reformers backed union demands, calling themselves the National Industrial Congress and demanding the ten-hour day. The popular radical novelist George Lippard declared in 1852, "Land Freedom, Labor's Rights and

Universal Happiness—The first two must be obtained before the last can be consummated."[31] In 1859 a commentator on the U.S. political scene wrote in the *Atlantic Monthly* that "the word Agrarians comprehends [Socialists, Communists, Fourierites, and so forth]."[32]

Especially during the two years preceding the 1846 revision of the New York State Constitution, there was widespread agitation for land limitation and land reform. The conservative press warned that calling a Constitutional convention in 1845 would be a public danger, since the land reformers were advocating measures that were "wild," "utterly senseless," "fatal to society," and "destructive to all social and civil purposes."[33] Melville's lawyer, harboring his own personal grievance, remembers the Constitutional revision for its abolition of the Chancery courts. Far more significant in the public debate over the New York State Constitution, however, was the issue of who should have the title to land.[34]

A chapter in the debate over land rights in New York that bears specific relevance to **"Bartleby"** is the scandal that erupted in 1846-1847 over the Episcopal diocese's management of its real estate. Trinity Church—situated on Broadway at the foot of Wall Street—was the headquarters of the diocese and gave it its name. A wealthy institution and a major owner of real estate throughout lower Manhattan, Trinity began in the mid-1840s to be heavily burdened with debts incurred in constructing both a new building at the Trinity site and Grace Church, a luxurious church at Broadway and Tenth Street that was to be patronized by wealthy parishioners. Trinity had, moreover, extended long-term leases at below-market rates to a few affluent New Yorkers—central among these the Astor family, which "paid $269 a year for some 350 lots on a lease that would not expire until 1866." There occurred a public outcry when, in the mid-1840s, Trinity retrenched by closing down a number of its missions in the poorer parts of the city, such as the Bowery and Five Points. Some ministers—including a relative of Melville's friend Richard Henry Dana Jr.—quit the diocese in protest. In 1846 some church members charged that Trinity had failed to use its wealth "to sustain the feeble, and to supply the destitute"; taking their own church fathers to court, they challenged Trinity's "moral and legal right to its lands." In 1847, the courts upheld Trinity's title—but "not before the public was treated to the spectacle of a high-toned brawl over the use and abuse of wealth." Radicals of the time added their commentary, verbal and symbolic. Mike Walsh, whose two "pet evils" were Trinity and Astor, "declared that Trinity's property, 'enough to make every person in the United States comfortable and happy,' should be confiscated for public use, and then followed this up by urging the city to take over St. John's Park on the grounds that it was an exclusive and privileged preserve from which the laboring class was excluded. Walsh demonstrated his contempt for Trinity's exclusiveness by climbing over the park's fence and walking on the forbidden ground."[35] Squatting, a time-honored practice in rural Anti-Rent movements, was also, it would appear, a weapon in the arsenal of urban radicals.

Astor and Trinity are thus implicated in **"Bartleby"** not only ideologically but also geographically. For the overwhelming probability is that No. _ Wall Street is either owned and rented by Astor; or owned and rented by Trinity; or leased at low cost to Astor, who then rents it out to the lawyer's landlord, who in turn rents office space to the lawyer. When the lawyer challenges Bartleby's right to remain in the office—"'Do you pay any rent? Do you pay my taxes? Or is this property yours?'" (35)—he invokes a language hardly innocent of political overtones. In the talk of the town, both Trinity and Astor were, in the late 1840s, repeatedly the target of similar questions about the legitimacy of their titles and business practices.

Bartleby's conduct becomes less freakish and idiosyncratic, more plausible and historically significant, I would argue, when seen in the full context of contemporaneous struggles and discourses over property rights. Any reader familiar with the Trinity controversy would not miss the irony inherent in the narrator's passing, en route to a sermon by a "celebrated preacher" at the power nexus of the Episcopal diocese, through a Wall Street "deserted as Petra" (26-27) and finding a homeless worker squatting in his chambers. Not only was Petra—"at one time . . . the Wall Street of Arabia"—familiar to many readers through contemporaneous travelers' accounts,[36] any reader knowledgeable about the dual campaign against land monopoly and wage slavery in the strategy and discourse of contemporaneous radicalism would recognize the appropriateness of Bartleby's chosen mode of rebellion. For Bartleby both withholds his labor power and asserts his right to terrain. Bartleby remains enclosed within the walls erected by privilege, while Mike Walsh scales them.[37] Both, however, challenge the existing state of property rights by asserting a prior and unconditional doctrine of human rights. Invoking a symbolic discourse current in the 1840s, both engage in an occupation of space that is, simultaneously, an assertion of humanity. As a "Story of Wall Street," then, **"Bartleby"** addresses not only the market in labor but also that in land, not only exploitation but also homelessness. Its portrait of alienation is devastatingly complete.

* * *

Thus far I have been arguing that an awareness of certain features of New York social history of the 1840s and 1850s validates—indeed, expands—the Marxist line of interpretation on **"Bartleby."** Implicit in this argument, however, has been the assumption that Melville's repression of history to the margins of the tale is, in the broadest sense, *intentional*. That is, Melville is consciously ironizing his narrator: the historically informed reader sees, but the lawyer does not, the fuller meaning of the text's references to Astor, Trinity, and the revised New York Constitution, as well as to mobs, taxes, rights, and rents. The text's apparent projection of Bartleby as a metaphysical creature, rootless and timeless, functions primarily as a revelation of the narrator's false consciousness, pointing to what Michael Paul Rogin calls "the historical triumph of abstraction" in the era of capitalist market relations.[38] Like Captain Delano in **"Benito Cereno,"** the lawyer-narrator in **"Bartleby"** exhibits a consciousness that cannot think concretely because it cannot afford to face the exploitative basis of social relations—for reasons that ring unto bullion.[39] The lawyer's comment that the walls of his office building have closed off "a lateral view of certain grimy backyards and bricks" (16) can thus be taken as Melville's oblique commentary on his narrator's own fetishized consciousness.

What I would like to suggest now—and here, admittedly, the entire tenor of my argument becomes a good deal more provisional and hypothetical—is that there is another historical subtext in **"Bartleby,"** one that Melville cannot entirely control because he is not fully aware of it. The nodal event in this repressed narrative is the Astor Place riot of 1849, which is denied direct articulation for reasons that ring not of bullion but (if I may be pardoned the pun) of bullets. Clustered about Melville's immediate reaction to and later memory of the 1849 riot, I suggest, are political conflicts and ambiguities so intensely troubling as to require expression in displaced and symptomatic form. In order to argue for the central importance of the 1849 riot as an absent presence in Melville's tale, however, I shall have to triangulate among various pieces of "evidence": certain known facts about Melville's life, the events of the riot itself, and Melville's 1854 diptych tale, **"The Two Temples."** The "proof" for my argument, I am aware, will consist in its plausibility and interpretive suggestiveness rather than in its empirical verifiability.

Melville was hunting whales on the *Acushnet* when John Colt came to trial for the murder of Adams and Monroe Edwards came to trial for forgery. By 1847, however, the recently married Melville was living at 103 Fourth Avenue, two blocks from Astor Place, a few short blocks from the house of John Jacob Astor, and right behind Grace Church. Until the fall of 1849, Melville lived in New York, writing in the mornings, walking down to the New York Society Library every afternoon to peruse the newspapers (of which he was an avid reader),[40] and taking in occasional performances at the newly constructed Astor Place Opera House. Apart from his family (he lived with his married brother Al-

lan—who was, incidentally, a Wall Street lawyer—in order to share household expenses for the large number of dependents), Melville at this time associated primarily with the literary wing of the Young America movement, which included such figures as the novelist Cornelius Mathews and the editors and literary publicists George and Evert Duyckinck. Self-styled literary nationalists, the adherents of Young America supported and promoted Melville in the early phases of his career. The literary Young Americans were progressive in some respects: Evert Duyckinck listened with delight to Melville's reading of a parody of Astor's will that appeared in the *Herald* in April 1848 and approved the reworking of this and similarly satiric political material in *Mardi,* of which Duyckinck wrote one of the few favorable reviews appearing in the spring of 1849.[41]

But Mathews and the Duyckincks were conservatives in other respects. Where the political wing of Young America "welcomed the 1848 revolutions," notes Rogin, the European uprisings made Evert Duyckinck "nervous"; "[h]is fear of disorder placed him closer to his northeastern Whig enemies than to the Democracy."[42] Evert Duyckinck was also "a good, active Episcopalian," Hershel Parker observes, one who "bridled at whatever favored airy transcendentalisms or slighted organized Christianity."[43] Duyckinck even attempted to warn Melville off Emerson.[44] As early as November 1848, Parker asserts, Melville, while grateful for the Duyckincks' publicizing efforts, was beginning to chafe against their continuing expectation that he would bury his views and perform literary hackwork for them.[45] Moreover, even as he was consorting with this socially conservative cultural elite, Melville was writing novels—*Mardi, Redburn,* and *White-Jacket*—manifesting his profound discomfort with elites and hierarchies of various kinds. By the late 1840s, Melville was living an increasingly intolerable contradiction.

In the fall of 1849—after purchasing two volumes of the Episcopal *Book of Common Prayer*—Melville traveled to England and the Continent.[46] Returning in early 1850, he began work on *Moby-Dick* and *Pierre,* settled in the Berkshires, and formed his intense friendship with Hawthorne. Evert Duyckinck, Mathews, the historian Joel C. Headley, and other Young Americans were present at the famous expedition up Monument Mountain in the summer of 1850 when Melville met Hawthorne and debated cultural politics with Oliver Wendell Holmes and other Bostonians. But Melville was gradually becoming more distant from the New York crowd in the early 1850s. Indeed, Parker opines that Melville may have moved to the Berkshires to "get away from the pettiness of the New York literati."[47] Melville dropped his subscription to the *Literary World* in February 1852;[48] in August of that year the Duyckincks published a "shocked review" of *Pierre.* Yet the Melville who in 1853 turned to the composition of magazine stories and sketches—of which **"Bartleby"** was the earliest published piece—was still in many respects living the conventional life of a middle-class man of letters. Indeed, because of the poor sales of *Moby-Dick* and *Pierre,* Melville had become more dependent than ever on the generosity of a father-in-law with whose politics, Carolyn Karcher argues, he must have been in deep conflict on many key points.[49] Even though Melville had broken with some of his more conservative literary associates by the time he began work on **"Bartleby"** in the summer of 1853, then, he continued to inhabit a conflicted social and political position.

Our story now shifts back some four years. On 10 May 1849 New York was shaken by the violence of the Astor Place riot. The high-toned British tragedian William Charles Macready had been invited to play Macbeth at the Astor Place Opera House at the same time that a popular American actor, Edwin Forrest, was scheduled to act the same role at a theater in the Bowery. A long-brewing rivalry between the two actors was readily incorporated into preexisting discourses of class and nation in a city already polarized by the labor struggles of the late 1840s. Proponents of Forrest crowded into the Astor Place Opera House on 7 May, and when Macready appeared, they drowned out his lines and pelted him with rotten eggs, vegetables, coins, and bottles of assafoetida. According to the *Tribune,* Macready reacted with aplomb: he "picked up one of the pennies and very coolly placed it in his bosom."[50] The demonstrators' slogans reflected the contradictory impulses of contemporaneous working-class consciousness: castigations of the white-shirted, white-gloved rich blended with the ironic salute, "Three cheers for Macready and Nigger Douglass!"[51] The next day, a portion of the same group, "still glowing with their success at the Opera House the night before, broke up the anniversary meeting of the American Anti-Slavery Society at the Broadway Tabernacle [and] . . . made an unsuccessful attempt to disrupt the proceedings of the American and Foreign Anti-Slavery Society in the same building."[52]

The city's elite reacted in dismay to the attack on Macready. In the *Literary World,* The Duyckincks praised Macready for conducting himself with "the highest magnanimity" and condemned the incident as a "gross and unprovoked . . . outrage" perpetrated by a "brutal mob." Dealing with the consequences of the disruption, they concluded, "is a matter for the police not for the critic."[53] A group of forty-seven prominent citizens published an open letter to Macready in the *Herald,* urging him to continue his performances:

> DEAR SIR: The undersigned, having heard that the outrage at the Astor Place Opera House, on Monday evening, is likely to have the effect of preventing you from concluding your intended farewell engagement on the American stage, take this public method of requesting you to reconsider your decision, and of assuring you that the good sense and respect for order prevailing in this community, will sustain you on the subsequent nights of your performance.[54]

This letter, which amounted to a guarantee of police protection, was signed by the Duyckincks, Washington Irving, and Mathews, as well as a number of leading municipal figures, including Francis B. Cutting, Mordecai M. Noah, and Samuel M. Ruggles. Also among the signatories was Herman Melville.[55]

When the letter appeared, anonymous threats were made to several of the signers who lived north of the Opera House around Union Square. A countermanifesto was issued by the supporters of Forrest:

> WORKINGMEN
> SHALL
> AMERICANS OR ENGLISH RULE
> IN THIS CITY?
>
> The crew of the English steamer has threatened all Americans who shall dare to express their opinion this night at the English Aristocratic Opera House! We advocate no violence, but a free expression of opinion to all public men!
>
> WORKINGMEN! FREEMEN!
> STAND BY YOUR
> LAWFUL RIGHTS.[56]

When Macready decided that the show must go on, the *Herald* editors, anticipating further disturbances, gleefully noted, "The rioters will be well-licked tonight, or the city again disgraced."[57]

Macready returned to the stage on 10 May. Once again, a disturbance erupted inside the theater. This time, however, the police were prepared: the demonstrators were pushed out to join the thousands thronged in the street. After members of the crowd tossed a few volleys of rocks, the police fired on them, killing twenty-two people, including an eight-year-old boy. Another nine people subsequently died of wounds, and as many as forty-eight more civilians were injured by the police, including a Wall Street lawyer who was crossing Lafayette Place at the wrong time and an elderly woman "sitting in her own room at the corner of Lafayette-Place, [who] was shot in the side."[58]

Nothing daunted, Macready attempted to rehearse *Richelieu* the next day, but the Opera House was closed; he rapidly left New York. There was a massive rally at City Hall Park, at which Mike Walsh proclaimed that "[n]ot in the whole history of the civilized world has there ever been committed an atrocity equal to that which was perpetrated last night. . . . If such a thing had occurred in Paris, the streets would have been soon filled with barricades raised against the cut-throats, with the Mayor at their head."[59] The press was sharply divided in its response to the riot. The Duyckincks, in the *Literary World,* bemoaned the "[m]elancholy circumstances under which Mr. Macready leaves the country" and praised the open letter as a tribute to "Mr. Macready and his honored position, gained by the most noble devotion to his Art." The *Literary World* further opined, the "Astor Opera House Riot will be remembered in connexion with a great principle—that of the supremacy of law over brute violence."[60] The *Herald,* on 16 May, fulminated against Greeley's *Tribune* as an "organ of French socialism and kindred abominations" and meditated on how much mischief "may have been wrought amongst ourselves, by this continual harping upon the tyranny and oppression of the rich." On 29 May, however, the *Herald* also noted, "We advise the proprietors of the Massacre Place Opera House to convert it into a church—into a place for hearing sermons, and singing of psalms, and making prayers, and repenting of sin, for assuredly there has been enough of sin committed in that region to be repented of in sackcloth and ashes." The Philadelphia *Ledger* asserted that the riot proved that there was in New York "what every patriot has considered it his duty to deny—a *high* and a *low* class." Horace Greeley's *Tribune* interpreted the riot as the outgrowth of the class antagonisms resulting from rapid urbanization: "Is there no means," Greeley asked, "of preventing so many young men from rushing to the cities, of giving the less fortunate, the poor, a direct personal interest in the property and order of society, so that when it is attacked they shall feel that they are themselves attacked?" The *Journal of Commerce,* arguing that the Opera House should have been closed after the events of 8 May, made the provocative charge that the signers of the open letter to Macready "were mainly instrumental in bringing this calamity on our city."[61]

Although Melville lived only two blocks from the site where twenty-five thousand demonstrators gathered on 10 May, his papers contain no direct reference to the Astor Place riot. Nor do they mention his role in signing the open letter or his reaction to the press coverage of the incident. There is no "mea culpa" on record. We can therefore only speculate about what his reactions might have been. There is no reason to assume that Melville signed the open letter under duress. Quite possibly the racism and nativism of the demonstrators repelled the imagination that would figure the *Pequod* as the ship of mankind. Possibly he found this mob, like other mobs, terrifying. The representation of the grotesque starving throng receiving the leavings of the Lord Mayor's banquet in **"Poor Man's Pudding and Rich Man's Crumbs"** (1854), while reverberating with moral outrage, also reveals not a little fear of the uncontrolled masses. **"The House-Top,"** written in reaction to the 1863 draft riot, proclaims that "[t]he Town is taken by its rats" and expresses revulsion at the "Atheist roar of riot."[62]

All the same, it is difficult to believe that the novelist who in the spring of 1849 was writing so angrily of class polarization in *Redburn* and planning his condemnation of flogging in *White-Jacket* could have been unaware of and untroubled by the implications of the position he had taken. Most of those killed by the police at Astor Place had not, after all, been involved in the attacks on antislavery meetings on 8 May; some were just bystanders.[63] Almost all were the sorts of workers or self-employed laborers celebrated in Whitman's "Song of Occupations": "machinists, butchers, clerks, marble cutters, plumbers, cork merchants, shoemakers, paper folders, carpenters, and gunsmiths." Moreover, the open letter that Melville had signed in the company of New York's literary and social elite was subsequently viewed by at least one newspaper—the *Journal of Commerce*—as a death warrant. The Melville who had lampooned Astor's will the year before was now aligning himself with Washington Irving, whose popular *Astoria; or, Anecdotes of an Enterprise beyond the Rocky Mountains* (1836) saw the expression of manifest destiny in Astor's fur-trading empire.[64] In short, Melville had joined ranks with those who had contributed to and then defended the conversion of Astor Place into "Massacre Place." It is difficult to believe that Melville did not experience at least some feelings of guilt and regret about the side that he had ended up taking in what proved to be one of the sharpest manifestations of class conflict in the New York of the 1840s—at least in terms of violence—indeed, perhaps the closest U.S. equivalent to the Paris barricades of 1848.

"Bartleby," I am suggesting, is, in disguised and displaced form, the missing "mea culpa" in the corpus of Melville's works. Consider the parallels between the situations of the lawyer and Melville. Both are identified with the power and prestige of the name of Astor. Both encounter indecorous behavior on the part of a proletariat refusing to quit the premises. Both entertain "fears of a mob." Both succumb to pressure from peers and endorse the summoning of state power. Both indirectly contribute to the deaths of those who have defied accepted standards of property, "right," and conduct. In his satirical portrait of the lawyer in **"Bartleby,"** Melville is not simply exposing the ideological blindness and moral failure of a typical citizen of Wall Street; he is also, I suggest, working through his ambivalence about his complicity in the events that transpired at "Massacre Place." Indeed, this ambivalence may help to illuminate a key point of contention among critics of **"Bartleby"**—namely, the extent to which Melville ironizes his narrator's would-be humanism or, conversely, appears to sympathize with his narrator's situation. Reading **"Bartleby"** in the context of the urban struggles of the 1840s—specifically, of the Astor Place riot—enables us to understand the tale as simultaneously an expression of Melville's contempt for bourgeois moral cowardice and an admission of his own identification with this quality. Melville knows his narrator so well because he carries aspects of the lawyer within himself.[65]

This reading of **"Bartleby"** as an expression of Melville's uneasiness with his class partisanship in these events of 1849 is corroborated when another of his magazine sketches of the early 1850s—**"The Two Temples"**—is read in the same historical context. **"The Two Temples,"** a diptych Melville wrote in 1854, was rejected for publication because of its harsh and pointed satire of New York's Episcopalian elite. In this sketch, Melville contrasts his first-person narrator's humiliating experience in being excluded from a wealthy Episcopal church (its location three miles north of the Battery marks it as Grace Church) with his sense of ease in the inexpensive working-class section of the Royal Lyceum theater in London, where he is the recipient of various small gestures of welcome and kindness from other occupants of the gallery. The sketch patently sets up an opposition between the cold and unchristian behavior of the Episcopalian elite, whose beadle denies the narrator entry to the church because of his shabby clothing, and the generosity of the "quiet, well-pleased working-men, and their glad wives and sisters" who are willing to share what little they have. The narrator concludes by contrasting his reception in the two "temples": "a stranger in a strange land, I found sterling charity in the one; and at home, in my own land, was thrust out from the other."[66]

In **"The Two Temples,"** as in **"Bartleby,"** Melville explores issues of charity and hypocrisy that will receive their fullest treatment in *The Confidence-Man.* But the two short pieces are linked not only by this general thematic convergence but also by multiple narrative parallels. In the first part of **"The Two Temples,"** the narrator specifies that in order to reach the church he had to "tram[p] this blessed Sunday morning, all the way from the Battery, three long miles, . . . prayerbook under arm" (303). Denied entry because of his shabby appearance, the narrator sneaks up to the bell tower past the "great, fat-paunched, beadle-faced man" (313) who guards the door. Up in the porch, the narrator is directly exposed to the brilliant light streaming through the stained-glass windows but is prevented from seeing the people below because of the "fine-woven, gauzy wire-work" (305) of an obstructing screen. He muses, "[I]t was but a gorgeous dungeon, for I couldn't look out, any more than if I had been the occupant of a basement cell in 'the Tombs'" (305). Even though he has been excluded, the narrator participates privately in the church service: "Though an insider in one respect, yet am I but an outsider in another. But for all that, I will not be defrauded of my natural rights" (305). Viewing "the theatric wonder of the populous spectacle of this sumptuous sanctuary" through the filter of the screen,

he sees the white-robed priest read from the text, leave the altar, and reenter wearing black. "Book in hand, responses on my tongue, standing in the very posture of devotion," the narrator remarks, "I could not rid my soul of the intrusive thought that, through some necromancer's glass, I looked down upon some sly enchanter's show" (306). The priest proceeds to deliver to his wealthy parishioners a sermon based on the text, "Ye are the salt of the earth." When the congregation leaves, the narrator realizes that he has been locked in, "left alone and solitary in a temple which but a moment before was more populous than many villages" (307). To gain release from his prison, he sets up a riot in the bells, prompting the beadle to have him arrested as a "lawless violator, and a remorseless disturber of the Sunday peace" (309).

The connections between the first part of **"The Two Temples"** and **"Bartleby"** are rich and suggestive. To begin with, Grace Church was centrally implicated in the Trinity scandal, since it was one of the lavish buildings constructed from the sacrifice of Trinity's missions at the Bowery and Five Points. Living in the posh area around Astor Place, Melville was dwelling in the shadow of Grace Church—in more senses than one—at the moment when the Episcopal diocese's financial and moral affairs were figuring prominently in the newspapers that he habitually read. The description of the fat "beadle-faced" man guarding the first "temple" apparently captured without ambiguity the physical appearance of Isaac Brown, sexton of Grace Church. Charles F. Briggs, explaining to Melville his reason for rejecting the sketch at *Putnam's,* noted that "the moral of the 'Two Temples' would array against us the whole power of the pulpit, to say nothing of Brown, and the congregation of Grace Church."[67] Yet in **"The Two Temples"** Grace Church is also defamiliarized and resituated in its relation to Wall Street. The narrator is not a neighbor of the church, but an alien: he ascends from the Battery, the lower tip of Manhattan, close in fact to Wall Street, where Bartleby makes his lonely domicile. In his shabby coat, the narrator in **"The Two Temples"** might be Bartleby—or Turkey or Nippers, for that matter—trying to visit Trinity. Moreover, the description of the interior of the church in **"The Two Temples"** recalls the plan not of Grace Church but of Trinity Church. According to Beryl Rowland, various features of the building in the sketch—the location and height of the platform, the stained-glass windows, the view of the altar available from the tower—bear no resemblance to any features of Grace Church but are virtually identical with those of Trinity Church, where Melville visited and climbed around with his brother-in-law in January of 1848. By collapsing Grace and Trinity, Melville manages, Rowland notes, "to assail simultaneously the ostentation and the superficial Christianity of the two newest and most Fashionable churches in New York."[68] But Melville also slyly links the church located around the corner from the site of the Astor Place riot with the church where the lawyer in **"Bartleby"** goes to get his weekly dose of morality, as well as where Mike Walsh scaled the fence and performed his squatter's sit-in.

What happens inside the church also meaningfully parallels what happens in **"Bartleby"**—with the signal difference that the narrator here takes the position not of the defender of the "Sunday peace" but of the invader. In fact, the narrator in **"The Two Temples"** resembles Bartleby in several ways. Like Bartleby, he finds himself sealed off from the rest of humanity by a screen, one that permits sound but limits vision. Just as Bartleby continually faces walls—the black and white walls outside the Wall Street office windows, the "Egyptian masonry" of the Tombs—the narrator in **"The Two Temples"** has his view blocked and compares his perch with "a basement cell in the Tombs."[69] In insisting upon occupying his isolated space, the narrator acknowledges his "outsider" status but, in a phrase invoking the rhetoric of contemporaneous radicalism from Skidmore to Walsh, asserts his "natural rights." When he is left alone in the church, the **"Two Temples"** narrator, like Bartleby on a Sunday, finds himself inhabiting a deserted scene formerly "more populous than many villages." And, as in Bartleby's case, the narrator's attempt to occupy a space that is socially used but privately owned leads to his being branded "lawless" and handed over to the state.

In other words, in a number of its key narrative details, as well as in its paradigmatic structure, the first part of **"The Two Temples"** offers Melville the opportunity to retell the events in the earlier tale—this time, however, from the point of view of the disenfranchised. The identification with Bartleby is by no means complete, for the narrator in the later sketch retains a degree of class privilege: when he goes to court, he notes, "my rather gentlemanly appearance procured me a private hearing from the judge" (309). Apparently the shabby coat is not the only one the narrator owns.[70] Moreover, he retains the air of wondering naïveté that Melville assigns to other quasi-autobiographical speakers in the diptych sketches: the author who frames the text's multiple ironies knows much more than the narrator who experiences them. If the narrator in **"Bartleby"** articulates the aspect of Melville that is acquainted with bourgeois complacency and cowardice from the inside, then the narrator in **"The Two Temples"** articulates the Melville who is alien, subversive, and slightly manic, setting up a clamorous alarm of whose full meaning he seems not fully aware.

The first part of **"The Two Temples"** expands the critique of Trinity adumbrated in **"Bartleby"**; it corroborates those readings of the tale that stress Melville's de-

testation of oppressive hierarchy and his sympathy with aliens and rebels. The second part of **"The Two Temples"** draws on contemporaneous history in a different way; it introduces a key figure in the repressed subtext of the Astor Place riot—namely, the tragedian Macready. For when the narrator attends the Royal Lyceum theater in London, the actor on the stage is none other than "the stately Macready in the part of Cardinal Richelieu" (311). Looking around the theater, the narrator notes with pleasure that "[s]uch was the decorum of this special theater, that nothing objectionable was admitted within its walls" (314). Moreover, he praises Macready as "an amiable gentleman, combining the finest qualities of social and Christian respectability, with the highest excellence in his particular profession, for which last he had conscientiously done much, in many ways, to refine, elevate, and chasten" (314). Yet, when Macready begins to speak, the narrator experiences a sense of *deja vu*:

> How marvellous this personal resemblance! He looks every inch to be the self-same, stately priest I saw irradiated by the glow-worm dyes of the pictured windows from my high tower-pew. And shining as he does, in the rosy reflexes of these stained walls and gorgeous galleries, the mimic priest down there; he too seems lit by Gothic blazonings.—Hark! the same measured, courtly, noble tone. See! the same imposing attitude. Excellent actor is this Richelieu!
>
> (315)

Watching Macready, the narrator muses, "Do I dream, or is it genuine memory that recalls some similar thing seen through the woven wires?" (315). When Macready finishes his performance, the narrator notes approvingly: "[T]he enraptured thousands sound their responses, deafeningly; unmistakably sincere. Right from the undoubted heart" (315).

Critics of **"The Two Temples"** routinely treat as unproblematic the narrator's claim to have found true charity and community in the London theater. The "similar thing" that the narrator discerns in the priest and the tragedian is read as heightening the contrast between essence and appearance: the priest flatters his wealthy listeners into believing they are the "salt of the earth," while the actor, unabashed in his pretense, delivers genuine human value to those who genuinely are the salt of the earth. It is pointed out, moreover, that Melville dedicated the sketch to the actor Sheridan Knowles—a gesture indicating his respect for the tragedian's art.[71] But what this line of interpretation overlooks is historical context. For *Richelieu,* we will recall, was the play that Macready, in a gesture of remarkable coldheartedness, attempted to rehearse at the Opera House the morning after the murderous police attack at Astor Place. Even if Melville admired great tragedians, it is difficult to believe that he did not intend an oblique reference to the events of 1849 in specifying Richelieu as the role played by Macready in this sketch of 1854.

What is more, Melville's own experiences in London theaters in the fall of 1849 diverge significantly from his delineation of them in **"The Two Temples."** Melville visited the Royal Lyceum Theatre on 7 November and bought a shilling ticket in the gallery, which he enjoyed for its "quite decent people" and the presence of a "fellow going round with a coffee pot & mugs crying 'Porter, gents, porter!'" The performers at the Lyceum, however, were Madame Vestris and Charles Mathews. Melville saw Macready—not in *Richelieu* but in *Othello*—on 19 November at the Haymarket Theatre.[72] He wrote of this performance in his journal: "McReady [*sic*] painted hideously. Didn't like him very much upon the whole—bad voice, it seemed."[73] Thus the narrator's praise of Macready in **"The Two Temples"** for his "qualities of Christian respectability," "noble tone," and "imposing attitude" runs directly counter to Melville's own impressions of the actor. The narrator's language echoes, if anything, the lofty estimate of Macready and Macready's art that accompanied the Duyckincks' castigation of the Bowery's citizenry for their behavior on 8 and 10 May 1849. The narratorial voice speaking approvingly of the lack of anything "objectionable" at Macready's London *Richelieu* performance therefore invites an at least partially ironic reading. Like the narrator of **"The Paradise of Bachelors and the Tartarus of Maids,"** who fails to analyze the "inverted similitude" that he discerns between the lawyers who consume and the millworkers who produce, the man who addresses the reader in **"The Two Temples"** comes nowhere near understanding the "similar thing" he has intuited in the sexton of Part I and the actor of Part II.

The path from **"The Two Temples"** back to **"Bartleby"** is circuitous but worth treading. Part I of the sketch suggests the passion with which the Melville of 1854 had come to reject all that Trinity stood for; it is well-nigh impossible to picture the portrayer of the "beadle-faced man" going out and purchasing prayer books for christenings, as Melville in fact did in 1849. Moreover, the first section of the diptych places the narrator in a position analogous to Bartleby's and implies a strong identification with the outcast who asserts his "natural rights" and disrupts the Sunday peace. The second section, by contrast, offers an ironic representation of the "stately Macready" that may be read as Melville's repudiation of his earlier support for the actor and perhaps by extension of his partisanship in the Astor Place riot as well. From the vantage point of this rearticulation of Macready, the reading of the paradigmatic plot of **"Bartleby"** as a tale of betrayal and guilt—as an expression of Melville's inchoate and largely unacknowledged regret in having aligned himself, however inad-

vertently, with the resonant name of Astor—gains credibility. The lawyer's irrational clinging to the scrivener—"him whom I had so longed to be rid of" (39)—takes shape not only as a subliminal recognition of his felt moral implication in the scrivener's fate but also, we may speculate, as a covert expression of the author's own implication in the fates of those who died at Astor Place.

"Bartleby" is a "Story of Wall Street," I hope I have shown, not only in its allusions to specific persons and events connected to conflicts between the rulers and the ruled in midcentury New York but also in its participation in contemporaneous discourses about class relations and property rights. In part these allusions and this participation are directed and deliberate, producing a controlled ironic framework within which the reader is invited to judge the inadequacies and hypocrisies of the tale's narrator. In part, however, Melville's treatment of this material is displaced and fragmentary, producing an irony and an ambiguity that are not always guided by a consistent authorial perspective. Just as there are issues of ethics and social responsibility that the Wall Street lawyer feels compelled to raise but cannot fully face, there are comparable moral—indeed political—issues that Melville himself allows to surface but then drives to the corners of his text. **"Bartleby"** gains in richness and complexity when read, in the context of 1840s New York social history, as Melville's ringing of the bells—both purposive and manic—against Astor and Trinity.

Notes

For many biographical, textual, and historical points, I am indebted to my friend and former colleague Harrison Hayford. I also wish to thank David Reynolds and Carl Smith, both also former colleagues at Northwestern, as well as Heyward Ehrlich and Sheila Post-Lauria, a current and former colleague, respectively, at Rutgers University-Newark.

1. John McWilliams, "The Rationale for 'The American Romance,'" *boundary 2* 17 (spring 1990): 81; George Dekker, "Once More: Hawthorne and the Genealogy of American Romance," *ESQ* 35 (first quarter 1989): 82.

2. The first grouping of critics is represented by Lewis Mumford, "Melville's Miserable Years," in *Bartleby the Inscrutable: A Collection of Commentary on Herman Melville's Tale "Bartleby, the Scrivener,"* ed. M. Thomas Inge (Hamden, Conn.: Archon, 1979), 57-60; and Leo Marx, "Melville's Parable of the Walls," in Inge, 84-113. The second grouping is represented by Walter H. Eitner, "The Lawyer's Rockaway Trips in 'Bartleby, the Scrivener,'" *Melville Society Extracts* 78

(September 1989): 14-16; Charles Swann, "Dating the Action of 'Bartleby,'" *Notes and Queries* 32 (September 1985): 357-58; T. H. Giddings, "Melville, the Colt-Adams Murder, and 'Bartleby,'" *Studies in American Fiction* 2 (1974): 123-32; and Hans Bergmann, "'Turkey on His Back': 'Bartleby' and New York Words," *Melville Society Extracts* 90 (September 1992): 16-19. The third grouping is represented by Louise K. Barnett, "Bartleby as Alienated Worker," *Studies in Short Fiction* 11 (1974): 379-85; Michael T. Gilmore, *American Romanticism and the Marketplace* (Chicago: Univ. of Chicago Press, 1985); David Kuebrich, "Melville's Doctrine of Assumptions: The Hidden Ideology of Capitalist Production in 'Bartleby,'" *New England Quarterly* 69 (September 1996): 381-405; and James C. Wilson, "'Bartleby': The Walls of Wall Street," *Arizona Quarterly* 37 (winter 1981): 335-46.

3. Swann, "Dating the Action of 'Bartleby,'" 357-58.

4. Herman Melville, *The Piazza Tales and Other Prose Pieces, 1839-1869,* ed. Harrison Hayford, Alma A. MacDougall, G. Thomas Tanselle, et al. (Evanston and Chicago: Northwestern Univ. Press and The Newberry Library, 1987), 14; all subsequent quotations from "Bartleby" are from this edition and will be cited parenthetically in the text.

5. See Giddings, "Melville, the Colt-Adams Murder, and 'Bartleby,'" 123-32. The chronological placement of the main action of "Bartleby" in 1843 is supported by the dating of a source that some critics consider seminal to Melville's tale—namely, a short piece entitled "The Lawyer's Story, Or, the Wrongs of the Orphans; By a Member of the Bar," which appeared in both the *New-York Times* and the *New York Tribune* in February of 1853. The story begins, "In the summer of 1843, having an extraordinary quantity of deeds to copy, I engaged, temporarily, an extra copying clerk, who interested me considerably, in consequence of his modest, quiet, gentlemanly demeanor, and in his intense application to his duties" (cited in Johannes Dietrich Bergmann, "'Bartleby' and 'The Lawyer's Story,'" *American Literature* 47 [November 1975]: 433).

6. David S. Reynolds, *Beneath the American Renaissance: The Subversive Imagination in the Age of Emerson and Melville* (New York: Knopf, 1988), 296.

7. Harrison Hayford, letter to author, 16 December 1992.

8. Sean Wilentz, *Chants Democratic: New York City and the Rise of the American Working Class, 1788-1850* (New York: Oxford Univ. Press, 1984), 350.

9. See Richard Moody, *The Astor Place Riot* (Bloomington: Indiana Univ. Press, 1958), 177.

10. Helene Zahler, *Eastern Workingmen and National Land Policy, 1829-1862* (1941; reprint, New York: Greenwood, 1969), 69-70.

11. Walt Whitman, *The Correspondence of Walt Whitman,* 6 vols., ed. Haviland Miller (New York: New York Univ. Press, 1961-1977), 1:46.

12. Luc Sante, *Low Life: Lures and Snares of Old New York* (New York: Farrar, Straus & Giroux, 1991), 340.

13. Thomas Skidmore, *The Rights of Man to Property! Being a Proposition to Make It Equal among the Adults of the Present Generation* (1829; reprint, New York: Burt Franklin, n.d.), 5, 137-38.

14. Reynolds, *Beneath the American Renaissance,* 81.

15. Mike Walsh, quoted in Wilentz, *Chants Democratic,* 378, 331.

16. Thomas Pribek, "Melville's Copyists: The 'Bar-Tenders' of Wall Street," *Papers on Language and Literature* 22 (spring 1986): 176-86.

17. John M. Green, "Bartleby, the Perfect Pupil," *American Transcendental Quarterly* 7 (March 1993): 71.

18. See Allan Silver, "The Lawyer and the Scrivener," *Partisan Review* 48, No. 3 (1981): 409-24.

19. Kuebrich, "Melville's Doctrine of Assumptions," 381-405. While the lawyer represents his tolerance for his workers' idiosyncrasies as a function of his charitable spirit, it is worth noting that the labor market in the late 1840s and early 1850s was tight, and bosses often had no choice but to keep on workers who were alcoholic or otherwise less than fully productive; see Richard B. Stott, *Workers in the Metropolis: Class, Ethnicity, and Youth in Antebellum New York City* (Ithaca, N.Y.: Cornell Univ. Press, 1990), 148-49. Sheila Post-Lauria argues that an ironic reading of the narrator's closing words is supported by Melville's choice to send "Bartleby" to *Putnam's* rather than to *Harper's.* Stories in *Harper's,* she points out, typically "emphasize the abilities of characters to find contentment through the hardships they encounter by transforming social problems as literary issues into a celebration of the moralistic principles of toleration, acquiescence, and impoverished nobility." The "common stance" of stories in *Putnam's,* by contrast, was "against sentimental rhetoric." The narrator in "Bartleby," Post-Lauria suggests, is a satiric caricature of a typical narrator in a *Harper's* story; see Post-Lauria, "Canonical Text and Context: The Ex-

ample of Herman Melville's 'Bartleby, the Scrivener: A Story of Wall Street,'" *College Literature* 20 (June 1993): 196-205.

20. See Dan McCall, *The Silence of Bartleby* (Ithaca, N.Y.: Cornell Univ. Press, 1989), 61-63, 110-13; and Bruce L. Grenburg, *Some Other World to Find: Quest and Negation in the Works of Herman Melville* (Urbana: Univ. of Illinois Press, 1989), 169-70.

21. Edward K. Spann, *The New Metropolis: New York City, 1840-1857* (New York: Columbia Univ. Press, 1981), 233; Astor is quoted on 208.

22. Ibid., 233.

23. Arthur D. Howden Smith, *John Jacob Astor: Landlord of New York* (Philadelphia: J. B. Lippincott, 1929), 97.

24. Stephen Zelnick, "Melville's 'Bartleby': History, Ideology, and Literature," *Marxist Perspectives* 2 (winter 1979-80): 75.

25. Eitner, "The Lawyer's Rockaway Trips," 15.

26. Spann, *The New Metropolis*, 208.

27. Ibid., 211.

28. Ibid., 234.

29. Quoted in Smith, *John Jacob Astor,* 90-91.

30. Wilentz, *Chants Democratic,* 336.

31. George Evans, quoted in Zahler, *Eastern Workingmen and National Land Policy,* 34; George Lippard, quoted in Zahler, 53.

32. *Atlantic Monthly,* April 1859, 396.

33. Zahler, *Eastern Workingmen and National Land Policy,* 44.

34. Irving Adler, "Equity, Law, and Bartleby," *Science and Society* 51 (winter 1987-1988): 468-74.

35. Spann, *The New Metropolis,* 229, 230, 233.

36. James C. Wilson, "The Significance of Petra in 'Bartleby,'" *Melville Society Extracts* 57 (February 1984): 10.

37. Helen P. Trimpi notes that Mike Walsh's "character and views were undoubtedly known to Melville early, as a resident of New York City and as the brother of a Democratic politician. Gansevoort Melville had been popular as an orator with the Irish in New York and was actively involved in the New York City Democratic efforts in 1844 to sign up Irish voters for the party, even at the risk of illegally naturalizing them by the hundreds. This was at the same time as Walsh was establishing his newspaper and was winning his way in the

party, in his attempt to break the barriers of the Tammany hall electoral system for the Irish immigrants." Trimpi also notes that Melville mentioned Walsh in his 1855-1857 journal and argues that Walsh may be the prototype for the skeptical Irish voice heard in the closing scene of *The Confidence-Man*; see Trimpi, *Melville's Confidence Men and American Politics in the 1850s* (Hamden, Conn.: Archon, 1987), 240-41, 238-40.

38. Michael Paul Rogin, *Subversive Genealogy: The Politics and Art of Herman Melville* (New York: Knopf, 1983), 194.

39. See James H. Kavanagh, "'That Hive of Subtlety': 'Benito Cereno' as Ideological Critique," *Bucknell Review* 28, No. 1 (1984): 127-57.

40. Merton Sealts, *Melville's Reading,* rev. ed. (Columbia: Univ. of South Carolina Press, 1988), 38.

41. Leon Howard, *Herman Melville: A Biography* (Berkeley and Los Angeles: Univ. of California Press, 1951), 108-11, 120.

42. Rogin, *Subversive Genealogy,* 73.

43. Hershel Parker, "Melville and Politics: A Scrutiny of the Political Milieux of Herman Melville's Life and Works," (Ph.D. diss., Northwestern University, 1964), 598.

44. John Stafford, *The Literary Criticism of "Young America": A Study in the Relationship of Politics and Literature, 1837-1850* (1952; reprint, New York: Russell and Russell, 1967), 22-28.

45. Hershel Parker, "Historical Note—II," in Herman Melville, *Moby-Dick, or the Whale,* ed. Harrison Hayford, Hershel Parker, and G. Thomas Tanselle (Evanston and Chicago: Northwestern Univ. Press and The Newberry Library, 1988), 594.

46. Sealts, *Melville's Reading,* 46.

47. Parker, "Melville and Politics," 204.

48. Ibid., 222.

49. Carolyn L. Karcher, *Shadow over the Promised Land: Slavery, Race, and Violence in Melville's America* (Baton Rouge: Louisiana State Univ. Press, 1980), 8-11. See also John Stark, "Melville, Lemuel Shaw, and 'Bartleby,'" in *Bartleby the Inscrutable,* ed. Inge, 166-73. Scholars differ over Melville's attitude toward Hawthorne in the early 1850s. Rogin and Karcher assert that Melville's friendship with Hawthorne cooled soon after Hawthorne authored a campaign biography of Franklin Pierce, who supported the 1850 Compromise and, as President, used Federal troops to enforce the Fugitive Slave Law (Rogin, *Subversive Geneal-*

ogy, 219; Karcher, 12-13). Harrison Hayford, however, maintains that Melville had strong affection and respect for Hawthorne past the mid-decade (*Melville's "Monody": Really for Hawthorne?* [Evanston: Northwestern Univ. Press, 1990]).

50. *New York Tribune,* 8 May 1849, 2.

51. Alvin P. Harlow, *Old Bowery Days: The Chronicles of a Famous Street* (New York and London: D. Appleton, 1931), 326.

52. Moody, *The Astor Place Riot,* 114.

53. *Literary World,* 12 May 1849. The *Literary World* was a weekly, so presumably the Duyckincks wrote these words and sent the issue to press before the shootings at Astor Place occurred.

54. *New York Herald,* 9 May 1849, 4.

55. Alvin Harlow inaccurately asserts that "John Jacob Astor" signed the *Herald* open letter (*Old Bowery Days,* 323-31). The name of John Jacob Astor I could not have appeared, since the old man died in 1848; neither, however, do the names of John Jacob Astor II or William Astor appear. The view that Melville's Young America acquaintances took of the Astor Place riot is suggested by the account of the event offered by Joel C. Headley, the historian who accompanied Melville and the rest on the Monument Mountain hike of 1850. In his *The Great Riots of New York: 1712 to 1873,* Headley referred to the Astor Place demonstrators as "rabble" and "rowdies." He concluded that "when the public peace is broken, it matters not how great or insignificant the cause, it must be preserved; and if the police or military are called out to do it, and are attacked, they must defend themselves, and uphold the laws, or be false to their trust" (1873; reprint, Indianapolis, Ind.: Bobbs-Merrill, 1970), 127. The bystanders who were killed, Headley wrote, "fell victim, as they always must if they will hang on the skirts of a mob from curiosity. Men anxious to witness a fight must take the chances to getting hurt" (126). Melville's situation in relation to the literary establishment is tellingly signaled by two reviews appearing in the very issue of the *Tribune* (10 May 1849) in which the Astor Place riot was reported. Headley's *The Adirondack; or, Life in the Woods* received a sympathetic reading, whereas *Mardi* was summarily dismissed: "We have seldom found our reading faculty so near exhaustion or our good nature as critics so severely exercised, as in the attempt to get through this new work by the author of the fascinating *Typee* and *Omoo.*" In May 1849, Melville was clearly dependent upon the Young Americans for his continuing reputation.

56. Headley, *The Great Riots of New York,* 120.

57. *New York Herald,* 10 May 1849, 2.

58. *New York Tribune,* supplement, 11 May 1849, 1.

59. Moody, *The Astor Place Riot,* 193.

60. *Literary World,* 19 May 1849, 438, 437.

61. Moody, *The Astor Place Riot,* 229, 219, 224.

62. *The Battle-Pieces of Herman Melville,* ed. Hennig Cohen (New York: Thomas Yoseloff, 1963), 89. My colleague Heyward Ehrlich has pointed out that a letter from Melville to Evert Duyckinck of 16 August 1850 may be read as making an oblique reference to the Astor Place riot. Ostensibly pitying Duyckinck and Mathews for being stuck in the city ("drear regions which are Trans-Taconic to me"), Melville elaborates a fantasy of his two friends getting "a contract to pave Broadway between Clinton Place & Union-Square." (The Young Americans met at Duyckinck's basement at 20 Clinton Place.) Melville teasingly calls upon his friends to "come out from among those Hittites & Hodites [and] give up mortar forever," noting that "mortar was the *precipitate* of the Fall; & with a brickbat, or a cobblestone *boulder,* Cain killed Abel." He then asks, "Do you use brickbats for paper-weights in the office? Do you & Mathews pitch pavingstones, & play ball that way in the cool of the evening, opposite the Astor-House?" (*The Letters of Herman Melville,* ed. Merrill R. Davis and William H. Gilman [New Haven: Yale Univ. Press, 1960], 111-12). Since the missiles thrown by the rioters at Astor Place had consisted of pieces of rubble from a nearby sewer construction project (Harlow, *The Great Riots of New York,* 328), the reference to Duyckinck and Mathews pitching paving stones is provocative. Melville's tone is hard to pinpoint. In part he engages in fond joking and playful punning. But the assertion that Cain murdered Abel with "a brick-bat, or a cobble-stone boulder" may refer indirectly to the overwhelming force used by the police against the Astor Place rioters and situate the Astor Place killings in the context of primal murder. (In "Bartleby," the lawyer's moralistically self-serving statement that he and his scrivener are both "sons of Adam" may further echo this idea.) The reference to Mathews and Duyckinck getting a "contract" to pave Broadway implies the two *Literary Review* editors' close connection to the municipal authorities. Furthermore, the notion that Mathews and Duyckinck might use brickbats or paper-weights, as well as the image of them tossing paving-stones and playing ball in front of the Astor House, may be read as suggesting the Young Americans' patrician detachment from the conse-

quences of the state violence that, in their role as cultural arbiters, they helped to instigate and then condoned. While Melville had not yet broken with Mathews and Duyckinck in August 1850, his barbed tone and veiled innuendoes may signal the impending split, as well as intimate a causal relation between this split and the events at Astor Place.

63. Moody, *The Astor Place Riot,* 173.

64. Washington Irving, referring to Astor as "my friend," noted in the preface to *Astoria* that the millionaire had "expressed a regret that the true nature and extent of his enterprise and its national character and importance had never been understood, and a wish that I would undertake to give an account of it" (*Astoria; or, Anecdotes of an Enterprise beyond the Rocky Mountains,* ed. William Goetzmann, 2 vols. [Philadelphia: J. B. Lippincott, 1961], 1:xiv). *Astoria,* a "striking and immediate success on both sides of the Atlantic" (Goetzmann, ix), went through eleven editions in Irving's lifetime; it was surely current at the time of the Astor Place riot.

65. For the significance of the fact that Melville's brothers Gansevoort and Allan had both at one point been Masters in Chancery, see Rogin, *Subversive Genealogy,* 196.

66. Herman Melville, "The Two Temples," in *The Piazza Tales,* ed. Hayford, MacDougall, Tanselle, ct al., 313, 315; all subsequent quotations from this sketch are from this edition and will be cited parenthetically in the text.

67. Beryl Rowland attributes this statement to Putnam; Harrison Hayford, however, opines that it was made by Briggs; see Rowland, "Grace Church and Melville's Story of 'The Two Temples,'" *Nineteenth-Century Fiction* 8 (1973): 340; Hayford, letter to author.

68. Rowland, "Grace Church and Melville's Story," 346.

69. A detail too delicious to omit: Grace Church was built from stone quarried at Sing Sing.

70. Melville apparently knew what it was to be shamed by improper clothing. According to Howard, during his European trip in 1849-1850 Melville "was acutely self-conscious about his unfashionable green coat, which aroused amusement on board the *Southampton,* attracted attention on the London streets and caused people to stare in church, but which he could not afford to replace" (*Herman Melville,* 144).

71. See, for example, William B. Dillingham, *Melville's Short Fiction, 1853-1856* (Athens: Univ. of Georgia Press, 1977), 104-18; Marvin Fisher,

Going Under: Melville's Short Fiction and the American 1850s (Baton Rouge: Louisiana State Univ. Press, 1977), 51-61.

72. Jay Leyda, *The Melville Log: A Documentary Life of Herman Melville, 1819-1891,* rev. ed., vol. 1 (New York: Gordian Press, 1969), 337, 334.

73. Herman Melville, *Journals,* ed. Howard C. Horsford with Lynn Horth [Evanston and Chicago: Northwestern Univ. Press and The Newberry Library, 1989], 22. Eleanor Metcalf's 1948 edition misreads the phrase as "panted hideously" (Herman Melville, *Journal of a Visit to London and the Continent 1849-1850,* ed. Eleanor Melville Metcalf [Cambridge: Harvard Univ. Press, 1948], 38).

Jonathan Beecher (essay date spring 2000)

SOURCE: Beecher, Jonathan. "Variations on a Dystopian Theme: Melville's 'Encantadas.'" *Utopian Studies* 11, no. 2 (spring 2000): 88-95.

[*In the following essay, Beecher explicates Melville's dystopian perspective in "The Encantadas, or Enchanted Isles," observing the significance of the work's imagery, epigraphs, and structure.*]

When in the spring of 1856 Herman Melville published a volume of stories entitled ***The Piazza Tales,*** reviewers hailed it as "decidedly the most readable thing" Melville had written since the great days of *Typee* and *Omoo.* According to the Concord, New Hampshire *Patriot and State Gazette,* the old Melville was back—"he of Tahitian memory; he who [in his first two works] introduced us to many Polynesian delights; who initiated us into the mysteries of tabooing and tatooing—who fed our imaginations with glowing descriptions of feasts, fruits and Fayaway." After the "morbid" *Pierre,* Melville had recaptured the "freshness and vivacity" of his earliest writing; and according to one reviewer, "scarcely a pleasanter book for summer reading could be recommended."

Reviewers of ***The Piazza Tales*** appreciated the richness of Melville's language, the vividness of his descriptive writing, and as one of them put it, the "splendidly sombre" character of his imagination. "Melville is a kind of wizard," wrote the reviewer for the New Bedford *Mercury.* "He writes of strange and mysterious things that belong to other worlds beyond this tame and everyday place we live in." One of the best received of Melville's tales was **"The Encantadas, or Enchanted Isles,"** a series of ten sketches focusing on the Galapagos Islands. "A more vivid picture of the fire-and-barren cursed Gallipagos we have never read," wrote the reviewer for the New York *Atlas*; and Thomas Powell of the New York *News* described **"The Encantadas"** [**"The Encantadas, or Enchanted Isles"**] as a series of beautifully written sketches "exerting an indefinable but irresistible sway over the imagination." These sketches could be "read and dwelt upon again and again, like [the most] gorgeous poem," wrote Powell, adding that Melville's "magnificent description of scenery, sea and cloud-land" possessed "the glowing richness [and] exquisite coloring" that distinguished the poetry of Tennyson (Higgins and Parker, 469-83).

While no twentieth-century critic has pursued the comparison with Tennyson, modern readers continue to find **"The Encantadas"** to be a haunting work of extraordinary power and verbal beauty. For the poet Marsden Hartley the Melville of **"The Encantadas"** was an "electric necromancer" and the work itself a "desolating tapestry" (105-06). Newton Arvin, no great admirer of Melville's shorter prose works, could nonetheless write of the "extraordinary harmony of image and feeling, of matter and meaning, in the best passages of '**The Encantadas**,'" adding that "nowhere in Melville are there grander images of utter desolation than those evoked in the first three sketches" (241). And for Melville's biographer, Laurie Robertson-Lorant, "Melville reached a pinnacle of stylistic brilliance in **'The Encantadas.'** His tragic vision buoyed up by wonderfully poetic prose, at times he seems to cresting on the blank-verse line of English epic. . . . At other times he surges toward a longer, looser prose line that anticipates the free-verse line of Walt Whitman" (339).

Although there is broad agreement concerning the power and beauty of **"The Encantadas,"** there is no consensus concerning the sources of that power or the nature of Melville's achievement. Critics disagree about the structure of the work, the credibility of the narrator, the function of the epigraphs, the importance of Melville's borrowings, and the question of what binds the whole together. Even the genre of **"The Encantadas"** is not entirely clear. On the most basic level it is a collection of travel sketches of a sort popular in mid-nineteenth-century journalism. But the sketches clearly have an allegorical dimension. They are not merely about a place but also about a condition of existence. Exactly what the allegory points to, however, is not so clear. One of the most cogent commentaries on **"The Encantadas"** describes it as picturing a "fallen world" similar to Dante's *Inferno* (Newbery). Another reader finds in it "a token of the inscrutable wholeness of nature" (Seelye). For a third **"The Encantadas"** is a reminder of the many-sidedness of truth (Yarina 147). Others have found in it an argument with Darwin (Franklin) and an indictment of slavery (Karcher, 109). So varied are the interpretations that one is tempted to

regard **"The Encantadas"** as a palimpsest as inscrutable to its readers as was Ahab's doubloon to the crew of the *Pequod*.

One big problem posed by **"The Encantadas"** is what to make of its narrator. In its first publication in *Putnam's Magazine* its author was identified as Salvator R. Tarnmoor, a name which evokes both the words *tarn* and *moor* and the seventeenth-century Italian painter, Salvator Rosa, whose wild and romantic landscapes (and seascapes) were much admired by Melville. At the outset of the work the narrator reveals himself as a lover of the picturesque and as one whose imagination is particularly stirred by ruins, abandoned cemeteries, and "profound solitudes." He is somewhat sententious, prone to exaggeration and contradiction; and he has what John Bryant aptly describes as a "jokey" side (150). While attracted to the dark and sinister, he is also glib and given to facile uplifting exhortations. This comes out cryptically in his little dissertation on the "two sides to a tortoise" (130-33). With its dark back and its bright breast-plate, he tells us, the tortoise symbolizes the fact that there is a bright side to almost everything if one can find it. In fact, the narrator's sketches, while nuanced, depict a world in which "the bright side" is conspicuous by its absence. Nonetheless, the narrator plunges ahead, urging us to "enjoy the bright side, keep it turned up perpetually if you can, but be honest and don't deny the black."[1]

What theme or themes lie at the center of this fascinating and enigmatic work? This is not an easy question to answer since one of Melville's great gifts as a writer is precisely his ability to move a range of issues in and out of focus in a single work and to explore ambiguities and multiple meanings in several realms at once. No single reading could begin to exhaust **"The Encantadas."** Yet one approach that I find suggestive is to consider **"The Encantadas"** as a kind of dystopia—or, better perhaps, as a series of variations on the dystopian theme. From its inception the concept of utopia has had a double meaning: it is "the good place" (*eu-topos*), but it is also "noplace" (*u-topos*). A utopia for our purposes is a description of an imaginary world thought to embody a kind of perfection not found in the ordinary world.[2] The concept of dystopia is looser, harder to define. Some dystopias are stiflingly perfect worlds in which the achievement of utopian dreams is shown to be horrific. Other dystopias are parodies, mocking the whole utopian enterprise. Still others are dark pictures of the world, offering perspectives on the human condition which, if true, would make utopian dreaming an utter waste of time.[3]

"The Encantadas" is a dystopia of the third kind. It presents an image of nature as a wasteland utterly inhospitable to human purposes, of human beings as either predators or victims, and of existence as so painful that endurance is the sole virtue. What gives the work its extraordinary power is first of all the rich symbolic resonance of its images of the natural world: the tortoises whose "crowning curse is their impulse to straightforwardness in a belittered world" (132); Rock Rodondo with its strata evoking both the biological chain of being and the "thrones, princedoms [and] powers" of human society (135); the tricky tides and shifting winds which confuse sailors trying to approach these apparently "wandering" islands. Each of these images encapsulates a perspective on the human condition.

Another source of the power of **"The Encantadas"** is to be found in the juxtaposition of Melville's epigraphs—most of them taken from Spenser's *Faerie Queene*—and the body of Melville's text. Sometimes the epigraphs reinforce the impression created by the text itself, as for example in the epigraph to the first sketch where Spenser's ferryman warns the Red Cross Knight that the islands he wishes to visit are not firm land but "Wandering Islands which to and fro do ronne" and lure hapless visitors into "most deadly danger and distressed plight." This is followed by a passage from Book II of *The Faerie Queene* in which the description of Despair's cave—"Darke, dolefull, dreary, like a greedy grave"—foreshadows the account of the islands as "cast . . . into the very body of cadaverous death" (128). Sometimes the epigraphs have an ironic sense which underlies by contrast the dystopian character of the islands. In the fourth sketch, **"A Pisgah View from the Rock,"** the lines of the epigraph are from the passage in *The Faerie Queene* where the Red Cross Knight is led up to the Mount of Contemplation and granted a vision of the New Jerusalem. In Melville's text it is strongly suggested that Rock Rodondo cannot be climbed and that if it could we would see nothing but a burned out landscape. In both cases—whether the epigraph echoes or contrasts with the text itself—the meaning of the text is extended beyond the frame of the sketch, and a second system of resonances is set up to go along with the symbolic resonance that Melville gives to certain images of the natural world (Albrecht 473-74 and Moses 133-50).

The chief source of the power of **"The Encantadas"** is the complex pattern of connections that Melville establishes from one sketch to another. A number of efforts have been made to elicit this pattern, and I can make no special claims for mine. But it seems to me that two central features of the work are its division into five paired sketches and the overall movement of the work from images of a cursed and blasted nature to accounts of the doomed communities established on the islands by the human beings washed up on their shores.

The first four sketches focus on the natural world. In a series of unforgettable images the narrator evokes the parched, god-forsaken landscape of the islands whose "special curse" is that "to them change never comes; neither the change of seasons nor of sorrows." Rain never falls on the islands: "Like split Syrian gourds, left withering in the sun, they are cracked by an everlasting drought beneath a torrid sky." And these islands are so "emphatically uninhabitable" that apart from a few species of reptiles, they "refuse to harbor even the outcasts of the beasts." The lowing of cattle, the howling of wolves, and the voices of humans are not heard on the islands. "The chief sound of life here is a hiss" (126-27).

In describing the rock-bound coast Melville's narrator repeatedly endows the physical features of the islands with base human attributes or compares them to broken or spent human artifacts. The rocks are like "the dross of an iron-furnace," the mist is "gray and haggard," the vegetation "ungrateful," and the tangled thickets of nameless bushes "treacherously" mask deep fissures in the "Plutonian" rocks. The landscape as a whole is "woe-begone." It resembles "abandoned cemeteries of long ago" and "old cities by piecemeal tumbling to their ruin," and the most striking creatures on the islands are the tortoises—those images of "sorrow and penal hopelessness"—whose bodies are said to be inhabited by the souls of "wicked sea-officers"—captains, mates and commodores. (128)

The tortoise is the single most powerful image in the entire work. As William B. Dillingham has pointed out (81), the tortoise casts its shadow over **"The Encantadas"** just as the whale does over *Moby-Dick,* and its curse is the same as that which hangs over the islands themselves: its changelessness. The tortoises seem to live forever, but they grow no wiser. The great feeling they inspire is that of age—of "dateless, indefinite endurance." They will not, and cannot, change course to evade obstacles in their path. With this "strange infatuation of hapless toil," they are symbols of the ageless, blind struggle of all creatures to survive in an inhospitable universe (131-32).

In the last half of the cycle Melville turns from the natural world to the human, offering us a series of pictures of failed or broken or repressive communities—from the little family group left to starve on Norfolk Island to the tyrannical kingdom established by the hermit Oberlus on Hood's Isle. These descriptions of failed communities are, properly speaking, Melville's variations on the dystopian theme. But each of these communities is in some way identified with its physical setting, just as the hermit Oberlus has the appearance of "a volcanic creature thrown up by the same convulsion" as the island itself (163).

The other central feature of the work is its division into five paired sketches. The tortoise and the Rock constitute one such pair. Another consists of sketches four and five which contrast the "Pisgah view"—the view of the whole, the view from the top of a rock that can never be climbed—with the limited perspective of sailors caught in the winds and currents at the base of Rodondo. Sketches six and seven describe two contrasting communities—that of the buccaneers on Barrington Isle who rob and murder one day and turn poets and philosophers the next, and that of the despotic Dog-King whose eventual overthrow leads to the establishment of a lawless *Riotocracy*.

Each of these two sketches is, in its way, a burlesque or parody of the republican ideal of political community. The pirates on their island have created a safe haven which offers them the tranquillity that they have denied the rest of the world. It is a sort of republic of thieves which stands in contrast to the classical notion of a republic of virtuous citizens. In the republic of virtue each citizen spontaneously and consistently identified his purposes with those of the community as a whole. But the members of Melville's pirates' republic behave in seemingly contradictory ways. "Could it be possible," asks a "sentimental voyager" quoted by Melville's narrator, "that they robbed and murdered one day, revelled the next, and rested themselves by turning meditative philosophers, rural poets, and seat builders on the third?" The voyager finds this "not very improbable," given "the vacillations of a man." But then for no obvious reason he entertains the "more charitable thought" that "among these adventurers were some gentlemanly, companionable souls, capable of genuine tranquillity and virtue."[4] The simple-minded optimism of the voyager is hardly convincing however, and the reader is left with the sense that the members of the pirates' republic, like most other human beings, are just as capable of base actions as they are of "genuine tranquillity and virtue" (146).

The account of Charles' Isle and the Dog-King is a much more elaborate and fully worked out political parody. A Creole adventurer creates his own little despotic kingdom on Charles' Isle. Faced with isolated acts of insubordination among the eighty souls whom he has lured to his promised land, he declares martial law and rules tyrannically with the aid of "a disciplined cavalry company of large, grim dogs." Finally, revolt breaks out; the Dog-King is banished; and a republic is declared. In practice the democratic republic of the rebels proves to be "no democracy at all, but a permanent *Riotocracy*, which gloried in having no law but lawlessness" (149). Here in a nutshell, and in a manner reminiscent of the fable of the Troglodytes in Montesquieu's *Persian Letters*, Melville gives us a burlesque version of the cycle of political systems described by political theorists since the classical age. Plato, Aristotle, and Polybius all held to cyclical views of the rise and fall of governments, and each of them had been fascinated by the process by which democracy regularly

degenerates into a lawless state of license or (in Polybius' terms) of *ochlocracy* or mob rule. Writing in this tradition but creating a fable in the manner of Montesquieu, Melville depicts the ideal of the democratic republic as becoming real in riot and lawlessness.[5]

The longest and most memorable of the sketches, the eighth and ninth, describe two contradictory individual responses to adversity—the resignation and endurance of Hunilla, the Chola widow, who is the victim of both natural forces and human predators, and the malignancy of Oberlus who could not even plant potatoes without seeming to perform a sinister act. In Melville's gallery of renegades, castaways and petty despots, these two represent the best and the worst of which a beleaguered humanity is capable. Having been abandoned on Norfolk Island by a blithe and treacherous French sea captain, having watched helplessly as her husband and brother drowned at sea, and finally having been subjected to unspeakable abuse and then abandoned again by whaleboaters to whom she looked for rescue, Hunilla *endures* with dignity and without complaint. On the other hand, the hermit slave-master Oberlus, who possesses a nature "so warped and crooked . . . that the very handle of his hoe seemed gradually to have shrunk and twisted in his grasp," illustrates the depths to which a man can be reduced by adversity and by "the long habit of sole dominion over every object round him" (163-64).

The final pair, which frames the whole, consists of the first and last sketches—the one with its bleak topography of the islands and their "burned out" landscape, and the other focusing on the traces left by the human detritus washed up on the islands—the rotting cabins, broken jars, rusting cutlasses and burial mounds. In a few years all of this will be gone, and none of these traces will prove as permanent as the ruts worn into "the vitreous inland rocks by ages and ages of the slow dragging of tortoises in quest of ponds of scanty water." Does our life add up to anything more, Melville seems to be asking, than the scratches on the rock left by the Galapagos tortoises? If this is all we will leave behind us, utopian fantasies can only prove delusive.

Notes

This paper was originally presented at a conference on "Melville and the Sea" organized by the Melville Society at Mystic Seaport, Ct. on June 17-19, 1999. I wish to thank Mary K. Bercaw Edwards and Jill Gidmark for giving me the opportunity to try out my ideas on "The Encantadas" before a wonderfully responsive and informed audience. I am also most grateful to Laurie Robertson-Lorant for her guidance and encouragement and her critical reading of several drafts of this essay as I revised it for publication.

1. This famous passage has been read ironically by Stein (323) and others who argue that, when

turned on its back, with the bright side exposed, a tortoise is helpless. Bryant (295) notes that the irony does not seem intended since Melville "does not press or even allude to this natural fact." I would argue that the *tone* invites an ironic reading of the passage.

2. The literature on the definition of utopia is immense. Works that I have found particularly helpful are the books by Kumar, Levitas and Morson and the articles by Sargent and Suvin cited in the bibliography.

3. The terms "dystopia" and "anti-utopia" are often used to refer only or principally to my first category: the dream of felicity that has become a nightmare. See, for example, Kumar 99-130. Kumar does, however, describe Swift's *Gulliver's Travels,* with its satire and parody, as "the greatest of the older anti-utopias" (105). My third category—"dark pictures of the world . . ." obviously broadens the concept of dystopia considerably. In terms of the framework of definitions offered by Sargent, my third category might properly be described not as a "dystopia" but rather as an "anti-utopia": "a non-existent society described in considerable detail and normally located in time and space that the author intended a contemporary reader to view as a criticism of utopianism or of some particular eutopia." (Sargent 1992 188). Melville's "Encantadas" are not exactly non-existent, but they offer an image of the Galapagos islands so selective and so personal that it can be described as if it were an imaginary world.

4. Melville's description of the "sentimental voyager's" view as "charitable" is a significant tip-off to the alert reader. In another of the *Piazza Tales,* "Benito Cereno," the "charitable" views of Amasa Delano are shown to be a manifestation of his obtuseness; and in *The Confidence-Man* charity is repeatedly connected with bad faith and never with Christian *caritas.*

5. Montesquieu's fable of the Troglodytes was one of the most widely read eighteenth-century dramatizations of the working out of the cycle of political forms described in more abstract terms by Plato, Aristotle, and Polybius. There is no reason to believe that Melville ever read *The Persian Letters,* but he was most definitely familiar with Plato's *Republic* in which the degeneration of democratic government was attentively described (Plato 240-43). For Polybius see Von Fritz 60-75.

References

Albrecht, Robert C. "The Thematic Unity of Melville's 'The Encantadas.'" *Texas Studies in Literature and Language* 14 (Fall 1972): 473-74.

Arvin, Newton. *Herman Melville.* New York: Viking, 1950.

Bryant, John. "Toning Down the Green: Melville's Picturesque." In *Savage Eye: Melville and the Visual Arts.* Ed. Christopher Sten. Kent, Ohio: Kent State UP, 1991. 145-61.

Dillingham, William B. *Melville's Short Fiction: 1853-1856.* Athens: U of Georgia P, 1977.

Franklin, H. Bruce. "The Island Worlds of Darwin and Melville." *The Centennial Review* 3 (Summer 1967): 353-70.

Hartley, Marsden. "Melville (After Reading the 'Encantadas')." *Selected Poems.* New York: Viking, 1945. 105-06.

Higgins, Brian and Hershel Parker, eds. *Herman Melville: The Contemporary Reviews.* Cambridge UP, 1995. 469-83.

Karcher, Carolyn L. *Shadow over the Promised Land: Slavery, Race and Violence in Melville's America.* Baton Rouge: Louisiana State UP, 1980.

Kumar, Krishan. *Utopia and Anti-Utopia in Modern Times.* Oxford: Basil Blackwell, 1987.

Levitas, Ruth. *The Concept of Utopia.* Syracuse, NY: Syracuse UP, 1990.

Melville, Herman. "The Encantadas, or Enchanted Isles." In *The Piazza Tales and Other Prose Pieces, 1839-1860.* Vol. 9 of the Northwestern-Newberry edition of *The Writings of Herman Melville.* Ed. Harrison Hayford et al. Evanston and Chicago: Northwestern UP and Newberry Library, 1987.

Montesquieu. *Lettres persanes.* Ed. Paul Vernière. Paris: Garnier, 1992. Letters XI-XIV.

Morson, Gary Saul. *The Boundaries of Genre, Dostoevsky's "Diary of a Writer" and the Traditions of Literary Utopia.* Austin: U of Texas P, 1981.

Moses, Carole. *Melville's Use of Spenser.* New York: Peter Lang, 1989. 133-50.

Newbery, Ilse. "'The Encantadas': Melville's *Inferno.*" *American Literature* 38 (1966): 49-68.

Plato. *The Republic.* Tr. Alan Bloom. New York: Basic Books, 1968.

Robertson-Lorant, Laurie. *Melville: A Biography.* New York: Clarkson Potter, 1996.

Sargent, Lyman Tower. "Utopia: The Problem of Definition." *Extrapolation* 16.2 (1975): 137-48.

Sargent, Lyman Tower. "Political Dimensions of Utopianism with Special Reference to American Communitarianism." In *Per una definizione dell'utopia.* Ed. Nadia Minerva. Ravenna: Longo editore, 1992. 185-210.

Seelye, John Douglas. *Melville: The Ironic Diagram.* Evanston: Northwestern UP, 1970.

Stein, William Bysshe. "Melville's Comedy of Faith." *Journal of English Literary History* (1960): 315-33.

Suvin, Darko. "Defining the Literary Genre of Utopia." *Studies in the Literary Imagination* 6 (Fall 1973):121-45.

Von Fritz, Kurt. *The Theory of the Mixed Constitution in Antiquity.* New York: Columbia UP, 1954.

Yarina, Margaret. "The Dualistic Vision of Herman Melville's 'The Encantadas.'" *The Journal of Narrative Technique* 3 (1973): 141-48.

Maurice S. Lee (essay date September 2000)

SOURCE: Lee, Maurice S. "Melville's Subversive Political Philosophy: 'Benito Cereno' and the Fate of Speech." *American Literature* 72, no. 3 (September 2000): 495-519.

[In the following essay, Lee delineates the limitations of political discourse in "Benito Cereno," demonstrating how the text subverts the language of slavery and free speech within the context of American republicanism.]

Melville was stirred by the possibilities of transgression, and critics trace his career with the question: How does he speak the unspeakable? What one means by "unspeakable" makes a difference, for God, society, and language systems all potentially bowstring one's speech; and Melville, we are told, quarreled with each as blasphemer, rebel, and protodeconstructionist. I am interested here in the radical Melville who voiced unspeakable politics. From the start, this Melville ran afoul of his culture with *Typee*'s (1846) explicit criticism of missionaries. He then flirted time and again with taboo, enduring chastising review upon review, until he became a clandestine writer whose work turned increasingly private and bitter before collapsing into obscure ambiguities, masquerades, and eventual silence. Ann Douglas, Carolyn Karcher, and Michael Paul Rogin tell various political versions of this fall, though I offer two caveats that bear heavily on the wicked work of **"Benito Cereno"** (1855).[1]

The first is that Melville's magazine fiction is not the run-out of a tragic career, for Melville did not abandon America after *Moby-Dick*'s (1851) lukewarm reception, nor did the author who expurgated *Typee* descend step-by-step, rebuke-by-rebuke, to the self-destructive, labyrinthine quietism of *Pierre* (1852) and *The Confidence-Man* (1856). There remains a tendency to utterly alienate the later Melville from his culture—to forget, for instance, that *Moby-Dick* was not entirely misunderstood; to elide some evidence that even *Pierre* was at one time intended to both profit and please; to read the end of *The Confidence-Man* as only a parting, ironic shot; to ignore *Israel Potter* (1855) and *Battle-Pieces* (1866) as texts that pursue the meaning of America. Melville's short fiction is not optimistic, nor is it finally intended for a casual reader. But neither does it forsake democracy as a subject worthy of intelligible talk. **"Benito Cereno"** may seem to be a skeptical lock with no key, and yet it struggles to engage, and perhaps even "solve," the time's foremost political quandaries.[2]

Which introduces a second caveat: the work of subversive politics is inherently problematic. Here *subversive* implies not only opposition to prevailing ideologies but also a cunning use of narrative and tone that defies the public spirit of politics. In this sense, the more subversive a text, the less political it becomes, until at some degree of difficulty covert radicalism quietly slides into solipsistic despair. We should locate the politics of **"Benito Cereno"** upon this slippery slope—somewhere between the *San Dominick*'s allegory and the tale's unknowable silences, between Melville's penetrating social criticism and his desire to puncture the political. To do so with any precision, however, we must, like Melville, closely attend to the potential responses of readers; for subversive politics are semiprivate. They must fool a suppressive, dominant culture while speaking the unspeakable to someone. They must imagine a friendly and sensitive listener in a hostile political world. In what follows I argue that **"Benito Cereno"** is "about" the failure of political speech—as a critical issue in Melville's America, as a challenge to his "great Art of Telling the Truth,"[3] and as a theoretical inevitability founded in the political philosophies of Machiavelli and Hobbes, whose dark convictions undermine the principles of American republicanism.

* * *

No Melville text invites political analysis more than **"Benito Cereno,"** if only because it explicitly addresses issues of slavery and race. Yet after reconstructing multifarious discourses and identifying manifold allusions, political readings of the last half-century arrive at different ends. Melville is a racist or a protomulticulturalist. He is radical but bedeviled by conservative fears. He ultimately advises a political tack or skeptically leaves us adrift.[4] Compelling scholarship has winnowed these arguments to the point that we can say with some confidence that Melville's satire of the slavery debate does not clearly imply his own stance, nor can we limit his social concerns solely to the subject of slavery. To devotees of Melville this is hardly surprising, for his mysteries so often conceal new mysteries, just as **"Benito Cereno"** appears to climax in Amasa Delano's whale boat. Here Babo shows his daggered hand as the *San Dominick* erupts in open revolt. Here the "past, present, and future seemed one," and Melville's fore-shadowing makes wonderful sense, so much so that critics, at the story's request, tend to privilege this "flash of revelation."[5] The scene, after all, explains so much with fulgurous, tableau-like efficiency. Delano's foot "ground the prostrate negro." His left hand "clutched the half-reclined Don Benito." His "right arm pressed for added speed on the after oar, his eye bent forward, encouraging his men." Such emphatic prose, however, obscures a central irony: this is not Emanuel Leutze's painting, *Washington Crossing the Delaware* (1851), in which a self-possessed freedom fighter poses at the prow of his boat. Melville has already made ample reference to the past of New World bondage. The scene in the *Rover* can stand for a nation presently struggling with slavery.[6] And as Delano rows from the stern, he turns his back on the *San Dominick*'s past, fearfully, awkwardly, and even ridiculously propelling his disorderly ship-of-state into a future he can hardly discern.

It really is a striking paragraph—so good, in fact, that the next twenty pages may seem an anticlimax or over-lengthy denouement. We abandon Delano's shifty perspective for an ornate description of the ship's recapture, followed by a dozen pages of detailed deposition, followed in turn by the last few pages, which by now might feel a bit overdue, if not, as the story itself admits, somewhat "irregularly given" (114). George William Curtis, who read the manuscript for *Putnam's,* anticipated the view of many formalist critics: "It is a great pity [Melville] did not work it up as a connected tale," for the "dreary documents at the end" make the plot "a little spun out," enough to precipitate the cry, "Oh! dear, why can't Americans write good stories."[7] Indeed, with just a few editorial touches, the tale might end with the defeat of the revolt—no tonal shifts or intrusive insertions, no repetitions or chronological leaps, all mysteries explained, all conflicts resolved, everything over except the interpreting and the rights to a dynamite screenplay.

Yet Melville does more than dramatize George M. Frederickson's *The Black Image in the White Mind* (Harper & Row, 1971), for the most provocative readings of **"Benito Cereno"** see it as "a discourse about discourse" and find the tale's political climax where we might expect it: near the end.[8] This climax is no tableau. Delano is speaking with Don Benito and desperately seeking some closure, trying to convince his moribund friend that "the past is passed. . . . Forget it" (116). "You are saved," Delano insists; "[W]hat has cast such a shadow upon you?" "The negro," Cereno famously answers, and "[t]here was no more conversation that day." One paragraph later, Melville reveals the fate of his final player: "As for the black, . . . he uttered no sound" and came to "his voiceless end." This silence speaks volumes, though what we hear can range from despair to racist erasure to more sensitive thoughts on the poli-

tics of silence and open-ended narration.[9] It also points to the state of political discourse, for we can see the *San Dominick* as a society dominated by a problem it will not or can not bring itself to name—as an allegory of antebellum America where debate over slavery was often preempted, suppressed, and misunderstood.

Frederick Douglass charged in 1853 that a "cardinal object" of the "Slavery Party" was the "suppression of all anti-slavery discussion,"[10] and abolitionists often traced their movement in terms of the struggle for speech—from William Lloyd Garrison's *Liberator* to Theodore Weld's Lane Seminary to Elijah Lovejoy and the Gag rule to more personal moments of speech and suppression at variously contested public sites. Melville is keenly aware of this emphasis. John Quincy Adams tried the *Amistad* case during the heart of his Gag rule fight. The year 1799, the setting of our tale, witnessed not only Toussaint L'Ouverture's revolution but also the Alien and Sedition Acts, which used the "black Jacobins" of Santo Domingo to justify domestic attacks on free speech, a reference Melville sharpens in the cuddy by comparing Cereno to James I.[11]

At the same time, abolitionists and slaves are not the only parties suppressed, nor can one blame only anti-abolitionists for the silences aboard the *San Dominick*. It is, after all, the oakum-pickers who serve as "monitorial constables" (54), and it is Cereno who lacks the "power to tell a single word" (110). Nonetheless, the terror aboard the *San Dominick*—Nat Turner's axes, Denmark Vesey's poison, and the inverted hierarchy of Santo Domingo—is no more effective at quelling expression than the horrors of a Southern plantation. Delano notices clue upon clue, until we see that the good captain's dullness is not simply a function of racism, that his convenient misreadings keep him light of heart as he pursues quite commercial "ulterior plans" (95). Moreover, Delano betrays a failing that proslavery forces condemned in their enemies, for he so woefully misunderstands the political crisis he presumes to solve that he walks unwittingly right to the verge of deadly, incendiary speech. Thus Melville can seem to satirize abolitionists and fire-eaters alike. He may even appear to echo the more moderate pleas of Daniel Webster, Henry Clay, and other compromising men, who believed that what the nation needed was decorous discussion in reason's clear light.

But what happens when speech does become "free" for Cereno, Delano, and (to some extent) Babo? What happens when our three principal characters take their places in the *Rover*'s tableaux? Delano mistakes his friend for a villain; Babo struggles silently; and Cereno emerges from his "speechless faint" "half-choked" and croaking "husky words, incoherent to all but the Portuguese" (99). Even later aboard the *Bachelor's Delight,* while Delano and Cereno converse with a supposed "fraternal unreserve" (114), there remains a singular lack of commerce as the victors rehash their experience. "See, yon bright sun has forgotten it all" (116), a forward facing and vaguely transcendental Amasa Delano gushes. "Because [it has] no memory," Cereno replies, unable to shake his retrospective mood and the thought of Aranda's sepulcher. "You are saved," Delano cries, putting a providential Puritan spin on their lucky escape. "The negro" is Cereno's only answer, for his slavery-dominated view of the world has no place for Northern grace. These men are speaking different discourses, even as they share the same tongue; so much so that when Delano earlier wonders, "How unlike we are made!" (61), he seconds the sentiments of John Calhoun: "[I]t is difficult to see how two peoples so different . . . can exist together in a common Union."[12]

By 1855 the North and South preferred different dictionaries, read different textbooks, and had become largely separate literary markets, while the slavery "dialogue" had entered a stage where the most compelling political topic was at what point must endlessly repeated arguments finally give way to war. In **"Benito Cereno,"** Melville predicts that language will not solve sectional conflict, that whether mistranslated, ignored, or suppressed, words will eventually end in deeds, the dark prophecy of Babo's demise. More than most of his peers, Melville implicates both North and South in sectional misprision. He also notes the plight of blacks when Babo illustrates Douglass's charge that "you [white Americans] shut our mouths, and then ask why we don't speak."[13] We can even argue that **"Benito Cereno"** anticipates a revisionist version of the War, one that blames not the ethics or economics of slavery but the inability of two alien cultures to talk over differences peaceably. We can do all this with critical care and yet miss much of the tale, for when demographic types jump the *San Dominick,* our political allegory fails.

If Cereno's *San Dominick* is the South and Delano's ship the North, then is the *Rover* a border state or the District of Columbia? Considering the story's prairie imagery, we could be in bleeding Kansas, after all. Or, more likely, when Don Benito claims to "know nothing" of rebellion (89), we might recall the conspiratorial silences of Northern political discourse. In 1854 the Know-Nothings staged what Emerson called a "revolution," and their secret societies sparked "ridiculous gossip about guns, and poison, and massacre."[14] Allegory, as Melville knows, encourages a paranoid style, for the anxious reader, Delano-like, may watch a stiffened scabbard, all the while mistaking a slave rebellion for the mystery of iniquity. **"Benito Cereno,"** like the sperm whale's brow, invites an allegorical eye. Locks, knots, masks, tableaus—read them if you can, dear critic, construct a towering thesis, though the more weight you ask your allegory to bear, the less stable its empire be-

comes. Bannadonna of **"The Bell-Tower"** (1855) learns this lesson. So, too, perhaps, does Ahab. And as readers of **"Benito Cereno,"** we should learn that while its political types allegorize misprision, they themselves are also fictitious. They, too, are part of the problem. As both Nat Turner and Uncle Tom, Babo belies black stereotypes. Just as the Cavalier Don Benito is sickly Hamlet and "bitter hard master" (94), Delano conflates Yankee types as a pious idealist who minds the main chance. There are too many allusions, too many references, to surely determine political analogs, and in this sense the meaning of **"Benito Cereno"** is as much sunk in silent depths as drowned in a deluge of discourse. To be sure, Melville raises the issue of slavery and free speech, but his overabundance of political types forces us beyond antebellum concerns toward more dreary— and ultimately more universal—failures of political speech.

* * *

Let us briefly return to the start of the story to examine the relation of narrative and power in light of Curtis's complaint that **"Benito Cereno"** is not a "connected tale." When the "commanding" Delano boards the *San Dominick,* he hears "in one language, and as with one voice," its "common tale of suffering"; but being "impatient of the hubbub of voices," he ignores the "less conspicuous" scores (49-51). This is, of course, Delano's flaw. Despite an alleged "republican impartiality" (80), he thinks a "brother captain" (52) can tell the "whole story" (54), so that when the ship explodes in a "clattering hubbub" of hatchets (98), his hierarchical mind can only suppose that Cereno is faking an abduction. We know (or soon will) that Don Benito is in truth a "paper captain" (59), and we probably attribute such deception to the subversive work of Babo, who in the court's opinion served as "the helm and keel of the revolt" (112)—a description that points to the *San Dominick*'s hull and its motto, "*Follow your leader*" (99).

We should not, however, too quickly situate Babo at the forefront of things, for not only are some ships built with false keels, but a subtext suggests that Babo's command is not as sure as the court (and some critics) conclude. When Delano dispenses needful provisions with a supposed "good-natured authority" (79), his casual, "half-mirthful, half-menacing gesture" nearly sets off a second revolt. This is prevented when the oakum-pickers "[drop] down into the crowd" and "[force] every white and every negro back" with "gestures" that, like Delano's mirth, also threaten physical violence. The oakum-pickers and Ashantees are Babo's appointed authorities; and when at his word the most desirable goods are saved for the cabin table, we might wonder if some nameless African rebel feels a little put out, perhaps even as famished and dispossessed as that rebel Israel Potter. We know Melville alters his historical source to create a more masterful and more vicious Babo. But even as the fictional court lists crimes performed at his "command" (112), there are instances where he is not in control: where simply "the negroes" commit certain crimes; where "the negresses used their utmost influence"; where a suspicious reader can well imagine that a lone, diminutive slave from Senegal might struggle to convince Ashantees, ex-kings, and a "restless," "mutinous," perishing populace that he is, in fact, the leader to follow—and to *his* homeland, not theirs (105).[15] Which is to say that the militant Ashantees and judicious oakum-pickers keep tenuous control over white *and* black "pawns" (71), and that the executive "ringleader" Babo is at least as vexed as Delano (105), who leaves his ship to a rumored pirate and does not trust his men.

Delano, of course, shows remarkable pith when "issuing his orders" to the *San Dominick*'s crew. The imperialist American is almost too glad to take over for Benito Cereno (92). Suddenly, however, there is Babo "faithfully repeating his orders," playing the "part of captain of the slaves," Melville's nod toward our actual leader. And yet a wink follows this nod, because just when Babo seems truly in charge, Delano wonders, "[W]ho's at the helm," and finds still another tableau. A sailor we know as an experienced "tar" (72) grasps the head of a "cumbrous tiller" with two "subordinate" blacks manning a pulley that helps to handle the weight (92). Thus, after Delano replaces Cereno and after Babo in turn takes over, we are asked to follow one more lead, to note that if anyone steers the *San Dominick,* it is not any one person but rather two nameless African rebels, a ragged lifelong tar, and the men and women at the rigging and ropes who work to harness the breeze.

What does Melville hope to accomplish by subverting the command of his captains? He implicates his reader yet again in Delano-like blindness, for we focus so intently on Babo's play that we ignore the less prominent rebels, even to the point that, as with Cereno, one singular "negro" casts his shadow over every aspect of the tale. We also assent to an unjust verdict by placing Babo in utter command. The white deponents have various claims on the *San Dominick*'s human cargo, and the more Babo is held responsible, the more of his cohorts survive to be sold—a point Melville makes with a pun when the court's "partial renumeration of the negroes" brings a remuneration partial to the whites (111). Finally, by challenging his leaders' command, not only does Melville further belie his Negro, Yankee, and Cavalier types, he suggests that we seek another tale behind his foregrounded threesome, a common tale that might be called a People's History of the *San Dominick.*

When Cereno desperately jumps for the *Rover,* "three sailors, from three different and distant parts of the ship," also abandon the vessel (98), suggesting both the

presence and absence of simultaneous, alternative narratives—"bottom up" tales that seem most accessible when the sailors retake the *San Dominick* and we escape Delano's oppressive perspective. The battle, however, resembles the *Serapis* fighting the *Richard* in *Israel Potter,* for "[o]bjects before perceived with difficulty, now glimmered ambiguously."[16] Earlier, and through Delano's eyes, the rebels are described as dogs, sheep, deer, leopards, crows, and bats, just as the white sailors are compared to sheep, foxes, centaurs, and bears. The ship's recapture is no better, for the sailors become "submerged sword-fish rushing hither and thither through shoals of black-fish" who quickly become—in ironic, mixed metaphor—"wolf-like" with lolling "red tongues" (102). When the chief mate cries, "Follow your leader!" and the sailors rally into "a squad as one man," we might sense that Melville is waxing poetic, his rhetoric rising with the attackers' "huzza," until we watch them ply their swords like the "carters' whips" of a slave master and note that during their victorious surge "not a word was spoken."

With the rebels compared to Dominican inquisitors, and with the sailors, "one leg sideways flung," "fighting as troopers in the saddle," we should also recall Milton's plea for free speech in "Areopagitica" (1644):

> [T]hey [Parliament] will . . . execute the most *Dominican* part of the Inquisition over us, and are already with one foot in the stirrup so active at suppressing, it would be no unequall distribution . . . to suppresse the suppressors themselves; whom the change of their condition hath puft up, more then [sic] their late experience of harder times hath made wise.[17]

Like Parliament, the sailors of **"Benito Cereno"** are unimproved by their hard experience. Or, as Melville writes in *Mardi* (1849), despite "glorious Areopagiticas," "he who hated oppressors, is become an oppressor himself."[18] Thus "Follow your leader" takes a wicked spin in the *San Dominick*'s bloody recapture, for Melville suggests that both sailors and captains indulge fallacious perspectives, that both revolution and counterrevolution end with the violent suppression of speech, and that political divisions finally obviate any truthful story—whether that story be "common" or "whole" and regardless of who's at the helm.

The same is true of the subsequent legal records that pretend to objectivity. Like Curtis, we may think them "a little spun out," for Melville himself seems impatient. Editing catalogs, extracting portions, recounting the *prolonged and perplexed navigation* (108), he appears almost to complain toward the end: *And so the deposition goes on* (110). By the time we reach *various random disclosures referring to various periods of time* (112), we might—Oh! dear—think less well of the story as a dramatic and unified tale, and we might not give a wilted pumpkin for the names of minor rebels, any more than we give a basket of fish for the rest of the nobles and tars. The *Narrative* (1817) of the real Amasa Delano feared this very response: "It may be considered by some of my readers that I have been at times too minute in giving details . . . concerning officers and crews. . . . But notices of this kind are valuable to the cause of morality and humanity."[19] That our Duxbury captain is not particularly moral is an irony Melville indulges. Yet the elisions and inventions of **"Benito Cereno,"** so clear in the doctored court documents, actually slight Delano's egalitarian, if hypocritical and laborious, detail. In the absence of sustained characterization, the story's lesser figures remain stubbornly inaccessible, not only because they are obscured by Delano's vision and Babo's shadow but also because Melville is already too long in his trying depositions. He has his own plot concerns that preclude a more inclusive tale.

This is surprising in light of Melville's reputation as a democratic writer;[20] for with the exception of **"Benito Cereno,"** every one of his ocean texts includes a voice from before the mast. There may be, of course, a tyrannical Jackson or some not-so-innocent hazing, but the forecastles prior to **"Benito Cereno"** are often marked by humor, camaraderie, and loving squeezes of the hand that reveal a guarded optimism for the potential of civic humanism. However, in **"Benito Cereno"** revolution brings only new oppression. Melville does challenge race relations by inverting color supremacy, but class consciousness remains largely inchoate, even if Melville bemoans the ambivalence of antislavery and labor reform. More troubling than the failure of sailors and slaves to find common ground, however, is the fact that such ground does not exist, either between or within class and racial categories. What if the "one voice" of a connected tale is always an authoritarian plot? What if rallying together "as one man" is always mock-heroic? Are various stories always "hubbub"—and dreary hubbub, at that?[21] **"Benito Cereno"** is not Melville's first text to subvert the power of captains. But its view of the forecastle is originally cynical, for the voice of the people is not simply suppressed or potentially tyrannical. The voice of the people does not exist when it is too diverse to be represented, when the people suppress the Other people, and when impatient readers expect from their fictions more commanding and dramatic performances, even as they, like Captain Delano, consider themselves "republican."

* * *

Melville, then, is ill at ease with monolithic narrative, though he is sensitive to readers like Delano and Curtis who expect a connected and totalized tale. It may go too far to suggest that Melville knows what comes after the New Criticism. More surely, we should note that by 1855 few Americans could describe their political scene without dwelling on the more and more prevalent themes of fragmentation, degeneration, and apocalypse. This was especially true after Webster and Clay followed Calhoun to the grave, as bloodshed in Kansas came to prefigure a widely anticipated war, and when the Whig collapse of 1854 prompted cries from Northern observers that "we are to have political chaos—'confusion worse confounded.'"[22] While the organizing conflicts of Jacksonian America centered on tariffs and banks, it was slavery that became divisive enough to sever the bonds of Calhoun's union, to dissolve Van Buren's party connections, and to assemble platforms so evasive and specious that Thoreau, before calling his country a "slave-ship," would compare its cacophonous political conventions to "that universal aboriginal game . . . at which the Indians cried *hub, bub!*"[23] In its leaderless, violent, fractious confusion, **"Benito Cereno"** is timely indeed. But just as Thoreau knows that disorderly politics are not new under the sun, Melville steers the *San Dominick*'s course toward a more philosophical gloom.

In many ways, **"Benito Cereno"** is a cunning critique of a nation founded on a diverse and often incompatible body of political thought. Intellectual historians have done much to reconstruct the ideological origins of the United States, and for decades the terms of scholarly debate set the civic virtue of classical republicanism against a liberal individualism associated with Locke. Recent work, however, resists this duality, advancing instead what Daniel Rogers calls a "poststructuralist reaction" that allows into play "all the messy, multitudinous possibilities of speech and discourse."[24] Thus the intellectual plot of early national politics has become so thick that we cannot tell a unified or easily structured tale. This narrative crisis is also manifest in the antebellum era, where studies of political discourse discuss profound linguistic anxieties at the center of national debate.[25] As is so often the uncanny case, Melville anticipates this story. Isaac Kramnick notes, "There was a profusion and confusion of political tongues among the founders"; but if "[t]hey lived easily with the clatter,"[26] the author of **"Benito Cereno"** does not.

After Babo and his cohorts stage a revolution aboard the *San Dominick*, they kill the aristocratic Aranda so they can "be sure of their liberty" (106). Cereno then arranges to "draw up a paper signed by [himself] and the sailors who could write," as well as by Babo, "for himself and all the blacks," thus ceding the ship to the rebels (108). This mock constitution is surely coercive, only dubiously representative, and it helps to establish a three-branched regime not unlike the United States government. In *Clarel* (1876), Melville—like James Madison before him—compares the Constitution to a Gordian knot that "[s]ome cut but with the sword."[27] And in **"Benito Cereno,"** our ship's puzzling polity introduces a host of contractual tangles at a time when Garrisonians burned the Constitution, fire-eaters insisted on the right to secede, and women and blacks challenged the justice of virtual representation. Unionists like Daniel Webster placed the Constitution next to the Bible, while Richard Hildreth, the abolitionist political thinker, followed Locke in calling slavery "a permanent state of war" that "bears no resemblance to any thing like a social compact."[28] Melville, however, does not see slavery as so anomalous a condition; and he subverts the authority of social contracts by turning to the political philosophies of Machiavelli and Hobbes, who posed knotty problems for republican theories of viable representation.

J. G. A. Pocock and Frank Coleman have done much to reclaim Machiavelli and Hobbes as influential figures in the founding of America.[29] In the antebellum era, however, both philosophers were fairly notorious—Machiavelli for amorality, Hobbes for suspect piety, both for antidemocratic tendencies and cynical views of human nature. Both put survival and self-interest at the center of natural law. Both voiced misgivings about rational efforts to order the political world. They did advance a civic individualism that made republican theory possible, but they also called for a sovereign figure to prevent a tyranny of the masses. It is thus not surprising that Jefferson and Madison often preferred the more catholic contracts of Locke, Rousseau, and Montesquieu, who recognized the threat of political corruption but hoped that a virtuous, natural aristocracy could rationally resist the temptations of power. But when such leadership did not arise under the Articles of Confederation, the framers reached what Pocock calls a sudden "crisis of confidence,"[30] a crisis only partly allayed by placing sovereignty in "the people" and one that remained a serious concern for antebellum political thinkers.

Hildreth and the proslavery Frederick Grimké for the most part followed the *Federalist Papers* (1788), advocating an enlightened populace and an equitable balance of interests. But even the abolitionist Hildreth agreed with the "keen-sighted Machiavel" that virtue in the United States did not tend toward positions of power, while Calhoun (and also George Fitzhugh) used Machiavelli and especially Hobbes to contradict the "great and dangerous error . . . that all men are born free and equal."[31] Thus even if the Constitution signaled an "End of Classical Politics,"[32] and even if the 1840s witnessed a peak of civic optimism, the more cynical thought of Machiavelli and Hobbes survived in antebellum America, particularly as the nation followed the violent examples of Renaissance Florence and England in the throes of civil war. This was especially true for Southerners like Calhoun and Fitzhugh, who railed against the perfectionist urges of antislavery reform. It is also to a lesser extent true for Northern Whigs, who,

as much as expedience allowed, tended to mouth classical philosophy and bemoan democratic excess.[33] Melville, however, voices a skepticism no politician could match, for **"Benito Cereno"** slyly invokes Machiavelli and Hobbes to vex severely the possibility of any tenable republican politics.

In 1854 Bohn's Standard Library released a new version of Machiavelli's *The History of Florence, and of the Affairs of Italy . . . with The Prince and Various Historical Tracts.*[34] *The Prince* might well serve as Babo's advice manual, so explicit is it in describing the uses of murder, terror, and dissembling. Moreover, Melville's "centaur" at the tiller (72) and the "dark satyr" on the *San Dominick*'s stern (49), recall *The Prince*'s allegorical centaur and Machiavelli's infamous claim that wise men rule by both human law and vicious animal stealth. By making his tar a centaur, however, and by zoomorphically describing sailors and blacks, Melville takes the "double form of man and beast" that Machiavelli reserves for his leaders and applies it to every last sovereign, duplicitous soul aboard the *San Dominick*.[35] The very viability of American republicanism depends on a virtuous people, and so Melville's irony is brutal indeed when he describes the *San Dominick*'s animal masses as the ship's "republican element" (80).

If doubt remains that **"Benito Cereno"** represents a Machiavellian world, we may recall that in *The History of Florence* we see a disinterment, a tyrant who is cannibalized, a man who kills a prince then displays his head on a stick in the piazza, and one Francesco, yet another tyrannicide, who shares the name of a *San Dominick* rebel and before being executed cannot "be induced, by . . . words or deeds . . . to utter a syllable."[36] Perhaps the *San Dominick* is actually Florence, and in some senses it is. By calling the ship an "Italian palace" (48) and comparing the sea to a "Venetian canal" (49), Melville tricks both his captain and reader, for the proverbial stability of republican Venice will give way to Florentine violence. Typee or Happar? Venice or Florence? Such dualisms loom, especially in light of Karcher's conjecture that **"Benito Cereno"** and **"The Bell-Tower"** were originally written as a diptych.[37] In the end, however, as with all Melville diptychs, such seeming distinctions blur. The *San Dominick*'s fearfully balanced government is as Florentine as the supposed republic of **"The Bell-Tower,"** and the contract between Cereno and Babo is as defective as Bannadonna's bell, which, as a "triumph" of enlightenment reason forged in social oppression, can stand for the U.S. Constitution fatally flawed by slavery.[38] In this way, **"Benito Cereno"** offers a terrible truth: The people are all Machiavellian princes, and all the world's a Florence.[39]

Reading **"Benito Cereno"** with *Leviathan* (1651) furthers such radical claims, for aboard the *San Dominick* the "condition of Man . . . is a condition of Warre of every one against every one." The story's locks and keys recall Hobbes's introductory advice that in judging the "dissembling" doctrines of others, we should also consider our own "designe," lest we (like the designing Delano) "decypher without a key."[40] Most telling is the stern piece tableau—the prophetic "dark satyr in a mask, holding his foot on the prostrate neck of a writhing figure, likewise masked" (49). In a crucial section on political authority, Hobbes traces the word *"Person"* to *"Face"* and, because faces can be "counterfeited on the Stage," to that "which disguiseth the face, as a Mask." In this way, the Commonwealth is composed of "Persons Artificiall"; for "a *Person,* is the same that an *Actor* is," and on this basis an individual can *"Represent* himselfe, or an other," not only as a metonymic figure, but on "diverse occasions, diversly."[41] Interestingly, Hobbes uses this argument to establish the right of "Covenants," for "The Actor"—though inconstant, artificial, and masked—does, in fact, "acteth by Authority"; but by an authority seeking practical order more than essential truth, and one founded on an inseparable sovereignty, for *"a Kingdome divided in it selfe cannot stand."*[42]

Melville, however, has made up his mind to annihilate practical masks. When Madison scattered his notion of sovereignty amongst an ill-defined "people," he rejected Machiavelli, Hobbes, and every republican theorist who believed that a unified concept of power was a needed defense against faction. Madison was well aware that he walked a new and dangerous path. He writes in *Federalist 10* that the "causes of faction are . . . sown in the nature of man"; and he admits that "[e]nlightened statesmen will not always be at the helm." In such cases, national safety lies in a "scheme of representation" that balances interests so that any faction "will be unable to . . . mask its violence under the forms of the Constitution." The trick is in the division of powers, for a system of government must steer between "the cabals of a few" and "the confusion of a multitude," a feat the *San Dominick* cannot accomplish with no sovereign presence at the helm and no common story to share.

Accordingly, the ship finally erupts, "not in misrule, not in tumult," but "with mask torn away" in "piratical revolt" (99). We do not see undifferentiated chaos but rather the clattering hubbub of faction—the predicted result of a sovereign people lacking a chief representative, even if that Hobbesian Actor is thespian and agent, even if he is a paper captain or a literal figurehead such as Aranda. The Old World court misses this subtlety. By beheading Babo, "whose brain, not body, had schemed and led the revolt" (116), it forgets *Leviathan*'s frontispiece and Hobbes's not-wholly-monarchial arguments that the head of the state is a political construction and that revolution comes from below—points that *Billy*

Budd (1891) recalls when the sailors' "wedged mass of upturned faces" witness Billy's execution aboard a man-of-war. Thus decapitation will not dispel the murmurings of political upheaval, for, as Melville quotes Hobbes in *Moby-Dick,* the "Commonwealth or State . . . is but an artificial man."[43]

In this sense, then, **"Benito Cereno"** abides by a brutal Hobbesian logic, though Melville rejects the proslavery views of Hobbes, Calhoun, and Grimké—even while doubting the very existence of a monastic "people," even in affirming Grimké's allusion of 1848: "Men throw the mantle of politics over their faces and fight each other in masks."[44] Like Grimké, Webster also lamented the excess of factional strife, proclaiming in his celebrated speech "The Constitution and the Union" (1850) that no one held "the helm in this combat" and that "the vernacular tongue of the country [had] become greatly vitiated, depraved, and corrupted."[45] In many ways, Melville agrees, although he ultimately suggests that the Union will not be saved and that the terrible equipoise of slavery will finally give way to violence. **"Benito Cereno"** is thus a telling attack on American republican theory. By combining Machiavelli's centaur with Hobbes's mantled actor, Babo's "play" cuts to the quick of contractual civic humanism (87). For Melville, leaders always dissemble, political representation is false, political compacts are inherently flawed, and throwing off these republican fictions ends in factional strife that in 1799 or 1855 takes the likely form of a race war.

All of which poses a serious challenge to honest political discourse. Or, as Melville wrote in 1838 in precocious exception to enlightenment optimism, "What doth it avail a man, though he possess all the knowledge of a Locke or a Newton, if he know not how to communicate that knowledge."[46] For Machiavelli, speech is essentially a means of deception and influence. Hobbes warns that "man must take heed of words; which besides the signification of what we imagine . . . have a signification also of the . . . speaker."[47] Not precisely *différance,* but not bad for the seventeenth century. And as critics suggest, quite germane to an antebellum America beset with misprision and faulty typology, commanding hegemony and clattering hubbub.[48] This, in part, constitutes the local relevance of **"Benito Cereno,"** though Melville speaks also to the human condition when Don Benito tragically cries that his story is "[p]ast all speech" (81).

We cannot turn from the condition of "Warre" to a presocial state of humanity. Although Delano spies "pure tenderness and love" in the "naked nature" of a negress (73), we later learn that the women rebels are effective political actors. Hobbes can turn to a "perfect Speech" that is the sovereignty of God,[49] but when our captains cheat their death, Delano cannot rightfully point to "Providence," any more than Cereno can praise "the Prince of Heaven" without a Machiavellian twist (115). Nor can one turn to private relations in **"Benito Cereno."** We might watch the gregarious, needy Delano win over Cereno's reserve. We might even pitch a psychological thriller: Man who lost brother displaces affection on brother captain who has eaten a friend. But if Melville's buddy urge is strong, in the end politics rule. At the very height of "sympathetic experience" (61), Delano verges on the terrible truth that Cereno will "never divulge" (112), and Babo convinces him "not again to broach a theme so unspeakably distressing" (61). Indeed, Babo is always underfoot—in the lengthy hand-squeeze "across the black's body" (97), even aboard the *Bachelor's Delight* when the negro's shadow falls upon what should be a budding relationship. *Together we escaped a political plot but, well, we don't talk much anymore.*

Finally, then, there is silence. Babo's end may point to the fact that African Americans were not free to speak. Indeed, Melville may agree with Martin Delany, who claimed that Harriet Beecher Stowe *"knows nothing about us . . .* neither does any other white person."[50] But rather than style Babo's "hive of subtlety" an alien African mind (116), we should note that in **"Benito Cereno"** no one understands anyone and that Babo's hive most likely points to Bernard Mandeville's *Fable of the Bees* (1714)—a cynical work of political philosophy in the tradition of Machiavelli and Hobbes. Like Mandeville, Melville suggests that selfishness lies at the core of human interaction, for private relationships do not flourish when public masks are ostensibly dropped, and language falters even at the moment we seem free of devious discourse. As in his diptychs, Melville baits us again when Cereno and Delano's "fraternal unreserve" seems "in singular contrast with former withdrawments" (114), for Don Benito in his wordless exit "unconsciously gather[s] his mantle about him, as if it were a pall" (116). Black or white, who ain't masked?—even a dying "dear friend" (114). What if the Other of cultural difference is a more solipsistic Not Me? Thus we can trace by various paths a despairing, skeptical Melville who believes that the "truth" is past all words—whether because language always mistranslates, because "the self" is too total or splintered, or (more in line with the present argument, and borrowing Carlyle's ironic allusion to Christ) because "[w]heresoever two or three Living Men are gathered together, there is Society . . . with its cunning mechanisms."[51] If any two people constitute a state with all its dishonest implications, then the failings of political discourse pervade all human speech, be it antebellum or antediluvian, be it between leaders, followers, or friends. Such is Melville's cynical estimation of our ability to talk truthfully with anyone, for **"Benito Cereno"** richly describes the expanding reach and limited grasp of a fearfully politicized language. It quietly constructs a political philosophy beneath the *San Dominick*'s events to suggest that America's political estate is, in fact, a world of lies.

* * *

Which may or may not leave little to say. **"Benito Cereno"** can predict a politics of deconstruction, though it seems to me a keener pleasure to view Melville's mistrust of representation from the also indeterminate and historically available vantage point of Hobbes or Machiavelli. Either way—that is, whether one's skepticism is old-fashioned or new—we might ask if such social critique performs any political work. Eric Sundquist argues that the threat of revolt survives beyond Babo's demise. Others find that the tale resists readerly racism by exposing the Delano in all of us.[52] These arguments rely to varying degrees on the possible responses of readers, which makes excellent sense, for to judge a text's work is necessarily to consider its audience. And having traced Melville's radical message, we should ask, To whom does it speak?

One wonders how Melville, by 1855, could sneak the unspeakable past anyone. *Typee* may have driven him underground, but it also marked him for intensified scrutiny when he, in the words of Hershel Parker, became a "literary sex symbol."[53] By the time we arrive at *Pierre*'s incivilities, antebellum America was not much mistaken about the dark-eyed sailor Herman Melville. Thus he becomes an intriguing paradox: a famously subversive writer who was closely watched by pious reviewers and, accordingly, many find in Cereno (or Babo) the figure of a suppressed author who, seemingly destined for misunderstanding, slides into silent oblivion.[54] Less biographically, it would be no surprise if **"Benito Cereno"** despairs of reaching a sympathetic contemporary audience without also drawing hostile attention to Melville's antirepublican doubts. In many ways, readers of *Putnam's* were better equipped than modern academics to decipher Melville's allusions. For them, political discourse was all around, not something reconstructed from microfiche. Nonetheless, reviews of *The Piazza Tales* (1856) suggest that Melville's subversion "works"—at least insofar as he managed to escape the outrage of his readers, at least insofar as his radical politics survive to this later date. That is, when pressing political questions become tangled in metaphysical knots, Melville does not fall into skeptical silence. He defers, instead, to the future.

Before reader-response became a school, scholars recognized the lively relation between **"Benito Cereno"** and its audience. The story anticipates our reactions. It is sensitive to the psychology of Otherness. It is proleptic, highly satiric, preternaturally self-deconstructive—which displeases some readers, who feel tricked, usurped, or unsure of Melville's commitments. And yet despite all the implications of quietism, a wonderful irony remains: that a story about the failure of speech from so supposedly an alienated an author is remarkably engaging for students and teachers, for minds on both sides of the veil;[55] for scholars who feel—as if by revelation—that the past, present, and future are one:

> Melville's interest [in **"Benito Cereno"**] is in a vast section of the modern world, the backward peoples, and today, from the continents of Asia and Africa, their doings fill the front pages of our newspapers.
>
> 　　　　　　　　　　　　　　—C. L. R. James, 1953

> **"Benito Cereno"** is truly a story whose time has come, whose currency will not soon pass, and whose present readers must be encouraged to use their own knowledge and experience in undoing the knot that Melville's contemporaries were less equipped to handle.
>
> 　　　　　　　　　　　　　　—Marvin Fisher, 1977

> It took the urban rebellions of 1964-68, the Vietnam War, and the subsequent economic and moral decay of America during the period of its apparent global triumph to create an audience capable of comprehending the deadly message of **"Benito Cereno."**
>
> 　　　　　　　　　　　—H. Bruce Franklin, 1997[56]

Subversive politics include and exclude, and Melville apparently speaks to *us* at the expense of an earlier *them*. From a privileged "now" we descry—one almost whispers it—"meaning."

Perhaps there comes some "aha!" moment with every interpretive leap; but for many readers of **"Benito Cereno"** the sense of now is uncanny. That these "nows" occur decades apart is a measure of the story's ability to, as it were, preconstruct itself in the eyes of future readers—to reflect on its narrative in the same way Melville watches Florence, England, and Santo Domingo, and to extrapolate the gap of historical difference while at the same time speaking beyond it. The self-proclaimed "strange history" of **"Benito Cereno"** invites us to think diachronically (78), for the story insists with Don Benito on the tragic presence of memory. Like a dreamy Whitman in *Leaves of Grass* (1855), Melville endeavors "To think of time . . . to think through the retrospection, / To think of today," and in doing so, to think of "the ages continued henceforward."[57] Unlike so many politicians, however, Melville does not find present assurance by invoking coming generations. Indeed, Delano betrays an inadequacy cited by John Quincy Adams in 1833: "Democracy . . . is swallowed up in the present and thinks of nothing but itself."[58] Because it lacks immediate relevance, **"Benito Cereno"** is less inclined to wear the mask of democratic self-interest. Despite, or more accurately, because of Melville's lack of faith in political speech, **"Benito Cereno"** helps us to talk about how we talk about politics.

Silence, then, does not end the tale, for Melville's distrust of the political present and his abiding skepticism compel him to construct a future discourse in which, he hopes, speech is more profitably practiced and some truths are not literally beyond words. We may be surprised by Melville's speech, but this now is not ours alone; past, present, and future remain in constant, dynamic interaction. In this sense, Melville's hermeneutics lean more toward new than old, more toward a differentially interpreted past than any recoverable history. Such hermeneutics have done much mischief to the prospects of representation; yet Melville, almost despite himself, rises to the challenge of speech. His "answer" is optimistic insofar as he willfully suspends his disbelief. Although he takes no partisan side in antebellum political conflict, in a time when no one could solve slavery's knot without recourse to the sword, Melville as a writer at work imagines a future community, even if he found no connected story for 1855. Curtis liked **"Benito Cereno"** just enough to recommend publication, and his final complaint of the once great Melville was that "[h]e does everything too hurriedly now."[59] Perhaps it was Curtis who was too much hurried. And perhaps we, too, rush Melville's tale by seeking a harder and faster politics. It seems to me that one province of literature, and one labor of those who would read it, is to seek and imagine an honest speech—in the antebellum then, in our present now, and in the ongoing talk over **"Benito Cereno"** from which, if history is any indication, something further will follow.

Notes

I am grateful to Michael Colacurcio, as well as to Barbara Packer, Richard Yarborough, Brian Walker, Greg Jackson, and the readers from *American Literature* for their comments on an earlier draft of this article.

1. Ann Douglas, *The Feminization of American Culture* (New York: Doubleday, 1977), 289-326; Carolyn L. Karcher, *Shadow over the Promised Land: Slavery, Race, and Violence in Melville's America* (Baton Rouge: Louisiana State Univ. Press, 1980); Michael Paul Rogin, *Subversive Genealogy: The Politics and Art of Herman Melville* (New York: Knopf, 1979). See also Toni Morrison, "Unspeakable Things Unspoken: The Afro-American Presence in American Literature," *Michigan Quarterly Review* 28 (winter 1989): 1-34.

2. Marvin Fisher offers a sustained political reading of Melville's magazine fiction in *Going Under: Melville's Short Fiction and the American 1850s* (Baton Rouge: Louisiana State Univ. Press, 1977). For the place of Melville's short fiction within the context of his career, see Merton M. Sealts Jr.'s "Historical Note" in Herman Melville, *The Piazza Tales and Other Prose Pieces, 1839-1860*, ed. Har-

rison Hayford, Alma A. MacDougall, G. Thomas Tanselle, et al., vol. 9 of *The Writings of Herman Melville* (Evanston and Chicago: Northwestern Univ. Press and The Newberry Library, 1987), 457-533.

3. Herman Melville, "Hawthorne and His Mosses" (1850), in *The Piazza Tales and Other Prose Pieces,* 244.

4. See, for instance, Sidney Kaplan, "Herman Melville and the American National Sin: The Meaning of 'Benito Cereno,'" *Journal of Negro History* 41 (October 1956): 311-38, and *Journal of Negro History* 42 (January 1957): 11-37 (racist); John Bryant, "The Persistence of Melville: Representative Writer for a Multicultural Age," in *Melville's Evermoving Dawn: Centennial Essays,* ed. John Bryant and Robert Milder (Kent, Ohio: Kent State Univ. Press, 1997): 3-30 (protomulticulturalist); Eric J. Sundquist, *To Wake the Nations: Race in the Making of American Literature* (Cambridge: Belknap Press of Harvard Univ. Press, 1993), 135-82 (radical); Karcher, *Shadow over the Promised Land,* 127-59 (conservative fears); Jean Fagan Yellin, "Black Masks: Melville's 'Benito Cereno,'" *American Quarterly* 22 (fall 1970): 678-89 (racist); and Gloria Horsley-Meacham, "Bull of the Nile: Symbol, History, and Racial Myth in 'Benito Cereno,'" *New England Quarterly* 64 (June 1991): 225-42 (political tack); Rogin, *Subversive Genealogy,* 208-24; and Allan Moore Emery, "The Topicality of Depravity in 'Benito Cereno,'" *American Literature* 55 (October 1983): 316-31 (adrift). For an early and intriguing political account of "Benito Cereno," see Robert Lowell, *The Old Glory* (New York: Farrar, Strauss & Giroux, 1964), 135-214.

5. Herman Melville, "Benito Cereno" (1855), in *The Piazza Tales and Other Prose Pieces,* 98, 99. Hereafter this story will be cited parenthetically in the text.

6. See particularly Yellin, "Black Masks"; and Sundquist, *To Wake the Nations.*

7. G. W. Curtis to J. H. Dix, 19 April 1855 and 31 July 1855, in Jay Leyda, *The Melville Log: A Documentary Life of Herman Melville, 1819-1891, Volume 2* (New York: Harcourt, Brace, 1951), 500-501, 504.

8. James Kavanagh, "That Hive of Subtlety: 'Benito Cereno' and the Liberal Hero," in *Ideology and Classic American Literature,* ed. Sacvan Bercovitch and Myra Jehlen (Cambridge, Eng.: Cambridge Univ. Press, 1986), 357; see also Sundquist, *To Wake the Nations.*

9. The best discussions of silence and politics include Kavanagh, "Hive of Subtlety"; Sundquist, *To Wake the Nations*; and Yellin, "Black Masks."

10. Frederick Douglass, *My Bondage and My Freedom* (1855), in *Frederick Douglass: Autobiographies* (New York: Library of America, 1994), 440.

11. See, for instance, Jedidiah Morse, "The Present Dangers and Consequent Duties of the Citizens" (1799), in *The Fear of Conspiracy: Images of Un-American Subversion from the Revolution to the Present,* ed. David Brion Davis (Ithaca, N.Y.: Cornell Univ. Press, 1971), 45-48.

12. John C. Calhoun to Thomas G. Clemson, 10 March 1850, *Correspondence of John C. Calhoun,* ed. J. Franklin Jameson (Washington, D.C.: Annual Report of the American Historical Society, 1900), 784.

13. Frederick Douglass, "The Church and Prejudice" (1841), in *The Life and Writings of Frederick Douglass, Volume 1: The Early Years, 1817-1849,* ed. Philip S. Foner (New York: International Publishers, 1950), 104.

14. Ralph Waldo Emerson, "Lecture on Slavery" (1855), in *Emerson's Antislavery Writings,* ed. Len Gougeon and Joel Myerson (New Haven: Yale Univ. Press, 1995), 96; *The Boston Daily Advertiser,* 15 August 1854, quoted in John R. Mulkern, *The Know-Nothing Party in Massachusetts: The Rise and Fall of a People's Movement* (Boston: Northeastern Univ. Press, 1990), 72.

15. Gavin Jones discusses the diversity of the African rebels in "Dusky Comments of Silence: Language, Race, and Herman Melville's 'Benito Cereno,'" *Studies in Short Fiction* 32 (winter 1995): 39-50.

16. Herman Melville, *Israel Potter: His Fifty Years of Exile* (1855), in *Herman Melville:* Pierre; Israel Potter; The Piazza Tales; The Confidence-Man; Uncollected Prose; Billy Budd, Sailor (New York: Library of America, 1984), 564.

17. John Milton, "Areopagitica" (1644), in *John Milton: Selected Prose, New and Revised Edition,* ed. C. A. Patrides (Columbia: Univ. of Missouri Press, 1985), 246.

18. Herman Melville, *Mardi: And a Voyage Thither* (1849), in *Herman Melville:* Typee, Omoo, *and* Mardi (New York: Library of America, 1982), 1183.

19. Amasa Delano, *Narrative of Voyages and Travels in the Northern and Southern Hemispheres* (Upper Saddle River, N.J.: Gregg Press, 1970), 20.

20. See, for instance, Larzer Ziff, *Literary Democracy: The Declaration of Cultural Independence in America* (New York: Viking, 1981), 260-79;

David S. Reynolds, *Beneath the American Renaissance: The Subversive Imagination in the Age of Emerson and Melville* (Cambridge: Harvard Univ. Press, 1988), 135-65, 275-308; Nancy Fredricks, *Melville's Art of Democracy* (Athens: Univ. of Georgia Press, 1995); and Nicola Nixon, "Men and Coats; or, The Politics of the Dandiacal Body in Melville's 'Benito Cereno,'" *PMLA* 114 (May 1999): 359-72. For a recent challenge to these views, see Dennis Berthold, "Class Acts: The Astor Place Riots and Melville's 'Two Temples,'" *American Literature* 71 (September 1999), 429-61.

21. For a similar suggestion with an emphasis on Melville's sense of authorship, see Nina Baym, "Melville's Quarrel with Fiction," *PMLA* 94 (October 1979), 909-23.

22. Washington Hunt to Hamilton Fish, 2 August 1854, quoted in William E. Gienapp, *The Origins of the Republican Party, 1852-1856* (New York: Oxford Univ. Press, 1987), 129.

23. Henry David Thoreau, "A Plea for Captain John Brown" (1859), in *Walden and Other Writings,* ed. William Howarth (New York: Modern Library, 1981), 694, 693.

24. Daniel T. Rogers, "Republicanism: The Career of a Concept," *The Journal of American History* 79 (June 1992): 35. Other helpful redactions of the long-standing debate over the ideological origins of the United States include John Patrick Diggins, *The Lost Soul of American Politics: Virtue, Self-Interest, and the Foundations of Liberalism* (New York: Basic Books, 1984), 3-17; J. G. A. Pocock, "Between God and Magog: The Republican Thesis and the *Ideologia Americana,*" *Journal of the History of Ideas* 48 (April 1987): 325-46; and Jerome Huyler, *Locke in America: The Moral Philosophy of the Founding Era* (Lawrence: Univ. Press of Kansas, 1995), ix-28.

25. See Thomas Gustafson, *Representative Words: Politics, Literature, and the American Language, 1776-1865* (Cambridge, Eng.: Cambridge Univ. Press, 1992); Michael P. Kramer, *Imagining Language in America: From the Revolution to the Civil War* (Princeton, N.J.: Princeton Univ. Press, 1992); Kenneth Cmiel, *Democratic Eloquence: The Fight over Popular Speech in Nineteenth-Century America* (New York: William Morrow, 1990); David Simpson, *The Politics of American English, 1776-1850* (New York: Oxford Univ. Press, 1986); and Diggins, *Lost Soul of American Politics,* 85-99, 359-65. For other relevant accounts of antebellum political ideology, see Major Wilson, *Space, Time, and Freedom: The Quest for Nationality and the Irrepressible Conflict, 1815-1861* (Westport, Conn.: Greenwood, 1974); and Daniel Walker Howe, *The Political Culture of the American Whigs* (Chicago: Univ. of Chicago Press, 1979).

26. Isaac Kramnick, *Republicanism and Bourgeois Radicalism: Political Ideology in Late Eighteenth-Century England and America* (Ithaca, N.Y.: Cornell Univ. Press, 1990), 261.

27. Herman Melville, *Clarel: A Poem and Pilgrimage in the Holy Land,* ed. Harrison Hayford, Alma A. MacDougall, G. Thomas Tanselle, et al., vol. 12 of *The Writings of Herman Melville* (Evanston and Chicago: Northwestern Univ. Press and The Newberry Library, 1991), 402. The pairing of Madison and *Clarel* is suggested by Gustafson, *Representative Words,* 37, 57.

28. Richard Hildreth, *Despotism in America: An Inquiry into the Nature, Results, and Legal Basis of the Slave-Holding System in the United States* (Boston: John P. Jewett, 1854), 50, 39.

29. See J. G. A. Pocock, *The Machiavellian Moment: Florentine Political Thought and the Atlantic Republican Tradition* (Princeton, N.J.: Princeton Univ. Press, 1975); and Frank M. Coleman, *Hobbes and America: Exploring the Constitutional Foundations* (Toronto: Univ. of Toronto Press, 1977).

30. Pocock, *Machiavellian Moment,* 516.

31. Richard Hildreth, *Theory of Politics: An Inquiry into the Foundations of Governments and the Causes and Progress of the Political Revolutions* (1853; reprint, New York: Augustus M. Kelley, 1969), 47; John C. Calhoun, *"A Disquisition on Government" and Selections from the "Discourse,"* ed. C. Gordon Post (1853; New York: Liberal Arts Press, 1953), 44.

32. Gordon S. Wood, *The Creation of the American Republic, 1776-1787* (Chapel Hill: Univ. of North Carolina Press, 1969), 606-15.

33. Howe, *American Whigs,* 77-79.

34. Melville owned a copy of *The History of Florence* prior to 1851, and one assumes he had access to *The Prince*; see Merton M. Sealts Jr., *Melville's Reading: Revised and Enlarged Edition* (Columbia: Univ. of South Carolina Press, 1988), 92. For Machiavelli and "Benito Cereno," see John H. Schaar, *Legitimacy in the Modern State* (London: Transaction Books, 1981), 68-71; and Diggins, *Lost Soul of American Politics,* 281-86.

35. Niccoló Machiavelli, *The History of Florence, and of the Affairs of Italy, from the Earliest Times to the Death of Lorenzo the Magnificent; Together with The Prince and Various Historical Tracts* (London: Henry G. Bond, 1854), 459.

36. Ibid., 362.

37. Karcher, *Shadow over the Promised Land,* 144-46. William B. Dillingham makes a similar suggestion in *Melville's Short Fiction, 1853-56* (Athens: Univ. of Georgia Press, 1977), 9-13, 208. For Venice as political symbol, see Pocock, *Machiavellian Moment,* 100-2; and Diggins, *Lost Soul of American Politics,* 180-87.

38. For political readings of "The Bell-Tower," see Fisher, *Going Under,* 95-104; and H. Bruce Franklin, *Future Perfect: American Science Fiction of the Nineteenth Century* (New York: Oxford Univ. Press, 1966), 144-65.

39. For a similar conclusion with a theological emphasis, see Emery, "Topicality of Depravity."

40. Thomas Hobbes, *Leviathan,* ed. Richard Tuck (1651; Cambridge, Eng.: Cambridge Univ. Press, 1991), 91, 10.

41. Ibid., 112.

42. Ibid., 127.

43. Herman Melville, *Billy Budd, Sailor* (1891), in *Herman Melville:* Pierre; Israel Potter, etc., 1427; Herman Melville, *Moby-Dick; or, The Whale,* ed. Harrison Hayford, Hershel Parker, G. Thomas Tanselle, et al., vol. 6 of *The Writings of Herman Melville* (Evanston and Chicago: Northwestern Univ. Press and The Newberry Library, 1988), xx.

44. Frederick Grimké, *The Nature and Tendency of Free Institutions,* ed. John William Ward (Cambridge: Belknap Press of Harvard Univ. Press, 1968), 402.

45. Daniel Webster, "The Constitution and the Union" (1850), in *The Works of Daniel Webster, Volume V* (Boston: Little and Brown, 1890), 325, 358. For partisan strife in antebellum America, see Joel H. Silbey, *The Partisan Imperative: The Dynamics of American Politics before the Civil War* (New York: Oxford Univ. Press, 1985).

46. Herman Melville, quoted in Sealts, "Historical Note," 462.

47. Hobbes, *Leviathan,* 31.

48. See, for instance, Gustafson, *Representative Words,* and Cmiel, *Democratic Eloquence.* For Hobbes and language in American politics, see Gustafson, *Representative Words,* 144-49; and Simpson, *The Politics of American English,* 33-35.

49. Hobbes, *Leviathan,* 287.

50. Martin Delany, "Letter From M. R. Delany," 23 March 1853, in *The Life and Writings of Frederick Douglass, Volume 5* (New York: International Publishers, 1975), 274. Delany later qualified his comment in a letter printed in *Frederick Douglass' Paper* on 6 May 1853: "They [know] nothing, comparatively, about us."

51. Thomas Carlyle, *Sartor Resartus,* ed. Kerry McSweeney and Peter Sabor (1833; Oxford: Oxford Univ. Press, 1987), 179.

52. See Sundquist, *To Wake the Nations*; Yellin, "Black Masks"; Horsley-Meacham, "Bull of the Nile"; and Jones, "Dusky Comments."

53. Hershel Parker, *Herman Melville: A Biography, Volume I, 1819-1851* (Baltimore: Johns Hopkins Univ. Press, 1996), xii.

54. See Stephen Railton, *Authorship and Audience: Literary Performance in the American Renaissance* (Princeton, N.J.: Princeton Univ. Press, 1991), 192-95.

55. Arnold Rampersad, "Shadow and Veil: Melville and Modern Black Consciousness," in *Melville's Evermoving Dawn,* 162-80.

56. C. L. R. James, *Mariners, Renegades and Castaways: The Story of Herman Melville and the World We Live In* (New York: Allison & Busby, 1953), 119; Fisher, *Going Under,* 117; H. Bruce Franklin, "Slavery and Empire: Melville's 'Benito Cereno,'" in *Melville's Evermoving Dawn,* 158.

57. Walt Whitman, "To Think of Time" (1855), in *The Portable Walt Whitman,* ed. Mark Van Doren (New York: Penguin Books, 1945), 108; the ellipses are Whitman's.

58. John Quincy Adams, quoted in Jack N. Rakove, *Original Meanings: Politics and Ideas in the Making of the Constitution* (New York: Knopf, 1996), 366.

59. G. W. Curtis to J. H. Dix, 20 April 1855, in Leyda, *Melville Log,* 2:501.

Scott A. Kemp (essay date spring 2001)

SOURCE: Kemp, Scott A. "'They But Reflect the Things': Style and Rhetorical Purpose in Melville's 'The Piazza Tale.'" *Style* 35, no. 1 (spring 2001): 50-78.

[*In the following essay, Kemp probes Melville's technique in "The Piazza Tale," illustrating the relationship between the text's syntactical components and its rhetorical strategies.*]

That Herman Melville found a locus of generative power in language's multiple possibilities—uses, meanings, and expressions—is unquestioned. Curiously absent, however, among the major studies of Melville's short fiction is discussion of just that: how Melville's style relates to his larger rhetorical choices during the writing of his serialized fiction, 1853-56.[1] Only R. Bruce Bickley, in *The Method of Melville's Short Fiction,* declares to connect Melville's "fictional methods" with his overall artistic vision (x). Bickley's aim is not sentence style, however, but an examination of "structure, narration, and characterization" as those elements contribute to the "essential meanings of his tales" (xi). Though described differently, Bickley's discussion of Melville's "technique" is actually another analysis of the topical patterns in the tales exposing the ironic stance of Melville's first person narrators (126).

The lack of critical attention to Melville's style may be a matter of timing with regard to when he began writing his tales. Critically, it is the period just prior to 1853 that has been the focus of most scholarly attention to Melville's stylistic thrusts. In Brian Foley's words, "during the years 1848-51, while Melville's imagination was teeming with new ideas gleaned from his reading, he sought a new mode of expression, one that could encompass a multiplicity of modes" (267). With that backdrop, it's not surprising that *Mardi, Moby-Dick,* and *Pierre* have become central works in the Melville canon for examining Melville's stylistic concerns. As appropriate as that may be, it still does not fully explain why such inquiry would not be directed into what is Melville's most mature period as a publishing author. One obvious explanation is that Melville's *ideas* invite attention. That is, as John Bryant says in the introduction to *Melville's Evermoving Dawn* (1997), as "traveler, ethnographer, allegorist, humorist, tragedian, philosopher, closet dramatist, psychologist, biographer, novelist, talespinner, and poet," Melville "could speak volumes" (5). Two other reasons are implicitly manifest in Michael Kearns's analysis of Melville's style: "the critics who argue most persuasively recognize that Melville's style has a rhetorical effect that can be connected in some way to his interest in what's inexplicable, ineffable about human experience" (54). One, this suggests that because Melville scholars have historically connected his style to larger metaphysical concerns, we have come to accept benignly this relation without close analysis of the syntactical component in his sentences; and, two, because Melville's metaphysical "ideas" are seen as his most defining characteristic as an author, less emphasis is placed on his stylistic innovations. To these explanations I would like to add one more: the lack of analysis of Melville's style in his serialized fiction between 1853 and 1856 is due to the implicit yet prominently held belief that the hermeneutical key to understanding Melville's narrative artistry is best seen in analysis of his longer prose narratives.[2]

If style as a rhetorical choice is central to *Mardi, Moby-Dick,* and *Pierre,* then it is worth examining during Melville's tenure as a serial writer between 1853 and 1856. Indeed, from the linguistic minimalism of Bartleby in **"Bartleby, the Scrivener,"** the epitaph inscribed on Oberlus's gravestone in the **"Encantadas"** [**"The Encantadas, or Enchanted Isles"**], to the court documents in **"Benito Cereno,"** it is clear that Melville's concern with language uses, meanings, and expressions continues into his short fiction. For these reasons, Melville's short fiction is worth closer examination in the way his syntactical sentence structures inform an understanding of his larger rhetorical choices during the period 1853 through 1856.[3]

As arguably the most stylistically embellished tale in the Melville oeuvre, **"The Piazza Tale"** is exemplary for analysis. What makes **"The Piazza Tale"** unique in the context of the other stories in the *Piazza Tales* collection (1856) is that it was written exclusively to introduce the collection, and as an introduction it anticipates in rhetorical purpose many moves Melville makes in the other tales. By analyzing Melville's stylistic techniques in this tale, we may better appreciate how the syntactical components in his sentences reinforce how he establishes character tension and subverts the narrative voice so often associated with the tales in general. Ultimately, meaning in **"The Piazza Tale"** not only evolves out of an understanding of the manifold allusions and topical patterns evident in the text, but also in Melville's manipulation of style in the voices of both the narrator and Marianna.[4]

One passage located just three pages into the story ideally illustrates the stylistic excess of **"The Piazza Tale."**

> And then, in the cool elysium of my northern bower, I, Lazarus in Abraham's bosom, cast down the hill a pitying glance on poor old Dives, tormented in the purgatory of his piazza to the south.
>
> (3)

The passage reflects two rhetorical strategies central to Melville's critique of American culture. Both reveal the sailor-narrator's unwillingness to confront reality. First, based on Cicero's *genera* of style, the sentence is *grande*: ornamental, densely allusive, elaborately constructed, with an elevated diction.[5] "Elsium" and "bower," terms used in classic Renaissance texts (Shakespeare's *Henry VI* and Spenser's *Faerie Queene,* for example) and the long, convoluted sentence identifies the style as baroque, a term that connotes not just heavy embellishment, but also the Renaissance period. The style of the passage reveals the depth of the sailor-narrator's Old World preoccupations. In the narrator's equating his farmhouse perspective first to an "elysium," then a "northern bower," and finally to "Abraham's bosom," the sentence moves farther and farther away from reality, as it also regresses in history. Additionally, the sentence is heavily modified, not straightforward or typical of common speech rhythm. The kernel sentence is delayed, then interrupted by an appositive before the predicate is completed by yet another modifying phrase. Such an artificial sentence construction parallels the narrator's style of indirect communication. That he refers to himself as "Lazarus" and his neighbor as "Dives," names taken from Christ's parable "The Rich Man and Lazarus" in Luke, only reinforces his unwillingness to confront directly and accept *his* reality.

Second, the passage also reveals the narrator's preoccupation with material interests. The word "elysium" indicates his perspective is blissful and like that from a paradise. Yet, the reality of his circumstance conveys something different. No elaborate "Bower of Bliss," the narrator's farmhouse is "old-fashioned" with the "deficiency" of no piazza, something he "more regretted" (1). Moreover, if he were in the paradise of "Abraham's bosom," he would be content with his material situation, but he is not; rather, while he "casts a pitying glance" on Dives, he too seeks the "Potosi mine" that will improve his material reality (5). Living in an old farmhouse that admittedly had a least one deficiency, and with a "fortune narrow," the narrator cannot be content with reality; his addition of a piazza to the farmhouse serves as tangible proof of his desire to improve his lot.

In both the narrator's style and his preoccupation with material interests, Melville establishes two characteristics contrary to a "republican" definition of America, a prominent theme in other stories in the *Piazza Tales.* The narrator's style illustrates his difficulty in clear, direct, confrontational communication, attributes important in democratic public discourse; and his preoccupation with material interests illustrates that he is motivated by economic determinism, not by the virtue of self-sacrifice forwarded by the nation's framers and persistent in cultural discourse prior to the Civil War. Both economic determinism and the call for self-sacrifice invalidate the reality of lived experience in America. The narrator's Old World preoccupations ignore the reality of economic deprivation in New World capitalism, evident in his "narrow fortune" and eventually in Marianna's "fagged out" existence later in the story. And his self-serving material drive lacks the republican virtue of selflessness necessary in helping others. So it is no surprise that at the end of the story the narrator's meeting with Marianna results in nothing more than his return to the "illusions" that characterized the beginning. The end of **"The Piazza Tale"** reveals the effect of Melville's rhetorical strategies: he effec-

tively subverts the narrator's antirepublican perspective by showing how it is contrary to the maintenance of community, and in fact leads to its destruction.

I. 1856 REVIEWS OF *THE PIAZZA TALES*

Surveying the critical heritage of **The Piazza Tales** indicates today's academic scholars have neglected what initial reviewers foregrounded in assessing the collected stories: Melville's style as a writer. In 1856, American reviewers were clearly taken by phrases such as the one, "in the cool elysium of my northern bower," associating them with leisurely repose on a comfortable summer afternoon. In contrast, today we tend to focus less on the *feeling* intimated by the style of Melville's writing than on his ideas. A case in point, William Bysshe Stein, in "Melville's Comedy of Faith," argues that **"The Piazza Tale"** is about "the hero's quest for spiritual regeneration, a faith in divine light that will reconcile him to the dislocating polarities of good and evil in the world" (315). Such interpretations are common in Melville Studies, but in focusing on Melville's ideas exclusive of his style we are neglecting an essential part of Melville's methodology as a writer: his manipulation of style *to emphasize* his ideas. And no tale in the Melville canon demonstrates this emphasis more than **"The Piazza Tale."**

Three noticeable patterns of response emerge from analyzing the reviews of **The Piazza Tales** appearing immediately after the collection's publication in 1856. Although they all deal with the style of the tales, reviewers in 1856 had a difficult time characterizing it. More than once reviewers applied the adjective "peculiar" in labeling his exorbitant language: "all of [the tales] exhibit that peculiar richness of language, descriptive vitality, and splendidly imaginative" quality characteristic of Melville, wrote one reviewer (482).[6] Thomas Powell's depiction of the **Piazza Tales** in the *New York News* exemplifies the attitude of many reviewers in the early summer of 1856, just after the collection was published: "magnificent descriptions of scenery, sea and cloud-land, resembles Tennysonian verse" (470). Perhaps the poetic richness of Melville's language was Tennysonian, but American reviewers looked for comparisons among writers in the short tradition of American fiction. For one, Poe was the best association in descriptive power they could link with Melville: "The weird, fantastic fancy of Poe [. . .] is in reasonable measure shared by Melville" (474). For another, the "mysterious" and "strange" things Melville writes of could only be compared with Charles Brockden Brown (474). Hawthorne, by comparison, was considered more "dry, prosaic, and detailed," while Irving had a style more "elegant, careful, and popular" (474). Melville, conversely, seemed more of a "wizard" (474). Clearly, reviewers recognized that Melville's writing style was unique, but exactly how it was unique was less clear.

A second noticeable pattern relates to reviewer preference. Many reviewers highlighted for mention the stories that still command our attention today. They most overtly preferred **"Bartleby, the Scrivener," "Benito Cereno,"** and **"The Encantadas,"** particularly with regard to the stories' topics. That these stories have maintained importance in the Melville canon attests to how little reader expectations—at least in terms of topical interest—have changed from 1856 to today. But beneath the surface of the reviews—and important for my analysis here, it is the style or styles of **"The Piazza Tale,"** the introductory tale of the collection, that clearly attracted contemporary readers. Though not mentioned nearly as often as the other tales, **"The Piazza Tale"** was singularly highlighted by reviewers. Notice the effect consistently described in the following responses: the book "would be an excellent companion for a summer tour" (478); it's "a delightful companion for an afternoon lounge" (478); "each [tale] forms the feast of a long summer's noon" (482). That this effect can be linked with **"The Piazza Tale"** specifically is evident in statements made by various reviewers: says one, "All of [the tales] exhibit that peculiar richness of language, descriptive vitality" that awaken in the reader "a deep longing to gaze with him upon the sublime and lovely scenery which his words paint so well" (482). Melville, says another, "proves to travel into the mystic regions of fairy land, that it is very seldom he can be either appreciated or understood" (473). These are all direct references to the narrator's gazing from his piazza into the scenery of the Berkshire mountains and his eventual journey there represented in **"The Piazza Tale."** The reader's desiring to "lounge" directly parallels the disposition of the narrator, who in the tale chooses a "royal lounge of turf—a green velvet lounge, with long, moss-padded back" to "leisurely" gaze upon the mountains around his home (2).

While reviewers for the popular press often do not read an entire book, that they selected for comment passages from **"The Piazza Tale"** nonetheless indicates their attachment to the style of Melville's writing. Their comments suggest that Melville's style affected readers on an intuitive, psychological level. Indeed, it may be that the style affected readers in a way that the ideas in the tales did not. Only one reviewer, in writing that he knew not whether to laugh or cry in reading **"Bartleby"** [**"Bartleby the Scrivener"**], even hints at the "concealment" motif we attach to Melville's intentions as a writer. Instead, it was the poetic nature of **"The Piazza Tale"** itself that invited comment. As one reviewer described it, "the introduction is one of the most graceful specimens of writing we have seen from an American pen. It is a poem—essentially a poem—lacking only rhythm and form" (481).

If it was Melville's style that most affected reviewers in 1856, that suggests stylistic techniques might prove important in analyzing Melville's rhetorical strategies today. Indeed, this point is emphasized in a third pattern evident in the contemporary reviews. While nearly all reviewers recognized "a singularly graphic power" in Melville's descriptions, several particularly keen observers understood that Melville's "style" really was a conglomerate of many *styles*. Of the stories, Powell, in the review already mentioned, wrote, "they are, we admit, moulded in styles different from the peculiar setting of Typee, but that fact only proves the versatility of the pen which prepared them" (470). The reviewer for the *New York Churchman* echoed Powell: Melville is "remarkable for certain taking variety of style" (475), commenting that the tales lie between *Typee* and *Moby-Dick* in stylistic sensibility. In one analytical observation, a reviewer commented that "his style is felicitously adapted to the subject" (476). That even in 1856, after several books in between, *Typee* and *Omoo* were still the benchmarks for comparison of everything else Melville wrote confirms why some reviewers either hesitantly embraced the collection of tales or found their style(s) too difficult for reading. "Under the idea of being romantic and pictorial in style, [Melville] is sometimes barely intelligible" was the conclusion in the London *Athenaeum* (481). The review in the *Newark Daily Advertiser* conveyed that one "reads [the tales] with delight and rejoicing that the author has laid his rhapsoding aside, which seemed too much of Swift, Rabelais, and others" (479). It is the "rhapsoding" comment that most deserves attention. If reviewers liked **"Bartleby"** and similar stories, then they were apt to be predisposed to a well structured plot and dislike Melville's "rhapsoding" style. Nevertheless, other reviewers clearly were positively affected by just the reverse: the rich variety of Melville's *styles*.

More recent criticism has tended to neglect how Melville manipulates style to reinforce his ideas. Stein, previously mentioned, is a case in point. He emphasizes the topical patterns in the text, and how they suggest a unity in "narrative method" (315). This approach to Melville, one consistent with much scholarship in Melville Studies, is a holdover lingering from the reading tendencies of New Critics. For example, in his analysis of *Mardi*, Ray Browne comments, "In this work Melville is an immature bird trying too soon to fly into abstract symbolism and merely getting confused" (20). Obviously, Browne's comment assumes that formal consistency in a work is important. This presupposition has long held sway in Melville scholarship. That is, compared in terms of a consciously well ordered plot structure, Melville does not fare as well as a Flaubert, Henry James, or Charles Dickens.[7] Only recently has scholarship begun to embrace Melville's general style as a writer and his careful manipulation of character voice through specific stylistic shifts. Paul Lyons, in a stylis-

tic analysis of *Moby-Dick*, writes that "*Moby-Dick* demonstrates how technique becomes statement [. . .
Melville's] style entangles personality, epistemological
angle, and zeitgeist in ways that enrich its participation
in meaning" (446). To Lyons, Melville's leaving styles
distinct demonstrates a coherent methodology reflecting
positively on Melville's rhetorical strategies. In reading
Melville, these antithetical views suggest a need to re-
valuate our practices. If we apply Wayne Booth's model
for responsible ethical criticism to Melville scholarship,
we not only would complicate our understanding of
Melville's rhetorical intentions, but also include an
awareness of our own critical appraisals of what we
value in a text (Booth 8).

II. STYLISTIC PRECURSORS TO "THE PIAZZA
TALE"

It is important to emphasize the maturation of Melville's
understanding of how style relates to his larger rhetorical aims in the period between 1848 and 1852, prior to
the serialization of his fiction. Since *Mardi* and *Moby
-Dick* have garnered the most attention, I'd like to focus
on these works. *Mardi* prefigures Melville's commitment to a dialogically conceived rhetorical strategy.
And *Moby-Dick* explores the notion that an epistemological understanding of reality is necessarily grounded
in the nature of linguistic representation. Both the dia-
logical and the linguistic are issues that become central
for Melville as he subverts the sailor-narrator's perspective in **"The Piazza Tale."** To start, I want to reinforce
a claim made by Paul Lyons: "as Melville's enthusiasm
for books increased he became less interested in synthe-
sizing his materials, and more open about leaving literary and extra-literary styles distinct" (445). Thus, while
we should recognize that formal consistency in a work
is a value, we must also recognize that it may not be
the best criterion for evaluating Melville—or evaluating
Mardi.

Certainly the seeds for what Melville employs stylistically later can be seen as early as *Mardi*. Elizabeth Foster notes that the book "freed his imagination and intellect to roam the universe from the silliest custom of
man to Dantean heavens, to hobnob with the great writers and thinkers of the ages, to match wits with them
and learn to speak their language" (657). Her words
suggest just how we should read *Mardi*: not as product,
but as process, something many contemporary reviewers
could not do. A review in the *Athenaeum* called the
book "strange," noting that "the reader will be at once
struck by the affectation of its style, in which are
mingled many madnesses" (Leyda 1: 293). Confused
about the resulting "product"—"pleasantry, allegory, romance, prose-poem, and adventure," this reviewer saw
the book become "more and more foggy" until the end
seemed a "happy release." Once again, such commentary says more about reader expectations than it does

about *Mardi*. An important step in criticism of the book
was the movement away from seeing the book as product, and thus expecting formal consistency. Merrill
Davis may have been the first to note that the book
emerged as a process of change in Melville's literary
methods, but his analysis also recognizes the book's
"flaws." Even when the book is praised for its digressions, scholars seem still unable to let go of an interpretive model that expects unity. In *That Lonely Game*
(1975), Maxine Moore pays homage to the book's complexities, but still her emphasis, like that of others before her, is to find "unity" in the book, in her case, one
found in an astro-mythological "game." That this desire
for unity is still prevalent is seen in Parker's recent biography where the book is depicted as a product of
Melville's "reckless impulses," an "artistic compromise" for Melville to write a romance in defense of
validating the authenticity of his travel adventures (591).
Certainly Parker is commenting as much on Melville's
own indecision or uneasiness regarding reader expectations as he is on the ultimate product of *Mardi*. It is this
uneasiness that would make him see his works as
"botches" (Leyda 1: 412).

If Melville himself felt his works were "botches," it
should come as no surprise that we too, as readers,
should feel similarly torn when reading his works. But
the confusion we feel in reading *Mardi* is not just the
result of a writer learning his craft, as Parker, Browne,
and others imply; while certainly it is true that Melville
was expanding as an author, the "artistic compromise"
with which Parker suggests Melville was struggling in
Mardi actually never ceases in his writing. If we assume *Mardi* was the product of an immature author,
then we immediately invalidate the clear choices
Melville made in keeping various literary styles distinct—Yoomy's songs and the dramatic structure of
chapter 180 being good examples. If we accept, however, that Melville's rhetorical aim was intransigence,
then we can see the book in a different light. Michael
Kearns, in linking Melville's style with his overall rhetorical aims, sees Melville employing a generative
model of chaos in his writing. This model is specifically seen, says Kearns, at the syntactical level:
"Melville's intransigent sentences display anti-grammar,
for instance, when they play fast and loose with prepositions or mix transitive and intransitive senses of verbs"
(58). Although his focus is *Moby-Dick,* the stylistic
thrusts Kearns notes can later be seen in **"The Piazza
Tale"** and earlier in *Mardi*.

Whereas Bickley focuses on Babbalanja's speeches in
chapter 180 in showing Melville's "improvisational
method" for writing (3), I want to focus on chapter 155
to show a similar thrust, but one that may better explain
how we as readers should respond to knowledge or
coming to epistemological understanding (that is, as
process). I focus on this chapter not because Taji and

the others in their shallop reach landfall—that would be looking at plot—but because this chapter contains what may be seen as a template for how to read Melville's use of style later in his later works. To contemporary reviewers, chapter 155 must have seemed like another "rhaposoding" event in a very loosely knitted plot intertwined with metaphysical meanderings, yet here we get the "wild soup of Yoomy, the wild chronicles of Mohi, and wilder speculations of Babbalanja." They not only "divert" Media in smoking, but they also divert our attention away from the search for Yillah, which, as the story progresses, actually becomes ancillary to the discussions between the searching men. Curious about "neap tides" and their relationship to the moon, Media in this chapter "turned over Babbalanja for an encyclopaedia, however unreliable," for an answer. Quoting from an "older and better authority [Bardianna]," Babbalanja refers to a specific chapter titled "On Seeing Into Mysteries Through Mill Stones." That Media knew Babbalanja to be an unreliable source and still demanded the information of him may indicate "product" was not his goal. For Media, the information itself is not so important as the process of its delivery and the epistemological quest for the information. Moreover, Babbalanja understands this. Accused of not being patient for wisdom, he says, "Ay, keep moving is my motto," then follows with the story of "Midni the ontologist and entomologist" (504).

The story not only affirms what Media and Babbalanja know, that truth is an ongoing search, but it may be taken as a parable of how we should read *Mardi* itself: as a quest in which the journey means more than the end result. Indeed, as such a parable, it is the story of Midni that points to Melville's rhetorical aims. "Poring over the works of old logicians," the philosopher Midni read often by night, glow worm in hand, "tracing over his pages, line by line" (504). Unavoidably, as knowledge is contingent on factors beyond our control, "glow worms burn not long; and in the midst of some calm intricate thought, at some imminent comma, the insect often expired, and Midni groped for meaning" (504). Here, inextricably, meaning is tied closely with sentence syntax. Unable often to locate another glow worm, Midni "thus forever went halting and stumbling through his studies, and plunging through his quagmires after a glim" (504). What he lamented was that "for one instant of sun-light to see [his] way to a period" (504). This anecdote nicely illustrates just how aware Melville was of the relationship of syntactics to overall meaning making. Like the maddening search for Yillah, meaning cannot come from the complete sentence, period at the end; we are thus reduced to accepting only a fragmentary understanding of final product. The focus, then, should not be on an unattainable end, but on the epistemological process in searching itself. Babbalanja's final resolve to stay on Serenia—his attempt to "counsel" Taji to give up the fruitless search of Yillah—and Taji's

descent into the "hell of despair" that consumes him in the end all reinforce the parable of Midni earlier (637-54).

Certainly the passage can be read as not a discussion of style so much as the investigation of an idea. Melville's emphasis on "the works of old logicians" might be like his commentary on the guidebooks Redburn uses in that novel: they are useless. Yet the digressiveness of the chapter away from the central plot, Babbalanga's "unreliability" in knowing, and the unique approaches Yoomy, Media, Mohi, and Babbalanga each brings to an epistemological understanding of reality—all relate to what Melville will do later in **"The Piazza Tale."**

The remainder of chapter 155, though not as significant here as the story of Midni, nonetheless supports Melville's investigation of style as it reinforces ideas in writing. It is devoted to a discussion of evolution, and ends with Babbalanja discoursing on the virtues of plants versus humans. "Plants," he says, "elegantly inhale nourishment, without looking it up [. . .] Such nourishment we humans are always after" (508). And, indeed, it is that quest—represented physically (geographically), psychologically, and linguistically—which consumes the men as they search for Yillah. Ultimately, it is the process of the quest that is the essence of life, not the unattainable product itself. Yoomy's songs, Media's revelry, Babbalanja's philosophical wanderings, and Mohi's historiography all confirm this theme.

Here we see the rhetorical strategy Melville will employ later: using varying styles to replicate a "heteroglossia" of voices, a feature essential in America to a republican definition of nationhood.[8] Media and the rest all approach knowledge differently, and that no single voice quashes the rest underscores the importance of Media's decision at the outset of the journey to dethrone himself symbolically. That single act presages the pluralism Melville allows to pervade the text later. Dillingham notes the loss of narrative voice in the novel—and truly Taji is absent from many of the discussions that take place in the shallop and on the various islands; but we must recognize that narrative voice evolves for Melville out of the combination of voices of all the characters. Taji is somewhat a composite of voices of all the others. So while *Mardi* does not illustrate Melville's manipulation of different period-bound and generic allusions stylistically (seen later in *Moby-Dick* and **"The Piazza Tale"**), the novel nicely prefigures in the multivaried voices of the characters his later commitment to a dialogically conceived rhetorical strategy.

As John Bryant, in *Melville and Repose* (1993), superbly illustrates, style for Melville became a central concern in *Moby-Dick*. The "historical pluralism" associated with the creation of the text and its reception by the reading public provides a good backdrop to Bryant's discussion of Melville's manipulation of sources (such as Shakespeare) (viii-ix). The novel advances Melville's rhetorical aim of making "fiction argument" by not only contrasting Ishmael and Ahab epistemologically, but by tying that understanding to a linguistic representation. The novel draws attention to the self-conscious, artificial nature of language formation and use. It does not begin with the famous words, "Call me Ishmael" in chapter one; instead, the reader is first ushered into an "Etymology" section "(supplied by a Late Consumptive Usher to a Grammar School)," where the definition of "whale" is given from both *Webster's* and *Richardson's* dictionaries (xv). Then, an "Extracts" section, "(Supplied by a Sub Sub Librarian)," provides "what has been promiscuously said, thought, fancied and sung of Leviathan, by many nations and generations, including our own" (xvii). The prefatory remarks to these sections—in purpose not unlike Babbalanga's philosophical meanderings in *Mardi*—are set in brackets, and like the parentheses that surround the commentary just below the section titles, they serve to draw attention to a digressive meditation on the multivaried perspectives associated with "whale"—literal word, empirical fact, and symbolic idea. All this comes before a narrative that includes styles—literary and extra-literary—that stray from the central plot. Taken together, these rhetorical choices announce a primary preoccupation of the novel itself: that an epistemological understanding of reality is reflected in a linguistic representation that is arbitrary.

A dramatic illustration of Melville's understanding of the representation of language and its relationship to meaning is the famous "Doubloon" chapter. Here, while other characters try to imbue the doubloon with meaning, only Pip, "with that unearthly idiot face," resists: "I look, you look, he looks; we look, ye look, they look" (434). The other "interpreters" can only pity his attempt: "he's been studying Murray's Grammar! Improving his mind, poor fellow." As Mark Bauerlein notes, Melville's reference to *Murray's Grammar* is important: unlike *Webster's, An American Dictionary of the English Language,* a book with which it competed, *Murray's Grammar* is not as concerned with word etymology as with how base morphemes are made into other parts of speech in contemporary usage. Like the whale itself, the doubloon resists an epistemological understanding. Pip's conjugation shows its meaning is relative to the speaker (25-26). Meaning evolves dialogically. As in *Mardi,* Melville in *Moby-Dick* explores the futility in the quest for ultimate meaning. Moreover, while this scene may not explicitly illustrate Melville's growing rhetorical sensitivity to the relation of sentence style to ideas, it does show his understanding that language is the arbitrator for humans in negotiating reality. Ahab, like Taji, is the tragic figure—an aspect of all of us—that must search for resolution, but ultimately fails because human capability is limited.

III. STYLE AND RHETORICAL PURPOSE IN "THE PIAZZA TALE"

By the time Melville writes **"The Piazza Tale"** in 1856, he has matured from a writer exploring the impact of sentence style on meaning to employing period-bound and generic allusions for the purpose of advancing his rhetorical aims in *Moby-Dick, Pierre,* and even in the serialized tales thereafter. Because **"The Piazza Tale"** was written exclusively to introduce the larger collection of his collected short stories, and given the time in which it was written, it may reflect his most sophisticated understanding of the relation between sentence style and overall meaning in a text. Written in first person, the story is of a land-locked sailor who, by his own admission, wishes to forgo the reality of the world around him in favor of indulging his romantic ideations in a journey to see Marianna, the perceived embodiment and fulfillment of his ideations. Only she isn't. Despite his journey to see her, his idealism remains untainted, a choice he clearly makes at the end of the tale. Unable to incorporate reality in the form of Marianna's economic plight into his thinking, the narrator ultimately rejects her instead, returns home, and contents himself with the illusion that his ideations were never challenged by Marianna's condition.

In relating Melville's manipulation of sentence style to his ideas, I suggest **"The Piazza Tale"** critiques the narrator's antirepublican perspective, and in doing so the story critiques an America that had failed to overturn Old World abuses and implement lasting republican reform.[9] The stylistic excess of the narrator's sentences illustrates at once his Old World preoccupations and his unwillingness directly to confront reality, a reality materially defined by economic deprivation. Marianna functions as a New World *reality* in directly confronting his ideations; her sentences are syntactically void of excess, and her lived experience is one of economic hardship. In the end, the narrator's unwillingness to reform his Old World illusions and include Marianna's reality into his perception illustrates not only the fallibility of a self not dialogically conceived, but also the failure of America to incorporate truly republican reform in overthrowing Old World abuses. Melville's subversion of the narrator's perspective demonstrates his idea that in a contingent reality, only by reaching mutual agreement through language can we sustain community.[10] The isolated quest for knowledge, as Taji, Ahab, and the sailor-narrator here tragically show, is antithetical to a republican definition of community: it leads to individual alienation and community destruction. Only in a knowledge conceived dialogically, through mutual agreement, can a democratic American community sustain itself.

The first sentence of the story immediately establishes the sailor-narrator's Old-World preoccupations and his denial of a reality that is materially restricted.

> When I removed into the country, it was to occupy an old-fashioned farm-house, which had no piazza—a deficiency the more regretted, because not only did I like piazzas as somehow combining the coziness of in-doors with the freedom of out-doors, and it is so pleasant to inspect your thermometer there, but the country round about was such a picture, that in berry time no boy climbs hill or crosses vale without coming upon easels planted in every nook, and sun-burnt painters painting there.
>
> (1)

The sentence is heavily embellished with several subordinating and relative clauses, features we should identify as characteristic of the late Renaissance period. Several facts support this association. One, the diction is of that style. For example, the word "removed," used in this sentence, takes on the unfamiliar intransitive verb form (I *removed*) with the antiquated (even for 1855) definition of "to change location." Illustrated in Samuel Johnson's *A Dictionary of the English Language* of 1755, the word's primary usage was as a transitive verb with the more familiar definition of "to take away" (I *removed* the dishes). Similarly, the word "round" is notable for its Old World charm. As a preposition, it is superseded in use in America by "around," but in England the shortened form is preferred (*Webster's New World Dictionary*). When combined with "vale," the more poetical term for "valley," and "nook," these words are remote, antiquated, not characteristic of a New World reality. And when we notice that the narrator makes direct allusions to Spenser ("not even one Edmund Spencer, who had been [to fairy-land]"), Shakespeare ("Midsummer Night's Dream, and all about Titania"), and Cervantes ("At least, so says Don Quixote, that sagest sage that ever lived"), it is clear he is invested in ideations characteristic of Romance (5-6).

Not only in diction does the style of the passage reflect such ideations. A pattern that becomes evident throughout the tale is the narrator's characteristic delaying of the kernel sentence, in this case by beginning with a subordinate clause: "When I removed into the country." Two other examples from the first page are notable. In describing the house, the narrator says, "Seventy years since, from the heart of the Hearth Stone Hills, they quarried the Kaaba, or Holy Stone, to which, each Thanksgiving, the social pilgrims used to come." And later, in describing a lone tree spared by workmen's axes, he says, "Of that knit wood, but one survivor stands—an elm, lonely, through steadfastness" (1). In the first example, the narrator modifies the kernel sentence with two prepositional phrases, and in the second example with one. Such modifying phrases, set awk-

wardly as sentence modifiers in front of the kernel sentence, have the literal effect of slowing the reader down with junctures uncharacteristic of common speech rhythms. The sentences seem irregular, unnecessarily gaudy, and needlessly dense and entangled. Melville clearly wants to draw attention to the artificial nature of language construction. Not direct, the character of the sentence parallels that of a narrator who is uncomfortable with reality as it exists and so does not speak in a straightforward way.

In reviewing the syntactical components in the story, what becomes evident in just a few sentences is the issue of perspective. Just as in *Moby-Dick,* these rhetorical choices announce a primary preoccupation of the tale itself: human perception of reality is reflected by the arbitrariness of linguistic representation. The language of the unnamed narrator in **"The Piazza Tale"** is entangled, just as his perception is. So when he says the farmhouse he bought "had no piazza—a deficiency the more regretted," he is also speaking—in a nice representation of dramatic irony—of a "deficiency" he has with viewing the world around him, a deficiency in perspective. And as his baroque sentence style and direct allusions illustrate, that deficiency is not just physical; it is also psychological: he is embedded in romantic ideations that are at odds with his lived reality—a reality, due to his economic constraints, he seems unwilling to accept psychologically.

The stylistic excess of the narrator's sentences is also reflected in the tale's Renaissance allusions. One of the central allusions in the tale is to Cervantes' *Don Quixote.* Coming just after the speaker sets off on a quest to locate what he perceives as a "fairy-land," the allusion informs both the nature of the questor and the reading of his quest. Seeing "drowsy cattle" that "seemed to walk in sleep," the narrator says, "Browse, they did not—the enchanted never eat. At least, so says Don Quixote, that sagest sage that ever lived" (6). Characteristically, the narrator inverts the normal order of subject and verb, placing "browse" awkwardly at the beginning of the sentence. Additionally, the allusion illustrates to what extent he is immersed in the system of values that Don Quixote represents—one also commensurate with the baroque style of his sentences. It can be argued that the narrator is being self-mocking in saying Quixote is the "sagest sage who ever lived." But even if he is, he is lost on just how ironically influenced he is by Quixotic values. A passage from *Don Quixote* is illustrative. In the pitch black of night and hearing the banging of hydraulic hammers, Don Quixote, "fearless as ever, climbed up on Rocinante and, taking up his shield, set his lance" and in hyperdramatic fashion said,

> Let me tell you, Sancho, my friend, that I have been born in this Age of Iron, by the will of Heaven, in order to restore the Age of Gold—or the Golden Age, as

they usually call it. I am the man for whom all dangers are expressly reserved, and grand adventures, and brave deeds. I, let me say once more, am the man destined to resurrect the Knights of the Round Table, the twelve Peers of France and the Nine Worthies, and the man who will make the world forget the Platirs, the Olivantes and Tirants, the Phoebuses and Belianises, and the whole mob of once famous knights errant, by accomplishing such extraordinary things, in this Age in which I find myself, such wonders, such feats of arms, that they will forever darken the brightest of theirs.

(103)

What is conjured by Quixote here—in the *grande* style replicated by Melville's sailor-narrator—is a dissatisfaction with a world where the self is becoming liberated from the constraints of an historically conceived, static order of existence.[11] It is this fact that makes the episode of Quixote freeing the galley slaves so ironic; saying that "it is [his] obligation as a knight errant to intervene" on behalf of those held against "their own free will," Quixote believes he is acting in accordance with the mandates of chivalry: "I have no choice but to undo compulsion and give aid and assistance to all sufferers" (120). What Quixote doesn't understand is that just as he is operating on "the will of Heaven," so is the system of justice under which the criminals were being held. The result, of course, is that although Quixote frees the criminals, thus literally showing the liberation of the individual from past constraints in the Age of Iron, he feels he is fulfilling a code of conduct mandated by the Age of Gold.

The lack of self-recognition on the part of Don Quixote is what makes the novel as a whole so humorous, and it is this same quality that makes **"The Piazza Tale"** so tragic. Like Quixote, the narrator in **"The Piazza Tale"** is consumed with a desire to escape to a world where there is permanence.[12] William Stein has noted that the hero may be "enamored" by "Spenser's world of imperishable forms" (324). Like Don Quixote, he is certainly consumed with Romance. As his interest grows in the gleam on the mountain that will be the object of his quest, he immerses himself in Shakespeare's *Midsummer Night's Dream*: "Day after day, now, full of interest in my new discovery, what time I could spare from reading Midsummer Night's Dream, and all about Titania, wishfully I gazed off toward the hills" (5). The exchange between his already idealized ideations and the play tend to exacerbate his longing for other worldliness. His obsession seems consistent with what we know Melville considered Quixoticism. In a passing comment in a letter, Melville noted the strange behavior of a Quixotic friend: he had "Puritanical energy," "preposterous" ideas, and a "resolve" to see his goal to the end (Leyda 1: 549). Significant, though not overtly apparent, is that such a quest is futile because no matter how resolved one is, the combination of a single-minded zeal with a preposterous idea will inevitably lead to failure in the face of reality—see Taji and Ahab.

As the style of his sentences show, the narrator is deeply embedded in Old-World preoccupations and unwilling to accept his lived reality. But exactly what his perception of reality is has caused disagreement. Stein believes the narrator is unsettled in the "polarities of good and evil in the world," and in his "unfaith" and "skepticism" he feels discomfited by the "chaos and impermanence of history" (324). Dillingham sees the narrator as suffering from severe "weariness," an "emotional crisis" that can essentially be described as depression (321). Helmbrecht Breinig believes that this prototypical Melvillian protagonist simply lacks a secure faith in God (274). Judith Slater, like others, sees the narrator suffering from an "emotional equilibrium" upset by the realization that evil is at the core of existence (278). John Seelye seems to believe he is just bored or susceptible to fantasy (24). While all these views have some merit, that the exact cause of the narrator's dissatisfaction with reality may be something different, something more economic in nature, is exemplified by an analysis of the following passage:

> The house was wide—my fortune narrow; so that, to build a panoramic piazza, one round and round, it could not be—although, indeed, considering the matter by rule and square, the carpenters, in the kindest way, were anxious to gratify my furthest wishes, at I've forgotten how much a foot.

(2)

This passage ideally fuses the exorbitant style of the first-person narrator with a topical pattern that has not been the focus of scholarship: economic circumstance. Ironically, the stylistic "wealth" of this passage, in all its denseness, is inconsistent with the narrator's lived economic reality. The dash between the first two clauses syntactically illustrates the semantic gulf between the narrator's desires and his economic circumstance. That "the house was wide" reflects the "wide" idealism associated with his placing there a piazza "round and round"—language indicative of the Old World charm seen by contemporary reviewers. Conversely, because of his "narrow" financial means, he is restricted in meeting his ideals. The result is a practical compromise that also has psychological implications: it is the feeling of economic restriction that motivates his eventual quest to the fairyland he perceives in the mountains. This psychological compromise is further illustrated in the syntactical arrangement of the sentence. Characteristic of the narrator, the main idea is subordinated to a number of conflicting thoughts, ones reflected by the various prepositional phrases and relative clauses evident in the passage. Not only is he disconsolate at not having the means to build an elaborate piazza, but he also feels the pangs of having to pay carpenters who seem ready to manipulate him for more money.

The conflation of the narrator's exorbitant style with allusions to the narrator's economic circumstance are spread throughout the tale. First evidence of the narrator's economic situation comes quite early in the story. Exactly why the narrator moved into the country to "occupy an old-fashioned farmhouse" is not clear (1). What is clear is that he didn't like the fact that it hadn't a piazza. At first he tries to do without one:

> During the first year of my residence, the more lei- surely to witness the coronation of Charlemagne [the mountain to the north of his farmhouse] (weather per- mitting, they crown him every sunrise and sunset), I chose me, on the hill-side bank near by, a royal lounge of turf.
>
> (2)

The style is characteristic of the narrator. The sentence beginning with a prepositional phrase is not unusual, but to delay the acting subject with two modifying ele- ments, one parenthetical, that should conventionally fol- low "royal lounge of turf" is unusual. That the adver- bial "more leisurely to witness" begins with an article complicates matters even more. Finally, the preposi- tional phrase set off in commas, "on the hill-side bank nearby," also belongs rightfully after "turf." In short, a straightforward rendering of the sentence would be:

> During the first year of my residence, I chose a royal lounge of turf on the hill-side bank near by to more lei- surely witness the coronation of Charlemagne (weather permitting).

Even the clarity of this sentence could be improved by eliminating the figurative language associated with roy- alty—"royal," "coronation," "Charlemagne"—and re- placing it with concrete description. But the figurative language demonstrates just how obsessed he is with his material reality. Now for the narrator to go without the "convenience" of a piazza for a year, "a deficiency" so pronounced that he mentions it first in his story before his beloved Charlemagne, may indicate that he lacks the financial means to build one. This fact is reinforced when he says it is because of his "narrow fortune" that he could not build a piazza around his entire farm- house—a dream in keeping with his romantic ideations (2). The result of his lack of wealth produces one of his most realistic statements in the whole story: "Upon but one of the four sides would prudence grant me what I wanted. Now, which side?" (2). Being forced to make a prudent financial decision would not set well with this narrator. It meant that he had to compromise his idealis- tic preoccupations of the whole "picture-gallery" all around his farmhouse in favor of just one side. Picking a side wasn't easy; each had its advantages: to the east were the "Stone hearth Hills"; to the south were "apple- trees"; to the west an "upland pasture, alleying away into a maple wood at the top"; but, as the narrator says, "to the north is Charlemagne" (3). By picking the north side of his farmhouse for the piazza, the narrator unwit- tingly plays into his romantic illusions; he strays farther into an interiority at odds with an ability to communi- cate with others in a dialogically conceived relation- ship.

Significantly, immediately after his discussion of where to build the piazza, the narrator reflects on how his neighbor, a man named Dives, "broke" into a laugh re- garding a piazza facing northerly weather. In essence, neighbor Dives is a part of the real world the narrator is trying to escape. Again, to him that real world is associ- ated with economic deprivation and a lack of romantic vision. Dives is exemplary of it; he chides the narra- tor's sense of vision by saying he no doubt wants to watch the "Aurora Borealis, I suppose; hope he's laid in good store of Polar muffs and mittens" (3). But the narrator's romantic vision is not as fleeting as the Au- rora Borealis, nor is it in need of home comforts like polar muffs and mittens. In essence, Dives juxtaposes literally and figuratively the narrator's romantic vision. That he "cast down the hill a pitying glance on poor old Dives, tormented in the purgatory of his piazza to the south" is indicative of the arrogance of his perception, a fact consistent with his affiliation with Don Quixote (3).

Of course, the purgatory of Dives's world is really eco- nomic in nature. The narrator disdains his sense of prac- ticality; this "work-a-day neighbor" is identified by how he juxtaposes the narrator's idealized perception. Think- ing the vision he sees is a fairy-land, the narrator rejects his neighbor's belief that "it was some old barn—an abandoned one, its broadside beaten in, the acclivity its background" (5). Of course, the egoistic narrator says such a view is false: "though I had never been there, I knew better" (5). By positioning himself and his value system above his neighbor, the narrator has effectively alienated himself from other people. So it is no wonder he suffers from depression, as other scholars have pointed out; but his "weariness" is symptomatic of a hostility to the practical, daily work habits that charac- terize the life of his neighbor. He would rather live a life of "convenience," one where he "leisurely" reclines in his "easy chair" while viewing his fairy land (2).

The solution for his "weariness," as he sees it, is to journey to his "one spot of radiance" (4). Again, the na- ture of the narrator's allusiveness (wide ranging) has given rise to the persistent belief that the narrator's quest is ultimately emblematic of an intellectualism equated with "enlightened ignorance," as Richard Fogle says (91). In this view, the quest is about the limitations of an intellectualism that privileges fancy to observa- tion. Perhaps so, but we cannot ignore the fact that the narrator associates his fairy land with economic salva- tion. He blatantly says that "viewed through the rain- bow's medium, it glowed like the Potosi mine." Once again, as with his other economically charged language in the story, this statement immediately elicits in his thoughts his "work-a-day neighbor" (5). It is important to emphasize that the narrator's illusory perception is also displayed syntactically. Both of the narrator's pre- ceding statements are highly figurative: not only does "glow" reflect the association he is making between the

Potosi mine and the glimmer on the mountain, it also represents the "glow" of his fancy with regard to that; and it is the "rainbow's medium"—figuratively—that also clouds his perception of reality. His escape is away, as Fogle rightly points out, from the "hard fact" of daily existence in favor of an "illusion" (91), but the nature of the illusion is economic: "remembering that rainbows bring out the blooms," the narrator says, he believes that "if one can get to the rainbow's end, his fortune is made in a bag of gold" (5). If the questor is a mouthpiece for Melville, as so many critics believe, it is a Melville concerned with a lot more than the nature of artistic representation or the creative imagination of the writer. That he is also concerned with a value system based on the individualistic desire to achieve a lifestyle of material wealth and ease is presented stylistically as well as topically.

Such a view is consistent with the way other protagonists throughout *The Piazza Tales* are represented in that they are unaware or fail to recognize the fallacy of their own positions. Whereas Judith Slater points to the "doubleness of vision" and "naivete" of the protagonists (279), Louise Barnett calls them "diminished" in perspective, or at most misguided (59). I would add that the problematic perspectives of these characters are seen stylistically in that their story telling replicates their values. In **"The Encantadas,"** the sailor-narrator is unreliable in his depiction of the setting and events of the Galapagos islands: "such is the vividness of my memory, or the magic of my fancy, that I know not whether I am not the occasional victim of optical illusion concerning the Gallipagos" (129). Like the sailor-narrator in **"The Piazza Tale,"** he uses a style that is excessive and language that is figurative. In **"Benito Cereno,"** Captain Delano, after being told that a "strange sail" was approaching, is described as having a "singularly undistrustful good nature" (47). But just as in **"The Encantadas"** and in **"Bartleby, the Scrivener,"** the reader is immediately alerted that what may appear to be true may actually turn out to be false: "Whether, in view of what humanity is capable, such a trait implies, along with a benevolent heart, more than ordinary quickness and accuracy of intellectual perception, may be left to the wise to determine" (47). Why the characters in these tales are so "blind" is their adherence to a value system that, like that of the narrator in **"The Piazza Tale,"** is defined by Old World characteristics. Ironically, while Delano considers himself "republican" in sentiment, it is his antirepublican upholding of slavery, the status quo, that leads to his misperception of events in that story. In **"Bartleby, the Scrivener,"** Bartleby's restrictedness is best evidenced by his unwillingness to go beyond the language of "I would prefer not to" (20).[13] As the first-person narrator, the lawyer privileges the language and encoded ideology of conformity and submission to a value system dominated by antirepublican paternalism and material

pursuits. He controls the narrative just as the sailor does in **"The Piazza Tale."** Just as submission to authority is established early in the story, so is the ideal of conformity. The office relationship between the narrator and his employees—Turkey, Nippers, and Ginger Nut—is based upon "mutually conferred" language (18). It is a community defined by the worldly business of Wall Street, "remunerative" financial reward, "vanity," and the worldly motto of "the easiest way of life is best" (14). The language is strikingly similar to that used in **"The Piazza Tale."** Only when Bartleby, a character antithetically defined by his lack of worldly possessions, enters the office community and says "I would prefer not to" does the stable, orderly world based upon "submission" to authority and "mutually conferred" language of conformity begin to break down. Then the central issue in the story is whether the narrator will reform his antirepublican ideas and admit to a dialogically conceived reality. It is upon the breakdown of the office community that the action in **"Bartleby, the Scrivener"** rests.

What's important to recognize in **"Bartleby"** is that the self-assured perspective of the narrator is challenged by Bartleby. Bartleby's fate represents the unwillingness of the lawyer-narrator to reform his perception to meet Bartleby's needs. That same unwillingness is evident in the sailor-narrator in **"The Piazza Tale."** In the stylistic excess of the narrator's language, two religious allusions reinforce the narrator's misguided perception of reality. While William Stein has already superbly analyzed the depth of the religious allusions in the tale, I want to highlight two, interestingly enough, that he does not, for they are significant.

In the first allusion, the narrator comments that the stone used for the foundation of his house was quarried from "the heart of the Hearth Stone Hills." He equates the stone with "the Kaaba, or Holy Stone, to which, each Thanksgiving, the social pilgrims used to come" (1). This phrase is indicative of the density of language evident in this tale and so noticed by critics. Figuratively, the phrase has a whole system of associations attached to it. Stein has adroitly noticed that "the Kaaba" is associated with Muslim piety, that "for the spiritual life of the Moslem remains incomplete until, on his day of Thanksgiving, he discharges the vow of a pilgrimage to Mecca in order to kiss the Kaaba and worship on the Hill of Mercy" (316). Such an act of piety forgoes his or her "self-indulgence." The association is an apt parallel to our questor. He believes piety is best done from "an easy chair" and that the piazza replaces dedicated worship, as was done in "cathedrals of those [past] ages" (2). Furthermore, he is self-indulgent, believing salvation for him lies in the "Potosi mine" that is his fairy land.

What is further—and significantly—conjured in our questor's language is his use of the words "social" and "thanksgiving." In American Puritan tradition, days of fast and thanksgiving were enormously important social occasions. On those days, entire communities would come together to hear a minister preach a jeremiad. In social terms, the importance of this event is emphasized by the belief that on the first nationally declared fast day in American history, July 20, 1775, more than two million colonists went to church. Of course, such a ritual of social bonding is foreign to the narrator in **"The Piazza Tale."** He is characterized by his alienation from others, his extreme isolation. And "fast"ing, in both the sense of community ritual and what Stein calls the act of "self-abnegation," is not consistent with the narrator's value system. Thus it is no surprise that in the second major religious reference, he forgoes fasting for the journey.

At the critical point in the story when the narrator initiates his quest, he comments that "further than to reach fairy-land, it must be voyaged to, and with faith" (6). Indeed, but it is not a faith consistent with Christian values that the narrator understands the terms of his journey. In fact, his act of leaving takes him farther away from the true source of his salvation: cordial relations with his "work-a-day" neighbors. Gathering himself together, rejecting the "convalescing" he was undergoing at home, he "cast off the fast," and ventured forth (6). Of course, he was not fasting in the Christian sense; no, his sense of fasting meant a deprivation from his fairy land. Such a conflation of religious terminology with his romantic ideations typifies his behavior and language use throughout the story.

Up to this point in the story, the narrator has indulged in baroque language indicative of an ethos inconsistent with his own lived reality of economic constraint. The question now is whether Marianna will truly "reflect" his ideations and satisfy them. Louise Barnett has noticed that speech in many of the *Piazza Tales* moves toward silence "because experience is too horrific or incomprehensible to find expression in words" (59). Articulated another way, we see the confrontation of different characters, represented stylistically, as the stories move on. **"Bartleby, the Scrivener"** clearly offers the most obvious confrontation between characters represented differently by their use of language. While the lawyer-narrator dominates the speech acts in the story, Bartleby ("I would prefer not") offers linguistic minimalism. The same pattern in the contrast between the sailor-narrator and Marianna plays out in **"The Piazza Tale."** While the speech of the narrator is characterized by long, convoluted sentences, the speech of Marianna is characteristically just the opposite: short and straightforward, as I will show. In **"The Piazza Tale,"** the narrator describes an "inland voyage to fairy-land" (empirically, a gleam of light he sees on a mountain off in the distance). Convinced this fairy-land is his "Potosi mine," the proverbial pot of gold at the end of the rain-

bow, he sets out in high hopes. Once he meets with Marianna, that Titania of his fantasy, she serves to confront his romantic ideas. Just as Dulcinea is not the beautiful and genteel damsel whom Don Quixote meets, neither is Marianna what the narrator in **"The Piazza Tale"** envisions. It is important to keep in mind exactly what he did expect: economic salvation. The narrator's emotional response to Marianna's condition demonstrates just how his "Potosi mine" fantasy eschewed reality. He describes Marianna as a "lonely girl, sewing at a lonely window" (8). Sadly, Marianna's humanity is compromised by the symbolism with which the narrator has imbued her. Materially deprived and lonely, Marianna seems much like the sailor-questor, but there are important differences.

Unlike the narrator's sentence style, Marianna's is not baroque. Typically, her sentences are more straightforward and direct. For example, Marianna mentions looking off in the distance and seeing what seems like a beautiful home, ironically his: "I have often wondered who lives there, but it must be some happy one; again this morning I was thinking so" (9). The sentence begins with the acting subject, not a modifying clause or phrase as is characteristic of the narrator's sentences. Though not stylistically excessive, Marianna's sentences do display elements that link her wishful thinking to the narrator's. The last independent clause contains inverted word order, and this inversion is characteristic of her expressions throughout this section. She also gives passing shadows the name of a dog, Tray, paralleling the narrator's illusory perception of the gleam of light he saw in the mountains. She, like the narrator, has dreams of something better.

Yet unlike the narrator who ventures off in search for his "Potosi mine," Marianna accepts her physical restrictedness. She realizes to "once get to yonder house, and but look upon whoever the happy being is that lives there" is a "foolish thought" (12). Her story is not of castles and bags of gold, but of how she and her brother were orphans and lived a piteous existence. Hers is a world best characterized by the drudgery of daily toil. Her brother works endlessly, "fagged out" often from work, presumably as a coal miner (9). Marianna's reality situates her as a victim in the story, and this role is reinforced by her being the recipient of the narrator's visit. The impetus for reformation in the story is with the narrator: he is the questor, and he knows the truth about the "yonder house." The question is whether he will actively engage such reformation or retreat into his illusions.

Ironically, while both Marianna and the narrator suffer from the same pain, they manifest different reactions to it. They both are products of an America that encourages desire, yet rejects charity. Melville's concern with the disparity between the rhetoric of promise bequeathed by the nation's framers and the reality of economic deprivation is evident throughout his 1850s fiction. A case in point is the Coulters in **"Poor Man's Pudding and Rich Man's Crumbs."** Their reality more than impinges on the Old World lifestyle of the narrator, Blandmour, and Squire Teamster, but the narrator's decision to leave without compensating Dame Coulter shows that those in wealth and status—though they recognize social and economic inequities—are not willingly going to participate in their reform. Thus we are left with an understanding of the distance between the two perspectives represented in **"Poor Man's Pudding and Rich Man's Crumbs"** (the narrator's and the Coulters'): one is able to transfer an Old-World paternalistic economic system, blessed by the rhetoric of the Revolution, onto the contemporary realities of 1850s America, while the other is able to participate only in the ideals of the Revolution by having "hope" in a better day. So it is apt when the narrator says upon leaving the Coulters that

> the American poor suffer more in mind than the poor of any other people in the world. Those peculiar social sensibilities nourished by our peculiar political principles, while they enhance the true dignity of a prosperous American, do but minister to the added wretchedness of the unfortunate; first, by prohibiting their acceptance of what little random relief charity may offer; and, second, by furnishing them with the keenest appreciation of the smarting distinction between their ideal of universal equality and their grind-stone experience of the practical misery and infamy of poverty.
>
> (296)

In "keenest appreciation" and "smarting distinction," the narrator appropriately illustrates the rigidity of the means which separate classes in American society. Here in a nutshell is one of Melville's boldest pronouncements showing the hypocrisy of an illusory rhetoric of promise and the reality of economic deprivation in America.

Both Marianna and the narrator in **"The Piazza Tale"** suffer like the Coulters do. Yet what is problematic is that the narrator proactively quests, and in doing so he must bear more responsibility than Marianna for altering his misguided illusions—and hers. She functions like Bartleby and Hunilla in other stories contained in the *Piazza Tales.* In each, the narrators would like to impose their realities on others, but in each case the objects of their imposition do not reciprocate. Instead, they tend to challenge the protagonists' perceptions. In **"Bartleby, the Scrivener,"** the narrator's initial reaction to Bartleby's refusal to work is one of shock: "rallying my stunned faculties [. . .,] it occurred to me that my ears deceived me" (20). Yet instead of dealing with Bartleby, he ignored the situation, saying, "But my business hurried me" (21). His business, predictably, is worldly material affairs. The dominant word used in

that story to describe Bartleby is "strange." It too is the dominant word used by the narrator in **"The Encantadas"** to describe Hunilla's story of being left on an island (152). And it is the way the narrator in **"The Piazza Tale"** describes Marianna's words: "Yours are strange fancies, Marianna," he says. Actually, because the strange fancies are the narrator's, when Marianna says, "They but reflect the things," only the questor himself loses its meaning (10).

At the end of the story, the narrator resists a dialogically conceived definition of self. Confronted with Marianna's plight, the narrator seems to have only two options at the end: in a truly republican act, he could try to help Marianna, and thus commit to changing his perception of reality, or he could retreat back into his romantic, Old-World ideations. That her condition made him "mute" signals his inability linguistically to bridge the gap between him and her (9). He tries to communicate, but wishes not to understand her perspective. Though he's been confronted with a reality that more than impinges on his romantic ideations, he still doesn't recognize that in her is a lesson. Instead, he goes home still willing to accept illusion: "I stick to my piazza" (12). Marianna's disillusionment with her world should affect the narrator like a mirror becoming clear from steam. Earlier, when the narrator says, "even in the common world, the soil, close up to farmhouses, as close up to pasture rocks, is, even though untended, ever richer than it is a few rods off—such gentle, nurturing heat is radiated there," he fails to grasp the fact that his salvation, human salvation, rests not in an external quest for romantic dreams but in humble, nurturing, active relationship-building (communication) with neighbors. Neither with Dives nor with Marianna has the narrator fostered a dialogic relationship. And worse, though he returns home, he still desires to participate in his romantic ideations.

When the narrator's baroque style returns at the end, it signals his unwillingness to change his reality, despite his confrontation with Marianna: "—Enough. Launching my yawl no more for fairy-land, I stick to the piazza. It is my box-royal; and this amphitheatre, my theatre of San Carlo. Yes, the scenery is magical—the illusion so complete" (12). His emphatic "enough" signals in language a psychological desire not to meditate further on Marianna's plight. Indeed, doing so would affect his "theatre of San Carlo," his willful participation in a material-driven play of his own creation. As earlier in the story, the word choice and specific allusion (San Carlo) illustrate his adherence to Old-World values. In short, he has chosen to maintain a perspective, literal and psychological (represented stylistically), that does not fully account for the reality around him. It can be argued that when the narrator says at the very end, "But, every night, when the curtain fall, truth comes in with the darkness," he has been affected by his visit with Marianna (12). Indeed, just as Bartleby's death makes the lawyer write about it later, so too is the sailor "haunted" by Marianna's condition. There is, however, a significant gap between feeling psychological pain and proactively altering reality. And this the sailor-narrator does not do. Melville has effectively shown here how sentence style can inform an overall thematic concern. The unwillingness of people to negotiate their perceptions to reach a level of agreement that maintains communal harmony can be as disastrous as the dissolution and utter destruction of the *Pequod* in *Moby-Dick* or as simple as two people in **"The Piazza Tale"** not being able to connect. Moreover, such unwillingness could also lead to the fall of a republic, as Melville shows in **"The Bell-Tower."** Bannadonna, in Frank Kermode's language, escaped into the destructive forces of myth, just as had the sailor in **"The Piazza Tale."** Ironically, while the protagonists in Melville's tales may be swept up in "fiction" of their own realities, the stories as fiction provoke a process of self-reflection in the reader. And therein lies Melville's "fiction as argument"—we must learn not to fall passively, unconsciously into the deception of myth and its destructive ends; we must actively, consciously engage others in such a way that communal interests are upheld, and the republic that America is supposed to be is maintained. Recognizing a dialogically conceived reality is that means.

Notes

1. Books analyzing Melville's fiction between 1853 and 1856 include Richard Fogle's *Melville's Shorter Tales* (1960), Marvin Fisher's *Going Under: Melville's Short Fiction and the American 1850s* (1977), William Dillingham's *Melville's Short Fiction 1853-1856* (1977), and R. Bruce Bickley's *The Method of Melville's Short Fiction* (1975). None of these studies considers style a focal point among Melville's other rhetorical choices. Only Bickley's book is unique in that it is a rhetorical analysis of the "techniques Melville experimented with during the four year period of literary reorientation" (xi) that followed *Pierre*. Unfortunately, Bickley's work does not address the complexity of Melville's style as a writer. Two other works, Helen Trimpi's *Melville's Confidence Men and American Politics in the 1850s* (1987) and Carolyn Karcher's *Shadow over the Promised Land* (1980), are particularly good books showing the intersection of politics and his 1850s fiction, but again, rhetorical analysis in these works locates the loci of Melville's generative power in contemporary allusions. There are numerous articles of distinction about single works within Melville's fiction of the 1850s, but like the aforementioned studies these do not speak to the relationship of sentence style to meaning in the texts.

2. John Wenke's justification for his focus in *Melville's Muse* is a case in point: "I have chosen to focus on those longer prose narratives that most clearly reveal Melville's attempt to marry fiction and philosophy" (xvii). Consequently, he does not "systematically examine" Melville's short fiction. Moreover, the "historical reconstruction" in *Israel Potter* makes that work tangential to his study. But he does acknowledge—importantly for my point here—that Melville was primarily an artist, not a metaphysician.

3. As the term "style" has a ubiquitous nature (in that it is used frequently, yet is often not even listed in the index of many grammar books), it is worth establishing the context of its use here. In "Nine Ideas About Language," Harvey Daniels writes that style is essentially a speech pattern of choice—informal, formal, etc.—that is a representation of "sociolinguistic rules which tell us what sort of speech is appropriate in differing social situations" (49). For a writer like Melville, we are better served to think of *style* as a conscious choice employed at the syntactical level in writing for the purpose of eliciting in the reader an awareness of a particular period-bound and generic allusion. As the argument here maintains that style is a statement of meaning within the context of other rhetorical choices made by Melville, we should be aware that Melville alters his style in writing to meet the rhetorical purpose(s) he intends. Thus, when critics note difficulty in locating a central "voice" in such texts as *Moby Dick* for example, it is often because Melville employs different styles for different characters (such as Ahab and Ishmael). Melville's "voice," then, emerges often out of the dialogue between competing styles. The example in this study is of the narrator and Marianna in "The Piazza Tale."

4. Historically, scholars have recognized the story as "unproportionally complex in imagery and symbolism," something not lost on original reviewers in late 1856 and early 1857 (Breinig 254). Interpretation of the tale, indicative of the "ambiguity" so attached to Melvillian scholarship (in more ways than one), has been diverse. The unreliability of perception, possibilities of creative imagination, and a reaction to the European romantic sublime have all been put forth as issues evident in the text. What persists as the most pervasive interpretation of the story is that it reveals a Melville in emotional crisis. Leon Howard may have been one of the first to raise this issue in 1951, but it hasn't lost its attraction. William B. Dillingham states in his 1977 *Melville's Short Fiction 1853-1856* that "'The Piazza' ["The Piazza Tale"] is not primarily a fictionalized treatment of a universal truth but a highly personalized account of an emo-

tional crisis" (320). References to "The Piazza Tale" are numerous throughout Melville scholarship, but for studies that specifically target "The Piazza Tale," see Breinig, Poenicke, and Stein. For other articles that contain interpretations relevant to "The Piazza Tale," see Slater, Barnett, and Donaldson. Book length studies of Melville's short fiction are listed in an earlier footnote.

5. While Cicero's rhetorical theory is spread among the great variety of his works, in the *Orator* he provides definitions for three styles used in *elocutio*: *genus tenue, genus medium,* and *genus grande.* Each style has particular aim suited to it: to instruct, to please, to win over, respectively. As will be shown, the passage from "The Piazza Tale" highlighted here clearly "won over" his reviewers.

6. All of the following reviews can be found collected in Higgins and Parker.

7. Early Melville scholarship particularly stressed the often inconsistent form of Melville's writing. And, indeed, the implied criterion of evaluation was the need for unity in a work. For elaboration of this perspective many works can be used. Although many others could be cited, I selected the works below because of their prominence in Melville scholarship. These authors listed here all posit unity as an important tool in determining the quality of a text, and their discussions of *Mardi* ideally exemplify the trend in seeing that book as having "many flaws" (Dillingham 111): Davis, *Melville's* Mardi: *A Chartless Voyage*; Stern, *The Fine Hammered Steel of Herman Melville*; and Dillingham, *An Artist in the Rigging.*

8. Here I follow Mikhail Bakhtin's position in *The Dialogic Imagination* that the stylistics of language contain a dialogized heteroglossia, one that is ideologically saturated with meaning, language as world view. So conceived, meaning in *Mardi* arises out of all the participants' speech acts on the journey to find Yillah. I tend to agree with Dorothy Finkelstein's idea that Taji is really a "composite figure," one encompassing "romantic, mythological, and mystical elements"—all the attributes of his other companions on the journey (197).

9. My argument presumes that Melville attempted to carry "republican progressiveness" into literature. In "Hawthorne and His Mosses" (1850), Melville teased those who believed in "Shakespeare's unapproachability." He wrote, "What sort of belief is this for an American, a man who is bound to carry republican progressiveness into Literature, as well as into Life?" (245). Throughout *The Piazza Tales,* and particularly in the serialized *Israel Potter* (1855), Melville critiques America's public defini-

tion of self as bequeathed by its framers. Revolutionary rhetoric promised an overthrow of Old World authority, dictatorial tyranny, and aristocratic corruption in favor of equality and individual liberty in a progressive democracy. To what extent such reform-laden principles took hold in the new republic is questionable. For a Melville who suffered through his own family's economic decline, his restrictedness as a commercial sailor, and his subsequent failure as a popular author, a discrepancy existed between the rhetoric of promise as bequeathed by the nation's framers and the reality of lived experience in America.

10. Informing my argument throughout is the application of the social theories of Jürgen Habermas. In one of his most celebrated works, *The Theory of Communicative Action* (1981), Habermas challenges a Western rationality, in place since the Enlightenment, that is based upon the Cartesian paradigm of the solitary thinker. At the root of Habermas's social theory is the assumption—quite antithetical to the Cartesian model—that our consciousness is socially conceived:

> If we assume that the human species maintains itself through the socially coordinated activities of its members and that this coordination is established through communication—and in certain spheres of life, through communication aimed at reaching agreement—then the reproduction of the species also requires satisfying the conditions of a rationality inherent in communicative action.
>
> (1: 397)

A monological approach to philosophy, the Cartesian model posed certain ways of seeing problems: subject versus object, reason versus sense, mind versus body, and self versus other. Because the model is rooted in a subjective, individualistic consciousness, it denies a socially conceived self. To Habermas, this assumption leads to the radical individualism associated with Western rationalism, an individualism Habermas identifies as anthropocentric, egoistic, possessive, and domineering—all characteristics of the narrator in "The Piazza Tale." Essentially, Habermas wants to ground rationality in communicative action, and thus a central concern of his is how language is used in culture. If we assume a contingent reality and reject truth claims, we then are left with the necessity of coming into mutual agreement through language. Habermas's theory of communicative action provides a way to avoid the individual's subjective claim to truth in favor of a socially conceived agreement in reality based upon people satisfying conditions for language use.

11. In linking the narrator in "The Piazza Tale" to Don Quixote, I argue that like Quixote he is repre-

sentative of a static mindset opposed to a progress (in the overthrow of history) that is, in America's case, associated with the Revolution and the overthrow of "tyranny" in the symbolic representation of England. Indeed, in this light, the project Melville undertakes in this story can be linked to his other serialized fiction, most notably, *Israel Potter.* I agree with Bernhard Radloff in *Melville's Critique of Modernity* (1996) that in *Moby-Dick* and beyond, Melville systematically attacks Enlightenment claims that posit "the economic enterprise and the atomistic social order of Lockean isolatoes defining modern democracy" (2).

12. As Frank Kermode says in *The Sense of an Ending* (1967), "myths are agents of stability, fictions the agents of change. [. . .] Myths make sense in terms of a lost order of time" (72). The narrator's desire to escape is inconsistent with the conscious awareness that his ideations are fiction; the result, as Kermode illustrates, is that in being unable to confront himself—a confrontation essential in understanding fiction, the narrator dips into myth, as the allusions to Quixote illustrate. The result of unconsciously falling into myth, seen in this tale and in *Don Quixote,* is the degeneration of social communication. Kermode's example of such degeneration is Nazism and its correlating belief systems.

13. Why this story has taken such a prominent place in the Melville canon may not be entirely based upon its tightly bound plot structure. The first sentence, "I am a rather elderly man," mirrors Ishmael's opening words in *Moby-Dick.* Straightforward, the syntactical component of such statements immediately encourage the credibility of the narrating perspective, something that the exorbitant language of the narrator in the opening of "The Piazza Tale" does not. As a result, the lawyer-narrator in "Bartleby" seems more honest, and thus more believable. And it is his believable "character" that really makes the tension with Bartleby so gripping in the story.

Works Cited

Bakhtin, Mikhail. *The Dialogic Imagination.* Ed. Michael Holquist. Trans. Caryl Emerson and Michael Holquist. Austin: U of Texas P, 1981.

Barnett, Louise. "'Truth is Voiceless': Speech and Silence in Melville's *Piazza Tales.*" *Papers on Language and Literature* 25 (1989): 59-66.

Bauerlein, Mark. "Grammar and Etymology in *Moby Dick.*" *Arizona Quarterly* 46 (1990): 17-32.

Bickley, R. Bruce, *The Method of Melville's Short Fiction.* Durham: Duke UP, 1975.

Booth, Wayne. *The Rhetoric of Fiction.* Chicago: U of Chicago P, 1961.

Breinig, Helmbrecht. "The Destruction of Fairyland: Melville's 'Piazza' in the Tradition of the American Imagination." *ELH* 35 (1968): 254-83.

Bryant, John, ed. *Melville's Evermoving Dawn.* Kent: Kent State UP, 1997.

Cervantes, Miguel. *Don Quixote.* Trans. Burton Raffel. New York: Norton, 1995.

Chomsky, Noam. *Syntactic Structures.* The Hague: Mouton, 1957.

Cicero, Marcus. *De Oratore: Landmarks in Rhetoric and Public Address.* Ed. J. S. Watson. Carbondale: Southern Illinois UP, 1970.

Daniels, Harvey. "Nine Ideas about Language." *Language: Readings in Language and Culture.* Ed. Virginia Clark et al. 6th ed. New York: St. Martin's, 1998.

Davis, Merrill. *Melville's* Mardi: *A Chartless Voyage.* New Haven: Yale UP, 1952.

Dillingham, William. *Melville's Short Fiction: 1853-1856.* Athens: U of Georgia P, 1977.

———. *An Artist in the Rigging.* Athens: U of Georgia P, 1972.

Donaldson, Scott. "The Dark Truth of the *Piazza Tales.*" *PMLA* 85 (1970): 1082-86.

Finkelstein, Dorothy. *Melville's Orienda.* New Haven: Yale UP, 1961.

Fisher, Marvin. *Going Under: Melville's Short Fiction and the American 1850s.* Baton Rouge: Louisiana State UP, 1977.

Fogle, Richard. *Melville's Shorter Tales.* Norman: U of Oklahoma P, 1960.

Foley, Brian. "Herman Melville and the Example of Sir Thomas Browne." *Modern Philology* 81 (1984): 265-77.

Habermas, Jürgen. *Theory of Communicative Action.* Trans. Thomas McCarthy. 2 vols. Boston: Beacon Press, 1984.

Higgins, Brian, and Hershel Parker, eds. *Herman Melville: The Contemporary Reviews.* Boston: Cambridge UP, 1995.

Johnson, Samuel. *A Dictionary of the English Language.* 1755. New York: AMS Press, 1967.

Karcher, Carolyn L. *Shadow Over the Promised Land.* Baton Rouge: Louisiana State UP, 1980.

Kearns, Michael. "Melville's Chaotic Style and the Use of Generative Models: An Essay in Method." *Style* 30 (1996): 50-68.

Kermode, Frank. *The Sense of an Ending: Studies in the Theory of Fiction.* Oxford: Oxford UP, 1967.

Leyda, Jay. *The Melville Log.* 2 vols. New York: Harcourt Brace, 1951.

Lyons, Paul. "Melville and His Precursers: Styles as Metastyle and Allusion." *American Literature* 62 (1990): 445-63.

Melville, Herman. *Mardi.* Ed. Harrison Hayford et al. Vol. 3. Evanston: Northwestern UP-Newberry, 1970.

———. *Moby-Dick. The Writings of Herman Melville.* Ed. Harrison Hayford et al. Vol. 6. Evanston: Northwestern UP-Newberry, 1988.

———. *The Piazza Tales. The Writings of Herman Melville.* Ed. Harrison Hayford et al. Vol. 9. Evanston: Northwestern UP-Newberry, 1987.

Moore, Maxine. *That Lonely Game.* Missouri: U of Missouri P, 1975.

Parker, Hershel. *Melville: A Biography.* Baltimore: John Hopkins UP, 1996.

Poenicke, Klaus. "A View from the Piazza: Herman Melville and the Legacy of the European Sublime." *Comparative Literary Studies* 4 (1967): 267-81.

Radloff, Bernhard. *Cosmopolis and Truth: Melville's Critique of Modernity. Studies in Themes and Motifs in Literature.* Vol. 16. Ed. Horst S. Daemmrich. New York: Peter Lang, 1996.

Seelye, John. *The Ironic Diagram.* Evanston: Northwestern UP, 1970.

Slater, Judith. "The Domestic Adventurer in Melville's Tales." *American Literature* 37 (1965): 267-79.

Stein, William. "Melville's Comedy of Faith." *ELH* 27 (1960): 315-33.

Stern, Milton. *The Fine Hammered Steel of Herman Melville.* Urbana: U of Illinois P, 1957.

Trimpi, Helen P. *Melville's Confidence Men and American Politics in the 1850s.* Hamden: Archon Books, 1987.

Webster's New World Dictionary. Ed. Victoria Neufeldt and David Guralnik. New York: Webster's, 1988.

Wenke, John. *Melville's Muse: Literary Creation & the Forms of Philosophical Fiction.* Kent: Kent State UP, 1995.

Thomas Dilworth (essay date winter 2002)

SOURCE: Dilworth, Thomas. "Narrator of 'Bartleby': The Christian-Humanist Acquaintance of John Jacob Astor." *Papers on Language & Literature* 38, no. 1 (winter 2002): 49-75.

[*In the following essay, Dilworth appraises the guilt felt by the anonymous lawyer-narrator of "Bartleby the Scrivener," tracing its origins to classical, Christian, and nineteenth-century moral philosophies.*]

Despite half a century of modern criticism, the intriguing constellation of images, actions, and choices in Melville's **"Bartleby the Scrivener"** remains inadequately charted, owing largely to the title of the story, which is misleading. What the narrator calls the "chief character" (635) is not Bartleby but the anonymous lawyer who is the narrator.[1] Aspects of the story that require further interpretation in relation to one another are the narrator's repeated references to Cicero, his biblical evocations, his references to Trinity Church, his pride of association with John Jacob Astor, his reading of works by Edwards and Priestly, his supposed (by the prison grub-man) acquaintanceship with a forger, the physical layout of his office, and his ultimate determination not to expel Bartleby from that office. All of these have as their primary focus the lawyer's relationship with Bartleby, but one element—the lawyer's having been "not unemployed . . . by the late John Jacob Astor" (636)—makes this a story like that described by Joseph Conrad, in which "the meaning of an episode was not inside like a kernel but outside, enveloping the tale which brought it out only as a glow brings out a haze" (7). The inner story—the lawyer's relationship with Bartleby and perhaps even Bartleby's famous 'preferring not to' work—can only be fully understood in relation to the outer story, which involves the lawyer's "snug business among rich men's bonds, and mortgages, and title-deeds" (635) and his holding—before, during, and after his acquaintanceship with Bartleby—the office of Master in Chancery.

An important key to interpreting **"Bartleby the Scrivener"** is the guilt the lawyer feels, which may explain his wish for anonymity. In his narration, he is conducting his own defense, and, as with any defense, it is a response to accusation of guilt.[2] A similar impulse motivates his summoning the other two scriveners in his office, Turkey and Nippers, to judge his request that Bartleby assist in verifying accuracy of copy—a task that scriveners are obliged, although not strictly speaking paid, to do. "What do you think," the lawyer asks them, "am I right?" Implicitly the same question underlies his extended narrative: "am I right?" The imputation of guilt, to which he responds, comes from within himself—as when, while moving to a new office, he looked back at Bartleby: "something from within me upbraided me" (664). His feeling of guilt is doubtless aggravated by Bartleby in prison telling him, "I know you . . . and I want nothing to say to you" (669). There may be no sure way to determine whether this rejection is based on accurate intuition or mental derangement in Bartleby—we shall see how and why it may express a moral judgment. But that begs the more important, though related, question: why might the narrator feel guilty?

This question is not, I think, an invitation to moralist criticism, which has too often blunted interpretation of the story. Blaming the narrator or defending him precludes analytical penetration.[3] If his guilt is moral, it is also psychological, and in that respect a matter for understanding rather than blame. Whether moral or psychological, however, the question 'why does the narrator feel guilty' is difficult to answer, which is precisely why it must be asked with some rigor.

As many interpreters have noted, the lawyer goes to extreme lengths to accommodate Bartleby.[4] Repeatedly the clerk "prefers not to" carry out the lawyer's orders to verify accuracy of copy and to perform simple errands. Verbally this is not outright refusal, but it amounts to that, and, after receiving clarification from Bartleby, the lawyer understands it as such.[5] After discovering Bartleby living night and day in his (the lawyer's) office, and after hearing his decision to give up copying for good, the lawyer dismisses him, offering him, in addition to salary owed, twenty dollars—at that time a large amount. Whether a bribe or a kindness (the lawyer calls it a bribe [664]), Bartleby refuses the entire sum, including the salary owed him. Eventually the narrator allows him to stay on, a sort of rentless tenant, until the "unsolicited and uncharitable remarks" of "professional friends" begin "scandalizing" his "professional reputation" (663). Rather than have Bartleby ejected by police, the lawyer himself departs, removing his office to another building. When the new occupants of his former building complain of Bartleby's lingering presence, the lawyer visits Bartleby and proposes possible alternative jobs. Exasperated by Bartleby declining these suggestions, he advises him to seek employment "as a companion to Europe, to entertain some young gentleman with your conversation"—a weak and only slightly unkind attempt at humor—but he then invites Bartleby to come home with him until they can make some other "convenient arrangement" (667). The lawyer's overall benignity towards Bartleby is emphasized by contrast with Bartleby's behavior. As Thomas Mitchell rightly puts it, "Bartleby's refusal to connect with others, his decision to isolate himself behind a wall of silent despair, rejecting any and all overtures of kindness and help, is in dramatic contrast . . . to the narrator's . . . failed efforts to find an accommodation with Bartleby and later to understand and help him" (332-3).

What more can the lawyer do or offer to do? Among critics of the story, the practical moralists contend that if he were more virtuous, he could help Bartleby (e.g. Schechter 360-1, 365, 369; Knox 30; Silver 423), yet no critic has been able to suggest a specific form such help might take. There seems nothing more that the lawyer or anyone else can do or offer to do. Is the lawyer, then, afflicted with a guilt as neurotic as Bartleby's passive noncommunication? Anyone might feel irrational guilt who has heard the words "I want nothing to say to you" from someone in the process of committing suicide by starvation. But what, precisely, might the lawyer feel guilty about?

A clue to an answer may be found in the range of allusions he makes. Approximately one half of these are Classical; the other half, Christian. The balanced proportion suggests that he is what has been called, since the Renaissance, a Christian humanist—someone who (like Erasmus and like Thomas More, another lawyer) incorporates in his philosophy and behavior the values of both Christianity and Classical antiquity.

Here are the Classical allusions. When the lawyer learns that the scrivener is living in the office, he thinks of Wall Street as "Petra," the Arab city deserted after Roman occupation in 106 AD, and he considers Bartleby "a sort of innocent and transformed Marius," a second-century BC Roman general in exile, "brooding among the ruins of Carthage" (651). Later he thinks Bartleby resembles the "last column of some ruined temple" (658). When Bartleby first prefers not to correct copy, he speaks so calmly that his employer does not dismiss him. The lawyer says, "I should have as soon thought of turning my pale plaster-of-paris bust of Cicero out of doors" (643-44). After Bartleby has ceased copying and while the lawyer interrogates him to no avail, Bartleby "did not," he writes, "look at me while I spoke, but kept his glance fixed upon my bust of Cicero, which, as I then sat, was directly behind me, some six inches above my head" (654). Cicero is the only Classical reference repeated and, therefore, emphasized. The famous Roman lawyer is known chiefly for his essay on friendship and his orations denouncing Cataline for treason to the state.

Public treachery or betrayal may, as we shall see, be intimated, but the most immediate issue seems to be friendship. Before the second reference to Cicero, the lawyer asks Bartleby, "what reasonable objection can you have to speak to me? I feel friendly towards you," and he goes on to "entreat" him "as a friend" (654). Later, when the prison grub-man asks "Is that your friend?" the lawyer replies "Yes," and he subsequently refers to Bartleby as "my friend" (669). But they are not friends. For Cicero, friendship involves genuine, deeply felt affection, which he repeatedly calls "love," using the Latin *caritas* and *amor.* Between the lawyer and Bartleby there is no love. There is no evidence that Bartleby loves the lawyer—quite the contrary, in fact—and although the lawyer's behavior may suggest love for Bartleby, his interior disclosures indicate, as we shall see, that he feels no love for Bartleby. Neither man qualifies, according to Cicero, to be or to have a friend. Cicero writes that friendship is a combination of "good will and love" in response to "virtue. . . . There is no way friendship can exist without virtue" (51).[6] Although Bartleby is, the lawyer says, financially trustworthy, there seems little else in him that Cicero or any other Classical author (or, I think, anyone else) would consider virtuous. Since there is so little apparent virtue in Bartleby, the lawyer cannot be faulted as a humanist for not loving him as a friend. (Later we shall see that Bartleby may be virtuous in a way that the narrator cannot appreciate and critics of the story have not noticed.) For Cicero there is no moral obligation to be anyone's friend, no guilt in the absence or failure of friendship. Why then does the lawyer make the false claim to be Bartleby's friend? One reason may be that the lawyer is a Christian as well as a humanist and that Christianity obliges him to love Bartleby whether Bartleby deserves it, in the view of Cicero, or not.

The Christian-humanist synthesis extended beyond the Renaissance in the writings of the Scottish moral philosophers, which had currency in mid-nineteenth century America, and even in Adam Smith, for whom benevolence combines with terms such as "justice" and "prudence." As these terms may suggest, however, there is a certain incompatibility between Classical humanism and Christianity. The narrator mentally incorporates this contradiction, although he attempts to solve it by privileging the great Christian imperative of charity over Classical freedom. Otherwise, he seems to live, think, and feel wholly within the Classical tradition. That tradition certainly values loving affection, but he is especially faithful to its fundamental emphasis on reason. All his repeated "assumptions"—he uses forms of the verb "to assume" ten times on pages 658-60—are reasonable. In not really loving Bartleby he is, as a Classical humanist might say, eminently reasonable.

Chief among the lawyer's Christian references are his twice mentioning Trinity Church (650, 653) and four times referring to charity, the primary Christian virtue (647, 661, 662), once quoting Jesus giving the "new commandment" of love (661).[7] For Jesus, and therefore for Christians, love is basic, indispensable, and not to be bestowed selectively.

Narrative motive seems largely determined by Jesus's commandment of love and the guilt that may accrue from noncompliance. Leaving aside the question of whether the lawyer pays a just wage or provides good working conditions—and that is leaving aside a good deal—his behavior towards the clerk is entirely compatible with Christianity. His actions could well have Christian charity as their motive, but they do not, which has been noticed by a few discerning critics. The narrator is only "superficially charitable" (Morgan 263). His "charitable actions" are imbued with "a distinct element of self-interest" (Schechter 360), so that he is "not as altruistic as we might wish him" (Pribeck 132). William Bysshe Stein sees him as a hypocrite, his "common sense" at odds with charity, and vehemently disparages him (105, 108). Absence of charity may not be blame-

worthy, however, and readers and critics might be wise to maintain moral neutrality in hopes of psychological and moral understanding. The lawyer is himself in agreement with Stein and other moralists, however, for, at some level, he, too, blames himself. However charitable his actions may seem, we know, because he tells us, that there is very little and usually no charity in his heart. Within the Classical tradition, especially as represented by Cicero, this involves no guilt; but within the Christian tradition, it renders the lawyer morally at fault, disqualifying him from being a good Christian.

The distinction between action and internal disposition is important in Christianity: if you give alms without feeling love, the act is morally and spiritually worthless. Behind such giving might be desire to avoid guilt-feelings or to maintain an ideal self-image, neither of which has spiritual currency. About this, St. Paul is quite clear: "though I bestow all my goods to fed the poor . . . and have not charity, it profiteth me nothing" (I Corinthians 13:3). Charity is not a kind of action; it is a virtue involving feeling. In this respect, it resembles Ciceronian friendship. A great problem for Christianity has always been that it enjoins charity without teaching how to attain it as an interior condition. Modern psychology or eastern meditative practice may solve this problem for modern Christians, but such solutions are unavailable to the lawyer. The problem for him is the same for any Christian who acts charitably but feels no love. It is a discrepancy between behavior and motivation of which the lawyer has every reason to be painfully aware. His narrative is largely, if inadvertently, a confession of it.

What chiefly governs his behavior is the desire to have a good opinion of himself. He first indicates this desire when determining to "endeavor charitably to construe in his imagination" Bartleby's declining to help correct his own copying (647). "Here," he comments, "I can cheaply purchase a delicious self-approval. To befriend Bartleby, to humor him in his strange willfulness, will cost me little or nothing, while I *lay up* in my soul what will eventually prove a sweet morsel for my conscience" (647, my italics). Melville, and perhaps the lawyer, is alluding to a scriptural text that bears on the outer story as well as on the inner story, which we are now considering: Jesus enjoins his followers, "Lay not up for yourselves treasures upon earth, where moth and rust doth corrupt and where thieves break through and steal, but lay up for yourselves treasures in heaven" (Matthew 7: 19-20). Instead of laying up treasures in heaven, the lawyer is preserving an ideal self-image in his "conscience." He remembers that after Bartleby first declined to vacate the office:

> when this old Adam of resentment rose in me and
> tempted me concerning Bartleby, I grappled him and
> threw him. How? Why, simply by recalling the divine

injunction: "A new commandment give I unto you, that
ye love one another." Yes, this it was that saved me.
Aside from higher considerations, charity often operates as a vastly wise and prudent principle—a great
safeguard to its possessor. . . . Mere self-interest, then
if no better motive can be enlisted, should, especially
with high-tempered men, prompt all beings to charity
and philanthropy.

(661)

Melville must have written this with a strong sense of
irony, since self-interest cannot prompt men to charity.
Nor is charity a "prudent principle." As G. K. Chesterton said of that other virtue honesty, it "is not a policy."
The lawyer has done and offered to do everything he
can to help Bartleby, but he has not loved him. In virtually admitting this here, he expresses no feelings of
guilt, but his continual, implied defense of himself suggests that he does feel guilty about it.

The Classical and Christian traditions overlap considerably and are not limited to the virtues they prioritize,
but they do prioritize different virtues. The Classical
tradition prioritizes reason; the Christian tradition, love.
The lawyer is inwardly divided between these virtues.
He embodies the preeminent Classical value but not the
preeminent Christian value. His actions and words to
Bartleby and the grub-man suggest charity and friendship, but his disclosures about how he thinks and feels
reveal that he is loveless. He is, therefore, more a humanist than a Christian—though not, perhaps, a humanist of whom Cicero or any other Classical author would
whole-heartedly approve. As a Christian certainly, and,
therefore as a Christian humanist, he is a failure.

As a failed Christian who does not acknowledge or admit his failing, the lawyer is a pretender. He is also, in
Ciceronian terms, a pretend friend. Though no critic has
suggested it, all this gives symbolic meaning to the
grub-man associating the lawyer with "genteel-like . . .
forgers": "Did you know Monroe Edwards? . . . he
died of consumption at Sing-Sing. So you weren't acquainted with Monroe?" The lawyer replies, "No, I was
never socially acquainted with any forgers" (670). For
one who sets such store at the start of the story by professional acquaintanceship with "the late John Jacob
Astor" (636) as indicative of the soundness of his reputation as "an eminently *safe* man" (635), this imputed
association with forgers is symbolically telling. Though
apparently mistaken in thinking Bartleby a forger, the
grub-man implies that the lawyer is himself one. As a
false Christian and non-friend, the lawyer is a forger
and also a forgery, although if he intends to deceive the
reader, he also apparently wants to deceive himself.

In being true to humanist reason but lacking in Christian love, the lawyer is divided in a way that corresponds to the layout of his office—with physical divi-

sions that allow for only partial awareness. The lawyer
and Bartleby are separated from the others in the office
by ground-glass folding doors that obscure vision and
allow for some vocal communication. On his own side
of these doors, the lawyer is separated from Bartleby by
a green folding screen that allows easy vocal communication but precludes visual observation. There are several ways in which his psyche corresponds to his divided office, as we shall see, but one psychological
barrier is implied by the lawyer's revelation of a division in himself between compassionate sympathy and
"prudential feeling." Upon discovering that Bartleby
lives in his office, the lawyer feels "overpowering stinging melancholy" at his awareness, or assumption, of
Bartleby's "misery" and even has a presentiment of
Bartleby's body "laid out, among uncaring strangers, in
its shivering winding sheet" (652). This side of the lawyer's consciousness is Christian. The other, the humanist, rational, more self-interested side quickly takes
over:

> a prudential feeling began to steal over me. My first
> emotions had been those of pure melancholy and sin-
> cerest pity; but just in proportion as the forlornness of
> Bartleby grew and grew to my imagination, did that
> same melancholy merge into fear, that pity into repul-
> sion. So true it is, and so terrible, too, that *up to a cer-*
> *tain* point the thought or sight of misery enlists our
> best affections; but, in certain special cases, *beyond*
> *that point* it does not. They err who would assert that
> invariably this is owing to the inherent selfishness of
> the human heart. It rather proceeds from a certain hope-
> lessness of remedying excessive and organic ill. To a
> sensitive human being, pity is not seldom pain. And
> when at last it is perceived that such pity cannot lend
> to effectual succor, common sense bids the soul be rid
> of it. What I saw that morning persuaded me that the
> scrivener was the victim of innate and incurable disor-
> der. I might give alms to his body; but his body did not
> pain him; it was his soul that suffered, and his soul I
> could not reach.

(653; my italics)

Up to a point, he feels pity; beyond that point, "common sense" or reason takes over. Significantly, he then
recalls, "I did not accomplish the purpose of going to
Trinity Church that morning. Somehow, the things I had
seen disqualified me for the time from church-going"
(653). He is blocking awareness of his real motive, for
nothing externally seen disqualifies him from church-
going. What does disqualify him is seen, only to be denied, within himself—lack of love, what he calls the
"selfishness of the human heart." In other words, rightly
or wrongly he feels guilty for not loving Bartleby. This
feeling may be, as we shall see, the tip of an iceberg of
guilt occasioned by past and present performance of duties as Master in Chancery and stirred by his having intended to attend a service at Trinity Church.

The narrator's inauthentic Christianity is dramatized in
what amounts to an evocation of the three Petrine deni-

als. On the night of Jesus's arrest, Peter follows the arrest-party to the courtyard of Caiaphas, where a servant-girl notices him and says, "Thou also was with Jesus of Galilee," to which Peter replies, "I know not what thou sayest." Then another says, "This fellow was also with Jesus of Nazareth," to which Peter replies, "I do not know the man." Then others say to him, "Surely thou also are one of them; for thy speech betrayeth thee" and swearing he replies, "I know not the man" (Matthew 26: 69-74). In Melville's story, the new occupant of the office vacated by the lawyer visits him to complain about Bartleby, saying "you are responsible for the man," and the lawyer replies, "I am very sorry, sir, . . . but, really, the man you allude to is nothing to me—he is no relation or apprentice of mine, that you should hold me responsible for him."[8] The visitor then asks who Bartleby is, and the lawyer answers, "I certainly cannot inform you. I know nothing about him." Subsequently the lawyer is confronted by the landlord and tenants of his former building complaining that, ejected from the office, Bartleby now haunts the stairway by day and sleeps in the entrance at night. To this, the lawyer persists, Bartleby is "nothing to me" (665).[9] No cock crows except, perhaps, in the mind of the reader, but the evocation does seem to be of the three denials of Jesus. The meaning here is not necessarily denial of Bartleby. He is not, as some have insisted, a simple, straight-forward Christ-figure.[10] There seems, in fact, nothing Christ-like about him. Instead, the motif of denial has as its meaning the lawyer's non-compliance with Jesus's new commandment of love. Only in this sense are the lawyer's disavowals denials of Jesus. In this sense also, the motif may resonate with the Ciceronian association of betrayal, although the lawyer is certainly no Cataline.

The narrator's guilt-feeling over lack of charity is complicated. He does not consciously feel responsible for Bartleby's suicide by starvation. Nevertheless, not to love may seem symbolically murderous if the person you fail to love dies. The narrator suggests homicidal guilt when he says, "both I and Bartleby were sons of Adam" (652). He means that both are human, but Melville is referring to Cain and Abel, the first murderer and his victim. The lawyer subsequently checks in himself the impulse that led to Colt's murder of Adams—an actual murder, committed in 1842, involving men whose names begin with the initials of 'Cain' and 'Abel' (Forst 265). Symbolic murderousness is evoked, a final time, when the lawyer first visits Bartleby in prison:

> I found him there, standing all alone in the quietest of the yards, his face towards a high wall, while all around, from the narrow slits of the jail windows, I thought I saw peering out from him the eyes of murderers and thieves.
>
> "Bartleby!"

"I know you," he said. . . .

                                                                (669)

The affinity between the narrator and criminals is emphasized by an implied correspondence between his office and the prison. Both are places of walls and restricted views, and in each place someone, whom the lawyer employs, procures food: in the office, Ginger Nut; in the prison, the grub-man.

Because he resembles Bartleby, the lawyer may feel strongly his failure to love Bartleby. The lawyer is "an eminently *safe* man" (635, his italics), as can sometimes be seen in his non-committal, self-protective rhetoric. Bartleby is also safe. The narrator has "singular confidence in his honesty" (649). Both men lost jobs owing to political change. For the narrator, this was the "abrogation of the office of Master in Chancery, by the new Constitution" (636). For Bartleby, it is his sudden removal from the Dead Letter Office in Washington "by a change in the administration" (672). This change occurred in November 1840 with the presidential inauguration of William Henry Harrison, a Whig, whose predecessors in office had been Democrats. (The temporal setting of the story is autumn sometime between 1841 and 1845.)[11] After trying in vain to convince Bartleby to leave the building and come home with him, he drives "for a few days" through upper New York City, into Jersey City and Hoboken, Manhatanville and Astoria. This last is geographical reaffirmation of his connection with John Jacob Astor, which is so good, he thinks (naively, as we shall see), for his reputation. He says, "I almost lived in my rockaway for the time" (668). In this, he resembles Bartleby who did live, day and night, in the office and afterwards in the office building, sleeping at its entrance. The similarities between the lawyer and his clerk reflect ironically on Cicero's statement that "a true friend is, so to speak, another self" (81) and emphasize the lawyer's failure to obey Jesus, who said, "Thou shalt love thy neighbor as thyself" (Matthew 19:19).

The principal evidence in the lawyer's defense against the guilt he feels is the information that, before coming to him, Bartleby had worked in the Dead Letter Office. It is only a rumor, but it provides a psychological explanation for Bartleby's depression and suicide that, the lawyer thinks (but apparently does not feel), absolves him from guilt. The information finally allows him to deny any practical consequence of his failure to love Bartleby. It enables him consciously to preserve for himself and, he expects, for the reader the image of himself as a Christian humanist. But he would never have told the story in the first place if he did not realize, at some level, that pragmatism is not morality, and that no matter what the consequences of his action, the awful and potentially damning truth is that, in his mind and heart, he did not love his neighbor.

About moral efficacy there has been considerable critical confusion. One aspect of the confusion, which the lawyer shares, is the assumption that love necessarily has practical consequences. Walter Anderson thinks that the lawyer fails in not selling "all that he has" and distributing it "to the poor," meaning to Bartleby (392), but Bartleby has already refused the lawyer's offer of money. Also thinking that total altruism might save Bartleby, William Schechter sees the lawyer as lacking "total selflessness and self-sacrifice," which, he says, is impossible, however, for limited, earthly men (265). Norman Springer thinks the story demonstrates "that the possibility of infinite pity . . . is absolutely outside the realm of this world" (413). Less absolute, G. A. Knox writes, "Christ's admonitions are sometimes literally impossible and . . . the lawyer goes as far as is humanly feasible" (29). But the admonition of Jesus is simply that people "love one another." In some instances, this may entail heroic sacrifice but not usually and apparently not here. Only a fundamentalist Freudian would maintain that simple love or charity is impossible in this world. J. Hillis Miller absolves the lawyer (and, for some reason, the reader) because, he says, "we cannot identify our ethical responsibility to a person we cannot identify, whose story we cannot tell" (174-5). Apparently Miller is unimpressed with the parable of the Good Samaritan who helps an anonymous, unconscious man, about whom he knows only one thing, which he is predisposed to dislike, that he is a Jew. Bartleby is precisely what the teller of that parable would mean by the lawyer's "neighbor." Bartleby may not be helpable in practical terms, but love is not reducible to effective aid. Like any person, Bartleby is, according to Jesus, worthy of love. It might conceivably take the form now called 'tough love,' though that, too, would probably not have helped him. Richard Abcarian thinks that the story is chiefly about "the inability of love and compassion to reach those to whom it [sic] is proffered" (214). He is wrong, I think, but he has a point. Love might not have helped Bartleby, but since there is none in the lawyer, or too little, we shall never know. Not that it matters. The lawyer's loving Bartleby would have been enough—for the reader if not for Bartleby. Love is gratuitous, a value in itself, good regardless of its effects.

The inner story, the lawyer's relationship to Bartleby, is the main narrative focus, and achieving that focus may be the lawyer's principal, because unnoticed, rhetorical triumph. He promotes a sort of myopia to distract from a larger, related, social-economic occasion for guilt. This occasion involves his reference to "mortgages and title-deeds" (635), his being Master in Chancery, and his association with the recently deceased John Jacob Astor (630).

The lawyer's relationship with Astor is far more significant than any interpreter has previously noticed, and it is a relationship that indirectly involves Trinity Church—historically, the first-established of all Wall-Street institutions. Near the start of his story, the lawyer pronounces the triple name of John Jacob Astor three times in quick succession (636), possibly to correspond (for Melville and for us) to his subsequently related enactment of the three Petrine denials. Melville may be suggesting that the narrator's denial of Jesus corresponds to his affirmation of what the name Astor represents, a name that "rings like unto bullion" (636). Jesus says that you cannot serve God and Mammon (Matthew 6:24; for Mammon read 'wealth').[12] As Master in Chancery, the narrator has served Mammon in the person of Astor, who was then, with a fortune exceeding $20,000,000, the richest American and one of the five or six richest people in the world.

Known as "the Landlord of New York," Astor had amassed most of his fortune through transactions in Manhattan real estate. The basis of many of these transactions was his leasing Trinity Church land from the Protestant Episcopal Trinity Corporation. The church and its Corporation were legally limited to $12,000 in annual income from its many Manhattan holdings (Porter 919), which allowed Astor cheaply to take out long-term leases on Trinity holdings and then lease them to others at a huge profit. Beginning in 1820, he secured possession of much of Manhattan by means of these and other lease-holdings plus land he bought outright, which he then leased. While acquiring wealth in this way, Astor made many people suffer. In the last twenty years of his life and for long after his death in 1848, he was widely despised for having gained most of his real estate by foreclosing the mortgages of widows with large families of young children (Porter 918, 931). Most New Yorkers shared this opinion of Astor at the time of the first publication of Melville's story in *Putnam's Monthly Magazine* (November and December, 1853). The popular judgment against Astor was not entirely fair. By the end of his life, he owned 500 mortgages of which he had foreclosed seventy—hardly 'most' of them although a substantial number. Astor was not as ruthless as generally supposed. He did foreclose for failure to pay principal, but he often extended mortgages for several times the prescribed period. When a mortgagor failed to pay interest on debt, however, he always promptly foreclosed (Porter 931). Astor made most of his foreclosures when real estate and securities values crashed in the panic of 1837. These foreclosures allowed him to acquire land at rock-bottom prices and many buildings at no cost, since, by the terms of Astor's leases, buildings built by the leasors were forfeit to Astor as lease-holder.

As Master in Chancery for New York City, the lawyer narrating **"Bartleby"** [**"Bartleby the Scrivener"**] has been facilitating Astor's foreclosures. Melville had good reason to know about the Court of Chancery. All three of his brothers—Gansevoort, Allan, and Thomas—had been Examiners in Chancery between 1842 and 1844. His youngest brother, Thomas, writes in October 1844 that his duty as examiner "consists in taking the testimony of witnesses in writing when attended by counsel in suits in chancery—a very fair office and one which pays quite well" (*Correspondence* 567)—words echoed by Melville's fictional lawyer saying that his "was not a very arduous office, but very pleasantly remunerative" (636). The Master in Chancery was "usually employed to take and state accounts, to take and report testimony, and to perform such duties as require computation of interest, the value of annuities, the amount of damages in particular cases, the auditing and ascertaining of liens upon property, and similar services" (Henderson 160). His office was ministerial and advisory rather than juridical, yet he often acted as a judge. He heard testimony, made rulings upon the admission of evidence, and, after the conclusion of evidence, heard the arguments of counsel and determined what facts were proven, what the law was, and how it applied to the facts determined. Rather than entering decrees or making judgments as would a judge, however, he reported his conclusions to the court for approval or disapproval. In other words, he had all of the determining influence of a principal advisor but none of the ultimate responsibility of juridical authority (Henderson 161)—a position suited to "an eminently *safe* man." Melville's lawyer may have been Master in Chancery during the panic of 1837. He says that for "some time prior to the period at which this little history begins," he held that office—until its "sudden and violent abrogation . . . by the new Constitution" (636). This was the New York State Constitution of 1846, which abolished the office of Master in Chancery nine years after the panic of '37 and two years prior to Astor's death (Chester 380). Those seven years or some portion of them were, therefore, among the "few short years" (636) of the lawyer's tenure as Master in Chancery. It was owing to being Master in Chancery that the lawyer hired Bartleby, to help handle paperwork that had increased because the lawyer's "original business—that of conveyancer and title hunter, and drawer up of recondite documents of all sorts—was considerably increased by receiving the master's office" (641). Between 1837 and Astor's death, Astor acquired by forfeiture fifty-eight conveyances (properties legally transferred) through the sheriff or the Master in Chancery (Porter 931). For all or some of those years, as Master in Chancery, the lawyer-narrator had been instrumental in dispossessing people and transferring to Astor the land on which they lived or had done business and the buildings they had erected on that land. In other words, the association with Astor, of which the narrator is so proud, implicates him in the very activity for which Astor was despised, and would continue to be despised, by the common people of New York City.

The symbolic interrelationship of the narrator with Trinity Church and the economic relationship of these with Astor and foreclosures will arm Marxist and other socioeconomic critics eager morally to attack the narrator or the legal system. Fair enough, but this interrelationship may also seem to implicate Christianity in systemic exploitation. Trinity Church and its Corporation and properties were, however, merely an occasion rather than a cause of the suffering Astor inflicted. He exploited the law that restricted the income of the Trinity Corporation; the church and Corporation gained virtually nothing in return. They might be blamed for having dealings with a man like Astor, but anyone leasing the land might, and probably would, foreclose as Astor did; and, once Astor had leased the land, it could not legally be taken back before the end of the term of the lease, which was always, Astor ensured, long-term: he leased the Trinity land for sixty years. For these reasons, the church shared no responsibility for Astor's foreclosures, although it might well be associated symbolically with these foreclosures in the mind of the Master in Chancery. This would explain his disinclination to attend the service there on the morning he discovers Bartleby living in his office and first resolves to expel him.

As Master in Chancery, the lawyer-narrator has been benefiting from condoning and assisting in the systemic disadvantaging of others—he says it was a "very pleasantly remunerative" office (636). In this regard, the reference to the "new Constitution" of 1846 is pointedly significant. Strongly influenced by a powerful 'Anti-Rent Movement,' this constitution instituted major reforms, protecting the rights of leasors by restricting the causes for foreclosure, discouraging long leases by taxing rents, and limiting leases of agricultural land to ten years (Dougherty 164-5). The new constitution was political acknowledgement of the corruption of that aspect of the legal system from which the lawyer had profited. In telling the story, the lawyer is consciously concerned primarily not with his public, professional life but with his personal relationship with Bartleby. In this instance, however, professional and personal lives are symbolically joined. Paradoxically, the lawyer's involvement in foreclosures may well account for his extraordinary accommodations of Bartleby, which he rightly calls "undeniable good usage and indulgence" (654). He does not expel him from the office after Bartleby declines to work for him—behavior by the lawyer that has astonished generations of readers. Certainly this behavior establishes a fascinating contrast, if not contradiction: the lawyer who professionally participates in foreclosing on so many of what Jesus would call his neighbors declines to 'foreclose' on Bartleby.

Hints at reasons for the contrast may be gleaned by seeing the lawyer and Astor as foils. If anything, the lawyer morally benefits by comparison to Astor, who is easily blamed for more than acquiring real estate through foreclosures.¹³ The lawyer is far more sensitive and less self-enriching at the expense of others. (But then, it might be asked, who isn't?) As an educated man, which Astor was not, he strives to embody Classical humanist values. As a thinking and perhaps actively practicing Christian—which nominally German-Calvinist Astor was not—the narrator is concerned about conscience and the requirements of charity. (The lawyer may not, however, be a regular church-goer, since he intended, on the Sunday morning he mentions, "to hear a celebrated preacher" [650], which suggests non-attendance when the preacher is not celebrated.) Certainly the narrator feels an underlying guilt the likes of which Astor, by all accounts, never felt. Astor was insensitive to the welfare of others in general, including his employees, but kindly disposed to those of his employees whom he knew personally and financially generous to some of them and their widows. Melville's lawyer knows all his employees and is certainly generous to them. He keeps on Turkey and Nippers to do the work virtually of one man, and we have noted his extreme kindnesses to Bartleby. Neither Astor nor the narrator is a conscious hypocrite, but each is morally and spiritually handicapped: Astor by an inability to imagine the suffering he caused anyone whom he did not personally know and by an evaluation of most people that was strictly utilitarian (Porter 931). There is certainly a streak of pragmatism in the lawyer—though few, if any, would think him practical in his relations with employees—and he, too, seems impervious, as we have begun to see, to the suffering of people he does not personally know.¹⁴

The form of the lawyer's kindness to Bartleby suggests an otherwise unexpressed guilt over the foreclosures that he facilitates as Master in Chancery. That he associates his office with foreclosures is indicated by his seeing himself as metaphorically a victim of foreclosure: it was an office, he says, in which "I had counted upon a life-*lease* of profits, whereas I only received those of a few short years" (636, my italics). This Master in Chancery apparently associates his office with his initial attempt to dismiss Bartleby, for he remembers, "I could not but highly plume myself on my *masterly* management in getting rid of Bartleby. *Masterly* I call it, and such it must appear to any dispassionate thinker" (658, my italics). Though literally no tenant, Bartleby "ate, dressed, and slept" in the lawyer's office (651), metaphorically "tenanting" it (650), "his constant abiding place and home" (653). Bartleby is ripe for expulsion. The lawyer asks rhetorically, "What earthly right have you to stay here? Do you pay any rent? Do you pay my taxes? Or is the property yours?" (660). As Master in Chancery, he forecloses leases, expelling tenants-in-default, but what he does by virtue of his public office, he cannot bear to do in private. He decides, "my mission in this world, Bartleby, is to furnish you with office-room for such period as you may see fit

to remain" (662), and he says to himself, "You will not thrust him, the poor, pale, passive mortal,—you will not thrust such a helpless creature out of your door? You will not dishonor yourself by such cruelty? No, I will not, I cannot do that" (664). As Master in Chancery, however, he does precisely that, though to people with whom he is not personally acquainted.

The narrator allows Bartleby to stay because he cannot bear to experience up close and personally what he is doing professionally. 'Foreclosing' on Bartleby would make too painfully real the activity he is performing for Astor and other landlords, activity he manages to hide—to wall off—from his conscience. One way he hides it from himself and the reader is by pampering Bartleby in what amounts to reverse-scapegoating. If the lawyer was not assisting in foreclosures or if they were not, at some level, troubling his Christian conscience, he might well be able to expel Bartleby immediately and with impunity. Instead, Bartleby symbolizes for him all those who have suffered, who are suffering, and who will suffer by the lawyer's participation in a system that allows the sort of expulsion he insists on sparing Bartleby. Being kind to the one compensates for unkindness to the many—at least this is the balance he unconsciously attempts to achieve.

The narrator is divided then, as Astor was, between the public man and the private man. The barriers in the narrator's office that suggest the division between humanist and Christian also correspond to this division between professional self and private self. The former is a heartless functionary, a legal tool; the latter is hypersensitive and exceptionally generous in dealings with subordinates. By concentrating on the personal side of the division, he avoids painful awareness of the professional side. His singleness of narrative focus, and the interior barrier it helps to maintain, is an expression of denial, which is the strongest of psychological mechanisms.

The power of his mental concentration in the service of denial is finally indicated by his meditation on Bartleby working in the Dead Letter Office. The lawyer dwells on kinds of letters that fail to reach people because they have died. The last kind mentioned comes close to implicating him as an agent of foreclosure: "good tidings for those who died stifled by unrelieved calamities" (672). More significant is his failing to consider the most common reason for a dead letter, which is not the death of the intended recipient but delivery to an address from which he or she has moved without leaving a forwarding address—which is often the case with people expelled by foreclosure.

Like the divisions in the lawyer's office, the wall of denial allows some communication, blocking conscious awareness but not feelings. Guilt penetrates the barriers between humanism and Christianity and between public and private life. In both instances, it is guilt over not loving. All that he does for Bartleby is praiseworthy. What he does professionally is legally correct. He has to do it by virtue of the "remunerative" office he holds, his only freedom in this regard being whether or not to hold the office. If he did not, someone else would. No wonder he takes refuge in "'Edwards on the Will' and 'Priestly on Necessity,'" works that argue against free will in favor, respectively, of Calvinist predestination and philosophical determinism. They "induced a salutary feeling" and help him, he says, "penetrate to the predestined purpose of my life" (662).[15] It may be no coincidence, for Melville and for us, that Edwards who writes about the will shares his surname with the forger named Monroe. To contend that human life is devoid of freedom, and therefore of responsibility, may be to perpetuate what is, for the lawyer, a comforting falsehood. By the power of denial, he remains consciously untroubled, but he nevertheless fails to love Bartleby just as much as he has failed to love the victims of foreclosure.

In his relationship with Bartleby, he may have good psychological reasons for feeling little, if any, love. That he does not disclose them hardly means they do not exist. He is probably unaware of them. To the degree that he is unable, rather than unwilling, to love, he is morally innocent of not loving. Feelings of guilt about not loving would, to that degree, be neurotic. This may apply equally to his professional participation in foreclosures. If he were able to disclose psychological reasons for inability to love, his argument in his own defense might be stronger. Many of the critics cited above have argued the case for the prosecution, but there is, I think, too little psychological evidence to eliminate reasonable doubt. In this case, the best moral approach may be that enjoined by Jesus, "Judge not." Rather than a villain, the lawyer might best be regarded as morally and psychologically weak.

The narrator's professional involvement in foreclosures, which I call the outer story, suggests a reason for Bartleby's refusal to work. Most commentators assume that if there is an objective reason for his "passive resistance" (646) it is Bartleby's reaction to the lawyer's attitude or behavior towards him or to the conditions of his employment. But the reason may lie, instead, in the nature of the documents Bartleby is copying. He first refuses to review the copy done by another while himself copying "four lengthy documents, being quadruplicates of a week's testimony"—in "an important suit," the lawyer says—"taken before me in my High Court of Chancery" (644). This suit may well require foreclosure to which Bartleby morally objects. Bartleby's second refusal is to help examine the documents he has copied for this suit. When he finally refuses to do any more copying, the lawyer remembers,

"Why, how now? What next" exclaimed I, "do no more writing?"

"No more."

"And what is the reason?"

"Do you not see the reason for yourself," he indifferently replied.

(656)

Bartleby may be declining further complicity in the suffering of those losing homes and property. Behind such a reaction may lie a Christian belief held by Bartleby, which is hinted at in the text.[16] We might be sure his refusal is an act of conscience if he had replied above 'indignantly' rather than "indifferently." Nevertheless, his refusal to copy may be the only act of love of which he is capable, based on a moral disapproval that underlies his implied harsh judgment of the lawyer: "I know you . . . and I want nothing to say to you" (669). However appealing, the possibility of such moral clarity is undermined by Bartleby's evident lunacy: his subsequent refusal to leave the lawyer's office and, once the lawyer leaves, his refusal to leave the building; his refusal to consider other ways of earning a living; and, finally, his refusal to go on living. Nevertheless, Bartleby's initial refusals may be acts of conscience. If so, Bartleby is the frailest of moral heroes, a pathetic Gandhi who cannot, or will not, name what he objects to, so that his protest is ineffectual—or it has been, at least, till now.

Notes

1. Among critics who agree are: Bruce R. Bickley, Jr. (*The Method of Melville's Short Fiction.* Durham, NC: Duke UP, 1975. [30]); Marvin Felheim ("Meaning and Structure in 'Bartleby.'" *College English* 23 [1962]: 369-76. [370]); Winifred Morgan (257); Michael Murphy ("'Bartleby the Scrivener': A Simple Reading." *Arizona Quarterly* 61 [Summer 1985]: 143-51. [143]); and Kingsley Widmer (*The Ways of Nihilism.* Los Angeles: California State College, 1970. [104]). J. Hillis Miller's recent, extended analysis (141-78) founders in deconstructive enigma largely because he assumes that the story is about Bartleby.

2. Only Thomas Mitchell asks why the narrator tells the story, though he does not conclude that guilt is the motive. He thinks the lawyer writes generously to affirm life and to save Bartleby from the oblivion of his own silence (338).

3. As a prelude to his own defense of the narrator, Dan McCall, in *The Silence of Bartleby,* lists many of the blamers, who include the majority of critics (Ithaca: Cornell UP, 1989. 99-112, 123-30).

4. These include the following: Anderson, who explains that the lawyer does everything he possibly can for Bartleby (387, 392); Donald H. Craver

and Patricia R. Plante, who write that the lawyer's actions are virtuous to the point of "heroism" ("Bartleby, or, the Ambiguities." *Studies in Short Fiction* 20 [Spring-Summer 1983]: 132-36. [133-34]); Mitchell, who accurately recounts the lawyer's exceptional kindnesses to Bartleby and also his amazing tolerance of the other scriveners (334-6); Schechter, who points out "how good the lawyer is" to "one of the most infuriating characters in . . . fiction," displaying "uncommon kindness and indulgence towards his impossible employee" (361-2); and Springer, who writes that the lawyer is "'more generous' in the highest sense than most men" (413).

5. When Bartleby "prefers not to" review copy done by one of the other scriveners, the lawyer says, "you are decided, then, not to comply with my request," and Bartleby "briefly gave me to understand that on that point my judgment was sound. Yes: his decision was irreversible" (645). Even about reviewing his own copying, the lawyer soon understood "that he would prefer not to—in other words, that he would refuse point-blank" (649).

6. Cicero repeatedly asserts that friendship is a natural response to virtue (29, 30, 48, 79). His main narrative persona, Laelius, says of his friend Scipio Africanus, "I loved him because of a certain amazement at his virtue" (30, see also 102). It is Virtue responding to Virtue: "when she has revealed herself and shone forth her light and when she has discerned and acknowledged the same in another, she gravitates toward this other and receives in turn that which is in the other; from this there takes fire either love or friendship" (100).

7. Other Judeo-Christian biblical references include those to "Adam" (661) and other allusions discussed below.

8. This is also an echo of Cain's response to God after murdering Abel, as Morgan (265) and Walter E. Anderson (391) have noticed.

9. The correspondence between the narrator's three denials and those of Peter was first noted in print by Bruce H. Franklin (*The Wake of the Gods: Melville's Mythology.* Stanford: Stanford UP, 1963. [132]). Without acknowledging Franklin, Morgan hears in the narrator's second denial an echo of Peter denying Jesus (265), and Gordon E. Bigelow mentions in passing that the narrator is like Peter in thrice denying Jesus ("The Problem of Symbolist Form in Melville's 'Bartleby the Scrivener.'" *MLQ* 31 [1970]: 345-56. [351]).

10. Fiene (21), Forst (265-6), and Franklin (128-36) see Bartleby as a Christ figure. Gerard McGowan argues more interestingly that Melville's evoca-

tions of Jesus, including any resemblances of Bartleby to Jesus, involve "dislocation" and "disfigurement in meaning" that "effectively brings us to the brink of the 'void'" (92-4).

11. It is autumn because the narrator refers to "an election day . . . for the mayoralty" (659). For reasons evident below, the year cannot be later than 1845. The reference to the mayoral election day does not locate the year more precisely because mayors of New York were then elected annually.

12. 'Mammon' derives from a late Latin transliteration of the Aramaic word meaning 'profit, wealth.'

13. Astor was the first monopolist, as the head of the American Fur Company, forcing out of business the Nor'west Company and wrecking the government trading houses that furnished goods to the Indians at fair prices, far higher than Astor subsequently paid. His agents got Indians drunk in order to cheat them. He paid his *voyageurs* low wages, sold them necessary equipment at exorbitant rates, and charged goods to his subordinate traders at such high prices that they had to mortgage their lands to his company in order to buy them (Porter 1046).

14. In a note focusing on Astor's bequest of money to fund a library for "useful knowledge" on "useful subjects," D'Avanzo fails to discriminate between Astor and the lawyer when he writes that they have the same "utilitarian attitude" (261).

15. Emery notes the arguments of Jonathan Edwards in *Freedom of the Will* (1754) and Joseph Priestly in *Doctrine of Philosophical Necessity Illustrated* (1778) but relates them not to the narrator but to Bartleby as a free and "exceedingly willful individual" (172).

16. On the Sunday morning that Bartleby is discovered living in the office, the lawyer returns after a short while to discover him gone, which mystifies him: "I was quite sure he never visited any refectory or eating house," and he "never went any where in particular that I could learn; never went out for a walk, unless indeed that was the case at present" (652). If not out for a walk, which he "never" did, where else might he have gone on a Sunday morning but to church, possibly to the very church—it is close by—to which the lawyer had intended going before feeling "disqualified . . . for the time from church-going" (652)? If Bartleby regularly attends Trinity Church and the lawyer goes only when he can hear a celebrated preacher, the lawyer would easily be unaware of Bartleby's devotions.

Works Cited

Abcarian, Richard. "The World of Love and the Spheres of Fright: Melville's 'Bartleby the Scrivener.'" *Studies in Short Fiction* 1 (1964): 203-215.

Anderson, Walter E. "Form and Meaning in 'Bartleby the Scrivener.'" *Studies in Short Fiction* 18 (Fall 1981): 383-93.

Chester, Alden, ed. *Legal and Juridical History of New York State.* Vol. 1. New York: National Americana Society, 1911.

Cicero, Marcus Tullius. *On Old Age, On Friendship.* Trans. Harry Edinger. New York: Bobbs-Merrill, 1967.

Conrad, Joseph. *Heart of Darkness.* New York: Bantam, 1969.

D'Avanzo, Mario. "Melville's Bartleby and John Jacob Astor." *New England Quarterly* 41 (June 1968): 259-64.

Dougherty, J. Hampden. *Legal and Juridical History of New York State.* Vol. 2. New York: National Americana Society, 1911.

Emery, Alan Moore. "The Alternatives of Melville's 'Bartleby.'" *Nineteenth-Century Fiction* 31 (1976): 170-87.

Forst, Graham Nicol. "Up Wall Street towards Broadway: The Narrator's Pilgrimage in Melville's 'Bartleby the Scrivener.'" *Studies in Short Fiction* 24 (Summer 1987): 263-70.

Henderson, John G. *Chancery Practice.* Chicago: T. H. Flood & Co., 1904.

Knox, G. A. "Communication and Communion in Melville." *Renascence* 9 (1956): 26-31.

McGowan, Gerard. "Christian Masochism and Melville." *Proceedings, Northeast Regional Meeting of the Conference on Christianity and Culture.* Ed. Joan F. Hallisey and Mary-Anne Vetterling. Weston, MA: Regis College, 1996. 91-96.

Melville, Herman, "Bartleby the Scrivener," *Pierre, Israel Potter, The Piazza Tales, The Confidence Man, Uncollected Prose, Billy Budd, Sailor.* Ed. Harrison Hayford. New York: The Library of America, 1984. 635-672.

———. *Correspondence.* Ed. Lynn Horth. Chicago: Northwestern UP, 1993.

Miller, J. Hillis. *Versions of Pygmalion.* Cambridge: Cambridge UP, 1990.

Mitchell, Thomas. "Dead Letters and Dead Men: Narrative Purpose in 'Bartleby the Scrivener.'" *Studies in Short Fiction* 27 (Summer 1990): 329-38.

Morgan, Winifred. "'Bartleby' and the Failure of Conventional Virtue." *Renascence* 45 (Summer 1993): 257-71.

Porter, Kenneth Wiggins. *John Jacob Astor, Business Man.* New York: Russell and Russell, 1966.

Pribeck, Thomas. "An Assumption of Naivete: The Tone of Melville's Lawyer." *Arizona Quarterly* 41 (Summer 1985): 131-42.

Schechter, Harold. "Bartleby the Chronometer." *Studies in Short Fiction* 18 (Fall 1982): 383-93.

Silver, Alan. "The Lawyer and the Scrivener." *Partisan Review* XLVII (1981): 409-24.

Springer, Norman. "Bartleby and the Terror of Limitation." *PMLA* 80 (1965): 410-18.

Stein, William Bysshe. "Bartleby: the Christian Conscience." *Bartleby the Scrivener, a Symposium.* Ed. Howard P. Vincent. Oberlin: Kent State, 1966. 104-112.

Peter Coviello (essay date autumn 2002)

SOURCE: Coviello, Peter. "The American in Charity: 'Benito Cereno' and Gothic Anti-Sentimentality." *Studies in American Fiction* 30, no. 2 (autumn 2002): 155-80.

[*In the following essay, Coviello interprets "Benito Cereno" as Melville's gothic response to the American reading public and its preference for antebellum romantic literature, explaining how this appetite for sentimentality co-opts ignorance about racism and its effects.*]

In 1852, a year after the publication and rather tepid reception of *Moby-Dick,* Herman Melville released to the world a novel he had promised was "much more calculated for popularity." "A regular romance," he called it in a letter to his publisher, though the romance that followed—the novel *Pierre, or the Ambiguities*—is anything but regular.[1] It is a novel in which, among other things, an amplifying strain of gothicism, and of gothic opacity, comes gradually to consume the plot, the major characters, and finally the narrative voice itself, much to the predictable dismay of the author's contemporaries. (One newspaper, the New York *Day Book,* gave its notice the pithy title, "HERMAN MELVILLE CRAZY."[2]) Still, before the novel's incest and murder plots are fully ripened, Melville pauses to consider young Pierre Glendinning's fate as an author, and the more general fate of authorship in America. In a chapter called "Young America in Literature," he writes:

> Pierre himself had written many a fugitive thing, which had brought him, not only vast credit and compliments from his more immediate acquaintances, but the less

partial applauses of the always intelligent, and extremely discriminating public. In short, Pierre had done that, which many other boys have done—published.[3]

For Melville, this is irony so broad and unregulated it might as well be called sarcasm; and the clear bitterness he felt over the treatment of *Moby-Dick,* particularly at the hands of the "Young America" clan of authors and editors, is on uncomfortably naked display here. That nakedness is probably what motivated one critic to aver that "whether the satire has the serious political implications which have been attributed to it may be doubtful."[4] We might have reason to be a bit more credulous than this, since the anger here, uncontoured though it may be, is directed not just at what this critic calls a "literary clique" but at, precisely, "the public"—the very same "public" who, as Melville goes on to write, "had applauded [Pierre's] gemmed little sketches of thought and fancy." At issue, in other words, is more than any literary clique, more than that "high and mighty Campbell clan of editors" who so unabashedly overpraise Pierre, but a specifically *civic* body, a "public" whose capacity for literacy, and aptitude for literary responsiveness, Melville wishes to worry over. And this makes sense, since the question of literacy—of a person or group's fluency with a variety of communicative acts and interpretive tools—is, for Melville, ever a matter of dramatic and necessarily civic consequence. We need only think of all the scenes of failed reading, impotent silence, and interpretation gone awry on that floating allegory of national fate, the *Pequod.* The moral is difficult to miss: civic health, in Melville's fictional cosmos, requires able readership.

Pierre appears in 1852, and the years immediately following do nothing to allay Melville's anxieties about the readerly capacities of the American public. But the events of those years do, it seems, focus his misgivings. Melville's breath, we might say, had time to straighten, his brain to bubble cool, so that what would come from him by 1855 was no longer that sneering broadside vitriol, but the rigidly controlled, exactingly apportioned anger of a writer who has passed beyond wounded authorial pride into a vastly more embracing fatalism. In the essay that follows, I want to contend that the vehicle Melville fashions to carry this anger, this furious dismay before a direly inept and seemingly ineducable American readership, is the great novella of slave revolt **"Benito Cereno"**; that its method is, in a complicated way, gothic; and that what not indirectly inspires and crystallizes this anger—what transpires so momentously between *Moby-Dick* and **"Benito Cereno"**—is the publication and unprecedented reception of Harriet Beecher Stowe's sentimental epic, *Uncle Tom's Cabin,* in 1852.[5] **"Benito Cereno"** responds to *Uncle Tom's Cabin* in at least two ways. It does so, first, in its assault on the self-satisfied and pointedly sentimental mode of reading emblematized by the guileless American ship captain,

Amasa Delano; and it does so, second, in the very locutions, the very turns of diction and syntax, it borrows from Stowe, and then calculatedly re-deploys. Trading on Stowe's use of a kind of offhand racial knowingness, a casually assured knowledge of black traits and black life, Melville assumes exactly this rhetorical posture in several conspicuously racist passages of unclearly indirect discourse—passages in which, as I hope to show, what is at stake is *any* reader's capacity to withstand authorial invitations to credulity. And it is precisely *this* literacy, this capacity to resist easy credulity and complacent self-assurance, which Melville fears sentimentality, as exemplified by Stowe, has been working assiduously to erode in American readers.

This line of argument goes slightly against the grain of recent movements in antebellum literary scholarship, particularly where race and genre are concerned. In much strong new work, we have been asked to reconsider the role of the gothic—of gothic forms, characterizations, figures, and rhetorics—within ostensibly sentimental genres. Works like *Incidents in the Life of a Slave Girl, Our Nig,* and *Uncle Tom's Cabin* itself have been shown to make strident use of gothic motifs as a counterpoint, or complicating addendum, to their markedly sentimental strains: maternal affection has been shown to be crossed with a violent fear of loss, filial obedience cut with rage, and so on. One fine example of this is Julia Stern's reading of *Our Nig,* in which she argues that the domestic spaces of the book—kitchens, dining rooms: usually sentimental safe-havens—are the sites of the novel's most gothic scenes of rivalry, fury, violence, and terror.[6] The gothic, in such an account, implicitly critiques the sentimental, though without abandoning it: more accurately, it *completes* the sentimental, enhancing its efficacy by extending the range of its sanctioned affects.

"Benito Cereno," I am suggesting, makes a different kind of argument, one that pits gothic occlusion and opacity against sentimental modes of reading and response, and sentimental readers, the better to show how easily sentimentality consorts with a particularly American racism. This reading is aligned with accounts of Melville's career by Ann Douglas and Gillian Brown, both of whom argue (with differing emphases) that after *Moby-Dick* Melville turns dramatically against the American reading public, and particularly against its seemingly insatiable appetite for "feminized," sentimental literatures. What results from this anti-sentimentalism, they contend, is an aggrieved "revolt against the reader" in Melville, and a more widely thematized "misanthropy"—a contention seemingly embodied to perfection by **"Benito Cereno,"** a text more vengefully disposed toward its readers, and more thoroughgoing in its misanthropy, than anything else Melville would produce. But I believe that the blistering assaults on readership in **"Benito Cereno"**—a text neither Douglas nor Brown takes up—show Melville's hostility toward sentimentalism to proceed on significantly different grounds than these critics suggest. For **"Benito Cereno"** is not a text unduly dismayed by effeminacy or "feminization" (as Douglas has it), or by the de-individuating caprices of the marketplace, for which women were so often made an emblem (as Brown argues). Much more directly and urgently, **"Benito Cereno"** arraigns sentimentality for the profound and self-exculpatory misapprehensions of an explosive, inhumane, and unsustainable racial standoff that it sponsors.[7] Sentimentality, the work finally suggests, is an American way of reading the gothic text of race in the New World—gothic in its violence, in its atmosphere of dread, and not least in its unyielding opacity, its resistance to easy legibility.[8] Or rather, sentimentality is, for Melville, a way of *misrecognizing* that text, of subsisting in a state of often grossly self-satisfied ignorance of its most dire aspects and consequences. There are many figures in **"Benito Cereno"** around whom such ominous ignorances revolve, but the one to whom we, as readers, are most intimately, exasperatingly tied is, of course, the cheery and indefatigably good-hearted Captain Amasa Delano.

THE GENEROSITY AND PIETY OF CAPTAIN AMASA DELANO

What sort of reader, then, is Amasa Delano, of Duxbury, Massachusetts? In the broadest view, he is plainly a *bad* one, which fact the narrative voice shares with us early on, in terms not very uncertain. We are introduced to Delano as he spies a ship, flying no flag to announce its origins or intentions, coming into an isolated harbor:

> Considering the lawlessness and loneliness of the spot, and the sort of stories, at that day, associated with those seas, Captain Delano's surprise might have deepened into some uneasiness had he not been a person of singularly undistrustful good nature, not liable, except on extraordinary and repeated incentives, and hardly then, to indulge in personal alarms, any way involving the imputation of malign evil in man. Whether, in view of what humanity is capable, such a trait implies, along with a benevolent heart, more than ordinary quickness and accuracy of intellectual perception, may be left to the wise to determine.[9]

We will return to this intensely provoking passage shortly, but for now I would note only that Delano's not more than ordinary intellectual acuity is presented here in relation to his capacity as a *reader*: that is, to his understanding and use (or misunderstanding and misuse) of "the sort of stories . . . associated with those seas." There is perhaps the solace of his "benevolence of heart," but this passing approbation—backhanded, we will later learn—only mildly mitigates, without at all canceling, the charge against him, as clearly put here as it ever will be, of dimwittedness and a more particular readerly incompetence.[10] And of course the plot of the

novella, once it is fully revealed, bears out exactly this condemnation. Delano has moments of seeming fluency, to be sure: he successfully interprets the "baked" lips of the slaves as evidence of the ship's lack of water (49); he even reads the person of Captain Benito Cereno with close-grained scrutiny: "Eyeing Don Benito's small, yellow hands, he *easily inferred* that the young captain had not got into command at the hawsehole, but the cabin-window" (58, emphasis added). But despite these brief interpretive successes, or the appearance of them, what Delano suffers on board the *San Dominick* is no general incompetency but, precisely, a catastrophic failure of reading. Confronted with a veritable crush of signs and portents—the frail captain, the vigilant Babo, chained Atufal, the oakum-pickers and hatchet-polishers, the flaring moments of violence and unease—he is unable to arrange them accurately or truthfully. As a reader of the text of the *San Dominick,* he fails to discern that the Spanish vessel is in fact in the grips of a complex, meticulously plotted mutiny, that the slaves have successfully revolted, and that the dutiful Babo is in fact the revolutionary in command.[11] Delano's illiteracy in this regard is very nearly fatal, and in a way that the text again renders plain, and that critics have frequently described, it is his cheery, unselfconscious, absolutely intractable racism—his offhand white supremacism—that drives and sustains this illiteracy. For most of what prevents him from discovering the plot, even despite his several moments of deep suspicion, is his unruffled confidence that a slave like Babo, so naturally docile, so ideally suited to those watchful and pleasant "avocations about one's person," could never surpass the "unaspiring contentment of a limited mind" common to all Africans (83, 84). The blacks in league with a piratical Cereno? "But they were too stupid," Delano reminds himself (75). Believing this, he cannot see what's before him. As Jean Fagan Yellin has it, "Because he is incapable of imagining the Negro in any but a passive role—devoted servant, victimized savage, exotic primitive—Delano cannot perceive the true situation on the *San Dominick.*"[12]

This much, by now, we know. More remarkable, I think, is that this pervasive racial illiteracy is linked explicitly to Delano's winning "benevolence of heart," and that this peculiar "benevolence" is equally a matter of reading and readerly aptitude. For Delano's failure as a reader is accretive; it comes slowly, and in stages. It is not so much that Delano cannot make any order or coherent narrative out of the portents he fronts; he does so, in fact, doggedly. The problem is more that the order he gives them, or rather the *genre* in which he narrates the scene back to himself, continually misapprehends it.

The text before him, could he but read it, is in fact relentlessly gothic. Packed extraordinarily densely into the opening of the tale, for instance, are a series of characteristically gothic emblems of aristocratic decay and decadent or declined Catholicism. When first viewed, the Spanish ship "appeared like a white-washed monastery after a thunder-storm, seen perched upon some dun cliff among the Pyrenees. But it was no purely fanciful resemblance which now, for a moment, almost led Captain Delano to think that nothing less than a ship-load of monks was before him" (48). We are told, too, that the ship has the distinct aspect of "superannuated Italian palaces . . . under a decline of masters" (48). In case we've missed the point, the narrator continues to paint the vessel as completely in the image of that central gothic set-piece, the ruined castle, as strained verisimilitude will allow:

> Battered and mouldy, the castellated forecastle seemed some ancient turret, long ago taken by assault, and then left to decay. Toward the stern, two high-raised quarter galleries—the balustrades here and there covered with dry, tindery sea-moss—opening out from the unoccupied state-cabin, whose dead lights, for all the mild weather, were hermetically closed and calked—these tenantless balconies hung over the sea as if it were the grand Venetian canal.

(48-49)

And while Eric Sundquist and H. Bruce Franklin are correct to note the salience of Catholicism, and of the papacy, as culpable authorizing agents of the New World slavery that is the novella's subject, we ought not to forget that the Catholicism mantling the Spanish Captain Cereno and his ship—like the repeated references to Venice—functions as a steady harbinger of, if not the fact, the *possibility* of a specifically gothic style of intrigue, conspiracy, and violence.[13] "These Spaniards are all an odd set," Delano muses to himself; "the very word Spaniard has a curious, conspirator, Guy-Fawkish twang to it" (79). In setting as in cast, as Delano himself notices, the *San Dominick* is a thoroughly gothic *mise en scéne*.

There is more than this, especially if we shift our interest in the gothic from what it is (the standard inventory of gothic conventions) to what it *does*. Beyond the text's other gothic topoi (encrypted texts, scenes of subjection and dominance, the unclearly violent or affectionate interdependency of two male leads, Babo and Cereno), it is invested throughout—again in a way Delano remarks—with a disquieting sense of the unspoken or unspeakable, somehow silently orchestrating the movements of all. As Eve Sedgwick remarks, "Of all the Gothic conventions dealing with the sudden, mysterious, seemingly arbitrary, but massive inaccessibility of those things that should normally be most accessible, the difficulty the story has in getting itself told is of the most obvious structural significance."[14] The gothic, she observes, is characteristically fascinated with the limits and aporias of communication, with the varied liabilities and often terrorizing difficulties of speech, writing,

and reading. And it is of course exactly the difficulty Sedgwick specifies, the difficulty the story of the *San Dominick* and its peculiarities has in telling itself coherently to Delano, that most unsettles the good captain. Noticing a young Spaniard on board whose fine linen undershirt is masked by the garb of a common sailor, Delano senses, not for the first time, the presence of a narrative not fully accessible to him: "At this moment the young sailor's eye was again fixed on the whisperers, and Captain Delano thought he observed a lurking significance in it, as if silent signs of some Freemason sort had that instant been interchanged" (66). Delano experiences here, as he does with even greater intensity elsewhere, what Eugenia C. DeLamotte describes as "the vague premonition, the indefinable feeling of dread" that characterizes the traditional gothic heroine's response to her environment.[15] In a real sense, Delano himself becomes still another gothic figure. Trapped in an environment whose whole aspect is distinctively gothic, Delano responds exactly in kind: with the inarticulable, premonitory dread of the conventional gothic protagonist.

These generic codings, as strident as they often are, are not lost Amasa Delano. He actually comes to suspect as much, and it is in fact the very thought of himself *as* a gothic protagonist—or rather, the thought that he has been imagining himself at the center of a gothic tale—that often facilitates his return to ease and suspicionlessness. Indeed, he tends to arrive at a self-castigating distrust of his own suspiciousness precisely by opposing the gothic to an altogether different genre of imagining. After the incident with the old Spanish seaman and the knot Delano once again feels "a qualmish sort of emotion," but is again, in a peculiar fashion, put back at his ease by the sight of his own boat, Rover, coming back from the *Bachelor's Delight*:

> The sight of that household boat evoked a thousand trustful associations, which, contrasted with previous suspicions, filled him not only with lightsome confidence, but somehow with half-humorous self-reproaches at his former lack of it.
>
> "What, I, Amasa Delano—Jack of the Beach, as they called me when a lad . . . I, little Jack of the Beach, that used to go berrying with cousin Nat and the rest; I to be murdered here at the ends of the earth, on board a haunted pirate-ship by a horrible Spaniard?—Too nonsensical to think of!"

(77)

What is nonsensical to Delano here is that he has, despite himself, credited gothic tale-telling—the sorts of stories associated with those seas—enough to be dispossessed of his good sense. And that good sense clearly resides for him in the "trustful associations" of the domestic and the familial: the "household boat," "cousin Nat," "berrying," all these domestic pleasures and securities draw him back from his gothic imaginings of conspiracy and secret murder, here made to seem patently burlesque in their contrast to the dreamy and trustful pleasantries of homelife.

This rhythm of suspicion and domestication reaches a crescendo late in the text as, finding himself entombed in the "subterranean vault" of the *San Dominick*'s below-deck corridors, "his mind . . . swarmed with superstitious suspicions":

> Hitherto, credulous good-nature had been too ready to furnish excuses for reasonable fears . . . What imported all those day-long enigmas and contradictions, except they were intended to mystify, preliminary to some stealthy blow? Atufal, the pretended rebel, but punctual shadow, that moment lurked by the threshold without. He seemed a sentry, and more. Who, by his own confession, had stationed him there? Was the negro now lying in wait?
>
> (96)

But watch how Delano reorganizes these threateningly opaque and occluded narrative elements:

> As he saw his trim ship lying peacefully at anchor, and almost within ordinary call; as he saw his household boat, with familiar faces in it, patiently rising and falling on the short waves by the San Dominick's side . . . and more than all, as he saw the benign aspect of nature, taking her innocent repose in the evening . . . as charmed eye and ear took in all these, with the chained figure of the black, clenched jaw and hand relaxed. Once again he smiled at the phantoms which had mocked him, and felt something like a tinge of remorse, that, by harboring them even for a moment, he should by implication, have betrayed an atheist doubt of the ever-watchful Providence above.
>
> There was a few minutes' delay, while, in obedience to his orders, the boat was being hooked along to the gangway. During the interval, a sort of saddened satisfaction stole over Captain Delano, at thinking of the kindly offices he had that day discharged for a stranger. Ah, thought he, after good actions one's conscience is never ungrateful, however much so the benefited party may be.
>
> (96-97)

Part of the brutal and oft-remarked irony here, to be sure, is that for Delano "the chained figure of the black" in no way unsettles or makes less idyllic "the benign aspect of nature," black subjection for him being simply a part of nature's order. But Melville's satire has other targets as well: for Delano is also acutely aware of the reward, to his own self-regard, of interpreting the world in this way. Here, as several times previously in the story, we watch Delano "drowning criticism in compassion, after a fresh repetition of his sympathies" (58). The pleasure, the "saddened satisfaction" he takes in what he calls his acts of conscience and "sympathetic conjectures"—in knowing himself to be possessed, if

not of acuity, than of a uniquely "benevolent heart"—is evident: for these "good actions" of his, Delano is grateful *to himself*. The very lexicon Melville persistently circulates around him (benevolent, sympathetic, generous, compassionate) serves to remind us further that this self-pleasing mode of reading has particular generic affiliations.[16] Indeed, the generic oppositions at play in Delano's imagination now come into sharper focus. For Delano continues to see on deck insinuations of a gothic tale—one of an encrypted and unspeakable terror and suffering—but the gothic, he repeatedly decides, is a genre too malign, too filled with phantoms and superstition and atheist doubt of watchful Providence, to be credited. Instead, he gathers in all the ship's gothic intimations, and there are many, and tirelessly insists on rearranging them into a manifestly sentimental textual order: suspicions gives way to "compassion," pirate ships turn into household boats, and the "ugly passions" slavery breeds become for Delano, in a twinkling, "but a sort of love-quarrel, after all" (88).[17]

The matter, then, is not just that Delano is a bad reader, and not just that Delano is a racist reader. This much, again, is by now clear enough. The underemphasized point, I think, is that for Melville Delano is first and foremost a sentimental reader, whose racism and incompetence in fact follow from his sentimentality. This sentimental reading practice ramifies in a number of telling ways in the tale. First, as we have already begun to see, it is a readerly disposition that sponsors in Delano what we might call a misapprehension of the nature of Nature, allowing him to ascribe to a benign and providentially-ordained Nature an alarmingly indiscriminate array of more properly human and social acts and practices, including those of racial terror and subjection. In local terms, by refusing to impute malign evil to any man or to watchful Providence—to do so would show him less than completely "generous" and "benevolent"—he cannot then think of human enslavement as an act of malignity; or, he cannot do so in any but the most saccharine, self-exculpatory terms ("Ah, this slavery breeds ugly passions in man," he muses momentarily, and with condescending detachment [88]). Relatedly, that intractable "benevolence of heart" convinces him that *human* nature is all nurturance and compassion, which makes it difficult in turn for him to imagine that it might also have much to do with a fervent, unrelenting drive to be free and self-determining. This is the category confusion at play in Delano's encounter with the "slumbering negress," a child at her breast:

> His attention had been drawn to a slumbering negress, partly disclosed through the lace-work of some rigging, lying, with youthful limbs carelessly disposed, under the lee of the bulwarks, like a doe in the shade of a woodland rock. Sprawling at her lapped breasts was her wide-awake fawn, stark naked, its black little body half lifted from the deck, crosswise with its dam's; its hands, like two paws, clambering upon her; its mouth

and nose ineffectually rooting to get at the mark; and meantime giving a vexatious half-grunt, blending with the composed snore of the negress.

The uncommon vigor of the child at length roused the mother. She started up, at distance facing Captain Delano. But as if not at all concerned at the attitude in which she had been caught, delightedly she caught the child up, with maternal transports, covering it with kisses.

There's naked nature, now; pure tenderness and love, thought Captain Delano, well pleased.

(73)

Delano cannot but read this scene as a kind of sentimental apotheosis, an image of human benignity at its most naked and pure, and carried, appropriately, by the transports of the "maternal." That there is more than a hint of defiance in the mother's regard for Delano—she knows it is not she who has been "caught"[18]—is a point obscured for him not least by the keen pleasure he takes in his own capacity to find and appreciate a scene of such sentimental confirmation, even on a strange ship half-way around the world.

Delano's preferred mode of reading provides him simultaneously with a misguided sense of his own capacity to know, thoroughly and accurately, the quality of another's suffering. Such misunderstanding is of course writ large across the whole of his engagement with the slaves, and with Babo in particular, but it has more local expressions as well. After Cereno haltingly tells him the falsified tale of his friend Aranda's death on board, Delano interjects:

Pardon me . . . but I think that, by a sympathetic experience, I conjecture, Don Benito, what it is that gives the keener edge to your grief. It was once my hard fortune to lose at sea a dear friend, my own brother, then supercargo. Assured of the welfare of his spirit, its departure I could have borne like a man; but that honest eye, that honest hand—both of which had so often met mine—and that warm heart; all, all—like scraps to the dogs!—to throw all to the sharks!

(61)

What Delano expresses here, along with his less than sterling tact, is his unshaken belief in a sentimental logic of equivalence: his intuition, in other words, that an experience of suffering and loss, of any kind, puts one in unlimited identification with any and all others who have suffered, in any way. This is of course part of sentimentality's utopian democratic appeal, what Glenn Hendler calls its "fantasy of experiential equivalence": because we all suffer and feel grief, the argument goes, we can therefore feel *for* each other, and in so doing know ourselves bound together by a common humanity greater than any division of wealth or race or sex, our common vulnerability to pain and bereavement.[19] Delano's ill-thought sympathetic conjectures mark, at the

least, Melville's rather withering regard for such a vision of harmonious mutual legibility. The text's alternate model of sympathy is of course Cereno himself, who in the end cannot face Babo at his trial, not because he sympathizes with or can conjecture about the state of slavery, but because he now knows, existentially, what it is to be enslaved. (Delano's observation is more suggestive than he knows when he thinks of Cereno, "He is like one flayed alive" [93].) And the knowledge of having been enslaved, which he knows he shares with "the Negro," is precisely what casts such a deathly shadow upon Cereno at the end. When he tells Delano that the sun and sky and winds are all untroubled, "because they have no memory . . . because they are not human" (116), he is insisting both that the memory of having been enslaved cannot be eradicated in him, and that, correlatively, one would finally have to believe "the Negro" not human—incapable even of memory—to imagine slaves might live unprotestingly with their enslavement, or let it pass unrevenged. At the same time, he is reminding Delano, with a pointedness the American seems not to notice, of the limitedness of his own sympathetic conjectures: "So far may even the best man err," Cereno says, "in judging the conduct of one with the recesses of whose condition he is not acquainted" (115).[20] The sentimental logic of suffering's equivalences, he obliquely but firmly recalls to the uncomprehending Delano, is a lie.

Finally, though, what most conspicuously—and, for Melville, most damningly—marks Delano as an emblem of a misbegotten sentimentality is his unhesitating use of the suffering of others. In this text, a generous contemplation of the suffering of others forever occasions a confirmation of the observer's own capacity for sympathetic self-extension—for exactly those sympathetic conjectures and acts of conscience which Delano finds so deeply rewarding. We have seen how Delano finds himself "well pleased" before the naked hungry slave child and its mother, before Babo's dutiful attentiveness, and most of all before his own generosity of disposition toward Cereno, whom Delano repeatedly exonerates for his minor affronts to his American benefactor on the grounds that the poor Spaniard has suffered so greatly. What becomes increasingly unmistakable over the course of the tale, though, is that Delano's interpretive disposition allows him to translate, repeatedly and seamlessly, the suffering of others into a mode of self-regard that is exclusively self-amplifying. The tale's conclusion turns on exactly this point: "The temper of my mind that morning," he explains to Cereno afterwards, "was more than commonly pleasant, while the sight of so much suffering, more apparent than real, added to my good-nature, compassion, and charity, happily interweaving the three" (115). The moment is striking, and clear: suffering adds to Delano's good nature, amplifies it, and contributes "happily" to his already more than commonly pleasant temper of mind. Such are the ethics of his reading, and this after all its mis-perceptions, hollow securities, and nearly catastrophic failures have been revealed. In **"Benito Cereno"**—a text introduced to a literary marketplace utterly convulsed by the massive success, three years earlier, of *Uncle Tom's Cabin*[21]—this is what sentimental reading looks like.

HERMAN MELVILLE HATES YOU

We miss a great deal, however, if we presume too hastily that Melville's anger in the tale is simply with Delano and the self-congratulatory sympathy for which he stands. On this point, Robert S. Levine is right to observe that readings which rush to take Melville's side against Delano are apt to forget that, for most of the story, Melville places *us*—his audience, past, present, and future—in a queasy, unstable, but nevertheless unyielding identification with Delano.[22] If the narrative does indeed have such brutally satirical designs on its anti-hero—if it hates Delano and his hollow sympathies as much as I, and many others, have suggested—it has designs no less hostile and accusatory on each and every one of its readers. To miss this is to miss much of the tale's drama, as well as its acute anxiety about, precisely, readership and the state of American civic life.

Melville's strategy of oblique readerly solicitation begins early on. Recall that at the outset the narrative voice takes pains to note for us Delano's dimwittedness. I have called that opening passage provoking, because it establishes from the first a hierarchy of knowingness and, with it, an economy of readerly positions. Here again is the narrative voice characterizing for us the man who will be, but is not here, the narrative's center of consciousness:

> Considering the lawlessness and loneliness of the spot, and the sort of stories, at that day, associated with those seas, Captain Delano's surprise might have deepened into some uneasiness had he not been a person of singularly undistrustful good nature, not liable, except on extraordinary and repeated incentives, and hardly then, to indulge in personal alarms, any way involving the imputation of malign evil in man. Whether, in view of what humanity is capable, such a trait implies, along with a benevolent heart, more than ordinary quickness and accuracy of intellectual perception, may be left to the wise to determine.
>
> (47)

As readers, we are in this moment given to understand ourselves as smarter than the narrated Delano, but only inasmuch as we identify with and stick close by the omniscient narrative voice itself, which has promised to collude with us, to share with us its worldly, knowing perspective, and in effect to whisper to us behind Delano's back. Inasmuch as we are *with* the narrative voice, that is, we are safe from its accusations of ignorance

and unworldliness. That omniscient voice is never more our friend and our confidant than at this moment, and the effect of this is complex.

If the narrative in this way solicitously assures us, at the start, that it will distinguish itself and its vantage from that of Delano, the better to allow us the enjoyment of feeling confidently more knowing than he is, it gradually turns that promise into a trap—what Carolyn Karcher aptly calls "a literary mantrap."[23] It does so, in essence, by allowing the narrative perspective and Delano's perspective to mingle more and more indeterminately, and in passages that are increasingly crucial to the reader's understanding of the events and characters of the narrative. When, with deadpan and unblinking cunning, Melville offers us these progressively more lengthy passages which *may* be indirect discourse, but with virtually no textual indication that they are anything other than omniscient narration, he is essentially confronting us with a kind of dare: where do you identify? How badly, how cravenly do you wish to be solaced by knowing yourself in tune with a narrative authority? And how much will you swallow in order to be so soothed? Note in these narratologically ambiguous passages, which bristle with self-assurance and worldly-wise certainties, exactly what we are being asked to swallow:

> the hatchet-polishers . . . sat intent upon their task, except at intervals, when, with the peculiar love in negroes of uniting industry with pastime, two and two they sideways clashed their hatches together, like cymbals, with a barbarous din. All six, unlike the generality, had the raw aspect of unsophisticated Africans.
>
> (50)

> Sometimes the negro gave his master his arm, or took his handkerchief out of his pocket for him; performing these and similar offices with that affectionate zeal which transmutes into something filial or fraternal acts in themselves but menial; and which has gained for the negro the repute of making the most pleasing body-servant in the world.
>
> (52)

> "Master wouldn't part with Babo for a thousand doubloons," murmured the black, overhearing the offer, and taking it in earnest, and, with the strange vanity of a faithful slave appreciated by his master, scorning to hear so paltry a valuation put upon him by a stranger.
>
> (71)

These moments are brief enough that we might pass them over without worrying too much over whose thoughts they are, those of the ironized Delano or the authorized narrative voice. (They are more or less of a piece with the narrative's references to "sight-loving Africans" [80] and "the African love of bright colors and fine shows" [84].) But how do we approach the rather different movements of this passage, which needs to be quoted at length:

Here the servant, napkin on arm, made a motion as if waiting his master's good pleasure. Don Benito signified his readiness, when, seating him in the malacca arm-chair, and for the guest's convenience drawing opposite it one of the settees, the servant commenced operations by throwing back his master's collar and loosening his cravat.

There is something in the negro which, in a peculiar way, fits him for avocations about one's person. Most negroes are natural valets and hair-dressers, taking to the comb and brush congenially as to the castinets, and flourishing them apparently with almost equal satisfaction. There is, too, a smooth tact about them in this employment, with a marvelous, noiseless, gliding briskness, not ungraceful in its way, singularly pleasing to behold, and still more so to be the manipulated subject of. And above all is the great gift of good-humor. Not the mere grin or laugh is here meant. Those were unsuitable. But a certain easy cheerfulness, harmonious in every glance and gesture; as though God had set the whole negro to some pleasant tune.

When to all this is added the docility arising from the unaspiring contentment of a limited mind, and that susceptibility of bland attachment sometimes inhering in indisputable inferiors, one readily perceives why those hypochondriacs, Johnson and Byron—it may be something like the hypochondriac, Benito Cereno—took to their hearts, almost to the exclusion of the entire white race, their serving men, the negroes, Barber and Fletcher. But if there be that in the negro which exempts him from the inflicted sourness of the morbid and cynical mind, how, in his most prepossessing aspect, must he appear to a benevolent one? When at ease with respect to exterior things, Captain Delano's nature was not only benign, but familiarly and humorously so.

(83-84)

Spoken to us in the very omniscient voice with which we have been encouraged to align ourselves—for it knows better than the hapless Delano—the passage invites us to weigh the eagerness of our identification with this worldly, confidently knowing voice against whatever suspicion we might (or might not) be able to muster with regard to its offhand and easily assured racial pronouncements. (The tone of assurance throughout these passages rests in the diction, particularly in the nominating locutions: "*the* peculiar love in negroes," "*that* affectionate zeal," "*that* susceptibility," all usages that deliberately draw on a knowledge assumed to be shared.) What's more, in this latter passage the narrative voice not only refuses to identify itself explicitly with Delano's vantage, it actually seems to announce a shift *back* to Delano and *from* omniscience ("But if there be that in the negro which exempts him from the inflicted sourness of the morbid and cynical mind, how, in his most prepossessing aspect, must he appear to a benevolent one?")—a movement that only heightens the quality of omniscience announced in a phrase like, "Not the mere grin or laugh *is here meant,*" which has every mark of a piece of narratorial instruction. Given the

readerly economy established so decisively at the outset, in which we are encouraged to hunger for the security and wisdom of the omniscient perspective, we might well wonder if it is so much as possible to divine immediately that this is, narratively speaking, a bit of perspectival foolery, a burlesque of Delano's racism later to be exposed.[24] But of course to the degree that any of us fails from the first moment to distance ourselves from this ambiguously unmarked perspective and recognize it as satirical indirect discourse, then to exactly that degree are our condemnations of Delano painfully hypocritical, since he too has allowed his own incuriousness about racial presumption to prevent him from suspecting irony where he had not expected to find it. If we haven't pegged these passages immediately as indirect discourse, then we, like Delano, have been the not sufficiently perceptive victims of a narrative ruse. That the deck is, narratologically speaking, stacked against us, is part of Melville's point. Such, I would say, is Melville's venomous regard for his readers, and their piteous credulity, in 1855.[25]

Just as crucially, Melville also seems in these passages to be marking the specific kinds of pronouncements his readers will, with only a little provocation, let pass all too incuriously. That offhand racial knowingness is not a tone he invents. Another writer, much more widely read than himself, had only recently written passages such as these:

> There were others, which made incessant mention of "Jordan's banks" and "Canaan's fields," and the "New Jerusalem;" for the negro mind, impassioned and imaginative, always attaches itself to hymns and expressions of a vivid and pictorial nature.[26]

> Tom got down from the carriage, and looked about with an air of calm, still enjoyment. The negro, it must be remembered, is an exotic of the most gorgeous and superb countries of the world, and he has, deep in his heart, a passion for all that is splendid, rich, and fanciful; a passion which, rudely indulged by an untrained taste, draws on them the ridicule of the colder and more correct white race.
>
> (253)

> It is impossible to describe the scene, as, with tears and sobs, they gathered round the little creature, and took from her hands what seemed to them a last mark of her love. They fell on their knees; they sobbed, and prayed, and kissed the hem of her garment; and the elder ones poured forth words of endearment, mingled in prayers and blessings, after the manner of their susceptible race.
>
> (419)

What these verbal gestures are all about—as, by incorporating them, Melville's text tries to show—is mutuality and assurance, collusion, the quiet insistence upon a knowledge that is presented as so effortlessly shared that any desire to substantiate it can only read as a mark of one's ineptness, one's exclusion from the deftly formed circle of those who know. They trade upon a kind of untroubled transparency, both of character to omniscient observation and judgment, and of that judgment to readers.[27]

This rhetorical tactic is so prevalent in Harriet Beecher Stowe's strongest work it might be called her stylistic signature, and is surely part of what lends to her narrative voice its oft-described authoritativeness.[28] Here is *Uncle Tom's Cabin*'s opening page, second paragraph:

> For convenience sake, we have said, hitherto, two *gentlemen*. One of the parties, however, when critically examined, did not seem, strictly speaking, to come under the species. He was a short, thickset man, with coarse, commonplace features, and that swaggering air of pretension which marks a low man who is trying to elbow his way upward in the world.
>
> (41)

With the flourish of a phrase like "*that* swaggering air . . . which marks a low man," Stowe here establishes for us not only the whole of Haley's character, but also the absolute command and fluency of her mastery over all the taxonomies of evaluation and all the avenues of moral judgment. As readers, we are both alerted to the fact of categorical judgment, and tacitly advised to protect ourselves from such judgment by practicing a conscientious openness to the narrator's assurance, and to the narrative's corresponding moral transparency. We are wise, then, to be at once alert and docile: to read attentively, and await instruction.

"**Benito Cereno,**" which cannibalizes exactly Stowe's signature locutions of knowingness, attacks both the ideal of transparency and the acquiescent readerly credulity that accompanies it—and attacks them as *civic* maladies, prone to exacerbating rather than ameliorating the increasingly dire racial crisis in which the nation finds itself. Delano's unflustered racial certainties, even in the midst of his gravest suspicions, prevent him from recognizing that there is a crisis afoot, but the crime Melville wishes to expose in the tale is not simply Delano's, or Cereno's, or the departed Aranda's. As against sentimental transparency, Melville offers instead an extended form of gothic occlusion and opacity, prosecuted not only diegetically but meta-textually. That is, the strength—or rather, the spite and the malice—of Melville's attack on the reader who is too credulous and wishes only to await transparent instruction comes less in his withering portrayal of Delano the incompetent reader than in his deliberate disorientation (Douglass would say "dispossession") of us, the readers who cannot read his story.[29] (Perhaps critics rush to take Melville's side against Delano in part to erase the stain of having been, at least once, locked into exactly the state of readerly uncertainty that afflicts the hapless

Captain.) Melville opens the text with an oblique promise of at least one kind of narrative transparency—the narrator offers to side with us against the dim Delano—and is betting that our acquiescence to that beguiling promise will be such that even the grossest forms of racist burlesque will not disabuse us of our desire to be instructed, as promised, by the voice of knowing omniscience. We await the authority of omniscience, and when it comes, as in those passages of unclearly indirect discourse, it is counterfeit, as false as a gentleman pretending to be a sailor, or a master playing the slave.

The problem with sentimental readers of Stowe, then, is not merely that they aggrandize themselves in fulsome contemplation of the suffering of others. The wild approbation for *Uncle Tom's Cabin* suggests to Melville that they have also nursed in themselves a tolerance, and perhaps even an appetite, for the very racial knowingness that prevents Delano, so guilelessly assured, from reading the actual text before him; and so it is exactly that tolerance that he sets out to test. It is as if Melville draws upon all the narrative tools he has at his disposal solely to ensnare and to castigate his readers, purposefully enticing them narratologically to suspend their disbelief in these gestures of racial knowingness—for he suspects, from Stowe, that his readers are in fact more than willing to suspend that disbelief, if they have any to begin with—only so that he may then expose the blindnesses and human cruelty that follow in their wake. Sentimental reading, Melville suggests, has trained American readers in exactly the kinds of self-pleasing acquiescent credulity, *racial* credulity, that make Delano so hapless and ethically bankrupt. "**Benito Cereno,**" with its gothic opacities and instigations to misreading, is the punishment he feels those American readers have earned for themselves. As Michael Rogin frames the matter, "The dreamlike reveries of the antebellum sentimental novel have been seen as escapes from the ineradicable horror of slavery." In "**Benito Cereno,**" "Melville turned the dreams . . . against the dreamers."[30]

This is, of course, a less than generous reading of *Uncle Tom's Cabin*. Stowe's narrative authority may indeed rest in her ability to persuade her readers, with a variety of narrative incentives, of the moral transparency, to her, of the world she describes. This does not mean, however, that the text she produces is as perfectly transparent, or as morally legible, as an instruction manual. If *Uncle Tom's Cabin* is abidingly compelling, it is not least because its vast range of moral propositions and clear-cut authorial judgments of taste and character and policy cannot be made to square with one another. The pious condescension that seems at the outset to be the narrator's is later lampooned in Miss Ophelia (272-74); the aristocratic contempt for the "vulgar" (like Haley and his circle) is troubled deeply by St. Clare's neo-Marxian prophecy of a grand revolution in which the low shall be raised up (390-96); and even the racial assurances the narrative offers come to be, at the very least, unsettled by the self-possessed and revolutionary aspect of George, whose homespun American heroism (he offers what the narrative calls his own "Declaration of Independence" [298-99]) is itself unraveled in its turn by his eventual removal far from the shores of America, to the African colony of Liberia (a solution itself made the object of satire earlier by St. Clare). In all, one of the most remarkable things about the book, which draws so much narrative force from its authorial promises of transparency, is its final inability actually to sustain a coherent moral vision of the nation and of the nation's future, despite laboring so strenuously to do so. Antebellum America and its contradictions expand beyond the perimeter of any one position of judgment Stowe can offer, and this terrifying, uncontainable excess—this tangle of human needs and possibilities with no clear path through it—is what Stowe's novel most succeeds in representing. The matters of race and slavery may not be opaque to the organizing consciousness of *Uncle Tom's Cabin*, and Melville may rightly object to this, but the matter of the fate of America itself most certainly is.

Still, the opacities of **"Benito Cereno"** are of an appreciably different order. The thematics of silence which pervade the text are one prominent expression of this difference. As Maurice Lee has persuasively shown, even after the plot has been revealed, even after the voice of authority (in the form of a legal deposition) has spoken, the text resolves into a series of ominous, death-like silences. There is of course Babo, who—very like Iago, another famed conspirator in a Venetian setting—refuses to divulge himself to his captors, and whose "voiceless end" (116) reminds us of the profound absences, the unrecuperated elisions, in the official archives of national and New World history.[31] So too is Cereno's end virtually voiceless:

> "You are saved," cried Captain Delano, more and more astonished and pained; "you are saved; what has cast such a shadow upon you?"
>
> "The negro."
>
> There was silence, while the moody man sat, slowly and unconsciously gathering his mantle about him, as if it were a pall.
>
> There was no more conversation that day.
>
> But if the Spaniard's melancholy sometimes ended in muteness upon topics like the above, there were others upon which he never spoke at all; on which, indeed, all his old reserves were piled.
>
> (116)

By the end of the tale the gothic motif of the unspeakable is literalized into a kind of contagion of muteness, a progressive abandonment of speech itself. Lee reads

this as clear evidence that "the failings of political discourse pervade all human speech, be it antebellum or antediluvian, be it between leaders, followers, or friends. Such is Melville's cynical estimation of our ability to talk truthfully with anyone." This is not the accretively contradictory, though still quite undeterred moral exposition of *Uncle Tom's Cabin*, but the voice of "a despairing, skeptical Melville" whose "mistrust of representation" is so thorough and exacting that he finds no refuge whatever from the bloody calamities he predicts within the range of the communicable.[32]

And yet the disastrous failings Melville's gothicism points to may not be those of "political speech" *per se,* and to describe what I have called the tale's anger in terms of Melville's thoroughgoing "distrust of representation" may be to misperceive it. The communicable, after all, seems for him substantially more variegated than the term "representation" allows—it exists, for instance, in particular assemblages, which can be recognized as *genres,* and all genres, to Melville, are not created equal. Melville's anger, in other words, may be less with "representation" than with the particular *kinds* of representation that were flourishing around him, and which in his view reflected pronounced and worrying debilities in the American public's aptitude for reading and, by extension, for good citizenship. To suggest that for Melville the grave problem is with language itself—that the text is finally a "discourse about discourse"[33]—is tacitly to exonerate all the acts of readerly incompetence he so meticulously enumerates. That language itself is the true *saboteur* of civic harmony seems, in all, an odd conclusion to draw from a text in which so much energy is expended anatomizing the methods and motives of misreading.

Such a qualification does not make the tale any less dire in its outlook or, in its procedures, any less vengeful. I have said already that the text aims to punish, but this puts the matter perhaps too diffusely. Lee writes that "subversive politics," to proceed, "must imagine a friendly and sensitive listener in a hostile political world," but this seems off the mark, especially in the case of **"Benito Cereno."**[34] For after the middling and then vitriolic receptions of *Moby-Dick* and *Pierre,* respectively—alongside the runaway popularity of Stowe—Melville offers in **"Benito Cereno"** one of the few texts that might be said, in conception and execution, actually to *hate* its readers, and to unfold according to the workings of that hostility. I am not the first to point out that you cannot read **"Benito Cereno,"** the best you can do is reread it. Readership in the text (our own, as well as Delano's) can only fail, or rather, can never sufficiently succeed, and this is what makes the text finally and unassailably gothic: this sustained refusal to divulge itself, to offer any but distorted and crazed surfaces (no matter how neatly its surfaces might be made to cohere in subsequent readings). But whatever Melville's pleasure in exposing to his audience the ease with which they, too, might be duped by the assured tones of racial sentimentalism, the tale offers only the bleakest form of social prophecy.

Of course, the coming of the Civil War, and more particularly the declension of national contestation over slavery into an impossibly dead-locked Manichaean feud between unbending absolutes, indelibly mark Melville's text as, precisely, prophetic.[35] For as Melville had only recently spent over six hundred pages of whaling lore, Shakespearean rhetoric, and cribbed philosophy attempting to demonstrate, a wise and healthy republic *demands* good readers, who can make truthful sense of the omens and portents, the mysterious characters and charismatic leaders which come before it. On the *Pequod,* misreading—Ishmael's of many portents, Ahab's of prophecy, the crew's of him—means disaster. But as **"Benito Cereno"** powerfully suggests, the knotted, devious, unresolvingly gothic text of race in the American New World only begins to come clear upon re-reading, and scarcely then. Unhappily, as Melville knew, out here in the current of history, where past, present, and future perpetually seem one, our only option is to make what we can of the text that unfolds before us, moment by vanishing moment.

Notes

1. Herman Melville, "Letter to Richard Bentley," April 16, 1852, in *Correspondence,* ed. Lynn Horth, Vol. 14 of *The Writings of Herman Melville* (Evanston: Northwestern Univ. Press and The Newberry Library, 1993), 226. Pertinent as well is Melville's letter to Sophia Peaboy Hawthorne of January 8, 1852, in which he promises her an antidote to the unappetizing "bowl of salt water" that was *Moby-Dick.* Thinking of *Pierre,* he writes, "The next chalice I shall commend, will be a rural bowl of milk" (*Correspondence,* 219).

2. Quoted in Hershel Parker's "Historical Note (II)," in Herman Melville, *Pierre, or the Ambiguities,* ed. Harrison Hayford, Hershel Parker, and G. Thomas Tanselle (Evanston: Northwestern Univ. Press, 1995), 380.

3. *Pierre, or the Ambiguities,* 245.

4. See Leon Howard, "Historical Note (I)," in *Pierre, or the Ambiguities,* 376.

5. This argument, which obviously underscores the literary history of the 1850s, does not seem to me to countervail the claim that in "Benito Cereno" Melville offers his response to the Fugitive Slave crisis, the northern vacillation on the matter of slavery (especially as exemplified by then-president Franklin Pierce), or the increasingly imperialist rhetoric of the 1850s. On these points see

especially Michael Rogin, *Subversive Genealogy: The Politics and Art of Herman Melville* (New York: Knopf, 1983), 208-20, and Eric Sundquist, *To Wake the Nations: Race in the Making of American Literature* (Cambridge: Harvard Univ. Press, 1993), 136-64. Rather, my sense has been that, as an author, Melville responds to these very matters as crises of *literacy:* momentous national dilemmas requiring at once a literary engagement adequate to their complexity and urgency, and a citizenry equipped with sufficient readerly dexterity to apprehend the true nature of their civic peril. (For Melville, the popularity of *Uncle Tom's Cabin* bodes ill, on both counts.) In this way, Melville's fears for the fate of the republic, so resonant throughout *Moby-Dick,* begin to dovetail in the early 1850s with the increasing dismay he felt over his inability to reach a wide and responsive American audience. "Benito Cereno," of 1855, marks the full convergence of these twin obsessions: it is a text in which the concerns of history and of literacy interlock with stunning seamlessness, and where, as Frederick Busch observes, "fiction is a matter of life and death." Introduction, *Billy Budd and Other Stories* (New York: Penguin, 1986), xviii.

6. See Julia Stern, "Excavating Genre in *Our Nig,*" *American Literature* 67 (1995), 439-66. On gothic aspects of Stowe's *Uncle Tom's Cabin,* see Eva Cherniavsky, *That Pale Mother Rising: Sentimental Discourses and the Imitation of Motherhood in Nineteenth-Century America* (Bloomington: Indiana Univ. Press, 1995), 41-60; on collisions of the gothic and the sentimental, see Jonathan Elmer, "Terminate or Liquidate? Poe, Sentimentalism, and the Sentimental Tradition," *The American Face of Edgar Allan Poe,* ed. Shawn Rosenhem and Stephen Rachman (Baltimore: The Johns Hopkins Univ. Press, 1995), 108-18; and Marianne Noble, *The Masochistic Pleasures of Sentimental Literature* (Princeton: Princeton Univ. Press, 2000), 71-73.

7. Both Douglas and Brown offer immensely persuasive accounts of Melville's career, and of the tenor of his anti-sentimentality. But to the degree that we accept it as one of Melville's principal major works, "Benito Cereno" does significantly inflect, and alter, their theses. Though part of Melville's animus in the mid-1850s may involve the decline of Calvinism and the intellectual rigor for which it stood; and though an even larger part may involve his horror before the evacuations and displacements of the authorial self required by the antebellum literary marketplace which, as a marketplace at all, he codes as feminine—still, these matters are clearly not the most pressing concerns of a work like "Benito Cereno," a text which quite

graphically takes up "the crimes of sentimentality" (in Douglas' phrase) but chiefly in the context of its catastrophically misbegotten visions of race, enslavement, and the state of the racially-divided American ship of state. See Douglas, *The Feminization of American Culture* (New York: Knopf, 1977), 294, 289-329; and Brown, *Domestic Individualism: Imagining Self in Nineteenth-Century America* (Berkeley: Univ. of California Press, 1990), 135-69. John Carlos Rowe and Stephen Railton offer additional compelling accounts of Melville's growing dislocation from his American readership, though I think both underplay the degree to which that readership is defined for Melville, both aesthetically and politically, by the voraciousness of its appetite for sentimental fare. See Rowe, *At Emerson's Tomb: The Politics of Classic American Literature* (New York: Columbia Univ. Press, 1997), 63-95; and Railton, *Authorship and Audience: Literary Performance in the American Renaissance* (Princeton: Princeton Univ. Press, 1991), 178-201. A keener approach to the effortful production of sentiment in *Pierre,* and of its relation to the matter of writing and audience, appears in Samuel Otter's *Melville's Anatomies* (Berkeley: Univ. of California Press, 1999), 211, 208-54.

8. The critical proposition that race in America partakes of an elementally gothic textuality originates with Leslie Fiedler, who wrote, "The gothic provides a way into . . . certain areas of our social life where nightmare violence and guilt actually exist. To discuss, for instance, the Negro problem in the United States is to falsify its essential mystery and unreality; it is a gothic horror of our daily lives." *Love and Death in the American Novel* (1960; New York: Stein and Day, 1966), 493. Teresa A. Goddu offers a strong updating of Fiedler's suggestion in *Gothic America: Narrative, History, and Nation* (New York: Columbia Univ. Press, 1997), especially 52-96.

9. Herman Melville, "Benito Cereno," in *The Piazza Tales and Other Prose Pieces, 1839-1869,* ed. Harrison Hayford, Alma A. MacDougall, G. Thomas Tanselle, *et al.,* Vol. 9 of *The Writings of Herman Melville* (Evanston: Northwestern Univ. Press and the Newberry Library, 1987), 47. Hereafter cited parenthetically.

10. In a way that sheds some light on Melville's devious use of qualifying phrases and successive dependent clauses that reframe but do not erase his sentences' initial, usually more fearful and damning speculations, Carolyn Karcher writes of how the narrative "cyclically lulls the reader, then alarms him, then at length reassures him, yet hardly allows his trepidations to subside before arousing them anew." See Karcher's *Shadow over the Promised Land: Slavery, Race, and Violence in Melville's America* (Baton Rogue: Louisiana State Univ. Press, 1980), 131.

11. Eric Sundquist argues compellingly that by setting the tale in 1799—as opposed to 1805, when the real-life Amasa Delano came upon the imperiled Benito Cereno—Melville underlines the revolutionary character of Babo's revolt. "In altering the date of Amasa Delano's encounter with Benito Cereno from 1805 to 1799," Sundquist writes, "Melville accentuated the fact that his tale belonged to the Age of Revolution, in particular the period of violent struggle leading to Haitian independence presided over by the heroic black general Toussaint L'Ouverture, which prompted Jefferson to remark in 1797 that 'the revolutionary storm, now sweeping the globe,' shall, if nothing prevents it, make us 'the murderers of our children'" (Sundquist, 140).

12. Jean Fagan Yellin, "Black Masks: Melville's 'Benito Cereno,'" *American Quarterly* 22 (Fall 1970), 685. For related accounts of Delano see James Kavanaugh, "That Hive of Subtlety: 'Benito Cereno' and the Liberal Hero," in *Ideology and Classic American Literature,* ed. Sacvan Bercovitch and Myra Jehlen (Cambridge: Cambridge Univ. Press, 1986), 352-83; and Karcher, 127-59.

13. Sundquist, 136-39, 148; H. Bruce Franklin, "Slavery and Empire: Melville's 'Benito Cereno,'" *Melville's Evermoving Dawn: Centennial Essays,* ed. John Bryant and Robert Milder (Kent: Kent State Univ. Press, 1997), 147-49.

14. Eve Kosofsky Sedgwick, *The Coherence of Gothic Conventions* (New York: Arno Press, 1980), 14.

15. Eugenia C. DeLamotte, *Perils of the Night: A Feminist Study of Nineteenth-Century Gothic* (New York: Oxford Univ. Press, 1990), 16. That the role Delano inhabits in the submerged tale of "Benito Cereno" is that of a gothic *heroine* accords well with the emblematic position Melville will have him occupy when he wishes to convince himself he is in fact *not* ensnared in gothic conspiracies—that of a sentimental reader. In both cases, Delano appears as a man whom Melville codes as neither effeminate nor even unmanly, but whose textual roles are decisively feminine. In this attenuated sense, Ann Douglas is right to suggest that Melville despairs over a "feminization" of the American reading public.

16. For more on the "astonishing frequency" with which Americans in the years before the Civil War "used the terms *benevolence* and *benevolent,*" and the relation of this discourse of "benevolent

citizenship" to Stowe's sentimental politics, see Susan M. Ryan, "Charity Begins at Home: Stowe's Antislavery Novels and the Forms of Benevolent Citizenship," *American Literature* 72 (2000), 751-82.

17. Kavanagh describes the rhythm of Delano's self-perception nicely, and in terms that are, I would argue, generically salient: "Delano's ruminations shift in a near schizophrenic pattern from a belief that everyone is conspiring to kill him to a satisfied certainty that everyone loves him too much to do him any harm" (363).

18. According to H. Bruce Franklin, Delano "has no inkling that the woman's snore may be 'composed' in a more sophisticated sense" (157).

19. Glenn Hendler, *Public Sentiments: Structures of Feeling in Nineteenth-Century American Literature* (Chapel Hill: Univ. of North Carolina Press, 2001), 7. The logic of equivalence and equivalent legibility in suffering is, for Melville, the underside of sentimentality's utopian project. Lauren Berlant cogently argues that it is one of the utopian aims of antebellum American sentimentality to fashion a viable form of national belonging—a mode of national citizenship—which might sidestep the brutal exclusions and inequities of the prevailing models of American citizenship and nationality, built as they were around whiteness, the privileges of masculinity, and the privileges of property. Sentimentality offers a different vision of the nation's coherence, one in which, as Berlant writes, "the sentimental subject is connected to others who share the same feeling." Here, the universal susceptibility to suffering, bereavement, and pain makes a kind of kin of all, and promises an absolutely inclusive form of belonging: we can belong together, all of us, in the fact that we all may suffer. But for Melville, this vision of mutuality presumes too easily the legibility, to all, of any kind of suffering. We may all suffer our private pains, Melville suggests through Delano's ignorances, but this does not mean we comprehend one another's suffering, or that one soul's suffering communicates itself in any way to another consciousness. Mutuality, for Melville, requires a kind of *reading* between selves, and in "Benito Cereno" reading is never a matter of untroubled legibility. See Berlant, "Poor Eliza," *American Literature* 70 (1998), 646, 635-68.

20. So too is there an oblique pointedness in the deposition's dirge-like refrain of the phrase "the generous Captain Amasa Delano." There are, in all, six full reiterations of the exact phrase "the generous Captain Amasa Delano," punctuated by a final and not-so-faintly damning reference to "the generosity and piety of Amasa Delano incapable of sound-

ing such wickedness" (108-12). By the end it resonates as accusingly as "and Brutus is an honorable man."

21. Stephen Railton reminds us that in 1852 "*Uncle Tom's Cabin* sold five thousand copies in two days, fifty thousand in six weeks, well over three hundred thousand by the end of the year, and more than half a million before the panic of 1857 depressed the book market" (Railton, 74).

22. "Reading *Benito Cereno*," Levine argued in 1989, "has become an exercise in certainty, in literary mastery, an occasion to offer pious denunciations of Delano and Cereno and fraternal embraces to Babo and his fellow conspirators. As a result, a dynamic and threatening text has been almost entirely stripped of any felt anxiety [and] implicating presence." Melville's attack on Delano's haplessness and self-satisfaction, his egalitarianism as Carolyn Karcher calls it, may be the major point we take with us from subsequent readings of the narrative; but to rest upon this point, Levine rightly suggests, is to forget our own confusion and disorientation in the first reading. Such deliberate acts of readerly disorientation, as both Ann Douglas and Gillian Brown have shown with regard to texts like *Pierre* and *The Confidence Man*, are very much a part of Melville's point in the later work. See Robert S. Levine, *Conspiracy and Romance: Studies in Brockden Brown, Cooper, Hawthorne, and Melville* (Cambridge: Cambridge Univ. Press, 1989), 166, 199-210. On Melville's egalitarianism, see Carolyn Karcher, *Shadow Over the Promised Land,* 158; Gloria Horsley-Meacham, "Bull of the Nile: Symbol, History, and Racial Myth in 'Benito Cereno,'" *The New England Quarterly* 64 (1991), 225-42, 226; and Franklin, 154-65.

23. Karcher, 131.

24. On the workings of this exposure, see also Karcher: Levine, *Conspiracy and Romance,* 211-15; Kavanagh, 366-88; and Franklin, 154-56.

25. Levine frames the matter nicely: "Melville enacts a double plot—one against Delano, another against the reader—that means to ambush both unawares" (199).

26. Harriet Beecher Stowe, *Uncle Tom's Cabin; or, Life Among the Lowly,* ed. Ann Douglas (New York: Penguin Books, 1981), 77-78. Hereafter cited parenthetically.

27. This racial assurance—at once earnestly heroicizing and ruthlessly belittling—reaches a kind of peak in the peroration of Chapter XVI, in which Stowe adumbrates when and how "Africa shall show an elevated and cultivated race": "Certainly

they will, in their gentleness, their lowly docility of heart, their aptitude to repose on a superior mind and rest on a higher power, their childlike simplicity of affection, and facility of forgiveness. In all these they will exhibit the highest form of the peculiarly *Christian life*" (*Uncle Tom's Cabin,* 275).

28. For a vivid example, see Jane Tompkins, *Sensational Designs: The Cultural Work of American Fiction, 1790-1860* (New York: Oxford Univ. Press, 1985), 122-46.

29. Of *Pierre,* Douglass writes, "Melville has dispossessed his readers without totally destroying his own rationale for writing: indeed, the dispossession itself becomes his motivation" (314). This elegant formulation is more accurately applied, I would argue, to "Benito Cereno."

30. Rogin, 220.

31. Maurice S. Lee, "Melville's Subversive Political Philosophy: 'Benito Cereno' and the Fate of Speech," *American Literature* 72 (2000): 496-99. On silence, slavery, and the historical archive see also Yellin, 687-88; and Gavin Jones, "Dusky Comments of Silence: Language, Race, and Herman Melville's 'Benito Cereno,'" *Studies in Short Fiction* 32 (1995), 39-50.

32. Lee, 511.

33. Kavanagh, 357.

34. Lee, 496.

35. Robert A. Ferguson observes that, as sectional conflict intensified through the 1850s, "eloquence itself appeared a source of disruption." *Law and Letters in American Culture* (Cambridge: Harvard Univ. Press, 1984), 229. On the melodramatic, Manichaean nature of civic discourse around slavery in the 1850s, see also Julia Stern, "Double Talk: The Rhetoric of the Whisper in Poe's 'William Wilson,'" *ESQ* 40 (1994), 185-87, 211-12.

D. S. Neff (essay date winter 2003)

SOURCE: Neff, D. S. "'A Spiritual Sphere Wholly Obscure': 'Lunacy,' the *Orlando Furioso,* and 'the Incident at the Mess' in *Billy Budd.*" *ANQ* 16, no. 1 (winter 2003): 28-33.

[*In the following essay, Neff assesses the importance of an image from the 34th canto of Ludovico Ariosto's* Orlando Furioso *as a direct source for the confrontation between Claggart and Billy in* Billy Budd *and for the narrator's subsequent ruminations on the causes and effects of mental instability.*]

Critics have found great psychological, symbolic, and allegorical significance in "the affair of the spilled soup" in *Billy Budd,* Melville's often perplexing final novel (73).[1] This affair recalls a memorable glimpse of some spilled soup in the 34th canto of Ariosto's *Orlando Furioso,* which has never been examined as a possible direct source for that fateful confrontation between Claggart and Billy. Although there is no specific record of Melville's ever having read or owned the *Furioso,* the first American edition of Leigh Hunt's *Stories from the Italian Poets,* which contains a prose translation of the episode in question, was published in 1846 by Wiley and Putnam. A new edition followed in 1848, only a short time after Melville joined, in 1847, the literary circle of Evert Duyckinck, editor for Wiley and Putnam. During that period in his life, Melville began purchasing and reading books from Wiley and Putnam's store (where he had a professional discount) and browsing in Duyckinck's well-stocked library (Barbour 6-7, Sealts 46-49). The discovery of spilled soup is a small, but not insignificant, allegorical detail in Ariosto's larger examination of humanity's propensity to madness, but the parallel incident in *Billy Budd* acquires an even greater importance. A *Furioso*-based reading of "the incident at the mess" (77), and of the resulting meditation on mental instability that that episode engenders, can offer more insight into how and why things went so wrong aboard the *Bellipotent.*

Near the center of Ariosto's romance epic, in an episode that is also excerpted in Hunt's prose summary, Orlando, nephew of Charlemagne, learns that Angelica, a princess of Cathay, has spurned his love and eloped with Medoro, an African soldier. The young Christian hero, distraught, falls into the insane fury that gives the poem its title. Later, Astolfo, an English knight, ascends to the Terrestrial Paradise, where he encounters St. John the Evangelist, who lives there with Elijah and Enoch. As the "only three mortals who never tasted death," those three men are characterized as "the elect of Paradise," prophets with a uniquely clear view of human folly. St. John then reveals that Astolfo has been permitted to visit the Terrestrial Paradise "by the favour of God, for the purpose of fetching away to earth the lost wits of Orlando, [. . .] which had been attracted out of his brains to the neighbouring sphere, the Moon." When Astolfo and his sagacious guide reach the moon, they find "vials of greater or less size" containing "a subtle fluid, apt to evaporate if not kept closely," a substance described as "sense," or "wit," something "which none of us ever prayed God to bestow, for we fancy we possess it in superabundance." Astolfo is amazed to find that there are "multitudes of the vials almost full to the stopper, which bore the names of men [including himself] whom he had supposed to enjoy their senses in perfection." In a valley on the lunar surface they also find "in one miraculous collection, whatsoever had been lost or wasted on earth." One of those items is "a great heap of overturned soup [. . .] found to be alms to the poor, which had been delayed till the giver's death." In his footnote to this passage, Hunt surmises that pots of soup were often left at convent gates to feed the indigent, which seems to suggest that the spilled soup on the moon represents an abject failure of charity—sustenance provided too late for those who may have starved throughout the life of someone who could only give when such giving involved absolutely no sacrifice on his part (370-75).[2]

How Melville may have employed elements from Astolfo's journey to the moon during the composition of **Billy Budd** is suggested by two assertions in the narrator's attempted explanation of what exactly transpired in the mess. In the opinion of the narrator, "the Hebrew prophets" are those who can "shed so much light into [such] obscure spiritual places" as human madness (75-76). He also implies that Claggart is a "peculiar human creature the direct reverse of a saint" (74). In the *Furioso,* St. John connects spilled soup with failed charity as part of a lesson on earthly folly and madness. In **Billy Budd,** however, Claggart's calling attention to the soup spilled accidentally by Billy (when the master-at-arms says, "Handsomely done, my lad! And handsome is as handsome did it, too!" [72-73]) is seen by the narrator as an example of the "lunacy" plaguing Claggart (76). According to the narrator, Claggart's madness stems from "envy and antipathy," emotions that are quite antithetical to charitable feelings and actions. Inordinately swayed by those feelings, Claggart takes the spilling of the soup "not for the mere accident it assuredly was, but for the sly escape of a spontaneous feeling on Billy's part more or less answering to the antipathy on his own" (77-79). Such madmen, in the narrator's view, have minds "peculiarly subject to the law of reason" and hearts that "would seem to riot in complete exemption from that law." Indeed, those individuals have "apparently little to do with reason further than to employ it as an ambidexter implement for effecting the irrational."[3] Such insanity is "of the most dangerous sort," because it is "not continuous, but occasional, evoked by some special object" (in Claggart's case, Billy Budd) and an "external provocation" (the accidental spilling of the soup [76, 79]).

The notion of Claggart as an evil, ironic version of Ariosto's St. John is supported further by another parallel. Near the conclusion of Astolfo's lunar trek, St. John, his eyes growing "so inflamed with anger, that they sparkled like two fires," delivers a brief but vituperative attack on a world so overfilled with folly that poets can do nothing but replicate it in their writings. Homer and Virgil are attacked for inflating the virtues and omitting the often very considerable shortcomings of emperors and heroes whom they choose to immortalize, while ignoring or falsely slandering those who do not catch their fancy (375-76). Claggart, like St. John, has eyes

that radiate "a quick, fierce light," a "red light [that . . .] flash[es] forth [. . .] like a spark from an anvil in a dark smithy" (88). Unfortunately, Claggart, unlike St. John, sows falsehood instead of truth because he sees the world through the distorting lens of a "mania of an evil nature" (76), remaining in resolute opposition against Billy, an orphan whom almost everyone else reveres as the proverbial "Handsome Sailor" (43-47).[4] Rather than give Billy the benefit of the doubt, Claggart makes "ogres of trifles," effecting a "retaliation [. . .] apt to be in monstrous disproportion to the supposed offense" (980). St. John, not suffering the trauma of death, ascends to heaven alive in a blaze of light as a reward for an exceptionally moral life. Claggart, however, dies ignominiously, his death likened by Captain Vere to the "divine judgment on Ananias [who was struck dead by God for lying to the Apostles (KJV— Acts 5.1-6)]" (99-100).

There is also a distinct possibility that Claggart, whose uncovered dead face is described as "the moon emerging from eclipse" and "reappear[ing] with quite another aspect than that which had gone into hiding" (99-100), brings out the incipient madness, resulting from normally hidden, but nonetheless irresolvable, conflicts between passion and reason, or the heart and the mind, within Billy and Captain Vere. Just as in Claggart's case, those men's psychological instability is triggered by an "external provocation" and a "special object," transforming them into very imperfect counterparts of the remaining two members of Ariosto's deathless prophetic triumvirate.[5]

Billy can be viewed as a failed Elijah who, unlike the prophet who so eloquently defended the ways of God before the idolatrous King Ahab (1 Kings 17-19), inexplicably does not speak up and report a developing mutiny plot when he himself is in danger of being implicated in it (80-85). The doomed foretopman has a "bonfire in his heart" that illumines his "heroic form" (77), but it is under the "sudden provocation of strong heart-feeling" that his desire and ability to speak his mind are thwarted (53), and he falls victim to stuttering under Claggart's penetrating gaze. The master-at-arms's unjust accusation of conspiracy to mutiny constitutes the "external provocation" for Billy's "agony of ineffectual eagerness to obey [. . . Vere's] injunction to speak and defend himself," and it is Vere, whose obvious belief in Billy's innocence and kindly manner touches "Billy's heart to the quick," who serves as the "special object" "confirming the [vocal] paralysis" and engendering the blow that kills Claggart (98-99). That Billy's fateful act is the result of "lunacy" is suggested by his "agony" on "the starboard side of the *Bellipotent*'s upper gun deck." During that time, "the skeleton in [. . . Billy's] cheekbone" is "just beginning delicately to be defined under the warm-tinted skin" by "pale moonshine" polluted by "flickering splashes of dirty yellow light" (118-19)—a detail that is later romanticized in "Billy in the Darbies" (132). The narrator begins the account of Billy's hanging by comparing the night's withdrawal to Elijah's directly entering heaven alive, riding on "a chariot of fire" (2 Kings 2.11-13). Billy, however, is ultimately "pinioned [. . .] at the yard-end," probably dead a moment before the hanging begins, his "will power" (at least in the Purser's opinion) triumphing over his heart. That victory, however, occurs much too late, resulting in what might be euthanasia, rather than a long, fulfilling life, for Billy (122-25).

Captain Vere is a good candidate for a spoiled Enoch (whose name means "teacher" [*Bible Almanac* 626]). Vere, a man displaying "a marked leaning toward everything intellectual," sometimes betrays "a certain dreaminess of mood" and is beset by "strange dubieties" that undermine his suspicion of Claggart during the attempt to "verify" the master-at-arms's charges against Billy (60-62, 96-100). This troublesome split within Vere's personality is described by the narrator, who explains that the captain is motivated not only by "philosophic austerity" but also, perhaps, by "the most secret of all passions, ambition" (129).⁶ If that surmise is correct, Vere's ambition disrupts his normally exceptional powers of reason after an "external provocation," Billy's killing of Claggart, forces him to, in the words of the ship's surgeon, become "unhinged" by the sight of Claggart's corpse (100-02). A secret desire to become another Nelson may cause the captain to employ his normally reliable powers of reason to settle any potential unrest aboard the *Bellipotent* as quickly as possible. Whatever Vere's reasons for doing so, Billy's fate is sealed when his captain adopts the role of witness, judge, and unofficial jury member at the drumhead court (104-14), and it seems entirely appropriate that the deck of the ship is flooded by moonlight when Vere gives his highly selective explanation to the crew concerning what occurred in his cabin between Claggart and Billy (116). Summing up what he cannot, or will not, explain in the Budd affair as "a 'mystery of iniquity [2 Thess. 2.7],' a matter for psychologic theologians to discuss" (107-08), Vere, unlike Enoch, who was taken up by God after a long life of 365 years (Gen. 5.23-24), is "cut off too early for the Nile and Trafalgar," never achieving "the fulness of fame" (128-29).

Norman Holmes Pearson is correct when he argues that the idea of "earth as the shadow of Heaven," which Melville acquired from "Milton's poetry and the Bible," is central to an understanding of *Billy Budd* (107). If St. John, Elijah, and Enoch were the "psychologic theologians" in Melville's thoughts during the writing of *Billy Budd,* the *Orlando Furioso* would also deserve some credit for inspiring such a central theme. Ariosto's romance epic helps readers of Melville's final novel understand how Claggart's charity, Billy's words of de-

fense, and Vere's wise lessons on unavoidable and ineradicable human weakness can be seen as resting ineffectually in a lunar valley amidst all other earthly "lost time and deeds" (374). Even if the line between "sanity and insanity," like the line in the rainbow "where the violet tint ends and the orange tint begins," ultimately constitutes "nothing" quite "namable" for the narrator of *Billy Budd* (102), Astolfo's journey to the moon offers an increased understanding of, if not very much hope for a way out from, Melville's troubling "labyrinth" of human madness (74).

Notes

Quotations in the title are from Melville (76-77, 107).

1. Some have detected occulted homosexual tendencies in Claggart's response to Billy's spilling of the soup (Watson 324-25; Auden 144-46; Miller 34, 360-61; Martin 111-13; Phillips). Others have seen Claggart as "a human scorpion" who "yearns to sting Billy with an awareness of the essential malignity of earthly life" (Seelye 164); a demonic serpent that will be eventually slain in the "central act in the sun-god myth" (Franklin 188-206); or "a personification of ambiguity and ambivalence," of "the very functioning of *difference*" in "an opposition [. . .] between two conceptions of language, or between two types of reading" (Johnson 83-85).

2. It seems entirely appropriate for St. John to employ the spilled soup as a lesson on failed charity, because Christian tradition portrays him as being particularly concerned with charity. In an anecdote related in Jacobus de Voragine's *Legenda Sanctorum* (also known as *The Golden Legend*), St. John chides a philosopher who has taught his pupils to despise their wealth by first exchanging it for diamonds and then destroying the diamonds. Explaining that "the contempt of riches is meritorious only when the rejected riches benefit the poor," St. John then "gathered the fragments of the diamonds in his hand, and prayed; and instantly the stones took the form which they had had before being broken." Afterwards, "the diamonds were sold, and the proceeds given to the poor" (59, 63-64).

3. My discussion of "lunacy" in *Billy Budd,* which concentrates on interactions between reason and emotion, differs somewhat from Scorza's insightful analysis of Claggart's insanity (65-88), which emphasizes the intellect's role in madness.

4. Christ's eyes are described as "a flame of fire" in Rev. 1.14, and Ariosto is almost certainly endowing St. John with the same quality. It is entirely possible, then, that Claggart's red eyes are ironic versions of the all-seeing eyes of Christ and St.

John and not automatically as Satanic as some might wish to see them.

5. McCarthy (127-35) states that "three figures aboard the *Bellipotent* disclose some degree of mental aberration": Claggart, Vere, and the ship's surgeon. While I agree with McCarthy concerning the first two characters, I tend to side with commentators such as Dillingham (375) who sees no such debility in the surgeon.

6. Dryden (212) argues convincingly that Vere is unduly influenced by ambition in the Budd case.

Works Cited

Auden, W. H. *The Enchafed Flood; or, The Romantic Iconography of the Sea.* New York: Vintage, 1950.

Barbour, James. "Melville Biography: A Life and the Lives." *A Companion to Melville Studies.* Ed. John Bryant. New York: Greenwood, 1986. 3-34.

The Bible Almanac. Ed. James I. Packer, Merrill C. Tenney, and William White, Jr. Nashville: Nelson, 1980.

de Voragine, Jacobus. *The Golden Legend of Jacobus de Voragine.* Trans. Granger Ryan and Helmut Ripperger. 1941. New York: Arno, 1969.

Dillingham, William B. *Melville's Later Novels.* Athens: U of Georgia P, 1986.

Dryden, Edgar A. *Melville's Thematics of Form: The Great Art of Telling the Truth.* Baltimore: Johns Hopkins UP, 1968.

Franklin, H. Bruce. *The Wake of the Gods: Melville's Mythology.* 1963. Stanford: Stanford UP, 1966.

Hunt, Leigh. *Stories from the Italian Poets: Being a Summary in Prose of the Poems of Dante, Pulci, Boiardo, Ariosto and Tasso; with Comments Throughout, Occasional Passages Versified, and Critical Notices of the Lives and Genius of the Authors.* New ed. 1846. New York: Putnam, 1848.

Johnson, Barbara. "Melville's Fist: The Execution of Billy Budd." *The Critical Difference: Essays in the Contemporary Rhetoric of Reading.* 1979. Baltimore: Johns Hopkins UP, 1980. 79-109.

Martin, Robert K. *Hero, Captain, and Stranger: Male Friendship, Social Critique, and Literary Form in the Sea Novels of Herman Melville.* Chapel Hill: U of North Carolina P, 1986.

McCarthy, Paul. *"The Twisted Mind": Madness in Herman Melville's Fiction.* Iowa City: U of Iowa P, 1990.

Melville, Herman. *Billy Budd, Sailor (An Inside Narrative).* Ed. Harrison Hayford and Merton M. Sealts, Jr. Chicago: U of Chicago P, 1962.

Miller, Edwin Haviland. *Melville.* New York: Braziller, 1975.

Pearson, Norman Holmes. "Billy Budd: 'The King's Yarn.'" *American Quarterly* 3 (1951): 99-114.

Phillips, Kathy J. "*Billy Budd* as Anti-Homophobic Text." *College English* 56 (1994): 896-910.

Scorza, Thomas J. *In the Time Before Steamships:* Billy Budd, *The Limits of Politics, and Modernity.* De Kalb: Northern Illinois UP, 1979.

Sealts, Merton M., Jr. "The Records of Melville's Reading." *Pursuing Melville, 1940-1980.* Madison: U of Wisconsin P, 1982. 31-57.

Seelye, John. *Melville: The Ironic Diagram.* Evanston: Northwestern UP, 1970.

Watson, E. L. Grant. "Melville's Testament of Acceptance." *New England Quarterly* 6 (1933): 319-27.

Corey Evan Thompson (essay date March 2003)

SOURCE: Thompson, Corey Evan. "Melville's 'Cock-A-Doodle-Doo!': A Case Study in Bipolar Disorder." *ATQ* n.s. 17, no. 1 (March 2003): 43-53.

[*In the following essay, Thompson diagnoses the narrator of "Cock-A-Doodle-Doo!" with manic depression, drawing parallels between Melville's frequent descriptions of mental instabilities in his fiction and the author's intimate acquaintance with mental illness.*]

Shortly after returning home from New York City in December 1831, Herman Melville's father, Allan, fell deathly ill. He had walked the final leg of his journey home across the frozen Hudson River after the *Constellation* was forced to pull ashore in Poughkeepsie due to heavy ice. Subsequent to his return home, Allan failed to allow himself adequate recuperation time, and by January of the following year he became delirious with fever. On 15 January 1832, extremely concerned about his brother's condition, Thomas Melvill, Jr.[1] wrote a letter to Lemuel Shaw (Allan's friend, the Chief Justice of Massachusetts, and Herman's future father-in-law) describing just how dire Allan's mental state was: "in short my dear sir, Hope, is no longer permitted of his recovery, in the opinion of the attending Physicians and indeed,—oh, how hard for a brother to say!—I *ought not* to hope it.—for,—in all human probability—he would live, *a Maniac!*" (Leyda, *Log* 52). Allan succumbed to his illness thirteen days later in the throes of wild delirium.

While losing his father would have been scarring enough, the ordeal was made much worse as Melville witnessed his father's mental breakdown and subsequent death first-hand. As Hershel Parker notes in the first volume of his exhaustive two-volume work *Herman Melville: A Biography,* young Herman, twelve years old, was in the house during the final weeks of his father's life. Unlike two of his sisters, Helen and Augusta, he had been withdrawn from school the previous October (Parker 1: 57). Some critics have gone even further by speculating that Melville had gained unattended access to his father's room and had seen him in a state of mental derangement (McCarthy 2). It is of little significance, however, if Melville had actually seen his father during his final days. All that matters is that he had undoubtedly heard his father's maniacal rants and that these memories would haunt him for the rest of his life.

Although this was Melville's first and most significant encounter with mental illness, it would certainly not be his last. His older brother Gansevoort demonstrated erratic behavior before his death in 1846, and shortly thereafter Melville's mother Maria, distraught over the death of her favorite son, experienced severe bouts of depression. Three years later, Melville received more devastating news: his friend and fellow contributor to literary magazines, Charles Fenno Hoffman, suffered a mental breakdown. Even when Melville, like Ishmael, quietly took to the ship, he was unable to escape episodes of others' mental derangement. Most notably, as Melville recounts in a 13 October 1849 journal entry, a man who "was crazy" jumped overboard on a voyage from New York to London on the *Independence,* thereby committing suicide (Melville, *Journals* 5).[2]

In his introduction to **The Portable Melville,** eminent Melville scholar Jay Leyda eloquently states that "There is a link between Melville's experiences and his works, which are all a transmutation, to some degree, of a reality he had observed or lived" (xi). Melville's frequent encounters with mental derangement are certainly no exception. As Paul McCarthy astutely argues in his pioneering 1990 study *"The Twisted Mind": Madness in Herman Melville's Fiction,* all of Melville's novels minus *Israel Potter* (1855), in addition to such shorter works as **"Bartleby, the Scrivener"** (1853), **"The Encantadas"** (1854), **"Benito Cereno"** (1855), and the posthumously published **Billy Budd, Sailor** (1924), contain characters who suffer from such mental disorders as madness, insanity, monomania, delirium, and depression. As McCarthy notes in his opening chapter, this is a direct result of Melville's frequent exposure to mental illness. While *"The Twisted Mind"* is undoubtedly the most comprehensive examination of Melville's engagement with mental abnormality, by no means does it fully exhaust the Melville canon of such works. One text that has yet to be adequately considered in the light of mental abnormality is the 1853 short story **"Cock-A-Doodle-Doo!"**

Like the vast majority of Melville's works, **"Cock-A-Doodle-Doo!"** has received countless varying interpretations. Although the story is certainly a symbolically-rich tale that legitimizes a wealth of differing readings, it is truly as much about mental abnormality as it is anything else. Melville himself, in fact, emphasizes this through his explicit use of the words "madness" and "asylum" (272, 276). Early in the story, the narrator refers to his mental illness: he is a self-professed hypochondriac (268). The text suggests, however, that this is an erroneous diagnosis. By definition, "hypochondria" is "a morbid state of mind, characterized by general depression, melancholy, or low spirits, for which there is no real cause." Yet the narrator has more than enough reason for his dejection and, therefore, cannot be legitimately classified as a hypochondriac. Early in the story, for instance, the narrator admits that his "own private affairs were also full of despotisms, casualties, and knockings on the head" (268). Moreover, he lives in "[a] miserable world" (269), a "divided empire" (268) that "call[s] the facilitation of death and murder an improvement" (270). The town's children are plagued with "measles, mumps, croup, scarlet fever, chickenpox, cholera morbus" (270), and the narrator himself suffers from rheumatics and dyspepsia (270-71). Furthermore, the "cool and misty, damp, disagreeable air" (268) can only make the narrator's "doleful dumps" (271) worse. These circumstances weigh so heavily on the narrator that they thrust him into an existential crisis in which he questions man's entire existence: "My eyes ranged over the capacious rolling country, and over the mountains, and over the village, and over a farmhouse here and there, and over woods, groves, streams, rocks, fells—and I thought to myself, what a slight mark, after all, does man make on this huge great earth. Yet the earth makes a mark on him" (269). The serious nature of these factors suggests that the narrator suffers from something much more nefarious than the "hypoes" (268).

If hypochondria is a faulty diagnosis, then we are presented with a perplexing question: from what type of mental condition does the narrator suffer? To date, Marvin Fisher is one of few critics to contemplate this. In his 1977 book *Going Under: Melville's Short Fiction and the American 1850s,* Fisher concludes with limited substantiated evidence that the narrator is not solely a hypochondriac, but that he is a "functioning schizophrenic" (164). While such a reading is provocative, I share Philip Young's assessment that "the psychiatry introduced to establish [Fisher's] claim is not at all persuasive" (348). As recent clinical research has shown, such psychotic features as paranoia, delusions, and hallucinations, the symptoms on which Fisher bases his diagnosis, are not strictly characteristic of schizophrenia (Jamison 59-60).

Fisher's inability to diagnose the narrator's condition accurately not only stems from his reliance on the faulty medical evidence available to him, but from his fundamental misreading of the narrator's development over the course of the story. He inaccurately maintains that the narrator progresses directly from depression to jubilation: "[The narrator] begins in a mood of deep depression and exhibits unmistakable symptoms of paranoia until he is shocked into apparent soundness by the invigorating crow of an unseen cock. His mood swings to the opposite extreme" (163-64).[3] As noted, Young vehemently disagrees with Fisher's final diagnosis of schizophrenia, yet he reiterates Fisher's statement concerning the narrator's progression. In "Experimental Melville: 'Cockeye-Doodle-Dee!,'" Young summarizes, and oversimplifies, the story as "[e]arly depression taken for a walk, heartening cockcrow rushing good spirits back to the walker" (346). More recently, Clark Davis provides an almost identical, and equally faulty, reading of the narrator's development in his otherwise perceptive study *After the Whale: Melville in the Wake of Moby-Dick.* As Davis argues, by the end of the story the narrator "has himself been converted; he now crows the language of optimism, [and] avoids the 'doleful dumps'" (68). Despite established criticism, however, the narrator's progression is not linear. He does not experience melancholy early in the story and then make an immediate and permanent reversal towards optimism in the end. From his initial moment of melancholy to his final ambiguous act of continuous crowing, the narrator oscillates between states of depression and mania, neither of which fully lasts. These elementary symptoms are a fundamental signpost of what is currently known as bipolar disorder, or manic depression, an illness that is frequently mis-diagnosed as schizophrenia (Jamison 3).

As defined by current medical literature, bipolar disorder is "an episodic (that is, recurrent) disorder" that consists of two primary states: a high state, mania, and a low one, depression (*Bipolar Disorder* 3). Each of these states is also characterized by specific symptoms. While experiencing mania, for example, an individual must also exhibit such symptoms as an exaggerated sense of self-esteem or feelings of grandeur, increased talking, and poor judgment (*BD* 5-6). The depressive state is marked by a depressed mood, loss of appetite, insomnia, feelings of worthlessness, and psychotic symptoms, which may include hallucinations (*BD* 7-8). Although it would have been impossible for Melville to be cognizant of the terms "bipolar disorder" or "manic depression," as they are twentieth-century terms, it is certainly possible that he was well aware of the condition itself. *La folie circulaire,* the original term for bipolar disorder, was introduced by Jules Falret in 1851 (Mendels 21), only two years prior to **"Cock-A-Doodle-Doo!"**'s publication in *Harpers New Monthly Magazine.* Moreover, Melville had access to numerous medical books during his various sea adventures on board

such ships as the *United States* and the *Lucy Anne,* and "seems to have been" familiar with Thomas Upham's *Outlines of Imperfect and Disordered Mental Action,* a book that contains valuable information on various kinds of mental defects (McCarthy 13). This, paired with Melville's intimate encounters with mental abnormality, increases the likelihood that he was fully aware of such a condition. In any case, the narrator consistently exhibits manic depressive symptoms, thereby becoming yet another example of a Melvillean character afflicted with mental illness.

In the outset of the story, the narrator is in the midst of one of his low states. It is more than mere melancholy, however, as he immediately exhibits manic depressive symptoms. He is clearly in a depressed mood and, as he himself tells us, suffers from insomnia (268). Moreover, his depression prevents him from being capable of functioning in society as he is unable to pay off his mounting debts. This takes on larger significance once we are told that he lives in a time when "money was never so plentiful" (270). The narrator soon hears the cock's crow, however, which marks his first transition from pessimism to optimism, depression to mania.

The narrator's next stage can be accurately classified not solely as optimism but as sheer mania as he immediately exhibits numerous symptoms of the manic state. His description of the cock's initial crow, for example, is marked by hyperbolic and repetitive language: "Hark! There again! Did ever such a blessed cock-crow so ring out over the earth before! Clear, shrill, full of pluck, full of fire, full of fun, full of glee. It plainly says—'*Never say die!*' My friends, it is extraordinary, is it not?" (271). In addition to evoking repetitive language, this initial crow makes the narrator feel "wild" (271) and restores his appetite, as he himself tells us: "Well, I have an appetite for my breakfast this morning, if I have not had it for a week" (272). This admission further reinforces the likelihood that the narrator's previous depressive state was, in fact, a part of his manic depression as a lack of appetite is also characteristic of the low state.

Shortly following the narrator's significant admission, the dun, or bill collector, visits him to collect his debt, at which point the narrator exhibits further characteristics of the manic state. Most notably, he behaves in an irrational and violent manner: "Without more ado, I seized that insolent dun by the slack of his coat—(and being a lean shad-bellied wretch, there was plenty of slack to it)—I seized him that way, tied him with a sailor-knot, and, thrusting his bill between his teeth, introduced him to the open country lying round about my place of abode" (273). After claiming further that he could have "fought an army of [duns]" (273), the narrator again hears the cock's crowing and ventures out on a quest to find it. While his search is unsuccessful, the narrator is nevertheless inspired by the cock's crowing as he returns "home once more full of reinvigorated spirits, with a dauntless sort of feeling" (274). This "dauntless" feeling manifests itself most significantly as a characteristic of mania when he contemplates his financial difficulties, an episode that demonstrates his feelings of power and grandeur:

> I thought over my debts and other troubles, and over the unlucky risings of the poor oppressed *peoples* abroad, and over the railroad and steamboat accidents, and over even the loss of my dear friend, with a calm, good-natured rapture of defiance, which astounded myself. I felt as though I could meet Death, and invite him to dinner.
>
> (274)

The final event that supports this phase as one of mania occurs when the narrator, who believes that the cock is the key to his manic state, claims that he will buy it even if he has to "clap another mortgage on [his] land" (275). This comment, when considering that he is already deeply in debt, certainly attests to his poor judgment.

As a typical manic depressive, however, the narrator eventually returns to his initial state of depression, in which his behavior again fully adheres to the symptoms of the depressive, or low, state. After another unsuccessful attempt to locate the cock, for instance, the narrator returns home feeling a "twinge of melancholy" (279). This melancholy causes the narrator to demonstrate severe manic depressive symptoms as he explicitly expresses his feelings of worthlessness:

> Here I am, as good a fellow as ever lived—hospitable—open-hearted-generous to a fault: and the Fates forbid that I should possess the fortune to bless the country with my bounteousness. Nay, while many a stingy curmudgeon rolls in idle gold, I, heart of nobleness as I am, I have civil-processes served on me! I bowed my head, and felt forlorn—unjustly used—abused—unappreciated—in short, miserable.
>
> (279)

Almost immediately following this utterance, the cock crows again and transforms the narrator back to the manic state, prompting him to describe the crowing in the most hyperbolic passage to date: "Hark! like a clarion! yea, like a jolly bolt of thunder with bells to it—came the all-glorious and defiant crow! Ye gods, how it set me up again! Right on my pins! Yea, verily on stilts! Oh, noble cock!" (279). More notably, the narrator's mania becomes more severe than it has heretofore been as he experiences an hallucination, an extreme symptom of the manic state. He believes that Signor Beneventano is talking directly to him. More importantly, he believes that the rooster is prompting him to resort to violence. These instructions, in fact,

border on murder: "Hark! the crow again. Plain as cock could speak it, it said, 'Hang the process, and hang the fellow that sent it! If you have not land or cash, go and thrash the fellow, and tell him you never mean to pay him'" (279).

Still inspired by the cock's crow, the narrator continues his quest to find it, which eventually ends in success and, in turn, allows him to meet Merrymusk. Upon his initial encounter with him, the narrator demonstrates even more mania-related poor judgment. Despite his aforementioned financial difficulties, the narrator stays true to his previous statement concerning buying the cock as he offers to pay up to five hundred dollars for the rooster, a ten-fold increase of what he had initially proposed (283). His offer is denied, however, and the narrator lapses back into depression and returns home "in a deep mood" (286). Yet thanks to another crow, the narrator's mania is quickly restored, an event followed by yet another demonstration of poor financial judgment: "My own frame of mind remained a rejoicing one. The cock still inspired me. I saw another mortgage piled on my plantation; but only bought another dozen of stout, and a dozen dozen of Philadelphia porter" (286).

Although the narrator's bibulousness has received scant attention from critics, it can be interpreted as yet another manifestation of manic depression. The narrator openly admits that he is a heavy drinker: "Some of my relatives died; I wore no mourning, but for three days drank stout in preference to porter, stout being the darker color" (286). The excess to which he drinks, drinking until he feels "as stout as Samson" (272), can be classified as comorbid disorder, "an illness or medical condition that occurs together with another illness or medical condition" (*BD* 9). Comorbid disorders occur frequently in manic depressives during the high state, and one of the most common accompanying conditions is alcohol abuse (*BD* 10). In **"Cock-A-Doodle-Doo!,"** the narrator drinks excessively only while he is experiencing mania.

Shortly following his admission about his drinking, the narrator decides to call on Merrymusk for what will eventually be the final time. During this visit, the narrator witnesses the death of Merrymusk, his family, and Signor Beneventano. Established criticism has almost unanimously regarded the story's final moments in an optimistic light.[4] The narrator, however, is not "redeemed," as Robert Milder suggests, "through the life-affirming crow of a marvellous cock" (xiii). Rather, the narrator's condition deteriorates from manic depression to sheer madness, an extreme yet possible end for manic depressives (Jamison 6). He is deprived of what he perceives to be the key to his optimistic state, namely the rooster. This, paired with the trauma of witnessing Merrymusk's death, for whom the narrator has great admiration (286), causes the narrator to take on the persona of Signor Beneventano as he "under all circumstances crow[s] late and early with a continual crow. COCK-A-DOODLE-DOO! - OO! - OO! - OO! - OO!" (288). The narrator is left to crow continually, forever trapped in a futile attempt to restore his sanity. While the narrator admits that "never since then ha[s] [he] felt the doleful dumps" (288), it is likely that the narrator has not felt them because he *cannot* feel them; he has lost all touch with reality.

Herman Melville has been described as a man who "dared to peer into the abysses of his own troubled, sensitive nature and to examine old wounds and old hurts" (E. H. Miller 16). His frequent portrayal of mental abnormality is arguably the most notable example of this claim; the "old wounds and old hurts" caused by his intimate acquaintance with those suffering from mental illness were impossible for him to escape. *Pierre* is frequently cited as a prime example; however, "Cock-A-Doodle-Doo!" is arguably more complex in this regard.[5] It is apparent that the story's narrator is based on—and his insanity inspired by that of—both Melville's father and Melville's friend Charles Fenno Hoffman. Consider, for instance, the parallels between the time of Allan's death and the story's seemingly vague temporal setting. The narrator goes insane in a time when various diseases including cholera are rampant. Had Allan survived his physical illness and gone insane, as his brother feared, then he would have lived a maniac during the cholera epidemic of 1832, a crisis that prompted Melville's mother to take all of her eight children to Pittsfield.

Perhaps more striking are the parallels between the narrator and Hoffman. When Melville was informed of Hoffman's mental breakdown, he wrote a letter to the *Literary World*'s editor Evert A. Duyckinck in which he maintained that Hoffman was a prime candidate for insanity: "Poor Hoffman—I remember the shock I had when I first saw the mention of his madness.—But he was just the man to go mad—. . . poor, unemployed, in the race of life distanced by his inferiors, unmarried—without a port or haven in the universe to make" (*Correspondence* 128). It must be noted that all of these characteristics aptly apply to "Cock-A-Doodle-Doo!"'s narrator. He is certainly poor, and laments the fact that he is "distanced by his inferiors."[6] Moreover, there is no evidence anywhere in the text to suggest that the narrator is, or has been, married. Similarities can also be drawn between the two men's physical disabilities. The narrator clearly suffers from a leg injury, which is "an insistent theme in Melville's work" (Adamson 315n4), as he frequently walks with a cane (268, 275). Hoffman also had difficulty walking as he lost one of his legs in an accident in 1817 (Parker 1: 471). Although Melville's observations on mental illness contributed to his frequent, detailed, and at times compassionate portrayal of

it, there is another factor that may account for his interest in the theme: his own state of mind.

After *Pierre* was published in 1852, there were many reports that Melville had gone insane (Peck 317; Leyda, *Log* 462-63; Greene 294-95). It was not just his reviewers who suggested this, however. His publishers, friends, and family were equally fearful (Parker 2: 88; McCarthy 125; Parker, "Damned by Dollars" 724). Such claims were so frequent, in fact, that Melville felt obliged to defend himself, maintaining that he was not "crazy" (*Correspondence* 454). Recent scholars have tended to agree; most have divorced themselves from the notion that Melville was clinically insane. Rather, it has been suggested that he, like "Cock-A-Doodle-Doo!"'s narrator, was bipolar (Jamison 269; Updike xiv). Melville's mental state will always be a point of contention, yet if he did suffer from manic depression, then it would not only explain further his interest in mental abnormality but may elucidate the disparity that exists between *Moby-Dick* and some of his other works.

Almost thirty years ago, in his seminal study *Creative Malady,* George Pickering argued that psychological or mental illness "may sometimes be an aid to creative work" (17). This concept has been examined more recently, and more specifically with regard to manic depression, by Kay Redfield Jamison. In her book *Touched with Fire: Manic-Depressive Illness and the Artistic Temperament,* Jamison claims that the "changes in mood, thinking, personality, and behavior" that occur during bipolar disorder's manic state may be advantageous for writers: it may enable them to "add depth, fire, and understanding to artistic imagination" (102). Perhaps Melville's masterpiece was written during such manic phases. More research is certainly needed, and a definitive answer may never be achieved. Yet if critics are correct in maintaining that "Cock-A-Doodle-Doo!" is indicative of Melville's state of mind (Sedgwick 173; Milder xiii; Parker 2: 168), then Melville's short story may provide us with the most conclusive evidence about the nature of the "doleful dumps" that he experienced from the 1850s onward.

Notes

1. Melville's mother, Maria, added an "e" to "Melvill" after her husband's death. Some have argued that it was merely to add an aristocratic flourish (Parker 1: 67), whereas others have speculated that it was "an attempt to give her first-born son, Gansevoort, a fresh start in the business world by thus distancing him from the debt and other improprieties associated with his father's business dealings" (Rollyson and Paddock 115).

2. There are other notable examples of mental illness in Melville's extended family. His grandmother, Priscilla Melvill, appeared unstable in 1833. His

cousin, Henry, was regarded by some as "insane," as was his niece, Lucy, who was committed to an asylum in 1870 (McCarthy 7). There is also controversy surrounding the mental health of his first son, Malcolm, who died in an apparent suicide in 1867. For the most detailed account of Melville's experiences with mental illness, see the opening chapter of Paul McCarthy's *"The Twisted Mind": Madness in Herman Melville's Fiction*. Kay Redfield Jamison's pithy section on Melville also contains valuable information on the history of mental illness in Melville's family (216-19).

3. While I single Fisher out in this instance, I do not mean to imply that he was the first to express this faulty view. James E. Miller, Jr., for instance, makes a similar claim in his 1962 publication *A Reader's Guide to Herman Melville* (166).

4. As mentioned, Fisher, Young, and Davis all hold this view. Other critics who have expressed a similar reading over the past fifty years include Newton Arvin (234-35), Sidney P. Moss (192), Beryl Rowland (597), and Hershel Parker (2: 168).

5. For instance Pierre's witnessing his father in a deranged state (70) is reminiscent of Melville's experiences in January 1832.

6. Recall the narrator's previously cited remark: "Here I am, as good a fellow as ever lived—hospitable—open-hearted—generous to a fault: and the Fates forbid that I should possess the fortune to bless the country with my bounteousness. Nay, while many a stingy curmudgeon rolls in idle gold, I, heart of nobleness as I am, I have civil-processes served on me!" (279).

Works Cited

Adamson, Joseph. *Melville, Shame, and the Evil Eye*. Albany: State U of New York P, 1997.

Arvin, Newton. *Herman Melville*. New York: Viking, 1950.

Bipolar Disorder. Toronto: Centre for Addiction and Mental Health, 2000.

Davis, Clark. *After the Whale: Melville in the Wake of Moby-Dick*. Tuscaloosa: U of Alabama P, 1995.

Fisher, Marvin. *Going Under: Melville's Short Fiction and the American 1850s*. Baton Rouge: Louisiana State UP, 1977.

Greene, Charles Gordon. "Review of *Pierre*." 1852. *Herman Melville: The Critical Heritage*. Ed. Watson G. Branch. London: Routledge, 1997. 294-96.

Jamison, Kay Redfield. *Touched with Fire: Manic-Depressive Illness and the Artistic Temperament*. New York: The Free Press, 1993.

Leyda, Jay. Introduction. *The Portable Melville*. Ed. Jay Leyda. New York: Viking, 1952. xi-xxii.

———. *The Melville Log: A Documentary Life of Herman Melville, 1819-1891*. 1951. Vol. 1. New York: Gordian P, 1969 (with supplement).

McCarthy, Paul. *"The Twisted Mind": Madness in Herman Melville's Fiction*. Iowa City: U of Iowa P, 1990.

Melville, Herman. "Cock-A-Doodle-Doo!" 1853. *The Piazza Tales and Other Prose Pieces: 1839-1860*. Ed. Harrison Hayford et al. Evanston: Northwestern UP, 1987. 268-88.

———. *Correspondence*. Ed. Lynn Horth. Evanston: Northwestern UP, 1993.

———. *Journals*. Ed. Howard C. Horsford with Lynn Horth. Evanston: Northwestern UP, 1989.

———. *Pierre*. 1852. Ed. Harrison Hayford, Hershel Parker, and G. Thomas Tanselle. Evanston: Northwestern UP, 1971.

Mendels, Joseph. *Concepts of Depression*. New York: John Wiley & Sons, 1970.

Milder, Robert. Introduction. *Billy Budd, Sailor and Selected Tales*. By Herman Melville. Ed. Robert Milder. Oxford: Oxford UP, 1997. vii-xxxix.

Miller, Edwin Haviland. *Melville*. New York: George Braziller, 1975.

Miller, James E., Jr. *A Reader's Guide to Herman Melville*. New York: Noonday, 1962.

Moss, Sidney P. "'Cock-A-Doodle-Doo!' and Some Legends in Melville Scholarship." *American Literature* 40 (1968): 192-210.

Parker, Hershel. "Damned by Dollars: *Moby-Dick* and the Price of Genius." *Moby-Dick*. 1851. By Herman Melville. Ed. Hershel Parker and Harrison Hayford. New York: Norton, 2002. 713-24.

———. *Herman Melville: A Biography*. 2 vols. Baltimore: Johns Hopkins UP, 1996-2002.

Peck, George Washington. "Review of *Pierre*." 1852. *Herman Melville: The Critical Heritage*. Ed. Watson G. Branch. London: Routledge, 1997. 314-21.

Pickering, George. *Creative Malady*. London: George Allen & Unwin Ltd., 1974.

Rollyson, Carl and Lisa Paddock. *Herman Melville A to Z: The Essential Reference to his Life and Work*. New York: Checkmark Books, 2001.

Rowland, Beryl. "Melville and the Cock that Crew." *American Literature* 52 (1981): 597-606.

Sedgwick, William Ellery. *Herman Melville: The Tragedy of Mind*. 1944. New York: Russell & Russell, 1962.

Updike, John. Introduction. *Herman Melville: The Complete Shorter Fiction.* By Herman Melville. New York: Knopf, 1997. xi-xxxiv.

Young, Philip. "Experimental Melville: 'Cockeye-Doodle-Dee!'" *ATQ* 4.4 (1990): 343-52.

Tom Allen (essay date spring 2003)

SOURCE: Allen, Tom. "Melville's 'Factory Girls': Feminizing the Future." *Studies in American Fiction* 31, no. 1 (spring 2003): 45-71.

[*In the following essay, Allen explores the ways "The Paradise of Bachelors and the Tartarus of Maids" exploits the conventions of popular fictional representations of young female factory workers, illuminating the conflict between the technological and pastoral ideals that inform the ideology of production in modern American culture.*]

> Of a sudden, the Factories burst upon him, or their windows did,—hundreds of bright windows, illuminated every night in honor of Toil,—and which neither the darkness of night, nor the wilderness of the storm, could obscure, and which never bent or blinked before the rage and violence around. The Factories, and factory life,—how it glowed at that moment to his eye! And even his own ideal notions thereof were more than transfigured before him, and he envied the girls, some of whom he knew, who, through that troubled winter night, were tending their looms as in the warmth, beauty, and quietness of a summer-day.
>
> —Sylvester Judd, *Richard Edney and the Governor's Family* (1850)

"Why is it, sir," the narrator of Melville's 1855 *Harper's Monthly* piece **"The Paradise of Bachelors and the Tartarus of Maids"** asks the owner of the paper mill he is touring, "that in most factories, female operatives, of whatever age, are indiscriminately called girls, never women?"[1] The proprietor's answer, that the operatives are all unmarried, "all maids," has informed a tradition of critical commentary that reads Melville's story in terms of the desexualizing effects of industrial labor. Marvin Fisher, for example, finds that "the world of the paper factory is the antithesis of sex," and Michael Rogin glosses the story's dominant image as "white-faced humans reduced to sterility."[2] According to such views, the desexing of the adult factory women into "factory girls" represents Melville's critique of the dehumanizing power of industrial modernization and his concern that, as Fisher puts it, "machine production is not reconcilable with human production." The images of female sterility in **"The Tartarus of Maids"** [**"The Paradise of Bachelors and the Tartarus of Maids"**] would, then, seem to contrast unfavorably with the riotous fecundity of the men represented in its companion

piece, **"The Paradise of Bachelors."** Sex appears to stand for a kind of fertile personhood, the ability to produce oneself in "health and beauty" through acts of "free will," as Fisher would have it.[3] In this dichotomous scheme, the bachelors possess such power, while the "factory girls" do not.

But the loss or rejection of a particular form of sexuality—and, by implication, humanity—need not imply the loss of all. What Fisher and Rogin perceive as desexing may, in fact, be read as resexing—the reconfiguration of sexuality, and hence personhood, into forms consonant with the modern social, economic, and technological environment represented by the conditions of labor and production in the factory. Tartarus' many images of fertility—from the tour guide named "Cupid" to the menstrual "Blood River" that runs through the mill—undermine the notion of a clean dichotomy between sexless maids and over-sexed bachelors, and point instead toward a more uncertain and fluid relationship between different versions of sexuality.[4] And if sex really does stand, synecdochically, for personhood, then this uncertainty about sex must imply a deeper ambiguity about just what sort of persons these mill workers might be. The "factory girls" represent experimental sketches of modern personhood, efforts to imagine what a human being might look like if established notions of "health and beauty," or even "free will," were to be abandoned or lose their currency. As such, they embody the "pattern of contradiction" that Leo Marx identifies in Melville's response to modernization.[5] If, as Marx argues, Americans at midcentury felt conscious of "two kingdoms of force," technology and nature, then Melville's factory girls incorporate both America's celebration of technological progress and its deeply felt attachment to an anti-technological pastoral ideal into their own inscrutable bodies.

The story's full interest as an exploration of America's conflicted attitude toward modern forms of production has largely been missed in the existing scholarship because of an unacknowledged assumption that journalistic and other nonfictional accounts of factory labor constitute its only possible literary context. When viewed in such a context, the story quite reasonably appears to be a protest against modern industry that incorporates what Kristie Hamilton describes as "the tactics of social and political resistance publicized in the sketches of activist labor writers."[6] However, the fictional factory girls who were stock characters in antebellum novels and periodical literature provided Melville with source material for a more ambiguous, less didactic exploration of the cultural conflict over the social effects of technology.[7] As this essay's epigraph from Sylvester Judd's then well-known novel *Richard Edney and the Governor's Family* (1850) suggests, fictional representations of young women working in the factory setting carried tremendous imaginative force among mid- nineteenth-century Americans, metaphorically glowing before their eyes in Judd's description. The passage quoted comes from a scene early in the novel when the young male protagonist, leaving his country home to seek his fortune, first encounters a modern urban environment through this symbolically charged imagery of industrial power.[8] What is most significant about Judd's description, in this context, is the fecundity it associates with the factory and the "girls . . . tending their looms as in the warmth, beauty, and quietness of a summer-day."[9] The contrast between the summer within the factory and the winter without might be described as unnatural, but summer, not winter, is the season of fertility and life. New forms of power create the conditions for new forms of production and growth, even as they distance human beings from what was previously understood as the "natural" environment.

In Melville's reworking of this popular genre, he takes note of how the conflict between technological and pastoral ideals becomes, itself, a productive ideological force in American culture. The popular narratives exhibit a range of responses to industrialization, from sanguine attempts to contain this new form of productive power by illustrating its compatibility with an (ostensibly traditional) pastoral way of life to more ambivalent efforts to suggest how modernization has changed America and separated the present and future from the past. Melville's tale synthesizes this whole range of conflicted attitudes, and hence produces a familiar yet new version of the factory girl, an overtly ideological figure whose precise meaning must remain unknown until the future her labor will produce can actually arrive. To be sure, Melville's account is harsher and more ironic than Judd's, replacing summer-like warmth with faces "pale with work, and blue with cold" (327). But in Melville's version as well, machine production turns out to be compatible with human production, as long as human production adapts itself to the new kind of power residing in the machine. The tale's bachelor narrator describes himself as a seed salesman; he uses the paper produced in the mill to wrap and disseminate his seeds. One of the first scenes he encounters in his tour of the mill is of a female operative feeding rose-colored note paper into a "piston-like machine" that stamps each sheet of paper with "the impress of a wreath of roses" (328). The production of these paper roses goes on independently of the male seed salesman; indeed, confronted by the machine's sexually suggestive stamping motion, the narrator looks on but relates that he "said nothing" (328). In response to this vision of a different kind of productive power, one that generates roses without recourse to his seeds, the narrator is able to produce only an impotent silence. Far from sterile, the female operatives have been integrated into a new regime of production that is both mechanical and feminine; they nurse the machinery until the "moist, warm sheets" are delivered into their hands (333). The

machinery has not replaced the fertility of the maids, but transformed and enhanced it, turning out paper in a gestational "nine minutes" while the male employees are engaged in the fatherly business of "doing nothing in particular" (329). The mill derives all of its power from the "Blood River," and, as Robyn Wiegman has pointed out, the surrounding landscape of the "Black Notch" and "Devil's Dungeon" resembles nothing so much as a "grotesque female body" (742).[10] The fact that Melville's naïve narrator finds this scene strange and unsettling is precisely the point; here is a new form of power that not only surpasses what he can accomplish by spreading his seeds but also threatens to render the masculine "paradise" of the "band of brothers" at Temple Bar obsolete (322).

It is this new way of understanding human growth and development in the context of modern, potentially "unnatural" forms of labor and economic relationships that Melville mined from fiction like Judd's. Factory fiction as a genre responded to a particularly intense moment of change in American social history. Though confined mostly to New England and employing relatively few people as a percentage of the total population of the United States, the factories and their workers came to symbolize the way that the accelerating processes of modernization promised to alter American life as a whole. As historian Jack Larkin notes, factories were "the most dramatically new work-places in the United States," and their newness provided a concrete and even spectacular sign of the changes that all Americans felt occurring in their lives as capitalism inexorably transformed the largely agricultural world of the eighteenth century into a bustling commercial nation.[11] The first American textile mills had opened in the 1790s, and by the 1830s there were dozens of factories spread across New England and the rest of the United States; to many Americans, the potential for the growth of industry seemed unlimited.[12] Because of its famous textile mills, Lowell, Massachusetts, had acquired the nickname "City of Spindles," an appellation that suggests the power of the factory to capture the imagination of progress-minded Americans. In a Fourth of July address delivered at Lowell in 1830, Edward Everett called the establishment of manufacturing in that city a "peculiar triumph of our political independence" and praised the "spirit of a free country which animates and gives energy to its labor . . . subdues to its command all the powers of nature, and enlists in its service an army of machines that do all but think and talk."[13]

Many antebellum Americans joined Everett in perceiving manufacturing centers like Lowell as symbols of national power and development. Others wondered whether human beings would, in the end, serve the machines. What is at issue in these debates, as Everett's millennial tone makes clear, is the impact of modernization on the future direction of American society. As

David Nye relates, "for many the most impressive fact of the mills was not the architecture, the intricate machinery, or the vast production, but the cohorts of workers who seemed to be marshalled into an ideal order."[14] Although machinery itself could evoke the feeling of awe that Nye (following Marx) calls the "technological sublime," what captured the public imagination most was the potential for dramatically new forms of identity and social affiliation created by new modes of labor and new economic relationships between human beings—symbolized by the "factory girls."

Of course, factory labor was also hard work, both physically demanding and mentally taxing. As historian Thomas Dublin explains, after the introduction of the power loom in the early 1820s, mill workers typically "were employed for an average of 12 hours a day, 6 days a week, 309 days a year," for wages averaging between forty and eighty cents per day.[15] Yet Dublin also documents how many mill workers felt positively about their careers. Although scholars have tended to discount the rosy pictures of mill life painted in the *Lowell Offering* as industry-sponsored propaganda, the private correspondence of individual operatives reveals that many appreciated the economic independence that wage labor provided. In 1830, Sarah Hodgdon wrote to her mother that "I have gone into the mill and like it very well," while Mary Paul wrote to her father in 1845 that "We found a place in a spinning room and the next morning I went to work. I like very well have 50 cts first payment increasing every payment as I get along in work have a first rate overseer and a very good boarding place."[16] And for the public at large, most of whom knew little about the realities of factory work, the "mill girl" came to stand for a newly independent and self-sufficient woman—indeed, person—able to take advantage of new possibilities for self-invention in a more modern world.

Harriet Robinson, who worked in the Lowell mills in the 1830s and 1840s, captures this sense of the transformative power of factory labor in her retrospective volume *Loom and Spindle; Or, Life among the Early Mill Girls* (1898). Robinson recalls how new workers would come from the country with peculiar dress, peculiar dialect, and peculiar names: "Samantha, Triphena, Plumy, Kezia, Aseneth, Elgardy, Leafy, Ruhamah, Lovey, Almaretta, Sarepta, and Florilla were among them." Through the floral names, Robinson represents the premodern in terms of the pastoral. The country girls' rustic apparel also evokes the idea of the disappearing past, being "of the plainest homespun, cut in such a fashion that each young girl looked as if she had borrowed her grandmother's gown."[17] Literally clothed in the past, the country girls are strange and unintelligible to those who have already been transformed by the experience of modern life. Robinson explains that upon commencing their work in the mills these country

girls immediately began assimilating into modern culture: "the severe discipline and ridicule which met them was as good as a school education, and they were soon taught the 'city way of speaking'" (40). The new girls were equally quick to adopt modern dress. Robinson observes that when they first arrived, typically their "only head-covering was a shawl," but that "after the first payday, a 'shaker' (or 'scooter') sunbonnet usually replaced this primitive head gear of their rural life" (40). Like the adoption of new, urban language, the new clothing symbolizes the transformation of the self into a modern form.

The reference to pay and clothing is especially important because it links the independent income of mill workers to the freedom to recreate themselves as modern women. By the 1840s, a consumer culture had emerged in the United States in which the capacity to purchase commodities was predicated upon the ability to earn cash.[18] Because they were paid in cash, mill workers became known to the public as much for their production of new lifestyles for themselves as for the commodities they produced. In her analysis of the nonfiction prose of the *Lowell Offering,* Elizabeth Freeman calls this phenomenon a "process of mass self-fabrication newly available to American women."[19] In Freeman's analysis, capitalism offers tremendous possibilities for invention and expansion of the self in return for submission to the logic of consumer culture, in which identity becomes defined in terms of commodities such as clothing and fashion. Crucially, in Robinson's portrait it was precisely because of the work discipline of the factory that these women learned to use their newly acquired freedom well. Even after leaving factory work, they continued to benefit from the transformation it had wrought in their characters: "Into whatever vocation they entered they made practical use of the habits of industry and perseverance learned during those early years" (57). The country girls who arrived were transformed into capable, mature women by the work discipline of the factory: "I know that they will join with me," Robinson declares, "in saying that the discipline of their youth helped to make them what they are; and that the cotton factory was to them the means of education, their preparatory school, in which they learned the alphabet of their life-work" (58). Hence, modern forms of labor provide the basis for the creation of modern selves; those who are best able to adapt themselves to modern modes of production will thrive in the modernizing world of the nineteenth century.

These cultural tensions over modernization and the accompanying social changes structure the plots of representative popular fiction published in the decade before Melville's tale, such as Ariel Cummings's *The Factory Girl; Or, Gardez la Coeur* (1847). Cummings's narrator invites readers to sympathetic identification with the painful transience of the novel's protagonist, Calliste, on her first journey away from her rural village: "Ye, who have learned by experience what it is to leave the paternal roof, for the first time, to mingle with strangers, you can tell the feelings of the subject of our narrative, on her journey to the place of her future abode."[20] The novel's plot, typical of antebellum factory fiction, follows the uncertain but ultimately successful efforts of the heroine to earn enough money working as a factory operative to support her brother's studies in divinity school. The dramatic tension of the narrative comes from Calliste's efforts to negotiate the social world of the modern urban environment while maintaining the traditional virtues of a country girl, virtues essential to her dream of marrying her lover, Marcus Hartwell, after he finishes medical school. But more importantly, the narrator's assumption that readers will sympathize with the novel's female protagonist, Calliste, because they must themselves have experienced similar episodes of transience and estrangement, implicitly generalizes her tale into a collective American story, crystallizing what it feels like to live through an epoch of historical change marked in particular ways by feelings of displacement.

In describing what is being left behind when Calliste leaves home, Cummings emphasizes not only the rustic charm of Calliste's native village but also the pastoral quality of traditional forms of labor in the village setting. For example, when Calliste takes a walk through the countryside before departing, the narrator describes hearing "the merry notes of some favorite air, as the farmer, whistling joyfully . . . took his way to the field, to commence the labors of the day, and animated nature in all its varieties, found a tone to echo in the glad strains which characterize rural life" (17). The bucolic harmony of such descriptions provides a resonant counterpoint to the clang of machinery and "noise and jar of a bustling town" that Calliste will encounter in the city (14). The point of the contrast seems to be not so much a critique of the unnaturalness of the factory as a sentimental homage to a way of life that the narrator acknowledges has been superceded. The culmination of this sentimental longing for what must be left behind occurs when, before leaving her village, Calliste arises at dawn to "catch the rich perfumes of myriads of flowers, borne on etherial wings" and seeks the "invigorating and salutary influence of the salubrious atmosphere of her native hills, once again, ere she left them for other scenes" (18).

The repeated use of words such as "home" and "native" to describe this rural setting emphasizes Calliste's emotional and psychological connection to place. As her "native" place, the rural village contributes to her sense of identity. The specific qualities attributed to this place, then, suggest those aspects of self-identity that might be lost in a more modern environment. The home that she leaves behind is not only a world of traditional labor and economics but also a world of known social rela-

tionships and cultural traditions. Calliste's journey to the city to find more lucrative employment maps the sense of loss of a known social world onto the economic transformations accompanying the transition to capitalism. Before leaving, she feels a "mixture of joy and grief . . . joy in anticipation of the accomplishment of her object,—and grief at the thought of the separation which much take place between herself and those near and dear to her heart; and in consideration of the many temptations and dangers to which a city life renders the young and inexperienced subjects" (18). As the narrator's ominous foreshadowing would lead us to expect, the world of the factory town turns out to be populated by human beings as strange and inscrutable as the factories themselves.

Although Calliste finds a true friend in Louisa, the daughter of her landlady, she is also exposed to peril in the form of two seducers, Cassius Wilson and Alfred Boyden, wealthy and indolent young men who represent the corruption stemming from inherited wealth and aristocratic social position. Shortly after these rakes are introduced, the narrator informs us that "Evil does not present itself, save under a mask—generally the most comely that can be devised" (61). The seducers, who portray themselves as friends to the poor and lonely Calliste even while they lay plans for "the accomplishment of their hellish purposes" (59), represent the threat of hypocrisy that Karen Halttunen has identified in the mid-century "confidence man." As Halttunen observes, antebellum Americans invested the figure of the confidence man with the principal danger posed by the modern city—the possibility of deception and manipulation in a world of strangers. The narrator of *The Factory Girl* warns readers that in the city "appearances are deceptive; hence the necessity of accurate observation, with an apt and discriminating eye, that we may be prepared to withstand the machinations of the adversary" (62). Over the course of the novel, Calliste's progress in learning to interpret the urban social world parallels her progress as a factory operative; as she becomes more successful economically, she becomes more secure socially. Indeed, these two plot lines are so closely intertwined in the text that it would be too simple to say that one concern represents the other tropically; rather, they are two aspects of the same problem, that of refashioning the self to survive in a new and different world.

For this reason, it is essential that the very modernizing forces that bring about the threat to Calliste's selfhood also prove to contain her salvation. It is through the discipline that Calliste acquires in her work as an operative that she finds the strength to withstand the advances of the seducers, who, themselves, represent the modern world in which it is possible for Calliste to become an operative. The narrator describes her acquisition of work skills in terms of a transition from strangeness to familiarity: "Though the hum of business was new to her, yet she soon became accustomed to it, and her daily labors were less and less irksome" (49). At the same time, she learns to interpret her social environment accurately, so that the true nature of rakes such as Alfred and Cassius becomes clear to her. In *The Factory Girl,* knowledge and virtue intersect; the most important form of knowledge is not knowledge of manufacturing processes per se, but knowledge of the modern world, both social and technological, and one's place in it. This knowledge enables virtuous behavior and the maintenance of integrity.

Ultimately, the multiple plot lines of separation—from family and from betrothed—resolve themselves into return and union, as Edwin becomes a minister and Calliste returns to the village to get married. The concluding chapters feature repetitions of imagery from the beginning of the book, emphasizing how things have changed but also remained the same. For example, Edwin becomes pastor of the "same old church" that he and Calliste had attended as children. The narrator emphasizes that it is Calliste's work in the factory that enables this outcome: "And this, fair reader, was to a great degree, the result of the labors of a *Factory Girl.* But for her, Edwin had never been able to prepare for the duties of his holy calling. But for her, he had not that day stood in the sacred desk in his own native village" (120). Calliste's quintessentially modern employment as a factory operative makes possible Edwin's redemption of the pulpit of "his own native village"; mastering the logic of the modern world facilitates the reclamation of tradition and return from separation. The fact that Edwin returns to the village as a minister only adds to the sense that this is a public, social form of redemption—it is not simply Edwin and Calliste's story, but the story of the entire village.

Calliste herself is also able to return to the village and marry Marcus, from whom she has been separated over the course of the novel. As in the depiction of Edwin's return, the narrator describes Calliste's homecoming in terms that explicitly connect the present to the past. Calliste returns in the late spring of the year, while the novel had opened in mid-summer. Although more than one year has passed, the movement from summer to spring emphasizes the cyclical quality of the plot of departure and return.[21] In addition, we encounter Calliste in the same place in which we had seen her with Marcus early in the narrative: "A Saturday evening, at this season, found Calliste again beside the gentle rolling stream near her father's residence—at which place we first introduced her to our readers, and, as then, Marcus, (now Dr. Hartwell) was at her side" (154). This redemption of the past leads to a middle-class domesticity whose security and stability contrast with the restless movement and separation depicted throughout most of the novel: "Our humble *Factory Girl* had found a home

in the midst of the brightest prospects, and in the bosom of time and faithful affection" (158). While going to the factory to seek employment at first had seemed to separate Calliste from home, it now appears to have enabled the possession of home. To a certain extent, of course, this outcome means that her identity has become instrumentalized; by acquiring the proper psychological affect and relation to the world, Calliste obtains a desirable social and economic place in that world. But the novel decidedly represents becoming "Mrs. Hartwell" as an authentic process that is its own reward.

Indeed, in the novel's concluding domestic imagery, "home" becomes a way of imagining authenticity, appealing to a longing for certainty in a shifting world. *The Factory Girl* affirms the possibilities of modernity, the hope that change, properly mastered, could lead to security. Through hard work, economy, and self-discipline, Calliste finally marries and reestablishes herself in a comforting domestic environment much like that she had known as a girl. Hence, by remaking herself into a modern person, Calliste is able not only to attain a stable, controlled life for herself in the modern world, but also to redeem her premodern origins. Evoking the culturally central tropes of domesticity and the maternal bosom in terms of time itself, *The Factory Girl* invites readers to imagine the bright prospect that history might be not only moral but even affectionate.

As Cummings's example demonstrates, the operatives imagined by the public were not only female but also distinctively Protestant and middle-class in affect. While it would be too simple to assign these characters unambiguously to a particular class, given especially that financial need is, as in Calliste's case, often the initial motivation for them to seek factory work, it is clear that in their modes of speech and decorous, sentimental attitudes they reveal an affinity with idealized middle-class mores. This was true despite the fact that by the 1840s the initial wave of white Protestant operatives was already being replaced by a new generation of ethnic immigrant workers.[22] Because the predominantly middle-class reading public understood that such "true women," to borrow Barbara Welter's phrase, were to be assigned to the domestic sphere, and because their highest calling was understood to be motherhood, tales of young women leaving home and working in a factory elicited a culturally resonant drama of displacement.[23] Fictions of "factory girls" could end in one of the two ways: the resolution of this displacement through the marriage plot, and the heroine's ultimate return to the familiar domestic environment, or the seduction and death of the heroine in the strange, unfamiliar world of the factory town or city.[24] Laura Hapke notes that in this respect the fictional "factory girls" are the "successors" of the imperiled heroines of sensation novels like Susanna Rowson's *Charlotte Temple* (1791).[25] But in these works the heroine of the seduction novel has been thoroughly modernized and her story invested with new significance. Both of these potential fates, marriage and seduction, seem imminent for Calliste at various points in *The Factory Girl,* and her ability to acquire the domestic security of marriage through mastery of her experience in the factory provides a comforting allegory of survival in the future world that factory represents.

If Cummings domesticates history within the familiar confines of the marriage plot, Melville might be read as historicizing domesticity by showing how time's passage renders the equivalent fraternal comfort of Temple Bar obsolete. The bachelors display many of the qualities Americans of the period associated with idealized domesticity. Their "snug cells" in Temple Bar are places where "sweet hours" are passed in "genial hospitality" (319). The furniture in the "sedate apartment" where the narrator dines is "wonderfully unpretending, old, and snug" (320). The bachelors who attend the dinner evince "the most tender concern for each other's health" and display "perfect genialness and unconstraint" in their manners. It is, the narrator concludes, "the very perfection of quiet absorption of good living, good drinking, good feeling, and good talk" whose "grand trait" is "fraternal, household comfort" (322). However, "bachelors' dinners, like bachelors' lives, cannot endure forever," and the evening comes to a somewhat melancholy close as the bachelors go their separate ways (323).

This lugubrious conclusion is foreshadowed throughout the Paradise portion of the diptych by images of antiquity and suggestions that Temple Bar possesses at best a tenuous connection to the modern world around it. Unlike the commercial "din" and "mud" of Fleet Street, where the "Benedick [that is, married] tradesmen are hurrying by, with ledger-lines ruled along their brows," the "cloisters" of the bachelors are a "cool, deep glen, shady among harboring hills." Adding to the sense of unreality and detachment, the way thither is "dim" and "monastic," the Paradise itself is "dreamy," and its library is "ancient" (316). The narrator expounds upon the medieval history of the Templars, calling them "romantic" and remarking that a "monk-knight were a curious sight picking his way along the Strand, his gleaming corslet and snowy surtout spattered by an omnibus" (317). Clearly Melville intends a joke at the expense of the lawyers by portraying them as diminished descendants of the outmoded Templars, "struck by Time's enchanter's wand" (317). But the more serious point to be made is that the idealized domestic world that the bachelors inhabit is not real, and, indeed, contributes nothing to the real world around it.

This sense of unreality is evoked especially through the use of pastoral imagery akin to that which Cummings uses to characterize traditional life in *The Factory Girl.*

Unlike the sexually charged "Blood River" of Tartarus, the bachelors enjoy a Thames that is innocent as the "mild Euphrates" flowing through "Eden's primal garden." Echoing the slow pace of life in the "native hills" that Calliste leaves behind, the bachelors "lounge on benches beneath the trees" in the Edenic "Temple Garden" (318). Though Melville locates the antiquated pastoral world in England, when considered in the context of American culture in the antebellum, and other factory narratives especially, the "Temple Garden" clearly evokes the idea of America's traditional rural culture. But while Cummings reassuringly proposes that this traditional culture can be redeemed through mastery of modern modes of production, Melville characteristically hints that what seems more desirable must be sacrificed in favor of something more grim. While Paradise may be more appealing than Tartarus, it is clearly oriented toward the past rather than the future, and just as the bachelor dinner must come to an end, so must Paradise be superceded by something more viable. This critique of domesticity is, indeed, perhaps Melville's most radical gesture in the story, suggesting as it does that the moral and emotional center of middle-class life in the Victorian age is already out-moded in the very moment of its cultural ascendancy.

This reading might seem to put Melville on familiar ground as a trenchant but lonely critic of a naïve American optimism represented by factory fiction such as Cummings's novel. But other writers before Melville had also taken a more ambivalent view of modernization and the kinds of sacrifices such historical change might require. Day Kellogg Lee's *Merrimack; Or, Life at the Loom* (1854) eschews "rural romance" in favor of a more bittersweet meditation on separation and loss.[26] Like *The Factory Girl, Merrimack* focuses on the experiences of a young woman who makes a transition from traditional small town life to life in the urban world of the factory (in this case, the eponymous New Hampshire city of Merrimack). Unlike Calliste, though, Mercy is an orphan, symbolically cut off from any traditional roots to which she might return, and, despite her middle-class diction and manners, forced by poverty to move to the city. The orphan as heroine appears in many antebellum factory fictions, and these works typically evince a darker tone than works like *The Factory Girl* in which the protagonist voluntarily leaves a stable family situation in the native village. Instead of redemption and reunion, orphan novels seek forms of solace for the painful disjunction between self and origin that seems to characterize the modern experience.

Much like *The Factory Girl, Merrimack* begins with a pastoral vision of Mercy's life in her hometown, Salem, before she is orphaned and leaves to work in the textile mills. Her family life revolves around picnics on "The Juniper," a wooded peninsula near town, and visits with the friendly neighbors who mostly get their livelihood from traditional occupations such as farming or artisanship. This pastoral idyll is abruptly interrupted, however, by the deaths of Mercy's parents: her father, a merchant ship captain, takes ill and dies, and her mother dies of consumption brought on by grief not long after.[27] In the meantime, the family has lost all their savings because they invested their money with a smooth-tongued but unscrupulous speculator whose business fails. Because these events happen quickly and contemporaneously, Mercy's status as an orphan adds symbolic emphasis to the way that she is rendered insecure and adrift by the capricious forces of the modern economy.

Still in Salem, the now-orphaned and impoverished Mercy is taken in by a Quaker family, the Buxtons, who continue her education in the traditional virtues of good housekeeping. This period is an intermediate one in Mercy's life, for although the Buxtons provide a surrogate family for her, it is a family she is only contingently a part of, and one that she is free to leave if she can find a better place. Indeed, while Mercy is happy with the Buxtons, she is tempted to move to Merrimack when her friend Amelia Dorlon finds work there in a textile mill. Amelia's father has also died, and "Mrs. Dorlon removed to Merrimack, and placed Amelia in a mill. Amelia was pleased with her employment; it gave her an independence she had not enjoyed in Salem, and she was able to clothe herself better and help her mother more" (70). Life at the loom thus promises to compensate for the absence of their fathers by enabling these young girls to provide for themselves. By precipitating a move to a more urban environment and a place in the modern economy, the deaths of the fathers symbolize the end of the premodern way of life and the passage into the modern world.

Significantly, the real antebellum "mill girl" Lucy Larcom, in her 1889 memoir *A New England Girlhood*, would attach the same symbolic import to the death of her own father. Describing his death, an event which spurred the family's move to Lowell, Larcom recounts how "my father had believed in the near millennium. His very last writing, in his sick-room, was a penciled computation, from the prophets, of the time when it would begin."[28] In Larcom's narrative, her father's death signals the death of the millennial world view in which he believed, making way for the modernity of factory life. Larcom adds further symbolic emphasis to the passing of traditional ways of life when she describes how her family's church burned down, an event that "seemed to me almost the end of the world."[29] Like the fictional Mercy, Larcom experiences the transition from one historical world to another. Yet by writing her book, Larcom revives a trace of premodern consciousness, and, indeed, shows how it had persisted all along in her own memory (the subtitle of Larcom's book is "Outlined from Memory"). In this respect, too, Larcom's story mirrors that of Mercy, for, even as she embraces

the challenges of her new modern life, Mercy's guiding dream, which remains unrealized throughout the novel, is to be reunited with her family in Heaven and to redeem her past by mastering her present and future.

This complex relationship between past, present and future is packed into the dense patterns of imagery surrounding Mercy's departure from Salem. Before leaving Salem, Mercy wakes up before dawn and walks down to the shore to revisit her favorite natural places, taking "a shell and some pebbles and mosses, to keep in remembrance of that tender hour" (71). After this pastoral farewell to premodern life, she returns to town where "at 9:00 the stage-coach wheeled up to the door, and I started for Merrimack" (75). The precise time of arrival of the stage-coach foreshadows the modernity of the new world to which she is going. Life at the mill will be regulated by the bells and clocks of industry, rather than by the natural phenomena of daylight and seasons.[30] After setting out, Mercy contemplates the prospects of her new modern life and wonders whether she will ever be able to recapture what she is leaving behind:

> Then I indulged in a reverie, and brought up months and years of the future to my gaze; with the toils and triumphs of factory life, and the mental culture, and nobler womanhood I resolved to attain. Then my sweet Quaker home had a tear of remembrance. Then the forms of my friends thronged around me, repeating their tender good-byes. Then my father, mother and brothers smiled upon my dream, and my spirit inquired, as it clasped them, if I might not meet them in heaven!
>
> (76)

This reverie integrates the prospects of self-discipline through factory labor with the ultimate hope of a heavenly reunion with the parents who have died and left her to make her own way in the modern world. By spending the months and years of labor in acquiring the nobility requisite to secure God's grace, she hopes to redeem the past that the transition to modern life is forcing her to leave behind.

Upon arriving at the Merrimack home of Amelia and Mrs. Dorlon, Mercy is immediately struck by the contrast between the industrial urban scene and her pastoral small-town home. "Chestnut Hill may have been worthy of its name when the Indian built his wigwam there," she remarks, "but to tell the truth, it was far from any rural romance now" (77). The only signs of nature present are a few small trees in front of the house, which look as though they are not thriving. A lone cedar particularly catches her attention, for it looks "as if it was dying of homesickness in such a barren and ungenial spot." Identifying with the struggling, lonely cedar, Mercy resolves that "the first thing I would do after tea would be to bring out a pail of water and refresh the poor sapling, and see if I could not restore its hopes" (77). Lee depicts Mercy's separation from her past life in Salem as a separation from nature, and the emotional identification with the struggling tree symbolizes the way that Mercy sees herself as a natural being transplanted into an unnatural urban environment. Yet Mercy maintains a hopeful attitude, and is even excited to begin her new life as a "mill girl."

When she begins her new vocation the following day, she immediately learns that working at a loom instills a virtuous self-discipline in the laborers. The superintendent, Mr. Olney, tells her that "it would be good for every girl, rich or poor, to spend a year in a mill. It is a good physical discipline. It may even invigorate the mind, while it puts every heart in communication with our age, and its possession of an independent and progressive spirit" (91). In Mr. Olney's exemplary philosophy, the self-discipline that one can acquire through factory work connects the individual's life to that of the modern age by making individual progress a part of the larger progress of the age. That night Mercy falls into an exhausted slumber, in which "the mill seemed still to be roaring around me, and I worked all night in my dreams" (92). The discipline of working at the loom has impressed itself upon her mind, so that even her dreams reflect her entrance into modern life through the internalized work discipline of the factory.

After a few months have passed, Mercy perceives that her new life as a factory worker has enabled her to improve her time more effectively than she ever had before, for "though the days and weeks were fleeting, in their time, yet as I recall that year to remembrance, it seems the longest of all my life." The work she engages in during these days and weeks transforms her character: "During that year I did something, I fancy, to invigorate my feeble powers, and quicken the activity of my being. . . . I lived in a new and more animated world" (108). The quality of newness and difference from the past that Mercy experiences gives her a more vital sense of being alive. She is awakening to the progressive spirit of modernity, and realizing the power to create herself as a modern person.

This process of self-creation allows Mercy to apply the discipline she has acquired from factory work to cultivating the very traditional virtues that her parents and the Buxtons had taught her to value. Explaining that the "duty of improvement called to me day and night, with its eloquent voice" (109), Mercy embarks upon a course of edifying reading during her free time. Rather than detracting from her ability to find time for self-culture, mill work helps her achieve the self-discipline necessary to use her free time efficiently. Mercy connects this self-discipline back to a sense of the eternal significance of using secular time well: "The course of time and the plane of eternity opened before me as one end-

less scale, which might be to me a scale of progression" (109). The spirit of progress of the modern age enables her to improve her everyday, secular time, so that she ensures her progress in the eternal time that is of spiritual significance. In *Merrimack,* these two forms of progress do not compete with each other but rather are complementary.

Paradoxically, modern life also produces the greatest threat to this disciplined moral progress in the form of the luxuries that are available to tempt the mill workers. "Temptations of which I had been ignorant, I often met," Mercy relates, such as "temptations in the shops and stores, to inflame my love of dress, and steal away my earnings" (110). The negative aspect of modern progress is its creation of excessive wealth and corrupting luxury items. In contrast, Mercy consistently associates the positive aspects of modern life with the discipline to avoid such temptations and practice self-denial. The friends Mercy makes among the mill workers exemplify different possible responses to these modern temptations. She has one friend who is flawed by a love of finery, while in contrast another merits praise because she "loved her work for the discipline it gave her" (113). Part of what makes the mill an improving place to work is that the superintendent, Mr. Olney, "was very strict in his discipline, and free to rebuke any error or vanity that he saw in us" (115). Indeed, Mr. Olney does not simply enforce discipline on the workers, he helps them internalize the values of self-discipline. Mr. Olney's teachings help the young women navigate the perils of modernity, and Mercy explains that the workers are actually fond of him because of his strictness.

Despite her enthusiasm for modern life, however, Mercy also expresses a poignant sense of longing for the previous existence she had as a girl in Salem. She probes the loss of this earlier way of life through fantasies of reunion with her parents, as in the following passage:

> I sometimes dreamed that father returned from his voyages, and built a fine cottage in South Salem, and mother and all were still alive, and happy to enjoy it. Night after night I returned to that home, and passed into the summer-house, and through the grape-arbor, and round among the maples, pines, and larches, which he talked so much of planting in his grounds; then visited the parlor and kitchen, and all the chambers, and found them so pleasant, and father and mother so young and happy! Then I dreamed that I was dreaming, and had no father, mother, or home, and woke and found my heart throbbing with anguish and my pillow drenched with tears.
>
> (146)

The pastoral imagery of her dream of returning to Salem reflects Mercy's feeling of disconnection from nature in her life as a factory worker. Mercy's dreams associate the loss of the pastoral world with her status as an orphan, symbolically emphasizing the sense of isolation and loneliness of modern life. To be modern is to be independent, as Mr. Olney says, but this independence comes at the price of those close connections to family and community that might have been left behind in the premodern world.[31]

As a method of assuaging these feelings of loneliness, Mercy reiterates again and again her need for the discipline of factory work. In reference to her orphanage and poverty, she explains that in her independent life, "I found that my afflictions, severe as they had been, were not without their blessing. I needed the very discipline which they were sent to give" (147). This discipline is then continuously reinforced by her labor in the factory. Factory discipline enables the mill workers to survive the challenges of modern life, as when economic depression sets in. Then Mercy explains that "I myself felt the reverse severely, but the fruits of a stern economy remained to support me now, and I was enabled to live, and do something for the relief of others more needy" (184). Of course, since Mercy's parents were ruined by a speculator, Mercy has now overcome their failings in her own life. They were unable to cope with modern economic fluctuations; she is. The other mill workers have also been well-prepared for such a turn by the discipline instilled through their labor: "There was great and grievous suffering. A large majority, however, had practiced such economy, that they met the crisis with very good success, and took some discipline from it" (185). Later, Mercy explains that "I was but one of many in Merrimack who loved employment,—who admired examples of labor. I needed still more of its discipline" (247). Again, after she has been away from the factory for a time she describes how "I returned to my looms once more, and their cheerful clack was music to my ears. . . . I worked a number of weeks and found my moral strength and serenity more than I anticipated" (345). Throughout the novel, whenever she suffers a trial, she returns to the idea of life at the loom as a source of moral strength.

At the conclusion of the novel Mercy leaves the loom for good when she marries a Merrimack lawyer and finds domestic happiness. At this point, she finally achieves the return to her pastoral childhood that she had longed for even in the midst of her new existence. She and her husband live in a small cottage where "We have shadows with our sunshine, and troubles with our peace; and yet we are far more happy than I used to fancy wedded life could be" (352). She describes a pleasant visit from Mr. and Mrs. Buxton, the Quaker couple who took her in when she was first orphaned, and notes that she and her husband are planning to visit Salem and have "a pic-nic on the Juniper," the wooded peninsula that was one of her favorite places as a child.

Through this plot structure of loss, trial, and redemption, *Merrimack* represents the transition to modernity in hopeful but also ambivalent terms. Mercy is happy with her new life in the modern world but the pain of her orphanage remains just beneath the surface of this life. Eventually, she finds happiness when the strength she has gained from the adversity of modern life enables her to redeem her connection to the pastoral, premodern world she left behind. Yet this connection is still tenuous, for now she will only visit Salem, but remain living in Merrimack where her husband's work is. And because she is an orphan, she is able to redeem her connection to family only in the substitute form of the Buxtons. The conclusion of the novel thus represents only a partial, incomplete version of the redemption of the past that Mercy had dreamed of when she first departed Salem in the stage-coach.

In its concluding picture of incomplete, ambiguous redemption, *Merrimack* synthesizes the competing feelings of hope and fear that nineteenth-century American writers invested in the concept of modernity. Even as many American writers advocated mastery of the future through the modernization of everyday life, others emphasized the loneliness and contingency of human existence within these modern conditions. To be, metaphorically, an orphan provided the opportunity to fashion oneself in a new world but also meant loss of the security of tradition and connection to the kinds of communities that had sustained previous generations. As Dublin notes, "For many, work in Lowell proved to be a first, and an irreversible, step away from the rural, agricultural lives of their parents. . . . The world of their parents was the world of their past; they had moved beyond."[32] The plot of *Merrimack* stages the process of adapting oneself psychologically to a new order based on wage labor and advancing technology. The feelings of loss that accompany Mercy's departure from the rural village represent, in part, the feeling of loss of self, the necessity to leave some part of the self behind in history.

If Calliste and Mercy represent increasingly ambivalent variations on the generic story of estrangement from home, then the maids of Tartarus introduce an even more problematic version in which any return home is perpetually forestalled—frozen in the icy plotlessness of Melville's tale. Like Mercy and Calliste, the anonymous maids come from "far-off villages" (334). However, since nothing changes in Tartarus, the sense of displacement that other factory fictions resolve through the marriage plot becomes a permanent condition. Laboring in the shadow of Woedolor ("pain and suffering") Mountain, these maids seem destined to share the ultimate fate of the "crazy spinster" whose hut is said to have "long ago stood somewhere hereabouts" (323).

Hence, while Mercy and Calliste illustrate strategies for recuperating traditional version of the self and rehabilitating them for a modern environment, Melville's heroines make estrangement itself a distinguishing mark of identity.

"The Paradise of Bachelors and the Tartarus of Maids" thus shares with contemporary factory fiction the sense that the most profound problem of modernity resides in its threat to previously coherent ways of imagining human identity. Melville pushes this theme farther than other writers by sketching a far more frightening vision of what human beings might look like if given over wholly to modernity, to become "mere cogs to the wheels" of modern production (328). Furthermore, the maids' story, like the stories of all "factory girls," may be more generalizable than the bachelor narrator would like to acknowledge. While the maids' seemingly inhuman coldness and abject suffering initially repel the narrator, he finds himself inexorably drawn to them in the same imaginative way in which readers are invited to identify with heroines such as Calliste and Mercy. Upon hearing that these women are required to sacrifice the comfort of domesticity in order to become the "steady workers" the factory requires, the narrator relates that "some pained homage to their pale virginity made me involuntarily bow" (334). Then, as his cheeks turn "whitish" like those of the maids, he is filled with a "strange emotion" (334). While Melville's narrator is more effusive about his feelings of connection to the other bachelors in Paradise, part of what frightens him about Tartarus is his recognition of kinship with the "factory girls."

Indeed, all of the bachelors are so implicated, as their shirts are used as raw material in the factory's paper-making process. When approaching the factory, the narrator notes an "inverted similitude" between the landscape around the factory and Temple Bar, and remarks, "This is the very counterpart of the Paradise of Bachelors, but snowed upon, and frost painted to a sepulcher" (326-27). The apparent inhumanity of Tartarus has become the human. Just as the bachelor's clothing goes to make blank sheets of paper, so too do human beings who resemble the bachelors enter the factory to be transformed into "rows of blank-looking girls" (328), while the waters of the Blood River, source of human life and productive power, have "not changed their hue by coming under the use of man" (329). If, as Wiegman argues, the bachelors represent the patriarchal fantasy of reproduction without women, "women's exclusion" from and exploitation by the politically and economically powerful bachelors, then the Blood River's undiminished feminine potency suggests that this fantasy is a naïve illusion.[33] While the bachelors pretend that their antiquated world is perfect and complete, the maids display the sacrifice of health and beauty required by modernity.

In the end, it does not seem to matter much whether the bachelor narrator approves of, or feels affection for, or would willingly choose the vision of humanity he discovers in Tartarus, for Melville casts this bleak future in terms of inevitability. Hamilton reads the maids' threat to the narrator in terms of their possibly "enslaving" him, but the fate of the bachelors' shirts suggests that what the narrator fears more is their consuming and re-fashioning him into a new and inscrutable form.[34] This new kind of humanity, represented by the maids, is already spreading everywhere. The married and procreant "Benedick tradesmen" of Fleet Street, who have the "rise of bread and fall of babies" on their minds, possess brows that are "ruled" with "ledger-lines," just as one of the first factory workers Melville sees possesses a "ruled and wrinkled" brow that duplicates the "ruled" sheets of paper she withdraws from the end of a machine (316, 328). Tartarus has arrived on the doorstep of Paradise, conveyed by the power of modern production and commerce. "Pacing slowly to and fro along the involved machine," the narrator recounts, "I was struck as well by the inevitability as the evolvement-power in all its motions." "It *must* go," Cupid tells him. "The machinery makes it go just so; just that very way, and at that very pace you there plainly see it go. The pulp can't help going" (333). Just as bachelors' shirts are inexorably pulped and turned into white paper, so too must bachelors be remade into blank people.

Many critics have noted the similarity between the last line of this tale—"Oh! Paradise of Bachelors! And oh! Tartarus of Maids!"—and the final line of **"Bartleby, the Scrivener"** (1853)—"Ah Bartleby! Ah humanity!" (335, 45). In the same way that the anonymous narrator of **"Bartleby"** reluctantly comes to recognize that his pallid clerk makes visible the poverty of humanity in the law office, the narrator of the factory tale recognizes that the maids express the real conditions of modern life for all human beings, not merely for themselves. In much of his fiction, Melville associates the kind of fraternal affection the bachelors exemplify with a warm humanity and almost utopian freedom from social and historical constraints. But as **"Bartleby"** illustrates, by the time he turned to writing magazine fiction Melville had become deeply skeptical of such fantasies. Representing Tartarus in terms of feminine reproductive power may be a way of acknowledging the fundamental strangeness and unknowability of the social world of the future—a future whose feminine vitality signifies not weakness, but rather the awesome power of the machinery of historical change, and "the metallic necessity, the unbudging fatality which governed it" (333).

Notes

1. Herman Melville, *The Piazza Tales and Other Prose Pieces, 1839-1860* (Evanston: Northwestern University Press, 1987), 334. Hereafter cited parenthetically.

2. Marvin Fisher, *Going Under: Melville's Short Fiction and the American 1850s* (Baton Rouge: Louisiana State Univ. Press, 1977), 92; Michael Paul Rogin, *Subversive Genealogy: The Politics and Art of Herman Melville* (New York: Knopf, 1983), 204.

3. Fisher, 93.

4. There is a tradition of criticism that views the mill as a sexually fertile environment, but these interpretations tend to deemphasize the Melville's interest in industrialization and modernization in order to foreground more traditional understandings of sexuality. Beryl Rowland, for example, argues that Melville intended his readers to understand "mill" as a slang term for a brothel, and hence views the story as a critique of women's sexual exploitation by men that is timeless rather than specifically modern in import. Philip Young also treats modern industrial production as incidental to Melville's purpose when he explicates the story's depiction of fertile female sexuality exclusively in terms of "classical myth and Christian allegory" while dismissing "critics who manage to read the story sociologically." Beryl Rowland, "Melville's Bachelors and Maids: Interpretation through Symbol and Metaphor," *American Literature* 41 (1969), 390-91; Philip Young, "The Machine in Tartarus: Melville's Inferno," *American Literature* 63 (1991), 209, 213.

5. Leo Marx, *The Machine in the Garden: Technology and the Pastoral Ideal in America,* 35th anniversary ed. (New York: Oxford Univ. Press, 2000), 278.

6. Kristie Hamilton, *America's Sketchbook: The Cultural Life of a Nineteenth-Century Literary Genre* (Athens: Ohio Univ. Press, 1998), 119.

7. The first full-length American novel to feature an operative as a protagonist, Sarah Savage's *The Factory Girl,* appeared as early as 1814. By the late 1850s dozens of factory-related novels and short stories had been published, almost invariable featuring female protagonists. It is difficult to determine the number of such publications with precision, due to the fact that so many of them, published in periodicals or as pulp novels, have been lost to time. Judith A. Ranta's annotated bibliography, the most comprehensive overview of the textile mill literature published in nineteenth-century America, lists several dozen works of fiction from the antebellum period. This bibliography covers only textile mill literature, however, rather than all types of factories, and, as Ranta notes, "There are undoubtedly more writings, especially in periodicals and non-English publications, yet to be examined by scholars." *Women and Children of the Mills: An Annotated Guide to Nineteenth-Century American Textile Factory Literature* (Westport: Greenwood, 1999), xi. On Savage's *The Factory Girl,* see Thomas B. Lovell, "Separate Spheres and Extensive Circles: Sarah Savage's *The Factory Girl* and the Celebration of Industry in the Early Republic," *Early American Literature* 31 (1996), 1-24.

8. As if to dramatize the extent of the psychological transformations mapped onto the historical sense of place, in factory fiction the factory is almost always located in a vaguely described but clearly urban setting that contrasts sharply with the protagonist's rural place of origin. In reality, factories were located in a variety of settings ranging from village to city. See Walter Licht, *Industrializing America: The Nineteenth Century* (Baltimore: Johns Hopkins Univ. Press, 1995), 21-45.

9. Sylvester Judd, *Richard Edney and the Governor's Family* (Boston: Phillips, 1850), 10.

10. Robyn Wiegman, "Melville's Geography of Gender," *American Literary History* 1 (1989), 742.

11. Jack Larkin, *The Reshaping of Everyday Life, 1790-1840* (New York: Harper and Row, 1988), 55.

12. Although New England was the center of industrialization, there were factories in other parts of the country, including the South; see Robert S. Starobin, *Industrial Slavery in the Old South* (New York: Oxford Univ. Press, 1970), and Licht, 35-38.

13. Edward Everett, "Fourth of July at Lowell," in *The Philosophy of Manufactures: Early Debates over Industrialization in the United States,* ed. Michael Brewster Folsom and Steven D. Lubar (Cambridge: MIT Press, 1982), 282-83.

14. David E. Nye, *American Technological Sublime* (Cambridge: MIT Press, 1994), 115.

15. Thomas Dublin, *Women at Work: The Transformation of Work and Community in Lowell, Massachusetts, 1826-1860* (New York: Columbia Univ. Press, 1979), 59, 66.

16. *Farm to Factory: Women's Letters, 1830-1860,* ed. Thomas Dublin (New York: Columbia Univ. Press, 1981), 42, 101.

17. Harriet H. Robinson, *Loom and Spindle; Or, Life among the Early Mill Girls* (Hawaii: Pacifica, 1976), 40. Hereafter cited parenthetically.

18. For examples of the voluminous scholarship on nineteenth-century consumerism, see Larkin, *The Reshaping of Everyday Life,* 53; Charles Sellers,

The Market Revolution: Jacksonian America, 1815-1846 (New York: Oxford Univ. Press, 1991), 154-57; Stuart Blumin, The Emergence of the Middle Class: Social Experience in the American City, 1760-1900 (New York: Cambridge Univ. Press, 1989), 140-46, and passim; and Katherine C. Grier, Culture and Comfort: Parlor Making and Middle-Class Identity, 1850-1930 (Washington: Smithsonian, 1988).

19. Elizabeth Freeman, "'What Factory Girls Had Power to Do': The Technologic of Working-Class Feminine Publicity in The Lowell Offering," Arizona Quarterly 50 (1994), 121.

20. Ariel Ivers Cummings, The Factory Girl; Or, Gardez la Coeur (Lowell: Short, 1847), 21. Hereafter cited parenthetically.

21. This seasonal structure of course anticipates Walden, in which Thoreau moves into his cabin on the fourth of July and ends his narrative after the coming of spring. Thoreau redacts events from the time he spent at Walden, which actually ran from summer of 1845 until early fall of 1847, into a single summer-to-spring cycle.

22. For the social history and demographics of the industrial workforce, see Dublin, Women at Work; Jonathan Prude, The Coming of Industrial Order: Town and Factory Life in Rural Massachusetts, 1810-1860 (New York: Cambridge Univ. Press, 1983); and Christopher Clark, The Roots of Rural Capitalism: Western Massachusetts, 1780-1860 (Ithaca: Cornell Univ. Press, 1990). Elizabeth Stuart Phelps's novel The Silent Partner (1871) departs from the antebellum tradition of the "factory girl" discussed here, depicting an experience of industrial labor in which immigrants had come to comprise much of the workforce, and in which entire families were often rendered transient together. As Mr. Mell tells Perley, "He'd been turned out o' mills in this country twice for goin' into a ten-hour strike; once to Lawrence and once up to New Hampshire." Elizabeth Stuart Phelps, The Silent Partner (New York: The Feminist Press, 1983), 111.

23. Barbara Welter, "The Cult of True Womanhood: 1820-1860," American Quarterly 18 (1966), 151-74.

24. In addition to purely fictional representations of the dangers of seduction of the "factory girl," there were numerous semi-fictional or journalistic accounts of scandalous and tragic episodes involving the seduction of female operatives by unscrupulous men. See, for example, George Thompson, Catharine and Clara; Or, The Double Suicide; A True Tale of Disappointed Love (New York: Hill,

1853), and Catharine Williams, Fall River: An Authentic Narrative (1833; repr. New York: Oxford Univ. Press, 1993). The latter is one of numerous literary responses to the story of Sarah Maria Cornell, an itinerant mill worker whose pregnant body was found hanged from a haystack roof in Tiverton, Rhode Island, in December of 1832. The subsequent investigation pointed toward a Methodist minister, Ephraim Avery, whom Cornell had met while working in Lowell and who may have had an affair with Cornell when she was employed in Fall River, Rhode Island. Avery was acquitted; see Caldwell's introduction for details of the case. See Ranta, Women and Children of the Mills, for a selection of songs, poems, and stories about Cornell, as well as Jeanne Elders DeWaard, "'Indelicate Exposure': Sentiment and Law in Fall River: An Authentic Narrative," American Literature 74 (2002), 373-401.

25. Laura Hapke, Labor's Text: The Worker in American Fiction (New Brunswick: Rutgers Univ. Press, 2001), 69.

26. Day Kellogg Lee, Merrimack; Or, Life at the Loom: A Tale (New York: Redfield, 1854), 77; hereafter cited parenthetically. Lee, who was a Universalist minister and pastor of various churches in New York State, wrote two other novels concerned with labor: Summerfield; Or, Life on a Farm (1852), and The Master Builder; Or, Life at a Trade (1854).

27. It is perhaps significant that Lee makes Mercy's father a merchant ship captain, for mercantilism gave way to capitalism in the nineteenth century. Sellers notes that in the Revolutionary period, "Some of the biggest merchants lost out by taking the Loyalist side, and all lost their privileged access to British and West Indian markets." Merrimack is set considerably later than this, and Lee makes no reference to Mr. Winthrop's political persuasion, but it is possible that Lee intends a symbolic commentary on the passing of the old economic order. See Sellers, 21-23.

28. Lucy Larcom, A New England Girlhood: Outlined from Memory (Cambridge: Riverside, 1889), 141.

29. Larcom, A New England Girlhood, 145.

30. As Michael O'Malley notes, the "imposition of clock time through the factory system constituted one of the central conflicts of industrialization" in the United States. Michael O'Malley, Keeping Watch: A History of American Time (Washington: Smithsonian Institution Press, 1990), 39.

31. In reality, most women who left their homes to work in factories kept in close contact with their families and friends. Dublin observes that "The

letters they wrote indicate that even when work in the mills took women away from family and friends, they continued to feel strong affection and concern for those at home. They felt distant but by no means estranged from loved ones" (*Women at Work,* 47). This discrepancy between the real experience of women factory workers and Lee's fictional representation of that experience is important, for it suggests the extent to which the "mill girl" provided a symbol for the loss of past associations, a loss that the nation as a whole experienced as part of the ongoing process of modernization, even if individual women who really worked in the mills might not have felt such alienation from their origins to the same degree.

32. Dublin, *Women at Work,* 57.

33. Wiegman, 746.

34. Hamilton, 127.

Naomi C. Reed (essay date June 2004)

SOURCE: Reed, Naomi C. "The Specter of Wall Street: 'Bartleby, the Scrivener' and the Language of Commodities." *American Literature* 76, no. 2 (June 2004): 247-73.

[*In the following essay, Reed re-examines the Marxist context of "Bartleby the Scrivener," paying attention not only to the materialistic view of commodity but also to an immaterial dimension of capitalism itself.*]

"Ere introducing the scrivener, as he first appeared to me," writes the lawyer in Herman Melville's **"Bartleby, the Scrivener"** (1853), "it is fit I make some mention of myself, my *employés,* my business, my chambers, and general surroundings."[1] Intriguingly, the lawyer does not say he met Bartleby; instead, Bartleby "appeared" to him. We might read the word *appeared* as the diction of a man who has practiced law for many years, a profession in which the presence of individuals is often referred to as an "appearance." Yet in legal phraseology the verb *to appear* is typically followed by the preposition *before*: one always appears before the bench, the judge, or the jury. Bartleby, however, does not appear before the lawyer but, in a crucial change of prepositions, *to* him. Bartleby's appearance, of course, creates a subtle, dramatic tension, setting up the eventual climax in which he is shown to be quite different from the person he first appears to be. Yet the word *appeared* suggests a stranger possibility: perhaps Bartleby quite literally appeared, as would an apparition.

But what would it mean to take Melville at his word and read Bartleby as an apparition? We would be reminded of what current critics of the story seem to have

forgotten: Bartleby is strange. Contemporaneous reviewers certainly saw the story's occult possibilities. One wrote of Bartleby's "ghost-like taciturnity"; another called the story a "weird tale," reminiscent of the eeriness of Poe.[2] Yet for the most part, this sense of the story's weirdness has been lost. Nearly all current work on **"Bartleby"** [**"Bartleby the Scrivener"**] follows from another critical genealogy—not the occult but the quotidian, with one early reviewer going so far as to call the story "a portrait from life."[3] Marxist criticism of **"Bartleby,"** in particular, takes its cue from this sense of the tale as a story of the everyday, casting it as a realistic story, with an emphasis on working life.[4] This line of criticism began with Louise K. Barnett's seminal essay "Bartleby as Alienated Worker" (1974), in which, as the title suggests, Bartleby is the "perfect exemplum" of Marx's alienated worker and Melville's story a parable of the heartlessness of capitalism.[5]

This early Marxist criticism of **"Bartleby"** has come under fire from several critics. Pointing to the fact that the lawyer continues to pay Bartleby's salary and to help him even after he has stopped working, Dan McCall suggests that readings of **"Bartleby"** as a parable of the dangers of capitalism hinge on a fundamental misreading of the text, and of the lawyer in particular, who cannot easily be put into the mold of a typical heartless capitalist.[6] While McCall seems not to recognize that the motor of capital is the systemic exploitation of the worker to produce surplus value and thus does not depend on the personal characteristics of any one individual, he does point to the problem in early Marxist criticism of **"Bartleby"**: reading the story as a simple parable of the alienated worker cannot account for a number of its aspects, such as Bartleby's ghostlike presence, the sequel of the Dead Letter Office, and the fact that Bartleby refuses many things other than work.

In recent years, Marxist criticism of **"Bartleby"** has moved from this more thematic approach, which presents the story as illustrative of Marxist concepts, to rigorously historicist readings. While Marx is present methodologically in this later criticism, Marxism's relationship to Melville's critique of capitalism tends not, for historical reasons, to be an overt subject of discussion, since there is no real evidence that Melville was familiar with Marx's writings at the time he composed **"Bartleby."** Instead, these critical interventions root **"Bartleby"** in labor debates going on in New York City at the time of the story's composition and publication. The subtitle itself seems to suggest such a reading, offering this strange, inexplicable scrivener as "A Story of Wall Street." As David Kuebrich has shown, Melville was well aware that Wall Street was a hotbed of labor activism and knew of political debates about the rights of workers. The decision to situate Bartleby's story on Wall Street, Kuebrich suggests, was Melville's deliberate and politically inflected choice.[7] Along similar lines, Barbara Foley skillfully argues that the story cannot be understood without "a familiarity with mid-nineteenth-century class struggles in New York—and with the contemporaneous discourse about those struggles"—suggesting that the Astor Place riot of 1849 "provides a covert historical subtext" to the story.[8] Sheila Post-Lauria, unearthing the labor history of the text in a different way, relates its publication history. **"Bartleby"**'s publisher, *Putnam's Monthly,* in contrast to its competitor *Harper's Magazine,* featured stories that uncovered "'characteristic life in the cities'"; as a result, "many stories [in *Putnam's*] discussed the plight of employees."[9]

Whether consciously or not, this recent historical work responds to criticism of the earlier Marxist interventions by providing a context for **"Bartleby"** that convincingly suggests its investment in labor politics. This rich historicization points emphatically toward the plight of the worker, yet if the earlier criticism levied against Marxist readings of the story has shown us anything, it is that we cannot read **"Bartleby"** simply as a Marxist parable. Nevertheless, the long critical history that puts Marx and Melville into conversation, albeit often a one-sided one, means that **"Bartleby"** provides a framework and a language to rethink these Marxist projects of the 1970s. That is, if the criticism of **"Bartleby"** offers a way of understanding Melville's story through Marxism—however problematically—perhaps a return to the text of **"Bartleby"** can contribute to current work on Marx.

In returning to **"Bartleby"** as a "weird tale," I hope to allow a reading of Marx that attends not only to the material but also the immaterial in his analysis of the commodity and of capitalism. This reading of Marx will help us understand what seems to be a jarring contradiction: how can **"Bartleby"** be both a "weird tale" and simultaneously a "portrait from life"? By reading **"Bartleby"** and Marx against and through one another, I will ultimately suggest that Melville's **"Bartleby"** is more than just a parable of the heartlessness of capitalism. The story is a complex meditation on the structure and workings of capitalism and of circulation under capitalism, in which this strange apparition of Bartleby allows us to reconsider Marx's analysis of the commodity in terms of the spectrality of capitalism itself.

"A MILDLY CADAVEROUS REPLY"

From the beginning of **"Bartleby,"** it is clear that something about this new scrivener is amiss. Answering the lawyer's advertisement for copyists, Bartleby arrives on the doorstep of the law office as "a motionless young man" (19). Bartleby's strange inertness quickly transforms into an eerie question of life and death, for soon Bartleby, summoned by the lawyer, responds "[l]ike a

very ghost, agreeably to the laws of magical invocation" and "appear[s] at the entrance of his hermitage" (25). Once Bartleby has been compared to a ghost, he begins to act like one. Stopping by the office on a Sunday, the lawyer knocks on the door and "the apparition of Bartleby appear[s]," the significance of "appear" emphasized by the lexical tautology of an apparition's appearing (26).

Yet Bartleby is not just an apparition; he is also a corpse. The lawyer further describes Bartleby on that Sunday morning as having a "cadaverously gentlemanly *nonchalance*" (27). Melville's descriptors here are remarkably specific. Bartleby's demeanor is not that of a cadaver who is (or, more properly, was) a gentleman. Instead, Bartleby is gentlemanly *in a cadaverous way*. We cannot read this description as simply pointing to a past state—Bartleby as a gentleman before he died (ignoring here, if possible, the fact that he has not died). Clearly the thrust is that Bartleby is still a gentleman (or gentlemanly, at least) while simultaneously being cadaverous. We might say that Bartleby is deadly alive, or alively dead. Either way, Melville presents a conundrum. Bartleby is both an apparition and a gentlemanly cadaver. In fact, it is the apparition of Bartleby that carries itself in such a cadaverously gentlemanly way. If Bartleby is an apparition, he is not a mere ghost. He is an apparition of something in between life and death: a gentlemanly cadaver. **"Bartleby"** is thus no simple ghost story, for the specter of Bartleby is a strange admixture of the bodily and the ghostly. Bartleby is no more properly a spirit than he is a run-of-the-mill scrivener; he is an apparition *and* a scrivener, a cadaver *and* a gentleman, and he is "haunting the building generally" (40).

Melville renders the strange amalgam that is Bartleby as particularly figural. The lawyer, after Bartleby's first refusal to proofread his own copy, complains: "I should have violently dismissed him from the premises. But as it was, I should have as soon thought of turning my pale plaster-of-paris bust of Cicero out of doors" (21). The lawyer is not alone in his equation of Bartleby and Cicero, the historical figure perhaps most associated with rhetoric. Bartleby himself, it seems, identifies with Cicero: ostensibly listening to the lawyer's reasoned pleadings about work, Bartleby instead "kept his glance fixed upon [the lawyer's] bust of Cicero" (30). This kinship between Bartleby and Cicero is strengthened by its context, for it emerges at moments when Bartleby is at odds with the lawyer. Bartleby's "rhetoricality" thus stands in opposition to the reason of the lawyer, suggesting that the text juxtaposes the rhetorical—as it comes to be signaled by Cicero—to the logical (or at least the lawyer's logic):

> "These are your own copies we are about to examine.
> It is labor saving to you, because one examination will

answer for your four papers. It is common usage. Every copyist is bound to help examine his copy. Is it not so? Will you not speak? Answer!"

"I prefer not to," he replied in a flute-like tone. It seemed to me that while I had been addressing him, he carefully revolved every statement that I made; fully comprehended the meaning; could not gainsay the irresistible conclusion; but, at the same time, some paramount consideration prevailed with him to reply as he did.

"You are decided, then, not to comply with my request—a request made according to common usage and common sense?"

He briefly gave me to understand that on that point my judgement was sound. Yes: his decision was irreversible.

(22)

Bartleby does not reach a different conclusion about the common usage and common sense of checking his copy; indeed, he "fully comprehend[s] the meaning" of the lawyer's logic and its "irresistible conclusion." But Bartleby responds to another consideration. The lawyer's arguments are sound—as both he and Bartleby agree—yet Bartleby, as so many critics have noted, is not a man of reason but a man of preferences. We can perhaps call these preferences "rhetoric," but if they are marked textually as rhetorical, they are also specifically figural, for Bartleby's relationship to Cicero is established through the plaster-of-paris bust of Cicero that sits in the lawyer's office. The text thus defines Bartleby's preferences as rhetorical through a figure—the metaphoric relationship of Bartleby to Cicero—but also renders rhetoric itself through a figure: the bust of Cicero metonymically figures rhetoric, even as it synecdochically figures Cicero himself. If Bartleby is a man of preferences, he is, consequently, a man of figures.

Recalling Bartleby's first appearance at the door of the law office, the lawyer exclaims: "I can see that figure now—pallidly neat, pitiably respectable, incurably forlorn!" (19). Bartleby enters the narrative as a figure, and while the lawyer's choice of words might be accidental, the description sticks, becoming more pronounced as the text progresses, resulting in Bartleby's transformation into what Marvin Hunt calls "a pure semiological event":

[T]he remarkably swift devolution from functioning scrivener to starved corpse represents a shift of value from the factual to the symbolic, from Bartleby as flesh-and-blood reference to Bartleby as verbal sign. Starvation is the final stage of a progressive dematerialization that reduces all things to language.[10]

While Hunt rightly points to the semiological in the figure of Bartleby, this movement is not accompanied by any simple progression from Bartleby as "flesh-and-blood reference" to Bartleby as "verbal sign." For

Bartleby never simply dematerializes; he remains always somewhere between the material and the immaterial. He is a ghost who haunts, but one who can still be imprisoned by the law. He is a corpse that will not eat even as corpses cannot eat. That is, while Bartleby the figure might certainly be thought of only as a verbal sign, Bartleby the amalgam of apparition and gentlemanly cadaver always retains his physical self, however tenuously. What must be made sense of is Bartleby as both a figure and the apparition of the gentlemanly cadaver.

While these strange goings-on might seem at first to show the limits of a Marxist reading of **"Bartleby,"** I take them as provocation for a return to Marx, in search of a subtler understanding of his concept of alienation than those suggested so far by critics of the story. I return to Marx not only because the critical history of **"Bartleby"** places these two texts into conversation but also because *Capital* too is rife with apparitions and specters. Marx's portrait of capitalism is as strangely haunted as "#___ Wall Street." Returning to *Capital* can help us make sense of Bartleby the worker through Bartleby the apparition of a gentlemanly cadaver, a relationship we can begin to see by attending to the role of the figural in Marx's analysis of value.

"A STORY OF WALL STREET"

Reading **"Bartleby"** as the story of an apparition leads me to read *Capital* as another weird tale, another story of an apparition, a reading that begins with a linguistic coincidence. Just as Melville's story opens with the appearance of Bartleby at "#___ Wall Street," *Capital* opens with the appearance of the commodity. Neither Bartleby nor the commodity proves to be what it seems at first. Early in the first volume of *Capital,* Marx states: "The wealth of societies in which the capitalist mode of production prevails appears as an 'immense collection of commodities.'"[11] Marx's use of *appears* is quite deliberate. His point is that the commodity is more than just a simple, sensuous thing (thus more than it appears) and, further, that this "more" is something that can be described only with a rhetoric of appearance. For Marx, the commodity is thus more than a "plain, homely" use-value. Marx's insistence on the appearance of the commodity gestures toward the history of abstraction and reincorporation that is not physically visible within or on the commodity (except perhaps in the form of a price tag), but which constitutes it as such.

My analysis of the apparition of the commodity is routed first through Marx's explanation of value, which begins with what he calls the accidental form of value. His analysis could be summarized in the statement "*linen = coat,*" for that is "the basis of the equation." His task is to explain the process that makes the statement "*linen = coat*" not only possible but also sensical:

how can linen and the coat be simultaneously different (linen and coat) and equal (*C* [Karl Marx, *Capital,* Vol 1, translated by Ben Fawkes, 1990], 141, 138)? The answer lies in abstraction from use-values, which allows the linen and the coat to be related qualitatively (as abstract labor time, they become qualitatively the same) and thus quantitatively (hence moving from *linen = coat* to *20 yards of linen = 1 coat*).[12] In Marx's formulation, value is thus always an abstraction of the particular qualities of use-values.

But Marx does not stop at abstraction: "The value of the commodity linen is therefore expressed by the physical body of the commodity coat, the value of one by the use-value of the other." Even as value is necessarily an abstraction from use-value, it must still have a body—the use-value of the equivalent form, or exchange-value. "[I]n other words," writes Marx, "the physical body of commodity B [the coat] becomes a mirror for the value of commodity A [the linen]" (*C*, 143, 144). Because exchange-value comes to represent the value of other use-values, it enables an alienation: the representation of linen's value in an object that is not linen at all. Marx establishes here that value is a category with no physical reality; it is a pure abstraction. His critical move is to insist upon value's reincorporation, its becoming physical again after abstraction.[13] Thus, the value of linen comes to be represented not by some abstract, intangible idea but by the *body* of the coat.[14] The coat as use-value that serves as the mirror for the value of linen is thus not exactly the coat with which we began—it is a coat we have returned to after abstraction—hence, its "phantom-like objectivity." The coat is, Marx asserts in a deliberate paradox, something "sensuous" but is "at the same time suprasensible or social" (*C*, 128, 165). Neither solely a physical object nor solely an abstraction, it is something entirely different.

In arguing that the "physical body of commodity B becomes a mirror for the value of commodity A," Marx insists on the *specular* nature of value. Yet while he insists that in this specular relation the linen and the coat are "as like as two peas," he just as insistently reminds us that the relationship springs up precisely because the linen and the coat are not as like as two peas (*C*, 144). The linen must see itself in the coat despite the fact that they are different things. In order for this relation of equivalence to be established, exchange must be understood as, in Thomas Keenan's words, "a matter of signification, expression, substitution, and hence something that must be read."[15] If this mirror is reflecting, it must be reflecting something other than a physical existence. The linen and the coat can only be mirror images of one another after they have been abstracted from their physical forms and reduced to a common substance. Yet this commonality, while it most certainly exists, is not a visible quality—for value is "a purely verbal 'like.'"[16] Thus, the relations of equivalence proffered in exchange are figural because value necessarily puts things into metaphoric, and thus substitutable, relationships. Value itself functions as a process of figuration; it is what Werner Hamacher calls the "metaphor of a general substance, of labor."[17]

In *Specters of Marx,* Jacques Derrida extends the discussion of figuration at the heart of the value form by making reference to the "*revenant*" or specter. Both spirit and body—or something in between the two—the specter, described by Derrida as a "proper body without flesh," corresponds in Marx's analysis to exchange-value.[18] Derrida's analysis of the logic of the "*sensuous non-sensuous*" (his formulation of Marx's suggestion that exchange-value is both sensuous and suprasensible) lays out the structure of exchange-value, in particular, its salient differences from use-value.[19] While exchange-value, as the physical form of value, comes to look much like use-value, it is spectral because it must always retain a trace of its journey through abstraction—of its bodiless existence as value. It is spectral because it is both spirit and body, neither one nor the other but some combination of the two: "sensuous non-sensuous." If value is an act of figuration, then exchange-value becomes the figure that gives that process a recognizable, "physical" form, but that physical form is a monstrous amalgam of body and spirit, both material and immaterial.

This reading of Marx's theory of value as a theory of figuration thus enables a Marxist understanding of **"Bartleby"** that avoids the pitfalls of the first wave of such interpretations because it allows us to see the relationship between the eeriness of Bartleby and the story's portrayal of the everyday. The figure of Bartleby, that amalgam of spirit and body, apparition and gentlemanly cadaver, suggests that a Marxist reading of **"Bartleby"** must not simply account for a worker's resistance but must attend as well to the spectrality of capitalism, its complex intertwining of the material and the immaterial. Such a reading will allow us to see in **"Bartleby"** a critique not only of dehumanizing labor but of capitalism more broadly.

"I WOULD PREFER NOT TO"

Bartleby's critique of labor and capitalism is registered through his varied refusals. Of course Bartleby refuses to do his job as a copyist, but his refusals go far beyond that, taken to their most extreme in his refusal to eat. While haunting the office, Bartleby lives only on ginger nuts. By the end of the story, when Bartleby has been imprisoned in the prophetically named Tombs, the grubman asks of the lawyer: "'His dinner is ready. Won't he dine to-day, either? Or does he live without dining?' 'Lives without dining,' said [the lawyer], and closed the eyes" (45). Gillian Brown diagnoses Bartleby's refusal to eat as anorexia, which she suggests is a "radical refusal to partake of, and participate in, the world," concluding that "anorexia secures the agoraphobic division of self from world, home from market." Brown ultimately reads Bartleby's behavior as "a repudiation of the market-place and an expression of self-control."[20]

In pointing to the substance of Bartleby's refusal to eat, Brown also implicitly points to the substance of each of his refusals: they are refusals of circulation. After Bartleby has stopped working altogether, the lawyer tries to remove him from his premises. Implementing his doctrine of assumptions, the lawyer leaves Bartleby his remaining wages and, unexpectedly, an "odd twenty" to ensure that Bartleby is not "entirely" destitute (33).[21] When Bartleby refuses to take the bait, the lawyer responds:

> "I am seriously displeased. I am pained, Bartleby. I had thought better of you. I had imagined you of such a gentlemanly organization, that in any delicate dilemma a slight hint would suffice—in short, an assumption. But it appears I am deceived. Why," I added, unaffectedly starting, "you have not even touched that money yet," pointing to it, just where I had left it the evening previous.
>
> (35)

Bartleby thus becomes a particularly troubling puzzle to the lawyer; he seems to want nothing to do with the money at all, even though the wages are rightfully his. But Bartleby's puzzling behavior does not end there, for just as he refuses to take the money, he also refuses to leave the building:

> He answered nothing.
>
> "Will you, or will you not, quit me?" I now demanded in a sudden passion, advancing close to him.
>
> "I would prefer *not* to quit you," he replied, gently emphasizing the *not*.
>
> (35)

While a cursory reading might suggest that the lawyer is requesting that Bartleby quit his job, he has, in fact, asked Bartleby to leave the office (asking him to quit his job being a redundancy since he does no work). Bartleby's refusal is a refusal to quit, that is, to leave. It is, further, a refusal to accept his wages. He will not quit the office nor will he quit—settle accounts—with the lawyer. Bartleby thus refuses to work, to eat, to leave, and even to handle money, and with each refusal he maintains his motionless, emotionless manner, as if refusing as well both movement and affect.[22] Bartleby, in short, refuses every form of circulation in which he is pushed to participate, and his incredible stillness is both part and product of these repeated refusals.

Bartleby's string of refusals is catalyzed by a very specific demand of his job. As a scrivener, Bartleby's job is to reproduce faithfully the documents entrusted to

him and, once those documents are copied, to ensure their accuracy. At the outset of the story, Bartleby does at least part of his job very well: he is a voracious copier. What he prefers not to do, however, is check his own copy or any copy at all. John Carlos Rowe suggests that Bartleby refuses this task because he understands the impossibility of fulfilling the lawyer's demand. For the lawyer, "[a]ll the copies produced in his offices may be reduced to a single purpose that does not change. . . . Every legal document is part of an ideal representational system."[23] In short, the lawyer believes in the idea of an accurate copy. Bartleby, however, seems to think that this "ideal representational system" is a dream, or at least it is not something for which he will vouch. He will produce copies, but he refuses to verify their substitutability for the original.

What Bartleby first prefers not to do, then, is certify relations of equivalence.[24] Indeed, a refusal of circulation is necessarily a refusal of equivalence, for as Marx illustrates through the expanded form of value, circulation is predicated on the infinite substitutability of one commodity for another: "'There can be no exchange without equality.'"[25] In resisting circulation, what Bartleby avoids are these relationships of equality. Thus, we should not understand Bartleby as an alienated worker unless we understand alienation itself as his complaint. Alienation is the representation of one thing's value in something else, which is possible only if these two things can be equated and thus substituted; Bartleby's desire to escape these relations of equivalence, though never overtly declared, is evident in the common core of his various refusals.[26]

It is Bartleby's attempt to break out of these circuits of exchange, to disrupt circulation, that brings me back to the figure of Bartleby, the apparition of the gentlemanly cadaver. Here we can see the stakes of a reading of Marx's theory of value as a theory of figuration. Bartleby is rendered as a figure precisely because of and through his refusal to acquiesce to the equivalent relationships at the heart of circulation, for the figural registers the tropic work necessary to produce the appearance of equivalence. The specters that haunt *Capital* and "#___ Wall Street" are the eerie reminders of all that must be effaced to establish abstract equivalence; they are the "sensuous-nonsensuous" remnants of the production of equivalence through abstraction and reincorporation.

The figure of Bartleby thus disrupts what Marx calls the *warensprache,* the language of the commodity. The warensprache is a simple language, for it is "restricted to a grammatical-syntactic minimum in which only propositions of equality can be formed."[27] Commodity-language thus has but one representation: the equal sign. *Linen = coat* because the two items have been abstracted from sensible things into the suprasensible; they can be equated only because they have been reduced to their lowest common denominator: abstract labor time. The linen and the coat can be so resolutely equated because of the relentless movement of the logic of capital to homogenize the heterogeneous—to produce relations of equivalence.[28] This is precisely the rub of capitalism. Because workers sell their labor power, and not themselves, to the capitalist, the relationship between capitalist and worker is, on its face, a fair one. Marx forcefully asserts that the worker and the capitalist "exchange equivalent for equivalent" (*C,* 280).[29] Marx's "rhetoric of appearance" thus attempts to reveal the injustice of transactions even as they appear, in a capitalist context and logic, to be wholly fair and just. By refusing relations of equivalence, and thereby implying that these equal exchanges are, in fact, unequal, Bartleby denaturalizes these seemingly smooth operations of circulation.

While Bartleby's refusals foreground the spectral at work in the mundane, they are not aimed solely at revealing the disequivalence at work in capitalism, for Bartleby is quite intent on another, related goal: to get out of circulation entirely. Yet if Bartleby's resistance cuts through the logic of capital, Bartleby can never fully escape that logic. Bartleby's desire to get out of circulation ultimately proves impossible, an impossibility shown even in his most direct (and most repeated) refusal: "I would prefer not to." A deferral is embedded in the very grammar of the phrase. "I would prefer not to" is spoken in the conditional. Bartleby never states his preferences so much as states what they *would* be.[30] As a result, "I would prefer not to" becomes what Giorgio Agamben calls the "formula of potentiality."[31] We must surmise that Bartleby imagines this potentiality to be a space outside or beyond circulation. But if "I would prefer not to" expresses a formula of potentiality, it also simultaneously expresses its impossibility. The auxiliary verb "would" defers the action in the sentence, but it also constitutes the statement as a speculative-conditional one. As such, it necessarily implies the logic of the "if . . . then" statement: if such conditions existed, I would prefer X. Such conditional statements indicate specifically those things that are improbable or contrary to fact. Thus, while the conditional allows Bartleby to resist circulation on a grammatical level (through the deferral embedded in the phrase), it simultaneously marks the near impossibility of that resistance.[32]

There is no stronger illustration of this impossibility than Bartleby's ultimate fate. Bartleby's attempt to escape circulation and the relations of equivalence it implies results in his forced inclusion, guaranteed by the secure walls of the Tombs. While it would seem that Bartleby's imprisonment is a kind of fulfilled wish (prisons are designed precisely to prevent the circulation of criminals in the general populace), he clearly

does not read it in this manner, for when the lawyer comes to see him, Bartleby greets him with an "implied suspicion": "'I know you,' he said, without looking round,—'and I want nothing to say to you'" (43). While the penal system may offer what at first appears to be a form of noncirculation, it emerges here as a means of enforcing adherence to the other forms of circulation that Bartleby resists.

The apparent noncirculation in the Tombs, then, should not be misread as the fulfillment of Bartleby's preferences. Indeed, Bartleby's physical imprisonment comes with a fair amount of freedom, for the prison staff "had permitted him freely to wander about the prison, and especially in the inclosed grass-platted yards thereof" (43). Yet even in the relative freedom of this prison, Bartleby chooses again his own version of noncirculation. Rather than walking around the open grass, he turns "his face towards a high wall," in the posture, now so familiar, that he often kept in the offices on Wall Street (43). Bartleby's commitment to his preferences ultimately proves fatal: he dies (presumably of starvation) facing the high prison wall. Crucially, it is not the force of law that kills Bartleby (he would certainly have survived his sentence in the Tombs, particularly after the lawyer bribes the grub-man); it is his own continued commitment to refuse circulation.

We can, in this light, begin to understand the meaning of the Dead Letter Office. **"Bartleby"** ends with "one little item of rumor" offered by the lawyer to readers who have a remaining and pressing "curiosity as to who Bartleby was, and what manner of life he led prior to the present narrator's making his acquaintance" (45). Bartleby "had been a subordinate clerk in the Dead Letter Office at Washington" where letters that have not reached their destination are burned (45). The Dead Letter Office seems to be punishment for those missives that can not be delivered. The logic of the Dead Letter Office insists that those letters that have failed to circulate properly must be destroyed, that is, they must cease to be letters at all. As the lawyer, in a rare moment of perceptiveness, exclaims: "Dead letters! does it not sound like dead men?" (45). Bartleby's sad fate is another lesson in capitalism, one Bartleby himself never learns. If the seemingly equal exchanges of circulation conceal injustices, we cannot respond to these injustices by attempting to get out of circulation. Bartleby's fate makes his critique of circulation all the more pressing, for the story reminds us that a response to the capitalist logic of the lawyer lies not beyond circulation but within it.

"A Rounded and Orbicular Sound"

While we can clearly discern a sense of Bartleby's preferences by looking at his refusals and his ultimate fate, everything we learn about Bartleby comes through the narration of the lawyer. Writing the narrative some years after Bartleby's death, the lawyer is still confused by his strange scrivener and pens his narrative in yet another attempt to make sense of him. In the end, the lawyer will fail spectacularly to understand his scrivener, but this failure itself will help to clarify both Bartleby and **"Bartleby."**

If ultimately the lawyer cannot understand Bartleby, he must be credited with the attempt; in fact, he puts up with a great deal of Bartleby's preferences before leaving him to the punishment of the authorities. He gives Bartleby a prized place in the office; he continues to pay Bartleby for a time even though he does no work; he offers on more than one occasion to help get Bartleby a new job. It cannot be denied that Bartleby has an effect, and a significant one, on the lawyer, and there are moments when the lawyer even seems dimly to understand his strange scrivener.

Musing on his "doctrine of assumptions," the lawyer begins to realize that Bartleby feels no obligation to it:

> The more I thought over my procedure, the more I was charmed with it. Nevertheless, next morning, upon awakening, I had my doubts. . . . It was truly a beautiful thought to have assumed Bartleby's departure; but, after all, that assumption was simply my own, and none of Bartleby's. The great point was, not whether I had assumed that he would quit me, but whether he would prefer so to do. He was more a man of preferences than assumptions.
>
> (34)

Even as the lawyer tries hard not to let Bartleby shake him, his confidence in his "doctrine of assumptions" ultimately gives way to a resigned conclusion that his assumptions are simply his own. "It was hardly possible," the lawyer reasons, "that Bartleby could withstand such an application of the doctrine of assumptions. But upon second thoughts the success of the plan seemed rather dubious" (35). Bartleby's preferences have made their way into the lawyer's psyche to the degree that he finds "[he] had got into the way of involuntarily using this word 'prefer' upon all sorts of not exactly suitable occasions" (31). Despite his own best efforts, the lawyer himself is becoming a man of preferences.

It is not such a surprise that the lawyer finds himself beginning to understand, and even emulate, Bartleby. During Bartleby's employment at the law office, part of the lawyer's income comes from his position as a Master of Chancery. Chancery courts dealt not with questions of law but of equity, of "[j]ustice administered according to fairness as contrasted with the strictly formulated rules of common law." Guided by principles of equity, Chancery judges ruled "based on what was fair in a particular situation" rather than on the more regulated legal code.[33] The difference between the two

courts can be understood as the difference between equality and equity. The law promises equality. Its claim to justice comes from the fact that it "tends to group similar and dissimilar elements together, to decide like and unlike cases by a single standard."[34] Equity, in contrast, involves deciding each case based on its individual circumstances and peculiarities. As a Master of Chancery, then, the lawyer must have some special skill in understanding the uniqueness of a situation. The skills necessary to be a Master of Chancery include the ability to imagine people, events, and concepts in relationships other than simple equality, for it is precisely to remedy the doctrine of sameness under the law that Courts of Equity emerge.[35]

While the lawyer is a Master of Chancery during his interactions with Bartleby, he tells us at the time of the narrative that the "good old office" is "now extinct in the State of New-York" (14).[36] The lawyer's narrative is thus symbolically situated in a space not of equity but of equality. The closing of the Chancery courts prefigures the lawyer's ultimate approach to understanding Bartleby, best represented by his closing salvo: "Ah Bartleby! Ah Humanity!" (45). While Bartleby may begin the text as "a scrivener the strangest [the lawyer] ever saw or heard of," by the end of the text the lawyer, with apparent ease, places Bartleby in a simple synecdochal relationship with humanity at large (13). This relationship suggests that for all his attempts to understand and to come to terms with Bartleby in his strangeness, finally the lawyer can make sense of him only through the logic of the law rather than the logic of equity. The final line is the lawyer's ultimate attempt to account for Bartleby, to bring Bartleby into circuits of meaning that are legible and comfortable to him. Bartleby is transformed into a representative for each of us, his story rendered as a lesson for one and all.[37]

Why is it that the lawyer can finally see in Bartleby not the strange apparition haunting his office but only a representative of and for humanity? To find an answer to this question, I turn to the lawyer's introduction of himself to his readers, for it is in the lawyer's attempt to establish his credibility as a narrator that the root of his inability to understand Bartleby can be unearthed. He boasts that "[a]ll who know me, consider me an eminently *safe* man," suggesting that we too, as readers, should consider him safe and, as a consequence, trust that his narrative does not err or exaggerate. Offered as evidence of this statement is the testimony of John Jacob Astor, who confirms that the lawyer is prudent and methodical. But tellingly, the mention of John Jacob Astor disrupts the lawyer's composed narrative about himself, for he pauses inexplicably to ruminate on the name John Jacob Astor, "a name which, I admit, I love to repeat, for it hath a rounded and orbicular sound to it, and rings like unto bullion" (14).

In this rumination, the lawyer asserts a connection between the name John Jacob Astor and the condition of precious metals prior to their coining. The bullion to which the lawyer refers must be either gold or silver, the two metals used for coin at the time. It seems more probable that he implies gold, however, considering the obvious resonances between John Jacob Astor, the richest man in the United States at the time, and the idea of a gold standard, a standard of value by which to judge all others. In his comparison of John Jacob Astor to bullion, the lawyer seems to want to collapse the two lives of gold—as a precious metal and as money—for bullion is a liminal substance between gold as gold (as a commodity among other commodities) and gold as money. Bullion is, peculiarly, no longer only gold, earmarked as it is for coining, nor is it yet coin, having not yet borne the imprint or inscription that will transform it from a commodity into money.[38] Yet the lawyer's own construction seems intent on fixing the identity of bullion, for he asserts not only that the name John Jacob Astor "rings like unto bullion" but also that it has a "rounded and orbicular" sound. The lawyer thinks of language as a kind of money—specifically, he thinks of words as coins, for he speaks of the sound of Astor's name in figurative language that conjures up an image of coinage. The figure is strange and complex, mixing the aural and the visual, for John Jacob Astor's name sounds the way coins look (and the way bullion certainly does not). The lawyer's collapsing of bullion into coin is evinced in the very structure of the sentence: the oblique reference to coin precedes the reference to bullion. "John Jacob Astor" has "a rounded and orbicular sound" before it is even compared to bullion. For the lawyer, then, the relationship of bullion to coin can be assumed, even as, for the reader, that relationship must work through a different logical progression—we do not read the "rounded and orbicular sound" as coin except insofar as we re-read it. Only when returning to the phrase after reading the bullion simile does the imagery become clear. This is, perhaps, a modified form of the very doctrine of assumptions so often associated with the lawyer. Debating whether Bartleby will have left the office after being instructed to do so, the lawyer asserts: "Yes, as before I had prospectively assumed that Bartleby would depart, so now I might retrospectively assume that departed he was" (35). For the lawyer, there is absolutely no possibility for disconnection in his logic: I assumed that he will depart and thus I can assume that he has departed. Foresight seamlessly becomes hindsight, and assumptions can be taken as facts. Just as the lawyer rhetorically erases the gap between assumption and fact—or between copy and original—so too he erases the gap between bullion and coin.

What the lawyer does not see, of course, is that bullion is not yet money precisely because it has not yet been coined. It does not yet bear the symbolic imprint of the State (traditionally a visual depiction of the sovereign)

that guarantees its value. The lawyer imagines either that he does not need any symbol to transform bullion into coin or that there is no possibility for error in the transformation of bullion into coin, believing, as he does, in a kind of teleological fallacy wherein bullion is always already coin. In so doing, the lawyer elides the specifically figural genesis of money.[39] The lawyer has been mesmerized by this "dazzling money-form" and thus misunderstands the genealogy of money or, rather, refuses to admit that money has a genealogy at all (*C*, 139). When the lawyer asserts that bullion is coin, he short-circuits the very processes of figuration that enable bullion to *become* coin.[40]

Bartleby is thus unreadable to the lawyer precisely because he, too, is a figure. For the lawyer, Bartleby will always be the "unaccountable Bartleby": the lawyer's system of reasoning cannot *account* for him, cannot insert him into a system of economic calculation (37). Bartleby does not and cannot make sense within the lawyer's system of reasoning because the lawyer can speak only the warensprache, which denies, even as it relies on, the figural. Bartleby is ultimately so troubling to the lawyer because he suggests that the lawyer's logic—the logic of capitalism—is not as consistent and seamless as it appears.[41] As in Marx's *Capital*, the specter embodies the necessary figuration in the production of value, a figuration that must be effaced, but that can never fully be effaced. Thus, when the specter of Bartleby throws the lawyer's logic into crisis by refusing to be accounted for, the lawyer resorts to his own act of figuration, which functions only to reinstitute the warensprache through abstract equivalence: "Ah Bartleby! Ah Humanity!"

POSTSCRIPT: "ONE LITTLE ITEM OF RUMOR"

We should be cautious of the Dead Letter Office. The questionable genealogy of the story the lawyer tells in his postscript suggests that its meaning is up for grabs. And the lawyer makes the most of his opportunity. He seems to imagine in the Dead Letter Office not the charred remains of misdirected missives but wholly and completely legible objects that find, in the lawyer, perhaps not their intended reader but a reader nonetheless:

> Sometimes from out of the folded paper the pale clerk takes a ring:—the finger it was meant for, perhaps, moulders in the grave; a bank-note sent in swiftest charity:—he whom it would relieve, nor eats nor hungers any more; pardon for those who died despairing; hope for those who died unhoping; good tidings for those who died stifled by unrelieved calamities.

(45)

In constructing a series of tragic scenarios of letters sent and never received, the lawyer inserts himself into this postal circuit of his own design. In his imagined Dead Letter Office, a dead letter never fully falls out of circulation; someone, in this case the lawyer himself, will intercept and make meaning of the waylaid missive. For the lawyer, these circuits of exchange may not operate as planned, but they will not break down. The lawyer cannot help but try to make these lost letters meaningful, just as he cannot help but try to make sense of Bartleby.

I want to close, however, by offering a different Dead Letter Office, where the letters really are dead, where the letters remain unread, where their messages remain untransmitted. I want, that is, to work against the lawyer's desire for legibility both of the letters and of Bartleby himself. Bartleby's desire not to circulate extends to the sphere of interpretation, and the Dead Letter Office marks his desire to remain the "unaccountable" Bartleby, not to be brought into circuits of recognizable meaning. The desire, as it seems with all Bartleby's desires, is an impossible one, an impossibility marked by the structure of the story itself, for we have Bartleby's story only through the meaning-making efforts of the lawyer. (The predicament, of course, is only redoubled by my own, or any, reading of the text.) This desire for illegibility is another manifestation of Bartleby's resistance to relations of equivalence, and it reminds us that we cannot easily or carelessly make Bartleby into a representative, for Bartleby is, to put it mildly, an unwilling delegate. We should be all the more cautious of making Bartleby a representative when we consider that the lawyer uses the Dead Letter Office to explain his strange scrivener once and for all as the ultimate representative: "Ah Bartleby! Ah Humanity!" This language of abstract equivalence transforms Bartleby's strangeness into the commonplace; it obscures the fact that Bartleby is a weird figure, and that **"Bartleby"** is a weird tale. The lawyer's move is instructive, suggesting that it is precisely in making Bartleby into a representative of or for someone or something that we are in danger of losing his strangeness, and thereby of losing precisely what makes Bartleby, Bartleby.

While those readings of the story that see in the scrivener simply a representative of and for alienated workers surely have political aims at odds with the lawyer's, they too sacrifice Bartleby's strangeness by making him into a representative. In this respect, they recapitulate the lawyer's attempts to return Bartleby to seamless circuits of equivalence and, as a result, remain unable to make sense of Bartleby himself. More broadly, this mode of reading unwittingly recapitulates the gestures of abstract equivalence used in the service of capital, and thus cannot help but be invested in the very same seamless logic that the lawyer holds so dear. Like the lawyer, this reading takes the process of abstraction as perfect, in which bullion is always already coin and the "weird" Bartleby can ultimately be recuperated back into "a portrait from life."

Reading Marx's theory of value as a theory of figuration allows us to retain, as much as possible, the eeriness of Bartleby, to avoid making him into something he is not, for whatever political goals—to avoid, in other words, a kind of exploitation of representation. In this reading of Marx, a portrait of life under capitalism is necessarily also a weird tale, one in which we are constantly haunted by the specters of abstraction and incorporation, and things are never as they seem. And while Bartleby himself can never get out of circulation (except, of course, through death), the story testifies to the success, even if only partial, of his resistance. For if Bartleby's aim is to disrupt the apparently smooth running of a logic of abstract equivalence, the story itself records and reenacts just such a disruption, giving us the story of how a strange scrivener turns the "snug retreat" of the lawyer upside down (14). If, then, we are to continue to think of **"Bartleby"** as a text in conversation with Marxism—as I think we should—we must begin to look inside the four claustrophobic walls of "#___ Wall Street" and see the specters that haunt it.

Notes

I am deeply indebted to several people whose thoughtful comments on this essay greatly improved it: David Eng, Stephanie Foote, David Kazanjian, Rosalind Morris, and Joseph Valente. For his tireless commitment to seeing this essay through, I am particularly grateful to Zachary Lesser.

1. Herman Melville, "Bartleby, the Scrivener: A Story of Wall Street," in *The Piazza Tales and Other Prose Pieces, 1839-1860,* vol. 9 of *The Writings of Herman Melville,* ed. Harrison Hayford, Alma A. MacDougall, and G. Thomas Tanselle (Chicago: Northwestern Univ. Press and the Newberry Library, 1987), 13; further references to "Bartleby, the Scrivener" are to this edition and will be cited parenthetically.

2. *Boston Evening Traveller,* 3 June 1856; *United States Magazine and Democratic Review,* September 1836; both reprinted in *Herman Melville: The Contemporary Reviews,* ed. Brian Higgins and Hershel Parker (New York: Cambridge Univ. Press, 1995), 473, 482, respectively.

3. J. E. A. Smith, *(Pittsfield, Mass.) Berkshire County Eagle,* 30 May 1856; reprinted in *Herman Melville: The Contemporary Reviews,* ed. Higgins and Parker, 472.

4. For other Marxist readings of the text, see Michael T. Gilmore, *American Romanticism and the Marketplace* (Chicago: Univ. of Chicago Press, 1985), 132-45; and James C. Wilson, "'Bartleby': The Walls of Wall Street," *Arizona Quarterly* 37 (winter 1981): 335-46.

5. Louise K. Barnett, "Bartleby as Alienated Worker," *Studies in Short Fiction* 11 (fall 1974): 379.

6. Dan McCall, *The Silence of Bartleby* (Ithaca, N.Y.: Cornell Univ. Press, 1989), 61-63, 110-13.

7. David Kuebrich, "Melville's Doctrine of Assumptions: The Hidden Ideology of Capitalist Production in 'Bartleby,'" *New England Quarterly* 69 (September 1996): 381-84.

8. Barbara Foley, "From Wall Street to Astor Place: Historicizing Melville's 'Bartleby,'" *American Literature* 72 (March 2000): 88.

9. Sheila Post-Lauria, "Canonical Texts and Context: The Example of Herman Melville's 'Bartleby, the Scrivener: A Story of Wall Street,'" *College Literature* 20 (June 1993): 198.

10. Marvin Hunt, "'That's the Word': Turning Tongues and Heads in 'Bartleby, the Scrivener,'" *ESQ: A Journal of the American Renaissance* 40 (fourth quarter, 1994): 278, 277.

11. Karl Marx, *Capital: Volume 1,* trans. Ben Fowkes (New York: Penguin, 1990), 125. Further references are to this edition and will be cited parenthetically as *C.*

12. Diane Elson chastises theorists who see value as a theory of labor time, a construction in which value is determined by the amount of labor put into an individual object. Such a notion fails to attend to Marx's insistence on value as a measure of *abstract* social labor. The value of a commodity is not determined by the individual labor manifested in the thing itself but by the amount of labor considered socially necessary to produce the commodity. Perhaps a weaver is able to produce linen in five hours, but the socially necessary labor time to produce the same amount is six hours. The weaver is thus more efficient than the standard. Yet when that linen goes on the market, it will sell at the six-hour price, not at the five-hour price. Marx's point is that price is determined (though not guaranteed) by the abstract social labor time in the commodity, a figure determined in very small part by the particular labor in the commodity, insofar as it is itself labor and so factored into abstract labor. The correspondence between individual labor and price exists but is difficult to discern, giving rise to the idea that the system itself controls values, rather than the individual labor of the producers ("The Value Theory of Labour," in *Value: The Representation of Labour in Capitalism,* ed. Diane Elson [London: CSE Books, 1979], 115-80).

13. Marx's insistence on a form of value apart from value itself comes from Hegel. Jairus Banaji notes that in his *Science of Logic,* Hegel asserts that we must think of a thing as a combination of what he calls essence and form. "Precisely," Hegel writes,

"because *form is as essential to essence* as essence to itself, essence must not be grasped and expressed merely as essence . . . but as form also" (quoted in "From the Commodity to Capital: Hegel's Dialectic in Marx's *Capital,*" in *Value,* ed. Elson, 19). Hegel's formulation suggests that essence understood without form "remains devoid of any form of appearance, hence something purely abstract and hypothetical." Further, if essence is understood without form, there can be no bridge between form and essence, leaving "a world of appearances, divorced from any principle." Hegel's formulation thus allows one to conceptualize both a realm of abstraction and its relationship to the world of appearance, to the material (Banaji, "From the Commodity to Capital," 21).

14. Once relations of equivalence are made in the abstract, they must then carry over into material reality. This material reality, however, cannot be mistaken for value. Value remains, resolutely, in the abstract. The material form, the "form of appearance" of value, is exchange-value. Value and exchange-value are therefore not synonyms, though exchange-value is determined by value. The process by which value is transformed into exchange-value is by no means easily determined. Called the "transformation problem," it has long puzzled and motivated Marxist theorists of value (see Paul Sweezy, "Marxian Value Theory and Crises," *The Value Controversy,* ed. Ian Steedman [London: Verso, 1981], 25).

15. Thomas Keenan, "The Point Is to (Ex)Change It: Reading *Capital,* Rhetorically," in *Fetishism as Cultural Discourse,* ed. Emily Apter and William Pietz (Ithaca, N.Y.: Cornell Univ. Press, 1993), 174.

16. Ibid., 176.

17. Werner Hamacher, "Lingua Amissa: The Messianism of Commodity-Language and Derrida's *Specters of Marx,*" trans. Kelly Barry, in *Ghostly Demarcations: A Symposium on Jacques Derrida's* Specters of Marx, ed. Michael Sprinker (New York: Verso, 1999), 171.

18. Jacques Derrida, *Specters of Marx,* trans. Peggy Kamuf (New York: Routledge, 1994), 7. For Derrida, the figure of the specter offers a critique of ontology by offering a somewhat tongue-in-cheek "hauntology." The specter returns from where— the future? the past? We cannot be certain, and it is this uncertainty that implicitly critiques any notion of presence. Derrida critiques Marx in particular by suggesting that Marx believes the advent of communism will be a time when we shall be, as Aijaz Ahmad describes it, "free of all social contradictions, [when] the self shall fully coincide

with itself, and being and consciousness shall be one and the same" ("Reconciling Derrida: 'Specters of Marx' and Deconstructive Politics," in *Ghostly Demarcations,* ed. Sprinker, 94). Gayatri Chakravorty Spivak critiques Derrida's reading of Marx, charging that Derrida attends only to the Marx before *Grundrisse* and *Capital,* before, that is, Marx had "discovered the secret of industrial capitalism: the creation of surplus value through labor-power as commodity." She further suggests that Derrida portrays "a silly Marx, who thinks use is good and exchange bad, that use-value is 'proper to man.'" Spivak suggests instead that Marx understood that the social *is* spectral—and that communism is not about propriety or a space without spectrality but about using the spectrality of the social to benefit all rather than a select few. "In capital's subject," Spivak explains, "[the ghostliness is] poison; for the social subject, medicine" ("Ghostwriting," *Diacritics* 25 [summer 1995]: 72, 74, 75).

19. Derrida, *Specters,* 150.

20. Gillian Brown, "The Empire of Agoraphobia," *Representations* 20 (fall 1987): 147, 149. Brown also incisively links agoraphobia with the development of the market economy. Looking at psychological case histories from Melville's time, she notes a preponderance of instances in which growing technological advances, particularly in transportation and communication, are cited as the causes of agoraphobia. "In this context," she concludes, "agoraphobia, the anxiety and immobility occasioned by the space and scope of streets, by the appurtenances and avenues of traffic, is an anticommercial condition—literally, fear of the marketplace" (136).

21. We should not take the lawyer's charity as pure generosity. He helps Bartleby, if not wholly then at least in part, because he imagines it to be a smart economic transaction: "If I turn him away, the chances are he will fall in with some less indulgent employer, and then he will be rudely treated, and perhaps driven forth miserably to starve. Yes. Here I can cheaply purchase a delicious self-approval. To befriend Bartleby; to humor him in his strange willfulness, will cost me little or nothing" (23). The lawyer's charity is a profit-making enterprise: "delicious self-approval" for little or no cost.

22. Bartleby does have a "savings' bank" that the lawyer finds when rummaging through Bartleby's desk (28). Yet while the lawyer imagines this to be a savings bank, it seems probable that Bartleby would not characterize it in the same way. A savings bank implies the saving of money for future use. Since Bartleby stops using money altogether,

it would seem that he has a collection of money only because he refuses to use it *as* money, not because he is saving it for future use. Strictly speaking, then, Bartleby's collection of coins is not a savings bank, if a savings bank is a way of saving money. Because Bartleby seems to have no intention of using the money, the coins have stopped being money (at least while Bartleby holds onto them), in the same way that collectible coins are not money for the collector, their having been withdrawn from circulation.

23. John Carlos Rowe, *Through the Custom-House: Nineteenth-Century American Fiction and Modern Theory* (Baltimore: Johns Hopkins Univ. Press, 1982), 122. Rowe notes as well that the copying that the lawyer asks Bartleby to do "substitutes a writing of pure repetition in order to control the subversive movement of signification that relies on the absence of a signified and thus denies any pure mastery or original authority" (122).

24. It is telling, then, that the grub-man in the Tombs confesses to the lawyer: "Well now, upon my word, I thought that friend of yourn was a gentleman forger; they are always pale and genteel-like, them forgers" (44). In some sense, Bartleby is a forger, at least when evaluated by the logic of the lawyer. If Bartleby produces copies that are meant to be perfect substitutes for originals (an ideal copy is not recognizable as such) but refuses to verify their authenticity, perhaps he is guilty of a kind of forgery, of attempting to pass off "bad" copies as "good" ones, or, certain to be even more troubling to the lawyer, of refusing to recognize any difference between the two.

25. Aristotle, quoted in Marx, *Capital,* 151.

26. Indeed, we cannot understand Bartleby's refusal as a refusal simply of work, for when the lawyer offers to find Bartleby other employment, Bartleby rejects his ideas not on the grounds that he does not want to work but, rather, that the work the lawyer proposes is unsuitable to him. When asked if he would like to be a bartender, Bartleby replies: "I would not like it at all; though, as I said before, I am not particular." Asked by the lawyer about being a bill collector, he hones his objection: "No, I would prefer to be doing something else" (41). Bartleby's resistance is thus not a resistance to work per se—for he would prefer to do "something else," a something that is, presumably, work—but a resistance, if we can take his other refusals as evidence, to entering into the economy, into circulation.

27. Hamacher, "Lingua Amissa," 170.

28. As Gayatri Spivak notes, "Money conceals the heterogeneity of social relations irretrievably by substituting the category of (mis)-substitution for

(necessarily asymmetrical) exchange" ("Marx after Derrida," in *Philosophical Approaches to Literature: New Essays on Nineteenth- and Twentieth-Century Texts,* ed. William E. Cain [Lewisburg, Pa.: Bucknell Univ. Press, 1984], 231-32).

29. In Spivak's reading of *Capital* and of Marx more generally, she suggests that the disequivalence at the heart of capitalism is predicated on the super-adequation of laborers to themselves. The fact that laborers can produce more value than they consume is the basis for surplus and thus profit ("Marx after Derrida," 240-41).

30. This grammatical construction is ideal for Bartleby, as it allows him to refuse without refusing, to act without acting; his preferences are themselves refusals of any form of action. There are several moments in the text when Bartleby alters his phrase, uttering "I prefer not" instead. He uses this modified phrase only when pushed by the lawyer to answer in some language other than preference. Bartleby thus drops the "would" in order to placate the lawyer, suggesting that "would" indeed functions to make Bartleby's response as inactive as possible.

31. Giorgio Agamben, "Bartleby, or On Contingency," *Potentialities: Collected Essays in Philosophy,* trans. Daniel Heller-Roazen (Stanford, Calif.: Stanford Univ. Press), 255. Agamben analyzes Bartleby's preferences in opposition to the philosophical tradition of will. The lawyer, after Bartleby refuses to go to the post office, asks him: "You *will* not?" Bartleby, however, refuses not only the request but also the grammatical construction: "I *prefer* not," he replies (25). Agamben suggests that Bartleby's refusal of the verb *will* "calls into question precisely this supremacy of the will over potentiality" (254). In preferring rather than willing, Bartleby remains wholly outside the logic of the lawyer, so much so that Agamben suggests that Bartleby's potentiality "creates its own ontology" (259). Such a reading, while persuasive in some respects, is ultimately at odds with mine. While perhaps Bartleby imagines he will exist in a state of pure potentiality, this desire is proven by the text to be a fantasy.

32. "I would prefer not to" undoes Bartleby's preferences in another way as well. As Ann Smock notes, "[I]f *to prefer* means to incline toward one thing rather than another . . . it also means to pay one among a number of creditors before, or even to the exclusion of, all others. *Preference* means the act of so quitting a particular debt first, or the right to receive what is owed you before any other creditor does" ("Quiet," *Qui Parle* 2 [fall 1988]: 71). The OED gives a definition of *to prefer,* in addition to its more commonplace one, as "To give preference to as a creditor" (7b), a definition in working use in England until at least 1885. This double meaning of "to prefer" means that at those moments when Bartleby fashions himself as most outside circuits of exchange he is also squarely within them. Smock points specifically to Nipper's use of the term to illustrate this usage in the text: "Nippers exclaims . . . 'I'd prefer *him* [Bartleby]! I'd give him *his* preferences!' Nippers would pay Bartleby, straight away, everything he has coming to him" ("Quiet," 71).

33. *Black's Law Dictionary,* 5th ed. (1979), s.v. "Equity." A Master of Chancery serves as an investigator for such cases, helping the judge of the court render fair decisions based on the facts the Master uncovers. The investigatory aspect of the lawyer's role as Master of Chancery can be read back onto the story itself. The lawyer throughout the story investigates Bartleby; the text is the "report" of his investigations.

34. Joseph Valente, *James Joyce and the Problem of Justice: Negotiating Sexual and Colonial Difference* (New York: Cambridge Univ. Press, 1995), 2. Valente convincingly argues that justice should be understood as the perpetual oscillation between the law and equity, which he discusses as a difference between equity under the law and equity of the law (1-48).

35. *Black's Law Dictionary* states that the object of courts of equity is "to render the administration of justice more complete, by affording relief where the courts of law are incompetent to give it, or to give it with effect, or by exercising certain branches of jurisdiction independently of them" (s.v. "Equity").

36. Barbara Foley notes that the Chancery courts were abolished in 1846 when the New York state constitution was revised. They closed the following year when the new constitution went into effect ("From Wall Street to Astor Place," 89).

37. For it to be legible in some way, the story of Bartleby must be a story told by the lawyer, for Bartleby's continued attempts to withdraw himself from multiple economies mean that he must also withdraw from the linguistic one. He cannot narrate his own preferences in order to remain faithful to them. When pressed by the lawyer to detail what he would like to do if not copying, Bartleby is unable to articulate any alternative desires—indeed, his desire is illegible insofar as it is a desire to exist outside the common systems of circulation, which include language.

38. Barbara Foley suggests, based on historical references in the text, that the action of "Bartleby" must have taken place in New York City in the

1840s ("From Wall Street to Astor Place"). According to Margaret G. Myers, in the 1840s the currency was composed "largely of bank notes so subject to depreciation that no merchant could safely accept them before consulting his 'Banknote Detector' to determine their probable value." After the collapse of the Second Bank of the United States, there was no central authority that issued currency; so each state bank issued its own. In 1847, Congress passed a bill mandating that government officers accept only gold and silver coin as part of an attempt by "hard-money" Democrats to ensure that the currency of the nation did not become wholly paper. Clearly, the lawyer was not alone in his belief in gold (*Financial History of the United States* [New York: Columbia Univ. Press, 1970], 121, 131-34).

39. With money, as Marx points out, the specter of exchange-value develops into a further spectralized form and is "replaced by a symbol of itself." Whereas exchange-value hides a history of abstraction, we can speak of money as figural in that it hides its own history as a body, as a material commodity like any other (*Grundrisse,* trans. Martin Nicolaus [New York: Penguin, 1993], 144).

40. The lawyer thus engages in a kind of revisionist history similar to the approach of metaphysical philosophers to language that Derrida critiques in "White Mythology." Derrida compares the erosion of philosophical language to the erosion of the imprint on a coin, a process that allows the figuration inherent in philosophical language to be "no longer noticed." Metaphorical meaning is then taken for "proper meaning," through a deliberate forgetting that allows one to think of language (or economic value) "not as a displacement with breaks, as reinscriptions in a heterogeneous system, mutations, separations without origin" but as a continuous system (in *Margins of Philosophy,* trans. Alan Bass [Chicago: Univ. of Chicago Press, 1982], 211, 215). The lawyer's logic can only function within a belief in such a continuous system, for only if this system is continuous can he regularly elide it: bullion *is* coin.

41. Such a charge would be particularly troubling to the lawyer, convinced as he is of his fairness. The lawyer is so committed to his own self-image as fair—and thus not exploitative—that he is quite bothered not only by Bartleby's refusal to work but also by Bartleby as a voracious copier. The motionlessness of Bartleby—so pronounced as to be the first detail the lawyer notices—contrasts sharply with his performance on the job, for "[a]t first Bartleby did an extraordinary quantity of writing. As if long famishing for something to copy, he seemed to gorge himself on my documents.

There was no pause for digestion. He ran a day and night line, copying by sun-light and by candle-light" (19). Bartleby is, strangely, both motionless and a voracious copier: a motionless, voracious copier. It is not that Bartleby is motionless only when not copying; rather, the lawyer complains of Bartleby's work precisely through the qualities of his motion: "he wrote on silently, palely, mechanically" (20). Bartleby may have to move to copy, but he does so as little—and as inhumanly—as possible. In cataloging his dissatisfaction with Bartleby, the lawyer complains of Bartleby's motionless copying on an emotional register: "I should have been quite delighted with his application, had he been cheerfully industrious" (19-20). It is not that the lawyer feels that Bartleby is sullen rather than cheerful, angry rather than happy, but that he expresses no emotion whatsoever. Bartleby is as "unaffected" when he is a voracious copier as when he stops copying altogether. It is wholly plausible—in fact, probable—that on first encountering Bartleby, one would associate his endless copying and his lack of affect not with a resistant worker but with a kind of ideal—even if monstrous—one. Bartleby works tirelessly without any emotions that might distract him. In fact, Bartleby seems never to leave the office (he copies "a day and night line, copying by sun-light and candle-light"). And yet the lawyer finds this ideal worker unsettling, for through Bartleby-the-voracious-copier, the lawyer sees what he imagines to be the naturalness of capitalism pushed to its logical extreme, an extreme that reveals not the "Eden of the innate rights of man" that capitalism appears to be (*C,* 280) but a worker so single-minded and tireless that he has become almost inhuman.

Corey Evan Thompson (essay date summer 2004)

SOURCE: Thompson, Corey Evan. "Melville's 'Cock-A-Doodle-Doo!.'" *Explicator* 62, no. 4 (summer 2004): 201-04.

[*In the following essay, Thompson deduces that the narrator murdered Merrymusk in "Cock-A-Doodle-Doo!" during a manic phase of bipolar disorder.*]

In his 1990 essay on Herman Melville's short story **"Cock-A-Doodle-Doo!"** (1853), Philip Young poses a vital yet largely unconsidered and heretofore unanswered question concerning the conclusion of Melville's tale (Young 346): What is the cause of Merrymusk's death? The most logical postmortem analysis would be to suggest some type of degenerative illness or perhaps old age, a vague and largely unsubstantiated diagnosis that has been embraced by critics including Richard Harter Fogle (30). Upon closer examination, however, the text dismisses such conclusions. Although his wife is an invalid and their children are ill—"one child had the white-swelling, and the rest were rickety" (Melville 89)—Merrymusk appears in relatively good health. After all, "his family never suffered for lack of food. He worked hard and brought it to them" (95). It seems illogical that someone suffering from a terminal illness, or even old age, would be able to perform tasks requiring such constant physical exertion. Merrymusk's death, therefore, must be caused by something other than an unnamed illness or natural causes.

Understanding the narrator and his condition is vital for understanding the cause of Merrymusk's death. In the early moments of the story, the narrator claims that he suffers from hypochondria (75), a condition that the *OED* defines as "a morbid state of mind, characterized by general depression, melancholy, or low spirits, for which there is no real cause." As I have argued elsewhere, however, "the narrator has more than enough reason for his dejection and, therefore, cannot be legitimately classified as a hypochondriac" (Thompson 44-45). As opposed to hypochondria, as I have argued further, the narrator exhibits all of the unmistakable symptoms of what is currently known as bipolar disorder, or manic depression. This diagnosis may provide valuable insight into the cause of Merrymusk's death.

As Thomas Freeman's research on bipolar disorder demonstrates, manic depressives may become excessively violent in word or action when they are frustrated (257). Throughout **"Cock-A-Doodle-Doo!"** the narrator is extremely frustrated because his offers to buy the rooster from Merrymusk are continually denied (90, 92). As would be expected, this frustration causes him to become verbally abusive. After Merrymusk refuses to sell the rooster to the narrator for $500, for instance, a ten-fold increase of the narrator's initial offer, the narrator shouts at Merrymusk "in a rage" (92). Although this episode clearly demonstrates that the narrator is verbally abusive, I would argue that the narrator is physically abusive as well and that the physical abuse he performs causes Merrymusk's death. At the story's conclusion, the narrator, in a state of mania and filled with frustration, commits murder.

In addition to his manic depression, a variety of other factors may explain the narrator's action. For the three days preceding Merrymusk's death, for instance, the narrator continually drinks stout (95) and, as a result, presumably arrives at Merrymusk's house inebriated. Moreover, earlier in the tale the narrator experiences an hallucination, another key indicator of manic depression (*Bipolar Disorder* 7-8), that urges him to murder the dun, or bill collector: "Hark! the crow again. Plain as cock could speak, it said, 'Hang the process, and hang

the fellow that sent it! If you have not land or cash, go and thrash the fellow, and tell him you never mean to pay him'" (87). All of these factors inhibit the narrator's ability to think rationally and, in the end, cause him to exert his frustration in a psychotic and homicidal episode.

When the narrator arrives at Merrymusk's home, he sees him lying on a heap of old clothes (95). With no apparent justification, the narrator subsequently states, not asks: "'You are sick, Merrymusk'" (95). Merrymusk's response, however, is "'No, I am well'" (95). He later asserts that his family is also well, words that are, as the narrator tells us, "shouted forth in a kind of wild ecstasy of *triumph over ill*" (95, emphasis added), a statement suggesting that Merrymusk is in good health. After the narrator hears these words and recognizes the forcefulness with which they are uttered, he claims that "[i]t was too much" (95). Is it possible that the narrator, out of sheer frustration, in a state of mania, and under the influence of a hallucination that already prompted him to murder (80), proceeds to murder Merrymusk? The narrator's behavior subsequent to this event suggests that he realizes that he has done something horrible. Once we learn that "Merrymusk was dead" (95), for instance, the narrator is seized by an "awful fear" (95).

Other notable episodes near the story's conclusion support the claim of murder. In addition to having motive, not being able to obtain the rooster, the narrator has ample opportunity for committing this heinous crime. Merrymusk's house, for instance, is isolated from civilization. In fact, we are told that "[n]o one seemed to know where it was exactly" (90). Moreover, the narrator has detailed knowledge of their remote burial site: "If you visit that hilly region, you will see, nigh the railroad track, just beneath October Mountain, on the other side of the swamp—there you will see a gravestone, not with skull and cross-bones, but with a lusty cock in act of crowing" (96). This is the place where, as the narrator himself tells us in a seemingly inadvertent admission, "[he] buried them" (96). Burying Merrymusk and his family in such isolation seems like a curious decision. A curious decision, that is, unless he is attempting to hide a crime.

Works Cited

Centre for Addiction and Mental Health. *Bipolar Disorder.* Toronto: Centre for Addiction and Mental Health, 2000.

Compact Edition of the Oxford English Dictionary. Vol. 1. Oxford: Oxford UP, 1989.

Freeman, Thomas. "Observations on Mania." *Manic-Depressive Illness: History of a Syndrome.* Ed. Edward A. Wolpert. New York: International Universities Press, 1977. 257-70.

Fogle, Richard Harter. *Melville's Shorter Tales*. Norman: U of Oklahoma P, 1960.

Melville, Herman. "Cock-A-Doodle-Doo!" 1853. *Great Short Works of Herman Melville*. Ed. and intro. Warner Berthoff. New York: Harper and Row, 1969. 75-97.

Thompson, Corey Evan. "Melville's 'Cock-A-Doodle-Doo!': A Case Study in Bipolar Disorder." *American Transcendental Quarterly* 17 (2003): 43-53.

Young, Philip. "Experimental Melville: 'Cock-Eye-Doodle-Dee!'" *American Transcendental Quarterly* 4 (1990): 343-52.

Corey Thompson (essay date spring 2005)

SOURCE: Thompson, Corey. "Did Melville Write 'The Death Craft'?" *ANQ* 18, no. 2 (spring 2005): 41-5.

[*In the following essay, Thompson provides further evidence of Melville's authorship of the pseudonymously published "The Death Craft" based on narrative and phrasing affinities between that text and* Moby-Dick.]

The Gothic-inspired short story **"The Death Craft"** was published under the pseudonym Harry the Reefer on 16 November 1839 in Lansingburgh, New York's *Democratic Press*. It has since come to be regarded by some as the work of Herman Melville.[1] Those who accept and promote this ascription include Martin Leonard Pops, who believes that Melville "undoubtedly" wrote the story (327), Leon Howard (29), Harry Levin (168), and Edwin Haviland Miller (69, 109, 114, 302).[2] As is sometimes the case when authorship is assigned to a pseudonymously published work, however, not all scholars unequivocally agree with this attribution. Newton Arvin, James E. Miller, Jr., Victor-Lévy Beaulieu, and David Kirby, for instance, all fail to discuss the story in any capacity in their respective biographical and critical Melville studies. In *Melville's Early Life and* Reburn, William H. Gilman describes the possibility that Melville wrote **"The Death Craft"** as "unlikely" (327-84). Although Jay Leyda reprints an excerpt from the story and lists it as Melville's in *The Melville Log*, he does so hesitantly (97).[3] Most recently, Hershel Parker refuses to assign definitive authorship to anyone: "Whoever wrote ['**The Death Craft**'] probably took no more time on it than Herman would have taken; there is no reason it could not have been his and no reason to think no one else could have written it" (154).

Although the authorship of **"The Death Craft"** has elicited frequent commentary among Melville scholars, only Warren F. Broderick, in his 1986 publication "'Their Snowy Whiteness Dazzled My Eyes': 'The Death Craft'—Melville's First Maritime Story," and

Merton M. Sealts, Jr., in his pithy 1987 "Notes on 'The Death Craft,'" provide any substantial evidence to justify the story's ascription to Melville. Both Broderick and Sealts lend their support on the premise that "the case for attributing **'The Death Craft'** to Melville must necessarily rest chiefly on parallels in theme and especially in phraseology with the earlier **'Fragments [from a Writing Desk]**,'" Melville's first publication that also appeared in the *Democratic Press* six months prior to **"The Death Craft,"** "and also with later works such as *Mardi* (1849), *Redburn* (1849), and **'Benito Cereno'** (1855)" (Sealts 782). Broderick and Sealts certainly strengthen Melville's case through their cogent delineation of the incontrovertible similarities between **"The Death Craft"** and Melville's works; however, a comprehensive examination of the short story's undeniable relationship to *Moby-Dick* is notably lacking.[4] Therefore, following the example of Broderick and Sealts, I seek to provide further evidence of Melville's authorship of **"The Death Craft."**

"The Death Craft" and *Moby-Dick* contain undeniable affinities in narrative and phraseology. Both narrators, for instance, are deeply affected by whiteness. The unnamed narrator of **"The Death Craft"** is "dazzled" by the whiteness of the ship's sail (424), whereas Ishmael is "appalled" by the whiteness of the whale (188). Storms also occur in **"The Death Craft"** and *Moby-Dick,* as they do in such works as *Redburn* and *White-Jacket*; however, the way in which the ship in **"The Death Craft"** and the *Pequod* are affected by the storms are highly correlative. After being battered by the winds, the ship in **"The Death Craft"** "made a tremendous lurch to port and lay trembling on her beam-ends" (426). This is analogous to the *Pequod*'s near sinking in "The Musket" (chapter 123) as the storm's gales reduce it to "a tossed shuttle-cock" (513). Moreover, the tempestuous sea in **"The Death Craft"** is described as "milk-white" (426), which is nearly identical to its depiction in "The Whiteness of the Whale" (chapter 42), where it is described as a "milky sea" (194) with "milky whiteness" (193).[5] Furthermore, the "milk white crest" of the sea's waves in **"The Death Craft"** conjures up the image of Moby Dick's "hump like a snow-hill" (547) rising from the water in "The Chase—First Day" (chapter 133).

Although such parallels are suggestive of Melville's authorship, more striking ones exist between **"The Death Craft"** and *Moby-Dick*'s ninety-sixth chapter, "The Try-Works." They are so similar in terms of narrative and phraseology, in fact, that they not only attest to Melville's authorship but also suggest that the former is an early, albeit juvenile, version of the latter. Early in **"The Death Craft,"** for instance, the narrator stands on the ship's deck under the sun that is "pouring forth a heat only known in torrid climes" (424). The heat is so intense that it causes him to feel as though he has "coals of fire [. . .] in [his eye] sockets" (425). Shortly thereafter, he passes under the ship's helm and observes "the helmsman lying athwartships abaft the wheel" (425). Ishmael experiences similar events in "The Try-Works." He feels "the red heat of the fire" of the trying-out process and remarks that his shipmates stared into it "till their eyes felt scorched in their heads" (423). He also advises himself against doing what the helmsman in **"The Death Craft"** does; namely, he cautions himself from abandoning his post: "Look not too long in the face of the fire, O man! Never dream with thy hand on the helm!" (424).

In **"The Death Craft,"** the intense heat and the horrific sight of the *Death Craft* cause the narrator to fall into a "trance" (425), as he calls it, during which he comes into contact with madness. This not only links **"The Death Craft"** to *Moby-Dick* but also to much of Melville's other works for, as Paul McCarthy astutely argues in his pioneering 1990 study, madness is a common theme in Melville's writing (xiii). In an episode eerily prophetic of one Melville himself would witness in 1849, the narrator of **"The Death Craft"** is an onlooker as the ship's first mate sees the *Death Craft* and "with a long, long, shriek [. . .] wildly flung himself into the sea" (425).[6] Moreover, after witnessing "the frightful apparition" of the *Death Craft* for himself, the narrator rolls on the deck "with the laugh of wild delirium" (427). The fire in "The Try-Works" causes Ishmael to experience an "unnatural hallucination" (424) during which he also comes into contact with madness. During his trance, for instance, he contemplates "the redness, the madness, the ghastliness of others" (423) and comes to the realization that "there is a wisdom that is woe; but there is a woe that is madness" (425). Finally, both men are uncertain about the true nature of their trances. The narrator of **"The Death Craft"** does not know precisely how long his has lasted (425); in fact, he is unsure whether or not he actually experienced the ordeal or merely dreamed it (427). Ishmael is equally uncertain as he describes his experience as "inexplicable" (423).

Undeniable parallels also can be drawn between the *Death Craft* and the *Pequod*. On the basis of its description, the *Death Craft* certainly lives up to its name:

> Great God! there she lay, covered with barnacles, the formation of years—her sails unbent—a blood-red flag streaming from her mast-head—at her jib-boom-end hanging suspended by its long, dark hair, a human head covered with congealed gore and firmly griping between its teeth a rusty cutlass! Her yards were painted black, and at each of their arms hung dangling a human skeleton, whiter than polished ivory and glistening in the fierce rays of the sun!
>
> (425)

In "The Try-Works," the *Pequod* is described as a "burning ship [. . .] commissioned to some vengeful deed" (422) that is "laden with fire, and burning a

corpse" (423). Furthermore, Ishmael listens to his ship mates' "unholy adventures, their tales of terror" (423) and watches the "ghastly [. . .] flashes of redness" (424), the "snaky flames" (423) that "forked forth" to lick up the darkness (422). These images create an environment reminiscent of hell. For Ishmael, the *Pequod* becomes—quite literally—a Death Craft.[7]

No known manuscript of **"The Death Craft"** exists, it was never reprinted during Melville's lifetime, and there is no mention of it in any of his surviving papers: Therefore, the only known evidence on which scholars can rely to assign authorship to Melville is its incontestable parallels with his other works. This logic certainly holds as many of Melville's works are similar to, or continuations of, ones that preceded them. *Omoo* followed what he had done in *Typee*; **"The Fiddler"** engages with failure in much the same way as **"The Happy Failure"**; **"The Apple-Tree Table"** is similar in theme, or a companion piece, to **"I and My Chimney"**; *Billy Budd, Sailor* takes its lead from many of the conflicts, such as mutiny and rebellion, found in **"Benito Cereno."** **"The Death Craft"** is more notably linked to a large portion of the total body of Melville's work than any of the aforementioned texts.[8] These parallels must be more than a coincidence; it is highly likely that Melville wrote **"The Death Craft."**

Notes

1. An excerpt from "The Death Craft" was included in Jay Leyda's *The Melville Log*. It has only been reprinted in full as Melville's on three occasions: First, as an appendix to Martin Leonard Pops's *The Melville Archetype*, subsequently in Warren F. Broderick's "'Their Snowy Whiteness Dazzled My Eyes': 'The Death Craft'—Melville's First Maritime Story"; and, most recently, in the "Attributed Pieces" section of *The Piazza Tales and Other Prose Pieces, 1839-1860*.

2. Pops clearly accepts this attribution; I argue that Howard, Levin, and E. Miller unequivocally accept its ascription to Melville as they all discuss the story in their respective Melville studies, yet fail to document that uncertainty concerning its authorship exists.

3. After citing "The Death Craft" as Melville's, Leyda, in an aside, questions whether or not Melville actually wrote it.

4. Sealts does not mention *Moby-Dick* in his brief study; it is only a minor component of Broderick's.

5. The sea also is described in identical terms in chapter 22 of *Redburn,* when the *Highlander* is caught in a ferocious storm and must plow through the sea's "milk-white waves" (116), and in chapter 26 of *White-Jacket,* as the *Neversink* is "undulated" by the "milk-white billows of foam" (108).

6. As Melville recounts in his 13 October 1849 journal entry from his voyage to London on board the *Independence,* one of his shipmates jumped overboard in a fit of madness and drowned (*Journals* 5). The identical event occurs in chapter 10 of *Redburn* (56). It is more than likely, however, that the *Redburn* incident is based on his firsthand account of the suicide on the *Independence* as opposed to the similar episode in "The Death Craft."

7. In "Benito Cereno," the *San Dominick* also is described in similar terms as the *Death Craft* (37).

8. As Broderick, Sealts, and I have demonstrated, "The Death Craft" contains significant parallels with Melville's "Fragments from a Writing Desk," his first six novels, and "Benito Cereno."

Works Cited

Arvin, Newton. *Herman Melville.* New York: Viking, 1950.

Beaulieu, Victor-Lévy. *Monsieur Melville.* 3 vols. Trans. Ray Chamberlain. Toronto: Coach House, 1984.

Broderick, Warren F. "'Their Snowy Whiteness Dazzled My Eyes': 'The Death Craft'—Melville's First Maritime Story." *The Hudson Valley Regional Review* 3 (1986): 90-106.

Gilman, William H. *Melville's Early Life and* Redburn. New York: New York UP, 1951.

Howard, Leon. *Herman Melville: A Biography.* 1951. Berkeley: U of California P, 1958.

Kirby, David. *Herman Melville.* New York: Continuum, 1993.

Levin, Harry. *The Power of Blackness: Hawthorne, Poe, Melville.* 1958. New York: Knopf, 1970.

Leyda, Jay. *The Melville Log: A Documentary Life of Herman Melville, 1819-1891.* 1951. Vol. 1. New York: Gordian, 1969.

McCarthy, Paul. *"The Twisted Mind": Madness in Herman Melville's Fiction.* Iowa City: U of Iowa P, 1990.

Melville, Herman. "Benito Cereno." 1855. *Melville's Short Novels.* Ed. Dan McCall. New York: Norton, 2002. 34-102.

———. "The Death Craft." 1839. *The Piazza Tales and Other Prose Pieces, 1839-1860.* Ed. Harrison Hayford, Hershel Parker, and G. Thomas Tanselle. Evanston, IL: Northwestern UP, 1987. 424-27.

———. *Journals.* Ed. Harrison Hayford et al. Evanston, IL: Northwestern UP, 1989.

———. *Moby-Dick.* 1851. Ed. Harrison Hayford et al. Evanston, IL: Northwestern UP, 2001.

———. *Redburn.* 1849. Ed. and intro. Raymond M. Weaver. New York: Boni, 1924.

———. *White-Jacket.* 1850. Oxford: Oxford UP, 1995.

Miller, Edwin Haviland. *Melville.* New York: Braziller, 1975.

Miller, James E., Jr. *A Reader's Guide to Herman Melville.* New York: Noonday, 1962.

Parker, Hershel. *Herman Melville: A Biography.* Vol. 1. Baltimore: Johns Hopkins UP, 1996.

Pops, Martin Leonard. *The Melville Archetype.* Kent, OH: Kent State UP, 1970.

Sealts, Merton M., Jr. "Notes on 'The Death Craft.'" *The Piazza Tales and Other Prose Pieces, 1839-1860.* Ed. Harrison Hayford, Hershel Parker, and G. Thomas Tanselle. Evanston, IL: Northwestern UP, 1987. 782-83.

Corey Evan Thompson (essay date fall 2005)

SOURCE: Thompson, Corey Evan. "Melville's 'The Apple-Tree Table.'" *Explicator* 64, no. 1 (fall 2005): 38-41.

[*In the following essay, Thompson examines "The Apple-Tree Table" in the light of Melville's misogynistic reputation.*]

Herman Melville's role as an activist for female emancipation in mid-nineteenth-century America has gone largely unnoted by critics. In fact, many have implied that he directly contributed to the subordination of women by insinuating, with limited evidence, that he was abusive toward his wife, Elizabeth (Renker 123-50; Robertson-Lorant xi-xiii; Hardwick 51-52), and by describing the portrayal of women in his works as misogynistic (Adamson 26; Brown 160; Rollyson and Paddock 219-20). Contrary to such frequent yet largely unsubstantiated claims, Melville, in his 1856 short story **"The Apple-Tree Table,"** is an active voice in the call for women's liberation from patriarchal authority and, more specifically, from many of the ideals of domesticity that permeated mid-nineteenth-century American society. Although such an examination of only one of Melville's stories will not fully exonerate him from the largely unjustified label of wife-beater or misogynist, it will provide critics further reason "to modify," as Richard Chase has argued with regard to Melville's diptych **"The Paradise of Bachelors and the Tartarus of Maids"** (1855), "the commonly expressed idea that Melville's writing displays no closely sympathetic understanding of women" (xi).

Stemming from the changing notions of the home that accompanied burgeoning industrial America, there developed an ideal of domesticity, or "cult of true womanhood." This new ideal, which was evident in the era's women's magazines and religious journals, provided a new view of women's roles in society. As many have noted, this ideal identified certain fundamental virtues that "true" women possessed (Davidson et al. 302). Whereas men were believed to be naturally active, dominant, assertive, and materialistic, women served as their more refined counterparts. They "inherently" possessed such virtues as piety, submissiveness, and domesticity. **"The Apple-Tree Table,"** however, is rife with antipathy to many of the era's traditional views regarding the domestic ideals imposed on women. Throughout the story, the narrator's wife eschews many of the ideals of domesticity by portraying more masculine characteristics than her narrator-husband and by refusing to exhibit the supposedly inherent virtues prescribed by them. In doing so, the narrator's wife becomes arguably the most progressive female character in the Melville canon.

The ideals of domesticity maintained that women had a particular propensity for religion. Pious women were expected to attend church and to perform church work on a daily basis. Such actions would demonstrate their devout reverence of God. During the five days over which the story occurs (the five days commence on pages 378, 385, 390, 393, and 395), however, the narrator's wife does not attend a sermon, nor does she ever refer to the scripture, which is also in opposition to the cult's requirements, as women were expected to be handmaids to the Bible. In fact, other than the wife's hope that her children are all "good Christians" (Melville 387), which is expressed in a more colloquial than formally religious tone, there is no explicit reference to formal religion in the story. With regard to the narrator's wife, then, piety is only notable by its absence.

It is ironic that piety was regarded as the source of women's strength because it also provided justification for the virtue of submissiveness. Pious women who attended church regularly, as required, would frequently hear sermons providing biblical justification for their need to be submissive. Many passages, such as Ephesians 5.22-23, state this explicitly: "Wives, be in subjection unto your own husbands, as unto the Lord. For the husband is the head of the wife, as Christ also is head of the church, being himself the saviour of the body." The narrator's wife, however, heeds no such command. She is the furthest thing from submissive, in fact, as she is "not wanting in firmness and energy" (381) and is dominant over her husband and children: she frequently scolds them (385-86), addresses them in a "frightful business-like manner" (386), and has a propensity toward violence, which is a dominant and therefore masculine trait, as she threatens to "whip that [ticking] out of [the table]" (392).

Stemming from piety and submissiveness, domesticity was also an integral component of the cult of true womanhood. As part of their domestic role, women were expected to perform household work joyfully and to provide comfort and cheer to everyone who lived in and entered their homes. Yet, the narrator's wife does not perform any housework over the course of the story. The closest she comes is when she states that she wishes to have the titular table waxed (392). Immediately following this remark, however, she orders her housemaid, Biddy, to get wax and a brush and to give the table a "vigorous manipulation" (392). Biddy is also responsible for all other household chores, as she sets the table for the family's dinner and carries the dishes back to the kitchen, where she will be responsible for their washing (385-86). It is also difficult to imagine that the wife's house would be filled with the requisite comfort and cheer. She certainly makes no serious attempt to create such ambience, as she frequently speaks "indignantly" (382, 390), "contemptuously" (386), with "high displeasure" (391), and refers to her family as a group of "fools" (395).

Domesticity also required women to avoid the pleasures and values of "a materialistic society" (Welter 38). Yet, the narrator's wife is solely interested in material possessions. After the narrator discovers the "dingy and dusty table" (379) and brings it down from the garret and into the cedar parlor, his wife takes "little interest" in it because it is not an ostentatious piece of furniture. In fact, "[s]he disrelished the idea of so unfashionable and indigent-looking a stranger as the table intruding into the polished society of more prosperous furniture" (381). After the narrator has the table appraised and refurbished at the cabinetmaker's shop, however, her attitude toward it alters substantially. Once the table is "varnished over, bright as a guinea" and subsequently brought back home, the wife sees its natural beauty and only then places it in "an honorable position" in the cedar parlor (381).

As the 1860s approached, there were many forces at work that impelled women to change: "The movements for social reform, westward migration, missionary activity, utopian communities, industrialism, the Civil War—all called forth responses from woman which differed from those she was trained to believe were hers by nature and divine decree" (Welter 40-41). It is surely more than a coincidence that the composition and publication of **"The Apple-Tree Table"** coincided with these events. Melville was well aware, as Ann Douglas and Laurie Robertson-Lorant have noted, that his American reading public consisted largely of middle-class women (294; 137), those who were most familiar with and affected by the cult of true womanhood. It is possible that Melville wrote **"The Apple-Tree Table"** for his female audience, who would have possibly noticed the story's inverted domestic world. It is all the more plausible that this was Melville's intention, as he, through the narrator's voice, directly refers to his female readers in the story's concluding paragraph (397). By presenting a liberal female character who eschews the ideals of domesticity, Melville demonstrates his knowledge of and support for the emerging cultural shift from the cult's "true" woman to the less domestic and somewhat liberated "new" woman that began to emerge in the latter half of the nineteenth century.

Works Cited

Adamson, Joseph. *Melville, Shame, and the Evil Eye.* Albany: SUNY P, 1997.

Brown, Gillian. *Domestic Individualism: Imagining Self in Nineteenth-Century America.* Berkeley: U of California P, 1990.

Chase, Richard. Introduction. *Herman Melville: Selected Tales and Poems.* 1950. Ed. Richard Chase. New York: Holt, 1968. v-xix.

Davidson, James West, et al. *Nation of Nations: A Concise History of the American Republic.* New York: Overture, 1996.

Douglas, Ann. *The Feminization of American Culture.* 1977. New York: Knopf, 1978.

Hardwick, Elizabeth. *Herman Melville.* New York: Viking, 2000.

Melville, Herman. "The Apple-Tree Table." 1856. *The Piazza Tales and Other Prose Pieces, 1839-1860.* Ed. Harrison Hayford et al. Evanston: Northwestern UP, 1987. 378-97.

Renker, Elizabeth. "Herman Melville, Wife Beating, and the Written Page." *American Literature* 66 (1994): 123-50.

Robertson-Lorant, Laurie. *Herman Melville: A Biography.* 1996. Amherst: U of Massachusetts P, 1998.

Rollyson, Carl, and Lisa Paddock. *Herman Melville A to Z: The Essential Reference to His Life and Work.* New York: Checkmark, 2001.

Welter, Barbara. *Dimity Convictions: The American Woman in the Nineteenth Century.* Athens: Ohio UP, 1976.

Sean R. Silver (essay date spring 2006)

SOURCE: Silver, Sean R. "The Temporality of Allegory: Melville's 'The Lightning-Rod Man.'" *Arizona Quarterly* 62, no. 1 (spring 2006): 1-33.

[*In the following essay, Silver studies the ethical implications of the lightning-rod metaphor in "The Lightning-Rod Man," explicating the story's particular mode of New England allegory and underscoring the thematic relationship between post-Calvinist theology and responsible consumerism.*]

Poised between **"Benito Cereno"** and **"The Encantadas,"** two of Melville's most mature works of short fiction, is an innocuous little story about a peddler: **"The Lightning-Rod Man."** Though mostly unread and uncollected now, it was one of his most popular short stories during his lifetime; it was, in fact, Melville's only story that remained in print until his death.[1] After appearing first in *Putnam's Monthly* (in July, 1854) and then in *The Piazza Tales* (1856), **"The Lightning-Rod Man"** was collected in William E. Burton's *Cyclopaedia of Wit and Humor* (1857), and was regularly reprinted in similar compendia thereafter.[2] Its circulation outlived, even, the life of its author; though Melville died in 1891, **"The Lightning-Rod Man"** was reprinted, in 1895, in *Capital Stories by American Authors.*

Melville's tale probably found such persistent acceptance because it is generically recognizable. It is a salesman story, what Hershel Parker identifies as a "little Berkshire salesman story," and it is as a salesman story that it seems to have found its immediate legacy: bound up in anthologies like Burton's *Cyclopaedia* that recycled compact stories with a singleness of plot and a clear thematic task. As with the other salesman stories in such collections, the straightforward thematic tension of **"The Lightning-Rod Man"** develops between a hard-sell door-to-door peddler and an acute consumer; the trick, in the salesman story, is for the prospective buyer to figure out what the salesman is really selling; they are parables of alert consumerism. The moral of the tale is always *caveat emptor.*[3]

On the other hand, for all its historical popularity, the experience of reading **"The Lightning-Rod Man,"** if a survey of the critical response is any indication, is characterized by nothing so much as the sense that all is not as it seems, here.[4] For one thing, the salesman and his buyer are talking about a lightning-rod, but their dialogue seems to be orbiting into vocabularies not properly about lightning-rods: about Catholic indulgences, or rosaries, or scepters, tri-forked things, and Leyden jars. And, more telling, the sale of the rod never seems to turn on questions appropriate to the purchase of a lightning-rod; questions of voltage differentials and electrical resistance, of conductivity and the strange logic of electric "fluid" never quite come up. This is partly to say that thematic desire is very much like the critical desire that is implied in it; they both turn on a question first put by Melville's narrator in the opening paragraph of the tale: "what is that strange-looking walking-stick he carries?" (118, 122). Whatever it is, it is more than just an every-day lightning-rod. In Ben Kimpel's words, "obviously there is some allegory here" (30).[5]

Yet, if it is an allegory, it is an allegory of a particularly New England sort, allegory of the right sort, the Puritan sort of allegory. For **"The Lightning-Rod Man"** declines to invent a fiction out of the raw material of fancy. Instead, it insists on the literal fact of the lightning-rod as a lightning-rod just as it insists on the historicity of its figures; it is as much about the history of New England Protestantism as it is about one of the principle challenges to New England Protestant theology: the advent of the lightning-rod itself. Melville would have us know that a lightning-rod is very much like an idol, and the lightning-rod consumer is vulnerable to the charge of idolatry; placing trust in a lightning-rod is very much like putting one's refuge in means and creatures rather than in God.[6] As such, an ethical consideration of the lightning-rod, in the New England tradition of allegory, finds its most proper language in the rhetoric of post-Calvinist theology.[7]

And so in consideration of this question—this question of Reformed Christianity displaced onto the issue of responsible consumerism—Melville's narrator will insist on returning it to its historical precedents; an "allegorical" meditation on a present problem will turn on the types of its own figured past. The narrator's struggle to refuse the lightning-rod will become an ethical problem positioned around the historical threshold moments that anticipate it, around three crises of representation: Caesar Augustus's near electrocution, Martin Luther and Johann Tetzel's debates in sixteenth-century Saxony, and Cotton Mather's defense of the practice of inoculation during the small-pox crisis of 1721. Positioned against this background, the narrator's rejection of the lightning-rod is a rejection of an entire method of figuration, a rejection of a Protestant history rewritten as a history of progressive adaptation to a series of increasingly sophisticated idols and indulgences. Though this might at first seem astonishing—that Melville, and his interlocutor, would consider a discussion of inoculation to be the best way of settling issues of lightning-rods, and that both of these questions will fall under the sign of larger ethical concerns—it is in fact a strategy absolutely characteristic of what I want to suggest is the particularly New England mode of allegory. Before returning to **"The Lightning-Rod Man,"** then, it may help to start by clearing up a persistent blind spot in critical treatments of Melville's most allusive texts: what, exactly, we mean by "allegory."

* * *

For Cicero and Quintillian—the principal classical theorists of allegory—allegory is only "continued metaphor"; as Angus Fletcher describes it, the "analogical symbolism," which is allegory in the classical mode, is "the gathering of many little metaphors into the scope of one larger unifying figure which is also a metaphor" (71).[8] In this sense, the principal metaphor of the alle-

gory, extended, is the disciplining logic that governs the relation between the occurrence of a thing in allegorical narrative and its corresponding idea. It is sequence rather than series, a static and hierarchical arrangement of rhetorical kosmoi, which makes "only the slightest gestures towards full-scale narrative progress" (Fineman 7). In other words, the overdetermining metaphor of an allegory, understood in its classical mode, is the structuring principle in a cosmology. As Abraham Fraunce tells us, in the proper allegory "with what thing it begin, with the same it also end" (3-4). Such an allegory in the classical mode begins, ends, and turns timelessly on the same ordering relation that sponsored it.

But **"The Lightning-Rod Man"** doesn't seem to work this way. If it did—if **"The Lightning-Rod Man"** were only a little "Berkshire salesman story in which a fear-instilling religionist plays the role of the peddler" (Parker, *Melville* 2:216)—then we could expect something very much formally like, for example, Nathaniel Hawthorne's "The Celestial Railroad." It's worth noting that these two New England tales share a New England philosophical obsession; they both meditate on religion in the low state of the Antebellum New England world. But while we are meant to understand Hawthorne's "Railroad" as not a railroad itself—not an indictment of railroads and the riding of railroads—but instead an allegorical indictment of an easy and conformable Unitarian revision of the pilgrim's progress, in **"The Lightning-Rod Man,"** the lightning-rod clearly remains a lightning-rod; it is the lightning-rod itself which poses, considered ethically and historically, a problem to New England Calvinism.[9] The theological problem is grounded, as it were, in its own literal representation, a current new New England device characteristic of what might be called Franklinian optimism.[10]

Of course, we'd be wrong to think that all allegory is only a matter of the obsessive repetition of a single idea. As Fletcher begins to signal, allegory is also, under the right conditions, the trope that allows an idea—a cosmic vision, a political struggle, a theology, whatever—to govern narrative action; it is *ethical* in this way (147-80). Understood as the driving principle of narrative, allegory is metaphor extended under the pressure of time; it is a working-out of the ramified terms of a sponsoring, or "threshold," metaphor that propagates itself forward through a typology of charged and related allusions; type gives way to antitype, always gesturing to some satisfying resolution that will make sense of the whole. The threshold metaphor, in other words, is the formal opening or rupture that enables the problem of plot to emerge into a symbolic idiom, and to be resolved, as a symbolic question. It is the opening of form that allows the introduction of history into the allegorical mode.

Protestant theology has always been—ever since Luther's foundational rupture with Catholic orthodoxy—

about breaking from the excesses of Catholic allegorical hermeneutics. Martin Luther, for instance, denounced the "idle and unlettered monks and scholastic doctors [who] taught that there are four senses of Scripture—the literal, the tropological, the allegorical, and the anagogical" with which they "misinterpreted almost every word of Scripture." "With these awkward and foolish fables," Luther continues, "they tore Scripture apart into many meanings and robbed themselves of the ability to give sure instruction to human consciences" (*Lectures* 26:440).[11] Luther was speaking, of course, of allegory classically understood—as an ordering cosmology. And it is excesses of this sort of allegorical exegesis, Luther continues, that involve the invention of meaning; it is a creation of a fiction under rules too liberal that results in a surplus of signification at the cost of the proper, or literal, sense of the text. It is the work of Protestant exegesis to return the text to its historical and literal sense, to maintain the strict sense that "spiritual things are distinct from physical or earthly things" (26:440). In order for "doctrine" to have any "certainty," then, it must be grounded in historical fact. As Calvin, after Luther, tells us,

> representations are of two classes—viz. historical, which give a representation of events, and pictorial, which merely exhibit shapes and figures. The former are of some use for instruction and admonition. The latter, so far as I can see, are fitted only for amusement.
>
> (1:133)[12]

History, for Calvin, is the fit source for ethical instruction; allegory, on the other hand, is only the construction of "pictures." Such a taking of means into the hands of men—however penetrating or learned—earns the characteristic distrust of the Protestant moment: such a technique is fit only "for amusement," but not for the serious task of "instruction and admonition." In order for "figures" to have any doctrinal value, they must be positioned in a realized history.

But I also want to insist that classical allegory, to the Protestant after Luther, starts to look very much like a kind of idolatry. "It is not safe," Samuel Mather warns, "for Men to form Allegories out of their own Fancies" (129)—not safe because it, at some fundamental and formal level, idolizes the object, which is very much like idolizing or fetishizing the flesh which the object, Calvin tells us, stands in to represent. In Luther's words, again, "spiritual things" must be kept "distinct from physical or earthly things." Or, as the narrator of **"The Lightning-Rod Man"** formulates it, it is the "*false* negotiator," the "*pretended* envoy extraordinary," who would "put [his] pipestem between clay and sky" (124, emphasis added).

Instead, the post-Calvin allegorical vision regards itself as only the literal truth of literal history: what might be called a typological cosmic vision—typological not in the limited sense of the New Testament authors who recouped the Law for their own Spiritual purposes, but in the broader, applied sense that "typological exegesis is a method of reading history; it is centrally rooted in history itself" (Davis 17). It is fundamentally typological inasmuch as it can read history under the sign of a Providential intention, a string of historically true figures that relate one to another as progressive types anticipating the same antitype which is often the present moment. This, indeed, may be the principal contribution of Puritan theology to typological exegesis; it was Puritanism, and mostly New England Puritanism, that adapted biblical hermeneutics to the specular consideration of contemporary history as only the continuing antitypes of Providential wisdom prefigured in the paired Testaments.[13]

Readings of the state of things as they are, in such a typological or "figural" mode, do double work: they read history under the aspect of the present moment—as types to the present antitype—and the present moment as only the redaction of moments historically true.[14] This is to say that allegory of the typological stamp is always about a "recuperative originology," as Joel Fineman puts it (6), but it is also to say that readings of the present state of things, in order for them to have any philosophical weight, necessarily situate themselves against the backdrop of past instantiations of related "types." In the typological mode, moments in time are mutually referential: the antitype can only be made sense of by the history that has produced it, but types are only tentative instances that promise future clarification.

What emerges as the characteristic New England allegorical mode, then, is not what would have been recognized as allegory by Dante, for instance, or Spenser, or even, surprisingly, John Bunyan (whose "fall into allegory" has been impressively documented by Thomas Luxon [131]). Instead, **"The Lightning-Rod Man"**—inasmuch as it is allegorical as a theological form adapted to the demands of the novelistic chronotope—is an allegory of the sort of *The Scarlet Letter*. It is *The Scarlet Letter* that is the representative example of the New England allegorical vision, and as such, Hawthorne's novel provides much of the vocabulary for thinking about Calvinist typology as an artistic mode.

It is from *The Scarlet Letter* that Edwin Honig develops the concept of the threshold metaphor. *The Scarlet Letter* is an "allegory," he argues, initiated by the rupture of the first return of Hester Prynne to Salem. This threshold metaphor is poised on a literal threshold; it is a red rosebush on the threshold of the prisonhouse from which Prynne emerges, holding her illegitimate daughter Pearl. This rosebush, Hawthorne informs his reader, is said to have sprung from the footsteps of the sainted Anne Hutchinson; complicating matters, and speaking, already, in the symbolic mode that enables allegory, Pearl herself is said to have sprung, new-formed, from just such a rosebush. In this way, the bush of red roses, understood as metaphorical or symbolic, enables the emergence of the observable problem of the illegitimate child into the symbolic code, preformed, of the negotiated community that doesn't quite welcome Prynne back. It is through the threshold metaphor of the rosebush that she emerges from the prisonhouse of Salem into the prisonhouse of language; she emerges from the spectacular icon of social control—the prison—to find what she certainly already knew: that sexual love has always already been politicized in a long and complicated history of discipline and punishment, and that it is in this politicized code that her story will be worked out.

And so the rosebush, as a key type already situated against the historical type of Anne Hutchinson, also propagates itself forward: through Pearl, and the scarlet letter, and portents in the sky, the bit of red tape in the Custom House that ties the letter to its documents. It is what initiates and enables an allegorical discourse turning on ethical questions—love, sex, and even Antinomianism—that drives the plot of the story. *The Scarlet Letter,* understood as a representative American allegory, is about the resolution of the rupture signaled by Hester's emergence. **"The Lightning-Rod Man,"** I will demonstrate, works in the same way. Allegory of this type, like allegory classically understood, "with what thing it begin, with the same it also end" (Fraunce 4). Yet, it does not become frozen in "the petrified, primordial landscape" (Benjamin 166) of its own timeless, overdetermining vision. Instead, allegory, in this typological model, is the organizing principle of thematic desire; plot is the promise of resolution of the ethical questions introduced at the threshold of plot. In the typological allegory, thematic resolution is about ethical resolution; it is about defining and correcting the rupture created on the threshold of the story.

* * *

The threshold is where the business of allegory is established; it is also quite literally where the plot of the salesman story is transacted. Melville's **"The Lightning-Rod Man"** starts in a snug Berkshire cottage. His bachelor narrator is meditating on the grandness of thunder in the mode, for instance, of Ik Marvel's *Reveries of a Bachelor.*[15] This could go on forever; the story can only begin with an interruption. A "singular" visitor arrives; he crosses the threshold of the cottage, carrying a "strange-looking walking-stick" (118). With reference to this walking-stick the bachelor narrator—like the rest of us after him—begins building his sense of what the stranger might represent. Through this walking-stick, a sort of talisman, the narrator is (we are) "drawn into an iconographic frame of mind"

(Fletcher 217). Without answering the question of what, exactly, the walking-stick is—we will find out a couple of pages later that it is his "specimen-rod"—the narrator instead begins framing the terms of what the stranger represents, built around the totem that will become his talismanic representation. It is a lightning-rod. He is a lightning-rod man:

> "Sir," said I, bowing politely, "have I the honor of a visit from that illustrious god, Jupiter Tonans? So stood he in the Greek statue of old, grasping the lightning-bolt. If you be he, or his viceroy, I have to thank you for this noble storm you have brewed among our mountains. Listen: That was a glorious peal. Ah, to a lover of the majestic, it is a good thing to have the Thunderer himself in one's cottage. The thunder grows finer for that. But pray be seated. This old rush-bottomed arm-chair, I grant, is a poor substitute for your evergreen throne on Olympus; but, condescend to be seated."
>
> (432)

By the time we realize that this rod—this curious copper rod—is a lightning-rod adapted for the traveler-on-foot, it is already something else: it is already, itself, a lightning-rod and a lightning-bolt, and the lightning-rod man is already both himself and the god that the narrator suggests he represents. In fact, even the storm outside has recentered itself; it is only an effect—allegorically speaking—of the ethical cause to be resolved between the narrator and the visitor to which, retrospectively, he ascribes the effect of the "noble storm."

The narrator, in other words, is beginning to position the lightning-rod man in an ethical tradition, a modern-day antitype (for salesmen were evidently a common feature of the New England landscape) of a historically disposed series of types.[16] In naming him "Jupiter Tonans," or envoy of Jupiter Tonans, the narrator is gesturing, as one figure always gestures to another, to the tradition of Jupiter Tonans in Roman theology, to the "Greek [*sic*] statue of old" erected to Jupiter in his aspect as "Thunderer." We might glance at Suetonius, who records that Caesar Augustus

> dedicated the shrine to Jupiter the Thunderer (*Jupiter Tonans*) because of a narrow escape; for on his Cantabrian expedition during a march by night, a flash of lightning grazed his litter and struck the slave dead who was carrying a torch before him.
>
> (1:167-69)

After having been spared once, Suetonius records, Augustus erected a temple, with a massive copper statue, high atop Capitol Hill. But Augustus was doing more than expressing gratitude for having his life spared; he was also doing more than playing the part of a "lover of the majestic." Augustus's dedication seems to have been intended to ward off future strikes as well. For while this near-electrocution "badly frightened" him, this wasn't an isolated incident (1:167). Suetonius records that he had always been "somewhat weak in his fear of thunder and lightning," and "he always carried a seal-skin about with him everywhere as a protection" (1:259).[17] His life had always already been interwoven with the alien agency of lightning: his birth augured by a lightning-strike in his home town, and his father's dream of Jupiter wielding a thunder-bolt (1:265). The Cantabrian episode only reconfirmed that his life was specially marked by signs and portents, that the universe was specially legible in lightning-bolts disposed according to his own experience and conduct. As these convictions became figured in practice, Augustus made constant, even guilty visits to the temple of the Thunderer (1:261), for this temple was the first lightning-rod; its copper statue was the first lightning-rod man (Pliny 6:185-87). And as such, Augustus's statue is the threshold type that introduces the terms of the theological tradition of lightning-rods.

Appropriate to the life-long trope, to Augustus's heightened sense of allegorical reading, it was by lightning that Augustus was deified. As Cassius tells us,

> A thunderbolt fell upon his statue that stood upon the capitol and blotted out the first letter of the name "Caesar." This led the seers to declare that on the hundredth day after that he should attain some divine state. They deduced this from the fact that the letter "C" signifies "one hundred" among the Latin, and the remainder of the word means "god" among the Etruscans.
>
> (7:67)

Lightning, then, is both an object of dread and means of deification; evidently (at least partly) through the agency of idols Augustus both conciliated his household gods and became, himself, a god among their number. He may even have intended, slyly, to remind the Roman populace of his own special prerogative as descendent of Jupiter; Augustus, being in the line of the Caesars, claimed a descent from the gods similar to the Greek Kings' descent from Zeus recorded by Ovid— Augustus was their "envoy extraordinary" (**"Lightning-Rod Man"** 124), the personal representative of the body of God.[18] Thus, the lightning rod is more than just a pragmatic insurance policy; for Caesar Augustus, it was magical in its powers in exactly the way that allegory is magical—as a legible and symbolic mediator poised between human agency and Providential intention, hinging on the ability of seers to parse it into its senses. In this sense, god, statue, and emperor are all bound in an economy of relations that, through the fact of the lightning-rod statue (agent and original and representation or reminder of both Jupiter and Caesar Augustus), at least rhetorically—or allegorically—folded power proper to the gods back on a human actor.

Protestant orthodoxy would have recognized this as the wrong sort of representation. "The flesh is always restless until it has obtained some figment like itself,"

Calvin suggests, "with which it may vainly solace itself as a representation of God" (1:124). Caesar with his statue of Jupiter (or himself) would certainly look to Calvin like the flesh that is like the figment that seeks, however "vainly," to stand in as that divine representation. But, what's more, the strange presumption of Augustus's behavior wasn't lost on his contemporaries. Pliny may even have been thinking of Augustus's shrine on the Capitol when he denounced idolatry of all sorts— denouncing those "in the very Capitol" who "swear (false) oaths by Jupiter who wields the thunder-bolts." All such pretenders, he continues, "indeed make a profit out of their crimes." Idolaters, we might say, in the tradition sponsored by Augustus (but which will be picked up by Tetzel), are salesmen. The alternative is charity: "for mortal to aid mortal—this is god" (Pliny 1:179-81).

Thus, a species of representation of the wrong sort opens up the allegorical possibilities of the lightning-rod for **"The Lightning-Rod Man,"** by grounding it in an episode with historical specificity that shadows forth the problem of the lightning-rod for the narrator and his own more particular salesman. Both the salesman and his prospective consumer realize that the temple to Jupiter Tonans is only a tentative figure, only a promise of additional clarification, because name-calling—labeling each other infidel—won't settle anything. The issue, it seems, for the ethical resolution of the problem of the lightning-rod, is how to position it in a more specifically Christian theological landscape—a theology that has always had a vexed relationship with the graven images and representative icons it both declines and relies upon, the move itself allegorical that it both depends upon and rejects. The problem becomes how to reposition what we now know are the revenants of Augustan idolatry in the thematic space of a New England salesman story—how to talk about the lightning-rod without, as the lightning-rod man accuses the narrator, being only inappropriately "profane in this time of terror" (120).

Allegory, in other words, is only of value inasmuch as it returns to the present time: as *allegoria* responds to the pressures of time to adapt history to the moment of the present marketplace, the Old Testament to the New, for example, or the mythic past to the realized present. Allegory is always "directed to critical or polemical ends"; the "motive to allegoricize emerges out of recuperative originology" (Fineman 6). And so allegory, for it to have any meaning, is always about adapting a shared history, a community vision, for its explanatory and polemic value, to the present moment; **"The Lightning-Rod Man"** is only a surprisingly literalized instance of an essential feature of the form.

It's also worth noting that this strategy of figuration, at the moment it recognizes past figures in present narrative, threatens by its very form to lapse into irony. We are not meant seriously to believe, after all, that the narrator considers the lightning-rod man actually to be Jupiter Tonans, somehow emerging, even through the trope of the figure, across space and time, and across his actual threshold. For certainly, though the serious issue of idolatry is at stake, the narrator is speaking ironically when he calls the lightning-rod man "Mr. Jupiter Tonans"; the mere juxtaposition between the mundane "Mr." and the mythic "Jupiter" is itself ironic. Likewise, the equation of mythic and profane, which reveals the lightning-rod for the idol that the narrator senses it to be, begins to reveal an internal ironic difference, a presumptuous disagreement, within the lightning-rod man's implicit theology.

The problem isn't just, as Martin Luther reminds us, that "spiritual things must be kept distinct from physical or earthly things." For in naming him "Mr. Jupiter Tonans," the narrator is not calling him the god of thunder, but, instead, something like Caesar Augustus: a mortal with pretensions to divine agency very like the lightning-rod man himself. And the narrator will clarify this later, will recast the epithet as "pretended envoy extraordinary and minister plenipotentiary to and from Jupiter Tonans" (124) for which "Mr. Jupiter Tonans" seems to be shorthand. The problem here, the evident disjunction that looms up from the structure of the typological form itself, is instead a problem of temporality; the narrator is aware of history in a way that the lightning-rod man is not. The strategy assumed by the narrator, then, is to illuminate the anachronistic structure that inhabits the figural vision—the evident impossibility of being both the type which defines the antitype and the antitype itself.

The structure of irony may formally be very like the structure of a typological narrative. For "in the world of allegory," Paul de Man recognizes, speaking of the sort of figural or typological allegory that drives the ethical tension of **"The Lightning-Rod Man,"** "time is the originary constitutive category." As such, the allegorical type or figure

> designates primarily a distance in relation to its own origin, and, renouncing the nostalgia and the desire to coincide, it establishes its language in the void of this temporal difference. In so doing, it prevents the self from an illusory identification with the non-self, which is now fully, though painfully, recognized as a non-self.
>
> (207)

Allegorical language, then, witnesses and is constituted upon its own internal difference, on the primitive doubleness between type and antitype. It is in the recognition of this difference, lurking in the language applied to the present, that the specter of irony threatens to emerge. For like typological experience, irony is about a doubling, what de Man (212-13), quoting Baudelaire (26), calls a *"dédoublement."*[19] But whereas the figure is constituted across time, irony is constructed in the existential moment: irony is the recognition of the difference between an existential self that postulates, recognizes, and writes an inauthentically historical self. In this way, writes de Man, "allegory and irony are . . . linked in their common discovery of a truly temporal predicament" (222). In our terms, irony is what happens when the figural past is written into the narrative present; it is what happens when the figure in a tale becomes aware that he is also—and maybe even principally—a figure in a figural history that encompasses the present moment. The unstable mode of irony, then, is that knife-edge vertigo that happens when the subject occupies—and is aware of occupying—both his narrative and prefigural (antitypical and typical) identities. And so, "it is a historical fact," continues de Man, that an ironic structure (such as the typological form) is illuminated "in the course of demonstrating the impossibility of our being historical" (211). It remains to be seen how the allegorist after Calvin can enter fully aware into a typological vision without irony; this will be the work of Melville's conclusion.

In one sense, then, it might even be said that as soon as one turns from a faith in the efficacy of idols, the problem of irony, of ironic knowledge, turns up. Formally speaking, the salesman's resistance of the narrator's ironic awareness drives the narrative tension of **"The Lightning-Rod Man."** In their strange transaction, which is quickly becoming a theological discussion, the narrator and salesman adopt and abandon other mutually unsatisfactory exemplary idols by way of comparison: the Catholic cathedral, a Quebecois maid at her rosary. All this is by way of looking forward to the present moment: towards updating the problem of the lightning-rod in the realized theology of New England practice. What gives meaning and thematic logic to a wide-ranging discussion of mutually recognized idols—graven images, and so forth—is the promise that the fact of the lightning-rod will both be revealed in its ethical dimension by, and give form and logic to, the handed-on history of idols and icons as they have been understood in the Protestant mind.

* * *

What threads together and underwrites this New England history is the shared vocabulary and social history of a covenanted community that has experienced its most pressing trials under times of contagion and epidemic. New England Calvinism had no clear, evolved position on the use of lightning-rods; if anything, the lightning-rod, as the salesman points out, seems to be an accepted part of church architecture, an integral part of church thinking. After all, the Church seems to be one of the lightning-rod man's best and most faithful clients. This, in fact, might be the problem. But the Calvinist church did have an established, embattled history of thinking about plague. The project of returning the lightning-rod to its theological present involves working it through the already available community symbolic code—returning it to the similar idiom that can either be adapted to accept it, or imagined as already anticipating it. And so, curiously, a history of inoculation—the figure of the inoculation—will inhabit the rupture opened up by the problem of the lightning-rod on the threshold of plot.

This move is not as idiosyncratic as it, at first, might seem. There is a certain amount of compulsive thinking going on here, and allegory—or the experience of living under the tyrannical logic of allegory—always has an element of compulsion.[20] And what's more, lightning and plague share imaginative similarities as the principal scourges in the divine arsenal. Because of this, plague, and the language used to describe plague, are mutually substitutive with lightning and the language used to describe lightning. A man struck by the plague, as Defoe suggests in the *Journal of a Plague Year,* is killed by the plague "as Men are kill'd by a flash of Lightning." Elsewhere, Defoe's narrator notes, again in the language of lightning, that plague victims are "struck from Heaven"; "'tis therefore the Hand of God" (162, 185).[21] Lurking under the comparison is the insistence that as lightning rods are to lightning, so inoculation is to disease; the ethical questions of inoculation are the ethical questions of the lightning-rod. And so for the New Englander—or, at least, for Protestants emerging from the broader Puritan tradition that includes Defoe—the move is a natural one. Almost certainly without knowing it, the salesman—a New England salesman, inhabiting a New England mode of thought—is repeating the compulsive rituals of a characteristically Protestant mode of dealing with divine displeasure. In order to "sell" the lightning-rod, the salesman ends up repeating older types and figures elaborately established in a violent controversy over a century before.

Most of the work positioning lightning in a Calvinist cosmic vision—without thinking through lightning-rods, which had not been invented yet—was developed by Cotton Mather. Indeed, by alluding to the "Acroceraunian hills" in the first page of **"The Lightning-Rod Man,"** Jay Leyda argues, Melville "can allude only to" Mather's chapter in *Magnalia Christi Americana*: "Ceraunius: Relating remarkables done by thunder."[22] Mather's call in this chapter—in the sermon he copies—is a signal example of hard-line Calvinist resignation, a wish that "the *thunder* awaken you to turn from every vanity to God in Christ without any delay, lest by the *thunder* it self it come quickly to be too late. . . . Man, what if the *thunder* should kill thee in the dead sleep of thy unregeneracy?" (319). In this way, Mather

would seem to be a Calvinist theologian of the old school, of a high Calvinist acceptance of the justice of divine displeasure, expressed in lightning; one who would, by extension, had the lightning-rod been invented, interpret the lightning-rod as blasphemy, if not outright idolatry.

But Mather was poised on the edge of two traditions: he was the grandson of John Cotton and Richard Mather who authored the definitive history of the Puritan project; but he also struggled, in *The Christian Philosopher,* to adapt Puritanism of the New England stamp to the pressures of experimental philosophy. He was not, in this way, the last of the Puritans of the type of first generation Puritans, but he was the first of a new school: the first major American Puritan to grapple significantly with the implications of medical science for Protestant theology. And he might be, as a thinker poised at such a moment, interpreted as the marker of a significant departure from the Protestant project; though a devout (if troubled) Puritan in the theological tradition after Calvin, he was, nevertheless, also working towards the decline of high Calvinism that deposited itself, finally, in something like the lapsed state of the Christian religion that Melville knew in Massachusetts and New York.

Mather was the surprising defender (and even champion) of the untried medical practice of inoculation. Thus the same thinker that interpreted a scourge like lightning as a benevolent reminder of an appointed task, even a sort of marker of special favor for a chosen people, pioneered the medical technology that seeks, at least outwardly, to neutralize another similarly spectacular scourge.[23] Mather probably first considered the practicability of inoculation about the time he was working on *The Christian Philosopher.* And later, he certainly would have read the Royal Society's 1714 and 1716 studies published in the *Philosophical Transactions* (Pylarinum and Timonius)—indeed, in 1716, he addressed the Royal Society with an essay entitled "Curiosities of the Smallpox"—but he had already heard rumors about inoculation from his African housekeeper Onesimus.[24] Inoculation had been in the air, as it were, for some time; the first trials were already quietly underway in London (though Mather could not have known it), with belletrist and intellectual Lady Mary Wortley Montagu covertly performing the operation on her daughter, and a doctor at Newgate publicly demonstrating the technique on eight (conditionally) pardoned inmates.[25] But when plague, in 1721, began to break out in Boston, Mather became himself publicly involved: first by inoculating members of his own family, and later by urging more general adoption of the practice.

Indeed, Mather became the foremost figure in what was to be an intense and anxious controversy. Because of the relative newness of the procedure—it was not in general use in Europe—he met nearly general resistance from the medical community; only forward-thinking surgeon and apothecary Zabdiel Boylston and a handful of Mather's followers among the clergy could be convinced to join his project. And because, as well, of the acrimonious and unstable political climate of Boston, Mather found himself isolated, cast out alike by Boston intellectuals, politicians, and physicians.[26] As one historical account has it: "here was a strange spectacle indeed. On the one side, it was the physicians who opposed the advent of preventive medicine . . . on religious as well as scientific grounds. On the other, it was the clergy who not only aided Boylston, but who also defended a liberal theology against the doctors and the populace at large" (Beall and Shryock 106). Even Mather was aware of this curious situation, objecting that his opponents seemed to be usurping his role of champion of theological orthodoxy; he found it "very strange and ridiculous, to see the Satyrists play the Divine."[27]

Strangely, as a historical question, the inoculation controversy was mostly a controversy over its medical implications. But Mather had, as well, members of his congregation and community members at large who felt betrayed by his evident desertion of orthodox Calvinism. Inoculation looks dangerously like an attempt to short-circuit Providence by deflecting the "second causes" concomitant to the "first cause" of righteous Divine judgment. Boylston was regularly denounced as one who proceeded to "contaminate the community"—in Perry Miller's words, "to commit, in short, exactly what every jeremiad held was the supreme violation of covenant" (351).[28] But closer to the point, Boston residents also recognized that inoculation at least outwardly seemed like idolatry; Adam Winthrop, as one example out of many, concluded in a letter to his son that the strategy of inoculation championed by Mather was "placing your Refuge in means and creatures rather than in God" (qtd. in P. Miller 348).

Thus, most of the fallout in the years after the epidemic was obsessed with trying to figure out what just happened: trying to position the fact of inoculation as an ethical or theological issue, what would become, in the sense I'm developing here, an idol. And if inoculation is an idol, what Melville's narrator will come to specify as an "indulgence," it is an idol lurking in a strategy of figuration. As one critic notes, because Mather recognized the plague as "a symbolic event, so too his view of the cure for Smallpox was symbol-fraught" (Breitweiser 119).[29] He justified the strategy of inoculation through what might strike us as a strangely vexed claim. After discussing its medical virtues, he lapses into language *almost* more proper to the pulpit:

> This practice . . . is a safe and sure method of delivering ourselves and our children from going down into

the pit by the stroke of a distemper which dispatches mankind thither by millions.

> (*Selected Letters* 364)

The grave polynomasia hinges on "pit"; the pit seems to be both the visible token of the disease itself—a disease he elsewhere calls the "horrible pit"—and eternal punishment (ibid.). In the same letter, he calls Smallpox "the *destroyer*," the "leviathan . . . who makes our blood boil as a pot," and opponents of inoculation "satanic," and the "Beasts [of] Ephesus." To suffer from the small-pox, he claims, is to "burn . . . for many days"; it is a "fiery trial" (360-61). Or, to die of small-pox, he seems to be saying, is bound up in the etiology of deserved perdition. In other words, Mather seems to be reading the small-pox allegorically. Inoculation, one might object, seems only the more idolatrous: like combating an allegorically disposed disease with an allegorically efficacious cure.

The clue to Mather's defense of inoculation lies in his understanding of the theological implications of post-Cartesian dualism, and it is here, as well, that Mather might be accused of adopting an idolatrous strategy of representation. Mather believed in the basic correspondence of the moral world and its physical, observable counterpart, a type to its metaphorable antitype, linked, perhaps, by a "Vital Ty," the "Nishmath Chajim" (Mather, *Angel* 40, 67). Speaking of the duality of mind and body, Mather suggests that

> there is a Spirit in Man . . . which may be of a Middle Nature, between the Rational Soul and the Corporeal mass; but may be the medium of Communication, by which they work upon one another.
>
> (40)

This is the *Nishmath Chajim*; this "Vital Ty" is Mather's version of Descartes's theory of the Pineal Gland. And it is this (only hypothesized, of course) scientific fact that allows the mind to operate on the body, and to allow the body to operate on the mind. One is legible on the other, by means of the *Nishmath Chajim*. Inoculation, according to this logic, is more than just an adventitious invention; it is a divine appointment. It is one's duty to mete out a dose of the scourge to oneself, by way of purging oneself of latent humors; it is a cleansing operation:

> Here the Man *makes himself Sick,* while he is well; and thinks that he is not *the whole who has no need of a Physician,* while he has the *Humours* in him which render him obnoxious to a *Deadly Sickness. . . .* He most properly takes GOD's Time to fall Sick: He does it seasonably, and in the *Time* when God has *commanded* him to do it.
>
> ("Sentiments" 2)

As Mitchell Breitweiser suggests, the inoculation was only one way of leveraging a created universe that Mather believed to be organized by the logic of analogy and allegory, what were, for him, the principles that "structured . . . creation." For Mather, again in the words of Breitweiser, "the body is analogous to the soul and the human community, all three of which were fields in which one might inquire into the etiology of the Lord's wrath" (119). Thus, sin—even Original Sin—is a sickness of the spirit which causes a concomitant sickness of the body; plague and Pride are convertible specie traded through an exchange rate governed by this "Vital Ty."

Yet, for all his justifications—in the defense, after all, of an important humanitarian agenda—one might still see Cotton Mather, in his handling of fresh samples of smallpox effluvia, as very much like Caesar Augustus with his handling of lightning. One might suspect that Cotton Mather, the Divine Doctor, in seizing the live strain of smallpox in order to avert future epidemics, looks very much like Caesar Augustus, with his copper statue, holding a lightning-bolt in order to avert future lightning-bolts. More to the point, both Cotton Mather and Caesar Augustus adopt a theory of allegorical figuration to read, explain, and maybe even control legible marks or pits: Mather's "pit" is very like Augustus's blotted CAESAR. It is a problem, in this sense, of idolatry—the wrong sort of representation, of the production of the flesh of a "figment like itself," in Calvin's words, with which it "solaces itself" as though God exerted his power through representations (1:124, 131).

That Melville's narrator is thinking the lightning-rod through the idiom of inoculation developed by Mather is first signaled by his description of the lightning-rod man: "His sunken pitfalls of eyes were ringed by indigo halos, and played with an innocuous sort of lightning: the gleam without the bolt" (118-19). This line—among the most quoted and puzzling in the story—is the kind of line that causes us to sense that there is "some allegory" lurking immediately under the skin of the literal narrative. The pun on innocuous, which shares sound (but not sense) with "inoculation," is only part of what is going on here. "Innocuous," of course, stems from the Latin (*innocuous: in-*, not; + *nocuus,* harmful); and this is a pun that Cotton Mather himself seems elsewhere to have heard, as Breitweiser notes, while he is speaking of inoculation in *The Christian Philosopher*:

> An excellent *Fellow of the College of Physicians* makes a just remark: ". . . it is probable that the most dangerous *Poisons,* skillfully managed, may not only be innocuous, but of all other Medicines the most effectual."
>
> (134, qtd. in Breitweiser 121)

But this doesn't account for the full complexity of the word-play. By pointing us to the salesman's eyes, Melville also indicates the etymological sense of inocu-

lation (*in-*, in; + *oculus,* eye): the horticultural insertion of a bud, or "eye," under the skin of another plant for propagation. **"The Lightning-Rod Man"** is an inoculation of inoculation; an insertion of an aggressive "eye" in the host genre of the salesman story, for the purposes of propagation of the sponsoring idea. If we understand the premise of the allusion, the rest of the medical image explicates itself; the "indigo halos" are the areolae which form the local phenomena of the normal inoculation; the areolae, in turn, surround the "pock," or "pit."[30] This is a pun, of course, that we have heard before—a pun turned back on Mather, with his parsing of smallpox as itself a pit or pitfall; for the salesman's eyes are not "sunken pits" but "sunken pitfalls." What is visible on the surface of the lightning-rod salesman's phiz is his own moral failure—and even the seductiveness of its own "pitfall," something like the easy indulgence that Melville's interlocutor will later (allusively) denounce.

But what is important for a story that seems to call out to be read "allegorically" is not in its particularities, but in its relations; indeed, the differences in unique technologies—protections against lightning and plague—collapse around their intentional similarities, anyway. The salesman is as much a mountebank of physic during times of plague as he is a lightning-rod salesman during times of thunder. For example, the salesman's technique for gauging his safety during a thunderstorm—gauging the proximity of lightning strikes by taking his pulse—is more than just curiously reminiscent of the technique employed for measuring the health of one who is afraid he might have contracted an infection. Likewise, according to the logic of lightning, the salesman's policy of "avoid[ing] a crowd of men" during a thunderstorm is absurd. It misses the point. It isn't community that is dangerous when it is storming. It is during times of "Distress" of the contagious variety, Defoe's interlocutor notes in his *Journal of a Plague Year,* that people "shut up [their] Compassion." In times of contagion, in other words, people "[begin] to be jealous of every Body, and a vast Number of People lock . . . themselves up, so as not to come abroad into any Company at all, nor suffer any . . . to come into their Houses, or near them." In so "dangerous a Time" as the plague year people "shun . . . one another, and fle[e] from one another" (133, 201, 218, 216).

As Hershel Parker puts it, **"The Lightning-Rod Man"** is a salesman story, with a "fear-instilling religionist playing the part of the peddler" ("Salesman" 154); this is how the problem of the lightning-rod writes itself back on the fear-instilling religionist that was Cotton Mather. But it might be more precise to suggest that the peddler is playing the part of the "fear-instilling religionist" as the only idiom of ethical persuasion he knows. Melville's narrator senses this, senses that the right way to talk about lightning-rods with a compulsively New England salesman is to talk about them as the visible icons of the mode of thinking that they seem already to be representing. He locates the most apt theological analog for the consideration of Franklinian optimism in the struggles of high Calvinism to adapt to the pressures of inoculation. He sees, in other words, that the lightning-rod salesman's thinking is already somehow in the allegorical mode, that the lightning-rod man has taken "particular precautions" (121). In terms that could only be opposable in New England (but that might remind us of Pliny) the narrator of **"The Lightning-Rod Man"** chooses charity instead of lightning-rods.

With this choice the narrator hits—somewhat too late, we might think—on the perfect idiom for the problem of the lightning-rod; in doing so, he reverts to the foundational episode of the Protestant moment. If "Jupiter Tonans" opens up the possibility of a theological reading of the lightning-rod, opens the allegorical and hence ethical plot of his encounter with the Berkshire peddler, it is "Tetzel" that closes it:

> "You pretended envoy extraordinary and minister plenipotentiary to and from Jupiter Tonans," laughed I; "you mere man who come here to put you and your pipestem between clay and sky, do you think that because you can strike a bit of green light from the Leyden jar, that you can thoroughly avert the supernal bolt? Who has empowered you, you Tetzel, to peddle round your indulgences from divine ordinations? The hairs of our heads are numbered, and the days of our lives. In thunder as in sunshine, I stand at ease in the hands of my God. False negotiator, away! See, the scroll of the storm is rolled back; the house is unharmed; and in the blue heavens I read in the rainbow, that the Deity will not, of purpose, make war on man's earth."
>
> (124)

Jupiter Tonans is on the entry threshold of the problem of the indulgence; Johann Tetzel is on its exit. This is a rupture and resolution negotiated entirely in the symbolic; other than the shared initials, which, talismanic, may summon the one from the other, Caesar Augustus's self-proclaimed ally and the Indulgence Commissar for Wittenberg share no common history except their history in the mutual negotiation of a problem—a particularly Romish problem, maybe—of idolatry. Johann Tetzel was the foil to Martin Luther's foundational 95 theses nailed on the door of the Wittenberg Castle Cathedral that launched the Protestant Reformation. The Indulgence, the narrator seems to say, is only clarified in its theological aspect by gesturing to the lightning-rod; the lightning-rod is only illuminated in its ethical ramifications by the history of the Indulgence. Inasmuch as the Protestant movement is the protestation of abuses of the Catholic Church, it fundamentally protests idolatrous thinking, the placing of faith in the devices of mankind. This, then, is what the narrator has been saying all along; he has been imagining Luther's forty-

fifth thesis: "Christians are to be taught that he who sees a man in need, and passes him by to purchase pardons, bargains not for the Indulgences of the Pope, but for the indignation of God."[31] The allusion to Luther, by way of Tetzel, is not at all frivolous; it conforms to the logic of the type. Luther, himself, gave his life over to God after narrowly escaping electrocution during a thunderstorm.[32]

* * *

I have traced the history of allegory as it appears in a story that is itself a history of allegory—of allegorical figuration that comes to look like idolatry—but there remains something to be said about the problems that emerge from the experience of living under the aspect of such a figural vision. For, as we have seen, the typological narrative threatens, by its very form, to lapse into irony, but irony is a poor mode for resolving the ethical claims that the typological narrative is summoned up to address in the first place. We would not, I think, accuse the narrator of speaking ironically as he rejects the lightning-rod man and his typical talisman. He seems, instead, as he casts out the "false negotiator" (124), to be speaking from a position of genuine authority.

But his position is not at all like the lightning-rod man's. The lightning-rod man finds a way out of the narrator's ironic position by refusing the awareness of history. One way, in other words, out of the *dédoublement* which triggers the ironic mode, is to refuse the historical self, and leap, instead, into a kind of faith. This is a faith in idols—a lightning-rod, or a copper statue, or an Indulgence—which is also a faith in allegorical reading. This is the solution of the lightning-rod man, and Caesar Augustus and Johann Tetzel. These technologies, evidently intended unironically, insist on the power of the icon, of itself, to bind mortal and divine around their own rates of exchange. They refuse, however, the form of the type itself, by refusing the overdetermining ordering mind of Providence which binds the figure in the "overwhelming allegorical force of . . . history" (Luxon 42).

The other, more satisfactory but difficult mode of escaping the vertigo of irony while maintaining an awareness of the ordering mind of Providence is to refuse the existential, autonomous self. This is the choice of Martin Luther, for example; it is also the choice of Jonathan Edwards. Martin Luther's experience of near-electrocution—a direct experience of the insignificance of the existential self—is what produces what we might call the first protestant conversion: Luther giving himself into a monastery.[33] But it is Jonathan Edwards's piety, as Marvin Fisher has demonstrated, that provides the model for the narrator's own conversion experience.[34] Edwards expanded the claims of typology to include the grand scope of creation as its encompassing objects:

under the right conditions of resignation, the hand of God is immediately legible on the book of Nature. As Edwards puts it, "the material and natural world is typical of the moral, spiritual, and intelligent world, or the city of God . . . as things belonging to the state of the church under the Old Testament were typical of things belonging to the church and kingdom of God under the New Testament" ("Types of the Messiah" 191). This is to say that events today are only events situated in a historical field under the aspect of an ordering teleology. To be a regenerated Christian is to be invited into a new Israel. Events, in the cosmos of the new Israel, are significant in just the same way that "all things," Edwards continues, "that pertained to the affairs of the children of Israel in the wilderness were typical, were ordered of God to be types of spiritual and eternal things."[35]

Edwards's thoughts on thunder make clear the connection between the event of the conversion and the new mode of seeing the typological and historical cosmos:

> Scarce anything, among all the works of nature, was so sweet to me as thunder and lightning. Formerly, nothing had been so terrible to me. I used to be a person uncommonly terrified with thunder, and it used to strike me with terror, when I saw a thunderstorm rising. But now, on the contrary, it rejoiced me. I felt God at the first appearance of a thunderstorm. And used to take the opportunity at such times, to fix myself to view the clouds, and see the lightnings play and hear the majestic and awful voice of God's thunder, which oftentimes was exceeding entertaining, leading me to sweet contemplations of my great and glorious God.
>
> ("Personal Narrative" 794)[36]

The retrospective construction of Edwards's piety is composed around two distinct stages or epochs of consciousness—two modes of knowing—punctuated by a transformative conversion experience. In the first, thunder was a strange and alien thing: it was "terrible," it "terrified"; it would "strike . . . with terror." In the second, however, the experience of thunder is the opportunity for rejoicing, for experiencing the mind of God directly in his ubiquitous figurations. What, exactly, triggers this conversion experience falls, in fact, outside the immediate text, but it hinges, as a question internal to the textual construction of the event, on the moment "now," the sudden intrusion of the epic present—what Edwards might call the Providential present—into what is a past-tense autobiographical recollection. This "now" is not the present—or, it includes the present moment, but is not limited to it. It is, instead, a "now" that sees no distinction between history and the existential moment; it hears no tense disagreement in "now . . . it rejoiced me." To return to de Man, such a speaker "who exists in [such a] 'now,' is that of a subject whose insight is no longer in doubt and who is no longer vulnerable to irony. It could be called, if one so wished, a stance of wisdom" (224).[37]

This moment of greatest existential joy, the "now" of Edwards's "rejoicing," is only experienced at the sacrifice of the authentic self—of the authentic (authorial) subject as distinct from the mind of God—and of the figures of the past that inform it, sacrificed in the construction of a subject that can only experience personal history as the syntactic object of the figure in history: "[thunder] rejoiced me." This, after all, is the mind of Edwards as he puts pen to paper; after the pivotal "now," his personal agency is limited to putting himself in a position to allow the thunder to be "leading . . . him to sweet contemplations"—contemplations which presumably included the one he was then composing.

The narrator, then, gestures to a pattern of Edwardsian experience to underwrite his own already-converted and unironic existential experience. It is at the moment that he ceases disputing that he sacrifices his existential self to the consciousness of his own historical and typological situation. It is a sort of conversion, much as Jonathan Edwards's or Martin Luther's before his. Implicated in the surrender of conversion is a new mode of reading, the kind of insight of Luther and Edwards, which is only the literal truth of the literal mind of God revealed "in thunder as in sunshine" (124). After the conversion—the critical event of Edwards's "Personal Narrative"—everything changes: there is no room for irony between the historical self and its seamless perception of historical events. Edwards can see "God's excellency, his wisdom, his purity and love . . . in everything; in the sun, moon and stars; in the clouds, and blue sky; in the grass, flowers, trees; in the water, and all nature; which used greatly to fix my mind" ("Personal Narrative" 794). For the narrator, this new sense provides a genuine certainty instantly available from the knowledge of the universe; he can "read" the Hand of Providence on the legible "scroll of the storm," can "read" "the blue heavens . . . in the rainbow" (124). He knows, in a leap of figural logic not available to the idolatrous faith of the lightning-rod man, that "the Deity will not, of purpose, make war on man's earth."

Notes

I wish to thank Michael Colacurcio, Anne Myers, and my anonymous reader at the *Arizona Quarterly* for their assistance with drafts of this essay.

1. As Hayford notes, "The Lightning-Rod Man" was "the one Melville tale regularly in print and available to the public throughout the remainder of this lifetime" (600).

2. The best discussions of the history of the production of "The Lightning-Rod Man" outside of Hayford's Notes are two studies by Parker: "Melville's Salesman Story," and *Herman Melville: A Biography,* 216. Burton's *Cyclopaedia,* noted by Hay-

ford, is an idiosyncratic collection: a large, bound anthology of contemporary "wit" in double-columns on inexpensive paper. It begins, apt to its explicit purpose of cataloguing historical and contemporary examples of wit, with "The Maypole" from Thomas Morton's *New England Canaan* (1625) and includes reprinted tales and poems from Hawthorne, Lowell, Holmes, Briggs, Burton himself, and, buried deep between "Negro Philosophy: A Fish Story" (by Dr. James S. Peacock) and "Two Days at Clichy, by Horace Greely" (432-34), Melville's "The Lightning-Rod Man."

3. See, for instance, Parker, "Melville's Salesman Story." One salient example of the form is John G. Whittier's "The Yankee Zincali," reprinted in Burton's *Cyclopaedia*. It begins, like "The Lightning-Rod Man," with a penny-ante confidence man walking into a bachelor's apartment out of the rain—includes, even, much of the same evidently formulaic language—and ends without him getting any money.

4. The first modern treatment of "The Lightning-Rod Man" sets the terms of later criticism by observing "obviously there is some allegory here" (Kimpel 30). Some later examples answering Kimpel's call include Verdier and Fisher. Fisher notes that the comic guise of the story might be Melville's own lightning-rod to deflect critical attention. Dillingham suggests that the "return-stroke" of lightning becomes symbolic of the narrator's act of defiance. Also, see Parker's "Melville's Salesman Story," which invites us "to share Melville's joke in palming off on the genteel *Putnam's Monthly* a scathing denunciation of one manifestation of nineteenth-century American Christianity, the fire-and-brimstone salvation salesman" (157-58).

5. Or, as Verdier puts it, "Who Is the Lightning-Rod Man?"

6. The lightning-rod is a figure that Melville already had in hand; Ahab characterizes his project as a cosmic lightning-rod raised over the "Himmalehs and Andes" (*Moby-Dick* 505, 511) to make (in the language of "The Lightning-Rod Man") a "Gibraltar" (120) of the world.

7. The reason for Melville's reversion to allegory is probably biographical. Melville had been thinking about idolatry in 1854 when he penned—in a period of extensive but hasty literary production—"The Lightning-Rod Man." Charles F. Briggs, the editor of *Putnam's Monthly* had just rejected "The Two Temples"; he was "very loth to reject" the tale, but the "point of [Melville's] sketch" might be distasteful or disturbing to "some of our church readers" (Melville, *Correspondence* 636). He was

almost certainly right. In "Temple First," the narrator visits and is turned away from an Episcopalian church that seems to meld architectural and historical details from two recent New York cathedrals: Grace and Trinity Churches. These were churches in the "Flamboyant Gothic" style, ostentatious and fashionable icons of sectarian power. Not only does Melville denounce the combined congregations of the Grace and Trinity Churches as a host of "Pharisees," he also complicates their implicit fascination with idols by comparing their Grace Church to a playhouse (in "Temple Second"), and their minister to an actor playing Cardinal Richelieu. Fearing that Melville's "pungent satire" would "offend . . . the religious sensibilities of the public," Putnam and Briggs rejected his manuscript (636). But instead of rewriting it, or placing it elsewhere, Melville turned his attention to a compact little story about a salesman. Though Melville couldn't explicitly discuss charged religious issues and expect publication, he could bury them in the overcharged earth of "The Lightning-Rod Man." Briggs becomes an accomplice in "publishing [Melville's] infidel notions" (Melville "Lightning-Rod Man" 124). For analysis of "The Two Temples," see Rowland, Berthold, Horner, and Cook. For details on the correspondence between Melville and *Putnam's*, see Melville, *Correspondence* 636-37. Also see Hayford's "Note" (Melville *Correspondence* 636); Leyda *The Melville Log* 1:491; and Parker, *Melville* 2:216-22. In reaction to *Putnam's* rejection of Melville's "Two Temples," Melville suggests "Ere long I will send down some other things," to which "no objections will be made on the score of tender consciences of the public" (*Correspondence* 261). Editors and critics alike have commonly understood these "other things" to indicate sixty pages of *Israel Potter* sent shortly thereafter to the editors, but it might also embrace Melville's concurrent "The Lightning-Rod Man." Melville was paid for the sixty manuscript pages of *Israel Potter* and those of "The Lightning-Rod Man" in the same remission (266).

8. See Quintilian 8:6.44, and Cicero 27:94. Some major studies of allegory, classically understood, include Benjamin, Fletcher, Tuve 99-109.

9. For a transitional example, an example poised between these two modes, one might consider "The Tartarus of Maids," an allegory about the work of art in the age of human reproduction.

10. The best discussion of this tradition in "The Lightning-Rod Man" is Emery.

11. Lewalski identifies this passage as foundational in rescuing typology of the Pauline model from the allegorical hermeneutical tradition (117).

12. Luther had already suggested that proper allegory is only "a kind of illumination of an oration or of a case that has already been established on other grounds." However, "not everyone has the skill to play around with allegories. For a pretty external appearance will impress a person in such a way that he will go astray" (*Lectures* 26:236, 438).

13. The best study of this is probably still Perry Miller's *The New England Mind*. Returns to the problems of American typology raised by Miller include Bercovitch (ed), and Lewalski's early transatlantic project.

14. This observation is adapted from Erich Auerbach's theory of figural poetics. "Figural interpretation establishes a connection between two events or persons, the first of which signifies not only itself but also the second, while the second encompasses or fulfills the first" (53).

15. An excerpt from Marvel's *Reveries,* a cultural sensation in its own right, also turns up in Burton's *Cyclopaedia of Wit and Humor.*

16. Leyda remarks that Helen Morewood, Melville's great-niece, suggested that "The Lightning-Rod Man" was based on an actual encounter with an actual salesman during an actual thunderstorm (Foreword xxvi-xxvii). While this is not at all important to the tale considered in itself, it is germane to note Melville's figure, here, may be more "real" than even the tale itself can possibly represent. In any case, while scholars would almost certainly never think to try to locate a real railroad as a precedent to Hawthorne's railroad, for example, it is not at all unreasonable to think to look for a real lightning-rod salesman as a precedent for Melville's fictional representation. This fact, as much as anything else, points towards the essential difference between these two strategies of figuration.

17. He planted laurels in front of his home (Cassius 6:233)—partly as a sign of his status, no doubt, but perhaps also to ward off electrocution, because seal-skins and laurel trees were well-known never to be struck (Pliny 1:283).

18. As Suetonius has it, Augustus was descended of Apollo—also a wielder of thunderbolts (1:265-67). But Augustus was certainly leveraging an older political theology; Frazer's classic and monumental study of Greek culture identifies a similar cosmic and even political vision. When Greek rulers claimed their special prerogative as "viceroys" of Zeus, Frazer tells us, and even, in so doing, blurred the line between mortal and immortal by suggesting kinship, they also "attempted to exercise his divine functions by making thunder and rain for the good of their people or the terror and confusion of their foes" (2:177, 361).

19. For Baudelaire, irony is always an internal dialectic in the first-person narrative subject. This, clearly, is not what is going on in "The Lightning-Rod Man"; the object of irony here is certainly the salesman. But this may be a case where the narrator most fully talks about himself by describing a representative episode, when he is most truthful about himself by talking about someone else. The real threat is that, by naming the salesman a "Jupiter," or a Caesar, he realizes the he is claiming himself as a Pliny; by calling him a Mather, he becomes a Winthrop; or, as we will see, by naming him a Tetzel, he calls himself a Luther. As de Man reminds us, "The moment the innocence or authenticity of our sense of being in the world is put into question, a far from harmless process gets underway" (215). This "process" is what Baudelaire calls the *vertige de l'hyperbole,* the threat of irony to unravel the entire web of consciousness (259).

20. For Fletcher, "compulsion" is an integral part of the allegorical mode; what seems like a digression is actually the assumption of yet another set of symbolic relations under the principal metaphor that drives the allegory in the first place. "Compulsive rituals have an infinite number of kinds of materials. Almost any object, any image, any word or words, any icon will do for this purpose, since what makes something a ritual is not a particular substance, but a particular order and repetition of parts" (292).

21. Fletcher suggests that "Contagion is the primary symbol of Christian allegory since that allegory is chiefly concerned with sin and redemption." In a note, developing this claim, he gestures to both Hawthorne's "Fancy's Show Box" and Defoe's *Journal of a Plague Year.* Defoe's *Journal,* written uncannily at the same time as the Boston small-pox epidemic was developing, is allegorical in the limited sense that it seeks to return a historical crisis to a contemporary political purpose.

22. Leyda interprets this clue in the "mythic" mode, arguing that Melville was alluding to Mather as the exemplar of "a troubling and frightening record of religion in its most fiercely bullying and bigoted aspect" (Foreword xxvi-xxvii).

23. While Benjamin Franklin had to leave Mather's parish in order to be Benjamin Franklin, he might not have had to leave to invent the lightning-rod. While Mather was a student of the Calvinist insistence that such scourges as lightning and plague were divine appointments, he also saw no problem with inoculating his parishioners; one might *almost* imagine that one of the churches that the lightning-rod salesman indemnifies in Melville's tale was Mather's old North Church in Boston,

and that Mather would have approved of the lightning-rod for the same reason that he would fight for the general acceptance of inoculation.

24. "Inquiring of my Negro-man Onesimus, who is a pretty Intelligent Fellow, Whether he ever had the Small-Pox; he answered, both, Yes, and No; and then told me, that he had undergone an Operation, which had given him something of the Small-Pox, & would forever preserve him from it. . . . His Description of it, made it the same, that afterwards I found related [in the *Philosophical Transactions*]" (*Selected Letters* 362). Also see Silverman's *Life* 336-63.

25. See, for instance, Montagu, and G. Miller. Also see Beall and Shryock 137-38; P. Miller 345-66; and Blake 489.

26. According to Shryock (137), Mather was "probably more widely read in medicine" than his chief antagonist, William Douglass, who had earned an M.D. in London. His continued interest following the subsidence of the epidemic also followed the techniques of empirical philosophy; Dr. Boylston and Cotton Mather's studies demonstrating the effectiveness of the medical practice of inoculation were some of the earliest examples of statistical studies employing mortality rates. See Mather's anonymous pamphlet *An Account of the Methods and Success of Inoculating,* and Boylston.

27. See the *Vindication of the Ministers of Boston.* That this anonymous pamphlet was composed (at least in part) by Mather, see Kittredge, 418-79.

28. Also see the anonymous pamphlet, "A Letter from one in the Country," which makes a similar contention.

29. Also see Levin, who shares Breitweiser's assessment that Mather's response to Smallpox was, strangely, essentially semiotic (and, hence, in our terms, allegorical).

30. See Dimsdale. Dimsdale's description chiefly tracks the evolution of the inflammation around the immediate incisions made to facilitate the inoculation.

31. See *Werke* 1:235: "Docendi sunt christiani, quod, qui videt egenum et neglecto eo dat pro veniis, non indulgentias Pape sed indignationem dei sibi vindicat."

32. See *Werke: Tischreden* 4:440 and 5:99. I am grateful to Anne Myers for this observation.

33. I owe this phrase—the "first Protestant conversion"—to Holly Crawford Pickett.

34. Like Mather, Edwards was a transitional figure whose life stood at the actual intersection of lightning and plague in a way that Mather stood only

at the imaginative junction. Though Edwards's conversion indirectly involves lightning, he died directly after a botched inoculation.

35. See Lowance and Watters 162, who quotes an undated sermon (from 1731 or 1732) on Corinthians 10:8-11, currently in the Beinecke Rare Book and Manuscript Library, Yale University (MS # 252). Also see Edwards's "Types": "I believe that the whole universe, heaven and earth, air and seas, and the divine constitution and history of the holy Scriptures, be full of images of divine things, as full as a language is of words" (152).

36. Still, we have to be careful not to read Edwards's thoughts as an example of unalloyed religious optimism, or religious optimism of the lightning-rod man's stamp, for example. Elsewhere, in a manuscript note, Edwards suggests that "The extreme fierceness and extraordinary power of the heat of lightning is an intimation of the exceeding power and terribleness of the wrath of God" ("Images" 59).

37. De Man continues "There is no real disjunction of the subject; the [narrative] is written from the point of view of a unified self that fully recognizes a past condition as one of error and stands in a present that, however painful, sees things as they actually are" (224). My reading of Edwards, which returns to Melville, is heavily dependent on de Man's reading of William Wordsworth's "A slumber did my spirit seal" (de Man 223-27).

Works Cited

Auerbach, Erich. *Scenes from the Drama of European Literature.* Trans. Ralph Manheim. New York: Meridian, 1959.

Baudelaire, Charles. "De l'essence du rire." *Curiosités esthétiques: L'Art romantique et autres Oeuvres critiques.* Ed. H. Lemaître. Paris: Garnier, 1962.

Beall, Otho T., and Richard H. Shryock. *Cotton Mather: First Significant Figure in American Medicine.* Baltimore: Johns Hopkins University Press, 1954.

Benjamin, Walter. "Allegory and Trauerspiel." *The Origin of German Tragic Drama.* Trans. John Osborn. London: Verso, 1998. 159-235.

Bercovitch, Sacvan, ed. *Typology and Early American Literature.* Amherst: University of Massachusetts Press, 1972.

Berthold, Dennis. "Class Acts: The Astor Place Riots and Melville's 'The Two Temples.'" *American Literature* 71 (1999): 429-61.

Blake, John B. "The Inoculation Controversy in Boston: 1721-1722." *New England Quarterly* 25 (1952): 489-506.

Boylston, Zabdiel. *An Historical Account of the Small-Pox Inoculated in New England.* London, 1726.

Breitweiser, Mitchell. *Cotton Mather and Benjamin Franklin: The Price of Representative Personality.* Cambridge: Cambridge University Press, 1984.

Burton, William E., ed. *Cyclopaedia of Wit and Humour.* New York: D. Appleton and Company, 1857.

Calvin, John. *Institutes of the Christian Religion.* Trans. Henry Beveridge. Edinburgh: Calvin Translation Society, 1845.

Capital Stories by American Authors. New York: The Christian Herald, 1895.

Cassius Dio Cocceianus. *Roman History.* 9 vols. Trans. Earnest Cary. Cambridge: Harvard University Press, 1960.

Cicero. *De Oratore.* Ed. and trans. E. Sutton and H. Rackham. London: Loeb Classics, 1948.

Cook, Clarence. "New York Church Architecture." *Putnam's Monthly Magazine* (Sept. 1853): 247.

Davis, Thomas M. "The Traditions of Puritan Typology." Bercovitch 11-46.

Defoe, Daniel. *Journal of a Plague Year.* Ed. Cynthia Wall. London: Penguin, 2003.

de Man, Paul. "The Rhetoric of Temporality." *Blindness and Insight.* Minneapolis: University of Minnesota Press, 1983. 187-228.

Dillingham, William. *Melville's Short Fiction: 1853-'56.* Athens: University of Georgia Press, 1977.

Dimsdale, Thomas. *Tracts on Inoculation: Written and Published at St. Petersburg in the Year 1768.* London, 1781.

Edwards, Jonathan. "Images of Divine Things." Ed. Wallace E. Anderson. *Typological Writings. The Works of Jonathan Edwards.* Vol. 11. New Haven: Yale University Press, 1993. 50-130.

———. "Personal Narrative." *Letters and Personal Writings.* Ed. George S. Claghorn. *The Works of Jonathan Edwards.* Vol. 16. New Haven: Yale University Press, 1998. 790-804.

———. "Types." Ed. Wallace E. Anderson. *Typological Writings. The Works of Jonathan Edwards.* Vol. 11. New Haven: Yale University Press, 1993. 146-53.

———. "Types of the Messiah," or "Miscellany 1069." Ed. Mason I. Lowance and David H. Watters. *Typological Writings. The Works of Jonathan Edwards.* Vol. 11. New Haven: Yale University Press, 1993. 191-324.

Emery, Allan Moore. "Melville on Science: 'The Lightning-Rod Man.'" *New England Quarterly* 56 (1983): 555-68.

Fineman, Joel. "The Structure of Allegorical Desire." *The Subjectivity Effect in Western Literary Tradition: Essays Towards the Release of Shakespeare's Will.* Cambridge: MIT Press, 1991. 3-31.

Fisher, Marvin. "'The Lightning-Rod Man': Melville's Testament of Rejection." *Studies in Short Fiction* 7 (1970): 433-38.

Fletcher, Angus. *Allegory: The Theory of a Symbolic Mode.* Ithaca: Cornell University Press, 1964.

Fraunce, Abraham. *The Arcadian Rhetorike.* Ed. Ethel Seaton. Oxford: Basil Blackwell, 1950.

Frazer, Sir James George. *The Golden Bough.* 8 vols. New York: St. Martins Press, 1976.

Hayford, Harrison, et al., eds. "Notes on 'Lightning-Rod Man.'" *The Piazza Tales and Other Prose Pieces, 1839-1860.* Evanston: Northwestern University Press, 1987. 600-02.

Honig, Edwin. *Dark Conceit: The Making of Allegory.* Evanston: Northwestern University Press, 1959.

Horner, Charles R. "Isaac Brown: Melville's 'Beadle-Faced Man.'" *Melville Society Extracts* 26 (1976): 11-13.

Kimpel, Ben D. "Two Notes on Melville." *American Literature* 16 (1944): 29-32.

Kittredge, George Lyman. "Some Lost Works of Cotton Mather." *Publications of the Massachusetts Historical Society* 45 (1911-12): 418-79.

"A Letter from One in the Country, to His Friend in the City." Boston: 1721.

Levin, David. *Cotton Mather: The Young Life of the Lord's Remembrancer.* Cambridge: Harvard University Press, 1978.

Lewalski, Barbara Kiefer. *Protestant Poetics and the Seventeenth-Century Religious Lyric.* Princeton: Princeton University Press, 1979.

Leyda, Jay. Foreword. *The Complete Stories of Herman Melville.* New York: Random House, 1949.

———. *The Melville Log: A Documentary Life of Herman Melville.* 2 vols. New York: Harcourt, 1951.

Lowance, Mason I. and David H. Watters. Introduction. "Types of the Messiah." *Typological Writings. The Works of Jonathan Edwards.* Vol. 11. New Haven: Yale University Press, 1993. 157-82.

Luther, Martin. *Lectures on Galatians. Works.* Vol. 26-27. Ed. and trans. Jaroslav Pelikan. St. Louis: Concordia, 1963.

———. *D. Martin Luther Werke: Tischreden.* 6 vols. Ed. K. Drescher and G. Krofer. Weimar: H. Böhlaus Nachfolger, 1912.

————. *D. Martin Luther Werke.* 69 vols. Weimar: H. Böhlaus Nachfolger, 1883.

Luxon, Thomas H. *Literal Figures: Puritan Allegory and the Reformation Crisis in Representation.* Chicago: University of Chicago Press, 1995.

Marvel, Ik. *Reveries of a Bachelor; or, a Book of the Heart.* New York: Baker and Scribner, 1850.

Mather, Cotton. *An Account of the Methods and Success of Inoculating.* Boston, 1721.

————. *The Angel of Bethesda.* Ed. Gordon W. Jones. Barre, MA: American Antiquarian Society and Barre Publishers, 1972.

————. *The Christian Philosopher.* London, 1721.

————. *Magnalia Christi Americana; or, the Ecclesiastical History of New-England.* 1702. Hartford, 1820.

————. *Selected Letters of Cotton Mather.* Ed. Kenneth Silverman. Baton Rouge: Louisiana State University Press, 1971.

————. "Sentiments on the Small Pox Inoculated." 1721. Cleveland: "Printed for Private Distribution," 1921.

Mather, Cotton, et. al. *Vindication of the Ministers of Boston.* Boston, 1722.

Mather, Samuel. *The Figures or Types of the Old Testament.* 1705. New York: Johnson Reprint Corporation, 1969.

Melville, Herman. *Correspondence.* Ed. Harrison Hayford, et. al. Evanston: Northwestern University Press, 1993.

————. "The Lightning-Rod Man." *The Piazza Tales and Other Prose Pieces: 1839-1860.* Ed. Harrison Hayford, et. al. Evanston: Northwestern University Press, 1987. 118-24.

————. *Moby-Dick; or, the Whale.* Ed. Harrison Hayford, et. al. Evanston: Northwestern University Press, 1988.

Miller, Genevieve. "Smallpox Inoculation in England and America: a Reappraisal." *William and Mary Quarterly* 13 (1956): 476-92.

Miller, Perry. *The New England Mind: From Colony to Province.* Boston: Beacon Press, 1953.

Montagu, Lady Mary Wortley. *Letters of the Right Honourable Lady M—y W—y M—e. . . .* London, 1763.

Parker, Hershel. "Melville's Salesman Story." *Studies in Short Fiction* 1.2 (1964): 154-58.

————. *Herman Melville: A Biography.* 2 vols. Baltimore: Johns Hopkins University Press, 2002.

Pliny. *Natural History.* 10 vols. Trans. H. Rackham. Ed. G. P. Goold. Cambridge: Harvard University Press, 1997.

Pylarinum, Jacobum (Jacob Pylarinus). "Nova & Tuta Variolas Excitandi per Transplantationem Methodus, Nuper Inventa & in Usum Tracta." *Philosophical Transactions* 347 (1716): 393-99.

Quintilian. *Istitutio Oratoria.* Trans. H. E. Butler. London: Loeb Classics, 1953.

Rowland, Beryl. "Grace Church and Melville's Story of 'The Two Temples.'" *Nineteenth-Century Fiction* 28 (1973): 339-46.

Shryock, R. H. *Development of Modern Medicine.* Madison: University of Wisconsin Press, 1979.

Shusterman, Alan. "Melville's 'The Lightning-Rod Man': A Reading." *Studies in Short Fiction* 9 (1972): 165-74.

Silverman, Kenneth. *The Life and Times of Cotton Mather.* New York: Harper & Row, 1984.

Suetonius. "The Deified Augustus." *The Lives of the Caesars.* 2 vols. Trans. J. C. Rolfe. Cambridge: Harvard University Press, 1951.

Timonius, Emanuel. "An Account, or History, of the Procuring the Small Pox by Incision, or Inoculation. . . ." *Philosophical Transactions* 339 (1714): 72-82.

Tuve, Rosemond. *Elizabethan and Metaphysical Imagery.* Chicago: University of Chicago Press, 1947.

Verdier, Douglas L. "Who Is the Lightning-Rod Man?" *Studies in Short Fiction* 18 (1981): 273-79.

FURTHER READING

Criticism

Bosworth, David. "Two Sides of a Tortoise: Melville, Dickens, and the Eclipse of the West's Moral Imagination." *Georgia Review* 58, no. 4 (winter 2004): 855-83.

  Explores notions of morality and industrialization in "Bartleby the Scrivener."

Colatrella, Carol. "The Significant Silence of Race: *La Cousine Bette* and 'Benito Cereno.'" *Comparative Literature* 46, no. 3 (summer 1994): 240-66.

  Discusses how Honoré de Balzac's *La Cousine Bette* and "Benito Cereno" exploit the interaction between reader and text in order to reveal the significance of racial difference.

Desmarais, Jane. "Preferring Not to: The Paradox of Passive Resistance in Herman Melville's 'Bartleby.'" *Journal of the Short Story in English* 36 (spring 2001): 25-39.

> Examines the psychological and political implications of Bartleby's behavior in "Bartleby the Scrivener."

Laufer, Matt. "'You Cannot Run and Read It': Melville's Search for the Right Reader." *Leviathan* 6, no. 2 (October 2004): 17-38.

> Applies reader-response theory to "The Piazza Tale."

Serlin, David Harley. "The Dialogue of Gender in Melville's 'The Paradise of Bachelors and the Tartarus of Maids.'" *Modern Language Studies* 25, no. 2 (spring 1995): 80-7.

> Examines how the narrator of "The Paradise of Bachelors and the Tartarus of Maids" facilitates the ideological power struggles among the story's range of gendered discourses.

Wertheimer, Eric. "Jupiter Underwritten: Melville's Unsafe Home." *Nineteenth-Century Literature* 58, no. 2 (September 2003): 176-201.

> Discusses themes of accident and loss in "The Lightning-Rod Man."

Additional coverage of Melville's life and career is contained in the following sources published by Thomson Gale: *American Writers*; *American Writers Retrospective Supplement,* **Vol. 1;** *Authors and Artists for Young Adults,* **Vol. 25;** *Concise Dictionary of American Literary Biography,* **1640-1865;** *Dictionary of Literary Biography,* **Vols. 3, 74, 250, 254;** *DISCovering Authors*; *DISCovering Authors: British Edition*; *DISCovering Authors: Canadian Edition*; *DISCovering Authors Modules: Most-Studied Authors* **and** *Novelists*; *DISCovering Authors 3.0*; *Exploring Novels*; *Exploring Short Stories*; *Gothic Literature: A Gale Critical Companion,* **Ed. 3;** *Literature and Its Times,* **Vols. 1, 2;** *Literature Resource Center*; *Nineteenth-Century Literature Criticism,* **Vols. 3, 12, 29, 45, 49, 91, 93, 123, 157;** *Novels for Students,* **Vols. 7, 9;** *Reference Guide to American Literature,* **Ed. 4;** *Reference Guide to Short Fiction,* **Ed. 2;** *Short Stories for Students,* **Vol. 3;** *Short Story Criticism,* **Vols. 1, 17, 46;** *Something about the Author,* **Vol. 59;** *Twayne's United States Authors*; **and** *World Literature Criticism,* **Vol. 4.**

Alice Munro
1931-

(Born Alice Anne Laidlaw) Canadian short story writer.

The following entry provides an overview of Munro's short fiction. For additional information on her short fiction career, see *SSC,* Volume 3.

INTRODUCTION

Munro is revered as one of Canada's leading literary figures. Her short stories have drawn comparisons to the work of Anton Chekhov and have been featured in such prestigious periodicals as the *Atlantic Monthly, New Yorker,* and *Paris Review.* Known for delving into the hidden passions of seemingly unremarkable people, Munro has explored the connection between memory, storytelling, and personal identity through her fiction. Although most of her stories focus on the lives of rural Canadians and involve issues of gender, Munro's unique insight into the human condition lends a universal appeal to her highly celebrated body of work.

BIOGRAPHICAL INFORMATION

Munro was born in Wingham, Ontario. Her father, Robert Eric Laidlaw, was a farmer. Her mother, Anne Clarke Laidlaw, was a schoolteacher who succumbed to Parkinson's disease in 1959. Although her family struggled financially, Munro earned a scholarship to the University of Western Ontario in 1949. Her first short story, "The Dimensions of a Shadow," was published in an undergraduate magazine in 1950. After marrying James Munro in 1951, she left school and settled in Vancouver, British Columbia, where she eventually gave birth to three daughters. Together with her husband, Munro opened a bookstore in Victoria, British Columbia, in 1963. Her debut collection of stories, *Dance of the Happy Shades,* appeared in 1968, earning Munro the Governor General's Award, Canada's top literary prize. After divorcing her husband in 1972, Munro was appointed writer-in-residence at the University of Western Ontario. She remarried in 1976 and received the prestigious Canada-Australia Literary Prize the following year. From 1979 to 1982 Munro toured throughout China, Scandinavia, and Australia while serving as writer-in-residence at the University of British Columbia and the University of Queensland. In 1986 she became the inaugural winner of the Marian Engel Award

for *The Progress of Love* (1986). Munro garnered the Trillium Book Award and the Canada Council Molson Prize, both in 1990, for *Friend of My Youth* (1990); she received the Lannan Literary Award for Fiction in 1995. The National Book Critics Circle Award for Fiction was bestowed upon Munro in 1998 for *The Love of a Good Woman* (1998), and her literary accomplishments were celebrated in 2001 with the Rea Award for the Short Story. Her 2004 collection of short fiction, *Runaway,* won the 2004 Giller Prize for excellence in Canadian letters.

MAJOR WORKS OF SHORT FICTION

Munro's stories examine the lives of ordinary people with compassion and objectivity, frequently centering on the emotional universe of children and interfamily relationships. *Dance of the Happy Shades* deals with the sense of personal isolation caused by insecurity, fear, and the inability to communicate. The narrator of "Day of the Butterfly," for example, is haunted by feelings of guilt surrounding her mistreatment of a foreign student during her childhood. As in many of Munro's stories, the events of "Day of the Butterfly" take place in the past, with the narrator seeking to make peace with her experiences through the process of storytelling. Although *Lives of Girls and Women* (1971) is subtitled *A Novel,* it consists of a series of loosely linked stories that trace the emotional maturation of Del Jordan, a woman coming of age in a small town. This semi-autobiographical book calls attention to the idealized perceptions of childhood while addressing the sexual anxieties of adolescence. The quiet, everyday struggles between family members and lovers inform *Something I've Been Meaning to Tell You* (1974), a collection of thirteen stories that reflects upon the trauma and mystery of past experiences. *Who Do You Think You Are?* (1978; published in America as *The Beggar Maid* in 1979) is a cycle of stories similar in structure to *Lives of Girls and Women.* Detailing the relationship between a stepdaughter and stepmother over the course of nearly forty years, *Who Do You Think You Are?* relies upon a non-chronological narrative approach to offer a dynamic presentation of its protagonists.

The Moons of Jupiter (1982) concentrates on sexual relationships more explicitly than Munro's earlier work. After a brief affair with a married man, the narrator of "Bardon Bus" becomes obsessed with her memories of the event, while the two women in "Hard-Luck Stories" relive their shared erotic longing for a man they met on a trip abroad by telling each other anecdotes about him. The tales in *The Progress of Love* revisit the emotionally intense bonds between families and lovers, the solitude of social outcasts, and the link between memory and identity. The title story of *Friend of My Youth* consists of a daughter's commentary on the veracity of her mother's memories of the past, reinforcing familiar motifs of narrative subjectivity and time. In the same collection, "Pictures of the Ice" evaluates the personal cost of following one's inner passion, and the voluntary exile that such a sacrifice sometimes requires. Winner of the W. H. Smith Literary Award in 1995, *Open Secrets* (1994) presents eight stories, half of which are told in the form of letters. Tales such as the labyrinthine "Carried Away" are notable for their elaborate structure, while others in this volume are distinguished by a dark tone, including "Vandals," a harrowing account of the psychological repercussions of child abuse. Dark secrets and betrayal underlie *The Love of a Good Woman*, particularly in the title story. Divided into three parts, "The Love of a Good Woman" concerns the murder of an optometrist, tracing its effects upon the people of a small town. *Hateship, Friendship, Courtship, Loveship, Marriage* (2001) and *Runaway* further examine the secret lives and private memories of inhabitants of rural Canadian communities, often encapsulating a novelistic scope within the short story format.

CRITICAL RECEPTION

A primary topic of critical interest in Munro's stories is her treatment of gender issues. Specifically, such elements as the intersection of geographic and fictional space and the act of storytelling have been viewed as symbolic representations of the struggle for sexual identity. Similarly, as scholar Ella Soper-Jones noted in her exploration of *Open Secrets,* Munro's protagonists are characterized by a propensity to "confront a societal consensus regarding the untenability of women's independence." Additionally, Munro's portrayal of intimate relationships has been studied according to the linguistic theories of Jacques Lacan, the literary concepts of Louis Marin, and Sigmund Freud's psychoanalysis of eroticism. Commentators have considered her innovative use of subjective narrative strategies integral to the personal quests for transformation and self-knowledge undertaken by her characters. Moreover, Munro's fiction has been compared favorably with the work of such renowned authors as Thomas Hardy, Eleanor Estes, and the brothers Grimm, and critics have recognized a classical strain in her overarching storytelling aesthetic. For example, reviewers have elucidated thematic and structural similarities between Munro's "Hold Me Fast, Don't Let Me Pass" and the traditional Scottish legend, "Tam Lin." While some scholars have noted

the tension between objective reality and the creative imagination in her short fiction, others, like Karen E. Smythe, have contended that "Munro entreats us not to separate life and art, not to reject the real in favour of the aesthetic, but instead to use one to illuminate the other."

PRINCIPAL WORKS

Short Fiction

Dance of the Happy Shades 1968

Lives of Girls and Women 1971

Something I've Been Meaning to Tell You . . . : Thirteen Stories 1974

Who Do You Think You Are? 1978; also published as *The Beggar Maid: Stories of Flo and Rose,* 1979

The Moons of Jupiter 1982

The Progress of Love 1986

Friend of My Youth 1990

Open Secrets 1994

Selected Stories 1996

The Love of a Good Woman 1998

Queenie: A Story 1999

Hateship, Friendship, Courtship, Loveship, Marriage 2001

Runaway 2004

Carried Away: A Selection of Stories 2006

The View from Castle Rock 2006

CRITICISM

Linda Weinhouse (essay date winter 1995)

SOURCE: Weinhouse, Linda. "Alice Munro: Hard-Luck Stories or There Is No Sexual Relation." *Critique* 36, no. 2 (winter 1995): 121-29.

[In the following essay, Weinhouse studies the gender dynamics in "Hard-Luck Stories" according to French psychoanalyst Jacques Lacan's theories of love.]

We recognize that we all, daily, tell historical and autobiographical stories about ourselves. But Freud and Lacan have changed forever the way we tell, write, and interpret these stories. Now we ask, for instance, who is telling the story to whom and who overhears it; what is being veiled that the gaps and errors in the narrative demonstrate is there; and what is the connection between discourse and sexuality?

In her collection of short fiction, *The Moons of Jupiter*, the Canadian writer Alice Munro has a story entitled **"Hard Luck Stories"** that offers an enlightening example of Lacan's theories of love in the analytic discourse. In that tale there is a framing story in which two women meet, bring each other up to date on their lives, and refer briefly to a trip they took together with a man named Douglas Reider, and a story within the story in which one of the women describes that trip. In the course of the trip that is described, one woman, Julie, tells stories, directed primarily at the man, in the presence of the narrator who has already heard them; and the narrator tells Julie a story in the presence of the man, who already knows the story because he took part in it. Through the story-telling, as in a good joke, the teller of the tale overcomes a series of adverse romantic encounters and achieves a happy ending that seems ironical in the circumstances. This ironical twist at the end is reminiscent of Freud's description of the joke as a triangular love story. According to Freud, a boy desires a girl; but because his desire is frustrated, he tells an obscene joke in her presence to another male. The joking triangle consists of a desiring subject, male, a desired female-butt of the joke, and an intruder-accomplice joke hearer, who is also male and who will eventually go on to repeat the joke to others.

Feminist readers have questioned whether, in such triangular situations, gender is a linguistic or biological distinction (Flieger 962). This is the question that Jerry Aline Flieger asks in her essay, "The Purloined Punchline: Joke as Textual Paradigm." In Lacan's view, which is central to his understanding of "The Purloined Letter," femininity is a "symptom signifying a vulnerability or privation which may be passed from player to player" (Flieger 958). Thus, as Flieger writes:

> In Lacan's version . . . it becomes obvious that the supposedly distinct and gender-identified roles of the joking triangle are not only often exchangeable but are actually coincidental or superimposed: each player is active and passive, desiring and desired, giver and receiver.
>
> (960)

Although Lacan suggests that anyone who becomes the butt of the joke or the one who is fooled becomes "female," it is not clear that the woman can become "the agent of desire, the active player, the joker" (Flieger 960). Flieger raises the question because, as she states, ". . . as long as woman cannot speak, as long as she is excluded from the subjective roles in the desiring triangle (poles one and three, joker and future joker), she is condemned to her role as 'wanted woman,' the object

of the hunt for the feminine subject" (961). This problem, inherent in Lacan's definition of femininity, appears in the dialogue between "I" and "She" in Miller's introduction to *Television*:

> I: . . . I mentioned courtly love, so far from us now as a practice, to simply indicate to what lengths men can go to . . . make Woman exist.
>
> She: Oh that is enough of this "Woman"! It is meaningless, and if it is not its meaning it totally—how shall I say?—unstable.
>
> (xv)

In **"Hard-Luck Stories"** it is "man" who masquerades and whose meaning is unstable; the women speak and eventually control their own destinies through speech. They are the jokers, and in all probability the future jokers.

Becoming the subject of one's own narration is, as Lacan recognizes in *Television*, a risky business (24). The first time the narrator of **"Hard-Luck Stories"** hears her friend Julie's sad love stories she remarks, "I think that I am in some ways a braver person than Julie, because I have taken the risk. I have taken more than one risk" (184). Of course, she may be referring to her decision years before to leave her husband, a decision Julie continues to put off; but in this context she may very well be referring, too, to her assumption of the role of subject in the narrative she is about to create. Later on in the narrative, Julie takes a similar risk by seeking love through story-telling. For both women, particularly Julie, speech becomes, as Lacan states, "essentially the means of gaining recognition" (*The Seminar* 240).

After the introductory framing story, in which the two women meet two months after their trip together, the woman who is the narrator begins to relate the story of that journey. Following a conference for librarians, the narrator offers the other woman, Julie, a ride home to Toronto with her friend, Douglas Reider. On the way, Julie tells two stories meant to demonstrate her hard luck in the area of romance. In one she tells how, in the early years of her marriage, suffering from a tendency to bake elaborate desserts, eat them, and purge, she fled to the beach one day with a cake to avoid eating it by throwing it into the ocean. There she meets a young man to whom she finds herself describing her symptoms. He claims to be a psychology student; and for a time, they meet once a week to neck at the beach, until she discovers that he is really a mental patient recovering from an attempted suicide who is meeting her on his one day out. Her second story involves an experience that she has later in the 1960s with a psychologist who runs encounter groups. He writes her letters expressing his adoration, which she ignores but comes to depend on. This involvement ends when it is discovered that he is having an affair with one woman in each of his groups.

The narrator then tells her own story. In it she accompanies a man she loves to the home of a rich couple, Keith and Caroline, who have also invited Caroline's latest lover, a pseudo-artist named Martin. Sometime during the visit, in the middle of the night to be precise, the narrator suddenly becomes sure that the man she is with, whom she never names, is in love with Caroline despite his claims to dislike her. It becomes clear to us that this man is Douglas; but although he listens to the story, he fails to confirm or refute her understanding of that visit. In fact, Douglas says very little, but we find out from the framing narrative that after the journey he and Julie become lovers.

In a talk, "The Beginning of the Cure," given at Barnard College on 15 April 1990, Carmen Gallano described the ways in which the patient may approach the psychoanalyst and in which the true beginning of analysis may be recognized. She mentioned the following approaches: patients may come desiring to be cured of a symptom, wanting to overcome the obstacles in their lives that are preventing them from succeeding, from being able to work things out; they may come wanting to understand their lives that appear to make no sense; they may come wanting to be relieved of their suffering, or they may simply want to complain and release their feelings.

The three stories in **"Hard-Luck Stories"** demonstrate these different approaches to analysis and the similarities between the approaches the female characters make to their therapist-lovers. Julie approaches her first psychologist-lover-disguised mental patient just after her marriage, with her symptom in her hands—the rich cake that she must throw into the water to prevent herself from consuming it. She tells Douglas and the narrator:

> I was one of those who gorge then purge . . . So I put the whole mess in a brown paper bag and I went down to the rocky end of the beach and heaved it into the sea. But—this boy saw me . . . Then within fifteen minutes' conversation I was telling him the truth, which I never dreamed of telling anybody. He told me he was a psychology student at U.B.C. but he had dropped out because they were all behaviorists there . . . I didn't know what a behaviorist was . . . So, he became my boyfriend . . . He could only meet me one day a week, always the same day. We didn't progress very far. The upshot was—well the upshot was really that I discovered he was in a mental hospital. That was his day out. I don't know if I discovered that first or the scars on his neck. Did I say he had a beard? Beards were very unusual then . . . He'd tried to cut his throat.

(188)

When Douglas asks her what happened to her symptom after she stopped seeing this seventeen-year-old patient masquerading as a nonbehaviorist psychologist, Julie answers simply, "I got over it. I think when I got pregnant."

She meets her second would-be lover-therapist years later. She goes to an encounter group that she says was designed for "ordinary functioning miserable mixed-up people." It is run by a man named Stanley, a psychologist who also has what is, by then, a fashionable beard. Before long Stanley begins writing her letters in which he expresses his love and his appreciation of her mental, physical, and spiritual qualities. Julie tells her listeners, "What rot. I knew it was all ludicrous but I won't deny I got to depend on it, in a way. I knew the exact time of day the postman came" (190).

The men to whom she entrusts her mental well-being are both punctual and reliable in their way, and both validate Lacan's judgment. Replying to a question, recorded in *Television,* about his opinion of psychologists, psychiatrists, and other mental health workers, the rank-and-file workers who take the burdens of the world's misery on their shoulders, Lacan replies: "One thing is certain: to take the misery onto one's shoulders, as you put it, is to enter into the discourse that determines it, even if only in protest." They are "collaborators" according to Lacan. Julie's first almost-lover is a patient, and the second is forced to leave town because his "patients" discover that he is sleeping with one woman in every group.

When the narrator first introduces Julie in the story within the story she briefly refers to her romantic adventures, which we have not yet heard, and remarks: "I've asked her, has she ever been in love, in love with somebody else? She says she once thought she was, with a boy she met on the beach, but it was all nonsense, it all evaporated. And once in recent years a man thought he was in love with her, but that was nonsense too, nothing came of it" (184). The recurrence of the appellate, "nonsense" is significant. In *Television* Lacan says:

> There are, insofar as the unconscious is implicated, two sides presented by the structure, by language.
>
> The side of meaning, the side we would identify as that of analysis, which pours out a flood of meaning to float the sexual boat.
>
> It is striking that this meaning reduces to non-sense the non-sense of the sexual relation, something that love stories have, throughout time, made obvious. . . . There is moreover the meaning that is taken for good sense, that even asserts itself as common sense. This is the high-point of comedy, except that in comedy the awareness of the nonrelation involved in getting it off, getting it off sexually, must be included. Thereby our dignity is recharged, even relieved.

(8)

This difficult and complex passage has a number of parallels in **"Hard-Luck Stories."** To begin, in the framing story with which **"Hard-Luck Stories"** opens, Julie tells the narrator:

Do you remember you said then about there being the two kinds of love, and the one kind nobody wants to think they've missed out on? Well I was thinking then, have I missed out on every kind? I haven't even got to tell the different kinds apart.

(182)

Julie is referring to the narrator's story in which she defines two kinds of love, the one she feels her lover has for Caroline, and the one she feels he has for her. She realizes that the man she loves, whom we presume to be Douglas, is in love with Caroline, whom he calls a "sexual monster." At the time she is overcome with frustration at the thought that she is "his sensible choice." As she relates:

"And I thought, why should I be surprised? Isn't this just what you always hear? How love isn't rational, or in one's best interests, it doesn't have anything to do with normal preferences?"

"Where do you always hear that?" Douglas said.

"It's standard. There's the intelligent sort of love that makes an intelligent choice. That's the kind you're supposed to get married on. Then there's the kind that's anything but intelligent, that's like a possession. And that's the one, that's the one, everybody really values. That's the one nobody wants to have missed out on."

"Standard," said Douglas.

"You know what I mean. You know it's true. All sorts of hackneyed notions are true."

"Hackneyed," he said. "That's a word you don't often hear."

(195)

The intelligent sort of love roughly corresponds to Lacan's good sense, and the other kind of love to the non-sense of the sexual relation. The love stories the women tell have no sense, but in telling them, as in the telling of a joke, they achieve what Lacan says is achieved by comedy; their "dignity is recharged, even relieved." In telling and retelling they find "hackneyed notions" that are "true." As Lacan, using that word that one does not often hear, says in *Encore,* "It is necessary to hackney thoroughly things like that" (56).

At this juncture it is useful to take a look at the reactions, in the story, to the narrator's hard-luck tale. Julie asks the narrator, "Did you ask him if he was in love with her?" To which the narrator answers, "Asking wouldn't have got me anywhere." But we soon realize that in telling the story while he, Douglas, cannot help but listen, she is asking him. She is asking him to validate what her unconscious, suddenly in the middle of the night, revealed to her. Thus, she places Douglas in the position of the men in Julie's life; he is lover and, as many of the details of Munro's characterization reveal, he can also be viewed as the analyst. For example,

at first the narrator had worried about introducing him to Julie, who bakes her own bread and takes hiking vacations, because she says he is "driven by any display of virtue into the most extraordinary provocations" (183). I am reminded of Lacan's remark in "Freud's Papers on Technique" that "all you have to do is read Freud's biography and be aware of the brutality of his responses to those people who came to him with their hearts of gold" (*The Seminar* 270). More important, Douglas

. . . is in charge of collecting, buying up for the Provincial Archives, all sorts of old diaries, letters, records, that would otherwise perish . . . He pursues various clues and hunches and when he finds a treasure it is not always his immediately. He often has to persuade reticent or suspicious or greedy owners, and to outwit private dealers . . . In this, as in any other enterprise where there is the promise of money, intrigues and lies and hoodwinking and bullying around. . . .

(184-185)

Between Julie's stories and the narrator's, Douglas sidetracks to drive them through a village where he had once got his hands on a valuable diary that the owner, an old woman, eventually burnt because it contained scandalous parts and she dreaded exposure. Julie contrasts this woman with herself because she has just lain bare her own affairs. Thus, Munro explicitly compares Julie's revelations with the material Douglas seeks and discovers. At this point the narrator decides to "lay bare" and Douglas says, "Will we risk it?" Again the risk of opening the unconscious and the parallel, beginning a narrative, is emphasized. Once the narrator has completed her story they stop at an old country church. Inside, Douglas puts his hand on the narrator's shoulder blade in such a way that Julie will not notice. As she tells it,

He brushed his hand down my back and settled at my waist, applying a slight pressure to the ribs before he passed me and walked up the outer aisle, ready to explain something to Julie . . . I hadn't expected there would be any announcement from him either while I was telling the story, or after it was over. I did not think that he would tell me that I was right, or that I was wrong. I heard him translating, Julie laughing, but I couldn't attend. I felt that I had been overtaken—stumped by a truth about myself, or at least a fact, that I couldn't do anything about. A pressure of the hand, with no promise about it, could admonish and comfort me. Something unresolved could become permanent. I could be always bent on knowing and always in the dark. . . .

(197)

The narrator then pays attention to each of the signs embroidered on the kneeling stools in the church: a dove on a blue ground with an olive branch in its mouth, a lamp with lines of straight golden stitching like rays, a trillium that looks at first like a white lily. When she shows them to Julie and Douglas they all become quite boisterous, and she remarks that it was as if "we had each one, secretly, come upon an unacknowledged spring of hopefulness."

According to Lacan, the "subject who comes into analysis places himself, as such, in the position of someone who is in ignorance" (*Seminar* 271). The narrator of **"Hard-Luck Stories"** comes to Douglas, lover, analyst, and as his name implies, reader, with her love and with her ignorance. But, as Jacques-Alain Miller writes in the Introduction to *Television,* "The analyst is not Dionysus. He cannot ensure you the peaceful jouissance of an accomplished sexual relationship" (xii). He is, rather, "that silence in the name of which the patient speaks. But he must be there; he provides his body; and he holds the place of what cannot be said" (xxx). The narrator accepts the hand on her back, the fact that something unresolved could become permanent; she is "overtaken by a truth about herself" (197). And somehow that truth alerts her to the chain of signifiers represented by the kneeling stools in the church and brings her and the others joy. As Jacqueline Rose states in her introduction in *Feminine Sexuality,* "The concept of jouissance (what escapes in sexuality) and the concept of significance (what shifts within language) are inseparable" (52). At Barnard College on 15 April 1990, Jacques-Alain Miller spoke of the jouissance that emerges when Freud takes us through the path of the dream, the translation of the text. In Munro's story, as the narrator comes to accept her own truth, Douglas is said to be "translating for Julie" (197). In *Television* Lacan described this jouissance:

> To see also that by making his way through a tissue of puns, metaphors, metonymies, Freud evokes a substance, a fluidic myth titrated for what he calls libido.
>
> But what he is really performing, there right before our very eyes glued to the text, is a translation that reveals that the jouissance that Freud implies through the term primary process properly consists in the logical straits through which he so artfully leads us.
>
> (9)

Munro's hard-luck stories are pleasurable despite the fact that there is no satisfying sexual relation. And the narrator is satisfied despite the fact that she remains ignorant as to what actually happened at the home of Keith and Caroline. Lacan explains how it is possible, in fact necessary, to learn from ignorance:

> . . . one never understands anything but one's fantasies. And one is never taught by anything other than what one doesn't understand, i.e. by nonsense. If the psychoanalyst holds in abeyance his understanding of what you say, that gives you the chance to do the same, and it is from that you may learn something—to the extent to which you take a distance from your fantasies.
>
> (*Television* xxvi)

Still, there does seem to be an actual sexual relation in Munro's story; after all, following the journey Julie and Douglas become lovers. This is the reason why Julie labels the story of their journey, "one of those ironical-twist-at-the-end sort of stories" (181). She discerns irony in the fact that she originally believed she was asked along as a buffer in the relationship of the narrator and Douglas and she became the subject of the love story herself. In the context of analytic discourse, the outcome is ironic because it reveals Julie's misreading of her own history. She tells her stories to indicate her recurrent failure in love and in the telling discovers her own aptitude for it. Through the act of retelling her hard-luck stories, Julie changes her luck. According to Lacan the aim of analysis is to have the subject create something new, to have as its goal "the advent of an authentic speech and the realization by the subject of his history in relation to a future" (*Encore* 302). Both Julie and the narrator, through speech, assume their own history, accept, and endorse their own destiny. They, especially the narrator, are able to acknowledge, "responsibility for the discourse of the Other in oneself, but also the forgiving of this discourse" (1027). Without rancor, the narrator declares: "I could be always bent on knowing, and always in the dark about what was important to him and what was not" (197).

Yet another question remains regarding this newly created idyll, the Julie and Douglas relation. We have every reason to assume, given Julie's repeatedly demonstrated vulnerability and Douglas's aptitude for deceit, that this affair will also become one of Julie's "hard-luck" tales, that like the recipient of the joke, she will go on to repeat. Barbara Johnson makes the relevant remark: ". . . it is the frame that makes it impossible for us to know where to begin and when to stop" (338). In going beyond the narrative to speculate that the hard luck will repeat itself, we enter the realm of *Beyond the Pleasure Principle.* Lacan insists on the importance of this "culminating point of Freud's doctrine" in more ways than it is possible to enumerate here. Because the main focus here has been on the relationship between Munro's narrative and analytic discourse, I shall borrow from Felman's summary of the importance of *Beyond the Pleasure Principle* to an understanding of the way in which signification repeats in a text or in a life. Felman writes:

> Since the compulsion to repeat is, in Lacan's view, the compulsion to repeat a signifier, *Beyond the Pleasure Principle* holds the key not just to history or to the transference but, specifically, to the textual functioning of signification, that is, to the insistence of the signifier in a signifying chain (that of a text, or of a life).
>
> What is then, psychoanalysis if not, precisely, a life-usage of the death-instinct—a practical, productive usage of the compulsion to repeat, through a replaying of the symbolic meaning of the death the subject has repeatedly experienced, and through a recognition and

assumption of the meaning of this death (separation, loss) by the subject, as a symbolic means of his coming to terms not with death but, precisely, with his life?

(1034)

In "The Purloined Letter" in which Lacan reads the story of analysis, Dupin finds the letter because he knows how to repeat the original theft. As Johnson states: "His 'analysis' is the repetition of the scene that led to the necessity of analysis . . . the analyst does not intervene by giving meaning, but by effecting a denouement" (348). So we may infer that just as the narrator comes to terms with "something unresolved" that "could become permanent" Julie may well be able to cope with her future by retelling it. As Lacan writes, "The game is already played, the dice are already thrown, with this one exception, that we can take them once more in our hand, and throw them once again" (SII 256).

Works Cited

Felman, Shoshana, "Beyond Oedipus: The Specimen Story of Psychoanalysis." In *Lacan and Narration: The Psychoanalytic Difference in Narrative Theory*. Ed. Robert Con Davis. Baltimore: Johns Hopkins UP, 1983. 1021-54.

Flieger, Jerry Aline. "The Purloined Punchline: Joke as Textual Paradigm." In *Lacan and Narration: The Psychoanalytic Difference in Narrative Theory*. Ed. Robert Con Davis. Baltimore: Johns Hopkins UP, 1983. 941-67.

Johnson, Barbara. "The Frame of Reference: Poe, Lacan, Derrida." In *The Purloined Poe*. Ed. John P. Muller and William J. Richardson. Baltimore: Johns Hopkins UP, 1988. 213-51.

Lacan, Jacques. *Encore: Le Seminaire XX*, 1972-73. Paris: Seuil, 1975.

———. *Feminine Sexuality*. Ed. Juliet Mitchell and Jacqueline Rose. New York: Norton, 1985.

———. *Le Seminaire, livre II: Le Moi dans la theorie de Freud et dans la technique psychoanalytique*. Paris: Seuil, 1975.

———. *The Seminar of Jacques Lacan*. Book I. New York: Norton, 1988.

———. *Television*. New York: Norton, 1990.

Munro, Alice. "Hard-Luck Stories." In *The Moons of Jupiter*. London: Penguin, 1984.

Gayle Elliott (essay date summer 1996)

SOURCE: Elliott, Gayle. "'A Different Tack': Feminist Meta-Narrative in Alice Munro's 'Friend of My Youth.'" *Journal of Modern Literature* 20, no. 1 (summer 1996): 75-84.

[*In the following essay, Elliott investigates the ability of storytelling and narrative interpretation to define gender identity in "Friend of My Youth."*]

I had my own ideas about Flora's story. I didn't think that I could have written a novel but that I would write one. I would take a different tack. I saw through my mother's story and put in what she left out. . . .

—Alice Munro, **"Friend of My Youth"**

"Friend of My Youth" is both the title story and a recurrent theme in a collection in which Alice Munro explores the nature of female friendships which either survive or fail to survive the tests of time. The women in these stories—in which narrative is embedded within narrative, fiction within metafiction—seek to retrieve meaning from a recollected past, while in the process denying their own inclinations to revise their stories; nevertheless, they manage to explore, together, the enticements and disappointments of sexual and romantic love, the compromises within marriage, and the pain of conflicting loyalties. **"Friend of My Youth"** is emblematic of Munro's vision of the nature of narrative and of the limitations imposed upon its practitioners. I approach Munro's work as both storyteller and critic; as a fiction writer myself, I am particularly interested in the ways in which women writers attempt to transform the structures of narrative, reshaping at once the concept of the short story and the aesthetic evaluations which define the genre.[1]

Women writers have shared with feminist critics both an interest in and a distrust of the notion of feminine writing. Yet, while loathe to delimit narrative strategies as either "male" or "female," women writers continue to articulate a theory of "women's writing," not so much, perhaps, to set it apart from the writing of men, but in order to empower themselves with a more extensive knowledge of their craft and a deeper sense of the contributions made by women to the evolution of modern fiction. Without reconstructing feminist debates about *l'écriture feminine*, it is nonetheless possible to explore Munro's work in terms of distinctions frequently made between "masculine" and "feminine" modes of writing, recognizing from the first that such binary oppositions immediately impose limits at which most writers would, justifiably, balk. My purpose is not to relegate the writing of either men or women to any easily classifiable milieu—Virginia Woolf characterized the writer's imagination as androgynous, after all—but instead to consider Munro's writing in the broader context of women's writing and, in so doing, to discover in her work the strategies that have enabled her so confidently to take "a different tack" in her own approach to fiction.

Pam Houston begins her discussion of Munro's **"Meneseteung"** by relaying the frustration expressed by male students in her Twentieth-Century Short Story course. Why (the men wanted to know) are summaries of males in contemporary stories so abrupt and dismissive? Why does short fiction make such short work of men? Houston, in attempting to address such questions, draws distinctions between the ways in which men and women think. Comparing the structures of thought to the structures of language, she asserts that meaning becomes available to women and to men in different ways. The male thought process, contends Houston, "moves in a straight line, forward, or sometimes even backward, but inevitably straight. From A to B to C to D. Often, by the time he is at D he has forgotten all about C (not to mention A and B), and all his energy is focused on E."[2] Her diagram of this male matrix resembles a vertical stack of building blocks, with A on the bottom and E on top; presumably, then, the male ascent to knowledge is vertical. Houston regards the male thought process as removed—by virtue of this verticality—from the immediate context and consequence of his actions. (One wonders how Houston's students took to this paradigm.) In contrast, Houston pictures the female matrix as a series of interconnecting loops placed horizontally across the page. "Each circle contains the next one, and the one before. Context is not just a small part of the system, it defines the system."[3]

Since the male sensibility has been the organizing principle upon which our language and institutions have been based, it is most familiar. Notes Houston: "The female matrix isn't inherently more difficult to understand than the male matrix, we just aren't used to describing it."[4] Houston (like Hélène Cixous and Luce Irigaray, influenced by Derrida's notion of logocentrism) sees language as an hierarchical and dualistic construction, one word or concept favored over the "other" as a means of organizing thought and, hence, culture.[5] What interests me, however, are the ways in which women writers—and particularly Munro—acknowledge the limitations of language. As Munro writes in **"Differently,"** "Trouble began, perhaps, as soon as they said that they loved each other. Why did they do that—defining, inflating, obscuring whatever it was they did feel?"[6]

Houston, aware of the pitfalls of stereotyping, frames her discussion in terms of masculine and feminine matrices rather than male and female practices. She never asserts that men and women adhere rigidly to gender-generated constructs when composing fiction; instead, she suggests that certain stories exist in a male sensibility, while others reflect a female sensibility. Women have often written narratives that reside within a male matrix, and, asserts Houston, "[T]here have been many narratives, historically, that reside inside the feminine matrix that have been written by men."[7] Houston offers Munro's metafictional **"Meneseteung"** as an example of a story which exists within a feminine matrix, and—although such distinctions often prove problematic—perhaps we can accept them, temporarily, as a means of examining metonymic meaning and meta-narrative in **"Friend of My Youth."**

In her analysis of Munro, Houston emphasizes the distinction between metaphor and metonymy as she considers men and women and the means by which each creates meaning in language:

> A metaphoric relationship is a relationship where one word is substituted for another, it is a relationship of analogy and it provides a totalizing view of narrative within a closed and complete system. A metonymic relationship is a relationship based on association, connection, proximity. It is a relationship by copresence, a relationship Lacan defines as "word by word," a relationship based on contiguity and context. Unlike the metaphoric relationship, with its verticality and self-containedness, a metonymic relationship is constructed horizontally.[8]

Houston's diagram of the feminine matrix might well be adapted to illustrate the narrative structure of **"Friend of My Youth,"** the plot progressing not in a linear fashion, like an arrow toward a target, but in recursive paths of connection and speculation. Meaning cannot be derived from any single story segment; it emerges, instead, from the shifting contexts in which the (multiple) stories are told. Seemingly unrelated fragments can be comprehended only in terms of their metonymic relationship, one to the other. Thus, Munro explores not only memory but the processes by which people account for and make sense of experience, examining in **"Friend of My Youth"**—as she does in **"Differently"** and **"Meneseteung"**—the nature of narration itself.

Storytelling, then, is central to Munro's fiction, the definitive task of characters who—intuiting a relationship between speaking and knowing—enter into narrative as a means of discovering truth. Yet, as Austin Wright asserts in his discussion of "Recalcitrance in the Short Story," the process of storytelling itself resists formal structure: "In every short story—indeed, in every formed work of fiction—two opposing forces are visible: the force of a shaping form and the resistance of the shaped materials."[9] The tensions between the potentialities of story and the language with which it is limited are readily apparent in Munro's fiction, which explores the incongruencies between primary and secondary narratives, memory and experience, chaos and resolution. Thus, **"Friend of My Youth"** is metafictional both in and of itself and also metonymically, in relation to other stories in the collection.

It is ironic that although Munro admits that the past can never be fully reclaimed, her protagonist's task in **"Friend"** [**"Friend of My Youth"**] is, nevertheless, the task of a storyteller. Her narrator—and, by extension, Munro, as author—must content herself with a story that tells not what happened, precisely, but what might have happened, instead. As Thomas Gullason observes, "in the hands of a first-rate talent, a story is not only dynamic and expanding, it is multiple in its effect, or layerings, as it mirrors and transforms a scene or episodes (cycles) from 'life.'"[10]

In **"Friend of My Youth,"** the unnamed narrator reconstructs, in a series of such "episodes," a story of two sisters with whom her schoolteacher mother boarded in the Ottawa Valley years before. The frugal Grieveses, who for religious reasons have foresworn modern conveniences (automobiles, electricity, telephones, even farm machinery), typify many Munro characters from rural Southern Ontario: reconciled to lives limited in both spiritual and material comfort, they stubbornly embrace the tenets of church and community, dismissed by the narrator as "[a]ll that configuration of the elect and the damned. . . . Doom and slippery redemption" (p. 12). The story of this family—of Flora and her sister, Ellie, and of Robert, the man loved by both—becomes the heart of a narrative passed along from narrator-mother to narrator-daughter and, finally, to the reader.

The title phrase, **"Friend of My Youth,"** is introduced as a salutation in a letter written by the narrator's dying mother. The daughter—embarrassed by the emotional excess in her mother's greetings to friends—admits to an "impatience with the flowery language, the direct appeal for love and pity," noting, "She would get more of that . . . if she could manage to withdraw with dignity . . ." (p. 24). The narrator might well be commenting upon the need for authorial restraint in the contemporary short story itself, which—intentionally leaving gaps and omissions—relies upon its reader to participate actively in "co-creating" the text. (Gone are direct appeals for pity or for love.) Indeed, the narrator herself seems well aware of the part that she will play in shaping Flora's story. The legatee of her mother's recollections of a now far-distant youth, the narrator-daughter seems confident that—when she recounts this story—the rules of narrative will change.

The daughter will reshape the narrative to accommodate her own version of events and of the mother who has related them: "I saw through my mother's story and put in what she left out" (p. 20). Such an assertion implies that the truth is obtainable, quantifiable, and that the daughter can comprehend it. Munro would suggest, instead, that neither narrator nor reader can know what the mother has left unsaid, and it is these lapses—in the story, in meaning, even in the typographical spacing between the sequencing of events—which Coral Ann Howells refers to as Munro's "Art of Indeterminacy." Writes Howells: "We still hear different voices insisting on the incompleteness of any story; it never contains the whole truth."[11] The fictional structures created by Munro "encourage multiple contradictory meanings" and resist easy closure. Characteristic of metafictional stories in particular, this final recalcitrance engages the reader in a struggle to find unity in narratives which steadfastly "evade any single meaning but allow room for the interplay of shifting multiple meanings and of multiple human interests."[12] Munro's characters search for truth, but their findings prove inconclusive. Perhaps,

speculates Howells, Munro feels at ease with this lack of resolution because of a "feminine preference for indeterminacy over the determinators of progress and mastery."[13]

If understanding can be found—if, occasionally, a Munro character experiences a moment of "accidental clarity" (p. 243)—it is not obtained at the sudden apprehension of a single, unitary Truth, but through participation in a narrative process which renders experience into speech, or—as Norman Friedman puts it—objectifies the subjective.[14] Indeed, Munro's careful attention to detail establishes us in the assumed real world and, at the same time, suggests a hidden reality just beyond its borders. Observes Friedman, "Thus the plot of the short story, however realistic on the surface—and, of course, it need not be—contains emotional depths relating it to myth and dream and thereby to the lyric."[15] Munro flawlessly depicts the detail of the physical world yet plumbs the depths of the unconscious as well, mediating between exterior and interior realities as gracefully as she mediates between mother and daughter narrative, personal and regional history, present and past event.

"Friend of My Youth" begins with—and is framed by—the narrator's recollection of a recurrent dream which she has about her mother. The life of the unconscious is not subject to the rules of the external world, of course, so the narrator finds herself transported in her dreams to the kitchen of her childhood, to visions of her mother rolling out piecrusts, washing dishes, or—on other occasions—meeting her unexpectedly on unfamiliar city streets, in hotel lobbies, and airports, her mother alive again, kind and forgiving. "[T]hough the details in the dream varied," reports the narrator, "the surprise in it was always the same" (p. 3). Dream events arrange themselves not according to logic or chronology, but in symbolic patterns that, taken together, convey to the dreamer suppressed or hidden meaning. It is no accident that these insights about her mother come to the narrator, then, through dream constructs while she is asleep.

The unconscious sifts through memory, then offers up details either strangely distorted or implausibly combined. As in art, as in story, dreams, too, render experience metonymically. It is this unconscious association of detail, this incongruous merging of memory and dream scene—and not any revelation from waking life—that provides the narrator's eventual insight into her mother. "I recovered then what in waking life I had lost" (p. 3). Munro's narrative structure provides the same sort of implausible juxtapositions that might be found in a dream: shifts in time, disparities of plot, a dreamlike intensity of imagery and sensory detail. Houston notes, "In a metonymic universe all symbology is constantly subject to change."[16] Dreamscapes, too, are subject to sudden alteration. So Munro's storytelling, while realistically chronicling farm life in rural Ontario, allows for the fluidity of memory and the intermingling of various sensibilities. Such imaginative constructs characterize works by both men and women authors, admittedly, but Houston's model of a feminine matrix—dependent upon metonymic meaning—aptly fits **"Friend of My Youth."**

Munro, resigned to the inevitable confines of her medium, responds by commenting upon—instead of attempting to disguise—its limitations. Narrative cannot conjure unitary meaning from what is, essentially, a formless and chaotic past, but telling and re-telling stories, from a variety of angles and viewpoints, affords opportunity for retrospection and, occasionally, for revelation. Yet it is the reader herself who must recognize the relationship among (the mother's, the narrator's, Ellie's, Flora's, Robert's) interconnecting stories. For **"Friend of My Youth,"** although first-person narrative, offers no single sensibility marshalling facts about characters' lives. Truth for Munro is not constant, but shifts and twists as the story progresses, evolving at last into a communal project—friends, neighbors, even strangers, contributing to the eventual recollection of one another's lives. (Ellie, Robert and Flora are, after all, subjected to smothering rural scrutiny.) The narrator, then, is limited in scope, for she can recount only what her mother has told her; necessarily, certain details are unobtainable or lost: "My mother could not say who the Cameronians were or why they were called that" (p. 5). The daughter—although ostensibly the narrative's "controlling" voice—is not the protagonist of the original story, nor is her mother, herself merely a secondary observer. The memories upon which the narrator reflects are not her own; thus, there can be no full disclosure: the daughter does not know the story.

The narrator must attempt to view her mother's past as it actually occurred rather than as her mother has imagined it—an impossibility, of course. The geography of her mother's youth has, in her memory, so "distinguished" itself that she recalls its textures and tastes as wholly unique. Wood in Southern Ontario weathers differently; sap rises more sweetly: "Houses turn black, maple syrup has a taste no maple syrup produced elsewhere can equal . . ." (p. 4). The Ottawa Valley visited by the daughter, then, cannot be the valley represented by the mother, but is, instead, "a scrambled, disarranged sort of country with no easy harmony about it, not yielding readily to any description" (p. 5). (This might serve as a description of Munro's fictive landscapes, as well.)

Certainly, there is no easy access in **"Friend of My Youth"** to a single truth about the Grieves sisters. We learn about them indirectly, the mother's recollection of the family coming to us through her daughter, who, in turn, relates the events of the story: the courtship of Flora by handyman Robert Deal; his eleventh-hour de-

fection to Flora's younger sister, Ellie; their marriage; Flora's division of the family home; Ellie's string of miscarriages; her eventual death; Robert's remarriage. Yet the narrator's knowledge of even these circumstances is limited; her mother's memory, and thus her daughter's narrative, must, by nature, be distorted or incomplete. Pieces of missing story, then, must be culled from a multiplicity of sources: from hints, confessions, gossip, news accounts, primary and secondary narrative, letters, photographs, even the telephone party line. Past and present interweave, as do the parallel narratives that account for them. "The story of Flora and Ellie and Robert had been told—or all that people knew of it—in various versions" (p. 8). The reader works to distill the metonymic meaning from the intersection of these stories. In the end, it is not resolution that is sought but understanding, knowledge not an end but an ongoing process: one experience touches upon and doubles back on the next, looping and threading together, very like Houston's diagram of the feminine thought process. ("Each circle contains the next one, and the one before. Context is not just a small part of the system, it defines the system.")

But if context "defines the system," then we must consider, too, the social and generational contexts in which stories are told. In relating the story of the Grieves sisters, Munro explores not only their personal histories, but the forces—both subtle and overt—that shape storytelling. Story—despite all a writer might do to resist this—can only be a product of its time. Ultimately, Munro's narrator recognizes the difference between her own and her mother's representation of Flora (and acknowledges the variance in the way each defines her heroine). Mother and daughter tell different tales, each uniquely shaped by the teller's own life and experience, and it is impossible to consider Flora's story apart from the context in which it is shaped. Observes the narrator:

> The odd thing is that my mother's ideas were in line with some progressive notions of her times, and mine echoes the notions that were favored in my time. This in spite of the fact that we both believed ourselves independent, and lived in backwaters that did not register such changes. It's as if tendencies that seem most deeply rooted in our minds, most private and singular, have come in as spores on the prevailing wind, looking for any likely place to land, any welcome.
>
> (pp. 22-23)

If there can be no shelter for the writer from such a powerful "prevailing wind," there is, at least, a means of acknowledging its presence and direction. By the narrator's own admission, she is (as is, presumably, Munro herself) subject also to the notions of her time. Women writers of her generation have taken up their mothers' stories and dramatically refashioned them, eschewing the "dainty tyranny" (p. 22) of literary conventions that reduced female characters to mere objects of moral example. Indeed, the narrator's mother is not un-aware of her own failings as storyteller; she counts among her regrets her inability to account properly for Flora. She tells her daughter, "If I could have been a writer—I do think I could have been; I could have been a writer—then I would have written the story of Flora's life. And do you know what I would have called it? 'The Maiden Lady'" (p. 19). Yet the narrator rejects this maidenly stereotype; Flora's self-denial, so much admired by the mother, is reviled by the daughter. "What made Flora evil in my story," declares the narrator, "was just what made her admirable in my mother's—her turning away from sex" (p. 22). The narrator dismisses the solemnity, the sentiment, with which her mother regards the abused and betrayed Flora: "[T]he stateliness and mystery. The hint of derision turning to reverence" (p. 19).

The self-sacrificing heroine, canonized by the mother's generation (and by its literature), is soundly rejected by the daughter's. The narrator sees Flora not in the rosy glow of perpetual renunciation, but in the barren after-math of years lived in service to a sexless, bloodless representation of idealized womanhood. Not only has Flora twice lost her lifelong love, she has even lost title to the family property, inherited not by her but by her sister's husband and (most unforgivably, perhaps) by Robert's second wife. Yet the narrator knows that her mother would refuse to cast Flora's story in any but a romantic light; she would insist upon refashioning it to suit the ethos of her time. "It is all right—the elect are veiled in patience and humility and lighted by a cer-tainty that events cannot disturb" (p. 20). So powerful is this forbearance that no vision of reality can mar it. "That was what I believed my mother would make of things," allows the narrator. "In her own plight her no-tions had turned mystical, and there was sometimes a hush, a solemn thrill in her voice that grated on me, alerted me to what seemed a personal danger" (p. 20). Indeed, the urge to impose upon story a restrictive moral imperative is one of the dangers faced by writers; Mun-ro's narrator resists any such temptation, observing of her mother, "I could see what she would do with Flora, what she had already done. She would make her into a noble figure . . ." (p. 19). Munro refuses to lend autho-rial sympathy to a character who never acts on her own behalf, and she urges the reader to disbelieve Flora's assertions about having lived a fulfilling life. "Flora said that she was happy and satisfied in her life, as she had always been, and she did not interfere with what others did or wanted, because such things did not con-cern her" (p. 19).

Although Flora's own accounting of her life must be read as unreliable, Munro acknowledges the fascination that the Grieves story—in all its variations—holds for other people. When Ellie loses Robert's baby after jumping from a barn beam, the narrator comments:

"Even if she hadn't done that, people would have ex-pected something to go wrong, with that child or maybe one that came later. God dealt out punishment for hurry-up marriages—not just Presbyterians but almost everybody believed that. God rewarded lust with dead babies, idiots, harelips, and withered limbs and club-feet" (p. 11). Once upon a time, such inevitable rewards were the concern of literature, too, the author meting out to wayward characters what was thought to be Old Testament retribution: there was a way such stories were supposed to turn out. Still, as Munro makes clear, although even the scandalous Grieves story has been told and retold, convention required that pertinent detail be deleted. "'My sister has a growth,' Flora said. No-body then spoke of cancer" (p. 8). Essential facts were to be read between the lines, obscured by euphemism, subterfuge, or deliberate silence. Narrative always meets with resistance.

Yet when a story contains holes, its audience rushes to fill them. **"Friend of My Youth"** is full of the specula-tions of townspeople, neighbors, and friends: "Some people thought . . ." (p. 5); "By the way people spoke . . ." (p. 6); "Such people would not mention . . ." (p. 6); "people saw . . ." (p. 9); "people would say . . ." (p. 25); "Some of the women thought . . ." (p. 18); "people knew . . ." (p. 8). Every story belongs to a community of stories related by a variety of narrators, and any story worth telling will surely be repeated. When Flora reveals the cause of Ellie's final illness, the narrator observes, "My mother had heard that before" (p. 8). This is, of course, expected, since everybody, in-cluding Ellie, has a story to tell. "If anybody came to visit, she would talk about the peculiarities of her head-aches or describe her latest fainting fit, or even—in front of men, in front of unmarried girls or children—go into bloody detail about what Flora called her 'disappointments.'" (p. 11).

Ellie either cannot—or refuses to—obey the rules of so-cial interaction, and she introduces into conversation ta-boo topics relating to her body (physical symptoms fol-lowing stillbirth and miscarriage, for instance); she has, or so it would seem, gone out of her senses. Madness is defined by social context, by the appropriateness, one might say, of story for audience. Our accounting of re-ality—and the responses of others to this account—becomes the final measure of our sanity. (Almeda Roth, in **"Meneseteung,"** reassures herself of her own mental balance by observing: "[S]he hasn't thought that cro-cheted roses could float away or that tombstones could hurry down the street. She doesn't mistake that for real-ity, and neither does she mistake anything else for real-ity, and that is how she knows that she is sane" (p. 71). Munro keeps us forever mindful of the artifice of art: a story may be an interpretation of reality but should never be mistaken for reality itself. This is, however, a distinction that few of the characters in **"Friend of My**

Youth" manage to make; each keeps repeating an endless round of stories, determined that her version of reality is true. "Everybody who came into the house had some story of that kind to tell" (p. 11).

Yet Munro instills in her reader a healthy skepticism about what is and is not true. Although the narrator's mother has cast Flora in the role of a classical, long-suffering heroine, a contemporary reader is suspicious of such unbridled generosity and temperance of spirit. Although we are told that ". . . Flora had behaved like a saint . . ." (p. 8), we suspect that there is a second, untold story embedded within the first, and that Flora's external actions mask an internal grief (hence, possibly, the surname "Grieve"). It is, after all, Flora who divides the family home, cutting herself off from what exists on the other side of partitions which she herself has helped to construct: sex, married life, the mental and physical disintegration of her sister. Flora lives a divided life, separate even from herself and her own desires.

Once her sister is bedridden, Flora does all the work of the household, earning her the respect of local folk, who champion her story. Yet we see in all her sacrificial fervor a preternatural energy: "She was up before daylight and never seemed to tire" (p. 7). Munro draws a clear distinction between Flora as presented by the narrator's mother—the tragic heroine—and as seen by the narrator herself, who views Flora with a far more critical eye. Calling attention to the contradictions in Flora's character, Munro describes the results of Flora's cleaning in unexpected and paradoxical terms: "Through the washed uncurtained windows came a torrent of unmerciful light" (p. 7); "The cleanliness was devastating" (p. 7). The freshly bleached sheets give the narrator's mother not a restful night's sleep but a rash, instead; Flora's household varnishes and cleansing powders make Ellie even more ill.

The narrator's writerly instinct is to appropriate Flora, to remove her from her mother's story and revise her, to reveal Flora more fully, to "take a different tack" (p. 20). Her version of Flora is all that her mother's was not: where her mother has been overly sympathetic, the daughter's story is devoid of sympathy. As she herself admits, "My Flora would be as black as hers was white" (p. 20). This Flora takes savage pleasure in the misfortunes that befall her; filled with lust and greed, she is eventually crippled by the passions which she suppresses. Clearly, the narrator-daughter is overcompensating for her mother's narrative transgressions; her Flora is as bad as her mother's was good, and—obviously—neither version is absolutely true. Yet the daughter has intuited that too much of the underside of Flora's character has been left out of her mother's version for Flora to be credible. And, although acknowledging that the art of storytelling lies as much in knowing what must be left out as put in ("Some things must

be disregarded," observes Almeda in **"Meneseteung"**), Munro is adamantly against sins of deliberate omission. A writer must never sanitize a character or attempt to mask her dark side simply to suit her own ends.

The narrator's developing awareness of the limits of narrative is what, ironically, frees her to re-imagine Flora in a more contemporary light. The narrator—by then a conscious deviser of her own fictions—has lost interest in the historical Flora. Aware of her own narrative power, the daughter at last moves into her own subjectivity. "I was always thinking of stories, and by this time I probably had a new one on my mind" (p. 24). The woman from her mother's past is displaced by a fictional construct, a character redrawn by the daughter and introduced to a new, more modern world in which Flora is portrayed as embracing her own physical, lived experience. Flora, then, at the end of this story, is all fiction. Her own account of her life differs widely from both mother's and daughter's, and is, finally, beside the point, as this imagined Flora is propelled by the narrator into a future of the narrator's speculation: "Would she get a permanent, paint her nails, put on lipstick? . . . How could she get to that out-of-the-way church unless she managed to buy a car and learned to drive it? And if she did that she might drive not only to church but to other places. . . . She might meet a man . . ." (p. 25).

Ironically, the narrator comes closest to the truth when, in her imagination, she comes face-to-face with her fictional version of Flora and assures her that she knows Flora's story. "I imagine myself trying to tell her," she says (p. 25). But Flora only shakes her head, weary, confesses the narrator, of "my notion that I can know anything about her" (p. 26). In this moment, the narrator thinks of her long dead mother, as Flora's story and the mother's story suddenly merge together. If the narrator at last finds solace—a sense of epiphany—it is where she least expects it. She cannot retrieve her mother's experience from the recalcitrance of the past; yet it is the process of storytelling that allows her valuable insight. In recognizing Flora as fictional character, the narrator realizes that she, too, has been living with a fiction of her mother. The paradoxes of storytelling have yielded a new perception of her mother's capacities and a deepening appreciation of their mother-daughter relationship. All this comes as a surprise: "My mother moving rather carelessly out of her old prison, showing options and powers I never dreamed she had, changes more than herself. She changes the bitter lump of love I have carried all this time into a phantom—something useless and uncalled for, like a phantom pregnancy" (p. 26).

Munro in her storytelling manages the same, delicate revelation described by the narrator: "My mother surprising me, and doing it almost indifferently" (p. 26).

At the same time, she continues to comment upon and to change the nature of fictional narrative, revising the story in order to accommodate women's ways of knowing and being.

In the story's final segment, Munro recounts the religious history of the Cameronian sect of which Flora was a member, leaving the reader to determine the metonymic relationship of this segment to those that came before. "One of their ministers, in a mood of firm rejoicing at his own hanging, excommunicated all the other preachers in the world" (p. 26). Certainly, the story of Richard Cameron might be read as a cautionary tale. Adherence to any single reality, an uncompromising belief in a monolithic and unitary truth, separates us not only from knowledge of ourselves but also from one another. Far better to release our fictions, to consider one another with that "astonishing lighthearted forgiveness" (p. 26) accorded the narrator by her mother.

Notes

1. Gayle Elliott, "'A Different Tack': Feminist Meta-Narrative in Alice Munro's 'Friend of My Youth,'" *Journal of Modern Literature*, XX, 1 (Summer 1996), pp. 75-84.

2. Pam Houston, "A Hopeful Sign: The Making of Metonymic Meaning in Munro's 'Meneseteung,'" *The Kenyon Review*, XIV (1992), p. 81.

3. Houston, p. 81.

4. Houston, p. 80.

5. Obviously, this is an over-simplification of what are, by now, widely discussed theories. I shall not concern myself here with providing an overview of an already familiar discourse; I wish only to enlist Houston's aid before I discuss Munro on my own terms.

6. Alice Munro, "Friend of My Youth," *Friend of My Youth* (Vintage, 1990), p. 233. All subsequent references are parenthetical.

7. Houston, p. 81.

8. Houston, p. 82.

9. Austin Wright, "Recalcitrance in the Short Story," *Short Story Theory at a Crossroads*, Susan Lohafer and Jo Ellyn Clarey, eds. (Louisiana State University Press, 1989), p. 115.

10. Thomas Gullason, "The Short Story: Revision and Renewal," *Studies in Short Fiction*, XIX (1982), p. 36.

11. Coral Ann Howells, "Alice Munro's Art of Indeterminacy: The Progress of Love," In *Gaining Ground*, (NeWest Press, 1985), p. 141.

12. Howells, p. 141.

13. Howells, p. 143.

14. Norman Friedman, "Recent Short Story Theories: Problems in Definition," in Lohafer and Clary, p. 21.

15. Friedman, p. 19.

16. Pam Houston, "A Hopeful Sign: The Making of Metonymic Meaning in Munro's 'Meneseteung,'" *The Kenyon Review*, XIV (1992), p. 85.

Darlene Kelly (essay date April 1998)

SOURCE: Kelly, Darlene. "Alice Munro's 'Day of the Butterfly': An American Source." *ARIEL* 29, no. 2 (April 1998): 115-28.

[*In the following essay, Kelly compares the portrayal of social estrangement in "Day of the Butterfly" with Eleanor Estes's 1944 novel for children,* The Hundred Dresses.]

In his autobiography, *A Sort of Life* (1971), Graham Greene gives an amusing account of how, years after it was written, he was startled to find in his short story "Under the Garden" an unlikely source: Beatrix Potter's *Squirrel Nutkin*. Quite unconsciously, as he explains, he had reworked into his own murder story that terrifying moment in Potter's miniature thriller when the hapless Tom Kitten is being "trounced up by the rats behind the skirting board and the sinister Anna Maria covering him with dough" (52). Clearly there is no way of predicting how and when in an author's mature writings material from the slagheap of childhood reading may assert itself.

Certainly in the case of Alice Munro, works she read as a child would seem to have infiltrated her stories. As her family and friends have noted, reading was an "addiction" to her (Ross 15). And she read widely and eclectically. Emily Brontë's *Wuthering Heights*, Tennyson's poetry, Dickens's *Child's History of England*, and L. M. Montgomery's novels, especially *Emily of New Moon*, captured her youthful imagination (Ross 14-16). Just as influential, however, were writers of a kind that clever people rarely mention when furbishing the child-prodigy part of their critical reputations:

> . . . behind all those childhood books I've mentioned, I was just reading anything and everything. When people talk about their reading, they tend to mention [only] the respectable books. I mentioned Tennyson, for instance, but at the same time I was reading *Gone with the Wind* compulsively. . . . I read everything we happened to have in the house, and the books that came

into our house all came in by accident. So my reading
was just here and there, and all over. I [also] read what
was in the Sunday school library.

(Ross 19)

Elsewhere she points out that authors "who have never
become very well known" because they wrote only "a
few marvellous stories" are unfortunately excluded from
a writer's list of literary mentors. "One tends not to
think of them," Munro told one interviewer, "when
you're on the spot with a question like this" (Struthers
11). The reason, then, for omitting such writers is not
their unimportance, but memory's inevitable gaps.

Difficult as it can be to remember what we read as
adults, it is harder yet to retrieve the name of every
book familiar to us in childhood. Yet these stories,
though immature, cannot be denied; they too leave their
mark. The persistent impression made by books read in
youth may account for the striking similarity between
Alice Munro's **"Day of the Butterfly,"** written in 1953,
and *The Hundred Dresses* (1944) by American juvenile
writer Eleanor Estes, best known for her award-winning
books about the Moffat family. Munro may have deliberately emulated Estes, a good possibility given her
habit of staging "imitations" of successful narratives in
her head, sometimes committing these works of dual
authorship to paper (Ross 20, 22). She defends this
early activity as a kind of apprenticeship: "There's nothing wrong with writing imitations. It's the only way, I
think, to learn" (Ross 22). Whether a writer is or is not
aware of copying others, Munro considers the practice
to be greatly beneficial:

> I'm not very often aware of influences, but I'm sure
> they're happening all the time. . . . I'm probably us-
> ing things that other people have used first without
> even realizing I'm doing it. I think many of us do that.
> Or we pick up a tone that seems appropriate to a cer-
> tain kind of material, and we try out that tone. Or per-
> haps we're given courage to go on using a kind of ap-
> proach or material when otherwise we might worry that
> too much had been done of this.

(Struthers 17)

Munro's admission that in the early stages of her career
she modelled her work on that of others makes her use
of *The Hundred Dresses* entirely plausible. Or perhaps
she wove strands from Estes's compelling tale into her
story all unconsciously, much as Graham Greene without realizing transposed elements of Beatrix Potter's
Squirrel Nutkin into his short story. In any case, if Munro had not read Estes's minor classic before writing
"Day of the Butterfly," then it is by an extraordinary
coincidence that two stories written less than a decade
apart should be almost mirror images of each other.

During the early 1940s, when the young Alice Munro
was reading all manner of books, Estes's novels were a
staple in North American libraries. Because Estes is not

a writer of the same rank, say as C. S. Lewis or Frances
Hodgson Burnett, a few words should be said about her
place in children's literature. In 1943, she won the Newbery Honor label for *Rufus M* and, in 1952, the Newbery Medal for *Ginger Pye,* two awards which established her reputation as one of America's finest
children's writers. Her books about the fatherless Moffat children were a perennial favourite with young readers, but adults were quick to see the greater sophistication of *The Hundred Dresses,* a sombre account of how
children of mainly Anglo-Saxon descent so persecute a
Polish classmate that her family has to move away.[1] In
a survey of children's books written between 1920 and
1950, Ruth Hill Viguers notes that "Among the few fine
stories of a child who is 'different,' one stands out for
its subtlety, its good writing and its perfect understanding of childhood. Eleanor Estes, in her *The Hundred
Dresses* (1944), has accomplished what only an artist in
the portrayal of children can do" (551). Critics writing
in another survey of children's literature make a case
for the book's uniqueness, saying that "Eleanor Estes's
The Hundred Dresses (1944) has some claim to be the
first story to deal with prejudice, [one which] is all the
more distinguished by its down-beat ending" (*Children's
Literature* 250). Estes can hardly be credited with having written the first story to deal with prejudice among
children—Mark Twain's *Huckleberry Finn* (1884) and
Katherine Mansfield's story "The Doll House" (1922),
for example, both preceded *The Hundred Dresses*—but
her sombre theme was indeed uncommon in literature
written expressly for children at that time.

Estes's controversial subject no doubt piqued the interest of Munro, whose stories often explore the dark side
of human motivation. She might also have been inclined to expose the evil of racism by her own dislike
of it, a dislike made clear by her remarks on the bias of
a juvenile encyclopedia called *The Book of Knowledge,*
which she had read uncritically as a child: "These books
have glaring faults—they're quite racist—and I would
never give them to children to read" (Ross 14). But Estes's skilful treatment of her subject in *The Hundred
Dresses* could alone have inspired Munro's respectful
imitation of it in **"Day of the Butterfly."** Mastering fictional techniques which had worked well for others was
very important to Munro in her days as a fledgling
writer. Her first stories, **"Day of the Butterfly"** among
them,[2] she herself compared to "paintings that are said
to be 'in the school of,' [or] 'after the manner'" of another artist (Struthers 23). Just how closely Munro emulated the "manner" or art of Estes in **"Day of the Butterfly"** can be inferred from its compelling resemblance
to *The Hundred Dresses.*

This paper documents the main parallels between the
two works. Both Munro and Estes convey the foreign
girl's suffering from a classmate's perspective. The two
stories begin the same way: the girl through whose eyes

we see events (a central consciousness in Estes, a first-person narrator in Munro) first describes the victim as a person who, before being harassed, was thought beneath everyone's notice, a subtle form of discrimination; then, noting those details which set the unfortunate child apart, this same observer makes clear to us, if not to herself, just why it was a young foreigner who was treated so cruelly. Estes's memorable character types will be shown to inhabit Munro's story as well, notably the immigrant friends and relations of the tiny pariah who worsen her social status, and also the young bullies who like a pendulum swing from abusing their strange classmate to doting on her. In Munro as in Estes, teachers accidentally initiate the youngster's misery and later preside over the group's act of collective restitution. The most remarkable similarity, however, is the shocking recognition by both Munro's narrator and Estes's observer that they are the victim's alter ego.

The Hundred Dresses opens with deceptive simplicity: "Today, Monday, Wanda Petronski was not in her seat. But nobody, not even Peggy and Madeline, the girls who started all the fun, noticed her absence" (1). The "fun" turns out to be the ritual mockery of Wanda for having once claimed to have one hundred dresses in a closet at home, despite her obvious poverty. This taunting is called the "hundred dresses game" and also "having fun with Wanda" by Madeline, or Maddie,[3] the girl who witnesses the events. Before the game ever started, no one had even noticed Wanda; outside of those moments when she is being persecuted, the children continue to ignore her; and when she stops coming to school altogether, no one remarks upon her absence for several days. In her understated way, Estes has captured society's attitude to the people it marginalizes. Neglect eventually gives way to persecution when Maddie's friend Peggy sets out to expose Wanda as a liar. Peggy daily cross-examines her in a "mock polite" voice (17), ostensibly to establish the truth of the matter: "Why did [Wanda] want to lie? And she wasn't just an ordinary person, else why would she have a name like that?" (16-17). The last line points to Wanda's ethnicity as the real irritant. Most of the children in the class do not have an unusual name like "Petronski," but rather "names [that were] easy to say, like Thomas, Smith, or Allen" (10). It comes as no surprise later that in a letter to the teacher Wanda's father should cite discrimination as the reason that he and his family are moving away: "Dear teacher: My Wanda will not come to your school any more. Jake also. Now we move away to big city. No more holler Polack. No more ask why funny name. Plenty of funny names in the big city" (47).

Mr. Petronski's broken English recalls details given earlier in the story that set Wanda herself apart. She too has trouble with English, as is shown by her painful failure to read aloud when called upon to do so and by her classmates' impatience with her on these occasions

(36). She makes herself noticeable by wearing the same worn, if clean, blue dress every day. Then there is the greasy sheen of her forehead. Maddie, herself a poor girl who wears other people's cast-off clothing, is very thankful that at least her own "forehead didn't shine the way Wanda's round one did. What did she use on it? Sapolio? That's what all the girls wanted to know" (17). In part, Wanda is reviled by others simply because of her greasy look, a stigma that Alice Munro's child-victim in **"Day of the Butterfly"** bears as well.

Wanda is also derided for living in a strange, run-down neighbourhood, a place made worse by its nearness to the house of another immigrant, an unemployed Swede who is known as "old man Svenson." Svenson's dilapidated house and property show the effects of his being out of a job. Maddie has heard people speak of him at best as an "'old good-for-nothing,'" at worst as someone who once shot a man (54). Yet these harsh judgements are based on nothing more substantial than poor Mr. Svenson's foreignness—he mumbles unintelligibly when addressed—and his offputting appearance, with his "drooping mustache and tangled hair, his hound loping behind him, and the long streams of tobacco juice [which] he expertly shot from between his scattered yellow teeth" (59). The book's illustrations reinforce this benign reading of Mr. Svenson's character.[4] The soft outlines of Louis Slobodkin's two sketches of him—seated innocuously on his porch in one and looking startled at the questions put to him by Peggy and Maddie in another—predispose us to see Mr. Svenson as a harmless man who has been badly treated by his American neighbours, and to regard Wanda the same way.

Like the young Polish victim in *The Hundred Dresses,* the foreign child in Munro's **"Day of the Butterfly"** at the outset is entirely ignored, confirming her status as a non-entity. The narrator Helen recalls barely noticing the girl whom she would later torment: "I do not remember when Myra Sayla came to town, though she must have been in our class at school for two or three years" (100). Prior to harassing her, the schoolchildren "had not paid much attention to Myra" (102); and when Myra stops coming to school, Helen cannot even say whether it was "the day . . . or the week after" another incident that Myra vanished, inconsequential as she was (106).

At first glance, the group's cruelty to Myra seems arbitrary, but Helen's careful noting of all the things that set Myra apart makes its own statement about why she is hounded, the same technique found in *The Hundred Dresses*. Even the minor details used to establish Myra's strangeness mimic those of Estes. Like Wanda, for example, Myra has trouble with English, being unable to spell and, when she speaks, sounding as if she were "wetting her lips with her tongue" (104-05). Her clothes are also as ill-fitting as those of her counterpart in *The Hundred Dresses*. Wanda always wore the same blue dress "that looked like a piece of the sky in summer" (24) but that "didn't hang right" (12), two details which are fused together in the reference to Myra's "glimmer-[ing] sadly in sky-blue taffeta, in dusty turquoise crepe, a grown woman's dress made over, weighted by a big bow at the V of the neck and folding empty over [her] narrow chest" (106). In short, she looks ridiculous.

Just as Wanda's social status suffers because of her proximity to the suspect Mr. Svenson, so too Myra's unfortunate connections make her lose caste in the eyes of her ruthless young critics. Deliberate mention is made of the fact that her aunt is a nun, for example, a reference that might seem innocent except that, in Munro's world, people's religious affiliation is so often a lightning rod, making them the object of discrimination.[5] Also, the unappetizing sight of Myra's father, a Svenson-like character who sits idly in his store all day chewing garlic, "with his shirt open over his swelling stomach and tufts of black hair showing around his belly button" (103), hardly enhances her social position. Significantly, the children find the daughter's own appearance as repellent as the father's. One compelling detail in Estes's work which becomes even more arresting when duplicated by Munro is the greasy look which stigmatizes both foreign girls. Myra's turban of "oily" hair recalls Wanda's forehead which looks as if she had rubbed Sapolio on it, in each case perhaps an oblique reference to their nationality, since many ethnic groups use creams and pomades to make skin supple and hair lustrous. This sign of obvious difference inspires Helen and her classmates to devise a "game," as they call it (103), a euphemism that also appears in *The Hundred Dresses*:

> . . . now a game developed; it started with saying, "Let's be nice to Myra!" Then we would walk up to her in formal groups of three or four and at a signal, say together, "Hel-lo Myra. Hello *My*-ra!" and follow up with something like, "What do you wash your hair in, Myra, it's so nice and shiny, Myra." "Oh she washes it in cod-liver oil, don't you Myra, she washes it in cod-liver oil, can't you smell it?"
>
> (103)

The songs and chants of childhood, as Iona and Peter Opie famously demonstrated in such books as *The Singing Game* (1985), *The Lore and Language of Schoolchildren* (1959), and *Children's Games in Street and Playground* (1969) are a universal part of growing up. As both Estes and Munro show, so is taunting.

What gives special interest to each author's depiction of schoolyard bullying is her emphasis on ritual. The teacher in both works, for example, like a shaman leads the group from guilt to atonement. In *The Hundred Dresses*, Miss Mason, in other respects a decent person,

is the first to discriminate against Wanda by relegating her to a corner of the room "where rough boys who did not make good marks on their report cards sat" (3), presumably because Wanda like the boys had mud on her shoes—in her case picked up from a long trek to school along country roads. The teacher no doubt simply wanted to keep the floor clean, but her segregation of Wanda still sets an unfortunate precedent. Similarly, in **"Day of the Butterfly,"** Myra's trials are also begun by her teacher. When Myra asks permission to take her little brother home because he has "wet himself" (100), Miss Darling forces her to put her request more euphemistically, making her ridiculous before the class. From that moment on Myra and her brother stand alone at recess on the school's back porch. In their isolation, they are strikingly like Wanda, who, while other children congregate in the playground, remains in her solitary place "by the ivy-covered brick wall of the school building" (14). Perceiving the misery of Myra and her brother, Miss Darling tries to scold the children into treating them better, a ploy that backfires with the invention of the taunting game. In the end, each girl finds asylum from the torture of school, Wanda in a larger city and Myra in a cancer ward.

The process of atonement in *The Hundred Dresses* begins when the teacher announces that Wanda has won an art contest with one hundred sketches of beautiful dresses, drawings which substantiate her once preposterous claim. This proclamation is followed by the news contained in Mr. Petronski's letter. Upon reading this document Miss Mason first adjusts her glasses, then removes and wipes them, a sign of clearer moral vision and perhaps even of regret for her part in Wanda's suffering. She is now fitted for the task of inspiring a similar change of heart in her students. Gently she tells them that their hurtful comments were probably made "in thoughtlessness" (48), but that they must examine their conscience all the same. Maddie and Peggy visit Wanda's house, hoping that she might still be there and that they might congratulate her; on finding it vacant, they send her a friendly letter praising her drawings (65). Wanda sends them a gracious (if unidiomatic) reply which the teacher reads aloud to the whole class. The children are now delighted to hear from the celebrated artist whom before they had mistreated. At the time of the class Christmas party, the ballet student Cecile, whose lovely red dress months earlier had provoked Wanda's boast, performs the "Passing of Autumn" for her classmates, a dance which becomes their favourite. This detail makes its point unobtrusively: the vile behaviour of the previous autumn is now a thing of the past for the children, who here undergo a ritual purgation.

In **"Day of the Butterfly,"** Munro enlarges upon Estes's idea of the teacher-guided ritual, giving it several complex twists. Miss Darling's attempted defence of

Myra and her brother makes them into living fetishes, or "small figures carved of wood, for worship or magic with faces smooth and aged" (101). Myra is later said to be "set apart for legendary uses" (103), but Miss Darling is incapable of understanding the scapegoating and victim worship that this term implies, far less her own role in expediting them. Like Miss Mason in *The Hundred Dresses*, she too is bespectacled, although her glasses are "fragile" and their rims "thin" (100, 101), two epithets which also describe her vision. Without realizing it she provokes the children into taunting Myra; with like incomprehension she inspires their collective atonement by organizing a fake birthday party for Myra in March in case she dies before her actual birthday in July. The idea of the party greatly appeals to the young bullies for whom Myra now becomes oddly enviable. Although she does not dazzle her classmates with a hundred beautiful drawings, Myra exudes all the same "the excitement of sickness and hospitals," within which context she is "impressively set free of all the rules and conditions of [her classmates'] lives" (107). The girls plan the party as if it were a "cause" (108) and decide that their gifts should exceed the twenty-five cent limit imposed by Miss Darling. In a striking phrase, they are said to discuss Myra "as if she were something [they] owned" (108). The earlier comparison of Myra to a small figure carved of wood now acquires a new, chilling significance: a human being must become an object, this time of worship, before the group can absolve itself.

The real awakening in each story, however, is not experienced by the group at all; rather, this improved moral vision is attributed solely to the girl from whose perspective the story is told, and then only when she comes to see herself as the victim's alter ego. Maddie's recognition of her kinship to Wanda begins on a bright October day when everyone seems more brightly arrayed than usual and even "Wanda looked pretty" (106). She sees that Wanda's claim on this occasion to have a hundred dresses is based on a simple desire to be like all the other girls who at that moment are admiring Cecile's red dress. With a piece of broken glass Maddie flashes a rainbow of the October colours onto nearby houses, trees, and telephone poles (23), a perfect symbol for herself as a reflector or mirror image of the bullied girl. Maddie always feels ill at ease when others harass Wanda, but her one attempt to stop Peggy from doing so ends abruptly when she perceives how much a target like Wanda she herself is:

Suddenly she paused and shuddered. She pictured herself in the school yard, a new target for Peggy and the girls. Peggy might ask her where she got the dress she had on, and Maddie would have to say that it was one of Peggy's old ones that Maddie's mother had tried to disguise with new trimmings so that no one in Room 13 would recognize it.

(35)

In Wanda's predicament, Maddie sees an image of her own. The very names "Wanda" and "Maddie"—their capital letters an inversion of each other, and the rest a trochaic assembly of like-sounding vowels and consonants—underline this identity. In the final analysis, Maddie's sense of kinship with Wanda impels her to make amends. Restitution takes the form of fantasies in which Maddie rescues her other self from various perils and, more concretely, of the friendly letter that she and Peggy write. Yet as the last paragraph of the novel makes clear, Maddie remains troubled by the memory of the persecuted girl:

. . . she blinked away the tears that came every time she thought of Wanda standing alone in that sunny spot in the school yard close to the wall, looking stolidly over at the group of laughing girls after she had walked off, after she had said, "Sure, a hundred of them—all lined up. . . ."

(80)

In **"Day of the Butterfly,"** the narrator retraces the journey to self-awareness made by Estes's Maddie. With adult hindsight, Helen presents at the story's end all the clues of her kinship with Myra, recalling uneasily, just as Maddie had done with Wanda, how her ostracized double used to stand alone against the school. Although not foreign like Myra, Helen has other liabilities. She lives outside the city limits, for example, which is presumably why her boots are encrusted with mud, a stigma in Estes's fictional world as well. Just as Maddie fears becoming the next Wanda, so too does Helen sense that her poverty will make her as inviting a target for bullying as Myra:

I was the only one in the class who carried a lunch pail and ate peanut-butter sandwiches in the high, bare, mustard-coloured cloakroom, the only one who had to wear rubber boots in the spring, when the roads were heavy with mud. I felt a little danger, on account of this; but I could not tell exactly what it was.

(103)

As a child Helen cannot entirely decipher her kinship with Myra, but she clearly senses it, as we see in the passage just quoted. This awareness of a common bond is reinforced by Helen's learning that Myra reads the same comics and popular fiction that she herself does (105). That Helen finally grasps what Maddie had plainly stated in *The Hundred Dresses*—that in her resemblance to the victim she herself might become the object of the next schoolyard game—is evident from her reaction when, in giving Myra the tin butterfly from her cracker jack box, she grazes Myra's hand: "I flushed but Myra did not. I realized the pledge as our fingers touched; I was panicky, but *all right*. I thought, I can come early and walk with her other mornings. I can go and talk to her at recess. Why not? *Why not?*" (106). She is relieved that Myra does not wear the butterfly and that she vanishes shortly afterwards into the hospital. Helen and her classmates write Myra a letter (just as Peggy and Maddie write to Wanda) and give her lavish presents. Helen refers to these gifts as "guilt-tinged offerings" (110), and she resolves to get rid of the one that Myra gives her. Like Maddie, Helen cannot escape the "treachery of [her] own heart" (110). The story ends exactly like *The Hundred Dresses,* with the sometime persecutor haunted by the image of the victim standing solitarily against the school:

> Did Myra ever say goodbye? Not likely. She sat in her high bed, her delicate brown neck, rising out of a hospital gown too big for her, her brown carved face immune to treachery, her offering perhaps already forgotten, prepared to be set apart for legendary uses, as she was even in the back porch at school.

(110)

In the first published version of **"Day of the Butterfly,"** which appeared in *Chatelaine* (July 1965) under the title **"Good-by Myra,"** the story had ended far more lamely: "At the door I had to pause once more and look back at her sitting in the high hospital bed. I thought that soon I would be outside. So I called back quickly, treacherously, almost gaily, 'Good-by!'" (58). In keeping with her early practice of imitating works she admired, Munro improved this conclusion by emulating Eleanor Estes's dramatic return to the time of past injury, an effective reminder in both works that the memory of cruel acts is not easily annulled.

To see *The Hundred Dresses* as the source of Munro's **"Day of the Butterfly"** heightens our appreciation of both texts, since each one casts a helpful light on the other. Such a study also illuminates the process by which texts are made of other texts. Finally, a comparison of the two works proves John Rowe Townsend's point that the boundaries between children's literature and adult fiction are shifting and elusive. Many books written for a mature audience—such as *Gulliver's Travels* and *Robinson Crusoe*—are often appropriated by youngsters, whereas children's works such as the Alice books and Tolkien's *The Lord of the Rings* can be popular with adults. No writer in any genre has a monopoly on the truth; and the truth buried deep in a child's heart, as Eleanor Estes and Alice Munro so movingly show, only the skill of a genuine storyteller is needed to reveal.

Notes

1. In "Eleanor Estes: A Study in Versatility," Mabel F. Rice tells of how a group of teachers taking summer school were held spellbound by their professor's reading of *The Hundred Dresses*:

> Toward the end of the morning session of a huge summer school course for teachers at Whittier College the visiting lecturer, Dr. Paul Witty, put

down his papers and picked up a thick colorful book. Sometimes he ended the period with a poem or a book review and the class looked forward to them. He stood silent for a moment, looking at the book before he announced the title. *The Hundred Dresses* by Eleanor Estes. Without preface or comment, he began to read. The large group sat silent, all eyes fixed intently on the reader. No proverbial pin dropped. People scarcely seemed to breathe. When he finished, he closed the book softly. . . . The class filed out silently, almost reverently. They must have scattered to libraries and book stores in their home towns across Southern California. The next morning one saw at the top of many a pile of notebooks and papers *The Hundred Dresses.*

(555-56)

In "Therapeutic Reading," Matilda Bailey recounts how a teacher of a racially mixed group of children saw in *The Hundred Dresses* a means of preventing discrimination:

> In an Anglo-Saxon community, the influx of "foreigners" often presents a problem in the school. One teacher wisely anticipated difficulty by reading aloud to her class Eleanor Estes's *The Hundred Dresses*. The pupils quickly recognized that the little girl in the story with her strange and almost unpronounceable name, was a very nice little girl made extremely unhappy by the Browns and Smiths and Joneses in her class.

> One girl said after the reading of the story, "I wish she were in our class. We'd be nice to her."

(32)

2. Munro admits that certain early stories, including "The Day of the Butterfly," were imitations of other works. At the time of her interview by Tim Struthers, she said that she couldn't recall just whom she was imitating in "Day of the Butterfly" because it was "*such* an early story" (Struthers 23). As she also said in the same interview, writers who have never become famous but who wrote one or two splendid stories are often forgotten when a writer is "put on the spot" with questions about influences (11).

3. This unusual nickname also appears in "The Peace of Utrecht" in *Dance of the Happy Shades,* a minor detail but one that nonetheless strengthens the case for Estes's influence on Munro.

4. Estes's book is made greatly appealing by Louis Slobodkin's whimsical sketches and watercolours. The smudged impression of his characters' faces, for example, is a perfect screen onto which young readers can project themselves; and his avoidance of period detail gives the story a timeless quality.

5. In "Friend of My Youth," the mother of the narrator dismisses the Cameronian sect as a "freak religion from Scotland" (*Friend of My Youth* 5), a

lofty judgment delivered from the "perch of her obedient and lighthearted Anglicanism" (5). One woman in "Accident" tells another of how a priest gave the last rites to, or "did the business" on, a Catholic boy after he died, a comment that elicits a censorious cluck from her listener: "There was not much hostility to Catholics in this disapproval, really; it was a courtesy Protestants were bound to pay to each other" (*The Moons of Jupiter* 93). The narrator of "Privilege" echoes this idea in observing that people of the town were "Catholics or fundamentalist Protestants, honour-bound to molest each other" (*Who Do You Think You Are?* 24). Such molestation sometimes took the form of preventing religious intermarriage. In "Walker Brothers Cowboy," a man's family rejects his sweetheart because she is a Catholic, or a person who "digs with the wrong foot" (*Dance of the Happy Shades* 14, 17). Similarly, in "Jesse and Meribeth," Floris had been courted by the local druggist, "but Aunt Ena objected to him: he drank (that is, he drank a little), and was a Catholic" (*The Progress of Love* 186). Clearly, to Aunt Ena, the druggist's being a Catholic was as bad as his being a drunkard.

Works Cited

Avery, Gillian, et al. "Children's Literature in America: 1870-1945." *Children's Literature: An Illustrated History*. Ed. Peter Hunt. Oxford: Oxford UP, 1995. 225-51.

Bailey, Matilda. "Therapeutic Reading." *Readings About Children's Literature*. Ed. Evelyn Rose Robinson. New York: David McKay, 1966. 31-40.

Estes, Eleanor. *The Hundred Dresses*. New York: Harcourt, 1944.

Munro, Alice. *Dance of the Happy Shades*. Toronto: McGraw-Hill Ryerson, 1968.

———. *Friend of My Youth*. Toronto: McClelland and Stewart, 1990.

———. "Good-by Myra." *Chatelaine* (July 1956): 17, 55-58.

———. *The Moons of Jupiter*. Toronto: Macmillan, 1982.

———. *The Progress of Love*. Toronto: McClelland and Stewart, 1986.

———. *Who Do You Think You Are?* Toronto: Macmillan, 1978.

Rice, Mabel F. "Eleanor Estes: A Study in Versatility." *Elementary English* (1968): 553-57.

Ross, Catherine. "An Interview with Alice Munro." *Canadian Children's Literature* 53 (1989): 14-24.

Struthers, Tim. "The Real Material: An Interview with Alice Munro." *Probable Fictions: Alice Munro's Narrative Acts*. Ed. Louis K. MacKendrick. Downsview, ON: ECW Press, 1983. 5-36.

Townsend, John Rowe. *A Sense of Story: Essays on Contemporary Writers for Children*. London: Longman, 1971.

Viguers, Ruth Hill. "The Golden Age 1920-1950." *A Critical History of Children's Literature*. Ed. Cornelia Meigs et al. New York: Macmillan, 1953. 427-604.

Robert Thacker (review date summer 1998)

SOURCE: Thacker, Robert. "What's 'Material'?: The Progress of Munro Criticism, Part 2." *Journal of Canadian Studies* 33, no. 2 (summer 1998): 196-210.

[*In the following review, Thacker surveys several critical works on Munro's fiction and concludes that reviewers tend to focus on aspects of her stories that support their own viewpoints and interpretations.*]

In one of the holograph drafts of Alice Munro's **"Dulse"** (1980), the narrator meets a "Mr. Middleton from Boston," Mr Stanley in the finished story, the man fixated on Willa Cather's writing, her person and the refuge that was hers there on Grand Manan Island. Hearing that Middleton has spent his life working on newspapers, she writes: "I was surprised, I had taken him for a university man, a professor of literature, I had thought that no other job in the world would allow him his pedantic preening [,] his serene absorption" (Papers 38.8.19.f1, 3). In what looks a subsequent typescript where the narrative has been shifted to third person, the now-named Lydia notes "the fact" of this man's "admiration, his adoration, of the chosen writer. It was not faked. It was true, fervent, engrossing. She thought he could not be a teacher, such worship being too far out of style, too unlikely even in his day" (Papers 38.8.20.f3). Also among the papers held at the University of Calgary is an autobiographical note in which Munro recounts the first time she heard from John Metcalf regarding her work; his letter buoyed her up because Munro was "reeling" from "a painful session with a man [at the University of Victoria] who told me that my work reminded him of the kind of thing he himself had been writing when he was fifteen and had abandoned with the first glimmerings of maturity." This view, she writes, "was damaging only because I had a most exaggerated respect, then, for academic opinion . . ." (6.6).

Beginning here, speaking for myself, this is the second time I have taken up a group of critical books focussed on Munro's writing. In the first review, I ended by citing a phrase from E. D. Blodgett's *Alice Munro* (1988) that asserts that Munro's "'unassailable moral integrity' is borne out in the fiction by the various shifts, doubts, and re-explanations she repeatedly offers, but always with an eye to discovering 'what is real,' and how can one really know, ever?" Concluding, I offered one of Munro's own doubts from her uncollected story, **"Home"** (1974): "*I want to do this with honour, if I possibly can*" and left readers with the perhaps wry, though still apt, invocation: "Go ask Alice" ("Go" 166).

Embarking on this second assay at Munro criticism, I am thinking about these threads: the compelling mass of Munro's *oeuvre,* emphatically including the still largely unstudied intricacies of the Munro archive in Calgary; "the preening absorption" of academics; the commonplace and not at all abandoned "adoration" many of us bring to "the chosen writer," Munro; and her author's own scepticism towards academics generally and literary critics in particular. She wrote, after all, the two scathing paragraphs that begin **"Material"** (1973) as well as—and here I am again reminding those of us who do this for a living—this notable trio of sentences from **"Goodness and Mercy"** (1989): "'Also, professors are dumb. They are dumber than ordinary. I could be nice and say they know about things we don't, but as far as I'm concerned they don't know shit'" (**Friend** [**Friend of My Youth**] 158). *I* want to do this with honour, if I possibly can.

OF CRITICAL AND "MUNROVIAN" CONTEXTS

One of the reviewers of two of these titles begins by asserting that they "belong to the 'second generation' of Munro criticism, one that is no longer in awe of the mimetic qualities detected by first-phase Munro critics but brings sophisticated theoretical frameworks to bear on her work" (Canitz). While I will address such matters as "mimesis," "awe" and "sophistication" presently, the notion of "second generation" seems a good point of departure for the examination of the current critical contexts surrounding Munro's writing. Clearly, the books reviewed in my first attempt—Blodgett, Carrington, Rasporich—had followed others published during the 1980s; together, they constituted the first extended attempts to evaluate Munro's writing (see Dahlie, MacKendrick, *Probable,* Martin, Miller, Pfaus). So the books taken up here do represent, as Canitz asserts, a second phase. What is more, they appear within a context in which Munro has been lionized—the reception accorded **Open Secrets** (1994) having surpassed those of her two previous books, however improbable that might have seemed. More broadly, critical articles abound and appear to be increasing in frequency. Alice Munro, most very clearly, has done far more than arrive: she has established herself as a writer of the very first rank—like, she knows very well, Willa Cather—and so, as "the chosen writer" herself, is more than fit

subject for adoration. And like Cather and others, she has been set upon by critics in a way which is daunting in its extent and in its intensity. Like Cather too, she is sceptical of such attention.[1]

And like the various quotations from the archives with which I began, this too is a necessary context here. There is more: apart from my previous review essay and various articles and bibliography I have contributed to Munro criticism myself, I bring to this task the perspective of a critic who has been working on Munro's fiction consistently since 1973 when I read my first Munro story, **"Material"** in *The Tamarack Review*; my MA thesis on her early stories and **Dance of the Happy Shades** (1968) was among the earliest critical assessments. While Canitz and others are free to identify and deprecate the "naïve awe" such critics as I putatively felt at Munro's mimesis in the first phase, I find myself equally dubious—and this while fully appreciative of its so-called "critical sophistication"—of much of what I have reviewed here. Together with many recent critical articles, some of these books—Heble's, and Smythe's, certainly, and perhaps even Carscallen's—are of doubtful worth; they establish their authors' presence and fulfil academic career needs—probably their most urgent function—but do very little for Munro studies. Indeed, much of Canitz's vaunted "second generation" criticism merely reiterates the first using other terms.

Before taking up each book and detailing such evaluation, a word of my own on Munro's fiction after reading these books and surveying journal articles from the late 1980s through 1996 (the most-recent article I found appeared in *Contemporary Literature* [Clark]). Reading over such a disparate grouping, one is struck by several things having to do with the relation of Munro's work to its critics. Foremost among these are the ways by which Munro's writing creates what amounts almost to an empathetic union among readers, critics most apparent among them. We are drawn to her writing by its verisimilitude—not of mimesis, so-called and much maligned by Heble as "realism"—but rather the feeling of being itself or, as I have said elsewhere in a review of **The Progress of Love** (1986), of just being a human being. Thus what seems to drive critics who have taken up Munro's work—and this is especially so of those who have embarked on book-length studies—is a desire to articulate some personal relation to the work, to replicate in the criticism our feelings upon reading Munro's work. I certainly feel this myself.[2]

What is more, a passage from **"Circle of Prayer"** (1986) that I quoted in the review of **Progress** [**The Progress of Love**] is relevant here: "What are those times that stand out, clear patches in your life—what do they have to do with it? They aren't exactly promises. Breathing spaces. Is that all?" (**Progress** 273). The beginnings of this passage are found in a draft holograph fragment of **"Dulse"** (38.11.7), by the way, and that relation encapsulates a quality in Munro which seems ever to beckon reader and critic alike. The "progress" of insight, from momentary vision to larger understanding, fleeting, tentative, illusory, yet powerful. Standing back from this recent body of Munro criticism, I am struck by this same quality, the desire of the critic to, as Redekop writes, identify "the story that I hear Munro telling *me*" (x). Each critic does this, of course, according to her or his lights—however bright or dim—seizing Munro's work most often at these very "clear patches"; that is, at those points of story at which her art is most evident, and most pointed. There is real consensus that it is never transparent, always elusive, with points of view and meanings compounding, patterns emerging out of other patterns. Katherine J. Mayberry has stated the matter succinctly:

> Munro's understanding of the function of narrative is mordantly paradoxical. Throughout her career, she has insisted on the existence of pre-linguistic experience, of a truth that originates outside of, independent of language. This truth is wholly experiential and wholly personal, never going beyond the bounds of individual perception. Particular and circumscribed, it would seem a simple truth, though as Munro's vision matures, its constitution grows increasingly intricate, its excision from the surrounding web of falsehoods, uncertainties, silence, and alternative perceptions increasingly difficult. But simple or complex, this truth admits little access. The approaches attempted by most of Munro's characters are memory and narrative—virtually equivalent faculties in that they both order past experience, re-collect lived moments within a chronological frame.

She concludes that in Munro "Narrative is finally not the province of truth; to tell is at best to revise, but never to perfectly revive" (540).[3]

What Mayberry calls "lived moments" here are Munro's "clear patches," "Breathing spaces"—insights based on moments or incidents that appear briefly in a draft or earlier story only to emerge as central in a later one.[4] This process—one which Carscallen balloons out of proportion in *The Other Country*—has resulted the emergence of a group of Munro stories which might themselves be seen as particularly indicative of her work's complexity. That is, owing to what seems their centrality to Munro's work—and one of the functions of this is the extent to which they attract critical attention—these most often serve as paradigmatic. **"Walker Brothers Cowboy"** (1968), **"Images"** (1968), **"Thanks for the Ride"** (1957), **"The Peace of Utrecht"** (1960) and **"Dance of the Happy Shades"** (1961) are arguably among this group in *Dance of the Happy Shades.* **"The Flats Road," "Changes and Ceremonies," "Baptizing"** and **"Epilogue: The Photographer"** from *Lives of Girls and Women* (1971). In *Something I've Been Meaning to Tell You* (1974), three stand out: the title story, **"Material,"** and most especially **"The Ot-**

tawa Valley" (1974). Most recently, **"Meneseteung"** (1988) and **"Carried Away"** (1991) appear to be qualifying. This is not the place to elaborate a theory of such selection; it is sufficient, however, to see such stories as embodying Munro's most urgent concerns and displaying her most artful effects—the very moments of being during which each of us, as readers more than as critics, recognizes as resonant. Such instances demand attention, as readers and as critics. Carscallen has this pointedly and well-articulated: "In a way opaque to ordinary logic, though implicit in it, we know that the one and the many, like truth and reality, do not ultimately shut each other out. We are our fully individual selves; we are also members of one another—participants in a humanity that is no bare abstraction" (88). What this has meant to Munro criticism, and especially in the instance which is Carscallen's *The Other Country,* is that beyond moments of epiphany—"clear patches"—Munro's art remains about "Connection. That was what it was all about" (**Moons** [**The Moons of Jupiter**] 6). Human connections, perceptual connections, echoes of other stories, other incidents, other characters, other scenes, other. . . . Alice Munro's art is shaped by a sensibility which ever sees, ever feels, the press of her own separateness, her own connection, her own being.

> "THIS IS NOT ENOUGH, HUGO. YOU THINK IT IS,
> BUT IT ISN'T." (*SOMETHING* [*SOMETHING I'VE
> BEEN MEANING TO TELL YOU*] 44)

In *Some Other Reality,* Louis K. MacKendrick challenges the view that **"Material"** is primarily Munro's own meditation on writing and writers; rather, he maintains, the unnamed narrator is a nasty person who has not forgiven her former husband, Hugo, and the story she writes is something of a calling him to reckoning (39-45). Thus the assertion used here as a section heading. However viewed, though, we need to remember that Hugo is a particular kind of writer: an *academic* writer—not, Munro ultimately implies, a "real" one. Hugo is one of those "vain quarrelsome men," she says, "Bloated, opinionated, untidy men . . . cosseted by the academic life, the literary life, by women" (24). Very clearly from this, Munro has thought about the university as a place in which people live lives, pursue careers, succeed and fail—as, I expect, have we all. Indeed, part of this calling to reckoning in **"Material"** is the narrator's wonder that someone as irresponsible, capricious, and incapable as Hugo has found a place in which he is able to not only survive, but thrive: "Do you wash, Hugo?" she asks, "Do you call your girl students fond exasperated dirty names, are there phone calls from insulted parents, does the Dean or somebody have to explain that no harm is meant, that writers are not as other men are?" (28-29).

Recognizing, as she does here, the hierarchy animating the academy, Munro provides fit point of departure for this review project; I wonder: What need do these books fill? What audience do they address? Do we need them? By my count, we now have 11 sole-author critical books on Munro's work—another, by Coral Ann Howells, is in press, a couple of collections of critical essays, one short biography, a monograph and about 100 critical essays and shorter pieces. Munro, of course, has herself published eight books, a dozen uncollected stories and some fugitive pieces. *Selected Stories* appeared in fall 1996 and fall 1998 will see the publication of another collection, *The Love of a Good Woman.* Given such a field, I have elected to approach these books sceptically, wondering in the first instance over their very existence.

Introducing his argument in *The Tumble of Reason,* Ajay Heble notes "a few revisionist studies which" he thinks "warrant consideration in the present context." Later, though, he complains about this, saying

> On the one hand, I ought, perhaps, to feel inconvenienced by the fact that I am no longer the only one to respond to Munro's fiction in the context of this renewed critical framework. On the other hand, of course, I am pleased to see that Munro's stories are finally beginning to receive the kind of critical attention they deserve.

> (15, 17)

My first response to these comments is, "Oh?," but then I see that Heble is attempting to assert "his Alice Munro." In any case, here is his argument:

> As a result we find Munro abandoning a kind of rational discourse—which assumes that reality is stable, intelligible, and masterable—and replacing it with an equivocal discourse which signifies on the level of the paradigm.

> * * *

> [Munro's] paradigmatic discourse enables us, as it often enables Munro's characters, to imagine *possible* correlations between sets of phenomena and consider how "reality" might be different if something absent or potential were substituted for the way things are. In making use of this kind of discourse, Munro will substitute direct refentiality with what contemporary critical theory might call "textuality." Her fiction, in part, attempts to force us to reconsider the metaphysical category of reality in textual terms. The world of facts, details, and objects, which, at first, serves to ground the reader in a safe and recognizable reality, is suddenly called into question as Munro makes us aware that we are reading only an attempt to represent these things in fiction, that language is being used to re-present reality.

> (6-7)

Thus there is disruption in Munro's writing in these terms—critically totted up for the present moment—and Heble demonstrates his case in seven chapters, one for each of the books in print up to *Friend of My Youth* (1990).

Intelligent, precise and thorough with respect to those of Munro's texts it examines, *The Tumble of Reason* need not have been a book; it should not have been a book. It was already a dissertation—one I have not read, though I have looked at its abstract—and what this book offers beyond that publication is not, likely, very much. Heble's introductory chapter posits his "corrective" theory well enough, and his readings of Munro's books demonstrate his ability, but they certainly do not challenge our understanding of Munro's writing in any way sufficient to justify another book. Heble's readings are selective, they are not based in the full scholarly record—archival, sequential or critical—and they do not advance understanding of Munro's art very much, if at all. This is a book that should have remained a dissertation and been published as one or two good articles. One need only read the last paragraph of each chapter: there is its point.

This same assessment is inescapable regarding Smythe's *Figuring Grief,* though, in her case she managed four published articles before the book. Smythe posits a theory of the "fiction-elegy" and argues that "in the late modern fiction of Gallant and Munro, the trust in language and art is questioned, and the exploration of grief and loss is conducted not only on the formal level of representation but also on the conceptual and tropological levels in terms of figuring memory, history, and the past" (21). (Given the context of this review, I will forebear any comment on Smythe's reading of Gallant, though I suspect that my comments, below, apply there as well.)

Smythe offers two chapters on Munro. The first, "Munro and Modern Elegy," suffices to demonstrate the limitations of her approach. Without question, Smythe is on to something: death—whether impending, recalled, actual or imagined—figures often and deeply in Munro's "material"; indeed, *how* it figures in a Munro story is often as interesting as its specifics. But Smythe's need to argue her theories and so develop a thesis in which an elegiac figuring is demonstrated in her writers' works is ever paramount. Thus in a subsection on "Munro and Modern Elegy" entitled "Shapes of Death: the Meaning of Loss in Munro's Early Stories" (112-22), Smythe treats the following stories in this order: **"Walker Brothers Cowboy"** (1968), **"Images"** (1968), **"Memorial"** (1974), **"The Time of Death"** (1956), **"Day of the Butterfly"** (1956), **"Winter Wind"** (1974), **"Material"** (1973) and **"Tell Me Yes or No"** (1974). It may be that my own work on these stories has valorized chronology, but I would not call stories written over nearly 20 years "early," nor would I treat the earliest stories within a frame later stories. Equally, here, Smythe manages to assign *Something I've Been Meaning to Tell You* (1974) the wrong year of publication.

When she turns, in the next subsection, to Munro's intervening volume, *Lives of Girls and Women,* Smythe makes no mention of Besner's book.

More than matters of scholarship and structure, what strikes me most in *Figuring Grief* is the drive to thesis. Smythe's reading of Munro is essentially a thematic overview. She sets out to illustrate her points; she treats Munro's stories seemingly randomly, out of any clear order, and all only with an eye toward her own thesis. The argument is well-informed by and rooted in relevant authorial statements and critical texts—though, as noted, there are lapses—but ultimately the whole is reductive. Smythe's own thesis is of far more importance than Munro's fiction which, to my mind, is frequently shoe-horned into some thesis-driven series of points. Overall, *Figuring Grief* reads like the academic exercise it was; like *The Tumble of Reason,* this should have remained a dissertation and its articles.

That this is the best I am able to offer regarding Heble and Smythe is unfortunate, and it reflects poorly on the present state of the profession of English. Readily conceding that others will disagree with my assessment of these two books—seeing them as effective, necessary critical texts—I nevertheless wonder how each of these authors came to be advised to publish them in their present form. True, they are published by reputable academic presses, but each author would have benefited from a few more years of post-PhD rumination, whether presses and granting agencies and mentors and authors think so or not. The smug self-congratulatoriness of Heble's comments on Munro criticism, quoted above, and the dissertationese of Smythe's writing, chock full as it is with "I argues" and "I perceives" (vii) fail to hide the fact that neither has much depth of understanding—theirs is quite appropriate for a doctoral degree which, still, should be the beginning of a career as a professional scholar and teacher, not the ending. Yet books like these, which many of us think are needed to ensure that our students do begin an academic career, are sad affairs. It may be that any bright PhD needs to have a book forthcoming to ensure any hope of a place in university, but it should not be.[5] Without question, each of these volumes testifies more to the currency of Munro's (and Gallant's, in Smythe's case) critical reputation than to the abilities of these critics.

"I RESPECT THE INTENTION AND THE EFFORT AND
THE RESULT" (*SOMETHING* 43)

Willa Cather, when writing about Sarah Orne Jewett (arguably the single-most important artistic influence on her own work), offers an observation which is an apt beginning for a consideration of Carscallen's *The Other Country* and Redekop's *Mothers and Other Clowns* in this section, and for the balance of these volumes in the next. If a writer

achieves anything noble, anything enduring, it must be by giving himself absolutely to his material. And this gift of sympathy is his great gift; is the fine thing in him that alone can make his work fine.

The artist spends a lifetime in pursuing the things that haunt him, in having his mind "teased" by them, in trying to get these conceptions down on paper exactly as they are to him and not in conventional poses supposed to reveal their character; trying this method and that, as a painter tries different lightings and different attitudes with his subject to catch the one that presents it more suggestively than any other. And at the end of a lifetime he emerges with much that is more or less happy experimenting, and comparatively little that is the very flower of himself and his genius.

(79-80)

Something of Cather's idea is working in each of the volumes yet to be considered, since each is the product of quite a number of years spent reading, ruminating and weighing Munro's substantive art, itself the product of just the sort of imaginative process Cather describes.

As he concludes his massive, delightful and peculiar book, *The Other Country,* Carscallen takes up a little-known piece Munro published in 1974, **"Everything Here Is Touchable and Mysterious,"** which deals with her sense of Huron County, particularly her "home place," "'Loretown'—a 'stragling, unincorporated, sometimes legendary non-part' of Wingham, Ontario. . . ." "'I am still partly convinced that this river'" he quotes Munro describing her hometown's river, the Maitland, "'not even the whole river, but this little stretch of it—will provide whatever myths you want, whatever adventures.'" Carscallen continues with a passage which bears quoting at length:

The same thing, as I have tried to indicate, is true of Munro's writing itself as it follows its not very extensive course. And while its adventures may often come to tragic ends—the river itself supposedly has "deep holes, ominous beckoning places," eerie enough to satisfy Uncle Benny—there is something here that transforms even the depths.

We saw how an unincorporated region like the Ottawa Valley can equally be the Church of St. John, where the Creator is celebrated for the bright and beautiful things he has made. Munro speaks with the same wonder of the living creatures along the river, or the names which they also are: "I name the plants, I name the fish, and every name seems to me triumphant, every leaf and quick fish remarkably valuable." And so, she concludes, "this ordinary place is sufficient, everything here touchable and mysterious." The touchability of things is their reality, the mystery of them is their truth—or, if we prefer, their truth is what can be grasped and their reality remains mysterious, as in a way reality always does; but in either case it is by the grace of naming, and its counterpart story-telling, that these contraries are gathered into one. Through names and stories, then, Munro offers us true reality: the ordinary made marvellous in its distinctness and the abundance of its life.

(534-35)

Before commenting on Carscallen's last words, here, I want to go back—over 535 pages back—to his first: "The following book is offered, not just to Munro specialists, but to anyone who has found her work enjoyable and moving" (vii). James Carscallen has been working on Munro, so far as I can tell, since the late 1970s; he published an early profile of Munro in 1980 and then two other essays a few years later. And judging by *The Other Country,* Munro's fiction has certainly "teased" his mind for some time, and to a *very* considerable extent.

I called this book "peculiar" for several different reasons. Though written in what he calls "plain English"—doubtless his rejection of the hipcrit jargon offered by others, such as Heble and Smythe, about University of Toronto's English Department—the density of language and, especially, that of argument, belie any hope that this book will be read in its entirety by anyone but Munro specialists. Indeed, such are the shifts, asides, allusions, promises, and recollections in *The Other Country* that even a person with a detailed command of Munro's writings has trouble following Carscallen's meanderings. (Indicative of this are the twin facts that I had trouble following his numerous arguments when reading the book towards the end of a semester-long seminar on Munro during which I reread the entire *oeuvre.*) Clearly peculiar, this approach may be a major problem. This is the more remarkable when one considers that Carscallen concerns himself wholly with the published works, generally eschewing archival materials and statements of authorial intention.

What Carscallen does do, and does very well indeed overall, is to have us take an entirely different tack towards Munro's work. Instead of theme, character, point-of-view, chronology, disruption, composition or other ways into the fiction, Carscallen sees patterns. By this he means the numerous ways texts reflect, elaborate and echo one another: "single stories seem to me to fit implicitly into a larger one of the same kind as themselves." "Thus pieces from anywhere in a book may help to illustrate a phase with which those in a particular location are linked in a more special way" (viii). A student of Frye, Carscallen displays that influence here in the ornate and detailed patterns he details in Munro. Offering an account of his own discovery of Munro's patterns, he takes up **Lives of Girls and Women,** noting that "Mrs. McQuade's whorehouse is located next to the B. A. service station. As I myself mused on this unremarkable but included fact, it first occurred to me that, in the world of the chapter, a whorehouse and a service station have somewhat the same function. . . ." He then goes from this to King Solomon, who "cultivated wisdom as well as arms and pleasure"—parallels he finds in Del and her mother's pursuit "of enlightenment"—and then goes on to note that there are two allusions to the biblical David. Though fearing that he

was engaging in "creative reading," Carscallen ultimately concludes—in a phrase which could be seen as having paradigmatic significance in relation to Munro's fiction—that "Once she has established a pattern by putting two worlds in parallel, the pattern assimilates whatever will fit into it" (10-11).

But this is not landmark Munro criticism. *The Other Country* is not a book for a general reader nor, even, for a interested undergraduate. Nevertheless, it offers a great many insights and bears scrutiny, contemplation and frequent consultation: Carscallen's is an intricate erudition. At the same time, the book's index of titles and characters, the daunting detail of the discussion—each chapter appears with scores of end notes—are well worth having. I have no quarrel with the approach Carscallen adopts, but I do wonder about the argument's extent and, as well, alternative explanations of what he sees. He takes the Bible as primary referent and, through an analysis of characters' names and a typing of stories—Apocalypse, Exodus, the Book of Judges—sees mythopoeic relation between, throughout and in great detail. Jumping back and forth between stories and other materials, promising to get into that later, weaving one interpretation of a story onto another, and then another, Carscallen offers a view of Munro's fiction like none seen before—though hard to follow, it is often quite worth the trouble.

Even so, a reader finds himself wondering over the degree to which connections are product of Carscallen's own proclivities—he has also written, one notes, on *The Faerie Queen*—and the degree to which this is a private system of meaning. As well, Carscallen's assertion that Munro thinks through charged images—this is evident, for example, in his fine discussion of the story of that title, **"Images,"** in relation to **"Monsieur Les Deux Chapeaux"** (1985) in terms of their "clear patch" scenes (107-17)—seems relevant too, and especially in light of Cather's point. While the notion that Munro—not, evidently, an especially religious person—would consistently use the Bible as analogue seems a bit farfetched, Carscallen's recognition really is an elaboration that her art is rooted in Huron County and in its Scots-Irish culture. That is, the patterns Carscallen finds are derived from the cultural images Munro inherited and has imaginatively dwelled upon and drawn upon for her fiction. These are patterns created by an imagination "teased" for years by her inherited cultural material, **"Material"** she has returned to repeatedly throughout her career. Part of that material, of course, are the biblical stories Carscallen elaborates, the names that resonate meaning and, most especially, the images that demand probing from Munro herself—one **"Carried Away"** by her **"Material,"** from Huron County where **"Everything . . . Is Touchable and Mysterious."**

Like her colleague Carscallen, Magdalene Redekop brings another sort of background to her work on Munro; she notes at the beginning of her book that **"The Progress of Love"** is, both ironically and appropriately, the title of a poem by Swift. By using "that phrase as a title, he initiated a satiric questioning and Munro pushes further with those questions." She does so, indeed, in a very seriously mocking way, also like Swift: thus Redekop's title, *Mothers and Other Clowns*: "Munro invokes details from her own life not as a traditional autobiographer would do, but as a clown would do" (xiii). While I wonder what Redekop means by "traditional autobiographer," the notion of clowning, like Carscallen's patterns, is an important one. So is this one:

> The narrator of **"Material,"** herself "pregnant with Clea" reproduces Dotty's litany of complaints. It includes three miscarriages. "My womb," says Dotty, "is in shreds. I use up three packs of Kotex every month." Our laughter cannot take away from the reality of Dotty's suffering, the material conditions of her life in "material" [sic]. The narrator of **"Material"** tries to write a letter to Hugo about his story. The letter is intercepted by the reader and here is what we read: *This is not enough, Hugo. You think it is, but it isn't. You are mistaken, Hugo.* I see Munro's stories as a response to the challenge issued by that jabbing sentence. It is not enough to see madonna and harlot as all dolled up to join the parade. They must be domesticated by being taken up into the family. How may a woman's reproductions act to resist a mimicry that is simply a burlesque, like Del's rag-doll dance? The question will partly turn itself into a question of how the woman can learn to *be* the clown instead of the rag-doll dummy used by the clown. The answer will lie . . . in Munro's focus on looking.
>
> (15-16)

As this suggests, *Mothers and Other Clowns* approaches Munro's work through an analysis of female perspective; as such, this book covers much of the same ground as Rasporich's *Dance of the Sexes* (1990). It does so, however, in a far better and more-informed way, certainly displacing the earlier book.

What Redekop offers is her own reading of Munro, to some degree an idiosyncratic one, but by no means as much so as Carscallen's. She is, as well, quite critically informed, and goes so far as to suggest that "Munro's stories have a lot to teach theorists writing today." Thus despite Munro's own disavowal of any aesthetic, Redekop has "excavated an aesthetic from Munro's stories" because she wanted to "invert" the premise of feminists "finding a vocabulary to explain what the storytellers are doing" (xii). This she does largely through the "Argument" section which makes up the first 40 pages of the book. Two quotations encapsulate the approach Redekop takes:

> The result of reading Munro's fiction is not to allow the reader—whether male or female—to be comfortable and smug. It is rather to find ourselves caught in the act of smugness—certainly defined as a part of a group. This is the most subtle of Munro's many tricks, to make us initially unaware of our participation, to lure us into a position where we settle into our own prejudices and stereotypes—then to follow this up by making us excruciatingly aware of our own self-deceptions.
>
> (30)

> Munro's own tricks do not stop with the thrill of power or even with the moment of ironic understanding. Her clowning offers comfort because it leads to a *mutual* failure. We read for enlightenment and arrive, repeatedly, at the point of recognized blindness. In this experience, however, we have company: reader and writer share this discovery of mutual foolishness.
>
> (34)

Redekop is arriving, in both of these comments, at the point at which the power of Munro's art is most deeply apparent: that is, when reader and writer—alike and together—are in an empathetic commingling. Thus she writes, again with reference to **"Material,"** that "At the deepest level of Munro's writing is her constant awareness that a writer, in the act of writing, is *using* people" (131).

As in Carscallen's book, there is an idiosyncratic density here. Yet, in contrast to his book where the connections leading to patterns threaten to envelope a reader, Redekop keeps her readings of Munro's stories balanced, and always in sight of her own argument. At the same time, and again like *The Other Country*, there is a leaping about within Munro's works that at times proves disconcerting: stories are discussed without reference to order of composition and, as well, Redekop has no apparent knowledge of the Calgary archives. And given the argument offered here, which has much to say about autobiography both in theory and in Munro's approach to it, about mothers and daughters, and about **"The Ottawa Valley"** in particular, the omission of any sustained reading of "Home"—despite its inclusion in the bibliography—seems singularly odd.

Not a great book, *Mother and Other Clowns* is a good one—its "Argument" section is much the best part of the book, theoretically alert and well-grounded in Munro's art. While I would have liked a cleaner rationale for the examination of the fiction—why these stories, greater awareness of provenance, and much more critique of other critics in light of her own readings—those found here are sustained, precise and convincing. Some of these deficiencies, I recognize, are those I noted above with reference to Heble's and Smythe's books. Yet the difference between the two pairs ought to be clear: the depth of understanding Carscallen and Redekop offer outweigh weaknesses. Theirs are books worth having.

"A FINE AND LUCKY BENEVOLENCE" (*SOMETHING*
43)

Early in *Some Other Reality* Louis K. MacKendrick
makes a point that bears echoing and is, indeed, one already made here; after surveying the various book-
length critical studies available to him, he concludes his
chapter by writing that "It may be evident that studies
of individual stories, not subject to large schematic argument, continue to reveal Alice Munro's truer achieve-
ments as a writer. Though this method has not been a
consistent practice in Canadian literary criticism, it suits
Munro's fictive particularities handsomely" (25). That
is, Munro's material—like her **"Material,"** of which
more in a moment—best lends itself to close textual
treatment on the same more narrow scale she adopts
herself. And as this assertion suggests, MacKendrick—
followed at only a slight distance by Neil Besner in his
Introducing Alice Munro's Lives of Girls and
Women—is by far the best critic of this group. His
knowledge of his subject is clearly as deep and precise
as any of the others', and the format he employs—one
book sharply focussed upon, thoroughly contextualized
and textualized—yields the best and most useful sustained criticism.

This, I confess, surprised me: I had not expected the
ECW series books—of which these are two from its
"Canadian Fiction Studies" series, now numbering over
30 volumes—to be as good as they are. By contrast,
and as I have said elsewhere, Catherine Sheldrick
Ross's *Alice Munro: A Double Life*—one of the first
volumes published in ECW's Canadian Biography series—shows the limitations of the series format. While
she has produced a very good and useful book—one
quite effective as a class text—Ross's biography is exceptionally constrained by the series format. In this regard, too, my survey of criticism here has confirmed
one particular need in Munro studies: an extended critical biography, one that shapes its material to its construction of Munro's writing life. Ross begins that process, but in her rush to fit into ECW's limitations this
book falls far short of the need.

I want to take up MacKendrick in more detail and consider, so as to conclude this—"*with honour, if I possibly
can*"—with the story which has been a mainstay
throughout my own "Munrovian" career and leitmotif
here, **"Material."** But before that, Besner's book,
briefly noted. His introduction to **Lives** [*Lives of Girls
and Women*] is excellent, thorough and precise. In keeping with the ECW format, he offers a chronology, addresses "The Importance of the Work," treats its critical
reception and stature, and then offers a detailed reading
of the book. Besner manages all of this in a balanced
way: showing a fine knowledge of the book's provenance, Munro's intentions and difficulties, and a rarely
equalled generosity in acknowledging the work of the

book's other critics. What is more, he manages to say
something original about a book that has received a dis-
proportionate share of critical attention.

Besner is at his very best when he discusses the ending
of **Lives,** particularly when he considers another leitmotif in Munro criticism: the difference between what is
real—the title of one of her essays—and what is true.
Having rejected Garnet French at the end of **"Baptizing,"** bereft of scholarship, Del confronts *"Real Life"*
(238). Carscallen attempts to meld the two in his final
sentence, "Through names and stories, then, Munro offers us true reality: the ordinary made marvellous in its
distinctness and the abundance of its life" (535). Contrasting the book we have in our hand with the "Hallo-
way novel" that Del writes, Besner asserts:

> The writer's art, regardless of its conventions, creates a
> reality which, regardless of its own "truth," is both au-
> tonomous *and* related to the world it refers to, however
> diffuse or symbolic this connection may be. Paradoxi-
> cally, it is in the Halloway novel that we (along with
> Del) may be able to see more clearly the relations be-
> tween the real world and the fictional world. In *Lives
> of Girls and Women* itself, the relations are more mys-
> terious, for all of realism's supposed mimetic proper-
> ties; and Del is discovering this mystery at the heart of
> what will be her art as she sits with Bobby Sheriff,
> who is himself only the last of the several Jubilee ec-
> centrics who have confronted Del with unknowable
> and yet alluring realities.

(109)[6]

Besner is asking, along with Munro, "What *is* Real?"
and, also along with her, he is acknowledging that in
the world, generally, and in Munro's Jubilee, particularly, "Everything *Is* Touchable and Mysterious." Besner continues, recognizing that **Who Do You Think
You Are?** (1978) amounts to Munro's return to many of
these same questions; he might have taken the ending
of **Lives**—with its tension between what is real to Del
and what is true, what is Munro's fiction and what is
Del's—stopped off for a bit at the ending of **Who [Who
Do You Think You Are?**], and continued on to **"Meneseteung,"** another of Munro's attempts at the Caroline-
Marion problem in **Lives.**

Early in her celebrity, Munro told an interviewer that
"writing is the act of approach and recognition," an act
of "just approaching something that is mysterious and
important." "I believe that we don't solve these
things—in fact or explanations take us further away"
(Gardiner 178). Thus Munro may be seen moving from
Del to Rose to Almeda, and the mystery continues, as
Pam Houston has argued about **"Meneseteung,"** a
"clear-patch story" *par excellence:*

> What is true is untrue, what is untrue is true. We have
> an hysterical bleeding woman inside an admittedly fic-
> titious account, written by a narrator who doesn't even

know her name. We have a distortion of reality within a distortion of reality, within a story that is also a poem, and sometimes a river. Nothing here will stay long enough to mean just one thing.

(90)

Welcome, one is tempted to say, to Alice Munro where everything is paradoxically touchable and mysterious—that is, not graspable. Explanations do take Munro—and us—"further away" and yet, as Redekop says, this is an author who has much to teach literary theorists: "Also, professors are dumb."

MacKendrick makes substantially the same point when he writes, early in his reading of the text of *Something I've Been Meaning to Tell You*:

> It is quite hopeless and redundant to expect an Alice Munro story to surrender a clear, indisputable, and singular "meaning." The language itself is the prime variable, and it is complicated by an almost predictable complexity of her first-person narrators, few of whom are able to remain disengaged from what they are relating. It is a little surprising, then, that given the possible permutations of language, character, and event, the critical interpretations of her writing should have such an occasional, but interdependent, element of repetition. This is no guarantee, however, that Munro's work will not be used to prove a prescriptive formula of fiction, or a single-minded argumentative philosophy.

(26)

Here MacKendrick has provided text to account for the several books reviewed here, plus those that proceeded them. The problem, of course, is in which Munro—by rendering in a long critical form "my" Munro, the authors of such texts are constructing her fiction along the lines of personal proclivities—theoretical, structural or linguistic. Even MacKendrick, here, tends to privilege "first-person narrators" who, until *Something* seemed to be increasing in frequency. Ever at the ready, Munro has since tended more towards third person, folding much of the first-person narrator's uncertainties into the narrative voice—as in **"Meneseteung."**

As he works his way through *Something*'s stories, MacKendrick offers readings of each story that are convincing, certainly, but more than that they show him ever alert to nuance—and in this Munro volume, which is transitional in several ways, that means looking back to earlier work as well as forward to more recent, and complex, renderings. Thus

> Munro's stories may have almost cheerful and unapologetic interruptions in any expected narrative line—generally by her preferred voice, a first-person narrator. Very often in reading a Munro story we become pleasantly aware that along with perfectly credible or "realistic" characters and situations we are also variously hearing echoes, reverberations, repetitions, ironies, juxtapositions, contrasts, digressions, interpolations. We

are hearing not only a storyteller's tricks but we are hearing them almost as a matter of narrative course. Very often we are hearing a truly oral narrative a distinctive and personalized voice.

(29)

While his reading of the collection's title story is especially fine—and complex—it is MacKendrick's reading of **"Material"** that interests me most here. Following on his final point, he concentrates on the oral quality of the narrative, saying that **"Material"** "is a thorough and consistently revealing self-portrait, with enough ramifications of character that the narrator, ranging through moods and tones, virtually comes to life beyond the confines of this chronicle." What is more, "In the story's present she is marking test papers in history, and Hugo is to be assigned a grade after all the material has been considered—after she has written her history of their relationship." Seeing this narrator's narrative as a "sometimes unflattering self-portrait," one that "is a contest" "between a professional creative writer and his ex-wife, a teacher and corrector, who has nothing to lose and everything to win, for she is the only one aware of the contest" (39).

As MacKendrick notes, "Some of Munro's critics believe the passage [in which she acknowledges Hugo's successful artistry] to be one of [Munro's] personal testaments about her fiction." (43) I have said so myself, and I still believe it is. But I also see the "real truth" of MacKendrick's careful close reading of Munro's text, one that ultimately sees this narrator as a nasty, vituperative person who does, indeed, both "envy and despise" the men in her life, Hugo and Gabriel both, for not being "*at the mercy*" (**Something** 44). Thus "her lingering past demons and lingering resentments have been once again been dealt with. Gabriel's discovery of Hugo's story has precipitated a farrago of memory, bitterness and self-justification, and an apparent summary confession of spite, jealousy and error. Yet the narrator continues to be a vigorous combatant in her own arena" (45). Writing of the same story, taking a very different tack, Redekop asks "Has the narrator appropriated some of the power invested in Hugo, the writer? She has, after all, written *this* story: the story '**Material**'" (31). "'Yes,' I said, instead of thank you" (**Lives** 250).

What the critic is asking, in both cases, though most thoroughly in MacKendrick's reading, is "What's '**Material**'?" What we have as critics, in the first instance and to use another phrase of MacKendrick's, are Alice Munro's "Narrative Acts." What we do with them, as MacKendrick asserts and I certainly echo based on what I have examined for this review essay, is largely whatever we want. Each of us shapes a Munro to suit—privileging this, downplaying that, exaggerating here, ignoring there—and we emerge (as I certainly do myself, here) having shaped a version of the Munro critique. Perhaps entertaining, perhaps wry, perhaps illuminating, perhaps dry: the answer to all this, again and ever, is the same as before: Go ask Alice, where "Everything *Is* Touchable and Mysterious."

Notes

I would like to express my appreciation to J. R. (Tim) Struthers, University of Guelph, for encouraging me to write a second essay on this subject.

1. Both Klaus P. Stich and I have examined the Munro-Cather relation in some detail. What it reveals, like other parallels between Munro and numerous other writers, particularly Eudora Welty, is that Alice Munro has a deep understanding of the writer's position *vis-à-vis* her self, her family, her society and her critics. As I suggest throughout this essay, Munro quite reasonably now puts critics at the end of this line, whatever her attitude was years ago in Victoria.

2. Although my focus here is on critical books on Munro's work published since 1990, I want to comment briefly on journal articles which, as I say, have appeared with increasing frequency. While doing the work for this review, I read my way through those articles which appeared during the same period as well as some from the 1980s I had missed.

   One is struck that hand in hand with her international celebrity, Munro has received attention from foreign critics—American and European alike. Much of this is of little worth, owing largely to the perspective of the critics or the peculiar approach taken—far too many critics, still, discover Munro and rush to print without doing the necessary scholarship; their insights are mundane, their arguments commonplace (Sturgess, Ventura, Seyersted). Equally, too, editors have discovered Munro and commissioned overview pieces that—though probably of some use to those who have never read any of her work—would be better off left to reference books (Ditsky). One of these, by Georgeann Murphy, is particularly troubling in that it includes a full bibliography of Munro's work without any acknowledgement of the various published bibliographical sources that, doubtless, were consulted in the compilation. Other foreign critics have contributed articles that have derived from reading and teaching individual stories, and are offered without reference to Canadian Literature as a subfield (Cam, Clark, Elliot, Goodman, Houston, Mayberry). At the same time, foreign critics who have established themselves as scholars of Canadian literature have continued to contribute; one, Carrington, has done so with her usual detail and zeal (see also Gilbert and Irvine).

Canadian critics, in the same vein, have continued to offer examinations of Munro that extend the theoretical and nationalist discourse with regard to her work (Canitz, Garson, Goldman, Hoy, McCarthy, Rooke, Seaman, Sellwood, Smythe, Stubbs). Others, most notably John Weaver, have approached Munro's work from an altogether new vantage point. As will become evident below, my own view is that given that Munro's form is the short story, articles are much the better format for criticism of her work than books. Indeed, since she published *Controlling the Uncontrollable,* Carrington's work has demonstrated the efficacy of the critical article to Munro abundantly; would that Smythe and Heble had done as much. And while some critics have availed themselves to the wealth of information available in the Calgary archives (Hoy, Tausky), this remains a largely untapped resource.

3. Even with this fine insight, Mayberry offers an example of the sort of blinkered scholarship I bemoan. In an excellent article she manages to discuss Munro's use of paradox without citing Helen Hoy's work in this area; though she does cite critics who acknowledge Hoy—Blodgett and Carrington—that hardly seems enough.

4. A most graphic instance of this is the recurrence of an industrial decapitation that first appeared in "Thanks for the Ride" (1957)—a story Munro submitted to Robert Weaver at the CBC in 1955—as the cause of Lois's father's death. There the incident is a brief description offered to Dick by Lois's mother (*Dance* [*Dance of the Happy Shades*] 51). It is a major focus in "Carried Away" (1991), where Louisa's imagined suitor, Jack Agnew, is killed in the same accident, his severed head being "carried away" by the factory owner, Arthur Doud, whom Louisa eventually marries. Such recurrent incidents seem more worth analysis than many, if not most, of the patterns Carscallen elaborates.

5. These two books, ironically, derive from dissertations submitted in 1990 to the University of Toronto's Department of English, the same department among whose members are Carscallen and Redekop. Largely regarded as the pre-eminent department in the country—at least by those associated with it—Toronto has been slow in establishing a hospitable environment for the critical study of Canadian writing; that history may enter into the phenomenon such books as these represent, since each author aspires to tie the argument to some discourse other than Canadian literature. However seen, such an assertion needs defence, certainly, especially when a reasonable response to it would be the three words "Frye," "Atwood"

and "Davies." See my "Gazing Through the One-Way Mirror" for a discussion of the historical contexts of Canadian writing in the Canadian academy generally, and in the English Department at Toronto particularly.

6. It may be worth noting that here, in 1990, Besner is critiquing mimesis in Munro, à la Canitz, without recourse to the current jargon used by Heble. It goes without saying, too, that Besner's "sophistication" outstrips Heble's and Carscallen's in my view.

Works Cited

The Alice Munro Papers: Second Accession. Comp. Jean M. Moore. Ed. Apollonia Steele and Jean F. Tener. Calgary: U Calgary P, 1987.

Beran, Carol L. "Images of Women's Power in Contemporary Canadian Fiction by Women." *Studies in Canadian Literature* 15.2 (1990): 55-76.

Blodgett, E. D. *Alice Munro.* Boston: Twayne, 1988.

Cam, Heather. "Learning From the Teacher: Alice Munro's Reworking of Eudora Welty's 'June Recital.'" *Span* 25 (1987): 16-30.

Canitz, A. E. Christa. Rev. of *The Other Country* by James Carscallen and *The Tumble of Reason* by Ajay Heble. *University of Toronto Quarterly* 65 (1995-96): 247-50.

Carrington, Ildikó de Papp. *Controlling the Uncontrollable: The Fiction of Alice Munro.* Dekalb: Northern Illinois UP, 1989.

———. "Talking Dirty: Alice Munro's 'Open Secrets' and John Steinbeck's *Of Mice and Men.*" *Studies in Short Fiction* 31 (1994): 595-606.

———. "What's in a Title?: Alice Munro's 'Carried Away.'" *Studies in Short Fiction* 30 (1993): 555-64.

Carscallen, James. "Alice Munro." *Profiles in Canadian Literature* 2. Ed. Jeffrey M. Heath. Toronto: Dundurn, 1980. 73-80.

———. "The Shining House: A Group of Stories." Miller 85-101.

———. "Three Jokers: The Shape of Alice Munro's Stories." *Centre and Labyrinth: Essays in Honour of Northrop Frye.* Ed. Eleanor Cook et al. Toronto: U Toronto P, 1983. 128-46.

Cather, Willa. "Miss Jewett." *Not Under Forty.* 1936. Lincoln: U Nebraska P, 1988. 76-95.

Clark, Miriam Marty. "Allegories of Reading in Alice Munro's 'Carried Away.'" *Contemporary Literature* 37 (1996): 49-61.

Dahlie, Hallvard. "Alice Munro and Her Works." *Canadian Writers and Their Works.* Eds. Robert Lecker, Jack David, and Ellen Quigley. Toronto: ECW, 1985. 213-54.

Ditsky, John. "The Figure in the Linoleum: The Fiction of Alice Munro." *The Hollins Critic* 22 (1985): 1-10.

Gilbert, Paula Ruth. "All Roads Pass Through Jubilee: Gabrielle Roy's *La Route d'Altmount* and Alice Munro's *Lives of Girls and Women.*" *Colby Quarterly* 29 (1993): 136-44.

Goldman, Marlene. "Penning in the Bodies: The Construction of Gendered Subjects in Alice Munro's 'Boys and Girls.'" *Studies in Canadian Literature* 15 (1990): 62-75.

Goodman, Charlotte. "Cinderella in the Classroom: (Mis)Reading Alice Munro's 'Red Dress—1946.'" *Reader* 30 (1993): 49-64.

Heble, Ajay. "The Tumble of Reason: Paradigmatic Reservoirs of Meaning in the Fiction of Alice Munro." Diss. U Toronto, 1990. DAI 52 (1991): 3416A.

Houston, Pam. "A Hopeful Sign: The Making of Metonymic Meaning in Munro's 'Meneseteung.'" *Kenyon Review* 14 (1992): 79-92.

Hoy, Helen. "'Dull, Simple, Amazing and Unfathomable': Paradox and Double Vision in Alice Munro's Fiction." *Studies in Canadian Literature* 5 (1980): 100-15.

———. "'Rose and Janet': Alice Munro's Metafiction." *Canadian Literature* 121 (1989): 59-83.

———. "Alice Munro: 'Unforgettable, Indigestible, Messages.'" *Journal of Canadian Studies* 26.1 (1991): 5-21.

Irvine, Lorna. "Questioning Authority: Alice Munro's Fiction." *CEA Critic* 50 (1987): 57-66.

MacKendrick, Louis K., ed. *Probable Fictions: Alice Munro's Narrative Acts.* Toronto: ECW, 1983.

Martin, W. R. *Alice Munro: Paradox and Parallel.* Edmonton: U Alberta P, 1987.

Mayberry, Katherine J. "'Every Last Thing . . . Everlasting': Alice Munro and the Limits of Narrative." *Studies in Short Fiction* 29 (1992): 531-41.

McCarthy, Dermot. "The Woman Out Back: Alice Munro's 'Meneseteung.'" *Studies in Canadian Literature* 19 (1994): 1-19.

Miller, Judith, ed. *The Art of Alice Munro: Saying the Unsayable.* Waterloo: U Waterloo P, 1984.

Munro, Alice. *Dance of the Happy Shades.* Fore. Hugh Garner. Toronto: McGraw-Hill Ryerson, 1968.

―――. *Friend of My Youth.* Toronto: McClelland & Stewart, 1990.

―――. "Home." *New Canadian Stories*: 74. Ed. David Helwig and Joan Harcourt. Ottawa: Oberon, 1974. 133-153.

―――. *Lives of Girls and Women.* New York: McGraw-Hill, 1971.

―――. *The Moons of Jupiter.* Toronto: Macmillan, 1982.

―――. *The Progress of Love.* Toronto: McClelland & Stewart, 1986.

―――. *Selected Stories.* Toronto: McClelland & Stewart, 1996.

―――. *Something I've Been Meaning to Tell You: Thirteen Stories.* Toronto: McGraw-Hill Ryerson, 1974.

―――. Untitled Interview. Appendix. "The Early Short Stories of Alice Munro." MA Thesis. New Brunswick, 1973. 169-82.

Murphy, Georgeann. "The Art of Alice Munro: Memory, Identity, and the Aesthetics of Connection." *Canadian Women Writing Fiction.* Ed. Mickey Pearlman. Jackson: UP Mississippi, 1993. 12-27, 155-56.

Pfaus, B. *Alice Munro.* Ottawa: Golden Dog, 1984.

Rasporich, Beverly J. *Dance of the Sexes: Art and Gender in the Fiction of Alice Munro.* Edmonton: U Alberta P, 1990.

Rooke, Constance. "Fear of the Open Heart." *A Mazing Space: Writing Canadian Women Writing.* Eds. Shirley Neuman and Smaro Kamboureli. Edmonton: Longspoon/NeWest, 1986.

Sellwood, Jane. "'Certain Vague Hopes of Disaster': A Psychosemiotic Reading of Alice Munro's 'The Flood Boat' as the Flooding Text." *Studies in Canadian Literature* 17 (1992): 1-16.

Seyersted, Per. "'Who Do You Think You Are?': Alice Munro and the Place of Origin." *American Studies in Scandinavia* 24 (1992): 17-23.

Smythe, Karen Elizabeth. "Late Modern Works of Mourning: The Elegiac Fiction of Mavis Gallant and Alice Munro." Diss. U of Toronto, 1990. DAI 51 (1991): 3416A.

―――. "Sad Stories: The Ethics of Epiphany in Munrovian Elegy." *University of Toronto Quarterly* 60 (1991): 493-506.

Stich, Klaus P. "The Cather Connection in Alice Munro's 'Dulse.'" *Modern Language Studies* 20.4 (1989): 102-11.

Stubbs, Andrew. "Fictional Landscape: Mythology and the Dialectic in the Fiction of Alice Munro." *World Literature Written in English* 23 (1984): 53-62.

Sturgess, Charlotte. "Alice Munro's 'The Progress of Love': Secrets, Continuity and Closure." *Etudes Canadiennes* 29 (1990): 223-33.

Tausky, Thomas E. "'What Happened to Marion?': Art and Reality in Lives of Girls and Women." *Studies in Canadian Literature* 11 (1986): 52-76.

Thacker, Robert. "Alice Munro: An Annotated Bibliography." *The Annotated Bibliography of Canada's Major Authors,* Volume 5. Ed. Robert Lecker and Jack David. Toronto: ECW, 1984. 354-414.

―――. "Alice Munro's Willa Cather." *Canadian Literature* 134 (1992): 42-57.

―――. "Gazing Through the One-Way Mirror: English-Canadian Literature and the American Presence." *Colby Quarterly* 29 (1993): 74-87.

―――. "Go Ask Alice: The Progress of Munro Criticism." *Journal of Canadian Studies* 26.2 (Summer 1991): 156-69.

―――. "Munro's Progress." Rev. of *The Progress of Love* by Alice Munro. *Canadian Literature* 115 (1987): 239-42.

―――. Rev. of *Stephen Leacock: The Sage of Orillia* by James Doyle, *k. d. lang: Carrying the Torch* by William Robertson, *Alice Munro: A Double Life,* by Catherine Sheldrick Ross, and *Dorothy Livesay: Patterns in a Poetic Life* by Peter Stevens. *Biography* 17 (1994): 66-68.

Ventura, Héliane. "Country Girls and City Girls in Alice Munro's 'The Progress of Love.'" *Etudes Canadiennes* 29 (1990): 223-33.

Weaver, John. "Society and Culture in Rural and Small-Town Ontario: Alice Munro's Testimony on the Last Forty Years." *Patterns of the Past: Interpreting Ontario's History.* Eds. Roger Hall, William Westfall and Laura Sefton MacDowell. Toronto: Dundurn, 1988. 381-402.

Judith Maclean Miller (essay date autumn 1998)

SOURCE: Miller, Judith Maclean. "An Inner Bell That Rings: The Craft of Alice Munro." *Antigonish Review,* no. 115 (autumn 1998): 157-76.

[*In the following essay, Miller explores Munro's statements concerning her writing style and storytelling aesthetic, citing interviews with the author.*]

> Freeman Patterson: The rapidly changing surface makes every image significantly different from all the others, and each contains an element of chance, because I cannot press the shutter release quickly enough to capture exactly what I've seen before it changes.
>
> (*Portraits of Earth* 90)

Patterson's statement has a lively life in my own mind. Too true. I have been reading interviews with Alice Munro—and her own statements on writing. I have also been working in my garden and browsing in my dictionary. "Craft" is an ancient word in the English language, closely connected to an Old Norse word meaning "strength." So I have been thinking about the strength of Alice Munro, about her ways of working, and about gardens. Images from all of it keep flickering and connecting in my mind. I have been feeling the need for a particularly quick shutter release.

Munro taught me to understand something of how the oblique, complicated language of southern Ontario works. When the aunts suggest to Del, in *Lives of Girls and Women,* that it must be nice that her mother has time to run around the countryside selling encyclopedias, I now know that they mean something altogether other than what they seem to be saying. Like Del, I knew that this way of speaking was powerful and dangerous. I did not know much about how it worked until Munro showed me. I will always be grateful.

It has been less clear to me that Munro has influenced me in lots of other ways as well. She describes her stories as houses, with places to wander in and out and around in. I was startled to recognize that I have constructed my garden that way. Lots of entry points. No single way of moving in it. No single viewing point. Above all, it is not constructed to sit back and look at. It is an invitation to participate, to move around in—in non-linear ways. I have been surprised to learn that I also write essays that way: lots of open spaces. Lots of recurring motifs, colours, to enjoy separately, in juxtaposition to one another, or as a whole: *essai*: a *process,* I have come to understand, instead of a *practice.* Munro has also fought a battle for femininity, for a direct and personal voice which does not have to take on some fashionable accent or other. It is what it is, grounded in her experience and observation. Delightful. Freeing. And it follows the directions of her interests.

It vastly *amuses* me to discover that reading Munro stories over the years has affected the way I have approached making a garden, and in turn has given me greater appreciation than I might otherwise have had for Munro's reflections on her writing. It also greatly *pleases* me to understand that Munro has had the courage to insist on her own processes, her forms, her designs. I would not have expected one of the positionings of a reader to be outside, in the garden, with a shovel. These stories do indeed go on working beyond the space/time of the reading act which turns their pages—in whatever sequence.

Mallow. Deeply cut, dark leaves, intricate and private, have sprung up around a birdbath. Their blossom will be violet or white, where buds are settling now among the leaves. I brought them here from a dusty ditch by the roadside, just outside of Elora, where they were wilting in the heat. Here they grow rich and plump. Malvaceous.

For a while, I puzzled about issues of readership in relation to these interviews with Munro. Author-Text-Reader? Who is author? Munro? The interviewer? The transcriber who listened painstakingly to a taped interview, trying to catch "the grain of the voice," and to reproduce it faithfully? Probably editing some as she went? What is the text? Transcribed orality: with all the rhythms of the spoken language, as opposed to the inscribed. Certainly, it is text: texture: weaving: of many strands, all put together for a reading pleasure. What is that pleasure? How am I positioned as reader? Eavesdropper? Privileged? Ignored? Addressed in some indirect way? Some other time I will think more about all that. This time, I wanted to know what Munro had to say about writing.

I have focused on three conversations—with Hancock, Rasporich, and Metcalf—with occasional digressions into other Munro statements about writing. For another time, there are lots of other conversations to consider. I was also—briefly—intrigued by the ways in which the speech of the questioner is always neat and tidy on the page: clear, direct, coherent. Munro's answers are full of open spaces: sets of dots to mark ellipses (of what? words left out? her breathing? her thinking?), occasional "um" as she pauses to choose a word, repetitions of words or corrections of them. The presentation on the page suggests a power relationship. The interviewer always speaks first, in clear ordered prose—and then Munro does her best to answer, reaching for words to express the deep processes of her writing. Somehow, through it all, Munro prevails.

With a gift certificate, I recently treated myself to Freeman Patterson's *Portraits of Earth.* For some time, there did not seem to be any connections between my browsing in Munro interviews, working in my garden, reading in the dictionary, and looking into Patterson's book. I was simply enjoying the images and patterns from each, until a central irritation became a place around which they all began to gather. That centre presented itself in the following exchange between Alice Munro and Geoff Hancock. The passage kept repeating in my mind, over and over, until I finally turned to look straight at it.

Hancock: So, you don't feel completely secure in your style. You are still working towards that.

Munro: No. That's not it. I don't want to work towards a style. I want to go with the story the way it has to be. I do feel a kind of inner bell that rings when something is okay. I'm never sure it's as it should be but I have a certain amount of confidence. It has never occurred to me to work towards a style. I don't think I have a style.

I don't recognize a style. I would probably call it something else. I would call it a way of telling a story. Or
something like that. There I like to be fairly flexible.

(Hancock, 1982 108)

Hancock's statement at first startled, even annoyed me.
It seemed a condescending thing to say to a writer who
had won two Governor General's awards for fiction and
who had published several impressive and successful
books. How dare he, I thought. But then I noticed that
his comment had brought a quick and direct answer
from Munro—and that both his implied question and
her answer have lingered with me. As an "interviewing
question," it worked well. I also acknowledge that he
was voicing what a good many people thought then—
and often still think. As Munro herself says, in the same
interview, people are always asking her about the next
book, and they all want to hear that the next one is a
novel. Many of her readers assume she is working toward somewhere. Why, I wondered. And I began to
think that it has something to do with what she says
about her ways of working with a story. She herself
says that she is often not sure that the story is done.
And it often is not finished. She takes it a certain distance and then it goes on developing in the mind of the
reader. What she does is uncannily effective. Is it style?
Maybe. In the very widest sense of that word. It is not,
as she suspected Hancock to mean, formula. She insists
on working from the inside of the story, following where
it leads. Instead of imposing a style or pattern onto material, she works at finding "A way of telling a story."
Process instead of practice.

What Munro has to say about her ways of telling a
story is endlessly interesting to me. I notice as I read
interviews with her, that I tend to skip over the bits
about her attitudes to men and women, whether or not
she is a feminist. Those passages are often marked in
the library books or journals I have been reading. I just
do not seem to care as much about those topics. I am
intrigued that she has told us over and over again how
she works, but we seem not to believe her—or at least
not to understand what she means. So we keep asking
her.

> Munro: What I want to get changes with different sto-
> ries. It's got to be dictated by the material itself. And
> sometimes I want to get something that is very grainy
> and I don't want any artifice at all. I don't want the
> choice of words to seem anywhere elegant. I want awk-
> wardness. I want to get a kind of plainness. And then I
> would be doing another story with different material
> and I want it to be, I feel that it should be, well, lush
> isn't the word I mean. But there should be a kind of
> luxuriance. The feeling of the story should be of lots
> and lots of words and resonance. Things level upon
> level. And this means the writing has to change com-
> pletely.

(Hancock 107)

As I read this conversation, I realize that my pleasure in
this text is not passive or dispassionately analytic but a
delight in a deep recognition which goes all the way
into muscles and joints and bones which still ache from
last summer's clearing away of underbrush and dead
wood, to make a garden. Is this part of what reading/
writing with the body means? Style, she is telling me,
is not a fixed and static thing. Style grows out of the
task. Intellectual awareness, analysis, which I confess I
delight in, is not all there is. Writing, reading, garden-
ing are processes which discover their own logic, their
own positioning, their own aesthetic, in response to
what is called for: grainy or elegant; plain or lush.

> Munro: Well, I read a bit in your interview with John
> (Metcalf). He knew why he was using words. He did. I
> was terribly impressed. That's like knowing carpentry
> or something. And I am really impressed by skills. Yes.
> And I thought, if I had written that, I wouldn't be able
> to explain why I used any of those words. I would
> have laboured over them. It wouldn't have come out in
> any divine flood of inspiration.

(Hancock 87)

The labour, for Munro, is not to theorize about why she
chooses specific words, but as she says, to find the right
resonance, the sound, the fit. Perhaps it is difficult for
academics to accept an explanation like that. We have
such an ingrained habit of watching with one hand
whatever it is that the other hand (or brain) is doing.
There is nothing naïve about the labour Munro is describing. Much of it is based in waiting—and in trust. It
is sophisticated, difficult, disciplined work.

Munro tells Hancock about overhearing a conversation
in China where one of the Canadian men explained to
their hosts that in Canada we have "serious writers and
popular writers. Alice is a popular writer" (Hancock
86). She was upset by that comment because she considers herself a serious writer. Is a person to be considered a serious writer only if no one wants to read his
books—or if he is theoretical and analytical about his
work? Munro is suspicious about such analysis: "I do
spend a lot of my time engaged at whatever this process is. If I'm called upon to back off and describe it,
not only do I do it badly but it doesn't help the process
at all" (Hancock 76).

Yes. I could never have described to anyone what I was
doing in the yard last year. I was making my way toward garden. I laboured over the placing of plants—
there was no flood of inspiration, but there was a trust
that it would all work out. If I placed plants respectfully
and carefully, they would be in the right place: after I
had moved them several times—and as I continue to
move them. Munro says she constantly edits and
changes a story—even after the story is published. During a reading, she says, she will change what is on the
page, because now she knows how "to do it better."

Munro tells Beverly Rasporich:

> But, you know I don't get into theoretical arguments because most of them seem ridiculous.
>
> [Rasporich:] Why?
>
> [Munro:] Because most arguments that pretend to be about, you know, intellectual topics, seem actually sort of simple ego struggles, simple one-up-manship. And I suppose I know that I'm not good at that, but I also don't see any need to do it. And I think many women are reacting this way so that in a way we castigate ourselves for not being assertive enough but we may just be unwilling to waste the time.
>
> (Rasporich 16)

Refusing to waste time in this sort of debate/discussion does not mean inferiority. Even if some male academics want to dismiss Munro as "a housewife writer" (Rasporich 3). As Rasporich asserts, ". . . she is neither the naïve intellectual nor casual artist she sometimes pretends to be. She is an extremely sophisticated, literate and literary woman, an obsessively dedicated writer who has served a long apprenticeship, writing continuously since she was fourteen years old, a woman with an exacting mind when it comes to a discussion of her work and the literary process, and however careful she is of others' feelings, quietly does not suffer either imprecise thinkers or pretentious people gladly" (Rasporich 3).

I know what Rasporich means, but I really do not think, having looked at many interviews, that Munro ever pretends to be a "naïve intellectual" or a "casual artist." That is a persona which has been constructed for her in some circles and she takes a wicked kind of glee in participating in it, parodying it, mimicking it. But only so far. She always defends the work and its way of happening. She never compromises the integrity of her artistry. Rasporich is absolutely right about the sophistication: a sophistication which insists on process rather than practice, a process which is never static, which constantly renews itself, which keeps Munro alive and growing as a writer and makes her difficult to label or pin into a place on a board, described as a particular kind of writer, with a certain style. Something about it all makes me want to laugh. Munro constantly repositions her reader, within a story and certainly from story to story, from book to book. I did not expect to be repositioned all the way out to the garden and a lot of hard work—but I am glad it happened.

As I read these interviews, parallel texts happen in my mind: passages from the fiction, a subtext of Freeman Patterson's comments and a surprising, unexpected, intertext of my own garden, with, I suspect, a kind of ghost-text of my reading in "high theory."

"Her solution to the problem of artist-as-female was quite naturally and bravely to become the female-as-artist, and as an interpreter and puzzling critic of the roles of women and codes of sexual conduct she knew and witnessed, a quiet revolutionary" (Rasporich 11). Rasporich appreciates Munro's celebration of "the feminine." Yes. Many women have striven for Virginia Woolf's ideal of the "incandescent mind," the mind free of all emotion, distraction and connection with the trials/insights of femininity or womanliness, of daily life. Woolf's advocacy of androgyny became, in some instances, a kind of castration, which insisted on an objectivity or distancing that was almost impossible to maintain. And which we have learned to distrust. Indeed, Woolf herself could not sustain it. Munro has been a vital part of our learning to accept our humanity, to work from where we find ourselves, as careful craftspeople who engage in the whole process from the inside out.

> Twigg: You're suspicious of spontaneity?
>
> Munro: I suppose so. I'm not afraid spontaneity would betray me because I've done some fairly self-exposing things. But I'm afraid it would be repetitious and boring if I wrote that way. It's as if I must take great care over everything. Instead of splashing the colours out and trusting they will all come together, I have to know the design.
>
> (Twigg 16)

Sigh. My friend is a wonderful gardener. She can grow all kinds of things. But she splashes the colour all around with no semblance of design. Some days, it hurts me to look at it. I am not anything like as good a gardener. Things don't grow or don't bloom as I expect them to, or as hers do, but I *make* my garden. I design it. I want a certain kind of atmosphere, a certain kind of space, and I do my best to create it. Over and over again. I move things around, I add new things. I give away plants. It is never done. I never get it right. But I keep working at it. Within an overall design or feeling that I want. Which has nothing to do with graph paper and planning it all out ahead of time on a piece of paper. Which a garden magazine recommends—and which idea horrifies me. I walk in it, I sit in it, I stare at it, and I keep working at it.

> Munro: So when I write a story I want to make a certain kind of structure, and I know the feeling I want to get from being inside that structure. This is the hard part of the explanation, where I have to use a word like "feeling," which is not very precise, because if I attempt to be more intellectually respectable I will have to be dishonest. "Feeling" will have to do.
>
> There is no blueprint for the structure. It's not a question of, "I'll make this kind of house because if I do it right it will have this effect." I've got to make, I've got to build up, a house, a story, to fit around the indescribable "feeling" that is like the soul of the story, and which I must insist upon in a dogged, embarrassed way, as being no more definable than that. And I don't know where it comes from. It seems to be already there and some unlikely clue, such as a shop window or a bit

of conversation, makes me aware of it. Then I start accumulating the material and putting it together. Some of the material I may have lying around already, in memories and observations, and some I invent, and some I have to go diligently looking for (factual details), while some is dumped in my lap (anecdotes, bits of speech). I see how this material might go together to make the shape I need, and I try it. I keep trying and seeing where I went wrong and trying again.

(Munro, "What Is Real?" 224)

I understand that process. I know what she is describing. It has nothing to do with style or theory and everything to do with the look and feel of the structure emerging, as it is faithful to that sense of the "soul" of the undertaking. Sometimes, a glimpse of it comes clear and then it can be worked toward. At least for a while. But then it may rain—and the whole process has to start all over again. Or the slugs may get it. Or it may collapse from lack of sun or from its own weight. But there are times when it works. Wonderfully.

> Munro: I don't mean that I don't learn form and style. I just don't know how to talk about it. I probably absorb it. I learn all the time from just about everybody I choose to read now. Because a lot of things I don't read any more. You know, I used to read everything I thought I was supposed to read. I think a writer is probably learning from everything they read from the age of fifteen on.
>
> (Hancock 92)

Munro ends her article, "What is Real," with a clear statement: "No, I am not concerned with using what is real to make any sort of record or prove any sort of point, and I am not concerned with any methods of selection but my own, which I can't fully explain. This is quite presumptuous, and if writers are not allowed to be so—and quite often, in many places, they are not—I see no point in the writing of fiction" (Munro 226). Testy. And true. And brave. Good for her, I think. And, I also think, one of the reasons it is so hard to explain is that we are used to "explanatory" language which takes a point of observation outside a finished product, rather than inside a process—"and we don't really try to explain because it is too difficult" (Munro 223). Fiction, I remind myself occasionally, comes from a Latin word meaning "to arrange." Which is exactly what Munro says she does: she observes, she selects, she arranges, she creates, and then she arranges again. Does that mean that my garden is a fiction? It may well be. In more ways than one.

> Munro: Other stories are just completely a feeling, as I've said. I want the characters and what happens subordinated to a climate.
>
> Hancock: How do you create that climate?
>
> Munro: That's what the whole story is trying to do. You don't do it by passages of descriptive writing or anything like that. It's the writer's angle of vision that will do it.
>
> (Hancock 82)

> Patterson: Depending on our mobility and our range of lenses, anything is possible.
>
> (91)

And Munro well knows that an angle of vision may be odd, peculiar, sometimes even dangerous:

> . . . the other problem I feel that is related to the woman's life as a woman and her life as an artist is that writing is dangerous to the psyche. It's unbalanced. It's like a trip you take alone, all serious writing is like this. Now this is something we are accustomed to thinking of the male artist as doing. It may not be very nice for his wife and kids but it is important that he do it. And we have a picture of woman which is very strong in our minds as being the person who doesn't go on journeys, the person who is there looking after the material wants but also providing a kind of unquestioning cushion.
>
> (Rasporich 21)

> Patterson: My most familiar waterscape is my bathtub. When it is filled to the usual level, my knees protrude through the water surface like two large triangular rocks, and an old brown bathsponge drifts like a mass of floating seaweed, while I observe everything from a position halfway up the island of my head. From here I gaze across a seemingly enormous expanse of water, watching as the visible dynamic of its surface changes with my activity, from placid to gently rippled, rough and textured or turbulent. Waves move in whatever direction I choose, whipping up foam that swirls around the islands to faraway coasts. Reflections vary with the calmness of the surface, the amount of light streaming through the window, and the nearby arrangement of bath towels, which occasionally appear as the warm rays of a sunrise or sunset on a glassy sea.
>
> (Patterson 91)

Patterson goes on to say that when he leaves his bath tub, he goes into the light and shadow of the St. John River close to his home, his second most familiar waterscape, or he wanders the world, finding such scapes in many widely differing settings. But they all come back, in some way, to that time in the bathtub. He works from the inside out, widening into an ever expanding world. He takes the physical voyages and also the other ones which Munro refers to. And he knows about creating "climate:"

> If we use the lens we already have on the camera and move a little closer to important foreground objects, perhaps some flowers, we can enlarge them enormously without noticeably increasing the size of the background—perhaps some hills—thus changing their relative size in the picture space and increasing the impression of distance between them.
>
> (Patterson 46)

A photographer discussing his craft. He makes decisions about composition, about what is given significance. And he often does that by concentrating on the foreground, understanding what he is doing, how it works. And each picture is different. He learns methods, but he then uses them. He does not simply repeat them. He approaches each photograph as a new project. Why is it so hard to believe that of Munro? Why would we assume that she is "working toward a style?"

Patterson describes his way of staring at a scene until he begins to "see" it, by which he means moving beyond a careless viewing, beginning to feel his way into the various elements which make up a situation which has caught his interest. What is there—and how can it best be shown? Not to duplicate it, but to demonstrate what is intrinsic to it, what is interesting. "Important foreground objects—" the things we fail to see as we contemplate the faraway hills. Patterson, like Munro, brings the focus in sharply to the foreground. And the paradox, of course, is that by doing so, they widen the sense of distance, they open up vistas to move in which we never imagined.

> Hancock: Do you try to make a scene like a photographer might?
>
> Munro: Well, I see the scene. I see it awfully clearly. And I want the reader to see it the way I see it. There's a story in the new book called **"Visitors,"** where there's an important scene for me. It's at the beginning of the story. It's where two women are sitting out in the shade of a driveway on little camp chairs, crocheting tablecloths on a hot summer afternoon. The story is around that scene and I want that scene there so strongly. But I don't do much with it. I just say that they were sitting out crocheting tablecloths. That's all. So, I don't know how a reader's going to see that. Maybe I've buried it. I would feel it was wrong for that story to tell any more detail about that scene. It's got to be just like that.
>
> (Hancock 107-108)

That angle of vision shifts with each story. Which is, of course, part of the reason why the "style" has to shift or change with each piece. These stories are not, as Munro has told us, about reconstructing reality. They are about conveying that angle which gives us vision, truth, insight, but not necessarily reality as we think we know it. No wonder Munro gets testy or irritated. It's hard to be asked over and over again to explain what she's doing. Why can't we get it? Why can't we see it? Or is it more that we just thoroughly enjoy hearing her talk? That we like to listen to her reach for the explanation of what she does and how she does it? Perhaps we simply enjoy hearing a writer talk about her craft.

I have always liked the description of the Photographer which Del was working out in *Lives of Girls and Women* to include in the novel she was writing about Jubilee. It has always seemed to me exactly a description of the artist and of the ways an artist looks at the world—or at least the way Del looks at the world, and I

confess, the way I think Munro does. Probably because this book seems to me not so much *bildungsroman* as *kunstlerroman,* the novel about the development of the artist-as-a-young-woman:

> One day a man came to take photographs at the high school. She saw him first shrouded in his photographer's black cloth, a hump of gray-black, shabby cloth behind the tripod, the big eye, the black accordion pleating of the old-fashioned camera. When he came out, what did he look like? Black hair parted in the middle, combed back in two wings, dandruff, rather narrow chest and shoulders, and a pasty, flaky skin— and in spite of his look of scruffiness and ill health, a wicked fluid energy about him, a bright unpitying smile.
>
> (*LGW* [*Lives of Girls and Women*] 205)

Munro knows what she is talking about when she describes the dangers of the artist's journey. She has decided not to be eccentric, not to drive around the countryside in "a high square car whose top was of flapping black cloth" (*LGW* 205), probably because, as she says, the price would be too high.

> Metcalf: Does it frighten you that many successful women writers have led very a-typical lives?
>
> Munro: Yes. It does frighten me because I'm a fairly security-demanding person. I don't think I'm in any danger of ever leading a bizarre life. I tend to be a person of rather dull habits just because I want to work so much. I don't endanger this by having an exciting life.
>
> (Metcalf 59)

We might understand her ways of working better, though. Sometimes I think part of the trouble people have reading Munro's work is that she seems so *normal.* She does not prepare observers for the kind of angle of vision which might seem more appropriate to this eccentric photographer. People were afraid of him and they did not like his work. But they went to him because he was inexpensive. And then wondered what to do with a photograph where someone's eyes were white. And then Del/Munro's wry voice: "I had not worked out all the implications of this myself, but felt they were varied and powerful" (205). As, indeed, they are.

> Metcalf: How far is your work autobiographical?
>
> Munro: Oh. Well. I guess I have a standard answer to this . . . in incident—no . . . in emotion—completely. In incident up to a point too but of course, in *Lives of Girls and Women* which is a . . . I suppose it could be called an autobiographical novel . . . most of the incidents are changed versions of real incidents. *Some* are completely invented but the emotional reality, the girl's feeling for her mother, for men, for life is all . . . it's all solidly autobiographical. I would not disclaim this at all.
>
> (Metcalf 58)

Munro is right to be suspicious about "style." Mavis Gallant decides it is the part of writing which writers themselves know least about. The word contains its own warnings within itself: it developed out of the Greek word for column or pedestal. And then it got tangled around the Latin word *stylus,* for a kind of pen, so that it came to be linked to what writers do. No one is more suspicious of pedestals than Munro. She knows how they sap the energy which needs to go into the work itself.

Themes and images repeat in my garden because they need to, because there is a space where something needs to be put. And the something suggests itself. It is not put there for reasons of some style or other, but because it balances something else—or it repeats something which needs repeating. Or I want it there. I have worked hard to make this garden a place to enter into, from any number of entry points, to move about in, in different directions, with wild places, where a hop toad lives and maybe other things. Sometimes people construct gardens to look at from a particular—single—vantage point. In this garden even the robin takes up the invitation to follow the stepping stones. Sometimes in one direction, sometimes in another. Pausing here and there to absorb climate or atmosphere or to pick up a worm. The dog and cat know how to do it too. The cat sits and smiles on a stepping stone, soaking up sun. The dog follows my latest way of walking the stones. None of them would ever expect to encounter the garden the same way twice. Even the stones themselves are moveable.

Reading in the ways Munro invites us to do is not easy to learn. Linearity has served us well for a long time. Munro, of course, is part of the postmodernist, post-structuralist way—which does not work toward a "well-wrought urn," finished and polished, to be admired from a distance. Her stories require moving around in, absorbing, constructing. Reader becomes subject rather than indirect object. It is still probably the case that most people read Munro's stories from the beginning, through the middle, to the end. It is pleasing to stand back to see the whole design. But it is even more gratifying to linger, to read back and forth, to let the stories poem.

> Munro: All pictures. The reasons for things happening I seemed vaguely to know, but could not explain; I expected all that would come clear later. The main thing was that it seemed true to me, not real but true, as if I had discovered, not made up such people and such a story, as if that town was lying close behind the one I walked through every day.
>
> (*LGW* 206)
>
> Hancock: You like the story to have several layers of meaning and intent.
>
> Munro: What I like is not to really know what the story is all about. And for me to keep trying to find out.

> Hancock: What makes a story interesting for you?
>
> Munro: The thing that I don't know and that I will discover as I go along.
>
> (Hancock 84)

Yes. I understand. I did not know that geranium (cranesbill—the real geranium) has purplish blue flowers and that it would add serenity to a place of shadow and texture. I did not know that a firm line around the garden, where it meets the lawn, would allow for more chaos within it. I still don't know what witchhazel will do in a garden. At one time, I might have thought that the associations with witchhazel were "varied and powerful," but now I will watch to see how it grows and how much water it needs.

> Hancock: Are there on-going mythic undertones in any of your stories?
>
> Munro: Not that I am aware of. No. It is what I keep returning to. That I don't get time to think about these things because I am always involved in this immediate task. It is almost as if I always write from that small place out. I never write from an idea, a myth or a pattern. Or any of the big perceptions.
>
> (Hancock 113)

Patterson in his bathtub. Probably I do not think much about Eden while I pick slugs off the hostas. Which, I suppose, is not to say that it is not there somewhere, lurking in the background. Munro does say, "the sight of the two women crocheting tablecloths can get me all excited—as if it is tied into something far bigger than itself" (Hancock 114), but she moves immediately, she says, into writing the story, into working with that "fluid energy," rather than distancing herself to think about its implications—which would kill the story.

Helene Cixous on myth and women:

So for the sons of the Book: research, the desert, inexhaustible space, encouraging, discouraging, the march straight ahead. For the daughters of the housewife: the straying into the forest. [Is that why I have left wild spaces in the garden?] Deceived, disappointed, but brimming with curiosity. Instead of the great enigmatic duel with the Sphinx, the dangerous questioning addressed to the body of the Wolf: What is the body for? Myths end up having our hides. Logos opens its great maw, and swallows us whole. (*Coming to Writing* 14-15)

Practice versus process. Talking with the wolf, dangerous as it might be, is at least conversation with a live animal. The winding paths of the forest are more complex than the straight ahead march on the desert. But I do not want to give up the Sphinx, either. Why should she be left to the "sons of the Book?"

> Astilbe. Perhaps the astilbe is my greatest love-among-loves in this garden. Maybe because I discovered one in a back corner of a nursery and brought it here to try,

to see if it could grow in this shadow, in this clay soil. In June, its feathery blooms rise through the garden like candles: mauve, pink, white, burgundy. But I would not care if it never bloomed. The stateliness of its branching would be enough. As would its name, from Greek words meaning "not glittering." Which reminds me that much of my pleasure in this garden comes from its not-glittering, its green and quiet presence, full of windsong, birdsong, and healing.

Close to the beginning of his conversation with Munro, Geoff Hancock says:

> I see you as much a poet as a short story writer.
>
> Munro: I like you saying that but I've written very little poetry. I began to write poetry when I was about— oh—twelve, I guess, and I wrote it all through my teens. And then during my first pregnancy I wrote a lot of poems which I sent off under an assumed name and they weren't very good. They were all sent back. That is the only time in my adult life that I've at all wanted to write poetry. What is the difference that makes you see me as a poet rather than a story writer?
>
> Hancock: I see you as a lyricist, as a songwriter. You give voice to our secret selves.
>
> Munro: That's absolutely what I think a short story can do.
>
> (Hancock 76)

They then leave the topic there, but I would agree with Hancock that it is easy to see Munro as a poet. Not only for the reasons they set out between them, but also because of the way the stories work, through juxtaposition, image, the rhythm of language, space, layers, the suggestive: all poetic uses of language. Munro talks about the whole process in the way a poet does—which may be one of the reasons why we find it hard to assimilate the things she tells us about her ways in to stories. They are like a poet's way. That deep entry into reverie, waiting *with* an idea, an image, until it begins to find its form seems to me a way closely associated with poetry. But then, it may be that, at base, the creative process is poetic, is "making:" why do we talk about a "poetics" of almost anything? Munro and Metcalf had an interesting exchange about language. I appreciated his way of offering her actual passages of her writing to talk about.

> Metcalf: There's a passage which struck me *very* forcibly when I was reading it in ***Lives of Girls and Women*** which describes one of the Aunts sitting on her verandah in a rocking chair. And if I could just read a very brief passage from that and explain to you the kind of thing that I mean . . .
>
> *She sat on the verandah in the wicker rocker, wearing, in spite of the hot weather, some stately, layered dress, dark and trembling with beads, a large hat like a turban, earth-coloured stockings which she would sometimes roll down, to let the bandages "breathe."*

Now, when I first read that, the word that leapt out at me was *earth-coloured*. The immediate thing is its accuracy of observation, of colour. But it seems to me that the word *earth-coloured* operates simultaneously on three or four levels. Well let me be very pedantic and boring and laborious about it but *earth-coloured* starting off primarily from the observation and then moving into the sort of earth mother idea almost . . . And earth in the sense of 'peasant like' and 'oppressed' and always when I read your writing I find it operates on me in very much the same way that poetry does . . . That there are levels of meaning and compression that are suddenly packed into something, yet, it all seems to flow very naturally from something acutely observed in the first place. Now what's *your* attitude to craft in your own writing?

Munro: Well, let's think about why . . . why one uses that word. If you think of the stockings they could be *clay* coloured, they could be *mud* coloured . . . um . . . when I choose a word . . . uh . . . I wouldn't, for instance think of the connotations of . . . peasant or earth mother or dirt or anything like that. But the quality of the word *earth* to me has a . . . I'm not able to say very well . . . It's something even about the vowels and the *r* sound that reaches something that I mean to say about this person . . . but that sounds ridiculous. That doesn't make any sense. It's the *sound, the sound* itself . . . And mud wouldn't do it. . . .

(Metcalf 55-56)

A brave articulation on Alice's part. And, of course, it does make sense. What she is describing is a poet's way of choosing words. Metcalf is right too, that the word as placed, in the end, has all those kinds of resonances for a reader. But for Munro, the sound, as it relates to the character is the primary concern. I suspect it also builds on the rhythm and sound of the rest of the passage. The phrase which stood out for me this time of reading was *trembling with beads*. It has the *r* sound, a bit lighter, which deepens almost into a grunt in *earth*— the kind of sound this woman would make as she stands up. The trembling with beads shows me a woman reaching for fashion, a slightly out-of-date fashion—like the black jet beads Victorian matrons wore—an attempt at a sort of grandeur, and it shows me a woman unsure of herself—the beads tremble with her breath—in a way, they betray her. "Style" encloses her—in stockings she has to roll down so that the bandages under them can "breathe—" in beads which give her away and in a too heavy layered dress: more weight for her to carry. Patterson's bare knees. He is not caught in this self-immolation caused by style. He—and Munro—are preoccupied with things beyond themselves, beyond style. There is no place in their world for trembling with beads or sweltering in too many clothes, worrying about fashion or style.

I like Metcalf's point about the "compression" of this writing, that it has the effects of poem. A person can linger a long time over a paragraph like this in Munro—which becomes like a stanza in a poem. It is part of the effect she says she wants when she invites a reader to enter these stories anywhere and linger in the "rooms" she has created. That cannot happen in a story which is driving itself forward, in one direction, along a plot line. Munro and Metcalf went on to talk further about words:

> Metcalf: Would you regard the way that I respond to that word as being ridiculous?
>
> Munro: No. No. You just analyse a bit further than I do. I know that it has to be that word for some reason that I don't go into. I'm just satisfied when I know the word is right.
>
> Metcalf: But when you are writing you have this extremely conscious care and choice about finding the exact word for an exact place within the rhythm?
>
> Munro: Yes. And it isn't so much exactness in the *meaning* sense. It's an *emotional* exactness . . . an exactness of resonance.
>
> Metcalf: It's *deliberate* but it's not *conscious*. Could we put it that way?
>
> Munro: Yes, I think so. Sometimes the word comes right away . . . the right word . . . you might say it's not deliberate. But in other cases the word has to be sought for . . . But not sought for in a dictionary or a thesaurus or anything like *that* or not sought for because of its official meaning.
>
> (Metcalf 56)

Such a hard thing to talk about. I admire both of them for trying. Curious that we have so little language to talk about these processes. Probably because most writers feel that too much talk about them scares them away, that words in the right place are a kind of gift to be accepted and treasured. Too much analysis of it seems disrespectful, somehow, like looking the proverbial gift horse in the mouth. There is a great deal of courage involved in waiting for or looking for, as Munro says, the right word: so that the small bell rings inside her and she knows that the word is right. It takes courage and discipline to hear that bell, to learn to trust it. It also requires the kind of stillness which Munro insists is essential to her.

> Metcalf: There was a very interesting passage which was quoted by various reviewers of **Lives of Girls and Women** . . . some of them admiringly, some of them pityingly . . . in the epilogue . . . where the heroine of the book talks about her desire to write down and capture the reality of Jubilee . . .
>
> *And no list could hold what I wanted, for what I wanted was every last thing, every layer of speech and thought, stroke of light on bark or walls, every smell, pothole, pain, crack, delusion, held still and held together— radiant, everlasting.*
>
> It seems that in all your writing you *glory* in the surfaces and textures. I don't know how to put this question to you without sounding philosophical or pompous but do you feel 'surfaces' not to *be* surfaces?

> Munro: Yes. Yes. I know exactly what you mean. I feel that everything . . . Yes. I don't know how to answer your question without sounding pompous or . . . pseudo-mystical . . . It's very easy to sound this way when you're trying to explain what you feel about the way things look and the tones in people's voices . . . and . . . it's probably . . . there's this kind of magic . . . you know . . . about everything.
>
> (Metcalf 56)

Yes. About Patterson's knees in the bathtub. About the light on my garden at 4:30 in the afternoon. About the bell inside that rings when the work is right. About the density of the words Munro discovers and places. About the wide spaces around and under the surfaces of our attempts to talk about these things. About the trickery of surfaces.

> Patterson: Water has a *graphic* dynamic as well. Its capacity for reflecting and blocking light is such an important characteristic that we can think of water surfaces as being constantly painted and repainted by light.
>
> (90)

Metcalf went on to ask Munro whether it is possible to gain the texture of a place as an adult—that texture which a writer has to have—or at least which Munro confirms that she has to have. Munro replies that she has not been able to, and that worries her some because in this time, a person should be able to write about anywhere—but she cannot—and so perhaps that makes her anachronistic . . . "but so what?" Sometimes, I think that is why I am making a garden: to learn the smells and textures of this earth, of this place where I did not grow up. And which Munro helps me to learn.

> Petunia. "One lonely little petunia in an onion patch:" song from when I was little. So that I find it hard to take this small flower seriously. Also the name of a solemn, droop-eared Bassett hound I knew in Montreal. But when there are no petunias in a summer, I miss them. This year, there is a gentle one, with a blush of yellow. It pleases me that its name comes from petyn, a South American Guarani word for tobacco, where the yn is pronounced in the way of the French "un."

> Munro: I wrote an essay several years ago for my friend John Metcalf, in which I said something that got a surprised reaction from readers—and their surprise surprised me. I said that I don't always, or even usually, read stories from beginning to end. I start anywhere and proceed in either direction. So it appears that I'm not reading—at least in an efficient way—to find out what happens. I do find out, and I'm interested in finding out, but there's much more to the experience. A story is not like a road to follow, I said, it's more like a house. You go inside and stay there for a while, wandering back and forth and settling where you like and discovering how the room and corridors relate to each other, how the world outside is altered by being viewed from these windows. And you, the visitor, the reader, are altered as well by being in this enclosed space, whether it is ample and easy or full of crooked turns,

or sparsely or opulently furnished. You can go back again and again, and the house, the story, always contains more than you saw the last time. It also has a sturdy sense of itself, of being built of its own necessity, not just to shelter or beguile you. To deliver a story like that, durable and freestanding, is what I'm always hoping for.

(*Selected Stories* xvii)

Style betrays. Pattern or blueprint proves inadequate. Surfaces are deceiving. Practice may not include enough dimensions. Process trusts winding paths—in houses, gardens, forests, stories. Fashion followed, "trembling with beads," has nothing to do with Munro or her stories. Munro has a stance to the world, an approach to writing, a way of seeing the graphics on surfaces and looking deep within them. And she shows us not a pre-chosen, fixed, un-changing way of writing or seeing, but a deep integrity which insists on finding its way into whatever is interesting, especially what is not well understood, or talked about, to find the angle of vision from which it can be experienced, and then to find the way to construct that: "a way of telling a story," "with a sturdy sense of itself." A task always changing, always shifting, always demanding different f-stops or lenses, waiting for the right light, listening for the right word. Daring the difficult journey, the trip taken alone.

Works Cited

Cixous, Helene. *"Coming to Writing" and Other Essays*. Cambridge, Massachusetts: Harvard University Press. 1991.

Hancock, Geoff. "An Interview with Alice Munro," *Canadian Fiction Magazine*. 43 (1982): 74-114.

Metcalf, John. "A Conversation with Alice Munro," *Journal of Canadian Fiction*. 1.4 (1972): 54-62.

Munro, Alice. *Lives of Girls and Women*. Toronto: Penguin, 1990. First published Toronto: McGraw-Hill-Ryerson, 1971.

———. "What Is Real?" *Making It New: Contemporary Canadian Stories*. Ed. John Metcalf. Toronto: Methuen, 1982. 223-26.

———. "Introduction," *Selected Stories*. Toronto: Penguin, 1998. First published as a Douglas Gibson Book by McClelland and Stewart, 1996.

Patterson, Freeman. *Portraits of Earth*. Toronto: Key Porter Books, 1997 (First published 1987).

Rasporich, Beverly. "Alice: the Woman behind the Art," *Dance of the Sexes: Art and Gender in the Fiction of Alice Munro*. Edmonton: University of Alberta Press, 1990. 1-31.

Twigg, Alan. "What Is," *For Openers: Conversations with 24 Canadian Writers*. Madeira Park, B.C.: Harbour Publishing, 1981. 13-20.

Brian Johnson (essay date autumn 1998)

SOURCE: Johnson, Brian. "Private Scandals/Public Selves: The Education of a Gossip in *Who Do You Think You Are?*." *Dalhousie Review* 78, no. 3 (autumn 1998): 415-35.

[*In the following essay, Johnson characterizes* Who Do You Think You Are? *as a "reflection on the ethics of gossip and the ambiguous virtues of privacy," terming Munro's collection a* Klatchmaulroman—*a work depicting the education of a gossip.*]

> In the prohibited transgression of the boundary into the sphere that the subject of gossip would claim as "private" . . . lies a constitutive element and at the same time essential stimulus to gossip.[2]
>
> If all truths became public, we would approach utopia.[3]

The longstanding conflict between gossip and privacy has recently entered a new and surprising phase.[1] After centuries of moral censure, gossip's reputation is on the upswing, while privacy has come increasingly to be regarded with suspicion and even hostility. The impetus behind this strange reversal of fortunes dates to the 1960s when anthropologists like Max Gluckman first proposed that "gossip, and even scandal, have important positive virtues."[4] In contrast to traditional condemnations which focused on gossip's violation of privacy and dissemination of secret information, Gluckman and his school[5] focused on its social function, arguing that gossip is a mechanism that maintains community norms and values by identifying transgressions, and that mediates communal discord by providing an outlet for the harmless discharge of conflict and hostility. Echoes of Gluckman's influential formulation are still audible in contemporary vindications of idle talk,[6] but what makes Gluckman's defence of gossip such a significant turning-point in the contest between gossip and privacy is the degree to which it succeeds in disengaging the analysis of gossip from questions relating to the privacy of those it violates. Even Robert Paine, Gluckman's principal sparring partner in the 1960s, was silent on the issue of privacy—despite its bearing on his theory that gossip is not a communal mechanism but "a cultural device used by the individual to forward his own interests" through the acquisition and management of information.[7]

The tendency of social scientists to celebrate gossip's power to reinforce communal values or to enhance individual status, while demurring on the question of its effects on individual privacy, received a radical twist by feminist critics[8] who began to deconstruct the stereotype of the female gossip in the 1980s. By exposing the patriarchal assumptions which support traditional attacks on "scandalmongering" and "idle talk," feminist reappraisals of gossip typically sought to revalue women's discourse and to reclaim gossip as a positive term, without acquiescing to the sexist claim that gossip is an exclusively female activity. As Patricia Meyer Spacks argues, "The ferocity of several centuries' attack on derogatory conversation about others probably reflects the justifiable anxiety of the dominant about the aggressive impulses of the submissive."[9] In light of such a critique, traditional appeals to the sanctity of privacy lose their moral heft and begin to sound suspiciously hollow. Conversely, gossip seems to promise not only a valuable means of consolidating a feminist community but, in its characteristic mode of undercutting authority by making public what those in power would prefer to conceal, may even provide a politically liberating practice.[10]

The growing mistrust of certain forms of privacy apparent in feminist discourses of gossip has recently been generalized in a provocative way by Ronald de Sousa. De Sousa agrees with Gluckman that gossip can promote community values by symbolically punishing those who violate them; but like the feminist critics, he "prize[s] the subversive element in gossip" and rejects the notion that community values are themselves intrinsically valuable. "Community," he warns, "is a Janus face: though one side wears the smile of social harmony, on the other lurks the scowl of fascism."[11] Arguing that "a world in which all information were universally available would be preferable to a world where immense power resides in the control of secrets," de Sousa celebrates gossip's "assault on the notion of a private sphere of life" as the triumph of the Kantian categorical imperative.[12]

Against this proliferation of defences of gossip, I wish to place Alice Munro's novelistic collection of interlinked short stories, *Who Do You Think You Are?*—a text that provides a nuanced and critical reflection on the ethics of gossip and the ambiguous virtues of privacy. As I will argue, *Who Do You Think You Are?* is neither a *Bildungsroman* as some critics maintain, nor even a *Künstlerroman* as others have argued, but a *Klatchmaulroman*: a novel of the education of a gossip. Peter Bergmann's analysis of gossip as "discreet indiscretion" suggests that such an education would be conducted as a tug-of-war between contradictory values, since the feelings of power gossip generates in the gossiper are at odds with the feelings of helplessness it can generate in the victim. In the first place, the gossip's education includes an initiation into a practice of gossiping that is performed unconsciously, "without having 'to call it by its proper name'"—what Schütz and Luckmann call "habitual knowledge."[13] Gossip's disrepute, however, means that learning to gossip is not only a matter of "knowing how" but also of "knowing that"—in other words, recognizing gossip as a morally problematic activity. Bergmann's sense that "gossip's significance has not begun to be clarified" thus rests on "the discrepancy that exists between talking about gos-

sip and its practice—the discrepancy between the collective public denunciation and the collective private practicing of gossip."[14] This division clearly begs larger questions about the responsibility of the gossip to the privacy of his or her victims, but also about the nature and value of privacy itself.

Munro's stories offer their own evaluation of gossip's significance in light of the pervasive discrepancy between public pronouncements and private practices by showing how gossip is central to the invention and management of their protagonist's identity, as well as to her ethical growth. Initially, Rose learns to gossip by emulating her stepmother Flo, approaching gossip as a discursive practice that allows her to assume the identity of "chronicler" with imaginative power over other people. Over the course of the stories, however, Rose becomes increasingly uncomfortable with a form of self-construction that depends on a structure which is itself reversible and, as such, can be turned against its user. By the end of the collection, Rose has radically revised her view of her own freedom as a gossip, finding her power not in its use but in its renunciation. Throughout this process of education, gossip becomes a trope for the interpenetration of private and public identities. The stories thus productively complicate both traditional dismissals and contemporary defences by dramatizing how identities are forged in the heat of gossiping about other people's private scandals.

2

Munro's exploration of gossip as a technique of self-fashioning in *Who Do You Think You Are?* foregrounds the gendered representation of gossip by revisiting an old stereotype of the crone in the character of Flo, Rose's wicked stepmother and spinner of "old wives tales." As Bergmann argues, the history of associating gossip with women has a "symbolic birth place" at the washing place,

> because while doing their wash, which contained the bodily dirt of its user, "revealing" stains and worn out places and holes, the women constantly came across traces of the private and intimate affairs of others. Washerwomen thereby structurally assumed the position of gossip producers who acquired morally contaminated information about the private affairs of others or at least could figure it out from traces (visible evidence). If the resounding slaps of the mallets and the voices and laughter of the women could be heard in the village then in time these sounds assumed for the villagers—especially for the men—a significantly threatening character, and "gossip" thereby became accepted as the designation for the socially condemned, feared, and specifically female form of conversation about the private affairs of others.[15]

When viewed from this perspective, Flo's impulse "to see people brought down to earth" that leads her to "make public what she finds in the laundry bag"[16] is emblematic of the gossip's function:

Late at night she or Rose, or both of them, would be out at the washing machine in the woodshed. Sometimes, Rose saw, her father's underwear was stained. She would not want to look, but Flo held it up, waved it almost under Rose's nose, cried out, "Lookit that again!" and made clucking noises that were a burlesque of disapproval.

(48)

However, the crone's subversive play with the father's unmentionables is not enough to make ***Who Do You Think You Are?*** into a feminist "crone-ography," in Mary Daly's sense of the term, since Flo's telling has little to do with "unmasking deceptive patriarchal history, rendering it obsolete."[17] Instead, Flo's performances tend to confirm social mores, turning patriarchal norms to her own advantage. Flo is thus "like Isis remaking the penis of Osiris" in that she "reinstates and reaffirms the patriarchy even as she appears to challenge it."[18] As Robert Paine argues, such choric reaffirmations are the cornerstone of gossip as a technique in which "morality and self-interest are brought extremely close to each other" in a competition for "moral status."[19] Gossipers thus raise their own status, or "generate an immediately satisfying sense of power," through "appropriate interpretations" of other people's behaviour.[20]

Flo's ribald accounts of scandalous goings-on in Hanratty exemplify this self-consolidating version of gossip which Rose herself later learns to employ. The story of the Tyde-family history, for instance, furnishes Flo with ample opportunity to secure her own moral status: the tyrant butcher-father; the deformed daughter Becky whom he supposedly beats ("they did not understand about polio," Flo tells us knowingly); rumours of an incestuous birth; the mock-trial and murder of the father that follow; the trial, sentencing, and eventual pardon of the young men involved ("A farce, said Flo"); and finally, Becky's ensuing "career of public sociability and display" (9). In Flo's catalogue of rural horrors, prohibition and transgression are two sides of the same coin. She admonishes herself to Rose, "I shouldn't even be telling you this stuff"; but the ironic narrator assures us, "More was to follow" (7). The conclusion of her story is marked by a similarly calculated ambivalence:

That was all. Flo put the lid down on the story as if she was sick of it. It reflected no good on anybody.

"Imagine," Flo said.

(9)

Flo's assessment that the story "reflected no good on anybody" may be reasonable within the narrative parameters she sets, but on a dramatic level it reflects very well on Flo herself. Occupying the dominant position of observer and judge, Flo distances herself from the transgressions she describes and identifies herself

with the power of social institutions. For the judgmental chronicler, the need to tell the tale is clearly as important as the need to censure it or, at least, to "be sorry for people like that" (45). The resulting ambivalence is succinctly rendered by Flo's concluding injunction, "Imagine," which, on the one hand typifies the function of the gossip to relish the contemplation of each scandal in scrupulous detail; and on the other, conveys the contempt and disbelief that accompany the exasperation of a scandalized arbiter of social norms.

Despite the imaginative power wielded by the gossip in the creation of a persona, the narrative does not romanticize that power by depicting her as an invulnerable figure. Flo's identity is always menaced by a counter-force that threatens to subvert her careful self-construction. According to Bergmann, the power to scandalize is ultimately rooted in "the specific *relational structure* of gossip"—"the gossip triad" consisting of the subject, producer, and recipient of gossip.[21] Because gossip's power depends largely on the absence of its subject, anyone can occupy any position within the gossip triad at any given moment. The gossiper always risks becoming the gossipee. The instability of this situation has a profound impact on the gossiper who would construct herself by telling stories about other people, since the implicit story of the self embedded in criticism of others must compete with a potential body of other stories about the gossiper that stretches beyond the horizon of authorial control. Consequently, the gossip is an anxious figure, typified by an alternation of curiosity and paranoia. The cost of self-aggrandizement is the stricter policing of private behaviours to ensure that one's reputation is beyond reproach, or at least beyond the public gaze.

For Flo, this contradictory position is manifested in an obsession with privacy and a constant fear of being overheard. Her admonition to Rose, for example, "You mind your own business" (1), rehearses the attitude that informs Flo's own frantic self-protection prior to Rose's "royal beating" at the hands of her father:

"Well we don't need the public in on this, that's for sure," Flo says, and she goes to lock the door of the store, putting in the store window the sign that says "Back Soon," a sign Rose had made for her with a great deal of fancy curving and shading of letters in black and red crayon. When she comes back she shuts the door to the store, then the door to the stairs, then the door to the woodshed.

(15)

Considering that she has just gossiped about another royal beating—the one received by Becky Tyde's father—Flo's attempts to "shut up" the beating she precipitates seem especially hypocritical. Tellingly, as Rose's beating nears a climax, Flo's anxiety intensifies: "She [Rose] has given up on words but is letting out a noise, the sort of noise that makes Flo cry, *Oh, what if people can hear?*" (17). Such hypocrisy casts doubt on the sociological cliché, first devised by E. A. Ross, that gossip functions as a social control for gossipers themselves since, the theory goes, the fear of being gossiped about pre-emptively ensures conformative behaviour.[22] Instead, Flo's antics emphasize the superficiality of an identity forged in the heat of gossip, exposing it as the mere veneer of respectability.

One of the principal ways in which the narrator undercuts Flo's pretentions is by identifying gossip with "dirty talk"—a strategy that recalls the scatological discourse of the washerwoman and implicitly reinscribes the moral critique of idle talk. The filth and impropriety that Flo attributes to others in order to create her own respectability reassert themselves as metaphors for her own discourse. This link between gossip and Rose's own favourite "toilet locale" (24) is established very early on in the text, when we are told that Flo had an indoor bathroom put into the kitchen:

> They were all familiar with each other's nether voices, not only in their most explosive moments but in their intimate sighs and growls and pleas and statements. And they were all most prudish people. So no one ever seemed to hear, or be listening, and no reference was made. The person creating the noises in the bathroom was not connected to the person who walked out.
>
>   (4)

The location of the toilet is significant since the kitchen, like the washing place, is a symbolic female space that is frequently seen as a locus for gossip.[23] Likewise, the metaphoric loquaciousness of these "nether voices" which produce "pleas" and "statements" involves a type of "body language" that, like gossip, is jettisoned from more acceptable ways of speaking. Most importantly, the division of domestic space into public and private realms emulates the structural conditions of gossip, whose "*central theme . . . lies precisely in* [a] *tense relationship between a revealed 'first' and a concealed 'second' world.*"[24]

The irreconcilable tension between "the person creating the noises in the bathroom" and "the person who walked out" perfectly describes the dynamic of Flo's scandalmongering:

> Present time and past, the shady melodramatic past of Flo's stories, were quite separate, at least for Rose. Present people could not be fitted into the past. Becky herself, town oddity and public pet, harmless and malicious, could never match the butcher's prisoner, the cripple daughter, a white streak at the window: mute, beaten, impregnated. As with the house, only a formal connection could be made.
>
>   (8)

Like the "bathroom noises," Flo's gossip depends on a rupture between past and present, public and private. Consequently, her histories resemble what Rose finds

"in the heaped snow under a glaze of ice, where the snow had melted and frozen again": "turds copious and lonesome, preserved as if under glass, bright and mustard or grimy as charcoal, with every shading in between" (24). Flo, who Rose fears "would show up at the school with a pail and shovel" to clean out the filthy outhouses, "lambasting everbody in the bargain" (24-25), is finally not so different from the "honey-dumper" whose job she nearly usurps. Her symbolic embodiment of his function offers a wry critique of the bullshit artist, even as the honey-dumper's permanent retirement, when "the School Board saw fit to put flush toilets in the cleaned-up basement" (38), anticipates the stories' final verdict on her "dirty talk."

3

If the glaring contradictions in Flo's discourse and practice typify the self-deceptive position of the gossip, critics have been anxious to confine the significance and influence of her strategies to the early stories in the collection. W. R. Martin leaves Rose curiously free of the charge of gossiping since his reading associates gossip exclusively with Flo. Viewing Flo as "a contrast to the sensitive, imaginative Rose," he suggests that the crone's weakness for sensationalism is only a foil for the real heroine, who "typically examines and ponders events more deeply."[25] Rose might tell stories, Martin concedes, but she certainly does not gossip. A closer analysis of Rose's discursive practices, however, seriously questions such a conclusion. For when we find that "Flo and Rose had switched roles," that "now Rose was the one bringing stories home, Flo was the one who knew the names of the characters and was waiting to hear" (41), the discursive register in which "stories" are told has not changed. Thus, "the sort of story Rose brought home" (42) about Muriel Mason's elusive Kotex and Ruby Carruthers's sexual misadventures precisely mirrors "the sort of story Flo told Rose" about Becky Tyde (43).

The narrative of Rose's story about Ruby Carruthers, one of her earliest attempts at gossip, emphasizes the fluidity of Rose and Flo's roles as gossip producer and recipient. As Flo—still the more sophisticated gossip—interjects with interpretations of Rose's gossip about "a slutty sort of girl" who keeps house for a local family, she foregrounds ways in which others' folly can furnish raw material for flattering self-comparisons:

> One time when [Ruby] was there alone three boys went over to see her. Del Fairbridge, Horse Nicholson, Runt Chesterton.
>
> *"To see what they could get," Flo put in.* She looked at the ceiling and told Rose to keep her voice down. Her father would not tolerate this sort of story.
>
> Del Fairbridge was a good-looking boy, conceited, and not very clever. He said he would go into the house and persuade Ruby with no trouble at all, and if he

could get her to do it with all three of them, he would. What he did not know was that Horse Nicholson had already arranged with Ruby to meet him under the veranda.

"Spiders in there, likely," said Flo. "I guess they don't care."

(42; my emphasis)

Rose still seems to be the apprentice telling this story, since Flo clearly anticipates its real significance: "'If you ever got up to any of that with a boy it would be the end of you,' she said. 'I mean it'" (43). Flo's vigilance about the differences that emerge in her dialogue with the story between "us" and "them" is less for her benefit than for her pupil's, for it is Rose who unexpectedly receives the moral of her own story. But she has already anticipated the lesson, for

> Rose would not have told her anything in which she did not play a superior, an onlooker's part. Pitfalls were for others, Flo and Rose agreed. The change in Rose, once she left the scene, crossed the bridge, changed herself into a chronicler, was remarkable. No nerves any more. A loud skeptical voice, some hip-swinging in a red and yellow plaid skirt, more than a hint of swaggering.
>
> (41)

Whereas Flo's self-dramatizations remained implicit in her gossip, Rose's storytelling suggests a deeper and more self-conscious commitment to gossip as a strategy and as an identity, even though her desire to legitimate her discourse with the title of "chronicler" betrays an anxiety about her chosen method of self-invention. For even at this early stage in her education, Rose is keenly aware of which details are worth emphasizing and which are better left unreported, as she demonstrates in her omission of the story's actual conclusion, which threatens to humanize Ruby and restore her lost dignity:

> Rose did not bother with the rest of the story, which was that Ruby got into a bad mood, sat on the veranda steps with the dirt from underneath all over her clothes and in her hair, refused to smoke a cigarette or share a package of cupcakes (now probably rather squashed) that Runt had swiped from the grocery store where he worked after school. They teased her to tell them what was the matter and at last she said, "I think I got a right to know who I'm doing it with."
>
> (43)

The inclusion of each new pathetic detail, from the dirt in Ruby's hair to the (probably) squashed cupcakes, increases the listener's sense of sympathy for Ruby. But when the subject is finally allowed to speak for herself, her affirmation of her human right "to know who I'm doing it with" moves the hearer from distant sympathy for Ruby to visceral empathy with her. For she has been violated by more than a callous group of boys; the gossiper has also violated her right to know what is being said about her.

Rose's omission of another story in which she herself is ridiculed for the pretentious claim that she eats half a grapefruit for breakfast—which Flo would have thought "as bad as drinking champagne" (40)—undercuts for us, but not for Flo, the impressiveness of her new-found swagger. Rose's hypocrisy is most glaring, however, in her account of the schoolgirl whose missing Kotex was "smuggled somehow into the trophy case in the main hall. There it came to public notice. Folding and carrying had spoiled its fresh look, rubbed its surface, so that it was possible to imagine it had been warmed against the body. A great scandal" (41). The incident is initially presented as part of the narration; only after it has been told is it dramatized as part of Rose's after-school gossip. This circuitous presentation foregrounds the differences between the event and its discursive repetition, which is meagerly described ("Flo enjoyed the episode of the Kotex") and thus highlights Rose's undisclosed reaction of sympathetic identification: "Rose could have been the girl who lost the Kotex. That was probably a country girl, carrying the Kotex in her pocket or in the back of her notebook, for use later in the day. Anybody who lived at a distance might have done that. Rose herself had done it" (40-41). In the ensuing scandal, however, "Rose was afraid that she might be the leading candidate for ownership, so was relieved when responsibility was fixed on a big sullen country girl named Muriel Mason, who wore slub rayon housedresses to school, and had B.O." (41). In light of Flo and Rose's maxim, "pitfalls are for others," the "episode of the Kotex" is particularly revealing of how intimately gossip links identity to the protection of one's own privacy at the expense of another's. For Rose's gossip about Muriel Mason does not only elide her identification with the victim in order to secure her superior position retrospectively; it also reproduces the likely method by which "responsibility was fixed" on Muriel rather than on Rose herself by their classmates. By implying that Rose has a vested interest in the gossip about Muriel because of the threat of ridicule represented by the Kotex to her own reputation at school, the narrator exposes the degree to which the gossip's identity is based on a competition for privacy, as it provides a stinging comment on Rose's self-protecting strategies.

For a gossip like Flo, a gap in space is more essential than a gap in time to her successful relation of self-aggrandizing scandal. Because Flo constructs herself at the expense of her neighbours, her gossip depends on metaphors of spatial difference between self and other, inside and outside. As an adult, Rose expands upon the strategies she learned from Flo by adapting the structure of her discursive inheritance to a gap in time. This new strategy allows her, paradoxically, to make a younger version of herself the subject of her own gossip. As a girl, listening to Flo's tall tales, Rose found that "present people could not be fitted into the past" (8). As an adult, however, she finds that she herself is capable of the same kind of splitting that she had once noticed in the subjects of Flo's gossip. When she tries to repeat the scandals she once shared with Flo, Rose discovers that she cannot fit her present self into the stories of her own past: "She had to swear they were true, she was not exaggerating" (28).

According to Phillipe Lejeune, such self-division is typical of the autobiographer, for whom difference from oneself is initially a function of time:

> The name is the guarantor of the unity of our multiplicity; it federates our complexity in the moment and our change in time. . . . [And yet] any speaking subject carries within himself that double split of addresser and addressee and of enunciation and utterance. . . . In general, these gaps, these divisions are both expressed and masked by the use of a single "I."[26]

Lejeune's theory of a subject who is temporally split— for whom "the first person always conceals . . . a secret third person"[27]—has important consequences for theories of gossip, a discourse which, as Roland Barthes warns, "reduces the other to *he/she* . . . the third person pronoun . . . the pronoun of the non-person."[28] For as soon as an autobiographer speaks of herself as an absent third-person, this pronominal shift means that the gossiper also carries within herself a younger gossipee whose absence fulfils the structural conditions of the triad. Throughout her adulthood, Rose exploits this structural self-division to assemble a public persona from the private details of her own past. Rather than effecting a reconciliation of past and present selves, as autobiography often seeks to, Rose's divulgences are primarily concerned with recreating the self-aggrandizing dynamic of her gossip: "Rose knew a lot of people who wished they had been born poor, and hadn't been. So she would queen it over them, offering various bits of squalor from her childhood" (24).

Although she finds this strategy useful for "intimidat-[ing] right-thinking people at dinner parties" (90), Rose's self-doubling is darkly reflected in the humiliation she feels at an earlier dinner party, when she brings her snobbish fiancé Patrick back to Hanratty to meet Flo:

> Patrick got to hear about a man who cut his own throat, *his own throat,* from ear to ear, a man who shot himself the first time and didn't do enough damage, so he loaded up and fired again and managed it, another man who hanged himself using a chain, the kind of chain you hook on a tractor with, so it was a wonder his head was not torn off.
>
> *Tore off,* Flo said.
>
> She went on to a woman who though not a suicide, had been dead in her house a week before she was found, and that was in the summer. She asked Patrick to imagine it. All this happened, said Flo, within five miles of

where she herself was born. She was presenting credentials, not trying to horrify Patrick, at least not more than was acceptable, in a social way; she did not mean to disconcert him.

(89-90)

Rose's real shame about her past in Hanratty, as she endures Flo's gossip from Patrick's priggish point of view, belies the apparent ease of her self-division later, when she cynically turns her childhood "squalor" into a kind of anti-cultural capital. But this chilling resumé of local suicides does not only prefigure Rose's habit of "presenting credentials" at dinner parties with a grim sense of irony; by linking public acts of self-construction to gossip about self-destruction it pinpoints the issues behind "the things she was ashamed of . . . the failure she couldn't seize upon or explain" that haunts Rose throughout her quest for identity in her adult life (207). As Lejeune's model insinuates, the gossip who would change herself into an object is always caught in precisely the same dialectic between creation and immolation because she must first make herself absent before she can "make" herself present.

Like Flo's attempts to elevate her moral status in the eyes of her listeners, Rose's desire to "queen" herself above her peers is undercut by the threat of imminent reversal that is constitutive of gossip's structure. This theme is developed in **"Simon's Luck,"** the story that is the "crucial link in the design of the volume: it provides the vital link between Rose's flounderings and her confident magnanimity at the end."[29] As the story begins, Rose finds herself at a party, fearing that "she might be doomed to hang out on the fringes of things, making judgments" (158), only to become the subject of malicious gossip among a group of young faculty members:

> They were talking in low, serious voices. One of them looked at her. She smiled. Her smile was not returned. A couple of others looked at her, and they went on talking. She was sure they were talking about her. . . .

(162)

Complementing the emphasis on self-construction in her own discourse, the junior faculty's gossip directly threatens Rose's identity, making her represent the "Fucked-up jealous establishment," and leaving her helplessly wanting "to state her case" (162):

> The years of work, the exhaustion, the travelling, the high school auditoriums, the nerves, the boredom, the never knowing where your next pay was coming from. She wanted to plead with them, so they would forgive her and love her *and take her on their side.*

(163)

If there is some poetic justice in this reversal that allows Rose to experience first-hand the reductive effects of gossip, it does not precipitate an immediate rehabilitation. Instead, Rose's response to becoming the subject of other people's smug judgements recalls Flo's urgency to withdraw from public scrutiny when scandal threatened during Rose's "royal beating."

Rose's intensified concern to defend her privacy emerges during her relationship with Simon, the man she meets at the same faculty party. When Rose buys groceries for their evening together, she discovers how easily her private desperation for love enters the sphere of public knowledge, even if it does not become the subject of malicious gossip *per se*:

> "You must have brought home some company," said the woman who kept the store. She spoke with no surprise or malice or censure, just a comradely sort of envy.
>
> "When I wasn't expecting it." Rose dumped more groceries on the counter. "What a lot of bother they are. Not to mention expense. Look at that bacon. And cream."
>
> "I could stand a bit of it," the woman said.
>
> (166)

As the narrator implies, Rose's misplaced anxiety about "malice or censure" reveals more about the impetus behind her own inclination to gossip than about the woman's "comradely" inquiries. Her transparent attempts to protect her privacy, moreover, recall her earliest fears of being gossiped about back in Hanratty when, as a teenager, she anticipates going to Toronto to "buy hair-remover to put on her arms and legs, and if possible an arrangement of inflatable cushions, supposed to reduce your hips and thighs" (59):

> She thought they probably had hair-remover in the drugstore in Hanratty, but the woman in there was a friend of Flo's and told everything. She told Flo who bought hair-dye and slimming medicine and French safes. As for the cushion business, you could send away for it but there was sure to be a comment at the Post Office, and Flo knew people there as well.
>
> (59)

Flo's contacts in the drugstore and the Post Office, like the woman who envies Rose at the grocery store, create for Rose the impression of being fully visible—always potentially an object of gossip. Consequently, she avoids the prying eyes of the envious woman by buying her groceries "at a supermarket several miles away" (168). When Simon does not arrive for dinner, "She put out the lights because she didn't want to be caught sitting up . . . what could be more desperate than a woman of Rose's age sitting up all night in her dark kitchen waiting for her lover?" (170). And finally, at the climax of the story, she gives up chasing after Simon because she fears that her vulnerability will become public knowledge: "she thought of how many crazy letters she had written, how many overblown excuses she had found,

having to leave a place, or being afraid to leave a place, on account of some man. Nobody knew the extent of her foolishness, friends who had known her for twenty years didn't know half of the flights she had been on, the money she had spent, and the risks she had taken" (172). Such a juxtaposition of Rose's public self-constructions with her private desires does more than simply ironize the protagonist's lack of self-knowledge. It also suggests that the danger of romanticizing privacy is commensurate with the danger of romanticizing gossip. For Rose's desire to preserve her privacy is directly proportional to her characteristic failure to consider the feelings and weaknesses of others, as the story's ending pointedly suggests.

In the final moments of **"Simon's Luck,"** Rose learns of Simon's death from a woman she had also met at the faculty party: "Poor Simon. You know he died. . . . Cancer of the pancreas. . . . Sad. He had it for a long time" (176-77). Ironically, through this bit of idle talk, Rose is roused from the feelings of powerlessness she associates with being publicly humiliated, to imagine someone else's vulnerability: "It was preposterous, it was unfair, that such a chunk of information should have been left out, and that Rose even at this late date could have thought herself the only person who could seriously lack power" (177). By making her aware of other people's lack of power, the gossip about Simon's "luck" finally enables Rose to question her own discourse of gossip—not simply in terms of its reversibility, that is to say, its disadvantages for her—but ethically, in terms of its effect on others.

4

Rose has been seeking transformation through the strategic use of gossip since her youth in Hanratty. In **"Wild Swans,"** for instance, Rose conflated Flo's gossip about the "White Slavers" she was to watch out for on the train to Toronto with her gossip about the undertaker who "drove the old hearse all over the country, looking for women" and sang about a girl whose *"throat is like a swan"* (58) to characterize her sexual encounter with a male passenger as a drama of seduction and transformation. Even in the final pages of the story, "She wanted to fill up in that magical, releasing way, transform herself; she wanted the courage and the power" (204). Throughout the collection of stories, however, gossip's transfiguring power has been ironized by a narrator who points out the superficiality and hypocrisy of a transformation in which the private and public identities of the gossip refuse to cohere. **"Who Do You Think You Are?,"** the final story of the collection, confirms this critique of gossip as an agent of self-transformation by suggesting that maturity results from an ethical engagement with the complexity and ineffability of other people's experience that can only be achieved by sacrificing the self-protecting pleasure gossip affords.

Initially, Rose's acceptance of the crone's voyeuristic language is signalled by the story's narrative frame: a gossipy conversation between Rose, her brother, and his wife about the "village idiot," Milton Homer. It is not, however, this gossip about Milton Homer's "scandalous behaviour" (198) that has a profound effect on Rose's education, but her memory of a chance encounter with Ralph Gillespie, a boy from her English class "who specialized in Milton Homer imitations" (202):

> when Rose remembered this unsatisfactory conversation she seemed to recall a wave of kindness, of sympathy and forgiveness, though certainly no words of that kind had been spoken. That peculiar shame which she had carried around with her seemed to have been eased. The thing that she was ashamed of, in acting, was that she might have been paying attention to the wrong things, reporting antics, when there was always something further, a tone, a depth, a light that she couldn't get and wouldn't get. Everything she had done could sometimes be seen as a mistake.

> (209)

Rose's habit of "reporting antics" to construct a persona is thrown seriously into question as a result of this seemingly idle conversation. For her inability to penetrate beyond its very idleness to recapture something of the profound connection they shared as schoolmates gives Rose a transforming insight into the difficulty of achieving human intimacy that has profound implications for her own discourse:

> There seemed to be feelings which could only be spoken of in translation; perhaps they could only be acted on in translation; not speaking of them and not acting on them is the right course to take because translation is dubious. Dangerous as well.

> For these reasons Rose did not explain anything further about Ralph Gillespie to Brian and Phoebe. . . .

> (210)

By making the Other the subject of concern, by giving Ralph the right, not of last word, but of first refusal, Rose renders the stories' judgement on the use of gossip as a means of self-construction: the gossip's education culminates in a rejection of her own "dangerous" voice. Rose finally seems to escape becoming a crone by embracing an ethic of privacy and a practice of silence.

This would be a strange conclusion for a novel of education to reach, however, particularly one as fascinated by gossip's generative powers as it is suspicious of its methods. To be sure, Flo's example and Rose's education exemplify Paine's thesis that gossip is self-interested. But *Who Do You Think You Are?* must still be distinguished from patriarchal condemnations of female gossip, in part because its ironic treatment of Flo nevertheless remains largely sympathetic and humaniz-

ing. Although I have emphasized the self-interested elements of her discourse, Ajay Heble is also correct to argue that Flo's "tales evolve out of a local community of gossip" that represents "the transforming, myth-making powers of memory."[30] Gossip's ambiguity lies precisely in its embodiment of such contradictory values. Rose's gossip too embodies these contradictions, but at a much deeper level than Flo's, because Rose's apparent rejection of gossip at the end of the story is not as straightforward as it seems. As Spacks suggests, "gossip provides a model for many operations of the novel [and] opens the way for a kind of interpretation that defines aspects of the text's relation to the reader and locates its roots in ordinary social discourse."[31] If Rose has been in command of her own story as a secret third-person narrator since the beginning, as Munro's most careful critics argue,[32] she has hardly embraced an ethic of silence as fully as the final story might suggest. Rose, in other words, might renounce one form of gossip only to take up another form which now implicates the reader. Transposing the gossip triad from thematic to formal concern, Rose's autobiographical narration turns the reader into the recipient of her literary gossip. Consequently, not Rose, but the reader, is revealed to have been the gossip's apprentice all along. If we are meant to be Rose's apprentices, however, we are clearly expected to learn that Rose's paean to privacy is only one element in a much larger story whose end is an ethical dialogue with others in the public domain. Such a dialogue may be achieved, Munro suggests, only if we are willing to sacrifice the protective shell of public identity and follow Rose's example of *self*-disclosure, turning gossip into open discourse, widely distributed and honestly attributed.

To the rising chorus of voices currently reassessing the conflict between gossip and privacy in favour of the former, Munro's stories lend a valuable sense of balance. Like the most radical critics of privacy, Munro is highly suspicious of its capacity "to promote self-deception and hypocrisy."[33] But she is equally suspicious of utopian appeals to "a universalized practice of radical and guiltless indiscretion, a world of transparent gossip."[34] At a time when we already seem to inhabit "a world of transparent gossip" in which privacy is in short supply, Munro's exhortation that we become ethical gossips is particularly welcome. What we might be expected to learn from her fiction is that we cannot escape from gossip, even if we finally make ourselves its object by implicating ourselves in a laying bare of such practices.

Notes

1. Jörg R. Bergmann, *Discreet Indiscretions: The Social Organization of Gossip,* trans. John Bednarz, Jr. (New York: Aldine de Gruyter, 1993) 54.

2. Ronald de Sousa, "In Praise of Gossip: Indiscretion as a Saintly Virtue," *Good Gossip,* ed. Robert

F. Goodman and Aaron Ben-Ze'ev (Kansas: UP of Kansas, 1994) 31.

3. This paper was written with the financial assistance of a doctoral fellowship from the Social Sciences and Humanities Research Council of Canada and an Izaak Walton Killam fellowship. I would like to thank David Williams of the Department of English at the University of Manitoba for his help and guidance during the development of this paper.

4. Max Gluckman, "Gossip and Scandal," *Current Anthropology* 4 (1963): 308.

5. See, for example, Elizabeth Colson, *The Makah Indians* (Minneapolis: U of Minnesota P, 1953); M. Herskovits, *Life in a Haitian Valley* (New York: Knopf, 1937) and *Trinidad Village* (New York: Knopf, 1947); James West, *Plainsville, USA* (New York: Columbia UP, 1945).

6. See Aaron Ben-Ze'ev, "The Vindication of Gossip," *Good Gossip* 11-24; Ferdinand Schoeman, "Gossip and Privacy," *Good Gossip* 72-82.

7. Robert Paine, "What is Gossip About? An Alternative Hypothesis," *Man* 2 (1967): 282.

8. See Patricia Meyer Spacks, *Gossip* (Chicago: U of Chicago P, 1986); Deborah Jones, "Gossip: Notes on Women's Oral Culture," *The Feminist Critique of Language: A Reader,* ed. Deborah Cameron (New York: Routledge, 1991) 242-50; Donna C. Stanton, "Recuperating Women and the Man Behind the Screen," *Sexuality and Gender in Early Modern Europe: Institutions, Texts, Images,* ed. James Grantham Turner (Cambridge: Cambridge UP, 1993) 247-65; Lorraine Code, "Gossip, or in Praise of Chaos," *Good Gossip* 100-105; Louise Collins, "Gossip: A Feminist Defence," *Good Gossip* 106-14.

9. Spacks, *Gossip* 30.

10. See the discussion of feminist revisions of Gluckman and Paine's theories of gossip in Brian Johnson, "Language, Power, and Responsibility in *The Handmaid's Tale*: Toward a Discourse of Literary Gossip," *Canadian Literature* 148 (1996): 39-55.

11. De Sousa, "In Praise of Gossip" 33.

12. De Sousa, "In Praise of Gossip" 32.

13. Bergmann, *Discreet Indiscretions* 20-21.

14. Bergmann, *Discreet Indiscretions* 21.

15. Bergmann, *Discreet Indiscretions* 63.

16. Alice Munro, *Who Do You Think You Are?* (Agincourt: Signet, 1978) 48. Subsequent references are to this edition.

17. Mary Daly, *Gyn/ecology: The Metaethics of Radical Feminism* (Boston: Beacon, 1978) 16.

18. Magdalene Redekop, *Mothers and Other Clowns: The Stories of Alice Munro* (New York: Routledge, 1992) 117.

19. Paine, "What is Gossip About?" 281.

20. Bergmann, *Discreet Indiscretions* 147.

21. Bergmann, *Discreet Indiscretions* 45-49.

22. Bergmann, *Discreet Indiscretions* 144.

23. See Jones, "Gossip: Notes on Women's Oral Culture."

24. Bergmann, *Discreet Indiscretions* 53.

25. W. R. Martin, *Alice Munro: Paradox and Parallel* (Edmonton: U of Alberta P, 1987) 106.

26. Phillipe Lejeune, *On Autobiography,* trans. Katherine Leary (Minneapolis: U of Minnesota P, 1989) 34.

27. Phillipe Lejeune, *On Autobiography* 35.

28. Roland Barthes, *A Lover's Discourse,* trans. Richard Howard (New York: Noonday, 1977) 185.

29. W. R. Martin, *Alice Munro: Paradox and Parallel* 101.

30. Ajay Heble, *The Tumble of Reason: Alice Munro's Discourse of Absence* (Toronto: U of Toronto P, 1994) 101-102.

31. Spacks, *Gossip* 12.

32. See Williams, *Confessional Fictions: A Portrait of the Artist in the Canadian Novel* (Toronto: U of Toronto P, 1991) 204; Heble, *The Tumble of Reason* 104.

33. De Sousa, "In Praise of Gossip" 32.

34. De Sousa, "In Praise of Gossip" 33.

W. R. Martin and Warren U. Ober (essay date summer 2000)

SOURCE: Martin, W. R. and Warren U. Ober. "Alice Munro's 'Hold Me Fast, Don't Let Me Pass' and 'Tam Lin.'" *ANQ* 13, no. 3 (summer 2000): 44-8.

[*In the following essay, Martin and Ober consider "Hold Me Fast, Don't Let Me Pass" an ironic reworking and modernization of the traditional Scottish ballad "Tam Lin."*]

Alice Munro's use of an earlier writer's work as a point of departure is nothing new in her stories. It has been obvious from the first that she is always keenly aware of literary history, the cultural heritage, and the tradition within which she writes, and her richly allusive work prompts the reader to ponder parallels and significances. But nothing of hers points as directly to another piece as **"Hold Me Fast, Don't Let Me Pass,"** a story from her 1990 volume *Friend of My Youth* (74-105), points to the old Scottish ballad "Tam Lin." Like "Tam Lin," all the characters in **"Hold Me Fast, Don't Let Me Pass"** are divided between two worlds, the one vital and alive, the other unfulfilling and sterile, but a fundamental difference between "Tam Lin and Munro's characters brings us to the nub of the story. This difference is a striking ironic reversal in which Munro turns the ballad upside down. Whereas in "Tam Lin" the desirable transition is downward from the phantom hills of fairyland to the world of flesh and blood, in the story the implication is that the passage should be upwards from the mundane commercial life of the town to the remote high hills of the Scottish Border, the locus of human passion and imagination.

"Tam Lin" is recited in full in the story, and Munro actually quotes several complete stanzas, generally from Sir Walter Scott's transcription in *Minstrelsy of the Scottish Border*. The ballad heroine, Jennet ("Janet" in Scott), despite stern warnings about the risks, goes out in her most fetching attire to Carterhaugh (at the junction of the Yarrow and Ettrick rivers). There she meets a gently bred knight, Tam Lin ("Tamlane" in Scott; unnamed in the story), who had been snatched away to "Fairy-Land" to become the lover of the Queen of Fairies but now longs to return to the world of flesh and blood.

The world of human passion and vitality is epitomized in the ballad by the "plain" of Carterhaugh (Scott 2: 188), the field on which Jennet and Tam Lin make love. There she wins and holds the soul of Tam, who, determined at last to break free from a bloodless existence that he has found enervating and treacherous, has descended from the hills of fairyland. He fathers a child by Jennet and tells her how to win him back from the Queen of Fairies. She must go to Miles Cross (a half mile from Carterhaugh), and there, as the fairy cavalcade passes, she must seize Tam Lin and hold fast to his body until the queen releases him to become Jennet's groom and "her bairn's father" (Scott 2: 203).

Munro has turned the ballad upside down. In her story the local habitation of the ethos of the ballad, now beleaguered and diminished, is the house of Miss Margaret Dobie. Still rooted in the Border hills and among the woods, Miss Dobie has retreated from the old family house. Unmarried and childless, this strange old woman has shut out the world and even her own personal past, but she has living with her Judy, a refugee from the town, with her love child, Tania, fathered by Dudley Brown. ("Tania" is the short form of "Tatiana" or "Tita-

nia," the name of a queen of the fairies.) Hazel Curtis, the center of consciousness in the story, hears Dudley ("Dudley" = "fair field" in Celtic) recite the ballad, and it is clear that his relation to Judy reflects, though inversely, the relation in the ballad between Tam Lin and Jennet. According to Hazel's version of Dudley's rendition, "the boy captured by fairies" grows "wary as he gets older," longs for "a human climate," seduces "a bold girl," and instructs her "how she can get him free. She has to do it by holding on to him . . ." (100-01). Dudley feels a powerful attraction to the vibrantly handsome Judy—a bold girl certainly—and to the geography of the ballad world, but he remains trapped within a banal and passionless affair with Antoinette, "queen" (99) not of fairyland but of the Royal Hotel (75) in town. Dudley's dilemma is similar to Tam Lin's, but inside out: he is living in the humdrum world, entangled with a mundane paramour from whom he can't escape.

With sedulous effort and desperate contrivance, Antoinette holds fast to Dudley. It is Judy Armstrong who commands his vital affection, but, despite her surname, she has not yet been able to hold him fast. Antoinette, although at the cost of great suffering to herself, goes out of her way to prevent Dudley from taking Hazel, the visitor from Canada, to visit the Dobie household, once a home away from home for Hazel's late husband. The ambience of Miss Dobie's house is so completely antipathetic to Antoinette's consciousness that she becomes physically sick. As she returns with Hazel from the visit, while pointing out "Cathaw"—i.e., Carterhaugh—"a low field by the river," where "the girl [in the ballad] goes out and loses her maidenhead, and so on," she speaks "hastily" and seems "afraid of being overtaken by further vomiting" (98). This is how Antoinette sees Carterhaugh, where Tam made love to Jennet and no doubt where lovers through the ages have met. "Cathaw" may be a popular contraction of the name, but it suggests that, in Antoinette's mind, the couplings now bear the stigma of animality and whoredom. Dudley later tells Hazel that Antoinette "doesn't know what she's talking about!" (101). To Dudley and Judy, as to Tam and Jennet, lovemaking has an altogether higher and more beautiful significance than it has to Antoinette. It seems likely then that Antoinette, who, as Hazel sees her, is a "pared-down, vigilant, stupid-shrewd woman, sprayed and painted and preserved to within an inch of her life" (82), will eventually give way to Judy Armstrong, who is "bursting with ballad fervor" (103) and endowed with "a ripply fan of red hair, shining over her shoulders" (91).

Besides Tam Lin and Dudley there's the case of Jack Curtis, which is skillfully built into the story, being relevant to the theme of longing for another, more desirable world. But Jack, probably because he does not recognize that world clearly, fails to hold it fast. A Canadian serving as a bomber pilot in the Second World

War and stationed in the heart of the industrial "Black Country," Jack escaped from the tawdriness of Wolverhampton to the Scottish hills to visit Miss Dobie, his mother's cousin. His response to the world of romance seems to have been erratic and unreliable: He used to hear instrumental music and voices inside his plane on the bombing raids (88), and in Scotland he became infatuated with Antoinette, then the sixteen-year-old daughter of a hotelkeeper. He mistook her garish—and presumably bleached—blonde hair for the striking natural yellowness of, for example, Jennet's hair in the ballad. Now, when Hazel sees her, Antoinette has, despite the "paraphernalia" on her dresser (99), nothing but "a puff of gilt hair" (75). Hazel, too, was apparently a blonde when Jack returned to Canada and married her in her teens, but now she "let her hair grow out whatever color it liked" (82). Neither Antoinette nor Hazel has hair like Jennet's or Judy's, aflame with vitality and passion.

Back in Canada, the uncertain Jack turns to the seventeen-year-old sensitive and imaginative Hazel to hold him fast. But marriage and children turn their life together to petty habit and routine. Hazel has a vision of Jack "gray and insubstantial" and "drained of power" in the front window of the "appliance-sales-and-repair business" where he worked and where he "slumped over" and died (76, 104). Hazel has more vitality than Jack: Instead of holding fast to the fading Jack, she "took hold of her life" (82-83) by qualifying as a high school teacher of biology. Though Jack was largely responsible for the lack of fulfillment in their marriage, Hazel herself appears to be aware of a shade of guilt for failing to hold him fast, and her trip to Scotland seems to be a kind of homage, a sort of restitution. She is sensitive to the world of the ballads and, like Dudley, lives ambivalently and incompletely in both the everyday and the imaginative worlds. When Dudley offers to take Hazel to see the enchanted field of Carterhaugh, she "could feel something, as if a cat had jumped into her lap. Sex." But she knows that he shares her realization that "all that was beyond them at present. They would let the attraction wash over them and ebb away" (101-02). Hazel understands the tug-of-war in the consciousness of Jack, Dudley, and Tam Lin, but she also knows that life in the real world, for the middle aged at least, is more complicated than it is in the ballads.

The setting of **"Hold Me Fast, Don't Let Me Pass,"** Selkirk and the valley of the Ettrick, has of course close associations with Sir Walter Scott, whose preeminent achievement was to preserve the political, cultural, and literary traditions of the heroic Border ethos that is under siege in Munro's story. Selkirkshire is, moreover, the part of Scotland that Munro's family, the Laidlaws, stem from, and it has strong associations for her. One of the Laidlaws, William (1780-1845), of Blackhouse-on-Yarrow (where both he and his distant cousin James

Hogg, the "Ettrick shepherd," worked for his father, a sheep farmer), went on to assist Walter Scott "in the preparation of the third volume of the 'Minstrelsy'" and to become Scott's steward at Abbotsford (Crockett 189-90; *DNB* 397-98).

Throughout the story "Tam Lin" is brought into the service of Munro's larger theme—that the romantic territory of the imagination and the culture embodied in the ballads are today fighting a rear-guard action against a heterogeneous and formless urban sprawl. Hazel's slip in recording the date of Philiphaugh, the great battle that was the decisive defeat of the Scottish Royalists in the Civil War, as 1945 instead of 1645 (75) suggests a subconscious awareness that the struggle of the Border culture for survival is not over yet. There are still pockets of resistance.

Works Cited

Crockett, W. S. *The Scott Country*. London: Black, 1905.

Dictionary of National Biography. Vol. 11. London: Oxford UP, 1921-22.

Munro, Alice. *Friend of My Youth*. Toronto: McClelland and Stewart, 1990.

Scott, Sir Walter. *Minstrelsy of the Scottish Border*. 5th ed. 3 vols. Edinburgh: Constable, 1812.

Judith McCombs (essay date autumn 2000)

SOURCE: McCombs, Judith. "Searching Bluebeard's Chambers: Grimm, Gothic, and Bible Mysteries in Alice Munro's 'The Love of a Good Woman.'" *American Review of Canadian Studies* 30, no. 3 (autumn 2000): 327-48.

[*In the following essay, McCombs probes the various literary and religious influences on Munro's "The Love of a Good Woman," describing the story as "simultaneously archetypal and documentary, revealing people's lives in exact and mythic detail."*]

Like her 1992 story, **"A Wilderness Station,"** Alice Munro's 1996 **"The Love of a Good Woman"** is a concealed murder mystery whose luminous, disturbing power emanates in great part from her transformations of Grimm's Bluebeard tales, compounded with other Grimm tales, Gothic romance, and Bible myths. Both stories are masterpieces of Munro's realism, simultaneously archetypal and documentary, revealing people's lives in exact and mythic detail. People's "lives," as she wrote in *Lives of Girls and Women,* are "dull, simple, amazing, and unfathomable—deep caves paved with kitchen linoleum" (210). Both **"Wilderness"** ["A Wilderness Station"] and "Love" ["The Love of a Good Woman"] are set in Walley, a small Ontario town whose name suggests a walleye with a skewed or wider vision; in both a brutal Bluebeard murder is revealed in secret by a woman who may be crazed or lying. In both stories elusive clues, illuminations, allusions, and archetypes lure the reader to search the Bluebeard's chambers of storytelling, sex, and death.[1]

"The Love of a Good Woman" opens with an objective yet image-laden and resonant description of things preserved for "the last couple of decades" in the local historical museum of Walley, Ontario; these include a red box of optometrist's implements that once, the label tells us, "belonged to Mr. D. M. Willens, who drowned in the Peregrine River, 1951. It escaped the catastrophe and was found, presumably by the anonymous donor, who dispatched it to be a feature of our collection" (3). There follows a description of Willens's ophthalmoscope, with its large and small top disks that "could make you think of a snowman," its lenses and "hole to look through," handle and electric batteries; then of his retinoscope, with its column from which "a tiny light is supposed to shine," and its flat glass face that "is a dark sort of mirror. Everything is black, but that is only paint. . . . [W]here the optometrist's hand must have rubbed most often, . . . you can see a patch of shiny silver metal" (3-4).

This present-time prologue is both overture and, we will later be able to see, conclusion to Munro's Bluebeard and Bible mysteries. Here is the clue that will solve the murder mystery: the red box that "escaped the catastrophe" and was anonymously "dispatched" some twenty years later. Here are the intimations of a gender- and otherwise-transformed Bluebeard tale to come: the victim, the red chamber-box, the hole he looked through. Here are the archetypal images from myth and Bible myth that structure Munro's setting and theme. The "snowman" suggested by the ophthalmoscope's disks is a winter man who will give way to the story's flowerings of spring and summer, childhood and adulthood; and, simultaneously, the "snowman" warns us of snow jobs—in the socially accepted story of Willens's drowning, and in the Bluebeard stories to come.

The "dark sort of mirror" is, as Dennis Duffy has pointed out, St. Paul's glass through which we now see darkly (183-84; 1 Corinthians 13:12). The tiny light that "is supposed to shine" evokes Christ's Sermon on the Mount ("Let your light so shine before men, that they may see your good works," Matthew 5:16), and the hymn Protestant children are taught to sing ("This little light of mine, I'm gonna let it shine"). On the level of the murder mystery, the blackness that "is only paint," except where Mr. Willens's hand rubbed, so that "a patch of shiny silver" can be seen, hints at the sexual rubbings that will lead to murder and dark, cover-up

paint. On the mythic and Bible mystery level, the same image intimates that out of our blackness and rubbing, shining patches of illumination will come, when we learn to see not darkly but clearly.

* * *

Munro's Bluebeard archetypes come primarily from two Grimm's tales, "Fitcher's Bird" and "The Robber Bridegroom." The essential Grimm's characters are three: the Bluebeard serial killer, who compels or lures maidens to his isolated dwelling; the dismembered victim maidens; and the surviving clever bride who by daring, trickery, lies and storytelling saves herself and ruins Bluebeard.

In "Fitcher's Bird" the Bluebeard is an evil wizard, or fitcher, who with his magic touch carries off a first sister, then a second, then a third, giving each in turn an egg to carry always and keep spotless, and a key to a forbidden chamber. Curiosity leads each sister in turn to open the forbidden chamber, where she finds a chopping block and axe, and a bloody basin full of dismembered bodies. Frightened, each of the first two sisters lets her egg slip into the basin; when she cannot wash the telltale blood from the egg, the wizard drags her to the bloody chamber and chops her into pieces. The third, clever sister puts her egg away, explores the forbidden chamber, and heals her two dismembered sisters by gathering and putting in order their severed parts. Tricked by her lies, the wizard loses his power; the clever bride compels him to carry his gold and her sisters home, while she prepares his house for a wedding feast. She places a flower-decked skull in the garret window, and greets the wizard and his friends disguised as a wondrous bird, singing of the young bride: "'From cellar to garret she's swept all clean / And now from the window she's peeping, I ween'" (219-20). When they go inside, her kinsmen lock the doors and burn them all.

In Grimm's "Robber Bridegroom" the clever bride feels "a secret horror" of her rich betrothed, and marks her way to his dark forest house with peas and lentils (200). Exploring all his empty house, she finds a caged bird who sings "'Turn back, turn back, young maiden dear / 'Tis a murderer's house you enter here'" (201). In the cellar an old, old woman warns "you will keep your wedding with death," for the robber bridegroom and his men "are eaters of human flesh" (201). Hidden behind a hogshead by the old woman, the bride sees the cannibal robbers kill and dismember another maiden, whose cut-off finger with a gold ring on it springs "up in the air" and lands in her bosom (202). When the robbers fall asleep, the bride and old woman help each other escape to her father's mill. At the wedding feast, the bride tells as if it were a dream her story of the singing bird, the old woman, the murder, and then the dismembering of the other maiden, following each of these four revelations with the tag line, "My darling, I only dreamt this," and at the climax producing the cut-off finger with its ring (204). So her father's guests send the robber and his crew to execution.

These Grimm's Bluebeard tales, then, are thrilling sex-and-death versions of the archetypal fairy-tale quest, where a young person goes out into the world, is tempted and threatened by evil, and must use courage and trickery to triumph. Other Bluebeard versions may be found in Perrault's "La Barbe bleüe," with its greedier bride and telltale bloodied key to the forbidden chamber, and the English tale of "Mr. Fox" (Opie 133-46). An asexual, childhood version may be found in Grimm's "Hansel and Gretel," with its cannibal witch and clever Gretel, who tricks the witch into the oven and rescues her brother, Hansel. An animal version may be found in "The Three Little Pigs," where a fairy-tale fox gets tricked and boiled by the clever pig, who then rescues his brother and sister; and in the very similar nursery tale, where a wolf eats the two stupid pigs, but is tricked and boiled by the third, clever pig.

Grimm's Bluebeard tales are often read as warnings to women to beware rapacious men and to keep their eggs clean, by remaining virgins or faithful, obedient wives; both "Fitcher's Bird" and "The Robber Bridegroom," however, clearly show the advantages of daring, lying, acting, and storytelling (see Bettelheim 299-303 and Wilson 259-62). And although these tales have been read as sexual polarizations of evil men versus innocent women, in the end good men and clever bride cooperate to destroy the Bluebeard: the bride's kinsmen and her society's executioners have the necessary power; the clever, daring bride has the trickster-hero role. And, in the animal versions as well as the human ones, it is the hungry, devouring Bluebeard, or witch, fox, or wolf who is never portrayed as a victim, only as a villain who has to lose possessions and power, and end up justly burnt or executed, roasted or boiled.

* * *

Although Munro's four main characters are fully made, fully believable inhabitants of her 1951 Huron County, Ontario, their stories rework much older archetypes, in which the dismembered Grimm elements are brought to life again, reversed, and recombined. The two men, Mr. Willens and Rupert Quinn, are each a Bluebeard *and* a Bluebeard's victim. Rupert's dying wife, Mrs. Quinn, and her home nurse, Enid, are each a victim *and* a clever bride; Mrs. Quinn is also something of a female Bluebeard or Atwoodian Robber Bride.

We know Mr. D. M. Willens as a drowned victim before we know him as a Bluebeard character; the first two of the story's four sections only hint at his ladykill-

ing ways. A short, hairy, unattractive optometrist in small-town Walley, Mr. Willens is a minor sexual predator who roams the countryside making house calls; sometimes, Mrs. Willens tells the authorities, he gets "held up" overnight (30). The name Willens suggests *will ends, will lens, willing;* the full name, D. M. Willens, may be a rough anagram for *demon.* The D. may hint ironically and pathetically at a first name of David, which means beloved.

Our first glimpses of Mr. Willens come by way of the three young boys who in the spring of 1951, we are told omnisciently, find his body caught in his car in the river, like a muskrat drowned in a trap.[2] They see his arm in its "hairy" sleeve pushing up through the car's open roof panel like a "dark and furry . . . big animal tail" (6). That description, a bestial, phallic image, suggests the wolf's tail in children's storybook illustrations for "Little Red Riding Hood."[3] The boys "picture" the Mr. Willens they know as a "grotesque" brassy-haired, caterpillar-eyebrowed "cartoon character," short and thick, large of shoulder and head, who in death as in life seems "crammed into his little [foreign] car as if it was a bursting suit of clothes" (7, 6)—a sort of animal, troll, or cramped giant—or overgrown child. His marriage is childless; Mrs. Willens is a harsh-voiced, androgynously dressed, "lumpy little woman" and a renowned, generous, shear-carrying gardener, whose house-high forsythia seems like a vision of joyous fertility and sexuality from Katherine Mansfield or Virginia Woolf: "it sprayed yellow into the air the way a fountain shoots water" (23).[4]

Enid, the thirty-seven-year-old home nurse who, with her widowed mother, lives next door to the Willenses, knows Mr. Willens as a bridge partner who with "jokey gallantry," offers her chocolates or a pink rose "to make up for his own inadequacies as a partner" (50, 41). Munro's sexual pun is obvious; her subtler pun contrasts the limited romantic possibilities among the Bridges of Huron County with the idealized love affair between a lonely farmwife and a photographer in the American *The Bridges of Madison County.*[5] Whether the Willens marriage is sexless as well as childless, and whether Mrs. Willens knows about his tomcatting, we cannot know: separately and together, the Willenses keep up the appearance of vigorous and reasonably happy lives.

Not until the third section of Munro's story, when on 9 July 1951 the dying Mrs. Quinn tells her home nurse, Enid, what happened in her front room, can we clearly see Mr. Willens's death that spring as no accident, no hushed-up suicide, but a Bluebeard-imaged murder. In Mrs. Quinn's deathbed narrative, Mr. Willens becomes an electrified magic-wand version of Grimm's magic-touch wizard, peering into her eye through the hole in his battery-powered ophthalmoscope while he kneels like a clumsy, off-balance suitor to grope her bare leg.

And Mrs. Quinn, like a mesmerized victim bride, cannot stop him because she has "to concentrate on keeping still" (57). This house call (which may have been arranged by telephone) happens at a time when her husband "was supposed to be cutting wood down by the river" (57).

But, almost immediately in Mrs. Quinn's narrative, her groping ladykiller lover becomes a helpless victim, "down before he knew it," bashed to death in a Bluebeard killing chamber (57). Rupert, her husband, sneaks in on the two of them when Mr. Willens's hand was on her bare leg: Rupert jumps on the kneeling Mr. Willens from behind "like a bolt of lightning. . . . Rupert banged his head up and down on the floor, Rupert banged the life out of him" (57). Like the severed gold-ringed finger flying through the air in Grimm's "Robber Bridegroom," everything "flew out of" Mr. Willens's knocked-over box. When Mrs. Quinn turns Mr. Willens over, "to get him right side up," he is dead or near death; his eyes are neither open nor shut, and dribbly "pink stuff," like the froth on boiling-down strawberry jam, "com[es] out of his mouth" (57). Although there is no sign that Mrs. Quinn intends to kill the battered Mr. Willens, it is quite possible that he does literally drown when she turns him over: "he made a sound. . . . *Glug-glug* and he was laid out like a stone" (57-58).

The Willens-Quinn foreplay was "the same game every time" (62), Mrs. Quinn says; that she builds her tale to four Bluebeard-female romance climaxes of helpless female passivity and increasingly rapacious male lust—first Mr. Willens's groping, then his dead foot nudging, then his dribbly kissing, then his battering sexual attack—may echo the four-times repeated passive female disclaimers ("My darling, I only dreamt this" [204]) with which the Grimm storytelling bride exposes the evil Robber Bridegroom.[6] And, in a perverse echo of the Fitcher's bride who brought her dismembered sisters back to life, Mrs. Quinn's tale does bring her battered lover back to lustful, demon-lover life: even dead he was still a "horny old devil," with "his dead old foot" nudging her between the legs as she helps Rupert carry him out (59). Her description of their kissing sounds like an unaroused woman's—or child's—disgust with an impotent or incontinent lover—or with a wolf's or wolf-child's grabbing and devouring: he was a "dribbly," "dirty old brute," "[s]ucking and chewing away at her lips and her tongue and pushing himself up at her and the corner of the [dark red optometrist's] box sticking into her and digging her behind" (60). And each time Mrs. Quinn, "so surprised" and trapped, is helpless as Yeats's high-art Leda with the Swan (60). The symbolically dismembering climax of their Bluebeard coupling was supposed to happen after he'd got "his fingers slicked" inside her and packed up his "looker thing" and she'd asked how much she owed for today? "And that was the signal for him to get her down

and thump her like an old billy goat . . . to knock her up and down [on the bare floor] and try to bash her into pieces. Dingey on him like a blowtorch" (62).

Mrs. Quinn's tale, then, like that of her precursor Annie Herron in **"A Wilderness Station,"** is a recognizable but radical transformation of the Grimm Bluebeard tales: Munro's triangle involves one woman and two men, rather than one man and what are essentially two women, the victim and the clever hero; and Munro's essential roles are divided, doubled, shared. Each of the three characters in Mrs. Quinn's killing chamber is some kind of killer and some kind of victim, is basher and bashed and, with genders transcended, some kind of Bluebeard and dismembered or clever maiden. Rupert, after "bang[ing] the life out of" Mr. Willens, goes to pieces mentally (57). Shocked and incoherent, he puts Mrs. Quinn's knocked-over chair right side up, then just sits there; then jumps up, and tries to fit "everything in right" in Mr. Willens's knocked-over red-plush-lined optometrist's box (58). Acting like the hapless Fitcher's brides who cannot wash the red blood from their eggs, and also like the clever bride who puts their dismembered parts in order, Rupert puts things right, and yet cannot put things right. Like a thwarted, overgrown child, he sits bashing himself, "pounding on his knees" and "banging his big flat hands" (58).

It is Mrs. Quinn who, like the clever bride healing her sisters, or the practical Lady Macbeth standing by her man, puts the incoherent killer back together—once she sees that he is not going to attack her. Munro has indicated that what fascinated her in the true murder story that stands behind **"Love"** is the "sudden switch from sex to murder to marital cooperation . . . one of those marvelous, unlikely, acrobatic pieces of human behavior" ("Contributors'" 443). If we read again slowly, and go beneath the overriding rhythms of Mrs. Quinn's salacious murder tale, we can see how the "sudden switch" begins nonverbally, in what child psychologists call parallel play: he jumps on Mr. Willens, she jumps up from the chair, knocking it over. He sets the chair right side up, she gets Mr. Willens "right side up" (a position which may finish what her husband started in killing Mr. Willens) (57).[7] Rupert then sits in the chair where his wife had sat, jumps up as she did, sits again, and pounds himself. Then, trying to spare them both, she covers up Mr. Willens's bloodied head with a tablecloth.

Soon the couple switch into step-by-step, verbal, complementary cooperation: she says to bury him and suggests where, he asks where can they bury his car; she "thought of him sitting in his car" in the river, he "thought up the rest of what to do" (58-59). She gets the keys to the car from the still-warm body and gives them to Rupert; together they carry out the body. Then, honoring the traditional female-indoors and male-outdoors division of labor, she cleans up inside while he drives Mr. Willens's car and body to a nearby little-used road that dead-ends at the river, and pushes them in. Rupert walks back home and tells his wife he did the job in his sock feet, to avoid leaving identifiable tracks; she tells him he "must have got [his] brains going again" (61). Both husband and wife, however, are more shaken than they realize, for both leave the tell-tale dark-red, red-plush-lined box out in plain sight on the front room table, like the Grimm's telltale bloodied egg; Mrs. Quinn finally sees it, many days after the murder, and hides it, in one place and then another; she will not tell where.

Like a Fitcher's victim bride or a Lady Macbeth, Mrs. Quinn tries to erase the telltale blood stains: she scrubs her shoes and the stained floor of the front room and burns the bloodied cloth with which she had covered Mr. Willens's smeared face; she burns her own front-smeared blouse; she paints over the still-stained front-room floor with leftover ugly brown paint. Then, like the Grimm's victims and Lady Macbeth, she goes to pieces: it was the smells of the burning cloth and of the paint that began her fatal sickness, she tells Enid. But, as we can infer from an earlier section of Munro's story, it is more likely that Mrs. Quinn is dying of kidney failure because, as Rupert's nosey, righteous sister suspects, Mrs. Quinn took pills to abort a fetus—probably, as Dennis Duffy has argued, Mrs. Quinn thought the fetus was Willens's child (182).[8] This aborted fetus would be a literal equivalent of Grimm's dirtied, bloodied egg.

* * *

Part of the disturbing power of Mrs. Quinn's salacious Bluebeard murder story is that it is formed from, and brings to shocking life the Grimm and Gothic elements in what we already know from the second section of Munro's story. Rupert Quinn is a big, shy, hardworking farmer. About thirty-seven now, he apparently married late, and "never had any kind of girlfriend before" he met a pretty, fair-haired, green-eyed girl who said she was an orphan from Montreal (33). Rupert was then working alone in the bush up north, and she was working as a chambermaid or something in a hotel, Rupert's sister tells Enid. As a young schoolboy, Rupert had been romantically "teased and tormented" by Enid and her girlfriends, who mocked his name to make him blush (33); later, as bright, studious seniors, Enid and Rupert had formed a shy, tenuous friendship. The name Rupert suggests both *rube* and the seventeenth-century hero/exile Prince Rupert, nephew to Charles of England and third son of an exiled Bohemian king, who became a Royalist cavalry leader known for his fiery charges, a general, an exile, an admiral—and the first governor of the Hudson's Bay Company. Rupert now keeps some distance from his dying wife. Though he seems concerned he also seems wary, paying her brief, late visits;

he sleeps and eats at his sister's, who arranged this os-tensibly to spare Enid, and he has to work later and later in the fields to save the rain-threatened crops that have ripened weeks early in the summer's heat wave. Some evenings, while his dying, drugged wife sleeps in the front room, Rupert sits quietly with Enid in the kitchen, sharing the newspaper's headlines and cross-word puzzle, much as the two had shared schoolwork in their senior year. As Duffy points out, the two are already "cohabiting" like an "old married couple" (176-75).

Should Rupert be seen as a Bluebeard who brought a young orphan to his lonely farmhouse, then trapped her in the chambers of murder and abortion? And now, as she lies dying in the next room, quietly courts a re-placement bride? Shy, wary Rupert is subtly but repeatedly associated with woodsmanship, chopping, and hatchets—in the bush up north, supposedly chopping wood the morning of Mr. Willens's visit, volunteering to cut back the berry canes from the road. Is Rupert a bride-dismembering Bluebeard? Or a rescuing hunts-man who came out of the woods to save his Little Red Riding Hood, first from orphanhood and later from a "wolf," Willens? A Prince-in-exile, who would hack through the thorns of the "Sleeping Beauty" story that Enid reads his daughters, to bring love to a lonely or-phan or an unawakened, virginal nurse? For us and for Enid, the archetypes arouse possibilities of death and desire, making shy Rupert a demon lover and Gothic hero/villain who might, like Brontë's Mr. Rochester, be hero, or villain, or victim of a bad, mad wife.

Throughout Munro's story, what we are told of Rupert and Mrs. Quinn is limited to and colored by what Enid sees, hears, and thinks, as selected, arranged, and re-ported by Munro's Joycean omniscient-subjective nar-rator, who shows us only Enid's thoughts. What Enid knows of Mrs. Quinn begins with suspicion, and soon gets worse. A green-eyed, once-pretty young woman, the dying Mrs. Quinn claims to be twenty-seven, though Enid would have thought her older. Rupert's sister, the childless Mrs. Olive Green, who covets the Quinn chil-dren and who Enid sees as bent on "sniffing out ram-pant impurity" (38), doubts Mrs. Quinn's Montreal-orphanage story and says she wrecked her kidneys by taking pills "for a bad purpose"—that is, an abortion (32). We learn Mrs. Quinn's first name only after her death, when Enid notes that it is Jeannette, which sounds French-Canadian. Munro's story may seem merely to follow Enid's professional courtesy in refer-ring to her patient as Mrs. Quinn; but the surname pairs Mrs. Quinn and Mr. Willens as unknowable, death-bound, corrupt Gothic elders, in opposition to the younger-seeming, nascent couple, Enid and Rupert. This effect must be deliberate, as it takes some maneuvering to have Rupert never once use his wife's name.

In this story called **"The Love of a Good Woman,"** the good nurse Enid sees Mrs. Quinn as a disturbingly bad and unloving woman. Poisoned and deformed by the wastes of her own body, suffering pain and torment, scarcely able to eat or drink or keep warm, often unable to bear light or sound, Mrs. Quinn resents her husband, her children, and Enid. She mocks Rupert's brief, late visits, complaining to Enid that he, Enid, and everyone think her better dead, and that he goes to other women after seeing her. When Enid says that as far as she knows, Rupert goes to his sister's house after his visit, Mrs. Quinn throws the words back at her: "'As far as you know. But you don't know much'" (36). She seems to Enid to be "without shame" in her vulgar sexual talk and in opening her legs to be washed (35). She doesn't want to see her seven- and six-year-old daughters, whom she has raised "wild as little barn cats," without manners or prayers (34). Her housekeeping is filthy and without order. She rejects Enid's offer of a minister or priest—"'Do I look like a Mick?'" with a slur that calls to mind Rupert's and his sister's round, snub-nosed, "'potato-Irish'" faces (54, 32). When Rupert comes early to visit his wife, because he will be away for two days at a stock auction, with the doctor's approval, eavesdropping Enid hears "Mrs. Quinn weakly laughing," and hears—or mishears—a vileness in that laughing, and then sees a shocked-looking Rupert come out of her room (56).

Enid, the thirty-seven-year-old home nurse who was Rupert's classmate, finds herself losing a contest of wills with this "doomed, miserable young woman" who seems filled with "spite and venom" (38, 36). Enid has been a compassionate, dedicated, hardworking, self-sacrificing home nurse for sixteen years, since she was twenty-one; she chose this calling as a way "to be good, and do good," but "not necessarily in the orderly, customary, wifely way" (41)—and to honor her father's dying wish that she foreswear hospital work, which he thought would be sexually coarsening. Celibate, or perhaps androgynous, Enid is known among patients and doctors as an "angel of mercy" (52), a gentle, generous female healer who spends most of her earnings on needy patients' children. Her name, Enid, is almost an anagram of *deny*; her namesake, "Enid the Good" in Tennyson's *Idylls of the King* (Book 4, line 963), is an exemplary long-suffering good woman whose love redeems her unjust and cruelly mistrustful husband.[9]

Against Mrs. Quinn's vulgar sexuality, her bitter mockery, her repudiations of conventional comfort, Enid feels her goodness and vocation fail. Reproaching herself, but increasingly unable to "conquer her dislike of this doomed, miserable young woman," Enid sees "a willed corruption" in Mrs. Quinn's diseased body, sees its nipples as "malignant-looking" and its teeth as "pathetic [and] ferretlike" (38). Worse still, Enid senses that Mrs. Quinn knows her revulsion, and "made know-

ing it her triumph" (39). Though naïve, repressed Enid consciously "didn't know why this was happening" (38), her shocked revulsion involves not only righteousness and prudery, but also sexual rivalry with Mrs. Quinn—as Munro's puns and juxtapositions make clear. Enid offers Rupert capable fuse-changing and calm candlelight against Mrs. Quinn's darkened room and weak, shocking laughter; mannerly Christian mothering of his children and orderly housekeeping against neglect, disorder, and filth; companionably shared crossword puzzles against cross, mocking words. The scene where Rupert gives Enid crossword clues of exotic foods—"'Manioc?'" "'Cassava?'" is immediately juxtaposed with Enid seeing Mrs. Quinn as "more capricious daily about her food," because the dying woman asks for but cannot eat simple foods when Enid has prepared them (48-49).

Beneath Mrs. Quinn's sufferings and mockery, and Enid's revulsion, are the Grimm Bluebeard patterns of a young orphan carried off by an older, foreign man to a lonely farmhouse where, her egg bloodied by a second man who is an ophthalmoscope-wielding wizard, she sickens and lies dying. Friendless and luckless as the substitute victim-bride in Grimm's "Robber Bridegroom," Mrs. Quinn is not healed by any stronger sister: instead, her husband's sister, like a bad Queen Mother, snoops around, keeps the Prince at her house, and plots to carry off the children; while Enid the good healer and Sleeping Beauty/self-imprisoned Rapunzel becomes a Grimm True Bride bent on reclaiming her first, tenuous bond with Rupert, and ministers to the dying first, False Bride with increasing hostility.[10]

Underneath the Grimm True Bride/False Bride struggle, and the Jane Eyre female Gothic mad wife story is, of course, an Electral story: a primal triangle of a good, strong daughter supplanting a bad, worn-out mother, and claiming the father for herself. Enid may be older than Mrs. Quinn, but Enid is fresh, full-breasted, virginal, and childlike; Mrs. Quinn is diseased and finished, her abdomen "swollen," her breasts shrunk to "malignant-looking," "dried-currant nipples" (35, 38). Under the Grimm and Gothic stories there is also, here and elsewhere in Munro, the story of a daughter's anger, fear, and desertion of a sick, pregnant, or dying mother: see especially the autobiographical **"The Peace of Utrecht,"** with the sisters' guilty rejection and resentment of "Our Gothic Mother" dying in a back room (200); and **"Images,"** the early Bluebeard story that is the first sketch and germinal core of **"Love"**'s essential Grimm and Gothic elements.

Sleeping on a couch in her patient's room, hearing Mrs. Quinn's "harsh and angry breathing," Enid wakes from shameful dreams of herself "trying to copulate with utterly forbidden and unthinkable partners"—babies, bandaged patients, "her own mother" (50-51). These dreams are obscene versions of Enid's daylit life where, honoring her father's deathbed wish, she meets only such partners: she washes Mrs. Quinn's exposed genitals, "do[es] without a man," and "tak[es] her father's place" in bridge games with her widowed mother and the Willenses (34, 41). In these dreams Enid's life is both corrupted and awakened by Mrs. Quinn's shameless, vulgar sexuality—and by Enid's own consciously denied attraction to Rupert. Afraid to sleep, Enid tries reason and religion, but her "hopeful and sensible" Protestant faith gives way to the cynical despair she hears from Mrs. Quinn: life's loveliness seems to lead to "[a]nimal horrors," and Enid's dedicated goodness seems despised foolishness (51-52). Seeking "to be penitent," Enid finds a female Protestant way; she gets up and works quietly "through the night," cleaning and restoring to order the filthy kitchen cupboards, trying to save the neglected "good house" (52-53).

In these dreams, as in the parts of Mrs. Quinn's subsequent Bluebeard story that cunningly amplify Enid's own thoughts of the shocked Rupert and the gallant Mr. Willens, the dying woman's sexuality, anger, and despair invade Enid's conscious and unconscious mind; as Coral Ann Howells says, Mrs. Quinn "becomes Enid's dark mirror" (152). It is as if the two women were secret sharers—or as if Jane Eyre were made the sister's keeper of Sandra M. Gilbert and Susan Gubar's Madwoman in the Attic, forced to sleep in her chamber, dream her vileness, wake to her despair. Or as if Mrs. Quinn were a trapped, amateur version of Margaret Atwood's Grimm-based Robber Bride, a malicious storyteller who preys on lonely, repressed good women, evoking their sexual and forbidden shadow sides; and Enid a professional version of Atwood's gentle would-be healer, Charis.[11]

* * *

The fourth and final section of Munro's story shows us, in evocative and tantalizingly cryptic flashes of illumination, the Grimm, Gothic, and Bible-imaged crises through which Enid passes in the three sleepless nights and days after she hears Mrs. Quinn's shocking Bluebeard story—interior crises, known only to Enid and us, that determine the course of her and Rupert's lives, love, and salvation.[12] Troubled and unsure after the first sleepless night, Enid, in a scene that replays Rochester's resolution scene in *Jane Eyre*,[13] goes out into the "[s]opping wet" meadow and along a "clear" path to see the mist-hidden river, where a tied-up rowboat that the current "lifted and let fall" seems to tell her "something gentle and final. *You know. You know*" (63-64). What Enid knows is "What had happened"—but did it happen?—and "What to do about it" (63)—but are these statements clues, or further mysteries? How can we know?

Secretly resolved, Enid sets to work like a Grimm's True Bride supplanting a ugly, luckless False Bride: knowing Mrs. Quinn will die after that "last" "wicked outpouring," Enid in "bountiful good spirits" lets her own "hair loose," suns her bare legs, and makes for the children special treats and memorable "holiday" games. While Mrs. Quinn's shrunken kidneys fail, Enid the good fairy godmother shows the children how to make, from bent-wire "bubble-wands" and soapsuds, "as large a shining bladder as possible." When the children scream with joy as they chase the shining bubbles, nurse Enid, who knows their mother's sensitivity to noise, "put[s] no restriction on the[ir] noise." Wanting the children to see the outcome of her plan, and "herself," "in a redeeming light"—but deciding that "nothing good" can come of their seeing their mother—Enid teaches them that you must always tell and "'be punished'" if you do a very bad thing, even if nobody knows, because if "'you are not punished you feel worse'" (64-66).

Insofar as she deems proper, Enid abandons her patient, "never sp[eaking] to her and never touch[ing] her hand, except with the cloth" (66).[14] Mrs. Quinn dies alone, her head "hanging over the side of the bed"; Enid gets "the body straightened out . . . and the bed put to rights before the doctor" comes (67). Like her partner the drowned Mr. Willens, whose furry and hairy-looking arm "got free" of the car (7), Mrs. Quinn has gone beyond propriety in death as in life: and Enid believes in putting things right.

Two days later Enid, resolved like Jane Eyre on Christian romantic sacrifice ("'your heart shall be the victim; and you, the priest, to transfix it'"), and rapt like Saul in a blinding vision followed by three sleepless, fasting days, returns to Rupert (Brontë 341; Acts 9:3-9). The funeral is over, Rupert's childless sister has taken the children away, and Rupert comes to the door with the "heavy, steady footsteps" of an unreadable hero/villain (69). Suddenly awkward, Enid twice avoids "look[ing] into his face"; he seems "bewilder[ed]" by her visit (69-70) until she takes refuge in talking about the shortening days. Enid has transformed herself—powdered her face, French-braided her hair, and dressed in what might be "the last clothes she would ever wear" (70), dark green silk and matching green suede shoes. Green suggests her naïveté and her fertility, in contrast to Mrs. Quinn's diseased browns and blood-smeared reds; but green also links Enid to Rupert's other women—his green-eyed wife, his sister Mrs. Green.

Seated at the table across from Rupert, facing Mrs. Quinn's shut door, Enid almost forgets her secret mission. Enid has planned—we learn only now—to risk her life to redeem Rupert: she will get him to row her out in the river, ostensibly so she can get a picture of the willows; then tell him she cannot swim, which is true; then ask him if Mrs. Quinn's story is true. If Rupert does not deny the story, or drown her, as he could easily do, Enid will guide him, "one step at a time," on the long journey of confession and jail, trial and punishment, with a pure, sexless, selfless "devotion . . . that is like love but beyond love" (73). Is naïve, reckless, devoted Enid bound for redemption or death?[15]

Now, when she asks to be rowed out, Rupert says "'All right.'" But Enid, distracted by Rupert's treating her as country people treat a visitor, "foolish[ly]" asks a housewife's question—have the quilts been taken down from the front windows? (73). Rupert offers to show her the room: "'It's all right,'" Rupert says, "'Come in'" (73). The room is empty of bed and coffin; the table that may have held Mr. Willens's dark-red box, that did hold Enid's supplies, holds only flowers now; the tall windows are filled with light.

Rupert is silent; but Enid hears, "out of all the words that Mrs. Quinn said in that room," the word *Lies*; and Enid asks herself whether such a "detailed and diabolical" story could have been made up (74). Remembering her own filthy, elaborate dreams in that haunted chamber, Enid answers, "yes" (74). Then Rupert, the front room, *lies* and dreams call up the childhood memory that will change Enid's life in an inner drama that Carrington calls "the story's central act of moral acrobatics," more central than the Quinns' switch from sex and murder to cooperation (168).

Once, when Enid was four or five, so young that she did not know the word for breasts, and called them fronts, Enid saw her father "behind his desk with a woman on his knee," her clothing unbuttoned, the tip of her bare breast "disappearing into Enid's father's mouth." Enid told her mother that "'One of her fronts was stuck in Daddy's mouth. . . . Like an ice-cream cone.'" The grown-up Enid can still see what she saw as a child, the "mound of vanilla ice cream squashed against the woman's chest and the wrong end sticking into her father's mouth." Enid's mother had pulled out her own dull, floppy breast to persuade Enid that it was all a silly dream, too silly to tell Daddy; and Enid as a child came to believe her mother, because ice-cream cones "were never so big" (74-75).

Now the scales fall from Enid's eyes, as they did from Saul's (Acts 9:18), and she sees clearly that the remembered scene is no childish dream, but a shocking truth: her father was toying with a woman, was nursing for sexual pleasure in an adulterous dalliance. Celibate, self-sacrificing Enid, with her "big udders," has nursed home patients instead of ever nursing a baby with her milk, or nursing a man for pleasure (36). But now it is as if a fairy-tale curse had been lifted, and Enid is freed, by seeing clearly her father's sexual coarseness and her mother's silencing complicity, from the "deathbed

promise" her father had exacted: Enid had given up her almost-completed nurse's training, and the hospital career and wider life that would have followed, because her father thought that "the familiarity [hospital] nurses had with men's bodies" would make a woman sexually "coarse" (40, 39).

Freed also from her mother-judging pride and her reliance on good works alone, the self-denying "angel of mercy" Enid opens her heart to a Joycean, human charity (52; cf. 1 Corinthians 13, Tindall 32) as she sees clearly now "an entirely different possibility" for her life: if she keeps silent about the murder, if she "collaborat[es] in a silence," what benefits could bloom. For others, and for herself" (75-76). The protagonist of Joyce's "A Painful Case," reseeing his life, saw too late that "venal and furtive loves" were love, and that his solitary righteous life made him an "outcast from life's feast" (*Dubliners* 146). But Enid sees in time to recant, inwardly, the "melodramatic fate" in which she had been inwardly "glorying" (76, 75).[16] She weeps with relief, and thinks she sees that Rupert too has wept.

"'I don't know what I was thinking of,'" she tells Rupert; "'I can't walk down to the river in these shoes'" (76). Rupert, reenacting the Cinderella shoe-test, finds in an old storage bin a pair of discarded boots for Enid to wear—not Mrs. Quinn's, which would be too small for Enid's big feet. When Rupert sets the boots before her, the freed Enid is aroused by his smell, and welcomes "something new and invasive about the smell of a body so distinctly not in her power or under her care" (77). But Enid, like the Grimm and Perrault Bluebeard brides and Jane Eyre, is also powerfully aroused by the prospect of hidden chambers: Rupert's neglected house "would have plenty of bins, drawers, shelves, suitcases, trunks, crawl spaces full of things that it would be up to Enid to sort out," to save and label, restore or send to the dump (77). Enid has taken Mrs. Quinn's bait: if there is a hidden, dark-red chamber in some hidden chamber, Enid will find it. Like a victorious True Bride or a Fitcher's Bride ("'From cellar to garret she's swept all clean'"), Enid will make this house into her realm, "a place that had no secrets from her and where all order was as she had decreed" (Grimm 219, **"Love"** 77).

"'See can you walk,'" says Rupert, and Enid can. Walking in what may be his boyhood boots, Enid follows Rupert into the cows' meadow as he chops at "the big fleshy thistles" with his hatchet, "to clear their path" (77). Sleeping Beauty/Rapunzel/Little Red Riding Hood Enid, compelled now by a vision of a different, secretly collaborative redemption, thinks that her earlier despair "had to seem childish to her now" (77). But is hero/villain Rupert the rescuing woodsman-Prince, and the agrarian Adam to this secretly knowing Eve—or the dangerous "bolt of lightning" killer (57) of his wife's Bluebeard story?

Following Rupert and his hatchet, Enid moves through clear, sunlit air and through clouds of bugs "no bigger than specks of dust . . . yet . . . together in the shape of a pillar or a cloud," as if she were moving towards a divinely Promised Land (78; Exodus 13.21). The "almost night" of the path under trees holds wild, post-Edenic, Darwinian obstacles of swelling roots and dangling vines; but opens into the "flash of water," "the trees still decked with light," and the oracular rowboat she had seen before, that holds her fate, still "riding in the shadows, just the same" (78).

Enid soon loses sight and sound of Rupert when he goes into the willow bushes to find the hidden oars. Alone, Enid goes "to the water's edge, where her boots sank into the mud a little and held her" (78)—compare Jane Eyre who, after discovering Rochester's secret lies, despaired: "'the waters came into my soul; I sank in deep mire; I felt no standing'" (340; Psalm 69, 1-2). Enid is about to submit herself to Conrad's "'destructive element,'" but she cannot rely on "'the exertions of [her] hands and feet'" to make the depths keep her up (*Lord Jim* 214)—she cannot swim. In the story's final lines, Enid can still hear Rupert if she tries, but like the bride-to-be at the end of Joyce's "Boarding House," Enid is at the fateful moment more tempted by reverie than reality: if she concentrates on the boat's "slight and secretive motion, she [can] feel as if everything for a long way around had gone quiet" (*Dubliners* 84; **"Love"** 78). Rupert remains hidden and unknown, to Enid and to us; and inwardly questing Enid has slipped once more into a secret vision that opens her to love, or to death.

*   *   *

We can know what happened in the murder chamber and thereafter only by returning to the prologue and considering the dark-red optometrist's box of Mr. D. M. Willens, that "escaped the catastrophe" of his 1951 drowning, and was found and anonymously dispatched to the local historical museum in Walley, which opened "a couple of decades" ago, in the 1970s (3). That the optometrist's dark-red box "escaped the catastrophe" surely means that it escaped undamaged—not battered, not stained, not water-marked or muddied as it would have been if it had gone into the river with Mr. Willens and his car in the spring of 1951.[17] "For the last couple of decades" the dark-red box has been a silent witness, like the severed finger or the bloodied egg of the Grimm Bluebeard tales, to the truth of Mrs. Quinn's story.

Enid did survive to marry Rupert, then, and to search in all his hidden chambers till she found the dark-red telltale box where Mrs. Quinn had hid it. (And, let's face it, being married to shy, "withholding" Rupert would be much enlivened by the dangerous mystery of his Bluebeard, hero/villain past [32].) Then, like the first Mrs.

Quinn, Enid neither threw the dark-red box into the river nor sent it to the dump: she kept it, "sav[ed] and labell[ed]" as she "decreed" (77). Perhaps Enid waited until Rupert died; perhaps until Mrs. Willens died. Or perhaps she waited only until there was a right place to put the saved red box—in the new museum in Walley.

Notes

An earlier version of this paper was presented at the ACSUS convention, Pittsburgh, PA, 17-21 November 1999.

1. I am indebted to Ildikó de Papp Carrington's authoritative explication of Munro's intensities, allusions, metaphors, "documentary realism," splits and "seismic shifts," in the 1989 *Controlling the Uncontrollable,* quoted page 4. For walleye, see Carrington, "Double-Talking" 78-79, 87.

2. Just before they find Mr. Willens, Cece Ferns and the two other boys talk of trapping muskrats; when they peer hard to see Mr. Willens's pale, drowned hand riding "tremulously and irresolutely, like a feather" in the water (7), that image reworks what the child narrator of Munro's early Bluebeard story, "Images," saw when she peered hard at the drowned muskrat "waving at the edge of the water, like . . . a dark fern" in her father's trap (36). Thus, *sees fern* becomes *Cece Ferns.*

In character, setting, archetypal images, and themes, Munro's 1968 story "Images" is prototype for the 1996 "The Love of a Good Woman." The child narrator of "Images," who learns in flashes something of the adult mysteries of birth and death, sex and violence, who treasures the electrifying thrill of a longed-for Bluebeard terror coming true, and then kept secret, prefigures the childlike home nurse who is the protagonist of "Love," Enid, as well as the three boys hesitating between childhood and adulthood. The vulgar, bossy home nurse of "Images" prefigures both the foul-mouthed Mrs. Quinn and the take-charge nurse Enid. The bedridden, unwelcoming, pregnancy-swollen mother of "Images," and the grandfather who lies dying in the dark and stifling-hot front room while she awaits the birth, prefigure the swollen, dying Mrs. Quinn in her dark, hot, blood-haunted front room. Both the muskrat-killing, secret-keeping father, and the semi-crazed man with the hatchet who comes through the riverbank bushes towards him, prefigure the wary, withholding, hatchet-bearing Rupert. In addition, James Joyce's story from *Dubliners,* "An Encounter," where young boys encounter adult lust and brutality, stands behind Munro's "Images" and is reworked in the boys' section of "Love"; but Munro, unlike Joyce, uses Bluebeard themes in both stories. J. R. (Tim) Struthers and Walter Martin have each discussed Munro's connections to Joyce.

3. See, for example, the wolf of Little Red Riding Hood, whose furry tail protrudes from his human clothes, in Zipes 248-49, 252-53, illustrations by Walter Crane 1870, unknown n.d., John B. Gruelle 1914, and for Encyclopedia Britannica Films, Inc. 1968; the 1870 Crane wolf is reproduced as the cover of the Opies's *Classic Fairy Tales.* In the Grimm's "Little Red-Cap," after the familiar story where the girl and her grandmother are saved from the wolf's belly by the huntsman, and the wolf dies with stones in his belly, there is another, shorter version, where grandmother and granddaughter cooperate to trick a second greedy wolf into falling into the grandmother's great trough, where he, like Mr. Willens, "was drowned" (143).

4. The tall, quivering, blossoming pear tree in Katherine Mansfield's 1918 "Bliss" helps awaken a childlike young woman to her own bisexual desires. Mrs. Ramsay, in Virginia Woolf's 1927 *To the Lighthouse,* "pour[s] erect into the air a rain of energy, a column of spray [. . . that is a male-nourishing, deliciously fecund] fountain and spray of life" (58); see Annis Pratt's explication of Mrs. Ramsay's nurturing, androgynous eroticism, 144-46. Munro's story is also about awakening sexuality, in the boys, Rupert, and her protagonist Enid; Enid's awakening and shameful, lustful dreams will be in part androgynous.

5. In "Save the Reaper," which is the fourth story in Munro's *Love of a Good Woman,* the temporarily reunited mother and daughter watch a videotape of *The Bridges of Madison County*; its simpler true-love story contrasts with their divided and unfulfilled yearnings (149).

6. Carrington, however, finds Mrs. Quinn's narrative unreliable, because her passivity is unconvincing and because Mr. Willens's lust changes and gets worse in each of the four times Mrs. Quinn tells it ("'Don't Tell'" 165). I agree that Mrs. Quinn is boasting to the naïve Enid, but I find that Mrs. Quinn's passive disclaimers and four increasingly salacious climaxes serve her storytelling purposes—to increase the shock, thrill, and horror.

7. In Munro's 1996 *New Yorker* story, Rupert "set the chair right side up" (130); in Munro's 1998 book version, Rupert "set the chair up" (57).

8. Mrs. Quinn's taking abortifacient pills, as Rupert's hostile sister suspects, is the only sufficient cause of her fatal illness mentioned in the story. The medically knowledgeable Enid avoids confirming the sister's suspicions, but does not contradict them. While it is true that the unmaternal Mrs. Quinn might not want more children, she would have a much stronger motive to abort a child fathered by the short, dark, hairy Mr. Willens, who looks quite unlike her tall, light-skinned husband.

9. Another namesake, Robert Thacker has suggested to me in conversation, is the sexually-repressed Enid Royce in Willa Cather's *One of Ours.* Thacker has discussed Munro's use of Cather's fiction.

10. For the Rapunzel syndrome, in which a woman imprisons herself in internalized walls, see Atwood's *Survival* 209-10. The best known of Grimm's True Bride versus False Bride tales is "Cinderella"; "The Robber Bridegroom" can also be read as a True versus False or substituted Bride. Grimm's less-known "Maid Maleen" is closest to Munro's story: there, after seven years in a Rapunzel tower, a loving maiden reclaims her curiously forgetful Prince from the ugly false bride in his bed. Grimm's "Brother and Sister," "The Three Little Men in the Wood," "The Goose-Girl," "The White Bride and the Black Bride," and "The True Bride" are also True versus False Bride tales.

11. Designed as a vampirish female equivalent of the Grimm cannibal robber bridegrooms, Atwood's modern Robber Bride, Zenia, is a con-artist predator who delights in wrecking the lives of good women, by gaining their trust and friendship, then stealing their goods and men. Like Atwood's Robber Bride, Mrs. Quinn is a foreigner of suspect, unverified origins, an openly sexual and defiant woman, and a gifted storyteller. Munro's sickroom struggle between Good Enid and Evil Mrs. Quinn strikingly reworks Atwood's duels between Zenia and the gentle Charis, who has repressed her abused, dangerous childhood self and renamed herself after 1 Corinthians 13.13, *charity* (*Robber Bride* 303). Charis tries and fails to heal the cynical, lying, supposedly dying Zenia; but false Zenia does awaken true Sleeping Beauty/Rapunzel Charis to orgasm and conception. Munro's story reverses Atwood's True Bride/mansealing False Bride romance to have the bad storyteller's man quietly drifting towards the good Sleeping Beauty. The creative and competitive metamorphoses between Munro's and Atwood's Muses go back decades, and at times involve Bluebeard elements (McCombs 1997, 1999).

12. As Robert Thacker has pointed out, Mrs. Quinn dies on Munro's birthday, 10 July (conversation). The autobiographical link would seem to be that Enid's rebirth, which involves her abandoning a diseased and dying mother, begins on that date (62-67).

13. Like Rochester walking in his "'dripping'" "'wet garden'" after a desperate night of his wife's maniac curses, gazing at blue water and "'clear prospects'" while the voice of Hope tells him he can leave his dishonorable wife, and have her cared for in secret, and be free to form a new tie (354), Enid in the wet meadow sees a "clear" path that, we later learn, parallels Rochester's: apparently the first wife's "wicked outpouring talk" justifies Enid secretly "absent[ing] herself," insofar as proper, from that wife's care, and seeking a new bond (63-64, 66).

14. In Munro's earlier "A Wilderness Station," the main character, Annie Herron, similarly withholds touch from her brutal, dead Bluebeard husband: as she washes his body she keeps "the rag between my hand and his skin" (208).

15. As Carrington points out, Enid's camera-boat-drowning scenario resembles the camera-drowning-murder scenario in Dreiser's 1925 *An American Tragedy* ("'Don't Tell'" 159-60, 166). A less similar drowning test of love, between two lovers who have murdered the wife's husband, occurs near the end of Tay Garnett's 1946 film, *The Postman Always Rings Twice*: there the widow persuades her lover to swim out with her to the point where she cannot get back without his help; proving his love, he helps her back. As Howells points out, *Postman* is a possible source of Mrs. Quinn's story (151-52). If Munro saw the film, she would have been quite interested in the lightning-like depiction of the short circuit that coincidentally strikes just as the adulterous, murder-minded wife hits her unsuspecting husband on the head.

16. Compare Jane Eyre's secret heroism as she confronts the dangerously angered Rochester: "I felt an inward power, a sense of resolution, which supported me. The crisis was perilous; but not without its charm: such as the Indian, perhaps, feels when he slips over the rapids in his canoe" (347).

17. Though I am indebted to Carrington's admirable explication of Enid's childhood memory, and much else, I cannot agree that Mr. Willens's box could have gone into the river and been washed up—or that Cece Ferns, whose hideaway cannot even keep cardboard safe over the winter, could have been hiding it there for years and years (see "Love" 3, 30; Carrington 168-69).

Works Cited

Atwood, Margaret. *The Robber Bride*. Toronto: McClelland and Stewart, 1993.

———. *Survival: A Thematic Guide to Canadian Literature*. Toronto: Anansi, 1972.

Bettelheim, Bruno. *The Uses of Enchantment: The Meaning and Importance of Fairy Tales*. New York: Vintage, 1977.

The Bridges of Madison County. Dir. Clint Eastwood. 1995.

Brontë, Charlotte. *Jane Eyre*. 1847. Ed. Michael Hulse. Köln, Ger.: Könemann, 1997.

Carrington, Ildikó de Papp. *Controlling the Uncontrollable: The Fiction of Alice Munro*. DeKalb: Northern Illinois University Press, 1989.

———. "'Don't Tell (on) Daddy': Narrative Complexity in Alice Munro's 'The Love of a Good Woman.'" *Studies in Short Fiction* 34 (1997): 159-70.

———. "Double-Talking Devils: Alice Munro's 'A Wilderness Station.'" *Essays on Canadian Writing* 58 (1996): 71-92.

The Complete Grimm's Fairy Tales. Trans. Margaret Hunt; rev. James Stern. New York: Pantheon, 1944.

Conrad, Joseph. *Lord Jim*. 1900. Ed. John Batchelor. Oxford: Oxford University Press, 1983.

———. "The Secret Sharer." 1912. *The Portable Conrad*. Ed. Morton Dauwen Zabel. New York: Viking, 1947. 648-99.

Dreiser, Theodore. *An American Tragedy*. 1925. New York: Signet, 1964.

Duffy, Dennis. "'A Dark Sort of Mirror': 'The Love of a Good Woman' as Pauline Poetic." *The Rest of the Story: Critical Essays on Alice Munro*. Ed. Robert Thacker. Toronto: ECW, 1999. 169-90.

Gilbert, Sandra M., and Susan Gubar. *The Madwoman in the Attic: The Woman Writer and the Nineteenth-Century Literary Imagination*. New Haven: Yale University Press, 1979.

Holy Bible. King James Version. Cleveland: World Publishing, 1945.

Howells, Coral Ann. *Alice Munro*. Manchester, England: Manchester University Press, 1998.

Joyce, James. *Dubliners*. 1914. New York: Modern Library, 1926.

Mansfield, Katherine. "Bliss." 1918. *The Short Stories of Katherine Mansfield*. 1937. New York: Knopf, 1961. 337-50.

McCombs, Judith. "'From Listening to the Stories of Others, We Learn to Tell Our Own': Southern Ontario Gothic in Alice Munro's 'Wilderness Station' and [Margaret Atwood's] *Alias Grace*." *Margaret Atwood Society Newsletter* 22-23 (Fall/Winter 1999): 32-33.

————. "Munro's and Atwood's Bloody Chambers: Epistolary Structure, Storytelling, Grace Notes and Grimm Archetypes in 'A Wilderness Station' and *Alias Grace.*" Paper presented at the biennial meeting of the Association for Canadian Studies in the United States, Minneapolis, MN, 22 November 1997.

Munro, Alice. Contributors' Notes. *Prize Stories 1997: The O. Henry Awards.* Ed. Larry Dark. New York: Anchor, 1997. 442-43.

————. "Images." *Dance of the Happy Shades and Other Stories.* Harmondsworth, Middlesex, England: Penguin, 1968. 30-43.

————. Introduction to the Vintage Edition. *Selected Stories.* By Munro. 1996. New York: Vintage, 1997. xiii-xxi.

————. *Lives of Girls and Women.* 1971. New York: Signet, 1974.

————. "The Love of a Good Woman." *The Love of a Good Woman.* New York: Knopf, 1998. 3-78.

————. "The Love of a Good Woman." *New Yorker* (23 and 30 December 1996): 102+.

————. "The Peace of Utrecht." *Dance of the Happy Shades and Other Stories.* Harmondsworth, Middlesex, England: Penguin, 1968. 190-210.

————. "Save the Reaper." *The Love of a Good Woman.* New York: Knopf, 1998. 146-80.

————. "A Wilderness Station." 1992. *Open Secrets.* Toronto: McClelland and Stewart, 1994. 190-225.

Opie, Iona and Peter. *The Classic Fairy Tales.* New York: Oxford University Press, 1974.

Perrault, Charles. "Bluebeard." ["La Barbe bleüe." 1697.] Trans. Robert Samber. 1729. *The Classic Fairy Tales.* Iona and Peter Opie. New York: Oxford University Press, 1974. 133-41.

The Postman Always Rings Twice. Dir. Tay Garnett. 1946.

Pratt, Annis. *Archetypal Patterns in Women's Fiction.* Bloomington: Indiana University Press, 1981.

Tennyson, Alfred Lord. *Idylls of the King.* 1859-72, 1885. *The Poems and Plays of Alfred, Lord Tennyson.* New York: Modern Library 1938. 433-664.

Thacker, Robert. "Alice Munro's Willa Cather." *Canadian Literature* 134 (1992): 42-57.

————. Conversation with author, Pittsburgh, PA, 18 November 1999.

"The Three Little Pigs." *The Green Fairy Book.* Circa 1892. Ed. Andrew Lang. New York: Dover, 1965. 100-05.

"The Three Little Pigs." *The Three Little Pigs and Other Favorite Nursery Stories.* Cambridge, MA: Candlewick, 1991. 82-93.

Tindall, William York. *A Reader's Guide to James Joyce.* New York: Noonday, 1959.

Wilson, Sharon Rose. *Margaret Atwood's Fairy-Tale Sexual Politics.* Jackson: University Press of Mississippi, 1993.

Woolf, Virginia. *To the Lighthouse.* New York: Harcourt, Brace, 1927.

Yeats, W. B. "Leda and the Swan." *The Collected Poems of W. B. Yeats.* New York: Macmillan, 1959. 211-12.

Zipes, Jack. "A Second Gaze at Little Red Riding Hood's Trials and Tribulations." *Don't Bet on the Prince: Contemporary Feminist Fairy Tales in North America and England.* 1987. Ed. Zipes. New York: Routledge, 1989. 227-60.

Héliane Ventura (essay date spring 2002)

SOURCE: Ventura, Héliane. "The Ordinary as Subterfuge: Alice Munro's 'Pictures of the Ice.'" *Journal of the Short Story in English,* no. 38 (spring 2002): 73-85.

[*In the following essay, Ventura evaluates "Pictures of the Ice" according to philosopher and critic Louis Marin's theories of deception and entrapment.*]

In his essay entitled «Le récit est un piège» («The tale is a trap») Louis Marin relies on the supposed evidence of a XVI century Venetian treatise on the composition and use of traps to distinguish between three types of entrapment. Through fantasy, through appetite, and through strength which he envisages respectively as the traps of the imagination, of need, and of movement, in French fables and histories of the XVII century, I use the theoretical framework proposed by Louis Marin, after Gian Battista de Contugi, to examine a story by Alice Munro from her 1990 collection *Friend of my Youth.* This story ["**Pictures of the Ice**"] is remarkable for its use of devices linked with deception and as such is emblematic of the work of this most Machiavellian of writers.

* * *

As often in a Munro story, one is confronted with two story lines which are partly an extension and partly a reflection of each other. The main story line apparently concerns Austin Cobbett, a retired minister who engineers a fake scenario to indulge his passion for self-sacrifice in secret. Austin tells his grown-up children and the community he has lived in for many years that he is about to get married again to a rich widow in Hawaii and live the well-earned leisurely existence of a contented pensioner, walking the sandy beach of an earthly, and mundane, paradise. Because this choice is out of character, the former minister takes great pains to establish the veracity of his tale, buying summer clothes, joking with the bank clerks, and showing likely photographs as material evidence. In reality, he is covering up for the fact that he is about to be hired as a minister for a godforsaken community in Northern Ontario, where he will live in a trailer, in sub-zero temperatures, dedicate himself to thankless people, and (as it turns out) get drowned in a treacherous lake.

The subsidiary story line, or what appears to be such, concerns his housekeeper, Karin Duprey, whose life is shadowed by a traumatic event the nature of which we only discover in the last pages: her baby died of meningitis during a winter storm when the road to the hospital was blocked. She is the only one to discover Austin's subterfuge and she equally indulges in deceptions of her own. Like the minister, she is about to embark on a new life, far from her original community, although her plans are only hinted at and not disclosed in the narrative.

Related to both story lines we find the character of Brent Duprey, Karin's former husband and Austin's former protégé. Brent is rescued from drunkenness by Austin. He becomes a hard-line teetotaller, makes final demands on Karin before separating from her, and eventually dispossesses Austin of the temperance house he had created in order to take full control of the renamed establishment.

The story could be regarded as an ordinary tale of human betrayal and deception except that it embeds treacherousness in such a way as to transform subterfuge into selflessness and ordinariness into transcendence. Such is the art of entrapment, says Louis Marin, that it relies on ordinariness:

> This is what is strange. It is not because this type of writing is ordinary that it is not strange. This is what the art of entrapment relies on: the ordinary. This is what, as a consequence, the art of deconstructing artifice must rely on: locating the strange in the ordinary.
>
> (Marin 75; my translation)

Louis Marin establishes a protocol for reading the story: no matter how ordinary the writing pretends to be, it is ciphered and requires to be treated like a cryptogram. Consider the opening paragraph of the story:

> Three weeks before he died—drowned in a boating accident in a lake whose name nobody had heard him mention—Austin Cobbett stood deep in the clasp of a three way mirror in Crawford's Men's Wear in Logan, looking at himself in a burgundy sports shirt and a pair of cream, brown, and burgundy plaid pants. Both permanent press.
>
> (Munro 137)

The painstaking attention to the different items of clothing worn by the main character, whose death is announced before the relation of his life has begun, immediately strikes a discordant note which hardly conceals the shafts of wit which surround the description or lie in the blanks, one of which being the suppressed name of the obscure lake: Shaft Lake, which also refers to Austin's «shafting» the community. The allusion to permanence with regard to the shirt and pants appears as an instance of ironic displacement which, «under cover» of ordinariness, metonymically points in the direction of the minister's lifelong commitment. It is also a profoundly ironic detail, particularly ill-fitted for a man who dedicated his life to the reformation of sinners and maintained his hope in the possibility of change by creating a house called «Turn-around House», not to mention the choice of colour for the shirt and the pants, extremely ironic for a man who encouraged abstinence from alcohol. The minister's reflection «in the clasp of the mirror» is equally proleptic and programmatic in its apparent ordinariness: one simultaneously perceives the clasp of ice which will seal his fate and the multi-faceted dimension of the character who indulges in deception.

The doubleness which results from the simultaneous presence of the character and of his reflections immediately points in the direction of duplicity, a duplicity openly acknowledged by Austin himself. His first words are: «Did you ever hear that expression 'mutton dressed as lamb'?» This reference to duplicitous metamorphosis is particularly ironic because Austin was a minister, in the service of the lamb of God. By choosing casual clothes for his Hawaiian retirement he seems to draw away from the lamb of God while pretending to be a lamb. This is the most significant clue given to the reader at the start: even though Austin pretends to have turned around and relinquished his religious commitments, he is not to be trusted. Once a minister, always a minister: his commitment is as permanent as the crease in his new pants. The minister's new vestments act as a lure or a decoy to convince the community that he is now different when he is essentially the same. According to Marin's terminology, supposedly borrowed from Gian Battista de Contugi, the type of entrapment represented here is the trap of fantasy:

> The trap of fantasy is the one through which the adversary finds himself confronted by his own image, one which is particularly pleasing. By making him stop, entranced, in front of his own image, one can easily and safely hit him. The principle of this type of trap is the appeal to sameness and the pleasure engendered by imitation. However, experience indicates that the efficacy of the trap does not lie in fantasy itself or in the images it creates. They are only the means that make the trap function. Efficacy lies in the appeal to sameness and the pleasure in likeness. Thus, the decoy carried by the hunter on his fist to call back his hawk, or the decoys that he sets up in marshes when the wild

ducks pass by; the female flies towards the image of
the male and the male towards the image of the female,
and both find themselves within reach of the swift arrow shot by the man who lies in wait.

(Marin 13; my translation)

The image in the mirror that Austin offers the community in Logan is the image of their expectations in terms
of retirement. The socially acceptable form of withdrawal from the sphere of work is linked with enjoyment of life. The ascetic minister offers a version of
himself as a consumer and hedonist. He covers up his
difference with counterfeit similarity to square with the
doxa, and the community is taken in precisely because
of the attraction to similarity and the pleasure in imitation. Austin pleases them by imitating their ways or doing what they would do if they were in his place.

Austin's self-transformation into a decoy meant to deceive people in Logan can also be deciphered through
the extended metaphor and the rhetorical internal rhyme
used by an authoritative narrator: «he was a stringy old
rooster—stringy but tough, and game enough to gear up
for a second marriage». It is also to be found in the explicit double-entendre: «Austin needed all the cover-up
he could get» (Munro 137). Not only do we find the
setting up of a trap in narrative utterance but we also
encounter it in the process of enunciation. In fact the
suggestion of entrapment through polysemy and metaphors precedes the discovery of the subterfuge. The
reader is confronted with a double-barreled process of
entrapment. She is shown the mechanism of the trap
before the revelation of the fake scenario is conveyed to
her. In other words she is alerted to the process of entrapment; she knows, being a Munro devotee, that she
is being led astray which triggers a desire to discover
other lures.

These lures can be perceived in photographs, which
supplement, in narrative economy, the initial mirror image. Like the mirror image, the photographs and postcard pictures belong in the category of traps of fantasy.
They rely on complacent stereotypes to delineate Austin's future existence in a Hawaiian town, the name of
which is written «in flowing letters like silk ribbon» on
the postcards that he shows Karin. Of this name the
narrator says: «the name floating in the sky looked as
possible as anything else about it.» (Munro 140) It is
precisely this assertion of likelihood which strikes up
the chord of suspicion and leads us to investigate a
striking stylistic feature linked with the description of
the pictures and the characters they display. «Fluffy
white hair, trim figure. Chic». «The town where he will
live in Hawaii. Also a photograph of her house».
(Munro 140) The ekphrastic narration is based on nominal sentences which, so structural grammar tells us,
give the text an appearance of irrefutability by identifying the embedded predicate with the subject. (Dupriez
306) As Louis Marin further develops:

What is strange is precisely this:

1—that «a minimal assertion should coincide with an item of
syntax which, from the morphological point of view, belongs to
the category of nouns», that «a form morphologically characterized as nominal should play the syntactic role of a verb»

2—that this assertion should in the present situation be a narration describing a way of being and a situation . . . Its use reveals something of great import: that the event, the way of being,
are in effect described in the present moment but as a complete
essence, an absolute truth, a permanent value, timeless and placeless, without any relationship with the one who speaks, describes,
or narrates; a final assertion, an authoritative argument.

The process of nominalization reinforces the power that
photographs have «to ratify what is represented.»
(Barthes 133) What matters in the photographs, as in
the nominal sentences which describe them, is the «certificate of presence», «the power of assertion» which
make this scenario exist as an indubitable reality.
(Barthes 135) The narrator joins hands with the character to try to authenticate the phony tale of the second
marriage in Hawaii by seemingly eliminating subjectivity. By conspicuously taking away from the sentence
part of the ordinary syntax, the narrator indulges in a
process of effacement which has far-reaching significance. It provides one with a morphological clue to the
presence of «holes» in the text, which gape open like so
many pitfalls to alert one to the fact that something is
missing, that some things are concealed in the textual
blanks that have been purposefully constructed.

Together with the strategy of depletion which curtails
sentences, one finds devices aimed at replenishment or
redundancy which are similarly suspicious and similarly
draw attention to the rhetorical nature of the process of
entrapment. Alliterations and consonance, for example,
are particularly conspicuous in the description of the
photographs: «a postcard picture», «a bit of balcony»,
«the jewel-bright waves breaking». The imitative value
of alliteration makes one hear the sound of waves
pounding on the shore, as if to reinforce the referential
illusion by buttressing images with sounds in the discourse of fantasy and simulacrum.

* * *

The traps of fantasy are set up on two levels: in discursive utterance they are set up by one character to entice
the other characters in the narrated world and, at the
level of enunciation, they are set up by the narrator to
lure the reader. The traps of appetite in Munro's story
differ from the previous ones in the sense that they are
apparently destined for one set of characters and do not
directly aim at taking in the reader. These traps consist
in baits and have to do with temptation:

The trap of appetite is the one through which the animal or human being that one wants to capture is shown
a thing he needs. The violent desire he has to acquire

it, whether spurred by hunger, thirst, or sex, or some other appetite, makes him powerless precisely because of his power and renders him defenseless in front of a lesser power. Thus, the lures of all kinds that the hunter or clever fisherman sets in his hoop nets. . . .

(Marin 13; my translation)

These traps, engineered by Austin, are apparently meant for Karin. Austin has made up his mind to donate his worldly possessions to Turnaround House, now controlled by Brent Duprey and renamed Lazarus House. Out of respect for other people's taste he has chosen to sell his goods by auction and present Lazarus House with the resulting amount in cash. He has entrusted Karin with clearing everything out but she feels the need to keep some of those things for herself. The things she hankers after are presented in the text through, once more, the use of a truncated syntax: «A willow-pattern plate. The blue-and-gray flowered curtains. A little, fat jug of ruby-colored glass with a silver lid.» (Munro 149) The nominal sentences endow the things that Karin has selected with the timelessness of art, they become things of beauty dispensing joy forever. «She can see her place transformed with these things in it. More than that she can feel the quiet and content they would extend to her». (Munro 149) Karin's appetite is definitely whetted by the thought of stealing, and the materialistic objects displayed in the house do function as baits, yet their status becomes somehow transmuted as Karin imagines that they will trigger off a change in her house and above all in herself. «Sitting in a room so furnished, she wouldn't need to go out. She would never need to think of Brent and ways to torment him». (Munro 149) These baits are depicted as playing a healing and compensatory part, as Karin's way to redemption. If she steals the minister's wife's valuables, she will lead a better life and be a better person. One should be aware of the fact that this construction of meaning is due to Karin's focalization. She is the one who is responsible for this casuistry, but far from appearing like an untenable proposition, it becomes more and more validated by the narrating agency, as forcefully exemplified in: «she feels approved of—a most unexpected thing». (Munro 155)

The trap of appetite set up by Austin for Karin has been converted into a bait for the reader, meant to make her accept a most unorthodox protocol. The way has been paved for this moral turnaround by the various instances of duplicitous conversion which precede Karin's smug decision to keep some of the valuables for herself, for example, Brent Duprey's conversion from an irresponsible alcoholic to a ferocious teetotaller, a process which hints at a total conversion, and his taking over Turnaround House to convert it into Lazarus House, a change of name which signifies conversion from the realm of the dead to the realm of the living. But, above all, semantic and stylistic parallelisms alert the reader

to the notion of turning around. For instance, Austin is first seen in Crawford's Men's Wear as he looked at himself in the mirror, or «turned around» to respond to a joke, while Karin is first encountered in a doughnut place where «she swung around» on the stool to address her acquaintances. And just as Austin's doubleness was revealed in the mirror, so Karin's is indicated by the double colour of her hair, the roots all black and the remaining part all blond.

The major instance of duplicitous transformation however, is in the title of the story and what it refers to: «**Pictures of the Ice**». The «unlikely formations» created by the snow and the ice covering the landscape represent a familiar topos in Munro's work. For instance, they are to be found in the story entitled «**Fits**» from *The Progress of Love* (1986), where they echo the cover-up for a double murder. Here their symbolic dimension is also unmistakable but here they are used to conjure up intimations of paradise through reference to pearly gates and honeycomb:

> Sheets of ice drop from the burdened branches of the willow trees to the ground, and the sun shines through them from the west; they're like walls of pearls. Ice is woven through the wire of the high fence to make it like a honeycomb.
>
> (Munro 151)

Austin captures these radiant moments with his camera the day before he leaves for his supposed retirement in Hawaii. He asks Karin to collect the pictures when they are developed and wait for his instructions. The instructions will never reach her since Austin dies in a boating accident on Shaft Lake. The pictures of the ice become Karin's implicit inheritance and are in sharp opposition to the objects she acquired by stealth, ethereal radiance set against the substantiality of materialism and the taint of theft. But the radiance acquires a supernatural dimension which qualifies the intimations of paradise and lends the pictures a sinister aspect:

> Karin looks at these pictures of the pale lumpy ice monstrosities, these pictures Austin took, so often that she gets the feeling that he is in them, after all. He's a blank in them, but bright.
>
> (Munro 155)

The bright blank does not seem to be constructed as the irradiating brightness of the godhead shining through the ice formation. What Karin sees is more akin to the sheen of glass covering up the monstrous shapes of traitors locked in ice, in Dante's ninth circle of hell:

> . . . e vidimi davante
> e sotto i piedi un lago che per gelo
> avea di vetro e non d'acqua sembiante.
>
> Canto XXXII 22-24[1]

Like the pictures of the ice, the frozen lake of Dante's inferno «has the appearance of glass and not of water», it is an abyss which constitutes the lowest point in the journey to hell. It seems to be present in Munro's short story under several guises, as a mirror in the initial paragraph, as Austin's final burial place in Northern Ontario and as a bright blank in the pictures of the ice.

The pictures of the ice are constructed in such a way as to allow room for the imagination to fill in the blank: «shapes of ice that might be people, animals, angels, monsters, left unfinished» (Munro 151). Their elliptical description makes room for the return of the missing, the effaced or the repressed: Austin is explicitly made to inhabit forever the bright blank. Other ghosts might implicitly be lurking: Karin's baby for instance who died during a snowstorm and seems to be superimposed upon the picture through the play of similes. When Brent, far advanced in drunkenness, finally realized that the baby was «like a hot coal», he wrapped him in wet towels with Karin's help and brought him to the hospital, but too late. The similes that are used to depict the baby's death coalesce polarities, the fire of coal and the wetness of towels. These polarities resonate against Austin's plot conjuring up the mock image of a Hawaiian paradise better to plunge into a frozen hell. They also resonate against the ambivalence of the pictures simultaneously evoking the pearly gates of Heaven and the abyssal lake of icy destruction. The metaphors of «the sheets of ice over pale lumpy monstrosities» provide an additional clue which suggests the unspeakable event repressed under these shrouds of memory, all the more so as what is «buried» in ice is precisely the children's playground: «And all the playground equipment, the children's swings and climbing bars, has been transformed by ice, hung with organ pipes or buried in what looks like half-carved statues» (Munro 151). The baby's death hovers about the bright blank which can be designated as Karin's private inferno. The pictures of the ice conjure up an empty and frozen universe which seems to encapsulate Austin's dereliction in the glacial solitude of Shaft Lake and the agonies of his self-sacrifice as well as Karin's mental torture and her sense of utter deprivation at the time of her baby's death.

* * *

The ambiguity of the pictures of the ice constitutes another trap or trick, less clearly designed but more powerfully constructed:

> The trap of strength or movement . . . is the one simultaneously set up and concealed on the path of the animal or man that one wants to capture, it is a mechanism that he encounters by chance, in which he will be caught, without being directed to it through a lure or a decoy . . . The essence of the trap is thus to create a place where and a moment when a small part of the adversary's strength or movement becomes the cause of the annihilation of his total strength and movement.
>
> (Marin 14; my translation)

What was Austin's intention when he entrusted Karin with the photographs? Did he really want to deploy another system of thought than the materialistic one? What is Karin's intention when she sends these pictures, without a note or a signature, to Austin's children, Don and Megan, and to Brent Duprey? The last line of the story provides a cryptic answer: «She just wants to make them wonder». To be wonder-struck is to be silenced and arrested in one's movement by the unexpected, unfamiliar or inexplicable. (OED) All three characters, Don, Megan, and Brent, are high achievers who will doubtless be stopped for a while in their race towards power and control by the sight of the unexplained and inexplicable pictures of the ice. They can be regarded as traps of force or movement leading those who contemplate them to the stasis of self-examination all the more so as, in their arrested dimension, they constitute a «freeze» in which past events are simultaneously crystallized and covered up.

Just as the characters will be made to wonder about the meaning of the pictures of the ice sent to them anonymously, so the reader is made to wonder about the questions they will ask themselves, perhaps one of them prompted by Umberto Eco in *The Name of The Rose*:

> Finally, the basic question of philosophy (as of psychoanalysis) is the same as in the detective novel: Whose fault is it?
>
> (Lits 211; my translation)

The pictures of the ice can be regarded as «a metonymy for the spiritual quest», as suggested by Mark Lits with reference to Umberto Eco's monk, William of Baskerville investigating the traces left on the fresh snow around the monastery, or with reference to Gaboriau, making Lecoq say:

> This waste land covered with snow is like an immense white sheet of paper where the people we are looking for have inscribed not only their movements and their strategy but also their secret thoughts, the hopes and fears which agitated them. What are they telling you these transient traces, Daddy? Nothing. For me they are alive, as the ones who left them there, they are palpitating, they are speaking, they are accusing.
>
> (Lits 237, my translation)

Palpitating with unknown forces and intent, the pictures of the ice might be regarded as an accusatory document which is all the more mysterious as it is simultaneously anonymous and silent. Who is guilty? What is one guilty of? The pictures point in the direction of a secret transgression. They transform those who send them into accusers, those who receive them into the accused and readers into investigators but the principle of conversion or turnaround which dominates the story prompts the reader to reverse roles and investigate the accuser's wrongdoing as much as the offences of the accused, only to discover that the categories coalesce. Transformation and tricks are so inextricably linked that deception becomes converted into innocence.

Austin's traps of fantasy, his fake scenario built on lies and equivocation, are an empowering strategy, destined to buttress his apostolic mission among the underprivileged in Shaft Lake. The traps of appetite which lead Karin to pilfer are presented as compensating for her loss and repairing her wounds. Although she is a prey to Austin's bait, she is constructed as having an interchangeable role with the minister. Like him she uses an empowering strategy which enables her to set up traps of force for other people. Like him she uses dubious double-dealing to try to awaken speculative enquiry or self-examination in the minds of people around her. Brent is equally presented as being condoned for his treachery in taking over Lazarus House. As Austin himself says «Who's to say whether Brent's way isn't closer to God than mine is, after all?» Disloyalty, theft, and fraudulent strategies become converted into Christian behaviour or selfless dedication to one's religious ideal. Thus the story sets up an apology for deception which is further validated by the implicit realization that the ways of God are impenetrable.

The transformation of heresy into orthodoxy is all the more slippery as it can also be read as an apology for revenge. Austin donating all his worldly possession to the «snake» who dispossessed him of the house he had created reads like an act of Christian forgiveness which is nonetheless destined to teach him a lesson. It is at the same time a selfless gesture of immense generosity and a retaliation of the most self-righteous kind, which defines Austin as an unrelenting forgiver, and a smug forger, tricking his community into believing in his saintly behaviour at the same time as in his mundane desires, giving away his possessions and remarrying in Hawaii: «Slipping out from under, fooling them, enjoying it». The process of nominalization captures the permanence of deception in the construction of the character and the metaphor likens him to a snake, the very image that Karin had used to depict Brent Duprey. Just as Karin's and Austin's roles are interchangeable, so Austin's and Brent's become reversible. Just as Karin and Austin carry echoing first names, which reinforce the possibilities of reversion, so Austin, Karin, and Brent are inextricably linked by the play on words involving their names, Duprey and Cobbett, in which one cannot help hearing a dupe, a prey and a bait, if not a co-bait. The interlaced structure of their stories has created a mesh, a tangled web of deception which renders each of them equally guilty or by the same token, equally innocent, reinforcing their status as confirmed sinners or saviours.

Ironically enough, by stressing the possibilities of reversibility, onomastic determinism simultaneously highlights and invalidates the very principle of conversion

upon which the story is built. The turning to God of sinners is an irreversible transformation, as exemplified for instance by the conversion of Saint Augustine. Austin, whose name is short for Augustine, falls short of his famous predecessor. Instead of walking the straight path of orthodoxy, he scuttles across the floors of frozen lakes in utter dereliction. As for Brent, whose name evokes migratory geese, he seems condemned to move back and forth according to genetic determinism. Karin's fate remains unspoken but there is a curse upon her quasi namesake. Karin did not kill her brother but will never forgive herself for her baby's death. The pictures of the ice are no ordinary snapshots. They are the unresolved enigma in which the characters' damnation or redemption are forever or momentarily suspended in the stasis of ice and art.

Note

1.　　. . . et je vis devant moi
　　　et sous mes pieds un lac à qui le gel
　　　donnait l'aspect du verre, et non de l'eau

Works Cited

Barthes, Roland. *La Chambre claire*. Paris: Seuil, 1980

Dante. *L'Enfer Inferno*. Paris: Flammarion, 1985. [1314]

Lits, Marc. «Herméneutique du déchiffrement dans le genre policier. De l'énigme cryptologique comme source du littéraire,» *Le roman policier, introduction à la théorie et à l'histoire d'un genre littéraire*. Liège: CEFAL, 1993.

Marin, Louis. *Le récit est un piège*. Paris: Minuit, 1978.

Munro, Alice. *Friend of my Youth*. London: Vintage, 1990.

Catherine Sheldrick Ross (essay date summer 2002)

SOURCE: Ross, Catherine Sheldrick. "'Too Many Things': Reading Alice Munro's 'The Love of a Good Woman.'" *University of Toronto Quarterly* 71, no. 3 (summer 2002): 786-810.

[In the following essay, Ross documents key images and details in "The Love of a Good Woman" that echo Munro's earlier stories and create a sense of Gothic mystery.]

The effect of a vintage Munro story resembles Italo Calvino's description of fable: '[T]he fable unwinds from sentence to sentence, and where is it leading? To the point at which something not yet said, something as yet only darkly felt by presentiment, suddenly appears and seizes us and tears us to pieces, like the fangs of a man-eating witch' (18). With *The Love of a Good Woman,* Munro offers her readers eight stories that seize us by the throat. How does she do it? She has returned to earlier material and rewritten it in a form that is more complex and multilayered. So, for example, **'Cortes Island'** seems to have swallowed up **'The Office'** as just one element among many, while **'The Love of a Good Woman'** can be read, in part, as a return to themes and characters that appeared in **'Images'** and **'Friend of My Youth.'** Readers can keep up with these dazzling new stories because Alice Munro has given us a long apprenticeship in reading her kind of story. Previous experience with earlier Munro stories, where the patterns are clearer, provides a sort of scaffolding helpful in making sense of these latest works. In the stories in this collection, I found myself digging down through layers and following threads backward through to earlier handlings of the same material. Underneath a reading of the current story are the contours of previous readings of earlier stories, in which some of the same material is handled but with variations. This seems to be especially true of **'The Love of a Good Woman,'** which Robert Thacker has called 'a central Munro text' with echoes of previous Munro stories (1) and Dennis Duffy has called a 'capstone' and 'pivotal work in the structure of her fiction' (169).

An apprenticeship in reading Munro teaches the importance of things that are off to the side, just out of our line of vision, innocent objects that we normally pass over. In **'The Love of a Good Woman,'** the reader is challenged to make sense of a text that contains so much and that refuses to subordinate the plurality of its detail within a single frame. One strategy for writers and readers is to work towards clarity by leaving out detail and emphasizing an overall design usually derived from the patterns of genre or of myth. An opposite approach is to work towards complexity by including details that don't fit patterns and often subvert them. Lorna Irvine argues, following Frank Kermode, 'The first process tends towards clarity and propriety . . . , the second toward secrecy, toward distortions which cover secrets' (104). In **'Differently'** from *Friend of My Youth,* Munro seems to be describing her own refusal to simplify. When Georgia took a creative writing course, the instructor told her that she was putting in 'Too many things. Too many things going on at the same time; also too many people. Think, he told her. What is the important thing? What do you want us to pay attention to?' So when Georgia wrote a story about her grandfather killing chickens, '[s]he made a long list of all the things that had been left out and handed it in as an appendix to the story' (*Friend* [*Friend of My Youth*], 216). A major effect in a Munro story is achieved by the reader's sense that Munro has included too many things to be held together in the same frame. Some overlooked thing can be expected to emerge from the shadows to overturn any achieved pattern. In **'The**

Love of a Good Woman,' the list of 'too many things going on at the same time' minimally includes the following:

• a red box fitted with special eye-examining instruments

• a pale hand floating up through the roof panel of an Austin submerged in the swollen spring river

• bouquets of forsythias carried in the arms of three boys

• ugly brown porch paint sloppily painted on a linoleum floor

• the weak laughter of a dying woman that is overheard by another woman who interprets the sound as 'something deliberately vile'

• a disturbing dream

• a little hatchet carried down towards a riverbank to cut down berry canes and thistles

• the secretive motion of a rowboat riding in the shadows of the river

THE RED BOX

Let's start with that red box, which is a powerful element of disruption and disorder in the story, linked with the invasive gaze, illicit sex, and violent death. Everyone associated with the red box eventually is silenced—the optometrist who carried it with him on his professional, and maybe not-so-professional, house-calls; Mrs Quinn, who on her deathbed told a story about it, which may be a malicious lie; and the anonymous donor who dispatched it to the museum, where it has been on display for several decades. It is tempting to see this box as the mysterious centre around which the whole story has been built.[1] Munro stories often grow from a visual seed, a very vivid scene—e.g., the mother sewing her daughter an elaborate red dress in **'Red Dress—1946,'** a man encountered in the woods coming down the riverbank carrying a hatchet in **'Images,'** the rope over the beam in **'The Progress of Love,'** the newspaper story about the vigilante group who blackened their faces and horsewhipped a man suspected of incest in **'Royal Beatings.'** In her often-quoted comparison between writing a story and exploring the inner spaces of a house, Munro has said that the horsewhippers story is 'the black room at the centre of the house' of **'Royal Beatings'** ('What Is Real?' 225). She says that she typically builds up a story in layers 'to fit around the indescribable "feeling" that is like the soul of the story. . . . Then I start accumulating the material and putting it together' ('What Is Real?' 224). The major task of writing the story is to get this initial scene adequately housed in a story that builds round it, often layering real and invented incident, past and present to convey the emotional reality, which is what the story is really about. As Munro remarked in a 1995 interview with

Boyce and Smith concerning the stories in *Open Secrets*, 'the stories . . . aren't about what they seem to be about' (225).

The first appearance of the red box is innocent enough. It is introduced in one of those typical Munrovian framing descriptions that start in the present and sweep backwards in time. For the 'last couple of decades,' we are told, there has been a historical museum in Walley that collects curiosities such as butter churns and horse harnesses and an old dentist's chair. 'Also there is a red box,' appearing in the second paragraph as an item with 'local significance, since it belonged to Mr. D. M. Willens, who drowned in the Peregrine River, 1951.' The provenance of the red box is helpfully provided in a museum note placed beside the box, which explains: 'It escaped the catastrophe and was found, presumably by the anonymous donor, who dispatched it to be a feature of our collection' (3). On my first reading of the story, my attention was drawn to the uneven style of the note with its odd mixture of dramatization ('escaped the catastrophe') and bland formality ('a feature of our collection'), and I didn't much notice the 'anonymous donor,' whose identity turns out to be a pivotal point of the story.

The red box itself has a smug, indestructible, empirical presence, but even in the opening preamble it is beginning to accumulate significance that goes beyond what can be known empirically. In its museum setting, the box is presumably open, since the narrator is able to describe its contents—the ophthalmoscope and the retinoscope that can be used to inspect interior places that are usually hidden. By the third paragraph, the descriptive language invites the reader to imagine extravagant transformations: 'The ophthalmoscope could make you think of a snowman' (2) and 'Underneath the round forehead clamp [of the retinoscope] is something like an elf's head' (3). The retinoscope, we are told, is black except where the paint has disappeared in 'some places where the optometrist's hand must have rubbed most often' (4). Pay attention to that rubbing hand that once carried the red box; that was described as grabbing the leg of Mrs Quinn; and that was spotted by three boys who saw it floating up through the Austen's skylight and drifting like a feather on the Peregrine River swollen by spring run-off. Its lineage in previous Munro stories includes the pumping hand of Mr Chamberlain in *Lives of Girls and Women,* the hand of the possibly disguised clergyman on the train in **'Wild Swans'** (*Who* [*Who Do You Think You Are?*]), and the hand moving among the feathers of a brown hat in **'Open Secrets'** that is transformed into the punished hand imagined as pressed down on the hot stove burner (*Open* [*Open Secrets*], 156, 158).[2]

In the inset story told in section 3 about a time that predates the finding of Mr Willens's body, Mrs Quinn provides three differing accounts of what the optometrist was doing in her house on the day when she alleges Rupert came back unexpectedly and saw her and Mr Willens together. In the first account, Rupert misinterprets behaviour during a purely professional visit. Mrs Quinn was innocently sitting in the rocking chair getting her eyes examined and Mr Willens was 'holding the thing up to her eye,' using the other hand 'to keep his balance' by grabbing her leg: 'she couldn't do a thing about it, she had to concentrate on keeping still' (57). In the second version, the grabbing is redescribed as deliberate, habitual, and opportunistic: 'Not that she ever let him do anything, but he was always ready to get a grab if he could. Like grabbing her leg up under her skirt when he had the thing to her eye and she couldn't stop him and Rupert had to come sneaking in and get the wrong idea' (59). In the third version, the sexual encounter is planned in advance, with Mr Willens leaving his hat in the car to make it easier to grab and kiss her: 'If you could call that kissing, all that pushing up against her with the box still in one hand and the other grabbing on . . . pushing himself up at her and the corner of the box sticking into her and digging her behind' (60). In this account, the box is initially a penetrating weapon and later a prop in a sexual game of Doctor and Patient, played according to a rehearsed script, in which Mrs Quinn's role is to be surprised: 'It was like the same game every time, and she wasn't supposed to suspect what was going on. . . . Her not supposed to say anything till he stops and gets the looker thing packed up in his box and all and then she's supposed to say, "Oh, Mr. Willens, now, how much do I owe you for today?"' That was his cue to get her down on the bare floor: 'Dingey on him like a blowtorch. How'd you've liked that?' (62).

If the solid presence of the red box in the museum seems to lend additional weight to Mrs Quinn's final version of the story, this is because of a reading strategy that readers normally bring to texts: we pay attention to repeated images and assume that if we keep reading long enough various highlighted, but disconnected, details will eventually come together and make interpretive sense. As readers, we have learned what Peter Rabinowitz has called the implicit 'rules of reading' that people follow in reading prose fiction: these rules 'serve as a kind of assumed contract between author and reader—they specify the grounds on which the intended reading should take place' (43). The first of these, the rules of notice, guide a reader in sorting out significant details from the myriad of less significant ones in any long narrative. According to Rabinowitz, texts that are successful in communicating with their audience have 'a hierarchical organization of details' (53) that provides a framework for understanding. Authors and readers, says Rabinowitz, agree to concentrate their attention on certain textual features. For example, the title, subtitle, and epigraph of a novel direct our attention to a significant theme or interpretive code. Italicized words or phrases are granted extra significance. Sentences or paragraphs at the beginning and the end of stories, or of sections within stories, occupy privileged positions. Threats, warnings, and promises deserve notice because they predict the likely shape of the plot, although reversals can be expected (a character who is asked to promise never to become a nurse and never to marry a farmer may end up doing both). Dreams are granted significance as a predictor of future events, a bearer of messages about past events, or an indicator of the inner lives and hidden desires of characters. We give weight to details that happen at climactic moments of the plot (reversals, discoveries, revelations, recognitions). We notice details that are repeated. When something is described in great detail, we expect that it will eventually turn out to be significant to the theme or plot. Also noticeable are disruptions, or breaks in textual continuity, such as inappropriate or uncharacteristic behaviour by characters, the inclusion of apparently irrelevant details, shifts in literary style or shifts in tone. Certain words such as 'suddenly' or 'realized' or 'surprising' are semantic markers of significance—the more so when phrased in striking formulations such as Munro's description of Rupert's last exit from his wife's sickroom: 'He looked as if he had caught hold of an electric wire' (56).

These rules of notice tell us *what* literary features to attend to, but we also need what Rabinowitz calls the rules of significance that help us know *how* to attend to these features. To judge ethical value and sort out good characters from bad ones, for example, readers rely on a variety of indicators such as the following: authorial statements about a character; references to legendary or mythical patterns; allegorical names; speech patterns of characters including contrasts between refined and non-standard English; and physical markers such as hair colour, eyes, and clothing. Notes Rabinowitz, 'In addition to metaphorical rules of appearance, which make it appropriate to assume that physical or verbal characteristics stand for moral qualities, we have metonymical rules of enchainment, which make it appropriate to assume that the presence of one moral quality is linked to the presence of another that lies more or less contiguous to it' (89). Third are the 'rules of configuration' that activate certain expectations in the reader about how a given work may be 'resolved' (111).

Our long apprenticeship in reading Alice Munro, however, warns us that following these 'rules of reading' with a Munro text will produce instabilities. In **'The Love of a Good Woman,'** reading strategies engender interpretations that, far from converging, are in conflict with each other. To take only the most obvious example, readers use genre expectations as one of the basic ways of bringing disparate elements into a coherent pattern. 'A murder, a mystery, a romance' was the subtitle for the *New Yorker* version of the story, though

omitted in the collected version. Read as romance, which is the dominant reading given by Ildiko de Papp Carrington ('Don't Tell') and Coral Ann Howells (*Alice Munro*), the story is about a woman who seems to have missed out on love until she reestablishes a connection with a man from her past. Read as Gothic murder, which is how Dennis Duffy interprets it, the story is about a woman with a fatal attraction for self-sacrifice who falls in love with a murderer and may be his next victim. Moreover, genre preferences are self-reinforcing. Using reading strategies appropriate for a love story encourages us to pay closer attention to details and images activated by that genre (in a love story, early hostility between a man and a woman is to be read as a sign that they will eventually fall in love). Using reading strategies appropriate for Gothic horror highlights quite different details and images (in Gothic horror, the appearance of low-key ordinariness may be a sign of repressed craziness about to run amok).

Readers pay attention to these genre cues, even while they acknowledge, as Howells does, that Munro's use of generic elements is 'slightly off-centre' (*Alice Munro*, 149)[3] and that in any case she has never been interested in providing the satisfactions of a traditional plot. Interpretive problems occur at every level of this story, not just when we try to decide *how* we should evaluate characters and events but also when we try to determine just *what* those events are. Did Mr Willens drown, as the note on the red box in the museum states, or did Rupert dispose of the already-dead body in the river to make murder look like suicide or an accident, as Mrs Quinn claimed in her shocking account to Enid?[4] Was Mrs Quinn's story that accused Rupert of murder to be given any credence or did she make up the whole story as a sort of poison pill to break up an anticipated romance between Rupert and Enid? What was the electrifying thing that Mrs Quinn said to Rupert in their final conversation when Enid overheard the weak laughter and interpreted it as 'something deliberately vile' (56): a threat to tell Enid about the murder (if it was a murder), or a taunt that Rupert's suspicions were right all along about Mr Willens and possibly even worse than he had supposed?[5] And does Enid ever reveal to Rupert what she has been told by Mrs Quinn, or does she keep her secrets to herself?[6]

One set of reading strategies encourages us to grant factual status to Mrs Quinn's account. The introduction of the red box as a real object in the opening vignette, together with the eight separate references to the box and its contents in section 3, establishes the box as a significant plot element in a way that, say, Mr Willens's hat, mentioned only once, is not. Repetition has turned the arrival of the red box at the museum into a problem that requires explanation. One rule of reading mystery stories is that anything that could be a murder *is* a murder and further that we should expect important acts of agency to be done by characters featured within the text. Therefore, if a particular reading adequately explains the arrival of the red box at the museum using clues supplied within the story, we are not to prefer a rival reading that presupposes another chain of events involving unidentified agents. This rule focuses attention on two clues—one more obvious than the other—positioned at the end of the story and offering alternative candidates for the identity of the anonymous donor. As Enid and Rupert are poking through bins in the woodshed looking for a pair of rubber boots to equip Enid for her trip to the river, Enid considers all the 'bins, drawers, shelves, suitcases, trunks, crawl spaces full of things that it would be up to Enid to sort out, saving and labeling some, restoring some to use, sending others by the boxload to the dump' (77). She thinks, 'She would make this house into a place that had no secrets from her and where all order was as she decreed' (77)—in fact, we can see that she is just the person, after her marriage to Rupert, to sort through bins and drawers and pack off to a historical museum any hidden agent of disorder. On the other hand, why hasn't she already found the red box in her extensive housecleaning efforts? Possibly because there was *one* bin she 'had never looked into,' wrongly thinking it contained firewood. Hence the second, less obvious clue. Rummaging in the bin for boots, Rupert remarks, 'Forgot all the stuff that was in here,' immediately throws back the items he has started to remove, drops the lid to close up the bin again, and gives 'a private, grieved, and formal-sounding sigh' (77). Perhaps after his boat ride with Enid, Rupert goes back to the bin to remove the last link that connects him to the murder.

However, another rule of reading requires us to give special weight to titles, subtitles, and opening and closing sentences and paragraphs, and this rule raises the possibility of a conflicting reading. Why, for example, is section 2 entitled 'Heart Failure' and not 'Kidney Failure'? Perhaps it is to suggest that a failure of the heart motivated Mrs Quinn's decision to tell her murder story (is it this failure that made her laughter sound 'deliberately vile'?). She segues into her story with the statement: 'I bet it's all lies. You know Mr. Willens was right here in this room?' (56). Similarly, 'Mistake' and 'Lies,' which are the titles for sections 3 and 4 respectively, foreground the possibility of error and duplicity. Returning to the front room/sick room after Mrs Quinn's funeral, Enid finds that the word that sticks in her mind is 'Lies.' 'Could a person make up something so detailed and diabolical?' she wonders, and answers yes: 'You can never say, "Nobody could make that up." Look how elaborate dreams are, layer over layer in them, so that the part you can remember and put into words is just the bit you can scratch off the top' (74). The impact of the title 'Lies' is heightened later in the section by the italicizing of two passages, '*Lies. I bet it's all lies*' (74) and '*Lies*' (75), and by their strategic positioning

at the end of two subsections. The title 'Lies' might refer to Mrs Quinn's story of murder; but then again it might refer to lies that Enid tells herself in order to 'keep the world habitable' (76). If so, Enid is belatedly learning a strategy for ignoring unpleasantness that was modelled for her years ago by her mother: 'Don't tell Daddy' (75). The interpretation of the story's events is radically unstable, as readers are invited to consider incompatible possibilities for the provenance of the red box.

FORSYTHIA

Just as problematic as the red box are the three armloads of cut forsythia that Mrs Willens gives to the three boys to take home to their mothers. Mrs Willens is already a widow, although she doesn't know it yet, since the boys have chosen not to tell her. Reflecting on the role this forsythia performs in the story, we might note how it works as a seasonal marker, since it is 'the very first thing in the spring' (23). The story starts when the snow is not quite off the ground and the river is flooding and it unfolds through the intense heat and humidity of a southern Ontario summer. Botanic references track the seasonal cycle from the marsh marigold and yellow forsythia of early spring in section 1 to the June berry canes and wild grapevines and ripening hay in section 2 to the crushed flowers dropped at the July funeral and the big fleshy thistles in section 4. Moreover the forsythias, carried reluctantly down the street, provide an ironic introduction to the wedding theme. Seeing the three boys with their bouquets, the sister of one of the boys and her friend hoot derisively, 'Oh, look at the flowers . . . Where's the wedding? Look at the beautiful bridesmaids' (24). Already the chain of events is beginning that allows the reader to link, in various ways, sexual transgression, murder, guilt, sickness, death of a wife, the sexual awakening of a good woman, and the poising of a man and a woman on the threshold of some momentous change.

But from another point of view, we could view the forsythia and the whole sequence of events in which the forsythia plays a part as posing an interpretive problem of relevance. It is only because the boys have already missed three opportunities to tell their news that the forsythia incident has an opportunity to occur. The longest of the story's four sections, 'Jutland' is a *tour de force* of deferral, in which the three boys who have found the body are *not* able to tell of their discovery to anyone who can hear it. Initially the boys have the idea that when they get close enough, they will start to shout out the terrible secret of what they have seen in the river: 'They would come into town yelling and waving their news around them' (12). But the moment passes, and the narrative takes an unexpected turn, elaborating on the way that the three boys go home to three very different families to eat their very different noontime dinners and in each case fail to mention what they have seen. Notable is the weight of detail given to establishing the three families for whom the forsythia bouquets were intended—Cece Ferns and his drunken, abusive father and defeated, exhausted mother; Bud Salter and his turbulent family of two older, appearance-obsessed sisters and a spoiled baby brother; and Jimmy Box and his extended family of people who bear up under burdens and are invariably polite.

The three accounts of the boys' dinners show enormous variety in specifics, but in the end they converge on the same silence, which is the reality that endures: 'Something was made of the boys' sitting down and eating their dinners and never saying a word . . . A new nickname—Deadman—was found and settled on each of them' (30). In total, there are five missed opportunities to tell their news: coming into town; at dinner with their families, repeated at three different dinner tables; receiving forsythia from Mrs Willens; at the police station; and sitting opposite Captain Tervitt, the crossing guard. The whole point of the repetition with variation of the same event—the failure to tell the news—must be that some things are untellable and some messages cannot be delivered. The central dilemma in what we might consider the story proper is a woman's decision whether or not to tell a terrible secret. How we decide to interpret her decision is shaped in our minds by the weighting we choose to give to the representation in section 1 of the silent boys and their bouquets of forsythia.

If we decide that **'The Love of a Good Woman'** is about ancient prohibitions, then the story invites comparison with all those other Munro stories about taboos of silence, starting in the first volume, **The Dance of the Happy Shades,** with **'Walker Brothers Cowboy,' 'The Peace of Utrecht,'** and **'Images.'** At the end of **'Walker Brothers Cowboy,'** the narrator comments, 'My father does not say anything to me about not mentioning things at home, but I know, just from the thoughtfulness, the pause when he passes the licorice, that there are things not to be mentioned. The whiskey, maybe the dancing' (18). At the beginning of **'The Peace of Utrecht,'** the narrator says, 'Silences disturb us. . . . I want to ask her . . . But I don't ask her; we never talk about any of that. No exorcising here, says Maddy' (190, 191). At the end of **'Images,'** the narrator reports that her father asks, '"What are you not going to mention about?" and I said, "The axe"'—'dazed and powerful with secrets, I never said a word' (42-43).

A GOOD WOMAN

But suppose we take a different thread: the good woman of the title. The title sounds vaguely familiar, as if taken from some quotation such as 'Be thankful for the love of a good woman' or 'There, but for the love of a good

woman, go I,' although no such quotations can be found in *Bartlett's*. Perhaps we are expected to hear an echo of the virtuous woman of Proverbs who is 'a crown to her husband' (12:4) with a price that is 'far above rubies' (31:10) and who makes a contrastive pair with the 'strange woman' whose 'feet go down to death' (5:5) and whose mouth is 'a deep pit' (22:14). The story invites us to think about different types of women—the good and the not-so-good daughters, wives, and mothers; the lucky and the unlucky.

Enid is the strongest candidate for the role of 'good woman.' She is one of those familiar Munro characters who are ambitious, cheerful, self-sufficient, sensible, managerial, energetic, high-minded, idealistic, and sexually prudish—somehow isolated and set apart from others, marked out as different, as missing some essential self-protective skin. Glorying in hardship and sacrificial gestures, Enid had once thought of becoming a missionary. When she eventually decided on nursing, '[h]er hope was to be good, and do good, and not necessarily in the orderly, customary, wifely way' (42). She is one of the *not* chosen. She is what the narrator of **'Red Dress—1946'** might have become had she not been unexpectedly rescued by Raymond Bolting and 'brought from Mary Fortune's territory into the ordinary world' (**Dance** [**Dance of the Happy Shades**], 160). Like a character in a fairy tale, Enid has made a deathbed vow to her dying father to sacrifice her career as a professional hospital nurse (according to her father, familiarity with men's bodies makes a woman 'coarse'). Instead she becomes a practical nurse, performing, as her disapproving mother put it, 'miserable backbreaking work in miserable primitive houses for next to no money' (43). She is an 'angel of mercy, as her mother had said, with less and less irony as time went on' (52).

Oddly enough in a story in which even minor female characters are closely described (Mrs Willens is 'a lumpy little woman' [23]; Jimmy Box's mother is 'a short woman' and when she stood tiptoe you could see 'the rosy plump cushions of her heels through her stockings' [25]; Mrs Quinn's sister-in-law Mrs Green is 'a tall, stout woman' with 'a round, snub-nosed, agreeably wrinkled face' [32]), we are told almost nothing about Enid's physical appearance. We have an impression of her as a physically healthy and attractive person in her late thirties, but is she tall or short, plump or slim? We learn indirectly that she is large-breasted, since Mrs Quinn says to her, 'I never had no big udders on me, like you' (36). One of the few concrete physical details provided by way of authorial description is that her long, wild, thick hair (but what colour?),[7] which is usually worn rolled, was carefully done up in a French braid in preparation for her intended confrontation of Rupert with Mrs Quinn's secret. The choice, so unusual for Munro, *not* to provide a complete physical description of the central character Enid prevents readers from using one of their most relied-upon strategies for evaluating characters and placing them in a moral universe. Enid's appearance, and by extension the way we evaluate Enid, are a gap that readers have to fill in.

Mrs Quinn, on the other hand, is abundantly described, although mostly through the hostile eyes of her nurse Enid. As so often in a Munro story, contrasting characters represent different life choices. In this case, Mrs Quinn, the not-so-good wife, careless housekeeper, and indifferent mother, is being nursed by the good woman through the last stages of kidney failure that is poisoning her body with toxins. With her narrow body, pale face, 'sparse, fair hair,' 'large greenish eyes,' 'childish translucent teeth and small stubborn chin' (36), she resembles other knowing characters in earlier stories who are disadvantaged by class and family background and have to fight for everything they get—for example, the 'cold and narrow and pale' Lois with her 'light-coloured eyes' in **'Thanks for the Ride'** (*Dance,* 49, 46); the 'pale shrewd' Patricia in **'Time of Death'** with 'her tiny pointed teeth . . . almost transparent . . . [that] made her look like a ferret, a wretched little animal insane with rage or fear' (*Dance,* 99); or the ferocious Madeleine from **'The Flats Road'** with her thin white face and long legs like scissors (*Lives* [*Lives of Girls and Women*], 14). Distantly shadowing these derisive, scornful characters are the trapped animals and captive foxes with their 'pointed, malevolent faces . . . drawn exquisitely sharp in pure hostility, and their golden eyes' that appear in **'Boys and Girls'** (*Dance,* 115) and those other early stories featuring the father with the fox farm or trapline. The imagery of the trapped animal that is about to die supports a reading of Mrs Quinn as a victim, a view that is strengthened by the sparse details provided about her childhood in a Montreal orphanage and the chambermaid job that she had when she first met Rupert. Mrs Green says, 'You'd expect her to speak French, but if she does she don't let on,' hinting at cumulative losses of family, language, and culture. Even her name has been erased: she is called Mrs Quinn throughout, and we learn her Christian name only from Enid's notation in her notebook after her patient's death: 'July 10. Patient Mrs Rupert (Jeannette) Quinn died today approx. 5 p.m. Heart failure due to uremia. (Glomerulonephritis)' (67). Rupert's own epitaph on his wife after the funeral is 'She wasn't lucky in her life' (76).

Nevertheless, in the darkened front room that has been turned into a sickroom, Mrs Quinn dominates the house with her sceptical and scornful presence. She follows in a line of mockers that can be traced from Lois in **'Thanks for the Ride'** through Flo in *Who Do You Think You Are?* Responding to Enid's comment that as far as she knew Mr and Mrs Willens 'got along beautifully,' Mrs Quinn says in derision of Enid's reserved, genteel tone, 'Oh, is that so? . . . Bee-you-tif-

ley' (50). Mrs Quinn is disturbing because she refuses to settle into the role of the good wife, mother, and patient. Instead she makes demands and complaints and speaks uncomfortable truths, culminating in that last 'great spurt of energy, that wicked outpouring talk' (64). In contrast to Enid, who holds sentimental and conventional views (such as it always does a patient good to have a visit from her husband), Mrs Quinn takes satisfaction in pointing out undercurrents of distaste and avoidance: 'Doesn't hang around here very long, does he? . . . Ha-ha-ha, how-are-you? Ha-ha-ha, off-we-go. Why don't we take her out and throw her on the manure heap? Why don't we just dump her out like a dead cat?' (35). Her taunting comments to Enid, 'Won't you be glad when I'm dead?' and 'Good riddance to bad rubbish' and 'As far as you know. But you don't know much' (36), are truer than Enid is prepared to admit.

When a fatal disease strikes down a young mother of twenty-seven, a caregiver is expected to feel compassion. One of the mysteries, at least to Enid, who is not especially self-reflective or in touch with her own feelings, is her own unconquerable dislike 'for this doomed, miserable young woman': 'She disliked this particular body, all the particular signs of its disease. The smell of it and the discoloration, the malignant-looking little nipples and the pathetic ferretlike teeth' (38). Enid's rejection of Mrs Quinn may owe something to the distinction of class: 'Mrs. Quinn reminded her somewhat of girls she had known in high school—cheaply dressed, sickly looking girls with dreary futures, who still displayed a hard-faced satisfaction with themselves' (38). But class rivalry in itself would not account for why a caregiver, for sixteen years a model of unjudgmental compassion, should in this one case read disease symptoms as signs of 'willed corruption' (38). Given this uncharacteristic hostility, we are entitled to wonder whether Enid might not be projecting her own feelings on her patient when she reports what she heard when Rupert visits his wife for the last time. Enid hears Mrs Quinn's weak laughter through the closed door and detects in the sound 'something she hadn't heard before, not in her life—something deliberately vile' (56).

Enid is not the only one to see Mrs Quinn's disease as a sign to be interpreted. The sister-in-law, the oddly named Mrs Olive Green, reads the illness as an indicator of sexual transgression and hints at a possible abortion: 'You hear that sometimes a woman might take some pills . . . if they take too many and for a bad purpose their kidneys are wrecked. Am I right?' (32). Mrs Quinn herself says that her illness coincided with her attempt to cover up the murder. The horrible smell when she burned fabrics stained with Mr Willens's blood and the smell of the brown paint that she claimed to have hastily applied to hide the bloodstains on the floor of the front room—that, she says, was 'the whole beginning of her being sick' (61). But this 'plausible connection' between Mrs Quinn's guilt in concealing a murder and her death by toxic poisoning is the sort of symmetry that previous reading of Munro stories has taught us to resist. For example, the narrator of 'The Stone in the Field,' reflecting on a newspaper account of the death of a hermit, remarks that she has grown to distrust the drive to narrative closure: 'If I had been younger, I would have figured out a story. I would have insisted on Mr. Black's being in love with one of my aunts [but never disclosing his feelings] . . . I would have made a horrible, plausible connection between that silence of his, and the manner of his death [cancer of the tongue]. Now I no longer believe that people's secrets are defined and communicable, or their feelings full-blown and easy to recognize. I don't believe so' (*Moons* [*The Moons of Jupiter*], 35).

Other ways of achieving reading closure are also disrupted. As mentioned previously, one method of reading the story is to try to subsume its details to the romance pattern, in which the focus is on the developing love relationship between two people (see Radway). One passage that invites this reading is the sequence with Rupert and Enid together in the evening after Mrs Quinn and the children are asleep (45-49)—Rupert's presentation of the ceiling fan and newspaper, the whispered conversation, the revival of shared memories from the past, Enid's offer of a cup of tea, and the cooperative work on the crossword puzzle that lets Rupert demonstrate his exotic knowledge ('Bread of the Amazon?' 'Manioc?' 'Cassava?'). But just when we think we are getting the good woman/bad woman polarities lined up satisfactorily, echoes from earlier stories set up an interference pattern. The character of Enid is attended by ghosts—for who is Enid, after all, but a variant of the practical nurse, who in previous stories is an invader who takes over the household, throws her weight around, and supplants the wife/mother figure?[8] The presentation of Enid as a threat is muted, but behind her angel-of-mercy role surely there is more than a whiff of Mary McQuade in 'Images' with her complaining voice and 'frizzy, glinting, naturally brass-coloured hair' and Nurse Audrey Atkinson in 'Friend of My Youth' with corsets as stiff as barrel hoops, marcelled hair the color of brass candlesticks' (*Friend,* 13). The parallels among Mary McQuade, Nurse Atkinson, and Enid draw attention to the menacing aspects of the good woman's role, which might otherwise be less noticeable. Consider. All three nurses arrive in springtime. Nurse Atkinson comes to nurse Robert's cancer-stricken wife Ellie, who has spent her entire married life broken down by one gynecological disaster after another. By midsummer both Ellie and Mrs Quinn are dead. Nurse Atkinson stays on to marry Robert, displace Ellie's sister Flora for a second time, and modernize the farmhouse. After the funeral,

Enid returns to the Quinn farm and begins to imagine herself marrying the widowed Rupert and bringing order to his house.

Differences in representation of the three practical nurses are in part a function of who is doing the looking (how might Enid appear in a story narrated by the Quinn children, Lois or Sylvie?). Most of the story proper of 'The Love of a Good Woman' is seen through the eyes of Enid, who naturally constructs events in terms sympathetic to herself—for example, the hostility of patients who 'detested the sight of Enid herself' is attributed to inexplicable fits that overcome people when they are seriously ill (37-38). In contrast, Nurse Atkinson is presented from the hostile perspective of the narrator's mother, who configures her as a brassy figure of greed and self-promotion. The menace of Mary McQuade is even more strongly exaggerated— she is 'the embodiment . . . of terror, to the child,' said Munro in a 1982 interview with Geoff Hancock (111). When Mary McQuade moved into the house in March, the narrator held her responsible for her mother's mysteriously invalided state, just as she had held the nurse responsible the previous summer for the grandfather's death: 'She came, and cooked what she liked and rearranged things to suit herself, complaining about draughts, and let her power loose in the house. If she had never come my mother would never have taken to her bed' (*Dance,* 32-33). Too young to know on a conscious level what was happening, the narrator nevertheless sensed a connection between the mystery of death and birth and the arrival of Mary McQuade. Looking at the gigantic shadows cast on the wall by Mary McQuade and her father talking together, the narrator says she was 'trying to understand the danger, to read the signs of invasion' (*Dance,* 35). Significantly, the opening sentences of 'Images' highlight the narrator's sense of menace: 'Now that Mary McQuade had come, I pretended not to remember her. It seemed the wisest thing to do' (*Dance,* 30). In 'The Love of a Good Woman,' the response to the threat of Enid's arrival is muted but similar: the wary Rupert pretends to have forgotten Enid and the humiliations of flirtatious teasing practised on him by Enid and her friends when they were at school together: 'Impossible that he would have forgotten. But he treated Enid as if she were a new acquaintance, his wife's nurse, come into his house from anywhere at all' (33-34).

The sequence of Rupert and Enid's cozy evenings together over newspaper and tea can be read as a stage in the invasion. Here Enid and Rupert are, as Dennis Duffy has pointed out, 'domesticating their relationship. They are now the old married couple, with the wife in her sickroom the excluded third' (175). Similarly open to a negative reading is Enid's behaviour on the day she expects her patient to die. She absents herself from her patient[9] to create a holiday atmosphere for the little girls Lois and Sylvie with Jell-O treats, sugared cook-ies, bubble-making, and improvised swimming pools. The explanation given for this celebratory activity is that 'She wanted them to hold something in their minds that could throw a redeeming light on whatever came later. On herself, that is, and whatever way she would affect their lives later on' (64). Enid's ambition to have some future connection with the little girls is apparent to Mrs Green, whose response is a pre-emptive strike: 'You must be wanting to get off home yourself' (68).

In this triangle of invader, displaced wife, and husband, the male figure is an ambiguous presence. In **'Friend of My Youth,'** Robert is initially engaged to marry Flora, but he passes over Flora not once but twice in favour of a more sexually generous partner. The narrator thinks, 'To me the really mysterious person in the story, as my mother told it, was Robert. He never has a word to say. He gets engaged to Flora. He is walking beside her along the river when Ellie leaps out at them. He finds Ellie's thistles in his bed . . . he was the one who started everything, in secret. He *did it to* Ellie. He did it to that skinny wild girl at a time when he was engaged to her sister' (*Friend,* 21). In **'The Love of a Good Woman,'** Rupert is a similarly mysterious character who doesn't explain himself. In his case what's hidden may be a capacity for sudden violence that can flash out like lightning. In **'Images,'** the character corre-sponding to the Robert/Rupert character is the narra-tor's father, who is associated with the dead trapped animals and 'the skinning knife, its slim bright blade' (36). The matchmaking role is displaced onto the series of 'preposterous imagined matings' that the narrator's father thinks up for Mary McQuade, culminating with Old Joe Phippen, the axe-wielding hermit who lives in an underground house with a whiskey-drinking cat: 'We found the one for you today, Mary' (*Dance,* 43). Joe Phippen, who is the father's dark double, is thus brought into alignment with Robert/Rupert in a way that alerts us to the unmentionable connection that all three char-acters have with sexuality and death—Old Joe with the axe that the narrator is not supposed to mention, Robert with that sad sequence of miscarried and dead babies fathered on Ellie, and Rupert, who has allegedly bat-tered Mr Willens to death.

And what about the third element in this triad—the pa-tient? At first glance there are more differences than similarities among the narrator's mother, Ellie, and Mrs Quinn. Yet considering the importance of the figure of the sick, abdicating mother throughout Munro's work, it is worth looking again at the treatment of the invalid in these stories. In **'Images,'** the narrator's 'own real, warm-necked, irascible and comforting human mother' has turned into a childish, indifferent figure who is no longer available to the narrator. In this story the expla-nation for the mother's absence is a pregnancy, but long-time readers of Munro know that the real cause of

abdication—the one that Munro can never forget—is Parkinson's disease. From her first appearance in **'The Peace of Utrecht,'** the mother with Parkinson's disease is the character, *par excellence,* who lies in a down-stairs room darkened against the summer heat and calls out her complaints and unmeetable demands. In the sto-ries that feature this stricken mother, the fact of her ill-ness evokes a complex mixture of love and guilt which is also infused with anger—anger because of the daugh-ter's irrational feeling that the mother has 'given her consent' (*Something* [*Something I've Been Meaning to Tell You*], 244) to this illness, given her consent, that is, to death and to the fact of death. A clue to obsession is the way the mother obtrudes herself into the daugh-ter's stories and dreams. **'Ottawa Valley'** concludes with the narrator's recognition, 'The problem, the only problem, is my mother. And she is the one of course that I am trying to get' (*Something,* 246). In the ending of **'Friend of My Youth'** Flora, who seems to survive because Ellie takes her place, gets transposed into the mother figure: 'Of course it's my mother I'm thinking of, my mother as she was in those dreams, saying, It's nothing, just this little tremor' (*Friend,* 26).

A Dream

As anticipated by Rabinowitz's 'rules of notice,' experi-enced readers of Munro short stories know that they should pay particular attention to reported dreams and visions. In **'Friend of My Youth'** and **'The Ottawa Valley,'** the dream figure is the mother who returns from a time when her illness was still mild—just this little tremor—to remind the narrator of something for-gotten or repressed (for an extensive analysis of this dream motif as wish-fulfilment, see Heller, 60-68). In **'Open Secrets,'** an almost hallucinatory image of a punished hand gives the main character the feeling of 'looking into an open secret, something not startling until you think of trying to tell it' (*Open,* 158). In the final story in *The Love of a Good Woman,* **'My Moth-er's Dream,'** the dream is the same one that haunted Alice Munro recurrently after the death of her second daughter, who was born without functioning kidneys and who died, like Mrs Quinn, of toxic poisoning. In her own dream, Munro has said, 'I was doing some-thing and had the feeling I was forgetting something very, very important. It was a baby. I had left it outside and forgotten about it, and it was out in the rain. By the time I remembered what it was, the baby was dead' (Ross, *Double Life,* 53). In all these stories, the dream can be seen to provide an interpretive key, introducing from another level of reality an element that has been forgotten or denied or can't be talked about or is not acknowledged in the conscious life.

Hence in **'The Love of a Good Woman'** notice is taken of Enid's disturbing dreams, which are so much at odds with her waking life. These dreams come to her when she is sleeping in the sickroom of the dying Mrs Quinn and reflect Enid's awareness of the current of sexuality in the house. Were this story written in the horror genre, the dreams could be explicitly identified as emanations from the sickroom, escaping from the hidden red box or given off by the blood concealed under the hastily applied brown paint. In any case, the dreams are horrifying enough. What gives these dreams their nightmare quality for Enid is the way they highlight her lack of control. Her response, characteristically, is a middle-of-the-night house-cleaning bee that resembles Flora's rearguard action against disorder in **'Friend of My Youth'** (*Friend,* 6-7). In the medicalized setting which is Enid's usual environment, Enid is the one in charge and naked bodies lose their power. Enid often says briskly to her patients, 'Do you think I haven't seen any bottom parts before? . . . Bottom parts, top parts, it's pretty boring after a while. You know, there's just the two ways we're made' (35). But in her dreams, she encounters bodies not under her care and control: 'In the dreams that came to her now she would be copulating or trying to copulate . . . with utterly forbidden and unthinkable partners. With fat squirmy babies or patients in bandages or her own mother. She would be slick with lust, hollow and groaning with it' (51). In the love-story genre, dreams may reveal the dreamer's unrecognized desire for the hero; in Gothic horror, dreams are warnings that the heroine's apparently safe environment is really a death-trap. Both genre-based strategies can be called upon here, each with different interpretive outcomes. So we can say that in Enid's dreams, the forbidden partner that Enid does not allow herself to think about is Rupert. Or we can see the dreams as an anticipation of death. With respect to the latter, the contrast is striking with **'Cortes Island,'** which uses the same triangle of murder in a quite different way. In **'Cortes Island'** the 'faithful, regularly satisfied' narrator has recurrent dreams of sex with a presumed murderer or murder accomplice, Mr Gorrie, on the island where the murder took place: 'Our bed—Mr. Gorrie's and mine—was the gravelly beach or the rough boat deck or the punishing coils of greasy rope. There was a relish in what you might call ugliness' (*Love* [*The Progress of Love*], 145). Whereas the narrator of **'Cortes Island'** welcomes 'the attack, the response, the possibilities [that] went beyond anything life offered,' Enid is left susceptible by her dreams to an ironic vision in which all human action winds down to death. She thinks, 'For everybody, though, the same thing. Evil grabs us when we are sleeping; pain and disintegration lie in wait. Animal horrors, all worse than you can imagine beforehand' (52).

A connection is explicitly made in the story between Enid's dreams, Mrs Quinn's story of transgressive sexuality and male violence, and Enid's memory of a childhood event that is said to be a dream. Enid puts them all in the same category of 'disgusting inventions': 'Lies

of that nature could be waiting around in the corners of a person's mind, hanging like bats in the corners, waiting to take advantage of any kind of darkness' (74). The third in this series of so-called lies is a remembered event from Enid's early childhood. When Enid reported to her mother that she had seen her father in his office sucking an unknown woman's nipple, her mother reframed the memory as a dream that can't be talked about: 'Dreams are sometimes downright silly. Don't tell Daddy about it. It's too silly' (75). The introduction of this third example doesn't strengthen Enid's developing argument that all three are inventions ('*Lies*') to be disregarded and erased, but it does prepare for the story's reversal—Enid's recognition of the benefits of secrecy. Previously Enid has been imagining a melodramatic scenario in which she invites Rupert to take her out in the rowboat, confronts him with Mrs Quinn's story, risks being drowned, urges a public confession ('You can't live with that kind of secret' [72]), and then, if all goes well, dedicates herself devotedly to a lifetime of visiting him in prison. Suddenly another future opens itself to her imagination. Enid discovers what everyone else, she thinks, has known all along—that silence is 'how to keep the world habitable': 'She hadn't asked him yet, she hadn't spoken. Nothing committed her to asking. It was still *before*. Mr. Willens had still driven himself into Jutland Pond, on purpose or by accident. . . . Through her silence, her collaboration in a silence, what benefits could bloom. For herself and for others' (75-76).

A LITTLE HATCHET

From the beginning, Munro's stories have pushed towards dark, hidden regions that are unexplored because as yet there are no words to get us there. Like Enid at the end of **'The Love of a Good Woman,'** the reader is brought along a tangled path and left on the threshold of a mystery. This long-standing feature in Munro's work of resisting closure seems to be related to her own deepest feelings about the enterprise of writing itself: on the one hand it is endlessly valuable to try to get it all down, to make connections, to attend to messages; on the other hand, the patterns may be wrong, the connections mistaken, and the attempt itself a sort of betrayal. As a way of saying the unsayable, Munro often, as one of her earliest critics put it, presents an 'essential tension between two sets of values, two ways of seeing, two worlds' (Macdonald, 335).[10] Munro's narrative interest in absences, gaps, discontinuity, disruption, fragmentation, parallel lives, 'funny jumps,' and missing chunks of information used to be called 'the art of disarrangement' (Mathews) and more recently has been called a postmodern rejection of totalizing systems and master narratives (Nunes). Characteristically Munro's stories pull back from clarity and end with a recognition of a mystery that changes the known landscape into something unfamiliar. A prototypical example is the often-quoted ending from **'Walker Brothers Cowboy,'** the first story from the first collection. After a journey during which a young girl learns something about her father's life that must be kept a secret from her mother, she feels her father's life 'flowing back . . . darkening and turning strange' (**Dance,** 18). The last paragraphs of **'The Love of a Good Woman'** achieve a similar effect with a description of Enid on the threshold of a new life. She is about to enter a boat and begin a journey, but the destination is uncertain. At dusk Enid and Rupert follow the path to the river, Rupert walking ahead with his little hatchet and clearing the path of thistles. They walk through swarms of tiny bugs that are constantly in motion yet keep together 'in the shape of a pillar or a cloud.' Their path is made hazardous by the tangle of roots underfoot and dangling vines. The boat is waiting 'riding in the shadows,' and Rupert goes out of sight to find the oars, which are hidden: 'If she tried to, she could still hear Rupert's movements in the bushes. But if she concentrated on the motion of the boat, a slight secretive motion, she could feel as if everything for a long way around had gone quiet' (78). There is nothing here, except for the description of the boat, that could not pass as a straight realistic description of a scene along the Maitland River in Huron County on one of those humid buggy evenings in July. Coral Ann Howells asks, 'Is this Munro at her most realistic or her most symbolic?' (**Alice Munro,** 153). But our readerly expectations require that final paragraphs be charged with meaning and so we puzzle over the little hatchet, the tangled path, the swarming formation of bugs, the river, the secretive motion of the boat, the concluding quiet. The meanings of some of these elements here have been shaped in our minds by previous appearances within this story and within other stories by Munro.

Take the river. When the river is introduced in section 1, it is associated with the three boys whose plans for swimming were cut short when they saw the submerged car and Mr Willens's floating hand. Enid, of course, can't swim—she had intended to reveal this to Rupert once they were out in the boat in deep water (if indeed there is any deep water in midsummer).[11] In section 2, the river is associated with mist and with the 'overflow and density of summer' (44-45) and in section 4 the boat is first introduced: 'Mist was rising so that you could hardly see the river. . . . There was a boat moving . . . Now that she had found it, she kept watching it, as if it could say something to her. And it did. It said something gentle and final. *You know. You know*' (63-64). In her 'Contributor's Notes,' in which she describes how she transferred the original incident from an island off the British Columbia coast to Huron County, Munro emphasizes the importance of the river: 'And there is the boat, still, waiting by the bank of the Maitland River.' Why does she need the river? Because of the special position that this river has always occupied in

Munro's imagination as a place that is both ominous and beckoning, legendary and ordinary, touchable and mysterious, a place associated with the source of writing itself.[12] In **'Meneseteung,'** the narrator imagines a visionary state in which Almeda Roth, a nineteenth-century poet, has a sense of the 'one very great poem that will contain everything': 'The name of the poem is the name of the river. No, in fact it is the river, the Meneseteung, that is the poem—with its deep holes and rapids and blissful pools under the summer trees and its grinding blocks of ice thrown up at the end of winter and its desolating spring floods' (**Friend,** 70).

In its appearance at the end of **'The Love of a Good Woman,'** the river landscape is similarly described as a place inclusive enough to encompass opposites: the feminine image of the gently rocking boat and the masculine image of the axe. The man with the axe has a long history in Munro's creative imagination. In **'Images,'** Old Joe Phippen with his axe is the personification, as we have seen, of the child's worst imaginings about death. In a commentary included in *The Narrative Voice,* Munro has said that this story 'started with the picture in my mind of the man met in the woods, coming obliquely down the riverbank, carrying the hatchet, and the child watching him, and the father unaware, bending over his traps. For a long time I was carrying this picture in my mind, as I am carrying various pictures now which may or may not turn into stories' ('Colonel's Hash,' 182). Munro was still carrying in her mind the picture of the menacing axe-man when she wrote **'Vandals,'** a story in which Ladner, a taxidermist who works with piles of animal skins and eyeless animal heads, turns out to be a child-abuser. The first time that the six- and seven-year old Kenny and Liza saw Ladner, we are told, 'He came out like a murderer on television, with a little axe, from behind a tree.' Like the little girl in **'Images,'** the young Liza learns from her encounter with the axe-man that some secrets can never be told: 'She learned not to talk so much about all she knew' (**Open,** 286). Having encountered this axe-man before, a long-time Munro reader can be expected to take special note of the little hatchet and the smell of whiskey on Rupert's breath and be reminded of Old Joe Phippen and hence of Rupert's connection with death.

But, as we might expect, this reading is not enough. We have left something out. The image of the hatchet is double-coded to evoke both Rupert the murderer and Rupert the lover. The latter reading has been prepared for as early as those three bouquets of yellow forsythia and the hooting girls yelling, 'Look at the beautiful bridesmaids.' With the benefit of hindsight, we can re-read section 2 and realize that the hatchet itself has been introduced, at least by implication, earlier in the story. As an example of the kind of detail recorded in her personal notebook, Enid tells Rupert that she wrote down something the other day that Lois had said: 'Lois and Sylvie came in when Mrs. Green was here and Mrs. Green was mentioning how the berry bushes were growing along the lane and stretching across the road, and Lois said, "It's like in 'Sleeping Beauty.'"' Because I'd read them the story. I made a note of that' (55). Rupert's response is to say, 'I'll have to get after those berry canes and cut them back.' 'Sleeping Beauty' is the best-known version of the story of the spring maiden who is pricked by the thorn of winter and sleeps on the heights in her ring of fire or in a castle enclosed in briars until the hero comes to hack through the briars and wake her with a kiss. In other versions, she appears as Briar Rose, the Princess on the Glass Hill, or the swan-maiden Brynhild rescued by Sigurd. At first glance, Rupert might seem like an unlikely Sigurd. But the ending highlights the hatchet in its benign aspect as a tool to cut through brambles, thorns, and thistles: 'he had brought a little hatchet from the woodshed, to clear their path' (77). Let's look again at Enid, associated both with the gently moving boat and with helping people die—the good woman begins to look like a swan-maiden, if we recall that in William Morris's *Sigurd* Brynhild is both 'she that loveth' and 'the chooser of the slain' who picks those to be slain on the battlefield and carried off to Valhalla.

And so by the end of this dazzling story, Munro has brought us face to face with a mysterious silence. Duffy calls it death; Howells calls it love. Generic expectations of Gothic horror and of romance allow for double readings of almost every incident, right up to Enid's sense that 'everything for a long way around had gone quiet.' This story—surely among Munro's most complex and suggestive—is a garden of forking paths. It turns into an encyclopaedic reservoir of stories, the particular one realized by any single reading depending on which echo of previous Munro stories the reader hears, which detail the reader chooses to foreground, and which patterns the reader is prepared to see.

Notes

This paper was first presented at the 1999 Conference 'A Visionary Tradition: Canadian Literature and Culture at the Turn of the Millennium' organized by J. R. (Tim) Struthers at the University of Guelph. A version of it was presented at the 2002 Indian Association of Canadian Studies conference in Haridwar, India.

1. When 'The Love of a Good Woman' was published in the volume of O. Henry Award stories for 1997, Munro discussed the origins of the story in her section of 'Contributors' Notes': 'What did I first know about this story? A man and woman disposing of her lover's body. This happened on an island off the B.C. coast—they put him in his own boat and towed him out into open water. . . .

The sudden switch from sex to murder to marital cooperation seemed to me one of those marvelous, unlikely, acrobatic pieces of human behavior. Then the lover got transferred into a car, and it all went on in Huron County, and the boys got into it, and their families, and Enid, who took over the story as insistently as she took over a sickroom. And there is the boat, still, waiting by the bank of the Maitland River' (443). A different treatment of the same episode can be found in 'Cortes Island' in *The Love of a Good Woman*, where a woman and her lover cover up the murder of the husband, not by water but by fire. According to a newspaper report of the inquest quoted in the text of 'Cortes Island,' 'The death of Mr. Wild was ruled to be an accident due to misadventure, its cause being a fire of origins unknown' (*Love*, 136).

2. Mr Willens, hardly a common name, was also the name given to a similarly opportunistic character in a very early short story, 'Story for Sunday,' published in April 1951 in the University of Western Ontario's literary magazine *Folio*. As described in Sheila Munro's *Lives of Mothers and Daughters* (8-9), this story is about a young, and not very attractive, girl, Evelyn, who becomes infatuated with the new Sunday school superintendent, Mr Willens, after he says flattering things to her and kisses her in the church vestry—until the next week when she overhears Mr Willens in the vestry saying the same words to, and kissing, someone else.

3. For example, Coral Ann Howells's reading gives priority to the love story, with the result that she anticipates a happy ending for Enid: 'The story opens out into the space for a love story as Enid waits for [Rupert] to find the oars. . . . The imagery suggests a journey to the promised land' (*Alice Munro*, 153). Dennis Duffy's reading foregrounds the elements of Gothic horror, so that for him the ending represents Enid as 'an imperilled gothic heroine' (177) 'in love with death as any gothic heroine' (182) and 'on the verge of embracing a demon lover. She is about to set out on a boat ride with the killer. . . . The message is clear. . . . Call it death' (184).

4. Howells finds support for the view that Mrs Quinn made up the murder story: 'Actually, Mrs. Quinn's scenario is very close to Tay Garnett's film *The Postman Always Rings Twice*, starring Lana Turner (1946) which she might well have seen . . . , but Enid does not think of that' (*Alice Munro*, 151-52). Duffy explicitly rejects the unreliable narrator explanation on various grounds, including the argument that 'Once all narrative reliability is dethroned, can anything in the story be saved? What else may be delusional?' (186-87). Carol Beran

accepts the authority of Mrs Quinn's story as the basis for what she thinks is the real mystery: 'The mystery of how Willens died seems to be solved in the story; the mystery of whether another murder is about to happen at the end of the story is not' (244).

5. Duffy says, 'there is a hint that her fatal illness originated in a reaction to the drugs that she swallowed in order to abort a foetus planted in her by the optometrist whom her husband killed' (182).

6. In my reading, the repeated instances in section 1 in which secrets cannot be told cue the reader to give considerable weight to the paragraph that starts: 'She hadn't asked him yet, she hadn't spoken. Nothing yet committed her to asking' (75). Similarly, Ildiko de Papp Carrington's excellent article 'Don't Tell (on) Daddy' sees Enid as belatedly learning the social advantage of collaborating in silence by not telling: 'Like her mother, Enid decides against confrontation. By telling Rupert nothing, she will let him believe that she accepts the official version of Mr. Willens's death, suicide or accident.' In contrast, in an article that is perceptive and compelling, Dennis Duffy's reading anticipates a risky disclosure: 'We are in Rocky Horrorland, where we shriek out a warning to the oblivious gothic heroine lurching toward disaster' (182). '[The story] closes with Enid alone on a riverbank with Rupert, uncertain of what the result will be of her planned disclosure to him of what she has heard from Jeannette' (186).

7. This omission of hair colour must surely be deliberate. In Duffy's listing of textual variants between the story that appeared in the *New Yorker* (NY) and the hardback (HB) version, he notes: 'HB 47 omits "dark" in "her dark thick hair" (NY 125)' (188). Unruly dark thick hair is a physical characteristic of Munro herself that she has repeatedly bestowed on female characters from the narrator of 'Red Dress—1946' in the first collection *Dance of the Happy Shades* to Pauline in 'The Children Stay' in *The Love of a Good Woman.*

8. Robert Thacker has noted the family resemblance among Mary McQuade, Audrey Atkinson, and Enid, significantly calling it 'another textual "progress" derived from the mother that ought to be traced further' (17).

9. Carol Beran even suggests that Enid's treatment of her patient constitutes 'a brutal form of euthanasia' (244), citing in evidence the nurse's failure at the end to call in the doctor and family members as well as her surreptitious tidying up of the traces of the patient's final death struggle.

10. Titles of Munro criticism have emphasized terms such as 'paradox,' 'oxymoron,' and 'double vision' or featured juxtaposed contraries such as the strange vs the familiar/deep caves vs kitchen linoleum/legendary patterns vs surface detail (e.g., Hoy's '"Dull, Simple, Amazing and Unfathomable": Paradox and Double Vision,' 1980; Djwa's 'Deep Caves and Kitchen Linoleum,' 1981; Ross's '"At Least Part Legend,"' 1983; Howells's 'Worlds Alongside: Contradictory Discourses . . . ,' 1985; Martin's *Alice Munro: Paradox and Parallel,* 1987; York's '"Gulfs" and "Connections,"' 1987; Carrington's *Controlling the Uncontrollable,* 1989; James Carscallen's *The Other Country,* 1993; Louis K. MacKendrick's *Some Other Reality,* 1993).

11. In *Lives of Girls and Women,* Miss Farris drowned in the high water of the Wawanash in springtime, a drowning that Del transfers to her fictional character Caroline, who 'walked into the Wawanash River' in midsummer (but how in the heat of summer, Del worries, 'was there going to be enough water. . . . Caroline would have to lie down on her face as if she was drowning herself in the bathtub' [*Lives,* 205-6]).

12. In a magazine article published in 1974, here's how Munro described the Maitland River: 'We believed there were deep holes in the river. We went looking for them, scared and hopeful, and never found them, but not stop believing for that. Even now I believe that there were deep holes, ominous beckoning places, but that they have probably silted up. But maybe not all. Because I am still partly convinced that this river—not even the whole river but this little stretch of it—will provide whatever myths you want, whatever adventures. I name the plants, I name the fish, and every name seems to me triumphant, every leaf and quick fish remarkably valuable. This ordinary place is sufficient, everything here touchable and mysterious' ('Everything Here,' 33).

Works Cited

Beran, Carol. 'The Luxury of Excellence: Alice Munro in the *New Yorker.' Essays on Canadian Writing* 66 (1998), 204-31

Boyce, Pleuke, and Ron Smith. 'A National Treasure: Interview with Alice Munro.' *Meanjin* 54 (1995), 222-32

Calvino, Italo. 'Cybernetics and Ghosts.' *The Uses of Literature: Essays.* Trans Patrick Creagh. San Diego and New York: Harcourt, Brace, Jovanovich 1986, 3-27

Carrington, Ildiko de Papp. *Controlling the Uncontrollable: The Fiction of Alice Munro.* DeKalb: Northern Illinois University Press 1989

———. '"Don't Tell (on) Daddy": Narrative Complexity in Alice Munro's "The Love of a Good Woman."' *Studies in Short Fiction* 34 (1999), 159-70

Carscallen, James. *The Other Country: Patterns in the Writing of Alice Munro.* Toronto: ECW 1993

Djwa, Sandra. 'Deep Caves and Kitchen Linoleum: Psychological Violence in the Fiction of Alice Munro.' *Violence in the Canadian Novel since 1960.* Ed Virginia Harger-Grinling and Terry Goldie. St John's: Memorial University Press 1981, 177-90

Duffy, Dennis. '"A Dark Sort of Mirror": "The Love of a Good Woman" as Pauline Poetic.' *Essays on Canadian Writing* 66 (1998), 169-90

Hancock, Geoff. 'An Interview with Alice Munro.' *Canadian Fiction Magazine* 43 (1982), 75-114

Heble, Ajay. *The Tumble of Reason: Alice Munro's Discourse of Absence.* Toronto: University of Toronto Press 1994

Heller, Deborah. 'Getting Loose: Women and Narration in Alice Munro's *Friend of My Youth.*' *Essays on Canadian Writing* 66 (1998), 60-80

Howells, Coral Ann. *Alice Munro.* Manchester and New York: Manchester University Press 1998

———. 'Worlds Alongside: Contradictory Discourses in Alice Munro and Margaret Atwood.' *Gaining Ground.* Ed R. Nischik and R. Kroetsch. Edmonton: NeWest 1985, 121-36

Hoy, Helen. '"Dull, Simple, Amazing and Unfathomable": Paradox and Double Vision in Alice Munro's Fiction.' *Studies in Canadian Literature* 5 (1980), 100-15

Irvine, Lorna. '"Changing is the Word I Want."' *Probable Fictions: Alice Munro's Narrative Acts.* Ed. Louis K. MacKendrick. Downsview, Ont: ECW 1983, 99-111

Macdonald, Rae McCarthy. 'A Madman Loose in the World: The Vision of Alice Munro.' *Modern Fiction Studies* 22 (1976), 365-74

MacKendrick, Louis K. *Some Other Reality: Alice Munro's 'Something I've Been Meaning To Tell You.'* Toronto: ECW 1993

Martin, W. R. *Alice Munro: Paradox and Parallel.* Edmonton: University of Alberta Press 1987

Mathews, Laurence. '*Who Do You Think You Are?*: Alice Munro's Art of Disarrangement.' *Probable Fictions: Alice Munro's Narrative Acts.* Ed Louis K. MacKendrick. Downsview, Ont: ECW 1983, 181-93

Munro, Alice. 'The Colonel's Hash Resettled.' *The Narrative Voice: Stories and Reflections by Canadian Authors.* Ed John Metcalf. Toronto: McGraw-Hill Ryerson 1972

———. 'Contributors' Notes.' *Prize Stories: The Best of 1997.* [The O. Henry Awards.] Ed Larry Dark. New York: Doubleday 1997, 442-43

———. *Dance of the Happy Shades.* Toronto: McGraw-Hill Ryerson 1968

———. 'Everything Here Is Touchable and Mysterious.' *Weekend Magazine* [*Toronto Star*], 11 May 1974, 33

———. *Friend of My Youth.* Toronto: McClelland and Stewart 1990

———. *Lives of Girls and Women.* Toronto: McGraw-Hill Ryerson 1971

———. *The Love of a Good Woman.* Toronto: McClelland and Stewart 1998

———. *The Moons of Jupiter.* Markham, Ont: Penguin, 1982

———. *Open Secrets.* Toronto: McClelland and Stewart 1994

———. *The Progress of Love.* Toronto: McClelland and Stewart 1986

———. *Something I've Been Meaning to Tell You.* Toronto: McGraw-Hill Ryerson 1974

———. 'What Is Real?' *Making It New: Contemporary Canadian Stories.* Ed John Metcalf. Toronto: Methuen 1982, 223-26

———. *Who Do You Think You Are?* Toronto: Macmillan 1978

Munro, Sheila. *Lives of Mothers and Daughters.* Toronto: McClelland and Stewart 2001

Nunes, Mark. 'Postmodern "Piecing": Alice Munro's Contingent Ontologies.' *Studies in Short Fiction* 34:1 (1997), 11-26

Rabinowitz, Peter. *Before Reading: Narrative Conventions and the Politics of Interpretation.* Ithaca and London: Cornell University Press 1987

Radway, Janice. *Reading the Romance: Women, Patriarchy and Popular Literature.* Chapel Hill: University of North Carolina Press 1984

Ross, Catherine Sheldrick. *Alice Munro: A Double Life.* Downsview, Ont: ECW 1992

———. '"At Least Part Legend": The Fiction of Alice Munro.' *Probable Fictions: Alice Munro's Narrative Acts.* Ed Louis K. MacKendrick. Downsview, Ont: ECW 1983, 112-26

Thacker, Robert. 'Introduction: Alice Munro, Writing "Home": "Seeing This Trickle in Time."' *Essays on Canadian Writing* 66 (1998), 1-20

York, Lorraine. '"Gulfs" and "Connections": The Fiction of Alice Munro.' *Essays on Canadian Writing* 35 (1987), 135-46

Robert McGill (essay date December 2002)

SOURCE: McGill, Robert. "Where Do You Think You Are?: Alice Munro's Open Houses." *Mosaic* 35, no. 4 (December 2002): 103-19.

[*In the following essay, McGill investigates the concept of "geographic metafiction" in Munro's work, maintaining that "Vandals" "makes use of its own spatiality to comment upon the places it evokes within its narrative, while those places in turn inform the space of the story."*]

> Compared to the other houses in town, hers appeared to have no secrets, no contradictions. What people said was, "It's such a pretty house, doesn't look real."
>
> —Alice Munro, *Lives of Girls and Women*

The conviction that literary criticism should develop a rigorous approach to space in fiction emerges from themes in many fields that indicate a shift in theoretical preoccupation from time to space. Postcolonial, neo-Marxist, and feminist studies are each in their way preoccupied with space, but terms such as *interstice* and *territory* are variously deployed, sometimes as metaphor and sometimes as direct referent to spatial problematics. Accordingly, the need has arisen for a hermeneutics of fictional space, that is, of the spaces in and of fiction. Literary hermeneutics must consider the spatial character of fiction: how it occupies and configures space, how geography and fiction intersect and inform one another, and how space is fundamental to reading. Linda Hutcheon has identified in postmodern fiction a tendency toward what she calls "historiographic metafiction," a fiction that, even as it tells a historical story, comments upon its own writing of history: its own involvements, its process, its limitations. In this essay I argue that in fiction such as Alice Munro's, there is also a geographic metafiction, a fiction that, even as it configures space and place, examines its own ability to do so. A reading of **"Vandals,"** the final story in Munro's 1994 collection ***Open Secrets,*** demonstrates that Munro's fiction makes use of its own spatiality to comment upon the places it evokes within its narrative, while those places in turn inform the space of the story.

To refer to Munro's stories as "open houses" is to nod to her title ***Open Secrets*** in the belief that the two phrases are often synonymous in her work. The house is frequently a central figure in Munro's fiction, and it appears as a place infused with secrets, as evidenced in the much-cited assertion in ***Lives of Girls and Women*** that people's lives are "deep caves paved with kitchen linoleum" (249). Moreover, the concept of the "open house" suggests that, like the writer, someone who holds an open house is making secrets available and knowable to all visitors. Such acts of exposure are not transparent but fraught with vested interests and limitations,

hiding some things even as they reveal others. Munro herself links the house to short fiction in her essay "What Is Real": "Everybody knows what a house does, how it encloses space and makes connections between one enclosed space and another and presents what is outside in a new way. This is the nearest I can come to explaining what a story does for me, and what I want my stories to do for other people" (224). Munro's house-fiction comparison insists on a relationship in which each co-constituent both defines itself in opposition to and shares characteristics with the other. Houses can be essentially fictional spaces, while the space of fiction is a manner of built form that offers conceptual and imaginative dwelling.

But, while houses are at the centre of Munro's art, they are often places of marginalization in her stories, especially with regard to the women who inhabit them. Accordingly, a consideration of the peripheral visions in Munro's fiction must take into account the connections between gender and space. Munro says that early in her career "there was a feeling that women could write about the freakish, the marginal. [. . .] I came to feel that was our territory, whereas the mainstream big novel about real life was men's territory. I don't know how I got that feeling of being on the margins; it wasn't that I was *pushed* there. Maybe it was because I grew up on a margin" ("Art" 255, emph. Munro's). The comment underscores Munro's persistent accentuation of the spatial aspect of concepts such as "territory" and "margin," which critics often deploy primarily as tropes. And, in **"Vandals"** and other stories, Munro extends the link between gendered and regional marginality to explore the peripheral enspacement of fiction itself, as well as the connections among stories, gender, and space. Munro asks readers to consider ways in which women might stage protest from the margins and what form that protest might take in fiction. Given Munro's house-fiction metonym, this request may even instigate a revision of contemporary spatial theory, which has tended to privilege tropes of mobility and deterritorialization.

* * *

Munro's **"Vandals"** tells the story of a young woman named Liza, who, with her husband, Warren, visits the empty house of her older friend Bea and goes on a rampage, mutilating the house's interior for reasons that are initially unclear. Through a series of flashbacks it becomes apparent that Liza and her brother Kenny used to visit Bea and her husband Ladner when they were children, and that Ladner repeatedly sexually abused them in the forest behind his house. At the most literal level, space is not simply a backdrop for the story; the traversing, invasion, and vandalizing of it are central.

The narrative is especially rife with excursions and tours, which are by no means innocuous but which appear as tools of an oppressive masculinity that controls and orders space. Ladner's books, which include *The Peninsular War* and *The Peloponnesian Wars,* are reminders that space is not only a site of dispute but an object and tool of it, while Warren's name doubly puns on "warring" and "warren" to underscore further the kinship of space and conflict. In **"Vandals,"** such hostilities arise when men enact their urge to define and dominate otherness through gestures of dividing and enclosing. In order for Ladner to define his own mobile subjectivity, he attempts to make the apiarian-named Bea like the dead animals he puts on display: inert and enclosed. Mobility represents agency in space, and in **"Vandals"** it is the privilege of men. Peter Parr brings Bea "into an orderly life" through his weekly driving tours (264), Liza's father moves his family nomadically from place to place, Warren drives "*his* snowmobile" while Liza rides (261, emph. mine), and Kenny notably dies in a car crash. Most conspicuously of all, Ladner uses his mobility and familiarity with land to assert authority and discipline others. The tour he gives Bea leaves her feeling lost and powerless; the two conditions often cognate in the story. Bea initially plans to introduce herself to Ladner with a story that she is lost, but her spatial helplessness becomes real when Ladner has her within his space: "He did not slow down for her or help her in any way" (270) and she "couldn't keep track of their direction or get any idea of the layout of the property" (272). Ladner takes pleasure in her vulnerability to a wilderness that he has subdued, consolidating his confidence and comfort in space. The fact that Ladner induces and perpetuates Bea's bewilderment underscores Henri Lefebvre's point that power deliberately confuses and deceives: "Dissimulation is necessarily part of any message from power. Thus space indeed 'speaks'—but it does not tell all. Above all, it prohibits" (142). Ladner is prohibitive in exactly this manner. His refusal to allow others knowledge of space frees him to operate within exclusive spaces of his own devising, such as the site where he abuses Liza and Kenny. His violations make Liza's violation of the house's space a symbolically appropriate retribution.

Moreover, Ladner's various inscriptions upon space imply that the narration of space is central to control of it. The topography in **"Vandals"** is everywhere written over with text. There are the posted quotations from Aristotle and Rousseau, the sign that names the "Lesser Dismal" swamp, labels on trees, Warren's tomato-sauce graffiti and Ladner's "No Trespassing" signs. Such inscriptions aid in ordering, naming, dividing, and enclosing, all subjective and often arbitrary interpretations of land and impositions upon it that can function as authoritative, colonizing gestures. Bea and Liza are trapped not only within a space but also within particular narratives that have produced and manipulated it. Throughout the story Munro depicts Ladner as an ironic God- and Adam-figure who has dominion in word as well as action to make, name, narrate, and control his

"territory," and even to separate the elect from the preterite in his space by declaring, "Sometimes I let people go through but they're the people I decide on" (268). Ladner lives in an A-frame, emphasizing his identification as Adam, the alpha-man who is also the alphabet man, ordering and classifying, in contrast with Bea, the beta-woman who follows and supplements him.

Because the land is very much Ladner's and Bea principally remains within the house, Liza's choice to attack the dwelling may seem strange, and critics have accordingly inferred that Liza is reacting against Bea's failure to protect her from Ladner. After all, criticism has identified an inclination in Canadian fiction to characterize the house as a feminine space: "The house is containing, nurturing, protecting, mothering" (Kroetsch, *Lovely* 80). But **"Vandals"** complicates such a generalization. Ladner's offer to make tea for Bea is the first sign that it is he who has dominion over the house, and later we hear that she has made only a few inroads there: "She had not brought much—just enough to make islands here and there among Ladner's skins and instruments" (293). A critic like Gaston Bachelard (who declares, "If I were asked to name the chief benefit of the house, I should say: the house shelters daydreaming, the house protects the dreamer, the house allows one to dream in peace" [6]) may posit the house as a safe dwelling, but for Munro the house can present women not with sanctuary but incarceration, and surveillance rather than solitude. For men, the idea of home may involve both a sense of ownership and of belonging to place, while women risk becoming only possessions and constituents. In *Who Do You Think You Are?* Patrick leads tours of his and Rose's home, while Rose has been "uneasy about these tours from the start, and tagged along in silence, or made deprecating remarks which Patrick did not like" (143). Women are outsiders even within the home, and Liza's attack on it confirms what has already been implied, that, far from aligning the house with female authority, the male has not simply invaded but has constructed the house as an oppressive, claustrophobic enclosure. **"Vandals"** challenges the traditional correlations of houses with safety, and Liza follows Annie Herron in **"A Wilderness Station"** (another story in *Open Secrets*) as a "wild woman" who trespasses into male space and threatens dominant masculinist views.

Liza's response to male ordering is a necessary disordering. Consider the etymology of the title **"Vandals."** It comes from the Germanic people of that name who destroyed books and works of art around the Mediterranean in the fourth and fifth centuries. Vandalism is a spatial transgression that violently rejects property claims and spatial uniformity, but Liza's vandalism is also a reaction against Ladner's dominant text, not unlike Rose's "deprecating remarks" during Patrick's tours. The final image of Liza in the vandalism scene is of her "pointed tongue" on Warren's neck (284), reminding readers that if her revenge has been spatial, it has also been discursive. She has betrayed Bea and taken revenge on Ladner not only by decimating the house but by reconstructing the act in words. Her ability to deceive is a sign of power as it was for Ladner. Meanwhile, Bea also has a fantasy of vandalism, writing: "I am tempted just to light a match and let everything go up in smoke" (262). Hers is a vision of self-expression reminiscent of Bertha Mason's last act in *Jane Eyre,* which is reconfigured as an anti-patriarchal gesture in Jean Rhys's *Wide Sargasso Sea.* Like Bertha, Bea has been a "kept woman," subject to the fickle whims of a stoic Englishman, and of course "Bea" is a manner of abbreviation of "Bertha." It is notable, then, that the story ends with "darkness collecting [. . .] like cold smoke coming off the snow" (294). The phrase suggests the smoke of arson, while the word "collecting" reminds us that we are reading a volume of stories, and that its author may also be engaging in her own acts of liberating vandalism.

* * *

So far I have argued that **"Vandals"** exhibits an interest in geography as a site and medium of power and identity, and that it construes space as intrinsic to gender relations, which are formed and maintained through the collusive actions of gendering spaces and enspacing genders—that is, ascribing an ontological space to them. These spatial preoccupations have ramifications not only for social praxis but also for writing fiction. For instance, perhaps **"Vandals"** is itself somehow vandalizing. In considering such possibilities, one must bear in mind that the relationship of fictional space to textual space is not merely incidental or metaphorical. Fiction transforms space, our awareness of it, and our relationship to it, while generating its own spaces, whether they be words on paper or maps in the mind.

A fundamental error on the part of critics has been to conflate different species of spaces. Metaphorical, cognitive, social, and physical all coalesce in a single spatial idiom, and it is not surprising that those who fail to appreciate the differences between these varieties might come to view space—in fiction or otherwise—as abstract and homogenous, and in turn transparent, universal, and placeless: no more than "setting." Neil Smith and Cindy Katz warn that "it is precisely this apparent familiarity of space, the givenness of space, its fixity and inertness, that makes a spatial grammar so fertile for metaphoric appropriation" (68). Such metaphorization is often evident in interpretation of Munro's texts. For example, to use geographical terminology in discussing concepts like Munro's "hidden territory of sexual desire" (Howells 27) is profitable if it recognizes Munro's attention to the spatial intricacies of sex, but it also risks conflating spaces and reducing all space to

the level of metaphor. Gillian Rose is critical of Smith and Katz's implication that physical space is the only "real" space (59), since—as we have seen in **"Vandals"**—ideological, symbolic, and physical space are intricately intertwined. However, Rose's argument that one space is not more real than another means that there is all the more need for a vocabulary capable of articulating the specificities and conjunctions of each.

Reduction of space to the status of psychological symbol can be just as misleading as its attenuation to metaphor. For instance, Beverly Rasporich discusses Munro's work by taking up Margaret Atwood's assertion in *Survival* that landscapes in literature often represent "interior landscapes; they are maps of a state of mind" (qtd. in Rasporich 122). To explicate Munro's landscapes in such a way is dangerously reductive, eliding not only important differences between mental and physical spaces but also interdependencies. This approach ostensibly seeks to foreground place in Munro's texts but actually draws attention away from it by assigning place the status of a vehicle in metaphor, thereby reducing it to instrumentality. Munro's use of space can be more fruitfully seen as metonymical. As Pam Houston argues, the metonymic relationship is "based on association, connection, proximity. It is a relationship by copresence, [. . .] a relationship based on contiguity and context" (82). For metonymy to function, neither co-constituent is simply a means to the other. To notice when landscape functions as metonym and not as metaphor is to be aware that space is not subordinate to character and plot but interconnected with them. Munro has said: "Fiction is all bound up in the local. The internal reason for that is surely that *feelings* are bound up in place. [. . .] The truth is, fiction depends for its life on place" (qtd. in Rasporich 122, emph. Munro's). In other words, physical space does not dissolve but is all the more important *as* space because of its relationship with human mental life. Munro insists that multiple discourses construct multiple modes of reality and that physical geography is at least implicated in all of them.

In addition to physical, mental, and social spaces, one might add the *fictional,* which is located within and between these fields. In the course of reading **"Vandals,"** we encounter or are reminded of multiple spaces with dynamic and mutually informing relationships to one another: the textual word-topography of Stratton Township, the mental map of the township that we compose from it, the (also-mental) map of the region where Munro resides—Huron County, Ontario—that we might overlay, and the physical terrain of that region, not to mention the (always-mediating) fact of our own spatial situatedness. Robert Kroetsch argues that "geography is also part of the text in a strange way, and I think geography is not fixed, it's changing—every journey across it or through it is another reading in a way" (*Labyrinths*

8). Henry James's "house of fiction" looks out upon the world (46), but in Munro's house-fiction metonym the fictional, social, and psychological commingle with no fixed boundary between them.

D. W. Meineg calls the geographer "a creator of literature" (318), while others reverse the comparison and identify writers as cartographers or geographers. One might circumvent these discussions by suggesting that Munro is a *geomancer*: one who organizes space to some apparent harmony. We might also notice the rhetorical aspect of such a role; Munro's organization of words in space evokes in readers a reaction toward space. In *Lives of Girls and Women,* Del acknowledges the particular hypnotic and disorienting potentials of communicating geography as she recalls Uncle Benny's relation of his trip to Toronto: "A map of the journey was burnt into his mind. And as he talked a different landscape [. . .] seemed to grow up around us created by his monotonous, meticulously remembering voice, and we could see it, we could see how it was to be lost there, how it was just not possible to find anything, or go on looking" (25). The power that the map-maker wields over her audience is both made possible and complicated by the fact that the reader is also involved in drawing the map. World and word may be conjoined, but they are "different landscapes," and in order to communicate, a story must necessarily warp just as a cartographic projection of the world distorts the globe. If cubism in visual art "deliberately shows up the contradictions which arise when a three-dimensional object is represented on a flat surface" (Butler 64), then how might a writer convey a three-dimensional world on the page? Fiction has its own codes and grammars of spatial representation that Munro employs and exploits.

* * *

While the connections between the physical space and meaning of poetry are a standard object of critical commentary, a common assumption is that fiction is transparently spatial, even a transcription of a quasi-oral event. However, the placement of text mediates our relationship to a story. It is a simple but important point that reading fiction is a journey across material space, and it is the artist's talent to exploit this fact in constructing the text. For example, it is not accidental that **"Vandals"** is the last story in *Open Secrets.* The fact that it features Bea Doud, whose family has appeared in several stories throughout the collection, suggests connections with the entire volume, and, accordingly, although one might approach **"Vandals"** as an enclosed and autonomous space, it offers a manner of back door through which to enter and re-enter the book. The "back door" metonym, which Munro's house-fiction metonym legitimizes and which the story itself suggests, underscores both the linear and non-linear possibilities inherent in reading such a collection.

Although, in one sense, text seems to be the arrest of lived experience into an immutable and static form, it is a process as much as a product, and to mistake the diachronic experience of text for the synchronic printed page is a synecdochal fallacy that ignores the dynamic processes of reading and writing and their circumscription of one's view of the text. It is impossible to see everything while being nowhere, and in terms of how readers configure space in a text, an apposite metonym is the walking tour, a metonym that is prominent in **"Vandals."** Michel de Certeau points out that maps of a journey "lose what existed: *the act of going by itself*" (129, emph. de Certeau's), but, in fiction, walks and their record are coeval. A story's mapping is performative; although ostensibly a reproduction, it enacts what it names, and what it creates is not only a journey for a character but for readers as well. In **"Vandals"** a number of topographical details appear in the course of Ladner's tour to emphasize that Bea feels lost, but, paradoxically, readers orient themselves and map Ladner's property with these same details even as they share in Bea's confusion. They are lost and found at the same time. Fiction territorializes and stages place by making landmarks and constructing relationships between them. It does not set down points according to constant, preexisting coordinates, but creates territory as needed, establishing certain sites that provide the references for further elaborations, after which readers might return to the initial point and know it for the first time.

In **"Vandals,"** Liza experiences the dazzling passage of landscape quite literally during her snowmobile ride: "Black trunks against the snow flashed by in a repetition that was faintly sickening" (277). The attention to black landmarks on a white surface, coming as it does after a poetic landscape description, reminds readers of the textual character of the space. They are literally reading the landscape. It also reminds them that the diachronic character of fiction can be disconcerting and disorienting, and Munro's mapping exploits these effects. **"Vandals"** cleverly manipulates its own physical space on the page to comment on space in ways that dovetail with issues that Munro explores through her narrative. One such strategy is enforced double vision. Consider this passage from **"Vandals"**:

> It was a wooden house with the top half painted white and the bottom half a glaring pink, like lipstick. That had been Liza's father's idea. Maybe he thought it would perk the place up. Maybe he thought pink would make it look as if it had a woman inside it.

> There is a mess in the kitchen—spilled cereal on the floor, puddles of milk on the counter. A pile of clothes from the Laundromat overflowing the corner armchair, and the dishcloth—Liza knows this without looking— all wadded up with the garbage in the sink. It is her job to clean all this up, and she had better do it before her father gets home.

(290)

The unexpected switch in tense between the paragraphs is confusing. Until this point in the story the third-person narrator has employed only the past tense, and the principle action closest to the "present" (i.e., the time of Bea's letter) is Liza's act of vandalism at Ladner's house. Accordingly, when we read about spills and messes, we expect to be reading about *Ladner*'s house, and we temporarily encounter a spatial jarring: we are not sure where we are. The result is a double exposure that causes us momentarily to live in both houses at once. Munro exploits the physical space of the text to nudge readers toward comparing spaces in the text and setting Liza's life in her father's house against her experiences in Ladner's territory. Moreover, Munro does not allow readers to remain complacent within the frame of fiction. Instead, she reminds them of fiction's material embeddedness in the world as something that is (dis)ordered on the page. Indeed, the text points to itself as *mise-en-abyme* in Liza's drawing of an Easter egg "(with a smaller egg inside it and a still smaller egg inside that)" (290). The image recalls the multiple-house *trompe-l'œil* that we have just experienced, while the typographical space created by the parentheses adds a further element of textual layering. Like Liza, Munro goes about making messes and cleaning them up. Using a strategy of fictional anamorphosis, she exploits the parallax of reading to reveal apparent distortions in the landscape as something other than what they first seem.

"Vandals" is an example of geographic metafiction in that it calls attention to the very gaps it creates, fragmenting a fictive architecture that in its original was never complete. Furthermore, it addresses readers in order to foreground the deterritorializing process that they undergo as the story territorializes its own topography. As Magdalene Redekop says, "Munro is not interested in showing us 'All' but she does take us beyond the blind spot of the pupil and captures the act of looking itself" (19-20). When Warren turns on the television in Ladner's house and says "Look at this" (280), the imperative is not explicitly directed to anyone, leaving open the possibility that he is speaking to the reader. If this sounds farfetched, juxtapose it with Munro's fondness for using the second person, and her purposefulness in doing so, in titles like *Who Do You Think You Are?* and *Something I've Been Meaning to Tell You*. The "you" is polyvalent, and it signals Munro's preoccupation with the rhetorical, communicative function of fiction and with the problems of establishing identity. For instance, the second person appears when Liza thinks that Ladner "could switch from one person to another and make it your fault if you remembered" (*Open* [*Open Secrets*] 289). The irony of Liza's thought is that she is herself switching "from one person to another," namely, from the first to the second. The second person is partly a defence mechanism that lends Liza distance from her own plight. She says "you" when she means

herself. But the second person also turns the readers' gaze back on themselves. Munro makes this transition provocatively again as Liza leaves her father's property: "No divisions over here, no secret places—everything is bare and simple. [. . .] But when you cross the road—as Liza is doing now, trotting on the gravel—when you cross into Ladner's territory, it's like coming into a world of different and distinct countries" (291). Here Munro stops just short of completely shifting the narrative voice out of Liza's consciousness. Instead, it is unclear whether or not it is some part of Liza's mind or a separate narrator who leads the reader into the hidden spaces of Ladner's territory. All traces of Liza disappear in the next paragraph, replaced only by references to "you." The diction is that of a tour guide, and readers are no longer separated from "that country" by a distanced narrator (277); "there" has become the demonstrative "here." The text both completely identifies readers with Liza as the "you" and utterly alienates them from her by eliding her. Liza's displacement seems to extend beyond the nominal to the geographical, and readers are similarly displaced.

In Bea's confusion as she follows Ladner, she wonders if "this tour, so strenuous physically and mentally, might be a joke on her" (272). The hint to readers is that they are as reliant on Munro for locating themselves in the topography as Bea is on Ladner. Readers might safely orient themselves using names in the text like Toronto and Sarnia, but once they enter the fictional Stratton Township—even though the story gives them fairly precise instructions on how to get there—they are within a territory created by Munro and subject to her whims. If one marvels at Munro's detail in her description of the vandalism scene, one should recognize the subsequent parody of it when Liza reconstructs for Bea the spatial record of the damage. It is most emphatically a performance and a lie: "She went on describing things, commiserating, making her voice quiver with misery and indignation" (283). Munro again generates scepticism about the storyteller's ability to achieve authenticity and sincerity. Her artist-characters recurrently fear misrepresenting what is "real" by reducing and enclosing it within the space of fiction, and **"Vandals"** cautions readers not to conclude from the topography they take from the text that they have witnessed all of the terrain worthy of attention. Ajay Heble identifies Munro's practice of "paradigmatic writing" ("tales that turn on what has been left out, or what cannot be told or written" [75]), and her evocation of geography is also as much a matter of admitting what space is absent or hidden as what is present. Munro forces readers to pay attention to the gaps in her fiction and to the process of filling them in.

Munro's textual tours have affinities with Ladner's bush: "Certain walks impose decorum and certain stones are set a jump apart so that they call out for craziness"

(291). Munro makes her readers take such jumps, looking and leaping simultaneously within the fictional space in the text, requiring them constantly to challenge their own perspective. One might tweak a familiar phrase to say that Munro asks her readers, "Where do you think you are?" The original phrase is a way of "putting people in their place," and Munro is fully aware of the multiple meanings of that cliché. In **"Connection,"** the narrator says of Cousin Iris, "I don't think she wanted to remind me of home, and put me in my place; I think she wanted to establish herself, to let me know that she belonged here, more than there" (**Moons** [**The Moons of Jupiter**] 15). Munro wants to put things in place, and she recognizes our "wanting to know," but she cautions readers that every entry into the house of fiction admits and installs new gaps even as it fills old ones. For Munro, the important spaces are noumenal and cannot be seen but only guessed at. Knowledge is sometimes a matter of recognizing what you do not know.

To answer the question of whether Munro might be considered to be committing her own kind of vandalism, we have needed an idea of how a story might even attempt to do this in some way that is not simply metaphorical. **"Vandals"** provides examples, performing the same kinds of spatial ordering, naming, dividing and enclosing that Ladner undertakes, but to different ends than his oppressive ones. Through the indeterminacies of the narrative voice and her jumps back and forth in space and time, as well as other techniques, Munro refuses to be authoritative even as she authors. In fact, **"Vandals"** further complicates her evocation of the story as a house, for if the house is ostensibly a form that men have circumscribed and controlled, the same may be said of the short story. Munro as vandal must act against the strictures of a male-dominated form of expression. In order to make the house of fiction a comfortable space, she needs to vandalize it and repudiate patriarchal smugness in the security of dwelling. Her subtle, ostensibly realist method allows her, like Liza, to go about her work in the enemy's house under the cover of performing expected roles. As a result, **"Vandals"** remains full of texts hidden in space and spaces hidden in text. The second person notably resurfaces in the text's last section, placed conspicuously in the first sentence—"Liza locked the door as you had to, from the outside" (**Open** 293)—and then the last, where "you could feel the darkness collecting" (294). In a story about hidden places and the impediments to understanding other people, Munro finishes by asking readers to question the extent of intimacy they really gain as readers. It could be that they have in fact been able to participate only "as you had to, from the outside." If Munro has led us into darkness, it is unclear whether we have been rewarded with another manner of sight. This very process of scotomization is potentially an alternative mode of knowledge-acquisition, forcing the gaze away from the immediate and straightforward to make it squint askance, engaging with those peripheral visions that are sometimes the most difficult and urgent to see.

* * *

A recent focus of many spatial theorists has been deterritorialization: a movement away from what Gilles Deleuze and Félix Guattari characterize as sedentary, arborescent, and striated space toward one that is nomadic, rhizomatic, and smooth. Homi Bhabha's sense of cultural hybridity is another gesture toward deterritorialization: his "third space" is the "interstitial passage between fixed identifications" (4). Hybridity and nomadology both refer to conceptual space, but conceptual practices inform spatial practices, and hence these frameworks have implications for geography. Steven Spalding reads nomadology as extolling the "outside": that which is beyond territorialized limits (48). Similarly, Bhabha seems to suggest an end of geography, both descriptively and prescriptively. He says that the "imaginary of spatial distance" is "to live somehow beyond the border of our times" (4), and the concomitant ontology is "unhomed" and "extra-territorial" (6).

In contrast with these theorists, Alice Munro seems to be the paragon of home and hearth. She has said as early as 1971: "I guess that maybe as a writer I'm kind of an anachronism [. . .] because I write about places where your roots are and most people don't live that kind of life any more at all" (**Lives** [**Lives of Girls and Women**], n. pag.). Such comments incline one to align her against nomadology and hybridity in a debate that might even contend human ontology: Does the nature of being tend toward the sedentary or the nomadic? The apparent rupture is between dwelling and wandering, between being home or on the road. But, although one interpretation might align Munro with the inside, arborescent and sedentary, her fiction refuses to respect the very formulation of arborescent-rhizomatic oppositions. The open house—the tour through the home—encapsulates the co-presence of the static and mobile in Munro's fiction. Lefebvre suggests that the house's space has a fluid relationship with the "outside," so that like the wave/particle duality of light, the house is both punctual and trajectoral—both a determined point and a fluid entity—and a smooth as well as a striated space (87). Under Spalding's conception, the house seems to be the epitome of the striated and the "inside," but in Munro's fiction it is a place of indeterminacy and subtle but fundamental flows.

Munro's stories demand a reinterpretation of the trope of stasis. They suggest the value of reconfiguring striation as embeddedness in a network of unfixed relationships, and they are sceptical of conceptions of striated and smooth spaces that characterize them as masculine and feminine, respectively. Such approaches construe masculine, striated space as rational, ordered, divisive, and static, while feminine, smooth space is seen as intuitive, curved, inclusive, and flowing. However, the desire to break free from striated space, to seek a life on the road and freedom from connection, is not incongruent with stereotypically masculinist attitudes, like that of Mr. Chamberlain in **Lives of Girls and Women**: "*I am taking off this evening in my trusty Pontiac and heading for points west. There is a lot of the world I haven't seen yet and no sense getting fenced in*" (168, emph. Munro's). Munro knows that this is a false utopia. She cautions elsewhere: "No place became real till you got out of the car" (**Progress** [**The Progress of Love**] 99). Writers like Rosi Braidotti have claimed nomadism as primarily metaphorical, arguing: "It is the subversion of set conventions that defines the nomadic state, not the literal act of traveling" (5). But the use of such a metaphor still implies a valorization of mobility and insists on the deterritorialized mind's triumph over embodiment, whereas Munro insists on the very opposite; she emphasizes the connections of cognitive and habitational embeddedness. Donna Haraway insists that "the only way to find a larger vision is to be somewhere in particular" (259). Nomadic thought is similarly also a situated one—a "tribe in the desert instead of a universal subject within the horizon of all-encompassing Being" (Deleuze and Guattari 379)—but in opposition to this model, Haraway and Munro's situatedness does not privilege the nomadic against the sedentary even at the metaphorical level. To celebrate the *nomos* assumes a rejection of home under the masculinist conception (stable, secure, and ordered), which is a model that Munro does not accept.

Munro admits both the home and the tour into her stories and does not set them against one another but observes their interactions and interdependencies. She shows that the homed and the unhomed are part of the same ontology. As Yi-Fu Tuan points out, "'home' is a meaningless word apart from 'journey' and 'foreign country'" (102). Bhabha's insistence on transnational, translational and hybrid cultures may appear to be antithetical to the communities that Munro portrays, but Munro's house-fiction metonym insists that one can celebrate the interstices between binaries such as home/ road from *within* the punctual. Her fiction deploys both arborescent and rhizomatic models: a flow between identity and hybridity, as people recognize the contingency and partiality of place-based identities yet continue to construct and cling to them. The concomitant provisionality and stubbornness of place is evident in **"Meneseteung"**: "The town has taken root, it's not going to vanish, yet it still has some of the look of an encampment" (**Friend** [**Friend of My Youth**] 54). If self-location is fundamental, for Munro home is always a reference point, not only physically but conceptually, although its location shifts and it is not always the

"here." Munro suggests that a substantial human project is not to travel over deterritorialized ground but to rediscover familiar places and to re-examine home. Munro's contribution to deterritorialization strategies is to emphasize the inside as the place of mystery and complex interrelations.

Munro supplies her own figure for the mystery of the inside, which we might place alongside the house as a recurring trope for her fiction: namely, the heaps of rubbish that appear throughout her stories, like the piles of wrecked automobiles that constitute Robert's mystical vision in **"Fits"** (in **The Progress of Love**). Coral Ann Howells argues that they "have very little if any meaning in a literal sense" (94) and interprets them as metaphors for the indeterminacy of meaning, but Lefebvre, writing in a non-literary context, suggests a different figure: "The *mundus*: a sacred or accursed place in the middle of the Italiot township. A pit, originally—a dust hole, a public rubbish dump. Into it were cast trash and filth of every kind. [. . .] A pit, then, 'deep' above all in meaning. It connected the city, the space above ground, land-as-soil and land-as-territory, to the hidden, clandestine, subterranean spaces which were those of fertility and death" (242). The *mundus* is a liminal monument, set below and reaching down. Instead of a transcendence of earth, it pays tribute to displacement of it, propinquity with it. Instead of focussing on horizons of vision, it emphasizes gaps between the self and the vanishing point. It suggests not a lack, but a whole: enspacement through absence; the promise of further inclusion rather than exclusion. Such a formation is neither rhizomatic nor arborescent as those attributes have been formulated. It is not rooted but excavated, yet it is not the hollow, negative space of the cavus. Rather, it is an array or texture. In Munro, monuments do not just mark what is buried but are themselves buried, like her "deep caves paved with kitchen linoleum." And in her stories, the house is not separate from such a texture but an example of it. Consider the piles of debris in and around Uncle Benny's house in **Lives of Girls and Women,** or Mrs. Fullerton's *mundus*-like residence in **"The Shining Houses"**: "The house and its surroundings were so self-sufficient, with their complicated and seemingly unalterable layout of vegetables and flower beds, apple and cherry trees, wired chicken-run, berry path and wooden walks, woodpile, a great many built dark little sheds, for hens or rabbits or a goat. Here was no open or straightforward plan, no order that an outsider could understand; yet what was haphazard time had made final" (**Dance** [**Dance of the Happy Shades**] 22). And compare that passage with Michel Foucault's description of the function of heterotopias: "Either their role is to create a space of illusion that exposes every real space, all the sites inside of which human life is partitioned, as still more illusory. [. . .] Or else, on the contrary, their role is to create a space that is other, another real space, as perfect, as meticulous, as well arranged as ours is messy, ill constructed, and jumbled" (27). Munro's fiction seems to achieve both sides of the heterotopic potential: meticulous and "real," it is at the same time filled with the "messy" jumbles that we witness in heaps and houses. Like the *mundus,* fiction is both part of and apart from the world, peripherally enspaced and fundamental to social processes, both static and defined by flows of changing content, space and meaning, composed of the world's materials and transforming them.

If Munro's house is her art, it is also an ark: a shifting *mundus* that is both potentially synecdochal of the world and discrete in itself. Instead of opposing caricatures of an inert house against a mobile vessel, Munro blends them to reconfigure the concept of the house itself: not as something static to be escaped but something smooth to revisit and transform from within. This project mirrors her use of realism, in which she does not abandon its conventions but subtly subverts them. In **"Vandals"** as elsewhere, Munro's geographic metafiction is a key constituent of a poetics that seeks to challenge the reader's very conception of what is real.

Works Cited

Atwood, Margaret. *Survival: A Thematic Guide to Canadian Literature.* Toronto: Anansi, 1972.

Bachelard, Gaston. *The Poetics of Space.* Trans. Maria Jolas. Boston: Beacon, 1994.

Bhabha, Homi K. *The Location of Culture.* London: Routledge, 1994.

Braidotti, Rosi. *Nomadic Subjects: Embodiment and Sexual Difference in Contemporary Feminist Theory.* New York: Columbia UP, 1994.

Brontë, Charlotte. *Jane Eyre.* 1847. Ed. Q. D. Leavis. London: Penguin, 2000.

Butler, Christopher. *Early Modernism: Literature, Music, and Painting in Europe, 1900-1916.* Oxford: Clarendon, 1994.

Certeau, Michel de. "Practices of Space." Trans. Richard Miller and Edward Schneider. *On Signs.* Ed. Marshall Blonsky. Oxford: Blackwell, 1985. 122-45.

Deleuze, Gilles, and Félix Guattari. *A Thousand Plateaus: Capitalism and Schizophrenia.* Trans. Brian Massumi. London: Athlone, 1999.

Foucault, Michel. "Of Other Spaces." Trans. Jay Miskowiec. *Diacritics* 16.1 (1986): 22-27.

Haraway, Donna. "Situated Knowledges: The Science Question in Feminism and the Privilege of Partial Perspective." *Feminism and Science.* Ed. Evelyn Fox Keller and Helen E. Longino. 1996. Oxford: Oxford UP, 1998. 249-63.

Heble, Ajay. *The Tumble of Reason: Alice Munro's Discourse of Absence.* Toronto: U of Toronto P, 1994.

Houston, Pam. "A Hopeful Sign: The Making of Metonymic Meaning in Munro's 'Meneseteung.'" *Kenyon Review* 14.4 (1992): 79-92.

Howells, Coral Ann. *Alice Munro.* Manchester: Manchester UP, 1998.

Hutcheon, Linda. *The Canadian Postmodern: A Study of Contemporary English-Canadian Fiction.* Toronto: Oxford UP, 1988.

James, Henry. *The Portrait of a Lady.* 1881. London: Penguin, 1984.

Kroetsch, Robert. *Labyrinths of Voice: Conversations with Robert Kroetsch.* Ed. Shirley Neuman and Robert Wilson. Edmonton: NeWest, 1982.

———. *The Lovely Treachery of Words: Essays Selected and New.* Oxford: Oxford UP, 1989.

Lefebvre, Henri. *The Production of Space.* Trans. Donald Nicholson-Smith. Oxford: Blackwell, 2000.

Meinig, D. W. "Geography As an Art." *Transactions of the Institute of British Geographers* N.S. 8 (1983): 314-28.

Munro, Alice. "The Art of Fiction CXXVII." Interview with Jeanne McCulloch and Mona Simpson. *Paris Review* 131 (1994): 227-64.

———. *Dance of the Happy Shades.* 1968. London: Vintage, 2000.

———. *Friend of My Youth.* 1990. Toronto: Penguin, 1991.

———. *Lives of Girls and Women.* 1971. London: Penguin, 1982.

———. *The Moons of Jupiter.* 1982. Toronto: Penguin, 1995.

———. *Open Secrets.* 1994. London: Vintage, 1995.

———. *The Progress of Love.* 1985. London: Vintage, 1996.

———. *Something I've Been Meaning to Tell You.* Scarborough, ON: McGraw-Hill Ryerson, 1974.

———. "What Is Real?" *Making It New: Contemporary Canadian Stories.* Ed. J. Metcalf. Toronto: Methuen, 1982. 223-26.

———. *Who Do You Think You Are?* 1978. Toronto: Penguin, 1995.

Rasporich, Beverly J. *Dance of the Sexes: Art and Gender in the Fiction of Alice Munro.* Edmonton: U of Alberta P, 1990.

Redekop, Magdalene. *Mothers and Other Clowns: The Stories of Alice Munro.* London: Routledge, 1992.

Rhys, Jean. *Wide Sargasso Sea.* 1966. London: Penguin, 2000.

Rose, Gillian. "As If the Mirrors Had Bled: Masculine Dwelling, Masculinist Theory and Feminist Masquerade." *BodySpace: Destabilizing Geographies of Gender and Sexuality.* Ed. Nancy Duncan. London: Routledge, 1996. 56-74.

Smith, Neil, and Cindy Katz. "Grounding Metaphor: Towards a Spatialized Politics." *Place and the Politics of Identity.* Ed. Michael Keith and Steve Pile. London: Routledge, 1993. 87-119.

Spalding, Steven D. "Travels in Theoretical Spaces: Deleuze, Guattari and Foucault." *Hybrid Spaces: Theory, Culture, Economy.* Ed. Johannes Angermüller et al. Hamburg: LIT, 2000. 37-48.

Tuan, Yi-Fu. *Topophilia: A Study of Environmental Perception, Attitudes, and Values.* Englewood Cliffs, NJ: Prentice-Hall, 1974.

JoAnn McCaig (essay date 2002)

SOURCE: McCaig, JoAnn. "'Short Story': Remaking Genre." In *Reading In: Alice Munro's Archives,* pp. 81-111. Waterloo, Ontario: Wilfrid Laurier University Press, 2002.

[*In the following essay, McCaig probes Munro's transformation and reinvention of the short story genre, underscoring ways in which the author's nationality and gender inform her style.*]

In a 1994 *Morningside* interview, Peter Gzowski credits Munro with reinventing the short story form with the dense, complex stories of **Open Secrets.** Critic Oakland Ross also suggests that she has transformed the cultural economy as well; Ross begins his review of *Strangers Are Like Children,* by Joan Baxter, as follows: "It's a sad truth of the literary marketplace in Canada that short-story collections don't sell, unless they are written by Alice Munro" (C8). If Munro has reinvented the genre and transformed the market, this feat is certainly due in part to her great gift and her persistence in cultivating it, but the achievement is also the result of long-term resistance to the more constricting rules of the field. Munro's nationality and gender certainly complicate her pursuit of authorship, but it is on the question of genre that Munro's formation as a writing subject meets its greatest challenges.

What is the actual status of the short story within the literary culture(s) where Munro seeks authority? On the one hand, Canada's burgeoning literary scene makes the genre reasonably lucrative, and the consecrating powers of the CBC and the literary magazines are con-

siderable. On the other hand, the audience in such venues is (in the imagination of the artistic community, if not in fact) so small that the producer/editor knows all of his listeners/subscribers by name. Likewise, in the United States, venues like the *New Yorker* or *McCall's* are rewarding both symbolically and financially. However, magazine pieces don't have the shelf life of books, and they rarely receive what Robert Lecker calls "the value conferred by prize-giving or other forms of certification" ("Anthologizing" 57). Anthology publication is a more durable venue, and a good means of academic exposure, but the financial rewards are mediocre. Finally, though the short story is Munro's genre, book publishers on both sides of the border are reluctant to publish a short story collection for market reasons. To reap the rewards of all three of these markets—magazine, anthology, and published collection—is, in a way, to "have it all," as a rather trite feminist slogan used to promise. Munro's choice of the marginalized but, in Canada at least, relatively marketable genre is severely tested in the years between 1976 and 1978, but she rises to the challenge magnificently in the production of her fourth book.

In "The Short Story: An Underrated Art," Thomas Gullason mentions Gustav Flaubert's *Madame Bovary* as the "impetus" for the privileging of the novel in the literary hierarchy of genres (13). Bourdieu, likewise, finds Flaubert's influence extremely significant, and his analysis of how the work of Flaubert changed the form of the novel in France provides a useful analogy to Munro's situation. Bourdieu observes:

> When Flaubert undertook to write *Madame Bovary* or *Sentimental Education,* he situated himself actively within the space of possibilities offered by the field. . . . In choosing to write these novels, Flaubert risked the inferior status associated with a minor genre. Above all, he condemned himself to take a place within a space that was already staked out with names of authors, names of sub-genres (the historical novel, the serial, and so on) and names of movements or schools (realism). Despite Balzac's prestige, the novel was indeed perceived as an inferior genre.
>
> (*Field* 203)

If one applied Bourdieu's analysis of a French nineteenth-century male novelist to our twentieth-century Canadian woman short story author, the analogy holds. For example, in choosing to write a book like **Who Do You Think You Are?,** Munro actively situates herself in the space of possibilities offered by the field; she attempts to produce a "story sequence," which appears to be one of the less desirable options available within "the universe of possible choices" (203). She risks "inferior status" because of her association with the "minor genre" of the short story, yet she also "condemns" herself to take a place in a space already staked out by authors such as Anne Tyler, whose novels are both literary and profitable, and a space structured by the subgenre of the modern "literary" (as opposed to "magazine") short story, as well as by the movement or school of "realism."

Pierre Bourdieu's concept of "habitus" provides a useful approach to understanding Munro's position in the cultural field. Bourdieu defines "habitus" as constituted by "schemes of perception and appreciation," as a "sense of social direction." The relationship between the habitus and the field is the result of

> the configuration, at the moment, and at the various critical turning points in each career, of the space of available possibilities (in particular, the economic and symbolic hierarchy of the genres, schools, styles, manners, subjects, etc.), the social value attached to each of them, and also the meaning and value they received for the different agents or classes of agents in terms of the socially constituted categories of perception and appreciation they applied to them.
>
> *(Field* 65)

Bourdieu shows how Flaubert, by virtue of his sociohistoricity and habitus was "predisposed . . . to experience at their strongest the force of contradictions inscribed in the position of the writer and in the position of the pure artist, where these contradictions attained their highest degree of intensity" (202). By "writer," Bourdieu refers to the artist in the marketplace, and by "pure artist" to the producer in the field of restricted production, that of "art for art's sake"; in short, he is saying that Flaubert found himself in the contradictory space between the real and the ideological.

Bourdieu suggests that Flaubert reinvented the novel, and that "what confers on his work an incomparable *value,* is his relationship, albeit negative, with the whole literary world in which he acted and whose contradictions and problems he assumed absolutely" (205). In a 1994 *Morningside* interview following the publication of *Open Secrets,* Peter Gzowski suggests that Munro has, with this new collection, reinvented the short story, "a new form that is between novel and short story . . . not novella but . . . in fact a short novel." However, the defensiveness of Munro's response to Gzowski's praise indicates how she "assumes absolutely" these "contradictions and problems": she says, "You mean, I could've written eight novels if I'd just set my mind to it?". The remark echoes Bourdieu's observation that "the whole time he was working on *Madame Bovary,* Flaubert never stopped talking about his suffering, even his despair . . . above all, he repeated over and over again that he did not, strictly speaking, know what he was doing" (204-205).

The history of the production of Munro's fourth book, *Who Do You Think You Are?,* is a complicated one. When the Canadian version of the book was in galleys,

Munro made drastic changes to the structure of the text, at her own expense, transforming it from a metafictional short story collection to a "story sequence" about a single character. In an interview with Tim Struthers, Munro explains the difficulties, negotiations, and last-minute changes in terms of her own "stupidity." She says it was "not a question of me being persuaded against my will. It's just a question of me being too stupid to see, or being not clear about what I would do next" (Struthers, "Real" 31). What Munro did do next, after this ideological struggle over the hierarchy of genres, was first to establish her own position by refusing to produce any more collections of linked stories, and second to reinvent the short story with each succeeding book, until by the time she produces *Open Secrets,* her transformation of the genre is acknowledged. It is this moment of intense struggle in the final arrangement of the stories in *Who Do You Think You Are?/The Beggar Maid* that shows Munro's most ambiguous, troubled, but very powerful negotiation with the construct of literary authorship.

In his discussion of the "hierarchy of genres," Pierre Bourdieu does not mention the short story. He does, however, situate the novel in the hierarchy with some implications that are useful to this discussion. Bourdieu differentiates two points of view in the hierarchization of the literary field. From the economic point of view, drama is at the top, poetry at the bottom. The novel he places in between, because it

> can secure big profits (in the case of some naturalist novels), and sometimes very big profits (some "popular" novels), for a relatively large number of producers, from an audience which may extend far beyond the audience made up of the writers themselves, as in the case of poetry, and beyond the bourgeois audience, as in the case of theatre, into the *petite bourgeoisie* or even, especially through municipal libraries, into the "labour aristocracy."
>
> *(Field* 48)

Thus the novel is a form whose profitability results from the breadth of its potential audience, which ranges from what Bourdieu has described earlier as "the field of restricted production," or production for other producers (and certainly the designation "a writers' writer" is often applied to Munro[1]), through the *bourgeois* and even including some members of the working class. However, according to Bourdieu, the hierarchy is reversed when one takes the symbolic point of view. Because the disavowal or repression of the economic increases symbolic capital, then poetry takes its place at the top of the symbolic hierarchy because of its small audience and its unprofitability, while drama (and film, in our century), with its larger audiences and larger profits, is at the bottom of the pile. The case for the novel, however, is more complex, because "the hierarchy of specialties"—that is, "the degree to which the authors and works conform to the specific demands of the genre"—"corresponds to the hierarchy of the audiences reached and also, fairly strictly, to the hierarchy of the social universes represented" (*Field* 48). The difference between a "literary" novel and a "bestseller" is a matter of subgenre, or "specialties." Certain features distinguish serious fiction, such as a tendency to prevalently anti-bourgeois attitudes, the "literary" use of language, metaphor, and symbol, as well as inclusion on academic syllabuses and attention from serious critical venues. Literary fiction does "cross over" in some cases, but a serious work that achieves commercial success risks being judged as "popular" or "commercial." In short, the smaller the audience and the lower the profits, the more "autonomy" the author supposedly enjoys, and thus the more symbolic capital inheres to his/her work.

The omission of the short story in Bourdieu's discussion of genre hierarchies is unsurprising. The neglect of the short story in literary criticism and theory has been noted by a variety of scholars. For example, in a collection of essays called *Short Story Theories,* editor Charles E. May asserts that, "Compared with the vast amount of theoretical criticism on the novel, serious approaches to the short story have been embarrassingly few" (xi). Likewise, in *Re-Reading the Short Story,* Clare Hanson remarks that "For a complex of reasons the short story has been largely excluded from the arena of contemporary critical debate" (1). The reasons for this neglect can be attributed to three factors. First, the short story has had a briefer history, as a literary form, than the novel, and thus has simply not had the time to achieve critical respect. Second, the short story is more "popular" than the novel, because of its marketability in magazines, and thus is deemed less worthy by critics, which is in accord with Bourdieu's view of the hierarchy of genres and the field of production. Third, the formal properties of the novel more closely inscribe the ideology of the dominant culture, thus making it a more central form.

In terms of its history, the short story is a twentieth-century phenomenon in the sense that serious critical and academic attention to the form is a relatively recent development, far more recent than for drama, poetry, and even the novel. North American short story theory begins with Poe's review of Hawthorne's *Twice-Told Tales* in 1842, in which the critic insists on the importance of "unity of effect or impression" (47). In 1901, Brander Matthews reiterates and expands upon Poe's ideas in his essay "The Philosophy of the Short Story," asserting that "The difference in spirit and in form between the Lyric and the Epic is scarcely greater than the difference between the Short-story and the Novel" (53), thus beginning a long line of defensive postures vis-à-vis the relative merits of the two genres. The modernist challenge to the realist model of Poe and Matthews is evident by the postwar period, and is detailed

in A. L. Bader's "The Structure of the Modern Short Story" (1945). Frank Davey asserts that the short story achieved academic acceptance in the postwar period not only because of the work of short story theorists and critics, but also for the very practical reason that it upheld the ideology of the current theoretical orthodoxy, namely the New Criticism. Following his survey of critics such as Poe, Matthews, and Bader, Davey suggests that: "An even stronger attempt to establish the unity of the short story, and to valorize the story as an object of high art, was made by the New Critics, who used it, along with the lyric poem, as a pedagogical tool in the attempt to teach literature and taste to the newly large and democratized freshman classes that came to U.S. universities following the Second World War" ("Writers" 139). Certainly, the short story would appear an ideal vehicle for the New Critical ideology of the "well-wrought urn," and it is an accessible form, pedagogically. This rise of the short story anthology in both the United States and Canada parallels the postwar democratization of the university. As Bourdieu remarks, "economic and social changes affect the literary field indirectly, through the growth in the cultivated audience, i.e. the potential readership, which is itself linked to increased schooling" (*Field* 54).

If the critical history of the short story and of short story criticism in the United States is brief, in Canada it is even briefer. When Robert Weaver published the World's Classics Series *Canadian Short Stories* in 1960, he asserted that "there have been so few collections of Canadian short stories that there is no tradition which an editor must either follow or explain away" (ix). In fact, there had been several anthologies published before this,[2] but the 1960 publication is regarded as a watershed by most Canadian literary historians. The work is a historical survey of sorts, including stories by Roberts, Haliburton, and Leacock, but Weaver states quite bluntly that few stories of merit, by his standards, were produced in Canada before 1920. Weaver's introduction to the collection concludes with a kind of apology, an admission that the stories which follow might be read as lacking in sophistication, as "naive"—a situation that Weaver hopes to see change, and that, indeed, he plays a key role in changing.[3]

In her discussion of canon and genre in Robert Lecker's *Canadian Canons,* Donna Bennett sees two historical factors that helped to establish the short story genre in Canada in the mid-twentieth century. First, she observes that poetry was the most prestigious genre until the mid-1960s after which "prose fiction [was seen] as the central form of contemporary literature" (136). Secondly, notes Bennett, "investment in radio and television broadcasting has greatly increased the importance of the short story as a canonical form, for writers can gain exposure as well as money by working in this genre. (In contrast, book publication privileges the novel as the only important literary form for financial return.)" (147). For Munro, at least in Canada, the privileging of the novel over the short story is partly mitigated by the short story's academic acceptance, its marketability to the public broadcasting service, and the relative youth of the Canadian literary culture as a whole.

The second factor in the deprivileging of the short story genre in literary culture is its "popular" appeal. As Bourdieu points out, there is an inverse relationship, in the literary field, between popular success and literary seriousness. In *The Culture and Commerce of the American Short Story,* Andrew Levy points to two significant periods in the development of the genre in the twentieth century. One is "the creation and popularity of a system of how-to handbooks and courses [on short story writing] during the period 1910-1935, concomitant with the period during which the short story had its highest value in the commercial market" (48). Levy reproduces a document in his text that lists the number of stories published in twenty-eight major American mass circulation magazines from August 1927 to June 1928. The figures are quite astonishing: 1,417 short stories appeared in the period, 334 of them in the *Saturday Evening Post* alone.[4] During the period 1910-35, which Levy describes as the point when the short story had its highest commercial value, the merit of magazine short fiction was called into question by critics, because of its "uneasy intersection of the fields of literature and commerce," in which "the physical configuration of the commercial magazine, which arranged fiction and advertising on the same page, represented a perfect example of the contamination that had taken place" (50).[5] Bourdieu notes that, "The opposition between the 'commercial' and the 'non-commercial' . . . is the generative principle of most of the judgements which, in the theatre, cinema, painting or literature, claim to establish the frontier between what is and what is not art" (*Field* 82).

The other significant period in the popularization of the short story, according to Levy, is that of the democratization of the producer him or herself. Levy observes that, while how-to handbooks proliferated in the early half of this century, the producibility of the short story was fostered in the latter half by the "development of the system of academic workshop and graduate programs, concomitant with the near-demise of the short story as a commercial product and its rebirth as an academic genre with second-hand commercial implications" (48). Levy remarks that creative writing programs are now found in one-third of all American high schools. Moreover, each year, the 250 graduate writing programs in American universities turn out 1,500 "would-be writers of *literature,* of whom approximately half will attempt to publish short stories" (48, n65). Obviously, whether the genre is identified with how-to manuals and handbooks or with workshops and academic programs, both developments lead to the damning conclusion that *anyone* can write a short story, that it is an "apprentice" form in which one works until ready to take on the challenge of the novel or more experimental prose modes. And, of course, according to the charismatic ideology of literary creation, if anyone can do it, then it can't be art.

Yet some commentators insist that the short story genre *is* high art. For example, Nobel Prize winner William Faulkner says that the short story is "the most demanding form after poetry" and ascribes his place as a novelist to his failure to master either of the other two genres (123). In "The Short Story and the Novel," Alberto Moravia compares the work of Maupassant and Chekhov to that of Flaubert and Dostoyevsky and argues that the short story writers present a world that is "wider and more varied," that they give the reader "an incomparable picture of life in France and Russia of their time" (47). Beyond breadth, Moravia defends the story as less structured, and more intuitive. In essence, he says, the story is less ideologically rigid than the novel. For Moravia, ideology is the most important structural difference between the short story and the novel, "that is the skeleton of the theme from which the flesh of the story takes its form. In other words the novel has a bone structure holding it together from top to toe, whereas the short story is, so to speak, boneless" (149). Furthermore, Moravia locates ideology in the plot and characterization of the novel as well as in its structure: "The twists and turns of the plot [of the novel] . . . are never due to extrinsic interventions by the author or to what we could call the inexhaustible resources of life, but to the dialectical and necessary development of the ideological themes" (150). Finally, he describes the characters in the short story as "lyrical intuitions" while those in the novel are "symbols" (150).

The ideological aspect of the novel/short story debate is especially pertinent to Munro. While Moravia hints at gender in his article, using the word "intuitive" (a word usually aligned with the "feminine") to describe the short story, Desmond Pacey articulates the ideological masculinist contours of the novel form very clearly in a disparaging review of a Morley Callaghan novel which the critic regards as inferior to the author's short stories. Pacey comments: "the short story can be made out of a moment of insight, a compassionate glimpse of suffering humanity. Of the novel, however, we demand a firm philosophy, a clearly articulated sense of values" (211). I'd like to draw attention to the "feminine" language used to describe the short story: adjectives like "compassionate" and "suffering," nouns like "insight" and "humanity," suggest the intuitive, the heart, while "glimpse" and "moment" give a sense of the formal brevity of the genre. Compare this to the words Pacey uses to define the novel: the descriptors are the no-nonsense, male-associated words "firm," "clear" and "articulate," while the nouns that describe the form are "values" and "philosophy," suggesting the head, the intellectual. Even the verbs Pacey uses are instructive; that which describes the short story is passive—"can be made"—while the novel requires the active verb "demand."

In fact, the relationship between (female) gender and (short story) genre is worth exploring. Clare Hanson suggests that "the short story has been from its inception a particularly appropriate vehicle for the expression of the ex-centric, alienated vision of women" (3). Gail Scott, in "Shaping a Vehicle for Her Use," undertakes to answer the question of why women writers are attracted to short fiction. For Scott, the most obvious reasons are time and money: "First, in terms of time, a woman's life is never simple; she must put aside her writing to do a million other things. Indeed, her socialization has taught her to keep her mind so cluttered with details that it is often difficult for her to concentrate for whole days at a time in order to deal with a longer work like a novel. Then too a story is easier to sell than a longer piece" (187).

The issue of time and money is particularly difficult for young mothers (which Munro was, for the first twenty or so years of her career).[6] Tillie Olsen points out that:

> Motherhood means being instantly interruptible, responsive, responsible. Children need one *now* (and remember, in our society, the family must often try to be the center for love and health the outside world is not). The very fact that there are needs of love, not duty, that one feels them as one's self; *that there is no one else to be responsible for these needs,* gives them primacy. It is distraction, not meditation, that becomes habitual; interruption, not continuity; spasmodic, not constant, toil.
>
> (33; emphasis in original)

Distraction, interruption, spasm versus meditation, continuity, constancy. It is easy to see how the circumstances of many women's lives do not translate too well into the ideological form of the novel. Munro has said, "When I think of male writers . . . I can't tell you how horrified I feel when I go to a male writer's house and see *the Study,* you know, the entire house set up for him to work." Interestingly, however, she goes on to suggest that the male writer's position is not particularly enviable: "I just can't help thinking *poor bugger.* What a load to carry, it's really got to work, that novel, if everybody else is sacrificing for it" ("Writing's Something I Did" E1). Obviously Munro, as a wife and mother, is accustomed to working around the family schedule, not asking others to "sacrifice" for her work—which gives her some leeway and allows for false starts and failures.

Scott likewise posits an ideological dimension to the attraction of women writers to the short story genre, namely that its relatively brief history makes it less rule-bound:

> The short story is one of the existing genres for which there are few firmly established conventions. This tends to confuse the little censor lurking within all of us, the little man who represents literary norms and criteria, thus giving us space to play with more feminine rhythms and concepts of time and space. . . . [It] gives us the latitude to avoid linear time, the cause-and-effect time of patriarchal logic.
>
> (187)

In the *Paris Review* interview, Munro makes a comment that certainly suggests her own awareness of that "little censor," when she recalls the day she began to write *Lives of Girls and Women:* "It was in January, a Sunday. I went down to the bookstore, which wasn't open Sundays, and locked myself in. My husband had said he would get dinner, so I had the afternoon. I remember looking around at all the great literature that was around me and thinking, 'You fool! What are you doing here?'" (237). However, Munro says, she overcame self-censorship, went up to the office, and began to write **"Princess Ida."** But then, once into the material, Munro confesses:

> I made a big mistake. I tried to make it a regular novel, an ordinary sort of childhood adolescence novel. About March I saw it wasn't working. It didn't *feel* right to me, and I thought I would have to abandon it. I was very depressed. Then it came to me that what I had to do was pull it apart and put it in the story form. Then I could handle it. That's when I learned that I was never going to write a real novel because I could not think that way.
>
> (237; my emphasis)

To Munro, the "ordinary" novel doesn't "feel" right, because she can't "think that way." To "think that way" is perhaps to think in a linear fashion, to articulate a "firm philosophy," as per Desmond Pacey. The opposition of the words "think" and "feel" is important in Munro's discussions of genre. For example, in an interview with Tim Struthers in *Probable Fictions,* Munro again discusses the moment when she decided that trying to write *Lives of Girls and Women* as a traditional novel was not working: "I didn't *think* about what I was doing. I just went back and started tearing it apart and putting it into these little sections, because that's the way I wanted to tell the story to myself" ("Real" 14). Munro's desire to "tell the story to" herself in a particular way is partly a function of what Bourdieu terms the "habitus," defined as: a "feel for the game," a "practical sense . . . that inclines agents to act and react in specific situations in a manner that is not always calculated and that is not simply a question of conscious obedience to rules. . . . The habitus is the result of a long process of inculcation, beginning in early childhood, which becomes a 'second sense' or a second nature" (Johnson 5). Certainly, in discussing her own work, and especially in pondering her difficulties in producing a novel, Munro's habitus is evident in the way she uses the words "think" and "feel," and in the metaphors she used to describe her understanding of the two different genres and her own writing process. In general, "think" is applied to what she "ought" to be doing, and "feel" pertains to what she actually does. For example, in attempting to write a novel, Munro says "I don't feel this pulling on a rope to get to the other side that I have to feel" (Struthers, "Real" 15). About composing a story, Munro opposes the images of a "road" (which is linear, like a rope) and a "house":

> So obviously I don't take up a story and follow it as if it were a road, taking me somewhere, with views and neat diversions along the way. I go into it, and move back and forth and settle here and there, and stay in it for a while. It's more like a house. . . . I want to make a certain kind of structure and I know the feeling I want to get from being inside that structure. This is the hard part of the explanation, where I have to use a word like "feeling," which is not very precise, because if I attempt to be more intellectually respectable I will have to be dishonest. "Feeling" will have to do.

(Munro, "What Is Real" 224)

For Munro, this "indescribable 'feeling' . . . is like the soul of the story" (224). The ideological implications of the novel form are apparent in these commentaries. A novel is linear, it is a road or a rope, a form for people who think a certain way, who accept what Scott calls "linear time, the cause-and-effect time of patriarchal logic" (187). Munro's habitus, however, leads her to a "feeling," which is her honest view of her process, but one that is not "intellectually respectable," not "precise." Her stories have a "soul," and the image of their construction is, for her, the domestic image of a house. The gender implications of the opposition of these two ways of describing the genres are obvious.

The implication of Canadian-ness is evident too, in a remark that Munro makes about another "failed" novel, *Something I've Been Meaning to Tell You*; the author says that this material began as a novel, but then it "all boiled down like maple syrup" (Twigg, "What Is" 16) to its present form—a short story. The image is not only domestic, but also suggestively Canadian. In interviews, Munro tends to list as her major influences writers who are, primarily, American, female, and "Southern" (as in "regional") practitioners of the short story such as Eudora Welty, Katherine Anne Porter, Flannery O'Connor, and Carson McCullers. She does this at least partially because "There was a *feeling* that women could write about the freakish and the marginal," and that the natural genre for this freakishness and marginality is the short story, described by Munro as "our territory, whereas the mainstream big novel about real life was men's territory" (McCulloch and Simpson 255; my emphasis).

Janice Kulyk Keefer alerts us, however, to the dangerous essentialism of suggesting that "the female mind

. . . is more at home in the short story, whereas the novel, with its wide range and scope, must be a more naturally male preserve" (170). It is fascinating to note how Keefer uses the domestic image of "home" juxtaposed with the sense of space and movement and the outdoors in her remarks on the novel's "wide range" and "scope." Keefer argues that it is not "habitus" or natural inclination but practical matters such as space and time that lead Canadian women writers like Munro and Gallant to the short story genre. She cites Munro's marriage and motherhood as factors, and Gallant's dependence on her writing "for her economic survival; in the days before mega-advances, short stories would have produced quicker economic results, more often" (170). Gallant was also a working journalist, and thus accustomed to writing short pieces.

While the practical is certainly a factor, and essentialism certainly risks a dangerous limitation on women's creativity, the evidence suggests that a part of women's attraction to the short story genre lies in its relative freedom from restraints of dominant ideology, as compared to the novel. Mary Eagleton, in "Gender and Genre," suggests that "Perhaps for some women writers their interest in this form has arisen, not from their belief that it is known and safe, but from their hope that the flexible, open-ended qualities of the short story may offer a transforming potential, an ability to ask the unspoken question, to raise new subject matter" (65). Eagleton thus posits a critical view of the short story that is "non-essentialist, non-reductive, yet subtly alive to the links between gender and genre" (66).

Though Canada may be considered a more welcoming market for the short story than the United States because of this country's relatively brief cultural history, its relatively small and well-educated audience, and its somewhat less entrenched literary ideology, genre privilege is still an issue. In "Calgary, Canonization, and Class," Lawrence Mathews explores the relation between issues of social class and the canon: he suggests that the novels selected as "most important" at the 1978 Calgary Conference on the Canadian Novel share not only a "conservatism of technique" but also a similarity in content:

> these novels tend to focus almost exclusively on the growth or development of an individual. The protagonist's success or failure turns on his or her ability to make correct choices according to a set of values which may vary slightly form [sic] novel to novel but is always (in the broad sense) humanist and is always clearly spelled out for the reader. Social or political reality, if it exists at all, is no more than a backdrop for the protagonist's quest for self-knowledge, self-fulfillment, or self-something else.

(165)

Obviously, this ideological conservatism impinges on the acceptability of the short story as well; it is difficult to describe a character's lifelong quest for self-realization within the limits of the short story.

Mathews also compares the way in which canonization occurs in the United States and Canada. He begins by citing Richard Ohmann's "The Shaping of a Canon: U.S. Fiction 1960-1975." Ohmann describes a two-stage process similar to that formulated by Andrew Levy. The first stage involves the world of commerce: "book buyers, agents, editors, advertisers, and reviewers, whose work, collectively, constitutes a screening process which resulted in the identification of a relatively small number of novels as 'compelling, important'" (qtd. in Mathews 154). Stage two involves the separation of popular and serious literature, the latter type receiving attention from "an elite group of about eight journals," which attracts the attention of academics, who thereupon place the text on their course syllabuses. In this second stage, "the college classroom and its counterpart, the academic journal, . . . have become in our society the final arbiters of literary merit" (qtd. in Mathews 154).[7] However, as Mathews observes, in Canada:

> Ohmann's first stage, preliminary commercial success, need not occur at all (*As For Me and My House*), or if it does, there need not be a demonstrable connection between bestsellerdom and canonization (*The Mountain and the Valley*). Nor is the first part of Ohmann's second stage, the singling out of the novel by an elite group of trend-setting journals, relevant. Virtually all of the action in Canada occurs at the very end of the process, the simultaneous embracing of a work by the classroom and the academic journal.
>
> (155)

Kent Thompson, in "The Canadian Short Story in English and the Little Magazines—1971," concurs in his examination of the short fiction scene in Canada. He notes the paucity of mass circulation markets, as well as the tendency of the little magazines to be either university affiliated, government subsidized, or both, and he concludes that while the lack of "a market, a large readership, or criticism" (18) may be liberating in some ways, still "in Canadian short story publishing, there is always an impulse toward an academy technique" (18).[8]

Unfortunately for Munro, one of the strongest academic constraints in Canada, as elsewhere, is the privileging of the novel over the short story. While the story is a good teaching tool, it is the study of the novel that is traditionally used to fully challenge students as prose readers; normally the syllabus of a first-year English course in the two genres includes four or five novels, and a selection of short stories presented through an anthology. Teaching a short story collection by a single author was—until quite recently—a rare choice.

In *Taking Stock*, the proceedings of the 1978 Calgary conference on the novel, the privileging of the longer work of fiction over the shorter is evident. Short story collections are not even included on the ballot, because as Hallvard Dahlie points out in his introduction, the goal of the conference was "to articulate and celebrate the stature that the Canadian *novel* had by virtue of its own intrinsic qualities already achieved" (3; emphasis mine). However, Dahlie then goes on, throughout his discussion, to use the words "fiction" and "novel" interchangeably, as in "What the conference articulated above all was the maturity and richness of Canadian *fiction*" (3; emphasis mine).

The ballot for List A, the top one hundred, includes Munro's *Lives of Girls and Women* and Gallant's *The Pegnitz Junction*. In the voting, Munro places eighteenth, and does not make it onto List B, the top ten; Gallant does not place on either list (Steele 151-54, 161-64).

Bourdieu has pointed out how difficult it is to pinpoint all the complex issues, impediments, and tensions implicit in any literary position-taking in the cultural field, but here, I think, is one very suggestive piece of evidence of the impact of genre bias on the work of an individual author. I can confirm that Munro was aware of the conference through a letter from Douglas Gibson, dated 7 February 1978, mentioning "you may see me at Calgary at this (irreverence surfaces) ridiculous conference on the novel" (MsC 38.1.75.2). The conference took place 16-18 February. My contention is that the Calgary Conference played a role in the production of Munro's fourth book, *Who Do You Think You Are?*. As part of the cultural milieu in which the work was produced, the way in which the Calgary Conference inscribed genre privilege must certainly have been a factor in what Helen Hoy calls "the complicated editorial history [of] this collection" (60). The details of this complex history are explored below, but first, the following example from Bourdieu is useful in understanding the relationship between "the unconscious strategies engendered by habitus and strategies consciously produced in response to a situation designed in accordance with the schemes of the habitus":

> The manuscripts a publisher receives are the product of a kind of pre-selection by the authors themselves according to their image of the publisher who occupies a specific position within the space of publishers. The authors' image of their publisher, which may have oriented the production, is itself a function of the objective relationship between the positions authors and publishers occupy in the field. The manuscripts are, moreover, coloured from the outset by a series of determinations . . . stemming from the relationship between the author's position in the field of production (unknown young author, consecrated author, house author, etc.) and the publisher's position within the system of production and circulation ("commercial" publisher, consecrated or avant-garde). They usually bear the marks of the intermediary whereby they came to the publisher . . . and whose authority, once again, is a

function of respective positions in the field. Because subjective intentions and unconscious dispositions contribute to the efficacy of the objective structures to which they are adjusted, their interlacing tends to guide agents to their 'natural niche' in the structure of the field.

(*Field* 133-34)

In early 1978, Munro finds herself occupying two very different positions in the cultural field at the same time. In Canada, she is an established author of three books, is the winner of a Governor General's Award, and is beginning to achieve academic consecration. Robert Thacker's bibliography of works on Alice Munro notes fifty-seven entries by February 1978, ranging from biographies in companions, surveys, bibliographies, and histories of Canadian literature to scholarly articles in such journals as *World Literature Written in English, Studies in Short Fiction, Canadian Fiction Magazine,* and *Modern Fiction Studies.* Also, between 1972 and 1978, Munro's work has also been the subject of eleven theses or dissertations (including Thacker's own MA thesis). In the United States, however, Munro is a beginner, a relative unknown who has not yet found her "natural niche." She is newly published in the *New Yorker,* certainly, but she has yet to produce her first book with an American publisher. Thus, the evolution of the text known as *Who Do You Think You Are?* in Canada and as *The Beggar Maid* in the United States is much affected by the competing requirements of these two different cultural fields. In fact, the Gibson correspondence provides a telling point of contrast between the Canadian market, in which Munro has a sure foothold, and the American market, which she has entered through her association with Barber less than eighteen months before, and in which the tension between the actual and the ideological aspects of the author function are more transparent.

After publishing her first three books with McGraw-Hill Ryerson, Munro, by the mid-seventies, is considering a change to Macmillan, after being approached to that end by Douglas Gibson. The archive contains a polite letter of introduction, dated August 1974, and then, six months later, a generous and open offer:

> We understand fully that your current position [as writer in residence at Western] makes demands on your time which will not allow you to begin work on your fiction at least until the summer. This does not deter us in any way; we are confident that you will produce a book in your own good time which we shall be proud to publish. Accordingly, if you could let me know what delivery date for the manuscript you consider reasonable and what you would expect by way of an advance.

(MsC 37.2.20.3)

For Munro to be invited to set her own completion date and to state her expectations of an advance is an indication of the power she has achieved on the Canadian

scene. No doubt because of his obvious eagerness to sign Munro, Gibson is also equable on the question of genre, though his letter of 23 December 1975 indicates an awareness of Munro's genre-anxiety in the following remark: "In the meantime please keep me posted on your feelings about the next batch (it's a lovely expression and has no hint of disrespect) of short stories. We'd be very pleased to draw up a contract at any time that the idea appeals to you" (MsC 37.2.20.5). Gibson is polite, but determined; in February 1976, he reminds Munro, "Anytime that you are far enough advanced with the writing to become formally involved with us, we, like Barkis, 'is willin''" (MsC 37.2.20.6). By 7 February 1978 Gibson is close to making a deal with Munro, but he must clear a couple of hurdles first. It is possible that she has asked for more money. Because financial information is restricted, I can't be sure of that, though according to Geoff Hancock, the paperback rights for Munro's second Macmillan book, *The Moons of Jupiter,* were sold for $45,000, the highest price for a work of Canadian fiction ever recorded (187). The Gibson correspondence for this period also mentions the forthcoming publication by Macmillan of a novel by Munro's father, Robert Laidlaw, titled *The McGregors* (MsC 38.1.75.2), as well as a job interview Gibson conducted with Munro's daughter (MsC 38.13.14). I mention these two items only to support my suggestion that, in Canada, Munro is negotiating with her new publisher from a position of relative power and authority—well-earned power resulting from her publishing history and the recognition her work has received. The above-mentioned letter turns out to be the penultimate letter before his contract with Munro is signed; after mentioned *The McGregors* and the job interview, Gibson returns to his familiar refrain: "I wonder if you are now close to having a book-length collection and therefore to drawing up a contract with us. I can think of no author I would rather have on Macmillan's list." Gibson's tenacity eventually pays off: A letter dated 28 April 1978, begins "Welcome to Macmillan" and invites Munro to leave the contractual details to publisher and agent, while he and Munro prepare the forthcoming book for a fall publication.

The book contracted to Macmillan is a short story collection. Gibson proposes the title "True Lies: Stories by Alice Munro," taken from a line in the story **"Providence."** From his discussion of the ordering of the stories, it's possible to guess that the collection comprises several "Rose" stories, some "Simon" stories, and other unrelated stories, including **"Accident," "Chaddeleys and Flemings,"** and **"Characters."** Gibson proposes putting the Rose stories at the end, in order to avoid confusing the reader; yet on the other hand, he does not want Munro to "anonymize" some of the Rose stories, which Munro must have been trying to do to make the book more of a collection and less of a story sequence. On this point, Gibson says: "The heroine of **'The Beg-**

gar Maid,' for example, is clearly Rose; I suggest that you should think twice before plucking too many Roses" (MsC 37.2.20.7b). What Gibson's letter makes clear is that the planned book is neither a novel nor a short story sequence, though several stories appear to be "linked" by focusing on the same character, either Rose or Simon. While Munro's habitus of the (sometimes linked) short story is acceptable to her Canadian publisher, the picture on the other side of the border is somewhat different, and the pressure from her American connections to produce a novel mounts as the year progresses.

As Frank Davey has commented, literary publishing in English Canada in the 1970s remained in the "petty-commodity" mode ("Writers" 95), in which publishers do not unduly influence the form and content of the text, or pay too much attention to its marketability. In the United States, however, the publishing game is not nearly so laissez-faire. In fact, Munro begins a working relationship with Norton editor Sherry Huber some time before signing a contract with the company. From 1976 to 1978, Barber has been busily circulating Munro's stories. When **"The Beggar Maid"** appears in the *New Yorker* in June 1977, it generates a great deal of interest. Though a formal contract between Munro and Norton is not signed until 19 May 1978, it is clear from correspondence in the archive that a dialogue between Huber and Munro about the shape of that book is already well underway. While Macmillan was happy to publish a collection of unrelated or partially linked short stories, Munro's American publisher was rather insistent that the stories be linked closely.

In "Rose and Janet: Alice Munro's Metafiction," Helen Hoy has produced a lengthy and meticulous study of the "tortuous" (69) publication history of Munro's fourth book. Hoy explains:

> Before Alice Munro's **Who Do You Think You Are?** appeared in the fall of 1978, her anticipated new collection of stories was announced as *Rose and Janet*. The first reviews, although about a book entitled **Who Do You Think You Are?**, described a collection unlike the one soon available in bookstores, the one we know. In *Books in Canada,* for example, Wayne Grady discussed the mirror stories of twin heroines, "Rose, who grows up in West Hanratty, Ont., the child of a defeated father and a powerless but compassionate stepmother named Flo; and Janet, who is from Dagleish [*sic*], the child of an equally ineffectual father and a somewhat non-existent mother."
>
> (59)

The title **Who Do You Think You Are?** takes on quite a different resonance when the book is described this way. In fact, Janet is a writer, and the closing stories suggest that she has been the "creator" of Rose, the actress. Why did this book not appear? In Hoy's account:

> Doug Gibson, Munro's editor, explained Munro's sudden decision to revise the book when she realized that Rose and Janet were the same person, a decision which meant literally stopping the presses one Monday morning in mid-September while Munro, who stayed in Toronto overnight, revised, copy-editors proof-read, the press rewrote the flap copy, and the printers ordered more paper. **Who Do You Think You Are?,** as we know it, with ten third-person stories about Rose, was off to press two days later, in time for its November 18 publication deadline. The decision cost Munro $1,864.
>
> (59)

Hoy identifies no less than seven different proposed forms of the book.. . . She comments that "The tension between a Rose version of the material and a 'Rose and other stories' arrangement, which almost culminated in two independent Norton and Macmillan publications, manifested itself time and again during the editing process" (60-1). But like Doug Gibson's explanation that Munro simply "realized that Rose and Janet were the same person," Hoy's analysis ultimately boils down to the mystery of the creative process: she says that in achieving the final version, "Munro had finally created the arrangement she felt to be artistically right" (69). Hoy acknowledges that "fortuitous factors extraneous to the individual stories . . . [such as] the inclinations of editors—may influence the direction of artistic revision and experimentation" (70), but given the evidence which she mentions, and which I discuss in detail, she severely understates the case.

The archive contains four letters from Munro to Sherry Huber at Norton. The first is undated; it is a brief note scribbled in Munro's hand on the torn-off front cover of a drugstore writing pad. It appears to have been sent to Huber in a box along with some revised manuscripts. I can safely assume a mid-May 1978 date for this document, because Munro refers to the recently sent box in her next two letters, both dated 19 May. I can also confirm that Huber received this first, undated, scribbled-on-cardboard letter, because several comments that appear to be Huber's are written there. All three letters propose somewhat different configurations for the book.[9]

Huber's notes on the undated letter suggest that Munro's attempts to make Rose the central character of all the stories have not worked (MsC 38.2.64.3). Obviously, Munro has been asked by Norton to make all the stories about Rose, but she is having difficulty doing so. In her marginalia, Huber plans her strategy: "be strong, sound positive with Alice. Call Ginger before final conference" (MsC 38.2.64.3). Apparently, Huber recognizes that Munro must be treated with firm resolve in this matter, must be encouraged to believe that she can "novelize" these stories. It is also clear that Barber is part of this negotiation, though, oddly, the six-month gap in the correspondence noted in the previous chapter occurs during this period.[10] To unearth this correspondence would be very useful, because when Barber writes to Munro four times in June 1978, the idea of a "novel-like" structure for the book is very much on her mind. For example, in a letter of 20 June, Barber sends Munro a copy of *Earthly Possessions,* and comments on how Anne Tyler created a novel out of a series of stories about a single character (MsC 38.2.63.12).

In the first of the dated letters to Huber, Munro asserts that while **"Royal Beatings," "Privilege," "Half a Grapefruit," "Characters," "Wild Swans," "Spelling,"** and **"Beggar Maid"** are stories about Rose, others—the central characters of **"Mischief"** and **"Providence"**—are not. The irony that these two stories are now very much about Rose in the "definitive" text is inescapable. However, it is also interesting to note that other stories proposed for this collection but later published in *The Moons of Jupiter* began as "Janet" stories and have remained so, namely **"Chaddeleys and Flemings,"** and **"The Moons of Jupiter,"** which feature a central character named Janet, who is a writer, divorced from Richard, and mother of Nichola and Judith.

The solution that Munro proposes is a split between Rose stories and Janet stories . . . in two almost equal parts. Munro tells Huber that Macmillan is doing this with the Canadian version, but with the story **"Accident"** in the middle, and **"Chaddeleys and Flemings"** divided into two stories. (MsC 38.2.64.4a-d).

Munro's second letter, of the same date, proposes a similar configuration, with the addition of **"Characters"** (an uncollected story) to the Rose section. Munro adds that she has mailed a rewrite of **"Simon's Luck,"** which has somehow changed, in her thinking, from a "Janet" story to a "Rose" story (MsC 38.2.64.5a).

These two letters raise several questions. How does one story become a "Rose" story and another a "Janet" story? Did Munro suddenly "realize" that Janet and Rose were "the same person"? If so, what external pressures and internalized beliefs combined to create this realization? Point of view is an interesting aspect; the archive reveals how Munro attempted to write the Rose and Janet stories in every possible configuration of narrative viewpoint—first/third, third/first, all first, all third. It's an amusing sidenote that the Norton version had been planned as first person, but the definitive text is in the third person because in September 1978, that's how Macmillan had already printed the first few stories of Rose and Janet, and to reprint those early stories in first person was simply too costly (Hoy 69).

Another question is which of these letters were ever sent. The Munro archive contains *no* outgoing correspondence at all, with the exception of these four letters. Obviously, the undated note must have been sent and received, because Huber's handwriting is visible on

the document. If so, was it sent back to Munro with the box of manuscripts? Otherwise, how could it be in the collection? Similarly, what about the other two long letters both dated 19 May? Were they ever sent, or are they present in the archive because another letter, describing a completely different book, was the one actually sent to Sherry Huber at Norton?

In Helen Hoy's examination of the editorial dialogue between Huber and Munro, she notes Huber's input on the ordering of the stories. Hoy asserts that the Norton version was to be *all* Rose, Huber having presumably rejected the Rose and Janet idea of the Macmillan version. Furthermore, Huber changed the title **"Wild Swans"** to "Nerve" because "she liked the *progression* from privilege to nerve to providence and luck in Rose's perception of life" (Hoy 68; my emphasis). Hoy notes Huber's preference for narrative linearity as well: "Uncomfortable with narrative gaps and discontinuities, Huber also suggested conventional transitions" (68). Finally, says Hoy, Huber also explicitly indicated a preference for the first person. All of these preferences point to the ideology of the conventional novel—continuity, first person, progression, linearity, connection—indicating the ideological struggle that underlies the supposedly "artistic" negotiation between author and editor. Hoy concludes, "Norton's never-published novel *The Beggar Maid*—its conventional structure deservedly abandoned—was the catalyst for Munro's sudden decision to stop the presses at Macmillan" (68).. . . I question the logic of this statement, because the version now deemed authoritative and definitive, and published by Macmillan in Canada in 1978 and Knopf in the United States in 1979, is far more like this "deservedly abandoned" "novel" than any of the previous configurations, though unlike the Norton version in that the text is written in third-person-focused point of view, and does not give conventional narrative transitions, so that each story is capable of standing on its own. Hoy cites a letter from Munro to Huber dated 19 September 1978,[11] in which the author says, "After you said you liked [the rewrite of] **'Simon's Luck,'** I got more and more convinced that the series of Rose stories was the only way to do this book and that the Macmillan book was a dreadful awkward waste of good material" (68-69). Munro apparently wrote these words to her American editor from the Macmillan offices where her last-minute transformation of the text was underway. After examining the archival evidence, I must disagree with Hoy's assertion that, in the published version, "Munro had finally created the arrangement she felt to be artistically right" (69). To me, the evidence points to a bewildering assortment of external pressures—the Calgary Conference and the equability of the Canadian market compared to the novelizing pressures from Huber and Barber—combined with internal forces such as Munro's own strong drive to achieve American publication, to work in the genre in which she "feels" at home, and to maintain her own position in the "hierarchically structured space" (Bourdieu, *Field* 95) of the cultural field. For one thing, what is the significance of the statement that Huber's liking for **"Simon's Luck"** suddenly made the Rose sequence fall into place?

The 19 September letter noted above is Munro's last communication with Sherry Huber, who left the employ of W. W. Norton early in the fall of 1978. Munro's contractual agreement to publish with Norton collapsed at around the same time, though the relationship between Huber's departure and the demise of the Norton deal is unclear. Munro's contract was then picked up by Knopf; Barber encloses the Norton release form and the Knopf contract in the same letter, dated 7 November 1978 (MsC 38.2.63.16), and the letter from Knopf editor Ann Close welcoming Munro to the company is dated 13 November (MsC 38.1.3.5). Barber's covering letter of 7 November mentions that Huber is looking for work and might need Munro to provide a reference. It's not unreasonable to speculate that for several weeks that fall, Munro was without an American publisher, a fact which may well have stimulated her to find the form of a story sequence "artistically right." Even more ironic is the fact that, after all of Huber's efforts, the Knopf editors chose the Canadian version of the book over Norton's (38.1.3.5). All they wanted to change was the title.

Who Do You Think You Are? is the last "linked" work Munro has produced. I would argue that this text is Munro's final and glorious bow to the privileging of the novel over the short story. Once she has fully entered into her habitus and located her art in the short story form, without defensiveness or apology (except occasionally on *Morningside*), she, like Flaubert in his own time, has transformed the field.

Hoy appears to put her faith in the concept of the authoritative text. She describes "the author's subjective experience of an abrupt and thoroughgoing flash of insight, the bathwater-displacing Eureka moment of revelation" (70) as the moment when Munro decides to make the text Rose-only, at her own expense. What such an analysis fails to take into account is that Munro was shut out of the Calgary Conference by virtue of genre; that Sherry Huber's departure from Norton seems to have left Munro temporarily without an American publisher; and that the Macmillan book had a looming deadline. As Munro points out to Tim Struthers: "A book cannot go on the Canadian market later than about mid-November, or its chances for Christmas sales are just dead. So we had to get it out by that time. All of which things, having been a bookseller, I understand" ("Real" 31). Bourdieu asserts that "to utter 'in public' the true nature of the field, and of its mechanisms, is sacrilege *par excellence,* the unforgivable sin which all

the censorships in the field seek to repress" (*Field* 73). Munro appears to realize that in the previous comment she has sinned against the field, because she then adds, haltingly,

> You see it was mostly a. . . . It wasn't an artistic decision as much. . . . Well, it was. In the end it was *my* decision for what the book had to be. But the decisions before that were made from a publishing point of view, with me going along with them because I couldn't, at that time, see how I could alter things. I couldn't see if I would ever get enough stories to make a Rose book. In this I was helped by the patience of my American publisher who seemed, with good reason, less commercially nervous than a Canadian publisher, and who was willing to wait to see what I could do.
>
> ("Real" 31-32)

Though both the Macmillan and Norton contracts were signed on 20 June 1978 (Hoy 67), the publication deadline for Macmillan was 18 November of that year, while the Americans required a completed draft by late September 1978 for a spring 1979 publication (MsC 38.2.64.9). The question, therefore, is whether the Americans are more patient or simply required a longer lead time for production and promotion in their far larger literary market. It is also possible that the longer production schedule reflected the American publisher's uncertainty about an unknown Canadian writer.

For Hoy, the received version is a "hurdle" that we see Munro "attempt . . . several times, each time acquiring new resources" (70) until she reaches "the conviction, sense of inevitability, and facility of the final creative leap" (70). Given the archival evidence I have presented, I would argue that the authoritative text is in itself a fiction, as are final creative leaps, at least leaps dissociated from cultural pressures to make money, crack the American market, write novels, think like a man, focus on the growth of the individual while subtly denouncing bourgeois values yet supporting the dominant ideology of secular humanism—all the while pretending to care only about "Art" and not at all about money.

Given the struggles Munro underwent to produce this text, the irony must have been delicious: in this year of canon-formation at Calgary, from which she was excluded by genre, the Governor General's Award for the best work of fiction in English was given to a short story sequence called ***Who Do You Think You Are?*** It might well have been a further and equally delicious irony for Munro that the American version of the text, ***The Beggar Maid,*** earned her a nomination for the Booker Prize the following year. Bourdieu defines successful cultural producers as those "who can *recognize* the specific demands of this universe [i.e., the cultural field] and who, by concealing from themselves and others the interest at stake in their practice, obtain the means of deriving profits from disinterestedness" (*Field* 75). Obviously, the production of ***Who Do You Think You Are?*** forced Munro to develop her recognition of the specific demands of the literary field. What is most intriguing and inspiring about the whole episode is that, following this highly successful story sequence, instead of slavishly attempting to repeat the success of ***Who Do You Think You Are?,*** Munro has never returned to the story sequence form.[12]

In closing his discussion of Flaubert, Bourdieu warns his reader that the now "familiar world" of Flaubert's work and influence "keeps us from understanding, among other things, the extraordinary effort that he had to make, the exceptional resistances that he had to surmount, beginning within himself, in order to produce and impose that which, largely because of him, we now take for granted" (205-206). Munro's effort in the creation of ***Who Do You Think You Are?*** is reflected in her defensive reaction to Gzowski's comment on how each of the stories in ***Open Secrets*** is a novel; the exceptional resistance she mounted in its creation is evident in the archive; and the way in which "we now take for granted" the results of Munro's struggles is obvious in the critical appraisal of her work: Gzowski cites a review of ***Open Secrets*** which lavishes praise on "the incomparable Alice Munro, who is not just a good writer but a great one, the first Canada has produced" (Oct. 94). However, it is not *only* Canada which "has produced" Alice Munro; in fact, I have shown that the author function, the "plurality of selves" known as Alice Munro, has been "produced":

—by Canada *and* the United States and their respective cultural fields;

—by Robert Weaver, Virginia Barber, Charles McGrath, Sherry Huber, and Ann Close, and all those "cultural bankers in whom art and business meet in practice" (Bourdieu, *Field* 75);

—by a patriarchy that subordinates women in language and thus produces particularly potent forms of resistance;

—by such canonizers as the academy and the Calgary conference;

—by the exigencies of the marketplace and the disavowal of the economic necessary to the "accumulation of symbolic capital" (Bourdieu 75); and

—finally, in response to and engagement with all these producers, by the active but not sovereign protagonist in the struggle, the author herself, who "reinvents" the short story form in her struggle to "remake" the individual short stories in ***Who Do You Think You Are?.***

Notes

1. See, for example, Wachtel, *Writers and Company,* CBC Radio, September 1991.

2. Including Raymond Knister, ed., *Canadian Short Stories* (Toronto: Macmillan, 1928); Desmond Pacey, ed., *Book of Canadian Stories* (Toronto: Ryerson, 1947); Robert Weaver and Helen James, eds., *Canadian Short Stories* (Toronto: Oxford University Press, 1952).

3. Five subsequent editions of this anthology have appeared since 1960, the most recent co-edited with Margaret Atwood.

4. The document, reproduced from a 1928 edition of *Best American Stories,* is also interesting for the way in which editor Edward J. O'Brien further categorizes the "distinctiveness" of the stories with a system of asterisks. Three-asterisk stories are judged by O'Brien to be "worth reprinting in book form" (Levy 39). For example, of the 334 *Saturday Evening Post* selections, only 2 per cent are "distinctive" enough to get three asterisks, while 64 percent of the 33 stories that appeared in *Harper's* achieved that level of distinction.

5. For a fascinating discussion of such "contamination" from a contemporary perspective, see Carole L. Beran, "The Luxury of Excellence: Alice Munro in the *New Yorker,*" *Essays on Canadian Writing* 66 (Winter 1998): *Alice Munro: Writing On.*

6. Munro's children were born in 1953, 1957, and 1966. In 1955 she gave birth to a daughter who lived only two days.

7. This is true not only of North America; in "A Neglected Responsibility: Contemporary Literary Manuscripts," Philip Larkin deplores the fact that reams of English literary papers are being purchased by American academies. In answer to the question of how archivists are to know which writer's archival materials should be considered valuable, Larkin responds: "Simple. We ask our English departments." See *Encounter* (July 1979): 33-41.

8. The thorny relationship between the writer and the academy is explored in detail in chapter 5, "Writer."

9. The fourth letter, dated 21 August 1978, encloses a rewritten version of "Simon's Luck" (MsC 38.2.64.8a).

10. In her study of an alternate manuscript for this book, Helen Hoy makes extensive use of the University of Calgary archival materials. She remarks that other correspondence between Barber and Munro is held by the Barber agency and is cur-

rently closed to researchers. Hoy expresses her hope, echoed by me, that these letters, "will become part of the Munro collection sometimes in the future"(p. 80, n. 14). This has not yet occurred. The recent Third Accession does contain 85 items of correspondence from the Barber Agency, but none dated prior to 1981.

11. Hoy p. 82, n. 50 Alice Munro file, W. W. Norton.

12. As mentioned, the character of "Janet" appears in the first, second, and final stories of *The Moons of Jupiter,* while the remaining stories all present different and unrelated characters. None of Munro's subsequent texts have been described, by herself or by critics, as a "novel" or "story sequence."

Works Cited

ARCHIVAL

Alice Munro Papers. Special Collections. University of Calgary Library. Acc. 396/87.3.

PUBLISHED

Bader, A. L. "The Structure of the Modern Short Story." May 107-15.

Bennett, Donna, and Russell Brown, eds. "Conflicted Vision: A Consideration of Canon and Genre in English-Canadian Literature." Lecker *Canadian Canons* 131-49.

Bourdieu, Pierre. *The Field of Cultural Production.* London: Columbia UP, 1993.

Dahlie, Hallvard. Introduction. Steele 1-5.

Davey, Frank. "Writers and Publishers in English-Canadian Literature." *Reading Canadian Reading.* 87-104.

Eagleton, Mary. "Gender and Genre." Hanson 55-68.

Faulkner, William. "The *Paris Review* Interview." *Writers at Work.* Ed. Malcolm Cowley. New York: Viking P, 1958. 119-42.

Gullason, Thomas A. "The Short Story: An Underrated Art." May 13-31.

Gzowski, Peter. Interview with Alice Munro. *Morningside.* CBC Radio. Oct. 1994

Hanson, Clare, ed. *Re-Reading the Short Story.* New York: St Martin's P, 1989. 1-9.

Hoy, Helen. "Rose and Janet: Alice Munro's Metafiction." *Canadian Literature* 121 (Summer 1989): 59-84.

Johnson, Randal. "Editor's Introduction: Pierre Bourdieu on Art, Literature, and Culture." Bourdieu, *The Field of Cultural Production.* 1-25.

Keefer, Janice Kulyk. "Gender, Language, Genre." *Language in Her Eye.* Ed. Libby Scheier, Sarah Sheard, and Eleanor Wachtel. Toronto: Coach House, 1990. 164-71.

Lecker, Robert. "Anthologizing English-Canadian Fiction: Some Canonical Trends." *Open Letter* 9.1 (Fall 1994): 25-80.

Levy, Andrew. *The Culture and Commerce of the American Short Story.* New York: Cambridge UP, 1993.

MacKendrick, Louis K., ed. *Probable Fictions: Alice Munro's Narrative Acts.* Downsview, ON: ECW Press, 1983.

Mathews, Lawrence. "Calgary, Canonization, and Class: Deciphering List B." Lecker, *Canadian Canons* 150-68.

Matthews, Brander. "The Philosophy of the Short Story." May 52-59.

May, Charles E., ed. *Short Story Theories.* Athens: Ohio UP, 1976.

McCulloch, Jeanne, and Mona Simpson. "Alice Munro: The Art of Fiction CXXXVII." *Paris Review* 131 (Summer 1994): 227-64.

Moravia, Alberto. "The Short Story and the Novel." May 147-52.

Munro, Alice. "The Beggar Maid." *Who Do You Think You Are?* 67-99.

———. *Lives of Girls and Women.* New York: Signet, 1974.

———. *The Moons of Jupiter.* Toronto: McClelland and Stewart, 1982.

———. *Open Secrets.* Toronto: McClelland and Stewart, 1994.

———. *Something I've Been Meaning to Tell You.* New York: Signet, 1975.

———. "What Is Real?" *Making It New: Contemporary Canadian Stories.* Ed. John Metcalf. Toronto: Methuen, 1982. 223-26.

———. *Who Do You Think You Are?* Scarborough, ON: Signet, 1979.

Olsen, Tillie. *Silences.* New York: Delacorte, 1978.

Pacey, Desmond. "Modern Canadian Fiction, 1920-1950." *Creative Writing in Canada.* 2nd. ed. Toronto: Ryerson, 1961. 186-229.

Poe, Edgar Allen. "Review of *Twice-Told Tales.*" May 45-51.

Ross, Oakland. Rev. of *Strangers Are Like Children* by Joan Baxter. *Globe and Mail* 10 Aug. 1996: C8.

Scott, Gail. "Shaping a Vehicle for Her Use: Women and the Short Story." *In the Feminine: Women and Words.* Ed. Ann Dybikowski et al. Edmonton: Longspoon P, 1985. 184-91.

Struthers, J. R. (Tim). "The Real Material: An Interview with Alice Munro." MacKendrick. 5-38.

Thacker, Robert. "Alice Munro: An Annotated Bibliography." *The Annotated Bibliography of Canada's Major Authors.* Ed. Jack David. Downsview, ON: ECW Press, 1984. 354-414.

Thompson, Kent. "The Canadian Short Story in English and the Little Magazines—1971." *World Literature Written in English* 11 (April 1972): 15-24.

Twigg, Alan. "What Is." *For Openers: Conversations with 24 Canadian Writers.* Madeira Park, BC: Harbour, 1981. 13-20.

Wachtel, Eleanor. "Alice Munro." *Writers and Company.* Toronto: Knopf, 1993. 101-12.

Weaver, Robert. Introduction. *Canadian Short Stories.* Ed. Robert Weaver. Toronto: Oxford UP, 1960. ix-xiii.

———. Preface. *Canadian Short Stories.* 5th Series. Ed. Robert Weaver. Toronto: Oxford UP, 1991. ix-xii.

"Writing's Something I Did Like the Ironing." *Globe and Mail* 11 Dec. 1982: E1.

Elizabeth A. Shih (essay date spring 2003)

SOURCE: Shih, Elizabeth A. "Phallicism and Ambivalence in Alice Munro's 'Bardon Bus.'" *Contemporary Literature* 44, no. 1 (spring 2003): 73-105.

[*In the following essay, Shih applies the psychoanalytical theories of Sigmund Freud to the intimate relationships in "Bardon Bus," emphasizing the role of parental influence on the characters' sexuality.*]

In a 1982 interview, Alice Munro commented on characterization in her short stories by saying: "[T]he whole mother-daughter relationship interests me a great deal. It probably obsesses me. The way fathers obsess some male writers" (Interview [Hancock] 215). Making that observation on the eve of the publication of *The Moons of Jupiter* (1982), a short-story collection whose treatment of female experience is frequently centered in mother-daughter relationships, Munro acknowledged her personal investment in one of the most fundamental psychoanalytic narratives of subjectivity—the loss of the mother and the necessary repudiation of that loss. While Munro's latest collection—*Hateship, Friendship, Courtship, Loveship, Marriage* (2001)—deals with the "stuff of adult life: love, sex, success, failure, hope, death" (McClelland and Stewart book jacket), I find an ambitious if under-appreciated discussion of the paradoxes of compulsory heterosexual and female gendering in **"Bardon Bus"** (*Moons* [*The Moons of Jupiter*]) that Munro herself dates to a more "autobiographical or personal" period of fiction (Interview [Wachtel]).[1]

"Bardon Bus" is the first-person testimony of an unnamed female freelance writer who returns to Toronto after a research trip in Australia, during which she had a casual affair with a married man of former acquaintance. The period and setting of the affair are described in florid detail. The narrator's subsequent obsession over her male lover, whom she calls X, is intense and compelling, implicating his friend, Dennis, and hers, Kay, in two barely intimated love triangles. The lovers' apparently sophisticated adult sexual relationship is prefigured by the narrator's unresolved oedipal loss, by which she and in fact all of the major characters in the story became gendered in the first place. Munro's self-acknowledged obsession about "mothers and daughters" is evident in ambivalently epiphanic moments of the narrator's testimony, by which the woman gradually recognizes that the source of her suffering is not her faithless lover. It lies instead in her melancholic incorporation of the absent mother in and as her own ego, a loss that has traumatically constituted the narrator's sexuality, and that she unconsciously repeats in the heterosexual bond.[2] The narrator's obsession over X is only the central conflict in a larger landscape of psychosexual crisis in **"Bardon Bus."**

Following Freud, classical psychoanalysis posits a "phallic" phase in infantile development that for children of both sexes follows the oral and anal phases but precedes the oedipal one (Freud, "Infantile" 139-45). During the phallic phase, the child (not yet a subject) takes as the primary erogenous zone the phallus that Freud problematically equates to the male penis. The unconscious fantasy of this period is that one's mother has the phallus (be it the penis or other site of ontological power) because her adaptation to the child's needs is so close that she seems to be omnipotent. The infant's fantasy lasts until sexual difference is discovered in the oedipal period. The concept of the phallic mother then becomes the child's defense against acknowledging the mother's lack and the threat to the self of a similar castration (Jacobus 105).[3] Phallicism conveys a sense of self-grandiosity, dominated by the blissful experience of being the center of all existence. The fantasy usually changes in the oedipal period, so that the phallus is seen for a time to be the father's and rivalry developed with the mother for it, until, if oedipalization is not resolved, the "phallic" figure is displaced to other women in the adult life of the child (Moore and Fine 143-44). The phallic phase, as object-relations theorists and self-psychologists argue, becomes "phallicism" when that early infantile self experiences instability and unreliability in the caregiver, who thwarts the child's needs for both dependence and independence (or, in classical terms, the need to release aggression for individuation), so that the oedipal phase becomes a fragmenting and traumatizing experience. As Mary Jacobus writes, "unless [the mother] is imagined as the phallic mother, the mother is always lost, the subject forever abroad" (105).

By her autobiographical testimony in **"Bardon Bus,"** the narrator scrutinizes female experiences of phallicism in herself and her friend Kay more intensely than she can the male ones of her lover, whom she calls X, and his friend, Dennis. But phallicism is central to the motivation of the characters' gendered behavior and to our understanding, particularly of the narrator's psychosexual identity conflict. When the narrator meditates on how she would have been an "old maid" in a previous generation, hoarding paltry trinkets as sexual fetishes, she reveals not only her capacity to fantasize about men in a "lifelong secret, lifelong dream-life" (110), but more importantly that in the fantasy she expresses feminine behavior she would have learned from her mother. When the narrator observes that she could make erotic the most mundane tasks of "polishing the stove, wiping the lamp chimneys [and] dipping water for tea from the drinking-pail" (110-11), these traditionally "female" chores are not neutral, but overdetermined with an infantile, pre-oedipal longing for plenitude with the mother.[4]

The narrator expresses this longing more clearly in a companion moment near the end of the story, when she recalls only a short-lived enchantment in the childhood game of dress up: at "ten or eleven years old," she unconsciously imitated her mother by masquerading "as the bride in old curtains, or as a lady in rouge and a feathered hat" (126). The narrator notes that after "all the effort and contriving . . . there was a considerable letdown. What are you supposed to do now?" and in the present moment asserts that "there is great fear and daring and disappointment" in the "display" of gender (126). The need and vulnerability that mark the narrator's "letdown" with her own specular reflection, and her later sense of the "fear, daring and disappointment" of gender, ontologically precede her affair with X and characterize the narcissistic wound she sustained in infancy, by losing the idealized object of her primary identification.

By describing her former lover, X, in melodramatically inflated language that betrays her psychological investment in him as a replacement for an absent, idealized mother, Munro's narrator most obviously demonstrates phallicism. X becomes the object of the "enchantment" the narrator felt fleetingly as a child, when she "dressed up" as a "bride" or a mature "lady" before the mirror (126).[5] Onboard the plane, after she departs from X and so ends their affair in Australia, she fantasizes that "the bulk of [him] was still beside me and when I woke I filled the space quickly with memories of his voice, looks, warmth, our scenes together" (123). Back in Toronto, the fantasy becomes embellished, so that what she

believes is "love" for X includes a "movie-dream of heaven" one night, in which their "innocent athletic underwear outfits . . . changed at some point into gauzy bright white clothes and these turned out to be . . . our substances . . . our souls. Embraces took place . . . with the usual urgency, but were transformed . . . into a rare state of content" (127). The "content" she dreams of is not a waking reality, for only in fantasy can the narrator's perceptions of X intensify despite the increasing distance between them. X becomes what Freud terms the "ideal ego," the reflection of the grandiose self she most wants to feel, a position originally occupied by the mother, and whose loss the narrator now defends against, not only as that of a lover, but as a lover overdetermined by her own preoedipal longing for wholeness.

The focus of the narrator's testimony on X conveys the sense that her life began, has entirely revolved around, and threatens to end with him. The narrator alludes only in the most cursory way to being divorced from her first husband at the time she reconnects with X (111). Yet that divorce itself has repeated the loss of the phallic mother, for although her husband gave her a baby at age twenty-one, it clearly was not the phallus she longed for: motherhood came with her husband's sexist expectation that she would nurse the baby "in the bushes" during a public picnic, so that years later when she recalls the marriage, she says, "[s]ex has not begun for me at all" (118). That particular assertion from the middle-aged narrator further reflects that sexuality has replaced maternity as the new mode of her phallicism. This early maternal scene of nursing her baby, which she recalls as one of lack, is also significantly the first occasion on which she spoke with X, and was "lightened" by "gratitude" for the attention he paid her. The scene presages his role as a phallic figure in their affair, twenty years later.[6]

Just as the narrator performs a masquerade of femininity before the mirror at "ten or eleven years old," and as an adult imagines herself as a sex-starved "old maid" ancestor, the narrator writes X into a private psychic fantasy, calling him "one of the letters of his name" less "because it suits him" than because "it seems to me expansive and secretive" and thus like a "character in an old-fashioned novel, that pretends to be true" (112). Although the letter x may in fact be secretive, signifying among other things an unknown algebraic quantity, it is the "expansive" potential of the letter as signifier that attracts the narrator: through it she can project onto X and their affair whatever qualities she desires—irrespective of his abandonment, and dismissing her own doubts in the affair, when she "had cried once, thought I was ugly, thought he was bored" (123).[7] The narrator's grandiose construction of her former lover aligns her with her imaginary "old maid" ancestors, for the "expansive-[ness]" she finds in the signifier "X" echoes the synecdochic structure of the older women's fetishes—the "piece" of Chinese silk ". . . worn by the touch of fingers in the dark," in which "a little go[es] a long way" and "a touch communicates a whole" (110).[8]

Through memory and dreams, two sites classically associated with the unconscious, the narrator forestalls the pain of maternal loss: she writes the character of "X" as the character in her own "old-fashioned novel" (112), dreams the elated "white" dream of the "bright . . . clothes" (127), the more tormented dream of the trip to Cuba (114), and compulsively replays her memory of sexual bliss with X. In the dream, when X proposes they go to Cuba, the narrator's ostensibly sexual desire only thinly veils her childhood desire for protection from the mother, a wish that is fulfilled when X claims "he did not want to interfere . . . but he did want to shelter me" (114). But before she awakens to feel that fulfillment "shrivel," the fantasy is disrupted when she finds herself unable to go because "it seemed I had the responsibility of a baby, asleep in a dresser drawer." By contrast to the picnic scene in which X speaks to her as she breastfeeds her baby in the bushes, in this maternal scene, her symbolic status as a mother herself precludes her from seeking with him the fulfillment of her childhood desire: her need for X as phallic mother is displaced and deferred to the baby's need for her.

That displacement continues in the yellow nightgown passage, in many ways an unrecoverable trauma of her adult womanhood and the outcome of the ten- or eleven-year-old child's memory of standing "letdown" before the mirror (126). In this passage, the narrator's postcoital turmoil seems to fulfill the "old maid" fantasies of "perfect mastery," as it reduces her to the "woman, who has almost lost consciousness, whose legs are open, arms flung out, head twisted to the side as if she has been struck down in the course of some natural disaster" and who "rouses herself . . . slops water . . . drinks, shudders, falls back" (123-24). While this memory replays in her head to the point of her "torment" (124), the narrator, by contrast, finds her other dream, of "white" clothing, "misplaced," and finds that "misplacement is the clue in love, the heart of the problem" (128). Her term "misplacement" is a syntactic variation of psychoanalytic "displacement," the associative or metonymic web of lack and desire for the (m)other, repeated in the heterosexual bond.[9] Clearly, the forms by which the narrator expresses her longing for X—dream and the autobiographical re-telling of memory—are laden with phallic longing and logic.

In particular, the narrator's disturbing memory of sex with X, by which the room was filled with "long subsiding spasms . . . a rich broth of love, a golden twilight of love" (124), demonstrates the narrator's version of the old maids' stubborn virgin's belief that "perfect mastery" in a man's hands is possible: she uncon-

sciously expects orgasmic bliss to repair her wounded femininity.[10] The term "perfect," both symptom of and synonym for the narrator's phallicism, recurs significantly to the narrator and X when she is most vulnerable—when they separate for her return to Canada. She recalls lying to him, "As it is, it's been perfect," and is surprised that he responds "Perfect" (123).[11] X's phallic view of sex as the means by which they "almost finished each other off" (124) reverberates through the narrator's psyche, so that she acknowledges in herself the old maid's fantasy that in sex "you give yourself up, give yourself over" to a man in an "assault which is guaranteed to *finish off* everything you've ever been before" (111; emphasis added). The grandiose self that the narrator maintains by keeping X as her fantasy lover makes him her phallic principle—the other or object who inherits the power she invested in and ceded to the phallic mother. Because the narrator merely repeats with X her melancholic longing without becoming able to move beyond it, her hope to stabilize her sense of femininity by relation to him is doomed to fail; her belief that X has had "perfect mastery" over her implicitly alludes to the goal of Freud's "pleasure principle," whereby the child compulsively repeats the trauma of the mother's departure in the vain effort to "master" it and so restore the illusion of self-plenitude (Freud, "Beyond the Pleasure Principle" 285).

Compulsory heterosexuality in **"Bardon Bus"** is predicated on the characters' incorporation of the phallic mother, and the presumption that gender is stabilized by heterosexuality; however, on the contrary, the story betrays widespread panic in gender-specific ways. X, who is in his third marriage by the time of the narrator's meditation, takes the narrator and eventually Kay as lovers. And although his psychological motivations are largely occluded from the narrator's testimony, his orgasmic exclamation "We almost finished each other off" and his willingness to affirm that their affair has been "perfect" evoke his reliance on women as phallic mother figures, just as he is for the narrator. X compensates for the lost mother with one woman from his female "army" until, when the illusion of plenitude she supports is spent, and when his identification with her overtakes his desire for her, he abandons her for another. In ironic contradiction to the meaning of "Alexander," X's full name (128), a "helper of mankind," he uses many and ever younger women: in Dennis's terms "having that nice young mirror to look in" (121), X reflects his gender anxiety as an aging man trying to return to the illusion of preoedipal union he had with the mother. The apparently infinite source of female lovers for X's serial monogamy helps him to deny the threat or lack he otherwise feels as a heterosexual man, of being "not total" (Gallop, *Daughter's Seduction* 25).

X's friend Dennis betrays a similarly panicked masculinity, while he practices his social equivalent of X's serial monogamy—visiting foreign countries as a tourist and exploiting the hospitality of acquaintances there. All the while, Dennis arrogantly dominates others with fragments of knowledge he presents as authoritative. His life as an opportunistic, serial tourist, with its egomaniacal talk, allows him unconsciously to compensate for his psychic castration. X is uncommonly able to assess Dennis's character, since it mirrors his own:

> Dennis always talked about the last place he'd been and the last people he'd seen, and never seemed to notice anything, but . . . would . . . be talking about us . . . to the next people he had dinner with, in the next city. . . . Dennis spent most of his life travelling, and talking about it, and . . . knew a lot of people just well enough that when he showed up he had to be asked to dinner.
>
> (119)

A throwback to the nineteenth-century imperialism, Dennis crosses the globe to repress his own lack.

But Dennis's gender panic motivates a more overt sadism than X's to repress his sense of failing masculinity: while ostensibly criticizing his friend for his philandery, Dennis comments that X's "army" of women "marches on" (119), and so objectifies the female narrator, who not only sits before him but also made the dinner he has just consumed. Dennis equates her sexual difference as a woman not merely with being "not total" but with being "not at all" (Gallop 22), and so with a sexual inferiority or castration more intense than his own. As such, the narrator's position bolsters his own faltering ego (Gallop 22). Dennis's cruelty is more obvious when he meets the narrator months later in Toronto, for then she recognizes that "He asked me [to dinner] so he would have somebody to talk to" (120). And that "talk"—an antifeminist diatribe—is again unconsciously motivated to console himself at her expense, for he claims women's lives, unlike men's, go "only . . . in one direction" (121)—to the grave—and disingenuously pronounces her to be "lucky" to be "forced to live in the world of loss and death" (122).[12] Dennis's sadism demonstrates more openly than X's serial monogamy a profound masculine anxiety against identifying with women, whose "castration" both may suspect but vociferously deny in themselves. Dennis in particular demonstrates Judith Butler's critique of the heterosexist male who since "he wouldn't be caught dead being her" must instead "want her" sexually, as the condition of his heterosexual identity (*Psychic Life* 137).

In fact, by equating his anatomical difference from the female narrator with gender superiority, and by conveniently repressing the hazards, such as sexual impotence, that aging men face, Dennis denies the reality of both sexes' ontological lack or castration.[13] He may function to prick the narcissistic bubble of the lovers' bliss in their Queensland house by exposing the tempo-

rariness of their affair, but he's also a "prick" who bases his theory of gender with symptomatic singularity on the "prick" (or penis). His argument that anatomy is destiny is neither "a new theory about the life of women" (121) nor an indisputable one, when psychoanalysts have long argued that the anatomical body may be no more accessible as biological artifact than the unconscious itself, always already mediated by cultural influences.[14] In fact, by making false concessions to the "suffering" of a sex whose experience he misappropriates, Dennis illustrates Jane Gallop's point that even the apparent "resenters" of phallocentric logic are in fact "the most obstinate of believers" (*Daughter's Seduction* 131). He deludes himself that his ostensible social mastery of others is phallic self-presence, even as he must move peripatetically and parasitically from one host to the next, before his illusion of plenitude can dissipate.

Yet for all this, female experiences of phallocentric logic feature more prominently in **"Bardon Bus"** than the male ones. Both Kay and the narrator are caught between the double bind of preoedipal longing for the mother and the desire to be seen by the male lover, in X's "mind and in his eyes" (127). If Dennis mirrors X in denying his castrated state by exploiting women, then Kay similarly mirrors the narrator by exhibiting her "masochistic compliance with her own humiliation" (Carrington 153). Masochism paradoxically may be the only way in which the narrator can sense the boundaries of her fragile ego and so be assured that she still exists; so too is it with Kay. Like Alexander, who is ironically named, Kay is named "pure one," when she is degraded and depleted by her own serial monogamy.[15] The narrator observes that serial pattern by finding on Kay's bookshelf "a history of her love affairs": "books on prison riots, autobiographies of prisoners, from the period of the parolee; this book on anatomy and others on occult phenomena, from the period of the artist; books on caves, books by Albert Speer, from the time of the wealthy German importer who taught her the word *spelunker*; books on revolution which date from the West Indian" (116).

The narrator's awareness of such a pattern in Kay's love life—the efforts at first "to disguise her condition, pretending to be prudent or ironic," and "soon a tremor, a sly flutter" (116)—enables the reader to recognize along with her at the end of the story that Kay has supplanted her in X's affections (128). What remains more disturbing, however, is the implication that compulsory heterosexuality (between Kay and X) will prelude the threat of homosocial or lesbian attachment between Kay and the narrator, when the homosocial bonding between Dennis and X evidently continues despite X's change in partners and Dennis's envy of him. Butler's point that the "'truest' lesbian melancholic" is the "strictly straight woman" applies to the women of **"Bardon Bus,"** because the foreclosure of lesbianism in the oedipal phase is the very mechanism that produces "un-livable passion and ungrievable loss" in the symbolic for the mother (Butler, *Psychic Life* 135).

In fact, the narrator's obsession over X is the central conflict in a larger landscape of psychosexual crisis in **"Bardon Bus"** in which gender is composed of what is repressed—not expressed—by oedipalized sexuality. Two parallel "love" triangles develop between, on one hand, the narrator, X, and K(ay); and, on the other, the narrator, X, and Dennis. Constituted on repressed homosexual desire (between the narrator and K[ay], between X and Dennis) and on correspondingly anxious serial heterosexual monogamy (between X and the narrator and later between X and K[ay]), both triangles perfectly allegorize Freud's neurotic model of oedipal conflict and its limits. In fact, by observing the very blind spots of his theory, we find a way through the story's persisting tension between the narrator's obsession over X, X's serial use of women, and the melancholic gender identifications of the characters.

The development of X's heterosexual affairs with the narrator and later with Kay is arrested on what Mikkel Borch-Jacobsen terms the "two scandals" of Freud's Oedipus: first, that characters view their desire for their lovers as separate from their identification with each other and their same-sex friends, when post-Freudian psychoanalysis has suggested that the first emotional connections of a child with others are not oriented around an a priori genital sexual difference; and secondly, that throughout Freud's writings on the Oedipus complex, he repressed identificatory ambivalence, when post-Freudian critique has found that the child's primal identification with the mother is "shot through" with "hatred and violence" as well as love (Borch-Jacobsen 298).

In the first "scandal," Freud argues that the subject's aim or cathexis and identification only converge in the formation of the oedipal triangle, but **"Bardon Bus"** demonstrates the two as intersecting forces throughout the narrator's adult life, in which the adults' relationships repeat their preoedipal ambivalence. The phallic mother and phallocentric logic form the basis of women's mimetic gender identification and of the melancholic, masochistic dynamic of their sexual desire for men. If, by compulsorily repudiating the loss of the mother, X and Dennis must want to have a "girl [*sic*]" so as not to be her, the narrator and Kay demonstrate their womanliness by not "want[ing] a girl because wanting a girl brings being a girl into question" (Butler, *Psychic Life* 137).[16]

Therefore, the narrator, Kay, X, and Dennis all share anxiety to be "proper" women and men, since threats to heterosexual relations with a phallicized object pathologically threaten heterosexual gender itself. The narra-

tor and Kay only become female by achieving heterosexuality, but femaleness is always and only unstable, contingent upon their dressing up to keep a man "from freeing himself" (116), more than upon being with him. The narrator's and Kay's rivalry for a love object in X to stabilize their unstable gender identities is preceded by Dennis's and X's implicit rivalry for power over the narrator in the story's first dinner scene. And here their unconscious goal is to shore up masculinity threatened by any sympathetic identification they feel with her.

By becoming obsessed with X, and without recognizing that she identifies with him as a substitute for the phallic mother, the narrator demonstrates the unconsciously antimimetic nature of Freud's Oedipus complex. Freud favored the erotic aim or cathexis of sexuality above the imitative process of the infant's identification, including its earliest, neuter preoedipal state. Unconsciously repressing both aim and the preoedipal state, he was able to find an easy symmetry between male and female heterosexual oedipal processes and to root that symmetry in genital sexuality. By contrast, the mere existence of homosexual object relations, in which identification and aim for a same-sex object are aligned, exposes Freud's scandalous repressions (Borch-Jacobsen 302).

In a crucial admission in "The Ego and the Id" (1923), Freud concedes that aim and object identification are "no doubt indistinguishable from each other," since the oedipus complex has its prehistory in the ambivalent incorporation of the mother. Asserting that the child's identity with the mother therefore precedes or coincides with desire for her, Freud nonetheless continues to separate libidinal aim from identification in his "official" theory. This practice reflects his desire to repress the homosexual and its power to panic heterosexual identity.

The second scandal of the oedipus complex for Freud, as Borch-Jacobsen explicates, also governs the characters of **"Bardon Bus"**—the possibility that the subject feels incestuous or aggressive desires toward the mother, which in combination with the arbitrary, nongenital basis of heterosexuality, threaten heterosexist culture and so must be repressed (Borch-Jacobsen 299). Sexual rivalry in Munro's story is only a displacement of the lasting influence of preoedipal ambivalence toward the mother. Therefore, the urgency of male partnership and the threat of competition "in love" take on great proportion in **"Bardon Bus,"** as symptoms of a fundamental anxiety of heterosexual gender identification.

In other words, it is not only the loss of the mother as identificatory object, but also the possibility that the ambivalence the characters feel for her could as likely be channeled into homosexual as into heterosexual love that motivates the two love triangles in **"Bardon Bus"** in the first place. If there is no anatomical or compulsory basis for genital heterosexuality, then the apparently homosocial ties in the story (the narrator with Kay, Dennis with X) could just as readily be homosexual. In fact, the lure of the homosexual aim and identification makes the narrator and Kay and also X and Dennis defensively heterosexual. For instance, when the narrator and Kay desperately seek to sustain their respective love affairs with men, that aim seems, as Freud argues, fully distinct from their feminine identification with the mother and each other: they commiserate over their similarly failing love lives (117), and Kay replaces X as the provider of "shelter" to the narrator (114). Yet the narrator not only identifies with Kay (enough to defend her manic behavior to others), but by the end of the story unconsciously wants her and becomes the initial audience for her new makeover. Certainly, when the adult, graying Kay parades in a "schoolgirl's tunic worn without a blouse or brassiere" that makes her arms look "soft and brown" (128), the masquerade resonates with the narrator's reversal of it, her memory of playing "grown-up" as a child, when she would "dress up as a bride in old curtains, or as a lady in rouge and a feathered hat" (126). But Kay also titillates the narrator, who affirms that the outfit looks "kinky" (128). The intensification of the women's mutual identification by their implied desire proves all the more devastating when the narrator realizes that Kay, in accord with compulsory heterosexuality, is performing for X's benefit, not hers (128). Kay's androgynous masquerade as the prepubescent "schoolgirl" disrupts heterosexual gender identity in a way parallel to the "pretty boy," whom the narrator sees, while in the throes of her own gender masquerade, earlier in the story.

What we might term characters' drag in **"Bardon Bus"** not only unveils the arbitrary performativity of gender as a series of imitations and repetitions without origin, but also performs, as a gendered identification, the subject's taboo sexual aim for the mother. The male drag queen becomes "femme," and Kay regresses to a prepubescent state of dependence on the mother. Therefore, when the narrator is titillated by Kay's boyish look (observing that her tunic is worn "without blouse or brassiere," and conceding that she looks "kinky") and observes that the "pretty boy," though "not a young lady at all but a pretty boy dressed up as a lady," is still the "prettiest . . . person she has seen all day" (125-26), she experiences the paradoxical coexistence of female gendered identification and homosexual aim that Freud could not bear to avow.[17]

Further, the panicking of gender by ungrieved homosexual aim is also evident in the male characters of **"Bardon Bus."** As we have seen, X's serial monogamy is panicked by the possibility that he could be a woman and therefore desire men. And Dennis is jealous of both X's success with women and of those women's close-ness to X, so that he insults both X and the narrator by claiming X has an "army" of women, "Row on row and always a new one appearing at the end of the line" (119). By his masculine aggressiveness in this scene and in the second dinner he shares with the narrator, Dennis demonstrates that the more defensive the gender identification, the more fierce the ungrieved homosexual aim.

By contrast to the male characters in **"Bardon Bus"** who experience oedipalization as a threat of being "not total," or the loss of the phallus they ostensibly have, the female narrator and Kay, who experience oedipalization as the fear that they do "not [exist] at all" (Gallop, *Daughter's Seduction* 146), display a nostalgic longing to return to the mother. For men, psychic desire "can be married to a threat," Gallop writes, but for women, according to Lacan, "it can join *nostalgia* instead. If the threat is understood as the male's castration anxiety, fear of losing what he has as the mother has lost hers, then perhaps the nostalgia is the female's regret for what she does not have (any longer). Man's desire will henceforth be linked by law to a menace; but women's desire will legally cohabit with nostalgia" (Gallop 145-46; emphasis added). Therefore, while X and Dennis attempt to dominate women sexually or socially to defend against their own castration anxiety, the narrator and Kay resort to "nostalgia" as a coping mechanism. A coding for feminine oedipal desire, nostalgia is for women a heterosexually permitted neurosis toward the mother and "the feminine articulation of what it means to become a gendered subject" (Jacobus 105). Kay's and the narrator's experiences "in love" paradoxically embody their longing for a mythical phallic mother whom no child ever has yet continues to long for, fulfilling Freud's observation in "Beyond the Pleasure Principle" that patients repeat repressed material in "reproductions, which . . . always have as their subject some portion of infantile sexual life—of the Oedipus complex" (288).

The narrator's affair with X is therefore less important for its own sake than for serving her fantasy of preoedipal unity with the phallic mother, demonstrating Kay's claim of men: "You don't want them, you want what you can get from them" (117). The narrator's oscillations between grandiosity ("hysterical eroticism") and despair (apparent "common sense") as she endures the loss of X are overdetermined by nostalgia for the lost mother. And although Kay's behavior is yet more exaggerated than the narrator's, the narrator unconsciously identifies her own nostalgia in Kay and so not only "joke[s] about" her but rationalizes that her "trust is total . . . miseries . . . sharp" (116), and that she "survives without visible damage" (117). By remembering their fragmented egos through affairs of the past in such hyperbolic terms, the female characters in **"Bardon Bus"** reveal that their nostalgia is "the retrospective form of desire which Freud defines, in 'The Uncanny,' as masculine homesickness for the maternal body" (Jacobus 94).[18] Indeed, as Jacobus writes, "If the mother has [the phallus], then there is only masculinity after all" (104).

Throughout the story, the narrator depicts moments of phallicism by rhetorical figures of the uncanny that mark the blurring of the boundary between the characters' fantasies of omnipotence and the reality of the loss of the mother. These moments consist of the contradiction between a sense of plenitude that is *heimlich,* or familiar to the womb, and the *unheimlich,* the unfamiliar or repressed loss. Although these moments often involve X, the observations and images are of the narrator's telling. For instance, she recalls in terms of the uncanny her visits with X to the Australian town near his house, when descending from the "half-wild hill villages into the central part of town, with its muddy river" was both "remarkably *familiar* and yet not to be confused with anything we had known in the past. . . . This *familiarity* was not oppressive but delightful, and there was a slight *strangeness* to it, as if we had come by it in a way we didn't understand" (112-113; emphasis added). This descent is couched in imagery reminiscent of a regression to the mother's womb, with the lovers' return to the womblike center or "muddy river" of the nearby town (112). And here alone does the narrator explain the name of the title bus as the one that transports them on this trip and so supports their state of denial. By naming the story **"Bardon Bus,"** Munro might seem to foreground the narrator's "system" (112) of using synecdoche to tell her story, in which the bus's name, like X's, stands for a whole: "I say to myself, 'Bardon Bus, No. 144,' and I see a whole succession of scenes . . . in detail" (112). Arguing that the Australian village, its "housewives" and "shuttered, sun-blistered houses" are familiar (113), the lovers demonstrate one such moment of denial when the situation is more invested than they realize with the loss of the mother.

Images that Freud enumerates in "The Uncanny" (1919), such as "dismembered limbs [and] a severed head," and especially those that seem capable of independent activity, further proliferate associations of oedipal castration throughout the narrator's story. When Dennis insults the narrator by commenting that X's "women aren't intact. Or not for long" (120), he compares them to the decapitated and dismembered terracotta soldiers in China: "Their legs and torsos and heads have to be matched up" (120). Virtually the same uncanny associations recur as the narrator compulsively and nostalgically repeats her yellow nightgown memory at X's hands, even if her reversion to a third-person voice here may represent a simultaneous disavowal of her disempowerment: "On the bed a woman . . . has almost lost consciousness, whose *legs* are open, *arms* flung out, *head* twisted to the side as if she has been

struck down in the course of some natural disaster" (123; emphasis added). Even as the narrator tries to substitute orgasmic sex with X for the mother, the uncanny underlies those moments metonymically, thereby transmitting the structure of loss that characterizes Lacanian desire. By the uncanny, the narrator's nostalgic memory of sex dismembers her, even as she would remember herself by it into a mythic phallic unity.

Uncanny images of beheading or headlessness recur elsewhere in **"Bardon Bus"**—for instance, by association with Sir Walter Raleigh, whose poem "on the eve of his execution" repeats in the narrator's head: "Even such is time, that takes in trust—" (122). Like Raleigh, who operated under the illusion of the power of England's phallic mother, Elizabeth the First, the narrator gains a false sense of omnipotence by being with X (himself the "ruler of an army"). Raleigh joins the metonymies of castration in **"Bardon Bus"** by his beheading and is historically associated with Queen Elizabeth—Munro's final pun on the term "queen." The historical "queen" join the *Queen*sland house where the narrator and X have their affair (119), Kay's apartment at the corner of *Queen* and Bathurst (114), and the drag "queen" or "pretty boy" in evoking scenes of impending loss or lack. The recurrence of the word is only one of several chains of metonymic play in **"Bardon Bus"** by which the narrator's unconscious strategies to disavow her castrated state are ingeniously transmitted throughout the story, as through her psyche.

Exploitation by men may have characterized the narrator's original experience of oedipalization and so predisposed her to comply with the abuse of X and Dennis in creating masochistic conditions by which she shores up her faltering identity. During the narrator's second dinner with Dennis, she complies with his need to "have somebody to talk to" (120), while feeding her own fantasy that she may learn of X's whereabouts or that Dennis may tell him "that I was charming" (120). For such emotional scraps, the narrator sits in silence, eats "pudding" suggestive of her childhood longing for the mother, and submits to Dennis's yet more overt cruelty in X's absence.[19] She says, "I feel him watching me" (122), and feels a gaze as brutal as the misogynistic diatribe he freely levels at her. Under the auspices of describing his "theory" of sexual difference, he says, disingenuously, "[w]omen are the lucky ones," because they are "forced to live in the world of loss and death," before openly charging that "The uterus dries up. The vagina dries up" (122). In both dinner scenes, the narrator is reduced to a child striving to please or submit to a cruel parental figure—not only the sadistic Dennis, but also the more insidious cruelty of X, who abandons the narrator to loneliness in Canada and to Dennis's insults.

Masochism reflects the perverse limit at which the narrator's search for self-coherence has become sexual-

ized. In the two dinner scenes, as in her compulsive replaying of the "yellow nightgown" memory, the narrator
unconsciously revels in her complete emotional and
physical helplessness, "drowning" in memories: the
process of individuation, which in early infancy had no
sexual content, has long since become erotically
charged, so that "sensations of pain, like other unplea-
surable sensations, trench upon sexual excitation and
produce a pleasurable condition" (Freud, "Instincts"
126). That pleasure is based on self-devastation: so un-
confident is the narrator of the boundaries differentiat-
ing herself from the mother and male lovers after her
that only the shattering of those boundaries enables her
to feel their existence in the first place, and so to distinguish herself from the use of others.[20] Masochism marks
the dynamic in which the aggression necessary for the
narrator's early individuation from the mother could not
safely be released in the face of the parents' own narcissism and so, according to Leo Bersani, it is turned
upon the self in self-shattering behavior she is compelled to repeat as the traumatic constitution of her
sexuality (Bersani 217-18).

Therefore, although the narrator achieves grandiosity
from the masochistic repetition of her "hysterically"
erotic fantasies of X, that self-inflation forms only one
side of her complicated defense against lost plenitude in
the mother. In a dialectic with grandiosity that ultimately constitutes her "profound ambivalence" toward
X, the narrator displays apparent rationalism that Munro terms the "survivor's common sense" (Interview
[Scobie] 12-13).[21] "Common sense" is evident when the
narrator assesses her predicament, saying casually:
"People have this problem frequently, and we know it
is their own fault and they have to change their way of
thinking, that's all. It is not an honorable problem"
(126). Elsewhere, she is sufficiently rational to identify
her "torment" (124) in her sexual fantasy of X, to align
herself with imaginary "old maid" ancestors, and to observe through her erotic obsession that "the language of
pornography and romance are alike[,] . . . seductive,
quickly leading to despair" (123). As the process of
self-narration enables her to gain some control over her
unconscious fantasies of X, she sensibly observes,
"There is a limit to the amount of misery and disarray
you will put up with, for love" (127). Yet the fact that
the narrator normalizes Kay's version of her own excessive behavior as "what women do" in love, and calls
the old maids' craziness "harmless," reveals that her
apparent "common sense" as much as her grandiosity
are distortions that defend her from the emotional "castration" of losing X. Munro therefore understates as
"common sense" her narrator's defense against the despair of maternal loss that she unconsciously seeks to
restore in the heterosexual bond.

In fact, the narrator's ambivalence between "hysterical
eroticism" and "common sense" is itself defensive, de-

nying the very denial of lack each represents, for she
assumes that her ability to recognize her self-
contradiction can resolve the profound psychic loss it
conceals. For instance, instead of feeling pain, she
quickly rationalizes that she finds "pleasure in taking
into account, all over again, everything that is contradictory and persistent and unaccommodating about life
. . . there's something in us wanting to be reassured
about all that, right alongside—and at war with—whatever there is that wants permanent vistas and a lot of
fine talk" (128). Similarly, she universalizes the childhood root of her melancholy and the havoc it wreaks in
her life by naming it "something in us" all (128), and
"not an honorable problem" (126), that can be consciously mastered by "chang[ing] [your] way of thinking, that's all." Such comments defend against the pain
at the root of her loss of the mother and X's failure to
replace her.

The narrator's apparently opposite responses of "hysterical eroticism" and "common sense" therefore merely
invert each other and, however anxiously repeated, cannot overcome the traumatic loss or absence in which
they are rooted.[22] Further, these defenses prove futile
before long, for she says, "I have tried vigilance and
reading serious books but I can still slide deep . . . before I know where I am" (123). By the end of **"Bardon
Bus,"** the narrator concedes of her loss that "likely
somebody drunk or high I can't quite get a grasp on
what I see" (128) and so is vulnerable to repeating the
obsession even at the end of her story.

The narrator's phallocentric sexual desire for X is
equally evident in her experience of gender. In another
interview, Munro identified the inspiration for **"Bardon
Bus"** as downtown Toronto, where she spent the summer of 1981 "getting a very strange feeling from Queen
Street. It was a kind of hysterical eroticism. It was
something about women's clothes and the very very
whorish makeup that women were wearing. And all this
was sort of nightmarish" (Rasporich 23). And elsewhere,
she clarified that the story is "to have a kind of feeling
of hysterical eroticism. Very edgy and sad. This came
to me from the feelings I get sometimes in women's
dress shops . . . about the masquerades and attempts to
attract love" (Interview [Hancock] 193-94). The apparently instinctive attraction the narrator feels toward X is
shown to be no more corporeally determined as a source
of self-plenitude than the gender she performs. Unable
to accept that X has not committed to her beyond their
casual liaison, the narrator plots to win him back, "devastating him" with a campy makeover that she fantasizes will demonstrate her "late-blooming splendor"
(125): a "deep-red satin blouse, a purple shawl, a dark-
blue skirt . . . a lilac lipstick, a brownish rouge" (124).
The excessively bright colors of her makeover ironically contrast with those of the simpler clothes she
wore in X's company, a "faded wraparound cotton skirt

and T-shirt" she now disparages as "appall[ing]" for leaving her "face bare" and "legs with the lumps of veins showing" (124). The narrator deludes herself that such a superficial change will make a difference, "that a more artful getup would have made a more powerful impression, more dramatic clothes might have made me less discardable" (124-25), when X seduced and abandoned her (as others before her) regardless. Phallicism underpins the narrator's "hysterically erotic" femininity as her effort "to attract love" (Interview [Hancock] 194).

The narrator's attempt to win X back through her own phallic fantasy of female identity is evident in her clothing fetish, when she grows obsessed over a pair of vintage silver earrings: "I can't find them, I can't find anything resembling them, and they seem more and more necessary" (125). The earrings, like the old maids' trinkets, are a fetish: according to Moore and Fine, "the woman's—usually the mother's—phallus" (77). In fact, the narrator's campy new appearance aligns her more than she realizes with the "absurdity" of the "old women on Queen Street"—with the "hysterical eroticism" of "the fat woman with pink hair; the eighty-year-old with painted-on black eyebrows; . . . the buttercup woman I saw a few days ago on the streetcar . . . [dressed] in a frilly yellow dress, well above the knees, a straw hat with yellow ribbons, yellow pumps dyed-to-match on her little fat feet" (125).

As Carrington observes, the intense "yellow" coloring of the latter woman resonates not only with the narrator's bright new clothes but more importantly with the "golden twilight" of the postcoital scene with X that she replays in her head, in which she lies "in a yellow nightgown which has not been torn but . . . pulled off her shoulders and twisted up around her waist" (123). As the narrator lies prostrate under X and his gaze, he seems to offer her both the penis and the phallus she values it to be. The "yellow nightgown" for the narrator and the elaborate costumes of the Queen Street women are also fetishes, conflating the maternity gown with sexy lingerie, and thereby "crystallizing . . . the last moment in which the woman could still be regarded as phallic" (Freud, "Fetishism" 135).[23] In her quintessentially female moments in the story, the narrator anxiously defends against maternal lack. By observing the "yellowness" of both her nightgown and the Queen Street "buttercup" woman, the narrator unconsciously connects her own delusional memory of sex with X with the old woman's illusion that self-coherence inheres in impossibly youthful beauty.

Yet the "pretty boy" whom the narrator encounters momentarily at the climax of the story startles her with evidence that gender is fraudulently performative and not intrinsic, for he exhibits femaleness more convincingly than any other woman in the story. He wears his "black velvet dress" and matching "pumps and gloves"

(125), all while concealing his anatomical maleness beneath. When he asks the narrator, "How do I look, momma" (126), he interpellates the narrator, not merely by staging the arbitrary nature of signification that comprises gender, but more importantly because, like her, he is unable to convince himself of a coherent gendered identity. Neither his vampy, hysterically erotic dress nor his penis gives him the phallus of self-plenitude. The narrator notes his anxiety when she observes that his face, though smiling, is "tense and tremulous." He is not only "brash" but also "timid" with his "boyish crackling voice." The possibility of the narrator's fantasy of phallicized sexuality is further undermined by his very act of dressing up before a "three-way mirror," a sign of the infinite regress of identity, which prompts the narrator to recall her own dissatisfying performance of gender before another mirror when she was "ten or eleven years old."[24]

In seeing the "pretty boy," the narrator more clearly glimpses the fallacy of the phallic logic that arrests her experience and development as a female subject: with his "black velvet dress with long sleeves and a black lace yoke; black pumps and gloves; a little black hat with a dotted veil," the narrator finds him the "most ladylike person" she has "seen all day" (125-26).[25] That a man appears to be so "ladylike" and so performs femaleness without any anatomical "core" of gender "beneath" foregrounds for the narrator that all gender is performative, a series of imitations and repetitions without origin. "Ladylikeness," in Butler's argument, can only ever be approximated, not expressed, because such imitations are interrupted and deferred, each repetition differing from the last and from those of other subjects of the same sex.[26] The revelation applies to all the performers of gender in **"Bardon Bus"**: to the "pretty boy" in black, as well as to the narrator with her "deep-red satin blouse . . . purple shawl . . . dark-blue skirt" (124); to Kay, whose disguises vary from "an old woman, with a gray wig and a tattered fur coat" (116) to the schoolgirl (128); and to the "Queen Street women" with "pink hair" or "painted-on black eyebrows" (125). The "pretty boy" exposes the *différance* of gender for the narrator—the argument Butler makes by citing Aretha Franklin, "You make me feel like a natural woman": Naturalness is only achieved by "a kind of metaphorical substitution," she writes ("Imitation" 27), so that feeling *like* a woman is not the same as being one and instead merely perpetuates the illusion of a coherent feminine identity. Drag, in Esther Newton's words, "is not an imitation or a copy of some prior and true gender . . . [but] enacts the very structure of impersonation by which *any gender* is assumed" (qtd. in Butler, "Imitation" 21).[27]

The fact that the best actor of femininity in **"Bardon Bus"** is a man allows the "pretty boy" momentarily to unveil the narrator's phallic logic of gender, her assumption that the signifiers of gender and especially male power are rooted in an authentic or original inwardness or anatomy, instead of in arbitrary and repeated imitations.[28] In him, the narrator sees that gender is enacted in action, speech, and gesture, by a "ritualized repetition of conventions" that are not originally unconscious but consciously repeated in childhood to produce "retroactively the illusion" of "an inner gender core," or a feminine "disposition" (Butler, *Psychic Life* 144). The narrator associates this momentary glimpse of truth with her childhood performance "as a bride in old curtains, or as a lady in rouge and a feathered hat" (126). By exposing the arbitrary performativity of gender, writes Adam Phillips in his response to Butler, the "pretty boy" displays that the "ego is always dressing up for somewhere to go," because "[i]nsofar as being is being like, there can be no place for true selves or core gender identities" (Butler, *Psychic Life* 151-52). The "pretty boy," then, even more than the Queen Street women, subverts the assumption of self-possession in gender and so may be "edgy and sad," and not only titillating, for the narrator (Interview [Hancock] 193-94).

But the narrator's encounter with him/her is ambivalent, for as much as the "pretty boy" destabilizes conventional notions of gender, his/her unveiling of its fraudulence awakens the narrator to her entitlement to power as a woman. For a moment, the image of the "pretty boy" seems to reverse the acute imbalance of power in the narrator's relationship with X: in contrast to the degrading repetition of the yellow nightgown scene, in which the narrator becomes the object of her own "male" gaze, the boy's "tense and tremulous" efforts to be "ladylike," and his interaction with the narrator, position her as the "male" viewer of his archly female masquerade and so disrupt her critical self-objectification. Furthermore, the boy's anxiety, like the narrator's, draws to her attention that he too, like her, seems to have lost sight of the impossible phallus/fallacy of coherent femininity, even as he strives to embody it. In Butler's term, drag "allegorizes" oedipal and "heterosexual melancholy" (*Psychic Life* 145), the truth that heterosexual gender is acquired by denying the ontological "castration" of the phallic mother, and by simultaneously repudiating that loss to foreclose the homosexual desire that results from it (Adam Phillips; in Butler 152).

Given the intensity of her phallicism from and ambivalence toward the mother, it would be falsely optimistic to assert that the narrator's glimpse of the drag queen near the end of **"Bardon Bus"** resolves her appalling predicament. The unveiling of the maternal phallus can only ever be fleeting in a heterosexist culture whose (especially female) melancholy toward the mother is a founding moment. The "pretty boy" nonetheless offers the narrator a glimpse of self-understanding that is valuable, however temporary, for exposing the phallocentric

fallacy of heterosexual gender identity. After months of replaying as desire for X a self-concept that is based on looking into the glass of gender darkly, the narrator glimpses in the "pretty boy," face to face, the truth that gender is performative, imitative, and predicated on a maternal loss she long ago repudiated. That glimpse is necessarily brief, for, as Marjorie Garber asserts, "the scandal of transvestism [is] that transvestism tells the truth about gender. Which is why . . . we cannot"—or not for long—"look it in the face" (250-51).

Finally, if we are to derive for the narrator anything as radically reevaluating and hopeful as what Dennis terms a "new theory about the life of women" (122), his sexist definition of femininity as "natural renunciation and . . . deprivation" and the narrator's and Kay's vulnerability to X are not it. By foregrounding the narrator's narcissistic defenses against the unveiling of her phallic fantasy life, and the oedipal coding of her nostalgia, I have argued instead that the birth into subjectivity is always already gendered subjectivity, and that its progress through oedipalization leaves both sexes, but women most intensely, homesick for the phallic mother. Such a reading provides one interpretation for Munro's claim that "the whole mother-daughter relationship interests me a great deal . . . probably obsesses me," which Julia Kristeva formulates: "That every subject poses him/herself in relation to the phallus has been understood. But that the phallus is the mother: it is said, but here we are all arrêtés" (204).

The characters in **"Bardon Bus"** repeat, through heterosexual object relations, melancholia over the loss of the mother and the illusion of plenitude they felt with her in infancy. The mythic concept of such a maternal bond is at the heart of compulsory heterosexuality and its gender codes. Part of the power of the narrator's obsession over X stems from the fact that the affair, however adulterous on his part, conforms to those compulsory gender roles and therefore makes socially respectable what is rooted in taboo preoedipal longing. When the alternative to compulsory heterosexuality is to feel that early maternal loss, the lure of the phallus becomes understandable: the "wish for the Phallus is great," because "[n]o matter how oppressive its reign, it's much more comforting than no one in command" (Gallop, *Daughter's Seduction* 130-31).

The emotionally charged nature of **"Bardon Bus"** has given it power to "go for the jugular" in readers, critics, and perhaps even Munro herself. Although letters of appreciation for the story fill her archive at the University of Calgary, **"Bardon Bus"** has elicited more affect than understanding, which may have contributed to Munro's own ambivalence toward the story. For instance, after hearing Munro read the story's opening passage during a radio interview in 1982, the young Canadian journalist Peter Gzowski commented, puritanically, "You just read a dirty passage!" (Interview [Gzowski]). Munro's editor at Knopf, Ann Close, reported to Munro that Douglas Gibson at McClelland and Stewart did not like the story but never explained (or perhaps could explain) why (Close 1).[29] Munro's own defensiveness about her narrator's predicament was evident in an interview with Stephen Scobie, when she euphemized the despair the narrator and Kay feel as "common sense" ("Visit" 12-13). She similarly understated the nature of the narrator's melancholia to Gzowski by describing it as a historical more than a psychological problem: "The narrator is living a modern woman's life of free choice and various experience . . . she's having this kind of intense response to experience, but she's living now in a context where you're expected to take things more lightly, so in a way there's no place, there's no room, to feel what she's feeling" (20 Oct. 1982). And further demonstrating her reticence toward **"Bardon Bus,"** in the year that *The Moons of Jupiter* was published, Munro dismissed it to Beverly Rasporich as one of the "florid" stories in a volume that was already "sort of past" (22).

The gender anxiety that plagues the characters of **"Bardon Bus,"** and which I earlier referred to as a "pseudohomosexual" conflict, is the legacy of feelings of inadequacy and lack of confidence that are the underside of the subject's belief in a phallic mother figure. Although Lionel Ovesey is quick to observe that pseudohomosexual conflict does not preclude the existence of true lesbian or gay desire, it *can* precipitate psychosis, which is demonstrated in the narrator's description, late in the story, of her mental state—one so overdetermined that "a poem or rhyme that I didn't even know I knew . . . has some relation to what is going on in my life. And that may not be what seems to be going on" (122). This florid state suggests in fact a kind of mania, counterposed in the narrator by its depressive opposite, earlier in the story, when the narrator claims to be "at a low point," unable "to deal with all that assails [her] . . . unless [she] exist[s] in X's mind and in his eyes" (126). I want to hypothesize, then, that Munro's narrator (if not the author herself) displays a bipolar psyche, and that the story's cycling between "hysterical eroticism" and "common sense" marks the psyche's manic and depressive phases respectively.

Munro's evident distaste for **"Bardon Bus"** upon its publication may reflect a retroactive defensiveness toward its reception by certain insensitive readers, all the more wounding if we at least consider that the story *may* reflect her own experience as a wounded daughter or lover. In a 1991 interview, Munro commented that by the time she was "eleven or twelve," her mother had contracted Parkinson's disease, so that the already "complex relationship" of mother and daughter "was made much more so by the fact that my mother was ill" ("Interview" [Wachtel] 49-50).

The author's later dislike for **"Bardon Bus"** may well be rooted in more personal pain and loss than the "strange feeling" she attributed to the women on Queen Street, in the summer of 1981. Certainly the unnamed status of the narrator invites, though it cannot define, identification with Munro herself. It may be the author's own romantic life that inspired the story, rather than the "lives of friends who are always either falling in love or recovering from a love affair and then going on to the next one [with] no time or energy for anything else" (Munro, "Great Dames" 38). Munro's assessment that by 1982 the story was already "sort of past" (Rasporich 22) evokes a sentiment similar to that which artist-survivors have shared in conversation with me, as they look back at the notes they have compulsively kept during phases of creative mania. At any rate, Munro's reticence toward **"Bardon Bus"** seems to have prompted her to exclude it from the 1996 edition of her *Selected Stories,* despite the laboriously revised nature of the original story.[30]

By rereading **"Bardon Bus,"** a story that Munro seems to have wanted to forget earlier than readers have, I am not proposing a nostalgic return of our own to her writing of the 1980s. But in light of recent accolades for the more distant, less structured nature of Munro's later work (Byatt), I hope to have demonstrated that we find an intensely complex vision of female (in fact, gendered) subjectivity at mid-career. The narrator's delight in **"Bardon Bus"** in all that is "contradictory and persistent and unaccommodating" in her life (128), although a means to defend against her pain, also makes a survival strategy out of her storytelling process. And although by the story's end this process seems doomed to another defeat, it is nonetheless remarkable for its simultaneous, if often unconscious, subversion of the female romance plot.

Notes

I wish to thank Apollonia Steele, Marlys Chevrefils, and the staff of the Alice Munro collection at the University of Calgary Library for assisting me in using the archive; the Virginia Barber Literary Agency, for granting me permission to quote from Munro's draft; and Barbara Brown, Keith Hart, and Gail Donald of the CBC Radio Archives, for allowing me to hear Peter Gzowski's five-part 1982 interview with Munro. Rowland Smith, Julian Patrick, Jane Campbell, Viviana Comensoli, Linda Hutcheon, and Naomi Morgenstern commented judiciously on earlier versions of this essay. The Social Sciences and Humanities Research Council of Canada funded its research.

1. I quote from a 1999 interview with Eleanor Wachtel (on the twentieth anniversary of the CBC Literary Awards), in which Munro comments that she has "always thought back" to the emotions of her

past: "Now I'm writing about . . . these days as a housewife, not quite so autobiographical or personal fiction [as before]."

2. Mikkel Borch-Jacobsen and Judith Butler provide two recent accounts of gender in which mimetic identification (being like) collapses into incorporation (the state of being itself), as a central mechanism of the trauma of subject formation. The prominence of oedipal conflict in childhood development means that the birth into subjectivity is always already a *gendered* subjectivity, which leaves for both sexes, but most intensely for women, homesickness for the mother as a phallic figure. I return to this point later in the essay.

3. This sense of the phallic mother reflects Jane Gallop's exposition of Lacan's "The Signification of the Phallus," of the ambivalence between fear and love for the mother as a woman of whom we are afraid (Gallop, *Reading Lacan* 148-49).

4. By finding that the narrator's gender identification and sexual aim betray their melancholy particularly over the phallic mother, I disagree with Magdalene Redekop's emphasis on the story's intense union between the "symbolic *father* and perfect lover" (157; emphasis added) and her "envision[ing] the father as a brutal lover" (158). The narrator's undescribed father may have been destructive, but the loss of the mother is the narrator's central psychic wound (see Clark 4, 12). While she does not address the narrator's masochism directly, Redekop acknowledges the narrator's desire for plenitude as "lust for her own elimination" (158).

5. Although Ildiko de Papp Carrington does not mention the prevalent connection of characters' gendered phallicism in the story, she observes parallels in the sexual desire between the imaginary "old maids" and the narrator's "yellow nightgown" scene with X (151).

6. Recall also the presence of children who "looked shocked and solemn" (112) in the scene onboard the excursion boat in Australia, when X first propositions the narrator. His extravagant behavior in the seduction scene, where he gets down on his knees, ironically parodies a proposal of marriage or more genuine commitment that he does not offer ("Come and live with me in my house," not Christopher Marlowe's "Come live with me and be my love"). The image also aligns X with a child, arrested by his own narcissistic needs, whom the narrator is reduced to mothering by reprimanding him, "Get up, behave!" (112). X has earlier played the mother to the narrator at the picnic where they meet, when his kind attentions and offer of the beer figuratively nurture the narra-

tor: "[D]rink up. Beer's supposed to be good for your milk, isn't it?" (118). Throughout "Bardon Bus," the presence of children and childlike behavior signifies the characters' profound oedipal conflicts.

7. On the multiple significations of the letter "X," see Heble (139), Rasporich (191), and Redekop (157-58). Although he does not discuss the ironic implications of his reading, Ajay Heble observes that "X" puts the narrator's lover "sous rature" (under erasure), by which the narrator reads Alex Walther as at once the unreliable (abandoning) and indispensable object of her fantasy life. The signifier "X" clearly exceeds the narrator's conscious control of it. The well-established reading of X as *ex*-lover foregrounds the identity X adopts in relation to his lovers by his serial monogamy, virtually before each affair begins. But "X" also marks the spot of a traumatic chiasmus of ambivalence between the reality of oedipal loss and the narrator's phallic fantasy, between having and not having the mother. The chiasmus of these two psychic spaces designates what the narrator must cross over to be a "survivor" of "love": she claims to Kay to be "getting over" X (117; "Getting Over" was a working title for earlier drafts of "Bardon Bus"), and later that she is "at a low point" that she must "get past" (126). Similarly relevant is the phrasing of Kay's sympathetic anecdote about the daughter of Victor Hugo, who, after years of living a romantic fantasy, "can't connect the real man any more with the person she loves, in her head. She can't connect him at all" (117). The need for "connection" between the fragments of the narrator's psyche in "Bardon Bus" thereby enriches one of Munro's key words with psychoanalytic meaning. On Munro's previous use of the term "connections," see York.

8. Fetishism is one form of addictive and compulsive sexuality that manifests in adulthood the phallicism of the child. I return to it and the narrator's compulsive sexuality later.

9. Although she does not discuss the narrator's underlying desire for plenitude, Carrington reads her "misplacement" as "paradoxically positioning herself on both sides of her internal argument . . . between her dreams and her compulsive sexual memories . . . and her waking actions and consciously formulated beliefs" (153).

10. In a review of *The Moons of Jupiter,* Anne Collins perceptively observes that the volume of stories is all about people "still caught in the fantasy of 'perfect mastery'" (74)—phallicisms—over their own lives.

11. Although the narrator's fantasies of X leave her blind to psychic motivation that prompts *him* to

start the affair and lie that he's found it "perfect" (123), one can sense that he lies in that moment to be rid of her before she creates another tearful scene ("I had cried once" [123]), even if that lie feeds the narrator's subsequent fantasy that he shares her "love" and will return to her. Compare, for instance, Munro's later draft of the story ("Bardon Bus, Revised Version"), in which the narrator cries over X's attractiveness to a younger woman who passes them in the street—crying that X passively appeases, without much evident interest or sympathy (3rd Accession 4.42).

12. By essentializing that "Munro even hazards a philosophic challenge through the male character, Dennis, that it is perhaps women who are most often granted" a "privileged sensitivity and understanding beyond Ego" (74), Rasporich overlooks the narrator's disempowerment and Dennis's sadism.

13. Impotence would be one great fear of a phallic narcissist like Dennis. Given the legalization of Viagra in North America in the late 1990s, it seems likely that Dennis today would harness evidence of the wide acceptance of the drug to his claim of male superiority (now that men can apparently "get it up" through old age). The manufacturers' caveats for the drug, restated in the media (that it is not an aphrodisiac, does not work for all men, and carries side effects), seem implicitly intended for consumers with Dennis's phallocentric logic. The variable effects of Viagra would in fact reinforce Dennis's gender anxiety especially well, when we recall Butler's point that gender is performative, repetitive, and therefore, by nature, a failure. Each repetition differs from the last and disrupts the ones that precede it.

14. Butler argues, for instance, that there is no easy correlation between "sex, gender presentation, sexual practice, fantasy and sexuality," despite Dennis's anxious insistence otherwise (Butler, "Imitation" 25).

15. The fact that Kay's name puns with its first letter, "K," unconsciously aligns her in the narrator's mind with [Ale]X[ander] and so foreshadows the connection between the two at the end of "Bardon Bus." More important to the argument that follows, however, is Kay's function as double to the narrator's experience of nostalgia. As the female coding of narcissism, nostalgia differs from X's and Dennis's narcissism, which is their defense against threatened masculinity.

16. Butler's argument "He wouldn't be caught dead being her: therefore he wants her" (137) borrows from Freud's point in "Findings, Ideas, Problems" that the man must "have" the breast to be able to

say, "I am not it" (299). The psychoanalyst Lionel Ovesey terms "pseudohomosexual anxiety" a neurosis that results from a patient's strivings for power over while conceding dependency on an (often idealized) other, which can be misinterpreted by that patient as fear of being homosexual—whether accompanied by same-sex desire or not (32). I return to this concept in my conclusion.

17. The narrator finds this coexistence as hard to bear as Freud did. Her response to the "pretty boy"— "You look very nice" (126)—is remarkably similar to her response to Kay's new masquerade (128). The affirmation in both cases reflects her disowned homosexual desire. The logical sequence of the narrator's pseudohomosexual anxiety after X abandons her would be, "I am a failure in heterosexual love = I am not a woman = I am like a man (in a woman's body) = I am a lesbian" (adapted from Ovesey 44). Kay's schoolgirl (boyish) look and her willingness to offer the narrator shelter allow her to become the man and the narrator the woman in a bond that is neither fully heterosexual nor homosexual (128).

18. By finding work in Australia, X and the narrator discover that their mother(land), Canada, lacks the phallus of knowledge. But then they immediately deny this by using "home" as the standard against which they colonize the sights before them: "we knew the insides of the shuttered, sun-blistered houses . . . we knew the streets we couldn't see" (113). To be a gendered subject is to be alienated from and homesick for the maternal womb.

19. Carrington links images of sweet food in Munro to women's sexuality and their masochistic submission to verbal and physical assault (45, 126, 174-76).

20. Beyond the Queen Street makeover and the "yellow nightgown," the sartorial is generally a source of masochism in the story; the narrator obsesses at the end of her affair with X that their "clothes that had shared drawers . . . tumbled together in the wash, and been pegged together . . . were all sorted and separated and would not rub together anymore" (123).

21. In a 1982 interview, Munro described the narrator's conflict between "hysterical eroticism" and "common sense," claiming that in the end, "common sense wins out" ("Visit" 12-13). But the margin of its success is negligible by the end of "Bardon Bus." Carrington describes the narrator's ambivalent feelings toward X as her predilection for "positioning herself on both sides of her internal argument" (153).

22. The connection between the narrator's "hysterical eroticism" and apparent "common sense" toward

X demonstrates what Andrew Morrison theorizes as the "janus-face of narcissism," in which both sides are dialectical or different manifestations of the same distorted defense against the pain of the psychic loss (64-66).

23. Fetishes proliferate metonymically throughout "Bardon Bus": intrauterine images—such as the marsupials at the animal reserve (the "wombats curled up like blood puddings" and the "koala bears" [112])—both embody the narrator's wish for phallic unity and imply its impossible status. The female breast is also fetishized against the loss of the mother, as the means to fuse maternity, infanthood, and sexuality: the narrator nurses her baby in the bushes (116), and years later, the narrator's breasts are exposed in the yellow nightgown scene (124); finally, in the story's ironic ending, Kay attracts X with a schoolgirl's tunic, worn "without a blouse or brassiere" (128). Sweet oral fetishes also recur, reminiscent of the preoedipal and its phallic illusions of plenitude, as the narrator remembers eating "licorice and chocolate ginger" with X and tries to tolerate Dennis's company by consuming "a rich creamy pudding with pureed chestnuts at the bottom . . . and fresh raspberries on top" (121).

24. Although she misses the deconstructive potential of the three-way mirror by arguing that "Munro reclaims the mirror image often used to condemn women to narcissism" (159), Redekop foregrounds the role of the "pretty boy" in the story.

25. Redekop identifies but does not engage the "blackness" of his "masquerade" as "a place where the woman can identify her oblivion" and ambivalently "step back from it" (160).

26. This of course is Derrida's point with "*différance,*" based in part on Saussure's argument that in language (and therefore in the realm of symbolic identity), there "are concepts defined not positively, in terms of their content, but negatively by contrast with other items in the same system" (115).

27. A more contemporary example that affirms the currency of Derrida's point and Butler's application of it to gender is Shania Twain's hit song, "Man! I Feel Like a Woman" (1999), which she performed by invitation at a recent Grammy Awards ceremony while dressed in a campy short skirt and tall leather boots. The song and similarly "hysterically erotic" photos of Twain have since become her logo as a Revlon poster girl.

28. The drag queen's "boyish crackling voice" (126), however, is part of what gives away his act. Terry Eagleton observes that the "best actor" of subjec-

tivity could also be considered the "worst," if one argues that s/he imitates fraudulently what appears to be a true or coherent female self (469-471).

29. Fellow writers, media personalities, and general readers have written to Munro to remark upon the psychological power of "Bardon Bus."

30. Even for as relentless a reviser as Munro, the working papers of "Bardon Bus" are extensive and particularly labor-intensive. A less successful second version of the story exists, which depicts the ending differently, changes Kay's name and life, refers to another lover the narrator takes and to the violence of the photographic images of the narrator's affair with X—details that serve to intensify the traumatic quality of the narrative, as it circles back upon itself (2nd Accession: 38.8.3.1-2). Munro acknowledged to Peter Gzowski that she relies on editors to help her choose the final version of a story, since she often lives too closely with the drafts to make the decision: interestingly, it is the handwriting of Virginia Barber, Munro's agent, that records which draft of "Bardon Bus" Munro sent to the press (4.41-4.42, 18 March 1982).

Works Cited

Bersani, Leo. "Is the Rectum a Grave?" *October* 43 (1988): 197-222.

Borch-Jacobsen, Mikkel. "The Oedipus Problem in Freud and Lacan." *Disseminating Lacan.* Ed. David Pettigrew and François Raffoul. Albany: State U of NY P, 1996. 295-314.

Butler, Judith. "Imitation and Gender Insubordination." *Inside/Out: Lesbian Theories, Gay Theories.* Ed. Diana Fuss. New York: Routledge, 1991. 13-31.

———. *The Psychic Life of Power: Theories in Subjection.* Stanford, CA: Stanford UP, 1997.

Byatt, A. S. "Munro: The Stuff of Life." Rev. of *The Love of a Good Woman,* by Alice Munro. *Globe and Mail* [Toronto] 26 Sept. 1998: D1.

Carrington, Ildikó de Papp. *Controlling the Uncontrollable: The Fiction of Alice Munro.* DeKalb: Northern Illinois UP, 1989.

Clark, Hilary. "Living with the Dead: Narrative and Memory in Woolf's 'A Sketch of the Past' and Marlatt's *How to Hug a Stone.*" *Signature: A Journal of Theory and Canadian Literature* 4 (1990): 1-12.

Close, Ann. Letter to Alice Munro. 2nd Accession. ts. 38.1.3. The Alice Munro Papers. U of Calgary Library, Calgary.

Collins, Anne. "The Fantasy of Perfect Mastery." Rev. of *The Moons of Jupiter,* by Alice Munro. *Maclean's* 18 Oct. 1982: 74-75.

Derrida, Jacques. *"Différance." Margins of Philosophy.* Trans. Alan Bass. Chicago: U of Chicago P, 1982. 1-28.

Eagleton, Terry. "Brecht and Rhetoric." *Contemporary Literary Criticism: Literary and Cultural Studies.* 1986. Ed. Robert Con Davis and Ronald Schleifer. New York: Longman, 1994. 468-71.

Freud, Sigmund. "Beyond the Pleasure Principle." 1920. *On Metapsychology* 269-338.

———. "The Ego and the Id." 1923. *On Metapsychology* 350-408.

———. "Fetishism." 1927. *Standard Edition* 21: 152-57.

———. "Findings, Ideas, Problems." 1941. *Standard Edition* 23: 299-300.

———. "The Infantile Genital Organization." 1923. *Standard Edition* 19: 141-45.

———. "Instincts and Their Vicissitudes." 1915. *Standard Edition* 14: 117-40.

———. "Mourning and Melancholia." 1915. *On Metapsychology* 245-68.

———. *On Metapsychology: The Theory of Psychoanalysis.* Trans. and ed. James Strachey. London: Penguin, 1981.

———. "The Psychopathology of Everyday Life." 1901. *Standard Edition* 6: 1-279.

———. *The Standard Edition of the Complete Works of Sigmund Freud.* Trans. and ed. James Strachey. London: Hogarth, 1955.

———. "The Uncanny." 1919. *Standard Edition* 17: 219-56.

Gallop, Jane. *The Daughter's Seduction: Feminism and Psychoanalysis.* Ithaca, NY: Cornell UP, 1982.

———. *Reading Lacan.* Ithaca, NY: Cornell UP, 1985.

Garber, Marjorie. *Vested Interests: Cross-Dressing and Cultural Anxiety.* New York: Routledge, 1992.

Gzowski, Peter. Interview with Alice Munro. *Morningside* CBC Radio 18-22 Oct. 1982.

Heble, Ajay. *The Tumble of Reason: Alice Munro's Discourse of Absence.* Toronto: U of Toronto P, 1994.

Jacobus, Mary. "'The Third Stroke': Reading Woolf with Freud." *Grafts: Feminist Cultural Criticism.* Ed. Susan Sheridan. London: Verso, 1988. 93-110.

Kristeva, Julia. *Polylogue.* Paris: Editions du Seuil, 1977. 173-222.

Moore, Burness E., and Bernard Fine, eds. *Psychoanalytic Terms and Concepts.* New Haven, CT: Yale UP, 1990.

Morrison, Andrew, ed. *Shame: The Underside of Narcissism.* Hillside, NJ: Analytic P, 1988.

Munro, Alice. "Bardon Bus." *The Moons of Jupiter.* Toronto: Penguin, 1982. 110-28.

———. "Bardon Bus. Revised Version." 2nd Accession. ts. 38.8.3.1-2. The Alice Munro Papers. U of Calgary Library, Calgary.

———. "Bardon Bus. Revised Version." 3rd Accession. ts. 4.41-4.42. The Alice Munro Papers. U of Calgary Library, Calgary.

———. "Great Dames." Interview with Barbara Frum. *Maclean's* Apr. 1973: 32-38.

———. *Hateship, Friendship, Courtship, Loveship, Marriage.* Toronto: McClelland and Stewart, 2001.

———. "An Interview with Alice Munro." With Eleanor Wachtel. *Brick* 40 (1991): 48-53.

———. Interview with Peter Gzowski. *Morningside* CBC Radio 18-22 Oct. 1982.

———. Interview with Geoff Hancock. *Canadian Writers at Work.* Toronto: Oxford UP, 1987. 187-224.

———. Interview with Eleanor Wachtel. *Writers and Company.* CBC Radio. 14 Feb. 1999.

———. "A Visit with Alice Munro." Interview with Stephen Scobie. *Monday Magazine* [Victoria, BC] 19-25 Nov. 1982: 12-13.

Ovesey, Lionel. *Homosexuality and Pseudohomosexuality.* New York: Science, 1969.

Raleigh, Walter. "The Author's Epitaph, Made by Himself." *Sixteenth Century English Poetry.* Ed. Norman McClure. New York: Harper, 1954. 321-22.

Rasporich, Beverly J. *Dance of the Sexes: Art and Gender in the Fiction of Alice Munro.* Edmonton: U of Alberta P, 1990.

Redekop, Magdalene. *Mothers and Other Clowns: The Stories of Alice Munro.* London: Routledge, 1992.

Saussure, Ferdinand de. *Course in General Linguistics.* 1972. Ed. Charles Bally and Albert Sechehaye. Trans. Roy Harris. London: Duckworth, 1983. 112-16.

York, Lorraine. "'Gulfs' and 'Connections': The Fiction of Alice Munro." *Essays in Canadian Writing* 35 (1987): 135-46.

Ella Soper-Jones (essay date spring 2003)

SOURCE: Soper-Jones, Ella. "Wilderness Stations: Peregrination and Homesickness in Alice Munro's *Open Secrets*." *Wascana Review of Contemporary Poetry and Short Fiction* 38, no. 1 (spring 2003): 29-50.

[*In the following essay, Soper-Jones centers on the "retrospective narrative form" of* Open Secrets, *specifically examining "how the changing landscapes of [Munro's] fiction reflect the status of her female characters" in three of the collection's stories.*]

The retrospective narrative form is a hallmark of Munro's fiction. A Munrovian narrator typically relates the story of her narrative foil—another woman of another time—retrospectively, interpolating her own temporal and spatial situation in the process. The retrospective narrative is like a palimpsest upon which the narrator's judgements are first inscribed, then qualified, and finally reevaluated; thus, the retrospective form registers the evolution of the narrator's values. Setting is the most common catalyst for memory in Munro's fiction and her landscapes, like the retrospective narrative form itself, are subject to change over time whether as a result of the forces of natural regeneration or those of urban development. Such changes, then, reflect and comment upon changing social and environmental ethics. The relationship between setting and narration is typological; the palimpsestic landscapes of Munro's fiction prefigure the palimpsestic quality of the retrospective narrative form itself. Keeping Munro's use of the retrospective narrative form in mind as we examine three stories in *Open Secrets* (1994) allows us to see how the changing landscapes of her fiction reflect the status of her female characters and enable their evolution.

In *Open Secrets* Munro examines the "wilderness station" as a *topos* of itinerancy for women; the "pseudo-wilderness" (Murray 75) settings on the outskirts of town are represented as "wilderness stations" through which her protagonists pass. The term "a wilderness station"—the title of one of the stories in the collection—is taken from a sermon by Thomas Boston. In his sermon, Boston uses wilderness as a metaphor for the world, and suggests that life is a process of exchanging one station in the secular wilderness for another (Munro 238-9). The attendant quality of life is especially true of the lives of the girls and women in Munro's collection. In **"Spaceships Have Landed," "A Real Life,"** and **"Open Secrets"**—three stories set over the course of more than half a century in the changing "wilderness" landscape around the fictional town of Carstairs—Munro depicts the "wilderness" sojourns of girls and women.[1] The "wildernesses" in which they sojourn are either socially devalued or environmentally degraded and such settings reflect the social devaluation and sexual degradation of their female counterparts. The protagonists' evolve in response to their devaluation through the figurative exchange of one "station" in life for another.

The landscapes on the outskirts of town in Munro's fiction are represented, to borrow a term from Robert Kroetsch, as "dangerous middles" (xi).[2] Their "dangerous middle" status prefigures the status of the women who inhabit them. Like their counterparts, the indigenous flora, Munro's characters thrive in the uncultivated terrain on the margins of town. Through these landscapes, the girls and women in the collection confront—and sometimes subvert—the social prejudices that denote

their status as subjects, and this confrontation is signaled by the motif of mock death and resurrection. Munro represents the "wilderness stations" of the three stories as liminal and the women who inhabit them as transient. Through these representations, she focuses the conflict between a woman's desire to construct a viable home and identity for herself on the one hand, and a societal consensus regarding the untenability of women's independence on the other.[3]

I

In **"Spaceships Have Landed"** the "dangerous middle" territory is the riverbank on the margins of town. The Peregrine River runs around the town of Carstairs and the river is represented as the primary source of environmental transformation in the collection. The river's periodic flooding is unpredictable, affecting the lives of the poorer families who reside along its banks. The river is thus symbolic of the permeability of the borders separating "town" and "country." The permeability of the river and that of the social classes associated with it speaks to the dangers such natural and social forces are seen to pose to the urbane ideals of the town.

At the riverbank, Rhea and Eunie are transformed through their "play" into Toms. Rhea describes this "play" as "the most serious part of their lives" (Munro 274). The personas the girls assume are informed by the characters of Mark Twain's Tom Sawyer and Huck Finn. Like Tom and Huck's, Rhea and Eunie's adventures are embedded in the riverbank landscape, beyond the town and its conventions. In this place of transformation they subvert the gender stereotypes that denote their subject status as girls:

> When they cut from Eunie's yard down to the riverbank, they became different people. Each of them was called Tom. The Two Toms. A Tom was a noun to them, not just a name. It was not male or female. It meant somebody exceptionally brave and clever but not always lucky, and—just barely—indestructible.
>
> (275)

Through their role-playing, Rhea and Eunie assume the power and sexual agency of their personas, Tom and Huck. When they return to Eunie's house for lunch, they swagger, stinking of "the river, of the wild garlic and mint they had squashed underfoot, of the hot rank grass and the foul mud where the drain emptied" (276). Though still ostensibly "wild," the banks of the river are depicted as degraded by urban development, as is suggested by the "foul" smell of the mud where the drain empties. The riverbank landscape thus mirrors Rhea and Eunie's marginality, but it also offers them the prospect of subverting the values that render them powerless subjects of their class and gender.[4]

Eunie and Rhea are depicted as "writhing and sweating down among the juicy weeds" at the riverbank's edge and pressing their bellies "into mud that was slightly soft and warm like just-made fudge" (275). In this passage, the girls' bodies imprint the mud and the girls are, in turn, imprinted—socially conditioned—by their "play." In studies of animal behaviour, imprinting refers to the process of social conditioning that begins with the establishment of trust and recognition (*OED*). In its strictest definition, the term refers to a young bird's attachment to a parent or a parental surrogate; however, the socially mediated nature of the girls' relationship is suggested by their status as friends and peers. Their "play" is a form of social conditioning; through their interactions with one another and with their landscape, Rhea and Eunie explore safely their burgeoning sexual desires and their constructions of female sexuality.[5] In the process, their bodies assume the traditionally male missionary position and the power that that role confers. Their mimetic acts thus subvert traditional representations of female sexual inertia and exploitation. That their assertion of sexual agency is enacted with the riverbank speaks to the ethological nature of their experiences.

As Toms, Rhea and Eunie assume the power their male persons confer and exert this power over other children through exclusion and violence. Such assertions of power reverse the pattern of their own victimization as girls, and later, as women. Though they let others in on their game, Rhea recalls, "they never let the others be Toms" (276). The control they exercise over other children through their acts of violence is symbolic, rather than real: "They laid traps and lay in ambush and tortured the children they had stolen. Sometimes Eunie and Rhea got some real children . . . and persuaded them to let themselves be tied up and thrashed with cattails" (275); however, the girls would let their captives escape when they "could not or would not submit themselves to the plot" (275).

Rhea and Eunie assert their power over the other children much as Wayne later symbolically brutalizes Rhea at the bootlegger's. The precise social geography of Monk's establishment mirrors Rhea's subject status.[6] Monk's is situated—not far from Rhea's family's chicken farm—on the margins of town, one in a row of houses along the river. Like the riverbank where the girls once played, Monk's "bare, narrow wooden house, soiled halfway up the walls by the periodic flooding of the river" (264) is a place of transformation, where the sons of the town's wealthy families take their "working class" (268) girlfriends. Like Rhea and Eunie's captives, Rhea "gives consent" (Munro **"Miles City"** 141); she allows Wayne to force her up against the wall of the house, where he whispers in her ear, *"I'd like to fuck you if you weren't so ugly"* (292 emphasis Munro's). Wayne's misogynistic slur is disturbing in its own right; more disturbing is Rhea's internalization of his judgement. She considers telling her mother about it, but she fears her mother would be incensed by the word "fuck," not by the word "ugly"; "she would miss the point entirely." Rhea's father, on the other hand, "would be ashamed of Rhea. He would be forever ashamed that a man had called her ugly" (293). Though Rhea ultimately confronts Wayne about the incident, rejects his appraisal of her (and eventually marries him), her anxiety about how she measures up to social evaluations of a woman's worth is evident. Rhea's anxiety betrays her ambition to cultivate the qualities desired by men, qualities that will elide the stigma of her "country" upbringing and secure her a husband.

Rhea's memories of Monk's are interpolated with memories of her childhood, in particular with those of her "serious" (274) tomfoolery with Eunie. This interpolation registers both the promises of Rhea's youth and the disillusionments of her maturity. The riverbank landscape figures as a palimpsest upon which is first inscribed Rhea's childhood hubris and later, her growing resignation to the social prejudices she once rejected.[7] Rhea accepts the town's values, as her anxiety about the veracity of Wayne's slur suggests she will, and this acceptance is marked by her movement away from the river and from the poverty of those who live along its banks. Rhea interprets this movement away from the river as "a banishment" (286) but in reality it is she who has banished—devalued—her rural background, and her girlish bravado in favour of the trappings of social "success."

In **"Open Secrets"** Munro uses retrospective third person narration to similar effect; in this case, to lament "the lost hope of girls" (162). The setting of the Falls at the Peregrine River is a catalyst for the narrator's memory. Her depiction of this setting resonates with a sense of the degeneration of social and environmental values. Maureen interpolates memories of her own childhood as a Canadian Girl in Training as she relates the story of a teenage girl's disappearance during a C.G.I.T camp outing. Maureen recalls fondly "the smell of girls" like herself "who had swum for hours in the river and run and hidden in the reeds along the banks and had to burn leeches off their legs" (161). Their boisterousness and daring contrasts with the modesty and reticence she recalls learning to cultivate; "qualities her husband would see and value when hiring and proposing" (162). Maureen envisions Heather Bell's disappearance as she sits on a hassock "at her husband's side" (162). The hassock—a cushion used to rest one's feet upon, and "especially in places of worship to kneel upon (*OED*)—illustrates Maureen's subservience to Lawyer Stephens. Seated upon it, she views a prospect of "old copper-beech trees, seeing behind them not the sunny lawn but the unruly trees along the river" (162). The shaded and "unruly" qualities of the view Maureen commands at her husband's side suggest that her perspective registers both the dangers of youth and those of maturity.

The dangers of youth are personified in **"Open Secrets"** by the "dangerous middle" status of the landscape at the Falls on the Peregrine River. The depiction of the well-traversed bushes near the Falls is inimical in its suggestion of darkness, secrecy and unruliness, and it serves to convey a moral regarding the dangers of female sexual transgression.[8] Female sexuality is represented in the story as both innocent and dangerous, naïve and collusive. Heather's lack of inhibition is seen to set her apart from the other girls: of all of those cooling themselves with the hose on the farmhouse lawn, Frances relates that Mary Kaye had said that Heather was the "worst one; the boldest, getting hold of the hose and shooting water on the rest of them in all the bad places" (150). Frances confides in Maureen, "They will try to make out she was some poor innocent, but the facts are dead different" (151). The "facts" themselves are slim; Heather left the other hikers and doubled back to camp to get her sweater, and she was never seen again. Frances's refusal to believe that the girl drowned suggests her suspicion of Heather's guilt in the matter. The townspeople of Carstairs are the real subjects of the narrative and their suspicion of Heather's culpability speaks to their compulsion to blame the victim.

The other campers search for Heather in the "love nests among the cedars," (157) which are littered with "French safes" (156). The references to the "love nests" and condoms suggest that such "nests" are the sites of consensual teenage lovemaking; the condoms indicate the "safe" nature of sexual experimentation and speak to the choices available to women regarding their reproductive control. This image is destabilized, however, by another, far darker one:

> . . . [of] dense cedars and shiny-leaved oaks and glittery poplars. A ragged sort of wall with hidden doorways, and hidden paths behind it where animals went, and lone humans sometimes, becoming different from what they were outside, charged with different responsibilities, certainties, intentions . . . there was always the other person on a path to intersect yours and his head was full of plans for you even before you met.
>
> (162)

Munro's choice of non-gendered nouns throughout the passage is notable; it suggests that such settings free men and women from social and sexual constraints in similar ways. The single instance of the possessive pronoun "his," however, suggests that though reproductive control and sexual inhibition may be liberating for women, a similar lack of inhibition can transform men into predators, and women into their victims.

The contrast between Heather's harmless play with the hose and the image of the man on the path whom she might have met as she doubled back to camp, "his head . . . full of plans for [her] even before [they] met"

(162), suggests that Heather's attempts to negotiate the terrain of teenage sexuality lead her into a compromising situation of some (unspecified) kind. The degraded status of the "love nests among the cedars," (157) littered with used condoms, beer bottles, and candy wrappers, is thus a metaphor for female sexuality. Teen sex is represented in the story as cheap and recreational, and while teenagers "use" one another, the young girls who allow themselves to be sexually compromised are represented as disposable. Heather's disappearance remains a mystery and her body is never found.

While Heather's disappearance is seen to illustrate the dangers of sexual promiscuity, Maureen's abusive marriage illustrates the dangers of a woman's silence and obedience—"feminine virtues" that were being interrogated in the mid 1960s, when the story is set. Miss Johnstone warns the C.G.I.T. girls about "boys and urges . . . And about liquor and cigarettes and how one thing could lead to another" (183), but nobody warns Maureen about miscarriage and tied tubes, about becoming the victim of her husband's emotional bullying and repeated sexual assaults. Maureen's lament for the "lost hope of girls" and for the carelessness and dauntlessness of youth (162) speaks, in this thwarted coming of age story, not only to Heather's lost hopes, but also to her own.

In **"A Real Life,"** the retrospective narration registers a similar sense of disillusionment. Over time, Millicent is less and less able to justify her invalidation of Dorrie's life as "a real life" (86). Many critics have commented on the discontinuities among the events in Munro's stories, the time of narration, and the geographical situation of the narrator.[9] As Janet Beer argues (in relation to Munro's *Lives of Girls and Women*), the retrospective view can underscore the obsolescence of superceded values (Beer 126). Millicent's retrospection works in this way: her narrative is a palimpsest upon which her judgements are inscribed, qualified, and reevaluated.

"A Real Life" is narrated in the third person by Porter's wife, Millicent. Millicent plays a central role in shaping Dorrie's future, and in (in)validating the choices available to her. Though they are peers, Millicent is a symbolic mother figure due to the (relative) stability of her subject status as a married woman. The events in the story begin in about 1918, when Albert returned to Carstairs from the War, and the story concludes when Millicent is well into what she refers to as her old age. The events in Dorrie's narrative, however, begin with Albert's death and end in the 1950s with her own. Albert's death signals the start of Dorrie's "real life"; it leaves her without an income, and she is compelled to earn money trapping in order to make ends meet. To the townspeople, Porter and Millicent included, Dorrie was "the lady who left skinned rabbits on doorsteps, who went through the fields and the woods with her dog and gun and waded along the flooded creeks in her high rubber boots" (Munro 80)—until that is, Millicent persuades her to accept Wilkie Speirs's proposal of marriage.

In the depiction of their courtship, Wilkie, a foreigner, is characterized by his silence and passivity, while Dorrie is characterized by her virility and control. Their symbolic reversal of gender roles is illustrated by the depiction of Dorrie's capability as a hunter and trapper and by Wilkie's name, a diminutive of Wilkinson, which bears a "feminine" ending. They meet for the first time at Porter and Millicent's, where Milkie sips fizzy lemonade on the veranda with the men. As Millicent explains, "drinking in the barn, abstinence in the house" was "a fairly common pattern at that time . . . Most men would have felt there was something the matter with a woman who didn't lay down such a law" (70). This "pattern" of men's obedience to women's "laws" underscores the reversal of traditional roles in the narrative, as does Muriel's cry: "Oh, my favourite . . . Gin and lemon!" (70), which leaves the men feeling disappointed and slightly emasculated by their drinks. When Dorrie arrives, flushed from her walk across the field, she excuses her tardiness for supper by stating that she had to shoot a feral cat. The warmth of her complexion contrasts with Wilkie's sallowness, and her talkativeness with his reticence.

Millicent suggests that Wilkie "saw Dorrie as a novelty, a Canadian wild woman who went around shooting things" (74). She describes the way he listens, "like an old dog, perhaps a hunting dog" that has gotten "a whiff of something nobody else can understand" as Dorrie talks "about the system of creeks she followed, tramping for miles day after day, after the snow was mostly melted but before the leaves came out, when the muskrats' fur was prime" (76). Dorrie's self-possession intrigues Wilkie. Noting his interest, she describes to him her hunting, trapping, and skinning abilities, wooing him with her assertion that "you needed a knife you could trust" (75). Though Millicent chalks Dorrie's success in captivating Wilkie up to "the way Dorrie used her knife and fork" (59), it is in fact Dorrie's use of her *skinning* knife that endears her to him.[10]

The creeks and fields that Dorrie traverses are "dangerous middles." Like the Peregrine River, such landscapes remind the Carstairs residents of the permeability of the borders between "town" and "country." While Wilkie admires Dorrie's vocation, to others her lifestyle speaks to a dangerous lack of social cultivation. Her gifts of skinned rabbits are spurned, for example, even by those on Relief because, "people thought [eating a rabbit] was as bad as eating a dog or a cat" (75). The townspeople's anxiety about consuming Dorrie's rabbits is xenophobic. Though Dorrie states, "people are prejudiced" (75), her own elision of cultural difference is

problematic: ". . . even that [eating dog or cat], she believed, was not considered out of the way in China" (75), as is her re-inscription of cultural stereotypes in this passage.

Millicent suggests that Dorrie and her dog, Delilah, have come "a little unhinged" (62) in the years succeeding Albert's death:

> Absences of such customary things—and the presence of others, such as Dorrie's traps and guns and the boards for stretching rabbit and muskrat skins—had made the rooms [of Dorrie's house] lose their designations, made the notion of cleaning them seem frivolous. Once, in the summer, Millicent saw a pile of dog dirt at the head of the stairs. She didn't see it while it was fresh, but it was fresh enough to seem an offense.
>
> (61)

Millicent recalls Dorrie once musing, "Albert always said people living alone are to be pitied" and adds, "as if she did not understand that she was now one of them" (63). Like the crazy woman on Albert's delivery route who tries to kill him with an axe, Dorrie is represented as feral in her isolation. Her lifestyle, which is predicated upon her love of the outdoors, her self-possession and her competency, is anomalous with constructions of feminine decorum in the late 1930s and early 1940s, when this portion of the narrative is set, and this lack of decorum speaks to Dorrie's "dangerous middle" status as a spinster.

In her widowhood, Millicent muses about her duplicity in encouraging Dorrie to accept Wilkie's proposal. Though she convinces herself of the benevolence of her intentions, she comes to accept that Dorrie could have lived the life of independence she had dreamed of; indeed, that now, at the time of her narration, such a life seemed not only feasible but also desirable. She recalls having listened in as Dorrie wooed Wilkie with talk of her work:

> [She] knew that Dorrie did these things but she had thought she did them to get a little money. To hear her talk . . . it would seem that she was truly fond of that life. The blackflies out already, the cold water over her boot tops, the drowned rats.
>
> (76)

As her concrete references to the blackflies, the drowned rats, and the "cold water over her boot tops" suggests, Millicent begins to imagine Dorrie's life as a "real" alternative to her own. Her growing acceptance of Dorrie's life is evident in her description of the dog dirt at the top of the stairs; she recalls, "Throughout the summer it changed, from brown to gray. It became stony, dignified, stable" (62). "Strangely" she remembers, she found "less and less need to see it as anything but something that had a right to be there" (62). Millicent's avowal of the dignity of Delilah's shit is tragic-comical in the contrast between its lofty tone and its "low" subject. Millicent's retrospection is as absurd as it is poignant; it destabilizes her sense of decorum and highlights the irrelevance of her judgements even as she is depicted in the act of forming them.

Millicent's retrospective narrative registers a growing sense of disillusionment with the convictions of her past and an incremental sense of personal loss. At the end of the story, she depicts Dorrie's "home" in a state of near ruinous disrepair:

> The house was not sold or rented. It was not torn down, either, and its construction was so sound that it did not readily give way. It was capable of standing for years and years and presenting a plausible appearance. A tree of cracks can branch out among the bricks, but the wall does not fall down. Window sashes settle at an angle, but the window does not fall out. The doors were locked, but it was probable that children got in, to write things on the walls and break up the crockery that Dorrie had left behind.
>
> (91)

The depiction of the house, undefended against the incursions of children and in the process of being reclaimed by the earth, illustrates the passage of time. Dorrie's tenacity is personified by the structural integrity of the building, and the dilapidation of her dreams by its "cracked face and [its] blank, slanted windows" (92). The house reminds Millicent of her intent to "knock [it] down and sell the bricks" (92), but her impulse to vandalize the house is balanced by an impulse to memorialize it.

Millicent's depiction of Dorrie's house, surrounded by walnuts lying uncounted in the grass, takes the form of a lament for Dorrie's exile and eventual death. Millicent recalls that Albert and Dorrie would collect and count the crop of walnuts every autumn, and write the total on the cellar wall. The walnut count, a custom thought to predict the harshness of the impending winter, goes unobserved in the years succeeding Dorrie's emigration. Millicent considers it "a useless chore" (92), but every year, "when the walnuts would by lying in the long grass, she would think of that custom, and how Dorrie must have expected to keep it up until she died" (92). The image of the fallen walnuts is elegiac in its suggestion of death, as is the depiction of the trees "losing again, again, their delicate canopy of leaves" (92). The repetition of "again, again" speaks to the palimpsestic quality of the seasons, whose continuation slowly obliterates the record of Dorrie's existence.

Millicent composes an informal epitaph for Dorrie: "A life of customs, of seasons. The walnuts drop, the muskrats swim in the creek" (92). "Dorrie must have believed that she was meant to live so," Millicent muses,

"in her reasonable eccentricity, her manageable loneliness. Probably she would have got another dog" (92). Millicent's qualification of Dorrie's eccentricity as "reasonable," and of her loneliness as "manageable" (92) speaks to her empathy with Dorrie's subject status as a middle-aged, unmarried woman. Millicent's narrative is thus a palimpsest upon which her changing evaluations of Dorrie's life are inscribed. Her retrospection conveys an incremental sense of disillusionment and loss, and the image of Dorrie's dilapidated "home" contributes to the elegiac tone of the narrative.

II

The "dangerous middle" status of Munro's "wilderness stations" prefigures the status of women in the collection. Through such settings, the protagonists in *Open Secrets* confront the social values that denote their "dangerous" and "middling" subject status. This confrontation is signalled by the motif of mock death and resurrection. Andrew Hiscock posits, "The ludic energy of many of Munro's short stories centres upon the detective obsessions of reader, narrator and character locked in a search for clues in a cryptically expressed reality" (28). Though Hiscock applies his hypothesis to Munro's *Friend of My Youth* (1990), it is equally applicable to **"Spaceships Have Landed," "A Real Life,"** and **"Open Secrets."** The "wilderness stations" in these stories are cryptic; they prefigure the status of women. This status is further underscored by the search for a female corpse, a motif that suggests a pattern of female victimization; however, Munro's characters are not victims of exposure, suicide, or murder. Though Heather's body is never found, the blunt refutations of Eunie's and Dorrie's deaths in **"Spaceships Have Landed"** and **"A Real Life"** are, as Hiscock suggests, ludic in their relief of narrative suspense. Eunie's and Dorrie's mock resurrections speak to their protean adaptability to poor social prospects.[11]

In **"Spaceships Have Landed"**—as in **"Open Secrets"**—the narrative is framed by the (presumed) abduction and (presumed) sexual assault of a young woman. In **"Spaceships Have Landed,"** Eunie disappears one hot summer night only to resurface the next morning with a tale of alien abduction, and later, details of her sexual exploitation. Eunie's mother is the first to discover that her daughter is missing. After searching the house, she summons her husband, who reluctantly helps her search the property. Together, they poke and peer among the currant and lilac bushes and the plum trees, "[t]heir trunks crowded in like watchers, crooked black animals" (Munro 273). They search the "wild growth along the riverbank," but they find "[n]othing there. Nobody" (272). This inimical setting is represented as somehow culpable in Eunie's disappearance. The shadowy garden and the "wild growth along the riverbank" (272) provide both atmospheric effect and ample means of hiding a corpse. At one point, Eunie's father inexplicably "lift[s] a great rhubarb leaf with his boot, [shines] the light under that. His wife ask[s] whether he had gone crazy" (273). The garden is represented as, if not culpable in their daughter's presumed murder, at least collusive in her disappearance. Their search is fruitless: "[n]othing there. *Nobody*" (272 emphasis mine).

Eunie's parents fail to find her body because Eunie isn't dead. Her friend Rhea, recovering from a hangover in her brothers' tree house, spies Eunie following the racetrack along the old fairgrounds the next morning:

> . . . with her white hair sticking up, her hair and pajamas catching the light. Like an angel in feathers. But walking in her usual awkward, assertive way . . . The sight of Eunie seemed both strange and natural to her.
>
> (295)

Rhea's numinous depiction of Eunie suggests not only that she survived her ordeal—whatever it was—but also that she was transformed by it. Eunie returns home to find her worried family and Billy Doud, Rhea's boyfriend and Eunie's future husband, waiting for her. With them is the Chief of Police, who "Of all the people waiting in the kitchen . . . might have been the happiest to see Eunie home safe, and to hear her story. It was right out of his jurisdiction. There was nothing to be followed up, nobody to be charged" (298). The Police Chief's relief mirrors the reader's own; the "resolution" of Eunie's disappearance is ludic in its element of surprise and its sheer incredibility.

In **"A Real Life,"** the reader is enticed to participate with Millicent in the search for Dorrie's corpse. When Dorrie fails to appear for dinner on the Sunday preceding her wedding, Millicent, fearing the worst, looks for her:

> What was in her mind was that Dorrie might have had an accident. Something to do with a gun. Maybe while cleaning her gun. That happened to people. Or she might be lying out in a field somewhere, lying in the woods among the old dead leaves and the new leeks and bloodroot.
>
> (83)

The suggestions of death and gore in the "old dead leaves" and the "bloodroot" embody Millicent's fears of what she might discover. Instead of the suicide victim she expects to find, however, Millicent finds Dorrie in her kitchen, very much alive, fixing herself a mess of fried onion, potato, and bacon. Dorrie's prodigious appetite is comic in its refutation of death; in no way does she suffer from a failure to thrive. Millicent's knees go "watery" (84) at the sight of Dorrie, and her relief signals the ludic redirection of energy in the narrative just as Eunie's reappearance does in **"Spaceships Have Landed."**

In **"Open Secrets"** Heather's disappearance is far less ludic—and far more cryptic—than in either of the other two stories because her body is never found. Despite the efforts of the campers and the police, who look for Heather in the pools and behind the curtain of water at the Falls and in the clusters of cedar bushes, all that remains of her is an elusive photograph:

> Heather Bell will not be found. *No body*, no trace. She has blown away like ashes. Her displayed photograph will fade in public places. Its tight-lipped smile, bitten in at one corner as if suppressing a disrespectful laugh, will seem to be connected with her disappearance rather than her mockery of the school photographer. There will always be a tiny suggestion, in that, of her own free will.
>
> (185 emphasis mine)

In **"Open Secrets"** the narrative suspense is not comically defused, nor are the reader's energies redirected. Narrative closure is deferred, and eventually subverted, and this subversion is destabilizing. The persistence of the reader's desire for closure is mirrored by the character of Mary Johnstone, who is advised to stop her public appeals for exoneration in the matter of Heather's disappearance: "Heather Bell is old news," the editor of the local paper informs her, "the story can't be rehashed forever" (186).

The stories in *Open Secrets* are disjunctive and open-ended, and these qualities are a product of narrative recalcitrance on Munro's part.[12] In each story this recalcitrance takes the form of a refusal to offer proof of female victimization in the form of a corpse. Eunie's and Dorrie's tenacity is illustrative of their ability to adapt to inclement prospects, prospects which are personified by their narrative counterparts, Rhea and Muriel respectively. The motif of mock death (and mock resurrection) signals Eunie's and Dorrie's survival through adaptation and transformation. In each case, the liminal "wilderness" through which the protagonist sojourns enables her to exchange one "station" in life for another.

In **"Spaceships Have Landed"** Eunie is transformed by her "abduction." When she emerges from the riverbank path, she is scratched and smeared with blood, and there are "bits of leaves caught in her hair. One side of her face was dirty, too, from being pressed against the ground" (297). Rhea depicts Eunie's transformation as something that might have been foreseen. Her evolution from a child who "claim[ed] attention from the moment of her birth" (274) to "a character" (278), and finally to "a calm, preposterous creature" (300) is depicted as a natural process, one agented by the landscape at the old fairgrounds.

Like Rhea's, Eunie's subject status is mirrored by the social typography of her family's home, located near the riverbank and the old fairgrounds. Eunie's poverty and her physical eccentricity—her height, her "fuzzy" whitish hair, her "long, heavy jaw," and "the thickness, the phlegmy growl, of her voice" (278)—render her a social pariah. Her status is underscored by her occupation as a seamstress at the glove factory: "[the women who worked there] were supposed to be of a lower class than waitresses, much lower than store clerks . . . They spread disorder as if they had every right" (279). The suggestion of the "disorder" the women spread betrays an upper-class fear of contamination. Significantly, this fear is betrayed by Rhea, herself a poor young woman of the same area as Eunie. Unlike Rhea, who can "trade up" on her looks, Eunie has no such wealth-in-kind with which to barter; her future is bleak and her prospects of reinventing herself slim—until, that is, she requires pity and protection. Her vulnerability, a quality decorous with constructions of femininity in the 1950s, when the first part of the story is set, redeems her. Billy listens, "enchanted" (300), as Eunie relates the story of her abduction:

> Eunie's singular revelations, her flushed and dirty face, her somewhat arrogant tone of voice appeared to give Billy Doud the greatest pleasure . . . It did not occur to her to ask that anybody take charge of her, and try to protect her, give her respect and kindness through whatever lay ahead. But Billy Doud had already made up his mind to do that.
>
> (300-301)

Through her "abduction," Eunie is transformed from a social pariah into the object of Billy's affection; from a person "close to the bottom" to one, like Billy, "right at the top" (279) of Carstairs society.

In **"A Real Life,"** Dorrie's transformation is mediated by the country to which she emigrates. Dorrie moves with Wilkie to Australia, but she does not sacrifice her independence as a result. Unlike Muriel, another of her narrative foils, she does not abdicate her power. Rather, she lives something like the life of independence she enjoyed on her southwestern Ontario property after Albert's death, only this time one modeled by a different geography. Dorrie's adaptation to her new life in a foreign country speaks to her Darwinian ability to accommodate herself to new circumstances. "I have grown as fat as the Queen of Tonga," she writes to Millicent:

> A photograph showed that she was not exaggerating. Her hair was white, her skin brown, as if all her freckles had got loose and run together. She wore a vast garment, colored like tropical flowers. The war had come and put an end to any idea of traveling, and then when it was over, Wilkie was dying. Dorrie stayed on, in Queensland, on a great property where she grew sugarcane and pineapples, cotton, peanuts, tobacco. She rode horses, in spite of her size, and had learned to fly an airplane. She took up some travels of her own in that part of the world. She had shot crocodiles. She died in the fifties, in New Zealand, climbing up to look at a volcano.
>
> (90)

Muriel, on the other hand, is transformed through her marriage of desperation to a "Christian minister" (90) into a shadow of her former self. Whereas Dorrie grows vast and brown and colourful, Muriel grows colourless and wan: "[s]he wore any color at all and had a bad permanent—her hair, going gray, stood up from her forehead in frizzy bunches" (91). Whereas Dorrie is presented in sharp focus and high definition, Muriel has blurred about the edges; she has lost the qualities of liberality and danger that set her apart in her youth.

In **"Open Secrets,"** Heather's transformation is agented by the landscape at the Falls on the Peregrine River. The mystery goes unsolved. Critics have proposed some ingenious solutions, but an alternative one is readily available: Heather has run away.[13] This interpretation is offered as a distinct possibility at various points and it co-exists with other clues that likewise suggest the plausibility of her survival:

> *I dare you to run away.* Was it possible? There are times when girls are inspired, when they want the risks to go on and on. They want to be heroines, regardless. They want to take a joke beyond where anybody has ever taken it before. To be careless, dauntless, to create havoc—that was the lost hope of girls . . . A light-haired young girl had been seen getting into a black car on the Bluewater Highway north of Walley at about one o'clock on Sunday afternoon. She might have been hitchhiking. Or waiting for just one car. That was twenty miles away from the Falls, and it would take about five hours to walk it, across the country. It could be done. Or she could have got a ride in another car.
>
> (162-3)

The suggestion of Heather's "own free will" (185) likewise attests to her agency and viability. These speculations are presented alongside various *refutatio* and contentions, none of them incontrovertible.

A close reading of the animal imagery in **"Open Secrets"** yields a suggestion of Heather's potential transformation.[14] The narrator states that some people working "in a forsaken country churchyard in the swampy northeastern corner of the country" on the day in question reported hearing something, "a cry, a scream, in the middle of the afternoon" (163). But they couldn't agree about the nature of the sound they heard: "Who was that? they remembered saying to one another. Not *what* but *who. Who was that?* But later on they thought that it might have been a fox" (163). A linguistic tension is conveyed by the words "cry" and "scream." Cries and screams are utterances attributed to both humans and animals, whereas "shout," a word that conveys similar properties of surprise, distress, or fear, is an utterance attributed specifically to humans.[15] "Not *what* but *who*" conveys a similar sense of linguistic and biological indeterminacy in this passage.[16]

Heather survives to haunt her narrative, and the name of the Peregrine River alludes to the nature of her transformation. Like the river, Heather is peregrine, a displaced person sojourning in perpetuity. Like Heather, Eunie and Dorrie are also rendered transient. In **"Spaceships Have Landed," "A Real Life,"** and **"Open Secrets,"** the female protagonists are married off, moved off, and "killed" off respectively. In each case, the protagonists evolve in response to the pattern of their victimization; spectral in their transformations, they "survive" to haunt their respective narratives.

III

Through her depiction of the transformative relationship between the women in the collection and the environments within which they sojourn, Munro focuses the conflict between a woman's desire to construct a viable home and identity for herself on the one hand, and a societal consensus regarding the untenability of women's independence on the other. In the prologue to *The Politics of Home: Postcolonial Relocations and Twentieth-Century Fiction*, Rosemary Marangoly George posits: "All fiction is homesickness" (1). She maintains, "The search for the location in which the self is 'at home' is one of the primary projects of twentieth-century fiction in English" (3). Such literature concerns itself, she argues, "with the search for viable homes for viable selves" (5). Though George refers throughout her book to global colonial and postcolonial literatures, the theory she proposes is equally applicable to Canadian literature in general and to the stories in *Open Secrets* in particular.

In **"Spaceships Have Landed," "A Real Life"** and **"Open Secrets,"** the primary action of each narrative occurs in the past. Munro documents changing attitudes towards women's independence by contrasting the perspectives of the narrators with those of their narrative foils. The subject status of the women in the three stories correlates with the status of the men to whom they are related; however, the narrators come to share with their narrative foils a sense of their subaltern status as women. The affliction that allows the narrators to identify with their narrative counterparts is homesickness.

Homesickness informs the depiction of Eunie's dysfunctional relationship with her parents in **"Spaceships Have Landed."** Eunie's parents are *laissez-faire* to the point of negligence. Their attitude toward her is one of dangerous liberality: "Eunie never seemed subject to her parents, or even connected to them, in the way of other children. Rhea was struck by the way she ruled her own life, the careless power she had in the house" (Munro 277). Eunie's independence is represented as both an asset and a liability; it is the cause of her eccentricity, but her self-determination also enables her to adapt to changing circumstances. In its sheer implausibility, her abduction story suggests that she—like Dorrie—has come "a little unhinged" (62). The possibility of mental impairment renders her vulnerable, and her

vulnerability enchants Billy. His sudden attraction to Eunie speaks to conventional depictions of female victimization; however, the strength of Eunie's character and that of Billy's devotion to her characterize their relationship as entirely unconventional, even unique in its poignancy. Rhea refers to the Douds's as "a special friendship" (304). When Billy proposes, Eunie warns: "I wouldn't want for there to be anything going on, or anything." Billy responds: "Oh, my dear! . . . Oh, my dear, dear Eunie!" (304).

Unlike Eunie, Rhea finds that she cannot adapt to change. Eunie's view is prospective; Rhea's is retrospective. When Rhea and Wayne return to Carstairs toward the end of the narrative, Billy and Eunie accompany them to the site of the old fairgrounds. Rhea's depiction of the site is elegiac, and it signals the end of what she perceives to have been a golden era:

> The river houses all gone. The Morgans' house, the Monks' house—everything gone of that first mistaken settlement. The land is now a floodplain, under the control of the Peregrine River Authority. Nothing can be built there anymore. A spacious parkland, a shorn and civilized riverbank—nothing left but a few of the same old trees standing around, their leaves still green but weighted down by a diffuse golden moisture that is in the air, on this September afternoon not many years before the end of the century.
>
> (303)

Rhea represents the floodplain as a palimpsest upon which nothing will ever be written again. The millenarian quality of her retrospection lends the description of the fairgrounds its air of lament. Unlike Eunie, who has evolved, Rhea's refrain, "I can't get used to it" (302) firmly identifies her with the obsolescence of the turning century. Whereas Eunie has found a relationship that values her "reasonable eccentricity" (92), Rhea has settled for a life riddled with turmoil and uncertainty. Unlike Eunie's, Rhea's life is not emotionally viable, as the infidelities of her marriage suggest: "And now abruptly, surprisingly, all this turbulence and fruitfulness and uncertain but lively expectation has receded and she knows that they are beginning to be old" (302).

In **"A Real Life,"** Millicent's retrospection reveals a similarly incremental sense of loss. As she relates Dorrie's narrative, Millicent begins to understand the enormity of Dorrie's sacrifices, and the nature of her own. Millicent recalls that Dorrie told Wilkie about her dreams of moving to the Arctic. She notes the way "Her voice thickened for the first time, with embarrassment—or excitement. 'I thought I could live in a cabin and trap all winter. But I had my brother, I couldn't leave my brother'" (77). Millicent recalls how, during their argument before the wedding, she had responded to Dorrie's statement, "I can't leave" as she would have "a child's announcement that she could not go to school" (85). Millicent invalidates Dorrie's argument as an exasperated parent might a child's fears. Though she convinces Dorrie of the rationality and inevitability of marriage, she lives to regret her actions. She recalls how Dorrie had stood by the window:

> . . . mulish, obedient, childish, female—a most mysterious and maddening person whom Millicent seemed now to have conquered, to be sending away. At greater cost to herself, Millicent was thinking—greater cost than she had understood.
>
> (88)

The progression from "mulish" to "female" suggests Millicent's growing identification with Dorrie's despair. Like Rhea, Millicent "suffers a banishment" (286), and like Rhea's, Millicent's is a product of her own orchestration. Millicent's regret speaks to her acknowledgment that she too has suffered for her sacrifices.

Millicent suggests that sacrifice, displacement, and homesickness are common features of a woman's life. She recalls having thought, "And what did Dorrie mean by 'here'? If she meant that she would be homesick, let her be! Homesickness was never anything you couldn't get over" (87). Millicent's diminishment of the pain of homesickness suggests that she has experienced such pain herself. She recalls that when Dorrie removed Albert's coat after her walk to the church on her wedding day, "she was gleaming, miraculous, like the Pillar of Salt in the Bible" (89). Like Lot's wife, Dorrie has already looked back, as the allusion to her transfiguration suggests. The fact that Millicent finds Dorrie the more beautiful for her sacrifices speaks to her sense that homesickness is a right of passage for women.

As the name of the Peregrine River—the site of girls' incursions for so many years—suggests, homesickness is represented as a ubiquitous condition in women. The theme recurs in **"Open Secrets"** with the portrait of Heather's absent mother. Like the vandalized houses such as Dorrie's and Ladner's that appear throughout the collection, Heather's is a "broken" home in a figurative sense. Heather is raised by her mother, a single parent, who is represented as careless and preoccupied with herself. Her mother's namelessness underscores her absence from the narrative. Like many other mothers in the collection, Heather's mother fails, in her absence, to be a role model for her daughter. Frances indicts Ms. Bell's absence on the weekend of her daughter's disappearance: ". . . her mother away on the weekend herself—yes, she was taking the opportunity. Getting off on an expedition of her own" (152).

Working mothers like Heather's are lumped together in the narrative with other morally corrupting influences such as "television" and "laxity in the home" (156). The story, set in 1965, thus depicts a fear of the changes being wrought by the Women's Independence Movement. Significantly, women like Frances and Miss Johnstone are the ones to vocalize such fears. Frances tells Maureen that when the constable went to inform Ms. Bell of her daughter's disappearance, he was shocked to find her "just back from her own weekend, wearing a backless sundress and high heels. 'Well, you better find her,' she said. 'That's your job'" (158). Frances sees Ms. Bell's sexual agency and her blunt abdication of responsibility for her daughter as endemic of a broader pattern of social degeneration.

Ms. Bell is not a positive role model for women; neither is Maureen. Maureen's narrative is an "open secret" warning women about the disappointments and dangers of marriage. Maureen is barren; her infertility renders her a failure in society's eyes, and a whore in her husband's. A subaltern in her marriage, Maureen's homesickness is illustrated by her perpetual sense of displacement: "This was Maureen's home . . . She had been living in the house for eight years, but she still felt as if she got around it on fairly narrow tracks, from one spot where she felt at home to another" (153). Like Heather, Maureen is peregrine, wandering through life, through "new places and houses . . . hundreds and thousands of miles away" (186) in search of a viable home and identity.

"Home is a place to escape to and a place to escape from" George asserts. She maintains that the importance of "home" "lies in the fact that it is not equally available to all" (9). George's assertion has profound implications in the context of Munro's fiction. Munro illustrates, through the contrast between the subject positions of narrator and narrative foil, the inequality George cites. Robert McGill argues, "while houses are at the centre of Munro's art, they are often places of marginalization in her stories, especially with regard to the women who inhabit them" ("Where" 104). McGill's observation certainly applies to the situation of characters like Maureen who speaks ironically of her subaltern status from within the "security" of her "own" "home."

"Home," George concludes, "is not a neutral place. It is community" (9). The sojourning women in Munro's collection explore, then, the feasibility of dwelling within society, rather than beyond its constraints. The Munrovian character's search for a "viable home" involves not only her search for a physical structure within which she might dwell peaceably and securely, but also her search for an inclusive community, one sympathetic to the issue of women's self-determination.

Munro explores a productive tension between itinerancy and stasis in *Open Secrets*. The representation of the "wilderness stations" through which her protagonists sojourn and the "homes" within which their narrative counterparts dwell is oppositional, but the dichotomy is a false one. In each of the stories we have examined, the narrator confronts her own subaltern status as she constructs another woman's narrative. The retrospective narrative form registers a sense of identification over time and across social classes; homesickness cuts across both. In each case, Munro's characters desire to construct viable homes and identities for themselves. In each case, the narrators and protagonists confront a societal consensus regarding the untenability of women's independence: the protagonists through their figurative exchange of one "station" in life for another—signalled by the motif of mock death and resurrection—and the narrators through the reevaluation of their past convictions. Moreover, these processes of transformation and identification are mirrored, mediated, and enabled by the "wildernesses" within which the narratives are set.

Rhododendron, spirea, lilac, oak, and maple: in Munro's fiction these trees and flowering shrubs are emblematic of the genteel towns in which they flourish, whereas wild grape, sword grass, pine, and chokecherries almost always signify the "dangerous middle" status of the outskirts of town. The environmentally degraded "wildernesses" on the margins of town prefigure the "dangerous" status and "middling" worth of girls and women. Like the "broken," abandoned, and vandalized homes that recur throughout the collection, the environmentally degraded "wildernesses" in the stories we have examined speak to the degeneration of social and environmental ethics. Through the elegiac depiction of such landscapes, Munro's narrators lament the "lost hope of girls" (Munro 162) and women like themselves. In **"Spaceships Have Landed," "A Real Life,"** and **"Open Secrets,"** then, Munro examines the changes wrought not only by the forces of urban development and moral decay, but also, and more optimistically, those wrought by the Women's Independence Movement.

Notes

1. I use the term "wilderness" in quotations to signal the contested and changing status of these landscapes as "wild." Heather Murray uses the term "pseudo-wilderness" to refer to similar spaces (now commonly known as "green belts") that signal the progression from urban space to wilderness; see "Women in the Wilderness," *A Mazing Space: Writing Canadian Women Writing,* Ed. Shirley Neuman and Smaro Kamboureli (Edmonton: Longspoon/NeWest, 1986): 75.

2. Heather Murray uses Kroetsch's term as well; she posits, ". . . women's writing is characteristic of English-Canadian fiction in which, as Robert Kroetsch has observed, stories of unalloyed wilderness experience are surprisingly rare; it is, instead, a 'literature of dangerous middles'" (75).

3. See Rosemary Marangoly George, *The Politics of Home: Postcolonial Relocations and Twentieth-Century Fiction* (Cambridge: Cambridge UP, 1996) for a discussion of the way in which contemporary literatures in English concern themselves with "the search for viable homes for viable selves" (5).

4. Dermot McCarthy's article about another story of Munro's considers the way "wild zones" in "Meneseteung" demarcate "woman's potential freedom, as well as her actual exclusion, from patriarchal order" to similar effect (5); see "The Woman Out Back: Alice Munro's 'Meneseteung,'" *Studies in Canadian Literature/Études en litérature canadienne* 19.1 (1994): 1-19.

5. For further consideration of role-playing and the construction of sexual identity, see Judith Butler, *Gender Trouble: Feminism and the Subversion of Identity* (New York: Routledge, 1990).

6. Gianfranca Balestra makes a similar point about the social typography of Almeda's home in Munro's "Meneseteung"; see "Alice Munro as Historian and Geographer: A Reading of *Meneseteung,*" *Intersections: la narrativa canadese tra storia e geographia,* Ed. Liana Nissim and Carlo Pagetti (Bologna: Cisalpino, 1999): 129.

7. Robert McGill makes a similar point about the palimpsestic nature of the countryside in "Spaceships Have Landed"; he suggests that the presence of "derelict or dismantled" structures in Munro's fiction indicate "the immanence of space's past in the present." See "Somewhere I've Been Meaning to Tell You: Alice Munro's Fiction of Distance," *Journal of Commonwealth Literature* 37.1 (2002): 12.

8. For further consideration of the personification of "nature" as malevolent in Canadian literature, see Margaret Atwood, *Survival: a Thematic Guide to Canadian Literature* (Toronto: Anansi, 1972) and Gaile McGregor, *The Wacousta Syndrome: Explorations in the Canadian Landscape* (Toronto: UTP, 1985).

9. See, for example, Marlene Goldman, "Penning in the Bodies: The Construction of Gendered Subjects in Alice Munro's Boys and Girls," *SCL/ÉLC* 15.1 (1990): 73; Balestra (122); and Janet Beer, "Short Fiction with Attitude: The Lives of Boys and Men in the *Lives of Girls and Women,*" *Yearbook of English Studies* 31 (2002): 126, 131.

10. Carol Beran's article considers similar (traditionally male) emblems of power in Munro's *Who Do You Think You Are?* and "Lichen"; see "Images of Women's Power in Contemporary Canadian Fiction by Women," *SCL/ÉLC* 15.2 (1990): 55-76.

11. For further consideration of mock deaths and "farcical resurrections" (224) in Munro's fiction, see Maggie Redekop, *Mothers and Other Clowns: The Stories of Alice Munro* (London: Routledge, 1992).

12. Austin M. Wright posits various forms of narrative recalcitrance that he claims are unique to short fiction, many of which seem to apply to Munro's writing, especially "final recalcitrance" and "modal discontinuity." See "Recalcitrance in the Short Story," *Short Story Theory at a Crossroads,* ed. Susan Lohafer and Jo Ellyn Clarey (Baton Rouge: Louisiana State UP, 1989): 115-29.

13. See, for example, Ildiko de Papp Carrington, "Talking Dirty: Alice Munro's 'Open Secrets' and John Steinbeck's *Of Mice and Men,*" *Studies in Short Fiction* 31.4 (Fall, 1994): 595-606.

14. Rosalie Mary Weaver asserts that Munro's "Open Secrets" "talks back" to Margaret Atwood's "Death by Landscape," which relates a similar story of a young girl's disappearance during a camp outing. Weaver suggests that Atwood's "Death by Landscape" alludes to Lucy's transformation into a Raven or a tree much as I argue that Heather has been transformed into a fox; see Rosalie Mary Weaver, "Innovation within the Modern Short Story through the Interaction of Gender, Nationality, and Genre: Margaret Atwood's *Wilderness Tips* and Alice Munro's *Open Secrets,*" diss., U of Manitoba, 1997.

15. Shouts used to be attributed to animals, but this usage is now obsolete (*OED*). Incidentally, the "shout/scream/cry/bark" Lois hears in Atwood's "Death by Landscape" (123) shares a linguistic tension with Munro's depiction of the "cry" or "scream" the witnesses report hearing in "Open Secrets."

16. For further discussion of indeterminacy in Munro's fiction, see Coral Ann Howells, "Alice Munro's Art of Indeterminacy: *The Progress of Love,*" *Modes of Narrative: Approaches to American, Canadian and British Fiction,* ed. Reingard M. Nischik and Barbara Korte (Wurzburg: Kongishausen & Neumann, 1990): 141-52.

Works Cited

Atwood, Margaret. *Survival: A Thematic Guide to Canadian Literature.* Toronto: Anansi, 1972.

———. "Wilderness Tips." *Wilderness Tips.* Toronto: M & S, 1991.

Balestra, Gianfranca. "Alice Munro as Historian and Geographer: A Reading of Meneseteung." *Intersections: la narrativa canadese tra storia e geografia.* Ed. Liana Nissim and Carlo Pagetti. Bologna: Cisalpino, 1999. 119-36.

Beer, Janet. "Short Fiction with Attitude: The Lives of Boys and Men in the *Lives of Girls and Women.*" *Yearbook of English Studies* 31 (2001):125-32.

Beran, Carol L. "Images of Women's Power in Contemporary Canadian Fiction by Women." *Studies in Canadian Literature/Études en littérature canadienne* 15.2 (1990): 55-76.

Butler, Judith. *Gender Trouble: Feminism and the Subversion of Identity.* New York: Routledge, 1990.

Carrington, Ildiko de Papp. "Talking Dirty: Alice Munro's 'Open Secrets' and John Steinbeck's *Of Mice and Men.*" *Studies in Short Fiction* 31.4 (Fall 1994): 595-606.

George, Rosemary Marangoly. *The Politics of Home: Postcolonial Relocations and Twentieth-Century Fiction.* Cambridge: Cambridge UP, 1996.

Goldman, Marlene. "Penning in the Bodies: The Construction of Gendered Subjects in Alice Munro's 'Boys and Girls.'" *SCL/ÉLC* 15.1 (1990): 62-75.

Hiscock, Andrew. "Longing for a Human Climate." *Journal of Commonwealth Literature* 32.2 (1997): 17-34.

Howells, Coral Ann. "Alice Munro's Art of Indeterminacy: The Progress of Love." *Modes of Narrative: Approaches to American, Canadian and British Fiction.* Ed. Reingard M. Nischik and Barbara Korte. Wurzburg: Kongishausen & Neumann, 1990. 141-52.

Kroetsch, Robert. "Beyond Nationalism: a Prologue." *Beyond Nationalism: The Canadian Literary Scene in Global Perspective.* Special edition of *Mosaic* 14.2 (Spring 1981): v-xi.

McCarthy, Dermot. "The Woman Out Back: Alice Munro's 'Meneseteung.'" *SCL/ÉLC* 19.1 (1994): 1-19.

McGill, Robert. "Somewhere I've Been Meaning to Tell You: Alice Munro's Fiction of Distance." *Journal of Commonwealth Literature* 37.1 (2002): 9-29.

———. "Where Do You Think You Are? Alice Munro's Open Houses." *Mosaic* 35.4 (2002): 103-19.

McGregor, Gaile. *The Wacousta Syndrome: Explorations in the Canadian Langscape.* Toronto: U of Toronto P, 1985.

Munro, Alice. *Friend of My Youth.* 1990. Toronto: Penguin, 1991.

———. *Lives of Girls and Women.* 1971. Toronto: Penguin, 1997.

———. "Miles City, Montana." *The Progress of Love.* 1986. Markham: Penguin, 1987.

———. *Open Secrets.* 1994. Toronto: Penguin Books, 1995.

Murray, Heather. "Women in the Wilderness." *A Mazing Space: Writing Canadian Women Writing.* Ed. Shirley Neuman and Smaro Kamboureli. Edmonton: Longspoon/NeWest, 1986. 74-83.

Redekop, Magdalene. *Mothers and Other Clowns: The Stories of Alice Munro.* London: Routledge, 1992.

Weaver, Rosalie Mary. "Innovation Within the Modern Short Story Through the Interaction of Gender, Nationality, and Genre: Margaret Atwood's *Wilderness Tips* and Alice Munro's *Open Secrets.*" Diss. U of Manitoba, 1997.

Wright, Austin M. "Recalcitrance in the Short Story." *Short Story Theory at a Crossroads.* Ed. Susan Lohafer and Jo Ellyn Clarey. Baton Rouge, LA: Louisiana State UP, 1989. 115-29.

Mary Condé (essay date autumn 2003)

SOURCE: Condé, Mary. "Fathers in Alice Munro's 'Fathers.'" *Journal of the Short Story in English,* no. 41 (autumn 2003): 93-101.

[*In the following essay, Condé argues that Munro's choice of setting and narrative technique illuminates the unhealthy family dynamics in "Fathers."*]

'Fathers' is an as yet uncollected short story by Alice Munro published in *The New Yorker,* in August 2002. Set in the nineteen-forties, it uses the background of the second world war both implicitly and explicitly to plot the growth of the narrator.

It opens abruptly with an italicised paragraph:

> *On Friday morning last, Harvey Ryan Newcombe, a well-known farmer of Shelby Township, lost his life due to electrocution. The funeral was held Monday afternoon from Reavie Brothers Funeral Home and interment was in Bethel Cemetery. Come unto me, all ye that labor and are heavy-laden, and I will give you rest* (64).

This paragraph, presumably either from a local newspaper or a parish magazine (given the closing text), gives no indication of date, although we know the death was very recent. This, with the awkwardness of 'lost his life due to electrocution', and the specifying of the funeral home, even though as the funeral is already over it has no practical purpose, suggests the local and the obscure.

The absence of any comment on Newcombe except that he was 'a well-known farmer of Shelby Township' indicates both that he had no social existence outside his occupation and that there is absolutely nothing creditable that can be recorded about him; the latter is confirmed by the text from St. Matthew, 11.28, since

Christ's words refer to those who follow his teaching, not those who die. Dying, perhaps, is the best thing Newcombe ever did.

The opening of the second paragraph, 'Dahlia Newcombe could not possibly have had anything to do with her father's accident' (64), not only identifies Newcombe as the first of the fathers of the story, but is startling in its matter-of-fact allusion to the possibility of patricide, only explained later in the story, as it is explained to the narrator herself, by Dahlia's ambitions to kill her brutal father.

The narrative, except for its conclusion, runs backward from the beginning, and a consciousness of time is crucial to it, even to these ambitions. Watching her father come out of a stable carrying a pitchfork (suitable for his devilish nature), Dahlia remarks that if she had a gun she could kill him now: "'. . . I should do it while I'm still young enough. Then I don't get hung'" (66). The narrator, mulling over this, comes to an opposite conclusion:

> I had a strange idea that she was too young to do it—as if killing somebody were like driving a car or voting or getting married.
>
> (67)

On the other hand, she tersely attributes the improvement of her relationship with her own father, among other things, to the fact that 'I grew older' (71).

The ending of the story is a reflection on the 'horrid invasions' of fathers and of the ultimate effect on her:

> And, as the saying goes, about this matter of what molds or warps us, if it's not one thing it will be another. At least that was a saying of my elders in those days. Mysterious, uncomforting, unaccusing.
>
> (71)

The term 'invasions', as a military image, recalls the pervasive background of the second world war, first mentioned in the third paragraph of the story. The narrator speculates that the sound of farmers calling to their plough-horses, heard all over the countryside the spring that Newcombe died, but soon to disappear altogether, was a sound caused by the war, since farmers could not find tractors to buy or else could not find the fuel to run them. This sound, about to cease both because of cyclical and linear time, is presented neutrally and without a deciphering nostalgia. It was as enigmatic, we are told, as the conversations of seagulls or the arguments of crows, except that the tone of voice 'probably' told you when the farmers were swearing. The war, then, as a transient entity, is neither shown as having liberated a pleasant bucolic tradition nor as having imparted a specific meaning to the lives of Shelby Township. Nevertheless, it is explicitly part of the narrator's thinking when she contemplates betrayal—the true subject of the story. She reflects that Dahlia would be 'crazy' to tell her about her plans to kill her father if she were really serious about them, since, she reasons,

> I might betray her. I would not intend to, but somebody might get it out of me. Because of the war that was just ending that spring, I often thought about what it would be like to be tortured. How much would I be able to stand? At the dentist's, when he hit a nerve, I had asked myself, If a pain like that went on and on unless I betrayed where my father was hiding with the Resistance, what would I do?

(66)

The war, with its history of persecutions and ostracisms, is also implicit in the narrator's account of her relationship with Frances Wainwright, some four or five years before she met Dahlia Newcombe. With both of these girls she walks to and from school, but whereas walking with the sturdy, handsome Dahlia, once she has become the best player on the school basketball team, gives the narrator 'a feeling of distinction' (p. 65), she had previously disowned the small, thin, asthmatic Frances as soon as they got to school. She guiltily hides from Frances with her friend Wanda Louise when Frances comes looking for them so that they can eat their lunch together, and, shamefully, joins in the jeering at Frances, who is marked as an outsider because she comes from Chicago. In retrospect, the narrator is uncertain about exactly how shameful her behaviour has been, confessing that,

> I would like to think that it was Wanda Louise who pointed her out to our classmates, when we stood in line ready to march into the schoolroom, as the girl we were always trying to avoid. But I could have been the one that did that, and certainly I went along with the joke, and was glad to be on the side of those doing the giggling and excluding.

(68)

While she is 'ready to march' with her comrades, she does not have the courage to defend what might be worth marching for.

Frances does, in fact, begin to function as a kind of parody of a civilization worth marching for when the narrator realizes that Frances, coming from the much-mocked Chicago, where she could see movies every afternoon, is a rich source of information about movie stars—the narrator's own passion. They discuss Ziegfeld girls, Frances (appropriately, given her first name) preferring Judy Garland and the narrator Hedy Lamarr. The narrator chooses Hedy Lamarr for her beauty and Frances Judy Garland because she could sing, a choice clearly connected with her parents, who both used to sing in the Light Opera Society, and to whom she is very attached. When the narrator visits their house for a

farewell supper just before Christmas, Frances is dressed exactly like her mother, in an outfit which could have come out of a movie magazine, and has her hair done exactly the same way as her mother—a symptom of what the narrator finds a disquieting intimacy in the family.

In many ways the farewell supper is a magical one. The Christmas tree, 'smothered in tinsel, gold and silver beads, and beautiful intricate ornaments' (p. 69), is a 'fairy-tale tree' (p. 70), and the narrator is served rich, delicious, unfamiliar food, which casts a kind of spell on her:

> . . . I seemed to have entered a dream, in which everything I saw was both potent and benign.

(70)

But the fairy-tale element is introduced only to be negated. Years later, although previously in the story, Dahlia's 'fanciful' and 'lovely' name had held out the promise of the beautiful daughter of an ogre in a fairy tale, but she had disappointed expectations by not having 'rippling yellow hair and a sweetly pining expression' (64), in the narrator's view incorrectly, since this meant she was 'not my idea of an ogre's daughter'. Frances Wainwright's potentially magical party is contaminated by another failure to live up to expectations, by what the narrator perceives as the 'charade' of Frances' father acting as waiter. This father behaves incorrectly on all sorts of levels. First of all, he should have stayed in the kitchen and left the girls to enjoy the delicious food in peace. Secondly, he does not sound or smell as a father should: his eager breathing sounds like a dog's and his smell of talcum and lotion makes the narrator think of a baby's fresh diapers. Thirdly, to her alarm, he pretends that the lemonade he is serving is champagne: 'We never had such drinks in our house, and neither did anybody I knew' (69). Fourthly, he pretends to think that they are beautiful young ladies. All these elements offend the narrator's sense of decorum, and emphasize the Wainwrights' status as outsiders.

But far worse than all this is the behaviour of Frances' mother and father after a near-disaster with the fire: they kiss each other openly, and fondle each other's behinds. The 'creepy menace' of this is compounded by their assumption that the narrator has really been a friend to Frances, as she knew she had been asked to be. The consciousness of her own treachery, and her recognition that she is at their house under false pretences, spoils the occasion in any case, but she feels that they are to blame, 'corralling me into playing the role of little friend', and humiliating her, 'almost as if somebody had taken a peep into my pants' (70).

This is why the chronology of the story is disrupted, so that Frances' father and the narrator's father can be adjacent in her telling, with the reiterated story of Dahlia's father forming a kind of bridge. Although every aspect of the narrator's father's behaviour is completely different from that of Frances' father, the common denominator is humiliation:

> Shame. The shame of being beaten, and the shame of cringing from the beating. Perpetual shame. Exposure. And something connects this, as I feel it now, with the shame, the queasiness that crept up on me when I heard the padding of Mr. Wainwright's slippered feet and his breathing. There were demands that fathers made that seemed indecent, there were horrid invasions, both sneaky and straightforward.
>
> (71)

The reiterated story of Dahlia's father forms a kind of bridge in that it is discussed by the narrator's family, to her retrospective perplexity, as if no kind of animus had ever existed between herself and her father, as if he had never beaten her, as Dahlia had complained that her father did. The narrator's family is secure in their perception of themselves as 'decent people' (71), in no way to be compared with the brutality and vulgarity of the Newcombes, just as they take a superior attitude to the Wainwrights' inappropriate ambition to set up a local wallpapering business. (Both families' names are of course very apt.)

The narrator, who retails to her family the melodramatic story of Dahlia's spying on her father (an activity in which she herself had joined), and Dahlia's threats to murder her father, does not ever describe to them the farewell party at the Wainwrights', and the significance of this is that she subsequently learned how to cope with her family precisely by being a narrator.[1] It becomes the way in which she, so to speak, earns her keep, at the same time safeguarding herself by her particular narrative manner:

> I had mastered a deadpan, almost demure style that could make people laugh even when they thought they shouldn't and which made it hard to tell whether I was innocent or malicious.
>
> (71)

She cannot transmit the story of the Wainwrights because she has not yet achieved this mastery, and because it makes her feel 'off balance'. The story of Dahlia and her father, although disturbing, as a story of espionage and projected murder, is not only eminently suitable for wartime, but perfectly fits the stereotypes they have become in the popular imagination. As the narrator puts it,

> The undeviating style of Bunt Newcombe's behavior had made him—and his wife—into such caricatures that a story ought to confirm, to everybody's satisfaction, just how thoroughly and faithfully they played their roles.
>
> (71)

The story of a real-life ogre has its own rigid protocol, just as a fairy tale has. There now (as Munro's story nears its end) appears to be a particularly appropriate sense of closure in the opening paragraph which begins Munro's story and ends Bunt Newcombe's. He has been electrocuted, like a criminal brought to justice, and the text *Come unto me, all ye that labor and are heavy-laden, and I will give you rest* can now be seen to refer not to Bunt, but to his family, who can now relax and rejoice in his permanent absence. But, although we may in retrospect read the opening paragraph slightly differently, we do not at any point have to revise our idea of Bunt Newcombe, any more than the narrator's local community has to. (Our, and their, idea of him is made the more inflexible in that we, and they, are never given any insight into the causes of his characteristic domineering irascibility.) Our attention is specifically drawn to the fact that he and his mistreated wife might 'nowadays' be regarded differently:

> Nowadays, Mrs. Newcombe might be seen as a serious case, terminally depressed, and her husband, with his brutish ways, might be looked on with concern and compassion as someone who needed help. In those days, they were just taken as they were and allowed to live out their lives without a thought of intervention—regarded, in fact, as a source of interest and entertainment.
>
> (64)

But, as readers who do not intervene and who are being interested and entertained, we are in the nineteen-forties and not 'nowadays'. Bunt, then, although disturbing in his power and his cruelty, is the least unsettling of the three fathers, and the most straightforward in terms of the explanation of the second world war. The older generation oppresses because it can, and will continue to do so until brought to some kind of justice. No precise date can be assigned to this justice, and it may be perceived as arbitrary and accidental.

The two other fathers are unsettling because they both provoke a feeling of guilt and complicity in the younger generation, as represented by the narrator. She remarks quite casually of Frances' movie magazines that

> if she had taken it into her head to remove them I would have been more grief-stricken than when my father drowned the kittens I had found in the barn.
>
> (69)

Of course, this reference to her father's (probably pragmatic) unkindness is far from casual, as establishing a benchmark for the usual behaviour of fathers as far as she is concerned, in the context of a world of glamorous, powerful heroines to which he stands utterly opposed; almost immediately after the reference to the kittens we are told of a lamp with a lampshade like a lady's skirt, which Frances explains represents Scarlett

O'Hara, a present from her father and herself to her mother. The juxtaposition of something given with something taken away balances the juxtaposition of Frances' father, who is ignorant of the narrator's true nature, with her own father, who understands it all too well. As she says of his beatings of her,

> . . . I saw what he hated in me. A shaky arrogance in my nature, something brazen yet cowardly, was what awoke in him this fury.
>
> (71)

The guilt and shame which this ignorance and this understanding *both* arouse in the narrator suggest a darkness of the human heart already demonstrated and a darkness yet to be exposed, which not only account for the second world war, but identify war as a constantly recurring phenomenon.

The three daughters represent three attitudes to fathers: Frances seems uncomplicatedly to love and admire her father, the narrator is ambivalent about hers, and Dahlia explicitly wants to murder Bunt Newcombe. Indeed, it is the very explicitness of Dahlia's desire that makes the narrator doubt it—significantly, since she immediately goes on to speculate about whether she might betray her own father under torture, which is obviously, and yet not explicitly, a wish-fulfilment fantasy.

As a meditation set against the background of war, **'Fathers'** might at first sight seem oddly to choose daughters rather than sons to set against the fathers who have set the war in progress—even though none is shown as actually fighting in it.[2] But Munro is here particularly interested in the sexual implications of father-daughter relationships. The narrator wonders of Raymond, Dahlia's younger brother, who seems not to be at risk from his father: 'Perhaps a son was abhorred less than daughters?' (66) There is clearly a sexual tension between the narrator and her father, and, as already mentioned, Frances' father's 'slopping-over of attention' makes her feel 'almost as if somebody had taken a peep into my pants'. (This aspect of Munro's story is illustrated in *The New Yorker* by an accompanying photograph of two little girls laughing together, in which one of the little girls is quite unconsciously displaying her knickers.)

The incestuous elements in the story represent the ultimate intrusion of an older generation, the **'Fathers'**, on the younger. The intrusion on and betrayal of a younger generation on a global scale is also demonstrated by the backdrop of the war, 'just ending that spring', to the local and obscure action of the narrative. We always feel the presence of this larger story looming behind the smaller one.

We are also constantly made aware of the significance of audience, from the opening news paragraph about the first father, which suggests a certain complicity with its readership, to the shameless behaviour of the second father in front of his daughter and her guest, to the management of the third father through storytelling. The narrator recognizes that Dahlia needed an audience for her feelings about her father—'she had just wanted someone to see her hating' (67)—and she, in telling the story **'Fathers'**, feels compelled to consider her father himself as her audience, and concede that 'If he were alive now, I am sure my father would say that I exaggerate' (71). She sees that she cannot with a clear conscience blame him (and fathers in general) as much as she would like to do, so that this somewhat enigmatic story is itself described in its closing sentence: 'Mysterious, uncomforting, unaccusing.'

Notes

1. The importance of storytelling within the stories is a commonplace of Munro criticism: see e.g. Karen E. Smythe, *Figuring Grief: Gallant, Munro, and the Poetics of Elegy* (Montreal and Kingston, London, Buffalo: McGill-Queens UP, 1992) p. 129; Ajay Heble, *The Tumble of Reason: Alice Munro's Discourse of Absence* (Toronto, Buffalo, London: U of Toronto P, 1994), p. 6; Coral Ann Howells, *Alice Munro* (Manchester and New York: Manchester UP, 1998), p. 4.

2. Munro is also more usually thought to be fascinated by mothers. See e.g. Magdalene Redekop, *Mothers and Other Clowns: The Stories of Alice Munro* (London and New York: Routledge, 1992).

Works Cited

Heble, Ajay. *The Tumble of Reason: Alice Munro's Discourse of Absence* (Toronto, Buffalo, London: U of Toronto P, 1994).

Howells, Coral Ann. *Alice Munro* (Manchester and New York: Manchester UP, 1998).

Munro, Alice. 'Fathers'. *The New Yorker,* 5 August 2002, pp. 64-71.

Redekop, Magdalene. *Mothers and Other Clowns: The Stories of Alice Munro* (London and New York: Routledge, 1992).

Smythe, Karen E. *Figuring Grief: Gallant, Munro, and the Poetics of Elegy* (Montreal and Kingston, London, Buffalo: McGill-Queen's UP, 1992).

Alice Munro and Eleanor Wachtel (interview date summer 2005)

SOURCE: Munro, Alice, and Eleanor Wachtel. "Alice Munro: A Life in Writing—A Conversation with Eleanor Wachtel." *Queen's Quarterly* 112, no. 2 (summer 2005): 267-82.

[*In the following interview, Munro discusses her characters' need for change or escape, the impact of small-town life on her stories, and her personal growth as an author.*]

Alice Munro is described as "Canada's Chekhov," "Canada's Flaubert"—you name it. She is a wonderful storyteller who has been called a writer's writer—and many writers, both in Canada and internationally, do love and admire her work. But Alice Munro is also a reader's writer. She writes with intelligence, depth, and compassion, carrying her readers with her in her explorations of character, in search of some kind of understanding—no neat resolutions, just trying to figure things out in an elegant, moving way.

Alice Munro has won virtually every prize available to a Canadian short story writer. From three Governor-General's Awards, starting with her very first book, *Dance of the Happy Shades,* in 1968, to the American National Book Critics Circle Award, the Trillium and two Giller Prizes. She was the first Canadian to win both the PEN/Malamud Award for Excellence in short fiction, and the Rea Award for the Short Story.

Alice Munro was born in Wingham, in southwestern Ontario, in 1931. She studied at the University of Western Ontario for two years, then married at 20 and moved to Vancouver. In 1976, she returned to Ontario, settling in Clinton, not far from where she grew up. I spoke to her in Goderich, a slightly bigger town just up the road from Clinton—still in "Alice Munro Country"—at Bailey's restaurant. I would call it "Alice's Restaurant" if that didn't sound too much like an old song (and movie). But it's the place where she likes to have lunch and meet friends, as well as visiting journalists, biographers, whatever. She has a regular table at the back and a particular seat at the table.

[*Wachtel*]: *The title of your new book,* **Runaway,** *actually fits many of your stories. They're about women in flight, running to or from relationships or ways of living. Did you feel that current underneath the stories as you were writing them?*

[Munro]: No, I didn't feel that. I had another title picked. I was going to call the book *Powers,* which was a title I liked very much and the title of the last story. And then it occurred to my editor, Doug Gibson—and *then* to me—that *Runaway* had more life in it, and it did relate to each of the stories, which I hadn't noticed before.

In keeping with the idea of **Runaway,** *in your 1998 collection,* **The Love of a Good Woman,** *you had a line about a woman who flees a marriage for another man, and you write, "So her life was falling forward. She was becoming one of those people who ran away. A*

woman who shockingly and incomprehensibly gave everything up for love, other observers would say wryly, meaning sex." What is it that these women run away from? Are they fleeing convention and expectation?*

I think they run away from a life in which they can look ahead and see what that whole life is going to be. You wouldn't call that a prison exactly. They run away from some kind of predictability, not just about the things that will happen in their lives but the things that happen in *themselves*—although I don't think most of my characters plan to do this. People don't usually say, at a certain stage of their lives, "I'll get out of this." And, in fact, I think the people who run away are often the same people who got into that life most enthusiastically, thinking, "*This* is it!" But then they want more; they just demand more of life than is happening at the moment. And sometimes this is a great mistake. But this is something that women in my generation tended to do because we'd been married young. We'd been married with a very settled idea of what life was supposed to be like, and we were in a hurry to get to that safe married spot. Then something happened to us when we were around forty. And all sorts of women decided that life had to have a new pattern. And I don't know if that will happen to women of the next generation or the generation after that—because so many things will happen to them *before* they're forty. Maybe they'll decide that *enough* has happened. And they'll pick a life and go on with it without these rather girlish hopes of finding love, finding excitement.

Why "girlish" hopes?

Well, they seem to me, often, to be rather youthful ideas. Ideas that somewhere there is passion that will last, or there is the kind of passion that surpasses everything else in life—that you can just tear everything apart and pick up and go on somehow. I think that's rather a youthful idea. But I think women of my age didn't hit this youthful phase until we'd had our middle age first. We had our kids, and our homes, and our husbands, and our quite programmed lives. And then there was this thing about, "There's got to be more to my life than that."

Are men the main route of escape or transformation for these women?

In my generation they certainly were. We didn't, I think, see any other means—and they're a pretty traditional one too, you know. Men for women and women for men. Falling in love is still one of the big, big ways to change your life and to give yourself this tremendous charge of excitement and hope. It's still one of the most important things we have.

In several stories, a romantic connection is thwarted by circumstance, and what seems to be leading to a sexual union turns into something else entirely. But something emotionally important or even life-changing still happens.

Yes, I like that. I like that to work in stories. I like the change *not* to be the change that you thought you were finding—and for something to come that is completely unexpected, as if life had a mind of its own and would take hold of you and present you with something that you hadn't anticipated.

You're talking about the importance of falling in love. One reviewer of your last book noted that infidelity, romantic encounters outside marriage, occurred in seven of the nine stories. How does this work for the writer?

Writers are always writing about infidelity—it's so dramatic. Again, maybe this applies to writers of my generation because we didn't have as much adventure before we were married. And there's all this business of the *wickedness* of it, the secrecy, the complications . . . the finding out that you thought you were one person, and you are also this *other* person. The innocent life and the guilty life. My God, it's just full of stuff for a writer! I doubt if it will ever go out of fashion.

What about sex? Canadian writer Audrey Thomas says you're the only writer who really, truly examines women's sexuality. American novelist Mona Simpson says you've done for female sexuality what Philip Roth did for male sexuality.

Truly?

That's what she says, and she adds, "Although covering much the same period, it would seem they knew vastly different women." Does it surprise you that . . .

It surprises me mightily! I think I write about sex just the way almost everybody I read writes about sex. I try to write about it with a great deal of interest and try to be as truthful as I can—or to think about what people really go through and what they think and how they feel. But I think every writer does that. John Updike writes a lot about sex. Charlotte Brontë was writing about sex. I suppose Jane Austen was too.

In the story **"Passion"** I wanted to tell first about the girl's relationship with the family, and then about this wonderful moment when she runs away with a man who is married, and who has great problems of his own, and how during the course of that day she comes to understand what his problems are—the problems of not being able to bear a life.

And so I wanted to take her much further into what she understands about other people. And then, of course, there's turnaround at the end—and I like when stories turn out in an unexpected way that doesn't seem too forced. And that story pleased me because I thought it did.

You take her further than she expected to go—because the initial attraction is sexual. The brother is more attractive to her than her own fiancé.

Yes, and I think it's often true that women are attracted to a man who has troubles, a man who is brooding and dark and unhappy, because there's the feeling that you perhaps can make him happy. In this case, the man is full of mystery, and he's older. So she senses that something is going to happen, probably some sexual awakening that will prove to be the answer to her life's questions, and it's going to happen on *this* day. She doesn't think this too clearly, but her feelings are urging her that way.

In **Runaway,** *many of the stories are quite harrowing— the threat of violence, death, suicide, and other forms of terrible loss are frequently present. Do you have a sense that your stories are becoming darker?*

I think they are, and this is not at all on purpose. I would like to be writing very cheerful stories that would make people feel better when they read them. I hope that people *do* feel better when they read my stories. I don't think having this content means that the stories need to be depressing. I don't know why this is happening. I think it may be that as you become older, there are more things like this coming close to your life, and things you learn about. It could be that—but again, it's nothing I intended. In the story where the mother is losing her daughter, I was really trying to explore how this could be a quite natural thing. Some things that seem so tragic can also be just *things people do*. In that story, the daughter has a choice—she can live quite honestly, which means just ditching her mother. Or she can choose to live within her given conventions and to live with very mixed emotions—and that is the way most people live with their parents. Instead, she gets out. And she doesn't do this because her mother is a terrible person or because she has any great grievance against her mother—she just goes on to a different life. And this is a terrible blow to the mother, because it's when you get quite old that the bonds to your children become so central to your life. When you're in middle age, or a little younger than middle age, the bonds to your parents are there, but they often seem like nuisances. So that's what this story is really about.

Alice Munro, I'm sitting with you here in Goderich, a southwestern Ontario town on the shores of Lake Huron—near the heart of "Alice Munro country," as it's come to be called. You write about a lot of places, but you continue to set stories around this part of the world, where you were born and have lived for much of your life. How do you stand back and see the possibilities of a place, fictionally, when it's so familiar to you?

I just always feel there's more to be discovered about this place. I don't ever have to think that I've finished with it, with the changes in it and the things I know about it. I don't like to be described as a regional writer. I'm annoyed sometimes when people think I write about a sort of idyllic life or a sort of pastorale, because I'm seen as someone who writes about small towns in the country. It almost seems to be by accident that I write about those people, because I know their houses, and I know certain things about their lives. But I don't think of them as particularly different from people you might find elsewhere in the world. It's just something I do without thinking about it. Nearly everybody I write about lives in a place where I have once lived. So maybe I'm not very good about imagination . . . except that I once did a story about Albania, and I enjoyed that a lot. But usually I don't choose anything exotic. I might like to, but there's always something else that I have to do first that isn't exotic at all.

How has small-town life changed?

Oh, it's changed enormously. There's so much tolerance now. When I went to school, people laughed at anyone who was disadvantaged. Now everybody knows that you don't make fun of people for their problems—at least, you don't do it publicly, and you don't do it in any very obvious way. And in the old days, nobody would ever claim to be an agnostic in a small town. But now it's acceptable. And the rules about sex have changed completely—so that women my age live with their lovers! It's quite amazing. There's just a freedom to live a more pleasant life, I think. It's much more compassionate, much more understanding. You could probably even announce that you like poetry.

You lived in British Columbia for more than twenty years, and you still winter on Vancouver Island. Do different landscapes suggest different stories or characters for you?

No, I don't think about it—the whole story just comes all of a piece. When I wrote, say, **"The Children Stay,"** I just saw it happening on Vancouver Island, particularly at Miracle Beach. Because I had to have them go away to a place like that. And there it was. So I saw them there. But I don't know if a particular kind of story is written in those places or not—mainly because I'm simply not very analytical about what I do. When something comes and settles into place, that's it, and I don't think about why it's there or even what it's about. I'm telling you as if I knew what they were about, but this is all after the fact.

What was it like for you to move back to small-town southwestern Ontario after being away for twenty-odd years?

That's one thing that *did* influence my writing—because I had written about growing up here, and I thought I was finished with anything about this area. When I

moved back, I started seeing things entirely differently. I didn't see them right away in present-day time, but I saw a lot of things that had to do with social class and the way people behave towards one another—things a child doesn't see. So I wanted to go into that all over again. And that's what I did. For me, personally, it was surprising. It was unexpected.

But I liked a lot of things about this place very much. I loved the countryside, going cross-country skiing in the winter and all that kind of thing. I liked living with my husband and making our life here. I liked our house, our backyard—all kinds of things were good. And also, I was now an independent woman. I was not someone who had grown up here and stayed here. And if people were talking about me or judging me, I didn't know. So that was okay.

What about social class? Did you become aware that you wanted to deal with this in your writing?

I wanted to write more about the class I lived amongst when I went to school. It was in my fourth book, I guess, that I began to do this. When I started school in Wingham, there was an area outside of town that was full of people who were suffering the hardships of the Depression—only I didn't know that at the time. It was a very rough school, and as an adult I hadn't really thought about that for a long time. I hadn't thought about the way these people lived and the difference between them and the people who lived in the town, over the bridge, who had marginally better lives—some of them a good deal better.

I described that school because it was a pretty horrific place—and it was so richly interesting. There were boys attending school there until they were sixteen or seventeen years old because they just couldn't get jobs. I'm not talking about high school—I'm talking about junior school. So these older boys were pretty well running things. There was a great deal of physical violence. This was all pretty amazing to me because I was being raised at the edge of this community as a little middle-class girl, and I was an only child—or so I thought, being the eldest child in my family. To come into this environment was astonishing, and probably so painful that for a long time I didn't think about it.

But later I wanted to write about it, because there were some wonderful things about it. Our favourite game was "funeral." Somebody would act as the corpse, and that was a favourite role. The person would be lying out, and we would pick flowers—weeds, really—and go with great armfuls and put them on the corpse. This wasn't dreadful at all. It was rather touching. And we'd line up, and then we would all get a chance to march past the dead person and cry and carry on. But the trouble was that the most important people got to be the corpse first. And then everybody else got a turn. But by the time it was my turn, everyone had lost interest in the game, and the mourners were few, and the flowers were few, and the children would drift off and play something else.

I learned things that I wouldn't have learned so quickly any other way—about how people are, and about how some people are like this because they are leading lives of great deprivation. In those years, people who didn't have enough fuel for the winter might stay in bed all day. In some ways it was like a Chekhov village.

You were saying you were an only child because you were the eldest?

Yes, that's dreadful—the way an elder child talks: "I was an only child." I had a baby brother and a baby sister at home, but I wasn't counting them at the moment.

You do have a lot of empathy for your characters, the characters in your stories who are limited by their circumstances, whether it's a matter of economics or societal expectations or obligations to family.

I grew up with a lot of people like that. For most of the people I knew it was very difficult to get what most people would now think of as perfectly normal opportunities. For instance, when I finished high school, I got a scholarship, and I could go to university. But had I not got the scholarship and had decided instead to get a job in the city, there were many obstacles. First of all, you had to get *to* the city—and then you needed to be able to support yourself for several weeks while you hunted for a job. In those days, this could be next to impossible for an average person. So there are things about those times that people today find hard to understand. I didn't think any of this was particularly unfair. I still think of my life as very interesting, a great life for a writer. This life gave me a lot of confidence as a writer because I was the only person I knew who tried to write when I was a teenager, and I didn't know anybody else who read as much as I did. So I thought that I was a uniquely gifted person, and that it was only going to take until I was about 21 or 22 years old before the first novel would burst upon the world. If I'd been going to a high school like Jarvis Collegiate in Toronto I might have had a very different idea of what the competition would be like.

What did give you the ability to pursue your aspirations back then?

A big ego—it never occurred to me not to follow my ambitions. At first, when I was about eight, I planned to be a movie star. Then I slipped into writing, slightly downgrading my plans—because being a movie star would be more wonderful. But I wanted to make up

stories, and I was making up stories in my head. By the time I was about eleven, I really thought that I had to write them down. That was what you did with stories. You didn't just let them fade; you had to write them. It was not even the thought that other people would be reading the stories, that there would be books with your stories in them. And it really never occurred to me until much later, when I was around thirty, that I might *not* be able to do this. That confidence lasted for a long time. And then it just went with a big *whoosh*. It was hard when that confidence went away.

There was no problem with that confidence all the time I was growing up. Children who grow up in an environment where they feel strange and out of place can develop an alternative world that can be a great source of security for them—if they're lucky, and they don't have too many bad things happening to them. And I was lucky. I may have been beaten up at school, but I always had enough to eat. I was taken to the doctor when I was sick. Good things happened for me. I was allowed to go to high school at a time when many teenagers had to quit school and take whatever work was available. It never occurred to me how fortunate I was. I think gifted people are sometimes quite selfish. It never occurred to me that I should go and work in the glove factory or a department store in order to help my family. No, I was going to do this thing that was so important to me.

It also led to your leaving—going back to your theme right at the beginning of the conversation, about running away, in some sense, from family responsibility as the eldest daughter.

Yes, and this is the thing with which I'll be able to nourish my guilt for the rest of my life—that I did not stay home. I did not look after my mother [who was ill]. I did not keep house, though my brother and sister were still quite young. I just left them. I came home from university every couple of months and did major housecleaning jobs, but in the end I left—and without, at the time, any qualms. My parents were very good about it. They never asked me to stay.

When did the guilt come?

About the time I was feeling safe. You never feel guilty while there's still a possibility, an opportunity, to make up for what you've done. When I could have gone back home, I didn't feel guilty. But as soon as I was free, and nobody could make me go back, I did feel guilty. And I've felt guilty since. I say I feel guilty, but I'm glad I did what I did. If I had stayed and just become the housekeeper, my life would have ended—and certainly no one would have married me. I was too weird. And I would have become too frightened to leave by the time my mother died. I would have been too frightened to go out into the world.

This has become your subject.

This has become my subject, yes. Writers are very economical. Nothing is wasted.

And your mother became your subject.

Very much so, yes.

How about your father?

Well, fathers and mothers at that time were very separate—they had separate spheres. My father was outside, and I was inside with my mother, doing housework. So all my conflicts were with my mother. And my father was allowed to be a figure outside this. When I was older, I had a great relationship with my father because he also read, and he wrote a book when he was dying. We were terribly good friends, and he was very understanding. He never criticized anything I did. The first books were not easy for him to take, living still in the town where people didn't read fiction and didn't know where fiction was going. There was all this new language, and all this sex, and he had to put up with people's reaction to that—but he never blamed me for it. He liked my books.

Did it surprise you—did you have any idea he had a book in him?

I was beginning to when I got older. I didn't know him that well when I was a child. He wrote columns for a local magazine and things like that. Then he started to write this book, and he became really involved in it. The last time I visited him in the hospital, he was sitting up in bed in his pyjamas, saying, "Now, what do you think about that character so-and-so?" So I told him that if he didn't pull out of the operation, I would make sure that it got published. And I did. I was really happy about that. It gave him such delight. I think he wouldn't have believed that there could be a connection between him and that distant world—where there were publishers, and books were written—if he hadn't seen me enter it. Then he really thought that it was possible for anybody to do it. I remember telling him that Margaret Laurence was a friend of mine, because he'd been reading a book of hers that he'd borrowed from the library, and he said, "But Alice, she's a really good writer!" So he started to feel that there could be a connection to that world, that it was no longer something distant and unreal, and so he could try it himself.

Memory shapes many of these stories, and that relationship between the older and younger parts of a life. Grace in "Passion," for instance, is literally revisiting the places where she spent time with the Travers family. What do you find interesting about having a character look back and reconsider her past?

I suppose in that particular story I wanted to show where Grace had ended up. But I also wanted to show the differences people experience—I like to have people trying to find something of their past, and then they end up looking at what they *really* find. Sometimes they'll find that the old house is still there, but it doesn't mean anything anymore. I thought it was just a good way to get into the story. Also, I suppose I'm a little self-conscious writing about the past, so I anchor it in the present—because there is a feeling sometimes that people who write about the past are writing about a time that is much easier to understand, and is safer. A reviewer said that I chose to write about the past because I would be safe there. Now, I don't feel that I am safe there, but I know that people have this nostalgic idea of the past being a more pleasant, gentler time—although I think that's quite false.

What tense do you live in now? Do you live in the present, the past, the future? Where is it that you inhabit when you're not necessarily writing?

Oh . . . I inhabit the present now, and I inhabit it with a great sense of grabbing it. I don't inhabit the future much, for obvious reasons. I don't know how much there is of it. For the same reason, I want to—oh, this sounds very clichéd—I want to appreciate every bit of life I can. It's not that I do that all the time. But I'm conscious of wanting to do that and thinking . . . it's almost like another "I should." "I should" be perfectly happy because, after all, I'm not dying, and my heart is fixed, and I live in this nice place, and things like that. But I can be just as irritable, loaded with things to do, as I ever was—so life doesn't really change that much.

You've had 35 years of publishing books, and 50 of publishing stories. You are celebrated internationally by both critics and readers as someone who never disappoints. Does that help or hinder the writing for you?

Oh . . . hinders it. I think, "Wait till next time. Sometime, this is going to come crashing down." And I hope that I'll be so old, I won't care. Or that I will have reached a kind of wonderful plateau where I'll feel that I don't have to write anymore, where I will just be sort of happy all the time. What will I do there? Play golf? No, I can't play golf . . . so I don't know. Maybe just go for long walks, and really appreciate things. Isn't that an ideal state: to be only feeling the present, not to be thinking about or feeling anything else? Isn't that a kind of nirvana?

But you already do that.

Yes, but if I could be at that plateau we talked about.

Note

A version of this conversation was first broadcast on CBC Radio's *Writers & Company* and produced by Lisa Godfrey.

FURTHER READING

Criticism

Beran, Carol L. "Thomas Hardy, Alice Munro, and the Question of Influence." *American Review of Canadian Studies* 29, no. 2 (summer 1999): 237-58.

> Investigates Munro's short story "Carried Away" in relation to Thomas Hardy's "An Imaginative Woman," underscoring both Munro's role as a contemporary Canadian author and her position in the British literary tradition.

Carscallen, James. *The Other Country: Patterns in the Writing of Alice Munro.* Toronto: ECW Press, 1993, 581 p.

> Book-length analysis of Munro's writing style and major themes.

May, Charles E. "Why Does Alice Munro Write Short Stories?" *Wascana Review of Contemporary Poetry and Short Fiction* 38, no. 1 (spring 2003): 16-28.

> Extols the atmospheric subtlety and subversion of expectations in Munro's work.

Miller, Judith Maclean. "On Looking into Rifts and Crannies: Alice Munro's *Friend of My Youth.*" *Antigonish Review,* no. 120 (winter 2000): 205-26.

> Traces the plots and themes of the stories in *Friend of My Youth.*

Murphy, Georgeann. "The Art of Alice Munro: Memory, Identity, and the Aesthetics of Connection." In *Canadian Women Writing Fiction,* edited by Mickey Pearlman, pp. 12-27. Jackson: University Press of Mississippi, 1993.

> Stresses the significance of narrative perspective, personal transformation, and self-awareness in Munro's stories.

Rasporich, Beverly J. *Dance of the Sexes: Art and Gender in the Fiction of Alice Munro.* Edmonton: The University of Alberta Press, 1990, 223 p.

> Highlights the passage of time and the prevalence of symbolic imagery in Munro's handling of gender relations.

Smythe, Karen E. "Munrovian Melancholy." In *Figuring Grief: Gallant, Munro, and the Poetics of Elegy,* pp. 129-52. Montreal: McGill-Queen's University Press, 1992.

> Analyzes notions of loss and grief in Munro's short stories.

Additional coverage of Munro's life and career is contained in the following sources published by Thomson Gale: *Authors in the News,* **2;** *Beacham's Encyclopedia of Popular Fiction: Biography & Resources,* **Vol. 2;** *Contemporary Authors,* **Vols. 33-36R;** *Contemporary Authors New Revision Series,* **Vols. 33, 53, 75, 114;** *Contemporary Canadian Authors,* **Vol. 1;** *Contemporary Literary Criticism,* **Vols. 6, 10, 19, 50, 95, 222;** *Contemporary Novelists,* **Eds. 1, 2, 3, 4, 5, 6, 7;** *Dictionary of Literary Biography,* **Vol. 53;** *DISCovering Authors: Canadian Edition; DISCovering Authors Modules: Most-Studied Authors* **and** *Novelists; DISCovering Authors 3.0; Encyclopedia of World Literature in the 20th Century,* **Ed. 3;** *Literature Resource Center; Major 20th-Century Writers,* **Eds. 1, 2;** *Major 21st-Century Writers,* **eBook 2005;** *Reference Guide to English Literature,* **Ed. 2;** *Reference Guide to Short Fiction,* **Ed. 2;** *Short Stories for Students,* **Vols. 5, 13, 19;** *Short Story Criticism,* **Vol. 3;** *Something about the Author,* **Vol. 29;** *Twayne Companion to Contemporary Literature in English,* **Ed. 1:2;** *World Literature Criticism Supplement;* **and** *World Writers in English,* **Vol. 1.**

How to Use This Index

> **Calvino, Italo**
> 1923-1985 .... CLC 5, 8, 11, 22, 33, 39,
> 73; SSC 3, 48

list all author entries in the following Thomson Gale Literary Criticism series:

AAL = *Asian American Literature*
BG = *The Beat Generation: A Gale Critical Companion*
BLC = *Black Literature Criticism*
BLCS = *Black Literature Criticism Supplement*
CLC = *Contemporary Literary Criticism*
CLR = *Children's Literature Review*
CMLC = *Classical and Medieval Literature Criticism*
DC = *Drama Criticism*
FL = *Feminism in Literature: A Gale Critical Companion*
GL = *Gothic Literature: A Gale Critical Companion*
HLC = *Hispanic Literature Criticism*
HLCS = *Hispanic Literature Criticism Supplement*
HR = *Harlem Renaissance: A Gale Critical Companion*
LC = *Literature Criticism from 1400 to 1800*
NCLC = *Nineteenth-Century Literature Criticism*
NNAL = *Native North American Literature*
PC = *Poetry Criticism*
SSC = *Short Story Criticism*
TCLC = *Twentieth-Century Literary Criticism*
WLC = *World Literature Criticism, 1500 to the Present*
WLCS = *World Literature Criticism Supplement*

> See also CA 85-88, 116; CANR 23, 61;
> DAM NOV; DLB 196; EW 13; MTCW 1, 2;
> RGSF 2; RGWL 2; SFW 4; SSFS 12

list all author entries in the following Thomson Gale biographical and literary sources:

AAYA = *Authors & Artists for Young Adults*
AFAW = *African American Writers*
AFW = *African Writers*
AITN = *Authors in the News*
AMW = *American Writers*
AMWR = *American Writers Retrospective Supplement*
AMWS = *American Writers Supplement*
ANW = *American Nature Writers*
AW = *Ancient Writers*
BEST = *Bestsellers*
BPFB = *Beacham's Encyclopedia of Popular Fiction: Biography and Resources*
BRW = *British Writers*
BRWS = *British Writers Supplement*
BW = *Black Writers*
BYA = *Beacham's Guide to Literature for Young Adults*
CA = *Contemporary Authors*
CAAS = *Contemporary Authors Autobiography Series*
CABS = *Contemporary Authors Bibliographical Series*
CAD = *Contemporary American Dramatists*
CANR = *Contemporary Authors New Revision Series*
CAP = *Contemporary Authors Permanent Series*
CBD = *Contemporary British Dramatists*
CCA = *Contemporary Canadian Authors*
CD = *Contemporary Dramatists*
CDALB = *Concise Dictionary of American Literary Biography*

CDALBS = *Concise Dictionary of American Literary Biography Supplement*
CDBLB = *Concise Dictionary of British Literary Biography*
CMW = *St. James Guide to Crime & Mystery Writers*
CN = *Contemporary Novelists*
CP = *Contemporary Poets*
CPW = *Contemporary Popular Writers*
CSW = *Contemporary Southern Writers*
CWD = *Contemporary Women Dramatists*
CWP = *Contemporary Women Poets*
CWRI = *St. James Guide to Children's Writers*
CWW = *Contemporary World Writers*
DA = *DISCovering Authors*
DA3 = *DISCovering Authors 3.0*
DAB = *DISCovering Authors: British Edition*
DAC = *DISCovering Authors: Canadian Edition*
DAM = *DISCovering Authors: Modules*
  DRAM: *Dramatists Module;* **MST:** *Most-studied Authors Module;*
  MULT: *Multicultural Authors Module;* **NOV:** *Novelists Module;*
  POET: *Poets Module;* **POP:** *Popular Fiction and Genre Authors Module*
DFS = *Drama for Students*
DLB = *Dictionary of Literary Biography*
DLBD = *Dictionary of Literary Biography Documentary Series*
DLBY = *Dictionary of Literary Biography Yearbook*
DNFS = *Literature of Developing Nations for Students*
EFS = *Epics for Students*
EXPN = *Exploring Novels*
EXPP = *Exploring Poetry*
EXPS = *Exploring Short Stories*
EW = *European Writers*
FANT = *St. James Guide to Fantasy Writers*
FW = *Feminist Writers*
GFL = *Guide to French Literature,* Beginnings to 1789, 1798 to the Present
GLL = *Gay and Lesbian Literature*
HGG = *St. James Guide to Horror, Ghost & Gothic Writers*
HW = *Hispanic Writers*
IDFW = *International Dictionary of Films and Filmmakers: Writers and Production Artists*
IDTP = *International Dictionary of Theatre: Playwrights*
LAIT = *Literature and Its Times*
LAW = *Latin American Writers*
JRDA = *Junior DISCovering Authors*
MAICYA = *Major Authors and Illustrators for Children and Young Adults*
MAICYAS = *Major Authors and Illustrators for Children and Young Adults Supplement*
MAWW = *Modern American Women Writers*
MJW = *Modern Japanese Writers*
MTCW = *Major 20th-Century Writers*
NCFS = *Nonfiction Classics for Students*
NFS = *Novels for Students*
PAB = *Poets: American and British*
PFS = *Poetry for Students*
RGAL = *Reference Guide to American Literature*
RGEL = *Reference Guide to English Literature*
RGSF = *Reference Guide to Short Fiction*
RGWL = *Reference Guide to World Literature*
RHW = *Twentieth-Century Romance and Historical Writers*
SAAS = *Something about the Author Autobiography Series*
SATA = *Something about the Author*
SFW = *St. James Guide to Science Fiction Writers*
SSFS = *Short Stories for Students*
TCWW = *Twentieth-Century Western Writers*
WLIT = *World Literature and Its Times*
WP = *World Poets*
YABC = *Yesterday's Authors of Books for Children*
YAW = *St. James Guide to Young Adult Writers*

Literary Criticism Series
Cumulative Author Index

Atticus
See Fleming, Ian; Wilson, (Thomas) Woodrow

Atwood, Margaret 1939- . **CLC 2, 3, 4, 8, 13, 15, 25, 44, 84, 135; PC 8; SSC 2, 46; WLC 1**
See also AAYA 12, 47; AMWS 13; BEST 89:2; BPFB 1; CA 49-52; CANR 3, 24, 33, 59, 95, 133; CN 2, 3, 4, 5, 6, 7; CP 1, 2, 3, 4, 5, 6, 7; CPW; CWP; DA; DA3; DAB; DAC; DAM MST, NOV, POET; DLB 53, 251, 326; EWL 3; EXPN; FL 1:5; FW; GL 2; INT CANR-24; LAIT 5; MTCW 1, 2; MTFW 2005; NFS 4, 12, 13, 14, 19; PFS 7; RGSF 2; SATA 50, 170; SSFS 3, 13; TCLE 1:1; TWA; WWE 1; YAW

Atwood, Margaret Eleanor
See Atwood, Margaret

Aubigny, Pierre d'
See Mencken, H(enry) L(ouis)

Aubin, Penelope 1685-1731(?) .... **LC 9**
See also DLB 39

Auchincloss, Louis 1917- ..... **CLC 4, 6, 9, 18, 45; SSC 22**
See also AMWS 4; CA 1-4R; CANR 6, 29, 55, 87, 130; CN 1, 2, 3, 4, 5, 6, 7; DAM NOV; DLB 2, 244; DLBY 1980; EWL 3; INT CANR-29; MAL 5; MTCW 1; RGAL 4

Auchincloss, Louis Stanton
See Auchincloss, Louis

Auden, W(ystan) H(ugh) 1907-1973 . **CLC 1, 2, 3, 4, 6, 9, 11, 14, 43, 123; PC 1; WLC 1**
See also AAYA 18; AMWS 2; BRW 7; BRWR 1; CA 9-12R; 45-48; CANR 5, 61, 105; CDBLB 1914-1945; CP 1, 2; DA; DA3; DAB; DAC; DAM DRAM, MST, POET; DLB 10, 20; EWL 3; EXPP; MAL 5; MTCW 1, 2; MTFW 2005; PAB; PFS 1, 3, 4, 10; TUS; WP

Audiberti, Jacques 1899-1965 .... **CLC 38**
See also CA 25-28R; DAM DRAM; DLB 321; EWL 3

Audubon, John James 1785-1851 . **NCLC 47**
See also AMWS 16; ANW; DLB 248

Auel, Jean M(arie) 1936- .... **CLC 31, 107**
See also AAYA 7, 51; BEST 90:4; BPFB 1; CA 103; CANR 21, 64, 115; CPW; DA3; DAM POP; INT CANR-21; NFS 11; RHW; SATA 91

Auerbach, Berthold 1812-1882 .... **NCLC 171**
See also DLB 133

Auerbach, Erich 1892-1957 .... **TCLC 43**
See also CA 118; 155; EWL 3

Augier, Emile 1820-1889 .... **NCLC 31**
See also DLB 192; GFL 1789 to the Present

August, John
See De Voto, Bernard (Augustine)

Augustine, St. 354-430 .... **CMLC 6; WLCS**
See also DA; DA3; DAB; DAC; DAM MST; DLB 115; EW 1; RGWL 2, 3; WLIT 8

Aunt Belinda
See Braddon, Mary Elizabeth

Aunt Weedy
See Alcott, Louisa May

Aurelius
See Bourne, Randolph S(illiman)

Aurelius, Marcus 121-180 .... **CMLC 45**
See Marcus Aurelius
See also RGWL 2, 3

Aurobindo, Sri
See Ghose, Aurabinda

Aurobindo Ghose
See Ghose, Aurabinda

Austen, Jane 1775-1817 ...... **NCLC 1, 13, 19, 33, 51, 81, 95, 119, 150; WLC 1**
See also AAYA 19; BRW 4; BRWC 1; BRWR 2; BYA 3; CDBLB 1789-1832; DA; DA3; DAB; DAC; DAM MST, NOV; DLB 116; EXPN; FL 1:2; GL 2; LAIT 2; LATS 1:1; LMFS 1; NFS 1, 14, 18, 20, 21; TEA; WLIT 3; WYAS 1

Auster, Paul 1947- .... **CLC 47, 131, 227**
See also AMWS 12; CA 69-72; CANR 23, 52, 75, 129; CMW 4; CN 5, 6, 7; DA3; DLB 227; MAL 5; MTCW 2; MTFW 2005; SUFW 2; TCLE 1:1

Austin, Frank
See Faust, Frederick (Schiller)

Austin, Mary (Hunter) 1868-1934 . **TCLC 25**
See also ANW; CA 109; 178; DLB 9, 78, 206, 221, 275; FW; TCWW 1, 2

Averroes 1126-1198 .... **CMLC 7**
See also DLB 115

Avicenna 980-1037 .... **CMLC 16**
See also DLB 115

Avison, Margaret (Kirkland) 1918- .. **CLC 2, 4, 97**
See also CA 17-20R; CANR 134; CP 1, 2, 3, 4, 5, 6, 7; DAC; DAM POET; DLB 53; MTCW 1

Axton, David
See Koontz, Dean R.

Ayckbourn, Alan 1939- ...... **CLC 5, 8, 18, 33, 74; DC 13**
See also BRWS 5; CA 21-24R; CANR 31, 59, 118; CBD; CD 5, 6; DAB; DAM DRAM; DFS 7; DLB 13, 245; EWL 3; MTCW 1, 2; MTFW 2005

Aydy, Catherine
See Tennant, Emma (Christina)

Ayme, Marcel (Andre) 1902-1967 ... **CLC 11; SSC 41**
See also CA 89-92; CANR 67, 137; CLR 25; DLB 72; EW 12; EWL 3; GFL 1789 to the Present; RGSF 2; RGWL 2, 3; SATA 91

Ayrton, Michael 1921-1975 .... **CLC 7**
See also CA 5-8R; 61-64; CANR 9, 21

Aytmatov, Chingiz
See Aitmatov, Chingiz (Torekulovich)
See also EWL 3

Azorin .... **CLC 11**
See Martinez Ruiz, Jose
See also DLB 322; EW 9; EWL 3

Azuela, Mariano 1873-1952 .. **HLC 1; TCLC 3, 145**
See also CA 104; 131; CANR 81; DAM MULT; EWL 3; HW 1, 2; LAW; MTCW 1, 2; MTFW 2005

Ba, Mariama 1929-1981 .... **BLCS**
See also AFW; BW 2; CA 141; CANR 87; DNFS 2; WLIT 2

Baastad, Babbis Friis
See Friis-Baastad, Babbis Ellinor

Bab
See Gilbert, W(illiam) S(chwenck)

Babbis, Eleanor
See Friis-Baastad, Babbis Ellinor

Babel, Isaac
See Babel, Isaak (Emmanuilovich)
See also EW 11; SSFS 10

Babel, Isaak (Emmanuilovich) 1894-1941(?) . **SSC 16, 78; TCLC 2, 13, 171**
See Babel, Isaac
See also CA 104; 155; CANR 113; DLB 272; EWL 3; MTCW 2; MTFW 2005; RGSF 2; RGWL 2, 3; TWA

Babits, Mihaly 1883-1941 .... **TCLC 14**
See also CA 114; CDWLB 4; DLB 215; EWL 3

Babur 1483-1530 .... **LC 18**

Babylas 1898-1962
See Ghelderode, Michel de

Baca, Jimmy Santiago 1952- . **HLC 1; PC 41**
See also CA 131; CANR 81, 90, 146; CP 6, 7; DAM MULT; DLB 122; HW 1, 2; LLW; MAL 5

Baca, Jose Santiago
See Baca, Jimmy Santiago

Bacchelli, Riccardo 1891-1985 .... **CLC 19**
See also CA 29-32R; 117; DLB 264; EWL 3

Bach, Richard 1936- .... **CLC 14**
See also AITN 1; BEST 89:2; BPFB 1; BYA 5; CA 9-12R; CANR 18, 93, 151; CPW; DAM NOV, POP; FANT; MTCW 1; SATA 13

Bach, Richard David
See Bach, Richard

Bache, Benjamin Franklin 1769-1798 .... **LC 74**
See also DLB 43

Bachelard, Gaston 1884-1962 ...... **TCLC 128**
See also CA 97-100; 89-92; DLB 296; GFL 1789 to the Present

Bachman, Richard
See King, Stephen

Bachmann, Ingeborg 1926-1973 .... **CLC 69**
See also CA 93-96; 45-48; CANR 69; DLB 85; EWL 3; RGHL; RGWL 2, 3

Bacon, Francis 1561-1626 ..... **LC 18, 32, 131**
See also BRW 1; CDBLB Before 1660; DLB 151, 236, 252; RGEL 2; TEA

Bacon, Roger 1214(?)-1294 .... **CMLC 14**
See also DLB 115

Bacovia, George 1881-1957 .... **TCLC 24**
See Vasiliu, Gheorghe
See also CDWLB 4; DLB 220; EWL 3

Badanes, Jerome 1937-1995 .... **CLC 59**
See also CA 234

Bagehot, Walter 1826-1877 .... **NCLC 10**
See also DLB 55

Bagnold, Enid 1889-1981 .... **CLC 25**
See also BYA 2; CA 5-8R; 103; CANR 5, 40; CBD; CN 2; CWD; CWRI 5; DAM DRAM; DLB 13, 160, 191, 245; FW; MAICYA 1, 2; RGEL 2; SATA 1, 25

Bagritsky, Eduard .... **TCLC 60**
See Dzyubin, Eduard Georgievich

Bagrjana, Elisaveta
See Belcheva, Elisaveta Lyubomirova

Bagryana, Elisaveta .... **CLC 10**
See Belcheva, Elisaveta Lyubomirova
See also CA 178; CDWLB 4; DLB 147; EWL 3

Bailey, Paul 1937- .... **CLC 45**
See also CA 21-24R; CANR 16, 62, 124; CN 1, 2, 3, 4, 5, 6, 7; DLB 14, 271; GLL 2

Baillie, Joanna 1762-1851 ...... **NCLC 71, 151**
See also DLB 93; GL 2; RGEL 2

Bainbridge, Beryl 1934- ...... **CLC 4, 5, 8, 10, 14, 18, 22, 62, 130**
See also BRWS 6; CA 21-24R; CANR 24, 55, 75, 88, 128; CN 2, 3, 4, 5, 6, 7; DAM NOV; DLB 14, 231; EWL 3; MTCW 1, 2; MTFW 2005

Baker, Carlos (Heard) 1909-1987 .... **TCLC 119**
See also CA 5-8R; 122; CANR 3, 63; DLB 103

Baker, Elliott 1922- .... **CLC 8**
See also CA 45-48; CANR 2, 63; CN 1, 2, 3, 4, 5, 6, 7

Baker, Jean H. .... **TCLC 3, 10**
See Russell, George William

Baker, Nicholson 1957- .... **CLC 61, 165**
See also AMWS 13; CA 135; CANR 63, 120, 138; CN 6; CPW; DA3; DAM POP; DLB 227; MTFW 2005

Baker, Ray Stannard 1870-1946 .... **TCLC 47**
See also CA 118

Baker, Russell 1925- .... **CLC 31**
See also BEST 89:4; CA 57-60; CANR 11, 41, 59, 137; MTCW 1, 2; MTFW 2005

Bakhtin, M.
See Bakhtin, Mikhail Mikhailovich

Bakhtin, M. M.
See Bakhtin, Mikhail Mikhailovich

Bakhtin, Mikhail
See Bakhtin, Mikhail Mikhailovich

Bakhtin, Mikhail Mikhailovich
1895-1975 .... **CLC 83; TCLC 160**
See also CA 128; 113; DLB 242; EWL 3

Bakshi, Ralph 1938(?)- .... **CLC 26**
See also CA 112; 138; IDFW 3

Bakunin, Mikhail (Alexandrovich)
1814-1876 .... **NCLC 25, 58**
See also DLB 277

Baldwin, James 1924-1987 ... **BLC 1; CLC 1, 2, 3, 4, 5, 8, 13, 15, 17, 42, 50, 67, 90, 127; DC 1; SSC 10, 33; WLC 1**
See also AAYA 4, 34; AFAW 1, 2; AMWR 2; AMWS 1; BPFB 1; BW 1; CA 1-4R; 124; CABS 1; CAD; CANR 3; CDALB 1941-1968; CN 1, 2, 3, 4; CPW; DA; DA3; DAB; DAC; DAM MST, MULT, NOV, POP; DFS 11, 15; DLB 2, 7, 33, 249, 278; DLBY 1987; EWL 3; EXPS; LAIT 5; MAL 5; MTCW 1, 2; MTFW 2005; NCFS 4; NFS 4; RGAL 4; RGSF 2; SATA 9; SATA-Obit 54; SSFS 2, 18; TUS

Baldwin, William c. 1515-1563 .... **LC 113**
See also DLB 132

Bale, John 1495-1563 .... **LC 62**
See also DLB 132; RGEL 2; TEA

Ball, Hugo 1886-1927 .... **TCLC 104**

Ballard, J.G. 1930- .... **CLC 3, 6, 14, 36, 137; SSC 1, 53**
See also AAYA 3, 52; BRWS 5; CA 5-8R; CANR 15, 39, 65, 107, 133; CN 1, 2, 3, 4, 5, 6, 7; DA3; DAM NOV, POP; DLB 14, 207, 261, 319; EWL 3; HGG; MTCW 1, 2; MTFW 2005; NFS 8; RGEL 2; RGSF 2; SATA 93; SCFW 1, 2; SFW 4

Balmont, Konstantin (Dmitriyevich)
1867-1943 .... **TCLC 11**
See also CA 109; 155; DLB 295; EWL 3

Baltausis, Vincas 1847-1910
See Mikszath, Kalman

Balzac, Honore de 1799-1850 ... **NCLC 5, 35, 53, 153; SSC 5, 59; WLC 1**
See also DA; DA3; DAB; DAC; DAM MST, NOV; DLB 119; EW 5; GFL 1789 to the Present; LMFS 1; RGSF 2; RGWL 2, 3; SSFS 10; SUFW; TWA

Bambara, Toni Cade 1939-1995 .... **BLC 1; CLC 19, 88; SSC 35; TCLC 116; WLCS**
See also AAYA 5, 49; AFAW 2; AMWS 11; BW 2, 3; BYA 12, 14; CA 29-32R; 150; CANR 24, 49, 81; CDALBS; DA; DA3; DAC; DAM MST, MULT; DLB 38, 218; EXPS; MAL 5; MTCW 1, 2; MTFW 2005; RGAL 4; RGSF 2; SATA 112; SSFS 4, 7, 12, 21

Bamdad, A.
See Shamlu, Ahmad

Bamdad, Alef
See Shamlu, Ahmad

Banat, D. R.
See Bradbury, Ray

Bancroft, Laura
See Baum, L(yman) Frank

Banim, John 1798-1842 .... **NCLC 13**
See also DLB 116, 158, 159; RGEL 2

Banim, Michael 1796-1874 .... **NCLC 13**
See also DLB 158, 159

Banjo, The
See Paterson, A(ndrew) B(arton)

Banks, Iain
See Banks, Iain M.
See also BRWS 11

Banks, Iain M. 1954- .... **CLC 34**
See Banks, Iain
See also CA 123; 128; CANR 61, 106; DLB 194, 261; EWL 3; HGG; INT CA-128; MTFW 2005; SFW 4

Banks, Lynne Reid .... **CLC 23**
See Reid Banks, Lynne
See also AAYA 6; BYA 7; CLR 86; CN 4, 5, 6

Banks, Russell 1940- . **CLC 37, 72, 187; SSC 42**
See also AAYA 45; AMWS 5; CA 65-68; CAAS 15; CANR 19, 52, 73, 118; CN 4, 5, 6, 7; DLB 130, 278; EWL 3; MAL 5; MTCW 2; MTFW 2005; NFS 13

Banville, John 1945- .... **CLC 46, 118, 224**
See also CA 117; 128; CANR 104, 150; CN 4, 5, 6, 7; DLB 14, 271, 326; INT CA-128

Banville, Theodore (Faullain) de
1832-1891 .... **NCLC 9**
See also DLB 217; GFL 1789 to the Present

Baraka, Amiri 1934- .... **BLC 1; CLC 1, 2, 3, 5, 10, 14, 33, 115, 213; DC 6; PC 4; WLCS**
See Jones, LeRoi
See also AAYA 63; AFAW 1, 2; AMWS 2; BW 2, 3; CA 21-24R; CABS 3; CAD; CANR 27, 38, 61, 133; CD 3, 5, 6; CDALB 1941-1968; CP 4, 5, 6, 7; CPW; DA; DA3; DAC; DAM MST, MULT, POET, POP; DFS 3, 11, 16; DLB 5, 7, 16, 38; DLBD 8; EWL 3; MAL 5; MTCW 1, 2; MTFW 2005; PFS 9; RGAL 4; TCLE 1:1; TUS; WP

Baratynsky, Evgenii Abramovich
1800-1844 .... **NCLC 103**
See also DLB 205

Barbauld, Anna Laetitia
1743-1825 .... **NCLC 50**
See also DLB 107, 109, 142, 158; RGEL 2

Barbellion, W. N. P. .... **TCLC 24**
See Cummings, Bruce F(rederick)

Barber, Benjamin R. 1939- .... **CLC 141**
See also CA 29-32R; CANR 12, 32, 64, 119

Barbera, Jack (Vincent) 1945- .... **CLC 44**
See also CA 110; CANR 45

Barbey d'Aurevilly, Jules-Amedee
1808-1889 .... **NCLC 1; SSC 17**
See also DLB 119; GFL 1789 to the Present

Barbour, John c. 1316-1395 .... **CMLC 33**
See also DLB 146

Barbusse, Henri 1873-1935 .... **TCLC 5**
See also CA 105; 154; DLB 65; EWL 3; RGWL 2, 3

Barclay, Alexander c. 1475-1552 .... **LC 109**
See also DLB 132

Barclay, Bill
See Moorcock, Michael

Barclay, William Ewert
See Moorcock, Michael

Barea, Arturo 1897-1957 .... **TCLC 14**
See also CA 111; 201

Barfoot, Joan 1946- .... **CLC 18**
See also CA 105; CANR 141

Barham, Richard Harris
1788-1845 .... **NCLC 77**
See also DLB 159

Baring, Maurice 1874-1945 .... **TCLC 8**
See also CA 105; 168; DLB 34; HGG

Baring-Gould, Sabine 1834-1924 ... **TCLC 88**
See also DLB 156, 190

Barker, Clive 1952- .... **CLC 52, 205; SSC 53**
See also AAYA 10, 54; BEST 90:3; BPFB 1; CA 121; 129; CANR 71, 111, 133; CPW; DA3; DAM POP; DLB 261; HGG; INT CA-129; MTCW 1, 2; MTFW 2005; SUFW 2

Barker, George Granville
1913-1991 .... **CLC 8, 48**
See also CA 9-12R; 135; CANR 7, 38; CP 1, 2, 3, 4, 5; DAM POET; DLB 20; EWL 3; MTCW 1

Barker, Harley Granville
See Granville-Barker, Harley
See also DLB 10

Barker, Howard 1946- .... **CLC 37**
See also CA 102; CBD; CD 5, 6; DLB 13, 233

Barker, Jane 1652-1732 .... **LC 42, 82**
See also DLB 39, 131

Barker, Pat 1943- .... **CLC 32, 94, 146**
See also BRWS 4; CA 117; 122; CANR 50, 101, 148; CN 6, 7; DLB 271, 326; INT CA-122

Barker, Patricia
See Barker, Pat

Barlach, Ernst (Heinrich)
1870-1938 .... **TCLC 84**
See also CA 178; DLB 56, 118; EWL 3

Barlow, Joel 1754-1812 .... **NCLC 23**
See also AMWS 2; DLB 37; RGAL 4

Barnard, Mary (Ethel) 1909- .... **CLC 48**
See also CA 21-22; CAP 2; CP 1

Barnes, Djuna 1892-1982 .... **CLC 3, 4, 8, 11, 29, 127; SSC 3**
See Steptoe, Lydia
See also AMWS 3; CA 9-12R; 107; CAD; CANR 16, 55; CN 1, 2, 3; CWD; DLB 4, 9, 45; EWL 3; GLL 1; MAL 5; MTCW 1, 2; MTFW 2005; RGAL 4; TCLE 1:1; TUS

Barnes, Jim 1933- .... **NNAL**
See also CA 108, 175; CAAE 175; CAAS 28; DLB 175

Barnes, Julian 1946- .... **CLC 42, 141**
See also BRWS 4; CA 102; CANR 19, 54, 115, 137; CN 4, 5, 6, 7; DAB; DLB 194; DLBY 1993; EWL 3; MTCW 2; MTFW 2005; SSFS 24

Barnes, Julian Patrick
See Barnes, Julian

Barnes, Peter 1931-2004 .... **CLC 5, 56**
See also CA 65-68; 230; CAAS 12; CANR 33, 34, 64, 113; CBD; CD 5, 6; DFS 6; DLB 13, 233; MTCW 1

Barnes, William 1801-1886 .... **NCLC 75**
See also DLB 32

Baroja, Pio 1872-1956 .... **HLC 1; TCLC 8**
See also CA 104; 247; EW 9

Baroja y Nessi, Pio
See Baroja, Pio

Baron, David
See Pinter, Harold

Baron Corvo
See Rolfe, Frederick (William Serafino Austin Lewis Mary)

Barondess, Sue K(aufman)
1926-1977 .... **CLC 8**
See Kaufman, Sue
See also CA 1-4R; 69-72; CANR 1

Baron de Teive
See Pessoa, Fernando (Antonio Nogueira)

Baroness Von S.
See Zangwill, Israel

Barres, (Auguste-)Maurice
1862-1923 .... **TCLC 47**
See also CA 164; DLB 123; GFL 1789 to the Present

Author Index

Bedford, Denton R. 1907-(?) .... **NNAL**
Bedford, Donald F.
    See Fearing, Kenneth (Flexner)
Beecher, Catharine Esther
    1800-1878 .... **NCLC 30**
    See also DLB 1, 243
Beecher, John 1904-1980 .... **CLC 6**
    See also AITN 1; CA 5-8R; 105; CANR 8;
    CP 1, 2, 3
Beer, Johann 1655-1700 .... **LC 5**
    See also DLB 168
Beer, Patricia 1924- .... **CLC 58**
    See also CA 61-64; 183; CANR 13, 46; CP
    1, 2, 3, 4, 5, 6; CWP; DLB 40; FW
Beerbohm, Max
    See Beerbohm, (Henry) Max(imilian)
Beerbohm, (Henry) Max(imilian)
    1872-1956 .... **TCLC 1, 24**
    See also BRWS 2; CA 104; 154; CANR 79;
    DLB 34, 100; FANT; MTCW 2
Beer-Hofmann, Richard
    1866-1945 .... **TCLC 60**
    See also CA 160; DLB 81
Beg, Shemus
    See Stephens, James
Begiebing, Robert J(ohn) 1946- .... **CLC 70**
    See also CA 122; CANR 40, 88
Begley, Louis 1933- .... **CLC 197**
    See also CA 140; CANR 98; DLB 299;
    RGHL; TCLE 1:1
Behan, Brendan (Francis)
    1923-1964 .... **CLC 1, 8, 11, 15, 79**
    See also BRWS 2; CA 73-76; CANR 33,
    121; CBD; CDBLB 1945-1960; DAM
    DRAM; DFS 7; DLB 13, 233; EWL 3;
    MTCW 1, 2
Behn, Aphra 1640(?)-1689 .. **DC 4; LC 1, 30,
    42; PC 13; WLC 1**
    See also BRWS 3; DA; DA3; DAB; DAC;
    DAM DRAM, MST, NOV, POET; DFS
    16; DLB 39, 80, 131; FW; TEA; WLIT 3
Behrman, S(amuel) N(athaniel)
    1893-1973 .... **CLC 40**
    See also CA 13-16; 45-48; CAD; CAP 1;
    DLB 7, 44; IDFW 3; MAL 5; RGAL 4
Bekederemo, J. P. Clark
    See Clark Bekederemo, J.P.
    See also CD 6
Belasco, David 1853-1931 .... **TCLC 3**
    See also CA 104; 168; DLB 7; MAL 5;
    RGAL 4
Belcheva, Elisaveta Lyubomirova
    1893-1991 .... **CLC 10**
    See Bagryana, Elisaveta
Beldone, Phil "Cheech"
    See Ellison, Harlan
Beleno
    See Azuela, Mariano
Belinski, Vissarion Grigoryevich
    1811-1848 .... **NCLC 5**
    See also DLB 198
Belitt, Ben 1911- .... **CLC 22**
    See also CA 13-16R; CAAS 4; CANR 7,
    77; CP 1, 2, 3, 4, 5, 6; DLB 5
Belknap, Jeremy 1744-1798 .... **LC 115**
    See also DLB 30, 37
Bell, Gertrude (Margaret Lowthian)
    1868-1926 .... **TCLC 67**
    See also CA 167; CANR 110; DLB 174
Bell, J. Freeman
    See Zangwill, Israel
Bell, James Madison 1826-1902 .... **BLC 1;
    TCLC 43**
    See also BW 1; CA 122; 124; DAM MULT;
    DLB 50

Bell, Madison Smartt 1957- ..... **CLC 41, 102,
    223**
    See also AMWS 10; BPFB 1; CA 111, 183;
    CAAE 183; CANR 28, 54, 73, 134; CN
    5, 6, 7; CSW; DLB 218, 278; MTCW 2;
    MTFW 2005
Bell, Marvin (Hartley) 1937- .... **CLC 8, 31**
    See also CA 21-24R; CAAS 14; CANR 59,
    102; CP 1, 2, 3, 4, 5, 6, 7; DAM POET;
    DLB 5; MAL 5; MTCW 1
Bell, W. L. D.
    See Mencken, H(enry) L(ouis)
Bellamy, Atwood C.
    See Mencken, H(enry) L(ouis)
Bellamy, Edward 1850-1898 ..... **NCLC 4, 86,
    147**
    See also DLB 12; NFS 15; RGAL 4; SFW
    4
Belli, Gioconda 1948- .... **HLCS 1**
    See also CA 152; CANR 143; CWW 2;
    DLB 290; EWL 3; RGWL 3
Bellin, Edward J.
    See Kuttner, Henry
Bello, Andres 1781-1865 .... **NCLC 131**
    See also LAW
**Belloc, (Joseph) Hilaire (Pierre Sebastien
    Rene Swanton)** 1870-1953 .... **PC 24;
    TCLC 7, 18**
    See also CA 106; 152; CLR 102; CWRI 5;
    DAM POET; DLB 19, 100, 141, 174;
    EWL 3; MTCW 2; MTFW 2005; SATA
    112; WCH; YABC 1
Belloc, Joseph Peter Rene Hilaire
    See Belloc, (Joseph) Hilaire (Pierre Sebas-
    tien Rene Swanton)
Belloc, Joseph Pierre Hilaire
    See Belloc, (Joseph) Hilaire (Pierre Sebas-
    tien Rene Swanton)
Belloc, M. A.
    See Lowndes, Marie Adelaide (Belloc)
Belloc-Lowndes, Mrs.
    See Lowndes, Marie Adelaide (Belloc)
Bellow, Saul 1915-2005 ...... **CLC 1, 2, 3, 6, 8,
    10, 13, 15, 25, 33, 34, 63, 79, 190, 200;
    SSC 14; WLC 1**
    See also AITN 2; AMW; AMWC 2; AMWR
    2; BEST 89:3; BPFB 1; CA 5-8R; 238;
    CABS 1; CANR 29, 53, 95, 132; CDALB
    1941-1968; CN 1, 2, 3, 4, 5, 6, 7; DA;
    DA3; DAB; DAC; DAM MST, NOV,
    POP; DLB 2, 28, 299, 329; DLBD 3;
    DLBY 1982; EWL 3; MAL 5; MTCW 1,
    2; MTFW 2005; NFS 4, 14; RGAL 4;
    RGHL; RGSF 2; SSFS 12, 22; TUS
Belser, Reimond Karel Maria de 1929-
    See Ruyslinck, Ward
    See also CA 152
Bely, Andrey .... **PC 11; TCLC 7**
    See Bugayev, Boris Nikolayevich
    See also DLB 295; EW 9; EWL 3
Belyi, Andrei
    See Bugayev, Boris Nikolayevich
    See also RGWL 2, 3
Bembo, Pietro 1470-1547 .... **LC 79**
    See also RGWL 2, 3
Benary, Margot
    See Benary-Isbert, Margot
Benary-Isbert, Margot 1889-1979 .... **CLC 12**
    See also CA 5-8R; 89-92; CANR 4, 72;
    CLR 12; MAICYA 1, 2; SATA 2; SATA-
    Obit 21
Benavente (y Martinez), Jacinto
    1866-1954 .... **DC 26; HLCS 1; TCLC 3**
    See also CA 106; 131; CANR 81; DAM
    DRAM, MULT; DLB 329; EWL 3; GLL
    2; HW 1, 2; MTCW 1, 2

Benchley, Peter 1940-2006 .... **CLC 4, 8**
    See also AAYA 14; AITN 2; BPFB 1; CA
    17-20R; 248; CANR 12, 35, 66, 115;
    CPW; DAM NOV, POP; HGG; MTCW 1,
    2; MTFW 2005; SATA 3, 89, 164
Benchley, Peter Bradford
    See Benchley, Peter
Benchley, Robert (Charles)
    1889-1945 .... **TCLC 1, 55**
    See also CA 105; 153; DLB 11; MAL 5;
    RGAL 4
Benda, Julien 1867-1956 .... **TCLC 60**
    See also CA 120; 154; GFL 1789 to the
    Present
Benedict, Ruth 1887-1948 .... **TCLC 60**
    See also CA 158; CANR 146; DLB 246
Benedict, Ruth Fulton
    See Benedict, Ruth
Benedikt, Michael 1935- .... **CLC 4, 14**
    See also CA 13-16R; CANR 7; CP 1, 2, 3,
    4, 5, 6, 7; DLB 5
Benet, Juan 1927-1993 .... **CLC 28**
    See also CA 143; EWL 3
Benet, Stephen Vincent 1898-1943 ..... **PC 64;
    SSC 10, 86; TCLC 7**
    See also AMWS 11; CA 104; 152; DA3;
    DAM POET; DLB 4, 48, 102, 249, 284;
    DLBY 1997; EWL 3; HGG; MAL 5;
    MTCW 2; MTFW 2005; RGAL 4; RGSF
    2; SSFS 22; SUFW; WP; YABC 1
Benet, William Rose 1886-1950 ..... **TCLC 28**
    See also CA 118; 152; DAM POET; DLB
    45; RGAL 4
Benford, Gregory (Albert) 1941- ..... **CLC 52**
    See also BPFB 1; CA 69-72, 175; CAAE
    175; CAAS 27; CANR 12, 24, 49, 95,
    134; CN 7; CSW; DLBY 1982; MTFW
    2005; SCFW 2; SFW 4
Bengtsson, Frans (Gunnar)
    1894-1954 .... **TCLC 48**
    See also CA 170; EWL 3
Benjamin, David
    See Slavitt, David R(ytman)
Benjamin, Lois
    See Gould, Lois
Benjamin, Walter 1892-1940 .... **TCLC 39**
    See also CA 164; DLB 242; EW 11; EWL
    3
Ben Jelloun, Tahar 1944-
    See Jelloun, Tahar ben
    See also CA 135; CWW 2; EWL 3; RGWL
    3; WLIT 2
Benn, Gottfried 1886-1956 .. **PC 35; TCLC 3**
    See also CA 106; 153; DLB 56; EWL 3;
    RGWL 2, 3
Bennett, Alan 1934- .... **CLC 45, 77**
    See also BRWS 8; CA 103; CANR 35, 55,
    106, 157; CBD; CD 5, 6; DAB; DAM
    MST; DLB 310; MTCW 1, 2; MTFW
    2005
Bennett, (Enoch) Arnold
    1867-1931 .... **TCLC 5, 20**
    See also BRW 6; CA 106; 155; CDBLB
    1890-1914; DLB 10, 34, 98, 135; EWL 3;
    MTCW 2
Bennett, Elizabeth
    See Mitchell, Margaret (Munnerlyn)
Bennett, George Harold 1930-
    See Bennett, Hal
    See also BW 1; CA 97-100; CANR 87
Bennett, Gwendolyn B. 1902-1981 .... **HR 1:2**
    See also BW 1; CA 125; DLB 51; WP
Bennett, Hal .... **CLC 5**
    See Bennett, George Harold
    See also CAAS 13; DLB 33
Bennett, Jay 1912- .... **CLC 35**
    See also AAYA 10; CA 69-72; CANR 11,
    42, 79; JRDA; SAAS 4; SATA 41, 87;
    SATA-Brief 27; WYA; YAW

Bennett, Louise 1919-2006 .. **BLC 1; CLC 28**
See also BW 2, 3; CA 151; CDWLB 3; CP
1, 2, 3, 4, 5, 6, 7; DAM MULT; DLB 117;
EWL 3

Bennett-Coverley, Louise
See Bennett, Louise

Benson, A. C. 1862-1925 .... **TCLC 123**
See also DLB 98

Benson, E(dward) F(rederic)
1867-1940 .... **TCLC 27**
See also CA 114; 157; DLB 135, 153;
HGG; SUFW 1

Benson, Jackson J. 1930- .... **CLC 34**
See also CA 25-28R; DLB 111

Benson, Sally 1900-1972 .... **CLC 17**
See also CA 19-20; 37-40R; CAP 1; SATA
1, 35; SATA-Obit 27

Benson, Stella 1892-1933 .... **TCLC 17**
See also CA 117; 154, 155; DLB 36, 162;
FANT; TEA

Bentham, Jeremy 1748-1832 .... **NCLC 38**
See also DLB 107, 158, 252

Bentley, E(dmund) C(lerihew)
1875-1956 .... **TCLC 12**
See also CA 108; 232; DLB 70; MSW

Bentley, Eric 1916- .... **CLC 24**
See also CA 5-8R; CAD; CANR 6, 67;
CBD; CD 5, 6; INT CANR-6

Bentley, Eric Russell
See Bentley, Eric

ben Uzair, Salem
See Horne, Richard Henry Hengist

Beranger, Pierre Jean de
1780-1857 .... **NCLC 34**

Berdyaev, Nicolas
See Berdyaev, Nikolai (Aleksandrovich)

Berdyaev, Nikolai (Aleksandrovich)
1874-1948 .... **TCLC 67**
See also CA 120; 157

Berdyayev, Nikolai (Aleksandrovich)
See Berdyaev, Nikolai (Aleksandrovich)

Berendt, John 1939- .... **CLC 86**
See also CA 146; CANR 75, 83, 151

Berendt, John Lawrence
See Berendt, John

Beresford, J(ohn) D(avys)
1873-1947 .... **TCLC 81**
See also CA 112; 155; DLB 162, 178, 197;
SFW 4; SUFW 1

Bergelson, David (Rafailovich)
1884-1952 .... **TCLC 81**
See Bergelson, Dovid
See also CA 220

Bergelson, Dovid
See Bergelson, David (Rafailovich)
See also EWL 3

Berger, Colonel
See Malraux, (Georges-)Andre

Berger, John (Peter) 1926- .... **CLC 2, 19**
See also BRWS 4; CA 81-84; CANR 51,
78, 117; CN 1, 2, 3, 4, 5, 6, 7; DLB 14,
207, 319, 326

Berger, Melvin H. 1927- .... **CLC 12**
See also CA 5-8R; CANR 4, 142; CLR 32;
SAAS 2; SATA 5, 88, 158; SATA-Essay
124

Berger, Thomas 1924- .... **CLC 3, 5, 8, 11, 18,**
38
See also BPFB 1; CA 1-4R; CANR 5, 28,
51, 128; CN 1, 2, 3, 4, 5, 6, 7; DAM
NOV; DLB 2; DLBY 1980; EWL 3;
FANT; INT CANR-28; MAL 5; MTCW
1, 2; MTFW 2005; RHW; TCLE 1:1;
TCWW 1, 2

Bergman, (Ernst) Ingmar 1918- ...... **CLC 16,**
72, 210
See also AAYA 61; CA 81-84; CANR 33,
70; CWW 2; DLB 257; MTCW 2; MTFW
2005

Bergson, Henri(-Louis) 1859-1941 . **TCLC 32**
See also CA 164; DLB 329; EW 8; EWL 3;
GFL 1789 to the Present

Bergstein, Eleanor 1938- .... **CLC 4**
See also CA 53-56; CANR 5

Berkeley, George 1685-1753 .... **LC 65**
See also DLB 31, 101, 252

Berkoff, Steven 1937- .... **CLC 56**
See also CA 104; CANR 72; CBD; CD 5, 6

Berlin, Isaiah 1909-1997 .... **TCLC 105**
See also CA 85-88; 162

Bermant, Chaim (Icyk) 1929-1998 ... **CLC 40**
See also CA 57-60; CANR 6, 31, 57, 105;
CN 2, 3, 4, 5, 6

Bern, Victoria
See Fisher, M(ary) F(rances) K(ennedy)

Bernanos, (Paul Louis) Georges
1888-1948 .... **TCLC 3**
See also CA 104; 130; CANR 94; DLB 72;
EWL 3; GFL 1789 to the Present; RGWL
2, 3

Bernard, April 1956- .... **CLC 59**
See also CA 131; CANR 144

Bernard, Mary Ann
See Soderbergh, Steven

Bernard of Clairvaux 1090-1153 .. **CMLC 71**
See also DLB 208

Berne, Victoria
See Fisher, M(ary) F(rances) K(ennedy)

Bernhard, Thomas 1931-1989 ..... **CLC 3, 32,**
61; DC 14; TCLC 165
See also CA 85-88; 127; CANR 32, 57; CD-
WLB 2; DLB 85, 124; EWL 3; MTCW 1;
RGHL; RGWL 2, 3

Bernhardt, Sarah (Henriette Rosine)
1844-1923 .... **TCLC 75**
See also CA 157

Bernstein, Charles 1950- .... **CLC 142,**
See also CA 129; CAAS 24; CANR 90; CP
4, 5, 6, 7; DLB 169

Bernstein, Ingrid
See Kirsch, Sarah

Beroul fl. c. 12th cent. - .... **CMLC 75**

Berriault, Gina 1926-1999 .... **CLC 54, 109;**
SSC 30
See also CA 116; 129; 185; CANR 66; DLB
130; SSFS 7,11

Berrigan, Daniel 1921- .... **CLC 4**
See also CA 33-36R; 187; CAAE 187;
CAAS 1; CANR 11, 43, 78; CP 1, 2, 3, 4,
5, 6, 7; DLB 5

Berrigan, Edmund Joseph Michael, Jr.
1934-1983
See Berrigan, Ted
See also CA 61-64; 110; CANR 14, 102

Berrigan, Ted .... **CLC 37**
See Berrigan, Edmund Joseph Michael, Jr.
See also CP 1, 2, 3; DLB 5, 169; WP

Berry, Charles Edward Anderson 1931-
See Berry, Chuck
See also CA 115

Berry, Chuck .... **CLC 17**
See Berry, Charles Edward Anderson

Berry, Jonas
See Ashbery, John
See also GLL 1

Berry, Wendell 1934- .... **CLC 4, 6, 8, 27, 46;**
PC 28
See also AITN 1; AMWS 10; ANW; CA
73-76; CANR 50, 73, 101, 132; CP 1, 2,
3, 4, 5, 6, 7; CSW; DAM POET; DLB 5,
6, 234, 275; MTCW 2; MTFW 2005;
TCLE 1:1

Berryman, John 1914-1972 ... **CLC 1, 2, 3, 4,**
6, 8, 10, 13, 25, 62; PC 64
See also AMW; CA 13-16; 33-36R; CABS
2; CANR 35; CAP 1; CDALB 1941-1968;
CP 1; DAM POET; DLB 48; EWL 3;
MAL 5; MTCW 1, 2; MTFW 2005; PAB;
RGAL 4; WP

Bertolucci, Bernardo 1940- ...... **CLC 16, 157**
See also CA 106; CANR 125

Berton, Pierre (Francis de Marigny)
1920-2004 .... **CLC 104**
See also CA 1-4R; 233; CANR 2, 56, 144;
CPW; DLB 68; SATA 99; SATA-Obit 158

Bertrand, Aloysius 1807-1841 .... **NCLC 31**
See Bertrand, Louis oAloysiusc

Bertrand, Louis oAloysiusc
See Bertrand, Aloysius
See also DLB 217

Bertran de Born c. 1140-1215 .... **CMLC 5**

Besant, Annie (Wood) 1847-1933 ..... **TCLC 9**
See also CA 105; 185

Bessie, Alvah 1904-1985 .... **CLC 23**
See also CA 5-8R; 116; CANR 2, 80; DLB
26

Bestuzhev, Aleksandr Aleksandrovich
1797-1837 .... **NCLC 131**
See also DLB 198

Bethlen, T. D.
See Silverberg, Robert

Beti, Mongo .... **BLC 1; CLC 27**
See Biyidi, Alexandre
See also AFW; CANR 79; DAM MULT;
EWL 3; WLIT 2

Betjeman, John 1906-1984 ...... **CLC 2, 6, 10,**
34, 43
See also BRW 7; CA 9-12R; 112; CANR
33, 56; CDBLB 1945-1960; CP 1, 2, 3;
DA3; DAB; DAM MST, POET; DLB 20;
DLBY 1984; EWL 3; MTCW 1, 2

Bettelheim, Bruno 1903-1990 .... **CLC 79;**
TCLC 143
See also CA 81-84; 131; CANR 23, 61;
DA3; MTCW 1, 2; RGHL

Betti, Ugo 1892-1953 .... **TCLC 5**
See also CA 104; 155; EWL 3; RGWL 2, 3

Betts, Doris (Waugh) 1932- ..... **CLC 3, 6, 28;**
SSC 45
See also CA 13-16R; CANR 9, 66, 77; CN
6, 7; CSW; DLB 218; DLBY 1982; INT
CANR-9; RGAL 4

Bevan, Alistair
See Roberts, Keith (John Kingston)

Bey, Pilaff
See Douglas, (George) Norman

Bialik, Chaim Nachman
1873-1934 .... **TCLC 25**
See Bialik, Hayyim Nahman
See also CA 170; EWL 3

Bialik, Hayyim Nahman
See Bialik, Chaim Nachman
See also WLIT 6

Bickerstaff, Isaac
See Swift, Jonathan

Bidart, Frank 1939- .... **CLC 33**
See also AMWS 15; CA 140; CANR 106;
CP 5, 6, 7

Bienek, Horst 1930- .... **CLC 7, 11**
See also CA 73-76; DLB 75

Bierce, Ambrose (Gwinett)
1842-1914(?) ..... **SSC 9, 72; TCLC 1, 7,**
44; WLC 1
See also AAYA 55; AMW; BYA 11; CA
104; 139; CANR 78; CDALB 1865-1917;
DA; DA3; DAC; DAM MST; DLB 11,
12, 23, 71, 74, 186; EWL 3; EXPS; HGG;
LAIT 2; MAL 5; RGAL 4; RGSF 2; SSFS
9; SUFW 1

Biggers, Earl Derr 1884-1933 .... **TCLC 65**
See also CA 108; 153; DLB 306

Billiken, Bud
See Motley, Willard (Francis)

Billings, Josh
See Shaw, Henry Wheeler

Boyd, Nancy
See Millay, Edna St. Vincent
See also GLL 1

Boyd, Thomas (Alexander)
1898-1935 .... **TCLC 111**
See also CA 111; 183; DLB 9; DLBD 16, 316

Boyd, William (Andrew Murray)
1952- .... **CLC 28, 53, 70**
See also CA 114; 120; CANR 51, 71, 131; CN 4, 5, 6, 7; DLB 231

Boyesen, Hjalmar Hjorth
1848-1895 .... **NCLC 135**
See also DLB 12, 71; DLBD 13; RGAL 4

Boyle, Kay 1902-1992 .... **CLC 1, 5, 19, 58, 121; SSC 5**
See also CA 13-16R; 140; CAAS 1; CANR 29, 61, 110; CN 1, 2, 3, 4, 5; DLB 4, 9, 48, 86; DLBY 1993; EWL 3; MAL 5; MTCW 1, 2; MTFW 2005; RGAL 4; RGSF 2; SSFS 10, 13, 14

Boyle, Mark
See Kienzle, William X.

Boyle, Patrick 1905-1982 .... **CLC 19**
See also CA 127

Boyle, T. C.
See Boyle, T. Coraghessan
See also AMWS 8

Boyle, T. Coraghessan 1948- ..... **CLC 36, 55, 90; SSC 16**
See Boyle, T. C.
See also AAYA 47; BEST 90:4; BPFB 1; CA 120; CANR 44, 76, 89, 132; CN 6, 7; CPW; DA3; DAM POP; DLB 218, 278; DLBY 1986; EWL 3; MAL 5; MTCW 2; MTFW 2005; SSFS 13, 19

Boz
See Dickens, Charles (John Huffam)

Brackenridge, Hugh Henry
1748-1816 .... **NCLC 7**
See also DLB 11, 37; RGAL 4

Bradbury, Edward P.
See Moorcock, Michael
See also MTCW 2

Bradbury, Malcolm (Stanley)
1932-2000 .... **CLC 32, 61**
See also CA 1-4R; CANR 1, 33, 91, 98, 137; CN 1, 2, 3, 4, 5, 6, 7; CP 1; DA3; DAM NOV; DLB 14, 207; EWL 3; MTCW 1, 2; MTFW 2005

Bradbury, Ray 1920- ... **CLC 1, 3, 10, 15, 42, 98; SSC 29, 53; WLC 1**
See also AAYA 15; AITN 1, 2; AMWS 4; BPFB 1; BYA 4, 5, 11; CA 1-4R; CANR 2, 30, 75, 125; CDALB 1968-1988; CN 1, 2, 3, 4, 5, 6, 7; CPW; DA; DA3; DAB; DAC; DAM MST, NOV, POP; DLB 2, 8; EXPN; EXPS; HGG; LAIT 3, 5; LATS 1:2; LMFS 2; MAL 5; MTCW 1, 2; MTFW 2005; NFS 1, 22; RGAL 4; RGSF 2; SATA 11, 64, 123; SCFW 1, 2; SFW 4; SSFS 1, 20; SUFW 1, 2; TUS; YAW

Braddon, Mary Elizabeth
1837-1915 .... **TCLC 111**
See also BRWS 8; CA 108; 179; CMW 4; DLB 18, 70, 156; HGG

Bradfield, Scott 1955- .... **SSC 65**
See also CA 147; CANR 90; HGG; SUFW 2

Bradfield, Scott Michael
See Bradfield, Scott

Bradford, Gamaliel 1863-1932 .... **TCLC 36**
See also CA 160; DLB 17

Bradford, William 1590-1657 .... **LC 64**
See also DLB 24, 30; RGAL 4

Bradley, David (Henry), Jr. 1950- ... **BLC 1; CLC 23, 118**
See also BW 1, 3; CA 104; CANR 26, 81; CN 4, 5, 6, 7; DAM MULT; DLB 33

Bradley, John Ed 1958- .... **CLC 55**
See also CA 139; CANR 99; CN 6, 7; CSW

Bradley, John Edmund, Jr.
See Bradley, John Ed

Bradley, Marion Zimmer
1930-1999 .... **CLC 30**
See Chapman, Lee; Dexter, John; Gardner, Miriam; Ives, Morgan; Rivers, Elfrida
See also AAYA 40; BPFB 1; CA 57-60; 185; CAAS 10; CANR 7, 31, 51, 75, 107; CPW; DA3; DAM POP; DLB 8; FANT; FW; MTCW 1, 2; MTFW 2005; SATA 90, 139; SATA-Obit 116; SFW 4; SUFW 2; YAW

Bradshaw, John 1933- .... **CLC 70**
See also CA 138; CANR 61

Bradstreet, Anne 1612(?)-1672 .... **LC 4, 30, 130; PC 10**
See also AMWS 1; CDALB 1640-1865; DA; DA3; DAC; DAM MST, POET; DLB 24; EXPP; FW; PFS 6; RGAL 4; TUS; WP

Brady, Joan 1939- .... **CLC 86**
See also CA 141

Bragg, Melvyn 1939- .... **CLC 10**
See also BEST 89:3; CA 57-60; CANR 10, 48, 89; CN 1, 2, 3, 4, 5, 6, 7; DLB 14, 271; RHW

Brahe, Tycho 1546-1601 .... **LC 45**
See also DLB 300

Braine, John (Gerard) 1922-1986 . **CLC 1, 3, 41**
See also CA 1-4R; 120; CANR 1, 33; CDBLB 1945-1960; CN 1, 2, 3, 4; DLB 15; DLBY 1986; EWL 3; MTCW 1

Braithwaite, William Stanley (Beaumont)
1878-1962 .... **BLC 1; HR 1:2; PC 52**
See also BW 1; CA 125; DAM MULT; DLB 50, 54; MAL 5

Bramah, Ernest 1868-1942 .... **TCLC 72**
See also CA 156; CMW 4; DLB 70; FANT

Brammer, Billy Lee
See Brammer, William

Brammer, William 1929-1978 .... **CLC 31**
See also CA 235; 77-80

Brancati, Vitaliano 1907-1954 .... **TCLC 12**
See also CA 109; DLB 264; EWL 3

Brancato, Robin F(idler) 1936- .... **CLC 35**
See also AAYA 9, 68; BYA 6; CA 69-72; CANR 11, 45; CLR 32; JRDA; MAICYA 2; MAICYAS 1; SAAS 9; SATA 97; WYA; YAW

Brand, Dionne 1953- .... **CLC 192**
See also BW 2; CA 143; CANR 143; CWP

Brand, Max
See Faust, Frederick (Schiller)
See also BPFB 1; TCWW 1, 2

Brand, Millen 1906-1980 .... **CLC 7**
See also CA 21-24R; 97-100; CANR 72

Branden, Barbara .... **CLC 44**
See also CA 148

Brandes, Georg (Morris Cohen)
1842-1927 .... **TCLC 10**
See also CA 105; 189; DLB 300

Brandys, Kazimierz 1916-2000 .... **CLC 62**
See also CA 239; EWL 3

Branley, Franklyn M(ansfield)
1915-2002 .... **CLC 21**
See also CA 33-36R; 207; CANR 14, 39; CLR 13; MAICYA 1, 2; SAAS 16; SATA 4, 68, 136

Brant, Beth (E.) 1941- .... **NNAL**
See also CA 144; FW

Brant, Sebastian 1457-1521 .... **LC 112**
See also DLB 179; RGWL 2, 3

Brathwaite, Edward Kamau
1930- .... **BLCS; CLC 11; PC 56**
See also BRWS 12; BW 2, 3; CA 25-28R; CANR 11, 26, 47, 107; CDWLB 3; CP 1, 2, 3, 4, 5, 6, 7; DAM POET; DLB 125; EWL 3

Brathwaite, Kamau
See Brathwaite, Edward Kamau

Brautigan, Richard (Gary)
1935-1984 .... **CLC 1, 3, 5, 9, 12, 34, 42; TCLC 133**
See also BPFB 1; CA 53-56; 113; CANR 34; CN 1, 2, 3; CP 1, 2, 3, 4; DA3; DAM NOV; DLB 2, 5, 206; DLBY 1980, 1984; FANT; MAL 5; MTCW 1; RGAL 4; SATA 56

Brave Bird, Mary .... **NNAL**
See Crow Dog, Mary

Braverman, Kate 1950- .... **CLC 67**
See also CA 89-92; CANR 141

Brecht, (Eugen) Bertolt (Friedrich)
1898-1956 ..... **DC 3; TCLC 1, 6, 13, 35, 169; WLC 1**
See also CA 104; 133; CANR 62; CDWLB 2; DA; DA3; DAB; DAC; DAM DRAM, MST; DFS 4, 5, 9; DLB 56, 124; EW 11; EWL 3; IDTP; MTCW 1, 2; MTFW 2005; RGHL; RGWL 2, 3; TWA

Brecht, Eugen Berthold Friedrich
See Brecht, (Eugen) Bertolt (Friedrich)

Bremer, Fredrika 1801-1865 .... **NCLC 11**
See also DLB 254

Brennan, Christopher John
1870-1932 .... **TCLC 17**
See also CA 117; 188; DLB 230; EWL 3

Brennan, Maeve 1917-1993 ... **CLC 5; TCLC 124**
See also CA 81-84; CANR 72, 100

Brenner, Jozef 1887-1919
See Csath, Geza
See also CA 240

Brent, Linda
See Jacobs, Harriet A(nn)

Brentano, Clemens (Maria)
1778-1842 .... **NCLC 1**
See also DLB 90; RGWL 2, 3

Brent of Bin Bin
See Franklin, (Stella Maria Sarah) Miles (Lampe)

Brenton, Howard 1942- .... **CLC 31**
See also CA 69-72; CANR 33, 67; CBD; CD 5, 6; DLB 13; MTCW 1

Breslin, James 1930-
See Breslin, Jimmy
See also CA 73-76; CANR 31, 75, 139; DAM NOV; MTCW 1, 2; MTFW 2005

Breslin, Jimmy .... **CLC 4, 43**
See Breslin, James
See also AITN 1; DLB 185; MTCW 2

Bresson, Robert 1901(?)-1999 .... **CLC 16**
See also CA 110; 187; CANR 49

Breton, Andre 1896-1966 .. **CLC 2, 9, 15, 54; PC 15**
See also CA 19-20; 25-28R; CANR 40, 60; CAP 2; DLB 65, 258; EW 11; EWL 3; GFL 1789 to the Present; LMFS 2; MTCW 1, 2; MTFW 2005; RGWL 2, 3; TWA; WP

Breytenbach, Breyten 1939(?)- .. **CLC 23, 37, 126**
See also CA 113; 129; CANR 61, 122; CWW 2; DAM POET; DLB 225; EWL 3

Bridgers, Sue Ellen 1942- .... **CLC 26**
See also AAYA 8, 49; BYA 7, 8; CA 65-68; CANR 11, 36; CLR 18; DLB 52; JRDA; MAICYA 1, 2; SAAS 1; SATA 22, 90; SATA-Essay 109; WYA; YAW

Bridges, Robert (Seymour)
1844-1930 .... **PC 28; TCLC 1**
See also BRW 6; CA 104; 152; CDBLB
1890-1914; DAM POET; DLB 19, 98
Bridie, James .... **TCLC 3**
See Mavor, Osborne Henry
See also DLB 10; EWL 3
Brin, David 1950- .... **CLC 34**
See also AAYA 21; CA 102; CANR 24, 70,
125, 127; INT CANR-24; SATA 65;
SCFW 2; SFW 4
Brink, Andre 1935- .... **CLC 18, 36, 106**
See also AFW; BRWS 6; CA 104; CANR
39, 62, 109, 133; CN 4, 5, 6, 7; DLB 225;
EWL 3; INT CA-103; LATS 1:2; MTCW
1, 2; MTFW 2005; WLIT 2
Brinsmead, H. F.
See Brinsmead, H(esba) F(ay)
Brinsmead, H. F(ay)
See Brinsmead, H(esba) F(ay)
Brinsmead, H(esba) F(ay) 1922- ...... **CLC 21**
See also CA 21-24R; CANR 10; CLR 47;
CWRI 5; MAICYA 1, 2; SAAS 5; SATA
18, 78
Brittain, Vera (Mary) 1893(?)-1970 . **CLC 23**
See also BRWS 10; CA 13-16; 25-28R;
CANR 58; CAP 1; DLB 191; FW; MTCW
1, 2
Broch, Hermann 1886-1951 .... **TCLC 20**
See also CA 117; 211; CDWLB 2; DLB 85,
124; EW 10; EWL 3; RGWL 2, 3
Brock, Rose
See Hansen, Joseph
See also GLL 1
Brod, Max 1884-1968 .... **TCLC 115**
See also CA 5-8R; 25-28R; CANR 7; DLB
81; EWL 3
Brodkey, Harold (Roy) 1930-1996 .. **CLC 56;**
TCLC 123
See also CA 111; 151; CANR 71; CN 4, 5,
6; DLB 130
Brodsky, Iosif Alexandrovich 1940-1996
See Brodsky, Joseph
See also AITN 1; CA 41-44R; 151; CANR
37, 106; DA3; DAM POET; MTCW 1, 2;
MTFW 2005; RGWL 2, 3
Brodsky, Joseph . **CLC 4, 6, 13, 36, 100; PC**
9
See Brodsky, Iosif Alexandrovich
See also AAYA 71; AMWS 8; CWW 2;
DLB 285, 329; EWL 3; MTCW 1
Brodsky, Michael 1948- .... **CLC 19**
See also CA 102; CANR 18, 41, 58, 147;
DLB 244
Brodsky, Michael Mark
See Brodsky, Michael
Brodzki, Bella .... **CLC 65**
Brome, Richard 1590(?)-1652 .... **LC 61**
See also BRWS 10; DLB 58
Bromell, Henry 1947- .... **CLC 5**
See also CA 53-56; CANR 9, 115, 116
Bromfield, Louis (Brucker)
1896-1956 .... **TCLC 11**
See also CA 107; 155; DLB 4, 9, 86; RGAL
4; RHW
Broner, E(sther) M(asserman)
1930- .... **CLC 19**
See also CA 17-20R; CANR 8, 25, 72; CN
4, 5, 6; DLB 28
Bronk, William (M.) 1918-1999 .... **CLC 10**
See also CA 89-92; 177; CANR 23; CP 3,
4, 5, 6, 7; DLB 165
Bronstein, Lev Davidovich
See Trotsky, Leon
Bronte, Anne
See Bronte, Anne
Bronte, Anne 1820-1849 ..... **NCLC 4, 71, 102**
See also BRW 5; BRWR 1; DA3; DLB 21,
199; TEA

Bronte, (Patrick) Branwell
1817-1848 .... **NCLC 109**
Bronte, Charlotte
See Bronte, Charlotte
Bronte, Charlotte 1816-1855 ...... **NCLC 3, 8,**
33, 58, 105, 155; WLC 1
See also AAYA 17; BRW 5; BRWC 2;
BRWR 1; BYA 2; CDBLB 1832-1890;
DA; DA3; DAB; DAC; DAM MST, NOV;
DLB 21, 159, 199; EXPN; FL 1:2; GL 2;
LAIT 2; NFS 4; TEA; WLIT 4
Bronte, Emily
See Bronte, Emily (Jane)
Bronte, Emily (Jane) 1818-1848 ... **NCLC 16,**
35, 165; PC 8; WLC 1
See also AAYA 17; BPFB 1; BRW 5;
BRWC 1; BRWR 1; BYA 3; CDBLB
1832-1890; DA; DA3; DAB; DAC; DAM
MST, NOV, POET; DLB 21, 32, 199;
EXPN; FL 1:2; GL 2; LAIT 1; TEA;
WLIT 3
Brontes
See Bronte, Anne; Bronte, Charlotte; Bronte,
Emily (Jane)
Brooke, Frances 1724-1789 .... **LC 6, 48**
See also DLB 39, 99
Brooke, Henry 1703(?)-1783 .... **LC 1**
See also DLB 39
Brooke, Rupert (Chawner)
1887-1915 .. **PC 24; TCLC 2, 7; WLC 1**
See also BRWS 3; CA 104; 132; CANR 61;
CDBLB 1914-1945; DA; DAB; DAC;
DAM MST, POET; DLB 19, 216; EXPP;
GLL 2; MTCW 1, 2; MTFW 2005; PFS
7; TEA
Brooke-Haven, P.
See Wodehouse, P(elham) G(renville)
Brooke-Rose, Christine 1926(?)- ..... **CLC 40,**
184
See also BRWS 4; CA 13-16R; CANR 58,
118; CN 1, 2, 3, 4, 5, 6, 7; DLB 14, 231;
EWL 3; SFW 4
Brookner, Anita 1928- .. **CLC 32, 34, 51, 136**
See also BRWS 4; CA 114; 120; CANR 37,
56, 87, 130; CN 4, 5, 6, 7; CPW; DA3;
DAB; DAM POP; DLB 194, 326; DLBY
1987; EWL 3; MTCW 1, 2; MTFW 2005;
NFS 23; TEA
Brooks, Cleanth 1906-1994 . **CLC 24, 86, 110**
See also AMWS 14; CA 17-20R; 145;
CANR 33, 35; CSW; DLB 63; DLBY
1994; EWL 3; INT CANR-35; MAL 5;
MTCW 1, 2; MTFW 2005
Brooks, George
See Baum, L(yman) Frank
Brooks, Gwendolyn 1917-2000 .... **BLC 1;**
CLC 1, 2, 4, 5, 15, 49, 125; PC 7;
WLC 1
See also AAYA 20; AFAW 1, 2; AITN 1;
AMWS 3; BW 2, 3; CA 1-4R; 190; CANR
1, 27, 52, 75, 132; CDALB 1941-1968;
CLR 27; CP 1, 2, 3, 4, 5, 6, 7; CWP; DA;
DA3; DAC; DAM MST, MULT, POET;
DLB 5, 76, 165; EWL 3; EXPP; FL 1:5;
MAL 5; MBL; MTCW 1, 2; MTFW 2005;
PFS 1, 2, 4, 6; RGAL 4; SATA 6; SATA-
Obit 123; TUS; WP
Brooks, Mel 1926-
See Kaminsky, Melvin
See also CA 65-68; CANR 16; DFS 21
Brooks, Peter (Preston) 1938- .... **CLC 34**
See also CA 45-48; CANR 1, 107
Brooks, Van Wyck 1886-1963 .... **CLC 29**
See also AMW; CA 1-4R; CANR 6; DLB
45, 63, 103; MAL 5; TUS
Brophy, Brigid (Antonia)
1929-1995 .... **CLC 6, 11, 29, 105**
See also CA 5-8R; 149; CAAS 4; CANR
25, 53; CBD; CN 1, 2, 3, 4, 5, 6; CWD;
DA3; DLB 14, 271; EWL 3; MTCW 1, 2

Brosman, Catharine Savage 1934- ..... **CLC 9**
See also CA 61-64; CANR 21, 46, 149
Brossard, Nicole 1943- .... **CLC 115, 169**
See also CA 122; CAAS 16; CANR 140;
CCA 1; CWP; CWW 2; DLB 53; EWL 3;
FW; GLL 2; RGWL 3
Brother Antoninus
See Everson, William (Oliver)
Brothers Grimm
See Grimm, Jacob Ludwig Karl; Grimm,
Wilhelm Karl
The Brothers Quay
See Quay, Stephen; Quay, Timothy
Broughton, T(homas) Alan 1936- ..... **CLC 19**
See also CA 45-48; CANR 2, 23, 48, 111
Broumas, Olga 1949- .... **CLC 10, 73**
See also CA 85-88; CANR 20, 69, 110; CP
5, 6, 7; CWP; GLL 2
Broun, Heywood 1888-1939 .... **TCLC 104**
See also DLB 29, 171
Brown, Alan 1950- .... **CLC 99**
See also CA 156
Brown, Charles Brockden
1771-1810 .... **NCLC 22, 74, 122**
See also AMWS 1; CDALB 1640-1865;
DLB 37, 59, 73; FW; GL 2; HGG; LMFS
1; RGAL 4; TUS
Brown, Christy 1932-1981 .... **CLC 63**
See also BYA 13; CA 105; 104; CANR 72;
DLB 14
Brown, Claude 1937-2002 ... **BLC 1; CLC 30**
See also AAYA 7; BW 1, 3; CA 73-76; 205;
CANR 81; DAM MULT
Brown, Dan 1964- .... **CLC 209**
See also AAYA 55; CA 217; MTFW 2005
Brown, Dee 1908-2002 .... **CLC 18, 47**
See also AAYA 30; CA 13-16R; 212; CAAS
6; CANR 11, 45, 60, 150; CPW; CSW;
DA3; DAM POP; DLBY 1980; LAIT 2;
MTCW 1, 2; MTFW 2005; NCFS 5;
SATA 5, 110; SATA-Obit 141; TCWW 1,
2
Brown, Dee Alexander
See Brown, Dee
Brown, George
See Wertmueller, Lina
Brown, George Douglas
1869-1902 .... **TCLC 28**
See Douglas, George
See also CA 162
Brown, George Mackay 1921-1996 ... **CLC 5,**
48, 100
See also BRWS 6; CA 21-24R; 151; CAAS
6; CANR 12, 37, 67; CN 1, 2, 3, 4, 5, 6;
CP 1, 2, 3, 4, 5, 6; DLB 14, 27, 139, 271;
MTCW 1; RGSF 2; SATA 35
Brown, (William) Larry 1951-2004 . **CLC 73**
See also CA 130; 134; 233; CANR 117,
145; CSW; DLB 234; INT CA-134
Brown, Moses
See Barrett, William (Christopher)
Brown, Rita Mae 1944- .... **CLC 18, 43, 79**
See also BPFB 1; CA 45-48; CANR 2, 11,
35, 62, 95, 138; CN 5, 6, 7; CPW; CSW;
DA3; DAM NOV, POP; FW; INT CANR-
11; MAL 5; MTCW 1, 2; MTFW 2005;
NFS 9; RGAL 4; TUS
Brown, Roderick (Langmere) Haig-
See Haig-Brown, Roderick (Langmere)
Brown, Rosellen 1939- .... **CLC 32, 170**
See also CA 77-80; CAAS 10; CANR 14,
44, 98; CN 6, 7
Brown, Sterling Allen 1901-1989 ...... **BLC 1;**
CLC 1, 23, 59; HR 1:2; PC 55
See also AFAW 1, 2; BW 1, 3; CA 85-88;
127; CANR 26; CP 3, 4; DA3; DAM
MULT, POET; DLB 48, 51, 63; MAL 5;
MTCW 1, 2; MTFW 2005; RGAL 4; WP

Brown, Will
See Ainsworth, William Harrison

Brown, William Hill 1765-1793 .... **LC 93**
See also DLB 37

Brown, William Wells 1815-1884 ...... **BLC 1; DC 1; NCLC 2, 89**
See also DAM MULT; DLB 3, 50, 183, 248; RGAL 4

Browne, (Clyde) Jackson 1948(?)- ... **CLC 21**
See also CA 120

Browne, Sir Thomas 1605-1682 .... **LC 111**
See also BRW 2; DLB 151

Browning, Robert 1812-1889 . **NCLC 19, 79; PC 2, 61; WLCS**
See also BRW 4; BRWC 2; BRWR 2; CD-BLB 1832-1890; CLR 97; DA; DA3; DAB; DAC; DAM MST, POET; DLB 32, 163; EXPP; LATS 1:1; PAB; PFS 1, 15; RGEL 2; TEA; WLIT 4; WP; YABC 1

Browning, Tod 1882-1962 .... **CLC 16**
See also CA 141; 117

Brownmiller, Susan 1935- .... **CLC 159**
See also CA 103; CANR 35, 75, 137; DAM NOV; FW; MTCW 1, 2; MTFW 2005

Brownson, Orestes Augustus 1803-1876 .... **NCLC 50**
See also DLB 1, 59, 73, 243

Bruccoli, Matthew J(oseph) 1931- ... **CLC 34**
See also CA 9-12R; CANR 7, 87; DLB 103

Bruce, Lenny .... **CLC 21**
See Schneider, Leonard Alfred

Bruchac, Joseph 1942- .... **NNAL**
See also AAYA 19; CA 33-36R; CANR 13, 47, 75, 94, 137; CLR 46; CWRI 5; DAM MULT; JRDA; MAICYA 2; MAICYAS 1; MTCW 2; MTFW 2005; SATA 42, 89, 131, 172

Bruin, John
See Brutus, Dennis

Brulard, Henri
See Stendhal

Brulls, Christian
See Simenon, Georges (Jacques Christian)

Brunetto Latini c. 1220-1294 .... **CMLC 73**

Brunner, John (Kilian Houston) 1934-1995 .... **CLC 8, 10**
See also CA 1-4R; 149; CAAS 8; CANR 2, 37; CPW; DAM POP; DLB 261; MTCW 1, 2; SCFW 1, 2; SFW 4

Bruno, Giordano 1548-1600 .... **LC 27**
See also RGWL 2, 3

Brutus, Dennis 1924- ... **BLC 1; CLC 43; PC 24**
See also AFW; BW 2, 3; CA 49-52; CAAS 14; CANR 2, 27, 42, 81; CDWLB 3; CP 1, 2, 3, 4, 5, 6, 7; DAM MULT, POET; DLB 117, 225; EWL 3

Bryan, C(ourtlandt) D(ixon) B(arnes) 1936- .... **CLC 29**
See also CA 73-76; CANR 13, 68; DLB 185; INT CANR-13

Bryan, Michael
See Moore, Brian
See also CCA 1

Bryan, William Jennings 1860-1925 .... **TCLC 99**
See also DLB 303

Bryant, William Cullen 1794-1878 . **NCLC 6, 46; PC 20**
See also AMWS 1; CDALB 1640-1865; DA; DAB; DAC; DAM MST, POET; DLB 3, 43, 59, 189, 250; EXPP; PAB; RGAL 4; TUS

Bryusov, Valery Yakovlevich 1873-1924 .... **TCLC 10**
See also CA 107; 155; EWL 3; SFW 4

Buchan, John 1875-1940 .... **TCLC 41**
See also CA 108; 145; CMW 4; DAB; DAM POP; DLB 34, 70, 156; HGG; MSW; MTCW 2; RGEL 2; RHW; YABC 2

Buchanan, George 1506-1582 .... **LC 4**
See also DLB 132

Buchanan, Robert 1841-1901 .... **TCLC 107**
See also CA 179; DLB 18, 35

Buchheim, Lothar-Guenther 1918- .... **CLC 6**
See also CA 85-88

Buchner, (Karl) Georg 1813-1837 .... **NCLC 26, 146**
See also CDWLB 2; DLB 133; EW 6; RGSF 2; RGWL 2, 3; TWA

Buchwald, Art 1925- .... **CLC 33**
See also AITN 1; CA 5-8R; CANR 21, 67, 107; MTCW 1, 2; SATA 10

Buchwald, Arthur
See Buchwald, Art

Buck, Pearl S(ydenstricker) 1892-1973 .... **CLC 7, 11, 18, 127**
See also AAYA 42; AITN 1; AMWS 2; BPFB 1; CA 1-4R; 41-44R; CANR 1, 34; CDALBS; CN 1; DA; DA3; DAB; DAC; DAM MST, NOV; DLB 9, 102, 329; EWL 3; LAIT 3; MAL 5; MTCW 1, 2; MTFW 2005; RGAL 4; RHW; SATA 1, 25; TUS

Buckler, Ernest 1908-1984 .... **CLC 13**
See also CA 11-12; 114; CAP 1; CCA 1; CN 1, 2, 3; DAC; DAM MST; DLB 68; SATA 47

Buckley, Christopher 1952- .... **CLC 165**
See also CA 139; CANR 119

Buckley, Christopher Taylor
See Buckley, Christopher

Buckley, Vincent (Thomas) 1925-1988 .... **CLC 57**
See also CA 101; CP 1, 2, 3, 4; DLB 289

Buckley, William F., Jr. 1925- ..... **CLC 7, 18, 37**
See also AITN 1; BPFB 1; CA 1-4R; CANR 1, 24, 53, 93, 133; CMW 4; CPW; DA3; DAM POP; DLB 137; DLBY 1980; INT CANR-24; MTCW 1, 2; MTFW 2005; TUS

Buechner, Frederick 1926- ..... **CLC 2, 4, 6, 9**
See also AMWS 12; BPFB 1; CA 13-16R; CANR 11, 39, 64, 114, 138; CN 1, 2, 3, 4, 5, 6, 7; DAM NOV; DLBY 1980; INT CANR-11; MAL 5; MTCW 1, 2; MTFW 2005; TCLE 1:1

Buell, John (Edward) 1927- .... **CLC 10**
See also CA 1-4R; CANR 71; DLB 53

Buero Vallejo, Antonio 1916-2000 ... **CLC 15, 46, 139, 226; DC 18**
See also CA 106; 189; CANR 24, 49, 75; CWW 2; DFS 11; EWL 3; HW 1; MTCW 1, 2

Bufalino, Gesualdo 1920-1996 .... **CLC 74**
See also CA 209; CWW 2; DLB 196

Bugayev, Boris Nikolayevich 1880-1934 .... **PC 11; TCLC 7**
See Bely, Andrey; Belyi, Andrei
See also CA 104; 165; MTCW 2; MTFW 2005

Bukowski, Charles 1920-1994 ... **CLC 2, 5, 9, 41, 82, 108; PC 18; SSC 45**
See also CA 17-20R; 144; CANR 40, 62, 105; CN 4, 5; CP 1, 2, 3, 4, 5; CPW; DA3; DAM NOV, POET; DLB 5, 130, 169; EWL 3; MAL 5; MTCW 1, 2; MTFW 2005

Bulgakov, Mikhail 1891-1940 .... **SSC 18; TCLC 2, 16, 159**
See also BPFB 1; CA 105; 152; DAM DRAM, NOV; DLB 272; EWL 3; MTCW 2; MTFW 2005; NFS 8; RGSF 2; RGWL 2, 3; SFW 4; TWA

Bulgakov, Mikhail Afanasevich
See Bulgakov, Mikhail

Bulgya, Alexander Alexandrovich 1901-1956 .... **TCLC 53**
See Fadeev, Aleksandr Aleksandrovich; Fadeev, Alexandr Alexandrovich; Fadeyev, Alexander
See also CA 117; 181

Bullins, Ed 1935- ... **BLC 1; CLC 1, 5, 7; DC 6**
See also BW 2, 3; CA 49-52; CAAS 16; CAD; CANR 24, 46, 73, 134; CD 5, 6; DAM DRAM, MULT; DLB 7, 38, 249; EWL 3; MAL 5; MTCW 1, 2; MTFW 2005; RGAL 4

Bulosan, Carlos 1911-1956 .... **AAL**
See also CA 216; DLB 312; RGAL 4

Bulwer-Lytton, Edward (George Earle Lytton) 1803-1873 .... **NCLC 1, 45**
See also DLB 21; RGEL 2; SFW 4; SUFW 1; TEA

Bunin, Ivan
See Bunin, Ivan Alexeyevich

Bunin, Ivan Alekseevich
See Bunin, Ivan Alexeyevich

Bunin, Ivan Alexeyevich 1870-1953 ... **SSC 5; TCLC 6**
See also CA 104; DLB 317, 329; EWL 3; RGSF 2; RGWL 2, 3; TWA

Bunting, Basil 1900-1985 ...... **CLC 10, 39, 47**
See also BRWS 7; CA 53-56; 115; CANR 7; CP 1, 2, 3, 4; DAM POET; DLB 20; EWL 3; RGEL 2

Bunuel, Luis 1900-1983 ... **CLC 16, 80; HLC 1**
See also CA 101; 110; CANR 32, 77; DAM MULT; HW 1

Bunyan, John 1628-1688 ... **LC 4, 69; WLC 1**
See also BRW 2; BYA 5; CDBLB 1660-1789; DA; DAB; DAC; DAM MST; DLB 39; RGEL 2; TEA; WCH; WLIT 3

Buravsky, Alexandr .... **CLC 59**

Burckhardt, Jacob (Christoph) 1818-1897 .... **NCLC 49**
See also EW 6

Burford, Eleanor
See Hibbert, Eleanor Alice Burford

Burgess, Anthony . **CLC 1, 2, 4, 5, 8, 10, 13, 15, 22, 40, 62, 81, 94**
See Wilson, John (Anthony) Burgess
See also AAYA 25; AITN 1; BRWS 1; CD-BLB 1960 to Present; CN 1, 2, 3, 4, 5; DAB; DLB 14, 194, 261; DLBY 1998; EWL 3; RGEL 2; RHW; SFW 4; YAW

Burke, Edmund 1729(?)-1797 .... **LC 7, 36; WLC 1**
See also BRW 3; DA; DA3; DAB; DAC; DAM MST; DLB 104, 252; RGEL 2; TEA

Burke, Kenneth (Duva) 1897-1993 ... **CLC 2, 24**
See also AMW; CA 5-8R; 143; CANR 39, 74, 136; CN 1, 2; CP 1, 2, 3, 4, 5; DLB 45, 63; EWL 3; MAL 5; MTCW 1, 2; MTFW 2005; RGAL 4

Burke, Leda
See Garnett, David

Burke, Ralph
See Silverberg, Robert

Burke, Thomas 1886-1945 .... **TCLC 63**
See also CA 113; 155; CMW 4; DLB 197

Burney, Fanny 1752-1840 .... **NCLC 12, 54, 107**
See also BRWS 3; DLB 39; FL 1:2; NFS 16; RGEL 2; TEA

Burney, Frances
See Burney, Fanny

Burns, Robert 1759-1796 ... **LC 3, 29, 40; PC 6; WLC 1**
See also AAYA 51; BRW 3; CDBLB 1789-1832; DA; DA3; DAB; DAC; DAM MST, POET; DLB 109; EXPP; PAB; RGEL 2; TEA; WP

Burns, Tex
See L'Amour, Louis

Burnshaw, Stanley 1906-2005 ..... **CLC 3, 13, 44**
See also CA 9-12R; 243; CP 1, 2, 3, 4, 5, 6, 7; DLB 48; DLBY 1997

Burr, Anne 1937- .... **CLC 6**
See also CA 25-28R

Burroughs, Edgar Rice 1875-1950 . **TCLC 2, 32**
See also AAYA 11; BPFB 1; BYA 4, 9; CA 104; 132; CANR 131; DA3; DAM NOV; DLB 8; FANT; MTCW 1, 2; MTFW 2005; RGAL 4; SATA 41; SCFW 1, 2; SFW 4; TCWW 1, 2; TUS; YAW

Burroughs, William S. 1914-1997 . **CLC 1, 2, 5, 15, 22, 42, 75, 109; TCLC 121; WLC 1**
See Lee, William; Lee, Willy
See also AAYA 60; AITN 2; AMWS 3; BG 1:2; BPFB 1; CA 9-12R; 160; CANR 20, 52, 104; CN 1, 2, 3, 4, 5, 6; CPW; DA; DA3; DAB; DAC; DAM MST, NOV, POP; DLB 2, 8, 16, 152, 237; DLBY 1981, 1997; EWL 3; HGG; LMFS 2; MAL 5; MTCW 1, 2; MTFW 2005; RGAL 4; SFW 4

Burroughs, William Seward
See Burroughs, William S.

Burton, Sir Richard F(rancis) 1821-1890 .... **NCLC 42**
See also DLB 55, 166, 184; SSFS 21

Burton, Robert 1577-1640 .... **LC 74**
See also DLB 151; RGEL 2

Buruma, Ian 1951- .... **CLC 163**
See also CA 128; CANR 65, 141

Busch, Frederick 1941-2006 .. **CLC 7, 10, 18, 47, 166**
See also CA 33-36R; 248; CAAS 1; CANR 45, 73, 92, 157; CN 1, 2, 3, 4, 5, 6, 7; DLB 6, 218

Busch, Frederick Matthew
See Busch, Frederick

Bush, Barney (Furman) 1946- .... **NNAL**
See also CA 145

Bush, Ronald 1946- .... **CLC 34**
See also CA 136

Bustos, F(rancisco)
See Borges, Jorge Luis

Bustos Domecq, H(onorio)
See Bioy Casares, Adolfo; Borges, Jorge Luis

Butler, Octavia E. 1947-2006 .... **BLCS; CLC 38, 121, 230**
See also AAYA 18, 48; AFAW 2; AMWS 13; BPFB 1; BW 2, 3; CA 73-76; 248; CANR 12, 24, 38, 73, 145; CLR 65; CN 7; CPW; DA3; DAM MULT, POP; DLB 33; LATS 1:2; MTCW 1, 2; MTFW 2005; NFS 8, 21; SATA 84; SCFW 2; SFW 4; SSFS 6; TCLE 1:1; YAW

Butler, Octavia Estelle
See Butler, Octavia E.

Butler, Robert Olen, (Jr.) 1945- ...... **CLC 81, 162**
See also AMWS 12; BPFB 1; CA 112; CANR 66, 138; CN 7; CSW; DAM POP; DLB 173; INT CA-112; MAL 5; MTCW 2; MTFW 2005; SSFS 11, 22

Butler, Samuel 1612-1680 .... **LC 16, 43**
See also DLB 101, 126; RGEL 2

Butler, Samuel 1835-1902 .... **TCLC 1, 33; WLC 1**
See also BRWS 2; CA 143; CDBLB 1890-1914; DA; DA3; DAB; DAC; DAM MST, NOV; DLB 18, 57, 174; RGEL 2; SFW 4; TEA

Butler, Walter C.
See Faust, Frederick (Schiller)

Butor, Michel (Marie Francois) 1926- .... **CLC 1, 3, 8, 11, 15, 161**
See also CA 9-12R; CANR 33, 66; CWW 2; DLB 83; EW 13; EWL 3; GFL 1789 to the Present; MTCW 1, 2; MTFW 2005

Butts, Mary 1890(?)-1937 .... **TCLC 77**
See also CA 148; DLB 240

Buxton, Ralph
See Silverstein, Alvin; Silverstein, Virginia B(arbara Opshelor)

Buzo, Alex
See Buzo, Alexander (John)
See also DLB 289

Buzo, Alexander (John) 1944- .... **CLC 61**
See also CA 97-100; CANR 17, 39, 69; CD 5, 6

Buzzati, Dino 1906-1972 .... **CLC 36**
See also CA 160; 33-36R; DLB 177; RGWL 2, 3; SFW 4

Byars, Betsy 1928- .... **CLC 35**
See also AAYA 19; BYA 3; CA 33-36R; 183; CAAE 183; CANR 18, 36, 57, 102, 148; CLR 1, 16, 72; DLB 52; INT CANR-18; JRDA; MAICYA 1, 2; MAICYAS 1; MTCW 1; SAAS 1; SATA 4, 46, 80, 163; SATA-Essay 108; WYA; YAW

Byars, Betsy Cromer
See Byars, Betsy

Byatt, Antonia Susan Drabble
See Byatt, A.S.

Byatt, A.S. 1936- .... **CLC 19, 65, 136, 223; SSC 91**
See also BPFB 1; BRWC 2; BRWS 4; CA 13-16R; CANR 13, 33, 50, 75, 96, 133; CN 1, 2, 3, 4, 5, 6; DA3; DAM NOV, POP; DLB 14, 194, 319, 326; EWL 3; MTCW 1, 2; MTFW 2005; RGSF 2; RHW; TEA

Byrd, William II 1674-1744 .... **LC 112**
See also DLB 24, 140; RGAL 4

Byrne, David 1952- .... **CLC 26**
See also CA 127

Byrne, John Keyes 1926-
See Leonard, Hugh
See also CA 102; CANR 78, 140; INT CA-102

Byron, George Gordon (Noel) 1788-1824 ..... **DC 24; NCLC 2, 12, 109, 149; PC 16; WLC 1**
See also AAYA 64; BRW 4; BRWC 2; CD-BLB 1789-1832; DA; DA3; DAB; DAC; DAM MST, POET; DLB 96, 110; EXPP; LMFS 1; PAB; PFS 1, 14; RGEL 2; TEA; WLIT 3; WP

Byron, Robert 1905-1941 .... **TCLC 67**
See also CA 160; DLB 195

C. 3. 3.
See Wilde, Oscar (Fingal O'Flahertie Wills)

Caballero, Fernan 1796-1877 .... **NCLC 10**

Cabell, Branch
See Cabell, James Branch

Cabell, James Branch 1879-1958 .... **TCLC 6**
See also CA 105; 152; DLB 9, 78; FANT; MAL 5; MTCW 2; RGAL 4; SUFW 1

Cabeza de Vaca, Alvar Nunez 1490-1557(?) .... **LC 61**

Cable, George Washington 1844-1925 .... **SSC 4; TCLC 4**
See also CA 104; 155; DLB 12, 74; DLBD 13; RGAL 4; TUS

Cabral de Melo Neto, Joao 1920-1999 .... **CLC 76**
See Melo Neto, Joao Cabral de
See also CA 151; DAM MULT; DLB 307; LAW; LAWS 1

Cabrera Infante, G. 1929-2005 ... **CLC 5, 25, 45, 120; HLC 1; SSC 39**
See also CA 85-88; 236; CANR 29, 65, 110; CDWLB 3; CWW 2; DA3; DAM MULT; DLB 113; EWL 3; HW 1, 2; LAW; LAWS 1; MTCW 1, 2; MTFW 2005; RGSF 2; WLIT 1

Cade, Toni
See Bambara, Toni Cade

Cadmus and Harmonia
See Buchan, John

Caedmon fl. 658-680 .... **CMLC 7**
See also DLB 146

Caeiro, Alberto
See Pessoa, Fernando (Antonio Nogueira)

Caesar, Julius .... **CMLC 47**
See Julius Caesar
See also AW 1; RGWL 2, 3; WLIT 8

Cage, John (Milton), (Jr.) 1912-1992 .... **CLC 41; PC 58**
See also CA 13-16R; 169; CANR 9, 78; DLB 193; INT CANR-9; TCLE 1:1

Cahan, Abraham 1860-1951 .... **TCLC 71**
See also CA 108; 154; DLB 9, 25, 28; MAL 5; RGAL 4

Cain, G.
See Cabrera Infante, G.

Cain, Guillermo
See Cabrera Infante, G.

Cain, James M(allahan) 1892-1977 .. **CLC 3, 11, 28**
See also AITN 1; BPFB 1; CA 17-20R; 73-76; CANR 8, 34, 61; CMW 4; CN 1, 2; DLB 226; EWL 3; MAL 5; MSW; MTCW 1; RGAL 4

Caine, Hall 1853-1931 .... **TCLC 97**
See also RHW

Caine, Mark
See Raphael, Frederic (Michael)

Calasso, Roberto 1941- .... **CLC 81**
See also CA 143; CANR 89

Calderon de la Barca, Pedro 1600-1681 .... **DC 3; HLCS 1; LC 23**
See also DFS 23; EW 2; RGWL 2, 3; TWA

Caldwell, Erskine 1903-1987 ... **CLC 1, 8, 14, 50, 60; SSC 19; TCLC 117**
See also AITN 1; AMW; BPFB 1; CA 1-4R; 121; CAAS 1; CANR 2, 33; CN 1, 2, 3, 4; DA3; DAM NOV; DLB 9, 86; EWL 3; MAL 5; MTCW 1, 2; MTFW 2005; RGAL 4; RGSF 2; TUS

Caldwell, (Janet Miriam) Taylor (Holland) 1900-1985 .... **CLC 2, 28, 39**
See also BPFB 1; CA 5-8R; 116; CANR 5; DA3; DAM NOV, POP; DLBD 17; MTCW 2; RHW

Calhoun, John Caldwell 1782-1850 .... **NCLC 15**
See also DLB 3, 248

Calisher, Hortense 1911- ..... **CLC 2, 4, 8, 38, 134; SSC 15**
See also CA 1-4R; CANR 1, 22, 117; CN 1, 2, 3, 4, 5, 6, 7; DA3; DAM NOV; DLB 2, 218; INT CANR-22; MAL 5; MTCW 1, 2; MTFW 2005; RGAL 4; RGSF 2

Callaghan, Morley Edward 1903-1990 ..... **CLC 3, 14, 41, 65; TCLC 145**
See also CA 9-12R; 132; CANR 33, 73; CN 1, 2, 3, 4; DAC; DAM MST; DLB 68; EWL 3; MTCW 1, 2; MTFW 2005; RGEL 2; RGSF 2; SSFS 19

Cherryh, C.J. 1942-
See Cherry, Carolyn Janice
See also CA 65-68; CANR 10, 147; SATA
172

Chesnutt, Charles W(addell)
1858-1932 .... **BLC 1; SSC 7, 54; TCLC
5, 39**
See also AFAW 1, 2; AMWS 14; BW 1, 3;
CA 106; 125; CANR 76; DAM MULT;
DLB 12, 50, 78; EWL 3; MAL 5; MTCW
1, 2; MTFW 2005; RGAL 4; RGSF 2;
SSFS 11

Chester, Alfred 1929(?)-1971 .... **CLC 49**
See also CA 196; 33-36R; DLB 130; MAL
5

Chesterton, G(ilbert) K(eith)
1874-1936 . **PC 28; SSC 1, 46; TCLC 1,
6, 64**
See also AAYA 57; BRW 6; CA 104; 132;
CANR 73, 131; CDBLB 1914-1945;
CMW 4; DAM NOV, POET; DLB 10, 19,
34, 70, 98, 149, 178; EWL 3; FANT;
MSW; MTCW 1, 2; MTFW 2005; RGEL
2; RGSF 2; SATA 27; SUFW 1

Chettle, Henry 1560-1607(?) .... **LC 112**
See also DLB 136; RGEL 2

Chiang, Pin-chin 1904-1986
See Ding Ling
See also CA 118

Chief Joseph 1840-1904 .... **NNAL**
See also CA 152; DA3; DAM MULT

Chief Seattle 1786(?)-1866 .... **NNAL**
See also DA3; DAM MULT

Ch'ien, Chung-shu 1910-1998 .... **CLC 22**
See Qian Zhongshu
See also CA 130; CANR 73; MTCW 1, 2

Chikamatsu Monzaemon 1653-1724 ... **LC 66**
See also RGWL 2, 3

Child, Francis James 1825-1896 . **NCLC 173**
See also DLB 1, 64, 235

Child, L. Maria
See Child, Lydia Maria

Child, Lydia Maria 1802-1880 .. **NCLC 6, 73**
See also DLB 1, 74, 243; RGAL 4; SATA
67

Child, Mrs.
See Child, Lydia Maria

Child, Philip 1898-1978 .... **CLC 19, 68**
See also CA 13-14; CAP 1; CP 1; DLB 68;
RHW; SATA 47

Childers, (Robert) Erskine
1870-1922 .... **TCLC 65**
See also CA 113; 153; DLB 70

Childress, Alice 1920-1994 . **BLC 1; CLC 12,
15, 86, 96; DC 4; TCLC 116**
See also AAYA 8; BW 2, 3; BYA 2; CA 45-
48; 146; CAD; CANR 3, 27, 50, 74; CLR
14; CWD; DA3; DAM DRAM, MULT,
NOV; DFS 2, 8, 14; DLB 7, 38, 249;
JRDA; LAIT 5; MAICYA 1, 2; MAIC-
YAS 1; MTCW 1, 2; MTFW
2005; RGAL 4; SATA 7, 48, 81; TUS;
WYA; YAW

Chin, Frank (Chew, Jr.) 1940- .... **AAL; CLC
135; DC 7**
See also CA 33-36R; CAD; CANR 71; CD
5, 6; DAM MULT; DLB 206, 312; LAIT
5; RGAL 4

Chin, Marilyn (Mei Ling) 1955- .... **PC 40**
See also CA 129; CANR 70, 113; CWP;
DLB 312

Chislett, (Margaret) Anne 1943- ...... **CLC 34**
See also CA 151

Chitty, Thomas Willes 1926- .... **CLC 11**
See Hinde, Thomas
See also CA 5-8R; CN 7

Chivers, Thomas Holley
1809-1858 .... **NCLC 49**
See also DLB 3, 248; RGAL 4

Choi, Susan 1969- .... **CLC 119**
See also CA 223

Chomette, Rene Lucien 1898-1981
See Clair, Rene
See also CA 103

Chomsky, Avram Noam
See Chomsky, Noam

Chomsky, Noam 1928- .... **CLC 132**
See also CA 17-20R; CANR 28, 62, 110,
132; DA3; DLB 246; MTCW 1, 2; MTFW
2005

Chona, Maria 1845(?)-1936 .... **NNAL**
See also CA 144

Chopin, Kate .... **SSC 8, 68; TCLC 127;
WLCS**
See Chopin, Katherine
See also AAYA 33; AMWR 2; AMWS 1;
BYA 11, 15; CDALB 1865-1917; DA;
DAB; DLB 12, 78; EXPN; EXPS; FL 1:3;
FW; LAIT 3; MAL 5; MBL; NFS 3;
RGAL 4; RGSF 2; SSFS 2, 13, 17; TUS

Chopin, Katherine 1851-1904
See Chopin, Kate
See also CA 104; 122; DA3; DAC; DAM
MST, NOV

Chretien de Troyes c. 12th cent. - . **CMLC 10**
See also DLB 208; EW 1; RGWL 2, 3;
TWA

Christie
See Ichikawa, Kon

Christie, Agatha (Mary Clarissa)
1890-1976 .. **CLC 1, 6, 8, 12, 39, 48, 110**
See also AAYA 9; AITN 1, 2; BPFB 1;
BRWS 2; CA 17-20R; 61-64; CANR 10,
37, 108; CBD; CDBLB 1914-1945; CMW
4; CN 1, 2; CPW; CWD; DA3; DAB;
DAC; DAM NOV; DFS 2; DLB 13, 77,
245; MSW; MTCW 1, 2; MTFW 2005;
NFS 8; RGEL 2; RHW; SATA 36; TEA;
YAW

Christie, Philippa .... **CLC 21**
See Pearce, Philippa
See also BYA 5; CANR 109; CLR 9; DLB
161; MAICYA 1; SATA 1, 67, 129

Christine de Pisan
See Christine de Pizan
See also FW

Christine de Pizan 1365(?)-1431(?) ...... **LC 9,
130; PC 68**
See Christine de Pisan; de Pizan, Christine
See also DLB 208; FL 1:1; RGWL 2, 3

Chuang Tzu c. 369B.C.-c.
286B.C. .... **CMLC 57**

Chubb, Elmer
See Masters, Edgar Lee

Chulkov, Mikhail Dmitrievich
1743-1792 .... **LC 2**
See also DLB 150

Churchill, Caryl 1938- .... **CLC 31, 55, 157;
DC 5**
See Churchill, Chick
See also BRWS 4; CA 102; CANR 22, 46,
108; CBD; CD 6; CWD; DFS 12, 16;
DLB 13, 310; EWL 3; FW; MTCW 1;
RGEL 2

Churchill, Charles 1731-1764 .... **LC 3**
See also DLB 109; RGEL 2

Churchill, Chick
See Churchill, Caryl
See also CD 5

Churchill, Sir Winston (Leonard Spencer)
1874-1965 .... **TCLC 113**
See also BRW 6; CA 97-100; CDBLB
1890-1914; DA3; DLB 100, 329; DLBD
16; LAIT 4; MTCW 1, 2

Chute, Carolyn 1947- .... **CLC 39**
See also CA 123; CANR 135; CN 7

Ciardi, John (Anthony) 1916-1986 . **CLC 10,
40, 44, 129; PC 69**
See also CA 5-8R; 118; CAAS 2; CANR 5,
33; CLR 19; CP 1, 2, 3, 4; CWRI 5; DAM
POET; DLB 5; DLBY 1986; INT
CANR-5; MAICYA 1, 2; MAL 5; MTCW
1, 2; MTFW 2005; RGAL 4; SAAS 26;
SATA 1, 65; SATA-Obit 46

Cibber, Colley 1671-1757 .... **LC 66**
See also DLB 84; RGEL 2

Cicero, Marcus Tullius
106B.C.-43B.C. .... **CMLC 3, 81**
See also AW 1; CDWLB 1; DLB 211;
RGWL 2, 3; WLIT 8

Cimino, Michael 1943- .... **CLC 16**
See also CA 105

Cioran, E(mil) M. 1911-1995 .... **CLC 64**
See also CA 25-28R; 149; CANR 91; DLB
220; EWL 3

Cisneros, Sandra 1954- .... **CLC 69, 118, 193;
HLC 1; PC 52; SSC 32, 72**
See also AAYA 9, 53; AMWS 7; CA 131;
CANR 64, 118; CN 7; CWP; DA3; DAM
MULT; DLB 122, 152; EWL 3; EXPN;
FL 1:5; FW; HW 1, 2; LAIT 5; LATS 1:2;
LLW; MAICYA 2; MAL 5; MTCW 2;
MTFW 2005; NFS 2; PFS 19; RGAL 4;
RGSF 2; SSFS 3, 13; WLIT 1; YAW

Cixous, Helene 1937- .... **CLC 92**
See also CA 126; CANR 55, 123; CWW 2;
DLB 83, 242; EWL 3; FL 1:5; FW; GLL
2; MTCW 1, 2; MTFW 2005; TWA

Clair, Rene .... **CLC 20**
See Chomette, Rene Lucien

Clampitt, Amy 1920-1994 .... **CLC 32; PC 19**
See also AMWS 9; CA 110; 146; CANR
29, 79; CP 4, 5; DLB 105; MAL 5

Clancy, Thomas L., Jr. 1947-
See Clancy, Tom
See also CA 125; 131; CANR 62, 105;
DA3; INT CA-131; MTCW 1, 2; MTFW
2005

Clancy, Tom .... **CLC 45, 112**
See Clancy, Thomas L., Jr.
See also AAYA 9, 51; BEST 89:1, 90:1;
BPFB 1; BYA 10, 11; CANR 132; CMW
4; CPW; DAM NOV, POP; DLB 227

Clare, John 1793-1864 .. **NCLC 9, 86; PC 23**
See also BRWS 11; DAB; DAM POET;
DLB 55, 96; RGEL 2

Clarin
See Alas (y Urena), Leopoldo (Enrique
Garcia)

Clark, Al C.
See Goines, Donald

Clark, Brian (Robert)
See Clark, (Robert) Brian
See also CD 6

Clark, (Robert) Brian 1932- .... **CLC 29**
See Clark, Brian (Robert)
See also CA 41-44R; CANR 67; CBD; CD
5

Clark, Curt
See Westlake, Donald E.

Clark, Eleanor 1913-1996 .... **CLC 5, 19**
See also CA 9-12R; 151; CANR 41; CN 1,
2, 3, 4, 5, 6; DLB 6

Clark, J. P.
See Clark Bekederemo, J.P.
See also CDWLB 3; DLB 117

Clark, John Pepper
See Clark Bekederemo, J.P.
See also AFW; CD 5; CP 1, 2, 3, 4, 5, 6, 7;
RGEL 2

Clark, Kenneth (Mackenzie)
1903-1983 .... **TCLC 147**
See also CA 93-96; 109; CANR 36; MTCW
1, 2; MTFW 2005

Clark, M. R.
See Clark, Mavis Thorpe

Clark, Mavis Thorpe 1909-1999 ...... **CLC 12**
See also CA 57-60; CANR 8, 37, 107; CLR 30; CWRI 5; MAICYA 1, 2; SAAS 5; SATA 8, 74

Clark, Walter Van Tilburg
1909-1971 .... **CLC 28**
See also CA 9-12R; 33-36R; CANR 63, 113; CN 1; DLB 9, 206; LAIT 2; MAL 5; RGAL 4; SATA 8; TCWW 1, 2

Clark Bekederemo, J.P. 1935- . **BLC 1; CLC 38; DC 5**
See Bekederemo, J. P. Clark; Clark, J. P.; Clark, John Pepper
See also BW 1; CA 65-68; CANR 16, 72; DAM DRAM, MULT; DFS 13; EWL 3; MTCW 2; MTFW 2005

Clarke, Arthur C. 1917- .... **CLC 1, 4, 13, 18, 35, 136; SSC 3**
See also AAYA 4, 33; BPFB 1; BYA 13; CA 1-4R; CANR 2, 28, 55, 74, 130; CLR 119; CN 1, 2, 3, 4, 5, 6, 7; CPW; DA3; DAM POP; DLB 261; JRDA; LAIT 5; MAICYA 1, 2; MTCW 1, 2; MTFW 2005; SATA 13, 70, 115; SCFW 1, 2; SFW 4; SSFS 4, 18; TCLE 1:1; YAW

Clarke, Austin 1896-1974 .... **CLC 6, 9**
See also CA 29-32; 49-52; CAP 2; CP 1, 2; DAM POET; DLB 10, 20; EWL 3; RGEL 2

Clarke, Austin C. 1934- . **BLC 1; CLC 8, 53; SSC 45**
See also BW 1; CA 25-28R; CAAS 16; CANR 14, 32, 68, 140; CN 1, 2, 3, 4, 5, 6, 7; DAC; DAM MULT; DLB 53, 125; DNFS 2; MTCW 2; MTFW 2005; RGSF 2

Clarke, Gillian 1937- .... **CLC 61**
See also CA 106; CP 3, 4, 5, 6, 7; CWP; DLB 40

Clarke, Marcus (Andrew Hislop)
1846-1881 .... **NCLC 19; SSC 94**
See also DLB 230; RGEL 2; RGSF 2

Clarke, Shirley 1925-1997 .... **CLC 16**
See also CA 189

Clash, The
See Headon, (Nicky) Topper; Jones, Mick; Simonon, Paul; Strummer, Joe

Claudel, Paul (Louis Charles Marie)
1868-1955 .... **TCLC 2, 10**
See also CA 104; 165; DLB 192, 258, 321; EW 8; EWL 3; GFL 1789 to the Present; RGWL 2, 3; TWA

Claudian 370(?)-404(?) .... **CMLC 46**
See also RGWL 2, 3

Claudius, Matthias 1740-1815 .... **NCLC 75**
See also DLB 97

Clavell, James 1925-1994 .... **CLC 6, 25, 87**
See also BPFB 1; CA 25-28R; 146; CANR 26, 48; CN 5; CPW; DA3; DAM NOV, POP; MTCW 1, 2; MTFW 2005; NFS 10; RHW

Clayman, Gregory .... **CLC 65**

Cleaver, (Leroy) Eldridge
1935-1998 .... **BLC 1; CLC 30, 119**
See also BW 1, 3; CA 21-24R; 167; CANR 16, 75; DA3; DAM MULT; MTCW 2; YAW

Cleese, John (Marwood) 1939- .... **CLC 21**
See Monty Python
See also CA 112; 116; CANR 35; MTCW 1

Cleishbotham, Jebediah
See Scott, Sir Walter

Cleland, John 1710-1789 .... **LC 2, 48**
See also DLB 39; RGEL 2

Clemens, Samuel Langhorne 1835-1910
See Twain, Mark
See also CA 104; 135; CDALB 1865-1917; DA; DA3; DAB; DAC; DAM MST, NOV; DLB 12, 23, 64, 74, 186, 189; JRDA; LMFS 1; MAICYA 1, 2; NCFS 4; NFS 20; SATA 100; YABC 2

Clement of Alexandria
150(?)-215(?) .... **CMLC 41**

Cleophil
See Congreve, William

Clerihew, E.
See Bentley, E(dmund) C(lerihew)

Clerk, N. W.
See Lewis, C.S.

Cleveland, John 1613-1658 .... **LC 106**
See also DLB 126; RGEL 2

Cliff, Jimmy .... **CLC 21**
See Chambers, James
See also CA 193

Cliff, Michelle 1946- .... **BLCS; CLC 120**
See also BW 2; CA 116; CANR 39, 72; CD-WLB 3; DLB 157; FW; GLL 2

Clifford, Lady Anne 1590-1676 .... **LC 76**
See also DLB 151

Clifton, Lucille 1936- ... **BLC 1; CLC 19, 66, 162; PC 17**
See also AFAW 2; BW 2, 3; CA 49-52; CANR 2, 24, 42, 76, 97, 138; CLR 5; CP 2, 3, 4, 5, 6, 7; CSW; CWP; CWRI 5; DA3; DAM MULT, POET; DLB 5, 41; EXPP; MAICYA 1, 2; MTCW 1, 2; MTFW 2005; PFS 1, 14; SATA 20, 69, 128; WP

Clinton, Dirk
See Silverberg, Robert

Clough, Arthur Hugh 1819-1861 .. **NCLC 27, 163**
See also BRW 5; DLB 32; RGEL 2

Clutha, Janet Paterson Frame 1924-2004
See Frame, Janet
See also CA 1-4R; 224; CANR 2, 36, 76, 135; MTCW 1, 2; SATA 119

Clyne, Terence
See Blatty, William Peter

Cobalt, Martin
See Mayne, William (James Carter)

Cobb, Irvin S(hrewsbury)
1876-1944 .... **TCLC 77**
See also CA 175; DLB 11, 25, 86

Cobbett, William 1763-1835 .... **NCLC 49**
See also DLB 43, 107, 158; RGEL 2

Coburn, D(onald) L(ee) 1938- .... **CLC 10**
See also CA 89-92; DFS 23

Cocteau, Jean (Maurice Eugene Clement)
1889-1963 ...... **CLC 1, 8, 15, 16, 43; DC 17; TCLC 119; WLC 2**
See also CA 25-28; CANR 40; CAP 2; DA; DA3; DAB; DAC; DAM DRAM, MST, NOV; DLB 65, 258, 321; EW 10; EWL 3; GFL 1789 to the Present; MTCW 1, 2; RGWL 2, 3; TWA

Codrescu, Andrei 1946- .... **CLC 46, 121**
See also CA 33-36R; CAAS 19; CANR 13, 34, 53, 76, 125; CN 7; DA3; DAM POET; MAL 5; MTCW 2; MTFW 2005

Coe, Max
See Bourne, Randolph S(illiman)

Coe, Tucker
See Westlake, Donald E.

Coen, Ethan 1958- .... **CLC 108**
See also AAYA 54; CA 126; CANR 85

Coen, Joel 1955- .... **CLC 108**
See also AAYA 54; CA 126; CANR 119

The Coen Brothers
See Coen, Ethan; Coen, Joel

Coetzee, J.M. 1940- ...... **CLC 23, 33, 66, 117, 161, 162**
See also AAYA 37; AFW; BRWS 6; CA 77-80; CANR 41, 54, 74, 114, 133; CN 4, 5, 6, 7; DA3; DAM NOV; DLB 225, 326, 329; EWL 3; LMFS 2; MTCW 1, 2; MTFW 2005; NFS 21; WLIT 2; WWE 1

Coetzee, John Maxwell
See Coetzee, J.M.

Coffey, Brian
See Koontz, Dean R.

Coffin, Robert P(eter) Tristram
1892-1955 .... **TCLC 95**
See also CA 123; 169; DLB 45

Cohan, George M. 1878-1942 .... **TCLC 60**
See also CA 157; DLB 249; RGAL 4

Cohan, George Michael
See Cohan, George M.

Cohen, Arthur A(llen) 1928-1986 ...... **CLC 7, 31**
See also CA 1-4R; 120; CANR 1, 17, 42; DLB 28; RGHL

Cohen, Leonard 1934- .... **CLC 3, 38**
See also CA 21-24R; CANR 14, 69; CN 1, 2, 3, 4, 5, 6; CP 1, 2, 3, 4, 5, 6, 7; DAC; DAM MST; DLB 53; EWL 3; MTCW 1

Cohen, Leonard Norman
See Cohen, Leonard

Cohen, Matt(hew) 1942-1999 .... **CLC 19**
See also CA 61-64; 187; CAAS 18; CANR 40; CN 1, 2, 3, 4, 5, 6; DAC; DLB 53

Cohen-Solal, Annie 1948- .... **CLC 50**
See also CA 239

Colegate, Isabel 1931- .... **CLC 36**
See also CA 17-20R; CANR 8, 22, 74; CN 4, 5, 6, 7; DLB 14, 231; INT CANR-22; MTCW 1

Coleman, Emmett
See Reed, Ishmael

Coleridge, Hartley 1796-1849 .... **NCLC 90**
See also DLB 96

Coleridge, M. E.
See Coleridge, Mary E(lizabeth)

Coleridge, Mary E(lizabeth)
1861-1907 .... **TCLC 73**
See also CA 116; 166; DLB 19, 98

Coleridge, Samuel Taylor
1772-1834 ...... **NCLC 9, 54, 99, 111; PC 11, 39, 67; WLC 2**
See also AAYA 66; BRW 4; BRWR 2; BYA 4; CDBLB 1789-1832; DA; DA3; DAB; DAC; DAM MST, POET; DLB 93, 107; EXPP; LATS 1:1; LMFS 1; PAB; PFS 4, 5; RGEL 2; TEA; WLIT 3; WP

Coleridge, Sara 1802-1852 .... **NCLC 31**
See also DLB 199

Coles, Don 1928- .... **CLC 46**
See also CA 115; CANR 38; CP 5, 6, 7

Coles, Robert (Martin) 1929- .... **CLC 108**
See also CA 45-48; CANR 3, 32, 66, 70, 135; INT CANR-32; SATA 23

Colette, (Sidonie-Gabrielle)
1873-1954 .. **SSC 10, 93; TCLC 1, 5, 16**
See Willy, Colette
See also CA 104; 131; DA3; DAM NOV; DLB 65; EW 9; EWL 3; GFL 1789 to the Present; MTCW 1, 2; MTFW 2005; RGWL 2, 3; TWA

Collett, (Jacobine) Camilla (Wergeland)
1813-1895 .... **NCLC 22**

Collier, Christopher 1930- .... **CLC 30**
See also AAYA 13; BYA 2; CA 33-36R; CANR 13, 33, 102; JRDA; MAICYA 1, 2; SATA 16, 70; WYA; YAW 1

Collier, James Lincoln 1928- .... **CLC 30**
See also AAYA 13; BYA 2; CA 9-12R; CANR 4, 33, 60, 102; CLR 3; DAM POP; JRDA; MAICYA 1, 2; SAAS 21; SATA 8, 70, 166; WYA; YAW 1

Corinna c. 225B.C.-c. 305B.C. ...... **CMLC 72**

Corman, Cid .... **CLC 9**
See Corman, Sidney
See also CAAS 2; CP 1, 2, 3, 4, 5, 6, 7;
DLB 5, 193

Corman, Sidney 1924-2004
See Corman, Cid
See also CA 85-88; 225; CANR 44; DAM
POET

Cormier, Robert 1925-2000 .... **CLC 12, 30**
See also AAYA 3, 19; BYA 1, 2, 6, 8, 9;
CA 1-4R; CANR 5, 23, 76, 93; CDALB
1968-1988; CLR 12, 55; DA; DAB; DAC;
DAM MST, NOV; DLB 52; EXPN; INT
CANR-23; JRDA; LAIT 5; MAICYA 1,
2; MTCW 1, 2; MTFW 2005; NFS 2, 18;
SATA 10, 45, 83; SATA-Obit 122; WYA;
YAW

Corn, Alfred (DeWitt III) 1943- .... **CLC 33**
See also CA 179; CAAE 179; CAAS 25;
CANR 44; CP 3, 4, 5, 6, 7; CSW; DLB
120, 282; DLBY 1980

Corneille, Pierre 1606-1684 ... **DC 21; LC 28**
See also DAB; DAM MST; DFS 21; DLB
268; EW 3; GFL Beginnings to 1789;
RGWL 2, 3; TWA

Cornwell, David
See le Carre, John

Cornwell, Patricia 1956- .... **CLC 155**
See also AAYA 16, 56; BPFB 1; CA 134;
CANR 53, 131; CMW 4; CPW; CSW;
DAM POP; DLB 306; MSW; MTCW 2;
MTFW 2005

Cornwell, Patricia Daniels
See Cornwell, Patricia

Corso, Gregory 1930-2001 .... **CLC 1, 11; PC 33**
See also AMWS 12; BG 1:2; CA 5-8R; 193;
CANR 41, 76, 132; CP 1, 2, 3, 4, 5, 6, 7;
DA3; DLB 5, 16, 237; LMFS 2; MAL 5;
MTCW 1, 2; MTFW 2005; WP

Cortazar, Julio 1914-1984 ... **CLC 2, 3, 5, 10,
13, 15, 33, 34, 92; HLC 1; SSC 7, 76**
See also BPFB 1; CA 21-24R; CANR 12,
32, 81; CDWLB 3; DA3; DAM MULT,
NOV; DLB 113; EWL 3; EXPS; HW 1,
2; LAW; MTCW 1, 2; MTFW 2005;
RGSF 2; RGWL 2, 3; SSFS 3, 20; TWA;
WLIT 1

Cortes, Hernan 1485-1547 .... **LC 31**

Corvinus, Jakob
See Raabe, Wilhelm (Karl)

Corwin, Cecil
See Kornbluth, C(yril) M.

Cosic, Dobrica 1921- .... **CLC 14**
See also CA 122; 138; CDWLB 4; CWW
2; DLB 181; EWL 3

Costain, Thomas B(ertram)
1885-1965 .... **CLC 30**
See also BYA 3; CA 5-8R; 25-28R; DLB 9;
RHW

Costantini, Humberto 1924(?)-1987 . **CLC 49**
See also CA 131; 122; EWL 3; HW 1

Costello, Elvis 1954- .... **CLC 21**
See also CA 204

Costenoble, Philostene
See Ghelderode, Michel de

Cotes, Cecil V.
See Duncan, Sara Jeannette

Cotter, Joseph Seamon Sr.
1861-1949 .... **BLC 1; TCLC 28**
See also BW 1; CA 124; DAM MULT; DLB
50

Couch, Arthur Thomas Quiller
See Quiller-Couch, Sir Arthur (Thomas)

Coulton, James
See Hansen, Joseph

Couperus, Louis (Marie Anne)
1863-1923 .... **TCLC 15**
See also CA 115; EWL 3; RGWL 2, 3

Coupland, Douglas 1961- .... **CLC 85, 133**
See also AAYA 34; CA 142; CANR 57, 90,
130; CCA 1; CN 7; CPW; DAC; DAM
POP

Court, Wesli
See Turco, Lewis (Putnam)

Courtenay, Bryce 1933- .... **CLC 59**
See also CA 138; CPW

Courtney, Robert
See Ellison, Harlan

Cousteau, Jacques-Yves 1910-1997 .. **CLC 30**
See also CA 65-68; 159; CANR 15, 67;
MTCW 1; SATA 38, 98

Coventry, Francis 1725-1754 .... **LC 46**

Coverdale, Miles c. 1487-1569 .... **LC 77**
See also DLB 167

Cowan, Peter (Walkinshaw)
1914-2002 .... **SSC 28**
See also CA 21-24R; CANR 9, 25, 50, 83;
CN 1, 2, 3, 4, 5, 6, 7; DLB 260; RGSF 2

Coward, Noel (Peirce) 1899-1973 . **CLC 1, 9,
29, 51**
See also AITN 1; BRWS 2; CA 17-18; 41-
44R; CANR 35, 132; CAP 2; CBD; CD-
BLB 1914-1945; DA3; DAM DRAM;
DFS 3, 6; DLB 10, 245; EWL 3; IDFW
3, 4; MTCW 1, 2; MTFW 2005; RGEL 2;
TEA

Cowley, Abraham 1618-1667 .... **LC 43**
See also BRW 2; DLB 131, 151; PAB;
RGEL 2

Cowley, Malcolm 1898-1989 .... **CLC 39**
See also AMWS 2; CA 5-8R; 128; CANR
3, 55; CP 1, 2, 3, 4; DLB 4, 48; DLBY
1981, 1989; EWL 3; MAL 5; MTCW 1,
2; MTFW 2005

Cowper, William 1731-1800 ..... **NCLC 8, 94;
PC 40**
See also BRW 3; DA3; DAM POET; DLB
104, 109; RGEL 2

Cox, William Trevor 1928-
See Trevor, William
See also CA 9-12R; CANR 4, 37, 55, 76,
102, 139; DAM NOV; INT CANR-37;
MTCW 1, 2; MTFW 2005; TEA

Coyne, P. J.
See Masters, Hilary

Cozzens, James Gould 1903-1978 . **CLC 1, 4,
11, 92**
See also AMW; BPFB 1; CA 9-12R; 81-84;
CANR 19; CDALB 1941-1968; CN 1, 2;
DLB 9, 294; DLBD 2; DLBY 1984, 1997;
EWL 3; MAL 5; MTCW 1, 2; MTFW
2005; RGAL 4

Crabbe, George 1754-1832 .... **NCLC 26, 121**
See also BRW 3; DLB 93; RGEL 2

Crace, Jim 1946- .... **CLC 157; SSC 61**
See also CA 128; 135; CANR 55, 70, 123;
CN 5, 6, 7; DLB 231; INT CA-135

Craddock, Charles Egbert
See Murfree, Mary Noailles

Craig, A. A.
See Anderson, Poul

Craik, Mrs.
See Craik, Dinah Maria (Mulock)
See also RGEL 2

Craik, Dinah Maria (Mulock)
1826-1887 .... **NCLC 38**
See Craik, Mrs.; Mulock, Dinah Maria
See also DLB 35, 163; MAICYA 1, 2;
SATA 34

Cram, Ralph Adams 1863-1942 ..... **TCLC 45**
See also CA 160

Cranch, Christopher Pearse
1813-1892 .... **NCLC 115**
See also DLB 1, 42, 243

Crane, (Harold) Hart 1899-1932 .... **PC 3;
TCLC 2, 5, 80; WLC 2**
See also AMW; AMWR 2; CA 104; 127;
CDALB 1917-1929; DA; DA3; DAB;
DAC; DAM MST, POET; DLB 4, 48;
EWL 3; MAL 5; MTCW 1, 2; MTFW
2005; RGAL 4; TUS

Crane, R(onald) S(almon)
1886-1967 .... **CLC 27**
See also CA 85-88; DLB 63

Crane, Stephen (Townley)
1871-1900 ...... **SSC 7, 56, 70; TCLC 11,
17, 32; WLC 2**
See also AAYA 21; AMW; AMWC 1; BPFB
1; BYA 3; CA 109; 140; CANR 84;
CDALB 1865-1917; DA; DA3; DAB;
DAC; DAM MST, NOV, POET; DLB 12,
54, 78; EXPN; EXPS; LAIT 2; LMFS 2;
MAL 5; NFS 4, 20; PFS 9; RGAL 4;
RGSF 2; SSFS 4; TUS; WYA; YABC 2

Cranmer, Thomas 1489-1556 .... **LC 95**
See also DLB 132, 213

Cranshaw, Stanley
See Fisher, Dorothy (Frances) Canfield

Crase, Douglas 1944- .... **CLC 58**
See also CA 106

Crashaw, Richard 1612(?)-1649 .... **LC 24**
See also BRW 2; DLB 126; PAB; RGEL 2

Cratinus c. 519B.C.-c. 422B.C. ..... **CMLC 54**
See also LMFS 1

Craven, Margaret 1901-1980 .... **CLC 17**
See also BYA 2; CA 103; CCA 1; DAC;
LAIT 5

Crawford, F(rancis) Marion
1854-1909 .... **TCLC 10**
See also CA 107; 168; DLB 71; HGG;
RGAL 4; SUFW 1

Crawford, Isabella Valancy
1850-1887 .... **NCLC 12, 127**
See also DLB 92; RGEL 2

Crayon, Geoffrey
See Irving, Washington

Creasey, John 1908-1973 .... **CLC 11**
See Marric, J. J.
See also CA 5-8R; 41-44R; CANR 8, 59;
CMW 4; DLB 77; MTCW 1

Crebillon, Claude Prosper Jolyot de (fils)
1707-1777 .... **LC 1, 28**
See also DLB 313; GFL Beginnings to 1789

Credo
See Creasey, John

Credo, Alvaro J. de
See Prado (Calvo), Pedro

Creeley, Robert 1926-2005 .... **CLC 1, 2, 4, 8,
11, 15, 36, 78; PC 73**
See also AMWS 4; CA 1-4R; 237; CAAS
10; CANR 23, 43, 89, 137; CP 1, 2, 3, 4,
5, 6, 7; DA3; DAM POET; DLB 5, 16,
169; DLBD 17; EWL 3; MAL 5; MTCW
1, 2; MTFW 2005; PFS 21; RGAL 4; WP

Creeley, Robert White
See Creeley, Robert

Crenne, Helisenne de 1510-1560 .... **LC 113**
See also DLB 327

Crevecoeur, Hector St. John de
See Crevecoeur, Michel Guillaume Jean de
See also ANW

Crevecoeur, Michel Guillaume Jean de
1735-1813 .... **NCLC 105**
See Crevecoeur, Hector St. John de
See also AMWS 1; DLB 37

Crevel, Rene 1900-1935 .... **TCLC 112**
See also GLL 2

Crews, Harry 1935- .... **CLC 6, 23, 49**
See also AITN 1; AMWS 11; BPFB 1; CA
25-28R; CANR 20, 57; CN 3, 4, 5, 6, 7;
CSW; DA3; DLB 6, 143, 185; MTCW 1,
2; MTFW 2005; RGAL 4

Crichton, Michael 1942- ..... **CLC 2, 6, 54, 90**
See also AAYA 10, 49; AITN 2; BPFB 1;
CA 25-28R; CANR 13, 40, 54, 76, 127;
CMW 4; CN 2, 3, 6, 7; CPW; DA3; DAM
NOV, POP; DLB 292; DLBY 1981; INT
CANR-13; JRDA; MTCW 1, 2; MTFW
2005; SATA 9, 88; SFW 4; YAW

Crispin, Edmund .... **CLC 22**
See Montgomery, (Robert) Bruce
See also DLB 87; MSW

Cristina of Sweden 1626-1689 .... **LC 124**

Cristofer, Michael 1945(?)- .... **CLC 28**
See also CA 110; 152; CAD; CANR 150;
CD 5, 6; DAM DRAM; DFS 15; DLB 7

Cristofer, Michael Ivan
See Cristofer, Michael

Criton
See Alain

Croce, Benedetto 1866-1952 .... **TCLC 37**
See also CA 120; 155; EW 8; EWL 3;
WLIT 7

Crockett, David 1786-1836 .... **NCLC 8**
See also DLB 3, 11, 183, 248

Crockett, Davy
See Crockett, David

Crofts, Freeman Wills 1879-1957 .. **TCLC 55**
See also CA 115; 195; CMW 4; DLB 77;
MSW

Croker, John Wilson 1780-1857 .... **NCLC 10**
See also DLB 110

Crommelynck, Fernand 1885-1970 .. **CLC 75**
See also CA 189; 89-92; EWL 3

Cromwell, Oliver 1599-1658 .... **LC 43**

Cronenberg, David 1943- .... **CLC 143**
See also CA 138; CCA 1

Cronin, A(rchibald) J(oseph)
1896-1981 .... **CLC 32**
See also BPFB 1; CA 1-4R; 102; CANR 5;
CN 2; DLB 191; SATA 47; SATA-Obit 25

Cross, Amanda
See Heilbrun, Carolyn G(old)
See also BPFB 1; CMW; CPW; DLB 306;
MSW

Crothers, Rachel 1878-1958 .... **TCLC 19**
See also CA 113; 194; CAD; CWD; DLB
7, 266; RGAL 4

Croves, Hal
See Traven, B.

Crow Dog, Mary (?)- .... **CLC 93**
See Brave Bird, Mary
See also CA 154

Crowfield, Christopher
See Stowe, Harriet (Elizabeth) Beecher

Crowley, Aleister .... **TCLC 7**
See Crowley, Edward Alexander
See also GLL 1

Crowley, Edward Alexander 1875-1947
See Crowley, Aleister
See also CA 104; HGG

Crowley, John 1942- .... **CLC 57**
See also AAYA 57; BPFB 1; CA 61-64;
CANR 43, 98, 138; DLBY 1982; FANT;
MTFW 2005; SATA 65, 140; SFW 4;
SUFW 2

Crowne, John 1641-1712 .... **LC 104**
See also DLB 80; RGEL 2

Crud
See Crumb, R.

Crumarums
See Crumb, R.

Crumb, R. 1943- .... **CLC 17**
See also CA 106; CANR 107, 150

Crumb, Robert
See Crumb, R.

Crumbum
See Crumb, R.

Crumski
See Crumb, R.

Crum the Bum
See Crumb, R.

Crunk
See Crumb, R.

Crustt
See Crumb, R.

Crutchfield, Les
See Trumbo, Dalton

Cruz, Victor Hernandez 1949- ... **HLC 1; PC 37**
See also BW 2; CA 65-68; CAAS 17;
CANR 14, 32, 74, 132; CP 1, 2, 3, 4, 5,
6, 7; DAM MULT, POET; DLB 41; DNFS
1; EXPP; HW 1, 2; LLW; MTCW 2;
MTFW 2005; PFS 16; WP

Cryer, Gretchen (Kiger) 1935- .... **CLC 21**
See also CA 114; 123

Csath, Geza .... **TCLC 13**
See Brenner, Jozef
See also CA 111

Cudlip, David R(ockwell) 1933- .... **CLC 34**
See also CA 177

Cullen, Countee 1903-1946 . **BLC 1; HR 1:2; PC 20; TCLC 4, 37; WLCS**
See also AFAW 2; AMWS 4; BW 1; CA
108; 124; CDALB 1917-1929; DA; DA3;
DAC; DAM MST, MULT, POET; DLB 4,
48, 51; EWL 3; EXPP; LMFS 2; MAL 5;
MTCW 1, 2; MTFW 2005; PFS 3; RGAL
4; SATA 18; WP

Culleton, Beatrice 1949- .... **NNAL**
See also CA 120; CANR 83; DAC

Cum, R.
See Crumb, R.

Cumberland, Richard
1732-1811 .... **NCLC 167**
See also DLB 89; RGEL 2

Cummings, Bruce F(rederick) 1889-1919
See Barbellion, W. N. P.
See also CA 123

Cummings, E(dward) E(stlin)
1894-1962 .. **CLC 1, 3, 8, 12, 15, 68; PC 5; TCLC 137; WLC 2**
See also AAYA 41; AMW; CA 73-76;
CANR 31; CDALB 1929-1941; DA;
DA3; DAB; DAC; DAM MST, POET;
DLB 4, 48; EWL 3; EXPP; MAL 5;
MTCW 1, 2; MTFW 2005; PAB; PFS 1,
3, 12, 13, 19; RGAL 4; TUS; WP

Cummins, Maria Susanna
1827-1866 .... **NCLC 139**
See also DLB 42; YABC 1

Cunha, Euclides (Rodrigues Pimenta) da
1866-1909 .... **TCLC 24**
See also CA 123; 219; DLB 307; LAW;
WLIT 1

Cunningham, E. V.
See Fast, Howard

Cunningham, J(ames) V(incent)
1911-1985 .... **CLC 3, 31**
See also CA 1-4R; 115; CANR 1, 72; CP 1,
2, 3, 4; DLB 5

Cunningham, Julia (Woolfolk)
1916- .... **CLC 12**
See also CA 9-12R; CANR 4, 19, 36; CWRI
5; JRDA; MAICYA 1, 2; SAAS 2; SATA
1, 26, 132

Cunningham, Michael 1952- .... **CLC 34**
See also AMWS 15; CA 136; CANR 96;
CN 7; DLB 292; GLL 2; MTFW 2005;
NFS 23

Cunninghame Graham, R. B.
See Cunninghame Graham, Robert
(Gallnigad) Bontine

**Cunninghame Graham, Robert (Gallnigad)
Bontine** 1852-1936 .... **TCLC 19**
See Graham, R(obert) B(ontine) Cunning-
hame
See also CA 119; 184

Curnow, (Thomas) Allen (Monro)
1911-2001 .... **PC 48**
See also CA 69-72; 202; CANR 48, 99; CP
1, 2, 3, 4, 5, 6, 7; EWL 3; RGEL 2

Currie, Ellen 19(?)- .... **CLC 44**

Curtin, Philip
See Lowndes, Marie Adelaide (Belloc)

Curtin, Phillip
See Lowndes, Marie Adelaide (Belloc)

Curtis, Price
See Ellison, Harlan

Cusanus, Nicolaus 1401-1464 .... **LC 80**
See Nicholas of Cusa

Cutrate, Joe
See Spiegelman, Art

Cynewulf c. 770- .... **CMLC 23**
See also DLB 146; RGEL 2

Cyrano de Bergerac, Savinien de
1619-1655 .... **LC 65**
See also DLB 268; GFL Beginnings to
1789; RGWL 2, 3

Cyril of Alexandria c. 375-c. 430 . **CMLC 59**

Czaczkes, Shmuel Yosef Halevi
See Agnon, S(hmuel) Y(osef Halevi)

Dabrowska, Maria (Szumska)
1889-1965 .... **CLC 15**
See also CA 106; CDWLB 4; DLB 215;
EWL 3

Dabydeen, David 1955- .... **CLC 34**
See also BW 1; CA 125; CANR 56, 92; CN
6, 7; CP 5, 6, 7

Dacey, Philip 1939- .... **CLC 51**
See also CA 37-40R, 231; CAAE 231;
CAAS 17; CANR 14, 32, 64; CP 4, 5, 6,
7; DLB 105

Dacre, Charlotte c. 1772-1825(?) . **NCLC 151**

Dafydd ap Gwilym c. 1320-c. 1380 ..... **PC 56**

Dagerman, Stig (Halvard)
1923-1954 .... **TCLC 17**
See also CA 117; 155; DLB 259; EWL 3

D'Aguiar, Fred 1960- .... **CLC 145**
See also CA 148; CANR 83, 101; CN 7;
CP 5, 6, 7; DLB 157; EWL 3

Dahl, Roald 1916-1990 ...... **CLC 1, 6, 18, 79;
TCLC 173**
See also AAYA 15; BPFB 1; BRWS 4; BYA
5; CA 1-4R; 133; CANR 6, 32, 37, 62;
CLR 1, 7, 41, 111; CN 1, 2, 3, 4; CPW;
DA3; DAB; DAC; DAM MST, NOV,
POP; DLB 139, 255; HGG; JRDA; MAI-
CYA 1, 2; MTCW 1, 2; MTFW 2005;
RGSF 2; SATA 1, 26, 73; SATA-Obit 65;
SSFS 4; TEA; YAW

Dahlberg, Edward 1900-1977 .. **CLC 1, 7, 14**
See also CA 9-12R; 69-72; CANR 31, 62;
CN 1, 2; DLB 48; MAL 5; MTCW 1;
RGAL 4

Daitch, Susan 1954- .... **CLC 103**
See also CA 161

Dale, Colin .... **TCLC 18**
See Lawrence, T(homas) E(dward)

Dale, George E.
See Asimov, Isaac

d'Alembert, Jean Le Rond
1717-1783 .... **LC 126**

Dalton, Roque 1935-1975(?) ..... **HLCS 1; PC 36**
See also CA 176; DLB 283; HW 2

Daly, Elizabeth 1878-1967 .... **CLC 52**
See also CA 23-24; 25-28R; CANR 60;
CAP 2; CMW 4

Daly, Mary 1928- .... **CLC 173**
See also CA 25-28R; CANR 30, 62; FW;
GLL 1; MTCW 1

Daly, Maureen 1921-2006 .... **CLC 17**
See also AAYA 5, 58; BYA 6; CANR 37,
83, 108; CLR 96; JRDA; MAICYA 1, 2;
SAAS 1; SATA 2, 129; WYA; YAW

Derrida, Jacques 1930-2004 ...... **CLC 24, 87, 225**
See also CA 124; 127; 232; CANR 76, 98, 133; DLB 242; EWL 3; LMFS 2; MTCW 2; TWA

Derry Down Derry
See Lear, Edward

Dersonnes, Jacques
See Simenon, Georges (Jacques Christian)

Der Stricker c. 1190-c. 1250 .... **CMLC 75**
See also DLB 138

Desai, Anita 1937- .... **CLC 19, 37, 97, 175**
See also BRWS 5; CA 81-84; CANR 33, 53, 95, 133; CN 1, 2, 3, 4, 5, 6, 7; CWRI 5; DA3; DAB; DAM NOV; DLB 271, 323; DNFS 2; EWL 3; FW; MTCW 1, 2; MTFW 2005; SATA 63, 126

Desai, Kiran 1971- .... **CLC 119**
See also BYA 16; CA 171; CANR 127

de Saint-Luc, Jean
See Glassco, John

de Saint Roman, Arnaud
See Aragon, Louis

Desbordes-Valmore, Marceline
1786-1859 .... **NCLC 97**
See also DLB 217

Descartes, Rene 1596-1650 .... **LC 20, 35**
See also DLB 268; EW 3; GFL Beginnings to 1789

Deschamps, Eustache 1340(?)-1404 .. **LC 103**
See also DLB 208

De Sica, Vittorio 1901(?)-1974 .... **CLC 20**
See also CA 117

Desnos, Robert 1900-1945 .... **TCLC 22**
See also CA 121; 151; CANR 107; DLB 258; EWL 3; LMFS 2

Destouches, Louis-Ferdinand
1894-1961 .... **CLC 9, 15**
See Celine, Louis-Ferdinand
See also CA 85-88; CANR 28; MTCW 1

de Tolignac, Gaston
See Griffith, D(avid Lewelyn) W(ark)

Deutsch, Babette 1895-1982 .... **CLC 18**
See also BYA 3; CA 1-4R; 108; CANR 4, 79; CP 1, 2, 3; DLB 45; SATA 1; SATA-Obit 33

Devenant, William 1606-1649 .... **LC 13**

Devkota, Laxmiprasad 1909-1959 . **TCLC 23**
See also CA 123

De Voto, Bernard (Augustine)
1897-1955 .... **TCLC 29**
See also CA 113; 160; DLB 9, 256; MAL 5; TCWW 1, 2

De Vries, Peter 1910-1993 ..... **CLC 1, 2, 3, 7, 10, 28, 46**
See also CA 17-20R; 142; CANR 41; CN 1, 2, 3, 4, 5; DAM NOV; DLB 6; DLBY 1982; MAL 5; MTCW 1, 2; MTFW 2005

Dewey, John 1859-1952 .... **TCLC 95**
See also CA 114; 170; CANR 144; DLB 246, 270; RGAL 4

Dexter, John
See Bradley, Marion Zimmer
See also GLL 1

Dexter, Martin
See Faust, Frederick (Schiller)

Dexter, Pete 1943- .... **CLC 34, 55**
See also BEST 89:2; CA 127; 131; CANR 129; CPW; DAM POP; INT CA-131; MAL 5; MTCW 1; MTFW 2005

Diamano, Silmang
See Senghor, Leopold Sedar

Diamond, Neil 1941- .... **CLC 30**
See also CA 108

Diaz del Castillo, Bernal c.
1496-1584 .... **HLCS 1; LC 31**
See also DLB 318; LAW

di Bassetto, Corno
See Shaw, George Bernard

Dick, Philip K. 1928-1982 ... **CLC 10, 30, 72; SSC 57**
See also AAYA 24; BPFB 1; BYA 11; CA 49-52; 106; CANR 2, 16, 132; CN 2, 3; CPW; DA3; DAM NOV, POP; DLB 8; MTCW 1, 2; MTFW 2005; NFS 5; SCFW 1, 2; SFW 4

Dick, Philip Kindred
See Dick, Philip K.

Dickens, Charles (John Huffam)
1812-1870 .... **NCLC 3, 8, 18, 26, 37, 50, 86, 105, 113, 161; SSC 17, 49, 88; WLC 2**
See also AAYA 23; BRW 5; BRWC 1, 2; BYA 1, 2, 3, 13, 14; CDBLB 1832-1890; CLR 95; CMW 4; DA; DA3; DAB; DAC; DAM MST, NOV; DLB 21, 55, 70, 159, 166; EXPN; GL 2; HGG; JRDA; LAIT 1, 2; LATS 1:1; LMFS 1; MAICYA 1, 2; NFS 4, 5, 10, 14, 20; RGEL 2; RGSF 2; SATA 15; SUFW 1; TEA; WCH; WLIT 4; WYA

Dickey, James (Lafayette)
1923-1997 .... **CLC 1, 2, 4, 7, 10, 15, 47, 109; PC 40; TCLC 151**
See also AAYA 50; AITN 1, 2; AMWS 4; BPFB 1; CA 9-12R; 156; CABS 2; CANR 10, 48, 61, 105; CDALB 1968-1988; CP 1, 2, 3, 4, 5, 6; CPW; CSW; DA3; DAM NOV, POET, POP; DLB 5, 193; DLBD 7; DLBY 1982, 1993, 1996, 1997, 1998; EWL 3; INT CANR-10; MAL 5; MTCW 1, 2; NFS 9; PFS 6, 11; RGAL 4; TUS

Dickey, William 1928-1994 .... **CLC 3, 28**
See also CA 9-12R; 145; CANR 24, 79; CP 1, 2, 3, 4; DLB 5

Dickinson, Charles 1951- .... **CLC 49**
See also CA 128; CANR 141

Dickinson, Emily (Elizabeth)
1830-1886 ..... **NCLC 21, 77, 171; PC 1; WLC 2**
See also AAYA 22; AMW; AMWR 1; CDALB 1865-1917; DA; DA3; DAB; DAC; DAM MST, POET; DLB 1, 243; EXPP; FL 1:3; MBL; PFS 1, 2, 3, 4, 5, 6, 8, 10, 11, 13, 16; RGAL 4; SATA 29; TUS; WP; WYA

Dickinson, Mrs. Herbert Ward
See Phelps, Elizabeth Stuart

Dickinson, Peter (Malcolm de Brissac)
1927- .... **CLC 12, 35**
See also AAYA 9, 49; BYA 5; CA 41-44R; CANR 31, 58, 88, 134; CLR 29; CMW 4; DLB 87, 161, 276; JRDA; MAICYA 1, 2; SATA 5, 62, 95, 150; SFW 4; WYA; YAW

Dickson, Carr
See Carr, John Dickson

Dickson, Carter
See Carr, John Dickson

Diderot, Denis 1713-1784 .... **LC 26, 126**
See also DLB 313; EW 4; GFL Beginnings to 1789; LMFS 1; RGWL 2, 3

Didion, Joan 1934- . **CLC 1, 3, 8, 14, 32, 129**
See also AITN 1; AMWS 4; CA 5-8R; CANR 14, 52, 76, 125; CDALB 1968-1988; CN 2, 3, 4, 5, 6, 7; DA3; DAM NOV; DLB 2, 173, 185; DLBY 1981, 1986; EWL 3; MAL 5; MBL; MTCW 1, 2; MTFW 2005; NFS 3; RGAL 4; TCLE 1:1; TCWW 2; TUS

di Donato, Pietro 1911-1992 .... **TCLC 159**
See also CA 101; 136; DLB 9

Dietrich, Robert
See Hunt, E(verette) Howard, (Jr.)

Difusa, Pati
See Almodovar, Pedro

Dillard, Annie 1945- ...... **CLC 9, 60, 115, 216**
See also AAYA 6, 43; AMWS 6; ANW; CA 49-52; CANR 3, 43, 62, 90, 125; DA3; DAM NOV; DLB 275, 278; DLBY 1980; LAIT 4, 5; MAL 5; MTCW 1, 2; MTFW 2005; NCFS 1; RGAL 4; SATA 10, 140; TCLE 1:1; TUS

Dillard, R(ichard) H(enry) W(ilde)
1937- .... **CLC 5**
See also CA 21-24R; CAAS 7; CANR 10; CP 2, 3, 4, 5, 6, 7; CSW; DLB 5, 244

Dillon, Eilis 1920-1994 .... **CLC 17**
See also CA 9-12R, 182; 147; CAAE 182; CAAS 3; CANR 4, 38, 78; CLR 26; MAICYA 1, 2; MAICYAS 1; SATA 2, 74; SATA-Essay 105; SATA-Obit 83; YAW

Dimont, Penelope
See Mortimer, Penelope (Ruth)

Dinesen, Isak ..... **CLC 10, 29, 95; SSC 7, 75**
See Blixen, Karen (Christentze Dinesen)
See also EW 10; EWL 3; EXPS; FW; GL 2; HGG; LAIT 3; MTCW 1; NCFS 2; NFS 9; RGSF 2; RGWL 2, 3; SSFS 3, 6, 13; WLIT 2

Ding Ling .... **CLC 68**
See Chiang, Pin-chin
See also DLB 328; RGWL 3

Diphusa, Patty
See Almodovar, Pedro

Disch, Thomas M. 1940- .... **CLC 7, 36**
See Disch, Tom
See also AAYA 17; BPFB 1; CA 21-24R; CAAS 4; CANR 17, 36, 54, 89; CLR 18; CP 5, 6, 7; DA3; DLB 8; HGG; MAICYA 1, 2; MTCW 1, 2; MTFW 2005; SAAS 15; SATA 92; SCFW 1, 2; SFW 4; SUFW 2

Disch, Tom
See Disch, Thomas M.
See also DLB 282

d'Isly, Georges
See Simenon, Georges (Jacques Christian)

Disraeli, Benjamin 1804-1881 ... **NCLC 2, 39, 79**
See also BRW 4; DLB 21, 55; RGEL 2

Ditcum, Steve
See Crumb, R.

Dixon, Paige
See Corcoran, Barbara (Asenath)

Dixon, Stephen 1936- .... **CLC 52; SSC 16**
See also AMWS 12; CA 89-92; CANR 17, 40, 54, 91; CN 4, 5, 6, 7; DLB 130; MAL 5

Dixon, Thomas, Jr. 1864-1946 ..... **TCLC 163**
See also RHW

Djebar, Assia 1936- .... **CLC 182**
See also CA 188; EWL 3; RGWL 3; WLIT 2

Doak, Annie
See Dillard, Annie

Dobell, Sydney Thompson
1824-1874 .... **NCLC 43**
See also DLB 32; RGEL 2

Doblin, Alfred .... **TCLC 13**
See Doeblin, Alfred
See also CDWLB 2; EWL 3; RGWL 2, 3

Dobroliubov, Nikolai Aleksandrovich
See Dobrolyubov, Nikolai Alexandrovich
See also DLB 277

Dobrolyubov, Nikolai Alexandrovich
1836-1861 .... **NCLC 5**
See Dobroliubov, Nikolai Aleksandrovich

Dobson, Austin 1840-1921 .... **TCLC 79**
See also DLB 35, 144

Dobyns, Stephen 1941- .... **CLC 37**
See also AMWS 13; CA 45-48; CANR 2, 18, 99; CMW 4; CP 4, 5, 6, 7; PFS 23

Doctorow, Edgar Laurence
See Doctorow, E.L.

Doctorow, E.L. 1931- . CLC 6, 11, 15, 18, 37, 44, 65, 113, 214
See also AAYA 22; AITN 2; AMWS 4; BEST 89:3; BPFB 1; CA 45-48; CANR 2, 33, 51, 76, 97, 133; CDALB 1968-1988; CN 3, 4, 5, 6, 7; CPW; DA3; DAM NOV, POP; DLB 2, 28, 173; DLBY 1980; EWL 3; LAIT 3; MAL 5; MTCW 1, 2; MTFW 2005; NFS 6; RGAL 4; RGHL; RHW; TCLE 1:1; TCWW 1, 2; TUS

Dodgson, Charles L(utwidge) 1832-1898
See Carroll, Lewis
See also CLR 2; DA; DA3; DAB; DAC; DAM MST, NOV, POET; MAICYA 1, 2; SATA 100; YABC 2

Dodsley, Robert 1703-1764 .... LC 97
See also DLB 95; RGEL 2

Dodson, Owen (Vincent) 1914-1983 .. BLC 1; CLC 79
See also BW 1; CA 65-68; 110; CANR 24; DAM MULT; DLB 76

Doeblin, Alfred 1878-1957 .... TCLC 13
See Doblin, Alfred
See also CA 110; 141; DLB 66

Doerr, Harriet 1910-2002 .... CLC 34
See also CA 117; 122; 213; CANR 47; INT CA-122; LATS 1:2

Domecq, H(onorio Bustos)
See Bioy Casares, Adolfo

Domecq, H(onorio) Bustos
See Bioy Casares, Adolfo; Borges, Jorge Luis

Domini, Rey
See Lorde, Audre
See also GLL 1

Dominique
See Proust, (Valentin-Louis-George-Eugene) Marcel

Don, A
See Stephen, Sir Leslie

Donaldson, Stephen R(eeder) 1947- .... CLC 46, 138
See also AAYA 36; BPFB 1; CA 89-92; CANR 13, 55, 99; CPW; DAM POP; FANT; INT CANR-13; SATA 121; SFW 4; SUFW 1, 2

Donleavy, J(ames) P(atrick) 1926- .... CLC 1, 4, 6, 10, 45
See also AITN 2; BPFB 1; CA 9-12R; CANR 24, 49, 62, 80, 124; CBD; CD 5, 6; CN 1, 2, 3, 4, 5, 6, 7; DLB 6, 173; INT CANR-24; MAL 5; MTCW 1, 2; MTFW 2005; RGAL 4

Donnadieu, Marguerite
See Duras, Marguerite

Donne, John 1572-1631 ... LC 10, 24, 91; PC 1, 43; WLC 2
See also AAYA 67; BRW 1; BRWC 1; BRWR 2; CDBLB Before 1660; DA; DAB; DAC; DAM MST, POET; DLB 121, 151; EXPP; PAB; PFS 2, 11; RGEL 3; TEA; WLIT 3; WP

Donnell, David 1939(?)- .... CLC 34
See also CA 197

Donoghue, Denis 1928- .... CLC 209
See also CA 17-20R; CANR 16, 102

Donoghue, P. S.
See Hunt, E(verette) Howard, (Jr.)

Donoso (Yanez), Jose 1924-1996 ... CLC 4, 8, 11, 32, 99; HLC 1; SSC 34; TCLC 133
See also CA 81-84; 155; CANR 32, 73; CD-WLB 3; CWW 2; DAM MULT; DLB 113; EWL 3; HW 1, 2; LAW; LAWS 1; MTCW 1, 2; MTFW 2005; RGSF 2; WLIT 1

Donovan, John 1928-1992 .... CLC 35
See also AAYA 20; CA 97-100; 137; CLR 3; MAICYA 1, 2; SATA 72; SATA-Brief 29; YAW

Don Roberto
See Cunninghame Graham, Robert (Gallnigad) Bontine

Doolittle, Hilda 1886-1961 . CLC 3, 8, 14, 31, 34, 73; PC 5; WLC 3
See H. D.
See also AAYA 66; AMWS 1; CA 97-100; CANR 35, 131; DA; DAC; DAM MST, POET; DLB 4, 45; EWL 3; FW; GLL 1; LMFS 2; MAL 5; MBL; MTCW 1, 2; MTFW 2005; PFS 6; RGAL 4

Doppo, Kunikida .... TCLC 99
See Kunikida Doppo

Dorfman, Ariel 1942- .... CLC 48, 77, 189; HLC 1
See also CA 124; 130; CANR 67, 70, 135; CWW 2; DAM MULT; DFS 4; EWL 3; HW 1, 2; INT CA-130; WLIT 1

Dorn, Edward (Merton) 1929-1999 .... CLC 10, 18
See also CA 93-96; 187; CANR 42, 79; CP 1, 2, 3, 4, 5, 6, 7; DLB 5; INT CA-93-96; WP

Dor-Ner, Zvi .... CLC 70

Dorris, Michael 1945-1997 .... CLC 109; NNAL
See also AAYA 20; BEST 90:1; BYA 12; CA 102; 157; CANR 19, 46, 75; CLR 58; DA3; DAM MULT, NOV; DLB 175; LAIT 5; MTCW 2; MTFW 2005; NFS 3; RGAL 4; SATA 75; SATA-Obit 94; TCWW 2; YAW

Dorris, Michael A.
See Dorris, Michael

Dorsan, Luc
See Simenon, Georges (Jacques Christian)

Dorsange, Jean
See Simenon, Georges (Jacques Christian)

Dorset
See Sackville, Thomas

Dos Passos, John (Roderigo) 1896-1970 ... CLC 1, 4, 8, 11, 15, 25, 34, 82; WLC 2
See also AMW; BPFB 1; CA 1-4R; 29-32R; CANR 3; CDALB 1929-1941; DA; DA3; DAB; DAC; DAM MST, NOV; DLB 4, 9, 274, 316; DLBD 1, 15; DLBY 1996; EWL 3; MAL 5; MTCW 1, 2; MTFW 2005; NFS 14; RGAL 4; TUS

Dossage, Jean
See Simenon, Georges (Jacques Christian)

Dostoevsky, Fedor Mikhailovich 1821-1881 .. NCLC 2, 7, 21, 33, 43, 119, 167; SSC 2, 33, 44; WLC 2
See Dostoevsky, Fyodor
See also AAYA 40; DA; DA3; DAB; DAC; DAM MST, NOV; EW 7; EXPN; NFS 3, 8; RGSF 2; RGWL 2, 3; SSFS 8; TWA

Dostoevsky, Fyodor
See Dostoevsky, Fedor Mikhailovich
See also DLB 238; LATS 1:1; LMFS 1, 2

Doty, M. R.
See Doty, Mark (Alan)

Doty, Mark
See Doty, Mark (Alan)

Doty, Mark (Alan) 1953(?)- .... CLC 176; PC 53
See also AMWS 11; CA 161, 183; CAAE 183; CANR 110; CP 7

Doty, Mark A.
See Doty, Mark (Alan)

Doughty, Charles M(ontagu) 1843-1926 .... TCLC 27
See also CA 115; 178; DLB 19, 57, 174

Douglas, Ellen .... CLC 73
See Haxton, Josephine Ayres; Williamson, Ellen Douglas
See also CN 5, 6, 7; CSW; DLB 292

Douglas, Gavin 1475(?)-1522 .... LC 20
See also DLB 132; RGEL 2

Douglas, George
See Brown, George Douglas
See also RGEL 2

Douglas, Keith (Castellain) 1920-1944 .... TCLC 40
See also BRW 7; CA 160; DLB 27; EWL 3; PAB; RGEL 2

Douglas, Leonard
See Bradbury, Ray

Douglas, Michael
See Crichton, Michael

Douglas, (George) Norman 1868-1952 .... TCLC 68
See also BRW 6; CA 119; 157; DLB 34, 195; RGEL 2

Douglas, William
See Brown, George Douglas

Douglass, Frederick 1817(?)-1895 ..... BLC 1; NCLC 7, 55, 141; WLC 2
See also AAYA 48; AFAW 1, 2; AMWC 1; AMWS 3; CDALB 1640-1865; DA; DA3; DAC; DAM MST, MULT; DLB 1, 43, 50, 79, 243; FW; LAIT 2; NCFS 2; RGAL 4; SATA 29

Dourado, (Waldomiro Freitas) Autran 1926- .... CLC 23, 60
See also CA 25-28R; 179; CANR 34, 81; DLB 145, 307; HW 2

Dourado, Waldomiro Freitas Autran
See Dourado, (Waldomiro Freitas) Autran

Dove, Rita 1952- .. BLCS; CLC 50, 81; PC 6
See Dove, Rita Frances
See also AAYA 46; AMWS 4; BW 2; CA 109; CAAS 19; CANR 27, 42, 68, 76, 97, 132; CDALBS; CP 5, 6, 7; CSW; CWP; DA3; DAM MULT, POET; DLB 120; EWL 3; EXPP; MAL 5; MTCW 2; MTFW 2005; PFS 1, 15; RGAL 4

Doveglion
See Villa, Jose Garcia

Dowell, Coleman 1925-1985 .... CLC 60
See also CA 25-28R; 117; CANR 10; DLB 130; GLL 2

Dowson, Ernest (Christopher) 1867-1900 .... TCLC 4
See also CA 105; 150; DLB 19, 135; RGEL 2

Doyle, A. Conan
See Doyle, Sir Arthur Conan

Doyle, Sir Arthur Conan 1859-1930 ..... SSC 12, 83, 95; TCLC 7; WLC 2
See Conan Doyle, Arthur
See also AAYA 14; BRWS 2; CA 104; 122; CANR 131; CDBLB 1890-1914; CLR 106; CMW 4; DA; DA3; DAB; DAC; DAM MST, NOV; DLB 18, 70, 156, 178; EXPS; HGG; LAIT 2; MSW; MTCW 1, 2; MTFW 2005; RGEL 2; RGSF 2; RHW; SATA 24; SCFW 1, 2; SFW 4; SSFS 2; TEA; WCH; WLIT 4; WYA; YAW

Doyle, Conan
See Doyle, Sir Arthur Conan

Doyle, John
See Graves, Robert

Doyle, Roddy 1958- .... CLC 81, 178
See also AAYA 14; BRWS 5; CA 143; CANR 73, 128; CN 6, 7; DA3; DLB 194, 326; MTCW 2; MTFW 2005

Doyle, Sir A. Conan
See Doyle, Sir Arthur Conan

Dr. A
See Asimov, Isaac; Silverstein, Alvin; Silverstein, Virginia B(arbara Opshelor)

Drabble, Margaret 1939- ...... **CLC 2, 3, 5, 8, 10, 22, 53, 129**
See also BRWS 4; CA 13-16R; CANR 18, 35, 63, 112, 131; CDBLB 1960 to Present; CN 1, 2, 3, 4, 5, 6, 7; CPW; DA3; DAB; DAC; DAM MST, NOV, POP; DLB 14, 155, 231; EWL 3; FW; MTCW 1, 2; MTFW 2005; RGEL 2; SATA 48; TEA

Drakulic, Slavenka 1949- .... **CLC 173**
See also CA 144; CANR 92

Drakulic-Ilic, Slavenka
See Drakulic, Slavenka

Drapier, M. B.
See Swift, Jonathan

Drayham, James
See Mencken, H(enry) L(ouis)

Drayton, Michael 1563-1631 .... **LC 8**
See also DAM POET; DLB 121; RGEL 2

Dreadstone, Carl
See Campbell, (John) Ramsey

Dreiser, Theodore 1871-1945 .... **SSC 30; TCLC 10, 18, 35, 83; WLC 2**
See also AMW; AMWC 2; AMWR 2; BYA 15, 16; CA 106; 132; CDALB 1865-1917; DA; DA3; DAC; DAM MST, NOV; DLB 9, 12, 102, 137; DLBD 1; EWL 3; LAIT 2; LMFS 2; MAL 5; MTCW 1, 2; MTFW 2005; NFS 8, 17; RGAL 4; TUS

Dreiser, Theodore Herman Albert
See Dreiser, Theodore

Drexler, Rosalyn 1926- .... **CLC 2, 6**
See also CA 81-84; CAD; CANR 68, 124; CD 5, 6; CWD; MAL 5

Dreyer, Carl Theodor 1889-1968 ...... **CLC 16**
See also CA 116

Drieu la Rochelle, Pierre
1893-1945 .... **TCLC 21**
See also CA 117; 250; DLB 72; EWL 3; GFL 1789 to the Present

Drieu la Rochelle, Pierre-Eugene 1893-1945
See Drieu la Rochelle, Pierre

Drinkwater, John 1882-1937 .... **TCLC 57**
See also CA 109; 149; DLB 10, 19, 149; RGEL 2

Drop Shot
See Cable, George Washington

Droste-Hulshoff, Annette Freiin von
1797-1848 .... **NCLC 3, 133**
See also CDWLB 2; DLB 133; RGSF 2; RGWL 2, 3

Drummond, Walter
See Silverberg, Robert

Drummond, William Henry
1854-1907 .... **TCLC 25**
See also CA 160; DLB 92

Drummond de Andrade, Carlos
1902-1987 .... **CLC 18; TCLC 139**
See Andrade, Carlos Drummond de
See also CA 132; 123; DLB 307; LAW

Drummond of Hawthornden, William
1585-1649 .... **LC 83**
See also DLB 121, 213; RGEL 2

Drury, Allen (Stuart) 1918-1998 .... **CLC 37**
See also CA 57-60; 170; CANR 18, 52; CN 1, 2, 3, 4, 5, 6; INT CANR-18

Druse, Eleanor
See King, Stephen

Dryden, John 1631-1700 ..... **DC 3; LC 3, 21, 115; PC 25; WLC 2**
See also BRW 2; CDBLB 1660-1789; DA; DAB; DAC; DAM DRAM, MST, POET; DLB 80, 101, 131; EXPP; IDTP; LMFS 1; RGEL 2; TEA; WLIT 3

du Bellay, Joachim 1524-1560 .... **LC 92**
See also DLB 327; GFL Beginnings to 1789; RGWL 2, 3

Duberman, Martin (Bauml) 1930- ..... **CLC 8**
See also CA 1-4R; CAD; CANR 2, 63, 137; CD 5, 6

Dubie, Norman (Evans) 1945- .... **CLC 36**
See also CA 69-72; CANR 12, 115; CP 3, 4, 5, 6, 7; DLB 120; PFS 12

Du Bois, W(illiam) E(dward) B(urghardt)
1868-1963 ..... **BLC 1; CLC 1, 2, 13, 64, 96; HR 1:2; TCLC 169; WLC 2**
See also AAYA 40; AFAW 1, 2; AMWC 1; AMWS 2; BW 1, 3; CA 85-88; CANR 34, 82, 132; CDALB 1865-1917; DA; DA3; DAC; DAM MST, MULT, NOV; DLB 47, 50, 91, 246, 284; EWL 3; EXPP; LAIT 2; LMFS 2; MAL 5; MTCW 1, 2; MTFW 2005; NCFS 1; PFS 13; RGAL 4; SATA 42

Dubus, Andre 1936-1999 ..... **CLC 13, 36, 97; SSC 15**
See also AMWS 7; CA 21-24R; 177; CANR 17; CN 5, 6; CSW; DLB 130; INT CANR-17; RGAL 4; SSFS 10; TCLE 1:1

Duca Minimo
See D'Annunzio, Gabriele

Ducharme, Rejean 1941- .... **CLC 74**
See also CA 165; DLB 60

du Chatelet, Emilie 1706-1749 .... **LC 96**
See Chatelet, Gabrielle-Emilie Du

Duchen, Claire .... **CLC 65**

Duclos, Charles Pinot- 1704-1772 .... **LC 1**
See also GFL Beginnings to 1789

Dudek, Louis 1918-2001 .... **CLC 11, 19**
See also CA 45-48; 215; CAAS 14; CANR 1; CP 1, 2, 3, 4, 5, 6, 7; DLB 88

Duerrenmatt, Friedrich 1921-1990 ... **CLC 1, 4, 8, 11, 15, 43, 102**
See Durrenmatt, Friedrich
See also CA 17-20R; CANR 33; CMW 4; DAM DRAM; DLB 69, 124; MTCW 1, 2

Duffy, Bruce 1953(?)- .... **CLC 50**
See also CA 172

Duffy, Maureen (Patricia) 1933- ...... **CLC 37**
See also CA 25-28R; CANR 33, 68; CBD; CN 1, 2, 3, 4, 5, 6, 7; CP 5, 6, 7; CWD; CWP; DFS 15; DLB 14, 310; FW; MTCW 1

Du Fu
See Tu Fu
See also RGWL 2, 3

Dugan, Alan 1923-2003 .... **CLC 2, 6**
See also CA 81-84; 220; CANR 119; CP 1, 2, 3, 4, 5, 6, 7; DLB 5; MAL 5; PFS 10

du Gard, Roger Martin
See Martin du Gard, Roger

Duhamel, Georges 1884-1966 .... **CLC 8**
See also CA 81-84; 25-28R; CANR 35; DLB 65; EWL 3; GFL 1789 to the Present; MTCW 1

Dujardin, Edouard (Emile Louis)
1861-1949 .... **TCLC 13**
See also CA 109; DLB 123

Duke, Raoul
See Thompson, Hunter S.

Dulles, John Foster 1888-1959 .... **TCLC 72**
See also CA 115; 149

Dumas, Alexandre (pere)
1802-1870 .... **NCLC 11, 71; WLC 2**
See also AAYA 22; BYA 3; DA; DA3; DAB; DAC; DAM MST, NOV; DLB 119, 192; EW 6; GFL 1789 to the Present; LAIT 2; NFS 14, 19; RGWL 2, 3; SATA 18; TWA; WCH

Dumas, Alexandre (fils) 1824-1895 ...... **DC 1; NCLC 9**
See also DLB 192; GFL 1789 to the Present; RGWL 2, 3

Dumas, Claudine
See Malzberg, Barry N(athaniel)

Dumas, Henry L. 1934-1968 .... **CLC 6, 62**
See also BW 1; CA 85-88; DLB 41; RGAL 4

du Maurier, Daphne 1907-1989 .. **CLC 6, 11, 59; SSC 18**
See also AAYA 37; BPFB 1; BRWS 3; CA 5-8R; 128; CANR 6, 55; CMW 4; CN 1, 2, 3, 4; CPW; DA3; DAB; DAC; DAM MST, POP; DLB 191; GL 2; HGG; LAIT 3; MSW; MTCW 1, 2; NFS 12; RGEL 2; RGSF 2; RHW; SATA 27; SATA-Obit 60; SSFS 14, 16; TEA

Du Maurier, George 1834-1896 ..... **NCLC 86**
See also DLB 153, 178; RGEL 2

Dunbar, Paul Laurence 1872-1906 ... **BLC 1; PC 5; SSC 8; TCLC 2, 12; WLC 2**
See also AFAW 1, 2; AMWS 2; BW 1, 3; CA 104; 124; CANR 79; CDALB 1865-1917; DA; DA3; DAC; DAM MST, MULT, POET; DLB 50, 54, 78; EXPP; MAL 5; RGAL 4; SATA 34

Dunbar, William 1460(?)-1520(?) .... **LC 20; PC 67**
See also BRWS 8; DLB 132, 146; RGEL 2

Dunbar-Nelson, Alice .... **HR 1:2**
See Nelson, Alice Ruth Moore Dunbar

Duncan, Dora Angela
See Duncan, Isadora

Duncan, Isadora 1877(?)-1927 .... **TCLC 68**
See also CA 118; 149

Duncan, Lois 1934- .... **CLC 26**
See also AAYA 4, 34; BYA 6, 8; CA 1-4R; CANR 2, 23, 36, 111; CLR 29; JRDA; MAICYA 1, 2; MAICYAS 1; MTFW 2005; SAAS 2; SATA 1, 36, 75, 133, 141; SATA-Essay 141; WYA; YAW

Duncan, Robert 1919-1988 ... **CLC 1, 2, 4, 7, 15, 41, 55; PC 2**
See also BG 1:2; CA 9-12R; 124; CANR 28, 62; CP 1, 2, 3, 4; DAM POET; DLB 5, 16, 193; EWL 3; MAL 5; MTCW 1, 2; MTFW 2005; PFS 13; RGAL 4; WP

Duncan, Sara Jeannette
1861-1922 .... **TCLC 60**
See also CA 157; DLB 92

Dunlap, William 1766-1839 .... **NCLC 2**
See also DLB 30, 37, 59; RGAL 4

Dunn, Douglas (Eaglesham) 1942- .... **CLC 6, 40**
See also BRWS 10; CA 45-48; CANR 2, 33, 126; CP 1, 2, 3, 4, 5, 6, 7; DLB 40; MTCW 1

Dunn, Katherine 1945- .... **CLC 71**
See also CA 33-36R; CANR 72; HGG; MTCW 2; MTFW 2005

Dunn, Stephen 1939- .... **CLC 36, 206**
See also AMWS 11; CA 33-36R; CANR 12, 48, 53, 105; CP 3, 4, 5, 6, 7; DLB 105; PFS 21

Dunn, Stephen Elliott
See Dunn, Stephen

Dunne, Finley Peter 1867-1936 ...... **TCLC 28**
See also CA 108; 178; DLB 11, 23; RGAL 4

Dunne, John Gregory 1932-2003 ..... **CLC 28**
See also CA 25-28R; 222; CANR 14, 50; CN 5, 6, 7; DLBY 1980

Dunsany, Lord .... **TCLC 2, 59**
See Dunsany, Edward John Moreton Drax Plunkett
See also DLB 77, 153, 156, 255; FANT; IDTP; RGEL 2; SFW 4; SUFW 1

Dunsany, Edward John Moreton Drax Plunkett 1878-1957
See Dunsany, Lord
See also CA 104; 148; DLB 10; MTCW 2

Duns Scotus, John 1266(?)-1308 ... **CMLC 59**
See also DLB 115

du Perry, Jean
See Simenon, Georges (Jacques Christian)

Fargue, Leon-Paul 1876(?)-1947 .... **TCLC 11**
See also CA 109; CANR 107; DLB 258;
EWL 3
Farigoule, Louis
See Romains, Jules
Farina, Richard 1936(?)-1966 .... **CLC 9**
See also CA 81-84; 25-28R
Farley, Walter (Lorimer)
1915-1989 .... **CLC 17**
See also AAYA 58; BYA 14; CA 17-20R;
CANR 8, 29, 84; DLB 22; JRDA; MAI-
CYA 1, 2; SATA 2, 43, 132; YAW
Farmer, Philip Jose 1918- .... **CLC 1, 19**
See also AAYA 28; BPFB 1; CA 1-4R;
CANR 4, 35, 111; DLB 8; MTCW 1;
SATA 93; SCFW 1, 2; SFW 4
Farquhar, George 1677-1707 .... **LC 21**
See also BRW 2; DAM DRAM; DLB 84;
RGEL 2
Farrell, J(ames) G(ordon)
1935-1979 .... **CLC 6**
See also CA 73-76; 89-92; CANR 36; CN
1, 2; DLB 14, 271, 326; MTCW 1; RGEL
2; RHW; WLIT 4
Farrell, James T(homas) 1904-1979 . **CLC 1,
4, 8, 11, 66; SSC 28**
See also AMW; BPFB 1; CA 5-8R; 89-92;
CANR 9, 61; CN 1, 2; DLB 4, 9, 86;
DLBD 2; EWL 3; MAL 5; MTCW 1, 2;
MTFW 2005; RGAL 4
Farrell, Warren (Thomas) 1943- ...... **CLC 70**
See also CA 146; CANR 120
Farren, Richard J.
See Betjeman, John
Farren, Richard M.
See Betjeman, John
Fassbinder, Rainer Werner
1946-1982 .... **CLC 20**
See also CA 93-96; 106; CANR 31
Fast, Howard 1914-2003 .... **CLC 23, 131**
See also AAYA 16; BPFB 1; CA 1-4R, 181;
214; CAAE 181; CAAS 18; CANR 1, 33,
54, 75, 98, 140; CMW 4; CN 1, 2, 3, 4, 5,
6, 7; CPW; DAM NOV; DLB 9; INT
CANR-33; LATS 1:1; MAL 5; MTCW 2;
MTFW 2005; RHW; SATA 7; SATA-
Essay 107; TCWW 1, 2; YAW
Faulcon, Robert
See Holdstock, Robert P.
Faulkner, William (Cuthbert)
1897-1962 .... **CLC 1, 3, 6, 8, 9, 11, 14,
18, 28, 52, 68; SSC 1, 35, 42, 92;
TCLC 141; WLC 2**
See also AAYA 7; AMW; AMWR 1; BPFB
1; BYA 5, 15; CA 81-84; CANR 33;
CDALB 1929-1941; DA; DA3; DAB;
DAC; DAM MST, NOV; DLB 9, 11, 44,
102, 316, 330; DLBD 2; DLBY 1986,
1997; EWL 3; EXPN; EXPS; GL 2; LAIT
2; LATS 1:1; LMFS 2; MAL 5; MTCW
1, 2; MTFW 2005; NFS 4, 8, 13, 24;
RGAL 4; RGSF 2; SSFS 2, 5, 6, 12; TUS
Fauset, Jessie Redmon
1882(?)-1961 .. **BLC 2; CLC 19, 54; HR
1:2**
See also AFAW 2; BW 1; CA 109; CANR
83; DAM MULT; DLB 51; FW; LMFS 2;
MAL 5; MBL
Faust, Frederick (Schiller)
1892-1944 .... **TCLC 49**
See Brand, Max; Dawson, Peter; Frederick,
John
See also CA 108; 152; CANR 143; DAM
POP; DLB 256; TUS
Faust, Irvin 1924- .... **CLC 8**
See also CA 33-36R; CANR 28, 67; CN 1,
2, 3, 4, 5, 6, 7; DLB 2, 28, 218, 278;
DLBY 1980
Fawkes, Guy
See Benchley, Robert (Charles)

Fearing, Kenneth (Flexner)
1902-1961 .... **CLC 51**
See also CA 93-96; CANR 59; CMW 4;
DLB 9; MAL 5; RGAL 4
Fecamps, Elise
See Creasey, John
Federman, Raymond 1928- .... **CLC 6, 47**
See also CA 17-20R, 208; CAAE 208;
CAAS 8; CANR 10, 43, 83, 108; CN 3,
4, 5, 6; DLBY 1980
Federspiel, J(uerg) F. 1931- .... **CLC 42**
See also CA 146
Feiffer, Jules (Ralph) 1929- ...... **CLC 2, 8, 64**
See also AAYA 3, 62; CA 17-20R; CAD;
CANR 30, 59, 129; CD 5, 6; DAM
DRAM; DLB 7, 44; INT CANR-30;
MTCW 1; SATA 8, 61, 111, 157
Feige, Hermann Albert Otto Maximilian
See Traven, B.
Feinberg, David B. 1956-1994 .... **CLC 59**
See also CA 135; 147
Feinstein, Elaine 1930- .... **CLC 36**
See also CA 69-72; CAAS 1; CANR 31,
68, 121; CN 3, 4, 5, 6, 7; CP 2, 3, 4, 5, 6,
7; CWP; DLB 14, 40; MTCW 1
Feke, Gilbert David .... **CLC 65**
Feldman, Irving (Mordecai) 1928- ..... **CLC 7**
See also CA 1-4R; CANR 1; CP 1, 2, 3, 4,
5, 6, 7; DLB 169; TCLE 1:1
Felix-Tchicaya, Gerald
See Tchicaya, Gerald Felix
Fellini, Federico 1920-1993 .... **CLC 16, 85**
See also CA 65-68; 143; CANR 33
Felltham, Owen 1602(?)-1668 .... **LC 92**
See also DLB 126, 151
Felsen, Henry Gregor 1916-1995 ..... **CLC 17**
See also CA 1-4R; 180; CANR 1; SAAS 2;
SATA 1
Felski, Rita .... **CLC 65**
Fenno, Jack
See Calisher, Hortense
Fenollosa, Ernest (Francisco)
1853-1908 .... **TCLC 91**
Fenton, James Martin 1949- .... **CLC 32, 209**
See also CA 102; CANR 108; CP 2, 3, 4, 5,
6, 7; DLB 40; PFS 11
Ferber, Edna 1887-1968 .... **CLC 18, 93**
See also AITN 1; CA 5-8R; 25-28R; CANR
68, 105; DLB 9, 28, 86, 266; MAL 5;
MTCW 1, 2; MTFW 2005; RGAL 4;
RHW; SATA 7; TCWW 1, 2
Ferdowsi, Abu'l Qasem
940-1020(?) .... **CMLC 43**
See Firdawsi, Abu al-Qasim
See also RGWL 2, 3
Ferguson, Helen
See Kavan, Anna
Ferguson, Niall 1964- .... **CLC 134**
See also CA 190; CANR 154
Ferguson, Samuel 1810-1886 .... **NCLC 33**
See also DLB 32; RGEL 2
Fergusson, Robert 1750-1774 .... **LC 29**
See also DLB 109; RGEL 2
Ferling, Lawrence
See Ferlinghetti, Lawrence
Ferlinghetti, Lawrence 1919(?)- .... **CLC 2, 6,
10, 27, 111; PC 1**
See also BG 1:2; CA 5-8R; CAD; CANR 3,
41, 73, 125; CDALB 1941-1968; CP 1, 2,
3, 4, 5, 6, 7; DA3; DAM POET; DLB 5,
16; MAL 5; MTCW 1, 2; MTFW 2005;
RGAL 4; WP
Ferlinghetti, Lawrence Monsanto
See Ferlinghetti, Lawrence
Fern, Fanny
See Parton, Sara Payson Willis
Fernandez, Vicente Garcia Huidobro
See Huidobro Fernandez, Vicente Garcia

Fernandez-Armesto, Felipe .... **CLC 70**
See Fernandez-Armesto, Felipe Fermin
Ricardo
See also CANR 153
Fernandez-Armesto, Felipe Fermin Ricardo
1950-
See Fernandez-Armesto, Felipe
See also CA 142; CANR 93
Fernandez de Lizardi, Jose Joaquin
See Lizardi, Jose Joaquin Fernandez de
Ferre, Rosario 1938- ...... **CLC 139; HLCS 1;
SSC 36**
See also CA 131; CANR 55, 81, 134; CWW
2; DLB 145; EWL 3; HW 1, 2; LAWS 1;
MTCW 2; MTFW 2005; WLIT 1
Ferrer, Gabriel (Francisco Victor) Miro
See Miro (Ferrer), Gabriel (Francisco
Victor)
Ferrier, Susan (Edmonstone)
1782-1854 .... **NCLC 8**
See also DLB 116; RGEL 2
Ferrigno, Robert 1948(?)- .... **CLC 65**
See also CA 140; CANR 125
Ferron, Jacques 1921-1985 .... **CLC 94**
See also CA 117; 129; CCA 1; DAC; DLB
60; EWL 3
Feuchtwanger, Lion 1884-1958 .... **TCLC 3**
See also CA 104; 187; DLB 66; EWL 3;
RGHL
Feuerbach, Ludwig 1804-1872 ..... **NCLC 139**
See also DLB 133
Feuillet, Octave 1821-1890 .... **NCLC 45**
See also DLB 192
Feydeau, Georges (Leon Jules Marie)
1862-1921 .... **TCLC 22**
See also CA 113; 152; CANR 84; DAM
DRAM; DLB 192; EWL 3; GFL 1789 to
the Present; RGWL 2, 3
Fichte, Johann Gottlieb
1762-1814 .... **NCLC 62**
See also DLB 90
Ficino, Marsilio 1433-1499 .... **LC 12**
See also LMFS 1
Fiedeler, Hans
See Doeblin, Alfred
Fiedler, Leslie A(aron) 1917-2003 ..... **CLC 4,
13, 24**
See also AMWS 13; CA 9-12R; 212; CANR
7, 63; CN 1, 2, 3, 4, 5, 6; DLB 28, 67;
EWL 3; MAL 5; MTCW 1, 2; RGAL 4;
TUS
Field, Andrew 1938- .... **CLC 44**
See also CA 97-100; CANR 25
Field, Eugene 1850-1895 .... **NCLC 3**
See also DLB 23, 42, 140; DLBD 13; MAI-
CYA 1, 2; RGAL 4; SATA 16
Field, Gans T.
See Wellman, Manly Wade
Field, Michael 1915-1971 .... **TCLC 43**
See also CA 29-32R
Fielding, Helen 1958- .... **CLC 146, 217**
See also AAYA 65; CA 172; CANR 127;
DLB 231; MTFW 2005
Fielding, Henry 1707-1754 .... **LC 1, 46, 85;
WLC 2**
See also BRW 3; BRWR 1; CDBLB 1660-
1789; DA; DA3; DAB; DAC; DAM
DRAM, MST, NOV; DLB 39, 84, 101;
NFS 18; RGEL 2; TEA; WLIT 3
Fielding, Sarah 1710-1768 .... **LC 1, 44**
See also DLB 39; RGEL 2; TEA
Fields, W. C. 1880-1946 .... **TCLC 80**
See also DLB 44
Fierstein, Harvey (Forbes) 1954- ..... **CLC 33**
See also CA 123; 129; CAD; CD 5, 6;
CPW; DA3; DAM DRAM, POP; DFS 6;
DLB 266; GLL; MAL 5

Forez
See Mauriac, Francois (Charles)

Forman, James
See Forman, James D(ouglas)

Forman, James D(ouglas) 1932- .... **CLC 21**
See also AAYA 17; CA 9-12R; CANR 4, 19, 42; JRDA; MAICYA 1, 2; SATA 8, 70; YAW

Forman, Milos 1932- .... **CLC 164**
See also AAYA 63; CA 109

Fornes, Maria Irene 1930- .... **CLC 39, 61, 187; DC 10; HLCS 1**
See also CA 25-28R; CAD; CANR 28, 81; CD 5, 6; CWD; DLB 7; HW 1, 2; INT CANR-28; LLW; MAL 5; MTCW 1; RGAL 4

Forrest, Leon (Richard)
1937-1997 .... **BLCS; CLC 4**
See also AFAW 2; BW 2; CA 89-92; 162; CAAS 7; CANR 25, 52, 87; CN 4, 5, 6; DLB 33

Forster, E(dward) M(organ)
1879-1970 ...... **CLC 1, 2, 3, 4, 9, 10, 13, 15, 22, 45, 77; SSC 27; TCLC 125; WLC 2**
See also AAYA 2, 37; BRW 6; BRWR 2; BYA 12; CA 13-14; 25-28R; CANR 45; CAP 1; CDBLB 1914-1945; DA; DA3; DAB; DAC; DAM MST, NOV; DLB 34, 98, 162, 178, 195; DLBD 10; EWL 3; EXPN; LAIT 3; LMFS 1; MTCW 1, 2; MTFW 2005; NCFS 1; NFS 3, 10, 11; RGEL 2; RGSF 2; SATA 57; SUFW 1; TEA; WLIT 4

Forster, John 1812-1876 .... **NCLC 11**
See also DLB 144, 184

Forster, Margaret 1938- .... **CLC 149**
See also CA 133; CANR 62, 115; CN 4, 5, 6, 7; DLB 155, 271

Forsyth, Frederick 1938- .... **CLC 2, 5, 36**
See also BEST 89:4; CA 85-88; CANR 38, 62, 115, 137; CMW 4; CN 3, 4, 5, 6, 7; CPW; DAM NOV, POP; DLB 87; MTCW 1, 2; MTFW 2005

Forten, Charlotte L. 1837-1914 .... **BLC 2; TCLC 16**
See Grimke, Charlotte L(ottie) Forten
See also DLB 50, 239

Fortinbras
See Grieg, (Johan) Nordahl (Brun)

Foscolo, Ugo 1778-1827 .... **NCLC 8, 97**
See also EW 5; WLIT 7

Fosse, Bob 1927-1987
See Fosse, Robert L.
See also CA 110; 123

Fosse, Robert L. .... **CLC 20**
See Fosse, Bob

Foster, Hannah Webster
1758-1840 .... **NCLC 99**
See also DLB 37, 200; RGAL 4

Foster, Stephen Collins
1826-1864 .... **NCLC 26**
See also RGAL 4

Foucault, Michel 1926-1984 . **CLC 31, 34, 69**
See also CA 105; 113; CANR 34; DLB 242; EW 13; EWL 3; GFL 1789 to the Present; GLL 1; LMFS 2; MTCW 1, 2; TWA

Fouque, Friedrich (Heinrich Karl) de la
Motte 1777-1843 .... **NCLC 2**
See also DLB 90; RGWL 2, 3; SUFW 1

Fourier, Charles 1772-1837 .... **NCLC 51**

Fournier, Henri-Alban 1886-1914
See Alain-Fournier
See also CA 104; 179

Fournier, Pierre 1916-1997 .... **CLC 11**
See Gascar, Pierre
See also CA 89-92; CANR 16, 40

Fowles, John 1926-2005 .... **CLC 1, 2, 3, 4, 6, 9, 10, 15, 33, 87; SSC 33**
See also BPFB 1; BRWS 1; CA 5-8R; 245; CANR 25, 71, 103; CDBLB 1960 to Present; CN 1, 2, 3, 4, 5, 6, 7; DA3; DAB; DAC; DAM MST; DLB 14, 139, 207; EWL 3; HGG; MTCW 1, 2; MTFW 2005; NFS 21; RGEL 2; RHW; SATA 22; SATA-Obit 171; TEA; WLIT 4

Fowles, John Robert
See Fowles, John

Fox, Paula 1923- .... **CLC 2, 8, 121**
See also AAYA 3, 37; BYA 3, 8; CA 73-76; CANR 20, 36, 62, 105; CLR 1, 44, 96; DLB 52; JRDA; MAICYA 1, 2; MTCW 1; NFS 12; SATA 17, 60, 120, 167; WYA; YAW

Fox, William Price (Jr.) 1926- .... **CLC 22**
See also CA 17-20R; CAAS 19; CANR 11, 142; CSW; DLB 2; DLBY 1981

Foxe, John 1517(?)-1587 .... **LC 14**
See also DLB 132

Frame, Janet .. **CLC 2, 3, 6, 22, 66, 96; SSC 29**
See Clutha, Janet Paterson Frame
See also CN 1, 2, 3, 4, 5, 6, 7; CP 2, 3, 4; CWP; EWL 3; RGEL 2; RGSF 2; TWA

France, Anatole .... **TCLC 9**
See Thibault, Jacques Anatole Francois
See also DLB 123, 330; EWL 3; GFL 1789 to the Present; RGWL 2, 3; SUFW 1

Francis, Claude .... **CLC 50**
See also CA 192

Francis, Dick
See Francis, Richard Stanley
See also CN 2, 3, 4, 5, 6

Francis, Richard Stanley 1920- ... **CLC 2, 22, 42, 102**
See Francis, Dick
See also AAYA 5, 21; BEST 89:3; BPFB 1; CA 5-8R; CANR 9, 42, 68, 100, 141; CD-BLB 1960 to Present; CMW 4; CN 7; DA3; DAM POP; DLB 87; INT CANR-9; MSW; MTCW 1, 2; MTFW 2005

Francis, Robert (Churchill)
1901-1987 .... **CLC 15; PC 34**
See also AMWS 9; CA 1-4R; 123; CANR 1; CP 1, 2, 3, 4; EXPP; PFS 12; TCLE 1:1

Francis, Lord Jeffrey
See Jeffrey, Francis
See also DLB 107

Frank, Anne(lies Marie)
1929-1945 .... **TCLC 17; WLC 2**
See also AAYA 12; BYA 1; CA 113; 133; CANR 68; CLR 101; DA; DA3; DAB; DAC; DAM MST; LAIT 4; MAICYA 2; MAICYAS 1; MTCW 1, 2; MTFW 2005; NCFS 2; RGHL; SATA 87; SATA-Brief 42; WYA; YAW

Frank, Bruno 1887-1945 .... **TCLC 81**
See also CA 189; DLB 118; EWL 3

Frank, Elizabeth 1945- .... **CLC 39**
See also CA 121; 126; CANR 78, 150; INT CA-126

Frankl, Viktor E(mil) 1905-1997 ...... **CLC 93**
See also CA 65-68; 161; RGHL

Franklin, Benjamin
See Hasek, Jaroslav (Matej Frantisek)

Franklin, Benjamin 1706-1790 .... **LC 25; WLCS**
See also AMW; CDALB 1640-1865; DA; DA3; DAB; DAC; DAM MST; DLB 24, 43, 73, 183; LAIT 1; RGAL 4; TUS

Franklin, (Stella Maria Sarah) Miles (Lampe) 1879-1954 .... **TCLC 7**
See also CA 104; 164; DLB 230; FW; MTCW 2; RGEL 2; TWA

Franzen, Jonathan 1959- .... **CLC 202**
See also AAYA 65; CA 129; CANR 105

Fraser, Antonia 1932- .... **CLC 32, 107**
See also AAYA 57; CA 85-88; CANR 44, 65, 119; CMW; DLB 276; MTCW 1, 2; MTFW 2005; SATA-Brief 32

Fraser, George MacDonald 1925- ...... **CLC 7**
See also AAYA 48; CA 45-48, 180; CAAE 180; CANR 2, 48, 74; MTCW 2; RHW

Fraser, Sylvia 1935- .... **CLC 64**
See also CA 45-48; CANR 1, 16, 60; CCA 1

Frayn, Michael 1933- .... **CLC 3, 7, 31, 47, 176; DC 27**
See also AAYA 69; BRWC 2; BRWS 7; CA 5-8R; CANR 30, 69, 114, 133; CBD; CD 5, 6; CN 1, 2, 3, 4, 5, 6, 7; DAM DRAM, NOV; DFS 22; DLB 13, 14, 194, 245; FANT; MTCW 1, 2; MTFW 2005; SFW 4

Fraze, Candida (Merrill) 1945- .... **CLC 50**
See also CA 126

Frazer, Andrew
See Marlowe, Stephen

Frazer, J(ames) G(eorge)
1854-1941 .... **TCLC 32**
See also BRWS 3; CA 118; NCFS 5

Frazer, Robert Caine
See Creasey, John

Frazer, Sir James George
See Frazer, J(ames) G(eorge)

Frazier, Charles 1950- .... **CLC 109, 224**
See also AAYA 34; CA 161; CANR 126; CSW; DLB 292; MTFW 2005

Frazier, Ian 1951- .... **CLC 46**
See also CA 130; CANR 54, 93

Frederic, Harold 1856-1898 .... **NCLC 10, 175**
See also AMW; DLB 12, 23; DLBD 13; MAL 5; NFS 22; RGAL 4

Frederick, John
See Faust, Frederick (Schiller)
See also TCWW 2

Frederick the Great 1712-1786 .... **LC 14**

Fredro, Aleksander 1793-1876 .... **NCLC 8**

Freeling, Nicolas 1927-2003 .... **CLC 38**
See also CA 49-52; 218; CAAS 12; CANR 1, 17, 50, 84; CMW 4; CN 1, 2, 3, 4, 5, 6; DLB 87

Freeman, Douglas Southall
1886-1953 .... **TCLC 11**
See also CA 109; 195; DLB 17; DLBD 17

Freeman, Judith 1946- .... **CLC 55**
See also CA 148; CANR 120; DLB 256

Freeman, Mary E(leanor) Wilkins
1852-1930 .... **SSC 1, 47; TCLC 9**
See also CA 106; 177; DLB 12, 78, 221; EXPS; FW; HGG; MBL; RGAL 4; RGSF 2; SSFS 4, 8; SUFW 1; TUS

Freeman, R(ichard) Austin
1862-1943 .... **TCLC 21**
See also CA 113; CANR 84; CMW 4; DLB 70

French, Albert 1943- .... **CLC 86**
See also BW 3; CA 167

French, Antonia
See Kureishi, Hanif

French, Marilyn 1929- .. **CLC 10, 18, 60, 177**
See also BPFB 1; CA 69-72; CANR 3, 31, 134; CN 5, 6, 7; CPW; DAM DRAM, NOV, POP; FL 1:5; FW; INT CANR-31; MTCW 1, 2; MTFW 2005

French, Paul
See Asimov, Isaac

Freneau, Philip Morin 1752-1832 .. **NCLC 1, 111**
See also AMWS 2; DLB 37, 43; RGAL 4

Freud, Sigmund 1856-1939 .... **TCLC 52**
See also CA 115; 133; CANR 69; DLB 296; EW 8; EWL 3; LATS 1:1; MTCW 1, 2; MTFW 2005; NCFS 3; TWA

Galt, John 1779-1839 .... **NCLC 1, 110**
See also DLB 99, 116, 159; RGEL 2; RGSF 2

Galvin, James 1951- .... **CLC 38**
See also CA 108; CANR 26

Gamboa, Federico 1864-1939 .... **TCLC 36**
See also CA 167; HW 2; LAW

Gandhi, M. K.
See Gandhi, Mohandas Karamchand

Gandhi, Mahatma
See Gandhi, Mohandas Karamchand

Gandhi, Mohandas Karamchand
1869-1948 .... **TCLC 59**
See also CA 121; 132; DA3; DAM MULT; DLB 323; MTCW 1, 2

Gann, Ernest Kellogg 1910-1991 ..... **CLC 23**
See also AITN 1; BPFB 2; CA 1-4R; 136; CANR 1, 83; RHW

Gao Xingjian 1940- .... **CLC 167**
See Xingjian, Gao
See also MTFW 2005

Garber, Eric 1943(?)-
See Holleran, Andrew
See also CANR 89

Garcia, Cristina 1958- .... **CLC 76**
See also AMWS 11; CA 141; CANR 73, 130; CN 7; DLB 292; DNFS 1; EWL 3; HW 2; LLW; MTFW 2005

Garcia Lorca, Federico 1898-1936 ...... **DC 2; HLC 2; PC 3; TCLC 1, 7, 49, 181; WLC 2**
See Lorca, Federico Garcia
See also AAYA 46; CA 104; 131; CANR 81; DA; DA3; DAB; DAC; DAM DRAM, MST, MULT, POET; DFS 4, 10; DLB 108; EWL 3; HW 1, 2; LATS 1:2; MTCW 1, 2; MTFW 2005; TWA

Garcia Marquez, Gabriel 1928- .... **CLC 2, 3, 8, 10, 15, 27, 47, 55, 68, 170; HLC 1; SSC 8, 83; WLC 3**
See also AAYA 3, 33; BEST 89:1, 90:4; BPFB 2; BYA 12, 16; CA 33-36R; CANR 10, 28, 50, 75, 82, 128; CDWLB 3; CPW; CWW 2; DA; DA3; DAB; DAC; DAM MST, MULT, NOV, POP; DLB 113, 330; DNFS 1, 2; EWL 3; EXPN; EXPS; HW 1, 2; LAIT 2; LATS 1:2; LAW; LAWS 1; LMFS 2; MTCW 1, 2; MTFW 2005; NCFS 3; NFS 1, 5, 10; RGSF 2; RGWL 2, 3; SSFS 1, 6, 16, 21; TWA; WLIT 1

Garcia Marquez, Gabriel Jose
See Garcia Marquez, Gabriel

Garcilaso de la Vega, El Inca
1539-1616 .... **HLCS 1; LC 127**
See also DLB 318; LAW

Gard, Janice
See Latham, Jean Lee

Gard, Roger Martin du
See Martin du Gard, Roger

Gardam, Jane (Mary) 1928- .... **CLC 43**
See also CA 49-52; CANR 2, 18, 33, 54, 106; CLR 12; DLB 14, 161, 231; MAICYA 1, 2; MTCW 1; SAAS 9; SATA 39, 76, 130; SATA-Brief 28; YAW

Gardner, Herb(ert George)
1934-2003 .... **CLC 44**
See also CA 149; 220; CAD; CANR 119; CD 5, 6; DFS 18, 20

Gardner, John, Jr. 1933-1982 ... **CLC 2, 3, 5, 7, 8, 10, 18, 28, 34; SSC 7**
See also AAYA 45; AITN 1; AMWS 6; BPFB 2; CA 65-68; 107; CANR 33, 73; CDALBS; CN 2, 3; CPW; DA3; DAM NOV, POP; DLB 2; DLBY 1982; EWL 3; FANT; LATS 1:2; MAL 5; MTCW 1, 2; MTFW 2005; NFS 3; RGAL 4; RGSF 2; SATA 40; SATA-Obit 31; SSFS 8

Gardner, John (Edmund) 1926- .... **CLC 30**
See also CA 103; CANR 15, 69, 127; CMW 4; CPW; DAM POP; MTCW 1

Gardner, Miriam
See Bradley, Marion Zimmer
See also GLL 1

Gardner, Noel
See Kuttner, Henry

Gardons, S. S.
See Snodgrass, W.D.

Garfield, Leon 1921-1996 .... **CLC 12**
See also AAYA 8, 69; BYA 1, 3; CA 17-20R; 152; CANR 38, 41, 78; CLR 21; DLB 161; JRDA; MAICYA 1, 2; MAIC-YAS 1; SATA 1, 32, 76; SATA-Obit 90; TEA; WYA; YAW

Garland, (Hannibal) Hamlin
1860-1940 .... **SSC 18; TCLC 3**
See also CA 104; DLB 12, 71, 78, 186; MAL 5; RGAL 4; RGSF 2; TCWW 1, 2

Garneau, (Hector de) Saint-Denys
1912-1943 .... **TCLC 13**
See also CA 111; DLB 88

Garner, Alan 1934- .... **CLC 17**
See also AAYA 18; BYA 3, 5; CA 73-76, 178; CAAE 178; CANR 15, 64, 134; CLR 20; CPW; DAB; DAM POP; DLB 161, 261; FANT; MAICYA 1, 2; MTCW 1, 2; MTFW 2005; SATA 18, 69; SATA-Essay 108; SUFW 1, 2; YAW

Garner, Hugh 1913-1979 .... **CLC 13**
See Warwick, Jarvis
See also CA 69-72; CANR 31; CCA 1; CN 1, 2; DLB 68

Garnett, David 1892-1981 .... **CLC 3**
See also CA 5-8R; 103; CANR 17, 79; CN 1, 2; DLB 34; FANT; MTCW 2; RGEL 2; SFW 4; SUFW 1

Garnier, Robert c. 1545-1590 .... **LC 119**
See also DLB 327; GFL Beginnings to 1789

Garrett, George (Palmer, Jr.) 1929- . **CLC 3, 11, 51; SSC 30**
See also AMWS 7; BPFB 2; CA 1-4R, 202; CAAE 202; CAAS 5; CANR 1, 42, 67, 109; CN 1, 2, 3, 4, 5, 6, 7; CP 1, 2, 3, 4, 5, 6, 7; CSW; DLB 2, 5, 130, 152; DLBY 1983

Garrick, David 1717-1779 .... **LC 15**
See also DAM DRAM; DLB 84, 213; RGEL 2

Garrigue, Jean 1914-1972 .... **CLC 2, 8**
See also CA 5-8R; 37-40R; CANR 20; CP 1; MAL 5

Garrison, Frederick
See Sinclair, Upton

Garrison, William Lloyd
1805-1879 .... **NCLC 149**
See also CDALB 1640-1865; DLB 1, 43, 235

Garro, Elena 1920(?)-1998 .. **HLCS 1; TCLC 153**
See also CA 131; 169; CWW 2; DLB 145; EWL 3; HW 1; LAWS 1; WLIT 1

Garth, Will
See Hamilton, Edmond; Kuttner, Henry

Garvey, Marcus (Moziah, Jr.)
1887-1940 ... **BLC 2; HR 1:2; TCLC 41**
See also BW 1; CA 120; 124; CANR 79; DAM MULT

Gary, Romain .... **CLC 25**
See Kacew, Romain
See also DLB 83, 299; RGHL

Gascar, Pierre .... **CLC 11**
See Fournier, Pierre
See also EWL 3; RGHL

Gascoigne, George 1539-1577 .... **LC 108**
See also DLB 136; RGEL 2

Gascoyne, David (Emery)
1916-2001 .... **CLC 45**
See also CA 65-68; 200; CANR 10, 28, 54; CP 1, 2, 3, 4, 5, 6, 7; DLB 20; MTCW 1; RGEL 2

Gaskell, Elizabeth Cleghorn
1810-1865 .... **NCLC 5, 70, 97, 137; SSC 25**
See also BRW 5; CDBLB 1832-1890; DAB; DAM MST; DLB 21, 144, 159; RGEL 2; RGSF 2; TEA

Gass, William H. 1924- . **CLC 1, 2, 8, 11, 15, 39, 132; SSC 12**
See also AMWS 6; CA 17-20R; CANR 30, 71, 100; CN 1, 2, 3, 4, 5, 6, 7; DLB 2, 227; EWL 3; MAL 5; MTCW 1, 2; MTFW 2005; RGAL 4

Gassendi, Pierre 1592-1655 .... **LC 54**
See also GFL Beginnings to 1789

Gasset, Jose Ortega y
See Ortega y Gasset, Jose

Gates, Henry Louis, Jr. 1950- ... **BLCS; CLC 65**
See also BW 2, 3; CA 109; CANR 25, 53, 75, 125; CSW; DA3; DAM MULT; DLB 67; EWL 3; MAL 5; MTCW 2; MTFW 2005; RGAL 4

Gatos, Stephanie
See Katz, Steve

Gautier, Theophile 1811-1872 .. **NCLC 1, 59; PC 18; SSC 20**
See also DAM POET; DLB 119; EW 6; GFL 1789 to the Present; RGWL 2, 3; SUFW; TWA

Gay, John 1685-1732 .... **LC 49**
See also BRW 3; DAM DRAM; DLB 84, 95; RGEL 2; WLIT 3

Gay, Oliver
See Gogarty, Oliver St. John

Gay, Peter 1923- .... **CLC 158**
See also CA 13-16R; CANR 18, 41, 77, 147; INT CANR-18; RGHL

Gay, Peter Jack
See Gay, Peter

Gaye, Marvin (Pentz, Jr.)
1939-1984 .... **CLC 26**
See also CA 195; 112

Gebler, Carlo 1954- .... **CLC 39**
See also CA 119; 133; CANR 96; DLB 271

Gee, Maggie 1948- .... **CLC 57**
See also CA 130; CANR 125; CN 4, 5, 6, 7; DLB 207; MTFW 2005

Gee, Maurice 1931- .... **CLC 29**
See also AAYA 42; CA 97-100; CANR 67, 123; CLR 56; CN 2, 3, 4, 5, 6, 7; CWRI 5; EWL 3; MAICYA 2; RGSF 2; SATA 46, 101

Gee, Maurice Gough
See Gee, Maurice

Geiogamah, Hanay 1945- .... **NNAL**
See also CA 153; DAM MULT; DLB 175

Gelbart, Larry
See Gelbart, Larry (Simon)
See also CAD; CD 5, 6

Gelbart, Larry (Simon) 1928- .... **CLC 21, 61**
See Gelbart, Larry
See also CA 73-76; CANR 45, 94

Gelber, Jack 1932-2003 ...... **CLC 1, 6, 14, 79**
See also CA 1-4R; 216; CAD; CANR 2; DLB 7, 228; MAL 5

Gellhorn, Martha (Ellis)
1908-1998 .... **CLC 14, 60**
See also CA 77-80; 164; CANR 44; CN 1, 2, 3, 4, 5, 6 7; DLBY 1982, 1998

Genet, Jean 1910-1986 .. **CLC 1, 2, 5, 10, 14, 44, 46; DC 25; TCLC 128**
See also CA 13-16R; CANR 18; DA3; DAM DRAM; DFS 10; DLB 72, 321; DLBY 1986; EW 13; EWL 3; GFL 1789 to the Present; GLL 1; LMFS 2; MTCW 1, 2; MTFW 2005; RGWL 2, 3; TWA

Genlis, Stephanie-Felicite Ducrest
1746-1830 .... **NCLC 166**
See also DLB 313

Gladkov, Fyodor (Vasilyevich)
1883-1958 .... **TCLC 27**
See Gladkov, Fedor Vasil'evich
See also CA 170; EWL 3

Glancy, Diane 1941- .... **CLC 210; NNAL**
See also CA 136, 225; CAAE 225; CAAS
24; CANR 87; DLB 175

Glanville, Brian (Lester) 1931- .... **CLC 6**
See also CA 5-8R; CAAS 9; CANR 3, 70;
CN 1, 2, 3, 4, 5, 6, 7; DLB 15, 139; SATA
42

Glasgow, Ellen (Anderson Gholson)
1873-1945 .... **SSC 34; TCLC 2, 7**
See also AMW; CA 104; 164; DLB 9, 12;
MAL 5; MBL; MTCW 2; MTFW 2005;
RGAL 4; RHW; SSFS 9; TUS

Glaspell, Susan 1882(?)-1948 ..... **DC 10; SSC
41; TCLC 55, 175**
See also AMWS 3; CA 110; 154; DFS 8,
18; DLB 7, 9, 78, 228; MBL; RGAL 4;
SSFS 3; TCWW 2; TUS; YABC 2

Glassco, John 1909-1981 .... **CLC 9**
See also CA 13-16R; 102; CANR 15; CN
1, 2; CP 1, 2, 3; DLB 68

Glasscock, Amnesia
See Steinbeck, John (Ernst)

Glasser, Ronald J. 1940(?)- .... **CLC 37**
See also CA 209

Glassman, Joyce
See Johnson, Joyce

Gleick, James (W.) 1954- .... **CLC 147**
See also CA 131; 137; CANR 97; INT CA-
137

Glendinning, Victoria 1937- .... **CLC 50**
See also CA 120; 127; CANR 59, 89; DLB
155

Glissant, Edouard (Mathieu)
1928- .... **CLC 10, 68**
See also CA 153; CANR 111; CWW 2;
DAM MULT; EWL 3; RGWL 3

Gloag, Julian 1930- .... **CLC 40**
See also AITN 1; CA 65-68; CANR 10, 70;
CN 1, 2, 3, 4, 5, 6

Glowacki, Aleksander
See Prus, Boleslaw

Gluck, Louise 1943- .... **CLC 7, 22, 44, 81,
160; PC 16**
See also AMWS 5; CA 33-36R; CANR 40,
69, 108, 133; CP 1, 2, 3, 4, 5, 6, 7; CWP;
DA3; DAM POET; DLB 5; MAL 5;
MTCW 2; MTFW 2005; PFS 5, 15;
RGAL 4; TCLE 1:1

Glyn, Elinor 1864-1943 .... **TCLC 72**
See also DLB 153; RHW

Gobineau, Joseph-Arthur
1816-1882 .... **NCLC 17**
See also DLB 123; GFL 1789 to the Present

Godard, Jean-Luc 1930- .... **CLC 20**
See also CA 93-96

Godden, (Margaret) Rumer
1907-1998 .... **CLC 53**
See also AAYA 6; BPFB 2; BYA 2, 5; CA
5-8R; 172; CANR 4, 27, 36, 55, 80; CLR
20; CN 1, 2, 3, 4, 5, 6; CWRI 5; DLB
161; MAICYA 1, 2; RHW; SAAS 12;
SATA 3, 36; SATA-Obit 109; TEA

Godoy Alcayaga, Lucila 1899-1957 .. **HLC 2;
PC 32; TCLC 2**
See Mistral, Gabriela
See also BW 2; CA 104; 131; CANR 81;
DAM MULT; DNFS; HW 1, 2; MTCW 1,
2; MTFW 2005

Godwin, Gail 1937- ...... **CLC 5, 8, 22, 31, 69,
125**
See also BPFB 2; CA 29-32R; CANR 15,
43, 69, 132; CN 3, 4, 5, 6, 7; CPW; CSW;
DA3; DAM POP; DLB 6, 234; INT
CANR-15; MAL 5; MTCW 1, 2; MTFW
2005

Godwin, Gail Kathleen
See Godwin, Gail

Godwin, William 1756-1836 .. **NCLC 14, 130**
See also CDBLB 1789-1832; CMW 4; DLB
39, 104, 142, 158, 163, 262; GL 2; HGG;
RGEL 2

Goebbels, Josef
See Goebbels, (Paul) Joseph

Goebbels, (Paul) Joseph
1897-1945 .... **TCLC 68**
See also CA 115; 148

Goebbels, Joseph Paul
See Goebbels, (Paul) Joseph

Goethe, Johann Wolfgang von
1749-1832 . **DC 20; NCLC 4, 22, 34, 90,
154; PC 5; SSC 38; WLC 3**
See also CDWLB 2; DA; DA3; DAB;
DAC; DAM DRAM, MST, POET; DLB
94; EW 5; GL 2; LATS 1; LMFS 1:1;
RGWL 2, 3; TWA

Gogarty, Oliver St. John
1878-1957 .... **TCLC 15**
See also CA 109; 150; DLB 15, 19; RGEL
2

Gogol, Nikolai (Vasilyevich)
1809-1852 .... **DC 1; NCLC 5, 15, 31,
162; SSC 4, 29, 52; WLC 3**
See also DA; DAB; DAC; DAM DRAM,
MST; DFS 12; DLB 198; EW 6; EXPS;
RGSF 2; RGWL 2, 3; SSFS 7; TWA

Goines, Donald 1937(?)-1974 ... **BLC 2; CLC
80**
See also AITN 1; BW 1, 3; CA 124; 114;
CANR 82; CMW 4; DA3; DAM MULT,
POP; DLB 33

Gold, Herbert 1924- ... **CLC 4, 7, 14, 42, 152**
See also CA 9-12R; CANR 17, 45, 125; CN
1, 2, 3, 4, 5, 6, 7; DLB 2; DLBY 1981;
MAL 5

Goldbarth, Albert 1948- .... **CLC 5, 38**
See also AMWS 12; CA 53-56; CANR 6,
40; CP 3, 4, 5, 6, 7; DLB 120

Goldberg, Anatol 1910-1982 .... **CLC 34**
See also CA 131; 117

Goldemberg, Isaac 1945- .... **CLC 52**
See also CA 69-72; CAAS 12; CANR 11,
32; EWL 3; HW 1; WLIT 1

Golding, Arthur 1536-1606 .... **LC 101**
See also DLB 136

Golding, William 1911-1993 . **CLC 1, 2, 3, 8,
10, 17, 27, 58, 81; WLC 3**
See also AAYA 5, 44; BPFB 2; BRWR 1;
BRWS 1; BYA 2; CA 5-8R; 141; CANR
13, 33, 54; CD 5; CDBLB 1945-1960;
CLR 94; CN 1, 2, 3, 4; DA; DA3; DAB;
DAC; DAM MST, NOV; DLB 15, 100,
255, 326, 330; EWL 3; EXPN; HGG;
LAIT 4; MTCW 1, 2; MTFW 2005; NFS
2; RGEL 2; RHW; SFW 4; TEA; WLIT
4; YAW

Goldman, Emma 1869-1940 .... **TCLC 13**
See also CA 110; 150; DLB 221; FW;
RGAL 4; TUS

Goldman, Francisco 1954- .... **CLC 76**
See also CA 162

Goldman, William 1931- .... **CLC 1, 48**
See also BPFB 2; CA 9-12R; CANR 29,
69, 106; CN 1, 2, 3, 4, 5, 6, 7; DLB 44;
FANT; IDFW 3, 4

Goldman, William W.
See Goldman, William

Goldmann, Lucien 1913-1970 .... **CLC 24**
See also CA 25-28; CAP 2

Goldoni, Carlo 1707-1793 .... **LC 4**
See also DAM DRAM; EW 4; RGWL 2, 3;
WLIT 7

Goldsberry, Steven 1949- .... **CLC 34**
See also CA 131

Goldsmith, Oliver 1730-1774 .... **DC 8; LC 2,
48, 122; WLC 3**
See also BRW 3; CDBLB 1660-1789; DA;
DAB; DAC; DAM DRAM, MST, NOV,
POET; DFS 1; DLB 39, 89, 104, 109, 142;
IDTP; RGEL 2; SATA 26; TEA; WLIT 3

Goldsmith, Peter
See Priestley, J(ohn) B(oynton)

Gombrowicz, Witold 1904-1969 .... **CLC 4, 7,
11, 49**
See also CA 19-20; 25-28R; CANR 105;
CAP 2; CDWLB 4; DAM DRAM; DLB
215; EW 12; EWL 3; RGWL 2, 3; TWA

Gomez de Avellaneda, Gertrudis
1814-1873 .... **NCLC 111**
See also LAW

Gomez de la Serna, Ramon
1888-1963 .... **CLC 9**
See also CA 153; 116; CANR 79; EWL 3;
HW 1, 2

Goncharov, Ivan Alexandrovich
1812-1891 .... **NCLC 1, 63**
See also DLB 238; EW 6; RGWL 2, 3

Goncourt, Edmond (Louis Antoine Huot) de
1822-1896 .... **NCLC 7**
See also DLB 123; EW 7; GFL 1789 to the
Present; RGWL 2, 3

Goncourt, Jules (Alfred Huot) de
1830-1870 .... **NCLC 7**
See also DLB 123; EW 7; GFL 1789 to the
Present; RGWL 2, 3

Gongora (y Argote), Luis de
1561-1627 .... **LC 72**
See also RGWL 2, 3

Gontier, Fernande 19(?)- .... **CLC 50**

Gonzalez Martinez, Enrique
See Gonzalez Martinez, Enrique
See also DLB 290

Gonzalez Martinez, Enrique
1871-1952 .... **TCLC 72**
See Gonzalez Martinez, Enrique
See also CA 166; CANR 81; EWL 3; HW
1, 2

Goodison, Lorna 1947- .... **PC 36**
See also CA 142; CANR 88; CP 5, 6, 7;
CWP; DLB 157; EWL 3

Goodman, Paul 1911-1972 ..... **CLC 1, 2, 4, 7**
See also CA 19-20; 37-40R; CAD; CANR
34; CAP 2; CN 1; DLB 130, 246; MAL
5; MTCW 1; RGAL 4

GoodWeather, Harley
See King, Thomas

Googe, Barnabe 1540-1594 .... **LC 94**
See also DLB 132; RGEL 2

Gordimer, Nadine 1923- ...... **CLC 3, 5, 7, 10,
18, 33, 51, 70, 123, 160, 161; SSC 17,
80; WLCS**
See also AAYA 39; AFW; BRWS 2; CA
5-8R; CANR 3, 28, 56, 88, 131; CN 1, 2,
3, 4, 5, 6, 7; DA; DA3; DAB; DAC; DAM
MST, NOV; DLB 225, 326, 330; EWL 3;
EXPS; INT CANR-28; LATS 1:2; MTCW
1, 2; MTFW 2005; NFS 4; RGEL 2;
RGSF 2; SSFS 2, 14, 19; TWA; WLIT 2;
YAW

Gordon, Adam Lindsay
1833-1870 .... **NCLC 21**
See also DLB 230

Gordon, Caroline 1895-1981 . **CLC 6, 13, 29,
83; SSC 15**
See also AMW; CA 11-12; 103; CANR 36;
CAP 1; CN 1, 2; DLB 4, 9, 102; DLBD
17; DLBY 1981; EWL 3; MAL 5; MTCW
1, 2; MTFW 2005; RGAL 4; RGSF 2

Gordon, Charles William 1860-1937
See Connor, Ralph
See also CA 109

Gordon, Mary 1949- .. **CLC 13, 22, 128, 216; SSC 59**
See also AMWS 4; BPFB 2; CA 102; CANR 44, 92, 154; CN 4, 5, 6, 7; DLB 6; DLBY 1981; FW; INT CA-102; MAL 5; MTCW 1

Gordon, Mary Catherine
See Gordon, Mary

Gordon, N. J.
See Bosman, Herman Charles

Gordon, Sol 1923- .... **CLC 26**
See also CA 53-56; CANR 4; SATA 11

Gordone, Charles 1925-1995 .. **CLC 1, 4; DC 8**
See also BW 1, 3; CA 93-96; 180; 150; CAAE 180; CAD; CANR 55; DAM DRAM; DLB 7; INT CA-93-96; MTCW 1

Gore, Catherine 1800-1861 .... **NCLC 65**
See also DLB 116; RGEL 2

Gorenko, Anna Andreevna
See Akhmatova, Anna

Gorky, Maxim .... **SSC 28; TCLC 8; WLC 3**
See Peshkov, Alexei Maximovich
See also DAB; DFS 9; DLB 295; EW 8; EWL 3; TWA

Goryan, Sirak
See Saroyan, William

Gosse, Edmund (William)
1849-1928 .... **TCLC 28**
See also CA 117; DLB 57, 144, 184; RGEL 2

Gotlieb, Phyllis (Fay Bloom) 1926- .. **CLC 18**
See also CA 13-16R; CANR 7, 135; CN 7; CP 1, 2, 3, 4; DLB 88, 251; SFW 4

Gottesman, S. D.
See Kornbluth, C(yril) M.; Pohl, Frederik

Gottfried von Strassburg fl. c.
1170-1215 .... **CMLC 10**
See also CDWLB 2; DLB 138; EW 1; RGWL 2, 3

Gotthelf, Jeremias 1797-1854 .... **NCLC 117**
See also DLB 133; RGWL 2, 3

Gottschalk, Laura Riding
See Jackson, Laura (Riding)

Gould, Lois 1932(?)-2002 .... **CLC 4, 10**
See also CA 77-80; 208; CANR 29; MTCW 1

Gould, Stephen Jay 1941-2002 .... **CLC 163**
See also AAYA 26; BEST 90:2; CA 77-80; 205; CANR 10, 27, 56, 75, 125; CPW; INT CANR-27; MTCW 1, 2; MTFW 2005

Gourmont, Remy(-Marie-Charles) de
1858-1915 .... **TCLC 17**
See also CA 109; 150; GFL 1789 to the Present; MTCW 2

Gournay, Marie le Jars de
See de Gournay, Marie le Jars

Govier, Katherine 1948- .... **CLC 51**
See also CA 101; CANR 18, 40, 128; CCA 1

Gower, John c. 1330-1408 .... **LC 76; PC 59**
See also BRW 1; DLB 146; RGEL 2

Goyen, (Charles) William
1915-1983 .... **CLC 5, 8, 14, 40**
See also AITN 2; CA 5-8R; 110; CANR 6, 71; CN 1, 2, 3; DLB 2, 218; DLBY 1983; EWL 3; INT CANR-6; MAL 5

Goytisolo, Juan 1931- .... **CLC 5, 10, 23, 133; HLC 1**
See also CA 85-88; CANR 32, 61, 131; CWW 2; DAM MULT; DLB 322; EWL 3; GLL 2; HW 1, 2; MTCW 1, 2; MTFW 2005

Gozzano, Guido 1883-1916 .... **PC 10**
See also CA 154; DLB 114; EWL 3

Gozzi, (Conte) Carlo 1720-1806 .... **NCLC 23**

Grabbe, Christian Dietrich
1801-1836 .... **NCLC 2**
See also DLB 133; RGWL 2, 3

Grace, Patricia Frances 1937- .... **CLC 56**
See also CA 176; CANR 118; CN 4, 5, 6, 7; EWL 3; RGSF 2

Gracian y Morales, Baltasar
1601-1658 .... **LC 15**

Gracq, Julien .... **CLC 11, 48**
See Poirier, Louis
See also CWW 2; DLB 83; GFL 1789 to the Present

Grade, Chaim 1910-1982 .... **CLC 10**
See also CA 93-96; 107; EWL 3; RGHL

Graduate of Oxford, A
See Ruskin, John

Grafton, Garth
See Duncan, Sara Jeannette

Grafton, Sue 1940- .... **CLC 163**
See also AAYA 11, 49; BEST 90:3; CA 108; CANR 31, 55, 111, 134; CMW 4; CPW; CSW; DA3; DAM POP; DLB 226; FW; MSW; MTFW 2005

Graham, John
See Phillips, David Graham

Graham, Jorie 1950- .... **CLC 48, 118; PC 59**
See also AAYA 67; CA 111; CANR 63, 118; CP 4, 5, 6, 7; CWP; DLB 120; EWL 3; MTFW 2005; PFS 10, 17; TCLE 1:1

Graham, R(obert) B(ontine) Cunninghame
See Cunninghame Graham, Robert (Gallnigad) Bontine
See also DLB 98, 135, 174; RGEL 2; RGSF 2

Graham, Robert
See Haldeman, Joe

Graham, Tom
See Lewis, (Harry) Sinclair

Graham, W(illiam) S(idney)
1918-1986 .... **CLC 29**
See also BRWS 7; CA 73-76; 118; CP 1, 2, 3, 4; DLB 20; RGEL 2

Graham, Winston (Mawdsley)
1910-2003 .... **CLC 23**
See also CA 49-52; 218; CANR 2, 22, 45, 66; CMW 4; CN 1, 2, 3, 4, 5, 6, 7; DLB 77; RHW

Grahame, Kenneth 1859-1932 ...... **TCLC 64, 136**
See also BYA 5; CA 108; 136; CANR 80; CLR 5; CWRI 5; DA3; DAB; DLB 34, 141, 178; FANT; MAICYA 1, 2; MTCW 2; NFS 20; RGEL 2; SATA 100; TEA; WCH; YABC 1

Granger, Darius John
See Marlowe, Stephen

Granin, Daniil 1918- .... **CLC 59**
See also DLB 302

Granovsky, Timofei Nikolaevich
1813-1855 .... **NCLC 75**
See also DLB 198

Grant, Skeeter
See Spiegelman, Art

Granville-Barker, Harley
1877-1946 .... **TCLC 2**
See Barker, Harley Granville
See also CA 104; 204; DAM DRAM; RGEL 2

Granzotto, Gianni
See Granzotto, Giovanni Battista

Granzotto, Giovanni Battista
1914-1985 .... **CLC 70**
See also CA 166

Grass, Guenter
See Grass, Gunter
See also CWW 2; DLB 330; RGHL

Grass, Gunter 1927- .. **CLC 1, 2, 4, 6, 11, 15, 22, 32, 49, 88, 207; WLC 3**
See Grass, Guenter
See also BPFB 2; CA 13-16R; CANR 20, 75, 93, 133; CDWLB 2; DA; DA3; DAC; DAM MST, NOV; DLB 75, 124; EW 13; EWL 3; MTCW 1, 2; MTFW 2005; RGWL 2, 3; TWA

Grass, Gunter Wilhelm
See Grass, Gunter

Gratton, Thomas
See Hulme, T(homas) E(rnest)

Grau, Shirley Ann 1929- .... **CLC 4, 9, 146; SSC 15**
See also CA 89-92; CANR 22, 69; CN 1, 2, 3, 4, 5, 6, 7; CSW; DLB 2, 218; INT CA-89-92; CANR-22; MTCW 1

Gravel, Fern
See Hall, James Norman

Graver, Elizabeth 1964- .... **CLC 70**
See also CA 135; CANR 71, 129

Graves, Richard Perceval
1895-1985 .... **CLC 44**
See also CA 65-68; CANR 9, 26, 51

Graves, Robert 1895-1985 ... **CLC 1, 2, 6, 11, 39, 44, 45; PC 6**
See also BPFB 2; BRW 7; BYA 4; CA 5-8R; 117; CANR 5, 36; CDBLB 1914-1945; CN 1, 2, 3; CP 1, 2, 3, 4; DA3; DAB; DAC; DAM MST, POET; DLB 20, 100, 191; DLBD 18; DLBY 1985; EWL 3; LATS 1:1; MTCW 1, 2; MTFW 2005; NCFS 2; NFS 21; RGEL 2; RHW; SATA 45; TEA

Graves, Valerie
See Bradley, Marion Zimmer

Gray, Alasdair 1934- .... **CLC 41**
See also BRWS 9; CA 126; CANR 47, 69, 106, 140; CN 4, 5, 6, 7; DLB 194, 261, 319; HGG; INT CA-126; MTCW 1, 2; MTFW 2005; RGSF 2; SUFW 2

Gray, Amlin 1946- .... **CLC 29**
See also CA 138

Gray, Francine du Plessix 1930- ..... **CLC 22, 153**
See also BEST 90:3; CA 61-64; CAAS 2; CANR 11, 33, 75, 81; DAM NOV; INT CANR-11; MTCW 1, 2; MTFW 2005

Gray, John (Henry) 1866-1934 ...... **TCLC 19**
See also CA 119; 162; RGEL 2

Gray, John Lee
See Jakes, John

Gray, Simon (James Holliday)
1936- .... **CLC 9, 14, 36**
See also AITN 1; CA 21-24R; CAAS 3; CANR 32, 69; CBD; CD 5, 6; CN 1, 2, 3; DLB 13; EWL 3; MTCW 1; RGEL 2

Gray, Spalding 1941-2004 .... **CLC 49, 112; DC 7**
See also AAYA 62; CA 128; 225; CAD; CANR 74, 138; CD 5, 6; CPW; DAM POP; MTCW 2; MTFW 2005

Gray, Thomas 1716-1771 .... **LC 4, 40; PC 2; WLC 3**
See also BRW 3; CDBLB 1660-1789; DA; DA3; DAB; DAC; DAM MST; DLB 109; EXPP; PAB; PFS 9; RGEL 2; TEA; WP

Grayson, David
See Baker, Ray Stannard

Grayson, Richard (A.) 1951- .... **CLC 38**
See also CA 85-88; 210; CAAE 210; CANR 14, 31, 57; DLB 234

Greeley, Andrew M. 1928- .... **CLC 28**
See also BPFB 2; CA 5-8R; CAAS 7; CANR 7, 43, 69, 104, 136; CMW 4; CPW; DA3; DAM POP; MTCW 1, 2; MTFW 2005

330; DLBY 1995; EWL 3; EXPP; MTCW
1, 2; MTFW 2005; PAB; PFS 2, 5, 8, 17;
RGEL 2; TEA; WLIT 4

Hearn, (Patricio) Lafcadio (Tessima Carlos)
1850-1904 .... **TCLC 9**
See also CA 105; 166; DLB 12, 78, 189;
HGG; MAL 5; RGAL 4

Hearne, Samuel 1745-1792 .... **LC 95**
See also DLB 99

Hearne, Vicki 1946-2001 .... **CLC 56**
See also CA 139; 201

Hearon, Shelby 1931- .... **CLC 63**
See also AITN 2; AMWS 8; CA 25-28R;
CANR 18, 48, 103, 146; CSW

Heat-Moon, William Least .... **CLC 29**
See Trogdon, William (Lewis)
See also AAYA 9

Hebbel, Friedrich 1813-1863 . **DC 21; NCLC
43**
See also CDWLB 2; DAM DRAM; DLB
129; EW 6; RGWL 2, 3

Hebert, Anne 1916-2000 .... **CLC 4, 13, 29**
See also CA 85-88; 187; CANR 69, 126;
CCA 1; CWP; CWW 2; DA3; DAC;
DAM MST, POET; DLB 68; EWL 3; GFL
1789 to the Present; MTCW 1, 2; MTFW
2005; PFS 20

Hecht, Anthony (Evan) 1923-2004 .... **CLC 8,
13, 19; PC 70**
See also AMWS 10; CA 9-12R; 232; CANR
6, 108; CP 1, 2, 3, 4, 5, 6, 7; DAM POET;
DLB 5, 169; EWL 3; PFS 6; WP

Hecht, Ben 1894-1964 ..... **CLC 8; TCLC 101**
See also CA 85-88; DFS 9; DLB 7, 9, 25,
26, 28, 86; FANT; IDFW 3, 4; RGAL 4

Hedayat, Sadeq 1903-1951 .... **TCLC 21**
See also CA 120; EWL 3; RGSF 2

Hegel, Georg Wilhelm Friedrich
1770-1831 .... **NCLC 46, 151**
See also DLB 90; TWA

Heidegger, Martin 1889-1976 .... **CLC 24**
See also CA 81-84; 65-68; CANR 34; DLB
296; MTCW 1, 2; MTFW 2005

Heidenstam, (Carl Gustaf) Verner von
1859-1940 .... **TCLC 5**
See also CA 104; DLB 330

Heidi Louise
See Erdrich, Louise

Heifner, Jack 1946- .... **CLC 11**
See also CA 105; CANR 47

Heijermans, Herman 1864-1924 .... **TCLC 24**
See also CA 123; EWL 3

Heilbrun, Carolyn G(old)
1926-2003 .... **CLC 25, 173**
See Cross, Amanda
See also CA 45-48; 220; CANR 1, 28, 58,
94; FW

Hein, Christoph 1944- .... **CLC 154**
See also CA 158; CANR 108; CDWLB 2;
CWW 2; DLB 124

Heine, Heinrich 1797-1856 .... **NCLC 4, 54,
147; PC 25**
See also CDWLB 2; DLB 90; EW 5; RGWL
2, 3; TWA

Heinemann, Larry 1944- .... **CLC 50**
See also CA 110; CAAS 21; CANR 31, 81,
156; DLBD 9; INT CANR-31

Heinemann, Larry Curtiss
See Heinemann, Larry

Heiney, Donald (William) 1921-1993
See Harris, MacDonald
See also CA 1-4R; 142; CANR 3, 58; FANT

Heinlein, Robert A. 1907-1988 .. **CLC 1, 3, 8,
14, 26, 55; SSC 55**
See also AAYA 17; BPFB 2; BYA 4, 13;
CA 1-4R; 125; CANR 1, 20, 53; CLR 75;
CN 1, 2, 3, 4; CPW; DA3; DAM POP;
DLB 8; EXPS; JRDA; LAIT 5; LMFS 2;

MAICYA 1, 2; MTCW 1, 2; MTFW 2005;
RGAL 4; SATA 9, 69; SATA-Obit 56;
SCFW 1, 2; SFW 4; SSFS 7; YAW

Helforth, John
See Doolittle, Hilda

Heliodorus fl. 3rd cent. - .... **CMLC 52**
See also WLIT 8

Hellenhofferu, Vojtech Kapristian z
See Hasek, Jaroslav (Matej Frantisek)

Heller, Joseph 1923-1999 . **CLC 1, 3, 5, 8, 11,
36, 63; TCLC 131, 151; WLC 3**
See also AAYA 24; AITN 1; AMWS 4;
BPFB 2; BYA 1; CA 5-8R; 187; CABS 1;
CANR 8, 42, 66, 126; CN 1, 2, 3, 4, 5, 6;
CPW; DA; DA3; DAB; DAC; DAM MST,
NOV, POP; DLB 2, 28, 227; DLBY 1980,
2002; EWL 3; EXPN; INT CANR-8;
LAIT 4; MAL 5; MTCW 1, 2; MTFW
2005; NFS 1; RGAL 4; TUS; YAW

Hellman, Lillian 1906-1984 . **CLC 2, 4, 8, 14,
18, 34, 44, 52; DC 1; TCLC 119**
See also AAYA 47; AITN 1, 2; AMWS 1;
CA 13-16R; 112; CAD; CANR 33; CWD;
DA3; DAM DRAM; DFS 1, 3, 14; DLB
7, 228; DLBY 1984; EWL 3; FL 1:6; FW;
LAIT 3; MAL 5; MBL; MTCW 1, 2;
MTFW 2005; RGAL 4; TUS

Helprin, Mark 1947- .... **CLC 7, 10, 22, 32**
See also CA 81-84; CANR 47, 64, 124;
CDALBS; CN 7; CPW; DA3; DAM NOV,
POP; DLBY 1985; FANT; MAL 5;
MTCW 1, 2; MTFW 2005; SUFW 2

Helvetius, Claude-Adrien 1715-1771 .. **LC 26**
See also DLB 313

Helyar, Jane Penelope Josephine 1933-
See Poole, Josephine
See also CA 21-24R; CANR 10, 26; CWRI
5; SATA 82, 138; SATA-Essay 138

Hemans, Felicia 1793-1835 ...... **NCLC 29, 71**
See also DLB 96; RGEL 2

Hemingway, Ernest (Miller)
1899-1961 .... **CLC 1, 3, 6, 8, 10, 13, 19,
30, 34, 39, 41, 44, 50, 61, 80; SSC 1, 25,
36, 40, 63; TCLC 115; WLC 3**
See also AAYA 19; AMW; AMWC 1;
AMWR 1; BPFB 2; BYA 2, 3, 13, 15; CA
77-80; CANR 34; CDALB 1917-1929;
DA; DA3; DAB; DAC; DAM MST, NOV;
DLB 4, 9, 102, 210, 308, 316, 330; DLBD
1, 15, 16; DLBY 1981, 1987, 1996, 1998;
EWL 3; EXPN; EXPS; LAIT 3, 4; LATS
1:1; MAL 5; MTCW 1, 2; MTFW 2005;
NFS 1, 5, 6, 14; RGAL 4; RGSF 2; SSFS
17; TUS; WYA

Hempel, Amy 1951- .... **CLC 39**
See also CA 118; 137; CANR 70; DA3;
DLB 218; EXPS; MTCW 2; MTFW 2005;
SSFS 2

Henderson, F. C.
See Mencken, H(enry) L(ouis)

Henderson, Sylvia
See Ashton-Warner, Sylvia (Constance)

Henderson, Zenna (Chlarson)
1917-1983 .... **SSC 29**
See also CA 1-4R; 133; CANR 1, 84; DLB
8; SATA 5; SFW 4

Henkin, Joshua .... **CLC 119**
See also CA 161

Henley, Beth .... **CLC 23; DC 6, 14**
See Henley, Elizabeth Becker
See also AAYA 70; CABS 3; CAD; CD 5,
6; CSW; CWD; DFS 2, 21; DLBY 1986;
FW

Henley, Elizabeth Becker 1952-
See Henley, Beth
See also CA 107; CANR 32, 73, 140; DA3;
DAM DRAM, MST; MTCW 1, 2; MTFW
2005

Henley, William Ernest 1849-1903 .. **TCLC 8**
See also CA 105; 234; DLB 19; RGEL 2

Hennissart, Martha 1929-
See Lathen, Emma
See also CA 85-88; CANR 64

Henry VIII 1491-1547 .... **LC 10**
See also DLB 132

Henry, O. . **SSC 5, 49; TCLC 1, 19; WLC 3**
See Porter, William Sydney
See also AAYA 41; AMWS 2; EXPS; MAL
5; RGAL 4; RGSF 2; SSFS 2, 18; TCWW
1, 2

Henry, Patrick 1736-1799 .... **LC 25**
See also LAIT 1

Henryson, Robert 1430(?)-1506(?) ..... **LC 20,
110; PC 65**
See also BRWS 7; DLB 146; RGEL 2

Henschke, Alfred
See Klabund

Henson, Lance 1944- .... **NNAL**
See also CA 146; DLB 175

Hentoff, Nat(han Irving) 1925- .... **CLC 26**
See also AAYA 4, 42; BYA 6; CA 1-4R;
CAAS 6; CANR 5, 25, 77, 114; CLR 1,
52; INT CANR-25; JRDA; MAICYA 1,
2; SATA 42, 69, 133; SATA-Brief 27;
WYA; YAW

Heppenstall, (John) Rayner
1911-1981 .... **CLC 10**
See also CA 1-4R; 103; CANR 29; CN 1,
2; CP 1, 2, 3; EWL 3

Heraclitus c. 540B.C.-c. 450B.C. ... **CMLC 22**
See also DLB 176

Herbert, Frank 1920-1986 ... **CLC 12, 23, 35,
44, 85**
See also AAYA 21; BPFB 2; BYA 4, 14;
CA 53-56; 118; CANR 5, 43; CDALBS;
CPW; DAM POP; DLB 8; INT CANR-5;
LAIT 5; MTCW 1, 2; MTFW 2005; NFS
17; SATA 9, 37; SATA-Obit 47; SCFW 1,
2; SFW 4; YAW

Herbert, George 1593-1633 . **LC 24, 121; PC
4**
See also BRW 2; BRWR 2; CDBLB Before
1660; DAB; DAM POET; DLB 126;
EXPP; RGEL 2; TEA; WP

Herbert, Zbigniew 1924-1998 ..... **CLC 9, 43;
PC 50; TCLC 168**
See also CA 89-92; 169; CANR 36, 74; CD-
WLB 4; CWW 2; DAM POET; DLB 232;
EWL 3; MTCW 1; PFS 22

Herbst, Josephine (Frey)
1897-1969 .... **CLC 34**
See also CA 5-8R; 25-28R; DLB 9

Herder, Johann Gottfried von
1744-1803 .... **NCLC 8**
See also DLB 97; EW 4; TWA

Heredia, Jose Maria 1803-1839 .... **HLCS 2**
See also LAW

Hergesheimer, Joseph 1880-1954 ... **TCLC 11**
See also CA 109; 194; DLB 102, 9; RGAL
4

Herlihy, James Leo 1927-1993 .... **CLC 6**
See also CA 1-4R; 143; CAD; CANR 2;
CN 1, 2, 3, 4, 5

Herman, William
See Bierce, Ambrose (Gwinett)

Hermogenes fl. c. 175- .... **CMLC 6**

Hernandez, Jose 1834-1886 .... **NCLC 17**
See also LAW; RGWL 2, 3; WLIT 1

Herodotus c. 484B.C.-c. 420B.C. .. **CMLC 17**
See also AW 1; CDWLB 1; DLB 176;
RGWL 2, 3; TWA; WLIT 8

Herrick, Robert 1591-1674 .... **LC 13; PC 9**
See also BRW 2; BRWC 2; DA; DAB;
DAC; DAM MST, POP; DLB 126; EXPP;
PFS 13; RGAL 4; RGEL 2; TEA; WP

Herring, Guilles
See Somerville, Edith Oenone

Herriot, James 1916-1995 .... CLC **12**
  See Wight, James Alfred
    See also AAYA 1, 54; BPFB 2; CA 148;
    CANR 40; CLR 80; CPW; DAM POP;
    LAIT 3; MAICYA 2; MAICYAS 1;
    MTCW 2; SATA 86, 135; TEA; YAW
Herris, Violet
  See Hunt, Violet
Herrmann, Dorothy 1941- .... CLC **44**
  See also CA 107
Herrmann, Taffy
  See Herrmann, Dorothy
Hersey, John 1914-1993 .. CLC **1, 2, 7, 9, 40,**
    81, 97
    See also AAYA 29; BPFB 2; CA 17-20R;
    140; CANR 33; CDALBS; CN 1, 2, 3, 4,
    5; CPW; DAM POP; DLB 6, 185, 278,
    299; MAL 5; MTCW 1, 2; MTFW 2005;
    RGHL; SATA 25; SATA-Obit 76; TUS
Herzen, Aleksandr Ivanovich
    1812-1870 .... NCLC **10, 61**
  See Herzen, Alexander
Herzen, Alexander
  See Herzen, Aleksandr Ivanovich
  See also DLB 277
Herzl, Theodor 1860-1904 .... TCLC **36**
  See also CA 168
Herzog, Werner 1942- .... CLC **16**
  See also CA 89-92
Hesiod c. 8th cent. B.C.- .... CMLC **5**
  See also AW 1; DLB 176; RGWL 2, 3;
    WLIT 8
Hesse, Hermann 1877-1962 ... CLC **1, 2, 3, 6,**
    11, 17, 25, 69; SSC 9, 49; TCLC 148;
    WLC 3
    See also AAYA 43; BPFB 2; CA 17-18;
    CAP 2; CDWLB 2; DA; DA3; DAB;
    DAC; DAM MST, NOV; DLB 66, 330;
    EW 9; EWL 3; EXPN; LAIT 1; MTCW
    1, 2; MTFW 2005; NFS 6, 15, 24; RGWL
    2, 3; SATA 50; TWA
Hewes, Cady
  See De Voto, Bernard (Augustine)
Heyen, William 1940- .... CLC **13, 18**
  See also CA 33-36R; 220; CAAE 220;
    CAAS 9; CANR 98; CP 3, 4, 5, 6, 7; DLB
    5; RGHL
Heyerdahl, Thor 1914-2002 .... CLC **26**
  See also CA 5-8R; 207; CANR 5, 22, 66,
    73; LAIT 4; MTCW 1, 2; MTFW 2005;
    SATA 2, 52
Heym, Georg (Theodor Franz Arthur)
    1887-1912 .... TCLC **9**
  See also CA 106; 181
Heym, Stefan 1913-2001 .... CLC **41**
  See also CA 9-12R; 203; CANR 4; CWW
    2; DLB 69; EWL 3
Heyse, Paul (Johann Ludwig von)
    1830-1914 .... TCLC **8**
  See also CA 104; 209; DLB 129, 330
Heyward, (Edwin) DuBose
    1885-1940 .... HR **1:2;** TCLC **59**
  See also CA 108; 157; DLB 7, 9, 45, 249;
    MAL 5; SATA 21
Heywood, John 1497(?)-1580(?) .... LC **65**
  See also DLB 136; RGEL 2
Heywood, Thomas 1573(?)-1641 .... LC **111**
  See also DAM DRAM; DLB 62; LMFS 1;
    RGEL 2; TEA
Hibbert, Eleanor Alice Burford
    1906-1993 .... CLC **7**
  See Holt, Victoria
    See also BEST 90:4; CA 17-20R; 140;
    CANR 9, 28, 59; CMW 4; CPW; DAM
    POP; MTCW 2; MTFW 2005; RHW;
    SATA 2; SATA-Obit 74

Hichens, Robert (Smythe)
    1864-1950 .... TCLC **64**
  See also CA 162; DLB 153; HGG; RHW;
    SUFW
Higgins, Aidan 1927- .... SSC **68**
  See also CA 9-12R; CANR 70, 115, 148;
    CN 1, 2, 3, 4, 5, 6, 7; DLB 14
Higgins, George V(incent)
    1939-1999 .... CLC **4, 7, 10, 18**
  See also BPFB 2; CA 77-80; 186; CAAS 5;
    CANR 17, 51, 89, 96; CMW 4; CN 2, 3,
    4, 5, 6; DLB 2; DLBY 1981, 1998; INT
    CANR-17; MSW; MTCW 1
Higginson, Thomas Wentworth
    1823-1911 .... TCLC **36**
  See also CA 162; DLB 1, 64, 243
Higgonet, Margaret ed. .... CLC **65**
Highet, Helen
  See MacInnes, Helen (Clark)
Highsmith, Patricia 1921-1995 ...... CLC **2, 4,**
    14, 42, 102
  See Morgan, Claire
    See also AAYA 48; BRWS 5; CA 1-4R; 147;
    CANR 1, 20, 48, 62, 108; CMW 4; CN 1,
    2, 3, 4, 5; CPW; DA3; DAM NOV, POP;
    DLB 306; MSW; MTCW 1, 2; MTFW
    2005
Highwater, Jamake (Mamake)
    1942(?)-2001 .... CLC **12**
  See also AAYA 7, 69; BPFB 2; BYA 4; CA
    65-68; 199; CAAS 7; CANR 10, 34, 84;
    CLR 17; CWRI 5; DLB 52; DLBY 1985;
    JRDA; MAICYA 1, 2; SATA 32, 69;
    SATA-Brief 30
Highway, Tomson 1951- ...... CLC **92; NNAL**
  See also CA 151; CANR 75; CCA 1; CD 5,
    6; CN 7; DAC; DAM MULT; DFS 2;
    MTCW 2
Hijuelos, Oscar 1951- .... CLC **65; HLC 1**
  See also AAYA 25; AMWS 8; BEST 90:1;
    CA 123; CANR 50, 75, 125; CPW; DA3;
    DAM MULT, POP; DLB 145; HW 1, 2;
    LLW; MAL 5; MTCW 2; MTFW 2005;
    NFS 17; RGAL 4; WLIT 1
Hikmet, Nazim 1902-1963 .... CLC **40**
  See Nizami of Ganja
    See also CA 141; 93-96; EWL 3; WLIT 6
Hildegard von Bingen 1098-1179 . CMLC **20**
  See also DLB 148
Hildesheimer, Wolfgang 1916-1991 .. CLC **49**
  See also CA 101; 135; DLB 69, 124; EWL
    3; RGHL
Hill, Geoffrey (William) 1932- ...... CLC **5, 8,**
    18, 45
  See also BRWS 5; CA 81-84; CANR 21,
    89; CDBLB 1960 to Present; CP 1, 2, 3,
    4, 5, 6, 7; DAM POET; DLB 40; EWL 3;
    MTCW 1; RGEL 2; RGHL
Hill, George Roy 1921-2002 .... CLC **26**
  See also CA 110; 122; 213
Hill, John
  See Koontz, Dean R.
Hill, Susan (Elizabeth) 1942- ...... CLC **4, 113**
  See also CA 33-36R; CANR 29, 69, 129;
    CN 2, 3, 4, 5, 6, 7; DAB; DAM MST,
    NOV; DLB 14, 139; HGG; MTCW 1;
    RHW
Hillard, Asa G. III .... CLC **70**
Hillerman, Tony 1925- .... CLC **62, 170**
  See also AAYA 40; BEST 89:1; BPFB 2;
    CA 29-32R; CANR 21, 42, 65, 97, 134;
    CMW 4; CPW; DA3; DAM POP; DLB
    206, 306; MAL 5; MSW; MTCW 1, 2;
    MTFW 2005; RGAL 4; SATA 6; TCWW
    2; YAW
Hillesum, Etty 1914-1943 .... TCLC **49**
  See also CA 137; RGHL
Hilliard, Noel (Harvey) 1929-1996 ... CLC **15**
  See also CA 9-12R; CANR 7, 69; CN 1, 2,
    3, 4, 5, 6

Hillis, Rick 1956- .... CLC **66**
  See also CA 134
Hilton, James 1900-1954 .... TCLC **21**
  See also CA 108; 169; DLB 34, 77; FANT;
    SATA 34
Hilton, Walter (?)-1396 .... CMLC **58**
  See also DLB 146; RGEL 2
Himes, Chester (Bomar) 1909-1984 .. BLC **2;**
    CLC **2, 4, 7, 18, 58, 108;** TCLC **139**
  See also AFAW 2; AMWS 16; BPFB 2; BW
    2; CA 25-28R; 114; CANR 22, 89; CMW
    4; CN 1, 2, 3; DAM MULT; DLB 2, 76,
    143, 226; EWL 3; MAL 5; MSW; MTCW
    1, 2; MTFW 2005; RGAL 4
Himmelfarb, Gertrude 1922- .... CLC **202**
  See also CA 49-52; CANR 28, 66, 102
Hinde, Thomas .... CLC **6, 11**
  See Chitty, Thomas Willes
    See also CN 1, 2, 3, 4, 5, 6; EWL 3
Hine, (William) Daryl 1936- .... CLC **15**
  See also CA 1-4R; CAAS 15; CANR 1, 20;
    CP 1, 2, 3, 4, 5, 6, 7; DLB 60
Hinkson, Katharine Tynan
  See Tynan, Katharine
Hinojosa, Rolando 1929- .... HLC **1**
  See Hinojosa-Smith, Rolando
    See also CA 131; CAAS 16; CANR 62;
    DAM MULT; DLB 82; HW 1, 2; LLW;
    MTCW 2; MTFW 2005; RGAL 4
Hinton, S.E. 1950- .... CLC **30, 111**
  See also AAYA 2, 33; BPFB 2; BYA 2, 3;
    CA 81-84; CANR 32, 62, 92, 133;
    CDALBS; CLR 3, 23; CPW; DA; DA3;
    DAB; DAC; DAM MST, NOV; JRDA;
    LAIT 5; MAICYA 1, 2; MTCW 1, 2;
    MTFW 2005; NFS 5, 9, 15, 16; SATA 19,
    58, 115, 160; WYA; YAW
Hippius, Zinaida (Nikolaevna) .... TCLC **9**
  See Gippius, Zinaida (Nikolaevna)
    See also DLB 295; EWL 3
Hiraoka, Kimitake 1925-1970
  See Mishima, Yukio
    See also CA 97-100; 29-32R; DA3; DAM
    DRAM; GLL 1; MTCW 1, 2
Hirsch, E.D., Jr. 1928- .... CLC **79**
  See also CA 25-28R; CANR 27, 51, 146;
    DLB 67; INT CANR-27; MTCW 1
Hirsch, Edward 1950- .... CLC **31, 50**
  See also CA 104; CANR 20, 42, 102; CP 6,
    7; DLB 120; PFS 22
Hirsch, Eric Donald, Jr.
  See Hirsch, E.D., Jr.
Hitchcock, Alfred (Joseph)
    1899-1980 .... CLC **16**
  See also AAYA 22; CA 159; 97-100; SATA
    27; SATA-Obit 24
Hitchens, Christopher 1949- .... CLC **157**
  See also CA 152; CANR 89, 155
Hitchens, Christopher Eric
  See Hitchens, Christopher
Hitler, Adolf 1889-1945 .... TCLC **53**
  See also CA 117; 147
Hoagland, Edward (Morley) 1932- .. CLC **28**
  See also ANW; CA 1-4R; CANR 2, 31, 57,
    107; CN 1, 2, 3, 4, 5, 6, 7; DLB 6; SATA
    51; TCWW 2
Hoban, Russell 1925- .... CLC **7, 25**
  See also BPFB 2; CA 5-8R; CANR 23, 37,
    66, 114, 138; CLR 3, 69; CN 4, 5, 6, 7;
    CWRI 5; DAM NOV; DLB 52; FANT;
    MAICYA 1, 2; MTCW 1, 2; MTFW 2005;
    SATA 1, 40, 78, 136; SFW 4; SUFW 2;
    TCLE 1:1
Hobbes, Thomas 1588-1679 .... LC **36**
  See also DLB 151, 252, 281; RGEL 2
Hobbs, Perry
  See Blackmur, R(ichard) P(almer)

Hobson, Laura Z(ametkin)
1900-1986 .... **CLC 7, 25**
See also BPFB 2; CA 17-20R; 118; CANR
55; CN 1, 2, 3, 4; DLB 28; SATA 52

Hoccleve, Thomas c. 1368-c. 1437 ...... **LC 75**
See also DLB 146; RGEL 2

Hoch, Edward D(entinger) 1930-
See Queen, Ellery
See also CA 29-32R; CANR 11, 27, 51, 97;
CMW 4; DLB 306; SFW 4

Hochhuth, Rolf 1931- .... **CLC 4, 11, 18**
See also CA 5-8R; CANR 33, 75, 136;
CWW 2; DAM DRAM; DLB 124; EWL
3; MTCW 1, 2; MTFW 2005; RGHL

Hochman, Sandra 1936- .... **CLC 3, 8**
See also CA 5-8R; CP 1, 2, 3, 4, 5; DLB 5

Hochwaelder, Fritz 1911-1986 .... **CLC 36**
See Hochwalder, Fritz
See also CA 29-32R; 120; CANR 42; DAM
DRAM; MTCW 1; RGWL 3

Hochwalder, Fritz
See Hochwaelder, Fritz
See also EWL 3; RGWL 2

Hocking, Mary (Eunice) 1921- .... **CLC 13**
See also CA 101; CANR 18, 40

Hodgins, Jack 1938- .... **CLC 23**
See also CA 93-96; CN 4, 5, 6, 7; DLB 60

Hodgson, William Hope
1877(?)-1918 .... **TCLC 13**
See also CA 111; 164; CMW 4; DLB 70,
153, 156, 178; HGG; MTCW 2; SFW 4;
SUFW 1

Hoeg, Peter 1957- .... **CLC 95, 156**
See also CA 151; CANR 75; CMW 4; DA3;
DLB 214; EWL 3; MTCW 2; MTFW
2005; NFS 17; RGWL 3; SSFS 18

Hoffman, Alice 1952- .... **CLC 51**
See also AAYA 37; AMWS 10; CA 77-80;
CANR 34, 66, 100, 138; CN 4, 5, 6, 7;
CPW; DAM NOV; DLB 292; MAL 5;
MTCW 1, 2; MTFW 2005; TCLE 1:1

Hoffman, Daniel (Gerard) 1923- . **CLC 6, 13, 23**
See also CA 1-4R; CANR 4, 142; CP 1, 2,
3, 4, 5, 6, 7; DLB 5; TCLE 1:1

Hoffman, Eva 1945- .... **CLC 182**
See also AMWS 16; CA 132; CANR 146

Hoffman, Stanley 1944- .... **CLC 5**
See also CA 77-80

Hoffman, William 1925- .... **CLC 141**
See also CA 21-24R; CANR 9, 103; CSW;
DLB 234; TCLE 1:1

Hoffman, William M.
See Hoffman, William M(oses)
See also CAD; CD 5, 6

Hoffman, William M(oses) 1939- ..... **CLC 40**
See Hoffman, William M.
See also CA 57-60; CANR 11, 71

Hoffmann, E(rnst) T(heodor) A(madeus)
1776-1822 .... **NCLC 2; SSC 13, 92**
See also CDWLB 2; DLB 90; EW 5; GL 2;
RGSF 2; RGWL 2, 3; SATA 27; SUFW
1; WCH

Hofmann, Gert 1931-1993 .... **CLC 54**
See also CA 128; CANR 145; EWL 3;
RGHL

Hofmannsthal, Hugo von 1874-1929 ... **DC 4; TCLC 11**
See also CA 106; 153; CDWLB 2; DAM
DRAM; DFS 17; DLB 81, 118; EW 9;
EWL 3; RGWL 2, 3

Hogan, Linda 1947- ..... **CLC 73; NNAL; PC 35**
See also AMWS 4; ANW; BYA 12; CA 120;
226; CAAE 226; CANR 45, 73, 129;
CWP; DAM MULT; DLB 175; SATA
132; TCWW 2

Hogarth, Charles
See Creasey, John

Hogarth, Emmett
See Polonsky, Abraham (Lincoln)

Hogarth, William 1697-1764 .... **LC 112**
See also AAYA 56

Hogg, James 1770-1835 .... **NCLC 4, 109**
See also BRWS 10; DLB 93, 116, 159; GL
2; HGG; RGEL 2; SUFW 1

Holbach, Paul-Henri Thiry
1723-1789 .... **LC 14**
See also DLB 313

Holberg, Ludvig 1684-1754 .... **LC 6**
See also DLB 300; RGWL 2, 3

Holcroft, Thomas 1745-1809 .... **NCLC 85**
See also DLB 39, 89, 158; RGEL 2

Holden, Ursula 1921- .... **CLC 18**
See also CA 101; CAAS 8; CANR 22

Holderlin, (Johann Christian) Friedrich
1770-1843 .... **NCLC 16; PC 4**
See also CDWLB 2; DLB 90; EW 5; RGWL
2, 3

Holdstock, Robert
See Holdstock, Robert P.

Holdstock, Robert P. 1948- .... **CLC 39**
See also CA 131; CANR 81; DLB 261;
FANT; HGG; SFW 4; SUFW 2

Holinshed, Raphael fl. 1580- .... **LC 69**
See also DLB 167; RGEL 2

Holland, Isabelle (Christian)
1920-2002 .... **CLC 21**
See also AAYA 11, 64; CA 21-24R; 205;
CAAE 181; CANR 10, 25, 47; CLR 57;
CWRI 5; JRDA; LAIT 4; MAICYA 1, 2;
SATA 8, 70; SATA-Essay 103; SATA-Obit
132; WYA

Holland, Marcus
See Caldwell, (Janet Miriam) Taylor
(Holland)

Hollander, John 1929- .... **CLC 2, 5, 8, 14**
See also CA 1-4R; CANR 1, 52, 136; CP 1,
2, 3, 4, 5, 6, 7; DLB 5; MAL 5; SATA 13

Hollander, Paul
See Silverberg, Robert

Holleran, Andrew .... **CLC 38**
See Garber, Eric
See also CA 144; GLL 1

Holley, Marietta 1836(?)-1926 .... **TCLC 99**
See also CA 118; DLB 11; FL 1:3

Hollinghurst, Alan 1954- .... **CLC 55, 91**
See also BRWS 10; CA 114; CN 5, 6, 7;
DLB 207, 326; GLL 1

Hollis, Jim
See Summers, Hollis (Spurgeon, Jr.)

Holly, Buddy 1936-1959 .... **TCLC 65**
See also CA 213

Holmes, Gordon
See Shiel, M(atthew) P(hipps)

Holmes, John
See Souster, (Holmes) Raymond

Holmes, John Clellon 1926-1988 ...... **CLC 56**
See also BG 1:2; CA 9-12R; 125; CANR 4;
CN 1, 2, 3, 4; DLB 16, 237

Holmes, Oliver Wendell, Jr.
1841-1935 .... **TCLC 77**
See also CA 114; 186

Holmes, Oliver Wendell
1809-1894 .... **NCLC 14, 81; PC 71**
See also AMWS 1; CDALB 1640-1865;
DLB 1, 189, 235; EXPP; PFS 24; RGAL
4; SATA 34

Holmes, Raymond
See Souster, (Holmes) Raymond

Holt, Victoria
See Hibbert, Eleanor Alice Burford
See also BPFB 2

Holub, Miroslav 1923-1998 .... **CLC 4**
See also CA 21-24R; 169; CANR 10; CD-
WLB 4; CWW 2; DLB 232; EWL 3;
RGWL 3

Holz, Detlev
See Benjamin, Walter

Homer c. 8th cent. B.C.- .... **CMLC 1, 16, 61; PC 23; WLCS**
See also AW 1; CDWLB 1; DA; DA3;
DAB; DAC; DAM MST, POET; DLB
176; EFS 1; LAIT 1; LMFS 1; RGWL 2,
3; TWA; WLIT 8; WP

Hongo, Garrett Kaoru 1951- .... **PC 23**
See also CA 133; CAAS 22; CP 5, 6, 7;
DLB 120, 312; EWL 3; EXPP; RGAL 4

Honig, Edwin 1919- .... **CLC 33**
See also CA 5-8R; CAAS 8; CANR 4, 45,
144; CP 1, 2, 3, 4, 5, 6, 7; DLB 5

Hood, Hugh (John Blagdon) 1928- . **CLC 15, 28; SSC 42**
See also CA 49-52; CAAS 17; CANR 1,
33, 87; CN 1, 2, 3, 4, 5, 6, 7; DLB 53;
RGSF 2

Hood, Thomas 1799-1845 .... **NCLC 16**
See also BRW 4; DLB 96; RGEL 2

Hooker, (Peter) Jeremy 1941- .... **CLC 43**
See also CA 77-80; CANR 22; CP 2, 3, 4,
5, 6, 7; DLB 40

Hooker, Richard 1554-1600 .... **LC 95**
See also BRW 1; DLB 132; RGEL 2

hooks, bell 1952(?)- .... **CLC 94**
See also BW 2; CA 143; CANR 87, 126;
DLB 246; MTCW 2; MTFW 2005; SATA
115, 170

Hope, A(lec) D(erwent) 1907-2000 .... **CLC 3, 51; PC 56**
See also BRWS 7; CA 21-24R; 188; CANR
33, 74; CP 1, 2, 3, 4, 5; DLB 289; EWL
3; MTCW 1, 2; MTFW 2005; PFS 8;
RGEL 2

Hope, Anthony 1863-1933 .... **TCLC 83**
See also CA 157; DLB 153, 156; RGEL 2;
RHW

Hope, Brian
See Creasey, John

Hope, Christopher (David Tully)
1944- .... **CLC 52**
See also AFW; CA 106; CANR 47, 101;
CN 4, 5, 6, 7; DLB 225; SATA 62

Hopkins, Gerard Manley
1844-1889 .... **NCLC 17; PC 15; WLC 3**
See also BRW 5; BRWR 2; CDBLB 1890-
1914; DA; DA3; DAB; DAC; DAM MST,
POET; DLB 35, 57; EXPP; PAB; RGEL
2; TEA; WP

Hopkins, John (Richard) 1931-1998 .. **CLC 4**
See also CA 85-88; 169; CBD; CD 5, 6

Hopkins, Pauline Elizabeth
1859-1930 .... **BLC 2; TCLC 28**
See also AFAW 2; BW 2, 3; CA 141; CANR
82; DAM MULT; DLB 50

Hopkinson, Francis 1737-1791 .... **LC 25**
See also DLB 31; RGAL 4

Hopley-Woolrich, Cornell George 1903-1968
See Woolrich, Cornell
See also CA 13-14; CANR 58, 156; CAP 1;
CMW 4; DLB 226; MTCW 2

Horace 65B.C.-8B.C. .... **CMLC 39; PC 46**
See also AW 2; CDWLB 1; DLB 211;
RGWL 2, 3; WLIT 8

Horatio
See Proust, (Valentin-Louis-George-Eugene)
Marcel

Horgan, Paul (George Vincent
O'Shaughnessy) 1903-1995 .. **CLC 9, 53**
See also BPFB 2; CA 13-16R; 147; CANR
9, 35; CN 1, 2, 3, 4, 5; DAM NOV; DLB
102, 212; DLBY 1985; INT CANR-9;
MTCW 1, 2; MTFW 2005; SATA 13;
SATA-Obit 84; TCWW 1, 2

Horkheimer, Max 1895-1973 .... **TCLC 132**
See also CA 216; 41-44R; DLB 296

Kantor, MacKinlay 1904-1977 .... **CLC 7**
See also CA 61-64; 73-76; CANR 60, 63;
CN 1, 2; DLB 9, 102; MAL 5; MTCW 2;
RHW; TCWW 1, 2

Kanze Motokiyo
See Zeami

Kaplan, David Michael 1946- .... **CLC 50**
See also CA 187

Kaplan, James 1951- .... **CLC 59**
See also CA 135; CANR 121

Karadzic, Vuk Stefanovic
1787-1864 .... **NCLC 115**
See also CDWLB 4; DLB 147

Karageorge, Michael
See Anderson, Poul

Karamzin, Nikolai Mikhailovich
1766-1826 .... **NCLC 3, 173**
See also DLB 150; RGSF 2

Karapanou, Margarita 1946- .... **CLC 13**
See also CA 101

Karinthy, Frigyes 1887-1938 .... **TCLC 47**
See also CA 170; DLB 215; EWL 3

Karl, Frederick R(obert)
1927-2004 .... **CLC 34**
See also CA 5-8R; 226; CANR 3, 44, 143

Karr, Mary 1955- .... **CLC 188**
See also AMWS 11; CA 151; CANR 100;
MTFW 2005; NCFS 5

Kastel, Warren
See Silverberg, Robert

Kataev, Evgeny Petrovich 1903-1942
See Petrov, Evgeny
See also CA 120

Kataphusin
See Ruskin, John

Katz, Steve 1935- .... **CLC 47**
See also CA 25-28R; CAAS 14, 64; CANR
12; CN 4, 5, 6, 7; DLBY 1983

Kauffman, Janet 1945- .... **CLC 42**
See also CA 117; CANR 43, 84; DLB 218;
DLBY 1986

Kaufman, Bob (Garnell)
1925-1986 .... **CLC 49; PC 74**
See also BG 1:3; BW 1; CA 41-44R; 118;
CANR 22; CP 1; DLB 16, 41

Kaufman, George S. 1889-1961 ...... **CLC 38;
DC 17**
See also CA 108; 93-96; DAM DRAM;
DFS 1, 10; DLB 7; INT CA-108; MTCW
2; MTFW 2005; RGAL 4; TUS

Kaufman, Moises 1964- .... **DC 26**
See also CA 211; DFS 22; MTFW 2005

Kaufman, Sue .... **CLC 3, 8**
See Barondess, Sue K(aufman)

Kavafis, Konstantinos Petrou 1863-1933
See Cavafy, C(onstantine) P(eter)
See also CA 104

Kavan, Anna 1901-1968 .... **CLC 5, 13, 82**
See also BRWS 7; CA 5-8R; CANR 6, 57;
DLB 255; MTCW 1; RGEL 2; SFW 4

Kavanagh, Dan
See Barnes, Julian

Kavanagh, Julie 1952- .... **CLC 119**
See also CA 163

Kavanagh, Patrick (Joseph)
1904-1967 .... **CLC 22; PC 33**
See also BRWS 7; CA 123; 25-28R; DLB
15, 20; EWL 3; MTCW 1; RGEL 2

Kawabata, Yasunari 1899-1972 ..... **CLC 2, 5,
9, 18, 107; SSC 17**
See Kawabata Yasunari
See also CA 93-96; 33-36R; CANR 88;
DAM MULT; DLB 330; MJW; MTCW 2;
MTFW 2005; RGSF 2; RGWL 2, 3

Kawabata Yasunari
See Kawabata, Yasunari
See also DLB 180; EWL 3

Kaye, M.M. 1908-2004 .... **CLC 28**
See also CA 89-92; 223; CANR 24, 60, 102,
142; MTCW 1, 2; MTFW 2005; RHW;
SATA 62; SATA-Obit 152

Kaye, Mollie
See Kaye, M.M.

Kaye-Smith, Sheila 1887-1956 .... **TCLC 20**
See also CA 118; 203; DLB 36

Kaymor, Patrice Maguilene
See Senghor, Leopold Sedar

Kazakov, Iurii Pavlovich
See Kazakov, Yuri Pavlovich
See also DLB 302

Kazakov, Yuri Pavlovich 1927-1982 . **SSC 43**
See Kazakov, Iurii Pavlovich; Kazakov,
Yury
See also CA 5-8R; CANR 36; MTCW 1;
RGSF 2

Kazakov, Yury
See Kazakov, Yuri Pavlovich
See also EWL 3

Kazan, Elia 1909-2003 .... **CLC 6, 16, 63**
See also CA 21-24R; 220; CANR 32, 78

Kazantzakis, Nikos 1883(?)-1957 .... **TCLC 2,
5, 33, 181**
See also BPFB 2; CA 105; 132; DA3; EW
9; EWL 3; MTCW 1, 2; MTFW 2005;
RGWL 2, 3

Kazin, Alfred 1915-1998 ..... **CLC 34, 38, 119**
See also AMWS 8; CA 1-4R; CAAS 7;
CANR 1, 45, 79; DLB 67; EWL 3

Keane, Mary Nesta (Skrine) 1904-1996
See Keane, Molly
See also CA 108; 114; 151; RHW

Keane, Molly .... **CLC 31**
See Keane, Mary Nesta (Skrine)
See also CN 5, 6; INT CA-114; TCLE 1:1

Keates, Jonathan 1946(?)- .... **CLC 34**
See also CA 163; CANR 126

Keaton, Buster 1895-1966 .... **CLC 20**
See also CA 194

Keats, John 1795-1821 ...... **NCLC 8, 73, 121;
PC 1; WLC 3**
See also AAYA 58; BRW 4; BRWR 1; CD-
BLB 1789-1832; DA; DA3; DAB; DAC;
DAM MST, POET; DLB 96, 110; EXPP;
LMFS 1; PAB; PFS 1, 2, 3, 9, 17; RGEL
2; TEA; WLIT 3; WP

Keble, John 1792-1866 .... **NCLC 87**
See also DLB 32, 55; RGEL 2

Keene, Donald 1922- .... **CLC 34**
See also CA 1-4R; CANR 5, 119

Keillor, Garrison 1942- ..... **CLC 40, 115, 222**
See also AAYA 2, 62; AMWS 16; BEST
89:3; BPFB 2; CA 111; 117; CANR 36,
59, 124; CPW; DA3; DAM POP; DLBY
1987; EWL 3; MTCW 1, 2; MTFW 2005;
SATA 58; TUS

Keith, Carlos
See Lewton, Val

Keith, Michael
See Hubbard, L. Ron

Keller, Gottfried 1819-1890 .... **NCLC 2; SSC
26**
See also CDWLB 2; DLB 129; EW; RGSF
2; RGWL 2, 3

Keller, Nora Okja 1965- .... **CLC 109**
See also CA 187

Kellerman, Jonathan 1949- .... **CLC 44**
See also AAYA 35; BEST 90:1; CA 106;
CANR 29, 51, 150; CMW 4; CPW; DA3;
DAM POP; INT CANR-29

Kelley, William Melvin 1937- .... **CLC 22**
See also BW 1; CA 77-80; CANR 27, 83;
CN 1, 2, 3, 4, 5, 6, 7; DLB 33; EWL 3

Kellogg, Marjorie 1922-2005 .... **CLC 2**
See also CA 81-84; 246

Kellow, Kathleen
See Hibbert, Eleanor Alice Burford

Kelly, Lauren
See Oates, Joyce Carol

Kelly, M(ilton) T(errence) 1947- ...... **CLC 55**
See also CA 97-100; CAAS 22; CANR 19,
43, 84; CN 6

Kelly, Robert 1935- .... **SSC 50**
See also CA 17-20R; CAAS 19; CANR 47;
CP 1, 2, 3, 4, 5, 6, 7; DLB 5, 130, 165

Kelman, James 1946- .... **CLC 58, 86**
See also BRWS 5; CA 148; CANR 85, 130;
CN 5, 6, 7; DLB 194, 319, 326; RGSF 2;
WLIT 4

Kemal, Yasar
See Kemal, Yashar
See also CWW 2; EWL 3; WLIT 6

Kemal, Yashar 1923(?)- .... **CLC 14, 29**
See also CA 89-92; CANR 44

Kemble, Fanny 1809-1893 .... **NCLC 18**
See also DLB 32

Kemelman, Harry 1908-1996 .... **CLC 2**
See also AITN 1; BPFB 2; CA 9-12R; 155;
CANR 6, 71; CMW 4; DLB 28

Kempe, Margery 1373(?)-1440(?) ... **LC 6, 56**
See also BRWS 12; DLB 146; FL 1:1;
RGEL 2

Kempis, Thomas a 1380-1471 .... **LC 11**

Kendall, Henry 1839-1882 .... **NCLC 12**
See also DLB 230

Keneally, Thomas 1935- .... **CLC 5, 8, 10, 14,
19, 27, 43, 117**
See also BRWS 4; CA 85-88; CANR 10,
50, 74, 130; CN 1, 2, 3, 4, 5, 6, 7; CPW;
DA3; DAM NOV; DLB 289, 299, 326;
EWL 3; MTCW 1, 2; MTFW 2005; NFS
17; RGEL 2; RGHL; RHW

Kennedy, A(lison) L(ouise) 1965- ... **CLC 188**
See also CA 168, 213; CAAE 213; CANR
108; CD 5, 6; CN 6, 7; DLB 271; RGSF
2

Kennedy, Adrienne (Lita) 1931- .... **BLC 2;
CLC 66; DC 5**
See also AFAW 2; BW 2, 3; CA 103; CAAS
20; CABS 3; CAD; CANR 26, 53, 82;
CD 5, 6; DAM MULT; DFS 9; DLB 38;
FW; MAL 5

Kennedy, John Pendleton
1795-1870 .... **NCLC 2**
See also DLB 3, 248, 254; RGAL 4

Kennedy, Joseph Charles 1929-
See Kennedy, X. J.
See also CA 1-4R, 201; CAAE 201; CANR
4, 30, 40; CWRI 5; MAICYA 2; MAIC-
YAS 1; SATA 14, 86, 130; SATA-Essay
130

Kennedy, William 1928- ... **CLC 6, 28, 34, 53**
See also AAYA 1; AMWS 7; BPFB 2; CA
85-88; CANR 14, 31, 76, 134; CN 4, 5, 6,
7; DA3; DAM NOV; DLB 143; DLBY
1985; EWL 3; INT CANR-31; MAL 5;
MTCW 1, 2; MTFW 2005; SATA 57

Kennedy, X. J. .... **CLC 8, 42**
See Kennedy, Joseph Charles
See also AMWS 15; CAAS 9; CLR 27; CP
1, 2, 3, 4, 5, 6, 7; DLB 5; SAAS 22

Kenny, Maurice (Francis) 1929- ..... **CLC 87;
NNAL**
See also CA 144; CAAS 22; CANR 143;
DAM MULT; DLB 175

Kent, Kelvin
See Kuttner, Henry

Kenton, Maxwell
See Southern, Terry

Kenyon, Jane 1947-1995 .... **PC 57**
See also AAYA 63; AMWS 7; CA 118; 148;
CANR 44, 69; CP 6, 7; CWP; DLB 120;
PFS 9, 17; RGAL 4

Kenyon, Robert O.
See Kuttner, Henry

Kirkup, James 1918- .... **CLC 1**
See also CA 1-4R; CAAS 4; CANR 2; CP
1, 2, 3, 4, 5, 6, 7; DLB 27; SATA 12

Kirkwood, James 1930(?)-1989 .... **CLC 9**
See also AITN 2; CA 1-4R; 128; CANR 6,
40; GLL 2

Kirsch, Sarah 1935- .... **CLC 176**
See also CA 178; CWW 2; DLB 75; EWL
3

Kirshner, Sidney
See Kingsley, Sidney

Kis, Danilo 1935-1989 .... **CLC 57**
See also CA 109; 118; 129; CANR 61; CD-
WLB 4; DLB 181; EWL 3; MTCW 1;
RGSF 2; RGWL 2, 3

Kissinger, Henry A(lfred) 1923- ..... **CLC 137**
See also CA 1-4R; CANR 2, 33, 66, 109;
MTCW 1

Kittel, Frederick August
See Wilson, August

Kivi, Aleksis 1834-1872 .... **NCLC 30**

Kizer, Carolyn 1925- ..... **CLC 15, 39, 80; PC
66**
See also CA 65-68; CAAS 5; CANR 24,
70, 134; CP 1, 2, 3, 4, 5, 6, 7; CWP; DAM
POET; DLB 5, 169; EWL 3; MAL 5;
MTCW 2; MTFW 2005; PFS 18; TCLE
1:1

Klabund 1890-1928 .... **TCLC 44**
See also CA 162; DLB 66

Klappert, Peter 1942- .... **CLC 57**
See also CA 33-36R; CSW; DLB 5

Klein, A(braham) M(oses)
1909-1972 .... **CLC 19**
See also CA 101; 37-40R; CP 1; DAB;
DAC; DAM MST; DLB 68; EWL 3;
RGEL 2; RGHL

Klein, Joe
See Klein, Joseph

Klein, Joseph 1946- .... **CLC 154**
See also CA 85-88; CANR 55

Klein, Norma 1938-1989 .... **CLC 30**
See also AAYA 2, 35; BPFB 2; BYA 6, 7,
8; CA 41-44R; 128; CANR 15, 37; CLR
2, 19; INT CANR-15; JRDA; MAICYA
1, 2; SAAS 1; SATA 7, 57; WYA; YAW

Klein, T(heodore) E(ibon) D(onald)
1947- .... **CLC 34**
See also CA 119; CANR 44, 75; HGG

Kleist, Heinrich von 1777-1811 ...... **NCLC 2,
37; SSC 22**
See also CDWLB 2; DAM DRAM; DLB
90; EW 5; RGSF 2; RGWL 2, 3

Klima, Ivan 1931- .... **CLC 56, 172**
See also CA 25-28R; CANR 17, 50, 91;
CDWLB 4; CWW 2; DAM NOV; DLB
232; EWL 3; RGWL 3

Klimentev, Andrei Platonovich
See Klimentov, Andrei Platonovich

Klimentov, Andrei Platonovich
1899-1951 .... **SSC 42; TCLC 14**
See Platonov, Andrei Platonovich; Platonov,
Andrey Platonovich
See also CA 108; 232

Klinger, Friedrich Maximilian von
1752-1831 .... **NCLC 1**
See also DLB 94

Klingsor the Magician
See Hartmann, Sadakichi

Klopstock, Friedrich Gottlieb
1724-1803 .... **NCLC 11**
See also DLB 97; EW 4; RGWL 2, 3

Kluge, Alexander 1932- .... **SSC 61**
See also CA 81-84; DLB 75

Knapp, Caroline 1959-2002 .... **CLC 99**
See also CA 154; 207

Knebel, Fletcher 1911-1993 .... **CLC 14**
See also AITN 1; CA 1-4R; 140; CAAS 3;
CANR 1, 36; CN 1, 2, 3, 4, 5; SATA 36;
SATA-Obit 75

Knickerbocker, Diedrich
See Irving, Washington

Knight, Etheridge 1931-1991 ... **BLC 2; CLC
40; PC 14**
See also BW 1, 3; CA 21-24R; 133; CANR
23, 82; CP 1, 2, 3, 4, 5; DAM POET; DLB
41; MTCW 2; MTFW 2005; RGAL 4;
TCLE 1:1

Knight, Sarah Kemble 1666-1727 .... **LC 7**
See also DLB 24, 200

Knister, Raymond 1899-1932 .... **TCLC 56**
See also CA 186; DLB 68; RGEL 2

Knowles, John 1926-2001 ... **CLC 1, 4, 10, 26**
See also AAYA 10; AMWS 12; BPFB 2;
BYA 3; CA 17-20R; 203; CANR 40, 74,
76, 132; CDALB 1968-1988; CLR 98; CN
1, 2, 3, 4, 5, 6, 7; DA; DAC; DAM MST,
NOV; DLB 6; EXPN; MTCW 1, 2;
MTFW 2005; NFS 2; RGAL 4; SATA 8,
89; SATA-Obit 134; YAW

Knox, Calvin M.
See Silverberg, Robert

Knox, John c. 1505-1572 .... **LC 37**
See also DLB 132

Knye, Cassandra
See Disch, Thomas M.

Koch, C(hristopher) J(ohn) 1932- .... **CLC 42**
See also CA 127; CANR 84; CN 3, 4, 5, 6,
7; DLB 289

Koch, Christopher
See Koch, C(hristopher) J(ohn)

Koch, Kenneth 1925-2002 .... **CLC 5, 8, 44**
See also AMWS 15; CA 1-4R; 207; CAD;
CANR 6, 36, 57, 97, 131; CD 5, 6; CP 1,
2, 3, 4, 5, 6; DAM POET; DLB 5; INT
CANR-36; MAL 5; MTCW 2; MTFW
2005; PFS 20; SATA 65; WP

Kochanowski, Jan 1530-1584 .... **LC 10**
See also RGWL 2, 3

Kock, Charles Paul de 1794-1871 . **NCLC 16**

Koda Rohan
See Koda Shigeyuki

Koda Rohan
See Koda Shigeyuki
See also DLB 180

Koda Shigeyuki 1867-1947 .... **TCLC 22**
See Koda Rohan
See also CA 121; 183

Koestler, Arthur 1905-1983 ... **CLC 1, 3, 6, 8,
15, 33**
See also BRWS 1; CA 1-4R; 109; CANR 1,
33; CDBLB 1945-1960; CN 1, 2, 3;
DLBY 1983; EWL 3; MTCW 1, 2; MTFW
2005; NFS 19; RGEL 2

Kogawa, Joy Nozomi 1935- ...... **CLC 78, 129**
See also AAYA 47; CA 101; CANR 19, 62,
126; CN 6, 7; CP 1; CWP; DAC; DAM
MST, MULT; FW; MTCW 2; MTFW
2005; NFS 3; SATA 99

Kohout, Pavel 1928- .... **CLC 13**
See also CA 45-48; CANR 3

Koizumi, Yakumo
See Hearn, (Patricio) Lafcadio (Tessima
Carlos)

Kolmar, Gertrud 1894-1943 .... **TCLC 40**
See also CA 167; EWL 3; RGHL

Komunyakaa, Yusef 1947- .. **BLCS; CLC 86,
94, 207; PC 51**
See also AFAW 2; AMWS 13; CA 147;
CANR 83; CP 6, 7; CSW; DLB 120; EWL
3; PFS 5, 20; RGAL 4

Konrad, George
See Konrad, Gyorgy

Konrad, Gyorgy 1933- .... **CLC 4, 10, 73**
See also CA 85-88; CANR 97; CDWLB 4;
CWW 2; DLB 232; EWL 3

Konwicki, Tadeusz 1926- .... **CLC 8, 28, 54,
117**
See also CA 101; CAAS 9; CANR 39, 59;
CWW 2; DLB 232; EWL 3; IDFW 3;
MTCW 1

Koontz, Dean R. 1945- .... **CLC 78, 206**
See also AAYA 9, 31; BEST 89:3, 90:2; CA
108; CANR 19, 36, 52, 95, 138; CMW 4;
CPW; DA3; DAM NOV, POP; DLB 292;
HGG; MTCW 1; MTFW 2005; SATA 92,
165; SFW 4; SUFW 2; YAW

Koontz, Dean Ray
See Koontz, Dean R.

Kopernik, Mikolaj
See Copernicus, Nicolaus

Kopit, Arthur (Lee) 1937- ...... **CLC 1, 18, 33**
See also AITN 1; CA 81-84; CABS 3;
CAD; CD 5, 6; DAM DRAM; DFS 7, 14;
DLB 7; MAL 5; MTCW 1; RGAL 4

Kopitar, Jernej (Bartholomaus)
1780-1844 .... **NCLC 117**

Kops, Bernard 1926- .... **CLC 4**
See also CA 5-8R; CANR 84; CBD; CN 1,
2, 3, 4, 5, 6, 7; CP 1, 2, 3, 4, 5, 6, 7; DLB
13; RGHL

Kornbluth, C(yril) M. 1923-1958 .... **TCLC 8**
See also CA 105; 160; DLB 8; SCFW 1, 2;
SFW 4

Korolenko, V.G.
See Korolenko, Vladimir G.

Korolenko, Vladimir
See Korolenko, Vladimir G.

Korolenko, Vladimir G.
1853-1921 .... **TCLC 22**
See also CA 121; DLB 277

Korolenko, Vladimir Galaktionovich
See Korolenko, Vladimir G.

Korzybski, Alfred (Habdank Skarbek)
1879-1950 .... **TCLC 61**
See also CA 123; 160

Kosinski, Jerzy 1933-1991 ..... **CLC 1, 2, 3, 6,
10, 15, 53, 70**
See also AMWS 7; BPFB 2; CA 17-20R;
134; CANR 9, 46; CN 1, 2, 3, 4; DA3;
DAM NOV; DLB 2, 299; DLBY 1982;
EWL 3; HGG; MAL 5; MTCW 1, 2;
MTFW 2005; NFS 12; RGAL 4; RGHL;
TUS

Kostelanetz, Richard (Cory) 1940- .. **CLC 28**
See also CA 13-16R; CAAS 8; CANR 38,
77; CN 4, 5, 6; CP 2, 3, 4, 5, 6, 7

Kostrowitzki, Wilhelm Apollinaris de
1880-1918
See Apollinaire, Guillaume
See also CA 104

Kotlowitz, Robert 1924- .... **CLC 4**
See also CA 33-36R; CANR 36

Kotzebue, August (Friedrich Ferdinand) von
1761-1819 .... **NCLC 25**
See also DLB 94

Kotzwinkle, William 1938- ..... **CLC 5, 14, 35**
See also BPFB 2; CA 45-48; CANR 3, 44,
84, 129; CLR 6; CN 7; DLB 173; FANT;
MAICYA 1, 2; SATA 24, 70, 146; SFW
4; SUFW 2; YAW

Kowna, Stancy
See Szymborska, Wislawa

Kozol, Jonathan 1936- .... **CLC 17**
See also AAYA 46; CA 61-64; CANR 16,
45, 96; MTFW 2005

Kozoll, Michael 1940(?)- .... **CLC 35**

Kramer, Kathryn 19(?)- .... **CLC 34**

Kramer, Larry 1935- .... **CLC 42; DC 8**
See also CA 124; 126; CANR 60, 132;
DAM POP; DLB 249; GLL 1

Laishley, Alex
　　See Booth, Martin
Lamartine, Alphonse (Marie Louis Prat) de
　　1790-1869 .... **NCLC 11; PC 16**
　　See also DAM POET; DLB 217; GFL 1789
　　　to the Present; RGWL 2, 3
Lamb, Charles 1775-1834 ..... **NCLC 10, 113;**
　　WLC 3
　　See also BRW 4; CDBLB 1789-1832; DA;
　　　DAB; DAC; DAM MST; DLB 93, 107,
　　　163; RGEL 2; SATA 17; TEA
Lamb, Lady Caroline 1785-1828 ... **NCLC 38**
　　See also DLB 116
Lamb, Mary Ann 1764-1847 .... **NCLC 125**
　　See also DLB 163; SATA 17
Lame Deer 1903(?)-1976 .... **NNAL**
　　See also CA 69-72
Lamming, George (William) 1927- ... **BLC 2;**
　　CLC 2, 4, 66, 144
　　See also BW 2, 3; CA 85-88; CANR 26,
　　　76; CDWLB 3; CN 1, 2, 3, 4, 5, 6, 7; CP
　　　1; DAM MULT; DLB 125; EWL 3;
　　　MTCW 1, 2; MTFW 2005; NFS 15;
　　　RGEL 2
L'Amour, Louis 1908-1988 .... **CLC 25, 55**
　　See also AAYA 16; AITN 2; BEST 89:2;
　　　BPFB 2; CA 1-4R; 125; CANR 3, 25, 40;
　　　CPW; DA3; DAM NOV, POP; DLB 206;
　　　DLBY 1980; MTCW 1, 2; MTFW 2005;
　　　RGAL 4; TCWW 1, 2
Lampedusa, Giuseppe (Tomasi) di
　　... **TCLC 13**
　　See Tomasi di Lampedusa, Giuseppe
　　See also CA 164; EW 11; MTCW 2; MTFW
　　　2005; RGWL 2, 3
Lampman, Archibald 1861-1899 ... **NCLC 25**
　　See also DLB 92; RGEL 2; TWA
Lancaster, Bruce 1896-1963 .... **CLC 36**
　　See also CA 9-10; CANR 70; CAP 1; SATA
　　　9
Lanchester, John 1962- .... **CLC 99**
　　See also CA 194; DLB 267
Landau, Mark Alexandrovich
　　See Aldanov, Mark (Alexandrovich)
Landau-Aldanov, Mark Alexandrovich
　　See Aldanov, Mark (Alexandrovich)
Landis, Jerry
　　See Simon, Paul
Landis, John 1950- .... **CLC 26**
　　See also CA 112; 122; CANR 128
Landolfi, Tommaso 1908-1979 .... **CLC 11, 49**
　　See also CA 127; 117; DLB 177; EWL 3
Landon, Letitia Elizabeth
　　1802-1838 .... **NCLC 15**
　　See also DLB 96
Landor, Walter Savage
　　1775-1864 .... **NCLC 14**
　　See also BRW 4; DLB 93, 107; RGEL 2
Landwirth, Heinz 1927-
　　See Lind, Jakov
　　See also CA 9-12R; CANR 7
Lane, Patrick 1939- .... **CLC 25**
　　See also CA 97-100; CANR 54; CP 3, 4, 5,
　　　6, 7; DAM POET; DLB 53; INT CA-97-
　　　100
Lane, Rose Wilder 1887-1968 ...... **TCLC 177**
　　See also CA 102; CANR 63; SATA 29;
　　　SATA-Brief 28; TCWW 2
Lang, Andrew 1844-1912 .... **TCLC 16**
　　See also CA 114; 137; CANR 85; CLR 101;
　　　DLB 98, 141, 184; FANT; MAICYA 1, 2;
　　　RGEL 2; SATA 16; WCH
Lang, Fritz 1890-1976 .... **CLC 20, 103**
　　See also AAYA 65; CA 77-80; 69-72;
　　　CANR 30
Lange, John
　　See Crichton, Michael
Langer, Elinor 1939- .... **CLC 34**
　　See also CA 121

Langland, William 1332(?)-1400(?) .... **LC 19,**
　　120
　　See also BRW 1; DA; DAB; DAC; DAM
　　　MST, POET; DLB 146; RGEL 2; TEA;
　　　WLIT 3
Langstaff, Launcelot
　　See Irving, Washington
Lanier, Sidney 1842-1881 . **NCLC 6, 118; PC**
　　50
　　See also AMWS 1; DAM POET; DLB 64;
　　　DLBD 13; EXPP; MAICYA 1; PFS 14;
　　　RGAL 4; SATA 18
Lanyer, Aemilia 1569-1645 .... **LC 10, 30, 83;**
　　PC 60
　　See also DLB 121
Lao Tzu c. 6th cent. B.C.-3rd cent.
　　B.C. .... **CMLC 7**
Lao-Tzu
　　See Lao Tzu
Lapine, James (Elliot) 1949- .... **CLC 39**
　　See also CA 123; 130; CANR 54, 128; INT
　　　CA-130
Larbaud, Valery (Nicolas)
　　1881-1957 .... **TCLC 9**
　　See also CA 106; 152; EWL 3; GFL 1789
　　　to the Present
Lardner, Ring
　　See Lardner, Ring(gold) W(ilmer)
　　See also BPFB 2; CDALB 1917-1929; DLB
　　　11, 25, 86, 171; DLBD 16; MAL 5;
　　　RGAL 4; RGSF 2
Lardner, Ring W., Jr.
　　See Lardner, Ring(gold) W(ilmer)
Lardner, Ring(gold) W(ilmer)
　　1885-1933 .... **SSC 32; TCLC 2, 14**
　　See Lardner, Ring
　　See also AMW; CA 104; 131; MTCW 1, 2;
　　　MTFW 2005; TUS
Laredo, Betty
　　See Codrescu, Andrei
Larkin, Maia
　　See Wojciechowska, Maia (Teresa)
Larkin, Philip (Arthur) 1922-1985 ... **CLC 3,**
　　5, 8, 9, 13, 18, 33, 39, 64; PC 21
　　See also BRWS 1; CA 5-8R; 117; CANR
　　　24, 62; CDBLB 1960 to Present; CP 1, 2,
　　　3, 4; DA3; DAB; DAM MST, POET;
　　　DLB 27; EWL 3; MTCW 1, 2; MTFW
　　　2005; PFS 3, 4, 12; RGEL 2
La Roche, Sophie von
　　1730-1807 .... **NCLC 121**
　　See also DLB 94
La Rochefoucauld, Francois
　　1613-1680 .... **LC 108**
Larra (y Sanchez de Castro), Mariano Jose
　　de 1809-1837 .... **NCLC 17, 130**
Larsen, Eric 1941- .... **CLC 55**
　　See also CA 132
Larsen, Nella 1893(?)-1963 .... **BLC 2; CLC**
　　37; HR 1:3
　　See also AFAW 1, 2; BW 1; CA 125; CANR
　　　83; DAM MULT; DLB 51; FW; LATS
　　　1:1; LMFS 2
Larson, Charles R(aymond) 1938- ... **CLC 31**
　　See also CA 53-56; CANR 4, 121
Larson, Jonathan 1960-1996 .... **CLC 99**
　　See also AAYA 28; CA 156; DFS 23;
　　　MTFW 2005
La Sale, Antoine de c. 1386-1460(?) . **LC 104**
　　See also DLB 208
Las Casas, Bartolome de
　　1474-1566 .... **HLCS; LC 31**
　　See Casas, Bartolome de las
　　See also DLB 318; LAW
Lasch, Christopher 1932-1994 .... **CLC 102**
　　See also CA 73-76; 144; CANR 25, 118;
　　　DLB 246; MTCW 1, 2; MTFW 2005

Lasker-Schueler, Else 1869-1945 ... **TCLC 57**
　　See Lasker-Schuler, Else
　　See also CA 183; DLB 66, 124
Lasker-Schuler, Else
　　See Lasker-Schueler, Else
　　See also EWL 3
Laski, Harold J(oseph) 1893-1950 . **TCLC 79**
　　See also CA 188
Latham, Jean Lee 1902-1995 .... **CLC 12**
　　See also AITN 1; BYA 1; CA 5-8R; CANR
　　　7, 84; CLR 50; MAICYA 1, 2; SATA 2,
　　　68; YAW
Latham, Mavis
　　See Clark, Mavis Thorpe
Lathen, Emma .... **CLC 2**
　　See Hennissart, Martha; Latsis, Mary J(ane)
　　See also BPFB 2; CMW 4; DLB 306
Lathrop, Francis
　　See Leiber, Fritz (Reuter, Jr.)
Latsis, Mary J(ane) 1927-1997
　　See Lathen, Emma
　　See also CA 85-88; 162; CMW 4
Lattany, Kristin
　　See Lattany, Kristin (Elaine Eggleston)
　　　Hunter
Lattany, Kristin (Elaine Eggleston) Hunter
　　1931- .... **CLC 35**
　　See Hunter, Kristin
　　See also AITN 1; BW 1; BYA 3; CA 13-
　　　16R; CANR 13, 108; CLR 3; CN 7; DLB
　　　33; INT CANR-13; MAICYA 1, 2; SAAS
　　　10; SATA 12, 132; YAW
Lattimore, Richmond (Alexander)
　　1906-1984 .... **CLC 3**
　　See also CA 1-4R; 112; CANR 1; CP 1, 2,
　　　3; MAL 5
Laughlin, James 1914-1997 .... **CLC 49**
　　See also CA 21-24R; 162; CAAS 22; CANR
　　　9, 47; CP 1, 2, 3, 4, 5, 6; DLB 48; DLBY
　　　1996, 1997
Laurence, Margaret 1926-1987 ..... **CLC 3, 6,**
　　13, 50, 62; SSC 7
　　See also BYA 13; CA 5-8R; 121; CANR
　　　33; CN 1, 2, 3, 4; DAC; DAM MST; DLB
　　　53; EWL 3; FW; MTCW 1, 2; MTFW
　　　2005; NFS 11; RGEL 2; RGSF 2; SATA-
　　　Obit 50; TCWW 2
Laurent, Antoine 1952- .... **CLC 50**
Lauscher, Hermann
　　See Hesse, Hermann
Lautreamont 1846-1870 .. **NCLC 12; SSC 14**
　　See Lautreamont, Isidore Lucien Ducasse
　　See also GFL 1789 to the Present; RGWL
　　　2, 3
Lautreamont, Isidore Lucien Ducasse
　　See Lautreamont
　　See also DLB 217
Lavater, Johann Kaspar
　　1741-1801 .... **NCLC 142**
　　See also DLB 97
Laverty, Donald
　　See Blish, James (Benjamin)
Lavin, Mary 1912-1996 . **CLC 4, 18, 99; SSC**
　　4, 67
　　See also CA 9-12R; 151; CANR 33; CN 1,
　　　2, 3, 4, 5, 6; DLB 15, 319; FW; MTCW
　　　1; RGEL 2; RGSF 2; SSFS 23
Lavond, Paul Dennis
　　See Kornbluth, C(yril) M.; Pohl, Frederik
Lawes, Henry 1596-1662 .... **LC 113**
　　See also DLB 126
Lawler, Ray
　　See Lawler, Raymond Evenor
　　See also DLB 289
Lawler, Raymond Evenor 1922- .... **CLC 58**
　　See Lawler, Ray
　　See also CA 103; CD 5, 6; RGEL 2

Lawrence, D(avid) H(erbert Richards)
1885-1930 .... **PC 54; SSC 4, 19, 73;
TCLC 2, 9, 16, 33, 48, 61, 93; WLC 3**
See Chambers, Jessie
See also BPFB 2; BRW 7; BRWR 2; CA
104; 121; CANR 131; CDBLB 1914-
1945; DA; DA3; DAB; DAC; DAM MST,
NOV, POET; DLB 10, 19, 36, 98, 162,
195; EWL 3; EXPP; EXPS; LAIT 2, 3;
MTCW 1, 2; MTFW 2005; NFS 18; PFS
6; RGEL 2; RGSF 2; SSFS 2, 6; TEA;
WLIT 4; WP

Lawrence, T(homas) E(dward)
1888-1935 .... **TCLC 18**
See Dale, Colin
See also BRWS 2; CA 115; 167; DLB 195

Lawrence of Arabia
See Lawrence, T(homas) E(dward)

Lawson, Henry (Archibald Hertzberg)
1867-1922 .... **SSC 18; TCLC 27**
See also CA 120; 181; DLB 230; RGEL 2;
RGSF 2

Lawton, Dennis
See Faust, Frederick (Schiller)

Layamon fl. c. 1200- .... **CMLC 10**
See Laȝamon
See also DLB 146; RGEL 2

Laye, Camara 1928-1980 ..... **BLC 2; CLC 4,
38**
See Camara Laye
See also AFW; BW 1; CA 85-88; 97-100;
CANR 25; DAM MULT; MTCW 1, 2;
WLIT 2

Layton, Irving 1912-2006 ..... **CLC 2, 15, 164**
See also CA 1-4R; 247; CANR 2, 33, 43,
66, 129; CP 1, 2, 3, 4, 5, 6, 7; DAC; DAM
MST, POET; DLB 88; EWL 3; MTCW 1,
2; PFS 12; RGEL 2

Layton, Irving Peter
See Layton, Irving

Lazarus, Emma 1849-1887 ...... **NCLC 8, 109**

Lazarus, Felix
See Cable, George Washington

Lazarus, Henry
See Slavitt, David R(ytman)

Lea, Joan
See Neufeld, John (Arthur)

Leacock, Stephen (Butler)
1869-1944 .... **SSC 39; TCLC 2**
See also CA 104; 141; DAC; DAM MST;
DAM MST; DLB 92; EWL 3; MTCW 2;
MTFW 2005; RGEL 2; RGSF 2

Lead, Jane Ward 1623-1704 .... **LC 72**
See also DLB 131

Leapor, Mary 1722-1746 .... **LC 80**
See also DLB 109

Lear, Edward 1812-1888 ..... **NCLC 3; PC 65**
See also AAYA 48; BRW 5; CLR 1, 75;
DLB 32, 163, 166; MAICYA 1, 2; RGEL
2; SATA 18, 100; WCH; WP

Lear, Norman (Milton) 1922- .... **CLC 12**
See also CA 73-76

Leautaud, Paul 1872-1956 .... **TCLC 83**
See also CA 203; DLB 65; GFL 1789 to the
Present

Leavis, F(rank) R(aymond)
1895-1978 .... **CLC 24**
See also BRW 7; CA 21-24R; 77-80; CANR
44; DLB 242; EWL 3; MTCW 1, 2;
RGEL 2

Leavitt, David 1961- .... **CLC 34**
See also CA 116; 122; CANR 50, 62, 101,
134; CPW; DA3; DAM POP; DLB 130;
GLL 1; INT CA-122; MAL 5; MTCW 2;
MTFW 2005

Leblanc, Maurice (Marie Emile)
1864-1941 .... **TCLC 49**
See also CA 110; CMW 4

Lebowitz, Fran(ces Ann) 1951(?)- ... **CLC 11,
36**
See also CA 81-84; CANR 14, 60, 70; INT
CANR-14; MTCW 1

Lebrecht, Peter
See Tieck, (Johann) Ludwig

le Carre, John 1931- .... **CLC 9, 15**
See also AAYA 42; BEST 89:4; BPFB 2;
BRWS 2; CA 5-8R; CANR 13, 33, 59,
107, 132; CDBLB 1960 to Present; CMW
4; CN 1, 2, 3, 4, 5, 6, 7; CPW; DA3;
DAM POP; DLB 87; EWL 3; MSW;
MTCW 1, 2; MTFW 2005; RGEL 2; TEA

Le Clezio, J. M.G. 1940- .... **CLC 31, 155**
See also CA 116; 128; CANR 147; CWW
2; DLB 83; EWL 3; GFL 1789 to the
Present; RGSF 2

Le Clezio, Jean Marie Gustave
See Le Clezio, J. M.G.

Leconte de Lisle, Charles-Marie-Rene
1818-1894 .... **NCLC 29**
See also DLB 217; EW 6; GFL 1789 to the
Present

Le Coq, Monsieur
See Simenon, Georges (Jacques Christian)

Leduc, Violette 1907-1972 .... **CLC 22**
See also CA 13-14; 33-36R; CANR 69;
CAP 1; EWL 3; GFL 1789 to the Present;
GLL 1

Ledwidge, Francis 1887(?)-1917 .... **TCLC 23**
See also CA 123; 203; DLB 20

Lee, Andrea 1953- .... **BLC 2; CLC 36**
See also BW 1, 3; CA 125; CANR 82;
DAM MULT

Lee, Andrew
See Auchincloss, Louis

Lee, Chang-rae 1965- .... **CLC 91**
See also CA 148; CANR 89; CN 7; DLB
312; LATS 1:2

Lee, Don L. .... **CLC 2**
See Madhubuti, Haki R.
See also CP 2, 3, 4, 5

Lee, George W(ashington)
1894-1976 .... **BLC 2; CLC 52**
See also BW 1; CA 125; CANR 83; DAM
MULT; DLB 51

Lee, Harper 1926- ... **CLC 12, 60, 194; WLC
4**
See also AAYA 13; AMWS 8; BPFB 2;
BYA 3; CA 13-16R; CANR 51, 128;
CDALB 1941-1968; CSW; DA; DA3;
DAB; DAC; DAM MST, NOV; DLB 6;
EXPN; LAIT 3; MAL 5; MTCW 1, 2;
MTFW 2005; NFS 2; SATA 11; WYA;
YAW

Lee, Helen Elaine 1959(?)- .... **CLC 86**
See also CA 148

Lee, John .... **CLC 70**

Lee, Julian
See Latham, Jean Lee

Lee, Larry
See Lee, Lawrence

Lee, Laurie 1914-1997 .... **CLC 90**
See also CA 77-80; 158; CANR 33, 73; CP
1, 2, 3, 4, 5, 6; CPW; DAB; DAM POP;
DLB 27; MTCW 1; RGEL 2

Lee, Lawrence 1941-1990 .... **CLC 34**
See also CA 131; CANR 43

Lee, Li-Young 1957- .... **CLC 164; PC 24**
See also AMWS 15; CA 153; CANR 118;
CP 6, 7; DLB 165, 312; LMFS 2; PFS 11,
15, 17

Lee, Manfred B. 1905-1971 .... **CLC 11**
See Queen, Ellery
See also CA 1-4R; 29-32R; CANR 2, 150;
CMW 4; DLB 137

Lee, Manfred Bennington
See Lee, Manfred B.

Lee, Nathaniel 1645(?)-1692 .... **LC 103**
See also DLB 80; RGEL 2

Lee, Shelton Jackson
See Lee, Spike
See also AAYA 4, 29

Lee, Spike 1957(?)- .... **BLCS; CLC 105**
See Lee, Shelton Jackson
See also BW 2, 3; CA 125; CANR 42;
DAM MULT

Lee, Stan 1922- .... **CLC 17**
See also AAYA 5, 49; CA 108; 111; CANR
129; INT CA-111; MTFW 2005

Lee, Tanith 1947- .... **CLC 46**
See also AAYA 15; CA 37-40R; CANR 53,
102, 145; DLB 261; FANT; SATA 8, 88,
134; SFW 4; SUFW 1, 2; YAW

Lee, Vernon .... **SSC 33; TCLC 5**
See Paget, Violet
See also DLB 57, 153, 156, 174, 178; GLL
1; SUFW 1

Lee, William
See Burroughs, William S.
See also GLL 1

Lee, Willy
See Burroughs, William S.
See also GLL 1

Lee-Hamilton, Eugene (Jacob)
1845-1907 .... **TCLC 22**
See also CA 117; 234

Leet, Judith 1935- .... **CLC 11**
See also CA 187

Le Fanu, Joseph Sheridan
1814-1873 .... **NCLC 9, 58; SSC 14, 84**
See also CMW 4; DA3; DAM POP; DLB
21, 70, 159, 178; GL 3; HGG; RGEL 2;
RGSF 2; SUFW 1

Leffland, Ella 1931- .... **CLC 19**
See also CA 29-32R; CANR 35, 78, 82;
DLBY 1984; INT CANR-35; SATA 65;
SSFS 24

Leger, Alexis
See Leger, (Marie-Rene Auguste) Alexis
Saint-Leger

Leger, (Marie-Rene Auguste) Alexis
Saint-Leger 1887-1975 .. **CLC 4, 11, 46;
PC 23**
See Perse, Saint-John; Saint-John Perse
See also CA 13-16R; 61-64; CANR 43;
DAM POET; MTCW 1

Leger, Saintleger
See Leger, (Marie-Rene Auguste) Alexis
Saint-Leger

Le Guin, Ursula K. 1929- ...... **CLC 8, 13, 22,
45, 71, 136; SSC 12, 69**
See also AAYA 9, 27; AITN 1; BPFB 2;
BYA 5, 8, 11, 14; CA 21-24R; CANR 9,
32, 52, 74, 132; CDALB 1968-1988; CLR
3, 28, 91; CN 2, 3, 4, 5, 6, 7; CPW; DA3;
DAB; DAC; DAM MST, POP; DLB 8,
52, 256, 275; EXPS; FANT; FW; INT
CANR-32; JRDA; LAIT 5; MAICYA 1,
2; MAL 5; MTCW 1, 2; MTFW 2005;
NFS 6, 9; SATA 4, 52, 99, 149; SCFW 1,
2; SFW 4; SSFS 2; SUFW 1, 2; WYA;
YAW

Lehmann, Rosamond (Nina)
1901-1990 .... **CLC 5**
See also CA 77-80; 131; CANR 8, 73; CN
1, 2, 3, 4; DLB 15; MTCW 2; RGEL 2;
RHW

Leiber, Fritz (Reuter, Jr.)
1910-1992 .... **CLC 25**
See also AAYA 65; BPFB 2; CA 45-48; 139;
CANR 2, 40, 86; CN 2, 3, 4, 5; DLB 8;
FANT; HGG; MTCW 1, 2; MTFW 2005;
SATA 45; SATA-Obit 73; SCFW 1, 2;
SFW 4; SUFW 1, 2

Leibniz, Gottfried Wilhelm von
1646-1716 .... **LC 35**
See also DLB 168

Loewinsohn, Ron(ald William)
1937- .... **CLC 52**
See also CA 25-28R; CANR 71; CP 1, 2, 3, 4

Logan, Jake
See Smith, Martin Cruz

Logan, John (Burton) 1923-1987 .... **CLC 5**
See also CA 77-80; 124; CANR 45; CP 1, 2, 3, 4; DLB 5

Lo Kuan-chung 1330(?)-1400(?) .... **LC 12**

Lombard, Nap
See Johnson, Pamela Hansford

Lombard, Peter 1100(?)-1160(?) ... **CMLC 72**

Lombino, Salvatore
See Hunter, Evan

London, Jack 1876-1916 .. **SSC 4, 49; TCLC 9, 15, 39; WLC 4**
See London, John Griffith
See also AAYA 13; AITN 2; AMW; BPFB 2; BYA 4, 13; CDALB 1865-1917; CLR 108; DLB 8, 12, 78, 212; EWL 3; EXPS; LAIT 3; MAL 5; NFS 8; RGAL 4; RGSF 2; SATA 18; SFW 4; SSFS 7; TCWW 1, 2; TUS; WYA; YAW

London, John Griffith 1876-1916
See London, Jack
See also CA 110; 119; CANR 73; DA; DA3; DAB; DAC; DAM MST, NOV; JRDA; MAICYA 1, 2; MTCW 1, 2; MTFW 2005; NFS 19

Long, Emmett
See Leonard, Elmore

Longbaugh, Harry
See Goldman, William

Longfellow, Henry Wadsworth
1807-1882 .... **NCLC 2, 45, 101, 103; PC 30; WLCS**
See also AMW; AMWR 2; CDALB 1640-1865; CLR 99; DA; DA3; DAB; DAC; DAM MST, POET; DLB 1, 59, 235; EXPP; PAB; PFS 2, 7, 17; RGAL 4; SATA 19; TUS; WP

Longinus c. 1st cent. - .... **CMLC 27**
See also AW 2; DLB 176

Longley, Michael 1939- .... **CLC 29**
See also BRWS 8; CA 102; CP 1, 2, 3, 4, 5, 6, 7; DLB 40

Longstreet, Augustus Baldwin
1790-1870 .... **NCLC 159**
See also DLB 3, 11, 74, 248; RGAL 4

Longus fl. c. 2nd cent. - .... **CMLC 7**

Longway, A. Hugh
See Lang, Andrew

Lonnbohm, Armas Eino Leopold 1878-1926
See Leino, Eino
See also CA 123

Lonnrot, Elias 1802-1884 .... **NCLC 53**
See also EFS 1

Lonsdale, Roger ed. .... **CLC 65**

Lopate, Phillip 1943- .... **CLC 29**
See also CA 97-100; CANR 88, 157; DLBY 1980; INT CA-97-100

Lopez, Barry (Holstun) 1945- .... **CLC 70**
See also AAYA 9, 63; ANW; CA 65-68; CANR 7, 23, 47, 68, 92; DLB 256, 275; INT CANR-7, -23; MTCW 1; RGAL 4; SATA 67

Lopez de Mendoza, Inigo
See Santillana, Inigo Lopez de Mendoza, Marques de

Lopez Portillo (y Pacheco), Jose
1920-2004 .... **CLC 46**
See also CA 129; 224; HW 1

Lopez y Fuentes, Gregorio
1897(?)-1966 .... **CLC 32**
See also CA 131; EWL 3; HW 1

Lorca, Federico Garcia
See Garcia Lorca, Federico
See also DFS 4; EW 11; PFS 20; RGWL 2, 3; WP

Lord, Audre
See Lorde, Audre
See also EWL 3

Lord, Bette Bao 1938- .... **AAL; CLC 23**
See also BEST 90:3; BPFB 2; CA 107; CANR 41, 79; INT CA-107; SATA 58

Lord Auch
See Bataille, Georges

Lord Brooke
See Greville, Fulke

Lord Byron
See Byron, George Gordon (Noel)

Lorde, Audre 1934-1992 .... **BLC 2; CLC 18, 71; PC 12; TCLC 173**
See Domini, Rey; Lord, Audre
See also AFAW 1, 2; BW 1, 3; CA 25-28R; 142; CANR 16, 26, 46, 82; CP 2, 3, 4, 5; DA3; DAM MULT, POET; DLB 41; FW; MAL 5; MTCW 1, 2; MTFW 2005; PFS 16; RGAL 4

Lord Houghton
See Milnes, Richard Monckton

Lord Jeffrey
See Jeffrey, Francis

Loreaux, Nichol .... **CLC 65**

Lorenzini, Carlo 1826-1890
See Collodi, Carlo
See also MAICYA 1, 2; SATA 29, 100

Lorenzo, Heberto Padilla
See Padilla (Lorenzo), Heberto

Loris
See Hofmannsthal, Hugo von

Loti, Pierre .... **TCLC 11**
See Viaud, (Louis Marie) Julien
See also DLB 123; GFL 1789 to the Present

Lou, Henri
See Andreas-Salome, Lou

Louie, David Wong 1954- .... **CLC 70**
See also CA 139; CANR 120

Louis, Adrian C. .... **NNAL**
See also CA 223

Louis, Father M.
See Merton, Thomas (James)

Louise, Heidi
See Erdrich, Louise

Lovecraft, H. P. 1890-1937 .... **SSC 3, 52; TCLC 4, 22**
See also AAYA 14; BPFB 2; CA 104; 133; CANR 106; DA3; DAM POP; HGG; MTCW 1, 2; MTFW 2005; RGAL 4; SCFW 1, 2; SFW 4; SUFW

Lovecraft, Howard Phillips
See Lovecraft, H. P.

Lovelace, Earl 1935- .... **CLC 51**
See also BW 2; CA 77-80; CANR 41, 72, 114; CD 5, 6; CDWLB 3; CN 1, 2, 3, 4, 5, 6, 7; DLB 125; EWL 3; MTCW 1

Lovelace, Richard 1618-1657 . **LC 24; PC 69**
See also BRW 2; DLB 131; EXPP; PAB; RGEL 2

Lowe, Pardee 1904- .... **AAL**

Lowell, Amy 1874-1925 ... **PC 13; TCLC 1, 8**
See also AAYA 57; AMW; CA 104; 151; DAM POET; DLB 54, 140; EWL 3; EXPP; LMFS 2; MAL 5; MBL; MTCW 2; MTFW 2005; RGAL 4; TUS

Lowell, James Russell 1819-1891 ... **NCLC 2, 90**
See also AMWS 1; CDALB 1640-1865; DLB 1, 11, 64, 79, 189, 235; RGAL 4

Lowell, Robert (Traill Spence, Jr.)
1917-1977 .... **CLC 1, 2, 3, 4, 5, 8, 9, 11, 15, 37, 124; PC 3; WLC 4**
See also AMW; AMWC 2; AMWR 2; CA 9-12R; 73-76; CABS 2; CAD; CANR 26, 60; CDALBS; CP 1, 2; DA; DA3; DAB; DAC; DAM MST, NOV; DLB 5, 169; EWL 3; MAL 5; MTCW 1, 2; MTFW 2005; PAB; PFS 6, 7; RGAL 4; WP

Lowenthal, Michael (Francis)
1969- .... **CLC 119**
See also CA 150; CANR 115

Lowndes, Marie Adelaide (Belloc)
1868-1947 .... **TCLC 12**
See also CA 107; CMW 4; DLB 70; RHW

Lowry, (Clarence) Malcolm
1909-1957 .... **SSC 31; TCLC 6, 40**
See also BPFB 2; BRWS 3; CA 105; 131; CANR 62, 105; CDBLB 1945-1960; DLB 15; EWL 3; MTCW 1, 2; MTFW 2005; RGEL 2

Lowry, Mina Gertrude 1882-1966
See Loy, Mina
See also CA 113

Lowry, Sam
See Soderbergh, Steven

Loxsmith, John
See Brunner, John (Kilian Houston)

Loy, Mina .... **CLC 28; PC 16**
See Lowry, Mina Gertrude
See also DAM POET; DLB 4, 54; PFS 20

Loyson-Bridet
See Schwob, Marcel (Mayer Andre)

Lucan 39-65 .... **CMLC 33**
See also AW 2; DLB 211; EFS 2; RGWL 2, 3

Lucas, Craig 1951- .... **CLC 64**
See also CA 137; CAD; CANR 71, 109, 142; CD 5, 6; GLL 2; MTFW 2005

Lucas, E(dward) V(errall)
1868-1938 .... **TCLC 73**
See also CA 176; DLB 98, 149, 153; SATA 20

Lucas, George 1944- .... **CLC 16**
See also AAYA 1, 23; CA 77-80; CANR 30; SATA 56

Lucas, Hans
See Godard, Jean-Luc

Lucas, Victoria
See Plath, Sylvia

Lucian c. 125-c. 180 .... **CMLC 32**
See also AW 2; DLB 176; RGWL 2, 3

Lucilius c. 180B.C.-102B.C. .... **CMLC 82**
See also DLB 211

Lucretius c. 94B.C.-c. 49B.C. .... **CMLC 48**
See also AW 2; CDWLB 1; DLB 211; EFS 2; RGWL 2, 3; WLIT 8

Ludlam, Charles 1943-1987 .... **CLC 46, 50**
See also CA 85-88; 122; CAD; CANR 72, 86; DLB 266

Ludlum, Robert 1927-2001 .... **CLC 22, 43**
See also AAYA 10, 59; BEST 89:1, 90:3; BPFB 2; CA 33-36R; 195; CANR 25, 41, 68, 105, 131; CMW 4; CPW; DA3; DAM NOV, POP; DLBY 1982; MSW; MTCW 1, 2; MTFW 2005

Ludwig, Ken 1950- .... **CLC 60**
See also CA 195; CAD; CD 6

Ludwig, Otto 1813-1865 .... **NCLC 4**
See also DLB 129

Lugones, Leopoldo 1874-1938 .... **HLCS 2; TCLC 15**
See also CA 116; 131; CANR 104; DLB 283; EWL 3; HW 1; LAW

Lu Hsun .... **SSC 20; TCLC 3**
See Shu-Jen, Chou
See also EWL 3

Lukacs, George .... **CLC 24**
See Lukacs, Gyorgy (Szegeny von)

McNally, Thomas Michael
See McNally, T.M.
McNally, T.M. 1961- .... **CLC 82**
See also CA 246
McNamer, Deirdre 1950- .... **CLC 70**
McNeal, Tom .... **CLC 119**
McNeile, Herman Cyril 1888-1937
See Sapper
See also CA 184; CMW 4; DLB 77
McNickle, (William) D'Arcy
1904-1977 .... **CLC 89; NNAL**
See also CA 9-12R; 85-88; CANR 5, 45;
DAM MULT; DLB 175, 212; RGAL 4;
SATA-Obit 22; TCWW 1, 2
McPhee, John 1931- .... **CLC 36**
See also AAYA 61; AMWS 3; ANW; BEST
90:1; CA 65-68; CANR 20, 46, 64, 69,
121; CPW; DLB 185, 275; MTCW 1, 2;
MTFW 2005; TUS
McPherson, James Alan 1943- . **BLCS; CLC**
19, 77; SSC 95
See also BW 1, 3; CA 25-28R; CAAS 17;
CANR 24, 74, 140; CN 3, 4, 5, 6; CSW;
DLB 38, 244; EWL 3; MTCW 1, 2;
MTFW 2005; RGAL 4; RGSF 2; SSFS
23
McPherson, William (Alexander)
1933- .... **CLC 34**
See also CA 69-72; CANR 28; INT
CANR-28
McTaggart, J. McT. Ellis
See McTaggart, John McTaggart Ellis
McTaggart, John McTaggart Ellis
1866-1925 .... **TCLC 105**
See also CA 120; DLB 262
Mead, George Herbert 1863-1931 . **TCLC 89**
See also CA 212; DLB 270
Mead, Margaret 1901-1978 .... **CLC 37**
See also AITN 1; CA 1-4R; 81-84; CANR
4; DA3; FW; MTCW 1, 2; SATA-Obit 20
Meaker, Marijane 1927-
See Kerr, M. E.
See also CA 107; CANR 37, 63, 145; INT
CA-107; JRDA; MAICYA 1, 2; MAIC-
YAS 1; MTCW 1; SATA 20, 61, 99, 160;
SATA-Essay 111; YAW
Medoff, Mark (Howard) 1940- .... **CLC 6, 23**
See also AITN 1; CA 53-56; CAD; CANR
5; CD 5, 6; DAM DRAM; DFS 4; DLB
7; INT CANR-5
Medvedev, P. N.
See Bakhtin, Mikhail Mikhailovich
Meged, Aharon
See Megged, Aharon
Meged, Aron
See Megged, Aharon
Megged, Aharon 1920- .... **CLC 9**
See also CA 49-52; CAAS 13; CANR 1,
140; EWL 3; RGHL
Mehta, Deepa 1950- .... **CLC 208**
Mehta, Gita 1943- .... **CLC 179**
See also CA 225; CN 7; DNFS 2
Mehta, Ved 1934- .... **CLC 37**
See also CA 1-4R, 212; CAAE 212; CANR
2, 23, 69; DLB 323; MTCW 1; MTFW
2005
Melanchthon, Philipp 1497-1560 .... **LC 90**
See also DLB 179
Melanter
See Blackmore, R(ichard) D(oddridge)
Meleager c. 140B.C.-c. 70B.C. ...... **CMLC 53**
Melies, Georges 1861-1938 .... **TCLC 81**
Melikow, Loris
See Hofmannsthal, Hugo von
Melmoth, Sebastian
See Wilde, Oscar (Fingal O'Flahertie Wills)
Melo Neto, Joao Cabral de
See Cabral de Melo Neto, Joao
See also CWW 2; EWL 3

Meltzer, Milton 1915- .... **CLC 26**
See also AAYA 8, 45; BYA 2, 6; CA 13-
16R; CANR 38, 92, 107; CLR 13; DLB
61; JRDA; MAICYA 1, 2; SAAS 1; SATA
1, 50, 80, 128; SATA-Essay 124; WYA;
YAW
Melville, Herman 1819-1891 ..... **NCLC 3, 12,**
29, 45, 49, 91, 93, 123, 157; SSC 1, 17,
46, 95; WLC 4
See also AAYA 25; AMW; AMWR 1;
CDALB 1640-1865; DA; DA3; DAB;
DAC; DAM MST, NOV; DLB 3, 74, 250,
254; EXPN; EXPS; GL 3; LAIT 1, 2; NFS
7, 9; RGAL 4; RGSF 2; SATA 59; SSFS
3; TUS
Members, Mark
See Powell, Anthony
Membreno, Alejandro .... **CLC 59**
Menand, Louis 1952- .... **CLC 208**
See also CA 200
Menander c. 342B.C.-c. 293B.C. .... **CMLC 9,**
51; DC 3
See also AW 1; CDWLB 1; DAM DRAM;
DLB 176; LMFS 1; RGWL 2, 3
Menchu, Rigoberta 1959- .. **CLC 160; HLCS**
2
See also CA 175; CANR 135; DNFS 1;
WLIT 1
Mencken, H(enry) L(ouis)
1880-1956 .... **TCLC 13**
See also AMW; CA 105; 125; CDALB
1917-1929; DLB 11, 29, 63, 137, 222;
EWL 3; MAL 5; MTCW 1, 2; MTFW
2005; NCFS 4; RGAL 4; TUS
Mendelsohn, Jane 1965- .... **CLC 99**
See also CA 154; CANR 94
Mendoza, Inigo Lopez de
See Santillana, Inigo Lopez de Mendoza,
Marques de
Menton, Francisco de
See Chin, Frank (Chew, Jr.)
Mercer, David 1928-1980 .... **CLC 5**
See also CA 9-12R; 102; CANR 23; CBD;
DAM DRAM; DLB 13, 310; MTCW 1;
RGEL 2
Merchant, Paul
See Ellison, Harlan
Meredith, George 1828-1909 .. **PC 60; TCLC**
17, 43
See also CA 117; 153; CANR 80; CDBLB
1832-1890; DAM POET; DLB 18, 35, 57,
159; RGEL 2; TEA
Meredith, William (Morris) 1919- .... **CLC 4,**
13, 22, 55; PC 28
See also CA 9-12R; CAAS 14; CANR 6,
40, 129; CP 1, 2, 3, 4, 5, 6, 7; DAM
POET; DLB 5; MAL 5
Merezhkovsky, Dmitrii Sergeevich
See Merezhkovsky, Dmitry Sergeyevich
See also DLB 295
Merezhkovsky, Dmitry Sergeevich
See Merezhkovsky, Dmitry Sergeyevich
See also EWL 3
Merezhkovsky, Dmitry Sergeyevich
1865-1941 .... **TCLC 29**
See Merezhkovsky, Dmitrii Sergeevich;
Merezhkovsky, Dmitry Sergeevich
See also CA 169
Merimee, Prosper 1803-1870 ... **NCLC 6, 65;**
SSC 7, 77
See also DLB 119, 192; EW 6; EXPS; GFL
1789 to the Present; RGSF 2; RGWL 2,
3; SSFS 8; SUFW
Merkin, Daphne 1954- .... **CLC 44**
See also CA 123
Merleau-Ponty, Maurice
1908-1961 .... **TCLC 156**
See also CA 114; 89-92; DLB 296; GFL
1789 to the Present

Merlin, Arthur
See Blish, James (Benjamin)
Mernissi, Fatima 1940- .... **CLC 171**
See also CA 152; FW
Merrill, James 1926-1995 ...... **CLC 2, 3, 6, 8,**
13, 18, 34, 91; PC 28; TCLC 173
See also AMWS 3; CA 13-16R; 147; CANR
10, 49, 63, 108; CP 1, 2, 3, 4; DA3; DAM
POET; DLB 5, 165; DLBY 1985; EWL 3;
INT CANR-10; MAL 5; MTCW 1, 2;
MTFW 2005; PAB; PFS 23; RGAL 4
Merriman, Alex
See Silverberg, Robert
Merriman, Brian 1747-1805 .... **NCLC 70**
Merritt, E. B.
See Waddington, Miriam
Merton, Thomas (James)
1915-1968 . **CLC 1, 3, 11, 34, 83; PC 10**
See also AAYA 61; AMWS 8; CA 5-8R;
25-28R; CANR 22, 53, 111, 131; DA3;
DLB 48; DLBY 1981; MAL 5; MTCW 1,
2; MTFW 2005
Merwin, W.S. 1927- ..... **CLC 1, 2, 3, 5, 8, 13,**
18, 45, 88; PC 45
See also AMWS 3; CA 13-16R; CANR 15,
51, 112, 140; CP 1, 2, 3, 4, 5, 6, 7; DA3;
DAM POET; DLB 5; EWL 3; INT
CANR-15; MAL 5; MTCW 1, 2; MTFW
2005; PAB; PFS 5, 15; RGAL 4
Metastasio, Pietro 1698-1782 .... **LC 115**
See also RGWL 2, 3
Metcalf, John 1938- .... **CLC 37; SSC 43**
See also CA 113; CN 4, 5, 6, 7; DLB 60;
RGSF 2; TWA
Metcalf, Suzanne
See Baum, L(yman) Frank
Mew, Charlotte (Mary) 1870-1928 .. **TCLC 8**
See also CA 105; 189; DLB 19, 135; RGEL
2
Mewshaw, Michael 1943- .... **CLC 9**
See also CA 53-56; CANR 7, 47, 147;
DLBY 1980
Meyer, Conrad Ferdinand
1825-1898 .... **NCLC 81; SSC 30**
See also DLB 129; EW; RGWL 2, 3
Meyer, Gustav 1868-1932
See Meyrink, Gustav
See also CA 117; 190
Meyer, June
See Jordan, June
Meyer, Lynn
See Slavitt, David R(ytman)
Meyers, Jeffrey 1939- .... **CLC 39**
See also CA 73-76, 186; CAAE 186; CANR
54, 102; DLB 111
Meynell, Alice (Christina Gertrude
Thompson) 1847-1922 .... **TCLC 6**
See also CA 104; 177; DLB 19, 98; RGEL
2
Meyrink, Gustav .... **TCLC 21**
See Meyer, Gustav
See also DLB 81; EWL 3
Michaels, Leonard 1933-2003 ..... **CLC 6, 25;**
SSC 16
See also AMWS 16; CA 61-64; 216; CANR
21, 62, 119; CN 3, 45, 6, 7; DLB 130;
MTCW 1; TCLE 1:2
Michaux, Henri 1899-1984 .... **CLC 8, 19**
See also CA 85-88; 114; DLB 258; EWL 3;
GFL 1789 to the Present; RGWL 2, 3
Micheaux, Oscar (Devereaux)
1884-1951 .... **TCLC 76**
See also BW 3; CA 174; DLB 50; TCWW
2
Michelangelo 1475-1564 .... **LC 12**
See also AAYA 43
Michelet, Jules 1798-1874 .... **NCLC 31**
See also EW 5; GFL 1789 to the Present

Michels, Robert 1876-1936 .... **TCLC 88**
See also CA 212

Michener, James A. 1907(?)-1997 . **CLC 1, 5, 11, 29, 60, 109**
See also AAYA 27; AITN 1; BEST 90:1; BPFB 2; CA 5-8R; 161; CANR 21, 45, 68; CN 1, 2, 3, 4, 5, 6; CPW; DA3; DAM NOV, POP; DLB 6; MAL 5; MTCW 1, 2; MTFW 2005; RHW; TCWW 1, 2

Mickiewicz, Adam 1798-1855 . **NCLC 3, 101; PC 38**
See also EW 5; RGWL 2, 3

Middleton, (John) Christopher 1926- .... **CLC 13**
See also CA 13-16R; CANR 29, 54, 117; CP 1, 2, 3, 4, 5, 6, 7; DLB 40

Middleton, Richard (Barham) 1882-1911 .... **TCLC 56**
See also CA 187; DLB 156; HGG

Middleton, Stanley 1919- .... **CLC 7, 38**
See also CA 25-28R; CAAS 23; CANR 21, 46, 81, 157; CN 1, 2, 3, 4, 5, 6, 7; DLB 14, 326

Middleton, Thomas 1580-1627 ...... **DC 5; LC 33, 123**
See also BRW 2; DAM DRAM, MST; DFS 18, 22; DLB 58; RGEL 2

Migueis, Jose Rodrigues 1901-1980 . **CLC 10**
See also DLB 287

Mikszath, Kalman 1847-1910 .... **TCLC 31**
See also CA 170

Miles, Jack .... **CLC 100**
See also CA 200

Miles, John Russiano
See Miles, Jack

Miles, Josephine (Louise) 1911-1985 .... **CLC 1, 2, 14, 34, 39**
See also CA 1-4R; 116; CANR 2, 55; CP 1, 2, 3, 4; DAM POET; DLB 48; MAL 5; TCLE 1:2

Militant
See Sandburg, Carl (August)

Mill, Harriet (Hardy) Taylor 1807-1858 .... **NCLC 102**
See also FW

Mill, John Stuart 1806-1873 .... **NCLC 11, 58**
See also CDBLB 1832-1890; DLB 55, 190, 262; FW 1; RGEL 2; TEA

Millar, Kenneth 1915-1983 .... **CLC 14**
See Macdonald, Ross
See also CA 9-12R; 110; CANR 16, 63, 107; CMW 4; CPW; DA3; DAM POP; DLB 2, 226; DLBD 6; DLBY 1983; MTCW 1, 2; MTFW 2005

Millay, E. Vincent
See Millay, Edna St. Vincent

Millay, Edna St. Vincent 1892-1950 ..... **PC 6, 61; TCLC 4, 49, 169; WLCS**
See Boyd, Nancy
See also AMW; CA 104; 130; CDALB 1917-1929; DA; DA3; DAB; DAC; DAM MST, POET; DLB 45, 249; EWL 3; EXPP; FL 1:6; MAL 5; MBL; MTCW 1, 2; MTFW 2005; PAB; PFS 3, 17; RGAL 4; TUS; WP

Miller, Arthur 1915-2005 ..... **CLC 1, 2, 6, 10, 15, 26, 47, 78, 179; DC 1; WLC 4**
See also AAYA 15; AITN 1; AMW; AMWC 1; CA 1-4R; 236; CABS 3; CAD; CANR 2, 30, 54, 76, 132; CD 5, 6; CDALB 1941-1968; DA; DA3; DAB; DAC; DAM DRAM, MST; DFS 1, 3, 8; DLB 7, 266; EWL 3; LAIT 1, 4; LATS 1:2; MAL 5; MTCW 1, 2; MTFW 2005; RGAL 4; RGHL; TUS; WYAS 1

Miller, Henry (Valentine) 1891-1980 .... **CLC 1, 2, 4, 9, 14, 43, 84; WLC 4**
See also AMW; BPFB 2; CA 9-12R; 97-100; CANR 33, 64; CDALB 1929-1941;

CN 1, 2; DA; DA3; DAB; DAC; DAM MST, NOV; DLB 4, 9; DLBY 1980; EWL 3; MAL 5; MTCW 1, 2; MTFW 2005; RGAL 4; TUS

Miller, Hugh 1802-1856 .... **NCLC 143**
See also DLB 190

Miller, Jason 1939(?)-2001 .... **CLC 2**
See also AITN 1; CA 73-76; 197; CAD; CANR 130; DFS 12; DLB 7

Miller, Sue 1943- .... **CLC 44**
See also AMWS 12; BEST 90:3; CA 139; CANR 59, 91, 128; DA3; DAM POP; DLB 143

Miller, Walter M(ichael, Jr.) 1923-1996 .... **CLC 4, 30**
See also BPFB 2; CA 85-88; CANR 108; DLB 8; SCFW 1, 2; SFW 4

Millett, Kate 1934- .... **CLC 67**
See also AITN 1; CA 73-76; CANR 32, 53, 76, 110; DA3; DLB 246; FW; GLL 1; MTCW 1, 2; MTFW 2005

Millhauser, Steven 1943- ... **CLC 21, 54, 109; SSC 57**
See also CA 110; 111; CANR 63, 114, 133; CN 6, 7; DA3; DLB 2; FANT; INT CA-111; MAL 5; MTCW 2; MTFW 2005

Millhauser, Steven Lewis
See Millhauser, Steven

Millin, Sarah Gertrude 1889-1968 ... **CLC 49**
See also CA 102; 93-96; DLB 225; EWL 3

Milne, A. A. 1882-1956 .... **TCLC 6, 88**
See also BRWS 5; CA 104; 133; CLR 1, 26, 108; CMW 4; CWRI 5; DA3; DAB; DAC; DAM MST; DLB 10, 77, 100, 160; FANT; MAICYA 1, 2; MTCW 1, 2; MTFW 2005; RGEL 2; SATA 100; WCH; YABC 1

Milne, Alan Alexander
See Milne, A. A.

Milner, Ron(ald) 1938-2004 ..... **BLC 3; CLC 56**
See also AITN 1; BW 1; CA 73-76; 230; CAD; CANR 24, 81; CD 5, 6; DAM MULT; DLB 38; MAL 5; MTCW 1

Milnes, Richard Monckton 1809-1885 .... **NCLC 61**
See also DLB 32, 184

Milosz, Czeslaw 1911-2004 .... **CLC 5, 11, 22, 31, 56, 82; PC 8; WLCS**
See also AAYA 62; CA 81-84; 230; CANR 23, 51, 91, 126; CDWLB 4; CWW 2; DA3; DAM MST, POET; DLB 215; EW 13; EWL 3; MTCW 1, 2; MTFW 2005; PFS 16; RGHL; RGWL 2, 3

Milton, John 1608-1674 ..... **LC 9, 43, 92; PC 19, 29; WLC 4**
See also AAYA 65; BRW 2; BRWR 2; CD-BLB 1660-1789; DA; DA3; DAB; DAC; DAM MST, POET; DLB 131, 151, 281; EFS 1; EXPP; LAIT 1; PAB; PFS 3, 17; RGEL 2; TEA; WLIT 3; WP

Min, Anchee 1957- .... **CLC 86**
See also CA 146; CANR 94, 137; MTFW 2005

Minehaha, Cornelius
See Wedekind, Frank

Miner, Valerie 1947- .... **CLC 40**
See also CA 97-100; CANR 59; FW; GLL 2

Minimo, Duca
See D'Annunzio, Gabriele

Minot, Susan (Anderson) 1956- ...... **CLC 44, 159**
See also AMWS 6; CA 134; CANR 118; CN 6, 7

Minus, Ed 1938- .... **CLC 39**
See also CA 185

Mirabai 1498(?)-1550(?) .... **PC 48**
See also PFS 24

Miranda, Javier
See Bioy Casares, Adolfo
See also CWW 2

Mirbeau, Octave 1848-1917 .... **TCLC 55**
See also CA 216; DLB 123, 192; GFL 1789 to the Present

Mirikitani, Janice 1942- .... **AAL**
See also CA 211; DLB 312; RGAL 4

Mirk, John (?)-c. 1414 .... **LC 105**
See also DLB 146

Miro (Ferrer), Gabriel (Francisco Victor) 1879-1930 .... **TCLC 5**
See also CA 104; 185; DLB 322; EWL 3

Misharin, Alexandr .... **CLC 59**

Mishima, Yukio ... **CLC 2, 4, 6, 9, 27; DC 1; SSC 4; TCLC 161; WLC 4**
See Hiraoka, Kimitake
See also AAYA 50; BPFB 2; GLL 1; MJW; RGSF 2; RGWL 2, 3; SSFS 5, 12

Mistral, Frederic 1830-1914 .... **TCLC 51**
See also CA 122; 213; GFL 1789 to the Present

Mistral, Gabriela
See Godoy Alcayaga, Lucila
See also DLB 283; DNFS 1; EWL 3; LAW; RGWL 2, 3; WP

Mistry, Rohinton 1952- ... **CLC 71, 196; SSC 73**
See also BRWS 10; CA 141; CANR 86, 114; CCA 1; CN 6, 7; DAC; SSFS 6

Mitchell, Clyde
See Ellison, Harlan

Mitchell, Emerson Blackhorse Barney 1945- .... **NNAL**
See also CA 45-48

Mitchell, James Leslie 1901-1935
See Gibbon, Lewis Grassic
See also CA 104; 188; DLB 15

Mitchell, Joni 1943- .... **CLC 12**
See also CA 112; CCA 1

Mitchell, Joseph (Quincy) 1908-1996 .... **CLC 98**
See also CA 77-80; 152; CANR 69; CN 1, 2, 3, 4, 5, 6; CSW; DLB 185; DLBY 1996

Mitchell, Margaret (Munnerlyn) 1900-1949 .... **TCLC 11, 170**
See also AAYA 23; BPFB 2; BYA 1; CA 109; 125; CANR 55, 94; CDALBS; DA3; DAM NOV, POP; DLB 9; LAIT 2; MAL 5; MTCW 1, 2; MTFW 2005; NFS 9; RGAL 4; RHW; TUS; WYAS 1; YAW

Mitchell, Peggy
See Mitchell, Margaret (Munnerlyn)

Mitchell, S(ilas) Weir 1829-1914 .... **TCLC 36**
See also CA 165; DLB 202; RGAL 4

Mitchell, W(illiam) O(rmond) 1914-1998 .... **CLC 25**
See also CA 77-80; 165; CANR 15, 43; CN 1, 2, 3, 4, 5, 6; DAC; DAM MST; DLB 88; TCLE 1:2

Mitchell, William (Lendrum) 1879-1936 .... **TCLC 81**
See also CA 213

Mitford, Mary Russell 1787-1855 ... **NCLC 4**
See also DLB 110, 116; RGEL 2

Mitford, Nancy 1904-1973 .... **CLC 44**
See also BRWS 10; CA 9-12R; CN 1; DLB 191; RGEL 2

Miyamoto, (Chujo) Yuriko 1899-1951 .... **TCLC 37**
See Miyamoto Yuriko
See also CA 170, 174

Miyamoto Yuriko
See Miyamoto, (Chujo) Yuriko
See also DLB 180

Miyazawa, Kenji 1896-1933 .... **TCLC 76**
See Miyazawa Kenji
See also CA 157; RGWL 3

Miyazawa Kenji
See Miyazawa, Kenji
See also EWL 3

Mizoguchi, Kenji 1898-1956 .... **TCLC 72**
See also CA 167

Mo, Timothy (Peter) 1950- .... **CLC 46, 134**
See also CA 117; CANR 128; CN 5, 6, 7;
DLB 194; MTCW 1; WLIT 4; WWE 1

Modarressi, Taghi (M.) 1931-1997 ... **CLC 44**
See also CA 121; 134; INT CA-134

Modiano, Patrick (Jean) 1945- .... **CLC 18,
218**
See also CA 85-88; CANR 17, 40, 115;
CWW 2; DLB 83, 299; EWL 3; RGHL

Mofolo, Thomas (Mokopu)
1875(?)-1948 .... **BLC 3; TCLC 22**
See also AFW; CA 121; 153; CANR 83;
DAM MULT; DLB 225; EWL 3; MTCW
2; MTFW 2005; WLIT 2

Mohr, Nicholasa 1938- .... **CLC 12; HLC 2**
See also AAYA 8, 46; CA 49-52; CANR 1,
32, 64; CLR 22; DAM MULT; DLB 145;
HW 1, 2; JRDA; LAIT 5; LLW; MAICYA
2; MAICYAS 1; RGAL 4; SAAS 8; SATA
8, 97; SATA-Essay 113; WYA; YAW

Moi, Toril 1953- .... **CLC 172**
See also CA 154; CANR 102; FW

Mojtabai, A(nn) G(race) 1938- ..... **CLC 5, 9,
15, 29**
See also CA 85-88; CANR 88

Moliere 1622-1673 ..... **DC 13; LC 10, 28, 64,
125, 127; WLC 4**
See also DA; DA3; DAB; DAC; DAM
DRAM, MST; DFS 13, 18, 20; DLB 268;
EW 3; GFL Beginnings to 1789; LATS
1:1; RGWL 2, 3; TWA

Molin, Charles
See Mayne, William (James Carter)

Molnar, Ferenc 1878-1952 .... **TCLC 20**
See also CA 109; 153; CANR 83; CDWLB
4; DAM DRAM; DLB 215; EWL 3;
RGWL 2, 3

Momaday, N. Scott 1934- ...... **CLC 2, 19, 85,
95, 160; NNAL; PC 25; WLCS**
See also AAYA 11, 64; AMWS 4; ANW;
BPFB 2; BYA 12; CA 25-28R; CANR 14,
34, 68, 134; CDALBS; CN 2, 3, 4, 5, 6,
7; CPW; DA; DA3; DAB; DAC; DAM
MST, MULT, NOV, POP; DLB 143, 175,
256; EWL 3; EXPP; INT CANR-14;
LAIT 4; LATS 1:2; MAL 5; MTCW 1, 2;
MTFW 2005; NFS 10; PFS 2, 11; RGAL
4; SATA 48; SATA-Brief 30; TCWW 1,
2; WP; YAW

Monette, Paul 1945-1995 .... **CLC 82**
See also AMWS 10; CA 139; 147; CN 6;
GLL 1

Monroe, Harriet 1860-1936 .... **TCLC 12**
See also CA 109; 204; DLB 54, 91

Monroe, Lyle
See Heinlein, Robert A.

Montagu, Elizabeth 1720-1800 .... **NCLC 7,
117**
See also FW

Montagu, Mary (Pierrepont) Wortley
1689-1762 .... **LC 9, 57; PC 16**
See also DLB 95, 101; FL 1:1; RGEL 2

Montagu, W. H.
See Coleridge, Samuel Taylor

Montague, John (Patrick) 1929- ..... **CLC 13,
46**
See also CA 9-12R; CANR 9, 69, 121; CP
1, 2, 3, 4, 5, 6, 7; DLB 40; EWL 3;
MTCW 1; PFS 12; RGEL 2; TCLE 1:2

Montaigne, Michel (Eyquem) de
1533-1592 .... **LC 8, 105; WLC 4**
See also DA; DAB; DAC; DAM MST;
DLB 327; EW 2; GFL Beginnings to
1789; LMFS 1; RGWL 2, 3; TWA

Montale, Eugenio 1896-1981 ... **CLC 7, 9, 18;
PC 13**
See also CA 17-20R; 104; CANR 30; DLB
114; EW 11; EWL 3; MTCW 1; PFS 22;
RGWL 2, 3; TWA; WLIT 7

Montesquieu, Charles-Louis de Secondat
1689-1755 .... **LC 7, 69**
See also DLB 314; EW 3; GFL Beginnings
to 1789; TWA

Montessori, Maria 1870-1952 ...... **TCLC 103**
See also CA 115; 147

Montgomery, (Robert) Bruce 1921(?)-1978
See Crispin, Edmund
See also CA 179; 104; CMW 4

Montgomery, L(ucy) M(aud)
1874-1942 .... **TCLC 51, 140**
See also AAYA 12; BYA 1; CA 108; 137;
CLR 8, 91; DA3; DAC; DAM MST; DLB
92; DLBD 14; JRDA; MAICYA 1, 2;
MTCW 2; MTFW 2005; RGEL 2; SATA
100; TWA; WCH; WYA; YABC 1

Montgomery, Marion H., Jr. 1925- .... **CLC 7**
See also AITN 1; CA 1-4R; CANR 3, 48;
CSW; DLB 6

Montgomery, Max
See Davenport, Guy (Mattison, Jr.)

Montherlant, Henry (Milon) de
1896-1972 .... **CLC 8, 19**
See also CA 85-88; 37-40R; DAM DRAM;
DLB 72, 321; EW 11; EWL 3; GFL 1789
to the Present; MTCW 1

Monty Python
See Chapman, Graham; Cleese, John
(Marwood); Gilliam, Terry; Idle, Eric;
Jones, Terence Graham Parry; Palin,
Michael (Edward)
See also AAYA 7

Moodie, Susanna (Strickland)
1803-1885 .... **NCLC 14, 113**
See also DLB 99

Moody, Hiram 1961-
See Moody, Rick
See also CA 138; CANR 64, 112; MTFW
2005

Moody, Minerva
See Alcott, Louisa May

Moody, Rick .... **CLC 147**
See Moody, Hiram

Moody, William Vaughan
1869-1910 .... **TCLC 105**
See also CA 110; 178; DLB 7, 54; MAL 5;
RGAL 4

Mooney, Edward 1951-
See Mooney, Ted
See also CA 130

Mooney, Ted .... **CLC 25**
See Mooney, Edward

Moorcock, Michael 1939- .... **CLC 5, 27, 58**
See Bradbury, Edward P.
See also AAYA 26; CA 45-48; CAAS 5;
CANR 2, 17, 38, 64, 122; CN 5, 6, 7;
DLB 14, 231, 261, 319; FANT; MTCW 1,
2; MTFW 2005; SATA 93, 166; SCFW 1,
2; SFW 4; SUFW 1, 2

Moorcock, Michael John
See Moorcock, Michael

Moore, Alan 1953- .... **CLC 230**
See also AAYA 51; CA 204; CANR 138;
DLB 261; MTFW 2005; SFW 4

Moore, Brian 1921-1999 ... **CLC 1, 3, 5, 7, 8,
19, 32, 90**
See Bryan, Michael
See also BRWS 9; CA 1-4R; 174; CANR 1,
25, 42, 63; CCA 1; CN 1, 2, 3, 4, 5, 6;
DAB; DAC; DAM MST; DLB 251; EWL
3; FANT; MTCW 1, 2; MTFW 2005;
RGEL 2

Moore, Edward
See Muir, Edwin
See also RGEL 2

Moore, G. E. 1873-1958 .... **TCLC 89**
See also DLB 262

Moore, George Augustus
1852-1933 .... **SSC 19; TCLC 7**
See also BRW 6; CA 104; 177; DLB 10,
18, 57, 135; EWL 3; RGEL 2; RGSF 2

Moore, Lorrie .... **CLC 39, 45, 68**
See Moore, Marie Lorena
See also AMWS 10; CN 5, 6, 7; DLB 234;
SSFS 19

Moore, Marianne (Craig)
1887-1972 .... **CLC 1, 2, 4, 8, 10, 13, 19,
47; PC 4, 49; WLCS**
See also AMW; CA 1-4R; 33-36R; CANR
3, 61; CDALB 1929-1941; CP 1; DA;
DA3; DAB; DAC; DAM MST, POET;
DLB 45; DLBD 7; EWL 3; EXPP; FL 1:6;
MAL 5; MBL; MTCW 1, 2; MTFW 2005;
PAB; PFS 14, 17; RGAL 4; SATA 20;
TUS; WP

Moore, Marie Lorena 1957- .... **CLC 165**
See Moore, Lorrie
See also CA 116; CANR 39, 83, 139; DLB
234; MTFW 2005

Moore, Michael 1954- .... **CLC 218**
See also AAYA 53; CA 166; CANR 150

Moore, Thomas 1779-1852 .... **NCLC 6, 110**
See also DLB 96, 144; RGEL 2

Moorhouse, Frank 1938- .... **SSC 40**
See also CA 118; CANR 92; CN 3, 4, 5, 6,
7; DLB 289; RGSF 2

Mora, Pat 1942- .... **HLC 2**
See also AMWS 13; CA 129; CANR 57,
81, 112; CLR 58; DAM MULT; DLB 209;
HW 1, 2; LLW; MAICYA 2; MTFW
2005; SATA 92, 134

Moraga, Cherríe 1952- .... **CLC 126; DC 22**
See also CA 131; CANR 66, 154; DAM
MULT; DLB 82, 249; FW; GLL 1; HW 1,
2; LLW

Morand, Paul 1888-1976 .... **CLC 41; SSC 22**
See also CA 184; 69-72; DLB 65; EWL 3

Morante, Elsa 1918-1985 .... **CLC 8, 47**
See also CA 85-88; 117; CANR 35; DLB
177; EWL 3; MTCW 1, 2; MTFW 2005;
RGHL; RGWL 2, 3; WLIT 7

Moravia, Alberto .... **CLC 2, 7, 11, 27, 46;
SSC 26**
See Pincherle, Alberto
See also DLB 177; EW 12; EWL 3; MTCW
2; RGSF 2; RGWL 2, 3; WLIT 7

More, Hannah 1745-1833 .... **NCLC 27, 141**
See also DLB 107, 109, 116, 158; RGEL 2

More, Henry 1614-1687 .... **LC 9**
See also DLB 126, 252

More, Sir Thomas 1478(?)-1535 .... **LC 10, 32**
See also BRWC 1; BRWS 7; DLB 136, 281;
LMFS 1; RGEL 2; TEA

Moreas, Jean .... **TCLC 18**
See Papadiamantopoulos, Johannes
See also GFL 1789 to the Present

Moreton, Andrew Esq.
See Defoe, Daniel

Morgan, Berry 1919-2002 .... **CLC 6**
See also CA 49-52; 208; DLB 6

Morgan, Claire
See Highsmith, Patricia
See also GLL 1

Morgan, Edwin (George) 1920- .... **CLC 31**
See also BRWS 9; CA 5-8R; CANR 3, 43,
90; CP 1, 2, 3, 4, 5, 6, 7; DLB 27

Morgan, (George) Frederick
1922-2004 .... **CLC 23**
See also CA 17-20R; 224; CANR 21, 144;
CP 2, 3, 4, 5, 6, 7

Morgan, Harriet
See Mencken, H(enry) L(ouis)

Morgan, Jane
See Cooper, James Fenimore

NOV; DLB 53; EWL 3; MTCW 1, 2;
MTFW 2005; RGEL 2; RGSF 2; SATA
29; SSFS 5, 13, 19; TCLE 1:2; WWE 1

Munro, H(ector) H(ugh) 1870-1916
See Saki
See also AAYA 56; CA 104; 130; CANR
104; CDBLB 1890-1914; DA; DA3;
DAB; DAC; DAM MST, NOV; DLB 34,
162; EXPS; MTCW 1, 2; MTFW 2005;
RGEL 2; SSFS 15

Murakami, Haruki 1949- .... **CLC 150**
See Murakami Haruki
See also CA 165; CANR 102, 146; MJW;
RGWL 3; SFW 4; SSFS 23

Murakami Haruki
See Murakami, Haruki
See also CWW 2; DLB 182; EWL 3

Murasaki, Lady
See Murasaki Shikibu

Murasaki Shikibu 978(?)-1026(?) .. **CMLC 1, 79**
See also EFS 2; LATS 1:1; RGWL 2, 3

Murdoch, Iris 1919-1999 .. **CLC 1, 2, 3, 4, 6, 8, 11, 15, 22, 31, 51; TCLC 171**
See also BRWS 1; CA 13-16R; 179; CANR
8, 43, 68, 103, 142; CBD; CDBLB 1960
to Present; CN 1, 2, 3, 4, 5, 6; CWD;
DA3; DAB; DAC; DAM MST, NOV;
DLB 14, 194, 233, 326; EWL 3; INT
CANR-8; MTCW 1, 2; MTFW 2005; NFS
18; RGEL 2; TCLE 1:2; TEA; WLIT 4

Murfree, Mary Noailles 1850-1922 .. **SSC 22; TCLC 135**
See also CA 122; 176; DLB 12, 74; RGAL
4

Murglie
See Murnau, F.W.

Murnau, Friedrich Wilhelm
See Murnau, F.W.

Murnau, F.W. 1888-1931 .... **TCLC 53**
See also CA 112

Murphy, Richard 1927- .... **CLC 41**
See also BRWS 5; CA 29-32R; CP 1, 2, 3,
4, 5, 6, 7; DLB 40; EWL 3

Murphy, Sylvia 1937- .... **CLC 34**
See also CA 121

Murphy, Thomas (Bernard) 1935- ... **CLC 51**
See Murphy, Tom
See also CA 101

Murphy, Tom
See Murphy, Thomas (Bernard)
See also DLB 310

Murray, Albert L. 1916- .... **CLC 73**
See also BW 2; CA 49-52; CANR 26, 52,
78; CN 7; CSW; DLB 38; MTFW 2005

Murray, James Augustus Henry
1837-1915 .... **TCLC 117**

Murray, Judith Sargent
1751-1820 .... **NCLC 63**
See also DLB 37, 200

Murray, Les(lie Allan) 1938- .... **CLC 40**
See also BRWS 7; CA 21-24R; CANR 11,
27, 56, 103; CP 1, 2, 3, 4, 5, 6, 7; DAM
POET; DLB 289; DLBY 2001; EWL 3;
RGEL 2

Murry, J. Middleton
See Murry, John Middleton

Murry, John Middleton
1889-1957 .... **TCLC 16**
See also CA 118; 217; DLB 149

Musgrave, Susan 1951- .... **CLC 13, 54**
See also CA 69-72; CANR 45, 84; CCA 1;
CP 2, 3, 4, 5, 6, 7; CWP

Musil, Robert (Edler von)
1880-1942 .... **SSC 18; TCLC 12, 68**
See also CA 109; CANR 55, 84; CDWLB
2; DLB 81, 124; EW 9; EWL 3; MTCW
2; RGSF 2; RGWL 2, 3

Muske, Carol .... **CLC 90**
See Muske-Dukes, Carol (Anne)

Muske-Dukes, Carol (Anne) 1945-
See Muske, Carol
See also CA 65-68, 203; CAAE 203; CANR
32, 70; CWP; PFS 24

Musset, Alfred de 1810-1857 . **DC 27; NCLC 7, 150**
See also DLB 192, 217; EW 6; GFL 1789
to the Present; RGWL 2, 3; TWA

Musset, Louis Charles Alfred de
See Musset, Alfred de

Mussolini, Benito (Amilcare Andrea)
1883-1945 .... **TCLC 96**
See also CA 116

Mutanabbi, Al-
See al-Mutanabbi, Ahmad ibn al-Husayn
Abu al-Tayyib al-Jufi al-Kindi
See also WLIT 6

My Brother's Brother
See Chekhov, Anton (Pavlovich)

Myers, L(eopold) H(amilton)
1881-1944 .... **TCLC 59**
See also CA 157; DLB 15; EWL 3; RGEL
2

Myers, Walter Dean 1937- .. **BLC 3; CLC 35**
See Myers, Walter M.
See also AAYA 4, 23; BW 2; BYA 6, 8, 11;
CA 33-36R; CANR 20, 42, 67, 108; CLR
4, 16, 35, 110; DAM MULT, NOV; DLB
33; INT CANR-20; JRDA; LAIT 5; MAI-
CYA 1, 2; MAICYAS 1; MTCW 2;
MTFW 2005; SAAS 2; SATA 41, 71, 109,
157; SATA-Brief 27; WYA; YAW

Myers, Walter M.
See Myers, Walter Dean

Myles, Symon
See Follett, Ken

Nabokov, Vladimir (Vladimirovich)
1899-1977 .... **CLC 1, 2, 3, 6, 8, 11, 15,
23, 44, 46, 64; SSC 11, 86; TCLC 108;
WLC 4**
See also AAYA 45; AMW; AMWC 1;
AMWR 1; BPFB 2; CA 5-8R; 69-72;
CANR 20, 102; CDALB 1941-1968; CN
1, 2; CP 2; DA; DA3; DAB; DAC; DAM
MST, NOV; DLB 2, 244, 278, 317; DLBD
3; DLBY 1980, 1991; EWL 3; EXPS;
LATS 1:2; MAL 5; MTCW 1, 2; MTFW
2005; NCFS 4; NFS 9; RGAL 4; RGSF
2; SSFS 6, 15; TUS

Naevius c. 265B.C.-201B.C. .... **CMLC 37**
See also DLB 211

Nagai, Kafu .... **TCLC 51**
See Nagai, Sokichi
See also DLB 180

Nagai, Sokichi 1879-1959
See Nagai, Kafu
See also CA 117

Nagy, Laszlo 1925-1978 .... **CLC 7**
See also CA 129; 112

Naidu, Sarojini 1879-1949 .... **TCLC 80**
See also EWL 3; RGEL 2

Naipaul, Shiva 1945-1985 .... **CLC 32, 39; TCLC 153**
See also CA 110; 112; 116; CANR 33; CN
2, 3; DA3; DAM NOV; DLB 157; DLBY
1985; EWL 3; MTCW 1, 2; MTFW 2005

Naipaul, V.S. 1932- .. **CLC 4, 7, 9, 13, 18, 37, 105, 199; SSC 38**
See also BPFB 2; BRWS 1; CA 1-4R;
CANR 1, 33, 51, 91, 126; CDBLB 1960
to Present; CDWLB 3; CN 1, 2, 3, 4, 5,
6, 7; DA3; DAB; DAC; DAM MST,
NOV; DLB 125, 204, 207, 326; DLBY
1985, 2001; EWL 3; LATS 1:2; MTCW
1, 2; MTFW 2005; RGEL 2; RGSF 2;
TWA; WLIT 4; WWE 1

Nakos, Lilika 1903(?)-1989 .... **CLC 29**

Napoleon
See Yamamoto, Hisaye

Narayan, R.K. 1906-2001 ...... **CLC 7, 28, 47, 121, 211; SSC 25**
See also BPFB 2; CA 81-84; 196; CANR
33, 61, 112; CN 1, 2, 3, 4, 5, 6, 7; DA3;
DAM NOV; DLB 323; DNFS 1; EWL 3;
MTCW 1, 2; MTFW 2005; RGEL 2;
RGSF 2; SATA 62; SSFS 5; WWE 1

Nash, (Frediric) Ogden 1902-1971 . **CLC 23; PC 21; TCLC 109**
See also CA 13-14; 29-32R; CANR 34, 61;
CAP 1; CP 1; DAM POET; DLB 11;
MAICYA 1, 2; MAL 5; MTCW 1, 2;
RGAL 4; SATA 2, 46; WP

Nashe, Thomas 1567-1601(?) .... **LC 41, 89**
See also DLB 167; RGEL 2

Nathan, Daniel
See Dannay, Frederic

Nathan, George Jean 1882-1958 .... **TCLC 18**
See Hatteras, Owen
See also CA 114; 169; DLB 137; MAL 5

Natsume, Kinnosuke
See Natsume, Soseki

Natsume, Soseki 1867-1916 .... **TCLC 2, 10**
See Natsume Soseki; Soseki
See also CA 104; 195; RGWL 2, 3; TWA

Natsume Soseki
See Natsume, Soseki
See also DLB 180; EWL 3

Natti, (Mary) Lee 1919-
See Kingman, Lee
See also CA 5-8R; CANR 2

Navarre, Marguerite de
See de Navarre, Marguerite

Naylor, Gloria 1950- ..... **BLC 3; CLC 28, 52, 156; WLCS**
See also AAYA 6, 39; AFAW 1, 2; AMWS
8; BW 2, 3; CA 107; CANR 27, 51, 74,
130; CN 4, 5, 6, 7; CPW; DA; DA3;
DAC; DAM MST, MULT, NOV, POP;
DLB 173; EWL 3; FW; MAL 5; MTCW
1, 2; MTFW 2005; NFS 4, 7; RGAL 4;
TCLE 1:2; TUS

Neal, John 1793-1876 .... **NCLC 161**
See also DLB 1, 59, 243; FW; RGAL 4

Neff, Debra .... **CLC 59**

Neihardt, John Gneisenau
1881-1973 .... **CLC 32**
See also CA 13-14; CANR 65; CAP 1; DLB
9, 54, 256; LAIT 2; TCWW 1, 2

Nekrasov, Nikolai Alekseevich
1821-1878 .... **NCLC 11**
See also DLB 277

Nelligan, Emile 1879-1941 .... **TCLC 14**
See also CA 114; 204; DLB 92; EWL 3

Nelson, Willie 1933- .... **CLC 17**
See also CA 107; CANR 114

Nemerov, Howard 1920-1991 .... **CLC 2, 6, 9, 36; PC 24; TCLC 124**
See also AMW; CA 1-4R; 134; CABS 2;
CANR 1, 27, 53; CN 1, 2, 3; CP 1, 2, 3,
4, 5; DAM POET; DLB 5, 6; DLBY 1983;
EWL 3; INT CANR-27; MAL 5; MTCW
1, 2; MTFW 2005; PFS 10, 14; RGAL 4

Neruda, Pablo 1904-1973 .. **CLC 1, 2, 5, 7, 9, 28, 62; HLC 2; PC 4, 64; WLC 4**
See also CA 19-20; 45-48; CANR 131; CAP
2; DA; DA3; DAB; DAC; DAM MST,
MULT, POET; DLB 283; DNFS 2; EWL
3; HW 1; LAW; MTCW 1, 2; MTFW
2005; PFS 11; RGWL 2, 3; TWA; WLIT
1; WP

Nerval, Gerard de 1808-1855 ... **NCLC 1, 67; PC 13; SSC 18**
See also DLB 217; EW 6; GFL 1789 to the
Present; RGSF 2; RGWL 2, 3

Norway, Nevil Shute 1899-1960
See Shute, Nevil
See also CA 102; 93-96; CANR 85; MTCW 2

Norwid, Cyprian Kamil
1821-1883 .... **NCLC 17**
See also RGWL 3

Nosille, Nabrah
See Ellison, Harlan

Nossack, Hans Erich 1901-1977 .... **CLC 6**
See also CA 93-96; 85-88; CANR 156; DLB 69; EWL 3

Nostradamus 1503-1566 .... **LC 27**

Nosu, Chuji
See Ozu, Yasujiro

Notenburg, Eleanora (Genrikhovna) von
See Guro, Elena (Genrikhovna)

Nova, Craig 1945- .... **CLC 7, 31**
See also CA 45-48; CANR 2, 53, 127

Novak, Joseph
See Kosinski, Jerzy

Novalis 1772-1801 .... **NCLC 13**
See also CDWLB 2; DLB 90; EW 5; RGWL 2, 3

Novick, Peter 1934- .... **CLC 164**
See also CA 188

Novis, Emile
See Weil, Simone (Adolphine)

Nowlan, Alden (Albert) 1933-1983 ... **CLC 15**
See also CA 9-12R; CANR 5; CP 1, 2, 3; DAC; DAM MST; DLB 53; PFS 12

Noyes, Alfred 1880-1958 ...... **PC 27; TCLC 7**
See also CA 104; 188; DLB 20; EXPP; FANT; PFS 4; RGEL 2

Nugent, Richard Bruce
1906(?)-1987 .... **HR 1:3**
See also BW 1; CA 125; DLB 51; GLL 2

Nunn, Kem .... **CLC 34**
See also CA 159

Nussbaum, Martha Craven 1947- .. **CLC 203**
See also CA 134; CANR 102

Nwapa, Flora (Nwanzuruaha)
1931-1993 .... **BLCS; CLC 133**
See also BW 2; CA 143; CANR 83; CDWLB 3; CWRI 5; DLB 125; EWL 3; WLIT 2

Nye, Robert 1939- .... **CLC 13, 42**
See also BRWS 10; CA 33-36R; CANR 29, 67, 107; CN 1, 2, 3, 4, 5, 6, 7; CP 1, 2, 3, 4, 5, 6, 7; CWRI 5; DAM NOV; DLB 14, 271; FANT; HGG; MTCW 1; RHW; SATA 6

Nyro, Laura 1947-1997 .... **CLC 17**
See also CA 194

Oates, Joyce Carol 1938- .. **CLC 1, 2, 3, 6, 9, 11, 15, 19, 33, 52, 108, 134; SSC 6, 70; WLC 4**
See also AAYA 15, 52; AITN 1; AMWS 2; BEST 89:2; BPFB 2; BYA 11; CA 5-8R; CANR 25, 45, 74, 113, 129, 247; CDALB 1968-1988; CN 1, 2, 3, 4, 5, 6, 7; CP 5, 6, 7; CPW; CWP; DA; DA3; DAB; DAC; DAM MST, NOV, POP; DLB 2, 5, 130; DLBY 1981; EWL 3; EXPS; FL 1:6; FW; GL 3; HGG; INT CANR-25; LAIT 4; MAL 5; MBL; MTCW 1, 2; MTFW 2005; NFS 8, 24; RGAL 4; RGSF 2; SATA 159; SSFS 1, 8, 17; SUFW 2; TUS

O'Brian, E. G.
See Clarke, Arthur C.

O'Brian, Patrick 1914-2000 .... **CLC 152**
See also AAYA 55; BRWS 12; CA 144; 187; CANR 74; CPW; MTCW 2; MTFW 2005; RHW

O'Brien, Darcy 1939-1998 .... **CLC 11**
See also CA 21-24R; 167; CANR 8, 59

O'Brien, Edna 1932- ..... **CLC 3, 5, 8, 13, 36, 65, 116; SSC 10, 77**
See also BRWS 5; CA 1-4R; CANR 6, 41, 65, 102; CDBLB 1960 to Present; CN 1, 2, 3, 4, 5, 6, 7; DA3; DAM NOV; DLB 14, 231, 319; EWL 3; FW; MTCW 1, 2; MTFW 2005; RGSF 2; WLIT 4

O'Brien, Fitz-James 1828-1862 ..... **NCLC 21**
See also DLB 74; RGAL 4; SUFW

O'Brien, Flann .... **CLC 1, 4, 5, 7, 10, 47**
See O Nuallain, Brian
See also BRWS 2; DLB 231; EWL 3; RGEL 2

O'Brien, Richard 1942- .... **CLC 17**
See also CA 124

O'Brien, Tim 1946- .... **CLC 7, 19, 40, 103, 211; SSC 74**
See also AAYA 16; AMWS 5; CA 85-88; CANR 40, 58, 133; CDALBS; CN 5, 6, 7; CPW; DA3; DAM POP; DLB 152; DLBD 9; DLBY 1980; LATS 1:2; MAL 5; MTCW 2; MTFW 2005; RGAL 4; SSFS 5, 15; TCLE 1:2

Obstfelder, Sigbjoern 1866-1900 .... **TCLC 23**
See also CA 123

O'Casey, Sean 1880-1964 .... **CLC 1, 5, 9, 11, 15, 88; DC 12; WLCS**
See also BRW 7; CA 89-92; CANR 62; CBD; CDBLB 1914-1945; DA3; DAB; DAC; DAM DRAM, MST; DFS 19; DLB 10; EWL 3; MTCW 1, 2; MTFW 2005; RGEL 2; TEA; WLIT 4

O'Cathasaigh, Sean
See O'Casey, Sean

Occom, Samson 1723-1792 .... **LC 60; NNAL**
See also DLB 175

Occomy, Marita (Odette) Bonner
1899(?)-1971
See Bonner, Marita
See also BW 2; CA 142; DFS 13; DLB 51, 228

Ochs, Phil(ip David) 1940-1976 .... **CLC 17**
See also CA 185; 65-68

O'Connor, Edwin (Greene)
1918-1968 .... **CLC 14**
See also CA 93-96; 25-28R; MAL 5

O'Connor, (Mary) Flannery
1925-1964 .... **CLC 1, 2, 3, 6, 10, 13, 15, 21, 66, 104; SSC 1, 23, 61, 82; TCLC 132; WLC 4**
See also AAYA 7; AMW; AMWR 2; BPFB 3; BYA 16; CA 1-4R; CANR 3, 41; CDALB 1941-1968; DA; DA3; DAB; DAC; DAM MST, NOV; DLB 2, 152; DLBD 12; DLBY 1980; EWL 3; EXPS; LAIT 5; MAL 5; MBL; MTCW 1, 2; MTFW 2005; NFS 3, 21; RGAL 4; RGSF 2; SSFS 2, 7, 10, 19; TUS

O'Connor, Frank .... **CLC 23; SSC 5**
See O'Donovan, Michael Francis
See also DLB 162; EWL 3; RGSF 2; SSFS 5

O'Dell, Scott 1898-1989 .... **CLC 30**
See also AAYA 3, 44; BPFB 3; BYA 1, 2, 3, 5; CA 61-64; 129; CANR 12, 30, 112; CLR 1, 16; DLB 52; JRDA; MAICYA 1, 2; SATA 12, 60, 134; WYA; YAW

Odets, Clifford 1906-1963 ..... **CLC 2, 28, 98; DC 6**
See also AMWS 2; CA 85-88; CAD; CANR 62; DAM DRAM; DFS 3, 17, 20; DLB 7, 26; EWL 3; MAL 5; MTCW 1, 2; MTFW 2005; RGAL 4; TUS

O'Doherty, Brian 1928- .... **CLC 76**
See also CA 105; CANR 108

O'Donnell, K. M.
See Malzberg, Barry N(athaniel)

O'Donnell, Lawrence
See Kuttner, Henry

O'Donovan, Michael Francis
1903-1966 .... **CLC 14**
See O'Connor, Frank
See also CA 93-96; CANR 84

Oe, Kenzaburo 1935- .. **CLC 10, 36, 86, 187; SSC 20**
See Oe Kenzaburo
See also CA 97-100; CANR 36, 50, 74, 126; DA3; DAM NOV; DLB 182; DLBY 1994; LATS 1:2; MJW; MTCW 1, 2; MTFW 2005; RGSF 2; RGWL 2, 3

Oe Kenzaburo
See Oe, Kenzaburo
See also CWW 2; EWL 3

O'Faolain, Julia 1932- .... **CLC 6, 19, 47, 108**
See also CA 81-84; CAAS 2; CANR 12, 61; CN 2, 3, 4, 5, 6, 7; DLB 14, 231, 319; FW; MTCW 1; RHW

O'Faolain, Sean 1900-1991 ...... **CLC 1, 7, 14, 32, 70; SSC 13; TCLC 143**
See also CA 61-64; 134; CANR 12, 66; CN 1, 2, 3, 4; DLB 15, 162; MTCW 1, 2; MTFW 2005; RGEL 2; RGSF 2

O'Flaherty, Liam 1896-1984 .... **CLC 5, 34; SSC 6**
See also CA 101; 113; CANR 35; CN 1, 2, 3; DLB 36, 162; DLBY 1984; MTCW 1, 2; MTFW 2005; RGEL 2; RGSF 2; SSFS 5, 20

Ogai
See Mori Ogai
See also MJW

Ogilvy, Gavin
See Barrie, J(ames) M(atthew)

O'Grady, Standish (James)
1846-1928 .... **TCLC 5**
See also CA 104; 157

O'Grady, Timothy 1951- .... **CLC 59**
See also CA 138

O'Hara, Frank 1926-1966 .... **CLC 2, 5, 13, 78; PC 45**
See also CA 9-12R; 25-28R; CANR 33; DA3; DAM POET; DLB 5, 16, 193; EWL 3; MAL 5; MTCW 1, 2; MTFW 2005; PFS 8, 12; RGAL 4; WP

O'Hara, John (Henry) 1905-1970 . **CLC 1, 2, 3, 6, 11, 42; SSC 15**
See also AMW; BPFB 3; CA 5-8R; 25-28R; CANR 31, 60; CDALB 1929-1941; DAM NOV; DLB 9, 86, 324; DLBD 2; EWL 3; MAL 5; MTCW 1, 2; MTFW 2005; NFS 11; RGAL 4; RGSF 2

O'Hehir, Diana 1929- .... **CLC 41**
See also CA 245

Ohiyesa
See Eastman, Charles A(lexander)

Okada, John 1923-1971 .... **AAL**
See also BYA 14; CA 212; DLB 312

Okigbo, Christopher 1930-1967 .... **BLC 3; CLC 25, 84; PC 7; TCLC 171**
See also AFW; BW 1, 3; CA 77-80; CANR 74; CDWLB 3; DAM MULT, POET; DLB 125; EWL 3; MTCW 1, 2; MTFW 2005; RGEL 2

Okigbo, Christopher Ifenayichukwu
See Okigbo, Christopher

Okri, Ben 1959- .... **CLC 87, 223**
See also AFW; BRWS 5; BW 2, 3; CA 130; 138; CANR 65, 128; CN 5, 6, 7; DLB 157, 231, 319, 326; EWL 3; INT CA-138; MTCW 2; MTFW 2005; RGSF 2; SSFS 20; WLIT 2; WWE 1

Olds, Sharon 1942- .. **CLC 32, 39, 85; PC 22**
See also AMWS 10; CA 101; CANR 18, 41, 66, 98, 135; CP 5, 6, 7; CPW; CWP; DAM POET; DLB 120; MAL 5; MTCW 2; MTFW 2005; PFS 17

Oldstyle, Jonathan
See Irving, Washington

Oz, Amos 1939- ...... **CLC 5, 8, 11, 27, 33, 54; SSC 66**
See also CA 53-56; CANR 27, 47, 65, 113, 138; CWW 2; DAM NOV; EWL 3; MTCW 1, 2; MTFW 2005; RGHL; RGSF 2; RGWL 3; WLIT 6

Ozick, Cynthia 1928- .... **CLC 3, 7, 28, 62, 155; SSC 15, 60**
See also AMWS 5; BEST 90:1; CA 17-20R; CANR 23, 58, 116; CN 3, 4, 5, 6, 7; CPW; DA3; DAM NOV, POP; DLB 28, 152, 299; DLBY 1982; EWL 3; EXPS; INT CANR-23; MAL 5; MTCW 1, 2; MTFW 2005; RGAL 4; RGHL; RGSF 2; SSFS 3, 12, 22

Ozu, Yasujiro 1903-1963 .... **CLC 16**
See also CA 112

Pabst, G. W. 1885-1967 .... **TCLC 127**

Pacheco, C.
See Pessoa, Fernando (Antonio Nogueira)

Pacheco, Jose Emilio 1939- .... **HLC 2**
See also CA 111; 131; CANR 65; CWW 2; DAM MULT; DLB 290; EWL 3; HW 1, 2; RGSF 2

Pa Chin .... **CLC 18**
See Jin, Ba
See also EWL 3

Pack, Robert 1929- .... **CLC 13**
See also CA 1-4R; CANR 3, 44, 82; CP 1, 2, 3, 4, 5, 6, 7; DLB 5; SATA 118

Padgett, Lewis
See Kuttner, Henry

Padilla (Lorenzo), Heberto 1932-2000 .... **CLC 38**
See also AITN 1; CA 123; 131; 189; CWW 2; EWL 3; HW 1

Page, James Patrick 1944-
See Page, Jimmy
See also CA 204

Page, Jimmy 1944- .... **CLC 12**
See Page, James Patrick

Page, Louise 1955- .... **CLC 40**
See also CA 140; CANR 76; CBD; CD 5, 6; CWD; DLB 233

Page, P(atricia) K(athleen) 1916- ...... **CLC 7, 18; PC 12**
See Cape, Judith
See also CA 53-56; CANR 4, 22, 65; CP 1, 2, 3, 4, 5, 6, 7; DAC; DAM MST; DLB 68; MTCW 1; RGEL 2

Page, Stanton
See Fuller, Henry Blake

Page, Stanton
See Fuller, Henry Blake

Page, Thomas Nelson 1853-1922 .... **SSC 23**
See also CA 118; 177; DLB 12, 78; DLBD 13; RGAL 4

Pagels, Elaine
See Pagels, Elaine Hiesey

Pagels, Elaine Hiesey 1943- .... **CLC 104**
See also CA 45-48; CANR 2, 24, 51, 151; FW; NCFS 4

Paget, Violet 1856-1935
See Lee, Vernon
See also CA 104; 166; GLL 1; HGG

Paget-Lowe, Henry
See Lovecraft, H. P.

Paglia, Camille 1947- .... **CLC 68**
See also CA 140; CANR 72, 139; CPW; FW; GLL 2; MTCW 2; MTFW 2005

Paige, Richard
See Koontz, Dean R.

Paine, Thomas 1737-1809 .... **NCLC 62**
See also AMWS 1; CDALB 1640-1865; DLB 31, 43, 73, 158; LAIT 1; RGAL 4; RGEL 2; TUS

Pakenham, Antonia
See Fraser, Antonia

Palamas, Costis
See Palamas, Kostes

Palamas, Kostes 1859-1943 .... **TCLC 5**
See Palamas, Kostis
See also CA 105; 190; RGWL 2, 3

Palamas, Kostis
See Palamas, Kostes
See also EWL 3

Palazzeschi, Aldo 1885-1974 .... **CLC 11**
See also CA 89-92; 53-56; DLB 114, 264; EWL 3

Pales Matos, Luis 1898-1959 .... **HLCS 2**
See Pales Matos, Luis
See also DLB 290; HW 1; LAW

Paley, Grace 1922- .. **CLC 4, 6, 37, 140; SSC 8**
See also AMWS 6; CA 25-28R; CANR 13, 46, 74, 118; CN 2, 3, 4, 5, 6, 7; CPW; DA3; DAM POP; DLB 28, 218; EWL 3; EXPS; FW; INT CANR-13; MAL 5; MBL; MTCW 1, 2; MTFW 2005; RGAL 4; RGSF 2; SSFS 3, 20

Palin, Michael (Edward) 1943- .... **CLC 21**
See Monty Python
See also CA 107; CANR 35, 109; SATA 67

Palliser, Charles 1947- .... **CLC 65**
See also CA 136; CANR 76; CN 5, 6, 7

Palma, Ricardo 1833-1919 .... **TCLC 29**
See also CA 168; LAW

Pamuk, Orhan 1952- .... **CLC 185**
See also CA 142; CANR 75, 127; CWW 2; WLIT 6

Pancake, Breece Dexter 1952-1979
See Pancake, Breece D'J
See also CA 123; 109

Pancake, Breece D'J .... **CLC 29; SSC 61**
See Pancake, Breece Dexter
See also DLB 130

Panchenko, Nikolai .... **CLC 59**

Pankhurst, Emmeline (Goulden) 1858-1928 .... **TCLC 100**
See also CA 116; FW

Panko, Rudy
See Gogol, Nikolai (Vasilyevich)

Papadiamantis, Alexandros 1851-1911 .... **TCLC 29**
See also CA 168; EWL 3

Papadiamantopoulos, Johannes 1856-1910
See Moreas, Jean
See also CA 117; 242

Papini, Giovanni 1881-1956 .... **TCLC 22**
See also CA 121; 180; DLB 264

Paracelsus 1493-1541 .... **LC 14**
See also DLB 179

Parasol, Peter
See Stevens, Wallace

Pardo Bazan, Emilia 1851-1921 .... **SSC 30**
See also EWL 3; FW; RGSF 2; RGWL 2, 3

Pareto, Vilfredo 1848-1923 .... **TCLC 69**
See also CA 175

Paretsky, Sara 1947- .... **CLC 135**
See also AAYA 30; BEST 90:3; CA 125; 129; CANR 59, 95; CMW 4; CPW; DA3; DAM POP; DLB 306; INT CA-129; MSW; RGAL 4

Parfenie, Maria
See Codrescu, Andrei

Parini, Jay (Lee) 1948- .... **CLC 54, 133**
See also CA 97-100; 229; CAAE 229; CAAS 16; CANR 32, 87

Park, Jordan
See Kornbluth, C(yril) M.; Pohl, Frederik

Park, Robert E(zra) 1864-1944 ..... **TCLC 73**
See also CA 122; 165

Parker, Bert
See Ellison, Harlan

Parker, Dorothy (Rothschild) 1893-1967 . **CLC 15, 68; PC 28; SSC 2; TCLC 143**
See also AMWS 9; CA 19-20; 25-28R; CAP 2; DA3; DAM POET; DLB 11, 45, 86; EXPP; FW; MAL 5; MBL; MTCW 1, 2; MTFW 2005; PFS 18; RGAL 4; RGSF 2; TUS

Parker, Robert B. 1932- .... **CLC 27**
See also AAYA 28; BEST 89:4; BPFB 3; CA 49-52; CANR 1, 26, 52, 89, 128; CMW 4; CPW; DAM NOV, POP; DLB 306; INT CANR-26; MSW; MTCW 1; MTFW 2005

Parker, Robert Brown
See Parker, Robert B.

Parkin, Frank 1940- .... **CLC 43**
See also CA 147

Parkman, Francis, Jr. 1823-1893 .. **NCLC 12**
See also AMWS 2; DLB 1, 30, 183, 186, 235; RGAL 4

Parks, Gordon 1912-2006 .... **BLC 3; CLC 1, 16**
See also AAYA 36; AITN 2; BW 2, 3; CA 41-44R; 249; CANR 26, 66, 145; DA3; DAM MULT; DLB 33; MTCW 2; MTFW 2005; SATA 8, 108

Parks, Gordon Alexander Buchanan
See Parks, Gordon

Parks, Suzan-Lori 1964(?)- .... **DC 23**
See also AAYA 55; CA 201; CAD; CD 5, 6; CWD; DFS 22; RGAL 4

Parks, Tim(othy Harold) 1954- ...... **CLC 147**
See also CA 126; 131; CANR 77, 144; CN 7; DLB 231; INT CA-131

Parmenides c. 515B.C.-c. 450B.C. .... **CMLC 22**
See also DLB 176

Parnell, Thomas 1679-1718 .... **LC 3**
See also DLB 95; RGEL 2

Parr, Catherine c. 1513(?)-1548 .... **LC 86**
See also DLB 136

Parra, Nicanor 1914- ... **CLC 2, 102; HLC 2; PC 39**
See also CA 85-88; CANR 32; CWW 2; DAM MULT; DLB 283; EWL 3; HW 1; LAW; MTCW 1

Parra Sanojo, Ana Teresa de la 1890-1936 .... **HLCS 2**
See de la Parra, (Ana) Teresa (Sonojo)
See also LAW

Parrish, Mary Frances
See Fisher, M(ary) F(rances) K(ennedy)

Parshchikov, Aleksei 1954- .... **CLC 59**
See Parshchikov, Aleksei Maksimovich

Parshchikov, Aleksei Maksimovich
See Parshchikov, Aleksei
See also DLB 285

Parson, Professor
See Coleridge, Samuel Taylor

Parson Lot
See Kingsley, Charles

Parton, Sara Payson Willis 1811-1872 .... **NCLC 86**
See also DLB 43, 74, 239

Partridge, Anthony
See Oppenheim, E(dward) Phillips

Pascal, Blaise 1623-1662 .... **LC 35**
See also DLB 268; EW 3; GFL Beginnings to 1789; RGWL 2, 3; TWA

Pascoli, Giovanni 1855-1912 .... **TCLC 45**
See also CA 170; EW 7; EWL 3

Pasolini, Pier Paolo 1922-1975 .. **CLC 20, 37, 106; PC 17**
See also CA 93-96; 61-64; CANR 63; DLB 128, 177; EWL 3; MTCW 1; RGWL 2, 3

Pasquini
See Silone, Ignazio

Peretz, Yitzkhok Leibush
See Peretz, Isaac Loeb

Perez Galdos, Benito 1843-1920 ..... **HLCS 2; TCLC 27**
See Galdos, Benito Perez
See also CA 125; 153; EWL 3; HW 1; RGWL 2, 3

Peri Rossi, Cristina 1941- .. **CLC 156; HLCS 2**
See also CA 131; CANR 59, 81; CWW 2; DLB 145, 290; EWL 3; HW 1, 2

Perlata
See Peret, Benjamin

Perloff, Marjorie G(abrielle) 1931- .... **CLC 137**
See also CA 57-60; CANR 7, 22, 49, 104

Perrault, Charles 1628-1703 .... **LC 2, 56**
See also BYA 4; CLR 79; DLB 268; GFL Beginnings to 1789; MAICYA 1, 2; RGWL 2, 3; SATA 25; WCH

Perry, Anne 1938- .... **CLC 126**
See also CA 101; CANR 22, 50, 84, 150; CMW 4; CN 6, 7; CPW; DLB 276

Perry, Brighton
See Sherwood, Robert E(mmet)

Perse, St.-John
See Leger, (Marie-Rene Auguste) Alexis Saint-Leger

Perse, Saint-John
See Leger, (Marie-Rene Auguste) Alexis Saint-Leger
See also DLB 258; RGWL 3

Persius 34-62 .... **CMLC 74**
See also AW 2; DLB 211; RGWL 2, 3

Perutz, Leo(pold) 1882-1957 .... **TCLC 60**
See also CA 147; DLB 81

Peseenz, Tulio F.
See Lopez y Fuentes, Gregorio

Pesetsky, Bette 1932- .... **CLC 28**
See also CA 133; DLB 130

Peshkov, Alexei Maximovich 1868-1936
See Gorky, Maxim
See also CA 105; 141; CANR 83; DA; DAC; DAM DRAM, MST, NOV; MTCW 2; MTFW 2005

Pessoa, Fernando (Antonio Nogueira) 1888-1935 ..... **HLC 2; PC 20; TCLC 27**
See also CA 125; 183; DAM MULT; DLB 287; EW 10; EWL 3; RGWL 2, 3; WP

Peterkin, Julia Mood 1880-1961 ...... **CLC 31**
See also CA 102; DLB 9

Peters, Joan K(aren) 1945- .... **CLC 39**
See also CA 158; CANR 109

Peters, Robert L(ouis) 1924- .... **CLC 7**
See also CA 13-16R; CAAS 8; CP 1, 5, 6, 7; DLB 105

Petofi, Sandor 1823-1849 .... **NCLC 21**
See also RGWL 2, 3

Petrakis, Harry Mark 1923- .... **CLC 3**
See also CA 9-12R; CANR 4, 30, 85, 155; CN 1, 2, 3, 4, 5, 6, 7

Petrarch 1304-1374 .... **CMLC 20; PC 8**
See also DA3; DAM POET; EW 2; LMFS 1; RGWL 2, 3; WLIT 7

Petronius c. 20-66 .... **CMLC 34**
See also AW 2; CDWLB 1; DLB 211; RGWL 2, 3; WLIT 8

Petrov, Evgeny .... **TCLC 21**
See Kataev, Evgeny Petrovich

Petry, Ann (Lane) 1908-1997 .. **CLC 1, 7, 18; TCLC 112**
See also AFAW 1, 2; BPFB 3; BW 1, 3; BYA 2; CA 5-8R; 157; CAAS 6; CANR 4, 46; CLR 12; CN 1, 2, 3, 4, 5, 6; DLB 76; EWL 3; JRDA; LAIT 1; MAICYA 1, 2; MAICYAS 1; MTCW 1; RGAL 4; SATA 5; SATA-Obit 94; TUS

Petursson, Halligrimur 1614-1674 .... **LC 8**

Peychinovich
See Vazov, Ivan (Minchov)

Phaedrus c. 15B.C.-c. 50 .... **CMLC 25**
See also DLB 211

Phelps (Ward), Elizabeth Stuart
See Phelps, Elizabeth Stuart
See also FW

Phelps, Elizabeth Stuart 1844-1911 .... **TCLC 113**
See Phelps (Ward), Elizabeth Stuart
See also CA 242; DLB 74

Philips, Katherine 1632-1664 . **LC 30; PC 40**
See also DLB 131; RGEL 2

Philipson, Morris H. 1926- .... **CLC 53**
See also CA 1-4R; CANR 4

Phillips, Caryl 1958- ..... **BLCS; CLC 96, 224**
See also BRWS 5; BW 2; CA 141; CANR 63, 104, 140; CBD; CD 5, 6; CN 5, 6, 7; DA3; DAM MULT; DLB 157; EWL 3; MTCW 2; MTFW 2005; WLIT 4; WWE 1

Phillips, David Graham 1867-1911 .... **TCLC 44**
See also CA 108; 176; DLB 9, 12, 303; RGAL 4

Phillips, Jack
See Sandburg, Carl (August)

Phillips, Jayne Anne 1952- .... **CLC 15, 33, 139; SSC 16**
See also AAYA 57; BPFB 3; CA 101; CANR 24, 50, 96; CN 4, 5, 6, 7; CSW; DLBY 1980; INT CANR-24; MTCW 1, 2; MTFW 2005; RGAL 4; RGSF 2; SSFS 4

Phillips, Richard
See Dick, Philip K.

Phillips, Robert (Schaeffer) 1938- .... **CLC 28**
See also CA 17-20R; CAAS 13; CANR 8; DLB 105

Phillips, Ward
See Lovecraft, H. P.

Philostratus, Flavius c. 179-c. 244 .... **CMLC 62**

Piccolo, Lucio 1901-1969 .... **CLC 13**
See also CA 97-100; DLB 114; EWL 3

Pickthall, Marjorie L(owry) C(hristie) 1883-1922 .... **TCLC 21**
See also CA 107; DLB 92

Pico della Mirandola, Giovanni 1463-1494 .... **LC 15**
See also LMFS 1

Piercy, Marge 1936- .... **CLC 3, 6, 14, 18, 27, 62, 128; PC 29**
See also BPFB 3; CA 21-24R, 187; CAAE 187; CAAS 1; CANR 13, 43, 66, 111; CN 3, 4, 5, 6, 7; CP 1, 2, 3, 4, 5, 6, 7; CWP; DLB 120, 227; EXPP; FW; MAL 5; MTCW 1, 2; MTFW 2005; PFS 9, 22; SFW 4

Piers, Robert
See Anthony, Piers

Pieyre de Mandiargues, Andre 1909-1991
See Mandiargues, Andre Pieyre de
See also CA 103; 136; CANR 22, 82; EWL 3; GFL 1789 to the Present

Pilnyak, Boris 1894-1938 . **SSC 48; TCLC 23**
See Vogau, Boris Andreyevich
See also EWL 3

Pinchback, Eugene
See Toomer, Jean

Pincherle, Alberto 1907-1990 ...... **CLC 11, 18**
See Moravia, Alberto
See also CA 25-28R; 132; CANR 33, 63, 142; DAM NOV; MTCW 1; MTFW 2005

Pinckney, Darryl 1953- .... **CLC 76**
See also BW 2, 3; CA 143; CANR 79

Pindar 518(?)B.C.-438(?)B.C. ..... **CMLC 12; PC 19**
See also AW 1; CDWLB 1; DLB 176; RGWL 2

Pineda, Cecile 1942- .... **CLC 39**
See also CA 118; DLB 209

Pinero, Arthur Wing 1855-1934 .... **TCLC 32**
See also CA 110; 153; DAM DRAM; DLB 10; RGEL 2

Pinero, Miguel (Antonio Gomez) 1946-1988 .... **CLC 4, 55**
See also CA 61-64; 125; CAD; CANR 29, 90; DLB 266; HW 1; LLW

Pinget, Robert 1919-1997 .... **CLC 7, 13, 37**
See also CA 85-88; 160; CWW 2; DLB 83; EWL 3; GFL 1789 to the Present

Pink Floyd
See Barrett, (Roger) Syd; Gilmour, David; Mason, Nick; Waters, Roger; Wright, Rick

Pinkney, Edward 1802-1828 .... **NCLC 31**
See also DLB 248

Pinkwater, D. Manus
See Pinkwater, Daniel Manus

Pinkwater, Daniel
See Pinkwater, Daniel Manus

Pinkwater, Daniel M.
See Pinkwater, Daniel Manus

Pinkwater, Daniel Manus 1941- .... **CLC 35**
See also AAYA 1, 46; BYA 9; CA 29-32R; CANR 12, 38, 89, 143; CLR 4; CSW; FANT; JRDA; MAICYA 1, 2; SAAS 3; SATA 8, 46, 76, 114, 158; SFW 4; YAW

Pinkwater, Manus
See Pinkwater, Daniel Manus

Pinsky, Robert 1940- .... **CLC 9, 19, 38, 94, 121, 216; PC 27**
See also AMWS 6; CA 29-32R; CAAS 4; CANR 58, 97, 138; CP 3, 4, 5, 6, 7; DA3; DAM POET; DLBY 1982, 1998; MAL 5; MTCW 2; MTFW 2005; PFS 18; RGAL 4; TCLE 1:2

Pinta, Harold
See Pinter, Harold

Pinter, Harold 1930- .. **CLC 1, 3, 6, 9, 11, 15, 27, 58, 73, 199; DC 15; WLC 4**
See also BRWR 1; BRWS 1; CA 5-8R; CANR 33, 65, 112, 145; CBD; CD 5, 6; CDBLB 1960 to Present; CP 1; DA; DA3; DAB; DAC; DAM DRAM, MST; DFS 3, 5, 7, 14; DLB 13, 310; EWL 3; IDFW 3, 4; LMFS 2; MTCW 1, 2; MTFW 2005; RGEL 2; RGHL; TEA

Piozzi, Hester Lynch (Thrale) 1741-1821 .... **NCLC 57**
See also DLB 104, 142

Pirandello, Luigi 1867-1936 .. **DC 5; SSC 22; TCLC 4, 29, 172; WLC 4**
See also CA 104; 153; CANR 103; DA; DA3; DAB; DAC; DAM DRAM, MST; DFS 4, 9; DLB 264; EW 8; EWL 3; MTCW 2; MTFW 2005; RGSF 2; RGWL 2, 3; WLIT 7

Pirsig, Robert M(aynard) 1928- ... **CLC 4, 6, 73**
See also CA 53-56; CANR 42, 74; CPW 1; DA3; DAM POP; MTCW 1, 2; MTFW 2005; SATA 39

Pisan, Christine de
See Christine de Pizan

Pisarev, Dmitrii Ivanovich
See Pisarev, Dmitry Ivanovich
See also DLB 277

Pisarev, Dmitry Ivanovich 1840-1868 .... **NCLC 25**
See Pisarev, Dmitrii Ivanovich

Pix, Mary (Griffith) 1666-1709 .... **LC 8**
See also DLB 80

Rampling, Anne
See Rice, Anne
See also GLL 2

Ramsay, Allan 1686(?)-1758 .... **LC 29**
See also DLB 95; RGEL 2

Ramsay, Jay
See Campbell, (John) Ramsey

Ramuz, Charles-Ferdinand
1878-1947 .... **TCLC 33**
See also CA 165; EWL 3

Rand, Ayn 1905-1982 ...... **CLC 3, 30, 44, 79; WLC 5**
See also AAYA 10; AMWS 4; BPFB 3;
BYA 12; CA 13-16R; 105; CANR 27, 73;
CDALBS; CN 1, 2, 3; CPW; DA; DA3;
DAC; DAM MST, NOV, POP; DLB 227,
279; MTCW 1, 2; MTFW 2005; NFS 10,
16; RGAL 4; SFW 4; TUS; YAW

Randall, Dudley (Felker) 1914-2000 . **BLC 3; CLC 1, 135**
See also BW 1, 3; CA 25-28R; 189; CANR
23, 82; CP 1, 2, 3, 4, 5; DAM MULT;
DLB 41; PFS 5

Randall, Robert
See Silverberg, Robert

Ranger, Ken
See Creasey, John

Rank, Otto 1884-1939 .... **TCLC 115**

Ransom, John Crowe 1888-1974 .. **CLC 2, 4, 5, 11, 24; PC 61**
See also AMW; CA 5-8R; 49-52; CANR 6,
34; CDALBS; CP 1, 2; DA3; DAM POET;
DLB 45, 63; EWL 3; EXPP; MAL 5;
MTCW 1, 2; MTFW 2005; RGAL 4; TUS

Rao, Raja 1908-2006 .... **CLC 25, 56**
See also CA 73-76; CANR 51; CN 1, 2, 3,
4, 5, 6; DAM NOV; DLB 323; EWL 3;
MTCW 1, 2; MTFW 2005; RGEL 2;
RGSF 2

Raphael, Frederic (Michael) 1931- ... **CLC 2, 14**
See also CA 1-4R; CANR 1, 86; CN 1, 2,
3, 4, 5, 6, 7; DLB 14, 319; TCLE 1:2

Ratcliffe, James P.
See Mencken, H(enry) L(ouis)

Rathbone, Julian 1935- .... **CLC 41**
See also CA 101; CANR 34, 73, 152

Rattigan, Terence (Mervyn)
1911-1977 .... **CLC 7; DC 18**
See also BRWS 7; CA 85-88; 73-76; CBD;
CDBLB 1945-1960; DAM DRAM; DFS
8; DLB 13; IDFW 3, 4; MTCW 1, 2;
MTFW 2005; RGEL 2

Ratushinskaya, Irina 1954- .... **CLC 54**
See also CA 129; CANR 68; CWW 2

Raven, Simon (Arthur Noel)
1927-2001 .... **CLC 14**
See also CA 81-84; 197; CANR 86; CN 1,
2, 3, 4, 5, 6; DLB 271

Ravenna, Michael
See Welty, Eudora

Rawley, Callman 1903-2004
See Rakosi, Carl
See also CA 21-24R; 228; CANR 12, 32,
91

Rawlings, Marjorie Kinnan
1896-1953 .... **TCLC 4**
See also AAYA 20; AMWS 10; ANW;
BPFB 3; BYA 3; CA 104; 137; CANR 74;
CLR 63; DLB 9, 22, 102; DLBD 17;
JRDA; MAICYA 1, 2; MAL 5; MTCW 2;
MTFW 2005; RGAL 4; SATA 100; WCH;
YABC 1; YAW

Ray, Satyajit 1921-1992 .... **CLC 16, 76**
See also CA 114; 137; DAM MULT

Read, Herbert Edward 1893-1968 ..... **CLC 4**
See also BRW 6; CA 85-88; 25-28R; DLB
20, 149; EWL 3; PAB; RGEL 2

Read, Piers Paul 1941- .... **CLC 4, 10, 25**
See also CA 21-24R; CANR 38, 86, 150;
CN 2, 3, 4, 5, 6, 7; DLB 14; SATA 21

Reade, Charles 1814-1884 .... **NCLC 2, 74**
See also DLB 21; RGEL 2

Reade, Hamish
See Gray, Simon (James Holliday)

Reading, Peter 1946- .... **CLC 47**
See also BRWS 8; CA 103; CANR 46, 96;
CP 5, 6, 7; DLB 40

Reaney, James 1926- .... **CLC 13**
See also CA 41-44R; CAAS 15; CANR 42;
CD 5, 6; CP 1, 2, 3, 4, 5, 6, 7; DAC;
DAM MST; DLB 68; RGEL 2; SATA 43

Rebreanu, Liviu 1885-1944 .... **TCLC 28**
See also CA 165; DLB 220; EWL 3

Rechy, John 1934- ..... **CLC 1, 7, 14, 18, 107; HLC 2**
See also CA 5-8R, 195; CAAE 195; CAAS
4; CANR 6, 32, 64, 152; CN 1, 2, 3, 4, 5,
6, 7; DAM MULT; DLB 122, 278; DLBY
1982; HW 1, 2; INT CANR-6; LLW;
MAL 5; RGAL 4

Rechy, John Francisco
See Rechy, John

Redcam, Tom 1870-1933 .... **TCLC 25**

Reddin, Keith 1956- .... **CLC 67**
See also CAD; CD 6

Redgrove, Peter (William)
1932-2003 .... **CLC 6, 41**
See also BRWS 6; CA 1-4R; 217; CANR 3,
39, 77; CP 1, 2, 3, 4, 5, 6, 7; DLB 40;
TCLE 1:2

Redmon, Anne .... **CLC 22**
See Nightingale, Anne Redmon
See also DLBY 1986

Reed, Eliot
See Ambler, Eric

Reed, Ishmael 1938- ..... **BLC 3; CLC 2, 3, 5, 6, 13, 32, 60, 174; PC 68**
See also AFAW 1, 2; AMWS 10; BPFB 3;
BW 2, 3; CA 21-24R; CANR 25, 48, 74,
128; CN 1, 2, 3, 4, 5, 6, 7; CP 1, 2, 3, 4,
5, 6, 7; CSW; DA3; DAM MULT; DLB
2, 5, 33, 169, 227; DLBD 8; EWL 3;
LMFS 2; MAL 5; MSW; MTCW 1, 2;
MTFW 2005; PFS 6; RGAL 4; TCWW 2

Reed, John (Silas) 1887-1920 .... **TCLC 9**
See also CA 106; 195; MAL 5; TUS

Reed, Lou .... **CLC 21**
See Firbank, Louis

Reese, Lizette Woodworth
1856-1935 .... **PC 29; TCLC 181**
See also CA 180; DLB 54

Reeve, Clara 1729-1807 .... **NCLC 19**
See also DLB 39; RGEL 2

Reich, Wilhelm 1897-1957 .... **TCLC 57**
See also CA 199

Reid, Christopher (John) 1949- .... **CLC 33**
See also CA 140; CANR 89; CP 4, 5, 6, 7;
DLB 40; EWL 3

Reid, Desmond
See Moorcock, Michael

Reid Banks, Lynne 1929-
See Banks, Lynne Reid
See also AAYA 49; CA 1-4R; CANR 6, 22,
38, 87; CLR 24; CN 1, 2, 3, 7; JRDA;
MAICYA 1, 2; SATA 22, 75, 111, 165;
YAW

Reilly, William K.
See Creasey, John

Reiner, Max
See Caldwell, (Janet Miriam) Taylor
(Holland)

Reis, Ricardo
See Pessoa, Fernando (Antonio Nogueira)

Reizenstein, Elmer Leopold
See Rice, Elmer (Leopold)
See also EWL 3

Remarque, Erich Maria 1898-1970 . **CLC 21**
See also AAYA 27; BPFB 3; CA 77-80; 29-
32R; CDWLB 2; DA; DA3; DAB; DAC;
DAM MST, NOV; DLB 56; EWL 3;
EXPN; LAIT 3; MTCW 1, 2; MTFW
2005; NFS 4; RGHL; RGWL 2, 3

Remington, Frederic S(ackrider)
1861-1909 .... **TCLC 89**
See also CA 108; 169; DLB 12, 186, 188;
SATA 41; TCWW 2

Remizov, A.
See Remizov, Aleksei (Mikhailovich)

Remizov, A. M.
See Remizov, Aleksei (Mikhailovich)

Remizov, Aleksei (Mikhailovich)
1877-1957 .... **TCLC 27**
See Remizov, Alexey Mikhaylovich
See also CA 125; 133; DLB 295

Remizov, Alexey Mikhaylovich
See Remizov, Aleksei (Mikhailovich)
See also EWL 3

Renan, Joseph Ernest 1823-1892 . **NCLC 26, 145**
See also GFL 1789 to the Present

Renard, Jules(-Pierre) 1864-1910 .. **TCLC 17**
See also CA 117; 202; GFL 1789 to the
Present

Renart, Jean fl. 13th cent. - .... **CMLC 83**

Renault, Mary .... **CLC 3, 11, 17**
See Challans, Mary
See also BPFB 3; BYA 2; CN 1, 2, 3;
DLBY 1983; EWL 3; GLL 1; LAIT 1;
RGEL 2; RHW

Rendell, Ruth 1930- .... **CLC 28, 48**
See Vine, Barbara
See also BPFB 3; BRWS 9; CA 109; CANR
32, 52, 74, 127; CN 5, 6, 7; CPW; DAM
POP; DLB 87, 276; INT CANR-32;
MSW; MTCW 1, 2; MTFW 2005

Rendell, Ruth Barbara
See Rendell, Ruth

Renoir, Jean 1894-1979 .... **CLC 20**
See also CA 129; 85-88

Resnais, Alain 1922- .... **CLC 16**

Revard, Carter 1931- .... **NNAL**
See also CA 144; CANR 81, 153; PFS 5

Reverdy, Pierre 1889-1960 .... **CLC 53**
See also CA 97-100; 89-92; DLB 258; EWL
3; GFL 1789 to the Present

Rexroth, Kenneth 1905-1982 .... **CLC 1, 2, 6, 11, 22, 49, 112; PC 20**
See also BG 1:3; CA 5-8R; 107; CANR 14,
34, 63; CDALB 1941-1968; CP 1, 2, 3;
DAM POET; DLB 16, 48, 165, 212;
DLBY 1982; EWL 3; INT CANR-14;
MAL 5; MTCW 1, 2; MTFW 2005;
RGAL 4

Reyes, Alfonso 1889-1959 .... **HLCS 2; TCLC 33**
See also CA 131; EWL 3; HW 1; LAW

Reyes y Basoalto, Ricardo Eliecer Neftali
See Neruda, Pablo

Reymont, Wladyslaw (Stanislaw)
1868(?)-1925 .... **TCLC 5**
See also CA 104; EWL 3

Reynolds, John Hamilton
1794-1852 .... **NCLC 146**
See also DLB 96

Reynolds, Jonathan 1942- .... **CLC 6, 38**
See also CA 65-68; CANR 28

Reynolds, Joshua 1723-1792 .... **LC 15**
See also DLB 104

Reynolds, Michael S(hane)
1937-2000 .... **CLC 44**
See also CA 65-68; 189; CANR 9, 89, 97

Reznikoff, Charles 1894-1976 .... **CLC 9**
See also AMWS 14; CA 33-36; 61-64; CAP
2; CP 1, 2; DLB 28, 45; RGHL; WP

Rezzori, Gregor von
See Rezzori d'Arezzo, Gregor von
Rezzori d'Arezzo, Gregor von
1914-1998 .... **CLC 25**
See also CA 122; 136; 167
Rhine, Richard
See Silverstein, Alvin; Silverstein, Virginia
B(arbara Opshelor)
Rhodes, Eugene Manlove
1869-1934 .... **TCLC 53**
See also CA 198; DLB 256; TCWW 1, 2
R'hoone, Lord
See Balzac, Honore de
Rhys, Jean 1890-1979 .... **CLC 2, 4, 6, 14, 19,
51, 124; SSC 21, 76**
See also BRWS 2; CA 25-28R; 85-88;
CANR 35, 62; CDBLB 1945-1960; CD-
WLB 3; CN 1, 2; DA3; DAM NOV; DLB
36, 117, 162; DNFS 2; EWL 3; LATS 1:1;
MTCW 1, 2; MTFW 2005; NFS 19;
RGEL 2; RGSF 2; RHW; TEA; WWE 1
Ribeiro, Darcy 1922-1997 .... **CLC 34**
See also CA 33-36R; 156; EWL 3
Ribeiro, Joao Ubaldo (Osorio Pimentel)
1941- .... **CLC 10, 67**
See also CA 81-84; CWW 2; EWL 3
Ribman, Ronald (Burt) 1932- .... **CLC 7**
See also CA 21-24R; CAD; CANR 46, 80;
CD 5, 6
Ricci, Nino (Pio) 1959- .... **CLC 70**
See also CA 137; CANR 130; CCA 1
Rice, Anne 1941- .... **CLC 41, 128**
See Rampling, Anne
See also AAYA 9, 53; AMWS 7; BEST
89:2; BPFB 3; CA 65-68; CANR 12, 36,
53, 74, 100, 133; CN 6, 7; CPW; CSW;
DA3; DAM POP; DLB 292; GL 3; GLL
2; HGG; MTCW 2; MTFW 2005; SUFW
2; YAW
Rice, Elmer (Leopold) 1892-1967 ...... **CLC 7,
49**
See Reizenstein, Elmer Leopold
See also CA 21-22; 25-28R; CAP 2; DAM
DRAM; DFS 12; DLB 4, 7; IDTP; MAL
5; MTCW 1, 2; RGAL 4
Rice, Tim(othy Miles Bindon)
1944- .... **CLC 21**
See also CA 103; CANR 46; DFS 7
Rich, Adrienne 1929- ..... **CLC 3, 6, 7, 11, 18,
36, 73, 76, 125; PC 5**
See also AAYA 69; AMWR 2; AMWS 1;
CA 9-12R; CANR 20, 53, 74, 128;
CDALBS; CP 1, 2, 3, 4, 5, 6, 7; CSW;
CWP; DA3; DAM POET; DLB 5, 67;
EWL 3; EXPP; FL 1:6; FW; MAL 5;
MBL; MTCW 1, 2; MTFW 2005; PAB;
PFS 15; RGAL 4; RGHL; WP
Rich, Barbara
See Graves, Robert
Rich, Robert
See Trumbo, Dalton
Richard, Keith .... **CLC 17**
See Richards, Keith
Richards, David Adams 1950- .... **CLC 59**
See also CA 93-96; CANR 60, 110, 156;
CN 7; DAC; DLB 53; TCLE 1:2
Richards, I(vor) A(rmstrong)
1893-1979 .... **CLC 14, 24**
See also BRWS 2; CA 41-44R; 89-92;
CANR 34, 74; CP 1, 2; DLB 27; EWL 3;
MTCW 2; RGEL 2
Richards, Keith 1943-
See Richard, Keith
See also CA 107; CANR 77
Richardson, Anne
See Roiphe, Anne

Richardson, Dorothy Miller
1873-1957 .... **TCLC 3**
See also CA 104; 192; DLB 36; EWL 3;
FW; RGEL 2
**Richardson (Robertson), Ethel Florence
Lindesay** 1870-1946
See Richardson, Henry Handel
See also CA 105; 190; DLB 230; RHW
Richardson, Henry Handel .... **TCLC 4**
See Richardson (Robertson), Ethel Florence
Lindesay
See also DLB 197; EWL 3; RGEL 2; RGSF
2
Richardson, John 1796-1852 .... **NCLC 55**
See also CCA 1; DAC; DLB 99
Richardson, Samuel 1689-1761 ...... **LC 1, 44;
WLC 5**
See also BRW 3; CDBLB 1660-1789; DA;
DAB; DAC; DAM MST, NOV; DLB 39;
RGEL 2; TEA; WLIT 3
Richardson, Willis 1889-1977 .... **HR 1:3**
See also BW 1; CA 124; DLB 51; SATA 60
Richler, Mordecai 1931-2001 .... **CLC 3, 5, 9,
13, 18, 46, 70, 185**
See also AITN 1; CA 65-68; 201; CANR
31, 62, 111; CCA 1; CLR 17; CN 1, 2, 3,
4, 5, 7; CWRI 5; DAC; DAM MST, NOV;
DLB 53; EWL 3; MAICYA 1, 2; MTCW
1, 2; MTFW 2005; RGEL 2; RGHL;
SATA 44, 98; SATA-Brief 27; TWA
Richter, Conrad (Michael)
1890-1968 .... **CLC 30**
See also AAYA 21; BYA 2; CA 5-8R; 25-
28R; CANR 23; DLB 9, 212; LAIT 1;
MAL 5; MTCW 1, 2; MTFW 2005;
RGAL 4; SATA 3; TCWW 1, 2; TUS;
YAW
Ricostranza, Tom
See Ellis, Trey
Riddell, Charlotte 1832-1906 .... **TCLC 40**
See Riddell, Mrs. J. H.
See also CA 165; DLB 156
Riddell, Mrs. J. H.
See Riddell, Charlotte
See also HGG; SUFW
Ridge, John Rollin 1827-1867 ...... **NCLC 82;
NNAL**
See also CA 144; DAM MULT; DLB 175
Ridgeway, Jason
See Marlowe, Stephen
Ridgway, Keith 1965- .... **CLC 119**
See also CA 172; CANR 144
Riding, Laura .... **CLC 3, 7**
See Jackson, Laura (Riding)
See also CP 1, 2, 3, 4, 5; RGAL 4
Riefenstahl, Berta Helene Amalia 1902-2003
See Riefenstahl, Leni
See also CA 108; 220
Riefenstahl, Leni .... **CLC 16, 190**
See Riefenstahl, Berta Helene Amalia
Riffe, Ernest
See Bergman, (Ernst) Ingmar
Riggs, (Rolla) Lynn
1899-1954 .... **NNAL; TCLC 56**
See also CA 144; DAM MULT; DLB 175
Riis, Jacob A(ugust) 1849-1914 ..... **TCLC 80**
See also CA 113; 168; DLB 23
Riley, James Whitcomb 1849-1916 .... **PC 48;
TCLC 51**
See also CA 118; 137; DAM POET; MAI-
CYA 1, 2; RGAL 4; SATA 17
Riley, Tex
See Creasey, John
Rilke, Rainer Maria 1875-1926 .... **PC 2;
TCLC 1, 6, 19**
See also CA 104; 132; CANR 62, 99; CD-
WLB 2; DA3; DAM POET; DLB 81; EW
9; EWL 3; MTCW 1, 2; MTFW 2005;
PFS 19; RGWL 2, 3; TWA; WP

Rimbaud, (Jean Nicolas) Arthur
1854-1891 ... **NCLC 4, 35, 82; PC 3, 57;
WLC 5**
See also DA; DA3; DAB; DAC; DAM
MST, POET; DLB 217; EW 7; GFL 1789
to the Present; LMFS 2; RGWL 2, 3;
TWA; WP
Rinehart, Mary Roberts
1876-1958 .... **TCLC 52**
See also BPFB 3; CA 108; 166; RGAL 4;
RHW
Ringmaster, The
See Mencken, H(enry) L(ouis)
Ringwood, Gwen(dolyn Margaret) Pharis
1910-1984 .... **CLC 48**
See also CA 148; 112; DLB 88
Rio, Michel 1945(?)- .... **CLC 43**
See also CA 201
Rios, Alberto 1952- .... **PC 57**
See also AAYA 66; AMWS 4; CA 113;
CANR 34, 79, 137; CP 6, 7; DLB 122;
HW 2; MTFW 2005; PFS 11
Ritsos, Giannes
See Ritsos, Yannis
Ritsos, Yannis 1909-1990 .... **CLC 6, 13, 31**
See also CA 77-80; 133; CANR 39, 61; EW
12; EWL 3; MTCW 1; RGWL 2, 3
Ritter, Erika 1948(?)- .... **CLC 52**
See also CD 5, 6; CWD
Rivera, Jose Eustasio 1889-1928 ... **TCLC 35**
See also CA 162; EWL 3; HW 1, 2; LAW
Rivera, Tomas 1935-1984 .... **HLCS 2**
See also CA 49-52; CANR 32; DLB 82;
HW 1; LLW; RGAL 4; SSFS 15; TCWW
2; WLIT 1
Rivers, Conrad Kent 1933-1968 .... **CLC 1**
See also BW 1; CA 85-88; DLB 41
Rivers, Elfrida
See Bradley, Marion Zimmer
See also GLL 1
Riverside, John
See Heinlein, Robert A.
Rizal, Jose 1861-1896 .... **NCLC 27**
Roa Bastos, Augusto 1917-2005 ...... **CLC 45;
HLC 2**
See also CA 131; 238; CWW 2; DAM
MULT; DLB 113; EWL 3; HW 1; LAW;
RGSF 2; WLIT 1
Roa Bastos, Augusto Jose Antonio
See Roa Bastos, Augusto
Robbe-Grillet, Alain 1922- .... **CLC 1, 2, 4, 6,
8, 10, 14, 43, 128**
See also BPFB 3; CA 9-12R; CANR 33,
65, 115; CWW 2; DLB 83; EW 13; EWL
3; GFL 1789 to the Present; IDFW 3, 4;
MTCW 1, 2; MTFW 2005; RGWL 2, 3;
SSFS 15
Robbins, Harold 1916-1997 .... **CLC 5**
See also BPFB 3; CA 73-76; 162; CANR
26, 54, 112, 156; DA3; DAM NOV;
MTCW 1, 2
Robbins, Thomas Eugene 1936-
See Robbins, Tom
See also CA 81-84; CANR 29, 59, 95, 139;
CN 7; CPW; CSW; DA3; DAM NOV,
POP; MTCW 1, 2; MTFW 2005
Robbins, Tom .... **CLC 9, 32, 64**
See Robbins, Thomas Eugene
See also AAYA 32; AMWS 10; BEST 90:3;
BPFB 3; CN 3, 4, 5, 6, 7; DLBY 1980
Robbins, Trina 1938- .... **CLC 21**
See also AAYA 61; CA 128; CANR 152
Roberts, Charles G(eorge) D(ouglas)
1860-1943 .... **SSC 91; TCLC 8**
See also CA 105; 188; CLR 33; CWRI 5;
DLB 92; RGEL 2; RGSF 2; SATA 88;
SATA-Brief 29

Roberts, Elizabeth Madox
1886-1941 .... **TCLC 68**
See also CA 111; 166; CLR 100; CWRI 5;
DLB 9, 54, 102; RGAL 4; RHW; SATA
33; SATA-Brief 27; TCWW 2; WCH
Roberts, Kate 1891-1985 .... **CLC 15**
See also CA 107; 116; DLB 319
Roberts, Keith (John Kingston)
1935-2000 .... **CLC 14**
See also BRWS 10; CA 25-28R; CANR 46;
DLB 261; SFW 4
Roberts, Kenneth (Lewis)
1885-1957 .... **TCLC 23**
See also CA 109; 199; DLB 9; MAL 5;
RGAL 4; RHW
Roberts, Michele (Brigitte) 1949- .... **CLC 48,
178**
See also CA 115; CANR 58, 120; CN 6, 7;
DLB 231; FW
Robertson, Ellis
See Ellison, Harlan; Silverberg, Robert
Robertson, Thomas William
1829-1871 .... **NCLC 35**
See Robertson, Tom
See also DAM DRAM
Robertson, Tom
See Robertson, Thomas William
See also RGEL 2
Robeson, Kenneth
See Dent, Lester
Robinson, Edwin Arlington
1869-1935 .... **PC 1, 35; TCLC 5, 101**
See also AMW; CA 104; 133; CDALB
1865-1917; DA; DAC; DAM MST,
POET; DLB 54; EWL 3; EXPP; MAL 5;
MTCW 1, 2; MTFW 2005; PAB; PFS 4;
RGAL 4; WP
Robinson, Henry Crabb
1775-1867 .... **NCLC 15**
See also DLB 107
Robinson, Jill 1936- .... **CLC 10**
See also CA 102; CANR 120; INT CA-102
Robinson, Kim Stanley 1952- .... **CLC 34**
See also AAYA 26; CA 126; CANR 113,
139; CN 6, 7; MTFW 2005; SATA 109;
SCFW 2; SFW 4
Robinson, Lloyd
See Silverberg, Robert
Robinson, Marilynne 1944- ...... **CLC 25, 180**
See also AAYA 69; CA 116; CANR 80, 140;
CN 4, 5, 6, 7; DLB 206; MTFW 2005;
NFS 24
Robinson, Mary 1758-1800 .... **NCLC 142**
See also DLB 158; FW
Robinson, Smokey .... **CLC 21**
See Robinson, William, Jr.
Robinson, William, Jr. 1940-
See Robinson, Smokey
See also CA 116
Robison, Mary 1949- .... **CLC 42, 98**
See also CA 113; 116; CANR 87; CN 4, 5,
6, 7; DLB 130; INT CA-116; RGSF 2
Roches, Catherine des 1542-1587 ...... **LC 117**
See also DLB 327
Rochester
See Wilmot, John
See also RGEL 2
Rod, Edouard 1857-1910 .... **TCLC 52**
Roddenberry, Eugene Wesley 1921-1991
See Roddenberry, Gene
See also CA 110; 135; CANR 37; SATA 45;
SATA-Obit 69
Roddenberry, Gene .... **CLC 17**
See Roddenberry, Eugene Wesley
See also AAYA 5; SATA-Obit 69
Rodgers, Mary 1931- .... **CLC 12**
See also BYA 5; CA 49-52; CANR 8, 55,
90; CLR 20; CWRI 5; INT CANR-8;
JRDA; MAICYA 1, 2; SATA 8, 130

Rodgers, W(illiam) R(obert)
1909-1969 .... **CLC 7**
See also CA 85-88; DLB 20; RGEL 2
Rodman, Eric
See Silverberg, Robert
Rodman, Howard 1920(?)-1985 .... **CLC 65**
See also CA 118
Rodman, Maia
See Wojciechowska, Maia (Teresa)
Rodo, Jose Enrique 1871(?)-1917 .... **HLCS 2**
See also CA 178; EWL 3; HW 2; LAW
Rodolph, Utto
See Ouologuem, Yambo
Rodriguez, Claudio 1934-1999 .... **CLC 10**
See also CA 188; DLB 134
Rodriguez, Richard 1944- .... **CLC 155; HLC
2**
See also AMWS 14; CA 110; CANR 66,
116; DAM MULT; DLB 82, 256; HW 1,
2; LAIT 5; LLW; MTFW 2005; NCFS 3;
WLIT 1
Roelvaag, O(le) E(dvart) 1876-1931
See Rolvaag, O(le) E(dvart)
See also CA 117; 171
Roethke, Theodore (Huebner)
1908-1963 .... **CLC 1, 3, 8, 11, 19, 46,
101; PC 15**
See also AMW; CA 81-84; CABS 2;
CDALB 1941-1968; DA3; DAM POET;
DLB 5, 206; EWL 3; EXPP; MAL 5;
MTCW 1, 2; PAB; PFS 3; RGAL 4; WP
Rogers, Carl R(ansom)
1902-1987 .... **TCLC 125**
See also CA 1-4R; 121; CANR 1, 18;
MTCW 1
Rogers, Samuel 1763-1855 .... **NCLC 69**
See also DLB 93; RGEL 2
Rogers, Thomas Hunton 1927- .... **CLC 57**
See also CA 89-92; INT CA-89-92
Rogers, Will(iam Penn Adair)
1879-1935 .... **NNAL; TCLC 8, 71**
See also CA 105; 144; DA3; DAM MULT;
DLB 11; MTCW 2
Rogin, Gilbert 1929- .... **CLC 18**
See also CA 65-68; CANR 15
Rohan, Koda
See Koda Shigeyuki
Rohlfs, Anna Katharine Green
See Green, Anna Katharine
Rohmer, Eric .... **CLC 16**
See Scherer, Jean-Marie Maurice
Rohmer, Sax .... **TCLC 28**
See Ward, Arthur Henry Sarsfield
See also DLB 70; MSW; SUFW
Roiphe, Anne 1935- .... **CLC 3, 9**
See also CA 89-92; CANR 45, 73, 138;
DLBY 1980; INT CA-89-92
Roiphe, Anne Richardson
See Roiphe, Anne
Rojas, Fernando de 1475-1541 ... **HLCS 1, 2;
LC 23**
See also DLB 286; RGWL 2, 3
Rojas, Gonzalo 1917- .... **HLCS 2**
See also CA 178; HW 2; LAWS 1
Roland (de la Platiere), Marie-Jeanne
1754-1793 .... **LC 98**
See also DLB 314
**Rolfe, Frederick (William Serafino Austin
Lewis Mary)** 1860-1913 .... **TCLC 12**
See Al Siddik
See also CA 107; 210; DLB 34, 156; RGEL
2
Rolland, Romain 1866-1944 .... **TCLC 23**
See also CA 118; 197; DLB 65, 284; EWL
3; GFL 1789 to the Present; RGWL 2, 3
Rolle, Richard c. 1300-c. 1349 ...... **CMLC 21**
See also DLB 146; LMFS 1; RGEL 2

Rolvaag, O(le) E(dvart) .... **TCLC 17**
See Roelvaag, O(le) E(dvart)
See also DLB 9, 212; MAL 5; NFS 5;
RGAL 4
Romain Arnaud, Saint
See Aragon, Louis
Romains, Jules 1885-1972 .... **CLC 7**
See also CA 85-88; CANR 34; DLB 65,
321; EWL 3; GFL 1789 to the Present;
MTCW 1
Romero, Jose Ruben 1890-1952 .... **TCLC 14**
See also CA 114; 131; EWL 3; HW 1; LAW
Ronsard, Pierre de 1524-1585 . **LC 6, 54; PC
11**
See also DLB 327; EW 2; GFL Beginnings
to 1789; RGWL 2, 3; TWA
Rooke, Leon 1934- .... **CLC 25, 34**
See also CA 25-28R; CANR 23, 53; CCA
1; CPW; DAM POP
Roosevelt, Franklin Delano
1882-1945 .... **TCLC 93**
See also CA 116; 173; LAIT 3
Roosevelt, Theodore 1858-1919 ...... **TCLC 69**
See also CA 115; 170; DLB 47, 186, 275
Roper, William 1498-1578 .... **LC 10**
Roquelaure, A. N.
See Rice, Anne
Rosa, Joao Guimaraes 1908-1967 ... **CLC 23;
HLCS 1**
See Guimaraes Rosa, Joao
See also CA 89-92; DLB 113, 307; EWL 3;
WLIT 1
Rose, Wendy 1948- . **CLC 85; NNAL; PC 13**
See also CA 53-56; CANR 5, 51; CWP;
DAM MULT; DLB 175; PFS 13; RGAL
4; SATA 12
Rosen, R. D.
See Rosen, Richard (Dean)
Rosen, Richard (Dean) 1949- .... **CLC 39**
See also CA 77-80; CANR 62, 120; CMW
4; INT CANR-30
Rosenberg, Isaac 1890-1918 .... **TCLC 12**
See also BRW 6; CA 107; 188; DLB 20,
216; EWL 3; PAB; RGEL 2
Rosenblatt, Joe .... **CLC 15**
See Rosenblatt, Joseph
See also CP 3, 4, 5, 6, 7
Rosenblatt, Joseph 1933-
See Rosenblatt, Joe
See also CA 89-92; CP 1, 2; INT CA-89-92
Rosenfeld, Samuel
See Tzara, Tristan
Rosenstock, Sami
See Tzara, Tristan
Rosenstock, Samuel
See Tzara, Tristan
Rosenthal, M(acha) L(ouis)
1917-1996 .... **CLC 28**
See also CA 1-4R; 152; CAAS 6; CANR 4,
51; CP 1, 2, 3, 4, 5, 6; DLB 5; SATA 59
Ross, Barnaby
See Dannay, Frederic; Lee, Manfred B.
Ross, Bernard L.
See Follett, Ken
Ross, J. H.
See Lawrence, T(homas) E(dward)
Ross, John Hume
See Lawrence, T(homas) E(dward)
Ross, Martin 1862-1915
See Martin, Violet Florence
See also DLB 135; GLL 2; RGEL 2; RGSF
2
Ross, (James) Sinclair 1908-1996 ... **CLC 13;
SSC 24**
See also CA 73-76; CANR 81; CN 1, 2, 3,
4, 5, 6; DAC; DAM MST; DLB 88;
RGEL 2; RGSF 2; TCWW 1, 2

Schneider, Leonard Alfred 1925-1966
　　See Bruce, Lenny
　　See also CA 89-92
Schnitzler, Arthur 1862-1931 ..... **DC 17; SSC 15, 61; TCLC 4**
　　See also CA 104; CDWLB 2; DLB 81, 118; EW 8; EWL 3; RGSF 2; RGWL 2, 3
Schoenberg, Arnold Franz Walter
　　1874-1951 .... **TCLC 75**
　　See also CA 109; 188
Schonberg, Arnold
　　See Schoenberg, Arnold Franz Walter
Schopenhauer, Arthur 1788-1860 . **NCLC 51, 157**
　　See also DLB 90; EW 5
Schor, Sandra (M.) 1932(?)-1990 ..... **CLC 65**
　　See also CA 132
Schorer, Mark 1908-1977 .... **CLC 9**
　　See also CA 5-8R; 73-76; CANR 7; CN 1, 2; DLB 103
Schrader, Paul (Joseph) 1946- . **CLC 26, 212**
　　See also CA 37-40R; CANR 41; DLB 44
Schreber, Daniel 1842-1911 .... **TCLC 123**
Schreiner, Olive (Emilie Albertina)
　　1855-1920 .... **TCLC 9**
　　See also AFW; BRWS 2; CA 105; 154; DLB 18, 156, 190, 225; EWL 3; FW; RGEL 2; TWA; WLIT 2; WWE 1
Schulberg, Budd (Wilson) 1914- .. **CLC 7, 48**
　　See also BPFB 3; CA 25-28R; CANR 19, 87; CN 1, 2, 3, 4, 5, 6, 7; DLB 6, 26, 28; DLBY 1981, 2001; MAL 5
Schulman, Arnold
　　See Trumbo, Dalton
Schulz, Bruno 1892-1942 .. **SSC 13; TCLC 5, 51**
　　See also CA 115; 123; CANR 86; CDWLB 4; DLB 215; EWL 3; MTCW 2; MTFW 2005; RGSF 2; RGWL 2, 3
Schulz, Charles M. 1922-2000 .... **CLC 12**
　　See also AAYA 39; CA 9-12R; 187; CANR 6, 132; INT CANR-6; MTFW 2005; SATA 10; SATA-Obit 118
Schulz, Charles Monroe
　　See Schulz, Charles M.
Schumacher, E(rnst) F(riedrich)
　　1911-1977 .... **CLC 80**
　　See also CA 81-84; 73-76; CANR 34, 85
Schumann, Robert 1810-1856 ...... **NCLC 143**
Schuyler, George Samuel 1895-1977 . **HR 1:3**
　　See also BW 2; CA 81-84; 73-76; CANR 42; DLB 29, 51
Schuyler, James Marcus 1923-1991 .. **CLC 5, 23**
　　See also CA 101; 134; CP 1, 2, 3, 4, 5; DAM POET; DLB 5, 169; EWL 3; INT CA-101; MAL 5; WP
Schwartz, Delmore (David)
　　1913-1966 ... **CLC 2, 4, 10, 45, 87; PC 8**
　　See also AMWS 2; CA 17-18; 25-28R; CANR 35; CAP 2; DLB 28, 48; EWL 3; MAL 5; MTCW 1, 2; MTFW 2005; PAB; RGAL 4; TUS
Schwartz, Ernst
　　See Ozu, Yasujiro
Schwartz, John Burnham 1965- .... **CLC 59**
　　See also CA 132; CANR 116
Schwartz, Lynne Sharon 1939- .... **CLC 31**
　　See also CA 103; CANR 44, 89; DLB 218; MTCW 2; MTFW 2005
Schwartz, Muriel A.
　　See Eliot, T(homas) S(tearns)
Schwarz-Bart, Andre 1928-2006 .... **CLC 2, 4**
　　See also CA 89-92; CANR 109; DLB 299; RGHL
Schwarz-Bart, Simone 1938- . **BLCS; CLC 7**
　　See also BW 2; CA 97-100; CANR 117; EWL 3

Schwerner, Armand 1927-1999 .... **PC 42**
　　See also CA 9-12R; 179; CANR 50, 85; CP 2, 3, 4, 5, 6; DLB 165
Schwitters, Kurt (Hermann Edward Karl Julius) 1887-1948 .... **TCLC 95**
　　See also CA 158
Schwob, Marcel (Mayer Andre)
　　1867-1905 .... **TCLC 20**
　　See also CA 117; 168; DLB 123; GFL 1789 to the Present
Sciascia, Leonardo 1921-1989 .. **CLC 8, 9, 41**
　　See also CA 85-88; 130; CANR 35; DLB 177; EWL 3; MTCW 1; RGWL 2, 3
Scoppettone, Sandra 1936- .... **CLC 26**
　　See Early, Jack
　　See also AAYA 11, 65; BYA 8; CA 5-8R; CANR 41, 73, 157; GLL 1; MAICYA 2; MAICYAS 1; SATA 9, 92; WYA; YAW
Scorsese, Martin 1942- .... **CLC 20, 89, 207**
　　See also AAYA 38; CA 110; 114; CANR 46, 85
Scotland, Jay
　　See Jakes, John
Scott, Duncan Campbell
　　1862-1947 .... **TCLC 6**
　　See also CA 104; 153; DAC; DLB 92; RGEL 2
Scott, Evelyn 1893-1963 .... **CLC 43**
　　See also CA 104; 112; CANR 64; DLB 9, 48; RHW
Scott, F(rancis) R(eginald)
　　1899-1985 .... **CLC 22**
　　See also CA 101; 114; CANR 87; CP 1, 2, 3, 4; DLB 88; INT CA-101; RGEL 2
Scott, Frank
　　See Scott, F(rancis) R(eginald)
Scott, Joan .... **CLC 65**
Scott, Joanna 1960- .... **CLC 50**
　　See also CA 126; CANR 53, 92
Scott, Paul (Mark) 1920-1978 ...... **CLC 9, 60**
　　See also BRWS 1; CA 81-84; 77-80; CANR 33; CN 1, 2; DLB 14, 207, 326; EWL 3; MTCW 1; RGEL 2; RHW; WWE 1
Scott, Ridley 1937- .... **CLC 183**
　　See also AAYA 13, 43
Scott, Sarah 1723-1795 .... **LC 44**
　　See also DLB 39
Scott, Sir Walter 1771-1832 .... **NCLC 15, 69, 110; PC 13; SSC 32; WLC 5**
　　See also AAYA 22; BRW 4; BYA 2; CD-BLB 1789-1832; DA; DAB; DAC; DAM MST, NOV, POET; DLB 93, 107, 116, 144, 159; GL 3; HGG; LAIT 1; RGEL 2; RGSF 2; SSFS 10; SUFW 1; TEA; WLIT 3; YABC 2
Scribe, (Augustin) Eugene 1791-1861 . **DC 5; NCLC 16**
　　See also DAM DRAM; DLB 192; GFL 1789 to the Present; RGWL 2, 3
Scrum, R.
　　See Crumb, R.
Scudery, Georges de 1601-1667 .... **LC 75**
　　See also GFL Beginnings to 1789
Scudery, Madeleine de 1607-1701 .. **LC 2, 58**
　　See also DLB 268; GFL Beginnings to 1789
Scum
　　See Crumb, R.
Scumbag, Little Bobby
　　See Crumb, R.
Seabrook, John
　　See Hubbard, L. Ron
Seacole, Mary Jane Grant
　　1805-1881 .... **NCLC 147**
　　See also DLB 166
Sealy, I(rwin) Allan 1951- .... **CLC 55**
　　See also CA 136; CN 6, 7
Search, Alexander
　　See Pessoa, Fernando (Antonio Nogueira)

Sebald, W(infried) G(eorg)
　　1944-2001 .... **CLC 194**
　　See also BRWS 8; CA 159; 202; CANR 98; MTFW 2005; RGHL
Sebastian, Lee
　　See Silverberg, Robert
Sebastian Owl
　　See Thompson, Hunter S.
Sebestyen, Igen
　　See Sebestyen, Ouida
Sebestyen, Ouida 1924- .... **CLC 30**
　　See also AAYA 8; BYA 7; CA 107; CANR 40, 114; CLR 17; JRDA; MAICYA 1, 2; SAAS 10; SATA 39, 140; WYA; YAW
Sebold, Alice 1963(?)- .... **CLC 193**
　　See also AAYA 56; CA 203; MTFW 2005
Second Duke of Buckingham
　　See Villiers, George
Secundus, H. Scriblerus
　　See Fielding, Henry
Sedges, John
　　See Buck, Pearl S(ydenstricker)
Sedgwick, Catharine Maria
　　1789-1867 .... **NCLC 19, 98**
　　See also DLB 1, 74, 183, 239, 243, 254; FL 1:3; RGAL 4
Sedulius Scottus 9th cent. -c. 874 .. **CMLC 86**
Seelye, John (Douglas) 1931- .... **CLC 7**
　　See also CA 97-100; CANR 70; INT CA-97-100; TCWW 1, 2
Seferiades, Giorgos Stylianou 1900-1971
　　See Seferis, George
　　See also CA 5-8R; 33-36R; CANR 5, 36; MTCW 1
Seferis, George .... **CLC 5, 11; PC 66**
　　See Seferiades, Giorgos Stylianou
　　See also EW 12; EWL 3; RGWL 2, 3
Segal, Erich (Wolf) 1937- .... **CLC 3, 10**
　　See also BEST 89:1; BPFB 3; CA 25-28R; CANR 20, 36, 65, 113; CPW; DAM POP; DLBY 1986; INT CANR-20; MTCW 1
Seger, Bob 1945- .... **CLC 35**
Seghers, Anna .... **CLC 7**
　　See Radvanyi, Netty
　　See also CDWLB 2; DLB 69; EWL 3
Seidel, Frederick (Lewis) 1936- .... **CLC 18**
　　See also CA 13-16R; CANR 8, 99; CP 1, 2, 3, 4, 5, 6, 7; DLBY 1984
Seifert, Jaroslav 1901-1986 . **CLC 34, 44, 93; PC 47**
　　See also CA 127; CDWLB 4; DLB 215; EWL 3; MTCW 1, 2
Sei Shonagon c. 966-1017(?) .... **CMLC 6**
Sejour, Victor 1817-1874 .... **DC 10**
　　See also DLB 50
Sejour Marcou et Ferrand, Juan Victor
　　See Sejour, Victor
Selby, Hubert, Jr. 1928-2004 ..... **CLC 1, 2, 4, 8; SSC 20**
　　See also CA 13-16R; 226; CANR 33, 85; CN 1, 2, 3, 4, 5, 6, 7; DLB 2, 227; MAL 5
Selzer, Richard 1928- .... **CLC 74**
　　See also CA 65-68; CANR 14, 106
Sembene, Ousmane
　　See Ousmane, Sembene
　　See also AFW; EWL 3; WLIT 2
Senancour, Etienne Pivert de
　　1770-1846 .... **NCLC 16**
　　See also DLB 119; GFL 1789 to the Present
Sender, Ramon (Jose) 1902-1982 ...... **CLC 8; HLC 2; TCLC 136**
　　See also CA 5-8R; 105; CANR 8; DAM MULT; DLB 322; EWL 3; HW 1; MTCW 1; RGWL 2, 3
Seneca, Lucius Annaeus c. 4B.C.-c. 65 .... **CMLC 6; DC 5**
　　See also AW 2; CDWLB 1; DAM DRAM; DLB 211; RGWL 2, 3; TWA; WLIT 8

Shepard, Sam 1943- .... **CLC 4, 6, 17, 34, 41, 44, 169; DC 5**
  See also AAYA 1, 58; AMWS 3; CA 69-72; CABS 3; CAD; CANR 22, 120, 140; CD 5, 6; DA3; DAM DRAM; DFS 3, 6, 7, 14; DLB 7, 212; EWL 3; IDFW 3, 4; MAL 5; MTCW 1, 2; MTFW 2005; RGAL 4

Shepherd, Jean (Parker)
  1921-1999 .... **TCLC 177**
  See also AAYA 69; AITN 2; CA 77-80; 187

Shepherd, Michael
  See Ludlum, Robert

Sherburne, Zoa (Lillian Morin)
  1912-1995 .... **CLC 30**
  See also AAYA 13; CA 1-4R; 176; CANR 3, 37; MAICYA 1, 2; SAAS 18; SATA 3; YAW

Sheridan, Frances 1724-1766 .... **LC 7**
  See also DLB 39, 84

Sheridan, Richard Brinsley
  1751-1816 . **DC 1; NCLC 5, 91; WLC 5**
  See also BRW 3; CDBLB 1660-1789; DA; DAB; DAC; DAM DRAM, MST; DFS 15; DLB 89; WLIT 3

Sherman, Jonathan Marc 1968- .... **CLC 55**
  See also CA 230

Sherman, Martin 1941(?)- .... **CLC 19**
  See also CA 116; 123; CAD; CANR 86; CD 5, 6; DFS 20; DLB 228; GLL 1; IDTP; RGHL

Sherwin, Judith Johnson
  See Johnson, Judith (Emlyn)
  See also CANR 85; CP 2, 3, 4, 5; CWP

Sherwood, Frances 1940- .... **CLC 81**
  See also CA 146, 220; CAAE 220

Sherwood, Robert E(mmet)
  1896-1955 .... **TCLC 3**
  See also CA 104; 153; CANR 86; DAM DRAM; DFS 11, 15, 17; DLB 7, 26, 249; IDFW 3, 4; MAL 5; RGAL 4

Shestov, Lev 1866-1938 .... **TCLC 56**

Shevchenko, Taras 1814-1861 .... **NCLC 54**

Shiel, M(atthew) P(hipps)
  1865-1947 .... **TCLC 8**
  See Holmes, Gordon
  See also CA 106; 160; DLB 153; HGG; MTCW 2; MTFW 2005; SCFW 1, 2; SFW 4; SUFW

Shields, Carol 1935-2003 .. **CLC 91, 113, 193**
  See also AMWS 7; CA 81-84; 218; CANR 51, 74, 98, 133; CCA 1; CN 6, 7; CPW; DA3; DAC; MTCW 2; MTFW 2005; NFS 23

Shields, David 1956- .... **CLC 97**
  See also CA 124; CANR 48, 99, 112, 157

Shiga, Naoya 1883-1971 .... **CLC 33; SSC 23; TCLC 172**
  See Shiga Naoya
  See also CA 101; 33-36R; MJW; RGWL 3

Shiga Naoya
  See Shiga, Naoya
  See also DLB 180; EWL 3; RGWL 3

Shilts, Randy 1951-1994 .... **CLC 85**
  See also AAYA 19; CA 115; 127; 144; CANR 45; DA3; GLL 1; INT CA-127; MTCW 2; MTFW 2005

Shimazaki, Haruki 1872-1943
  See Shimazaki Toson
  See also CA 105; 134; CANR 84; RGWL 3

Shimazaki Toson .... **TCLC 5**
  See Shimazaki, Haruki
  See also DLB 180; EWL 3

Shirley, James 1596-1666 .... **DC 25; LC 96**
  See also DLB 58; RGEL 2

Sholokhov, Mikhail (Aleksandrovich)
  1905-1984 .... **CLC 7, 15**
  See also CA 101; 112; DLB 272; EWL 3; MTCW 1, 2; MTFW 2005; RGWL 2, 3; SATA-Obit 36

Shone, Patric
  See Hanley, James

Showalter, Elaine 1941- .... **CLC 169**
  See also CA 57-60; CANR 58, 106; DLB 67; FW; GLL 2

Shreve, Susan
  See Shreve, Susan Richards

Shreve, Susan Richards 1939- .... **CLC 23**
  See also CA 49-52; CAAS 5; CANR 5, 38, 69, 100; MAICYA 1, 2; SATA 46, 95, 152; SATA-Brief 41

Shue, Larry 1946-1985 .... **CLC 52**
  See also CA 145; 117; DAM DRAM; DFS 7

Shu-Jen, Chou 1881-1936
  See Lu Hsun
  See also CA 104

Shulman, Alix Kates 1932- .... **CLC 2, 10**
  See also CA 29-32R; CANR 43; FW; SATA 7

Shuster, Joe 1914-1992 .... **CLC 21**
  See also AAYA 50

Shute, Nevil .... **CLC 30**
  See Norway, Nevil Shute
  See also BPFB 3; DLB 255; NFS 9; RHW; SFW 4

Shuttle, Penelope (Diane) 1947- .... **CLC 7**
  See also CA 93-96; CANR 39, 84, 92, 108; CP 3, 4, 5, 6, 7; CWP; DLB 14, 40

Shvarts, Elena 1948- .... **PC 50**
  See also CA 147

Sidhwa, Bapsi 1939-
  See Sidhwa, Bapsy (N.)
  See also CN 6, 7; DLB 323

Sidhwa, Bapsy (N.) 1938- .... **CLC 168**
  See Sidhwa, Bapsi
  See also CA 108; CANR 25, 57; FW

Sidney, Mary 1561-1621 .... **LC 19, 39**
  See Sidney Herbert, Mary

Sidney, Sir Philip 1554-1586 .... **LC 19, 39, 131; PC 32**
  See also BRW 1; BRWR 2; CDBLB Before 1660; DA; DA3; DAB; DAC; DAM MST, POET; DLB 167; EXPP; PAB; RGEL 2; TEA; WP

Sidney Herbert, Mary
  See Sidney, Mary
  See also DLB 167

Siegel, Jerome 1914-1996 .... **CLC 21**
  See Siegel, Jerry
  See also CA 116; 169; 151

Siegel, Jerry
  See Siegel, Jerome
  See also AAYA 50

Sienkiewicz, Henryk (Adam Alexander Pius)
  1846-1916 .... **TCLC 3**
  See also CA 104; 134; CANR 84; EWL 3; RGSF 2; RGWL 2, 3

Sierra, Gregorio Martinez
  See Martinez Sierra, Gregorio

Sierra, Maria de la O'LeJarraga Martinez
  See Martinez Sierra, Maria

Sigal, Clancy 1926- .... **CLC 7**
  See also CA 1-4R; CANR 85; CN 1, 2, 3, 4, 5, 6, 7

Siger of Brabant 1240(?)-1284(?) . **CMLC 69**
  See also DLB 115

Sigourney, Lydia H.
  See Sigourney, Lydia Howard (Huntley)
  See also DLB 73, 183

Sigourney, Lydia Howard (Huntley)
  1791-1865 .... **NCLC 21, 87**
  See Sigourney, Lydia H.; Sigourney, Lydia Huntley
  See also DLB 1

Sigourney, Lydia Huntley
  See Sigourney, Lydia Howard (Huntley)
  See also DLB 42, 239, 243

Siguenza y Gongora, Carlos de
  1645-1700 .... **HLCS 2; LC 8**
  See also LAW

Sigurjonsson, Johann
  See Sigurjonsson, Johann

Sigurjonsson, Johann 1880-1919 ... **TCLC 27**
  See also CA 170; DLB 293; EWL 3

Sikelianos, Angelos 1884-1951 .... **PC 29; TCLC 39**
  See also EWL 3; RGWL 2, 3

Silkin, Jon 1930-1997 .... **CLC 2, 6, 43**
  See also CA 5-8R; CAAS 5; CANR 89; CP 1, 2, 3, 4, 5, 6; DLB 27

Silko, Leslie 1948- ...... **CLC 23, 74, 114, 211; NNAL; SSC 37, 66; WLCS**
  See also AAYA 14; AMWS 4; ANW; BYA 12; CA 115; 122; CANR 45, 65, 118; CN 4, 5, 6, 7; CP 4, 5, 6, 7; CPW 1; CWP; DA; DA3; DAC; DAM MST, MULT, POP; DLB 143, 175, 256, 275; EWL 3; EXPP; EXPS; LAIT 4; MAL 5; MTCW 2; MTFW 2005; NFS 4; PFS 9, 16; RGAL 4; RGSF 2; SSFS 4, 8, 10, 11; TCWW 1, 2

Sillanpaa, Frans Eemil 1888-1964 ... **CLC 19**
  See also CA 129; 93-96; EWL 3; MTCW 1

Sillitoe, Alan 1928- .. **CLC 1, 3, 6, 10, 19, 57, 148**
  See also AITN 1; BRWS 5; CA 9-12R, 191; CAAE 191; CAAS 2; CANR 8, 26, 55, 139; CDBLB 1960 to Present; CN 1, 2, 3, 4, 5, 6; CP 1, 2, 3, 4, 5; DLB 14, 139; EWL 3; MTCW 1, 2; MTFW 2005; RGEL 2; RGSF 2; SATA 61

Silone, Ignazio 1900-1978 .... **CLC 4**
  See also CA 25-28; 81-84; CANR 34; CAP 2; DLB 264; EW 12; EWL 3; MTCW 1; RGSF 2; RGWL 2, 3

Silone, Ignazione
  See Silone, Ignazio

Silver, Joan Micklin 1935- .... **CLC 20**
  See also CA 114; 121; INT CA-121

Silver, Nicholas
  See Faust, Frederick (Schiller)

Silverberg, Robert 1935- .... **CLC 7, 140**
  See also AAYA 24; BPFB 3; BYA 7, 9; CA 1-4R; CAAE 186; CAAS 3; CANR 1, 20, 36, 85, 140; CLR 59; CN 6, 7; CPW; DAM POP; DLB 8; INT CANR-20; MAICYA 1, 2; MTCW 1, 2; MTFW 2005; SATA 13, 91; SATA-Essay 104; SCFW 1, 2; SFW 4; SUFW 2

Silverstein, Alvin 1933- .... **CLC 17**
  See also CA 49-52; CANR 2; CLR 25; JRDA; MAICYA 1, 2; SATA 8, 69, 124

Silverstein, Shel 1932-1999 .... **PC 49**
  See also AAYA 40; BW 3; CA 107; 179; CANR 47, 74, 81; CLR 5, 96; CWRI 5; JRDA; MAICYA 1, 2; MTCW 2; MTFW 2005; SATA 33, 92; SATA-Brief 27; SATA-Obit 116

Silverstein, Virginia B(arbara Opshelor)
  1937- .... **CLC 17**
  See also CA 49-52; CANR 2; CLR 25; JRDA; MAICYA 1, 2; SATA 8, 69, 124

Sim, Georges
  See Simenon, Georges (Jacques Christian)

Simak, Clifford D(onald) 1904-1988 . **CLC 1, 55**
  See also CA 1-4R; 125; CANR 1, 35; DLB 8; MTCW 1; SATA-Obit 56; SCFW 1, 2; SFW 4

Stegner, Wallace (Earle) 1909-1993 .. **CLC 9, 49, 81; SSC 27**
See also AITN 1; AMWS 4; ANW; BEST 90:3; BPFB 3; CA 1-4R; 141; CAAS 9; CANR 1, 21, 46; CN 1, 2, 3, 4, 5; DAM NOV; DLB 9, 206, 275; DLBY 1993; EWL 3; MAL 5; MTCW 1, 2; MTFW 2005; RGAL 4; TCWW 1, 2; TUS

Stein, Gertrude 1874-1946 .... **DC 19; PC 18; SSC 42; TCLC 1, 6, 28, 48; WLC 5**
See also AAYA 64; AMW; AMWC 2; CA 104; 132; CANR 108; CDALB 1917-1929; DA; DA3; DAB; DAC; DAM MST, NOV; DLB 4, 54, 86, 228; DLBD 15; EWL 3; EXPS; FL 1:6; GLL 1; MAL 5; MBL; MTCW 1, 2; MTFW 2005; NCFS 4; RGAL 4; RGSF 2; SSFS 5; TUS; WP

Steinbeck, John (Ernst) 1902-1968 ... **CLC 1, 5, 9, 13, 21, 34, 45, 75, 124; SSC 11, 37, 77; TCLC 135; WLC 5**
See also AAYA 12; AMW; BPFB 3; BYA 2, 3, 13; CA 1-4R; CANR 1, 35; CDALB 1929-1941; DA; DA3; DAB; DAC; DAM DRAM, MST, NOV; DLB 7, 9, 212, 275, 309; DLBD 2; EWL 3; EXPS; LAIT 3; MAL 5; MTCW 1, 2; MTFW 2005; NFS 1, 5, 7, 17, 19; RGAL 4; RGSF 2; RHW; SATA 9; SSFS 3, 6, 22; TCWW 1, 2; TUS; WYA; YAW

Steinem, Gloria 1934- .... **CLC 63**
See also CA 53-56; CANR 28, 51, 139; DLB 246; FL 1:1; FW; MTCW 1, 2; MTFW 2005

Steiner, George 1929- .... **CLC 24, 221**
See also CA 73-76; CANR 31, 67, 108; DAM NOV; DLB 67, 299; EWL 3; MTCW 1, 2; MTFW 2005; RGHL; SATA 62

Steiner, K. Leslie
See Delany, Samuel R., Jr.

Steiner, Rudolf 1861-1925 .... **TCLC 13**
See also CA 107

Stendhal 1783-1842 .. **NCLC 23, 46; SSC 27; WLC 5**
See also DA; DA3; DAB; DAC; DAM MST, NOV; DLB 119; EW 5; GFL 1789 to the Present; RGWL 2, 3; TWA

Stephen, Adeline Virginia
See Woolf, (Adeline) Virginia

Stephen, Sir Leslie 1832-1904 .... **TCLC 23**
See also BRW 5; CA 123; DLB 57, 144, 190

Stephen, Sir Leslie
See Stephen, Sir Leslie

Stephen, Virginia
See Woolf, (Adeline) Virginia

Stephens, James 1882(?)-1950 .... **SSC 50; TCLC 4**
See also CA 104; 192; DLB 19, 153, 162; EWL 3; FANT; RGEL 2; SUFW

Stephens, Reed
See Donaldson, Stephen R(eeder)

Steptoe, Lydia
See Barnes, Djuna
See also GLL 1

Sterchi, Beat 1949- .... **CLC 65**
See also CA 203

Sterling, Brett
See Bradbury, Ray; Hamilton, Edmond

Sterling, Bruce 1954- .... **CLC 72**
See also CA 119; CANR 44, 135; CN 7; MTFW 2005; SCFW 2; SFW 4

Sterling, George 1869-1926 .... **TCLC 20**
See also CA 117; 165; DLB 54

Stern, Gerald 1925- .... **CLC 40, 100**
See also AMWS 9; CA 81-84; CANR 28, 94; CP 3, 4, 5, 6, 7; DLB 105; RGAL 4

Stern, Richard (Gustave) 1928- ... **CLC 4, 39**
See also CA 1-4R; CANR 1, 25, 52, 120; CN 1, 2, 3, 4, 5, 6, 7; DLB 218; DLBY 1987; INT CANR-25

Sternberg, Josef von 1894-1969 .... **CLC 20**
See also CA 81-84

Sterne, Laurence 1713-1768 .... **LC 2, 48; WLC 5**
See also BRW 3; BRWC 1; CDBLB 1660-1789; DA; DAB; DAC; DAM MST, NOV; DLB 39; RGEL 2; TEA

Sternheim, (William Adolf) Carl 1878-1942 .... **TCLC 8**
See also CA 105; 193; DLB 56, 118; EWL 3; IDTP; RGWL 2, 3

Stevens, Margaret Dean
See Aldrich, Bess Streeter

Stevens, Mark 1951- .... **CLC 34**
See also CA 122

Stevens, Wallace 1879-1955 . **PC 6; TCLC 3, 12, 45; WLC 5**
See also AMW; AMWR 1; CA 104; 124; CDALB 1929-1941; DA; DA3; DAB; DAC; DAM MST, POET; DLB 54; EWL 3; EXPP; MAL 5; MTCW 1, 2; PAB; PFS 13, 16; RGAL 4; TUS; WP

Stevenson, Anne (Katharine) 1933- .. **CLC 7, 33**
See also BRWS 6; CA 17-20R; CAAS 9; CANR 9, 33, 123; CP 3, 4, 5, 6, 7; CWP; DLB 40; MTCW 1; RHW

Stevenson, Robert Louis (Balfour) 1850-1894 ...... **NCLC 5, 14, 63; SSC 11, 51; WLC 5**
See also AAYA 24; BPFB 3; BRW 5; BRWC 1; BRWR 1; BYA 1, 2, 4, 13; CDBLB 1890-1914; CLR 10, 11, 107; DA; DA3; DAB; DAC; DAM MST, NOV; DLB 18, 57, 141, 156, 174; DLBD 13; GL 3; HGG; JRDA; LAIT 1, 3; MAICYA 1, 2; NFS 11, 20; RGEL 2; RGSF 2; SATA 100; SUFW; TEA; WCH; WLIT 4; WYA; YABC 2; YAW

Stewart, J(ohn) I(nnes) M(ackintosh) 1906-1994 .... **CLC 7, 14, 32**
See Innes, Michael
See also CA 85-88; 147; CAAS 3; CANR 47; CMW 4; CN 1, 2, 3, 4, 5; MTCW 1, 2

Stewart, Mary (Florence Elinor) 1916- .... **CLC 7, 35, 117**
See also AAYA 29; BPFB 3; CA 1-4R; CANR 1, 59, 130; CMW 4; CPW; DAB; FANT; RHW; SATA 12; YAW

Stewart, Mary Rainbow
See Stewart, Mary (Florence Elinor)

Stifle, June
See Campbell, Maria

Stifter, Adalbert 1805-1868 .. **NCLC 41; SSC 28**
See also CDWLB 2; DLB 133; RGSF 2; RGWL 2, 3

Still, James 1906-2001 .... **CLC 49**
See also CA 65-68; 195; CAAS 17; CANR 10, 26; CSW; DLB 9; DLBY 01; SATA 29; SATA-Obit 127

Sting 1951-
See Sumner, Gordon Matthew
See also CA 167

Stirling, Arthur
See Sinclair, Upton

Stitt, Milan 1941- .... **CLC 29**
See also CA 69-72

Stockton, Francis Richard 1834-1902
See Stockton, Frank R.
See also AAYA 68; CA 108; 137; MAICYA 1, 2; SATA 44; SFW 4

Stockton, Frank R. .... **TCLC 47**
See Stockton, Francis Richard
See also BYA 4, 13; DLB 42, 74; DLBD 13; EXPS; SATA-Brief 32; SSFS 3; SUFW; WCH

Stoddard, Charles
See Kuttner, Henry

Stoker, Abraham 1847-1912
See Stoker, Bram
See also CA 105; 150; DA; DA3; DAC; DAM MST, NOV; HGG; MTFW 2005; SATA 29

Stoker, Bram . **SSC 62; TCLC 8, 144; WLC 6**
See Stoker, Abraham
See also AAYA 23; BPFB 3; BRWS 3; BYA 5; CDBLB 1890-1914; DAB; DLB 304; GL 3; LATS 1:1; NFS 18; RGEL 2; SUFW; TEA; WLIT 4

Stolz, Mary (Slattery) 1920- .... **CLC 12**
See also AAYA 8; AITN 1; CA 5-8R; CANR 13, 41, 112; JRDA; MAICYA 1, 2; SAAS 3; SATA 10, 71, 133; YAW

Stone, Irving 1903-1989 .... **CLC 7**
See also AITN 1; BPFB 3; CA 1-4R; 129; CAAS 3; CANR 1, 23; CN 1, 2, 3, 4; CPW; DA3; DAM POP; INT CANR-23; MTCW 1, 2; MTFW 2005; RHW; SATA 3; SATA-Obit 64

Stone, Oliver 1946- .... **CLC 73**
See also AAYA 15, 64; CA 110; CANR 55, 125

Stone, Oliver William
See Stone, Oliver

Stone, Robert 1937- .... **CLC 5, 23, 42, 175**
See also AMWS 5; BPFB 3; CA 85-88; CANR 23, 66, 95; CN 4, 5, 6, 7; DLB 152; EWL 3; INT CANR-23; MAL 5; MTCW 1; MTFW 2005

Stone, Ruth 1915- .... **PC 53**
See also CA 45-48; CANR 2, 91; CP 5, 6, 7; CSW; DLB 105; PFS 19

Stone, Zachary
See Follett, Ken

Stoppard, Tom 1937- ... **CLC 1, 3, 4, 5, 8, 15, 29, 34, 63, 91; DC 6; WLC 6**
See also AAYA 63; BRWC 1; BRWR 2; BRWS 1; CA 81-84; CANR 39, 67, 125; CBD; CD 5, 6; CDBLB 1960 to Present; DA; DA3; DAB; DAC; DAM DRAM, MST; DFS 2, 5, 8, 11, 13, 16; DLB 13, 233; DLBY 1985; EWL 3; LATS 1:2; MTCW 1, 2; MTFW 2005; RGEL 2; TEA; WLIT 4

Storey, David (Malcolm) 1933- . **CLC 2, 4, 5, 8**
See also BRWS 1; CA 81-84; CANR 36; CBD; CD 5, 6; CN 1, 2, 3, 4, 5, 6; DAM DRAM; DLB 13, 14, 207, 245, 326; EWL 3; MTCW 1; RGEL 2

Storm, Hyemeyohsts 1935- ... **CLC 3; NNAL**
See also CA 81-84; CANR 45; DAM MULT

Storm, (Hans) Theodor (Woldsen) 1817-1888 .... **NCLC 1; SSC 27**
See also CDWLB 2; DLB 129; EW; RGSF 2; RGWL 2, 3

Storni, Alfonsina 1892-1938 . **HLC 2; PC 33; TCLC 5**
See also CA 104; 131; DAM MULT; DLB 283; HW 1; LAW

Stoughton, William 1631-1701 .... **LC 38**
See also DLB 24

Stout, Rex (Todhunter) 1886-1975 ..... **CLC 3**
See also AITN 2; BPFB 3; CA 61-64; CANR 71; CMW 4; CN 2; DLB 306; MSW; RGAL 4

Stow, (Julian) Randolph 1935- ... **CLC 23, 48**
See also CA 13-16R; CANR 33; CN 1, 2, 3, 4, 5, 6, 7; CP 1, 2, 3, 4; DLB 260; MTCW 1; RGEL 2

Swift, Graham 1949- .... **CLC 41, 88**
See also BRWC 2; BRWS 5; CA 117; 122; CANR 46, 71, 128; CN 4, 5, 6, 7; DLB 194, 326; MTCW 2; MTFW 2005; NFS 18; RGSF 2

Swift, Jonathan 1667-1745 ..... **LC 1, 42, 101; PC 9; WLC 6**
See also AAYA 41; BRW 3; BRWC 1; BRWR 1; BYA 5, 14; CDBLB 1660-1789; CLR 53; DA; DA3; DAB; DAC; DAM MST, NOV, POET; DLB 39, 95, 101; EXPN; LAIT 1; NFS 6; RGEL 2; SATA 19; TEA; WCH; WLIT 3

Swinburne, Algernon Charles
1837-1909 ... **PC 24; TCLC 8, 36; WLC 6**
See also BRW 5; CA 105; 140; CDBLB 1832-1890; DA; DA3; DAB; DAC; DAM MST, POET; DLB 35, 57; PAB; RGEL 2; TEA

Swinfen, Ann .... **CLC 34**
See also CA 202

Swinnerton, Frank (Arthur)
1884-1982 .... **CLC 31**
See also CA 202; 108; CN 1, 2, 3; DLB 34

Swinnerton, Frank Arthur
1884-1982 .... **CLC 31**
See also CA 108; DLB 34

Swithen, John
See King, Stephen

Sylvia
See Ashton-Warner, Sylvia (Constance)

Symmes, Robert Edward
See Duncan, Robert

Symonds, John Addington
1840-1893 .... **NCLC 34**
See also DLB 57, 144

Symons, Arthur 1865-1945 .... **TCLC 11**
See also CA 107; 189; DLB 19, 57, 149; RGEL 2

Symons, Julian (Gustave)
1912-1994 .... **CLC 2, 14, 32**
See also CA 49-52; 147; CAAS 3; CANR 3, 33, 59; CMW 4; CN 1, 2, 3, 4, 5; CP 1, 3, 4; DLB 87, 155; DLBY 1992; MSW; MTCW 1

Synge, (Edmund) J(ohn) M(illington)
1871-1909 .... **DC 2; TCLC 6, 37**
See also BRW 6; BRWR 1; CA 104; 141; CDBLB 1890-1914; DAM DRAM; DFS 18; DLB 10, 19; EWL 3; RGEL 2; TEA; WLIT 4

Syruc, J.
See Milosz, Czeslaw

Szirtes, George 1948- .... **CLC 46; PC 51**
See also CA 109; CANR 27, 61, 117; CP 4, 5, 6, 7

Szymborska, Wislawa 1923- ... **CLC 99, 190; PC 44**
See also CA 154; CANR 91, 133; CDWLB 4; CWP; CWW 2; DA3; DLB 232; DLBY 1996; EWL 3; MTCW 2; MTFW 2005; PFS 15; RGHL; RGWL 3

T. O., Nik
See Annensky, Innokenty (Fyodorovich)

Tabori, George 1914- .... **CLC 19**
See also CA 49-52; CANR 4, 69; CBD; CD 5, 6; DLB 245; RGHL

Tacitus c. 55-c. 117 .... **CMLC 56**
See also AW 2; CDWLB 1; DLB 211; RGWL 2, 3; WLIT 8

Tagore, Rabindranath 1861-1941 .... **PC 8; SSC 48; TCLC 3, 53**
See also CA 104; 120; DA3; DAM DRAM, POET; DLB 323; EWL 3; MTCW 1, 2; MTFW 2005; PFS 18; RGEL 2; RGSF 2; RGWL 2, 3; TWA

Taine, Hippolyte Adolphe
1828-1893 .... **NCLC 15**
See also EW 7; GFL 1789 to the Present

Talayesva, Don C. 1890-(?) .... **NNAL**

Talese, Gay 1932- .... **CLC 37**
See also AITN 1; CA 1-4R; CANR 9, 58, 137; DLB 185; INT CANR-9; MTCW 1, 2; MTFW 2005

Tallent, Elizabeth 1954- .... **CLC 45**
See also CA 117; CANR 72; DLB 130

Tallmountain, Mary 1918-1997 .... **NNAL**
See also CA 146; 161; DLB 193

Tally, Ted 1952- .... **CLC 42**
See also CA 120; 124; CAD; CANR 125; CD 5, 6; INT CA-124

Talvik, Heiti 1904-1947 .... **TCLC 87**
See also EWL 3

Tamayo y Baus, Manuel
1829-1898 .... **NCLC 1**

Tammsaare, A(nton) H(ansen)
1878-1940 .... **TCLC 27**
See also CA 164; CDWLB 4; DLB 220; EWL 3

Tam'si, Tchicaya U
See Tchicaya, Gerald Felix

Tan, Amy 1952- ...... **AAL; CLC 59, 120, 151**
See also AAYA 9, 48; AMWS 10; BEST 89:3; BPFB 3; CA 136; CANR 54, 105, 132; CDALBS; CN 6, 7; CPW 1; DA3; DAM MULT, NOV, POP; DLB 173, 312; EXPN; FL 1:6; FW; LAIT 3, 5; MAL 5; MTCW 2; MTFW 2005; NFS 1, 13, 16; RGAL 4; SATA 75; SSFS 9; YAW

Tandem, Carl Felix
See Spitteler, Carl

Tandem, Felix
See Spitteler, Carl

Tanizaki, Jun'ichiro 1886-1965 ... **CLC 8, 14, 28; SSC 21**
See Tanizaki Jun'ichiro
See also CA 93-96; 25-28R; MJW; MTCW 2; MTFW 2005; RGSF 2; RGWL 2

Tanizaki Jun'ichiro
See Tanizaki, Jun'ichiro
See also DLB 180; EWL 3

Tannen, Deborah 1945- .... **CLC 206**
See also CA 118; CANR 95

Tannen, Deborah Frances
See Tannen, Deborah

Tanner, William
See Amis, Kingsley

Tante, Dilly
See Kunitz, Stanley

Tao Lao
See Storni, Alfonsina

Tapahonso, Luci 1953- .... **NNAL; PC 65**
See also CA 145; CANR 72, 127; DLB 175

Tarantino, Quentin (Jerome)
1963- .... **CLC 125, 230**
See also AAYA 58; CA 171; CANR 125

Tarassoff, Lev
See Troyat, Henri

Tarbell, Ida M(inerva) 1857-1944 . **TCLC 40**
See also CA 122; 181; DLB 47

Tarkington, (Newton) Booth
1869-1946 .... **TCLC 9**
See also BPFB 3; BYA 3; CA 110; 143; CWRI 5; DLB 9, 102; MAL 5; MTCW 2; RGAL 4; SATA 17

Tarkovskii, Andrei Arsen'evich
See Tarkovsky, Andrei (Arsenyevich)

Tarkovsky, Andrei (Arsenyevich)
1932-1986 .... **CLC 75**
See also CA 127

Tartt, Donna 1964(?)- .... **CLC 76**
See also AAYA 56; CA 142; CANR 135; MTFW 2005

Tasso, Torquato 1544-1595 .... **LC 5, 94**
See also EFS 2; EW 2; RGWL 2, 3; WLIT 7

Tate, (John Orley) Allen 1899-1979 .. **CLC 2, 4, 6, 9, 11, 14, 24; PC 50**
See also AMW; CA 5-8R; 85-88; CANR 32, 108; CN 1, 2; CP 1, 2; DLB 4, 45, 63; DLBD 17; EWL 3; MAL 5; MTCW 1, 2; MTFW 2005; RGAL 4; RHW

Tate, Ellalice
See Hibbert, Eleanor Alice Burford

Tate, James (Vincent) 1943- ..... **CLC 2, 6, 25**
See also CA 21-24R; CANR 29, 57, 114; CP 1, 2, 3, 4, 5, 6, 7; DLB 5, 169; EWL 3; PFS 10, 15; RGAL 4; WP

Tate, Nahum 1652(?)-1715 .... **LC 109**
See also DLB 80; RGEL 2

Tauler, Johannes c. 1300-1361 ...... **CMLC 37**
See also DLB 179; LMFS 1

Tavel, Ronald 1940- .... **CLC 6**
See also CA 21-24R; CAD; CANR 33; CD 5, 6

Taviani, Paolo 1931- .... **CLC 70**
See also CA 153

Taylor, Bayard 1825-1878 .... **NCLC 89**
See also DLB 3, 189, 250, 254; RGAL 4

Taylor, C(ecil) P(hilip) 1929-1981 ... **CLC 27**
See also CA 25-28R; 105; CANR 47; CBD

Taylor, Edward 1642(?)-1729 . **LC 11; PC 63**
See also AMW; DA; DAB; DAC; DAM MST, POET; DLB 24; EXPP; RGAL 4; TUS

Taylor, Eleanor Ross 1920- .... **CLC 5**
See also CA 81-84; CANR 70

Taylor, Elizabeth 1912-1975 ..... **CLC 2, 4, 29**
See also CA 13-16R; CANR 9, 70; CN 1, 2; DLB 139; MTCW 1; RGEL 2; SATA 13

Taylor, Frederick Winslow
1856-1915 .... **TCLC 76**
See also CA 188

Taylor, Henry (Splawn) 1942- .... **CLC 44**
See also CA 33-36R; CAAS 7; CANR 31; CP 6, 7; DLB 5; PFS 10

Taylor, Kamala 1924-2004
See Markandaya, Kamala
See also CA 77-80; 227; MTFW 2005; NFS 13

Taylor, Mildred D. 1943- .... **CLC 21**
See also AAYA 10, 47; BW 1; BYA 3, 8; CA 85-88; CANR 25, 115, 136; CLR 9, 59, 90; CSW; DLB 52; JRDA; LAIT 3; MAICYA 1, 2; MTFW 2005; SAAS 5; SATA 135; WYA; YAW

Taylor, Peter (Hillsman) 1917-1994 .. **CLC 1, 4, 18, 37, 44, 50, 71; SSC 10, 84**
See also AMWS 5; BPFB 3; CA 13-16R; 147; CANR 9, 50; CN 1, 2, 3, 4, 5; CSW; DLB 218, 278; DLBY 1981, 1994; EWL 3; EXPS; INT CANR-9; MAL 5; MTCW 1, 2; MTFW 2005; RGSF 2; SSFS 9; TUS

Taylor, Robert Lewis 1912-1998 .... **CLC 14**
See also CA 1-4R; 170; CANR 3, 64; CN 1, 2; SATA 10; TCWW 1, 2

Tchekhov, Anton
See Chekhov, Anton (Pavlovich)

Tchicaya, Gerald Felix 1931-1988 .. **CLC 101**
See Tchicaya U Tam'si
See also CA 129; 125; CANR 81

Tchicaya U Tam'si
See Tchicaya, Gerald Felix
See also EWL 3

Teasdale, Sara 1884-1933 .... **PC 31; TCLC 4**
See also CA 104; 163; DLB 45; GLL 1; PFS 14; RGAL 4; SATA 32; TUS

Tecumseh 1768-1813 .... **NNAL**
See also DAM MULT

Tegner, Esaias 1782-1846 .... **NCLC 2**

Teilhard de Chardin, (Marie Joseph) Pierre
1881-1955 .... **TCLC 9**
See also CA 105; 210; GFL 1789 to the Present

Ticheburn, Cheviot
See Ainsworth, William Harrison
Tieck, (Johann) Ludwig
1773-1853 .... **NCLC 5, 46; SSC 31**
See also CDWLB 2; DLB 90; EW 5; IDTP;
RGSF 2; RGWL 2, 3; SUFW
Tiger, Derry
See Ellison, Harlan
Tilghman, Christopher 1946- .... **CLC 65**
See also CA 159; CANR 135, 151; CSW;
DLB 244
Tillich, Paul (Johannes)
1886-1965 .... **CLC 131**
See also CA 5-8R; 25-28R; CANR 33;
MTCW 1, 2
Tillinghast, Richard (Williford)
1940- .... **CLC 29**
See also CA 29-32R; CAAS 23; CANR 26,
51, 96; CP 2, 3, 4, 5, 6, 7; CSW
Timrod, Henry 1828-1867 .... **NCLC 25**
See also DLB 3, 248; RGAL 4
Tindall, Gillian (Elizabeth) 1938- ...... **CLC 7**
See also CA 21-24R; CANR 11, 65, 107;
CN 1, 2, 3, 4, 5, 6, 7
Tiptree, James, Jr. .... **CLC 48, 50**
See Sheldon, Alice Hastings Bradley
See also DLB 8; SCFW 1, 2; SFW 4
Tirone Smith, Mary-Ann 1944- .... **CLC 39**
See also CA 118; 136; CANR 113; SATA
143
Tirso de Molina 1580(?)-1648 .... **DC 13;**
HLCS 2; LC 73
See also RGWL 2, 3
Titmarsh, Michael Angelo
See Thackeray, William Makepeace
Tocqueville, Alexis (Charles Henri Maurice
Clerel Comte) de 1805-1859 .. **NCLC 7,**
63
See also EW 6; GFL 1789 to the Present;
TWA
Toer, Pramoedya Ananta
1925-2006 .... **CLC 186**
See also CA 197; 251; RGWL 3
Toffler, Alvin 1928- .... **CLC 168**
See also CA 13-16R; CANR 15, 46, 67;
CPW; DAM POP; MTCW 1, 2
Toibin, Colm 1955- .... **CLC 162**
See also CA 142; CANR 81, 149; CN 7;
DLB 271
Tolkien, J(ohn) R(onald) R(euel)
1892-1973 .... **CLC 1, 2, 3, 8, 12, 38;**
TCLC 137; WLC 6
See also AAYA 10; AITN 1; BPFB 3;
BRWC 2; BRWS 2; CA 17-18; 45-48;
CANR 36, 134; CAP 2; CDBLB 1914-
1945; CLR 56; CN 1; CPW 1; CWRI 5;
DA; DA3; DAB; DAC; DAM MST, NOV,
POP; DLB 15, 160, 255; EFS 2; EWL 3;
FANT; JRDA; LAIT 1; LATS 1:2; LMFS
2; MAICYA 1, 2; MTCW 1, 2; MTFW
2005; NFS 8; RGEL 2; SATA 2, 32, 100;
SATA-Obit 24; SFW 4; SUFW; TEA;
WCH; WYA; YAW
Toller, Ernst 1893-1939 .... **TCLC 10**
See also CA 107; 186; DLB 124; EWL 3;
RGWL 2, 3
Tolson, M. B.
See Tolson, Melvin B(eaunorus)
Tolson, Melvin B(eaunorus)
1898(?)-1966 .... **BLC 3; CLC 36, 105**
See also AFAW 1, 2; BW 1, 3; CA 124; 89-
92; CANR 80; DAM MULT, POET; DLB
48, 76; MAL 5; RGAL 4
Tolstoi, Aleksei Nikolaevich
See Tolstoy, Alexey Nikolaevich
Tolstoi, Lev
See Tolstoy, Leo (Nikolaevich)
See also RGSF 2; RGWL 2, 3

Tolstoy, Aleksei Nikolaevich
See Tolstoy, Alexey Nikolaevich
See also DLB 272
Tolstoy, Alexey Nikolaevich
1882-1945 .... **TCLC 18**
See Tolstoy, Aleksei Nikolaevich
See also CA 107; 158; EWL 3; SFW 4
Tolstoy, Leo (Nikolaevich)
1828-1910 . **SSC 9, 30, 45, 54; TCLC 4,**
11, 17, 28, 44, 79, 173; WLC 6
See Tolstoi, Lev
See also AAYA 56; CA 104; 123; DA; DA3;
DAB; DAC; DAM MST, NOV; DLB 238;
EFS 2; EW 7; EXPS; IDTP; LAIT 2;
LATS 1:1; LMFS 1; NFS 10; SATA 26;
SSFS 5; TWA
Tolstoy, Count Leo
See Tolstoy, Leo (Nikolaevich)
Tomalin, Claire 1933- .... **CLC 166**
See also CA 89-92; CANR 52, 88; DLB
155
Tomasi di Lampedusa, Giuseppe 1896-1957
See Lampedusa, Giuseppe (Tomasi) di
See also CA 111; DLB 177; EWL 3; WLIT
7
Tomlin, Lily 1939(?)-
See Tomlin, Mary Jean
See also CA 117
Tomlin, Mary Jean .... **CLC 17**
See Tomlin, Lily
Tomline, F. Latour
See Gilbert, W(illiam) S(chwenck)
Tomlinson, (Alfred) Charles 1927- .... **CLC 2,**
4, 6, 13, 45; PC 17
See also CA 5-8R; CANR 33; CP 1, 2, 3, 4,
5, 6, 7; DAM POET; DLB 40; TCLE 1:2
Tomlinson, H(enry) M(ajor)
1873-1958 .... **TCLC 71**
See also CA 118; 161; DLB 36, 100, 195
Tonna, Charlotte Elizabeth
1790-1846 .... **NCLC 135**
See also DLB 163
Tonson, Jacob fl. 1655(?)-1736 .... **LC 86**
See also DLB 170
Toole, John Kennedy 1937-1969 ..... **CLC 19,**
64
See also BPFB 3; CA 104; DLBY 1981;
MTCW 2; MTFW 2005
Toomer, Eugene
See Toomer, Jean
Toomer, Eugene Pinchback
See Toomer, Jean
Toomer, Jean 1894-1967 .. **BLC 3; CLC 1, 4,**
13, 22; HR 1:3; PC 7; SSC 1, 45;
TCLC 172; WLCS
See also AFAW 1, 2; AMWS 3, 9; BW 1;
CA 85-88; CDALB 1917-1929; DA3;
DAM MULT; DLB 45, 51; EWL 3; EXPP;
EXPS; LMFS 2; MAL 5; MTCW 1, 2;
MTFW 2005; NFS 11; RGAL 4; RGSF 2;
SSFS 5
Toomer, Nathan Jean
See Toomer, Jean
Toomer, Nathan Pinchback
See Toomer, Jean
Torley, Luke
See Blish, James (Benjamin)
Tornimparte, Alessandra
See Ginzburg, Natalia
Torre, Raoul della
See Mencken, H(enry) L(ouis)
Torrence, Ridgely 1874-1950 .... **TCLC 97**
See also DLB 54, 249; MAL 5
Torrey, E(dwin) Fuller 1937- .... **CLC 34**
See also CA 119; CANR 71
Torsvan, Ben Traven
See Traven, B.
Torsvan, Benno Traven
See Traven, B.

Torsvan, Berick Traven
See Traven, B.
Torsvan, Berwick Traven
See Traven, B.
Torsvan, Bruno Traven
See Traven, B.
Torsvan, Traven
See Traven, B.
Tourneur, Cyril 1575(?)-1626 .... **LC 66**
See also BRW 2; DAM DRAM; DLB 58;
RGEL 2
Tournier, Michel 1924- .... **CLC 6, 23, 36, 95;**
SSC 88
See also CA 49-52; CANR 3, 36, 74, 149;
CWW 2; DLB 83; EWL 3; GFL 1789 to
the Present; MTCW 1, 2; SATA 23
Tournier, Michel Edouard
See Tournier, Michel
Tournimparte, Alessandra
See Ginzburg, Natalia
Towers, Ivar
See Kornbluth, C(yril) M.
Towne, Robert (Burton) 1936(?)- ..... **CLC 87**
See also CA 108; DLB 44; IDFW 3, 4
Townsend, Sue .... **CLC 61**
See Townsend, Susan Lilian
See also AAYA 28; CA 119; 127; CANR
65, 107; CBD; CD 5, 6; CPW; CWD;
DAB; DAC; DAM MST; DLB 271; INT
CA-127; SATA 55, 93; SATA-Brief 48;
YAW
Townsend, Susan Lilian 1946-
See Townsend, Sue
Townshend, Pete
See Townshend, Peter (Dennis Blandford)
Townshend, Peter (Dennis Blandford)
1945- .... **CLC 17, 42**
See also CA 107
Tozzi, Federigo 1883-1920 .... **TCLC 31**
See also CA 160; CANR 110; DLB 264;
EWL 3; WLIT 7
Tracy, Don(ald Fiske) 1905-1970(?)
See Queen, Ellery
See also CA 1-4R; 176; CANR 2
Trafford, F. G.
See Riddell, Charlotte
Traherne, Thomas 1637(?)-1674 .. **LC 99; PC**
70
See also BRW 2; BRWS 11; DLB 131;
PAB; RGEL 2
Traill, Catharine Parr 1802-1899 .. **NCLC 31**
See also DLB 99
Trakl, Georg 1887-1914 .... **PC 20; TCLC 5**
See also CA 104; 165; EW 10; EWL 3;
LMFS 2; MTCW 2; RGWL 2, 3
Trambley, Estela Portillo .... **TCLC 163**
See Portillo Trambley, Estela
See also CA 77-80; RGAL 4
Tranquilli, Secondino
See Silone, Ignazio
Transtroemer, Tomas Gosta
See Transtromer, Tomas (Goesta)
Transtromer, Tomas (Gosta)
See Transtromer, Tomas (Goesta)
See also CWW 2
Transtromer, Tomas (Goesta)
1931- .... **CLC 52, 65**
See Transtromer, Tomas (Goesta)
See also CA 117; 129; CAAS 17; CANR
115; DAM POET; DLB 257; EWL 3; PFS
21
Transtromer, Tomas Gosta
See Transtromer, Tomas (Goesta)
Traven, B. 1882(?)-1969 .... **CLC 8, 11**
See also CA 19-20; 25-28R; CAP 2; DLB
9, 56; EWL 3; MTCW 1; RGAL 4
Trediakovsky, Vasilii Kirillovich
1703-1769 .... **LC 68**
See also DLB 150

von Horvath, Odon 1901-1938 .... **TCLC 45**
See von Horvath, Oedoen
See also CA 118; 194; DLB 85, 124; RGWL 2, 3

von Horvath, Oedoen
See von Horvath, Odon
See also CA 184

von Kleist, Heinrich
See Kleist, Heinrich von

Vonnegut, Kurt, Jr.
See Vonnegut, Kurt

Vonnegut, Kurt 1922- ... **CLC 1, 2, 3, 4, 5, 8, 12, 22, 40, 60, 111, 212; SSC 8; WLC 6**
See also AAYA 6, 44; AITN 1; AMWS 2; BEST 90:4; BPFB 3; BYA 3, 14; CA 1-4R; CANR 1, 25, 49, 75, 92; CDALB 1968-1988; CN 1, 2, 3, 4, 5, 6, 7; CPW 1; DA; DA3; DAB; DAC; DAM MST, NOV, POP; DLB 2, 8, 152; DLBD 3; DLBY 1980; EWL 3; EXPN; EXPS; LAIT 4; LMFS 2; MAL 5; MTCW 1, 2; MTFW 2005; NFS 3; RGAL 4; SCFW; SFW 4; SSFS 5; TUS; YAW

Von Rachen, Kurt
See Hubbard, L. Ron

von Sternberg, Josef
See Sternberg, Josef von

Vorster, Gordon 1924- .... **CLC 34**
See also CA 133

Vosce, Trudie
See Ozick, Cynthia

Voznesensky, Andrei (Andreievich) 1933- .... **CLC 1, 15, 57**
See Voznesensky, Andrey
See also CA 89-92; CANR 37; CWW 2; DAM POET; MTCW 1

Voznesensky, Andrey
See Voznesensky, Andrei (Andreievich)
See also EWL 3

Wace, Robert c. 1100-c. 1175 .... **CMLC 55**
See also DLB 146

Waddington, Miriam 1917-2004 .... **CLC 28**
See also CA 21-24R; 225; CANR 12, 30; CCA 1; CP 1, 2, 3, 4, 5, 6, 7; DLB 68

Wagman, Fredrica 1937- .... **CLC 7**
See also CA 97-100; INT CA-97-100

Wagner, Linda W.
See Wagner-Martin, Linda (C.)

Wagner, Linda Welshimer
See Wagner-Martin, Linda (C.)

Wagner, Richard 1813-1883 ..... **NCLC 9, 119**
See also DLB 129; EW 6

Wagner-Martin, Linda (C.) 1936- .... **CLC 50**
See also CA 159; CANR 135

Wagoner, David (Russell) 1926- .... **CLC 3, 5, 15; PC 33**
See also AMWS 9; CA 1-4R; CAAS 3; CANR 2, 71; CN 1, 2, 3, 4, 5, 6, 7; CP 1, 2, 3, 4, 5, 6, 7; DLB 5, 256; SATA 14; TCWW 1, 2

Wah, Fred(erick James) 1939- .... **CLC 44**
See also CA 107; 141; CP 1, 6, 7; DLB 60

Wahloo, Per 1926-1975 .... **CLC 7**
See also BPFB 3; CA 61-64; CANR 73; CMW 4; MSW

Wahloo, Peter
See Wahloo, Per

Wain, John (Barrington) 1925-1994 . **CLC 2, 11, 15, 46**
See also CA 5-8R; 145; CAAS 4; CANR 23, 54; CDBLB 1960 to Present; CN 1, 2, 3, 4, 5; CP 1, 2, 3, 4, 5; DLB 15, 27, 139, 155; EWL 3; MTCW 1, 2; MTFW 2005

Wajda, Andrzej 1926- .... **CLC 16, 219**
See also CA 102

Wakefield, Dan 1932- .... **CLC 7**
See also CA 21-24R; 211; CAAE 211; CAAS 7; CN 4, 5, 6, 7

Wakefield, Herbert Russell 1888-1965 .... **TCLC 120**
See also CA 5-8R; CANR 77; HGG; SUFW

Wakoski, Diane 1937- ...... **CLC 2, 4, 7, 9, 11, 40; PC 15**
See also CA 13-16R, 216; CAAE 216; CAAS 1; CANR 9, 60, 106; CP 1, 2, 3, 4, 5, 6, 7; CWP; DAM POET; DLB 5; INT CANR-9; MAL 5; MTCW 2; MTFW 2005

Wakoski-Sherbell, Diane
See Wakoski, Diane

Walcott, Derek 1930- ... **BLC 3; CLC 2, 4, 9, 14, 25, 42, 67, 76, 160; DC 7; PC 46**
See also BW 2; CA 89-92; CANR 26, 47, 75, 80, 130; CBD; CD 5, 6; CDWLB 3; CP 1, 2, 3, 4, 5, 6, 7; DA3; DAB; DAC; DAM MST, MULT, POET; DLB 117; DLBY 1981; DNFS 1; EFS 1; EWL 3; LMFS 2; MTCW 1, 2; MTFW 2005; PFS 6; RGEL 2; TWA; WWE 1

Waldman, Anne (Lesley) 1945- .... **CLC 7**
See also BG 1:3; CA 37-40R; CAAS 17; CANR 34, 69, 116; CP 1, 2, 3, 4, 5, 6, 7; CWP; DLB 16

Waldo, E. Hunter
See Sturgeon, Theodore (Hamilton)

Waldo, Edward Hamilton
See Sturgeon, Theodore (Hamilton)

Walker, Alice 1944- ...... **BLC 3; CLC 5, 6, 9, 19, 27, 46, 58, 103, 167; PC 30; SSC 5; WLCS**
See also AAYA 3, 33; AFAW 1, 2; AMWS 3; BEST 89:4; BPFB 3; BW 2, 3; CA 37-40R; CANR 9, 27, 49, 66, 82, 131; CDALB 1968-1988; CN 4, 5, 6, 7; CPW; CSW; DA; DA3; DAB; DAC; DAM MST, MULT, NOV, POET, POP; DLB 6, 33, 143; EWL 3; EXPN; EXPS; FL 1:6; FW; INT CANR-27; LAIT 3; MAL 5; MBL; MTCW 1, 2; MTFW 2005; NFS 5; RGAL 4; RGSF 2; SATA 31; SSFS 2, 11; TUS; YAW

Walker, Alice Malsenior
See Walker, Alice

Walker, David Harry 1911-1992 ...... **CLC 14**
See also CA 1-4R; 137; CANR 1; CN 1, 2; CWRI 5; SATA 8; SATA-Obit 71

Walker, Edward Joseph 1934-2004
See Walker, Ted
See also CA 21-24R; 226; CANR 12, 28, 53

Walker, George F(rederick) 1947- .. **CLC 44, 61**
See also CA 103; CANR 21, 43, 59; CD 5, 6; DAB; DAC; DAM MST; DLB 60

Walker, Joseph A. 1935-2003 .... **CLC 19**
See also BW 1, 3; CA 89-92; CAD; CANR 26, 143; CD 5, 6; DAM DRAM, MST; DFS 12; DLB 38

Walker, Margaret 1915-1998 .. **BLC; CLC 1, 6; PC 20; TCLC 129**
See also AFAW 1, 2; BW 2, 3; CA 73-76; 172; CANR 26, 54, 76, 136; CN 1, 2, 3, 4, 5, 6; CP 1, 2, 3, 4, 5, 6; CSW; DAM MULT; DLB 76, 152; EXPP; FW; MAL 5; MTCW 1, 2; MTFW 2005; RGAL 4; RHW

Walker, Ted .... **CLC 13**
See Walker, Edward Joseph
See also CP 1, 2, 3, 4, 5, 6, 7; DLB 40

Wallace, David Foster 1962- ... **CLC 50, 114; SSC 68**
See also AAYA 50; AMWS 10; CA 132; CANR 59, 133; CN 7; DA3; MTCW 2; MTFW 2005

Wallace, Dexter
See Masters, Edgar Lee

Wallace, (Richard Horatio) Edgar 1875-1932 .... **TCLC 57**
See also CA 115; 218; CMW 4; DLB 70; MSW; RGEL 2

Wallace, Irving 1916-1990 .... **CLC 7, 13**
See also AITN 1; BPFB 3; CA 1-4R; 132; CAAS 1; CANR 1, 27; CPW; DAM NOV, POP; INT CANR-27; MTCW 1, 2

Wallant, Edward Lewis 1926-1962 ... **CLC 5, 10**
See also CA 1-4R; CANR 22; DLB 2, 28, 143, 299; EWL 3; MAL 5; MTCW 1, 2; RGAL 4; RGHL

Wallas, Graham 1858-1932 .... **TCLC 91**

Waller, Edmund 1606-1687 .... **LC 86; PC 72**
See also BRW 2; DAM POET; DLB 126; PAB; RGEL 2

Walley, Byron
See Card, Orson Scott

Walpole, Horace 1717-1797 .... **LC 2, 49**
See also BRW 3; DLB 39, 104, 213; GL 3; HGG; LMFS 1; RGEL 2; SUFW 1; TEA

Walpole, Hugh (Seymour) 1884-1941 .... **TCLC 5**
See also CA 104; 165; DLB 34; HGG; MTCW 2; RGEL 2; RHW

Walrond, Eric (Derwent) 1898-1966 . **HR 1:3**
See also BW 1; CA 125; DLB 51

Walser, Martin 1927- .... **CLC 27, 183**
See also CA 57-60; CANR 8, 46, 145; CWW 2; DLB 75, 124; EWL 3

Walser, Robert 1878-1956 ..... **SSC 20; TCLC 18**
See also CA 118; 165; CANR 100; DLB 66; EWL 3

Walsh, Gillian Paton
See Paton Walsh, Gillian

Walsh, Jill Paton .... **CLC 35**
See Paton Walsh, Gillian
See also CLR 2, 65; WYA

Walter, Villiam Christian
See Andersen, Hans Christian

Walters, Anna L(ee) 1946- .... **NNAL**
See also CA 73-76

Walther von der Vogelweide c. 1170-1228 .... **CMLC 56**

Walton, Izaak 1593-1683 .... **LC 72**
See also BRW 2; CDBLB Before 1660; DLB 151, 213; RGEL 2

Wambaugh, Joseph (Aloysius), Jr. 1937- .... **CLC 3, 18**
See also AITN 1; BEST 89:3; BPFB 3; CA 33-36R; CANR 42, 65, 115; CMW 4; CPW 1; DA3; DAM NOV, POP; DLB 6; DLBY 1983; MSW; MTCW 1, 2

Wang Wei 699(?)-761(?) .... **PC 18**
See also TWA

Warburton, William 1698-1779 .... **LC 97**
See also DLB 104

Ward, Arthur Henry Sarsfield 1883-1959
See Rohmer, Sax
See also CA 108; 173; CMW 4; HGG

Ward, Douglas Turner 1930- .... **CLC 19**
See also BW 1; CA 81-84; CAD; CANR 27; CD 5, 6; DLB 7, 38

Ward, E. D.
See Lucas, E(dward) V(errall)

Ward, Mrs. Humphry 1851-1920
See Ward, Mary Augusta
See also RGEL 2

Ward, Mary Augusta 1851-1920 ... **TCLC 55**
See Ward, Mrs. Humphry
See also DLB 18

Ward, Nathaniel 1578(?)-1652 .... **LC 114**
See also DLB 24

Ward, Peter
See Faust, Frederick (Schiller)

Wellman, Mac .... **CLC 65**
See Wellman, John McDowell; Wellman, John McDowell
See also CAD; CD 6; RGAL 4

Wellman, Manly Wade 1903-1986 ... **CLC 49**
See also CA 1-4R; 118; CANR 6, 16, 44; FANT; SATA 6; SATA-Obit 47; SFW 4; SUFW

Wells, Carolyn 1869(?)-1942 .... **TCLC 35**
See also CA 113; 185; CMW 4; DLB 11

Wells, H(erbert) G(eorge) 1866-1946 . **SSC 6, 70; TCLC 6, 12, 19, 133; WLC 6**
See also AAYA 18; BPFB 3; BRW 6; CA 110; 121; CDBLB 1914-1945; CLR 64; DA; DA3; DAB; DAC; DAM MST, NOV; DLB 34, 70, 156, 178; EWL 3; EXPS; HGG; LAIT 3; LMFS 2; MTCW 1, 2; MTFW 2005; NFS 17, 20; RGEL 2; RGSF 2; SATA 20; SCFW 1, 2; SFW 4; SSFS 1; SUFW; TEA; WCH; WLIT 4; YAW

Wells, Rosemary 1943- .... **CLC 12**
See also AAYA 13; BYA 7, 8; CA 85-88; CANR 48, 120; CLR 16, 69; CWRI 5; MAICYA 1, 2; SAAS 1; SATA 18, 69, 114, 156; YAW

Wells-Barnett, Ida B(ell)
1862-1931 .... **TCLC 125**
See also CA 182; DLB 23, 221

Welsh, Irvine 1958- .... **CLC 144**
See also CA 173; CANR 146; CN 7; DLB 271

Welty, Eudora 1909-2001 .... **CLC 1, 2, 5, 14, 22, 33, 105, 220; SSC 1, 27, 51; WLC 6**
See also AAYA 48; AMW; AMWR 1; BPFB 3; CA 9-12R; 199; CABS 1; CANR 32, 65, 128; CDALB 1941-1968; CN 1, 2, 3, 4, 5, 6, 7; CSW; DA; DA3; DAB; DAC; DAM MST, NOV; DLB 2, 102, 143; DLBD 12; DLBY 1987, 2001; EWL 3; EXPS; HGG; LAIT 3; MAL 5; MBL; MTCW 1, 2; MTFW 2005; NFS 13, 15; RGAL 4; RGSF 2; RHW; SSFS 2, 10; TUS

Welty, Eudora Alice
See Welty, Eudora

Wen I-to 1899-1946 .... **TCLC 28**
See also EWL 3

Wentworth, Robert
See Hamilton, Edmond

Werfel, Franz (Viktor) 1890-1945 ... **TCLC 8**
See also CA 104; 161; DLB 81, 124; EWL 3; RGWL 2, 3

Wergeland, Henrik Arnold
1808-1845 .... **NCLC 5**

Wersba, Barbara 1932- .... **CLC 30**
See also AAYA 2, 30; BYA 6, 12, 13; CA 29-32R, 182; CAAE 182; CANR 16, 38; CLR 3, 78; DLB 52; JRDA; MAICYA 1, 2; SAAS 2; SATA 1, 58; SATA-Essay 103; WYA; YAW

Wertmueller, Lina 1928- .... **CLC 16**
See also CA 97-100; CANR 39, 78

Wescott, Glenway 1901-1987 .. **CLC 13; SSC 35**
See also CA 13-16R; 121; CANR 23, 70; CN 1, 2, 3, 4; DLB 4, 9, 102; MAL 5; RGAL 4

Wesker, Arnold 1932- .... **CLC 3, 5, 42**
See also CA 1-4R; CAAS 7; CANR 1, 33; CBD; CD 5, 6; CDBLB 1960 to Present; DAB; DAM DRAM; DLB 13, 310, 319; EWL 3; MTCW 1; RGEL 2; TEA

Wesley, Charles 1707-1788 .... **LC 128**
See also DLB 95; RGEL 2

Wesley, John 1703-1791 .... **LC 88**
See also DLB 104

Wesley, Richard (Errol) 1945- .... **CLC 7**
See also BW 1; CA 57-60; CAD; CANR 27; CD 5, 6; DLB 38

Wessel, Johan Herman 1742-1785 .... **LC 7**
See also DLB 300

West, Anthony (Panther)
1914-1987 .... **CLC 50**
See also CA 45-48; 124; CANR 3, 19; CN 1, 2, 3, 4; DLB 15

West, C. P.
See Wodehouse, P(elham) G(renville)

West, Cornel (Ronald) 1953- .... **BLCS; CLC 134**
See also CA 144; CANR 91; DLB 246

West, Delno C(loyde), Jr. 1936- .... **CLC 70**
See also CA 57-60

West, Dorothy 1907-1998 ...... **HR 1:3; TCLC 108**
See also BW 2; CA 143; 169; DLB 76

West, (Mary) Jessamyn 1902-1984 ... **CLC 7, 17**
See also CA 9-12R; 112; CANR 27; CN 1, 2, 3; DLB 6; DLBY 1984; MTCW 1, 2; RGAL 4; RHW; SATA-Obit 37; TCWW 2; TUS; YAW

West, Morris L(anglo) 1916-1999 ..... **CLC 6, 33**
See also BPFB 3; CA 5-8R; 187; CANR 24, 49, 64; CN 1, 2, 3, 4, 5, 6; CPW; DLB 289; MTCW 1, 2; MTFW 2005

West, Nathanael 1903-1940 .. **SSC 16; TCLC 1, 14, 44**
See also AMW; AMWR 2; BPFB 3; CA 104; 125; CDALB 1929-1941; DA3; DLB 4, 9, 28; EWL 3; MAL 5; MTCW 1, 2; MTFW 2005; NFS 16; RGAL 4; TUS

West, Owen
See Koontz, Dean R.

West, Paul 1930- .... **CLC 7, 14, 96, 226**
See also CA 13-16R; CAAS 7; CANR 22, 53, 76, 89, 136; CN 1, 2, 3, 4, 5, 6, 7; DLB 14; INT CANR-22; MTCW 2; MTFW 2005

West, Rebecca 1892-1983 ... **CLC 7, 9, 31, 50**
See also BPFB 3; BRWS 3; CA 5-8R; 109; CANR 19; CN 1, 2, 3; DLB 36; DLBY 1983; EWL 3; FW; MTCW 1, 2; MTFW 2005; NCFS 4; RGEL 2; TEA

Westall, Robert (Atkinson)
1929-1993 .... **CLC 17**
See also AAYA 12; BYA 2, 6, 7, 8, 9, 15; CA 69-72; 141; CANR 18, 68; CLR 13; FANT; JRDA; MAICYA 1, 2; MAICYAS 1; SAAS 2; SATA 23, 69; SATA-Obit 75; WYA; YAW

Westermarck, Edward 1862-1939 . **TCLC 87**

Westlake, Donald E. 1933- .... **CLC 7, 33**
See also BPFB 3; CA 17-20R; CAAS 13; CANR 16, 44, 65, 94, 137; CMW 4; CPW; DAM POP; INT CANR-16; MSW; MTCW 2; MTFW 2005

Westmacott, Mary
See Christie, Agatha (Mary Clarissa)

Weston, Allen
See Norton, Andre

Wetcheek, J. L.
See Feuchtwanger, Lion

Wetering, Janwillem van de
See van de Wetering, Janwillem

Wetherald, Agnes Ethelwyn
1857-1940 .... **TCLC 81**
See also CA 202; DLB 99

Wetherell, Elizabeth
See Warner, Susan (Bogert)

Whale, James 1889-1957 .... **TCLC 63**

Whalen, Philip (Glenn) 1923-2002 .... **CLC 6, 29**
See also BG 1:3; CA 9-12R; 209; CANR 5, 39; CP 1, 2, 3, 4, 5, 6, 7; DLB 16; WP

Wharton, Edith (Newbold Jones)
1862-1937 ... **SSC 6, 84; TCLC 3, 9, 27, 53, 129, 149; WLC 6**
See also AAYA 25; AMW; AMWC 2; AMWR 1; BPFB 3; CA 104; 132; CDALB 1865-1917; DA; DA3; DAB; DAC; DAM MST, NOV; DLB 4, 9, 12, 78, 189; DLBD 13; EWL 3; EXPS; FL 1:6; GL 3; HGG; LAIT 2, 3; LATS 1:1; MAL 5; MBL; MTCW 1, 2; MTFW 2005; NFS 5, 11, 15, 20; RGAL 4; RGSF 2; RHW; SSFS 6, 7; SUFW; TUS

Wharton, James
See Mencken, H(enry) L(ouis)

Wharton, William (a pseudonym)
1925- .... **CLC 18, 37**
See also CA 93-96; CN 4, 5, 6, 7; DLBY 1980; INT CA-93-96

Wheatley (Peters), Phillis
1753(?)-1784 ... **BLC 3; LC 3, 50; PC 3; WLC 6**
See also AFAW 1, 2; CDALB 1640-1865; DA; DA3; DAC; DAM MST, MULT, POET; DLB 31, 50; EXPP; FL 1:1; PFS 13; RGAL 4

Wheelock, John Hall 1886-1978 .... **CLC 14**
See also CA 13-16R; 77-80; CANR 14; CP 1, 2; DLB 45; MAL 5

Whim-Wham
See Curnow, (Thomas) Allen (Monro)

Whitaker, Rod 1931-2005
See Trevanian
See also CA 29-32R; 246; CANR 45, 153; CMW 4

White, Babington
See Braddon, Mary Elizabeth

White, E. B. 1899-1985 .... **CLC 10, 34, 39**
See also AAYA 62; AITN 2; AMWS 1; CA 13-16R; 116; CANR 16, 37; CDALBS; CLR 1, 21, 107; CPW; DA3; DAM POP; DLB 11, 22; EWL 3; FANT; MAICYA 1, 2; MAL 5; MTCW 1, 2; MTFW 2005; NCFS 5; RGAL 4; SATA 2, 29, 100; SATA-Obit 44; TUS

White, Edmund 1940- .... **CLC 27, 110**
See also AAYA 7; CA 45-48; CANR 3, 19, 36, 62, 107, 133; CN 5, 6, 7; DA3; DAM POP; DLB 227; MTCW 1, 2; MTFW 2005

White, Elwyn Brooks
See White, E. B.

White, Hayden V. 1928- .... **CLC 148**
See also CA 128; CANR 135; DLB 246

White, Patrick (Victor Martindale)
1912-1990 ...... **CLC 3, 4, 5, 7, 9, 18, 65, 69; SSC 39; TCLC 176**
See also BRWS 1; CA 81-84; 132; CANR 43; CN 1, 2, 3, 4; DLB 260; EWL 3; MTCW 1; RGEL 2; RGSF 2; RHW; TWA; WWE 1

White, Phyllis Dorothy James 1920-
See James, P. D.
See also CA 21-24R; CANR 17, 43, 65, 112; CMW 4; CN 7; CPW; DA3; DAM POP; MTCW 1, 2; MTFW 2005; TEA

White, T(erence) H(anbury)
1906-1964 .... **CLC 30**
See also AAYA 22; BPFB 3; BYA 4, 5; CA 73-76; CANR 37; DLB 160; FANT; JRDA; LAIT 1; MAICYA 1, 2; RGEL 2; SATA 12; SUFW 1; YAW

White, Terence de Vere 1912-1994 ... **CLC 49**
See also CA 49-52; 145; CANR 3

White, Walter
See White, Walter F(rancis)

White, Walter F(rancis) 1893-1955 ... **BLC 3; HR 1:3; TCLC 15**
See also BW 1; CA 115; 124; DAM MULT; DLB 51

White, William Hale 1831-1913
See Rutherford, Mark
See also CA 121; 189
Whitehead, Alfred North
1861-1947 .... **TCLC 97**
See also CA 117; 165; DLB 100, 262
Whitehead, E(dward) A(nthony)
1933- .... **CLC 5**
See Whitehead, Ted
See also CA 65-68; CANR 58, 118; CBD;
CD 5; DLB 310
Whitehead, Ted
See Whitehead, E(dward) A(nthony)
See also CD 6
Whiteman, Roberta J. Hill 1947- ...... **NNAL**
See also CA 146
Whitemore, Hugh (John) 1936- .... **CLC 37**
See also CA 132; CANR 77; CBD; CD 5,
6; INT CA-132
Whitman, Sarah Helen (Power)
1803-1878 .... **NCLC 19**
See also DLB 1, 243
Whitman, Walt(er) 1819-1892 .. **NCLC 4, 31,
81; PC 3; WLC 6**
See also AAYA 42; AMW; AMWR 1;
CDALB 1640-1865; DA; DA3; DAB;
DAC; DAM MST, POET; DLB 3, 64,
224, 250; EXPP; LAIT 2; LMFS 1; PAB;
PFS 2, 3, 13, 22; RGAL 4; SATA 20;
TUS; WP; WYAS 1
Whitney, Isabella fl. 1565-fl. 1575 ..... **LC 130**
See also DLB 136
Whitney, Phyllis A(yame) 1903- .... **CLC 42**
See also AAYA 36; AITN 2; BEST 90:3;
CA 1-4R; CANR 3, 25, 38, 60; CLR 59;
CMW; CPW; DA3; DAM POP; JRDA;
MAICYA 1, 2; MTCW 2; RHW; SATA 1,
30; YAW
Whittemore, (Edward) Reed, Jr.
1919- .... **CLC 4**
See also CA 9-12R, 219; CAAE 219; CAAS
8; CANR 4, 119; CP 1, 2, 3, 4, 5, 6, 7;
DLB 5; MAL 5
Whittier, John Greenleaf
1807-1892 .... **NCLC 8, 59**
See also AMWS 1; DLB 1, 243; RGAL 4
Whittlebot, Hernia
See Coward, Noel (Peirce)
Wicker, Thomas Grey 1926-
See Wicker, Tom
See also CA 65-68; CANR 21, 46, 141
Wicker, Tom .... **CLC 7**
See Wicker, Thomas Grey
Wideman, John Edgar 1941- ... **BLC 3; CLC
5, 34, 36, 67, 122; SSC 62**
See also AFAW 1, 2; AMWS 10; BPFB 4;
BW 2, 3; CA 85-88; CANR 14, 42, 67,
109, 140; CN 4, 5, 6, 7; DAM MULT;
DLB 33, 143; MAL 5; MTCW 2; MTFW
2005; RGAL 4; RGSF 2; SSFS 6, 12, 24;
TCLE 1:2
Wiebe, Rudy (Henry) 1934- .. **CLC 6, 11, 14,
138**
See also CA 37-40R; CANR 42, 67, 123;
CN 1, 2, 3, 4, 5, 6, 7; DAC; DAM MST;
DLB 60; RHW; SATA 156
Wieland, Christoph Martin
1733-1813 .... **NCLC 17**
See also DLB 97; EW 4; LMFS 1; RGWL
2, 3
Wiene, Robert 1881-1938 .... **TCLC 56**
Wieners, John 1934- .... **CLC 7**
See also BG 1:3; CA 13-16R; CP 1, 2, 3, 4,
5, 6, 7; DLB 16; WP
Wiesel, Elie 1928- ...... **CLC 3, 5, 11, 37, 165;
WLCS**
See also AAYA 7, 54; AITN 1; CA 5-8R;
CAAS 4; CANR 8, 40, 65, 125; CDALBS;
CWW 2; DA; DA3; DAB; DAC; DAM
MST, NOV; DLB 83, 299; DLBY 1987;

EWL 3; INT CANR-8; LAIT 4; MTCW
1, 2; MTFW 2005; NCFS 4; NFS 4;
RGHL; RGWL 3; SATA 56; YAW
Wiesel, Eliezer
See Wiesel, Elie
Wiggins, Marianne 1947- .... **CLC 57**
See also AAYA 70; BEST 89:3; CA 130;
CANR 60, 139; CN 7
Wigglesworth, Michael 1631-1705 .... **LC 106**
See also DLB 24; RGAL 4
Wiggs, Susan .... **CLC 70**
See also CA 201
Wight, James Alfred 1916-1995
See Herriot, James
See also CA 77-80; SATA 55; SATA-Brief
44
Wilbur, Richard 1921- .. **CLC 3, 6, 9, 14, 53,
110; PC 51**
See also AMWS 3; CA 1-4R; CABS 2;
CANR 2, 29, 76, 93, 139; CDALBS; CP
1, 2, 3, 4, 5, 6, 7; DA; DAB; DAC; DAM
MST, POET; DLB 5, 169; EWL 3; EXPP;
INT CANR-29; MAL 5; MTCW 1, 2;
MTFW 2005; PAB; PFS 11, 12, 16;
RGAL 4; SATA 9, 108; WP
Wild, Peter 1940- .... **CLC 14**
See also CA 37-40R; CP 1, 2, 3, 4, 5, 6, 7;
DLB 5
Wilde, Oscar (Fingal O'Flahertie Wills)
1854(?)-1900 .... **DC 17; SSC 11, 77;
TCLC 1, 8, 23, 41, 175; WLC 6**
See also AAYA 49; BRW 5; BRWC 1, 2;
BRWR 2; BYA 15; CA 104; 119; CANR
112; CDBLB 1890-1914; CLR 114; DA;
DA3; DAB; DAC; DAM DRAM, MST,
NOV; DFS 4, 8, 9, 21; DLB 10, 19, 34,
57, 141, 156, 190; EXPS; FANT; GL 3;
LATS 1:1; NFS 20; RGEL 2; RGSF 2;
SATA 24; SSFS 7; SUFW; TEA; WCH;
WLIT 4
Wilder, Billy .... **CLC 20**
See Wilder, Samuel
See also AAYA 66; DLB 26
Wilder, Samuel 1906-2002
See Wilder, Billy
See also CA 89-92; 205
Wilder, Stephen
See Marlowe, Stephen
Wilder, Thornton (Niven)
1897-1975 .. **CLC 1, 5, 6, 10, 15, 35, 82;
DC 1, 24; WLC 6**
See also AAYA 29; AITN 2; AMW; CA 13-
16R; 61-64; CAD; CANR 40, 132;
CDALBS; CN 1, 2; DA; DA3; DAB;
DAC; DAM DRAM, MST, NOV; DFS
4, 16; DLB 4, 7, 9, 228; DLBY 1997;
EWL 3; LAIT 3; MAL 5; MTCW 1, 2;
MTFW 2005; NFS 24; RGAL 4; RHW;
WYAS 1
Wilding, Michael 1942- ...... **CLC 73; SSC 50**
See also CA 104; CANR 24, 49, 106; CN
4, 5, 6, 7; DLB 325; RGSF 2
Wiley, Richard 1944- .... **CLC 44**
See also CA 121; 129; CANR 71
Wilhelm, Kate .... **CLC 7**
See Wilhelm, Katie
See also AAYA 20; BYA 16; CAAS 5; DLB
8; INT CANR-17; SCFW 2
Wilhelm, Katie 1928-
See Wilhelm, Kate
See also CA 37-40R; CANR 17, 36, 60, 94;
MTCW 1; SFW 4
Wilkins, Mary
See Freeman, Mary E(leanor) Wilkins
Willard, Nancy 1936- .... **CLC 7, 37**
See also BYA 5; CA 89-92; CANR 10, 39,
68, 107, 152; CLR 5; CP 2, 3, 4, 5; CWP;
CWRI 5; DLB 5, 52; FANT; MAICYA 1,
2; MTCW 1; SATA 37, 71, 127; SATA-
Brief 30; SUFW 2; TCLE 1:2

William of Malmesbury c. 1090B.C.-c.
1140B.C. .... **CMLC 57**
William of Ockham 1290-1349 ..... **CMLC 32**
Williams, Ben Ames 1889-1953 ..... **TCLC 89**
See also CA 183; DLB 102
Williams, Charles
See Collier, James Lincoln
Williams, Charles (Walter Stansby)
1886-1945 .... **TCLC 1, 11**
See also BRWS 9; CA 104; 163; DLB 100,
153, 255; FANT; RGEL 2; SUFW 1
Williams, C.K. 1936- .... **CLC 33, 56, 148**
See also CA 37-40R; CAAS 26; CANR 57,
106; CP 1, 2, 3, 4, 5, 6, 7; DAM POET;
DLB 5; MAL 5
Williams, Ella Gwendolen Rees
See Rhys, Jean
Williams, (George) Emlyn
1905-1987 .... **CLC 15**
See also CA 104; 123; CANR 36; DAM
DRAM; DLB 10, 77; IDTP; MTCW 1
Williams, Hank 1923-1953 .... **TCLC 81**
See Williams, Hiram King
Williams, Helen Maria
1761-1827 .... **NCLC 135**
See also DLB 158
Williams, Hiram Hank
See Williams, Hank
Williams, Hiram King
See Williams, Hank
See also CA 188
Williams, Hugo (Mordaunt) 1942- ... **CLC 42**
See also CA 17-20R; CANR 45, 119; CP 1,
2, 3, 4, 5, 6, 7; DLB 40
Williams, J. Walker
See Wodehouse, P(elham) G(renville)
Williams, John A(lfred) 1925- . **BLC 3; CLC
5, 13**
See also AFAW 2; BW 2, 3; CA 53-56; 195;
CAAE 195; CAAS 3; CANR 6, 26, 51,
118; CN 1, 2, 3, 4, 5, 6, 7; CSW; DAM
MULT; DLB 2, 33; EWL 3; INT CANR-6;
MAL 5; RGAL 4; SFW 4
Williams, Jonathan (Chamberlain)
1929- .... **CLC 13**
See also CA 9-12R; CAAS 12; CANR 8,
108; CP 1, 2, 3, 4, 5, 6, 7; DLB 5
Williams, Joy 1944- .... **CLC 31**
See also CA 41-44R; CANR 22, 48, 97
Williams, Norman 1952- .... **CLC 39**
See also CA 118
Williams, Roger 1603(?)-1683 .... **LC 129**
See also DLB 24
Williams, Sherley Anne 1944-1999 ... **BLC 3;
CLC 89**
See also AFAW 2; BW 2, 3; CA 73-76; 185;
CANR 25, 82; DAM MULT, POET; DLB
41; INT CANR-25; SATA 78; SATA-Obit
116
Williams, Shirley
See Williams, Sherley Anne
Williams, Tennessee 1911-1983 . **CLC 1, 2, 5,
7, 8, 11, 15, 19, 30, 39, 45, 71, 111; DC
4; SSC 81; WLC 6**
See also AAYA 31; AITN 1, 2; AMW;
AMWC 1; CA 5-8R; 108; CABS 3; CAD;
CANR 31, 132; CDALB 1941-1968; CN
1, 2, 3; DA; DA3; DAB; DAC; DAM
DRAM, MST; DFS 17; DLB 7; DLBD 4;
DLBY 1983; EWL 3; GLL 1; LAIT 4;
LATS 1:2; MAL 5; MTCW 1, 2; MTFW
2005; RGAL 4; TUS
Williams, Thomas (Alonzo)
1926-1990 .... **CLC 14**
See also CA 1-4R; 132; CANR 2
Williams, William C.
See Williams, William Carlos

Williams, William Carlos
1883-1963 .... **CLC 1, 2, 5, 9, 13, 22, 42, 67; PC 7; SSC 31; WLC 6**
See also AAYA 46; AMW; AMWR 1; CA 89-92; CANR 34; CDALB 1917-1929; DA; DA3; DAB; DAC; DAM MST, POET; DLB 4, 16, 54, 86; EWL 3; EXPP; MAL 5; MTCW 1, 2; MTFW 2005; NCFS 4; PAB; PFS 1, 6, 11; RGAL 4; RGSF 2; TUS; WP

Williamson, David (Keith) 1942- ..... **CLC 56**
See also CA 103; CANR 41; CD 5, 6; DLB 289

Williamson, Ellen Douglas 1905-1984
See Douglas, Ellen
See also CA 17-20R; 114; CANR 39

Williamson, Jack .... **CLC 29**
See Williamson, John Stewart
See also CAAS 8; DLB 8; SCFW 1, 2

Williamson, John Stewart 1908-2006
See Williamson, Jack
See also CA 17-20R; CANR 23, 70, 153; SFW 4

Willie, Frederick
See Lovecraft, H. P.

Willingham, Calder (Baynard, Jr.)
1922-1995 .... **CLC 5, 51**
See also CA 5-8R; 147; CANR 3; CN 1, 2, 3, 4, 5; CSW; DLB 2, 44; IDFW 3, 4; MTCW 1

Willis, Charles
See Clarke, Arthur C.

Willy
See Colette, (Sidonie-Gabrielle)

Willy, Colette
See Colette, (Sidonie-Gabrielle)
See also GLL 1

Wilmot, John 1647-1680 .... **LC 75; PC 66**
See Rochester
See also BRW 2; DLB 131; PAB

Wilson, A.N. 1950- .... **CLC 33**
See also BRWS 6; CA 112; 122; CANR 155; CN 4, 5, 6, 7; DLB 14, 155, 194; MTCW 2

Wilson, Andrew Norman
See Wilson, A.N.

Wilson, Angus (Frank Johnstone)
1913-1991 . **CLC 2, 3, 5, 25, 34; SSC 21**
See also BRWS 1; CA 5-8R; 134; CANR 21; CN 1, 2, 3, 4; DLB 15, 139, 155; EWL 3; MTCW 1, 2; MTFW 2005; RGEL 2; RGSF 2

Wilson, August 1945-2005 .. **BLC 3; CLC 39, 50, 63, 118, 222; DC 2; WLCS**
See also AAYA 16; AFAW 2; AMWS 8; BW 2, 3; CA 115; 122; 244; CAD; CANR 42, 54, 76, 128; CD 5, 6; DA; DA3; DAB; DAC; DAM DRAM, MST, MULT; DFS 3, 7, 15, 17; DLB 228; EWL 3; LAIT 4; LATS 1:2; MAL 5; MTCW 1, 2; MTFW 2005; RGAL 4

Wilson, Brian 1942- .... **CLC 12**

Wilson, Colin (Henry) 1931- .... **CLC 3, 14**
See also CA 1-4R; CAAS 5; CANR 1, 22, 33, 77; CMW 4; CN 1, 2, 3, 4, 5, 6; DLB 14, 194; HGG; MTCW 1; SFW 4

Wilson, Dirk
See Pohl, Frederik

Wilson, Edmund 1895-1972 .. **CLC 1, 2, 3, 8, 24**
See also AMW; CA 1-4R; 37-40R; CANR 1, 46, 110; CN 1; DLB 63; EWL 3; MAL 5; MTCW 1, 2; MTFW 2005; RGAL 4; TUS

Wilson, Ethel Davis (Bryant)
1888(?)-1980 .... **CLC 13**
See also CA 102; CN 1, 2; DAC; DAM POET; DLB 68; MTCW 1; RGEL 2

Wilson, Harriet
See Wilson, Harriet E. Adams
See also DLB 239

Wilson, Harriet E.
See Wilson, Harriet E. Adams
See also DLB 243

Wilson, Harriet E. Adams
1827(?)-1863(?) .... **BLC 3; NCLC 78**
See Wilson, Harriet; Wilson, Harriet E.
See also DAM MULT; DLB 50

Wilson, John 1785-1854 .... **NCLC 5**

Wilson, John (Anthony) Burgess 1917-1993
See Burgess, Anthony
See also CA 1-4R; 143; CANR 2, 46; DA3; DAC; DAM NOV; MTCW 1, 2; MTFW 2005; NFS 15; TEA

Wilson, Lanford 1937- .. **CLC 7, 14, 36, 197; DC 19**
See also CA 17-20R; CABS 3; CAD; CANR 45, 96; CD 5, 6; DAM DRAM; DFS 4, 9, 12, 16, 20; DLB 7; EWL 3; MAL 5; TUS

Wilson, Robert M. 1941- .... **CLC 7, 9**
See also CA 49-52; CAD; CANR 2, 41; CD 5, 6; MTCW 1

Wilson, Robert McLiam 1964- .... **CLC 59**
See also CA 132; DLB 267

Wilson, Sloan 1920-2003 .... **CLC 32**
See also CA 1-4R; 216; CANR 1, 44; CN 1, 2, 3, 4, 5, 6

Wilson, Snoo 1948- .... **CLC 33**
See also CA 69-72; CBD; CD 5, 6

Wilson, William S(mith) 1932- .... **CLC 49**
See also CA 81-84

Wilson, (Thomas) Woodrow
1856-1924 .... **TCLC 79**
See also CA 166; DLB 47

Wilson and Warnke eds. .... **CLC 65**

Winchilsea, Anne (Kingsmill) Finch
1661-1720
See Finch, Anne
See also RGEL 2

Winckelmann, Johann Joachim
1717-1768 .... **LC 129**
See also DLB 97

Windham, Basil
See Wodehouse, P(elham) G(renville)

Wingrove, David 1954- .... **CLC 68**
See also CA 133; SFW 4

Winnemucca, Sarah 1844-1891 .... **NCLC 79; NNAL**
See also DAM MULT; DLB 175; RGAL 4

Winstanley, Gerrard 1609-1676 .... **LC 52**

Wintergreen, Jane
See Duncan, Sara Jeannette

Winters, Arthur Yvor
See Winters, Yvor

Winters, Janet Lewis .... **CLC 41**
See Lewis, Janet
See also DLBY 1987

Winters, Yvor 1900-1968 .... **CLC 4, 8, 32**
See also AMWS 2; CA 11-12; 25-28R; CAP 1; DLB 48; EWL 3; MAL 5; MTCW 1; RGAL 4

Winterson, Jeanette 1959- .... **CLC 64, 158**
See also BRWS 4; CA 136; CANR 58, 116; CN 5, 6, 7; CPW; DA3; DAM POP; DLB 207, 261; FANT; FW; GLL 1; MTCW 2; MTFW 2005; RHW

Winthrop, John 1588-1649 .... **LC 31, 107**
See also DLB 24, 30

Wirth, Louis 1897-1952 .... **TCLC 92**
See also CA 210

Wiseman, Frederick 1930- .... **CLC 20**
See also CA 159

Wister, Owen 1860-1938 .... **TCLC 21**
See also BPFB 3; CA 108; 162; DLB 9, 78, 186; RGAL 4; SATA 62; TCWW 1, 2

Wither, George 1588-1667 .... **LC 96**
See also DLB 121; RGEL 2

Witkacy
See Witkiewicz, Stanislaw Ignacy

Witkiewicz, Stanislaw Ignacy
1885-1939 .... **TCLC 8**
See also CA 105; 162; CDWLB 4; DLB 215; EW 10; EWL 3; RGWL 2, 3; SFW 4

Wittgenstein, Ludwig (Josef Johann)
1889-1951 .... **TCLC 59**
See also CA 113; 164; DLB 262; MTCW 2

Wittig, Monique 1935-2003 .... **CLC 22**
See also CA 116; 135; 212; CANR 143; CWW 2; DLB 83; EWL 3; FW; GLL 1

Wittlin, Jozef 1896-1976 .... **CLC 25**
See also CA 49-52; 65-68; CANR 3; EWL 3

Wodehouse, P(elham) G(renville)
1881-1975 . **CLC 1, 2, 5, 10, 22; SSC 2; TCLC 108**
See also AAYA 65; AITN 2; BRWS 3; CA 45-48; 57-60; CANR 3, 33; CDBLB 1914-1945; CN 1, 2; CPW 1; DA3; DAB; DAC; DAM NOV; DLB 34, 162; EWL 3; MTCW 1, 2; MTFW 2005; RGEL 2; RGSF 2; SATA 22; SSFS 10

Woiwode, L.
See Woiwode, Larry (Alfred)

Woiwode, Larry (Alfred) 1941- ... **CLC 6, 10**
See also CA 73-76; CANR 16, 94; CN 3, 4, 5, 6, 7; DLB 6; INT CANR-16

Wojciechowska, Maia (Teresa)
1927-2002 .... **CLC 26**
See also AAYA 8, 46; BYA 3; CA 9-12R; 183; 209; CAAE 183; CANR 4, 41; CLR 1; JRDA; MAICYA 1, 2; SAAS 1; SATA 1, 28, 83; SATA-Essay 104; SATA-Obit 134; YAW

Wojtyla, Karol (Josef)
See John Paul II, Pope

Wojtyla, Karol (Jozef)
See John Paul II, Pope

Wolf, Christa 1929- .... **CLC 14, 29, 58, 150**
See also CA 85-88; CANR 45, 123; CDWLB 2; CWW 2; DLB 75; EWL 3; FW; MTCW 1; RGWL 2, 3; SSFS 14

Wolf, Naomi 1962- .... **CLC 157**
See also CA 141; CANR 110; FW; MTFW 2005

Wolfe, Gene 1931- .... **CLC 25**
See also AAYA 35; CA 57-60; CAAS 9; CANR 6, 32, 60, 152; CPW; DAM POP; DLB 8; FANT; MTCW 2; MTFW 2005; SATA 118, 165; SCFW 2; SFW 4; SUFW 2

Wolfe, Gene Rodman
See Wolfe, Gene

Wolfe, George C. 1954- .... **BLCS; CLC 49**
See also CA 149; CAD; CD 5, 6

Wolfe, Thomas (Clayton)
1900-1938 **SSC 33; TCLC 4, 13, 29, 61; WLC 6**
See also AMW; BPFB 3; CA 104; 132; CANR 102; CDALB 1929-1941; DA; DA3; DAB; DAC; DAM MST, NOV; DLB 9, 102, 229; DLBD 2, 16; DLBY 1985, 1997; EWL 3; MAL 5; MTCW 1, 2; NFS 18; RGAL 4; SSFS 18; TUS

Wolfe, Thomas Kennerly, Jr.
1931- .... **CLC 147**
See Wolfe, Tom
See also CA 13-16R; CANR 9, 33, 70, 104; DA3; DAM POP; DLB 185; INT CANR-9; MTCW 1, 2; MTFW 2005; TUS

Wolfe, Tom .... **CLC 1, 2, 9, 15, 35, 51**
See Wolfe, Thomas Kennerly, Jr.
See also AAYA 8, 67; AITN 2; AMWS 3; BEST 89:1; BPFB 3; CN 5, 6, 7; CPW; CSW; DLB 152; LAIT 5; RGAL 4

Wolff, Geoffrey 1937- .... **CLC 41**
See also CA 29-32R; CANR 29, 43, 78, 154

Wolff, Geoffrey Ansell
See Wolff, Geoffrey
Wolff, Sonia
See Levitin, Sonia (Wolff)
Wolff, Tobias 1945- .... **CLC 39, 64, 172; SSC 63**
See also AAYA 16; AMWS 7; BEST 90:2; BYA 12; CA 114; 117; CAAS 22; CANR 54, 76, 96; CN 5, 6, 7; CSW; DA3; DLB 130; EWL 3; INT CA-117; MTCW 2; MTFW 2005; RGAL 4; RGSF 2; SSFS 4, 11
Wolitzer, Hilma 1930- .... **CLC 17**
See also CA 65-68; CANR 18, 40; INT CANR-18; SATA 31; YAW
Wollstonecraft, Mary 1759-1797 .... **LC 5, 50, 90**
See also BRWS 3; CDBLB 1789-1832; DLB 39, 104, 158, 252; FL 1:1; FW; LAIT 1; RGEL 2; TEA; WLIT 3
Wonder, Stevie 1950- .... **CLC 12**
See also CA 111
Wong, Jade Snow 1922-2006 .... **CLC 17**
See also CA 109; 249; CANR 91; SATA 112
Woodberry, George Edward 1855-1930 .... **TCLC 73**
See also CA 165; DLB 71, 103
Woodcott, Keith
See Brunner, John (Kilian Houston)
Woodruff, Robert W.
See Mencken, H(enry) L(ouis)
Woolf, (Adeline) Virginia 1882-1941 .. **SSC 7, 79; TCLC 1, 5, 20, 43, 56, 101, 123, 128; WLC 6**
See also AAYA 44; BPFB 3; BRW 7; BRWC 2; BRWR 1; CA 104; 130; CANR 64, 132; CDBLB 1914-1945; DA; DA3; DAB; DAC; DAM MST, NOV; DLB 36, 100, 162; DLBD 10; EWL 3; EXPS; FL 1:6; FW; LAIT 3; LATS 1:1; LMFS 2; MTCW 1, 2; MTFW 2005; NCFS 2; NFS 8, 12; RGEL 2; RGSF 2; SSFS 4, 12; TEA; WLIT 4
Woollcott, Alexander (Humphreys) 1887-1943 .... **TCLC 5**
See also CA 105; 161; DLB 29
Woolrich, Cornell .... **CLC 77**
See Hopley-Woolrich, Cornell George
See also MSW
Woolson, Constance Fenimore 1840-1894 .... **NCLC 82; SSC 90**
See also DLB 12, 74, 189, 221; RGAL 4
Wordsworth, Dorothy 1771-1855 . **NCLC 25, 138**
See also DLB 107
Wordsworth, William 1770-1850 .. **NCLC 12, 38, 111, 166; PC 4, 67; WLC 6**
See also AAYA 70; BRW 4; BRWC 1; CD-BLB 1789-1832; DA; DA3; DAB; DAC; DAM MST, POET; DLB 93, 107; EXPP; LATS 1:1; LMFS 1; PAB; PFS 2; RGEL 2; TEA; WLIT 3; WP
Wotton, Sir Henry 1568-1639 .... **LC 68**
See also DLB 121; RGEL 2
Wouk, Herman 1915- .... **CLC 1, 9, 38**
See also BPFB 2, 3; CA 5-8R; CANR 6, 33, 67, 146; CDALBS; CN 1, 2, 3, 4, 5, 6; CPW; DA3; DAM NOV, POP; DLBY 1982; INT CANR-6; LAIT 4; MAL 5; MTCW 1, 2; MTFW 2005; NFS 7; TUS
Wright, Charles 1935- ... **CLC 6, 13, 28, 119, 146**
See also AMWS 5; CA 29-32R; CAAS 7; CANR 23, 36, 62, 88, 135; CP 3, 4, 5, 6, 7; DLB 165; DLBY 1982; EWL 3; MTCW 1, 2; MTFW 2005; PFS 10

Wright, Charles Stevenson 1932- ..... **BLC 3; CLC 49**
See also BW 1; CA 9-12R; CANR 26; CN 1, 2, 3, 4, 5, 6, 7; DAM MULT, POET; DLB 33
Wright, Frances 1795-1852 .... **NCLC 74**
See also DLB 73
Wright, Frank Lloyd 1867-1959 .... **TCLC 95**
See also AAYA 33; CA 174
Wright, Harold Bell 1872-1944 .... **TCLC 183**
See also BPFB 3; CA 110; DLB 9; TCWW 2
Wright, Jack R.
See Harris, Mark
Wright, James (Arlington) 1927-1980 .... **CLC 3, 5, 10, 28; PC 36**
See also AITN 2; AMWS 3; CA 49-52; 97-100; CANR 4, 34, 64; CDALBS; CP 1, 2; DAM POET; DLB 5, 169; EWL 3; EXPP; MAL 5; MTCW 1, 2; MTFW 2005; PFS 7, 8; RGAL 4; TUS; WP
Wright, Judith 1915-2000 ... **CLC 11, 53; PC 14**
See also CA 13-16R; 188; CANR 31, 76, 93; CP 1, 2, 3, 4, 5, 6, 7; CWP; DLB 260; EWL 3; MTCW 1, 2; MTFW 2005; PFS 8; RGEL 2; SATA 14; SATA-Obit 121
Wright, L(aurali) R. 1939- .... **CLC 44**
See also CA 138; CMW 4
Wright, Richard (Nathaniel) 1908-1960 ... **BLC 3; CLC 1, 3, 4, 9, 14, 21, 48, 74; SSC 2; TCLC 136, 180; WLC 6**
See also AAYA 5, 42; AFAW 1, 2; AMW; BPFB 3; BW 1; BYA 2; CA 108; CANR 64; CDALB 1929-1941; DA; DA3; DAB; DAC; DAM MST, MULT, NOV; DLB 76, 102; DLBD 2; EWL 3; EXPN; LAIT 3, 4; MAL 5; MTCW 1, 2; MTFW 2005; NCFS 1; NFS 1, 7; RGAL 4; RGSF 2; SSFS 3, 9, 15, 20; TUS; YAW
Wright, Richard B(ruce) 1937- .... **CLC 6**
See also CA 85-88; CANR 120; DLB 53
Wright, Rick 1945- .... **CLC 35**
Wright, Rowland
See Wells, Carolyn
Wright, Stephen 1946- .... **CLC 33**
See also CA 237
Wright, Willard Huntington 1888-1939
See Van Dine, S. S.
See also CA 115; 189; CMW 4; DLBD 16
Wright, William 1930- .... **CLC 44**
See also CA 53-56; CANR 7, 23, 154
Wroth, Lady Mary 1587-1653(?) .... **LC 30; PC 38**
See also DLB 121
Wu Ch'eng-en 1500(?)-1582(?) .... **LC 7**
Wu Ching-tzu 1701-1754 .... **LC 2**
Wulfstan c. 10th cent. -1023 .... **CMLC 59**
Wurlitzer, Rudolph 1938(?)- .... **CLC 2, 4, 15**
See also CA 85-88; CN 4, 5, 6, 7; DLB 173
Wyatt, Sir Thomas c. 1503-1542 . **LC 70; PC 27**
See also BRW 1; DLB 132; EXPP; RGEL 2; TEA
Wycherley, William 1640-1716 .... **LC 8, 21, 102**
See also BRW 2; CDBLB 1660-1789; DAM DRAM; DLB 80; RGEL 2
Wyclif, John c. 1330-1384 .... **CMLC 70**
See also DLB 146
Wylie, Elinor (Morton Hoyt) 1885-1928 .... **PC 23; TCLC 8**
See also AMWS 1; CA 105; 162; DLB 9, 45; EXPP; MAL 5; RGAL 4
Wylie, Philip (Gordon) 1902-1971 ... **CLC 43**
See also CA 21-22; 33-36R; CAP 2; CN 1; DLB 9; SFW 4

Wyndham, John .... **CLC 19**
See Harris, John (Wyndham Parkes Lucas) Beynon
See also DLB 255; SCFW 1, 2
Wyss, Johann David Von 1743-1818 .... **NCLC 10**
See also CLR 92; JRDA; MAICYA 1, 2; SATA 29; SATA-Brief 27
Xenophon c. 430B.C.-c. 354B.C. ... **CMLC 17**
See also AW 1; DLB 176; RGWL 2, 3; WLIT 8
Xingjian, Gao 1940-
See Gao Xingjian
See also CA 193; DFS 21; DLB 330; RGWL 3
Yakamochi 718-785 .... **CMLC 45; PC 48**
Yakumo Koizumi
See Hearn, (Patricio) Lafcadio (Tessima Carlos)
Yamada, Mitsuye (May) 1923- .... **PC 44**
See also CA 77-80
Yamamoto, Hisaye 1921- .... **AAL; SSC 34**
See also CA 214; DAM MULT; DLB 312; LAIT 4; SSFS 14
Yamauchi, Wakako 1924- .... **AAL**
See also CA 214; DLB 312
Yanez, Jose Donoso
See Donoso (Yanez), Jose
Yanovsky, Basile S.
See Yanovsky, V(assily) S(emenovich)
Yanovsky, V(assily) S(emenovich) 1906-1989 .... **CLC 2, 18**
See also CA 97-100; 129
Yates, Richard 1926-1992 .... **CLC 7, 8, 23**
See also AMWS 11; CA 5-8R; 139; CANR 10, 43; CN 1, 2, 3, 4, 5; DLB 2, 234; DLBY 1981, 1992; INT CANR-10; SSFS 24
Yau, John 1950- .... **PC 61**
See also CA 154; CANR 89; CP 4, 5, 6, 7; DLB 234, 312
Yearsley, Ann 1753-1806 .... **NCLC 174**
See also DLB 109
Yeats, W. B.
See Yeats, William Butler
Yeats, William Butler 1865-1939 . **PC 20, 51; TCLC 1, 11, 18, 31, 93, 116; WLC 6**
See also AAYA 48; BRW 6; BRWR 1; CA 104; 127; CANR 45; CDBLB 1890-1914; DA; DA3; DAB; DAC; DAM DRAM, MST, POET; DLB 10, 19, 98, 156; EWL 3; EXPP; MTCW 1, 2; MTFW 2005; NCFS 3; PAB; PFS 1, 2, 5, 7, 13, 15; RGEL 2; TEA; WLIT 4; WP
Yehoshua, A(braham) B. 1936- .. **CLC 13, 31**
See also CA 33-36R; CANR 43, 90, 145; CWW 2; EWL 3; RGHL; RGSF 2; RGWL 3; WLIT 6
Yellow Bird
See Ridge, John Rollin
Yep, Laurence Michael 1948- .... **CLC 35**
See also AAYA 5, 31; BYA 7; CA 49-52; CANR 1, 46, 92; CLR 3, 17, 54; DLB 52, 312; FANT; JRDA; MAICYA 1, 2; MAI-CYAS 1; SATA 7, 69, 123; WYA; YAW
Yerby, Frank G(arvin) 1916-1991 ..... **BLC 3; CLC 1, 7, 22**
See also BPFB 3; BW 1, 3; CA 9-12R; 136; CANR 16, 52; CN 1, 2, 3, 4, 5; DAM MULT; DLB 76; INT CANR-16; MTCW 1; RGAL 4; RHW
Yesenin, Sergei Aleksandrovich
See Esenin, Sergei
Yevtushenko, Yevgeny (Alexandrovich) 1933- ...... **CLC 1, 3, 13, 26, 51, 126; PC 40**
See Evtushenko, Evgenii Aleksandrovich
See also CA 81-84; CANR 33, 54; DAM POET; EWL 3; MTCW 1; RGHL

Literary Criticism Series
Cumulative Topic Index

This index lists all topic entries in Thompson Gale's *Children's Literature Review* (CLR), *Classical and Medieval Literature Criticism* (CMLC), *Contemporary Literary Criticism* (CLC), *Drama Criticism* (DC), *Literature Criticism from 1400 to 1800* (LC), *Nineteenth-Century Literature Criticism* (NCLC), *Short Story Criticism* (SSC), and *Twentieth-Century Literary Criticism* (TCLC). The index also lists topic entries in the Gale Critical Companion Collection, which includes the following publications: *The Beat Generation* (BG), *Feminism in Literature* (FL), *Gothic Literature* (GL), and *Harlem Renaissance* (HR).

SSC Cumulative Nationality Index

ALGERIAN

Camus, Albert **9**

AMERICAN

Abish, Walter **44**
Adams, Alice (Boyd) **24**
Aiken, Conrad (Potter) **9**
Alcott, Louisa May **27**
Algren, Nelson **33**
Anderson, Sherwood **1, 46, 91**
Apple, Max (Isaac) **50**
Auchincloss, Louis (Stanton) **22**
Baldwin, James (Arthur) **10, 33**
Bambara, Toni Cade **35**
Banks, Russell **42**
Barnes, Djuna **3**
Barth, John (Simmons) **10, 89**
Barthelme, Donald **2, 55**
Bass, Rick **60**
Beattie, Ann **11**
Bellow, Saul **14**
Benét, Stephen Vincent **10, 86**
Berriault, Gina **30**
Betts, Doris (Waugh) **45**
Bierce, Ambrose (Gwinett) **9, 72**
Bowles, Paul (Frederick) **3**
Boyle, Kay **5**
Boyle, T(homas) Coraghessan **16**
Bradbury, Ray (Douglas) **29, 53**
Bradfield, Scott **65**
Bukowski, Charles **45**
Cable, George Washington **4**
Caldwell, Erskine (Preston) **19**
Calisher, Hortense **15**
Canin, Ethan **70**
Capote, Truman **2, 47, 93**
Carver, Raymond **8, 51**
Cather, Willa (Sibert) **2, 50**
Chabon, Michael **59**
Chambers, Robert W. **92**
Chandler, Raymond (Thornton) **23**
Cheever, John **1, 38, 57**
Chesnutt, Charles W(addell) **7, 54**
Chopin, Kate **8, 68**
Cisneros, Sandra **32, 72**
Coover, Robert (Lowell) **15**
Cowan, Peter (Walkinshaw) **28**
Crane, Stephen (Townley) **7, 56, 70**
Davenport, Guy (Mattison Jr.) **16**
Davis, Rebecca (Blaine) Harding **38**
Dick, Philip K. **57**
Dixon, Stephen **16**
Dreiser, Theodore (Herman Albert) **30**
Dubus, André **15**
Dunbar, Paul Laurence **8**
Dybek, Stuart **55**
Elkin, Stanley L(awrence) **12**
Ellison, Harlan (Jay) **14**
Ellison, Ralph (Waldo) **26, 79**
Fante, John **65**
Farrell, James T(homas) **28**
Faulkner, William (Cuthbert) **1, 35, 42, 92**

Fisher, Rudolph **25**
Fitzgerald, F(rancis) Scott (Key) **6, 31, 75**
Ford, Richard **56**
Freeman, Mary E(leanor) Wilkins **1, 47**
Gaines, Ernest J. **68**
Gardner, John (Champlin) Jr. **7**
Garland, (Hannibal) Hamlin **18**
Garrett, George (Palmer) **30**
Gass, William H(oward) **12**
Gibson, William (Ford) **52**
Gilchrist, Ellen (Louise) **14, 63**
Gilman, Charlotte (Anna) Perkins (Stetson) **13, 62**
Glasgow, Ellen (Anderson Gholson) **34**
Glaspell, Susan **41**
Gordon, Caroline **15**
Gordon, Mary **59**
Grau, Shirley Ann **15**
Hammett, (Samuel) Dashiell **17**
Hannah, Barry **94**
Harris, Joel Chandler **19**
Harrison, James (Thomas) **19**
Harte, (Francis) Bret(t) **8, 59**
Hawthorne, Nathaniel **3, 29, 39, 89**
Heinlein, Robert A(nson) **55**
Hemingway, Ernest (Miller) **1, 25, 36, 40, 63**
Henderson, Zenna (Chlarson) **29**
Henry, O. **5, 49**
Howells, William Dean **36**
Hughes, (James) Langston **6, 90**
Hurston, Zora Neale **4, 80**
Huxley, Aldous (Leonard) **39**
Irving, Washington **2, 37**
Jackson, Shirley **9, 39**
James, Henry **8, 32, 47**
Jewett, (Theodora) Sarah Orne **6, 44**
Johnson, Denis **56**
Jones, Thom (Douglas) **56**
Kelly, Robert **50**
Kincaid, Jamaica **72**
King, Stephen (Edwin) **17, 55**
Lardner, Ring(gold) W(ilmer) **32**
Le Guin, Ursula K(roeber) **12, 69**
Ligotti, Thomas (Robert) **16**
Lish, Gordon (Jay) **18**
London, Jack **4, 49**
Lovecraft, H(oward) P(hillips) **3, 52**
Maclean, Norman (Fitzroy) **13**
Malamud, Bernard **15**
Marshall, Paule **3**
Mason, Bobbie Ann **4**
McCarthy, Mary (Therese) **24**
McCullers, (Lula) Carson (Smith) **9, 24**
McPherson, James Alan **95**
Melville, Herman **1, 17, 46, 95**
Michaels, Leonard **16**
Millhauser, Steven **57**
Mori, Toshio **83**
Murfree, Mary Noailles **22**
Nabokov, Vladimir (Vladimirovich) **11, 86**
Nin, Anaïs **10**
Norris, (Benjamin) Frank(lin Jr.) **28**
Oates, Joyce Carol **6, 70**

O'Brien, Tim **74**
O'Connor, Frank **5**
O'Connor, (Mary) Flannery **1, 23, 61, 82**
O'Hara, John (Henry) **15**
Olsen, Tillie **11**
Ozick, Cynthia **15, 60**
Page, Thomas Nelson **23**
Paley, Grace **8**
Pancake, Breece D'J **61**
Parker, Dorothy (Rothschild) **2**
Perelman, S(idney) J(oseph) **32**
Phillips, Jayne Anne **16**
Poe, Edgar Allan **1, 22, 34, 35, 54, 88**
Pohl, Frederik **25**
Porter, Katherine Anne **4, 31, 43**
Powers, J(ames) F(arl) **4**
Price, (Edward) Reynolds **22**
Pynchon, Thomas (Ruggles Jr.) **14, 84**
Roth, Philip (Milton) **26**
Salinger, J(erome) D(avid) **2, 28, 65**
Salter, James **58**
Saroyan, William **21**
Selby, Hubert Jr. **20**
Silko, Leslie (Marmon) **37, 66**
Singer, Isaac Bashevis **3, 53**
Spencer, Elizabeth **57**
Spofford, Harriet Prescott **87**
Stafford, Jean **26, 86**
Stegner, Wallace (Earle) **27**
Stein, Gertrude **42**
Steinbeck, John (Ernst) **11, 37, 77**
Stuart, Jesse (Hilton) **31**
Styron, William **25**
Suckow, Ruth **18**
Taylor, Peter (Hillsman) **10, 84**
Thomas, Audrey (Callahan) **20**
Thurber, James (Grover) **1, 47**
Toomer, Jean **1, 45**
Trilling, Lionel **75**
Twain, Mark (Clemens, Samuel) **6, 26, 34, 87**
Updike, John (Hoyer) **13, 27**
Vinge, Joan (Carol) D(ennison) **24**
Vonnegut, Kurt Jr. **8**
Walker, Alice (Malsenior) **5**
Wallace, David Foster **68**
Warren, Robert Penn **4, 58**
Welty, Eudora **1, 27, 51**
Wescott, Glenway **35**
West, Nathanael **16**
Wharton, Edith (Newbold Jones) **6, 84**
Wideman, John Edgar **62**
Williams, William Carlos **31**
Williams, Tennessee **81**
Wodehouse, P(elham) G(renville) **2**
Wolfe, Thomas (Clayton) **33**
Wolff, Tobias **63**
Woolson, Constance Fenimore **90**
Wright, Richard (Nathaniel) **2**
Yamamoto, Hisaye **34**

Nationality Index

SSC-95 Title Index

ISBN-13: 978-0-7876-8892-9
ISBN-10: 0-7876-8892-4